Problems in Contract Law

Aspen Casebook Series

Problems in Contract Law
Cases and Materials

NINTH EDITION

CHARLES L. KNAPP
Emeritus Joseph W. Cotchett Distinguished Professor of Law
University of California, Hastings College of the Law
Max E. Greenberg Professor Emeritus of Contract Law
New York University School of Law

NATHAN M. CRYSTAL
Adjunct Professor of Law
New York University School of Law
Distinguished Professor Emeritus
University of South Carolina School of Law

HARRY G. PRINCE
Emeritus Professor of Law
University of California, Hastings College of the Law

Published by Wolters Kluwer in New York.

Wolters Kluwer Legal & Regulatory U.S. serves customers worldwide with CCH, Aspen Publishers, and Kluwer Law International products. (www.WKLegaledu.com)

To contact Customer Service, e-mail customer.service@wolterskluwer.com, call 1-800-234-1660, fax 1-800-901-9075, or mail correspondence to:

Wolters Kluwer
Attn: Order Department
PO Box 990
Frederick, MD 21705

Printed in the United States of America.

3 4 5 6 7 8 9 0

ISBN 978-1-5438-0147-7

Library of Congress Cataloging-in-Publication Data

Names: Knapp, Charles L., author. | Crystal, Nathan M., author. | Prince, Harry G., author.
Title: Problems in contract law : cases and materials / Charles L. Knapp, Emeritus Joseph W. Cotchett, Distinguished Professor of Law, University of California, Hastings College of the Law, Max E. Greenberg, Professor Emeritus of Contract Law, New York University School of Law; Nathan M. Crystal, Adjunct Professor of Law, New York University School of Law, Distinguished Professor Emeritus, University of South Carolina School of Law; Harry G. Prince, Emeritus Professor of Law, University Of California, Hastings College of the Law.
Description: Ninth edition. | New York : Wolters Kluwer, [2019] | Series: Aspen casebook series | Includes bibliographical references and index.
Identifiers: LCCN 2018058787 | ISBN 9781543801477 (hard cover : alk. paper)
Subjects: LCSH: Contracts—United States. | LCGFT: Casebooks (Law)
Classification: LCC KF801.A7 K5 2019 | DDC 346.7302—dc23
LC record available at https://lccn.loc.gov/2018058787

Certified Chain of Custody
Promoting Sustainable Forestry
www.sfiprogram.org
SFI-01681

SFI label applies to the text stock

About Wolters Kluwer Legal & Regulatory U.S.

Wolters Kluwer Legal & Regulatory U.S. delivers expert content and solutions in the areas of law, corporate compliance, health compliance, reimbursement, and legal education. Its practical solutions help customers successfully navigate the demands of a changing environment to drive their daily activities, enhance decision quality and inspire confident outcomes.

Serving customers worldwide, its legal and regulatory portfolio includes products under the Aspen Publishers, CCH Incorporated, Kluwer Law International, ftwilliam .com, and MediRegs names. They are regarded as exceptional and trusted resources for general legal and practice-specific knowledge, compliance and risk management, dynamic workflow solutions, and expert commentary.

To my law-school and law-firm classmates, Walter McNeill and Bob Smith: excellent lawyers and lifelong faithful friends.

C.L.K.

To Chuck and H.G. — Great teachers, terrific scholars, and — most important — fine people.

N.M.C.

To Andrew, James and Callie — with love.

H.G.P.

SUMMARY OF CONTENTS

Contents *xi*
Preface *xxi*
Acknowledgments *xxv*

CHAPTER 1
An Introduction to the Study of Contract Law 1

CHAPTER 2
The Basis of Contractual Obligation:
Mutual Assent and Consideration 35

CHAPTER 3
Liability in the Absence of Bargained-for Exchange:
Reliance on Gratuitous Promises, Unaccepted Offers,
and the Principle of Restitution 225

CHAPTER 4
The Statute of Frauds 345

CHAPTER 5
The Meaning of the Agreement:
Principles of Interpretation and the Parol Evidence Rule 395

CHAPTER 6
Supplementing the Agreement:
Implied Terms, the Obligation of Good Faith, and Warranties 481

CHAPTER 7
Avoiding Enforcement:
Incapacity, Bargaining Misconduct, Unconscionability,
and Public Policy 571

CHAPTER 8
Justification for Nonperformance:
Mistake, Changed Circumstances, and Contractual
Modifications 719

CHAPTER 9
Consequences of Nonperformance:
Express Conditions, Material Breach,
and Anticipatory Repudiation 803

CHAPTER 10
Expectation Damages:
Principles and Limitations 873

CHAPTER 11
Alternatives to Expectation Damages:
Reliance and Restitutionary Damages, Specific Performance, and Agreed Remedies 1001

CHAPTER 12
Rights and Duties of Third Parties 1093

Appendix: Answers to Review Questions *1137*
Table of Cases *1151*
Table of Uniform Commercial Code Provisions (UCC) *1171*
Table of Provisions from Restatement (Second) of Contracts *1175*
Table of Provisions from Restatement (First) of Contracts *1179*
Table of Provisions from Other Restatements *1181*
Table of Other Acts, Codes, and Rules *1183*
Table of Secondary Authorities *1185*
Index *1195*

CONTENTS

Preface *xxi*
Acknowledgments *xxv*

CHAPTER 1
An Introduction to the Study of Contract Law 1
A. What Do We Mean When We Talk About "Contract Law"? 2
Problem 1-1 4
B. The Structure of Contract Law 5
1. Formation 6
2. Interpretation and Implication 6
3. Defenses to Enforcement 6
4. Nonperformance and its Consequences 7
5. Rights and Duties of Third Parties 7
C. The Sources of Contract Law 8
1. Judicial Opinions 8
2. Statutory Law 9
3. The Restatements 10
4. Legal Commentary 11
5. International Commercial Law 12
D. The Perspective of Contract Theory 12
E. The Lawyering Perspective 16
F. Contract Law Through Case Study: Two Examples from Different Periods in Time 18
Allen v. Bissinger & Co. 18
Meyer v. Uber Technologies, Inc. 21
Notes and Questions 32
REVIEW QUESTIONS 33

CHAPTER 2
The Basis of Contractual Obligation:
Mutual Assent and Consideration 35
A. Mutual Assent 35
1. Intention to be Bound: The Objective Theory of Contract 36
Ray v. William G. Eurice & Bros., Inc. 37
Notes and Questions 44
2. Offer and Acceptance in Bilateral Contracts 46
Lonergan v. Scolnick 47
Notes and Questions 49

Normile v. Miller 51
Notes and Questions 57
Comment: Remedies for Breach of Contract 59
3. Offer and Acceptance in Unilateral Contracts 60
Cook v. Coldwell Banker/Frank Laiben Realty Co. 61
Notes and Questions 64
Comment: Historical Development of the Law of Unilateral Contracts 65
Sateriale v. R.J. Reynolds Tobacco Co. 66
Notes and Questions 75
Problem 2-1 76
4. Postponed Bargaining: The "Agreement to Agree" 77
Walker v. Keith 78
Notes and Questions 84
Quake Construction, Inc. v. American Airlines, Inc. 86
Notes and Questions 93
Comment: Contracting to Bargain in Good Faith 96
Problem 2-2 98
Problem 2-3 99
Problem 2-4 101

B. Consideration 101
Hamer v. Sidway 102
Notes and Questions 106
Pennsy Supply, Inc. v. American Ash Recycling Corp. of Pennsylvania 107
Notes and Questions 111
Dougherty v. Salt 115
Notes and Questions 116
Comment: The Lawyer's Role in Counseling for Legal Effect 118
Plowman v. Indian Refining Co. 120
Notes and Questions 125
Comment: The Power of Agents to Bind Their Principals 127
Dohrmann v. Swaney 129
Notes and Questions 137
Marshall Durbin Food Corp. v. Baker 139
Notes and Questions 145

C. Contract Formation Under Article 2 of the Uniform Commercial Code 147
Comment on the History of the Uniform Commercial Code 147
1. Mutual Assent Under the Uniform Commercial Code 148
Jannusch v. Naffziger 149
Notes and Questions 153
E.C. Styberg Engineering Co. v. Eaton Corp. 154
Notes and Questions 159
Comment: Introduction to the CISG 160
Problem 2-5 161

2. Qualified Acceptance: The "Battle of Forms" 163
Princess Cruises, Inc. v. General Electric Co. 165
Notes and Questions 171
Brown Machine, Inc. v. Hercules, Inc. 174
Notes and Questions 180
Paul Gottlieb & Co., Inc. v. Alps South Corp. 184
Notes and Questions 190
Problem 2-6 193
D. Electronic and "Layered" Contracting 195
DeFontes v. Dell, Inc. 197
Notes and Questions 205
Long v. Provide Commerce, Inc. 209
Notes and Questions 218
Problem 2-7 219
REVIEW QUESTIONS 221

CHAPTER 3
Liability in the Absence of Bargained-for Exchange: Reliance on Gratuitous Promises, Unaccepted Offers, and the Principle of Restitution 225
A. Protection of Promisee Reliance: The Doctrine of Promissory Estoppel 225
1. Promises Within the Family 226
Kirksey v. Kirksey 227
Notes and Questions 227
Harvey v. Dow 228
Notes and Questions 233
2. Charitable Subscriptions 236
King v. Trustees of Boston University 237
Notes and Questions 243
Problem 3-1 246
3. Promises in a Commercial Context 247
Katz v. Danny Dare, Inc. 248
Notes and Questions 253
Aceves v. U.S. Bank, N.A. 255
Notes and Questions 262
Comment: The Status and Future of Promissory Estoppel 264
B. Liability in the Absence of Acceptance: Option Contracts, Offeree Reliance, and Statutory Limitations on Revocation 265
1. Option Contract 266
Berryman v. Kmoch 266
Notes and Questions 270
2. Offeree's Reliance on an Unaccepted Offer as Limitation on Revocability 274
James Baird Co. v. Gimbel Bros., Inc. 274

Notes and Questions 277
Drennan v. Star Paving Co. 277
Notes and Questions 282
Pop's Cones, Inc. v. Resorts International Hotel, Inc. 285
Notes and Questions 291
Problem 3-2 293
3. Statutory Limits on the Power of Revocation 294
Problem 3-3 296

C. Liability for Benefits Received: The Principle of Restitution 296
1. Restitution in the Absence of a Promise 297
Credit Bureau Enterprises, Inc. v. Pelo 297
Notes and Questions 304
Comment: Development of the Law of Restitution 307
Commerce Partnership 8098 Limited Partnership v. Equity Contracting Co. 309
Notes and Questions 314
Watts v. Watts 315
Notes and Questions 325
2. Promissory Restitution 327
Mills v. Wyman 328
Notes and Questions 331
Webb v. McGowin 333
Notes and Questions 336
Problem 3-4 340
Problem 3-5 341

REVIEW QUESTIONS 342

CHAPTER 4

The Statute of Frauds 345

A. General Principles: Scope and Application 347
Crabtree v. Elizabeth Arden Sales Corp. 347
Notes and Questions 352
Beaver v. Brumlow 357
Notes and Questions 364
Comment: The Historical Development of Law and Equity 366
Alaska Democratic Party v. Rice 368
Notes and Questions 374
Problem 4-1 377
Problem 4-2 380

B. The Sale of Goods Statute of Frauds: UCC §2-201 380
Buffaloe v. Hart 381
Notes and Questions 387
Problem 4-3 390

REVIEW QUESTIONS 391

CHAPTER 5

The Meaning of the Agreement:
Principles of Interpretation and the Parol Evidence Rule 395

A. Principles of Interpretation 396
Joyner v. Adams 399
Notes and Questions 402
Comment: Interpretive Principles 405
Frigaliment Importing Co. v. B.N.S. International Sales Corp. 408
Notes and Questions 412
C & J Fertilizer, Inc. v. Allied Mutual Insurance Co. 416
Notes and Questions 424

B. The Parol Evidence Rule 427
Thompson v. Libby 429
Notes and Questions 432
Taylor v. State Farm Mutual Automobile Insurance Co. 438
Notes and Questions 447
Sherrodd, Inc. v. Morrison-Knudsen Co. 451
Notes and Questions 457
Nanakuli Paving & Rock Co. v. Shell Oil Co. 460
Notes and Questions 471
Problem 5-1 473
Problem 5-2 475

REVIEW QUESTIONS 476

CHAPTER 6

Supplementing the Agreement:
Implied Terms, the Obligation of Good Faith, and Warranties 481

A. The Rationale for Implied Terms 481
Wood v. Lucy, Lady Duff-Gordon 482
Notes and Questions 484
Leibel v. Raynor Manufacturing Co. 486
Notes and Questions 489

B. The Implied Obligation of Good Faith 492
Seidenberg v. Summit Bank 494
Notes and Questions 503
Comment: Requirements and Output Contracts 505
Morin Building Products Co. v. Baystone Construction, Inc. 508
Notes and Questions 512
Locke v. Warner Bros., Inc. 513
Notes and Questions 521
Geysen v. Securitas Security Services, USA, Inc. 523
Notes and Questions 533
Problem 6-1 539
Problem 6-2 540
Problem 6-3 540

C. Warranties 546
Bayliner Marine Corp. v. Crow 548
Notes and Questions 552
Comment on the History of Warranty Law 556

Problem 6-4 557
Speight v. Walters Development Co. 558
Notes and Questions 564
REVIEW QUESTIONS 567

CHAPTER 7
Avoiding Enforcement:
Incapacity, Bargaining Misconduct, Unconscionability, and Public Policy 571

A. **Minority and Mental Incapacity** 572
Problem 7-1 572
Dodson v. Shrader 572
Notes and Questions 576
Sparrow v. Demonico 579
Notes and Questions 586
Comment: Historical Development of the Law of Contractual Capacity 589

B. **Duress and Undue Influence** 591
Totem Marine Tug & Barge, Inc. v. Alyeska Pipeline Service Co. 591
Notes and Questions 598
Odorizzi v. Bloomfield School District 601
Notes and Questions 607

C. **Misrepresentation and Nondisclosure** 610
Syester v. Banta 611
Notes and Questions 619
Hill v. Jones 622
Notes and Questions 628
Comment: Lawyers' Professional Ethics 632
Park 100 Investors, Inc. v. Kartes 634
Notes and Questions 637

D. **Unconscionability** 638
Williams v. Walker-Thomas Furniture Co. 639
Notes and Questions 643
Comment: Historical Development of the Doctrine of Unconscionability 649
Higgins v. Superior Court of Los Angeles County 650
Notes and Questions 659
Comment: Mandatory Arbitration and Unconscionability 662
McFarland v. Wells Fargo Bank, N.A. 664
Notes and Questions 673
Comment: Consumer Protection Legislation 677

E. **Public Policy** 680
Problem 7-2 680
Valley Medical Specialists v. Farber 681
Notes and Questions 691
P.M. v. T.B. 695
Notes and Questions 707

Problem 7-3 710
Problem 7-4 712
Problem 7-5 714
REVIEW QUESTIONS 715

CHAPTER 8
Justification for Nonperformance:
Mistake, Changed Circumstances, and Contractual Modifications 719
A. Mistake 720
Lenawee County Board of Health v. Messerly 720
Notes and Questions 727
BMW Financial Services NA, LLC v. Deloach 730
Notes and Questions 737
B. Changed Circumstances: Impossibility, Impracticability, and Frustration 741
Hemlock Semiconductor Operations, LLC v. Solarworld Industries Sachsen GmbH 744
Notes and Questions 752
Mel Frank Tool & Supply, Inc. v. Di-Chem Co. 757
Notes and Questions 766
Problem 8-1 768
Problem 8-2 769
Problem 8-3 769
C. Modification 771
Problem 8-4 771
Alaska Packers' Association v. Domenico 773
Notes and Questions 777
Kelsey-Hayes Co. v. Galtaco Redlaw Castings Corp. 782
Notes and Questions 787
Brookside Farms v. Mama Rizzo's, Inc. 789
Notes and Questions 796
REVIEW QUESTIONS 799

CHAPTER 9
Consequences of Nonperformance:
Express Conditions, Material Breach, and Anticipatory Repudiation 803
A. Express Conditions 805
enXco Development Corp. v. Northern States Power Co. 805
Notes and Questions 813
J. N. A. Realty Corp. v. Cross Bay Chelsea, Inc. 818
Notes and Questions 824
Problem 9-1 827
B. Material Breach 829
Jacob & Youngs, Inc. v. Kent 829
Notes and Questions 834
Comment: The Doctrine of Constructive Conditions 838
Sackett v. Spindler 841
Notes and Questions 845

C. Anticipatory Repudiation 849
Truman L. Flatt & Sons Co. v. Schupf 849
Notes and Questions 856
Hornell Brewing Co. v. Spry 858
Notes and Questions 864
Problem 9-2 867
Problem 9-3 868
REVIEW QUESTIONS 868

CHAPTER 10
Expectation Damages:
Principles and Limitations 873
A. Computing the Value of Plaintiff's Expectation 876
Crabby's, Inc. v. Hamilton 879
Notes and Questions 886
Handicapped Children's Education Board v. Lukaszewski 889
Notes and Questions 894
American Standard, Inc. v. Schectman 895
Notes and Questions 899
B. Restrictions on the Recovery of Expectation Damages: Foreseeability, Certainty, and Causation 902
Hadley v. Baxendale 903
Notes and Questions 905
Florafax International, Inc. v. GTE Market Resources, Inc. 909
Notes and Questions 917
C. Restrictions on The Recovery of Expectation Damages: Mitigation of Damages 921
Rockingham County v. Luten Bridge Co. 922
Notes and Questions 926
Maness v. Collins 926
Notes and Questions 937
Jetz Service Co. v. Salina Properties 941
Notes and Questions 946
D. Nonrecoverable Damages: Items Commonly Excluded from Plaintiff's Damages for Breach of Contract 948
Zapata Hermanos Sucesores, S.A. v. Hearthside Baking Company, Inc. 949
Notes and Questions 954
Erlich v. Menezes 957
Notes and Questions 966
Comment: Recovery of Punitive Damages for Bad Faith Breach of Contract 969
Problem 10-1 971
E. Buyers' and Sellers' Remedies Under the Uniform Commercial Code 973
1. Buyers' Remedies 973

a. Cover, UCC §2-712 974
b. Market Damages, UCC §2-713 975
c. Damages for Accepted Goods, UCC §2-714 976
d. Specific Performance, UCC §2-716 976
e. Incidental and Consequential Damages, UCC §2-715 977
Problem 10-2 977
2. Sellers' Remedies 978
a. Resale Damages, UCC §2-706 978
b. Market Damages, UCC §2-708(1) 979
c. Lost Profits, UCC §2-708(2) 979
d. Seller's Action for the Price, UCC §2-709 981
e. Seller's Incidental and Consequential Damages, UCC §2-710 981
Problem 10-3 981

F. Justifications for the Expectation Damage Rule 982
1. Protecting the Expectation Interest Under a Wholly Executory Contract 982
2. Encouraging or Deterring Breach of Contract: The Concepts of "Efficient Breach" and Disgorgement 985
Roth v. Speck 990
Notes and Questions 992
Problem 10-4 994

REVIEW QUESTIONS 995

CHAPTER 11
Alternatives to Expectation Damages:
Reliance and Restitutionary Damages, Specific Performance, and Agreed Remedies 1001

A. Reliance Damages 1001
Wartzman v. Hightower Productions, Ltd. 1001
Notes and Questions 1009
Walser v. Toyota Motor Sales, U.S.A., Inc. 1012
Notes and Questions 1017

B. Restitutionary Damages 1020
United States ex rel. Coastal Steel Erectors, Inc. v. Algernon Blair, Inc. 1020
Notes and Questions 1023
Lancellotti v. Thomas 1024
Notes and Questions 1030
Ventura v. Titan Sports, Inc. 1032
Notes and Questions 1042
Problem 11-1 1044

C. Specific Performance 1045
City Stores Co. v. Ammerman 1048
Notes and Questions 1055
Reier Broadcasting Company, Inc. v. Kramer 1059
Notes and Questions 1065

D. Agreed Remedies 1069
Barrie School v. Patch 1070

Notes and Questions 1080
Problem 11-2 1086
Problem 11-3 1086
Problem 11-4 1087
REVIEW QUESTIONS 1089

CHAPTER 12
Rights and Duties of Third Parties 1093
A. Rights of Third Parties as Contract Beneficiaries 1093
Vogan v. Hayes Appraisal Associates, Inc. 1096
Notes and Questions 1101
Chen v. Chen 1104
Notes and Questions 1112
Problem 12-1 1114
B. Assignment and Delegation of Contractual Rights and Duties 1115
Herzog v. Irace 1117
Notes and Questions 1120
Sally Beauty Co. v. Nexxus Products Co. 1123
Notes and Questions 1132
Problem 12-2 1134
REVIEW QUESTIONS 1135

Appendix: Answers to Review Questions *1137*
Table of Cases *1151*
Table of Uniform Commercial Code Provisions (UCC) *1171*
Table of Provisions from Restatement (Second) of Contracts *1175*
Table of Provisions from Restatement (First) of Contracts *1179*
Table of Provisions from Other Restatements *1181*
Table of Other Acts, Codes, and Rules *1183*
Table of Secondary Authorities *1185*
Index *1195*

PREFACE

The book you are holding (or perhaps reading in electronic form) is the ninth version of this collective work, which we call *Problems in Contract Law*. This book is "collective" not merely because it represents the long and happy collaboration of three friends and colleagues, but also "collective" because, like any law casebook, its content is the aggregate of the industry and insights of hundreds of judges, lawyers, and legal commentators, gathered from the accumulated wisdom of decades, even centuries. From the literally "cut-and-paste" days of the 1970s to the virtual world of the twenty-first century's second decade, we have seen information technology undergo vast, even cataclysmic, change. And although contract law is commonly considered one of the more stable areas of law, it too, has undergone tremendous change and remains today in a state of flux. Technological and sociopolitical developments are rapidly merging the American marketplace into a global one, and new forms of communication and data management have revolutionized the way contracts are made and administered, so much so that many now question whether the basic principles of the contract law of the last century can provide an adequate framework for the future. All of this makes a realistic survey of contract law for present-day law students a complicated and challenging undertaking.

To give the student some sense of the complexity of our legal world, this new edition attempts, like its predecessors, to sound several themes. The first and foremost of these, of course, is to give an overview of contract doctrine: the rules and principles, both common law and statutory, that make up what we think of as "contract law." For this purpose, we continue to present a varied collection of judicial opinions for study and analysis, and we have added seven new principal cases (plus citations to many more). As in previous editions, introductory text summarizes basic concepts, enabling the cases to focus on more challenging applications of doctrine, while the Notes and Questions after each case help the student to analyze that case and to place it in context with other parts of the material. Complementing case study with the problem method, we present throughout the book a series of lengthy, multi-issue Problems to help the student understand and apply the principles reflected in the text and cases studied. This edition includes eight new problems to offer teachers more flexibility in making assignments as well as provide more contemporary fact patterns. And through text, Notes, and occasional Comments, we point out some of the places where contract law overlaps with or is affected by other areas of law, such as Tort, Agency, Professional Responsibility, and forms of Alternate Dispute Resolution. Again in this edition, Review Questions at the end of each chapter enable students to test their understanding of the concepts and rules presented.

With contract law — as with all areas of law — knowledge of doctrine is not the end of study, but only the beginning. Starting with the introduction in Chapter 1 and continuing throughout the book, we urge the student to view the material from a variety of other perspectives. The first of these is *historical.* Text, cases, and Comments describe the development of our common law of contract in the English courts of Law and Equity, and trace the historical progression of American contract law from Holmes and Williston through Corbin and Llewellyn to the present day. With this added historical perspective, students may better see contract law for what it really is: not simply a collection of discrete rules, but a complex and constantly evolving system.

The second perspective these materials stress is the *theoretical* one. From the outset, the student encounters the various strands of modern academic thought about contract law. The materials present extended quotations from scholars representing all modern schools of analysis (some notion of their number and variety can be gained from the Acknowledgments, which follow this Preface), and text, Notes, and Comments provide citations to dozens of other scholarly works, for the guidance of instructors or students who wish to pursue these questions further. (For easy reference we have again included in the back of the book a table of scholarly authorities cited, along with the usual tables of cases and statutes.)

Besides the historical and theoretical aspects, these materials focus on the *lawyering* perspective, reminding the student repeatedly that the rules of law we encounter have an impact on real people in real disputes, and that creative lawyering in the contract area requires not merely knowledge of the rules of law but the ability to analyze and predict the effects of various courses of conduct that a client might undertake, in the light of those rules. Many of the Notes following the cases invite the student to consider two practice-related questions: How could an attorney have either prevented this dispute from arising or helped her client to obtain a better outcome than was achieved in the actual case? How will this decision affect attorneys in the future, in their roles as counselors, negotiators, and advocates? The Problems, which often cast the student in the role of an attorney at the pre-dispute stage, also raise questions of both law and lawyering, but without the benefit of already-reached judicial outcomes. The Problems can serve a number of functions for the student, such as integrating various strands of doctrine and providing a useful preparation for law school essay-type examinations. Probably their most important purpose, however, is to suggest that in real life there is likely to be not just one answer to a client's problem but a whole range of possible answers, some of which are clearly wrong, but many of which are at least plausibly right, in varying degrees. Living with ambivalence and uncertainty is not always pleasant, but the ability to do so is surely a more necessary lawyering skill than mastering the niceties of citation form.

The book is comprised of 12 chapters, which fall generally into the following parts:

Introduction	Chapter 1
Formation	Chapters 2-4
Interpretation and implication	Chapters 5-6
Defenses and grounds for nonenforcement	Chapters 7-8
Breach and remedies	Chapters 9-11
Third parties	Chapter 12

Material on the Uniform Commercial Code (UCC) is integrated throughout wherever it is relevant to our understanding of the general law of contract. A separate supplement, *Rules of Contract Law,* reprints important provisions and comments from Articles 1, 2, and 9 of the UCC, and the Restatement (Second) of Contracts and other relevant Restatement subjects, along with the Articles of the Convention on International Sales of Goods (CISG), the Principles of International Commercial Contracts, and other relevant statutes. It also presents material on contract drafting, a selection of sample law school examination questions (some with suggested answers), and additional background material on the arbitration of contract disputes.

The first edition of *Problems in Contract Law*, prepared by Professor Knapp, appeared more than forty years ago, in 1976, under the publishing imprint of Little, Brown and Company. Beginning with the second edition in 1987, Professor Crystal joined him as co-author, and made significant contributions to the book, both in substance and in style. With its third edition in 1993, the book first appeared — as it continues to do — under the auspices of the Aspen Casebook Series. In 1999, with the fourth edition, Professor Prince became the third co-author of the book, and made significant contributions of his own, both to the successive editions of the book itself and also to its supplement, Rules of Contract Law. Between the three of us, we thus have a combined total of over nine decades of experience in shaping and re-shaping the way that we present the body of contract law to successive generations of law students through these materials.

For each of us, collaboration on these materials has always been, and continues to be, not only an educational experience but a great pleasure as well. We hope that those who use this new volume will likewise find enjoyment as well as information in its pages. As our closing word to students and teachers about to embark on this journey with us, we sound once again the note that has introduced every edition of this book from the very start:

> No study of law is adequate if it loses sight of the fact that law operates first and last *for, upon,* and *through* individual human beings. This, of course, is what rescues law from the status of a science and makes its study so frustrating, and so fascinating.

It was true in 1976, and it still is today.

Charles L. Knapp
Nathan M. Crystal
Harry G. Prince

February 2019

Professors Knapp and Prince would like to thank the University of California Hastings College of the Law for its longstanding research support. Professor Crystal would like to thank his family for their support during this revision. We are grateful to our many colleagues who have used previous editions of this work and have been generous with their comments and suggestions for improvement.

We would like to thank the following authors and copyright holders for permission to reprint portions of their work:

Richard M. Alderman, Pre-Dispute Mandatory Arbitration in Consumer Contracts: A Call for Reform, 38 Hous. L. Rev. 1237-1238 (2001). Reprinted with permission.

P.S. Atiyah, Contracts, Promises and the Law of Obligations, 94 L.Q. Rev. 193, 211-212 (1978). Copyright © 1978. Reprinted with permission of Stevens & Maxwell, Ltd. and the author.

James T. Brennan, Injunction Against Professional Athletes' Breaching Their Contracts, 34 Brooklyn L. Rev. 61, 70 (1967). Copyright © 1967 Brooklyn Law School, Brooklyn Law Review. Reprinted with permission.

Carol L. Chomsky, Casebooks and the Future of Contracts Pedagogy, 66 Hastings L.J. 879, 884 (2015). Copyright © 2015 Hastings Law Journal. Used with permission of Hastings Law Journal and the author.

Arthur L. Corbin, Corbin on Contracts, Vol. 1, §29, at 82-85; Vol. 3, §539, at 81. Reprinted from Corbin on Contracts (1971) with permission of West Publishing Co.

William Dodge, Teaching the CISG in Contracts, 50 J. Leg. Ed. 72, 75, 82-83, 86-89 (2000). Copyright © 2002 by the Journal of Legal Education. Reprinted by permission.

E. Allan Farnsworth, Contracts §12.9, at 764-798 (4th ed. 2004). Copyright © 2004 by E. Allan Farnsworth. Published by Wolters Kluwer Legal Education. Reprinted with permission.

E. Allan Farnsworth, Legal Remedies for Breach of Contract, 70 Colum. L. Rev. 1145, 1149-1156 (1970). Copyright © 1970 by the Directors of the Columbia Law Review Association, Inc. All rights reserved. Reprinted by permission.

E. Allan Farnsworth, Your Loss or My Gain? The Dilemma of the Disgorgement Principle in Breach of Contract, 94 Yale L.J. 1339, 1382 (1985). Copyright © 1985. Reprinted with permission of the Yale Law Journal, Fred B. Rothman & Co., and the author.

Daniel Friedmann, Restitution of Benefits Obtained Through the Appropriation of Property or the Commission of a Wrong, 80 Colum. L. Rev.

504, 551, 553-554 (1980). Copyright © 1980 by the Directors of the Columbia Law Review Association, Inc. All rights reserved. Reprinted by permission.

Roger C. Henderson, The Doctrine of Reasonable Expectations in Insurance Law After Two Decades, 51 Ohio St. L.J. 823, 846-847, 853 (1990). Copyright © 1990 by the Ohio State University. Reprinted with permission.

Charles L. Knapp, Enforcing the Contract to Bargain, 44 N.Y.U. L. Rev. 673, 682-684 (1969). Copyright © 1969. Reprinted with permission of New York University Law Review and the author.

Charles L. Knapp, Rescuing Reliance: The Perils of Promissory Estoppel, 49 Hastings L.J. 1191, 1322-1323, 1325, 1334 (1998). Copyright © 1999 by the University of California, Hastings College of the Law. Reprinted with permission.

Charles L. Knapp, Unconscionability in American Contract Law: A Twenty-First Century Survey, from Commercial Contract Law: A Transatlantic Perspective, Cambridge University Press, Larry A. DiMatteo, Qi Zhou, Séverine Saintier, and Keith Rowley, Editors. Copyright © 2013 by Cambridge University Press. Reprinted with permission.

Arthur Allen Leff, Unconscionability and the Code — The Emperor's New Clause, 115 U. Pa. L. Rev. 485, 554-556 (1967). Copyright © 1967. Reprinted with permission of the University of Pennsylvania Law Review and Fred B. Rothman & Co.

Peter Linzer, The Decline of Assent: At-Will Employment as a Case Study of the Breakdown of Private Law Theory, 20 Ga. L. Rev. 323, 423 (1986). Copyright © 1986. Reprinted with permission of the University of Georgia Law Review and the author.

Ian R. Macneil, Efficient Breach of Contract: Circles in the Sky, 68 Va. L. Rev. 947, 968-969 (1982). Virginia Law Review, Copyright © 1982. Reproduced with permission of Virginia Law Review via Copyright Clearance Center.

Judith L. Maute, Peevyhouse v. Garland Coal & Mining Co. Revisited: The Ballad of Willie and Lucille, 89 Nw. U. L. Rev. 1341, 1358-1363 (1995). Copyright © 1995. Reprinted by special permission of Northwestern University School of Law, Law Review.

John E. Murray, Jr., Contracts §54, at 112-113 (2d ed. 1974). Copyright © 1974 Matthew Bender & Company, Inc., a LexisNexis company. Reprinted with permission. All rights reserved.

National Conference of Commissioners on Uniform State Laws, Uniform Premarital and Marital Agreements Act, Copyright © 2012 by National Conference of Commissioners on Uniform State Laws. Reprinted with permission.

Edwin Patterson, The Interpretation and Construction of Contracts, 64 Colum. L. Rev. 833, 853-854 (1964). Copyright © 1964 by the Directors of the Columbia Law Review Association, Inc. All rights reserved. Reprinted by permission.

Richard A. Posner, Economic Analysis of Law 128-132 (9th ed. 2014). Copyright © 2014 Richard A. Posner. Published by Wolters Kluwer Legal Education. Reprinted with permission of Wolters Kluwer and Richard A. Posner.

Harry G. Prince, Contract Interpretation in California: Plain Meaning, Parol Evidence and Use of the "Just Result" Principle, 31 Loy. L.A. L. Rev. 557, 619-620 (1998). Copyright © 1998. Reprinted with permission.

Geoffrey R. Watson, In the Tribunal of Conscience: Mills v. Wyman Reconsidered, 71 Tul. L. Rev. 1749, 1751 (1997). Copyright © 1997. Reprinted with the permission of the Tulane Law Review Association. All rights reserved.

Provisions, comments, and illustrations from the Restatement of the Law, Contracts (copyright © 1932), the Restatement of the Law (Second), Contracts (copyright © 1981), the Restatement of the Law, Restitution (copyright © 1937), and the Restatement of the Law (Second), Torts (copyright © 1965) are reprinted with permission of The American Law Institute. Portions of the comments to the Uniform Commercial Code, by the American Law Institute and the National Conference of Commissioners on Uniform State Laws (copyright © 1991), are reprinted with permission of the Permanent Editorial Board for the Uniform Commercial Code.

Unless otherwise indicated, references to Corbin on Contracts are to the revised edition, copyright dates from 1962 through 1971; references to Williston on Contracts are to the third edition (W. Jaeger ed.), copyright dates from 1957 through 1979. Footnotes from cases and other quoted material have been omitted without indication; where footnotes have been included, their original numbering has been retained.

We would also like to thank the following copyright holders for permission to reproduce the images in the book:

Amusement park, photograph copyright by elesi, reprinted with permission of 123RF.com.

Elizabeth Arden (neé Florence Nightingale Graham), photograph by Alan Fisher. Reproduced courtesy of the Library of Congress.

Camel Cash advertisement, courtesy of www.trinketsandtrash.org.

Crabby's Seafood Bar & Grill, photograph by Patrick Tuttle, reproduced with permission.

Lady Duff-Gordon, photograph from the George Grantham Bain Collection (Library of Congress). Reproduced courtesy of the Library of Congress.

Clint Eastwood and Sandra Locke during the filming of *The Outlaw Josey Wales*, photograph reproduced with permission of Pictorial Press Ltd / Alamy Stock Photo.

Joseph and Jonah Hadley's flour mill, photograph copyright © 2003-04 Hugh Conway-Jones, from http://www.gloucesterdocks.me.uk, reproduced with permission.

Highway along the coastline in Hawaii, photograph copyright by Steven Heap, reprinted with permission of 123RF.com.

Dr. & Mrs. Martin Luther King Jr., *World Telegram & Sun* photograph by Herman Hiller. Reproduced courtesy of the Library of Congress.

Mebane Bridge, photograph copyright © 2016 by Royce Haley, reproduced with permission.

N. Joseph Guidry tugboat, photograph by Glen Daigrepont, reprinted with permission.

Resorts Hotel in Atlantic City, NJ, photograph by B64 at English Wikipedia. Reprinted with permission through Creative Commons.

Ginger Rogers and Fred Astaire in a dance studio during the filming of *Swing Time*, photograph reproduced with permission of World History Archive / Alamy Stock Photo.

Sally Beauty Supply store, photograph by SallyBeautyPR via Wikimedia Commons. Reprinted with permission through Creative Commons.

Salmon cannery in Pyramid Harbor, circa 1912, University of Washington Libraries, Special Collections, Thwaites 247.32. Reproduced with permission of University of Washington Libraries.

SS Sky Princess, photograph by Aah-Yeah via Wikimedia Commons. Reprinted with permission through Creative Commons.

TCBY Yogurt franchise store, photograph copyright © 2014 by Kat Robinson/ Grav Weldon. Reproduced with permission.

Tobacco barns in Dunn, NC, photograph by Christopher E. Bickers, reprinted with permission.

W.T. Smith Lumber Company Saw Mill in Chapman, AL, circa 1930, image courtesy of Bendav Postcards.

Walker-Thomas Furniture storefront, photograph reproduced with permission of Dan Silverman/PoPville.com.

Problems in Contract Law

CHAPTER 1

An Introduction to the Study of Contract Law

Since you're reading this book, the odds are that you're a first-year student in an American law school. If so, you are about to embark on a task that will be long (probably three "academic years"), arduous (requiring a lot of reading and thinking and discussion), often rewarding, but inevitably sometimes discouraging as well. We—the authors of these materials—know that; we've been there too. First as law students ourselves, then as law teachers watching several generations of students wrestle with new and sometimes puzzling concepts, we are well aware that even to students with something of a "law background" (family members who are lawyers, work experience as a paralegal or in law-related activity, etc.), a lot of what lawyers think and talk about can seem complicated, confusing and—perhaps most troubling—often counter-intuitive.

Besides all that, the way in which law is traditionally taught and learned in American law schools may seem at first to be circuitous and inefficient. Instead of just reading and memorizing rules, we study "cases." Why should that be so? At least for some of the traditional first-year, "building block" subjects—such as Contracts, but also Torts and Property—it is for two reasons: One is because in the Anglo-American tradition the law in these areas developed from court decisions. This kind of law we traditionally call "common law"; it was created and shaped over time by judicial actions in individual cases, and in large measure remains so. And indeed, some of the decisions we will present for you to study have been landmarks in this process. By itself, however, that factor surely would not justify the degree of concentration on cases that this and other "casebooks" exhibit. There is another, stronger reason for studying the decisions of courts in actual cases: Reading and discussing opinions rather than merely reading "rules" enables us better to see that in the real world, *rules alone are often not determinative of outcomes*. There are plenty of easy cases, to be sure, where once you know the rule and the facts you will know (or should know, if you have been paying attention) the outcome of the case. But the case-disputes we will consider in these pages are not, by and large, of that kind. They are cases where reasonable persons—lawyers and judges—did *and reasonably could* disagree as to the proper outcome. It's not (just) the outcomes that we care about here, it's how the court got there. This is what is meant when people sometimes say that law school is about learning to "think like a lawyer": Not that law students should forget everything they knew before law school, but rather that they need to experience and master the process of reasoning toward a legal conclusion, using the modes of reasoning (and the terminology) that lawyers employ. And in the course of that study, hopefully, students can learn—*you* will learn—to understand and appreciate what the tools of lawyering feel like in the hand, and how to work with them.

Like other modern casebooks, these materials present not only case reports, but explanatory text, problems, and supplementary readings. (And our accompanying volume, Rules of Contract Law, contains other relevant and useful material as well.) Employing all these materials, we hope to stimulate you to think about both the theoretical and the practical side of contract law. We hope also to convey our shared sense that contract law is not merely a static set of rules. It is rather at any given moment a complex composite of what was in the past, what is now, and what is in the process of becoming. Law students of today will, when they enter practice, deal with lawyers and judges who recall clearly the last century's Seventies and Eighties, while themselves becoming the lawyers of this century's Twenties, Thirties, and beyond. We hope therefore to set before you at least some glimpses of the history of our law of contract, a reasonably accurate picture of its present state, and some suggestions of what a contract law of the future might look like.

A. WHAT DO WE MEAN WHEN WE TALK ABOUT "CONTRACT LAW"?

Certainly it is possible to talk for hours about something without ever defining it. Many terms in everyday use—"justice," "love," "medium-rare"—are notoriously elusive in meaning. Nevertheless, at the risk of spelling out what to many students may already be obvious, we would like at the outset to present some working definitions of terminology we will be using throughout these materials.

"Contract," as we will use that term, ordinarily means an *agreement* between two or more persons as to something that is to be done in the future by one or both of them. Sometimes, the word *contract* is used also to refer to a *document*—the set of papers in which such an agreement is set forth. For lawyers, *contract* usually is used to refer to an agreement that has *legal effect;* that is, it creates obligations for which some sort of legal enforcement will be available if performance is not forthcoming as promised. Thus, it will sometimes be necessary to distinguish among three elements in a transaction, each of which might be called a "contract": (1) the agreement *in fact* between the parties, (2) the agreement *as written* (which may or may not correspond accurately to the agreement-in-fact), and (3) the *set of rights and duties* created by (1) and (2). In these materials we will survey the ways in which such agreements are made and enforced in our legal system — the role of lawyers and judges in creating contracts, in deciding disputes that may arise with respect to their performance, and in fashioning appropriate remedies for their breach.

Contract law is but one of several subjects that make up the traditional first-year law curriculum. Besides the course in contracts, most law schools have first-year courses in torts, criminal law, and property (as well as courses in procedure — civil procedure and perhaps criminal procedure as well). Where does contract law fit into this pattern?

In the Anglo-American legal system, a great number of things — both tangible and intangible — are susceptible of "ownership." A diamond ring, the Empire State Building, "Spider-Man," computer software — all may be the "property" of one person or group of persons, which means that the state will protect the right of the owner to use, enjoy, and even consume that thing, to the exclusion of all other persons. The first-year property course traditionally focuses on the rules that in Anglo-American law govern the ownership of "real property" (land and the buildings on it), as well as some types of "personal" property, such as "goods" (tangible moveable property). Later you will have the opportunity to explore bodies of law relating to ownership of other, less tangible kinds of property, such as copyrights, patents, and shares of corporate stock.

Any society that recognizes property rights must also address the question of how it should respond when someone violates those rights. And property rights are not the only kind of individual rights that may need legal protection. Not all societies permit private ownership of wealth to the degree that ours does, but they are still likely to recognize the personal rights of individuals to be free from certain kinds of harmful conduct, such as the infliction of physical injury or other interferences with their individual freedom or dignity. The courses in criminal law and torts deal with different aspects of this question: Criminal law focuses on those violations of personal and property rights that society deems serious enough to be deterred by the threat of punishment for their commission (robbery, rape, and murder are obvious examples); tort law considers what remedy should be made available to the individuals who have been so injured. Because of the nature of the conduct regulated, criminal law and tort law overlap to a great degree, but they are not congruent. Many acts are criminal but not tortious, because they are offenses not against individuals but against the state — treason, for example, or tax evasion. Other acts, such as slander, may be tortious but not necessarily criminal.

Where does contract law fit into this picture? We have noted already that our society recognizes and protects a variety of types of property and personal rights. Ownership of property ordinarily includes the right to use and consume the thing owned, but in many cases it will be more to the advantage of the owner to transfer, or "convey," the right of ownership to some other person in exchange for something else of value (most likely money, but perhaps other goods or services). A piano is more valuable to one who can play it than to one who cannot, and two lots of adjoining real property may be worth much more when combined into one parcel than when held separately. Similarly, the ownership of factory machinery may be much more valuable when it is combined with a right to the work of skilled technicians and laborers, a dependable source of supply of raw materials, and licenses to use patented processes in the manufacturing of goods. Agreements for exchange are the means by which such resources are assembled and put to productive use. Some such agreements call for the immediate and simultaneous exchange of money for goods or services (your purchase of a newspaper, for instance, or of a hamburger). Where exchanges of any significant size are concerned, however, it is much more common for both the planning and the performance to be spread over a considerable period of time. The law of contracts is our society's legal mechanism for protecting the expectations that arise from the making of agreements for the future exchange of various types of performance, such as the conveyance of property (tangible and intangible), the performance of services, and the payment of money. (Agreements that call for future performance are often referred to as "executory" contracts, because their performance is not yet "executed"—i.e., not yet carried out.)

Before proceeding to examine contract law in more detail, we should point out that this description of the relationship between the various "substantive" bodies of law that you will be encountering this year is necessarily an oversimplified one. Legal problems do not always fit neatly into the pigeonholes that legal theorists have created; frequently they raise issues involving more than one body of law. For instance, you will learn in this course that some types of conduct that we call "fraud" can constitute both a breach of contract and a tort. Lease agreements between landlord and tenant have historically been governed by rules of property law, but recently courts have tended to analyze their legal effect more in the manner traditionally applied to contracts. The web of the law may not be quite as "seamless" as the old saying would have it, but students and teachers alike must beware of falling into the trap of believing that our various legal categories are ironclad and unchanging; they are not.

PROBLEM 1-1

The preceding text suggests that in these materials we will ordinarily use the term "contract" to mean an agreement between two or more persons, as to something that is to be done in the future by one or more of them, which potentially has legal enforceability.

(A) Think about your activities during the last week, before the first session of your contracts class. Using the above working definition, what types of contracts did you enter into?

(B) Consider the following hypothetical transactions. In which ones is a "contract" (again, using that term in the sense suggested above) involved?

1. Amalgamated Rubber Products, Inc., agrees to buy 35 percent (700,000 shares) of the outstanding common stock of Fargo Petroleum Corp. for $85 million.
2. Behnaz Salimian buys a used car from Tiptop Motors, Inc. She pays $2,500 down and agrees to pay the balance in installments of $300

per month for 24 months. Tiptop assigns its rights under that document to Sunshine Finance Corp. As required by the laws of her state, Salimian obtains a policy of auto liability insurance from Fidelity Underwriters Co.

3. Melissa Gant is hired as a driver for Interstate Motorfreight, Inc. The Teamsters Union acts as the bargaining representative of all employees of Interstate, and Gant becomes a dues-paying member of the union.
4. On her way to work on Monday morning, Darah Protas leaves an overcoat at the neighborhood laundry/dry-cleaning shop. The proprietor gives Protas a ticket with a serial number on it and says "Friday."
5. Avraham Hersh signs up for a free Facebook account, agreeing to Facebook's "Terms and Conditions," which allow Facebook to use his "likes" in marketing activity.
6. Sondra Michaels accepts Jay Krieger's proposal of marriage, and he gives her a lovely sapphire engagement ring. Sondra's parents send out invitations to 400 people, inviting them to the wedding on May 28. About 150 of those people are also invited to a reception, "R.S.V.P." Nearly 130 of the invitees do respond, indicating their intention to attend the reception. All the invited guests who attend the wedding send (or bring) presents to Sondra and Jay.
7. Before leaving for work in the morning, Kris Kovacks promises to take his entire family out to dinner that evening. Kris takes the family to a local fast-food restaurant for dinner. Numerous hamburgers, French fries, and sodas are consumed; the bill is $77.85, which Kris pays with a credit card.
8. Jack Clawson, a wealthy resident of Tucson, dies unexpectedly, leaving a will providing that his considerable estate is to go three-quarters to his daughter Maria and one-quarter to his son John. John is thinking of challenging the will because his father had told him that he was going to leave everything to his two children equally.
9. Aurooj Gulzar and Jennifer Lien, law students, decide to go skiing together over the weekend. Aurooj says she will drive her car, and Jennifer says that she will pay for gas and bring some snacks for the two-hour drive. They agree to split the hotel bill evenly.
10. Edelmira Diaz, a candidate for President, promises not to raise taxes. Diaz wins the election with more than 60 million votes.

B. THE STRUCTURE OF CONTRACT LAW

Unlike the law of torts or crimes, where the obligations imposed are defined by the state, contract law exists to enforce obligations created by individual persons (both flesh-and-blood people and corporations). Although many would argue that the state through its courts also plays a vital role in defining those obligations, nevertheless the core task of contract law is the enforcement of obligations voluntarily assumed by private agreement. So the body of principles and rules that we call "contract law" is essentially concerned with identifying and enforcing those agreements that do have legal effect.

Contract law has several principal divisions with which the student needs to become familiar. These materials will address them in the following order (although some instructors may choose a different arrangement):

1. Formation

Chronologically, the history of any particular contractual transaction begins with an agreement by the parties (there are usually two parties, but there may be more) that something will be done by one or more of them in the future. There are a variety of ways in which that sort of agreement can be reached. Sometimes the parties will negotiate by making "offers" and "counter-offers" back and forth until they reach an agreement sufficiently final and complete to form a basis for their future actions (and perhaps eventually for legal enforcement if necessary). Sometimes one party will prepare a form of agreement that it is willing to commit to without further negotiation, and invite the other party to express his/her assent to also being bound by it. Or perhaps one person—a "promisor"—will simply make a promise to another person in a form, or in circumstances, that make legal enforcement available to the "promisee" if that promise is not kept. There are a wide variety of kinds of agreements that have potential legal effect. Chapters 1-3 of these materials will survey some of the ways by which those agreements are formed, and some of the pitfalls along the way. Chapter 4 will consider a related topic—the possibility that some rule of law requires that an agreement be expressed in a writing or other kind of "record" to be legally enforceable.

2. Interpretation and Implication

Once it appears that an agreement susceptible of legal enforcement has been made, it is also necessary before enforcement takes place to know just what obligations the parties have undertaken. Of course that inquiry begins with the words that the parties have used, but often their conduct is also expressive of their intentions. Besides simply knowing the parties' own words and actions, it may be necessary for the court both to interpret those words and actions—they may be ambiguous or unclear—and to consider also whether there are additional rights or duties that the law might permit or even require a court to interpolate into that agreement. Chapter 5 will address some of the methods a court can use to give more precise meaning to the parties' own agreement. Chapter 6 considers a few of the principal "implied terms" that a court might find to be part of a contract.

3. Defenses to Enforcement

Even if the parties have apparently entered into the kind of agreement that a court could enforce applying the traditional rules of contract law, it may be that one of the parties claims to have some basis for avoiding enforcement against it. Those defenses are many and varied, but they fall into two main categories. One consists of defenses that are based either on some misconduct by one party in the making of the agreement that allows the other party to "avoid" the contract, or on some aspect of the agreement itself that violates a public policy strong enough to justify withholding enforcement. Chapter 7 addresses many defenses of this type. There are also defenses to enforcement based on events that take place after the agreement has been formed, events which affect the parties in a way that could justify a court in deciding to deny enforcement of their agreement. These defenses are not based on misconduct by either party, but simply on the failure of the parties to foresee and provide for events that alter the effect of their agreement. Although this latter group of defenses is applied relatively rarely, they are part of the body of contract law that a lawyer should be familiar with; they are considered in Chapter 8.

4. Nonperformance and its Consequences

If the parties have made a potentially enforceable agreement, and one (or perhaps both) of them fails wholly or in part to perform what that agreement calls for, what are the legal consequences? Sometimes the agreement itself provides that the duty of performance will not arise until certain circumstances—typically called "conditions" to performance—are met. In that case, failure of the condition to occur may simply mean that performance will not take place. If there is an unexcused failure to perform, however, this is typically regarded as a "breach," the consequences of which may vary depending on its seriousness and a variety of other factors. These matters are explored in Chapter 9. Once a court concludes that a wrongful nonperformance has taken place, it will face the question of what remedy is appropriate to compensate the party injured by that nonperformance, or to otherwise protect it from the consequences of the other party's breach. This most often consists of the award of money damages (discussed in Chapter 10), but it can also involve other remedies as well (some of which we will consider in Chapter 11). The question of what remedies should be available for the wrongful nonperformance of contractual obligations is so central to the social utility of contract law that many contracts teachers believe it should be studied first, even before the various other issues of formation, defenses, and the like. In these materials, the study of remedies is mostly left for the later chapters. It should be clear, however, that a general understanding of the scope and nature of contract remedies is essential to an appreciation of contract law as a whole.

5. Rights and Duties of Third Parties

Whatever their order of presentation, when a student has learned the essentials of the above four aspects of contract law, she will have "closed the circle," so to speak—acquired a sense of contract law as a coherent whole. There are other topics, however, that as a practical matter are significant parts of modern contract law. These involve the possibility that persons other than the original contracting parties may acquire rights and/or become subject to duties under that contract. One issue is whether as part of their contract the original parties intended to confer enforceable rights of some sort on one or more "third parties"—to make other persons "beneficiaries" of that contract. Sometimes this intent is clear from the parties' agreement, but it often involves a difficult judgment call for the court. Of considerably more commercial significance is the power that contracting parties often possess to transfer their rights under a contract (to "assign" those rights to someone else) or to arrange for someone else to perform their obligations (to "delegate" performance of their contractual duties). Much of our modern credit economy is based on the fact that many important types of contractual rights can be transferred from person to person—can be sold, in effect, or used as security ("collateral") for a loan. This collection of third-party doctrines (which we will explore in Chapter 12) is in a sense tangential to the theoretical structure that makes up the main body of contract law but, like the tail that transforms the letter "O" into the letter "Q," it makes a big difference.

C. THE SOURCES OF CONTRACT LAW

Having surveyed the components of general contract law, we next face the question: Where is this law to be found? From what sources—what "authority"—do courts derive the rules of law they apply to decide contract disputes? The types of authority we will consider fall generally into two categories: "primary" and "secondary." Primary authority, commonly viewed by lawyers and judges as "the law" itself, consists of prior judicial decisions (which collectively make up what we call the "common law") and statutes, ordinances, and the like (expressions of the will of a duly constituted legislative body on a subject within its proper sphere of action). Secondary authority might be very loosely defined as anything else that could appropriately influence a court; the examples we will consider, however, consist mainly of the two principal types of persuasive authority that have had marked influence on the common law of contract: commentary by legal scholars and the American Law Institute's Restatements of the Law.

1. Judicial Opinions

Historically, contract law developed in the Anglo-American system as judge-made law, rules distilled from a composite of court decisions in prior cases. Thus, one of your principal tasks in using these materials will be to learn how to read, understand, and apply judicial decisions. Our judicial system of decision making is commonly said to be one of *stare decisis*—adherence to past decisions, or "precedents." A precedent is a prior decision with facts sufficiently similar to the case *sub judice*—under adjudication—that the court feels obliged to follow it and to render a similar decision. A regime of law based primarily on precedent is commonly justified on two grounds. First, it offers a high degree of predictability of decision, enabling those who so desire to order their affairs in accordance with ascertainable rules of law. Second, it puts a rein on what might otherwise be the natural proclivity of judges to decide cases on the basis of prejudice, personal emotion, or other factors that we might regard as improper grounds for decision. Such a system also will obviously have the characteristic (which may sometimes be a virtue, sometimes a defect) of being static and conservative, generally oriented toward preservation of the status quo.

There will be times, however, when a common law judge concludes that blind adherence to precedent would produce an unjust result in the case presented for decision. There are a number of ways such a result may be avoided. To begin with, a precedent is considered to be "binding" on a court only if it was decided by that same court or by an appellate court of higher rank in the same jurisdiction. Other precedents — from lower courts or from other jurisdictions — are said to be merely "persuasive." If a precedent of the latter type is in fact *un*persuasive, the judge is free to disregard it. If the precedent is not merely persuasive, but binding, it cannot simply be ignored. It may, however, be avoided: If the facts of the present case do not include a fact that appears to have been necessary ("material") to the earlier decision, the court may "distinguish" the precedent and render a different decision. If the earlier precedent is indeed binding, but is difficult or impossible to distinguish, there is one other way to avoid its effect: If the court of decision is the one that created the precedent (or is a higher court), it can simply "overrule" the earlier decision. (This does not retroactively change the outcome for the parties to that earlier case, but it does change the rule for the case under decision and subsequent similar cases.) Overruling is considered a relatively drastic action and is usually reserved for instances in which the court feels that the rule established by the earlier precedent is simply wrong, that is, unjust in its general application because either it was ill conceived at the outset or it has been outmoded by later developments.

Some cases cannot be decided on the basis of precedent alone, either because no precedent exists (even in our litigious society it is surprising how often undecided issues arise) or because the applicability of precedent to the case at hand is unclear. In these cases, courts turn to "policy" to resolve the case. Policy may be regarded generally as any societal goal that will be furthered by a particular decision. These goals may be economic, political, social, moral, or some combination thereof, and may have to do with the particular parties themselves or the good of society as a whole (or of some definable segment of it). Lawyers and scholars often disagree on issues of policy (and you will soon find yourself engaging in this debate). As you review the court decisions in these materials and participate in class discussion, try to articulate the policy grounds for decisions or arguments that are being made.

2. Statutory Law

In 1677 the English Parliament enacted what is commonly referred to as the "statute of frauds." Subsequently adopted in virtually every American state, this statute requires certain types of contracts to be evidenced by a signed writing to be enforceable in court. With this notable exception, until the twentieth century, contract law was largely judge-made. As we shall see, even the statute of frauds has itself become so overlaid by court decisions that it has more of the quality of common law than of a modern statute.

The common law character of contract law changed significantly in the twentieth century, although it is still accurate to characterize contract law as predominantly judge-made rather than statutory. Probably the most important inroad on the historical character of contract law was the development of the Uniform Commercial Code ("UCC"), begun in the 1940s. (We will have much more to say about the UCC later in these materials.) In the 1960s, a wave of consumer-protection statutes at both the federal and state levels modified traditional contract principles. Other statutory influences on contract law will be mentioned throughout these materials. It should also be noted that in a few states (California is one important example), significant principles of the common law have been "codified," enacted into statutory form.

When a court decides a case governed by a statute, its reasoning differs from that used when common law principles are applied. If it chooses to do so, a legislature may if it wishes modify or eliminate any of the rules of common law. However, any court, even the highest court of the jurisdiction, is bound to follow the provisions of a valid statute that apply to the dispute before it. This duty stems from a fundamental political tenet of our society: The legislature has ultimate lawmaking power so long as it acts within the bounds of its constitutional authority. Sometimes, of course, the language of a statute may be subject to differing interpretations; in such cases, courts ordinarily seek to ascertain the legislature's purpose in enacting it, in order to adopt a construction that will best effectuate that purpose. Sometimes there is "legislative history" (legislative debates, committee reports, and the like) which sheds light on that purpose. It should be noted, however, that a few judges and scholars believe that courts should not resort to legislative history, but should only examine the text of a statute in deciding what it means. These critics of the use of legislative history argue that such sources are often self-serving and in any event only the language of the statute, not its history, has been enacted into law. See Antonin Scalia, A Matter of Interpretation: Federal Courts and the Law (1997). Nonetheless, most judges continue to resort to legislative history when interpreting statutes.

3. The Restatements

As we shall see, the UCC (as well as other "model" statutes) represented a response to the growing uncertainty and lack of uniformity in commercial law. In the early twentieth century, another institutional effort emerged to address these problems in a different way. In 1923, the American Law Institute (ALI) was formed. The major project undertaken by this organization was the preparation and promulgation of "Restatements of the Law"—what purported to be accurate and authoritative summaries of the rules of common law in various fields, including contracts, torts, and property. The first such Restatement to be issued was the Restatement of Contracts, officially adopted by the ALI in 1932. A revised version (the "Restatement (Second) of Contract Law") was promulgated in 1979. In form, the Restatements resemble a statute, consisting of "black-letter" statements of the "general rule" (or, where the cases appeared to conflict, the "better rule"), supported by commentary and illustrations. However, unlike a statute or a court decision, the ALI Restatements are only secondary authority, without the force of "law." Still, the Restatements have in fact proved to be remarkably persuasive; a court will often justify its decision of an issue of common law by simply citing and relying on the Restatement's rule on a given point.

4. Legal Commentary

Although they are only a secondary authority, the Restatements of Contracts have clearly had a powerful effect in shaping judicial views of what the common law of contract ought to be. Probably no other secondary authority has had quite that much impact on the law, but over the years a variety of published articles, textbooks, and treatises has been devoted to analyzing, evaluating, and synthesizing the immense body of contract cases that has accumulated in the reported decisions of American courts. Authors of these works have sought to clarify the law, to propose solutions for unresolved issues, and in some cases to argue strenuously and often effectively for legal change. In the aggregate, such commentary has been extremely influential in shaping the course of the common law of contract.

During the twentieth century, the most influential of these commentaries were clearly two multi-volume treatises, by Professors Samuel Williston and Arthur Corbin, respectively. Williston was the Reporter for the original Restatement of Contracts, and his ideas were reflected in its organization and content. Professor Corbin's treatise was not published until 1950, capping a long and distinguished scholarly career. Although he and Williston were friends and associates, and Corbin himself took part in the writing of the first Restatement, the two differed in fundamental philosophy. Williston tended to regard the law as a set of abstract rules that courts could by deduction use to decide individual cases; Corbin regarded his task as a legal scholar to be to discover what the courts were actually doing and to attempt to weave those findings into what he called "working rules" of law. The Williston treatise has been updated by Professor Richard A. Lord; the Corbin treatise has been revised and updated by scholars under the leadership of the late Professor Joseph M. Perillo.

Besides the works of these two giants of contract law, many shorter commentaries have appeared over the years. Among those currently in print, perhaps the most influential have been three one-volume treatises, originally written in the mid-twentieth century but periodically updated: one by the late Professor E. Allan Farnsworth, who served as Reporter for the Restatement (Second) of Contracts; one by the late Professor Joseph M. Perillo; and one by the late Professor John E. Murray, Jr. For issues arising under the UCC, lawyers and courts frequently turn to James J. White & Robert S. Summers, Uniform Commercial Code (6th ed. 2010).

5. International Commercial Law

Most transactions in which American lawyers are involved take place entirely within the United States, but international commercial transactions are of growing importance to our economy. Today, exports and imports of goods are a significant percentage of gross domestic product. Moreover, it is likely that international business will continue to grow in importance as various legal and technological barriers to cross-border dealings diminish. Students entering the practice of law in the twenty-first century must be familiar with the sources of law for international transactions.

Lack of uniformity of the rules governing international commercial transactions has been a major barrier to international trade. Attempts to overcome this problem go back at least to the 1930s. In 1980, under the sponsorship of the United Nations Commission on International Trade Law (UNCITRAL), a number of countries adopted a treaty, the United Nations Convention on the International Sale of Goods ("CISG"). The Convention formally became effective January 1, 1988. The CISG is analogous to the UCC. Like the UCC's Article 2 it applies to the sale of goods. Also, like the UCC it has the force of law, because it is a treaty. On the other hand, there are important differences between the CISG and the UCC. For example, the CISG does not apply to consumer transactions, while the UCC does. See CISG Article 2(a). The CISG generally applies when the parties to a contract have places of business in countries that have adopted the Convention. Thus, the CISG would apply to a sale of a machine from an American manufacturer to a French company, since both countries are parties to the CISG. The text of the CISG is reprinted in the Rules Supplement; we will also refer to various articles of the CISG throughout these materials to compare its provisions with domestic law.

The CISG does not purport to cover all issues of international contract law. To fill in the gaps left by the CISG, a private organization, the International Institute for the Unification of Private Law (UNIDROIT), has sponsored the preparation of Principles of International Commercial Contracts. Published in 1994, revised in 2004 and revised again in 2010, the Principles are analogous to the Restatements, providing scholarly opinion as to what the law is (or should be), but without the force of law that the CISG has. The Principles are also reprinted in the Supplement.

D. THE PERSPECTIVE OF CONTRACT THEORY

Throughout our study of contract law, we will of course be centrally concerned with learning to understand and apply the body of rules that courts and lawyers commonly regard as making up the present-day law of contract, both common law and statutory. At the same time, students and teachers should be aware that many commentators and analysts have tried over the years to go beyond mere identification and classification of such rules of law to examine the fundamental nature of contract law itself: what it consists of; how it has evolved; what goals and policies it serves; and where it fits into the broader picture of law as viewed through the lens of legal or moral philosophy, economics, political or social science, historiography, or any of the various other branches of inquiry into human life and thought.

From time to time in the course of these materials, we will attempt to paraphrase the conclusions of those writers or will present excerpts from their writings. Such descriptions and quotations will of necessity fail to do justice to the arguments and analyses presented in those works; the best evidence is always the original writings themselves. Any attempt at "thumbnail sketching" must be open to the charge that it omits significant matters and inaccurately summarizes or generalizes about the matters that it does include. Nevertheless, the following discussion is our attempt briefly to introduce you to some of the points of view you will see reflected in the commentaries that are cited and quoted in the chapters that follow.

During the Willistonian period, contract law was viewed as a set of universal rules distilled from decided cases; it did not appear necessary either to explain or to justify its existence. Because cases were to be decided by the virtually mechanical application of rules to reach a doctrinally "correct" result, judges had no need to use—indeed, were in effect forbidden to use—moral or political values in reaching their decisions. This "formalist" approach to law is initially identified with Christopher Columbus Langdell, Dean of Harvard Law School, father of the case method and author of the first legal casebook, on contracts. Professor Williston is usually regarded as the heir to the Langdellian tradition; his ideas, as we have seen, in turn permeated the original Restatement of Contracts.

In the early years of the twentieth century, legal scholars began to produce works that rejected the tenets of formalism. Dean Roscoe Pound of the Harvard Law School argued for a "sociological jurisprudence," in which rules of law would be evaluated on the basis of the social interests that they served. In the 1920s and 1930s, a group of scholars working in diverse fields of law called for a "realistic" jurisprudence. The "Legal Realists," as they came to be called, had a view of the legal system different from that of Langdell and Williston. They saw court decisions not as products of the application of neutral principles to given sets of facts, but rather as the end results of a decisionmaking process in which both the finding of facts and the application of rules were affected by the personalities, points of view, interests, and goals of the decisionmakers. Since all lawmaking was in effect policymaking, they argued, the formation of legal rules should be the result of a conscious application of all relevant knowledge of human affairs—including that furnished by other disciplines such as economics, political science, psychology, and anthropology—rather than a process (real or pretended) of "discovering" neutral principles from which abstract rules could be deduced.

Not surprisingly, the Realists were particularly critical of the "black-letter" law approach of the Restatements. One of the most influential of the Realists was Karl Llewellyn, who later became the principal drafter of the UCC. In his numerous books and articles, Llewellyn propounded the notion that judges should reach their decisions only after having immersed themselves in the factual details of the disputes before them. From this process, he believed, would come the "situation sense" that would lead to the right result. Llewellyn's influence on the UCC can be seen in its emphasis on general standards (such as "good faith" and "unconscionability") rather than on mechanical rules, and in the Code's reliance on such broad sources of "law" as trade custom and business practice.

Because they focused almost exclusively on the impossibility of achieving true objectivity in legal decisionmaking, the Realists were criticized by many — including even Dean Pound — for failing to address the social purposes and goals of the legal process. This criticism may not have been well founded, however, because at least some of the Realists appear to have had a social program of their own; they believed that by the application of "scientific" knowledge, the decisionmaking process could be tamed and (along with other social institutions) made to serve the ideal of a perfectible, "liberal" state. Events during and after World War II dealt a sharp blow to the liberal belief in the progressive improvement of human institutions, however, and the Vietnam War and the social ferment we know as "the Sixties" probably also contributed to this process. As a result, legal scholarship in general and contract scholarship in particular have appeared over the last several decades to be engaged in a process of deconstruction and reconstruction, attempting both to show the inherent failings of the old system and to find some new basis on which to give theoretical legitimacy to a body of legal principles applicable to contract disputes.

One school of thought that gained many adherents during this period advocates the application of methods of economic analysis to legal issues. Central to this economic approach to law is the notion of "efficiency." (While writers differ over the appropriate definition of "efficiency," generally efficiency is thought to be increased when the cost of transactions in society is reduced, and resources are allocated to their most highly valued uses.) Scholars identified with the economic-analysis school of legal thought ordinarily make two claims about the relationship between law and economics: (1) the "positive" or empirical argument that legal rules (particularly those of the common law) tend in general to reach "efficient" outcomes and (2) the "normative" claim that "inefficient" rules of law should be modified in the direction of greater efficiency.

Economic theorists differ among themselves on a number of issues in contract law. The predominant wing, the "Chicago school," led originally by former University of Chicago Professor (now Judge) Richard Posner, reached conclusions that are generally regarded as conservative, politically as well as economically. Thus, Chicago school theorists argued that courts should not refuse to enforce agreements merely because they are unfair or "unconscionable";

enforcement should be withheld only when an agreement is the product of such defined bargaining misconduct as "fraud" or "duress." However, other economic scholars have challenged the Chicago school's noninterventionist conclusions, arguing for statutes that require disclosure of information to consumers, regulate the language of contracts, and impose increased warranty obligations on manufacturers.

Other scholars, without necessarily rejecting the possibility that useful insights can be gained from economic analysis, argue that the focus on efficiency is much too narrow. Professor Ian Macneil claimed that most significant modern contracts arise in settings in which the parties have long-term commercial or personal relationships. Relying on this insight, Macneil and other scholars have argued that contract law should embody principles designed to preserve such relationships. Thus, relational scholars place emphasis on concepts such as good faith and fair dealing. Other scholars have turned to moral philosophy to construct principles of contract law. Professors Melvin Eisenberg, Charles Fried, and Randy Barnett—just to name three who have proceeded independently, and from diverse perspectives—have argued for principles of contract law based primarily on the concepts of fairness, morality, and consent.

Beginning in the 1970s, a loosely connected group of scholars engaged in work in a variety of fields of law that came to be known as "Critical Legal Studies" (CLS). Acknowledging a debt to the Legal Realists of an earlier day, the CLS scholars went even further with the process of deconstruction, to argue that attempts to justify the existing legal process are essentially a form of political ideology, mere rhetoric having as its consequence the preservation of existing distributions of power and wealth in society.

More recently, other scholars have expanded upon the insights of Critical Legal Studies. Arguing from perspectives of race and gender, these theorists have maintained that the law has often served the interests of white males at the expense of women and members of minority groups. This new group of critical scholars contends that both the substance and teaching of law should become more sensitive to the values and goals of these groups. By contrast, Professors Robert Scott, Lisa Bernstein, and Omri Ben-Shahar have recently argued for a return to formalism in contract law. Professor John Murray, on the other hand, finds that most theoretical scholarship creates "products that are useless to courts and practitioners." At the same time he finds "no redeeming virtue" in a revival of formalism because that approach would ignore the context in which disputes and transactional matters arise. John E. Murray, Jr., Contract Theories and the Rise of Neoformalism, 71 Fordham L. Rev. 869, 912 (2002). Murray argues instead for a return to the practical reasoning used by Corbin and Llewellyn.

Although standardized forms have been used in contractual transactions for well over a century, and the related problem of "contracts of adhesion" has received much attention from academics over the years, the explosive growth in online transactions since the turn of the century has engendered a sizeable literature addressing the many aspects of "boilerplate" contracting. Everyone agrees that boilerplate is entrenched in contracting behavior, and clearly here to stay, but there is less agreement about what that should mean to the legal system, both to contracting generally and to consumer contracting in particular. Authors who have confronted these issues in the past few years include Nancy S. Kim, Wrap Contracts: Foundations and Ramifications (Oxford Univ. Press 2013), Margaret Jane Radin, Boilerplate: The Fine Print, Vanishing Rights, and the Rule of Law (Princeton Univ. Press 2012), and Omri Ben-Shahar, Regulation Through Boilerplate: An Apologia, 112 Mich. L. Rev. 883 (2014).

E. THE LAWYERING PERSPECTIVE

As teachers, students, and scholars, it is necessary and appropriate for us to consider the theoretical bases that may explain, justify, or even help to create our law of contract. However, we assume that most readers of these materials will have the goal of becoming practicing attorneys. If you are indeed an aspiring lawyer, you should from the very beginning of your law studies be addressing the material not only from the perspective of a student or scholar, but also from the standpoint of what the law as you encounter it may mean to you as a practicing attorney, to your clients, and to the judges before whom you may appear.

As a practicing attorney, you can be sure that you will be called on to play all of the following roles:

Counselor. Your first task will invariably be to assist your client in identifying the nature and scope of her legal problem(s), ascertaining the client's legal position as objectively as you can. If your client is already a party to a dispute, this may involve predicting how a court is likely to respond to the case if presented; if the client is merely looking toward entering into a commercial transaction, this may mean exploring the legal consequences of the different forms that transaction might take. In any case, it will mean identifying the options available, making sure the client understands the legal and practical consequences of each, helping the client to choose between those alternatives, and then helping her to implement that choice.

Negotiator. You might be called on to represent your client in discussions looking toward an agreement with some other party. These might be attempts to reach an agreement on some sort of contractual arrangement, or they might be discussions aimed at settling a dispute that has already arisen. Negotiation requires first understanding the client's needs and aspirations, then working out with the client the parameters for an acceptable agreement; only then can you be ready to meet with the opposing party in an attempt to reach an agreement within those parameters. In negotiations, the lawyer's analytical skills will of course be called on, but rational legal analysis is only one aspect of negotiation. The skills of a bargainer include the ability to employ a variety of negotiating techniques. The skills of a negotiator may to some extent be inborn, but skills training programs in law school address the possibility that they can also be taught.

Drafter. Perhaps your client has already reached an agreement; perhaps your skill as a negotiator has produced an agreement on your client's behalf. In either case, it will ordinarily appear necessary for a variety of legal and practical reasons to reduce that agreement to a writing that the parties can adopt as the final and complete expression of their bargain. Here is perhaps the greatest call on the lawyer's skill with words—the ability to organize a complicated package into a coherent, accessible structure; the ability to write with economy, clarity, and precision; sometimes, the ability to say as little as possible on a point where this is preferable in the circumstances. For some types of agreement a "form book" or other source may supply a useful pattern, but even then the attorney must fully understand the ways in which the form needs to be modified to serve a client's own particular needs.

Advocate. For many years in the English system, certain attorneys served as "barristers" and argued cases in court; others were known as "solicitors" and had only an office practice. (Recent changes have modified this system.) Except in the largest of firms, law practice in the United States is usually not so specialized, so the chances are that you will from time to time find yourself in court. In approaching the case, you must of course engage in rigorous and completely objective analysis, in order to know what legal arguments there may be and the relative strengths and weaknesses of each. As an advocate, however, you will be required to present the most persuasive arguments you can on behalf of your client. While bound to represent your client's interests zealously, you may not engage in illegal or fraudulent conduct on your client's behalf. Your advocacy may take the form of oral argument or of written briefs and trial memoranda addressed to the court; you will also have to prepare formal written pleadings in the action.

We have stressed the role of the lawyer as counselor, negotiator, and drafter as well as advocate in the hope of making you aware from the outset of a very simple but important truth: Contract law in action is not just a body of rules. It is a complicated process by which attorneys and their clients make, perform (or sometimes fail to perform), and enforce exchange agreements. While contract litigation is an important component of practice for many attorneys, you should never forget that the vast majority of disputes that the rules of contract law *could* solve are *never submitted to a court for decision.* On any given day, the number of individual contracts entered into in even one of the United States must number in the millions. Of that huge total, a tiny fraction (but still a large number, in absolute terms) will eventually give rise to a dispute between the parties. Of these relatively few disputes, the overwhelming majority will be resolved without even coming to the threshold of a court, much less to judgment or a decision on appeal. The number of written opinions on which the common law is based, incredibly large though it may be, is to the commercial life of our country as is a sand castle, not just to the beach on which it sits, but to the globe of which that beach is a part.

This observation should not be taken to mean that case law is therefore irrelevant to commercial practice. Once a dispute has arisen, a lawyer's estimate of how that dispute would be resolved in court will be one of the most important factors she weighs in advising her client on what terms that dispute should be settled. It will not, however, be the only factor. Knowledge of the rules of law is an important, indeed indispensable, tool for the lawyer, but it may be no more important than a number of other ones, such as knowledge of business practices, human understanding, and simple common sense.

F. CONTRACT LAW THROUGH CASE STUDY: TWO EXAMPLES FROM DIFFERENT PERIODS IN TIME

We have suggested above a variety of perspectives from which the law student (as well as the law teacher, the lawyer, and the judge) can attempt to understand, evaluate, and apply the work of judges as expressed in the reports of decided cases. Reproduced below are two written opinions from different courts in different periods of time, one from the Supreme Court of Utah in 1923 and another from the Second Circuit federal appellate court in 2017. First read the opinions carefully, with an eye toward the following questions: (1) What happened between the parties that brought about the lawsuits? (2) What are the legal issues that each court is called on to decide? (3) How do the courts decide those issues, and why? And finally, (4) Does it appear that the passage of more than 90 years between these two decisions has resulted in changes in the manner in which the asserted contracts were made, or in the law that was applied? Then consider the Notes and Questions that follow the opinions in light of our discussions above.

Allen v. Bissinger & Co.

Supreme Court of Utah 62 Utah 226; 219 P. 539 (1923)

Before CHERRY, J., WEBER, C.J., and GIDEON, THURMAN, and FRICK, J.J.
CHERRY, J.

This is an action at law by the plaintiff to recover fees for furnishing defendant a copy of the official report of certain proceedings before the Interstate Commerce Commission. A trial before the court resulted in findings and judgment for the plaintiff, from which the defendant has appealed. The sufficiency of the evidence to support the findings is the only question to be determined. There is no substantial conflict in the evidence, the most important part of which consists of written communications between the parties.

The plaintiff resided in New York and was the official reporter for the Interstate Commerce Commission, and the defendant was a corporation engaged in buying and selling pelts, hides, and furs at Salt Lake City, Utah.

On July 20, 1918, plaintiff sent letters to various large shippers of freight, including defendant, as follows:

> "Re Consolidated Classification, Case No. 10204.
>
> Dear Sir: At the request of the Director General of Railroads the Interstate Commerce Commission will conduct an investigation concerning the reasonableness and propriety of the descriptions, rules, regulations, ratings, and

minimum weights provided in proposed consolidated freight classification No. 1, prepared by the special committee appointed by the United States Railroad Administration to consolidate the official, western, and southern classifications. Hearings will be held in several cities beginning at Boston, August 1, and concluding at Atlanta, September 19.

"A summary of the changes recommended in the proposed consolidated classification is inclosed. As these are of unusual interest and importance, those who want copies of the official reports of these hearings, which will be furnished at the usual rate fixed by the Commission, should advise us at once so that we may make enough to supply them without delay."

On July 31, 1918, the defendant wrote plaintiff:

"We will be interested in your official report of the different changes in the handling of freight and would ask you to put our name down for a copy of same."

On August 5, 1918, the plaintiff wrote defendant:

"Please accept our thanks for your order of July 31, for one copy of the official report of the proceedings in the Consolidated Classification Case No. 10204, which will have our prompt attention."

In pursuance of the correspondence, the plaintiff prepared a copy of the official report of the hearings held up to August 17, which was shipped to defendant by express on September 13, 1918; and later prepared a copy of the official report of the hearings held subsequently, which was shipped to defendant by express on October 5, 1918.

On October 10, 1918, the defendant wrote the plaintiff:

"We are just in receipt of another allotment of your Interstate Commerce Commission, and want to say to you that this is something that we cannot use at all and there is no use of you sending us anything further. We wish to return you what we have on hand at present and pay you anything that is reasonable for the trouble that you have been put to.

"In ordering these from you in the first place we expected to find all the information we wanted in one volume and did not think we were going to get a full library.

"Trusting you will look at this matter as a business proposition, with kindest regards."

To this the plaintiff replied on October 15, 1918:

"Replying to your letter of October 10, if agreeable to you, we will accept your cancellation effective at the end of the hearing of September 27. A copy of the report having already been made for you up to that point. We cannot accept cancellation of your order for that part of the report, because we cannot return to our employees and get credit for the labor which they have expended in making the copy for you." . . .

On November 4, 1918, and November 13, 1918, plaintiff prepared and shipped the copy of official reports of the remaining hearings had up to September 27, 1918, the various shipments together making one complete copy of the official reports of the hearings had between August 1, and September 27, aggregating 8,380 pages, for which plaintiff was permitted to charge at the rate of 12 1/2 cents per page. Plaintiff sent defendant a statement of the amount due, amounting to $1,047.50, and received in response the following letter dated December 20, 1918:

> "Your first and only statement of prices and account under date of December 14, just received. We are certainly surprised at the price you attempted to charge for same, and amount of these goods attempted to be put upon us. Referring once again to this matter, as stated before, these reports are absolutely useless to us, and we absolutely refuse to pay this account, and hold these goods subject to your orders."

On January 3, 1919, the plaintiff wrote:

> "Replying to your letter of December 20, our charge for these reports is the rate fixed by the Commission in the inclosed order, and no lower rate has been paid by any one for the official reports of hearings before the Commission in the last ten years.... Obviously no one could tell in advance how extensive the reports of this investigation would be, but our letter of July 27th gave you all the information we had, including the places of the hearings and the dates they were to begin, from which you must have seen that hearings were to be held all over the country and last a couple of months." . . .

It is insisted by appellant that the correspondence did not create a contract because the offer contained in plaintiff's letter was not accepted, and hence the minds of the parties never met. It is not contended that the letter relied upon as an acceptance contained anything which changed, added to, or qualified the terms of plaintiff's offer, but it is claimed that plaintiff offered to furnish a copy of the hearings, etc., of the Interstate Commerce Commission, and that the defendant agreed to take a copy of an "official report of the different changes in the handling of freight," and that therefore the parties did not refer to the same thing in the transaction, and never agreed upon the subject-matter of the contract. . . .

In 13 C. J. 265, the rule is stated as follows:

> "The apparent mutual assent of the parties, essential to the formation of a contract, must be gathered from the language employed by them, and the law imputes to a person an intention corresponding to the reasonable meaning of its words and acts. It judges of his intentions by his outward expressions and excludes all questions in regard to his unexpressed intention. If his words or acts, judged by a reasonable standard, manifest an intention to agree to the matter in question, that agreement is established, and it is immaterial what may be the real but unexpressed state of his mind upon the subject."

The offer of the plaintiff was to furnish one specific thing, viz. a copy of the official report of the hearings. There was no uncertainty or ambiguity in the offer. The thing offered was described with fairness and verity. The defendant's response to the offer was that —

> "We will be interested in your official report of the different changes in the handling of freight, and would ask that you put our name down for a copy of same."

The defendant's letter does not describe the official report with exactness. Considered by itself, its meaning in that respect might be doubtful. But viewed in the light of the plaintiff's offer the reply is responsive and relevant. Plaintiff described and offered but one official report. Defendant referred to and requested a copy of "your official report," etc., which phrase in ordinary commercial practice would be understood to sufficiently identify the matter referred to. The additional descriptive words used, "of different changes in the handling of freight," while lacking in precision, are fairly referable to the subject of the plaintiff's offer. Especially is this true, since it is not made to appear that there was any other official report known to the parties to which the acceptance could refer. Under the circumstances, we think the communications of the parties above referred to, judged by a reasonable standard, manifest an intention to agree upon the same thing, and that the evidence was sufficient, as a matter of law, to support the finding of the trial court that the plaintiff's offer was accepted by the defendant. . . .

The later complaints of defendant were that the reports were of no value to defendant, that it could not use them, and that the price charged was surprising. No objection upon the grounds that the defendant did not contract for the particular reports furnished was made until this action was filed. There is no claim of misrepresentation or fraud against the plaintiff. It may well be that the reports proved useless and of no value to defendant, and that in volume and price they exceeded its expectations, but, in the absence of some misconduct on the part of the plaintiff, the defendant cannot be relieved from the consequences of its improvidence, merely because the bargain is burdensome and unprofitable.

Judgment affirmed.

WEBER, C. J., and GIDEON, THURMAN, and FRICK, JJ., concur.

Meyer v. Uber Technologies, Inc.

United States Court of Appeals 868 F.3d 66 (2nd Cir. 2017)

CHIN, Circuit Judge:

OPINION

In 2014, plaintiff-counter-defendant-appellee Spencer Meyer downloaded onto his smartphone a software application offered by defendant-counter-claimant-appellant Uber Technologies, Inc. ("Uber"), a technology company that operates, among other things, a ride-hailing service. Meyer then registered for an Uber account with his smartphone. After using the application approximately ten times, Meyer brought this action on behalf of himself and other similarly situated Uber accountholders against Uber's co-founder and former Chief Executive Officer, defendant-appellant Travis Kalanick, alleging that the Uber application allows third-party drivers to illegally fix prices. The district court joined Uber as a defendant and denied motions by Kalanick and Uber to compel arbitration. In doing so, the district court concluded that Meyer did not have reasonably conspicuous notice of and did not unambiguously manifest assent to Uber's Terms of Service when he registered. The district court held that Meyer therefore was not bound by the mandatory arbitration provision contained in the Terms of Service.

For the reasons set forth below, we vacate and remand for further proceedings consistent with this opinion.

BACKGROUND

A. The Facts

The facts are undisputed and are summarized as follows:

Uber offers a software application for smartphones (the "Uber App") that allows riders to request rides from third-party drivers. On October 18, 2014, Meyer registered for an Uber account with the Uber App on a Samsung Galaxy S5 phone running an Android operating system. After registering, Meyer took ten rides with Uber drivers in New York, Connecticut, Washington, D.C., and Paris.

In support of its motion to compel arbitration, Uber submitted a declaration from Senior Software Engineer Vincent Mi, in which Mi represented that Uber maintained records of when and how its users registered for the service and that, from his review of those records, Mi was able to identify the dates and methods by which Meyer registered for a user account. Attached to the declaration were screenshots of the two screens that a user registering in October 2014 with an Android-operated smartphone would have seen during the registration process.

The first screen, at which the user arrives after downloading the application and clicking a button marked "Register," is labeled "Register" and includes fields for the user to enter his or her name, email address, phone number, and a password (the "Registration Screen"). The Registration Screen also offers the user the option to register via a Google+ or Facebook account. According to Uber's records, Meyer did not sign up using either Google+ or Facebook and would have had to enter manually his personal information.[2]

After completing the information on the Registration Screen and clicking "Next," the user advances to a second screen labeled "Payment" (the "Payment Screen"), on which the user can enter credit card details or elect to make payments using PayPal or Google Wallet, third-party payment services. According to Uber's records, Meyer entered his credit card information to pay for rides. To complete the process, the prospective user must click the button marked "REGISTER" in the middle of the Payment Screen.

Below the input fields and buttons on the Payment Screen is black text advising users that "[b]y creating an Uber account, you agree to the TERMS OF SERVICE & PRIVACY POLICY." *See* Addendum B. The capitalized phrase, which is bright blue and underlined, was a hyperlink that, when clicked, took the user to a third screen containing a button that, in turn, when clicked, would then

2. The screenshots attached to the Mi Declaration are larger than the actual size of the Samsung S5's screen, which is 5.1 inches, measured diagonally. The record does not contain accurately sized images of both screens. Uber submitted an accurately scaled screenshot of the Payment Screen with

display the current version of both Uber's Terms of Service and Privacy Policy.[3] Meyer recalls entering his contact information and credit card details before registering, but does not recall seeing or following the hyperlink to the Terms and Conditions. He declares that he did not read the Terms and Conditions, including the arbitration provision.

When Meyer registered for an account, the Terms of Service contained the following mandatory arbitration clause:

DISPUTE RESOLUTION

> You and Company agree that any dispute, claim or controversy arising out of or relating to this Agreement or the breach, termination, enforcement, interpretation or validity thereof or the use of the Service or Application (collectively, **"Disputes"**) will be settled by binding arbitration, except that each party retains the right to bring an individual action in small claims court and the right to seek injunctive or other equitable relief in a court of competent jurisdiction to prevent the actual or threatened infringement, misappropriation or violation of a party's copyrights, trademarks, trade secrets, patents or other intellectual property rights. **You acknowledge and agree that you and Company are each waiving the right to a trial by jury or to participate as a plaintiff or class User in any purported class action or representative proceeding**. Further, unless both you and Company otherwise agree in writing, the arbitrator may not consolidate more than one person's claims, and may not otherwise preside over any form of any class or representative proceeding. If this specific paragraph is held unenforceable, then the entirety of this "Dispute Resolution" section will be deemed void. Except as provided in the preceding sentence, this "Dispute Resolution" section will survive any termination of this Agreement.

Appellants' App. at 111-12.[4] The Terms of Service further provided that the American Arbitration Association ("AAA") would hear any dispute, and that the AAA Commercial Arbitration Rules would govern any arbitration proceeding.

B. The District Court Proceedings

. . .

After the parties began to exchange discovery materials, Kalanick and Uber filed motions to compel Meyer to arbitrate. The district court denied the

defendants' joint motion to stay the case pending appeal, which is reproduced below as Addendum A. In his brief on appeal, Meyer included what he represents are accurately scaled screenshots of both the Registration and Payment Screens. These are reproduced below as Addendum B. Although the parties have not challenged the accuracy of these images, we note that the screenshots in Meyer's brief are slightly smaller (approximately 4.8 inches, measured diagonally) than the screenshot of the Payment Screen in the record.

3. Although the hyperlink on the Payment Screen referenced "Terms of Service," the following screen referenced "Terms and Conditions." Because the initial hyperlink, which defendants argue notified Meyer of the arbitration clause, refers to the relevant agreement [as] the Terms of Service, we use that title throughout this opinion.

4. A copy of the Terms of Service in effect at the time Meyer registered for an account was attached to the declaration of Uber Operations Specialist Michael Colman, submitted in support of Kalanick's motion to dismiss the Amended Complaint. The applicable version of the Terms of Service had been updated last on May 17, 2013.

motions, concluding that Meyer did not have reasonably conspicuous notice of the Terms of Service and did not unambiguously manifest assent to the terms. *See Meyer v. Kalanick*, 200 F. Supp. 3d 408, 420 (S.D.N.Y. 2016). . . .

Defendants timely appealed the district court's July 29, 2016 order denying the motions to compel arbitration pursuant to 9 U.S.C. § 16, which permits interlocutory appeals from the denial of a motion to compel arbitration. The district court stayed the underlying action pending appeal on the joint motion of defendants, taking into account, *inter alia*, "the need for further appellate clarification of what constitutes adequate consent to so-called 'clickwrap,' 'browsewrap,' and other such website agreements." *Meyer v. Kalanick*, 203 F. Supp. 3d 393, 396 (S.D.N.Y. 2016).

DISCUSSION

We consider first whether there is a valid agreement to arbitrate between Meyer and Uber and then whether defendants have waived their right to enforce any such agreement to compel arbitration.

I. The Arbitration Agreement

We review *de novo* the denial of a motion to compel arbitration. *Specht v. Netscape Commc'ns Corp.*, 306 F.3d 17, 26 (2d Cir. 2002). The determination of whether parties have contractually bound themselves to arbitrate is a legal conclusion also subject to *de novo* review. *Id.* The factual findings upon which that conclusion is based, however, are reviewed for clear error. *Id.*

. . . Although determinations regarding mutual assent and reasonable notice usually involve questions of fact, . . . the facts in this case are undisputed, and the district court determined as a matter of law that no reasonable factfinder could have found that the notice was reasonably conspicuous and the assent unambiguous. *Cf. HM DG, Inc. v. Amini*, 219 Cal. App. 4th 1100, 162 Cal. Rptr. 3d 412, 418 (Cal. Ct. App. 2013) ("[I]f the material facts are certain or undisputed, the existence of a contract is a question for the court to decide." (citation and internal quotation omitted)).

We therefore review the district court's conclusions *de novo. See Specht*, 306 F.3d at 27-28; . . .

A. Applicable Law

1. Procedural Framework

Under the Federal Arbitration Act (the "FAA"), "[a] written provision in . . . a contract . . . to settle by arbitration a controversy thereafter arising out of such contract . . . shall be valid, irrevocable, and enforceable." 9 U.S.C. § 2. The FAA reflects "a liberal federal policy favoring arbitration agreements," *AT&T Mobility LLC v. Concepcion*, 563 U.S. 333 (2011) (quoting *Moses H. Cone Mem'l Hosp. v. Mercury Constr. Corp.*, 460 U.S. 1, 24 (1983)), and places arbitration agreements on "the same footing as other contracts," *Schnabel*, 697 F.3d at 118 (quoting *Scherk v. Alberto-Culver Co.*, 417 U.S. 506 (1974)). It thereby follows that parties are not required to arbitrate unless they have agreed to do so. *Id.*

Thus, before an agreement to arbitrate can be enforced, the district court must first determine whether such agreement exists between the parties. *Id.* This question is determined by state contract law. *Nicosia v. Amazon.com, Inc.*, 834 F.3d 220, 229 (2d Cir. 2016).

. . .

If the district court concludes that an agreement to arbitrate exists, "it should then consider whether the dispute falls within the scope of the arbitration agreement." *Specht*, 306 F.3d at 26 (quoting *Genesco, Inc. v. T. Kakiuchi & Co.*, 815 F.2d 840, 844 (2d Cir. 1987)). In this case, the parties do not dispute that Meyer's claims would be covered by the arbitration provision of the Terms of Service.

2. *State Contract Law*

"State law principles of contract formation govern the arbitrability question." *Nicosia*, 834 F.3d at 231. . . . We agree with the district court's determination that California state law applies, and note that New York and California apply "substantially similar rules for determining whether the parties have mutually assented to a contract term." *Schnabel*, 697 F.3d at 119.

To form a contract, there must be "[m]utual manifestation of assent, whether by written or spoken word or by conduct." *Specht*, 306 F.3d at 29. California law is clear, however, that "an offeree, regardless of apparent manifestation of his consent, is not bound by inconspicuous contractual provisions of which he is unaware, contained in a document whose contractual nature is not obvious." *Id.* at 30 (quoting *Windsor Mills, Inc. v. Collins & Aikman Corp.*, 25 Cal. App. 3d 987, 101 Cal. Rptr. 347, 351 (Cal. Ct. App. 1972)). "Thus, California contract law measures assent by an objective standard that takes into account both what the offeree said, wrote, or did and the transactional context in which the offeree verbalized or acted." *Id.* at 30.

Where there is no evidence that the offeree had actual notice of the terms of the agreement, the offeree will still be bound by the agreement if a reasonably prudent user would be on inquiry notice of the terms. *Schnabel*, 697 F.3d at 120; *Nguyen v. Barnes & Noble Inc.*, 763 F.3d 1171, 1177 (9th Cir. 2014). Whether a reasonably prudent user would be on inquiry notice turns on the "[c]larity and conspicuousness of arbitration terms," *Specht*, 306 F.3d at 30; in the context of web-based contracts, as discussed further below, clarity and conspicuousness are a function of the design and content of the relevant interface. *See Nicosia*, 834 F.3d at 233.

Thus, only if the undisputed facts establish that there is "[r]easonably conspicuous notice of the existence of contract terms and unambiguous manifestation of assent to those terms" will we find that a contract has been formed. *See Specht*, 306 F.3d at 35.

3. *Web-based Contracts*

"While new commerce on the Internet has exposed courts to many new situations, it has not fundamentally changed the principles of contract." *Register.com,*

Inc. v. Verio, Inc., 356 F.3d 393, 403 (2d Cir. 2004). "Courts around the country have recognized that [an] electronic 'click' can suffice to signify the acceptance of a contract," and that "[t]here is nothing automatically offensive about such agreements, as long as the layout and language of the site give the user reasonable notice that a click will manifest assent to an agreement." *Sgouros v. TransUnion Corp.*, 817 F.3d 1029, 1033-34 (7th Cir. 2016).

With these principles in mind, one way in which we have previously distinguished web-based contracts is the manner in which the user manifests assent — namely, "clickwrap" (or "click-through") agreements, which require users to click an "I agree" box after being presented with a list of terms and conditions of use, or "browsewrap" agreements, which generally post terms and conditions on a website via a hyperlink at the bottom of the screen. *See Nicosia*, 834 F.3d at 233; *see also Nguyen*, 763 F.3d at 1175-76.[7] Courts routinely uphold clickwrap agreements for the principal reason that the user has affirmatively assented to the terms of agreement by clicking "I agree." *See Fteja v. Facebook, Inc.*, 841 F. Supp. 2d 829, 837 (S.D.N.Y. 2012) (collecting cases). Browsewrap agreements, on the other hand, do not require the user to expressly assent. *See* Juliet M. Moringiello, *Signals, Assent and Internet Contracting*, 57 Rutgers L. Rev. 1307, 1318 (2005) ("[B]rowse-wrap encompasses all terms presented by a web site that do not solicit an explicit manifestation of assent."). "Because no affirmative action is required by the website user to agree to the terms of a contract other than his or her use of the website, the determination of the validity of the browsewrap contract depends on whether the user has actual or constructive knowledge of a website's terms and conditions." *Nguyen*, 763 F.3d at 1176 (citation omitted); *see also Schnabel*, 697 F.3d at 129 n.18; *Specht*, 306 F.3d at 32.

Of course, there are infinite ways to design a website or smartphone application, and not all interfaces fit neatly into the clickwrap or browsewrap categories. Some online agreements require the user to scroll through the terms before the user can indicate his or her assent by clicking "I agree." *See Berkson v. Gogo LLC*, 97 F. Supp. 3d 359, 386, 398 (E.D.N.Y. 2015) (terming such agreements "scrollwraps"). Other agreements notify the user of the existence of the website's terms of use and, instead of providing an "I agree" button, advise the user that he or she is agreeing to the terms of service when registering or signing up. *Id.* at 399 (describing such agreements as "sign-in-wraps").

In the interface at issue in this case, a putative user is not required to assent explicitly to the contract terms; instead, the user must click a button marked "Register," underneath which the screen states "By creating an Uber account, you agree to the TERMS OF SERVICE & PRIVACY POLICY," with hyperlinks to the Terms of Service and Privacy Policy. . . . [I]n *Nicosia*, we held that reasonable minds could disagree regarding the sufficiency of notice provided to Amazon.

7. This nomenclature derives from so-called 'shrinkwrap' licenses, in which a software consumer arguably assents to the license terms contained inside after breaking the shrinkwrap seal and using the enclosed software. *See Specht*, 306 F.3d at 22 n.4.

com customers when placing an order through the website. *Nicosia*, 834 F.3d at 237.[8]

Following our precedent, district courts considering similar agreements have found them valid where the existence of the terms was reasonably communicated to the user. . . .

B. Application

Meyer attests that he was not on actual notice of the hyperlink to the Terms of Service or the arbitration provision itself, and defendants do not point to evidence from which a jury could infer otherwise. Accordingly, we must consider whether Meyer was on inquiry notice of the arbitration provision by virtue of the hyperlink to the Terms of Service on the Payment Screen and, thus, manifested his assent to the agreement by clicking "Register."

. . .

1. Reasonably conspicuous notice

In considering the question of reasonable conspicuousness, precedent and basic principles of contract law instruct that we consider the perspective of a reasonably prudent smartphone user. *See Schnabel*, 697 F.3d at 124 ("[T]he touchstone of the analysis is whether reasonable people in the position of the parties would have known about the terms and the conduct that would be required to assent to them."). "[M]odern cell phones... are now such a pervasive and insistent part of daily life that the proverbial visitor from Mars might conclude they were an important feature of human anatomy." *Riley v. California*, 134 S. Ct. 2473, 2484 (2014). As of 2015, nearly two-thirds of American adults owned a smartphone, a figure that has almost doubled since 2011. *See* U.S. Smartphone Use in 2015, Pew Research Center, at 2 (Apr. 2015), http://assets.pewresearch.org/wp-content/uploads/sites/14/2015/03/PI_Smartphones_0401151.pdf (last visited Aug. 17, 2017). Consumers use their smartphones for, among other things, following the news, shopping, social networking, online banking, researching health conditions, and taking classes. *Id.* at 5. In a 2015 study, approximately 89 percent of smartphone users surveyed reported using the internet on their smartphones over the course of the weeklong study period. *Id.* at 33. A purchaser of a new smartphone has his or her choice of features, including operating systems, storage capacity, and screen size.

Smartphone users engage in these activities through mobile applications, or "apps," like the Uber App. To begin using an app, the consumers need to locate and download the app, often from an application store. Many apps then require potential users to sign up for an account to access the app's services. Accordingly, when considering the perspective of a reasonable smartphone user, we need not presume that the user has never before encountered

---

8. In *Nicosia*, the Amazon website stated on the left side of the page: "By placing your order, you agree to Amazon.com's privacy notice and conditions of use," with the latter phrases hyperlinked to the terms and conditions. *Nicosia*, 834 F.3d at 236. The user placed an order by clicking on a "Place your order" button on a different part of the page. *Id.*

an app or entered into a contract using a smartphone. Moreover, a reasonably prudent smartphone user knows that text that is highlighted in blue and underlined is hyperlinked to another webpage where additional information will be found.

Turning to the interface at issue in this case, we conclude that the design of the screen and language used render the notice provided reasonable as a matter of California law.[9] The Payment Screen is uncluttered, with only fields for the user to enter his or her credit card details, buttons to register for a user account or to connect the user's pre-existing PayPal account or Google Wallet to the Uber account, and the warning that "By creating an Uber account, you agree to the TERMS OF SERVICE & PRIVACY POLICY." The text, including the hyperlinks to the Terms and Conditions and Privacy Policy, appears directly below the buttons for registration. The entire screen is visible at once, and the user does not need to scroll beyond what is immediately visible to find notice of the Terms of Service. Although the sentence is in a small font, the dark print contrasts with the bright white background, and the hyperlinks are in blue and underlined. This presentation differs sharply from the screen we considered in *Nicosia*, which contained, among other things, summaries of the user's purchase and delivery information, "between fifteen and twenty-five links," "text... in at least four font sizes and six colors," and several buttons and advertisements. *Nicosia*, 834 F.3d at 236-37. Furthermore, the notice of the terms and conditions in *Nicosia* was "not directly adjacent" to the button intended to manifest assent to the terms, unlike the text and button at issue here. *Id.* at 236.

In addition to being spatially coupled with the mechanism for manifesting assent — *i.e.*, the register button — the notice is temporally coupled. As we observed in *Schnabel*,

> inasmuch as consumers are regularly and frequently confronted with non-negotiable contract terms, particularly when entering into transactions using the Internet, the presentation of these terms at a place and time that the consumer will associate with the initial purchase or enrollment, or the use of, the goods or services from which the recipient benefits at least indicates to the consumer that he or she is taking such goods or employing such services subject to additional terms and conditions that may one day affect him or her.

Schnabel, 697 F.3d at 127. Here, notice of the Terms of Service is provided simultaneously to enrollment, thereby connecting the contractual terms to the services to which they apply. We think that a reasonably prudent smartphone user would understand that the terms were connected to the creation of a user account.

That the Terms of Service were available only by hyperlink does not preclude a determination of reasonable notice. *See Fteja*, 841 F. Supp. 2d at 839 ("[C]licking [a] hyperlinked phrase is the twenty-first century equivalent of turning over the cruise ticket. In both cases, the consumer is prompted to examine terms of sale that are located somewhere else."). Moreover, the language

9. In evaluating the application interface, we use the actual-size screenshot of the last step in the registration process, as it would have appeared on Meyer's Samsung Galaxy S5.

"[b]y creating an Uber account, you agree" is a clear prompt directing users to read the Terms and Conditions and signaling that their acceptance of the benefit of registration would be subject to contractual terms. As long as the hyperlinked text was itself reasonably conspicuous — and we conclude that it was — a reasonably prudent smartphone user would have constructive notice of the terms. While it may be the case that many users will not bother reading the additional terms, that is the choice the user makes; the user is still on inquiry notice.

Finally, we disagree with the district court's determination that the location of the arbitration clause within the Terms and Conditions was itself a "barrier to reasonable notice." *Meyer*, 200 F. Supp. 3d at 421 (citing, *inter alia*, *Sgouros*, 817 F.3d at 1033). In *Sgouros*, the Seventh Circuit determined that the defendant's website actively misled users by "explicitly stating that a click on the button constituted assent for TransUnion to obtain access to the purchaser's personal information," without saying anything about "contractual terms," and without any indication that "the same click constituted acceptance of the Service Agreement." 817 F.3d at 1035-36. . . . Here, there is nothing misleading. Although the contract terms are lengthy and must be reached by a hyperlink, the instructions are clear and reasonably conspicuous. Once a user clicks through to the Terms of Service, the section heading ("Dispute Resolution") and the sentence waiving the user's right to a jury trial on relevant claims are both bolded.

Accordingly, we conclude that the Uber App provided reasonably conspicuous notice of the Terms of Service as a matter of California law and turn to the question of whether Meyer unambiguously manifested his assent to those terms.

2. *Manifestation of assent*

Although Meyer's assent to arbitration was not express, we are convinced that it was unambiguous in light of the objectively reasonable notice of the terms, as discussed in detail above. See *Register.com*, 356 F.3d at 403 ("[R]egardless whether [a user] did or did not say, "I agree" . . . [the user's] choice was either to accept the offer of contract, taking the information subject to the terms of the offer, or, if the terms were not acceptable, to decline to take the benefits."); *see also Schnabel*, 697 F.3d at 128 ("[A]cceptance need not be express, but where it is not, there must be evidence that the offeree knew or should have known of the terms and understood that acceptance of the benefit would be construed by the offeror as an agreement to be bound."). As we described above, there is ample evidence that a reasonable user would be on inquiry notice of the terms, and the spatial and temporal coupling of the terms with the registration button "indicate[d] to the consumer that he or she is . . . employing such services subject to additional terms and conditions that may one day affect him or her." *Schnabel*, 697 F.3d at 127. A reasonable user would know that by clicking the registration button, he was agreeing to the terms and conditions accessible via the hyperlink, whether he clicked on the hyperlink or not.

The fact that clicking the register button had two functions — creation of a user account and assent to the Terms of Service — does not render Meyer's assent ambiguous. The registration process allowed Meyer to review the Terms of Service prior to registration, unlike web platforms that provide notice of contract terms only after the user manifested his or her assent. . . .

The transactional context of the parties' dealings reinforces our conclusion. Meyer located and downloaded the Uber App, signed up for an account, and entered his credit card information with the intention of entering into a forward-looking relationship with Uber. The registration process clearly contemplated some sort of continuing relationship between the putative user and Uber, one that would require some terms and conditions, and the Payment Screen provided clear notice that there were terms that governed that relationship.

Accordingly, we conclude on the undisputed facts of this case that Meyer unambiguously manifested his assent to Uber's Terms of Service as a matter of California law.

3. *Remand for trial*

Finally, we see no need to remand this case for trial. Meyer offers no basis for his argument that we should remand for further factfinding if we vacate the district court's ruling, other than his assertion that no circuit has previously compelled arbitration in similar circumstances. Although Meyer purports to challenge the evidentiary foundation for the registration screens, defendants have submitted a declaration from an Uber engineer regarding Meyer's registration for and use of the Uber App, as well as the registration process and terms of use in effect at the time of his registration. Accordingly, we conclude on this record, as a matter of law, that Meyer agreed to arbitrate his claims with Uber.[11]

II. Waiver

[The appellate court held the trial court should decide whether the defendants had waived the right to arbitrate by litigating the dispute. — Eds.]

CONCLUSION

For the reasons set forth above, the order of the district court denying defendants' motions to compel arbitration is **VACATED**, and the case is **REMANDED** to the district court to consider whether defendants have waived their rights to arbitration and for any further proceedings consistent with this opinion.

---

11. Although Kalanick is not a party to the Terms and Conditions between Uber and Meyer, he is nonetheless protected by them. "Courts in this and other circuits consistently have held that employees or disclosed agents of an entity that is a party to an arbitration agreement are protected by that agreement." *See Roby v. Corp. of Lloyd's*, 996 F.2d 1353, 1360 (2d Cir. 1993) (holding that individual defendants were entitled to rely on arbitration provisions incorporated into their employers' agreements with investors notwithstanding that the individual defendants were not signatories to any of the agreements).

Addendum A (Appellants' App. 560)

Addendum B (Appellee's Br. at 38)

NOTES AND QUESTIONS

1. *Relevant legal standards.* You will soon study in more specific detail the law of contract formation and the meaning of the phrase "meeting of the minds." At this point does it appear to you that the courts in *Allen* and *Meyer* applied the same legal standard concerning the making of an enforceable agreement? Would you expect that the technological evolution that occurred between 1923 and 2017 would require that there be changes in the law as well? Even if the legal standards governing contract formation have not changed during this period, the context for applying those standards certainly has. What significant factual differences do you see when comparing *Allen* and *Meyer*?

2. *Assessing the merits of the customers' claims.* Both *Allen* and *Meyer* involve customers or buyers who were unhappy with the price charged and the product or service ultimately provided by the seller. How often do you think customers enter into a contract without knowing precisely what performance will be provided by the seller or the exact price to be paid? Should the courts be sympathetic to such customers?

3. *Applying an equitable resolution.* The customer in *Allen* stated repeatedly that the report held no value for it and proposed at one point in the correspondence to pay the seller some reduced price ostensibly to cover expenses. Do you think the court should have been open to some compromise solution short of requiring that the full price be paid?

4. *Questions of merit and procedure.* Note that the court in *Meyer* did not attempt to resolve the actual merits of the customer's claim. Rather, the court was deciding in what forum those claims would be resolved — either by a federal court or by an arbitration procedure before the American Arbitration Association. Why should it matter to the plaintiffs whether their case will be heard by a court or by arbitrators? Consider the bold face language in the arbitration clause quoted in *Meyer.*

5. *Choice of law.* The court in *Meyer* had to decide whether to apply New York or California law in analyzing whether Uber's terms and conditions, including the arbitration clause, were contractually binding on the plaintiffs. While the court concluded that the choice of law issue did not make a difference in this case because California and New York follow "substantially similar rules for determining whether the parties have mutually assented to a contract term," in other cases the choice of law may be determinative. In Cullinane v. Uber Techs., Inc., 893 F.3d 53 (1st Cir. 2018), the court, applying Massachusetts contract law, found that Uber's terms and conditions did not meet the Massachusetts standard of "conspicuousness." In addition, California courts have considered the context of the disclosure of contractual terms and conditions ("T&C") in deciding whether they are contractually binding. See Long v. Provide Commerce, Inc., 200 Cal. Rptr. 3d 117 (Ct. App. 2016), discussed in Chapter 2(D).

6. *Lawyering perspectives.* Throughout these materials we will raise "lawyering issues," questions that practicing lawyers will face in their roles as counselors, negotiators, drafters, and advocates. See section E above. *Meyer* presents

the obvious issue of the role that lawyers play as advocates for their clients, but less obviously the case raises questions of counseling and drafting. The Court in *Meyer* found that Uber's T&C were enforceable, but Uber prevailed only by convincing the Second Circuit to reverse the district court's decision. See also the *Cullinane* case in note 5, which decided against the enforceability of Uber's T&C. The court in *Meyer* held that the fact that clicking the register button had two functions — registration and assent to Uber's T&C — did not make Meyer's consent ambiguous, but the case could have easily gone the other way. As adviser to Uber, can you think of ways in which user assent to Uber's T&C could be improved? What reaction might you expect to receive from Uber to your suggestions?

7. *Theoretical perspectives.* As the introductory text indicated, you will find throughout these materials excerpts and summaries of scholarly perspectives on various issues of contract law. Presently you have been given only brief descriptions of these scholarly outlooks, but one way to distinguish among them is to consider the kinds of questions or concerns that a disciple of a particular scholarly method might raise about a court decision or holding. For example, a legal realist might ask for articulation and critical consideration of the social values a decision or rule promotes. Adherents of the economic approach to law will typically ask whether a decision or rule promotes or impedes efficiency. A supporter of relational contract theory will focus on whether the parties were engaged in either a discrete transaction or a long-term relationship and whether the existence of such a relationship should affect the decision in the case. Finally, a critical theorist might ask which social groups are benefitted or disadvantaged by a supposedly neutral rule. Would any of these questions seem helpful in understanding the decisions in *Allen* or *Meyer*?

REVIEW QUESTIONS – CHAPTER ONE

1. You are an attorney in a small American town. One of your clients asks you to represent her in dealing with a lawsuit being threatened by her next-door neighbor. The neighbor claims that your client promised to pay half the cost of trimming and maintaining several large trees on his property that overhang her property line, and that since that time he has paid a landscape expert several thousand dollars to do that work. She tells you that although they did discuss it, she never made such a promise. If you undertake to represent her in this matter, in what kinds of legal materials might you find it necessary or appropriate to do research?
   A. Court decisions in your jurisdiction.
   B. The Restatement (Second) of Contracts.
   C. Statutes in your jurisdiction applying to land use.
   D. The CISG.
2. Which—if any—of the following statements are definitely true?
   A. In our system of contract law, legislatures make "the law"; courts just apply it to resolve disputes.

B. Contract law is not concerned with "justice" or "fairness," but only with enforcing whatever agreement the parties have made.

C. Legal theory has no relation to the way that courts actually decide cases.

3. Which of the following statements is most likely to be true?

A. When analyzing a legal problem, an attorney always looks at things in the way most favorable to her client.

B. Many attorneys seldom if ever appear in court.

C. Attorneys don't negotiate deals for their clients, they just draft contracts for them.

D. When a contract dispute arises, it's likely to end up in court.

4. In *Allen v. Bissinger*, we have seen an example of a transaction conducted between parties separated by space, in which the U.S. mails were used to communicate. The only alternatives at that point in time (1918) would have been telegraph and long-distance telephone, because wireless cellphones and the Internet did not yet exist. Suppose they did, and the parties had been communicating with each other by e-mail. Would that have affected the outcome or the reasoning used by the court in the *Allen* case?

CHAPTER 2

The Basis of Contractual Obligation: Mutual Assent and Consideration

In this chapter, we will address the process which traditionally has been employed to create binding legal contractual obligations: The manifestation of two (or more) parties' mutual assent to an exchange of performances, supported by consideration. See, e.g., Restatement (Second) §17: Formation of a contract requires "a bargain in which there is a manifestation of mutual assent to the exchange and a consideration." Part A-1 of this chapter considers the extent to which the parties must actually intend their agreement to have legally binding effect. Part A-2 looks at some examples of the agreement-making process at work. Part B examines the element of "consideration," traditionally a requisite for the creation of a binding contractual obligation. Part C looks at the impact that the Uniform Commercial Code has had on the law of contract formation, beginning in the mid-twentieth century, and also notes the effect of international commercial law. Part D confronts the possibility that present-day technological innovation is currently in the process of transforming the rules of contract formation in fundamental ways.

A. MUTUAL ASSENT

Several points about the Restatement's requirements for formation of a contract should be noted at this point. First, the Restatement refers to the concept of a "bargain," to which the parties express their "mutual assent." Under the traditional model of contract formation, parties engage in the give-and-take of bargaining through a process of offer and acceptance, ultimately either reaching a deal or breaking off negotiations. It is important to recognize, however, that a contract can be formed even when the parties do not engage in a bargaining process. Noncommercial transactions involving family members, friends, or charitable entities may in some cases result in contracts even though the parties have not engaged in a formal negotiation. We will consider a number of such noncommercial transactions in this chapter.

Even within the commercial realm, contracts can arise despite the absence of back-and-forth bargaining between the parties. Consider, for example, the many contracts that you have entered into over the Internet, in which you checked a box stating "I agree" to various terms that you have scrolled through, probably without reading and almost certainly without bargaining. (We will see later in this chapter that substantial controversy exists over how the law should treat such "contracts." One of the principal reasons for this controversy is that these contracts typically involve some form of inequality of bargaining power between the parties.) An important thing to recognize at this stage of your studies is that a bargain resulting in mutual assent is the traditional and probably most important way in which a contract can be formed, but it is definitely not the *only* way.

Second, it is also possible that one person can incur legal obligations to another even though they have not entered into a consideration-supported contract. The doctrines of *restitution* and *promissory estoppel* involve possible liability between parties even though no contract in the traditional sense has been formed or even contemplated. We will examine these concepts in Chapter 3, and consider the policy reasons why contract law has come to recognize those additional bases of obligation.

Third, even if a contract has been formed, that is far from the end of the analysis. As we will see in later chapters, a party who has entered into a contract may be relieved of that obligation if the other party has engaged in some form of bargaining misconduct, such as fraud or duress (to name just some of the possibilities), or if circumstances that existed at the time of the contract have changed sufficiently to justify nonperformance.

1. Intention to be Bound: The Objective Theory of Contract

In applying the concept of mutual assent, many courts have stated that the formation of a contract requires a "meeting of the minds" between the parties. A subtle but important distinction exists, however, between the ideas of "mutual assent" and "meeting of the minds." Suppose S and B sign a written document which states that B agrees to buy a condominium in a new development that S is building. B later claims she did not understand that she was signing a contract — she had not yet decided to buy the condo, and thought that the document she signed simply "reserved" the condo for her without obligating her to buy it. S sues B for breach of contract, and the case goes to a trial before a jury. Suppose the jury believes that B is telling the truth and that she honestly did not understand that the document she signed obligated her to buy the property, but the jury also finds that S did honestly (and reasonably) think B was committing herself to the purchase. If contract law truly requires a "meeting of the minds" for contract formation, then the jury should decide for B. This view of contract formation has been described as "subjective" in that the actual intention of a party, rather than that party's conduct, determines the party's legal obligations. On the other hand, if contract law requires only a "manifestation of mutual assent," then (absent some fraud or other misconduct by S) the jury should decide for S, because both S and B did manifest their apparent assent by signing the contract of sale. The latter approach has been described as "objective," in that it looks at the conduct of the parties from the perspective of a hypothetical "reasonable person" rather than attempting to examine their actual, subjective intentions. Which approach should contract law use? Consider the following case.

Ray v. William G. Eurice & Bros., Inc.

Maryland Court of Appeals 201 Md. 115, 93 A.2d 272 (1952)

HAMMOND, Judge.

In an action in the Circuit Court for Baltimore County by the owners of an unimproved lot against a construction company for a complete breach of a written contract to build a house, the court, sitting without a jury, found for the defendant and the plaintiffs appealed.

Calvin T. Ray and Katherine S. J. Ray, his wife, own a lot on Dance Mill Road in Baltimore County. Late in 1950, they decided to build a home on it, and entered into negotiations with several builders, including William G. Eurice & Bros., Inc., the appellee, which had been recommended by friends. They submitted stock plans and asked for an estimate — not a bid — to see whether the contemplated house was within their financial resources. John M. Eurice, its President, acted for the Eurice Corporation. He indicated at the first meeting that the cost of the house would be about $16,000. Mr. Ray then employed an architect who redrew the plans and wrote a rough draft of specifications. Mr. Ray had copies of each mechanically reproduced, and in January, 1951, arranged a meeting with Mr. Eurice to go over them so that a final bid, as opposed to an estimate, could be arrived at. In the Ray living room, Mr. Ray and Mr. John Eurice went over the redrawn plans dated January 9, 1951, and the specifications prepared by the architect, consisting of seven pages and headed "Memorandum Specifications, Residence for Mr. and Mrs. C. T. Ray, Dance Mill Road, Baltimore County, Maryland, 9 January, 1951," and discussed each item. Mr. Eurice vetoed some items and suggested change in others. For example, foundation walls were specified to be of concrete block. Mr. Eurice wanted to pour concrete walls, as was his custom. Framing lumber was to be fir. Mr. Eurice wanted this to be fir or pine. In some instances, Mr. Eurice, wanting more latitude, asked that the phrase "or equivalent" be added after a specified product or brand make. All the changes agreed on were noted by Mr. Ray in green ink on the January 9th specifications, and Mr. Eurice was given a set of plans and a set of the specifications so that he could make a formal bid in writing. On February 14, the Eurice Corporation submitted unsigned, its typewritten three-page proposed contract to build a house for $16,300 "according to the following specifications." Most of the three pages consisted of specifications which did not agree in many, although often relatively unimportant, respects with those in the January 9th seven-page specifications. Mr. Ray advised Mr. Eurice that he would have his own lawyer draw the contract. This was done. In the contract, as prepared and as finally signed, the builder agrees to construct a house for $16,300 "strictly in accordance with the Plans hereto attached and designated residence for Mr. and Mrs. C. T. Ray, Dance Mill Road, Baltimore County, Maryland, Sheets 1 through 7 dated 9 January 1951 . . . and to supply and use only those materials and building supplies shown on the Specifications hereto attached and designated Memorandum Specifications — Residence for Mr. C. T. Ray, Dance Mill Road, Baltimore County, Maryland, Sheets 1 through 5 dated 14 February 1951 it being understood and agreed that any deviation from the said Plans shall be made only with the prior assent of the Owner. Deviations from the Specifications shall be made only in the event any of the items shown thereon is unavailable at the time its use is required, and then only after reasonable effort and diligence on the part of the Builder to obtain the specific item has failed and the owner has given his prior approval to the use of a substitute item."

The Memorandum Specifications referred to in the contract, consisting of five pages and dated February 14, 1951, had been prepared by Mr. and Mrs. Ray, the night of the day the Eurice Corporation delivered its three-page proposal, and after Mr. Ray had said that his own lawyer would draw the contract. On the 14th of February the January 9 seven pages, as they had emerged from the green ink deletions and additions made at the meeting in January, were retyped and from the stencil so cut at the Ray apartment, Mr. Ray had many copies mechanically reproduced at the Martin Plant where he is an aeronautical engineer. The rewritten specifications were identified as they are designated in the contract, namely as ". . . Sheets 1 through 5, dated 14 February 1951."

On February 22, at the office of the Eurice Corporation, on the Old Philadelphia Road, the contract was signed. Present, at the time, were Mr. Ray — Mrs. Ray was absent and had signed the contract earlier because she could not get a babysitter — Mr. John Eurice and Mr. Henry Eurice, who is Secretary of the Eurice Corporation. Mr. Ray relates the details of the meeting, as follows:

> I had copies, plans and specifications before me, as well as two copies of the contract. We sat down, Mr. John Eurice and I sat down and went over all of the items in the specifications. I volunteered to show him I had in fact changed the specifications to reflect their building idiosyncrasies, such as wanting to build the house with a poured cellar. We also went over the contract document item by item. Following that, we each signed the contract and Mr. Henry Eurice, being the other party there at the time, witnessed our signature. He was in the room during the entire discussion or review of the contract.

After the contract had been signed, Mr. Ray says he asked that the Eurice brothers help him fill out the F.H.A. form of specifications (required to obtain the mortgage he needed) since he was not familiar with the intricacies of that form. This they did, with Mr. Henry Eurice giving most of the aid. They used the memorandum specifications of February 14 where they corresponded with the F.H.A. form and in other instances, as where the memorandum specifications were not adequate, Mr. Henry Eurice gave the necessary information. After the F.H.A. specifications were completed, the meeting broke up and a copy of the signed contract and copies of the Plans and Specifications were retained by the Eurice Corporation.

Mr. Ray then obtained a loan from the Loyola Savings & Loan Association. To do this it was necessary that he furnish it with his copy of the contract as well as copies of the Plans, the specifications of February 14 and the F.H.A. specifications. Neither the plans nor specifications which were left with the Building Association were signed by the Eurice Corporation, nor, through a misunderstanding, had they been signed by either Mr. or Mrs. Ray. When they applied for the loan, Mr. and Mrs. Ray did sign the reverse side of each page of the drawings and of the contract specifications. Thereafter, in response to a call from the Building Association, Mr. John Eurice went to its office and signed the reverse side of each page of the contract, each page of the specifications of the five-page specifications of February 14, referred to in the contract, and each page of the plans dated January 9, and referred to in the contract, although he says that he did not look at any of these prior to signing them.

Settlement of the mortgage loan was made on April 19 and thereafter, Mr. Ray phoned Mr. John Eurice repeatedly in order to set a starting date for the construction work. He finally came to the Ray home on April 22 and indicated that he would start construction sometime about the middle of May. Other details of the work were discussed and Mr. Ray was given the names of a plumber and a supply company so that he could pick out and buy direct various products which would be incorporated in the house. Mr. Eurice, at that time, brought up the question of a dry well which had not been noted in the specifications, and which was required by the Baltimore County Building Code, and Mr. Ray agreed that he would make allowance for this, as he felt it was an honest mistake.

On May 8, Mr. Ray received urgent messages from the Eurice Corporation that his presence was desired for a conference. As he walked into the office, Mr. Henry Eurice picked up the drawings, specifications and the contract, and threw them across the desk at him, and onto the floor, with the announcement that he had never seen them, and that if he had to build according to those specifications he did not propose to go ahead. Attempts were made at the meeting to iron out the differences which apparently caused Mr. Henry Eurice to state that he would not live up to the contract. A second meeting was held at the Ray apartment several days later, and these efforts were continued by Mr. John Eurice, and that was the last contact that the Ray family had with any officer or agent of the Eurice Corporation. Realization that to build according to contract specifications would cost more than their usual "easy going, hatchet and saw manner" as Judge Gontrum described it, undoubtedly played a part in the refusal of the Eurice brothers to build the Ray house, although they testified that the excess cost would be only about $1,000. More decisive, in all probability, was Mr. Ray's precision and his insistence on absolute accuracy in the smallest details which certainly made the Eurices unhappy, and to them was the shadow cast by harassing and expensive events to come. For example, at the meeting where the specifications were thrown across the desk, Mr. Ray agreed that certain millwork and trim which the Eurices had on hand was the equal of the specified Morgan millwork. Mr. Henry Eurice testified as to this:

> He said that he thought ours were better. I said "if we put that in your house how will we determine it was right or not?" He said he would bring a camera and take a picture of the moldings in our shed and when they were constructed in the house take another picture, and see if it would correspond. I said, "Man we can't build you a house under those conditions. It is not reasonable." It created a heated argument for a while.

After written notice by Mr. Ray's lawyer to the lawyer for Eurice Corporation, that Mr. and Mrs. Ray considered that the contract had been breached and unless recognized within the week they would hold the Eurice Corporation "for any additional amount necessary to construct the house over and above the price called for in the agreement which has been breached by your client" had been ignored, suit was filed.

Mr. John Eurice agrees, in his testimony, that the Memorandum Sheets 1 to 7, dated January 9, had been gone over by him with Mr. and Mrs. Ray, but only as he says, to pick up "pointers." He also agrees that he had been told that the contract was to be drawn by Mr. Ray's lawyer, but says that he agreed only "so long as it is drawn up to our three page contract." He says that no specifications were attached to the contract which was signed, at the time it was signed, and Mr. and Mrs. Ray cannot say definitely that the specifications were physically attached, although both say that they were unquestionably in existence and Mr. Ray is unequivocal and positive in his statement that they were present, stapled together, and discussed at the time of signing the contract. Mr. John Eurice says that the first time he saw the specifications was when his brother Henry "chucked them out," and in response to a question as to where they came from, said: "They were laying on the desk on the opened mail." This, he says, was some two weeks after the signing of the contract. No effort has been made by the appellee to show how the specifications arrived in the office at this time, with the opened mail. No envelope, with what could be a significant postmark, was introduced. No stenographer or clerk was brought into court to say that the specifications had been received in the mail, or to say that they had been delivered by messenger, or by Mr. Ray. Mr. John Eurice does not deny that he signed the plans and specifications, as well as the back of the contract at the office of the Loyola Building and Loan Association, but dismisses this as a practice necessary in all cases where financing is to be obtained, which has no relation to or significance in connection with the actual agreement between builder and owner.

Mr. Henry Eurice says that, although he was present at the time the contract was signed, and signed as a witness, that no specifications were attached to either copy of the signed contract, and that he did not see Specifications 1 to 5 until "right smart later, maybe a month." When he did first see them "they were laying on the desk on the opened mail."

Mr. John Eurice says in his testimony that the contract which was signed February 22 was not the proposal the Eurice Corporation had made. He sets forth that he read the contract of February 22 before he signed it, and he admits that he read paragraph B, whereby the builder agreed to construct the building strictly in accordance with the plans and specifications identified by description and date. He says he thought that the specifications, although they referred to pages 1 through 5, were those in his proposal which covered only three pages. Mr. Henry Eurice says that he read the contract of February 22, and that he read the paragraph with respect to the plans and specifications, but that he, too, thought it referred to the three-page proposal. Both agree that the plans were present at the time of the signing of the contract.

On the basis of the testimony which has been cited at some length, Judge Gontrum found the following:

> The plaintiff, Mr. Ray, is an aeronautical engineer, a highly technical, precise gentleman, who has a truly remarkable memory for figures and dates and a meticulous regard for detail. Apparently, his profession and his training have schooled him to approach all problems in an exceedingly technical and probably very efficient manner. He testified with an exceptional fluency and plausibility. His mastery of language and recollection of dates and figures are phenomenal.
>
> The defendants in the case are what might be termed old fashioned country or community builders. Their work is technical but it doesn't call for the specialized ability that Mr. Ray's work demands. They conduct their business in a more easy going, hatchet and saw manner, and have apparently been successful in a small way in their field of home construction.
>
> The contract in question was entered into, in my judgment, in a hasty and rather careless fashion.

Judge Gontrum then cites the testimony of the Eurice Brothers that they had not seen Specifications 1 through 5 when they signed, and then says:

> . . . There is real doubt in my mind about the matter. Why the defendants signed the agreement without checking up on the specifications, I do not know, but they clearly were under the impression that the specifications referred to in the agreement were the specifications they had submitted some time prior and which they had permitted to be redrafted by the attorney for Mr. Ray. They both stated with absolute emphasis, and I do not question their veracity, that they were under the impression that the specifications in the agreement were the same which they had prepared.

He concludes by saying that he feels that Mr. and Mrs. Ray were under one impression, and that the Messrs. Eurice were under another impression, saying:

> . . . In my opinion there was an honest mistake; that there was no real meeting of the minds and that the plaintiffs and defendants had different sets of specifications in mind when this agreement was signed. The minds of the parties, so different in their approach, to use a mechanical phrase, did not mesh.

It is unnecessary to decide, as we see it, whether there was or was not a mistake on the part of the Eurice Corporation. It does strain credulity to hear that the Messrs. Eurice, builders all their adult lives and, on their own successful builders for fifteen years of some twenty houses a year, would sign a simple contract to build a house, after they had read it, without knowing exactly what obligations they were assuming as to specifications requirements. The contract clearly referred to the specifications by designation, by number of pages and by date. It permits, in terms, no deviations from the specified makes or brands to be incorporated in the house, without the express permission of the owner. This would have been unimportant if the Eurice three-page specifications had been intended, since generality and not particularity was the emphasis there. Again, the contract could scarcely have intended to incorporate by reference the specifications in the three-page proposal because they were not set forth in a separate writing, but were an integral part of a proposed contract, which itself was undated, and which was of *three* pages, while the specifications designated in the contract were dated and were stated to be in the contract, *five* pages. Further, it is undisputed that the five pages of February 14th were the seven pages of January 9, corrected to reflect the deletions and changes made and agreed to by Mr. Ray and Mr. John Eurice. The crowning challenge to credulity in finding mistake is the fact that admittedly the contract, the plans and the specifications were all signed at one sitting by the President of the Eurice Corporation at the Loyola Building Association, after they had been signed by Mr. and Mrs. Ray.

If we assume the view as to mistake held by Judge Gontrum, in effect the mistake in the written agreement which prevented its execution by the Eurice Corporation from making it a contract was an unilateral one. It consisted, in the opinion of the Court, in the Eurice Corporation thinking it was assenting to its own specifications, while in form it was assenting to the Ray specifications. If there was such a mistake, the legal result the Court found to follow, we think does not follow.

The law is clear, absent fraud, duress or mutual mistake, that one having the capacity to understand a written document who reads and signs it, or, without reading it or having it read to him, signs it, is bound by his signature in law, at least. . . .

Neither fraud nor duress are in the case. If there was mistake it was unilateral. The Rays intended their specifications to be a part of the contract, and the contract so stated, so the misconception, if it existed, was in the minds of the Messrs. Eurice.

Williston, Contracts (Rev. Ed.), Sec. 1577, says as to unilateral mistake:

> But if a man acts negligently, and in such a way as to justify others in supposing that the terms of the writing are assented to by him and the writing is accepted on that supposition, he will be bound both at law and in equity. Accordingly, even if an illiterate executes a deed under a mistake as to its contents, he is bound if he did not require it to be read to him or its object explained.

In Maryland there may be exceptions in proceedings for specific performance, but otherwise the rule is in accord. . . . See also the Restatement, Contracts, Section 70, where it is said:

> One who makes a written offer which is accepted, or who manifests acceptance of the terms of a writing which he should reasonably understand to be an offer or proposed contract, is bound by the contract, though ignorant of the terms of the writing or of its proper interpretation.

It does not lie in the mouth of the appellee, then, to say that it intended to be bound to build only according to its specifications. First, its claimed intent is immaterial, where it has agreed in writing to a clearly expressed and unambiguous intent to the contrary. Next, it may not vary that clearly expressed written intent by parol. And, finally, it may not put its own interpretation on the meaning of the written agreement it has executed. The Restatement, Contracts, Section 20, states the first proposition:

> A manifestation of mutual assent by the parties to an informal contract is essential to its formation and the acts by which such assent is manifested, must be done with the intent to do those acts, but neither mental assent to the promises in the contract nor real or apparent intent that the promises shall be legally binding, is essential.

Williston (work cited), Sec. 21, states the rule as follows: "The only intent of the parties to a contract which is essential, is an intent to say the words and do the acts which constitute their manifestation of assent." Judge Learned Hand expressed it in this wise: "A contract has, strictly speaking, nothing to do with the personal, or individual, intent of the parties. A contract is an obligation attached by the mere force of law to certain acts of the parties, usually words, which ordinarily accompany and represent a known intent. If, however, it were proved by twenty bishops that either party, when he used the words, intended something else than the usual meaning which the law imposes upon them, he would still be held, unless there were some mutual mistake, or something else of the sort." Hotchkiss v. National City Bank, D.C., 200 F. 287, 293.

. . . The test in such case is objective and not subjective. Restatement, Contracts, Sec. 230. . . . Williston (work cited), Sec. 94, page 294, says: "It follows that the test of a true interpretation of an offer or acceptance is not what the party making it thought it meant or intended it to mean, but what a reasonable person in the position of the parties would have thought it meant." . . .

We conclude that the appellee wrongfully breached its contract to build the plaintiffs a house for $16,300. The measure of damage in such a case presents no difficulty. Keystone Engineering Corp. v. Sutter, Md., 78 A.2d 191, 195. Here Judge Marbury said for the Court: "When a contractor on a building contract fails to perform, one of the remedies of the owner is to complete the contract, and charge the cost against the wrongdoer. Williston on Contracts, Rev. Ed. Vol. 5, §1363, p.3825, Restatement Contracts, ch. 12, §346, Subsec. (1)(a)(i), p.573 and Comment 1, p.576." See also, Carrig v. Gilbert-Varker Corp., 314 Mass. 351, 50 N.E.2d 59, 62, 147 A.L.R. 927. There the court said: "The owner was entitled to be put in the same position that he would have been in if the contractor had performed its contract . . . . We think the proper measure of damages was the cost in excess of the contract price that would be incurred by the owner in having the houses built . . . ." That figure is ascertainable with sufficient definiteness in the instant case. . . .

Judgment reversed with costs and judgment entered for appellants against appellee in the sum of $5,993.40.

NOTES AND QUESTIONS

1. *The objective theory of contractual intent.* At one point the law may have looked for a true, or "subjective" intention on the part of the promisor. In any event, at least since Oliver Wendell Holmes's lectures and writings in the 1880s began to have their effect, both the rhetoric and the actions of courts and writers have stressed an "objective theory" of contract obligation, by which one is ordinarily bound or not bound, not by her "secret intent" to that effect, but by the reasonable interpretation of her words and actions. Indeed, the objective approach to contract formation and interpretation was seen as one of the central tenets of classical contract law.

In his famous 1881 set of lectures, Holmes stated, "The law has nothing to do with the actual state of the parties' minds. In contract, as elsewhere, it must go by externals, and judge parties by their conduct." Oliver Wendell Holmes, The Common Law 242 (Mark DeWolfe Howe ed. 1963). Later Holmes offered what we would today call a policy justification for the objective approach, based on principles of efficiency and fairness: Inquiry into the subjective intentions of the parties would "greatly enhance the difficulty of enforcing contracts" (efficiency) and would be unfair because both parties are on notice that their words would be understood "according to usage of the normal speaker of English under the circumstance" (fairness). Oliver Wendell Holmes, The Theory of Legal Interpretation, 12 Harv. L. Rev. 417, 419 (1899).

Judge Learned Hand's "twenty bishops" observation, invoked by the court in *Ray*, has become the classic statement of the strict objectivist position, which as the *Ray* court indicates was espoused also by Williston. The Restatement (Second) rejects the subjective approach in §21. As we shall see, this does not mean that the promisor's intention to be bound (real or apparent) is never significant; in some situations it may be extremely relevant. For the most part, however, the law looks merely for a sufficient expression of apparent commitment to perform. Did the court in the Allen v. Bissinger case in Chapter 1 appear to apply this same legal standard?

Are the social policies served by the objective theory of contracts, as advocated by Holmes, Williston, and Hand reflected in the *Ray* decision? Does it appear to you that any important social goals would be served by using a subjective test, enforcing only those contracts that appear to reflect a true "meeting of the minds"?

2. *Credibility of the parties.* Does it appear to you that Judge Hammond, the author of the Maryland Court of Appeals' opinion in *Ray*, believed the Eurice brothers' testimony? Do you? Under the view of the case taken by the

Appellate Court, is the issue of their veracity material to the outcome of the case? Should it be?

3. *Nature of the parties.* Although contract law typically assumes the interaction of hypothetical individuals (e.g., the ubiquitous *A, B,* and sometimes *C* of the illustrations to both Restatements), in real life it is common for at least one of the contracting parties to be a business enterprise, conducting its affairs through the medium of a corporation. This was true in the *Ray* case, where the defendant was a corporation, although it seems to have been essentially the creature of the two Eurice brothers, John and Henry. Do you think John and Henry Eurice were equally involved in and aware of the negotiations with Calvin and Katherine Ray? If not, what effect might that fact have had on the progress of those negotiations?

4. *Disparity in bargaining power.* One of the central features of classical contract law was that it ignored any imbalances in bargaining power — in economic resources, knowledge, and a host of other factors — that might exist between the parties. In *Ray,* the Eurice brothers appear to have been knowledgeable in the construction business and the Rays were not (although Calvin Ray seems to have made up in compulsive attention to detail what he might have lacked in expertise), so it is perhaps not surprising if the court holds the Eurices to a high standard of self-protection in the bargaining process. But the principle applied against the defendant in *Ray* is not limited in its application to knowledgeable or powerful contractors. See Skrbina v. Fleming Cos., 53 Cal. Rptr. 2d 481, 485 (Ct. App. 1996) (applying the objective theory to an employee's signed writing that included release of his wrongful termination claims; employee asserted he understood signing was only a formality necessary to obtain his severance pay).

5. *Does the signing party have a "duty to read" what she signs?* In reaching results like those in the *Ray* and *Skrbina* cases, courts sometimes declare that the person who signs a document that was apparently intended to have legal effect should be held to its terms because she has a "duty to read" what she signs. In a recent article, Professor Knapp considers this proposition, and concludes that at most it should be limited to a "presumption of knowing assent," rebuttable by evidence to the contrary, and susceptible to being limited or overcome by other contract law principles such as duress, fraud, mistake, and unconscionability. Charles L. Knapp, Is There a "Duty to Read?", 66 Hastings L.J. 1083 (2015).

6. *Is the promisor serious?* Occasionally, the maker of a promise will claim that it was not made with serious intent — it was only a joke, and the other party either knew that, or at least reasonably *should have* known it. In Lucy v. Zehmer, 84 S.E.2d 516 (Va. 1954), a land-purchase contract was enforced by the buyer despite the seller's contention that he was only joking and had believed that the buyer was, too. The court found that, despite the setting (a conversation over drinks in a bar), the past dealings between the parties made it reasonable for the buyer to believe that the seller was serious, and the seller should reasonably have known that. See also Keith A. Rowley, You Asked for It, You Got It . . . Toy Yoda: Practical Jokes, Prizes, and Contract Law, 3 Nev. L.J. 526 (2003).

By contrast, the court in Leonard v. Pepsico, Inc., 88 F. Supp. 2d 116 (S.D.N.Y. 1999), *aff'd,* 210 F.3d 88 (2d Cir. 2000), found that the defendant was not bound contractually to sell plaintiff a Harrier jet plane worth $23 million even though the defendant had advertised the plane as available for purchase/redemption for 7 million "Pepsi points," which could be purchased for 10 cents a point (total of $700,000). The court found that no reasonable person would interpret the advertisement as having been seriously intended.

2. Offer and Acceptance in Bilateral Contracts

In the first chapter, we suggested that the notion of "contract" typically involves an element of futurity: a commitment to some course of action to be undertaken in the future. Although important types of transactions are exceptions, it also seems likely that most contracts of commercial importance will involve commitments on *both* sides: an exchange of promises in which each party promises to do something for the other. Such agreements have traditionally been referred to in the contract lexicon as "bilateral contracts." (Note: Our use of the term "bilateral" doesn't simply mean there are two parties; *every* contract involves at least two persons, and maybe more. The label "bilateral contract" is a legal "term of art," referring to a particular type of contract, one formed by the exchange of promises.) Since they involve an exchange of reciprocal commitments, bilateral contracts were seen by the classical theorists as typically being the product of a negotiating process often referred to as "offer and acceptance."

This process was envisioned as ordinarily involving something like the following: First, the parties engage in a period of preliminary negotiation, exchanging communications of a more or less detailed nature about the type of exchange of performances to which each would be willing to agree. Next, one party (the "offeror") makes an "offer" – a direct, complete proposal that a contract be entered into, providing for an exchange of defined performances. This has the effect of creating in the party to which that offer is addressed (the "offeree") a "power of acceptance." If that other party manifests her "acceptance" of the offer in a legally effective way, then at that moment a contract comes into being. If the initial offer is not acceptable, however, the offeree may respond by making a "counter-offer" of her own, which may in turn be accepted by the original offeror (thus giving rise to a contract different from the one he originally proposed). Of course, a contract may never come into being at all; the offeree may simply reject the original offer without making one of her own in return. Or, the offeree may delay too long in accepting, so that the power of acceptance created by the offer has been terminated, either by a time limit (explicit or implicit) contained in the offer itself, or by the offeror's withdrawal ("revocation") of his offer.

Such is the process of agreement-making on which the rules of classical contract law are premised. As succeeding chapters will demonstrate, it is no longer true – if it ever was – that this model of the bargaining process necessarily describes the way people actually behave. The number of types of exchange-agreements that fall within our definition of contract is staggeringly large, and in many instances the process of contract formation is radically different from the one described above. As a starting point, however, we will look at some characteristic applications of the traditional rules of contract law to disputes between persons who have engaged in the process of attempting to reach mutual agreement to a bargained-for exchange of promises — in other words, a "bilateral contract."

Lonergan v. Scolnick

California District Court of Appeal 129 Cal. App. 2d 179, 276 P.2d 8 (1954)

BARNARD, Presiding Justice.

This is an action for specific performance or for damages in the event specific performance was impossible.

The complaint alleged that on April 15, 1952, the parties entered into a contract whereby the defendant agreed to sell, and plaintiff agreed to buy a 40-acre tract of land for $2,500; that this was a fair, just and reasonable value of the property; that on April 28, 1952, the defendant repudiated the contract and refused to deliver a deed; that on April 28, 1952, the property was worth $6,081; and that plaintiff has been damaged in the amount of $3,581. The answer denied that any contract had been entered into, or that anything was due to the plaintiff.

By stipulation, the issue of whether or not a contract was entered into between the parties was first tried, reserving the other issues for a further trial if that became necessary. The issue as to the existence of a contract was submitted upon an agreed statement, including certain letters between the parties, without the introduction of other evidence.

The stipulated facts are as follows: During March, 1952, the defendant placed an ad in a Los Angeles paper reading, so far as material here, "Joshua Tree vic. 40 acres, . . . need cash, will sacrifice." In response to an inquiry resulting from this ad the defendant, who lived in New York, wrote a letter to the plaintiff dated March 26, briefly describing the property, giving directions as to how to get there, stating that his rock-bottom price was $2,500 cash, and further stating that "This is a form letter." On April 7, the plaintiff wrote a letter to the defendant saying that he was not sure he had found the property, asking for its legal description, asking whether the land was all level or whether it included certain jutting rock hills, and suggesting a certain bank as escrow agent "should I desire to purchase the land." On April 8, the defendant wrote to the plaintiff saying "From your description you have found the property"; that this bank "is O.K. for escrow agent"; that the land was fairly level; giving the legal description; and then saying, "If you are really interested, you will have to decide fast, as I expect to have a buyer in the next week or so." On April 12, the defendant sold the property to a third party for $2,500. The plaintiff received defendant's letter of April 8 on April 14. On April 15 he wrote to the defendant thanking him for his letter "confirming that I was on the right land," stating that he would immediately proceed to have the escrow opened and would deposit $2,500 therein "in conformity with your offer," and asking the defendant to forward a deed with his instructions to the escrow agent. On April 17, 1952, the plaintiff started an escrow and placed in the hands of the escrow agent $100, agreeing to furnish an additional $2,400 at an unspecified time, with the provision that if the escrow was not closed by May 15, 1952, it should be completed as soon thereafter as possible unless a written demand for a return of the money or instruments was made by either party after that date. It was further stipulated that the plaintiff was ready and willing at all times to deposit the $2,400.

The matter was submitted on June 11, 1953. On July 10, 1953, the judge filed a memorandum opinion stating that it was his opinion that the letter of April 8, 1952, when considered with the previous correspondence, constituted an offer of sale which offer was, however, qualified and conditioned upon prompt acceptance by the plaintiff; that in spite of the condition thus imposed, the plaintiff delayed more than a week before notifying the defendant of his acceptance; and that since the plaintiff was aware of the necessity of promptly communicating his acceptance to the defendant his delay was not the prompt action required by the terms of the offer. Findings of fact were filed on October 2, 1953, finding that each and all of the statements in the agreed statement are true, and that all allegations to the contrary in the complaint are untrue. As conclusions of law, it was found that the plaintiff and defendant did not enter into a contract as alleged in the complaint or otherwise, and that the defendant is entitled to judgment against the plaintiff. Judgment was entered accordingly, from which the plaintiff has appealed.

The appellant contends that the judgment is contrary to the evidence and to the law since the facts, as found, do not support the conclusions of law upon which the judgment is based. It is argued that there is no conflict in the evidence, and this court is not bound by the trial court's construction of the written instruments involved; that the evidence conclusively shows that an offer was made to the plaintiff by the defendant, which offer was accepted by the mailing of plaintiff's letter of April 15; that upon receipt of defendant's letter of April 8 the plaintiff had a reasonable time within which to accept the offer that had been made; that by his letter of April 15 and his starting of an escrow the plaintiff accepted said offer; and that the agreed statement of facts establishes that a valid contract was entered into between the parties. In his briefs the appellant assumes that an offer was made by the defendant, and confined his argument to contending that the evidence shows that he accepted that offer within a reasonable time.

There can be no contract unless the minds of the parties have met and mutually agreed upon some specific thing. This is usually evidenced by one party making an offer which is accepted by the other party. Section 25 of the Restatement of the Law on Contracts reads:

> If from a promise, or manifestation of intention, or from the circumstances existing at the time, the person to whom the promise or manifestation is addressed knows or has reason to know that the person making it does not

intend it as an expression of his fixed purpose until he has given a further expression of assent, he has not made an offer.

The language used in Niles v. Hancock, 140 Cal. 157, 73 P. 840, 842, "It is also clear from the correspondence that it was the intention of the defendant that the negotiations between him and the plaintiff were to be purely preliminary," is applicable here. The correspondence here indicates an intention on the part of the defendant to find out whether the plaintiff was interested, rather than an intention to make a definite offer to the plaintiff. The language used by the defendant in his letters of March 26 and April 8 rather clearly discloses that they were not intended as an expression of fixed purpose to make a definite offer, and was sufficient to advise the plaintiff that some further expression of assent on the part of the defendant was necessary.

The advertisement in the paper was a mere request for an offer. The letter of March 26 contains no definite offer, and clearly states that it is a form letter. It merely gives further particulars, in clarification of the advertisement, and tells the plaintiff how to locate the property if he was interested in looking into the matter. The letter of April 8 added nothing in the way of a definite offer. It merely answered some questions asked by the plaintiff, and stated that if the plaintiff was really interested he would have to act fast. The statement that he expected to have a buyer in the next week or so indicated that the defendant intended to sell to the first-comer, and was reserving the right to do so. From this statement, alone, the plaintiff knew or should have known that he was not being given time in which to accept an offer that was being made, but that some further assent on the part of the defendant was required. Under the language used the plaintiff was not being given a right to act within a reasonable time after receiving the letter; he was plainly told that the defendant intended to sell to another, if possible, and warned that he would have to act fast if he was interested in buying the land. . . .

The judgment is affirmed.

GRIFFIN and MUSSELL, JJ., concur.

NOTES AND QUESTIONS

1. *Was there an offer?* To the appellate court that decided *Lonergan,* the principal issue was whether an offer had been made. Many contract cases have turned on the question whether a given communication did amount in legal contemplation to an offer, or whether it was merely a "preliminary negotiation" or an "invitation for an offer." The words used by the parties will be relevant, but not necessarily decisive; even a communication that uses the word *offer* may not be held to be an offer in the legal sense. E.g., Moulton v. Kershaw, 18 N.W. 172 (Wis. 1884) ("we are authorized to offer Michigan fine salt, in full car-load lots of 80 to 95 bbls . . . at 85c. per bbl . . ." held to be only an invitation for offers). See Restatement (Second) §24 (an offer invites assent to conclude the bargain). Restatement (Second) §26 provides that a communication is not

an offer if the person making the communication does not intend to enter into a bargain until the person has made a "further manifestation of assent." See Kerns v. Range Res.-Appalachia, LLC, 2011 U.S. Dist. LEXIS 4473 (N.D.W. Va.) (holding that defendant's communication that it "would consider" a delayed lease did not constitute an offer under Restatement (Second) §§24, 26 and illustration 4). Applying §§24 and 26, what factors are relevant to resolution of this issue? Would you agree with the court in *Lonergan* that the defendant's letter of April 8 did not rise to the level of an offer?

2. *An alternate basis for the **Lonergan** result: The "mailbox rule."* In *Lonergan*, the trial court also held that the plaintiff could not recover, but not because the defendant never made an offer; it ruled that the plaintiff had failed to make a timely acceptance. Does the Appellate Court's basis for decision appear to you a better one? If the defendant's letter of April 8 had amounted legally to an offer, then it would be necessary to decide how long the plaintiff's power of acceptance lasted, and whether he effectively accepted before it terminated. The plaintiff responded by mailing a letter of attempted acceptance on April 15; if on that date there was actually an offer still open for acceptance, would plaintiff's act of mailing that letter have completed the formation of a contract?

Although Anglo-American common law has traditionally held that both an offer and a revocation (by the offeror) must be *received* to be effective, an acceptance (by the *offeree*) will in some circumstances be treated as effective as soon as it was dispatched (mailed, telegraphed, etc.) by the offeree. E.g., Morton's of Chicago/Great Neck LLC v. Crab House, Inc., 746 N.Y.S.2d 317 (App. Div. 2002) (oral acceptance of written lease renewal agreement effective; even if not, acceptor mailed written acceptance before offeror faxed its notice of revocation); compare Gibbs v. American Sav. & Loan Assn., 266 Cal. Rptr. 517 (Ct. App. 1990) (offer not accepted merely by plaintiff giving it to mail clerk in her office; acceptance would occur only when deposited in U.S. mail, by which time revocation had been received). See generally Restatement (Second) §§63 (basic rule, exception for option contracts), 65 (medium of acceptance must be reasonable in circumstances), 66 (only applies where acceptance properly stamped, addressed, etc.). This rule — commonly known as the "deposited acceptance," or "mailbox" rule — will not apply, however, if the offeror has stated (expressly or by implication) that he must *receive* the acceptance for it to be effective. Restatement (Second) §§30, 63. This rule follows from the general concept that the offeror is the "master of the offer." Id. §29, Comment *a*.

Should the mailbox rule apply to contracts formed over the Internet? See Amelia Rawls, Contract Formation in an Internet Age, 10 Colum. Sci. & Tech. L. Rev. 200 (2009) (arguing that in an era of "near-instantaneous" electronic communication, acceptances should be treated as valid on receipt).

3. *The deposited acceptance rule under the CISG.* We noted earlier that the United States is a party to the Convention on Contracts for the International Sale of Goods (CISG). In Article 16(1), the CISG adopts a version of the mailbox rule, by providing that an otherwise revocable offer cannot be revoked once an

acceptance has been dispatched. CISG Article 18(2) modifies the common law mailbox rule, however, by placing the risk of non-arrival of the acceptance on the offeree rather than the offeror. Thus, to be legally effective in concluding the bargain at the time of its dispatch, the acceptance must actually reach the offeror in a timely fashion. A "lost acceptance" would not have that effect. See William S. Dodge, Teaching the CISG in Contracts, 50 J. Leg. Ed. 72, 81 (2000) ("CISG's rule . . . places the risk of a lost communication on the party who is in the best position to prevent that loss by choosing a more reliable means of communication").

4. *Advertisements as invitations to receive offers.* The general rule is that advertisements constitute invitations to receive offers rather than actual offers. See Comment *b* to Restatement (Second) §26: "Advertisements of goods by display, sign, handbill, newspaper, radio or television are not ordinarily intended or understood as offers to sell. . . . [T]o make an offer by an advertisement . . . there must ordinarily be some language of commitment or some invitation to take action without further communication." See Zanakis-Pico v. Cutter Dodge, Inc., 47 P.3d 1222 (Haw. 2002) (following "well-established principles," advertisements are generally not offers unless they invite acceptance without further negotiations in clear, definite, express, and unconditional language). The leading case finding an advertisement to be an offer is Lefkowitz v. Great Minneapolis Surplus Store, 86 N.W.2d 689 (Minn. 1957) where the defendant advertised one or two items of each kind — fur coats, etc. — at extremely low prices, with the additional language "first come, first served." In addition, if the seller is apparently engaged in "bait and switch" or other deceptive conduct, the court may treat the advertisement as an offer or may subject the seller to liability under unfair trade practice or other consumer protection statutes. See Izadi v. Machado (Gus) Ford, Inc., 550 So. 2d 1135 (Fl. Dist. Ct. App. 1989).

Normile v. Miller

Supreme Court of North Carolina 313 N.C. 98, 326 S.E.2d 11 (1985)

FRYE, Justice.

Defendant Hazel Miller owned real estate located in Charlotte, North Carolina. On 4 August 1980, the property was listed for sale with a local realtor, Gladys Hawkins. On that same day, Richard Byer, a real estate broker with the realty firm Gallery of Homes, showed the property to the prospective purchasers, Plaintiffs Normile and Kurniawan. Afterwards, Byer helped plaintiffs prepare a written offer to purchase the property. A Gallery of Homes form, entitled "DEPOSIT RECEIPT AND CONTRACT FOR PURCHASE AND SALE OF REAL ESTATE," containing blanks for the insertion of terms pertinent to the purchasers' offer, was completed in quadruplicate and signed by Normile and Kurniawan. One specific standard provision in Paragraph 9 included a blank that was filled in with the time and date to read as follows: "OFFER & CLOSING DATE: Time is of the essence, therefore this offer must be accepted on or before *5:00 p.m. Aug. 5th 1980.* A signed copy shall be promptly returned to the purchaser."

Byer took the offer to purchase form to Gladys Hawkins, who presented it to defendant. Later that evening, Gladys Hawkins returned the executed form to Byer. It had been signed under seal by defendant, with several changes in the terms having been made thereon and initialed by defendant. The primary changes made by defendant were an increase in the earnest money deposit ($100 to $500); an increase in the down payment due at closing ($875 to $1,000); a decrease in the unpaid principal of the existing mortgage amount ($18,525 to $18,000); a decrease in the term of the loan from seller (25 years to 20 years); and a purchaser qualification contingency added in the outer margin of the form.

That same evening, Byer presented defendant's counteroffer to Plaintiff Normile. Byer testified in his deposition that Normile did not have $500 for the earnest money deposit, one of the requirements of defendant's counteroffer. Also, Byer stated that Normile did not "want to go 25 [sic] years because he wanted lower payments." Byer was under the impression at this point that Normile thought he had first option on the property and that "nobody else could put an offer in on it and buy it while he had this counteroffer, so he was going to wait awhile before he decided what to do with it." Normile, however, neither accepted or rejected the counteroffer at this point, according to Byer. When this meeting closed, Byer left the pink copy of the offer to purchase form containing defendant's counteroffer with Normile. Byer stated that he thought that Normile had rejected the counteroffer at this point.

At approximately 12:30 A.M. on 5 August, Byer went to the home of Plaintiff Segal, who signed an offer to purchase with terms very similar to those contained in defendant's counteroffer to Plaintiffs Normile and Kurniawan. This offer was accepted, without change, by defendant. Later that same day, at approximately 2:00 P.M., Byer informed Plaintiff Normile that defendant had revoked her counteroffer by commenting to Normile, "[Y]ou snooze, you lose; the property has been sold." Prior to 5:00 P.M. on that same day, Normile and Kurniawan initialed the offer to purchase form containing defendant's counteroffer and delivered the form to the Gallery of Homes' office, along with the earnest money deposit of $500.

Separate actions were filed by plaintiff-appellants and appellee seeking specific performance. Plaintiff Segal's motion for consolidation of the trials was granted. Defendant, in her answer, recognized the validity of the contract between her and Plaintiff Segal. However, because of the action for specific performance commenced by Plaintiffs Normile and Kurniawan, defendant contended that she was unable to legally convey title to Plaintiff Segal. Both plaintiffs filed a motion for summary judgment. Plaintiff Segal's motion for summary judgment was granted by the trial court, and defendant was ordered to specifically perform the contract to convey the property to Segal. Plaintiffs Normile and Kurniawan appealed to the Court of Appeals from the trial court's denial of their motion for summary judgment. That court unanimously affirmed the trial court's actions. Discretionary review was allowed by this Court on petition of Plaintiffs Normile and Kurniawan.

I

. . . [We] begin with a brief description of how a typical sale of real estate is consummated. The broker, whose primary duty is to secure a ready, willing, and able buyer for the seller's property, generally initiates a potential sale by procuring the prospective purchaser's signature on an offer to purchase instrument. J. Webster, North Carolina Real Estate for Brokers and Salesmen, §8.03 (1974). "An 'offer to purchase' is simply an offer by a purchaser to buy property, . . . " J. Webster, supra, §8.03. This instrument contains the prospective purchaser's "offer" of the terms he wishes to propose to the seller. Id.

Usually, this offer to purchase is a printed form with blanks that are filled in and completed by the broker. Among the various clauses contained in such an instrument, it is not uncommon for the form to contain "a clause stipulating that the seller must accept the offer and approve the sale within a certain specified period of time, . . . The inclusion of a date within which the seller must accept simply indicates that the offer will automatically expire at the termination of the named period if the seller does not accept before then." Id. §8.10. Such a clause is contained in Paragraph 9 of the offer to purchase form in the case *sub judice*.

In the instant case, the offerors, plaintiffs-appellants, submitted their offer to purchase defendant's property. This offer contained a Paragraph 9, requiring that "this offer must be accepted on or before 5:00 p.m. Aug. 5th 1980." Thus the offeree's, defendant-seller's, power of acceptance was controlled by the duration of time for acceptance of the offer. Restatement (Second) of Contracts §35 (1981). "The offeror is the creator of the power, and before it leaves his hands, he may fashion it to his will . . . if he names a specific period for its existence, the offeree can accept only during this period." Corbin, Offer and Acceptance, and Some of the Resulting Legal Relations, 26 Yale L.J. 169, at 183 (1917); see Restatement, supra, §41; S. Williston, A Treatise on the Law of Contracts §53 (1957).

This offer to purchase remains only an offer until the seller accepts it on the terms contained in the original offer by the prospective purchaser. J. Webster, supra, §8.10. If the seller does accept the terms in the purchaser's offer, he denotes this by signing the offer to purchase at the bottom, thus forming a valid, binding, and irrevocable purchase contract between the seller and purchaser. However, if the seller purports to accept but changes or modifies the terms of the offer, he makes what is generally referred to as a qualified or conditional acceptance. Richardson v. Greensboro Warehouse & Storage Co., 223 N.C. 344, 26 S.E.2d 897 (1943); Wilson v. W. M. Storey Lumber Co., 180 N.C. 271, 104 S.E. 531 (1920); 17 Am. Jur. 2d Contracts §62 (1964). "The effect of such an acceptance so conditioned is to make a new counter-proposal upon which the parties have not yet agreed, but which is open for acceptance or rejection." (Citations omitted.) *Richardson,* 223 N.C. at 347, 26 S.E.2d at 899. Such a reply from the seller is actually a counteroffer and a rejection of the buyer's offer. J. Webster, supra, §8.10.

These basic principles of contract law are recognized not only in real estate transactions but in bargaining situations generally. It is axiomatic that a valid contract between two parties can only exist when the parties "assent to the same thing in the same sense, and their minds meet as to all terms." Goeckel v. Stokely, 236 N.C. 604, 607, 73 S.E.2d 618, 620 (1952). This assent, or meeting of the minds, requires an offer and acceptance in the exact terms and that the acceptance must be communicated to the offeror. . . . "If the terms of the offer are changed or any new ones added by the acceptance, there is no meeting of the minds and, consequently, no contract." G. Thompson, supra, §4452. This counter-offer amounts to a rejection of the original offer. S. Williston, supra, §51. "The reason is that the counter-offer is interpreted as being in effect the statement by the offeree not only that he will enter into the transaction on the terms stated in his counteroffer, but also by implication that he will not assent to the terms of the original offer." Id. §36.

The question then becomes, did defendant-seller accept plaintiff-appellants' offer prior to the expiration of the time limit contained within the offer? We conclude that she did not. The offeree, defendant-seller, changed the original offer in several material respects, most notably in the terms regarding payment of the purchase price. S. Williston, supra, §77 (any alteration in the method of payment creates a conditional acceptance). This qualified acceptance was in reality a rejection of the plaintiff-appellants original offer because it was coupled with certain modifications or changes that were not contained in the original offer. G. Thompson, supra, §4452. Additionally, defendant-seller's conditional acceptance amounted to a counter-offer to plaintiff-appellants. "A counter-offer is an offer made by an offeree to his offeror relating to the same matter as the original offer and proposing a substituted bargain differing from that proposed by the original offer." Restatement, supra, §39. Between plaintiff-appellants and defendant-seller there was no meeting of the minds, since the parties failed to assent to the same thing in the same sense.

In substance, defendant's conditional acceptance modifying the original offer did not manifest any intent to accept the terms of the original offer, including the time-for-acceptance provision, unless and until the original offeror accepted the terms included in defendant's counteroffer. The offeree, by failing to unconditionally assent to the terms of the original offer and instead qualifying his acceptance with terms of his own, in effect says to the original offeror, "I will accept your offer, provided you [agree to my proposed terms]." Rucker v. Sanders, 182 N.C. 607, 609, 109 S.E. 857, 858 (1921). Thus, the time-for-acceptance provision contained in plaintiff-appellants' original offer did not become part of the terms of the counter-offer. And, of course, if they had accepted the counteroffer from defendant, a binding purchase contract, which would have included the terms of the original offer and counteroffer, would have then resulted. J. Webster, supra, §8.03. . . .

It is generally recognized that "[a]n 'option' is a contract by which the owner agrees to give another the exclusive right to buy property at a fixed price within a specified time." 8A G. Thompson, Commentaries on the Modern Law of Real Property, §4443 (1963); Sandlin v. Weaver, 240 N.C. 703, 83 S.E.2d 806 (1954). In effect, an owner of property agrees to hold his offer open for a specified period of time. G. Thompson, supra, §4443. This option contract must also be supported by valuable consideration. Id. Disregarding the issue of consideration, it is more significant that defendant's counteroffer did not contain any promise or agreement that her counteroffer would remain open for a specified period of time.

Several of the cases cited by plaintiff-appellants are useful in illustrating how a seller expressly agrees to hold his offer open. For instance, in Ward v. Albertson, 165 N.C. 218, 81 S.E. 168 (1914), this Court stated, "An option, in the proper sense, is a contract by which the owner of property agrees with another that he shall have the right to purchase the same at a fixed price within a certain time." Id at 222-23, 81 S.E. at 169. . . .

In each of these . . . cases, this Court recognized that the sellers had given the prospective purchasers a contractual option to purchase the seller's property. In the present case we find no comparable language within defendant-seller's counteroffer manifesting any similar agreement. There is no language indicating that defendant-seller in any way agreed to sell or convey her real property to plaintiff-appellants at their request within a specified period of time. There is, however, language contained within the prospective purchasers' offer to purchase that does state, "DESCRIPTION: I/we Michael M. Normile and Wawie Kurniawan hereby *agree to purchase* from the sellers, . . ." and "*this* offer must be accepted on or before 5:00 p.m. Aug. 5th 1980." (Emphasis added.) Nowhere is there companion language to the effect that Defendant Miller "hereby agrees to sell or convey to the purchasers" if they accept by a certain date.

Therefore, regardless of whether or not the seal imported the necessary consideration, we conclude that defendant-seller made no promise or agreement to hold her offer open. Thus, a necessary ingredient to the creation of an option contract, i.e., a promise to hold an offer open for a specified time, is not present. Accordingly, we hold that defendant's counteroffer was not transformed into an irrevocable offer for the time limit contained in the original offer because the defendant's conditional acceptance did not include the time-for-acceptance provision as part of its terms and because defendant did not make any promise to hold her counteroffer open for any stated time.

II

The foregoing preliminary analysis of both the Court of Appeals' opinion and plaintiff-appellants' argument in their brief prefaces what we consider to be decisive of the ultimate issue to be resolved. Basic contract principles effectively and logically answer the primary issue in this appeal. That is, if a seller rejects a prospective purchaser's offer to purchase but makes a counteroffer that is not accepted by the prospective purchaser, does the prospective purchaser have the power to accept after he receives notice that the counteroffer has been revoked? The answer is no. The net effect of defendant-seller's counteroffer and rejection is twofold. First, plaintiff-appellants' original offer was rejected and ceased to exist. S. Williston, supra, §51. Secondly, the counteroffer by the offeree requires the original offeror, plaintiff-appellants, to either accept or reject. Benya v. Stevens & Thompson Paper Co., Inc., 143 Vt. 521, 468 A.2d 929 (1983).

Accordingly, the next question is did plaintiff-appellants, the original offerors, accept or reject defendant-seller's counteroffer? Plaintiff-appellants in their brief seem to answer this question when they state, "At the time Byer presented the counteroffer to Normile, Normile neither accepted nor rejected it. . . ." Therefore, plaintiff-appellants did not manifest any intent to agree to or accept the terms contained in defendant's counteroffer. Normile instead advised Byer that he, though mistakenly, had an option on the property and that it was off the market for the duration of the time limitation contained in his original offer. As was stated by Justice Bobbitt in Howell v. Smith, 258 N.C. 150, 128 S.E.2d 144 (1962): " 'The question whether a contract has been made must be determined from a consideration of the expressed intention of the parties — that is from a consideration of their words and acts.' " Id. at 153, 128 S.E.2d at 146. Although Normile's mistaken belief that he had an option is unfortunate, he still failed to express to Byer his agreement to or rejection of the counteroffer made by defendant-seller. . . .

Plaintiff-appellants in the instant case . . . did not accept, either expressly or by conduct, defendant's counteroffer. In addition to disagreeing with the change in payment terms, Normile stated to Byer that "he was going to wait awhile before he decided what to do with [the counteroffer]." Neither did plaintiffs explicitly reject defendant's counteroffer. Instead, plaintiff-appellants in this case chose to operate under the impression, though mistaken, that they had an option to purchase and that the property was "off the market." Absent either an acceptance or rejection, there was no meeting of the minds or mutual assent between the parties, a fortiori, there was no contract. Horton v. Humble Oil & Refining Co., 255 N.C. 675, 122 S.E.2d 716 (1961); Goeckel, 236 N.C. 604, 73 S.E.2d 618 (1952).

It is evident from the record that after plaintiff-appellants failed to accept defendant's counteroffer, there was a second purchaser, Plaintiff-appellee Segal, who submitted an offer to defendant that was accepted. This offer and acceptance between the latter parties, together with consideration in the form of an earnest money deposit from plaintiff-appellee, ripened into a valid and binding purchase contract.

By entering into the contract with Plaintiff-appellee Segal, defendant manifested her intention to revoke her previous counteroffer to plaintiff-appellants. "It is a fundamental tenet of the common law that an offer is generally freely revocable and can be countermanded by the offeror at any time before it has been accepted by the offeree." E. Farnsworth, Contracts, §3.17 (1982); Restatement, supra, §42. The revocation of an offer terminates it, and the offeree has no power to revive the offer by any subsequent attempts to accept. G. Thompson, supra, §4452.

Generally, notice of the offeror's revocation must be communicated to the offeree to effectively terminate the offeree's power to accept the offer. It is enough that the offeree receives reliable information, even indirectly, "that the offeror had taken definite action inconsistent with an intention to make the contract." E. Farnsworth, supra, §3.17 (the author cites Dickinson v. Dodds, 2 Ch. Div. 463 (1876), a notorious English case, to support this proposition); Restatement, supra, §43.

In this case, plaintiff-appellants received notice of the offeror's revocation of the counteroffer in the afternoon of August 5, when Byer saw Normile and told him, "[Y]ou snooze, you lose; the property has been sold." Later that afternoon, plaintiff-appellants initialed the counteroffer and delivered it to the Gallery of Homes, along with their earnest money deposit of $500. These subsequent attempts by plaintiff-appellants to accept defendant's revoked counteroffer were fruitless, however, since their power of acceptance had been effectively terminated by the offeror's revocation. Restatement, supra, §36. Since defendant's counteroffer could not be revived, the practical effect of plaintiff-appellants' initialing defendant's counteroffer and leaving it at the broker's office before 5:00 P.M. on August 5 was to resubmit a new offer. This offer was not accepted by defendant since she had already contracted to sell her property by entering into a valid, binding, and irrevocable purchase contract with Plaintiff-appellee Segal.

For the reasons stated herein, the decision of the Court of Appeals is modified and affirmed.

NOTES AND QUESTIONS

1. *Classical principles of offer and acceptance.* The court in *Normile* cites and applies many classical rules of offer and acceptance, as expressed in the Restatement (Second) of Contracts, including the following:

- The power of acceptance created by an offer will be terminated by the offeree's rejection (as well as by other events, such as revocation by the offeror, or his death or incapacity). Restatement (Second) of Contracts §36.
- An acceptance must be unequivocal and unqualified in order for a contract to be formed. Restatement (Second) §§57 and 58. See, e.g., Beastie Boys v. Monster Energy Co., 983 F. Supp. 2d 338, 350 (S.D.N.Y. 2013) (in course of negotiation of contract for music license, word "Dope!" could conceivably signify acceptance of offer, but in context was not sufficiently "clear, unambiguous and unequivocal"); Confederate Motors, Inc. v. Terny, 831 F. Supp. 2d 414, 422 (D. Mass. 2011) (attorney's statement that his client was "prepared to accept" offer did not in the circumstances amount to present communication of acceptance). Note that silence by the offeree rarely amounts to acceptance, but in some limited circumstances an offeree's silence may result in the formation of a contract. See Restatement (Second) §69.
- A "qualified acceptance" constitutes only a counter-offer, Restatement (Second) §59, and as such will have the same effect as a rejection, insofar as the original power of acceptance is concerned. Restatement (Second) §39. E.g., Ehlen v. Melvin, 823 N.W.2d 780, 784 (N.D. 2012) (where offeree made substantive changes to agreement before signing it, mere fact that agreement stated "This is a legally binding contract" did not make it more than counter-offer).

2. *Policy analysis of classical rules.* What policy justifies the rule that the offeree's power of acceptance is terminated by his rejection of the offer? Does that policy apply with equal force to the case where the offeree makes a counter-offer? Professor Melvin Eisenberg has argued that the counter-offer-equals-rejection rule of Restatement (Second) §39(2) is not congruent with the normal understanding of most bargainers, and ought to be either abandoned entirely, or "dropped to the form of a maxim." Melvin A. Eisenberg, Expression Rules in Contract Law and Problems of Offer and Acceptance, 82 Cal. L. Rev. 1127, 1158-1161 (1994). Note, however, that the rule of termination-by-counter-offer is not stated as an inflexible one, but as a "default" principle; Restatement (Second) §39(2) indicates that effect should be given to the expressed intention of either offeror or offeree to the contrary.

3. *Option contracts.* Upon receiving the defendant's counter-offer, plaintiffs Normile and Kurniawan apparently believed they had "first option" on the property and that Miller had bound herself to sell to no one else until 5:00 P.M. the following day. Simply stated, an option contract involves a promise to keep an offer open, a promise that is binding on the offeror. See Restatement (Second) §25. However, to be binding on the offeror, the promise to keep the offer open must either be supported by "consideration" given by the offeree or have some other basis for enforcement. The *Normile* court found that the defendant had not made any promise to keep her offer open and thus Normile and Kurniawan for that reason could not have had an option. Moreover, even if Miller's counter-offer had included an express promise to keep that offer open, Normile and Kurniawan also would have needed to show that they gave "consideration" in exchange for Miller's promise not to revoke. Instead, Normile and Kurniawan apparently argued that enforcement was appropriate because the counter-offer was made under "seal," i.e., in a formalized document. The court never reached that question. We will examine those issues in more detail in Chapter 3. For now it is sufficient for us to know that under the modern theory of consideration a promise is generally enforceable only if the promisee has given either a performance or another promise in exchange for it, and that rule would apply to a promise not to revoke an offer.

4. *Possibility of multiple acceptances.* In the course of its opinion in *Normile,* the North Carolina Supreme Court indicated that because the parties "failed to assent to the same thing in the same sense" there was "no meeting of the minds," and hence no contract. Suppose, however, that the plaintiffs had signed and returned Miller's counter-offer before they learned from Byer that Miller had in the meantime contracted to sell the property to Segal. It seems at least possible that a binding contract between Miller and the plaintiffs would have been formed at that point. If so, what about the contract between Miller and Segal? Could *both* contracts have been enforced?

Once it appears that a contract has been formed between two parties, and has been breached by one of them without a legal excuse, the question is then presented: What is the appropriate remedy for that breach? The fact that a contract will be "enforced" by a court does not mean that the court will necessarily order a breaching party to actually carry out the actions that she had promised to perform. The following Comment provides some preliminary information on this general topic.

Comment: Remedies for Breach of Contract

As you are aware, we have chosen to postpone the full discussion of remedies for breach of contract until later, after the formation process and the principal defenses to contract enforcement have been surveyed. On the other hand, we do recognize that even at this early stage of your studies, the most elementary Legal Realism requires some awareness of what is — and what is *not* — ordinarily entailed in the judicial enforcement of binding contractual obligations.

The conventional approach to contract enforcement is to award relief that will protect the plaintiff's "expectation interest": the *net value* that the plaintiff expected to realize from due performance of the contract at issue, but which the defendant's breach has denied her. Computation of this remedy typically involves not only putting some sort of price tag on the value of the performance that the plaintiff failed to receive, but also taking into account any savings which the plaintiff might have realized from withholding any remaining performance of her own. Other "interests," which contract remedies may also attempt to protect, are the "restitution" and "reliance" interests — the extent to which the defendant has been enriched by, or the plaintiff has been injured by, the plaintiff's actions in reliance on the defendant's commitment to perform. (These three remedial interests will be more fully defined and explored in Chapters 10 and 11.)

The simplest form of relief to protect the plaintiff's expectation interest would be an award of "specific performance," ordering the defendant to cooperate with the plaintiff in exchanging performances as originally agreed to. As we shall see, however, such "specific" relief is often unavailable to the plaintiff in a contract action. Sometimes the defendant is simply unable to perform what she promised. We suggested in the Notes above that the defendant in *Normile* might have found herself bound by two valid contracts to different buyers. Both contracts might have been "enforceable," but only one buyer could have obtained specific performance; the other would have had to be content with a damage award. Even where actual performance by the defendant is still a practical possibility, specific relief in Anglo-American law is the exception, not the rule. For a combination of reasons — historical, theoretical, and practical — English and American courts traditionally have used as their primary vehicle for contract enforcement the award of money damages, computed if possible so as to give the plaintiff the economic equivalent of her net expectation under the contract. Only in certain situations will the court actually order the defendant to perform what he promised to do.

In some situations, the court's award of money damages will be the practical equivalent of specific performance anyway, because payment of money was the defendant's unperformed obligation under the contract. (An example is Cook v. Coldwell Banker, a case in the next section.) Where the defendant's obligation is something other than the payment of money, however, the court ordinarily will have to put some sort of price tag on the plaintiff's lost expectation. Thus, if a building contractor breaches a contract with the owner of property to construct a residence, the owner generally will be entitled to recover the difference between the price for which the breaching contractor had agreed to perform the work and the (higher) price that the owner was required to pay another contractor to perform the same work. Ray v. William G. Eurice Bros., Inc., which we considered earlier in this chapter, illustrates this type of expectation damages.

In Chapters 10 and 11 we will address directly some of the theoretical and practical problems involved in awarding remedies for breach of contract. In the meantime, as we continue to move through cases illustrating issues of formation, validation and excuse, keep an eye out for remedies issues as well. In the *Lonergan* case, for instance, the plaintiff lost because the court resolved the issues of offer and acceptance in favor of defendant Skolnick. Suppose instead that Lonergan had prevailed on those issues, so that Skolnick was indeed liable to Lonergan for wrongful breach of a contract to sell him Skolnick's property in California. From the information available in the court's opinion in that case, what remedy might the court have awarded Lonergan?

3. Offer and Acceptance in Unilateral Contracts

In the preceding section, we focused on the bilateral contract, the typical kind of contract that is formed when the parties exchange promises of future performance. As we will see later in this chapter when we address the concept of "consideration" as an additional requisite for contract formation, an exchange of mutual promises will satisfy that requirement for a binding contract.

But what if one of the parties is not willing to accept merely an assurance of future action, but insists on receiving actual performance before even *committing* herself to perform in return? In some types of situations, it is common for one party to "offer" (in the sense which we have learned to use that word) to commit herself to some performance if *and only if* the other party first "accepts" by *actually rendering his performance.* Classical contract law referred to such a proposal as an "offer for a unilateral contract," and viewed the offeree's rendering of the requested performance as serving both as the consideration for the offeror's promise and as his acceptance of her offer. In such a situation, the offeree may never bind himself by a promise to perform, so he is free not to perform at all (or fail to complete performance), without liability. But once he has completed the performance as requested, the offeror's commitment is a binding one.

In such a true unilateral-contract case, the offeror is protected against the risk of being obligated to perform without getting anything in return from the offeree. On the other hand, if the offeror is never bound to a contractual commitment until the offeree has completed performing, then the offeree runs a substantial risk — the risk that the offeror will revoke her offer before he has completed performance, leaving him without any remedy for the time and effort he has already expended. To remedy this imbalance, contract law over time developed ways of protecting the offeree, by limiting the offeror's power to withdraw once the offeree had begun performance. (These historical developments are discussed in more detail in the Comment on Development of the Law of Unilateral Contracts, after the *Cook* case, which follows.) The following cases illustrate the "unilateral contract" device at work.

Cook v. Coldwell Banker/Frank Laiben Realty Co.

Missouri Court of Appeals 967 S.W.2d 654 (1998)

KATHIANNE KNAUP CRANE, Presiding Judge.

Defendant real estate brokerage firm appeals from a judgment entered on a jury verdict awarding defendant's former salesperson $24,748.89 as damages for breach of a bonus agreement. Defendant claims that the salesperson failed to make a submissible case in that she did not accept the bonus offer before it was revoked. Defendant also asserts trial court errors relating to instructions, evidence, and closing argument. We affirm.

Plaintiff, Mary Ellen Cook, a licensed real estate agent, worked as a real estate salesperson or agent pursuant to a verbal agreement for defendant Coldwell Banker/Frank Laiben Realty Co. and its predecessors. Plaintiff listed and sold real estate for defendant as an independent contractor. Frank Laiben was a co-owner of defendant.

At a sales meeting in March, 1991, defendant, through Laiben, orally announced a bonus program in order to remain competitive with other local brokerage firms and to retain its agents. The bonus program provided that an agent earning $15,000.00 in commissions would receive a $500.00 bonus payable immediately, an agent earning $15,000.00 to $25,000.00 in commissions would receive a twenty-two percent bonus, and an agent earning above $25,000.00 in commissions would receive a thirty percent bonus. Bonuses over the first $500.00 were to be paid at the end of the year. The first year of the program would be January 1, 1991 to December 31, 1991 and it would continue on an annual basis after that. Laiben kept track of the agents' earnings in a separate bonus account.

At the end of April, 1991, plaintiff surpassed $15,000.00 in earnings, entitling her to a $500.00 bonus which defendant paid to her in September, 1991. By September, 1991 plaintiff surpassed $32,400.00 in commissions.

At another sales meeting in September, 1991, Laiben indicated that bonuses would be paid at a banquet to be held in March of the following year instead of at the end of the year. Plaintiff asked if that meant that an agent had to be "here" in March in order to collect the bonus. Laiben indicated that was what it meant. Plaintiff testified that, at the time of the change in the bonus agreement, she had no intention of leaving defendant, but stayed with defendant until the end of 1991 in reliance on the promise of a bonus.

During 1991 plaintiff was contacted about joining Remax, another real estate brokerage firm. Although she was not initially interested, in January,

1992 she accepted a position with Remax and advised Laiben of her departure. Laiben informed her that she would not be receiving her bonus. At the end of 1991, plaintiff had total earnings of $75,638.47, which made her eligible for a combined bonus of $17,391.54. After placing her license with Remax, plaintiff finished closing four or five contracts that she had been working on prior to leaving defendant. In March, 1992 plaintiff sent a demand letter to defendant, seeking payment for the bonus she believed she had earned. Defendant did not pay plaintiff.

On December 17, 1992 plaintiff filed an action against defendant for breach of a bonus contract, seeking damages in the amount of $18,404.31. She amended this petition to include prejudgment interest. At trial Laiben denied that at the March meeting he had stated the bonuses would be paid at the end of the year and testified that at that meeting he had told the agents the bonuses would not be paid until the following March. The jury returned a verdict in favor of plaintiff and awarded her damages in the amount of $24,748.89. The court entered judgment in this amount.

In its first point defendant contends that the trial court erred in overruling its motions for directed verdict because plaintiff failed to make a submissible case of breach of the bonus agreement. In particular, defendant argues that plaintiff did not adduce sufficient evidence to establish a reasonable inference that 1) she tendered consideration to support defendant's offer of a bonus, or that 2) she accepted defendant's offer to give a bonus.

A directed verdict is a drastic action and should only be granted where reasonable and honest persons could not differ on a correct disposition of the case. Seidel v. Gordon A. Gundaker Real Estate Co., 904 S.W.2d 357, 361 (Mo. App. 1995). In determining whether a plaintiff has made a submissible case in a contract action, we view the evidence in a light most favorable to plaintiff, presume plaintiff's evidence is true, and give plaintiff the benefit of all reasonable and favorable inferences to be drawn from the evidence. Gateway Exteriors Inc. v. Suntide Homes Inc., 882 S.W.2d 275, 279 (Mo. App. 1994).

Plaintiff adduced evidence of a unilateral contract offered in March, 1991 to pay a bonus under certain conditions at the end of the year. She also adduced evidence that in September, 1991 defendant attempted to revoke that offer and make the bonus contingent upon the agent's remaining until March of the following year.

A unilateral contract is a contract in which performance is based on the wish, will, or pleasure of one of the parties. Klamen v. Genuine Parts Co., 848 S.W.2d 38, 40 (Mo. App. 1993). A promisor does not receive a promise as consideration for his or her promise in a unilateral contract. Id. A unilateral contract lacks consideration for want of mutuality, but when the promisee performs, consideration is supplied, and the contract is enforceable to the extent performed. Leeson v. Etchison, 650 S.W.2d 681, 684 (Mo. App. 1983). An offer to make a unilateral contract is accepted when the requested performance is rendered. Nilsson v. Cherokee Candy & Tobacco Co., 639 S.W.2d 226, 228 (Mo. App. 1982). A promise to pay a bonus in return for an at-will employee's continued employment is an offer for a unilateral contract which becomes enforceable when accepted by the employee's performance. Id. at 228.

In the absence of any contract to the contrary, plaintiff could terminate her relationship with defendant at any time and was not obligated to earn a certain level of commissions. There was sufficient evidence that the bonus offer induced plaintiff to remain with defendant through the end of 1991 and to earn a high level of commissions for the court to submit the issue of acceptance by performance to the jury.

Defendant next argues that it was free to revoke the first offer with the second offer because, as of the time the second offer was made, plaintiff had not yet accepted the first offer. Defendant maintains that, because plaintiff did not stay until March, 1992, she did not accept the second offer and thus, did not earn the bonus.

Generally, an offeror may withdraw an offer at any time prior to acceptance unless the offer is supported by consideration. Coffman Industries, Inc. v. Gorman-Taber Co., 521 S.W.2d 763, 772 (Mo. App. 1975). However, an offeror may not revoke an offer where the offeree has made substantial performance. Id. (citing 1 Williston on Contracts, Third Edition Section 60A (1957)). *Coffman* set out the general rule of law as follows:

> Where one party makes a promissory offer in such form that it can be accepted by the rendition of the performance that is requested in exchange, without any express return promise or notice of acceptance in words, the offeror is bound by a contract just as soon as the offeree has rendered a substantial part of that requested performance.

1 Corbin on Contracts Section 49 (1952), quoted in *Coffman,* 521 S.W.2d at 772. The court stated the rationale for the rule as follows:

> The main offer includes a subsidiary promise, necessarily implied, that if part of the requested performance is given, the offeror will not revoke his offer, and that if tender is made it will be accepted. Part performance or tender may thus furnish consideration for the subsidiary promises. Moreover, merely acting in justifiable reliance on an offer may in some cases serve as sufficient reason for making a promise binding. (Emphasis supplied.)

Restatement [First] of Contracts Section 45 cmt. b (1932), quoted in *Coffman,* 521 S.W.2d at 772. Thus, in the context of an offer for unilateral contract, the offer may not be revoked where the offeree has accepted the offer by substantial performance. Id. at 771-72.

In this case there was evidence that, before the offer was modified in September, 1991, plaintiff had remained with defendant and had earned over $32,400.00 in commissions, making her eligible for the offered bonus. This constitutes sufficient evidence of substantial performance.

Plaintiff adduced evidence that defendant offered to pay a bonus at the end of 1991 if she would continue to work for it, that she stayed through 1991 with an intent to accept the offer, that she sold and listed enough property to qualify for all three bonus levels, that defendant knew of plaintiff's performance, that defendant paid $500.00 of the bonus but did not pay the remainder, and that she was damaged. This evidence was sufficient to make a submissible case for breach of a unilateral contract. Point one is denied.

. . .

MARY RHODES RUSSELL and JAMES R. DOWD, JJ., concur.

NOTES AND QUESTIONS

1. *The conceptual basis for protecting the offeree.* In the course of deciding for the plaintiff, the court cited the first Restatement of Contracts §45 and the comment to that section that protects the offeree from revocation of the offer for a unilateral contract by finding that the offeror has made a "subsidiary promise, necessarily implied," to hold the offer open. Restatement (Second) §45 protects the offeree by providing that when the offeror invites acceptance by performance, the beginning of performance creates an "option contract." While using different conceptual foundations – implied promise versus option contract – the results are the same: the offeror is precluded from revoking the offer once the offeree begins the requested performance. Note that if the offeree fails to complete performance, the offeror would be free to revoke the offer. See Restatement (Second) §45(2).

2. *Is substantial performance by the offeree necessary?* In *Cook* the court, relying on earlier case law as well as the writings of Professors Williston and Corbin, indicated that in order to convert the defendant's offer to an irrevocable one, plaintiff Cook had to have rendered "substantial" performance. Restatement (Second) §45 does not impose this requirement. Should it? Some courts will do so. See, e.g., the *Storti* case, discussed in Note 4 below.

3. *Offeree's implied promise to complete performance?* In Comment *d* to §45, the drafters of the Restatement (Second) suggest that in many cases the beginning of performance by the offeree "carries with it an express or implied promise [by the offeree] to complete performance," in which case the offeror also would be protected by a contract, which would be "bilateral" in nature. Could that analysis apply to the facts of the *Cook* case?

4. *Offeror's explicit reservation of power to revoke.* Here, as in most areas of contract law, the party who is aware of the general rules and has adequate counsel may be able to avoid contractual liability. In Storti v. University of Washington, 330 P. 3d 159 (Wash. 2014), the defendant university announced a "merit raise policy" for faculty members who qualified by virtue of their service, then later "suspended" the policy because of major budget cuts stemming from the deep recession. Faculty members sued to enforce their claims for wage increases under the merit raise policy, claiming it had not been suspended until after they had furnished substantial service, creating a unilateral contract enforceable against the university. A similar suspension in an earlier year, followed by a lawsuit, had resulted in liability on the university's part on an earlier version of the plan. This time, however, the Washington Supreme Court held that even though the plaintiff faculty members had sufficiently performed to create a unilateral contract between themselves and the defendant university with

respect to the merit raise program (citing Restatement §45), defendant's suspension of the raise program did not constitute a breach of contract, because the university had by the terms of its plan (together with relevant provisions of its faculty handbook) sufficiently reserved the power to reevaluate the policy in light of changing economic conditions.

Comment: Historical Development of the Law of Unilateral Contracts

In its original, "classical" form, an offer for a unilateral contract remained revocable until the offeree *completed* the act(s) called for in the offer. (The offeree's performance also constituted the consideration necessary to make the offeror's promise binding.) This free-revocability rule potentially could result in injustice to an offeree who had begun to perform in reliance on the offeror's expressed intention to contract, only to have that offer revoked — to have the rug pulled out from under his feet, as it were. Contracts scholars of this period (early twentieth century) typically illustrated the rule through unrealistic hypotheticals: A promises to pay B a sum of money if B walks across the Brooklyn Bridge, and then revokes just before B completes performance. Under the classical approach to contract law, which favored clear rules over considerations of justice, scholars argued in favor of the rule of free revocability and dismissed the offeree's reliance as "alleged fanciful hardship." See, e.g., I. Maurice Wormser, The True Conception of Unilateral Contracts, 26 Yale L.J. 136, 136-138 (1916).

The drafters of both the First and Second Restatements of Contracts attempted to ameliorate the harsh results sometimes reached under the classical analysis. In many cases, the words used by the offeror may leave in doubt whether she intends to make only a "true" unilateral-contract offer, or whether the offeree might also accept by making a promise of performance, thus forming a bilateral contract. Section 32 of the Restatement (Second) declares that in such cases of ambiguity, the court should assume that the offeror intended to allow the offeree to have the power to accept *either* by making a return promise or by rendering the performance requested by the offeror. (Cf. Uniform Commercial Code §2-206(1)(b), to similar effect.) However, section 32 would not protect the offeree when it is clear that the offeror sought an act *and only an act* in exchange for her promise of performance.

Responding to these concerns, the drafters of both the Restatements also included §45, which now provides that when an offeree tenders or begins the requested performance under a unilateral contract, the offeror cannot revoke her offer so long as the offeree timely completes performance in accordance with the terms of the offer. (The Restatement uses the concept of an "option" contract to reach this result, although the offeror's promise not to revoke is implied by the law, a "legal fiction.") We have seen §45 in operation in the *Cook* case, above.

Writing in 1938, shortly after the promulgation of the first Restatement of Contracts, Professor Karl Llewellyn sharply criticized the common law's traditional dichotomy between bilateral and unilateral contracts. He argued that in the real world "true" unilateral contracts are relatively rare and should not be treated as one-half of the contracting universe. Llewellyn conceded the existence of a few common examples of true offers for unilateral contracts — for example, offers of commissions to real estate brokers (as in the *Cook* case) and offers of rewards. However, what these offers have in common is not merely that acceptance is made by performance, but the speculative nature of the offeree's performance; when it is not at all certain that the offeree will be able to perform, *even if he wants to*, an offeror is unlikely to be interested in a mere promissory acceptance. See Karl Llewellyn, On Our Case-Law of Contract: Offer and Acceptance (Pts. 1 & 2), 48 Yale L.J. 1, 779 (1938-1939), quoted and summarized in Mark Pettit, Jr., Modern Unilateral Contracts, 63 B.U. L. Rev. 551, 552-556 (1983). Influenced by Llewellyn's argument, the drafters of the Second Restatement abandoned the classical terminological distinction, suggesting that the terms *unilateral* and *bilateral contract* generally should be avoided, as "productive of confusion." See the Reporter's Note to Restatement (Second) §1, Comment *f*.

In his 1983 article, cited in the preceding paragraph, Professor Mark Pettit also argued that the obituary for the unilateral contract delivered in Restatement (Second) was premature. Pettit noted that judges have persisted in using the unilateral contract analysis as a basis for decision. (See the *Sateriale* case that follows.) Having gone full circle from the classical days, however, courts are now using unilateral contract analysis not to avoid liability but to *enforce* it, by imposing liability on an offeror in cases where no promissory acceptance from the offeree was invited or required. These "new-style" unilateral contracts (Professor Pettit's phrase) do not involve a performance by the offeree that is inherently speculative; they are simply cases in which the offeree is not necessarily committed to full performance. See Mark Pettit, Jr., Modern Unilateral Contracts, 63 B.U. L. Rev. at 577-583 (discussing employee benefit cases).

Sateriale v. R.J. Reynolds Tobacco Co.

United States Court of Appeals, 697 F.3d 777 (9th Cir. 2012)

Before: JOHN T. NOONAN, JR., and RAYMOND C. FISHER, Circuit Judges, and KIMBERLY J. MULLER, District Judge.*

OPINION

FISHER, Circuit Judge:

R.J. Reynolds Tobacco Company (RJR) operated a customer rewards program, called Camel Cash, from 1991 to 2007. Under the terms of the program, RJR urged consumers to purchase Camel cigarettes, to save Camel Cash certificates included in packages of Camel cigarettes, to enroll in the program and, ultimately, to redeem their certificates for merchandise featured in catalogs distributed by RJR. The plaintiffs allege that, in reliance on RJR's actions, they purchased Camel cigarettes, enrolled in the program and saved their certificates for future redemption. They allege that in 2006 RJR abruptly ceased accepting certificates for redemption, making the plaintiffs' unredeemed certificates worthless. The plaintiffs brought this action for breach of contract, promissory estoppel and violation of two California consumer protection laws. The district court dismissed the action for failure to state a claim. We affirm in part, reverse in part and remand. We hold that the plaintiffs have adequately alleged claims for breach of contract and promissory estoppel, but affirm dismissal of the plaintiffs' claims under the Unfair Competition Law and the Consumer Legal Remedies Act.

A 1994 Camel Cash advertisement.

I. Background

The plaintiffs appeal from a dismissal for failure to state a claim. *See* Fed. R. Civ. P. 12(b)(6). For purposes of a motion to dismiss, we accept all well-pleaded allegations of material fact as true and construe them in the light most favorable to the nonmoving party. *See Daniels-Hall v. Nat'l Educ. Ass'n,* 629 F.3d 992, 998 (9th Cir. 2010). We thus recite the facts as they appear in the plaintiffs' third amended complaint. This factual background is based on the *allegations* of the plaintiffs' complaint. Whether the plaintiffs' allegations are true has not been decided.

RJR initiated the Camel Cash customer loyalty program in 1991. Compl. ¶ 24. RJR represented on Camel Cash certificates, packages of Camel cigarettes and in the media that customers who saved the certificates — called C-Notes — could exchange them for merchandise according to terms provided in a catalog. *Id.* The C-Notes stated:

> USE THIS NEW C-NOTE AND THE C-NOTES YOU'VE BEEN SAVING TO GET THE BEST GOODS CAMEL HAS TO OFFER. CALL 1-800-CAMEL CASH (1-800-266-3522) for a free catalog. Offer restricted to smokers 21 years of age or older. Value 1/1000 of 1¢. Offer good only in the USA, and void where restricted or prohibited by law. Check catalog for expiration date. Limit 5 requests for a catalog per household.

Id. ¶ 26. According to the complaint, "Certain (but not all) of the Camel Cash catalogs state[d] that Reynolds could terminate the Camel Cash program without notice." *Id.* ¶ 32.

The plaintiffs are 10 individuals who joined the Camel Cash program by purchasing RJR's products and filling out and submitting signed registration forms to RJR. *Id.* ¶¶ 27, 48. RJR sent each plaintiff a unique enrollment number that was used in communications between the parties. *Id.* ¶ 27. These communications included catalogs RJR distributed to the plaintiffs containing merchandise that could be obtained by redeeming Camel Cash certificates. *Id.*

From time to time, RJR issued a new catalog with merchandise offered in exchange for Camel Cash, either upon request, or by mailing catalogs to consumers enrolled in the program. *Id.* ¶ 28. The number of Camel Cash certificates needed to obtain merchandise varied from as little as 100 to many thousands. *Id.* ¶ 29. This encouraged consumers to buy more packages of cigarettes together with Camel Cash and also to save or obtain Camel Cash certificates to redeem them for more valuable items. *Id.*

RJR honored the program from 1991 to 2006, and during that time Camel's share of the cigarette market nearly doubled, from approximately 4 percent to more than 7 percent. *Id.* ¶¶ 3, 34. In October 2006, however, RJR mailed a notice to program members announcing that the program would terminate as of March 31, 2007. *Id.* ¶ 32. The termination notice stated:

> As a loyal Camel smoker, we [sic] wanted to tell you our Camel Cash program is expiring. C-Notes will no longer be included on packs, which means whatever Camel Cash you have is among the last of its kind.
>
> Now this isn't happening overnight — there'll be plenty of time to redeem your C-Notes before the program ends. In fact, you'll have from OCTOBER '06 though MARCH '07 to go to camelsmokes.com to redeem your C-Notes. Supplies will be limited, so it won't hurt to get there before the rush.

Id. ¶ 33 & ex. A.

The announcement advised members that they could continue to redeem their C-Notes until March 2007. Beginning in October 2006, however, RJR allegedly stopped printing and issuing catalogs and told consumers that it did not have any merchandise available for redemption. *Id.* ¶ 34, 48. Several of the plaintiffs attempted, without success, to redeem C-Notes or obtain a catalog during the final six months of the program. *Id.* ¶ 49. The plaintiffs had saved hundreds or thousands of Camel Cash certificates that they were unable to redeem. *Id.* ¶ 11.

In November 2009, the plaintiffs filed a class action complaint against RJR. They allege breach of contract, promissory estoppel and violations of two California consumer protection laws, the Unfair Competition Law (UCL), Cal. Bus. & Prof. Code § 17200 *et seq.*, and the Consumer Legal Remedies Act (CLRA), Cal. Civ. Code § 1750 *et seq.* The district court dismissed the action under Rule 12(b)(6), and the plaintiffs timely appealed.

II. Jurisdiction and Standard of Review

We have jurisdiction under 28 U.S.C. § 1291. We review de novo a district court's order granting a Rule 12(b)(6) motion to dismiss. . . . The parties agree that the plaintiffs' claims are governed by California law.

III. Breach of Contract

We begin by addressing whether the plaintiffs have stated a claim for breach of contract. The plaintiffs do not dispute that RJR had the right to terminate the Camel Cash program effective March 31, 2007, but allege that RJR breached a contract by refusing to redeem C-Notes during the six months preceding program termination. Compl. ¶¶ 6-7. RJR challenges the plaintiffs' contract claim on four grounds: the absence of an offer, indefiniteness, lack of mutuality of obligation (premised on RJR's right to terminate its contractual obligations) and untimeliness. We address RJR's contentions in turn.

A. Existence of an Offer

"An offer is the manifestation of willingness to enter into a bargain, so made as to justify another person in understanding that his assent to that bargain is invited and will conclude it." *Donovan v. RRL Corp.,* 26 Cal. 4th 261, 109 Cal. Rptr. 2d 807, 27 P.3d 702, 709 (2001) . . . . "The determination of whether a particular communication constitutes an operative offer, rather than an inoperative step in the preliminary negotiation of a contract, depends upon all the surrounding circumstances." *Id.* "[T]he pertinent inquiry is whether the individual to whom the communication was made had reason to believe that it was intended as an offer." *Id.* The issue here is whether the C-Notes, read in isolation or in combination with the catalogs, may have constituted an offer.

1. Bilateral Contract

As an initial matter, we are not persuaded that the plaintiffs have alleged the existence of an offer to enter into a *bilateral* contract. "A bilateral contract consists of mutual promises made in exchange for each other by each of the two contracting parties." *Sully-Miller Contracting Co. v. Gledson/Cashman Constr., Inc.,* 103 Cal. App. 4th 30, 126 Cal. Rptr. 2d 400, 403 (2002) (quoting Corbin on Contracts § 1.23 (rev. ed. 1993)) (internal quotation marks omitted). Both sides of the bargain must have made promises. Here, the plaintiffs have identified an alleged promise by RJR (to allow customers to redeem Camel Cash certificates for rewards), but they have not pointed to any promise they made to RJR. Nor do they argue that RJR sought a return promise in exchange for its own promise to allow consumers to exchange C-Notes for merchandise. . . . The plaintiffs have not alleged that they were bound to do anything. They therefore have not alleged the existence of an offer to enter into a bilateral contract.[1]

2. Unilateral Contract

We reach a different conclusion as to the plaintiffs' theory that RJR made an offer to enter into a *unilateral* contract. In contrast to a bilateral contract, a unilateral contract involves the exchange of a promise for a performance. *See Harris*

1. It is, of course, possible for a consumer rewards program to involve a bilateral contract. Frequent flyer programs, for example, may be governed by membership agreements that impose contractual duties on both sides of the bargain, exposing airlines and travelers alike to potential contractual liability. *See, e.g., Ginsberg v. Northwest, Inc.,* 653 F.3d 1033, 1035, 1040 (9th Cir. 2011); *Am. Airlines, Inc. v. Am. Coupon Exch., Inc.,* 721 F. Supp. 61, 63 (S.D.N.Y. 1989). Here, however, the plaintiffs have not alleged an offer or contract involving reciprocal duties, and therefore they have not alleged a bilateral contract.

v. Time, Inc., 191 Cal. App. 3d 449, 237 Cal. Rptr. 584, 587 (1987). The offer is accepted by rendering a performance rather than providing a promise. *See* Restatement § 45 cmt. a. "Typical illustrations are found in offers of rewards or prizes. . . ." *Id.*

RJR argues that its C-Notes, whether read in isolation or in combination with the catalogs, were not offers, but invitations to make an offer. RJR relies on the common law's general rule that "[a]dvertisements of goods by display, sign, handbill, newspaper, radio or television are not ordinarily intended or understood as offers to sell." *Id.* § 26 cmt. b. RJR emphasizes that two judicial decisions have applied this general rule to customer rewards programs similar to the Camel Cash program, *see Leonard v. Pepsico, Inc.,* 88 F. Supp. 2d 116, 122-27 (S.D.N.Y. 1999); *Alligood v. Procter & Gamble Co.,* 72 Ohio App. 3d 309, 594 N.E.2d 668, 668-70 (1991) (per curiam), and urges us to apply the rule here as well. We decline to do so.

First, it is not clear that the common law rule upon which RJR relies applies under California law. *See Donovan,* 109 Cal. Rptr. 2d 807, 27 P.3d at 710 (stating that "[t]his court has not previously applied the common law rules upon which defendant relies, including the rule that advertisements generally constitute invitations to negotiate rather than offers," observing that "such rules . . . have been criticized on the ground that they are inconsistent with the reasonable expectations of consumers and lead to haphazard results," citing Melvin Aron Eisenberg, *Expression Rules in Contract Law and Problems of Offer and Acceptance,* 82 Cal. L. Rev. 1127, 1166-72 (1994), and concluding that "[i]n the present case . . . we need not consider the viability of the black-letter rule regarding the interpretation of advertisements").

Second, even assuming California law incorporates the common law rule, that rule includes an exception for offers of a reward, including offers of a reward for the redemption of coupons. As a leading contract law treatise explains,

> It is very common, where one desires to induce many people to action, to offer a reward for such action by general publication in some form. A statement that plausibly makes an offer of this kind must be reasonably interpreted according to its terms and the surrounding circumstances. If the statement, properly interpreted, calls for the performance or commencement of performance of specific acts, action in accordance with such an interpretation will close a contract or make the offer irrevocable. There are many cases of an offer of a reward for the capture of a person charged with crime, for desired information, for the return of a lost article, for the winning of a contest, or *for the redemption of coupons.* In addition, advertisements placed by buyers inviting sellers to ship goods without prior communication are clear cases of offers. The contracts so made are almost always unilateral.

Corbin on Contracts (hereinafter Corbin) § 2.4 (2012) (emphasis added) (footnotes omitted). RJR does not discuss this exception, relying instead on *Leonard* and *Alligood.* Several courts, however, have applied the exception to customer rewards programs. *See, e.g.,* . . . *Wolens v. Am. Airlines, Inc.,* 157 Ill. 2d 466, 193 Ill. Dec. 172, 626 N.E.2d 205, 208 (1993) (reward miles awarded for flying on

American Airlines), *rev'd on other grounds,* 513 U.S. 219, 115 S. Ct. 817, 130 L. Ed. 2d 715 (1995).[2]

Like these courts, we see no justification for applying the general common law rule, rather than the common law exception, to circumstances such as those presented here. The common law rule that advertisements ordinarily do not constitute offers arose to address a specific problem — the potential for over-acceptance — not applicable here. Professor Farnsworth explains that an offer ordinarily does not exist

> when a proposal for a limited quantity has been sent to more persons than its maker could accommodate. . . . Otherwise, supposing a shopkeeper were sold out of a particular class of goods, thousands of members of the public might crowd into the shop and demand to be served, and each one would have a right of action against the proprietor for not performing his contract. A customer would not usually have reason to believe that the shopkeeper intended exposure to the risk of a multitude of acceptances resulting in a number of contracts exceeding the shopkeeper's inventory.

E. Allan Farnsworth, *Contracts* (hereinafter Farnsworth) § 3.10, at 134 (4th ed. 2004) (footnote and internal quotation marks omitted). This problem arises in the case of ordinary advertisements for the sale of goods or services, but not here. First, RJR's ostensible purpose in promoting the Camel Cash program was not to sell a limited inventory, but to induce as many consumers as possible to purchase Camel cigarettes. Second, RJR could not have been trapped into a situation in which acceptances exceeded inventory. RJR alone decided how many C-Notes to distribute, so it exercised absolute control over the number of acceptances. As Farnsworth explains, "if the very nature of a proposal restricts its maker's potential liability to a reasonable number of people, there is no reason why it cannot be an offer." *Id.* at 135.

For these reasons, we find no reason to presume that RJR's communications did not constitute an offer merely because they were addressed to the general public in the form of advertisements. The operative question under California law, therefore, is simply "whether the advertiser, in clear and positive terms, promised to render performance in exchange for something requested by the advertiser, and whether the recipient of the advertisement reasonably might have concluded that by acting in accordance with the request a contract would be formed." *Donovan,* 109 Cal. Rptr. 2d 807, 27 P.3d at 710. Construing the complaint in the light most favorable to the plaintiffs, and drawing all reasonable inferences from the complaint in the plaintiffs' favor, . . . we conclude that the plaintiffs have adequately alleged the existence of an offer to enter into a unilateral contract, whereby RJR promised to provide rewards to customers who purchased Camel cigarettes, saved Camel Cash certificates and redeemed their certificates in accordance with the catalogs' terms.

2. . . . In *Wolens,* the Illinois Supreme Court recognized a contractual relationship between American Airlines and members of its frequent flyer program, stating, "When a member earns frequent flyer miles by flying on American or by doing business with American affiliates, a contractual relationship is formed which vests the frequent flyer with the right to earn specific travel awards." 193 Ill. Dec. 172, 626 N.E.2d at 208.

We reach this conclusion in light of the totality of the circumstances surrounding RJR's communications to consumers: the repeated use of the word "offer" in the C-Notes; the absence of any language disclaiming the intent to be bound; the inclusion of specific restrictions in the C-Notes ("Offer restricted to smokers 21 years of age or older"; "Offer good only in the USA, and void where restricted or prohibited by law"; "Check catalog for expiration date"; "Limit 5 requests for a catalog per household"); the formal enrollment process, through which consumers submitted registration forms and RJR issued enrollment numbers; and the substantial reliance expected from consumers.[3] *Donovan* explains that under the common law "advertisements have been held to constitute offers where they invite the performance of a specific act without further communication and leave nothing for negotiation." 109 Cal. Rptr. 2d 807, 27 P.3d at 710. These requirements are satisfied here. RJR's alleged offer invited the performance of specific acts (saving C-Notes and redeeming them for rewards in accordance with the catalog) without further communication, and leaving nothing for negotiation.

RJR properly emphasizes that the alleged offer left aspects of RJR's performance to RJR's discretion. The offer did not specify when future catalogs would be issued, what rewards merchandise they would include, what quantities of merchandise would be available or how many C-Notes would be required to exchange for particular items. The plaintiffs, however, do not allege that these were essential terms. *See* Compl. ¶ 31 ("[I]t was not a contract to obtain a specific item or good, such as a 'Joe Camel' jacket or ashtray."). Instead, they allege a contract the essence of which was their general right to redeem their Camel Cash certificates, during the life of the program, for whatever rewards merchandise RJR made available, with RJR's discretion limited only by the implied duty of good faith performance. The presence of discretion thus does not preclude the existence of an offer.

B. Definiteness

RJR argues that, even if there was an offer, any contract arising from it would be too indefinite to be enforced. To be enforceable under California law, a contract must be sufficiently definite "for the court to ascertain the parties' obligations and to determine whether those obligations have been performed or breached." *Bustamante v. Intuit, Inc.*, 141 Cal. App. 4th 199, 45 Cal. Rptr. 3d 692, 699 (2006).

---

3. The plaintiffs' substantial reliance distinguishes this case from cases involving garden-variety advertisements. To take advantage of the Camel Cash program, consumers were expected to purchase Camel cigarettes and accumulate Camel Cash certificates for a period of weeks, months or even years. *See* Compl. ¶ 29 (alleging that "[t]he number of Camel Cash certificates needed to obtain merchandise . . . varied from as little as one hundred to many thousands," and noting that RJR "further encouraged plaintiffs and other Class members to collect their Camel Cash (as opposed to redeeming them as soon as possible) because merchandise listed in defendant's catalogs for redemption by a greater number of coupons was disproportionately more valuable than the merchandise which could be redeemed by fewer coupons"). Citing an offer for a reward as an example, Corbin explains that "a proposal is likely to be deemed to be an offer if it is foreseeable that the addressee of the proposal will rely upon it." Corbin §2.2. This is so because a member of the public is unlikely to undertake substantial reliance in the absence of a binding commitment from the offeror — i.e., on the mere chance that the offeror will perform.

. . . "The terms of a contract are reasonably certain if they provide a basis for determining the existence of a breach and for giving an appropriate remedy." *Id.* . . .

1. Existence of a Breach

The first of these requirements is satisfied here. The plaintiffs do not claim that they were entitled to particular merchandise, but that RJR was required to make reasonable quantities of rewards merchandise available during the life of the Camel Cash program — a duty RJR allegedly breached by failing to make *any* merchandise available after October 1, 2006. This alleged breach is readily discernible. *See* Restatement § 33 cmt. b ("[T]he degree of certainty required may be affected by the dispute which arises and by the remedy sought. Courts decide the disputes before them, not other hypothetical disputes which might have arisen.").[5]

2. Giving an Appropriate Remedy

The second requirement "that the contract provide a basis for giving an appropriate remedy" presents a closer question. As noted, RJR exercised considerable discretion in deciding what rewards would be offered. We cannot know precisely what merchandise the plaintiffs might have received had RJR fully performed its obligations, an uncertainty that could inhibit the process of determining a remedy. *See Bustamante,* 45 Cal. Rptr. 3d at 699 ("[T]he limits of performance must be sufficiently defined to provide a rational basis for the assessment of damages." . . .).

It is not clear, however, that damages could not be rationally assessed here. RJR's internal documents assigned C-Notes values, such as 15 cents per $1 note, that might afford a basis for assessing damages. In the alternative, RJR's final rewards catalog and pre-breach performance might provide a basis for giving an appropriate remedy.

We should not lightly conclude, especially at this early stage in the proceedings, that there is no basis for determining an appropriate remedy where, as here, the allegations suggest that the parties intended to contract. . . . The plaintiffs enrolled in the Camel Cash program, purchased Camel cigarettes and collected Camel Cash certificates. RJR accepted the plaintiffs' registration forms, issued them enrollment numbers, performed under the program for 15 years and, according to internal RJR documents, treated outstanding C-Notes as a binding obligation and an outstanding financial liability. According to the documents, RJR closely monitored its exposure under the program, and even went so far as to create a financial reserve to cover that exposure — actions consistent with a legally binding commitment.

5. That the alleged contract afforded RJR some discretion in performing does not compel the conclusion that the alleged contract is too indefinite to be enforced. See Restatement§ 34 cmt. a ("If the agreement is otherwise sufficiently definite to be a contract, it is not made invalid by the fact that it leaves particulars of performance to be specified by one of the parties."); Corbin §4.4 ("[T]he fact that one of the parties reserves the power of fixing or varying the price or other performance is not fatal if the exercise of this power is subject to prescribed or implied limitations, as that the variation . . . must be reasonable or in good faith." (footnote omitted)); *Cal. Lettuce Growers, Inc. v. Union Sugar Co.,* 45 Cal.2d 474, 289 P.2d 785, 791 (1955) ("[W]here a contract confers on one party a discretionary power affecting the rights of the other, a duty is imposed to exercise that discretion in good faith and in accordance with fair dealing.").

We also consider the plaintiffs' substantial reliance on RJR's promises, as well as the substantial benefits RJR accrued by virtue of consumers' reliance on the Camel Cash program. Corbin explains that, "[i]f one party has greatly benefited by part performance or if one party has relied extensively on the agreement, the court should go to great lengths to find a construction of the agreement that will salvage it." Corbin § 4.3 (footnotes omitted). For these reasons, dismissal for indefiniteness is unwarranted.

C. Mutuality of Obligation & RJR's Right to Terminate

RJR argues that the plaintiffs' contract claim must be dismissed for lack of mutuality of obligation because RJR had an unrestricted right to terminate the Camel Cash program at will, and without notice. . . .

Given our conclusion that the plaintiffs have alleged an offer to enter into a unilateral rather than a bilateral contract, RJR's reliance on mutuality of obligation necessarily fails: that doctrine does not apply to unilateral contracts. *See, e.g., Asmus v. Pac. Bell,* 23 Cal. 4th 1, 96 Cal. Rptr. 2d 179, 999 P.2d 71, 78 (2000) ("In the unilateral contract context, there is no mutuality of obligation."). RJR's argument nonetheless raises important questions about the viability of the plaintiffs' contract claim. If, in fact, RJR reserved an *unrestricted* right to terminate the Camel Cash program, *without notice,* then the plaintiffs' contract claim may well be untenable.

First, a reservation of an unrestricted right to terminate could have precluded RJR's communications from constituting an offer. As Corbin explains, if an offeror expressly reserves not only the right to revoke the offer at will and without notice, but also the *unrestricted right not to perform,* then the offer is not legally effective as an offer at all: "A purported offer that reserves the power to withdraw at will even after an acceptance should not be described as an offer at all, but as an invitation to submit an offer." Corbin § 2.19.

Second, if RJR reserved an unrestricted right to terminate the Camel Cash program at any time and without notice, then RJR's promise to perform could be deemed illusory, and hence unenforceable. As Farnsworth explains, when a promise "appears on its face to be so insubstantial as to impose no obligation at all on the promisor — who says, in effect, 'I will *if* I want to' — the promise is not enforceable." Farnsworth § 2.13, at 75. Accordingly, an enforceable termination clause that gives a promisor an unrestricted power to terminate a contract at any time, without notice, renders the promise illusory and unenforceable, at least so long as the purported contract remains wholly executory.

Either of the foregoing principles could possibly serve to defeat the plaintiffs' contract claim here. The complaint, however, does not definitively allege that RJR reserved an *unrestricted* right to terminate its duty to perform. The complaint alleges only that "[c]*ertain* (but not all) of the Camel Cash catalogs state that Reynolds could terminate the Camel Cash program without notice." Compl. ¶ 32 (emphasis added). The complaint, moreover, alleges that RJR "waived any right to terminate without notice when, on or about October 1, 2006, it announced by mailing a notice to program members, that the program would terminate as of March 31, 2007." *Id.* Dismissal is therefore unwarranted on the current record.

[In the balance of its opinion, the court rejects the defendant's argument that the statute of limitations applies to preclude the plaintiffs' actions, and concludes that the plaintiffs' claim of promissory estoppel should stand pending further proceedings. (Promissory estoppel is discussed in Chapter 3.) It does uphold the district court's dismissal of their statutory claims, for lack of sufficient proof of the defendant's fraud or the plaintiffs' reliance. — EDS.]

VIII. CONCLUSION

We affirm dismissal of the plaintiffs' UCL and CLRA claims. We reverse dismissal of the plaintiffs' breach of contract and promissory estoppel claims.

The parties shall bear their own costs on appeal.

AFFIRMED IN PART, REVERSED IN PART AND REMANDED.

NOTES AND QUESTIONS

1. *Did the defendant make an "offer" to its customers in the "Camel Cash" campaign?* The court in *Sateriale* considers the "an-ad-is-not-an-offer" position to be the "common law's general rule." See note 4 following *Lonergan.* Courts and writers disagree as to whether that "traditional" rule is in fact still the "majority view." Professor Farnsworth's discussion of the rationale behind the traditional rule — protection of sellers from "over acceptance" — quoted by the court, is helpful here; see also the court's footnote 3.

2. *Is the defendant's broad discretion consistent with contractual obligation?* The court also addresses the wide latitude that the terms of the defendant's campaign left it in shaping its performance, by invoking the existence of an "implied duty of good faith performance" as potentially curing that problem. See the court's footnote 5. We will consider in Chapter 6 the general nature of the implied duty of good faith, as found in general contract law and the Uniform Commercial Code. At this point, it is enough for us to note here that this principle can sometimes cure problems of indefiniteness in the contract-making area.

3. *The concept of "mutuality of obligation."* The court in *Sateriale* also addresses — but rejects — the argument that because the defendant reserved the freedom to terminate its "Camel Cash" campaign, its relationship with the plaintiffs was necessarily incapable of being a binding contract, because it was lacking in "mutuality of obligation." This concept can be briefly capsulized as "both parties must be bound or neither will be bound." While that makes a succinct statement at the "sound-bite" level, it is not at all clear that contract law actually incorporates this principle as a general rule. See the Restatement (Second) §79(c), which apparently views it merely as a corollary of the requirement of consideration; see also Joseph M. Perillo & Helen H. Bender, 2 Corbin on Contracts §6.1, at 197 (Perillo rev. ed. 1995) ("so-called requirement of mutuality of obligation is now widely discredited"). In any event, the court in *Sateriale* is correct in saying this principle should not apply to the unilateral contract, where one party (the offeree) is generally not bound to continue her performance.

4. *The "prove me wrong" case.* Another kind of pseudo-reward case involves a public challenge in which the speaker promises to pay a specified sum to anyone who can disprove the speaker's assertion. A recent example is Kolodziej v. Mason, 774 F.3d 736 (11th Cir. 2014). The defendant, an attorney whose client was on trial for murder, offered publicly — in the course of a television interview — to pay a million dollars to anyone who could prove that his client's alibi was not an airtight one. The issue was how long it would necessarily have taken for the accused to travel by car and plane to the murder scene, commit the crime and then return, as the prosecution was arguing he had. The defendant asserted this was not a practical possibility, but the plaintiff claimed to have shown it could be done. The lower court granted, and the appellate court upheld, summary judgment to the defendant. In the context, the court held, the plaintiff could not have reasonably understood the statement as an offer. Cf. Leonard v. Pepsico, discussed in Note 6 after the *Ray* case, above.

PROBLEM 2-1

Global Oil Corporation ("GOC") is a multinational oil company. On April 1, 2017, GOC began a nationwide advertising campaign using postings on gas pumps at service stations owned or affiliated with GOC throughout the United States. These pumps had the following advertisements:

> BUY 100 GALLONS OF FUEL, GET A FREE THREE-DAY PASS TO WALLEY WORLD (ORLANDO). WWW.GOC/WALLEYWORLD FOR DETAILS.

The website provided various details about the program, including the procedure for submission of receipts to obtain the Walley World pass. In bold large type at the beginning of the website, GOC made the following statement:

THIS PROGRAM IS AN INVITATION TO PARTICIPATE, NOT AN OFFER.

The website also provided: (a) Passes received under the program could only be used for personal or family purposes and not for commercial use; any such use voided the pass. (b) Passes could not be assigned or transferred except to family members. (c) By participating in the program, users agreed that they would comply with these restrictions.

On June 30, GOC terminated the advertising campaign, removed the advertisement from all pumps, and refused to honor any further submissions for Walley World passes.

A class action lawsuit has been filed against GOC. Members of the class accessed the GOC website before June 30 after making an initial purchase of gasoline. Members of the class fall into three categories, depending on their level of purchase:

1. Subclass 1 consists of consumers who purchased 100 gallons of fuel and who hold receipts for their purchases, but had not submitted their receipts before GOC terminated the program.
2. Subclass 2 consists of consumers who purchased at least 50 gallons of fuel and who hold receipts for their purchases before GOC terminated the program.
3. Subclass 3 consists of consumers who had made only one purchase of fuel before GOC terminated the program.

Prepare a memorandum discussing the contractual rights of the class members.

4. Postponed Bargaining: The "Agreement to Agree"

The contracts that we have studied so far appeared to be relatively complete, in that the parties presumably negotiated all of the terms regarded as necessary to reach an agreement, even though — as in *Sateriale* — leaving discretion to one or both parties as to the manner of performing. In many cases, however, a contract may be clearly incomplete — may not contain express terms governing various potentially important aspects of the parties' relationship. This can be true for a variety of reasons:

- The parties to a contract may not realize that they hold different understandings about the unaddressed terms;
- The costs of continued bargaining (in time, money, and the risk of losing the deal) may not appear justifiable in light of the relative infrequency with which disputes involving such omitted matters actually arise;
- A party's failure to pursue the bargaining farther may stem from her belief that if a dispute involving a particular type of unresolved issue were in fact to arise, she would prevail anyway, under terms that the law would imply;

- Finally, the parties themselves may by agreement have explicitly designated certain matters for postponed decision-making — for agreement at some future time.

Despite all these practical reasons why parties may create seemingly incomplete bargains, they posed serious legal problems under the classical system, as indicated by the following excerpt from Professor Corbin's treatise:

> Communications that include mutual expressions of agreement may fail to consummate a contract for the reason that they are not complete, some essential term not having been included. Frequently agreements are arrived at piecemeal, different terms and items being discussed and agreed upon separately. As long as the parties know that there is an essential term not yet agreed on, there is no contract; the preliminary agreements on specific items are mere preliminary negotiation building up the terms of the final offer that may or may not be made. Even though one of the parties may believe that the negotiation has been concluded, all items agreed upon, and the contract closed, there is still no contract unless he is reasonable in his belief and the other party ought to have known that he would so believe. . . .
>
> Further illustrations are to be found in the cases of a so-called contract to make a contract. It is quite possible for parties to make an enforceable contract binding them to prepare and execute a subsequent documentary agreement. In order that such may be the effect, it is necessary that agreement shall have been expressed on all essential terms that are to be incorporated in the document. That document is understood to be a mere memorial of the agreement already reached. If the document or contract that the parties agree to make is to contain any material term that is not already agreed on, no contract has yet been made; and the so-called "contract to make a contract" is not a contract at all.

1 Corbin on Contracts §29 (1950). The rules and principles discussed by Professor Corbin over a half-century ago have not disappeared from the scene; they can be and are employed by courts today. But they have been supplemented and in some cases substantially modified by new rules and principles, particularly those enunciated in the Uniform Commercial Code and echoed in the Restatement (Second) of Contracts. The materials that follow explore some of these developments.

Walker v. Keith

Kentucky Court of Appeals 382 S.W.2d 198 (1964)

CLAY, Commissioner.

In this declaratory judgment proceeding the plaintiff appellee sought an adjudication that he had effectively exercised an option to extend a lease, and a further determination of the amount of rent to be paid. The relief prayed was granted by the Chancellor. The principal issue is whether the option provision in the lease fixed the rent with sufficient certainty to constitute an enforceable contract between the parties.

In July 1951 appellants, the lessors, leased a small lot to appellee, the lessee, for a 10-year term at a rent of $100 per month. The lessee was given an option to extend the lease for an additional 10-year term, under the same terms and conditions except as to rental. The renewal option provided: "rental will be fixed in such amount as shall actually be agreed upon by the lessors and the lessee with the monthly rental fixed on the comparative basis of rental values as of the date of the renewal with rental values at this time reflected by the comparative business conditions of the two periods."

The lessee gave the proper notice to renew but the parties were unable to agree upon the rent. Preliminary court proceedings finally culminated in this lawsuit. Based upon the verdict of an advisory jury, the Chancellor fixed the new rent at $125 per month.

The question before us is whether the quoted provision is so indefinite and uncertain that the parties cannot be held to have agreed upon this essential rental term of the lease. There have been many cases from other jurisdictions passing on somewhat similar lease provisions and the decisions are in hopeless conflict. We have no authoritative Kentucky decision.

At the outset two observations may be made. One is that rental in the ordinary lease is a very uncomplicated item. It involves the number of dollars the lessee will pay. It, or a method of ascertaining it, can be so easily fixed with certainty. From the standpoint of stability in business transactions, it should be so fixed.

Secondly, as an original proposition, uncomplicated by subtle rules of law, the provision we have quoted, on its face, is ambiguous and indefinite. The language used is equivocal. It neither fixes the rent not furnishes a positive key to its establishment. The terminology is not only confusing but inherently unworkable as a formula.

The above observations should resolve the issue. Unfortunately it is not that simple. Many courts have become intrigued with the possible import of similar language and have interpolated into it a binding obligation. The lease renewal option has been treated as something different from an ordinary contract. The law has become woefully complicated. For this reason we consider it necessary and proper to examine this question in depth.

The following basic principles of law are generally accepted:

> It is a necessary requirement in the nature of things that an agreement in order to be binding must be sufficiently definite to enable a court to give it an exact meaning. Williston on Contracts (3d ed.) Vol. 1, section 37 (page 107).
>
> Like other contracts or agreements for a lease, the provision for a renewal must be certain in order to render it binding and enforceable. Indefiniteness, vagueness, and uncertainty in the terms of such a provision will render it void unless the parties, by their subsequent conduct or acts supplement the covenant and thus remove an alleged uncertainty. The certainty that is required is such as will enable a court to determine what has been agreed upon. 32 Am. Jur., Landlord and Tenant, section 958 (page 806).
>
> The terms of an extension or renewal, under an option therefor in a lease, may be left for future determination by a prescribed method, as by future

> arbitration or appraisal; but merely leaving the terms for future ascertainment, without providing a method for their determination, renders the agreement unenforceable for uncertainty. 51 C.J.S. Landlord and Tenant 56b (2), page 597.
>
> A renewal covenant in a lease which leaves the renewal rental to be fixed by future agreement between the parties has generally been held unenforceable and void for uncertainty and indefiniteness. Also, as a general rule, provisions for renewal rental dependent upon future valuation of premises without indicating when or how such valuation should be made have been held void for uncertainty and indefiniteness. 32 Am. Jur., Landlord and Tenant, section 965 (page 810).

Many decisions supporting these principles may be found in 30 A.L.R. 572; 68 A.L.R. 157; 166 A.L.R. 1237.

The degree of certainty is the controlling consideration. An example of an appropriate method by which a non-fixed rental could be determined appears in Jackson v. Pepper Gasoline Co., 280 Ky. 226, 133 S.W.2d 91, 126 A.L.R. 1370. The lessee, who operated an automobile service station, agreed to pay "an amount equal to one cent per gallon of gasoline delivered to said station." Observing that the parties had created *a definite objective standard* by which the rent could with certainty be *computed,* the court upheld the lease as against the contention that it was lacking in mutuality. (The Chancellor cited this case as authoritative on the issue before us, but we do not believe it is. Appellee apparently agrees because he does not even cite the case in his brief.)

On the face of the rent provision, the parties had not agreed upon a rent figure. They left the amount to future determination. If they had agreed upon a specific method of making the determination, such as by computation, the application of a formula, or the decision of an arbitrator, they could be said to have agreed upon whatever rent figure emerged from utilization of the method. This was not done.

It will be observed the rent provision expresses two ideas. The first is that the parties agree to agree. The second is that the future agreement will be based on a comparative adjustment in the light of "business conditions." We will examine separately these two concepts and then consider them as a whole.

The lease purports to fix the rent at such an amount as shall "actually be agreed upon." It should be obvious that an agreement to agree cannot constitute a binding contract. Williston on Contracts (3d ed.) Vol. 1, section 45 (page 149); Johnson v. Lowery, Ky., 270 S.W.2d 943; National Bank of Kentucky v. Louisville Trust Co., 6 Cir., 67 F.2d 97. . . .

As said in Williston on Contracts (3d ed.) Vol. 1, section 45 (page 149):

> Although a promise may be sufficiently definite when it contains an option given to the promisor, yet if an essential element is reserved for the future agreement of both parties, the promise gives rise to no legal obligation until such future agreement. Since either party, by the very terms of the agreement, may refuse to agree to anything the other party will agree to, it is impossible for the law to fix any obligation to such a promise.

We accept this because it is both sensible and basic to the enforcement of a written contract. We applied it in Johnson v. Lowery, Ky., 270 S.W.2d 943, page 946, wherein we said:

> To be enforceable and valid, a contract to enter into a future covenant must specify all material and essential terms and leave nothing to be agreed upon as a result of future negotiations.

This proposition is not universally accepted as it pertains to renewal options in a lease. Hall v. Weatherford, 32 Ariz. 370, 259 P. 282, 56 A.L.R. 903; Rainwater v. Hobeika, 208 S.C. 433, 38 S.E.2d 495, 166 A.L.R. 1228. We have examined the reasons set forth in those opinions and do not find them convincing. The view is taken that the renewal option is for the benefit of the lessee; that the parties intended something; and that the lessee should not be deprived of his right to enforce his contract. This reasoning seems to overlook the fact that a party must have an enforceable contract before he has a right to enforce it. We wonder if these courts would enforce an *original* lease in which the rent was not fixed, but agreed to be agreed upon.

Surely there are some limits to what equity can or should undertake to compel parties in their private affairs to do what the court thinks they should have done. See Slayter v. Pasley, Or., 199 Or. 616, 264 P.2d 444, 449; and dissenting opinion of Judge Weygandt in Moss v. Olson, 148 Ohio 625, 76 N.E.2d 875. In any event, we are not persuaded that renewal options in leases are of such an exceptional character as to justify emasculation of one of the basic rules of contract law. An agreement to agree simply does not fix an enforceable obligation.

As noted, however, the language of the renewal option incorporated a secondary stipulation. Reference was made to "comparative business conditions" which were to play some part in adjusting the new rental. It is contended this provides the necessary certainty, and we will examine a leading case which lends support to the argument.

In Edwards v. Tobin, 132 Or. 38, 284 P. 562, 68 A.L.R. 152, the court upheld and enforced a lease agreement which provided that the rent should be "determined" at the time of renewal, "said rental to be *a reasonable rental* under the then existing conditions." (Our emphasis.) Significance was attached to the last quoted language, the court reasoning that since the parties had agreed upon a reasonable rent, the court would hold the parties to the agreement by fixing it.

All rents tend to be reasonable. When parties are trying to reach an agreement, however, their ideas or claims of reasonableness may widely differ. In addition, they have a right to bargain. They cannot be said to be in *agreement* about what is a reasonable rent until they specify a figure or an exact method of determining it. The term "reasonable rent" is itself indefinite and uncertain. Would an original lease for a "reasonable rent" be enforceable by either party? The very purpose of a rental stipulation is to remove this item from an abstract area.

It is true courts often must *imply* such terms in a contract as "reasonable time" or "reasonable price." This is done when the parties fail to deal with such matters in an otherwise enforceable contract. Here the parties were undertaking to fix the terms rather than leave them to implication. Our problem is not what the law would imply if the contract did not purport to cover the subject matter, but whether the parties, in removing this material term from the field of implication, have fixed their mutual obligations.

We are seeking what the agreement actually was. When dealing with such a specific item as rent, to be payable in dollars, the area of possible agreement is quite limited. If the parties did not agree upon such an unequivocal item or upon a definite method of ascertaining it, then there is a clear case of nonagreement. The court, in fixing an obligation under a non-agreement, is not enforcing the contract but is binding the parties to something they were patently unable to agree to when writing the contract.

The opinion in the *Tobin* case, which purportedly was justifying the enforcement of a contractual obligation between the lessor and lessee, shows on its face the court was doing something entirely different. This question was posed in the opinion: "What logical reason is there for equity to refuse to act when the parties themselves *fail to agree* on the rental?" (Our emphasis.) The obvious logical answer is that even equity cannot enforce as a contract a nonagreement. No distortion of words can hide the fact that when the court admits the parties "fail to agree," then the contract it enforces is one it makes for the parties.

It has been suggested that rent is not a material term of a lease. It is said in the *Tobin* case: "The method of determining the rent pertains more to form than to substance. It was not the essence of the contract, but was merely incidental and ancillary thereto." This seems rather startling. Nothing could be more vital in a lease than the amount of rent. It is the price the lessee agrees to pay and the lessor agrees to accept for the use of the premises. Would a contract to buy a building at a "reasonable price" be enforceable? Would the method of determining the price be a matter of "form" and "incidental and ancillary" to the transaction? In truth it lies at the heart of it. This seems to us as no more than a grammatical means of sweeping the problem under the rug. It will not do to say that the establishment of the rent agreed upon is not of the essence of a lease contract. . . .

We do not think our problem can be solved by determining which is the "majority" rule and which is the "minority" rule. We are inclined, however, to adhere to a sound basic principle of contract law unless there are impelling reasons to depart from it, particularly so when the practical problems involved in such departure are so manifest. Let us briefly examine those practical problems.

What the law requires is an adequate key to a mutual agreement. If "comparative business conditions" afforded sufficient certainty, we might possibly surmount the obstacle of the unenforceable agreement to agree. This term, however, is very broad indeed. Did the parties have in mind local conditions, national conditions, or conditions affecting the lessee's particular business?

That a controversy, rather than a mutual agreement, exists on this very question is established in this case. One of the substantial issues on appeal is whether the Chancellor properly admitted in evidence the consumer price index of the United States Labor Department. At the trial the lessor was attempting to prove the change in local conditions and the lessee sought to prove changes in national conditions. Their minds to this day have never met on a criterion to determine the rent. It is pure fiction to say the court, in deciding upon some figure, is enforcing something the parties agreed to.

One aspect of this problem seems to have been overlooked by courts which have extended themselves to fix the rent and enforce the contract. This is the Statute of Frauds. The purpose of requiring a writing to evidence an agreement is to assure certainty of the essential terms thereof and to avoid controversy and litigation. See 49 Am. Jur., Statute of Frauds, section 313 (page 629); section 353 (page 663); section 354 (page 664). This very case is living proof of the difficulties encountered when a court undertakes to supply a missing essential term of a contract.

In the first place, when the parties failed to enter into a new agreement as the renewal option provided, their rights were no longer *fixed* by the contract. The determination of what they were was automatically shifted to the courtroom. There the court must determine the scope of relevant evidence to establish that certainty which obviously cannot be culled from the contract. Thereupon extensive proof must be taken concerning business conditions, valuations of property, and reasonable rentals. Serious controversies develop concerning the admissibility of evidence on the issue of whether "business conditions" referred to in the lease are those on the local or national level, or are those particularly affecting the lessee's business. An advisory jury is impaneled to express its opinion as to the proper rental figure. The judge then must decide whether the jury verdict conforms to the proof and to his concept of equity. On appeal the appellate court must examine alleged errors in the trial. Assuming some error in the trial (which appears likely on this record), the case may be reversed and the whole process begun anew. All of this time we are piously clinging to a concept that the contract itself fixed the rent with some degree of certainty.

We realize that litigation is oft times inevitable and courts should not shrink from the solution of difficult problems. On the other hand, courts should not expend their powers to establish contract rights which the parties, with an opportunity to do so, have failed to define. As said in Morrison v. Rossingnol, 5 Cal. 64, quoted in 30 A.L.R. at page 579:

> A court of equity is always chary of its power to decree specific performance, and will withhold the exercise of its jurisdiction in that respect, unless there is such a degree of certainty in the terms of the contract as will enable it at one view to do complete equity.

That cannot be done in this case.

Stipulations such as the one before us have been the source of interminable litigation. Courts are called upon not to enforce an agreement or to determine what the agreement was, but to write their own concept of what would constitute a proper one. Why this paternalistic task should be undertaken is difficult to understand when the parties could so easily provide any number of workable methods by which rents could be adjusted. As a practical matter, courts sometimes must assert their right not to be imposed upon. This thought was thus summed up in Slayter v. Pasley, Or., 264 P.2d 444, page 449:

> We should be hesitant about completing an apparently legally incomplete agreement made between persons sui juris enjoying freedom of contract and dealing at arms' length by arbitrarily interpolating into it our concept of the parties' intent merely to validate what would otherwise be an invalid instrument, lest we inadvertently commit them to an ostensible agreement which, in fact, is contrary to the deliberate design of all of them. It is a dangerous doctrine when examined in the light of reason. Judicial paternalism of this character should be as obnoxious to courts as is legislation by judicial fiat. Both import a quality of jural ego and superiority not consonant with long-accepted ideas of legistic propriety under a democratic form of government. If, however, we follow the urgings of the lessee in the instant matter, we will thereby establish a precedent which will open the door to repeated opportunities to do that which, in principle, courts should not do and, in any event, are not adequately equipped to do.

We think the basic principle of contract law that requires substantial certainty as to the material terms upon which the minds of the parties have met is a sound one and should be adhered to. A renewal option stands on the same footing as any other contract right. Rent is a material term of a lease. If the parties do not fix it with reasonable certainty, it is not the business of courts to do so.

The renewal provision before us was fatally defective in failing to specify either an agreed rental or an agreed method by which it could be fixed with certainty. Because of the lack of agreement, the lessee's option right was illusory. The Chancellor erred in undertaking to enforce it.

The judgment is reversed.

NOTES AND QUESTIONS

1. *Factors favoring the tenant.* It seems clear that the court that decided Walker v. Keith could, if it wished, have determined a "reasonable" rental for the renewal term and upheld the plaintiff tenant's right to renew on that basis (or simply affirmed the decision of the lower court, which appears to have done just that). What factors impelled its refusal to do so? In the course of its opinion, the *Walker* court concedes that other courts have enforced lease-extension agreements substantially similar to the one at issue in *Walker*, despite the incompleteness of the parties' agreement ("decisions are in hopeless conflict"). What considerations might lead a court to decide such a case in favor of enforcement? Should those factors have outweighed the ones that apparently actuated the court in *Walker*? In Cassinari v. Mapes, 542 P.2d 1069 (Nev. 1975), the plaintiff tenant sought damages for wrongful eviction from the premises on which he operated a restaurant business. The renewal option provision that the plaintiff sought to enforce stated that the five-year renewal term should be on "the same terms and conditions" as the original term, but "at a monthly rental to be determined" at the time of renewal. The court upheld the tenant's claim, on the following reasoning:

> It is appropriate to enforce such a provision since the clause for renewal constitutes part of the consideration for the original lease, and was without question intended by the parties to have meaning and to be effective. Surely we may not presume that one of the signatories agreed to the provision only in the secret belief that it would prove unenforceable. It is proper, then, to imply that the parties intended a reasonable rent for the extended period. If [they are] unable to agree, a court should be allowed to fix the rental since economic conditions are ascertainable with sufficient certainty to make the clause capable of enforcement. This view, we think, carries out the true intention of the parties, and does not constitute a making of a lease by the court in opposition to the desire of lessor and lessee.

Id. at 1071. Is this argument persuasive, given the facts of *Cassinari*? Would it be equally applicable to the *Walker* case? Why did the defendant landlord refuse to renew Walker's lease, and why did Walker care enough to attempt to legally enforce it? Although *Walker* is a mid-twentieth-century decision, its indifference to context and to potential equitable factors seems as "classical" as anything from the heyday of Langdell and Williston.

2. *Other decisions.* A number of courts have enforced lease-renewal option agreements despite the failure of the parties to agree on a rental figure in advance. See, e.g., Berrey v. Jeffcoat, 785 P.2d 20 (Alaska 1990) ("rent shall be renegotiated and determined according to existing conditions and cost of living increases as of that time"); Little Caesar Enterprises, Inc., v. Bell Canyon Shopping Center, L.C., 13 P.3d 600 (Utah 2000) ("When a bargained-for term of a renewal provision sets a range within which negotiations for a rental rate must take place, the lessor may not render the renewal provision unenforceable simply by refusing to negotiate within the specified range and insisting on rent exceeding the maximum allowed by the contract."). Other courts have disagreed, however, and take the same position as the court in *Walker*. See, e.g., Joseph Martin, Jr., Delicatessen, Inc. v. Schumacher, 417 N.E.2d 541, 544 (N.Y. 1981) ("annual rentals to be agreed upon"); Steffen v. Dumke, 2008 WL 2120012 (Wis. Ct. App.) (price "shall be negotiated" at time of renewal).

3. *Open price term agreements under the UCC.* Although *Walker* and the other cases cited in the Notes above involved leases, the common law generally has been resistant to the notion that an enforceable contract could result from an agreement in which the parties failed to agree on either a specific price or at least a method (specific formula, designated arbitrator, extrinsic market source, etc.) by which price could be ascertained. On this point, the Uniform Commercial Code takes a diametrically opposite position. Section 2-305 provides that an "open price term" will not necessarily prevent enforcement of a contract for the sale of goods. Whether the parties leave price for their later mutual determination or agree in advance that one of them shall have the power to fix a price, the court in either case may enforce the contract if it finds that the parties intended to be bound by their agreement. In that event, if the parties later fail to agree on price, the court may enforce a "reasonable price"; if one party has the power to fix price, he must do so "in good faith."

4. *Open price term agreements outside the UCC.* If UCC §2-305 makes sense in the context of Article 2, should the courts apply similar principles to "open price" contracts of other types? The Restatement (Second) in Comment *e* to §33 appears to endorse the notion that the principle of UCC §2-305 could be applied to contracts other than the sale of goods (although suggesting that the remedy might be limited to protection of the reliance or restitution interests). For example, in Arbitron, Inc. v. Tralyn Broadcasting, Inc., 400 F.3d 130 (2d Cir. 2005), the Second Circuit distinguished earlier New York cases, including *Joseph Martin*, cited in Note 2 above, and held that an escalation clause in a licensing agreement that allowed the licensor to adjust the monthly fee if the licensee acquired additional radio stations was not impermissibly vague even though it did not contain a definite price. The court held that the clause was not an unenforceable "agreement to agree," but instead allowed the licensor to set the price when stated conditions arose.

Quake Construction, Inc. v. American Airlines, Inc.

Supreme Court of Illinois 141 Ill.2d 281, 152 Ill. Dec. 308, 565 N.E.2d 990 (1990)

Justice CALVO delivered the opinion of the court:

Plaintiff, Quake Construction, Inc. (Quake), filed a four-count, third-amended complaint against defendants, American Airlines, Inc. (American), and Jones Brothers Construction Corporation (Jones). . . .

Quake alleged in its complaint the following facts. In February 1985, American hired Jones to prepare bid specifications, accept bids, and award contracts for construction of the expansion of American's facilities at O'Hare International Airport. Quake received an invitation to bid on the employee facilities and automotive maintenance shop project (hereinafter referred to as the project), and in April 1985 submitted its bid to Jones. Jones orally notified Quake that Quake had been awarded the contract for the project. Jones then asked Quake to provide the license numbers of the subcontractors Quake intended to use on the project. Quake notified Jones that the subcontractors would not allow Quake to use their license numbers until Quake submitted a signed subcontract agreement to them. Jones informed Quake that Quake would shortly receive a written contract for the project prepared by Jones. To induce Quake to enter into agreements with its subcontractors and to induce the subcontractors to provide Quake and Jones with their license numbers, Jones sent Quake the following letter of intent dated April 18, 1985:

> We have elected to award the contract for the subject project to your firm as we discussed on April 15, 1985. A contract agreement outlining the detailed terms and conditions is being prepared and will be available for your signature shortly.
>
> Your scope of work as the general contractor includes the complete installation of expanded lunchroom, restroom and locker facilities for American Airlines employees as well as an expansion of American Airlines existing Automotive

> Maintenance Shop. The project is located on the lower level of 'K' Concourse. A sixty (60) calendar day period shall be allowed for the construction of the locker room, lunchroom and restroom area beginning the week of April 22, 1985. The entire project shall be complete by August 15, 1985.
>
> Subject to negotiated modifications for exterior hollow metal doors and interior ceramic floor tile material as discussed, this notice of award authorizes the work set forth in the following documents at a lump sum price of $1,060,568.00.
>
> (a) Jones Brothers Invitation to Bid dated March 19, 1985.
> (b) Specifications as listed in the Invitation to Bid.
> (c) Drawings as listed in the Invitation to Bid.
> (d) Bid Addendum # 1 dated March 29, 1985.
>
> Quake Construction Inc. shall provide evidence of liability insurance in the amount of $5,000,000 umbrella coverage and 100% performance and payment bond to Jones Brothers Construction Corporation before commencement of the work. The contract shall include MBE, WBE and EEO goals as established by your bid proposal. Accomplishment of the City of Chicago's residency goals as cited in the Invitation to Bid is also required. As agreed, certificates of commitment from those MBE firms designated on your proposal modification submitted April 13, 1985, shall be provided to Jones Brothers Construction Corporation.
>
> Jones Brothers Construction Corporation reserves the right to cancel this letter of intent if the parties cannot agree on a fully executed subcontract agreement.

Jones and Quake thereafter discussed and orally agreed to certain changes in the written form contract. Handwritten delineations were made to the form contract by Jones and Quake to reflect these changes. Jones advised Quake it would prepare and send the written contract to Quake for Quake's signature. No such formal written contract, however, was entered into by the parties.

At a preconstruction meeting on April 25, 1985, Jones told Quake, Quake's subcontractors, and governmental officials present that Quake was the general contractor for the project. On that same date, immediately after the meeting, American informed Quake that Quake's involvement with the project was terminated. Jones confirmed Quake's termination by a letter dated April 25, 1985. The damages Quake allegedly suffered included the money it spent in procuring the contract and preparing to perform under the contract, and its loss of anticipated profit from the contract.

The main issue is whether the letter of intent from Jones to Quake is an enforceable contract such that a cause of action may be brought by Quake. This court has previously set forth the principles of law concerning the enforceability of letters of intent:

> The fact that parties contemplate that a formal agreement will eventually be executed does not necessarily render prior agreements mere negotiations, where it is clear that the ultimate contract will be substantially based upon the same terms as the previous document. [Citation.] If the parties . . . intended that the . . . document be contractually binding, that intention would not be

> defeated by the mere recitation in the writing that a more formal agreement was yet to be drawn. However, parties may specifically provide that negotiations are not binding until a formal agreement is in fact executed. [Citation.] If the parties construe the execution of a formal agreement as a condition precedent, then no contract arises unless and until that formal agreement is executed. Chicago Investment Corp. v. Dolins (1985), 107 Ill. 2d 120, 126-27, 89 Ill. Dec. 869, 481 N.E.2d 712.

See Ceres Illinois, Inc. v. Illinois Scrap Processing, Inc. (1986), 114 Ill. 2d 133, 143-44, 102 Ill. Dec. 379, 500 N.E.2d 1. . . . Thus, although letters of intent may be enforceable, such letters are not necessarily enforceable unless the parties intend them to be contractually binding. . . .

A circuit court must initially determine, as a question of law, whether the language of a purported contract is ambiguous as to the parties' intent. . . . If no ambiguity exists in the writing, the parties' intent must be derived by the circuit court, as a matter of law, solely from the writing itself. . . . If the terms of an alleged contract are ambiguous or capable of more than one interpretation, however, parol evidence is admissible to ascertain the parties' intent. (Borg-Warner Corp. v. Anchor Coupling Co. (1958), 16 Ill. 2d 234, 242, 156 N.E.2d 513; *Interway*, 85 Ill. App. 3d at 1098, 41 Ill. Dec. 117, 407 N.E.2d 615.) If the language of an alleged contract is ambiguous regarding the parties' intent, the interpretation of the language is a question of fact which a circuit court cannot properly determine on a motion to dismiss. . . .

In determining whether the parties intended to reduce their agreement to writing, the following factors may be considered: whether the type of agreement involved is one usually put into writing, whether the agreement contains many or few details, whether the agreement involves a large or small amount of money, whether the agreement requires a formal writing for the full expression of the covenants, and whether the negotiations indicated that a formal written document was contemplated at the completion of the negotiations. (*Ceres,* 114 Ill. 2d at 144, 102 Ill. Dec. 379, 500 N.E.2d 1; *Chicago,* 107 Ill. 2d at 124, 89 Ill. Dec. 869, 481 N.E.2d 712.) Other factors which may be considered are: "where in the negotiating process that process is abandoned, the reasons it is abandoned, the extent of the assurances previously given by the party which now disclaims any contract, and the other party's reliance upon the anticipated completed transaction." A/S Apothekernes Laboratorium for Specialpraeparater v. I.M.C. Chemical Group, Inc. (N.D. Ill. 1988), 678 F. Supp. 193, 196, *aff'd* (7th Cir. 1989), 873 F.2d 155.

. . .

The circuit court in the case at bar dismissed Quake's complaint, relying principally on the following sentence in the letter: "Jones Brothers Construction Corporation reserves the right to cancel this letter of intent if the parties cannot agree on a fully executed subcontract agreement" (hereinafter referred to as the cancellation clause). . . . The circuit court determined, based on the cancellation clause, that the parties agreed not to be bound until they entered into a formal written contract. Consequently, the circuit court held that the letter was not an enforceable contract and accordingly dismissed the complaint.

The appellate court, however, found the letter ambiguous. . . .

We agree with the appellate court majority's analysis and its conclusion that the letter was ambiguous. Consequently, we affirm the decision of the appellate court. The letter of intent included detailed terms of the parties' agreement. The letter stated that Jones awarded the contract for the project to Quake. The letter stated further "this notice of award authorizes the work." Moreover, the letter indicated the work was to commence approximately 4 to 11 days after the letter was written. This short period of time reveals the parties' intent to be bound by the letter so the work could begin on schedule. We also agree with the appellate court that the cancellation clause exhibited the parties' intent to be bound by the letter because no need would exist to provide for the cancellation of the letter unless the letter had some binding effect. The cancellation clause also implied the parties' intention to be bound by the letter at least until they entered into the formal contract. We agree with the appellate court that all of these factors evinced the parties' intent to be bound by the letter.

On the other hand, the letter referred several times to the execution of a formal contract by the parties, thus indicating the parties' intent not to be bound by the letter. The cancellation clause could be interpreted to mean that the parties did not intend to be bound until they entered into a formal agreement. Therefore, the appellate court correctly concluded that the letter was ambiguous regarding the parties' intent to be bound by it.

Defendants contend the letter of intent did not contain all of the terms necessary for the formation of a construction contract. Defendants assert construction contracts typically include terms regarding payment, damages and termination. Defendants argue the detail in the contract is usually extensive if the value and complexity of the construction project are great. Defendants also note the letter stated the contract would include the detailed terms and conditions of the parties' agreement. The letter indicated the contract would include the MBE, WBE and EEO (Minority Business Enterprise, Women's Business Enterprise, and Equal Employment Opportunity, respectively) goals established by Quake's bid proposal. Defendants point out the letter stated certain terms of the agreement still had to be negotiated. Without the formal contract, defendants assert, the parties could not have continued toward the completion of the project because the letter excluded many terms of the agreement which would have been included in the contract. Defendants thus argue the absence in the letter of all the terms of the agreement reveals the parties' intent not to be bound by the letter.

The appellate court stated the number and extent of the terms in the letter can indicate the parties' intent to be bound by the letter. The final contract only need be substantially based on the terms in the letter as long as the parties intended the letter to be binding. (Chicago, 107 Ill. 2d at 126-27, 89 Ill. Dec. 869, 481 N.E.2d 712.) Many of the details regarding the project were included in the letter. The letter adopted by reference the contents of certain documents which included even further details concerning the project. We agree Jones accepted the MBE, WBE and EEO goals established by Quake. The letter merely indicated that those goals would be reiterated in the contract. We acknowledge that the absence of certain terms in the letter indicates the parties' intent not to be bound by the letter. This only confirms our holding that the letter is ambiguous as to the parties' intent.

. . .

Defendants contend even if the letter contained all of the essential terms of a contract, the cancellation clause negated any inference that the parties intended to be bound by the letter. The clause, according to defendants, clearly established the parties' intent not to be so bound. . . .

We do not find defendants' argument persuasive. The appellate court stated that, in addition to the detailed terms of the parties' agreement, the letter also contained a sentence in which Jones said it awarded the contract for the project to Quake. Moreover, the letter stated "this notice of award *authorizes* the work." (Emphasis added.) Furthermore, the appellate court pointed out, the letter was dated April 18, while at the same time the letter indicated that Quake was to begin work the week of April 22 and complete the work by August 15. We agree with the appellate court's conclusion that a "reasonable inference from these facts is that the parties intended that work on the Project would begin prior to execution of a formal contract and would be governed by the terms of the 'Letter of Intent.' " (181 Ill. App. 3d at 914, 130 Ill. Dec. 534, 537 N.E.2d 863.) All of these factors indicate the negotiations were more than merely preliminary and the parties intended the letter to be binding. The factors muddle whatever otherwise "clear" intent may be derived from the cancellation clause.

Defendants acknowledge the letter was dated April 18 and it stated the work would commence the week of April 22. Defendants point out that the letter also indicated Jones would submit a formal contract to Quake "shortly." Defendants argue a contract could conceivably have been written and signed within that period of time. Defendants conclude the appellate court's assumption regarding the date of the letter and the commencement of the work was invalid. While defendants' interpretation of these facts is plausible, we believe it only lends credence to our conclusion the letter is ambiguous concerning the parties' intent. Thus, the trier of fact should decide which interpretation is valid.

. . .

Defendants further contend that the cancellation clause is not ambiguous. Defendants assert parties may agree, in a letter of intent, to the course of, and discontinuance of, their negotiations. Defendants argue the letter of intent in the case at bar merely reflects the parties' agreement regarding the course of their negotiations.

We, like the appellate court, find the cancellation clause itself ambiguous as to the parties' intent. We do not agree with defendants' assertion that the cancellation clause so clearly indicates the parties' intent not to be bound by the letter that the clause negates other evidence in the letter of the parties' intent to be bound. The clause can be construed as a condition precedent to the formation of a contract. The clause, however, also states that Jones can "cancel" the letter. As the appellate court noted, if the parties did not intend to be bound by the letter, they had no need to provide for its cancellation. We also agree with the appellate court that the cancellation clause "implies that the parties could be bound by the 'Letter of Intent' in the absence of a fully executed subcontract agreement." (181 Ill. App. 3d at 914, 130 Ill. Dec. 534, 537 N.E.2d 863.) Thus, the ambiguity within the cancellation clause itself enhances the other ambiguities in the letter.

. . .

Defendants allege that the appellate court's decision puts the continued viability of letters of intent at risk. Defendants contend if we uphold the appellate court's decision finding the cancellation clause ambiguous, negotiating parties will have difficulty finding limiting language which a court would unquestionably consider unambiguous. We disagree. Courts have found letters of intent unambiguous in several cases referred to in this opinion. . . . Thus, the existence or absence of particular language or words will not ensure that a letter of intent is unambiguous. Our decision here follows the settled law in Illinois concerning letters of intent: The intent of the parties is controlling.

Neither we nor the appellate court have decided whether in fact a contract exists, that is, whether the parties intended to be bound by the letter. We merely hold that the parties' intent, based on the letter alone, is ambiguous. Therefore, upon remand, the circuit court must allow the parties to present other evidence of their intent. The trier of fact should then determine, based on the evidence and the letter, whether the parties intended to be bound by the letter.

. . .

For the foregoing reasons, we affirm the decision of the appellate court.

Affirmed.

Justice STAMOS, specially concurring:

Because dismissal is unwarranted unless clearly no set of facts can be proved under the pleadings that will entitle a plaintiff to recover, I agree with the majority that the circuit court should not have dismissed . . . Quake's complaint. . . .

However, even though the Jones letter of intent is just ambiguous enough for Quake's complaint to survive a motion to dismiss, I consider that any interpretation of the letter's language as potentially establishing an underlying construction contract is far less plausible than the majority implies. . . .

Instead of weighing as heavily for as against a construction contract, in my judgment the cancellation clause powerfully militates against any finding of such contract. . . .

The cancellation clause refers expressly to cancelling the *letter*, not to cancelling the construction contract that the letter anticipates. A construction contract certainly would bind the parties to that contract's terms, but upon acceptance by Quake the letter here would much more plausibly be viewed as, at most, only binding the parties to efforts at achieving a construction contract on the terms outlined. See, e.g., Evans, Inc. v. Tiffany & Co. (N.D. Ill. 1976), 416 F. Supp. 224 (obligation to negotiate derived from unclear letter of intent); see also Farnsworth, Precontractual Liability, 87 Colum. L. Rev. at 250-69 (discussing letters of intent classified as "agreements with open terms" and "agreements to negotiate"); Knapp, Enforcing the Contract to Bargain, 44 N.Y.U. L. Rev. 673 (1969) (discussing need for recognizing good-faith bargaining duty as intermediate stage between ultimate contract and none); cf. Shell, Substituting Ethical

Standards for Common Law Rules in Commercial Cases: An Emerging Statutory Trend, 82 Nw. U.L. Rev. 1198, 1199 & n.7 (1988) (noting case law on duty of good-faith negotiation pursuant to letters of intent).

. . .

Hence, the letter itself, as distinguished from the anticipated construction contract, may be regarded as a contract in its own right: a contract to engage in negotiations. If so, it was this contract, not the anticipated construction contract, that might be canceled by Jones pursuant to the cancellation clause. Indeed, the notion of cancelling a construction contract not yet entered into lacks meaning.

. . .

. . . Yet, one might ask in reply: If the letter required only an effort to achieve a construction contract, and if failure of the effort would necessarily prevent any such contract from arising to bind the parties, how could the issue of cancelling a mere letter ever take on enough significance to explain inclusion of the cancellation clause? . . .

. . .

[S]everal hypotheses suggest themselves for explaining the present letter of intent's cancellation clause:

> Because the letter can be regarded as creating an obligation on Jones to attempt to achieve a construction contract, existence of the clause might be explained as a device by which Jones could put an end to its obligation to negotiate.
>
> The fact that this letter, like many others, was intended to induce action by third parties furnishes another possible explanation for including the cancellation clause: It would give Jones a way to put an end to any further inducement based on Jones' once-expressed intention.
>
> A third possible explanation lies in the possibility that, as a result of the parties' subsequent conduct (such as commencement of construction work by Quake), an uncancelled letter of intent might become a link in a chain leading to a finding of contract.
>
> Still another possible explanation lies in the fact that, commercially if not legally, letters of intent have a certain weight as trustworthy indicators of business decisions; accordingly, an issuer might wish to cancel a letter once a decision had changed, in order not to mislead those who might otherwise rely on it.

Any or all of these possibilities would adequately explain the clause, without any need whatever to conclude that the clause betokens an intent to be bound to a construction contract thought to be embodied in the letter. See also Precontractual Liability, 87 Colum. L. Rev. at 257-58 (discussing other possible rationales for clause).

If letters of intent are to be used, their drafters would be well advised to avoid ambiguity on the point of whether the issuers are bound. As ever, obscurantist language can produce desired practical effects in the short term, but can well lead eventually to litigation and undesired contractual obligations. Extreme examples exist. (See, e.g., Note, The $10.53 Billion Question — When Are the Parties Bound?: Pennzoil and the Use of Agreements in Principle in Mergers and Acquisitions, 40 Vand. L. Rev. 1367 (1987).) Some counsel and clients may opt for ambiguity on grounds of expediency and may account for the probability of resultant litigation costs in the clients' overall business decisionmaking, but many others could benefit from more precision. In turn, counsel for recipients of such letters should remain alert to the likelihood that the instruments lack contractual force.

. . .

NOTES AND QUESTIONS

1. *A lawyering question.* Both the majority and concurring opinions in *Quake* lament the letter of intent's lack of clarity on the issue of intention to be bound. Assuming that you represented Jones in the original negotiations, and foresaw the possibility of such a dispute as this, how could you have drafted the letter of intent to avoid the ambiguity found by the court and to protect your client's interests? Do you think Quake would have agreed to your version? Why or why not?

2. *Incomplete bargains: intention to be bound.* Analytically, it is useful to contrast different situations of incomplete bargaining. In one type of case, the "agreement to agree," the parties have reached accord on a number of important matters but have left one or more terms for future agreement (Walker v. Keith, the landlord-tenant dispute, was this type of case.) In the second situation, the "formal contract contemplated," the parties have reached agreement in principle on at least the major provisions of their agreement, but they contemplate the later execution of a formal written contract. See, e.g., Cochran v. Norkunas, 919 A.2d 700 (Md. 2007) (despite letter of intent, parties did not intend to be bound until standard form realty contract was executed). It is, of course, possible that a fact pattern could involve both of these – be an agreement to agree and also a formal-contract-contemplated case. For example, the parties might reach agreement on all material terms of their contract, except for delivery dates, which would expressly be left for future agreement; they could then express their agreement in principle in a brief letter of intent which contemplates the later execution of a more formal contract. Is *Quake* an example of an "agreement to agree"? A "formal contract contemplated"? Perhaps both?

Both the UCC and the Restatement recognize that parties may be bound contractually when they have reached agreement in principle, even though they contemplate either further negotiations on particular points ("agreement to agree") or the execution of a formal written contract ("formal contract contemplated"). UCC §2-204(3) states: "Even if one or more terms are left open a contract for sale does not fail for indefiniteness if the parties have intended to make a contract and there is a reasonably certain basis for giving an appropriate remedy." (UCC §2-204 is explored in more depth in Section C of this chapter.) Section 27 of the Restatement (Second) states: "Manifestations of assent that are in themselves sufficient to conclude a contract will not be prevented from so operating by the fact that the parties also manifest an intention to prepare and adopt a written memorial thereof; but the circumstances may show that the agreements are preliminary negotiations." Both the UCC and the Restatement thus agree with the *Quake* court that whether a contract is formed in such cases turns on the factual question of whether the parties intended to be contractually bound at the point when they agreed in principle, or only if further negotiations proved successful. The court in *Quake* identified a number of factors that would be relevant to a determination of the parties' intention. Restatement (Second) §27, Comment *c* contains a similar list. The *Quake* court remanded the case for trial on this factual issue. Based on the facts set forth in the opinion, how do you think the factual question of intention to be bound should be resolved? Note that in this area, at least, contract law does appear to make the result depend to some extent on the "subjective" issue of actual intent.

3. *A middle ground: the contract to bargain in good faith.* According to the majority's analysis only two possibilities exist: Either the parties did intend to be bound to a construction contract when they signed the letter of intent, or they didn't. As concurring Justice Stamos indicates, however, there is a third possibility — that by executing the letter of intent the parties bound themselves to negotiate in good faith to attempt to reach agreement on a construction contract, while also reserving the right to terminate their negotiations if they should be unable to reach agreement. In his concurrence, Justice Stamos refers to an article written by Professor Knapp in 1969. Charles L. Knapp, Enforcing the Contract to Bargain, 44 N.Y.U. L. Rev. 673 (1969). That article and the issues it discusses are further explored in the Comment below. If the court in *Quake* had recognized a cause of action for breach of the duty to bargain in good faith, should Jones have been held to have breached the duty? If so, what should Quake's remedy have been?

4. *Protection of reliance.* The court in *Quake* recognizes the possibility that promises contained in a letter of intent could induce a change of position by one of the parties, possibly giving rise to reliance-based protection. Other courts have also accepted this theory of recovery. In Arcadian Phosphates, Inc. v. Arcadian Corp., 884 F.2d 69 (2d Cir. 1989), the plaintiff sought to enforce what it asserted was a contract to bargain in good faith toward the purchase by the plaintiff of the defendant's phosphate fertilizer business. The parties' memorandum clearly contemplated the possibility that the parties would not reach a full and final agreement, which the court regarded as expressing their intent not to be bound by the memorandum. However, the evidence did indicate that the defendants insisted on a substantial change in the deal when market conditions altered, and that the defendants might have violated a promise to bargain in good faith. Such a promise might give rise to a duty to compensate the plaintiff on a "promissory estoppel" basis, the court held, particularly since the remedy for promissory estoppel could appropriately be limited to compensation of the plaintiff's out-of-pocket costs. Id. at 74, n.2. In Chapter 3 we discuss promissory estoppel as a possible basis for obligation when a traditional contract does not exist.

5. *Insight into the background of **Quake**.* Professor Judith Maute's recent article, Race Politics, O'Hare Airport Expansion, and Promissory Estoppel: The More Things Change, the More They Stay the Same, 69 Hastings L.J. 119 (2017), provides interesting insight into the political background of the case. She explains that Chicago political concerns created pressure to use minority-owned businesses, but American Airlines and Jones Construction thought Quake was fronting for a nonminority-owned business.

6. *The **Pennzoil/Texaco** case.* In 1984, the Board of Directors of Getty Oil Company voted to accept an offer from Pennzoil Company to merge Getty with Pennzoil, and Getty issued a press release declaring the existence of an "agreement in principle" between it, Pennzoil, and certain Getty stockholders. Drafting of implementation agreements between the parties proceeded expeditiously. At the same time, however, the Getty interests pursued the possibility of a better offer elsewhere, and in a few days announced their agreement to sell all the shares of Getty to Texaco, Inc., at a higher price per share than Pennzoil had agreed to pay. Pennzoil attempted unsuccessfully to enjoin in Delaware the consummation of the Texaco-Getty merger, after which it sued Texaco in the Texas courts for tortious interference with Pennzoil's asserted contractual right to acquire the Getty shares. A Texas civil jury found for Pennzoil, and awarded it actual damages of $7.53 billion, plus an additional $3 billion in punitive damages — a judgment that was said at the time to be "the largest civil judgment in history." Wall St. J., Nov. 20, 1985, at 3, col. 1. The lower court's judgment was affirmed by the Texas Court of Appeals in a 99-page opinion, 729 S.W.2d 768 (Tex. Ct. App. 1987). After other litigation in the federal courts, culminating in Pennzoil Co. v. Texaco, Inc., 481 U.S. 1 (1987), the case was finally closed by the payment to Pennzoil by Texaco of $3 billion in cash.

If only because of the sheer magnitude of the dollar amounts at stake, *Pennzoil v. Texaco* was the focus of much attention at the time, not merely from the business community but from the public in general. From a legal point of view, the case was just as notable for the variety and complexity of the legal issues it raised. These included not merely issues of contract and tort but complex questions of federal procedure, federalism and constitutional law, as well as the federal regulation of trading in securities (plus, in the final stages, federal bankruptcy law). For us at this point, however, the most interesting legal question was the threshold one faced initially by the Texas trial jury: Were the Getty interests bound by an agreement to sell their stock to Pennzoil? The trial court's instructions to the jury included the following:

INSTRUCTIONS

1. An agreement may be oral, it may be written or it may be partly written and partly oral. Where an agreement is fully or partially in writing, the law provides that persons may bind themselves to that agreement even though they do not sign it, where their assent is otherwise indicated.
2. In answering Issue No. 1, you should look to the intent of Pennzoil and the Getty entities as outwardly or objectively demonstrated to each other by their words and deeds. The question is not determined by the parties' secret, inward, or subjective intentions.

3. Persons may intend to be bound to an agreement even though they plan to sign a more formal and detailed document at a later time. On the other hand, parties may intend not to be bound until such a document is signed.
4. There is no legal requirement that parties agree on all the matters incidental to their agreement before they can intend to be bound. Thus, even if certain matters were left for future negotiations, those matters may not have been regarded by Pennzoil and the Getty entities as essential to their agreement, if any, on January 3. On the other hand, you may find that the parties did not intend to be bound until each and every term of their transaction was resolved.
5. Every binding agreement carries with it a duty of good faith performance. If Pennzoil and the Getty entities intended to be bound at the end of the Getty Oil board meeting on January 3, they were obliged to negotiate in good faith the terms of the definitive merger agreement and to carry out the transaction.

729 S.W.2d at 816.

Contemporary discussions of the effect of *Pennzoil/Texaco* on the general law applying to preliminary agreements of various kinds can be found in numerous articles, including Robert H. Mnookin & Robert B. Wilson, Rational Bargaining and Market Efficiency: Understanding *Pennzoil v. Texaco,* 75 Va. L. Rev. 295 (1989); Theodore H. Oldham, Letters of Intent in Business Transactions, 68 Mich. Bus. L.J. 524 (1989).

Comment: Contracting to Bargain in Good Faith

As the preceding Notes point out, the majority in the *Quake* case takes toward the issue of contract formation the same binary position that Professor Corbin took in the passage quoted at the beginning of this section: Either the parties intended to be completely bound by their letter of intent (in which case a court might have to "fill in the blanks" in order to enforce that contract), or they didn't (in which case neither party has any ongoing obligation to the other); a mere "agreement to agree," however, is not a binding contract. In his *Quake* concurrence, however, Justice Stamos suggests a third possibility: The parties' execution of the letter of intent bound the parties to negotiate in good faith to attempt to reach agreement on a construction contract, but the parties reserved the right to terminate the negotiations should they be unsuccessful in reaching agreement. Professor Knapp, in his 1969 article cited by Justice Stamos, advocated judicial recognition of the contract to bargain in good faith:

> In the typical "formal contract contemplated" case, the parties have clearly intended a bargain; they have also reached the stage of agreement on at least a number of the material terms of the proposed exchange. However, for some reason, they both apparently contemplate the later execution of a full, formal written document. At this stage of the negotiations, there are once again a number of possible views which the parties may entertain as to the extent to which each of them is "bound," by good business ethics, to the proposed exchange of performances:

(1) Each may regard himself as not bound to anything at all unless and until a formal writing is signed by him, and, further, as being free to refuse to sign that writing for any reason whatsoever. . . . There are many cases in which it is impossible to believe that the parties intended any liability to attach to either side until final execution of the contemplated formal document.

(2) Each party may really feel that the "formal" document is only a "formality" — some sort of ritual, desirable for one or more reasons, but in no sense a prerequisite to a "binding" agreement. . . .

In each of the two preceding characterizations of the "formal contract contemplated" situation, the parties may have actually reached agreement on every detail of their proposed exchange. In any such case where at the relevant point in negotiation there remain terms on which agreement has not been expressly reached, there is yet a third possibility:

(3) It is possible that the principals have carried the "deal" as far as they can, and that they are relying on their agents (almost always including lawyers, but possibly also accountants and other experts) to complete the process of agreement. In this view of the facts, the purpose of preparing the formal document is not simply to postpone creation of an obligation, or even to provide evidence of its existence or terms, but rather to afford these experts an opportunity to add to the total agreement such protection against various risks as they think necessary or prudent. On this assumption, the principals are likely to feel ethically bound to the outlines of the deal as they have hammered it out, the withdrawal of either one based simply on dissatisfaction with those outlines being regarded by both as admittedly unjustified. The principals, however, are likely to consider themselves still morally free to withdraw if and when it should appear that the "second team" of bargainers have raised a substantial issue on which they are unable to agree and which the principals, when apprised of the difficulty, are likewise unable to resolve.

Charles L. Knapp, Enforcing the Contract to Bargain, 44 N.Y.U. L. Rev. 673, 682-684 (1969). The article goes on to argue that where the true state of mind of the parties is the third of those described above, the court should regard them as bound by a contract to bargain in good faith. That contract should be potentially enforceable by damages or specific relief, if appropriate. However, if good faith bargaining should fail to yield a complete agreement, then each party should be free to withdraw from the transaction. In other words, the legal effect of the "agreement to agree" or "formal contract contemplated" should more closely reflect the actual intention of the parties: They should be neither completely free (to withdraw for any reason whatever), nor completely bound (should they later be unable to agree).

In a 1987 article (also cited by Justice Stamos), Professor E. Allan Farnsworth also found a middle ground between pure negotiation on the one hand and complete agreement on the other. He identified two forms of agreement in this middle area. One of these, which he called an "agreement to negotiate," is the substantial equivalent of Professor Knapp's "contract to bargain." E. Allan Farnsworth, Precontractual Liability and Preliminary Agreements: Fair Dealing and Failed Negotiations, 87 Colum. L. Rev. 217 (1987). The Farnsworth article contains a useful discussion of various bargaining tactics viewed through the lens of "fair dealing," and, in an Appendix, describes several common types of preliminary agreement, such as real estate binders, mortgage commitment letters, and letters of intent in mergers and acquisitions, indicating how each might be characterized using his mode of analysis.

A number of courts have recognized the concept of a contract to bargain in good faith. In Butler v. Balolia, 736 F.2d 609 (1st Cir. 2013), a federal appellate court had to decide whether a contract to negotiate would probably be enforceable under the law of Washington state. In the course of deciding that issue (in the affirmative), the court noted that many more jurisdictions had accepted the enforceability of contracts to negotiate than had repudiated that doctrine, and that the "trend line appears to be moving steadily" in that direction. Id. at 614. See, e.g., TRT Transportation, Inc. v. Aksoy, 506 Fed. Appx. 511 (7th Cir. 2013) (oral settlement agreement enforceable despite failure to reduce to writing; terms sufficiently definite to enforce despite parties failure to agree on other terms).

Of course, even if a particular court does recognize a duty to bargain in good faith, it will still be necessary for the plaintiff to establish a breach of that duty. E.g., see Venture Associates Corp. v. Zenith Data Systems Corp., 96 F.3d 275, 279 (7th Cir. 1996) (defendant was free to negotiate for new terms not mentioned in the letter of intent, or for changes in terms mentioned in the letter, including the price, so long as it "was not trying to scuttle the deal"); IDT Corp. v. Tyco Group, 918 N.E. 2d 913, 916 (N.Y. 2009) (parties negotiated open terms for almost three years; no evidence that party failed to act in good faith).

PROBLEM 2-2

You are vice president and general counsel of Super Comics, Inc., a company that publishes several popular comic magazines featuring a variety of comic and super-hero characters. Super's publications are of course copyrighted, and their principal recurring characters are also registered trademarks, which Super licenses to numerous manufacturers for use on merchandise of various kinds designed for the teen and pre-teen market. Recently Super has been engaged in a negotiation with JayRan Products, Inc., a maker of various toys and novelties, looking to the licensing of JayRan to use the names and pictures of "The Ribbets," a family of comic frogs featured in one of Super's publications, on a line of lunchboxes and related items (thermos bottles, plastic plates and utensils, etc.) for the back-to-school market. You recently met with the vice president and the chief legal counsel of JayRan to discuss this transaction. (Although Diana Hunter, the president of Super, customarily approves and signs such licensing agreements on behalf of Super, she usually delegates to you the task of negotiating and drafting the agreements.) At that meeting, you and they agreed on the essential terms of the proposed licensing agreement — the rate of royalty payments to be made by JayRan, the products on which the Ribbets would be featured, the length of time the licensing agreement would run (one year, commencing next June 1), the technical and design assistance to be provided by Super, the sales reports and other data to be provided by JayRan from which their royalty payments would be computed, and the circumstances under which one party or the other would have the right to terminate the agreement. At the conclusion of that meeting, it was agreed that you as counsel for Super would prepare a written agreement in form satisfactory to Super and forward it to JayRan's attorney, for approval and — if satisfactory to him — signing by Jay Randolph, the president of JayRan.

Three days ago you completed a draft of the agreement between Super and JayRan. (The drafting task was for you an easy one; the agreement is of a type entered into by Super many times every year and contains many — from your point of view — "standard" clauses.) You then sent (by messenger) four unsigned copies of the draft agreement to Marion Gerber, attorney for JayRan, along with the following letter (signed by you):

> Dear Marion:
>
> Here is the draft of our proposed license agreement, as promised. I think it fully incorporates our discussions, and contains (I hope) no surprises. If you and Mr. Randolph find it satisfactory, please return to me the enclosed four copies, signed by him. I will return to you two copies signed also by our president, Diana Hunter.

You have as yet received no reply from Gerber. This morning you have been called to Ms. Hunter's office. She informs you that she has just received from Octopus, Inc., owner of the national chain of "Octopus Garden" seafood restaurants, a proposal to use the Ribbet family on a series of novelty premiums to be given away with children's meals at the Octopus Garden restaurants, beginning next September. The Octopus proposal would require that Super grant it an exclusive license for a one-year period to feature the Ribbets in any manner on, connected with, or related to, food or food products. Hunter tells you she is very anxious to pursue the Octopus deal, which appears likely to be financially very attractive, but that she views the exclusivity clause that they have requested as inconsistent with the proposed licensing of the Ribbets for JayRan's lunchboxes. She asks you whether there is any reason at this point why the negotiations with JayRan cannot be suspended or simply broken off entirely with no liability on Super's part.

What do you tell her?

PROBLEM 2-3

Marigold Realty Corp. ("Marigold") is a corporation that owns a large tract of land in your city, on which is located a large shopping center known as Marigold Plaza. (Marigold has also developed Marigold Manor and Marigold Mountain, residential subdivisions that surround the land occupied by Marigold Plaza.) In Marigold Plaza are two retail shoe stores. One of these is operated by a local merchant; the other is currently occupied by a store that is part of a national chain of retail shoe stores. The local shoe merchant has recently decided to close out his business and retire at the expiration of his current lease. StepRite, Inc., the proprietor of another national shoe store chain, is interested in opening a store in the premises to be vacated, and is actively negotiating with Marigold to that end. Marigold has submitted to StepRite the form of lease used for the present tenant, and StepRite has concurred generally with its treatment of such issues as utilities, insurance, security, hours of operation, obligations of maintenance, and the like. The amount of the rent has yet to be agreed on, however. If the rent is to be a fixed monthly sum, Marigold has yet to agree to anything less than $10,000 per month, while StepRite has yet to offer more than $7,500. (Both parties agree that if the rent is to be a fixed sum per month, there will be an escalator clause for an annual percentage increase in rent; the amount of that percentage is as yet undetermined – the numbers discussed have ranged from 3 to 6 percent.) As an alternative, the parties have considered a rental based in part on a percentage of the tenant's gross receipts from sales; StepRite has suggested a fixed rental of $3,500 per month (again, subject to an annual percentage increase) plus 3 percent of the gross.

Besides the rental, several other terms remain to be agreed on. One is the duration of the lease. StepRite would like a five-year term with an option on its part to extend for another five years; Marigold is generally amenable to this, but would probably insist on some provision for renegotiation of the rent at the end of the first five-year term. Another point remaining to be settled relates to renovation of the leased premises. Ordinarily the lessee of such a store would itself bear the cost of whatever renovation might be needed, even though at the end of the lease term nonremovable improvements (such as painting, carpeting, lighting fixtures) would inure to the benefit of the landlord. StepRite is arguing, however, that because the store has been previously occupied, the cost of interior decoration will be higher than it would be in a new building, and that some of that cost should be absorbed in some manner by Marigold. While all these points remain the subject of active discussion and negotiation, StepRite and Marigold appear genuinely anxious to reach agreement with each other and to believe that such agreement is only a matter of time and some effort on their respective parts.

Until now, the negotiations between Marigold and StepRite have proceeded at a rather leisurely pace, because the expiration of the present tenant's lease is several months away. However, StepRite has just been presented with the opportunity to open a store in another local shopping center, in premises which have unexpectedly become vacant on short notice. StepRite has been given only a few days to consider whether it wants to avail itself of this other opportunity, after which that landlord will probably make arrangements with another tenant (one slightly less attractive than StepRite but ready to move quickly). StepRite would prefer to be in Marigold Plaza, and has no desire to operate more than one store in your city. However, it does not want to let this new opportunity go by unless it has assurances that the negotiations with Marigold are going to reach fruition.

(a) As attorney for StepRite, could you draft a "Memorandum of Intent" to be entered into by your client and Marigold, which would give StepRite the assurance it needs at this time? Would that memorandum, if executed, be legally binding on Marigold? On StepRite?

(b) As attorney for Marigold, would you advise your client to sign the memorandum prepared by StepRite's client pursuant to (a), above? Would you advise your client to insist on changes before signing? If so, what would they be? Would you advise your client not to sign *any* such memorandum? If so, what course of action would you propose?

PROBLEM 2-4

Herbert Ventor is a freelance scientist who owns numerous patents. One of his recently obtained patents is for a chemical additive (known as TZ 211) that increases the durability of exterior paint.

Ventor has agreed to grant DuraKote, a national paint manufacturer, an exclusive right for a period of one year to market paint containing his additive. DuraKote will pay Ventor $100,000 for this right. The parties have also agreed that DuraKote will have an option to market the additive on a long-term basis. Royalties and other terms of a long-term contract will be agreed on by the parties if DuraKote elects to exercise the option. DuraKote has asked you to draft a letter from it to Ventor setting forth the agreement of the parties. Prepare a draft of the letter.

B. CONSIDERATION

When lawyers and judges list the basic elements of a contract in the Anglo-American system, in addition to the requirement of agreement (perhaps referred to as "mutual assent" or "offer and acceptance"), they invariably speak of the requirement of "consideration." "A promise is not enforceable," judges have been routinely declaring for years, "unless it is supported by consideration." Because of its historical status as a long-standing common law doctrine, consideration traditionally has been one of the prominent ingredients of a course in basic American contract law. In recent years, however, its importance has been called into question, because of the relative rarity of real-world contract disputes in which the presence or absence of consideration is likely to be a decisive factor. Consideration, it is often asserted, should be de-emphasized or perhaps even ignored in the contracts classroom.

To understand why this is so, one needs to know how this element has been defined. In an earlier formulation, one which is still in widespread use today, consideration was defined in terms of either "benefit to the promisor" or "detriment to the promisee." The "promisor" in this case is the one who made the promise the enforcement of which is in question. (If the dispute has escalated into a lawsuit, that person is probably the defendant.) The "promisee" is thus the person to whom that promise was made (probably, the plaintiff). This version asks: Did the person making the promise get something for it ("receive a benefit")? Did the other person part with something ("suffer a detriment")? The "benefit/detriment" analysis can be seen in action in the courts' discussions in the *Hamer* and *Dougherty* cases, below, and its origins are explored in note 2 after *Hamer* and the Comment on the casebook website.

For over a century, however, it also has been common to define consideration in terms of "exchange." See, e.g., Restatement (Second) of Contracts §71. In this version, there is consideration for a promise if its performance would be part of a "bargained-for exchange," in which one party's performance is the "price" of the other's, and vice versa. Since the vast majority of significant commercial transactions do contemplate an exchange of something (goods, real estate, services, etc.) for something else (typically, but not necessarily, money), the requirement of consideration in most business contracts automatically will be satisfied. (There may still be commercial situations in which the presence or absence of consideration is more problematic, however; some of these are illustrated by the *Pennsy Supply* and *Marshall Durbin* cases, below.)

When the promise in question is not part of a commercial transaction, but is made by one family member to another, or grows out of a friendly (or even romantic) relationship, consideration may not be so obviously present. Certainly, family members and friends (romantic or otherwise) can and do engage in exchange transactions between themselves — transactions which courts can and ordinarily do regard as examples of conventional contract. But sometimes such a non-commercial promise is clearly gratuitous, not made in return for any "quid pro quo." In such cases, conventional-contract enforcement of that promise may not be available, although — as we shall see in Chapter 3 — there may be other bases on which the disappointed promisee can claim some remedial protection. In the main, however, contract law is concerned with exchange transactions, in which the possible absence of consideration is usually not a major issue.

Hamer v. Sidway

New York Court of Appeals 124 N.Y. 538, 27 N.E. 256 (1891)

Appeal from order of the General Term of the Supreme Court in the fourth judicial department, made July 1, 1890, which reversed a judgment in favor of plaintiff entered upon a decision of the court on trial at Special Term and granted a new trial.

This action was brought upon an alleged contract.

The plaintiff presented a claim to the executor of William E. Story, Sr., for $5,000 and interest from the 6th day of February, 1875. She acquired it through several mesne assignments from William E. Story, 2d. The claim being rejected by the executor, this action was brought. It appears that William E. Story, Sr., was the uncle of William E. Story, 2d; that at the celebration of the golden wedding of Samuel Story and wife, father and mother of William E. Story, Sr., on the 20th day of March, 1869, in the presence of the family and invited guests he promised his nephew that if he would refrain from drinking, using tobacco, swearing and playing cards or billiards for money until he became twenty-one years of age he would pay him a sum of $5,000. The nephew assented thereto and fully performed the conditions inducing the promise. When the nephew arrived at the age of twenty-one years and on the 31st day of January, 1875, he wrote to his uncle informing him that he had performed his part of the agreement and had thereby become entitled to the sum of $5,000. The uncle received the letter and a few days later and on the sixth of February, he wrote and mailed to his nephew the following letter:

> Buffalo, Feb. 6, 1875
>
> W. E. Story, Jr.:
>
> Dear Nephew — Your letter of the 31st ult. came to hand all right, saying that you had lived up to the promise made to me several years ago. I have no doubt but you have, for which you shall have five thousand dollars as I promised you. I had the money in the bank the day you was 21 years old that I intend for you, and you shall have the money certain. Now, Willie I do not intend to interfere with this money in any way till I think you are capable of taking care of it and the sooner that time comes the better it will please me. I would hate very much to have you start out in some adventure that you thought all right and lose this money in one year. . . . Willie, you are 21 and you have many a thing to learn yet. This money you have earned much easier than I did besides acquiring good habits at the same time and you are quite welcome to the money; hope you will make good use of it. I was ten long years getting this together after I was your age. Now, hoping this will be satisfactory, I stop. One thing more. Twenty-one years ago I bought you 15 sheep. These sheep were put out to double every four years. I kept track of them the first eight years; I have not heard much about them since. Your father and grandfather promised me that they would look after them till you were of age. Have they done so? I hope they have. By this time you have between five and six hundred sheep, worth a nice little income this spring. Willie, I have said much more than I expected to; hope you can make out what I have written. To-day is the seventeenth day that I have not been out of my room, and have had the doctor as many days. Am a little better to-day; think I will get out next week. You need not mention to father, as he always worries about small matters.
>
> Truly Yours
> *W. E. Story.*
>
> P.S. — You can consider this money on interest.

The nephew received the letter and thereafter consented that the money should remain with his uncle in accordance with the terms and conditions of the letters. The uncle died on the 29th day of January, 1887, without having paid over to his nephew any portion of the said $5,000 and interest.

Parker, J. The question which provoked the most discussion by counsel on this appeal, and which lies at the foundation of plaintiff's asserted right of recovery, is whether by virtue of a contract defendant's testator William E. Story became indebted to his nephew William E. Story, 2d, on his twenty-first birthday in the sum of five thousand dollars. The trial court found as a fact that "on the 20th day of March, 1869, . . . William E. Story agreed to and with William E. Story, 2d, that if he would refrain from drinking liquor, using tobacco, swearing, and playing cards or billiards for money until he should become 21 years of age then he, the said William E. Story, would at that time pay him, the said William E. Story, 2d, the sum of $5,000 for such refraining, to which the said William E. Story, 2d, agreed," and that he "in all things fully performed his part of said agreement."

The defendant contends that the contract was without consideration to support it, and, therefore, invalid. He asserts that the promisee by refraining from the use of liquor and tobacco was not harmed but benefited; that that which he did was best for him to do independently of his uncle's promise, and insists that it follows that unless the promisor was benefited, the contract was without consideration. A contention, which if well founded, would seem to leave open for controversy in many cases whether that which the promisee did or omitted to do was, in fact, of such benefit to him as to leave no consideration to support the enforcement of the promisor's agreement. Such a rule could not be tolerated, and is without foundation in the law. The Exchequer Chamber, in 1875, defined consideration as follows: "A valuable consideration in the sense of the law may consist either in some right, interest, profit or benefit accruing to the one party, or some forbearance, detriment, loss or responsibility given, suffered or undertaken by the other." Courts "will not ask whether the thing which forms the consideration does in fact benefit the promisee or a third party, or is of any substantial value to anyone. It is enough that something is promised, done, forborne or suffered by the party to whom the promise is made as consideration for the promise made to him." (Anson's Prin. of Con. 63.)

"In general a waiver of any legal right at the request of another party is a sufficient consideration for a promise." (Parsons on Contracts, 444.)

"Any damage, or suspension, or forbearance of a right will be sufficient to sustain a promise." (Kent, vol. 2, 465, 12th ed.)

Pollock, in his work on contracts, page 166, after citing the definition given by the Exchequer Chamber already quoted, says: "The second branch of this judicial description is really the most important one. Consideration means not so much that one party is profiting as that the other abandons some legal right in the present or limits his legal freedom of action in the future as an inducement for the promise of the first."

Now, applying this rule to the facts before us, the promisee used tobacco, occasionally drank liquor, and he had a legal right to do so. That right he abandoned for a period of years upon the strength of the promise of the testator that for such forbearance he would give him $5,000. We need not speculate on the effort which may have been required to give up the use of those stimulants. It is sufficient that he restricted his lawful freedom of action within certain prescribed limits upon the faith of his uncle's agreement, and now having fully performed the conditions imposed, it is of no moment whether such performance actually proved a benefit to the promisor, and the court will not inquire into it, but were it a proper subject of inquiry, we see nothing in this record that would permit a determination that the uncle was not benefited in a legal sense. Few cases have been found which may be said to be precisely in point, but such as have been support the position we have taken.

In Shadwell v. Shadwell (9 C.B. [N.S.] 159), an uncle wrote to his nephew as follows:

> My Dear Lancey —
>
> I am so glad to hear of your intended marriage with Ellen Nicholl, and as I promised to assist you at starting, I am happy to tell you that I will pay you 150 pounds yearly during my life and until your annual income derived from your profession of a chancery barrister shall amount to 600 guineas, of which your own admission will be the only evidence that I shall require.
>
> Your affectionate uncle,
> *Charles Shadwell.*

It was held that the promise was binding and made upon good consideration.

In Lakota v. Newton, an unreported case in the Superior Court of Worcester, Mass., the complaint averred defendant's promise that "if you (meaning plaintiff) will leave off drinking for a year I will give you $100," plaintiff's assent thereto, performance of the condition by him, and demanded judgment therefor. Defendant demurred on the ground, among others, that the plaintiff's declaration did not allege a valid and sufficient consideration for the agreement of the defendant. The demurrer was over-ruled.

In Talbott v. Stemmons (a Kentucky case not yet reported), the step-grandmother of the plaintiff made with him the following agreement: "I do promise and bind myself to give my grandson, Albert R. Talbott, $500 at my death, if he will never take another chew of tobacco or smoke another cigar during my life from this date up to my death, and if he breaks his pledge he is to refund double the amount to his mother." The executor of Mrs. Stemmons demurred to the complaint on the ground that the agreement was not based on a sufficient consideration. The demurrer was sustained and an appeal taken therefrom to the Court of Appeals, where the decision of the court below was reversed. In the opinion of the court it is said that "the right to use and enjoy the use of tobacco was a right that belonged to the plaintiff and not forbidden by law. The abandonment of its use may have saved him money or contributed to his health, nevertheless, the surrender of that right caused the promise, and having the right to contract with reference to the subject-matter, the abandonment of the use was a sufficient consideration to uphold the promise." Abstinence from the use of intoxicating liquors was held to furnish a good consideration for a promissory note in Lindell v. Rokes (60 Mo. 249). . . .

[The defendant also argued that even if the uncle's promise had originally given rise to an enforceable obligation, the plaintiff's action to enforce that promise was barred by the statute of limitations — too much time had passed since the cause of action arose. The court held, however, that the uncle's letter amounted to a "declaration of trust," making the uncle himself a "trustee" of the promised sum on behalf of his nephew as "beneficiary." The case thus was viewed not as the mere attempt to enforce an executory promise, but as an action to compel the delivery of a sum of money held in trust; the uncle's original promise was viewed as having in a legal sense already been performed. — EDS.]

The order appealed from should be reversed and the judgment of the Special Term affirmed, with costs payable out of the estate.

All concur.

Order reversed and judgment of Special Term affirmed.

NOTES AND QUESTIONS

1. *Hypothetical variations of* ***Hamer****.* Consider the following cases:

(a) Recall our earlier discussions of Lucy v. Zehmer and Leonard v. Pepsico, in the Notes following the *Ray* case. Suppose that when young Mr. Story turned 21 and wrote his uncle to request payment, the uncle had responded (truthfully) that his "promise" of $5,000 was not seriously intended — that it had been made only as a boast to impress the guests at the golden wedding celebration. Should the outcome of the case have been different?

(b) Suppose that when young Mr. Story reached the age of 20 years, he had written a note to his uncle William, in which he stated: "Only one more year to go, Uncle Bill! I've kept my promise and I intend to keep on doing that; I have big plans for investing the $5,000 you promised me." Suppose his uncle had written back, "Dear Nephew: I'm glad you're being an upright young man, but I don't think you can count on that $5,000 from me. I'm devoting my energy and my finances to some new business ventures of my own." At that point, would the uncle have had any legal obligation to his nephew? What legal remedies — if any — might have been available to young Will?

(c) It's 2019, and young Will Story, aged 21, has a serious drug problem. His loving Uncle Bill promises to pay Will $5,000 on his 25st birthday if Will abstains from using cocaine for the next four years. Will spends four years clean and sober, with no use of drugs or alcohol, and asks Uncle Bill for the money. Perhaps Uncle Bill will pay gladly, but if he doesn't, should Will be able to sue him for the money?

2. *Historical background.* As we noted in the introduction to this section, the test for consideration employed by the court in *Hamer* is not the only one a court might use; the Restatement uses a "bargained-for exchange" analysis, which we will address below. The "benefit/detriment" test used in *Hamer* has deep roots in Anglo-American contract law. The casebook website contains a Comment on the history of the consideration doctrine and the "benefit/detriment" test. As discussed in more detail in that Comment, early English courts did not recognize what we today would call a cause of action or a claim for relief. Instead, the courts used a "writ" system. To obtain a remedy from a court, the plaintiff had to show that his situation fit within one of a number of writs. Early "contract-like" writs — the writs of covenant and debt — had specific requirements: To obtain the writ of covenant, the plaintiff had to show that the defendant made a promise in a sealed instrument; the writ of debt was available if the defendant breached a promise to pay a sum-certain of money. By 1600 the

writ of assumpsit replaced covenant and debt and became the general writ to recover for breach or nonperformance of a promise. Unlike covenant or debt, assumpsit did not have specific requirements other than the defendant's breach or nonperformance of a promise. As assumpsit evolved, it became customary to plead the factors that the defendant had considered in making his promise. The concepts of detriment to the promisee and benefit to the promisor, which were used quite early, came to represent the paradigms of consideration. One in-depth exploration of the history of the consideration doctrine is contained in Alfred W. B. Simpson, A History of the Common Law of Contract (1987).

Pennsy Supply, Inc. v. American Ash Recycling Corp. of Pennsylvania

Pennsylvania Superior Court 895 A.2d 595 (2006)

Before: Joyce, Orie Melvin and Tamilia, JJ.

Opinion by Orie Melvin, J.:

1. Appellant, Pennsy Supply, Inc. ("Pennsy"), appeals from the grant of preliminary objections in the nature of a demurrer in favor of Appellee, American Ash Recycling Corp. of Pennsylvania ("American Ash"). We reverse and remand for further proceedings.

2. The trial court summarized the allegations of the complaint as follows:

> The instant case arises out of a construction project for Northern York High School (Project) owned by Northern York County School District (District) in York County, Pennsylvania. The District entered into a construction contract for the Project with a general contractor, Lobar, Inc. (Lobar). Lobar, in turn, subcontracted the paving of driveways and a parking lot to [Pennsy].
>
> The contract between Lobar and the District included Project Specifications for paving work which required Lobar, through its subcontractor Pennsy, to use certain base aggregates. The Project Specifications permitted substitution of the aggregates with an alternate material known as Treated Ash Aggregate (TAA) or AggRite.
>
> The Project Specifications included a "notice to bidders" of the availability of AggRite at no cost from [American Ash], a supplier of AggRite. The Project Specifications also included a letter to the Project architect from American Ash confirming the availability of a certain amount of free AggRite on a first come, first served basis.
>
> Pennsy contacted American Ash and informed American Ash that it would require approximately 11,000 tons of AggRite for the Project. Pennsy subsequently picked up the AggRite from American Ash and used it for the paving work, in accordance with the Project Specifications.
>
> Pennsy completed the paving work in December 2001. The pavement ultimately developed extensive cracking in February 2002. The District notified . . . Lobar[] as to the defects and Lobar in turn directed Pennsy to remedy the defective work. Pennsy performed the remedial work during summer 2003 at no cost to the District.
>
> The scope and cost of the remedial work included the removal and appropriate disposal of the AggRite, which is classified as a hazardous waste material by

> the Pennsylvania Department of Environmental Protection. Pennsy requested American Ash to arrange for the removal and disposal of the AggRite; however, American Ash did not do so. Pennsy provided notice to American Ash of its intention to recover costs.

Trial Court Opinion, 5/27/05, at 1-3 (footnote omitted). Pennsy also alleged that the remedial work cost it $251,940.20 to perform and that it expended an additional $133,777.48 to dispose of the AggRite it removed. Compl. ¶¶26, 29.

3. On November 18, 2004, Pennsy filed a five-count complaint against American Ash alleging breach of contract (Count I); breach of implied warranty of merchantability (Count II); breach of express warranty of merchantability (Count III); breach of warranty of fitness for a particular purpose (Count IV); and promissory estoppel (Count V). American Ash filed demurrers to all five counts. Pennsy responded and also sought leave to amend should any demurrer be sustained. The trial court sustained the demurrers by order and opinion dated May 25, 2005, and dismissed the complaint. This appeal followed.

4. Pennsy raises three questions for our review:

> . . .
>
> (2) Whether Pennsy's relief of [American Ash's] legal obligation to dispose of a material classified as hazardous waste, such that [American Ash] avoided the costs of disposal thereof at a hazardous waste site, is sufficient consideration to ground contract and warranty claims.
>
> . . .

Appellant's Brief at 3.

5. "Preliminary objections in the nature of a demurrer test the legal sufficiency of the complaint." Hospodar v. Schick, 885 A.2d 986, 988 (Pa. Super. 2005).

> When reviewing the dismissal of a complaint based upon preliminary objections in the nature of a demurrer, we treat as true all well-pleaded material, factual averments and all inferences fairly deducible therefrom. Where the preliminary objections will result in the dismissal of the action, the objections may be sustained only in cases that are clear and free from doubt. To be clear and free from doubt that dismissal is appropriate, it must appear with certainty that the law would not permit recovery by the plaintiff upon the facts averred. Any doubt should be resolved by a refusal to sustain the objections. Moreover, we review the trial court's decision for an abuse of discretion or an error of law.

Id. In applying this standard to the instant appeal, we deem it easiest to order our discussion by count.

6. Count I raises a breach of contract claim. "A cause of action for breach of contract must be established by pleading (1) the existence of a contract, including its essential terms, (2) a breach of a duty imposed by the contract and (3) resultant damages." Corestates Bank, N.A. v. Cutillo, 723 A.2d 1053, 1058 (Pa. Super. 1999). While not every term of a contract must be stated in complete detail, every element must be specifically pleaded. Id. at 1058. Clarity

is particularly important where an oral contract is alleged. Snaith v. Snaith, 422 A.2d 1379, 1382 (Pa. Super. 1980).

7. Instantly, the trial court determined that "any alleged agreement between the parties is unenforceable for lack of consideration." Trial Court Opinion, 5/27/05, at 5. The trial court also stated "the facts as pleaded do not support an inference that disposal costs were part of any bargaining process *or* that American Ash offered the AggRite with an intent to avoid disposal costs." Id. at 7 (emphasis added). Thus, we understand the trial court to have dismissed Count I for two reasons related to the necessary element of consideration: one, the allegations of the Complaint established that Pennsy had received a conditional gift from American Ash, see Id. 6, 8, and, two, there were no allegations in the Complaint to show that American Ash's avoidance of disposal costs was part of any bargaining process between the parties. See Id. at 7.

8. It is axiomatic that consideration is "an essential element of an enforceable contract." Stelmack v. Glen Alden Coal Co., 339 Pa. 410, 414-415, 14 A.2d 127, 128 (1940). See also Weavertown Transport Leasing, Inc v. Moran, 834 A.2d 1169, 1172 (Pa. Super. 2003) (stating, "[a] contract is formed when the parties to it (1) reach a mutual understanding, (2) exchange consideration, and (3) delineate the terms of their bargain with sufficient clarity"). Consideration consists of a benefit to the promisor or a detriment to the promisee."*Weavertown*, 834 A.2d at 1172 (citing *Stelmack*). "Consideration must actually be bargained for as the exchange for the promise." *Stelmack*, 339 Pa. at 414, 14 A.2d at 129.

> It is not enough, however, that the promisee has suffered a legal detriment at the request of the promisor. The detriment incurred must be the "quid pro quo", or the "price" of the promise, and the inducement for which it was made. . . . If the promisor merely intends to make a gift to the promisee upon the performance of a condition, the promise is gratuitous and the satisfaction of the condition is not consideration for a contract. The distinction between such a conditional gift and a contract is well illustrated in Williston on Contracts, Rev. Ed., Vol. 1, Section 112, where it is said: "If a benevolent man says to a tramp, 'If you go around the corner to the clothing shop there, you may purchase an overcoat on my credit,' no reasonable person would understand that the short walk was requested as the consideration for the promise, but that in the event of the tramp going to the shop the promisor would make him a gift."

Weavertown, 834 A.2d at 1172 (quoting *Stelmack*, 339 Pa. at 414, 14 A.2d at 128-29). Whether a contract is supported by consideration presents a question of law. Davis & Warde, Inc. v. Tripodi, 616 A.2d 1384 (Pa. Super. 1992).

9. The classic formula for the difficult concept of consideration was stated by Justice Oliver Wendell Holmes, Jr., as "the promise must induce the detriment and the detriment must induce the promise." John Edward Murray, Jr., Murray on Contracts §60 (3d. ed. 1990), at 227 (citing Wisconsin & Michigan Ry. v. Powers, 191 U.S. 379 (1903)). As explained by Professor Murray:

> If the promisor made the promise for the purpose of inducing the detriment, the detriment induced the promise. If, however, the promisor made the promise with no particular interest in the detriment that the promisee had to suffer to take advantage of the promised gift or other benefit, the detriment was

> incidental or conditional to the promisee's receipt of the benefit. Even though the promisee suffered a detriment induced by the promise, the purpose of the promisor was not to have the promisee suffer the detriment because she did not seek that detriment in exchange for her promise.

Id. §60.C, at 230 (emphasis added). This concept is also well summarized in American Jurisprudence:

> As to the distinction between consideration and a condition, it is often difficult to determine whether words of condition in a promise indicate a request for consideration or state a mere condition in a gratuitous promise. An aid, though not a conclusive test, in determining which construction of the promise is more reasonable is an inquiry into *whether the occurrence of the condition would benefit the promisor. If so, it is a fair inference that the occurrence was requested as consideration.* On the other hand, if the occurrence of the condition is no benefit to the promisor but is merely to enable the promisee to receive a gift, the occurrence of the event on which the promise is conditional, though brought about by the promisee in reliance on the promise, is not properly construed as consideration.

17A Am. Jur. 2d §104 (2004 & 2005 Supp.) (emphasis added). See also Restatement (Second) of Contracts §71 comment c (noting "the distinction between bargain and gift may be a fine one, depending on the motives manifested by the parties"); Carlisle v. T & R Excavating, Inc., 704 N.E.2d 39 (Ohio App. 1997) (discussing the difference between consideration and a conditional gift and finding no consideration where promisor who promised to do excavating work for preschool being built by ex-wife would receive no benefit from wife's reimbursement of his material costs).

10. Upon review, we disagree with the trial court that the allegations of the Complaint show only that American Ash made a conditional gift of the AggRite to Pennsy. In paragraphs 8 and 9 of the Complaint, Pennsy alleged:

> American Ash actively promotes the use of AggRite as a building material to be used in base course of paved structures, and provides the material free of charge, in an effort to have others dispose of the material and thereby avoid incurring the disposal costs itself . . . American Ash provided the AggRite to Pennsy for use on the Project, which saved American Ash thousands of dollars in disposal costs it otherwise would have incurred.

Compl. ¶¶8, 9. Accepting these allegations as true and using the Holmesian formula for consideration, it is a fair interpretation of the Complaint that American Ash's promise to supply AggRite free of charge induced Pennsy to assume the detriment of collecting and taking title to the material, and critically, that it was this very detriment, whether assumed by Pennsy or some other successful bidder to the paving subcontract, which induced American Ash to make the promise to provide free AggRite for the project. Paragraphs 8-9 of the Complaint simply belie the notion that American Ash offered AggRite as a conditional gift to the successful bidder on the paving subcontract for which American Ash desired and expected nothing in return.

11. We turn now to whether consideration is lacking because Pennsy did not allege that American Ash's avoidance of disposal costs was part of any

bargaining process between the parties. The Complaint does not allege that the parties discussed or even that Pennsy understood at the time it requested or accepted the AggRite that Pennsy's use of the AggRite would allow American Ash to avoid disposal costs.[5] However, we do not believe such is necessary. The bargain theory of consideration does not actually require that the parties bargain over the terms of the agreement. . . . According to Holmes, an influential advocate of the bargain theory, what is required [for consideration to exist] is that the promise and the consideration be in "the relation of reciprocal conventional inducement, each for the other." Allen Farnsworth, Farnsworth on Contracts §2.6 (1990) (citing O. Holmes, The Common Law 293-94 (1881)); see also Restatement (Second) of Contracts §71 (defining "bargained for" in terms of the Holmesian formula). Here, as explained above, the Complaint alleges facts which, if proven, would show the promise induced the detriment and the detriment induced the promise. This would be consideration. Accordingly, we reverse the dismissal of Count I.

[The court went on to hold that the trial court also erred in dismissing the counts for breach of warranty under the UCC and for promissory estoppel. — EDS.]

22. For all of the foregoing reasons, we reverse the trial court's order granting the demurrers and dismissing the Complaint and remand for further proceedings. Jurisdiction relinquished.

NOTES AND QUESTIONS

1. *Disposal costs.* It may seem odd that Pennsy Supply sought in this lawsuit to recover the costs it incurred to dispose of the AggRite, given its argument that the consideration for its contract with American Ash was that this arrangement relieved American Ash of disposal costs. However, Pennsy planned on using the AggRite in paving work, which should not have involved any disposal expenses. The only reason Pennsy incurred these costs was that the AggRite was defective, requiring that it be removed and disposed of. Put another way: Pennsy did agree to take the AggRite "off American Ash's hands," but it did not agree to dispose of the AggRite in a way that would have required it to pay the expenses of disposal.

2. *Pennsy's claims for breach of warranty under Article 2.* Pennsy's complaint alleged causes of action for breach of various warranties under Article 2 of the UCC. We examine these warranties in Chapter 6. Most courts have restricted Article 2 warranties to contracts for the sale of goods. (UCC Article 2A, dealing

---

5. Pennsy's complaint, by placing the allegation in ¶8 that American Ash promotes AggRite and provides it free of charge, before the allegations in ¶¶9-10 related to formation of the oral contract, is arguably structured to suggest Pennsy did contemplate American Ash's avoidance of disposal costs. We note also that during oral argument on the preliminary objections, Pennsy's counsel represented "it was understood by everybody that this [i.e., avoidance of disposal costs] was what American Ash was getting in return for [providing the AggRite for free]." Transcript of Proceedings, Feb. 1, 2005, at 14-15.

with goods-leasing transactions, imposes somewhat similar warranties.) If the court had accepted American Ash's contention that it made only a conditional gift to Pennsy, then Pennsy would have been unable to recover on these warranty theories. (However, it might still have had a claim for promissory estoppel, which, as we will see in the next chapter, does not depend on the existence of a contract between the parties.)

3. *Consideration? Or only a condition to a gift?* The trial court had held that Pennsy's disposal costs did not constitute consideration for any promise by American Ash, because those costs were a mere "condition" to American Ash's gift of the AggRite to Pennsy. The appellate court rejected this conclusion. (Notice that this court stated that the presence of consideration is a question of law for the court to decide; courts in other jurisdictions might treat such a case differently, leaving it up to the jury to decide whether a contract is present, based on the court's instructions about the requirements for contract formation.) The distinction between conduct that constitutes consideration and conduct that is a condition to a gift is not a clear one, because the very same conduct may be consideration or a condition to a gift depending on how the parties treat the conduct. To illustrate the distinction, the court invoked Professor Williston's "an overcoat for the tramp" hypothetical. (Williston's reference to a "tramp" sounds archaic today, and perhaps ambiguous as well. As Williston used that term, synonyms would be "hobo" or "vagrant"; today we would probably instead say "homeless person.") What test does the court use to distinguish between consideration and a condition to a gift? Does the test help you to understand the outcome in *Pennsy Supply*? Can you think of other factors that should be relevant in determining whether conduct constitutes consideration rather than a condition to a gift? We return in Chapter 9 to a fuller exploration of the role that "conditions" play in contract law.

4. *Relationship of the benefit/detriment test and bargain theory of consideration.* Citing prior case law, the court holds that consideration requires a benefit to the promisor or a detriment to the promise, but one that is bargained for. See also Meincke v. Northwest Bank & Trust Co., 756 N.W. 2d 223 (Iowa 2008) (benefit to promisor or detriment to promisee must "induce" the making of the promise to be bargained for); Cobaugh v. Klick-Lewis, Inc., 561 A.2d 1248, 1250 (Pa. Super. Ct. 1989) (golfer who shot hole-in-one entitled to car offered by defendant as prize; court applies both bargained-for-exchange and benefit/detriment tests for consideration). Notice, however, that according to the court in *Pennsy Supply* the requirement that consideration be bargained for does not require actual bargaining between the parties. The court uses the Holmesian test of "reciprocal conventional inducement, each for the other." Under this test, American Ash affirmatively sought companies to take AggRite so that American Ash could avoid the disposal costs of this material. Correspondingly, Pennsy's assumption of this disposal obligation induced American Ash to deliver AggRite to it. Thus, each party's promise and resulting performance induced the corresponding promise and performance by the other party.

The Restatement appears to agree with *Pennsy Supply* that actual negotiation is not required. Restatement §71(2) states simply that a "performance or return promise is bargained for if it is sought by the promisor in exchange for his promise and is given by the promisee in exchange for that promise." Comment *b* to §71 adopts the Holmesian test of a "reciprocal relation of motive or inducement." Which view on the issue of negotiation do you think is better as a matter of policy? Can a "bargain" be created without "bargaining"? And does that matter?

5. *Practical effect of different tests for consideration.* For the student attempting to grapple with the niceties of consideration theory, developed over centuries of obscure and often inconsistent case law and commentary, a spoonful of Legal Realism may at this point help the doctrinal medicine go down. As we suggested in the introduction to this section, in the vast majority of real-world cases it will be unnecessary to worry about whether a benefit/detriment or a bargained-for-exchange test for consideration is employed, because the ordinary commercial contract will pass both tests with flying colors. Take for example a contract to sell a parcel of real estate for cash, where the parties exchange promises that at some future date they will exchange performances – cash from the purchaser in return for a conveyance of land from the vendor. Will the parties at that point be bound by their promises? The law's traditional answer is yes, they will. Even if both parties do no more than exchange promises of future performance, the law regards the making of a promise as sufficient legal "detriment" to bind the promisee to perform a return promise of his own under the benefit/detriment test for consideration. (Of course, the purchaser at the time of signing such an agreement is likely also to pay the vendor a sum of money, either as a "down payment" or as "earnest money," but that payment, while it furnishes additional consideration for the vendor's promise to sell, is not necessary to bind the vendor to her bargain.) On the other hand, if the Holmes "bargain" test is applied, the answer is the same: This land-purchase transaction would obviously be viewed as a bargained-for exchange and thus would be supported by consideration. See Restatement (Second) §§71, 77.

In light of the above analysis, the choice between the "benefit/detriment" and "bargained-for exchange" tests for consideration will ordinarily have little effect on the outcome of the question: Is this promise enforceable? As Professor Farnsworth has pointed out, the principal effect of Holmes's doctrinal shift to the "bargain" test seems to be at the margin: Promises made in a family setting, or otherwise "on the periphery of the marketplace," might under the bargain theory be more likely to go unenforced, as being non-exchange transactions. By the same token, the promisee's reliance on a promise, even if truly "detrimental to the promisee" would fail the consideration test unless it was bargained for as the price of that promise. Such reliance would thus go uncompensated, unless some other theory of liability should apply. E. Allan Farnsworth, Contracts 48 (4th ed. 2004). In the next chapter we explore the concept of "promissory estoppel," which may protect detrimental reliance that was *not* bargained for.

6. *The functions of legal formality.* Although our legal system is less concerned in general with matters of "form" than was the old English common law, there are even today some formalities that do have a particular legal effect when properly employed. The execution of a will is one example; another is the marriage ceremony. In the early days of English law, the seal was employed as a means of creating a binding contractual obligation. Today, however, the seal has little or no force in most jurisdictions, and promises are generally not enforceable merely because "formally" expressed, with or without the presence of a seal. For a survey of the law regarding the use of seals, see Eric Mills Holmes, Stature and Status of a Promise under Seal as a Legal Formality, 29 Willamette L. Rev. 617 (1993). Although clearly out of fashion today, the seal in its heyday did offer a clearly defined method by which persons seeking to create a legally enforceable promise could do so with confidence in its effectiveness. Building on the notion that formality as a legal device does have its uses, Professor Lon Fuller offered the following analysis of the functions that a legal formality may serve:

THE FUNCTIONS PERFORMED BY LEGAL FORMALITIES

The Evidentiary Function. — The most obvious function of a legal formality is, to use Austin's words, that of providing "evidence of the existence and purport of the contract, in case of controversy." The need for evidentiary security may be satisfied in a variety of ways: by requiring a writing, or attestation, or the certification of a notary . . .

The Cautionary Function. — A formality may also perform a cautionary or deterrent function by acting as a check against inconsiderate action. The seal in its original form fulfilled this purpose remarkably well. The affixing and impressing of a wax wafer — symbol in the popular mind of legalism and weightiness — was an excellent device for inducing the circumspective frame of mind appropriate in one pledging his future. To a less extent any requirement of a writing, of course, serves the same purpose, as do requirements of attestation, notarization, etc.

The Channeling Function. — Though most discussions of the purposes served by formalities go no further than the analysis just presented, this analysis stops short of recognizing one of the most important functions of form. That a legal formality may perform a function not yet described can be shown by the seal. The seal not only insures a satisfactory memorial of the promise and induces deliberation in the making of it. It serves also to mark or signalize the enforceable promise; it furnishes a simple and external test of enforceability. This function of form Ihering described as "the facilitation of judicial diagnosis," and he employed the analogy of coinage in explaining it. . . .

Interrelations of the Three Functions. — Though I have stated the three functions of legal form separately, it is obvious that there is an intimate connection between them. Generally speaking, whatever tends to accomplish one of these purposes will also tend to accomplish the other two. He who is compelled to do something which will furnish a satisfactory memorial of his intention will be induced to deliberate. Conversely, devices which induce deliberation will usually have an evidentiary value. Devices which insure evidence or prevent inconsiderateness will normally advance the desideratum of channeling, in two different ways. In the first place, he who is compelled to formulate his intention carefully will tend to fit it into legal and business categories. In this way the party is induced to canalize his own intention.

> In the second place, wherever the requirement of a formality is backed by the sanction of the invalidity of the informal transaction (and this is the means by which requirements of form are normally made effective), a degree of channeling results automatically. Whatever may be its legislative motive, the formality in such a case tends to effect a categorization of transactions into legal and non-legal.

Lon L. Fuller, Consideration and Form, 41 Colum. L. Rev. 799, 800-803 (1941). Professor Fuller's article goes on to argue that although the seal for various reasons has "decayed," the doctrine of consideration can and often does serve one or all of the above functions that the seal used to serve. While Fuller's analysis seems to be a useful general discussion of the policies that might be served by a legal "formality," subsequent writers have been skeptical of Fuller's "functions of form" thesis as it relates to the doctrine of consideration. E.g., Andrew Kull, Reconsidering Gratuitous Promises, 21 J. Legal Stud. 39, 51-55 (1992) (seal may have served such functions well, but consideration doctrine does so poorly that the absence of consideration should not be a conclusive argument against enforcement of a promise). Does the requirement of consideration effectively serve the evidentiary, cautionary, and channeling functions? We will refer to Fuller's discussion of "form" in later sections of these materials that more obviously involve legal "formalities."

Dougherty v. Salt

New York Court of Appeals 227 N.Y. 200, 125 N.E. 94 (1919)

CARDOZO, J. The plaintiff, a boy of eight years, received from his aunt, the defendant's testatrix, a promissory note for $3,000 payable at her death or before. Use was made of a printed form, which contains the words "value received." How the note came to be given, was explained by the boy's guardian, who was a witness for his ward. The aunt was visiting her nephew. "When she saw Charley coming in, she said 'Isn't he a nice boy?' I answered her, yes, that he is getting along very nice, and getting along nice in school, and I showed where he had progressed in school, having good reports, and so forth, and she told me that she was going to take care of that child, that she loved him very much. I said, 'I know you do, Tillie, but your taking care of the child will be done probably like your brother and sister done, take it out in talk.' She said: 'I don't intend to take it out in talk, I would like to take care of him now.' I said, 'Well, that is up to you.' She said, 'Why can't I make out a note to him?' I said, 'You can, if you wish to.' She said, 'Would that be right?' And I said, 'I do not know, but I guess it would; I do not know why it would not.' And she said, 'Well, will you make out a note for me?' I said, 'Yes, if you wish me to,' and she said, 'Well, I wish you would.' " A blank was then produced, filled out, and signed. The aunt handed the note to her nephew with these words, "You have always done for me, and I have signed this note for you. Now, do not lose it. Some day it will be valuable."

The trial judge submitted to the jury the question whether there was any consideration for the promised payment. Afterwards, he set aside the verdict in favor of the plaintiff, and dismissed the complaint. The Appellate Division, by a divided court, reversed the judgment of dismissal, and reinstated the verdict on the ground that the note was sufficient evidence of consideration.

We reach a different conclusion. The inference of consideration to be drawn from the form of the note has been so overcome and rebutted as to leave no question for a jury. This is not a case where witnesses summoned by the defendant and friendly to the defendant's cause, supply the testimony in disproof of value (Strickland v. Henry, 175 N.Y. 372). This is a case where the testimony in disproof of value comes from the plaintiff's own witness, speaking at the plaintiff's instance. The transaction thus revealed admits of one interpretation, and one only. The note was the voluntary and unenforcible promise of an executory gift (Harris v. Clark, 3 N.Y. 93; Holmes v. Roper, 141 N.Y. 64, 66). This child of eight was not a creditor, nor dealt with as one. The aunt was not paying a debt. She was conferring a bounty (Fink v. Cox, 18 Johns. 145). The promise was neither offered nor accepted with any other purpose. "Nothing is consideration that is not regarded as such by both parties" (Philpot v. Gruninger, 14 Wall. 570, 577; Fire Ins. Assn. v. Wickham, 141 U.S. 564, 579; Wisconsin & M. Ry. Co. v. Powers, 191 U.S. 379, 386; DeCicco v. Schweizer, 221 N.Y. 431, 438). A note so given is not made for "value received," however its maker may have labeled it. The formula of the printed blank becomes, in the light of the conceded facts, a mere erroneous conclusion, which cannot overcome the inconsistent conclusion of the law (Blanshan v. Russell, 32 App. Div. 103; *affd., on opinion below,* 161 N.Y. 629; Kramer v. Kramer, 181 N.Y. 477; Bruyn v. Russell, 52 Hun. 17). The plaintiff, through his own witness, has explained the genesis of the promise, and consideration has been disproved (Neg. Instr. Law, sec. 54; Consol. Laws, chap. 43). . . .

Judgment accordingly.

NOTES AND QUESTIONS

1. ***Dougherty** compared with **Hamer**.* In *Dougherty,* as in *Hamer,* an older person made a promise to a younger relative; enforcement of that promise was resisted later, after the promisor died. The promise in *Dougherty* was made in a more formal manner than the one in *Hamer,* but the latter promise was enforced while the former was not. Why? The promissory note that was used in *Dougherty* is not reproduced in the opinion, but presumably it was a written, signed promise by the aunt to pay her nephew the stated sum at the designated time. There is no indication that the promise was stated to be conditional on anything other than the aunt's death (that being the event defining the time when payment would be due). Suppose, however, that the note had begun, "In consideration of my nephew Charley having been a good boy until the age of 21 or until my death (whichever shall first occur), I hereby promise. . . ." Should the promise in the note in that case have been an obligation enforceable against the aunt's estate, just as the uncle's promise was enforceable in *Hamer*?

In *Dougherty,* as in *Hamer,* suit was brought not against the individual promisor, but against the representative of the deceased promisor's estate. (The defendant in *Hamer* is referred to as the "executor" and the aunt in *Dougherty* as the "testatrix," in both cases the term used indicating that the decedent left a valid will. Where the decedent has died "intestate" – without a will – the representative of the estate is often referred to as the "administrator." Today the term "personal representative" is used in many jurisdictions to refer to all such representatives.) The *Hamer* case was further complicated by the fact that the plaintiff was not the promisee himself, but an "assignee" – someone to whom Story had transferred ("assigned") his right to payment. (The general topic of assignment of contract rights is addressed in Chapter 12.) That might have influenced defendant Sidway's unwillingness to pay. In *Dougherty,* however, the plaintiff was Charley himself. There seems to have been no real dispute about the genuineness of the aunt's promise; nor does it appear that the aunt had changed her mind about Charley's merits before she died. Why didn't defendant Salt simply pay the note when it was presented?

2. *Should donative promises be enforced?* The court in *Dougherty* indicated that the promise was not supported by any consideration because it was no more than the promise of an "executory gift" (i.e., a gift to be performed in the future). There was no value received by the aunt for her promise, and the mere recital of value would not suffice, where it was plain that no value had in fact been given. Such "donative" promises are frequently made, often by one family member to another and occasionally between persons bound to each other not by blood relationship but by other ties of affection. Such promises also often go unperformed, sometimes because the promisor changes his mind (or the promisee declines to press the point), and sometimes, as in *Dougherty,* because the promisor dies before she has carried out her intent. Should the law enforce the purely donative promise, without insisting that it be supported by consideration? Professor Melvin Eisenberg has made a survey of this area, concluding that generally enforcement of the purely donative promise seems unnecessary where the promise has not been substantially relied on by the promisee. (The possibility of enforcement in the event of reliance is addressed in the next chapter.) In addition to the substantive reason of lack of reliance, Eisenberg identifies a number of issues that courts would have to consider if they decided to enforce donative promises: how to distinguish a true donative promise from a statement of present intention; whether the law should inquire into the level of deliberation that the donor exercised before making the promise; and to what extent the law should recognize excuses against enforcement of donative promises, such as ingratitude by the donee and improvidence by the donor. Eisenberg concludes: "Thus, despite occasional protests that the law should put its weight behind all promises that are seriously made, there seems to be widespread agreement that informal unrelied-upon donative promises should not be legally enforced." Melvin A. Eisenberg, Donative Promises, 47 U. Chi. L. Rev. 1, 4-6 (1979). Are Eisenberg's arguments persuasive? Do they apply to *Dougherty*?

For a skeptical response to many of Professor Eisenberg's arguments, see Andrew Kull, Reconsidering Gratuitous Promises, 21 J. Legal Studies 39, 63 (1992) ("person who makes a serious gratuitous promise of a magnitude that will later justify litigation is particularly unlikely to do so except as a matter of conscious choice"); see also Jane B. Baron, Gifts, Bargains, and Form, 64 Ind. L.J. 155 (1988/89) (questioning the way in which contract and other areas of law tend to undervalue gratuitous transfers by insisting on distinguishing them from bargains and then according them disfavoring treatment).

3. *Counseling Aunt Tillie.* Charley's guardian was apparently the aunt's only source of legal advice in *Dougherty,* and he obviously was not reliable. If Charley's aunt had consulted an attorney, could she have accomplished her purpose? The Comment that follows explores some of the possibilities that a lawyer would consider.

Comment: The Lawyer's Role in Counseling for Legal Effect

Suppose a present-day Aunt Tillie comes to you as her attorney, seeking advice regarding how to best confer a future benefit on her nephew Charley. Given the aunt's objective of somehow presently effecting a gift that will benefit her nephew Charley at some future time, what legal devices could you suggest to accomplish for her the result she seeks?

Promissory Note. The device actually employed in the *Dougherty* case — a promissory note with a recital of consideration — would probably have no more success with a modern judge than it did with Judge Cardozo in 1919. Comment *b* to Restatement (Second) §71 states: "Moreover, a mere pretense of bargain does not suffice, as where there is a false recital of consideration or where the purported consideration is merely nominal." Suppose that instead of just reciting "value received," the aunt were to receive from her nephew a small amount of money (a dollar or so) in exchange for her promise? Given the minimal nature of the law's requirement of "legal detriment," would that supply sufficient consideration for enforcement of her promise? The first Restatement §75 appeared to sanction such "nominal consideration" as a device for making a promise enforceable, but Restatement (Second) §71 unequivocally rejects that possibility, in comment *b* and the illustration that follows:

> 5. *A* desires to make a binding promise to give $1000 to his son *B*. Being advised that a gratuitous promise is not binding, *A* offers to buy from *B* for $1000 a book worth less than $1. *B* accepts the offer knowing that the purchase of the book is a mere pretense. There is no consideration for *A*'s promise to pay *B* $1000.

See also Weed v. Weed, 968 A.2d 310 (Vt. 2008) (payment of $10 between family members did not induce "sale" of land and thus was a pretense). Assuming therefore that a mere written promise that recites consideration will probably not create an obligation enforceable against the promisor's estate, what other devices might you advise your client to employ?

Promise Under Seal. English common law enforced promises under seal, in the action of covenant, without requiring any showing of consideration. See the Comment on the History of the Consideration Doctrine on the casebook website. Could your client confer an enforceable right on her nephew by signing and delivering to him a *sealed* promissory note? Such a document will have varying effect today, depending on the jurisdiction involved. As the volume of commercial transactions increased over the years, the original formality of the seal was relaxed, so that it might be no more than a preprinted notation on a contract form ("under seal" or "L.S." — abbreviation for *locus sigilli* in Latin); as the seal thus came to be less and less "special," legislatures responded by depriving it of its special legal effect. Some states have abolished the device altogether; others have reduced its effect to a mere presumption of consideration. See Eric Mills Holmes, Stature and Status of a Promise under Seal as a Legal Formality, 29 Willamette L. Rev. 617 (1993). See also Knott v. Racicot, 812 N.E.2d 1207 (Mass. 2004) (discussing the history and declining importance of the seal; abolishing the common law rule that option contracts under seal import consideration). The Uniform Commercial Code abolished the significance of the seal in sales of goods (UCC §2-203). Restatement (Second) §95 states a rule for enforcement of instruments under seal, but that rule can have effect only where the common law relating to seals has not been displaced by statutes abolishing or weakening the seal's legal effect. Despite a few recent statutory attempts to create a comparable device, there is today in American law no generally available equivalent of the old English seal for use in creating binding gratuitous obligations.

Executed Gift. The surest way to guarantee that the intended beneficiary of the aunt's generosity ends up with the money would, obviously, be for her to simply give him (or his guardian, on his behalf) the money now, in cash. While a promise to make a gift in the future is not an enforceable obligation under contract law, property law provides generally that once a gift has been "executed" — delivered by the donor with the intent to make a gift, and accepted by the donee — it is irrevocable and may not be recovered by the donor. Ray A. Brown, The Law of Personal Property 77-78 (3d ed. 1975). However, a gift may be subject to a condition, the failure of which would allow the transferor to recover the property subject to the condition. See Campbell v. Robinson, 726 S.E.2d 221 (S.C. Ct. App. 2012) (holding that, while courts are divided, in South Carolina an "engagement ring" is given on the implied condition of marriage and may be recovered by donor if the marriage does not occur).

Testamentary Gift. In light of your client's expressed wish that her nephew receive the money at her death, it would seem logical to suggest that a "testamentary gift" be employed: She could make a will, a "last testament" of her desires as to the disposition of her property after death. If her will is made with such formality as the law requires (typical requirements include a signed writing and the presence of witnesses who also sign, attesting the genuineness of the document), its provisions would be carried out (executed) after her death by her personal representative, the executor of her estate. Assuming that sufficient assets remained after payment of any debts of the estate, the bequest to the nephew would be paid along with any other bequests. In this case, the absence of consideration for the gift would be legally irrelevant. The testamentary-gift option has the disadvantage of requiring somewhat more effort than the promissory note used in *Dougherty*, since a will must be formally signed and witnessed. On the other hand, it should achieve its purpose (assuming the aunt is presently of sufficient mental capacity as required by law). What are its drawbacks? Only two readily appear: This bequest, along with any others, will not be payable until the debts of the estate have been satisfied; should the estate have insufficient assets, an enforceable promissory note (along with any other enforceable debt of the estate) would take priority over a mere testamentary gift. Also, unlike an apparently unconditional promissory note, a testamentary gift is "ambulatory"; it may be freely revoked by a later will.

Gift in Trust. One other legal device merits mention here. You may recall that in *Hamer* the court seized on the fact that the uncle had assertedly set aside the money owed his nephew, in order to find that a "trust" had been created (thereby avoiding what would have otherwise been the bar of the statute of limitations, and allowing enforcement of the obligation). If your client presently has the funds to make the gift to her nephew, but does not wish to give him (or his guardian) present control over those funds, she could create a trust on his behalf. As a trust "beneficiary," he would eventually enjoy the benefits of the gift. For a variety of legal and practical reasons, such "inter vivos" trusts have become a frequently employed vehicle for the gratuitous transfer of wealth between family members. Courses in Trusts and Estate Planning will give you a chance to explore them in depth later in your legal studies.

Plowman v. Indian Refining Co.

United States District Court 20 F. Supp. 1 (E.D. Ill. 1937)

LINDLEY, District Judge.

Thirteen persons and the administrators of five deceased persons brought this suit, alleging that defendant, in 1930, made separate contracts to pay each of the individual plaintiffs and each of the deceased persons whose administrators sued, monthly sums equal to one-half of the wages formerly earned by such parties as employees of the defendant for life. Each of the claimants had been employed for some years at a fixed rate of wages, usually upon an hourly basis but payable monthly or semimonthly.

The theory of plaintiffs is that on July 28, 1930 (with two exceptions), the vice-president and general manager of the refinery plant called the employees, who had rendered long years of service separately into his office and made with each a contract, to pay him, for the rest of his natural life, a sum equal to one-half of the wages he was then being paid. The consideration for the contracts, it is said, arose out of the relationship then existing, the desire to provide for the future welfare of these comparatively aged employees and the provision in the alleged contracts that the employees would call at the office for their several checks each pay-day.

Most of the employees were participants in group insurance, the premiums for which had been paid approximately one-half by the employee and one-half by the company, and, according to plaintiffs, their parts of the premiums were to be deducted from their payments as formerly. This procedure was followed.

The employees were retained on the pay roll, but, according to their testimony, they were not to render any further services, their only obligation being to call at the office for their remittances. Most of them testified that it was agreed that the payments were to continue throughout the remainder of their lives. But two testified that nothing was said as to the time during which the payments were to continue. As to still others the record is silent as to direct testimony in this respect.

The payments were made regularly until June 1, 1931, when they were cut off and each of the employees previously receiving the same was advised by defendant's personnel officer that the arrangement was terminated.

Defendant does not controvert many of these facts, but insists that the whole arrangement was included in a letter sent to each of the employees as follows:

> Confirming our conversation of today, it is necessary with conditions as they are throughout the petroleum industry, to effect substantial economies throughout the plant operation. This necessitates the reducing of the working force to a minimum necessary to maintain operation. In view of your many years of faithful service, the management is desirous of shielding you as far as possible from the effect of reduced plant operation and has, therefore, placed you upon a retirement list which has just been established for this purpose.
>
> Effective August 1, 1930, you will be carried on our payroll at a rate of $______ per month. You will be relieved of all duties except that of reporting to Mr. T. E. Sullivan at the main office for the purpose of picking up your semi-monthly checks. Your group insurance will be maintained on the same basis as at present, unless you desire to have it cancelled. (Signed by the vice-president.)

It contends and offered evidence that nothing was said to any employee about continuing the payments for his natural life; that the payments were gratuitous, continuing at the pleasure and will of defendant; that the original arrangement was not authorized, approved, or ratified by the board of directors, the executive committee thereof, or any officer endowed with corporate authority to bind the company; that there was no consideration for the promise to make the payments; and that it was beyond the power of any of the persons alleged to have contracted to create by agreement or by estoppel any liability of the company to pay wages to employees during the remainders of their lives, if they did not render actual services. Defendant admits the payments as charged and the termination of the arrangement on June 1, 1931.

The employees assert that there was ample authority in the vice-president and general manager to make a binding contract of the kind alleged to have existed; that, irrespective of the existence or nonexistence of such authority, the conduct of the company in making payment was ratification of the original agreement and that defendant is now estopped to deny validity of the same.

Plaintiff Kogan, an employee aged 72, testified that for some years prior to July 28, 1930, he had been employed as a drill pressman and in general repair work in the machine shops; that on July 28, 1930, he talked to Mr. Anglin, the vice-president and general manager, in the latter's private office; that Anglin said then that the oil industry was in a deplorable condition; that the management found it necessary to cut down expenses, and therefore, to lay off certain employees; that the witness was to be relieved of his duties, but that he would receive one-half of his salary and would be retained upon the pay roll; that this was being done because of the witness' many years of services; that the company did not desire to discharge him without further compensation; that he would be excused from all labor and required only to report to the main office to get his checks; that the company would carry his insurance in accord with previous practice; and that he would have all the privileges of hospitalization and in other respects of regular employees. The witness said he expressed his preference to work, but was told that that was impossible. He says that he was told that the arrangement was permanent, that is, for as long as he lived; that he would receive a letter confirming this conversation, which he should keep; that his labor would end on July 31, 1930; that he received the letter within a day or two; that thereafter he reported regularly at the office and obtained the checks until May 29, 1931, when he was told by the personnel department that the check then received would be the last one. This action, he said he was then told, was taken because of the necessity for further retrenchment. He testified that he sought no other employment; that nothing was said to him about working or not working for other parties, and that when he received the letter he kept it without comment or objection.

Other claimants testified substantially the same. . . .

In behalf of defendant, the assistant secretary testified that there were no minutes showing any corporate action with regard to the arrangement and that there was nothing in the records of the corporation, in bylaws, resolution or minutes authorizing, directing, or ratifying the payments or giving anybody authority to make the same. Anglin, vice-president and general manager in charge of manufacturing at the Lawrenceville Refinery where these men were employed, testified that he said to Kogan that, due to depressed conditions the company found it necessary to reduce expenses and lay off certain men; that it had no pension plan; that in an effort to be perfectly fair the company would keep him on the pay roll but relieve him of all duties except to pick up his check; that he said that the arrangement was voluntary with the company, and terminable at its pleasure, and that he hoped it would last during Kogan's lifetime, but that there might be a change in the policy of the company. His testimony as to the other employees was the same. He denied promising any of them that the payments would persist so long as they lived. He sent the letters as he promised confirming the arrangement. He testified that the letters were in compliance with what he had said; that no complaint or demand for any additional provisions was thereafter made; that he himself was employed orally; that he had no written contract; that he had no authority from the directors to make the arrangement; that he hired and fired men in Lawrenceville upon recommendation of the foreman; that a change in the management occurred when the Indian Refining Company was purchased by the Texas Company between October, 1930, and January, 1931; and that after the latter date he was not general manager at Lawrenceville. . . .

The present vice-president and general manager testified that he came into office January, 1931; and that no complaint was received by him by any plaintiff until suit was started.

Thus it is undisputed that a separate arrangement was made by the local office with each of the claimants, most of them on July 28, 1930, to continue them upon the pay roll, deliver to them semimonthly a check, upon their calling for same, for one-half of the former wages; that this was done until June 1, 1931. It is also undisputed that the letters sent out said nothing about how long the payments should continue but were wholly silent in that respect. It is also undisputed that insurance payments were deducted from the checks that were delivered; that the employees were retained on the pay roll; that they did no active work after August 1, 1931 [sic; 1930?]; that they received their checks as mentioned; that the payments terminated on June 1, 1931; that most of them called at the office for their checks and received same; and that in at least two instances the checks were mailed. The controverted question of fact arises upon the testimony of most of the plaintiffs that each of them was told that the payments would continue until their death. This is denied.

Let us assume, without so deciding, for the purpose of disposition of this case, that each of the employees was told that the payments would continue for his lifetime. Then the questions remaining are legal in character. The arrangement was made by no corporate officer having authority to make such a contract. Under the bylaws, corporation transactions as recorded in the minutes, there was no authorization or ratification of any such contract. It is urged, however, that by continuing to pay the checks the corporation ratified the previously unauthorized action. The facts render such conclusion dubious. I am unable to see how knowledge of the mere fact that men's names were on the pay roll and checks paid to them could create any estoppel to deny authority, in the absence of proof of knowledge upon the part of the duly authorized officers of the company that the men were not working but were receiving in effect pensions or that they had been promised payments for life. Consequently, there was no ratification express or implied and no estoppel.

Presented also is the further question of whether, admitting the facts as alleged by plaintiffs, there was any consideration for a contract to pay a pension for life. However strongly a man may be bound in conscience to fulfill his engagements, the law does not recognize their sanctity or supply any means to compel their performance, except when founded upon a sufficient consideration. Volume 6, American & English Encyclopedia of Law, p.673 (2d Ed.)

The long and faithful services of the employees are relied upon as consideration; but past or executed consideration is a self-contradictory term. Consideration is something given in exchange for a promise or in a reliance upon the promise. Something which has been delivered before the promise is executed, and, therefore, made without reference to it, cannot properly be legal consideration. Williston on Contracts, vol. 1, §142; 13 Corpus Juris, 359; Shields v. Clifton Hill Land Co., 94 Tenn. 123, 28 S.W. 668, 26 L.R.A. 523, 45 Am. St. Rep. 700; Restatement of the Law of Contracts, vol. 1, p.88.

It is further contended that there was a moral consideration for the alleged contracts. The doctrine of validity of moral consideration has received approval in some courts, but quite generally it is condemned because it is contrary in character to actual consideration. . . . Thus in Hart v. Strong, 183 Ill. 349, 55 N.E. 629, 631, the court said: "The agreement to receive less than the amount due on the note was made upon the purely moral consideration that John W. Hart, believing himself about to die, thought he ought not to have exacted so large a consideration for the reconveyance. But such an obligation does not form a valid consideration unless the moral duty were once a legal one. 'But the morality of the promise, however certain or however urgent the duty, does not, of itself, suffice for a consideration.' 1 Pars. Cont. 434."

Upon the same ground, appreciation of past services or pleasure afforded the employer thereby is not a sufficient consideration. . . . So Williston says (Contracts, vol. 1, p. 230): ". . . if there be no legal consideration, no motive, such as love and respect, or affection for another or a desire to do justice, or fear of trouble, or a desire to equalize the shares in an estate, or to provide for a child, or regret for having advised an unfortunate investment, will support a promise."

Plaintiffs have proved that they were ready, willing, and able to travel to and report semimonthly to the main office. But this does not furnish a legal consideration. The act was simply a condition imposed upon them in obtaining gratuitous pensions and not a consideration. The employees went to the office to obtain their checks. Such acts were benefits to them and not detriments. They were detriments to defendant and not benefits. This is not consideration. Williston on Contracts, vol. 1, pp. 231-235, and cases cited; Restatement of Contracts, par. 75, Illus. 2.

In the absence of valid agreement to make payments for the rest of their natural lives, clearly the arrangement was one revocable at the pleasure of defendant. If defendant agreed to make the payments for life, then, fatal to plaintiffs' cases is the lack of consideration. We have merely a gratuitous arrangement without consideration, and therefore, void as a contract.

In this enlightened day, I am sure, no one controverts the wisdom, justice, and desirability of a policy, whether promoted and fostered by industry voluntarily or by state or federal government, looking to the promotion and assurance of financial protection of deserving employees in their old age. We have come to realize that the industry wherein the diligent worker labors for many years should bear the cost of his living in some degree of comfort through his declining years until the end of his life. To impose this expense upon the industry, to the creation of whose product he has contributed, is not unfair or unreasonable, for, eventually, obviously, under wise budgeting and cost accounting systems, this element of cost is passed on to the consumer of the product. The public bears the burden — as, indeed, it does eventually of all governmental expenditures and corporate costs, either in taxes or price of products purchased. Surely no one would have the temerity to urge that such a policy is not more fair and reasonable, more humane and beneficent, than the poorhouse system of our earlier days. The recognition of the soundness of this proposition is justified by the resulting contribution to the advance of standards of living, hygienic and sanitary environment, and, in some degree at least, of culture and civilization.

But, in the absence of statute creating it, such a policy does not enter into the relationship of employer or employee, except when so provided by contract of the parties. The court is endowed with no power of legislation; nor may it read into contracts provisions upon which the parties' minds have not met.

Viewing the testimony most favorably for the plaintiffs, despite the desirability of the practice of liberality between employer and employee, the court must decide a purely legal question — whether under plaintiffs' theory there were valid contracts. The obvious answer is in the negative. Consequently, there will be a decree in favor of defendant dismissing plaintiffs' bill for want of equity. The foregoing includes my findings of fact and conclusions of law.

NOTES AND QUESTIONS

1. *Consideration or condition?* The court holds in *Plowman* that the plaintiffs' travel to the defendant's office, to pick up their checks, did not constitute consideration; it was "simply a condition imposed upon them in obtaining gratuitous pensions." Do you agree? Recall the court's discussion of "legal detriment" in Hamer v. Sidway, and the "Williston's tramp" hypothetical discussed in *Pennsy Supply*, above. Did the company receive any benefit from the plaintiffs' actions? In Dulany Foods v. C.M. Ayers, Inc., 260 S.E.2d 196 (Va. 1979), the defendant promulgated a policy of making severance payments to employees who remained on its payroll as of a given date. In response to the company's argument that the employees' continued employment was only a condition, and not consideration for its promise, the Virginia Supreme Court stated:

> We observe that the memorandum, prepared by Whittington and amended and approved by MacCormack, was not executed in a vacuum. . . . The decision by Dulany to close its Eastern Shore plants and facilities was a major one for both management and employees. The livelihoods of a great number of employees in Virginia, Maryland, and Delaware were involved, and the owners had at stake a large investment in plants, equipment, and unsold food. The four months between the decision to close the plants and the time the Exmore facilities were taken over by Exmore Foods, Inc., were critical months for Dulany. Not only did the company have an unpleasant decision to make, implement, and communicate to its employees, it also had "to wind down" a vast manufacturing and refrigeration plant, an operation which included the repacking and refrigeration of millions of pounds of vegetables. Dulany needed the continued services of loyal and efficient employees to perform this task. It was vital to the company that its closing-out period be a peaceful one, and that favorable public relations and plant morale be maintained. These objectives were

> accomplished. . . . The company's termination pay policy brought it industrial peace, avoidance of unrest on the part of its employees, and consequently a smooth termination of operations.
>
> During the four-month span involved in this case Dulany was actively seeking a buyer for its plants. It is a matter of common knowledge that the most valuable attraction a manufacturing plant can offer a prospective purchaser is a well-trained, efficient, loyal, and contented group of employees. Dulany possessed this intangible asset, and it is reasonable to believe that it was a factor in the willingness of Exmore Foods, Inc., to purchase the plant. It is equally as reasonable to attribute the good will of the employees to the severance pay policy that was inaugurated by Dulany.

Id. at 199-200. Could any of these factors have been at work in *Plowman*?

2. *Hypothetical variations of* ***Plowman***. The judge also dismisses (quoting Williston) the possibility that "love and respect, . . . affection for another or a desire to do justice" could amount to consideration; "legal consideration," he says, is necessary. It is frequently stated, however, that where bargained-for consideration is present, the fact that the promisor may have had some other motive or inducement for making the promise will not of itself defeat the agreement. See Restatement (Second) §81, and Comment *b*. Assuming that the principal motive for the defendant's promise may have been the welfare of its senior employees, should the promise have been enforceable if any of the following had also been part of the case?

(a) Each pensioned employee was required, before receiving any payments, to submit a signed resignation, waiving all right to future employment with the defendant and any claim to wages or payments other than the promised "pension."

(b) Each promisee was required, before receiving payments, to sign an agreement that he would, on request, assist in training new employees of the defendant. (Would it matter whether the employees had ever been called on to do so?)

(c) Each promisee was required to pick up his check in person at the office of the defendant, at a time when the employees of the defendant would be picking up their regular paychecks.

3. *"Past consideration and moral obligation."* The court also rejects the possibility that the "long and faithful service" of the plaintiffs could constitute consideration, using two related arguments. Services already performed could be, at best, only "past consideration," which is a "self-contradictory" term: Something already done cannot constitute consideration for a later promise. See also Barton v. Sclafani Investments, Inc., 320 S.W. 3d 453 (Tex. App. 2010) (all brokerage services were rendered before making of promise to pay commission; it was past consideration and promise was not enforceable). Nor can any "moral obligation" arising out of past faithful service constitute consideration, unless the "moral" duty was also a "legal" one. If this is indeed the law, *should* it be? Professor Charles Fried has argued that the making of a promise is an act that of itself creates a moral obligation that the law should respect and enforce:

> The utilitarian counting the advantages affirms the general importance of enforcing *contracts.* The moralist of duty, however, sees *promising* as a device that free, moral individuals have fashioned on the premise of mutual trust, and which gathers its moral force from that premise. The moralist of duty thus posits a general obligation to keep promises, of which the obligation of contract will be only a special case — that special case in which certain promises have attained legal as well as moral force. But since a contract is first of all a promise, the contract must be kept because a promise must be kept.

Charles Fried, Contract as Promise 17 (1981). Do you agree with Fried's position? Even if you would stop short of enforcing the moral obligation implicit in *every* promise, would you as judge in *Plowman* have felt impelled to enforce the moral obligation of the Indian Refining Co.? We return later in this chapter to questions of "past consideration" and "moral obligation" as possible bases for promissory liability.

4. *The issue of authority.* Would the plaintiffs' legal position have been improved if the defendant's board of directors had adopted by formal resolution a plan to pay the disputed pensions to the plaintiffs, specifically providing that such payments should continue for the lives of the discharged employees? Although his opinion is perhaps slightly unclear on the point, Judge Lindley appears to find that the promises, even if they were made, were made by agents lacking in authority to bind the defendant, and were not made binding on the defendant by later events. The issue of whether a person or organization is legally responsible for the acts of an employee is one of the issues addressed by agency law. This body of law has, like contract law, been the subject of two ALI Restatements; agency law can be, and often is, the subject of a separate law school course. Agency issues frequently arise in contract cases, however, and not every law school today offers a separate agency course. The following Comment is therefore designed to provide a brief introduction to some basic agency concepts.

Comment: The Power of Agents to Bind Their Principals

Agency is a consensual relationship in which one person, the agent, agrees to act on behalf of, and subject to the control of, another person, the principal. Restatement (Third) of Agency §1.01. ("Person" in this context means a "legal" person, which can include corporations as well as individuals; corporations, being artificial persons, can act only through agents.) The agency relationship is often described as "fiduciary," because it involves a relationship of trust and confidence in which one person is bound to act in the interests of another. Id. §8.01. The principal's right to control the agent is the essence of the relationship. As indicated, the agency relationship is a consensual one; it is usually created by contract between the principal and its agent, although agency may also be gratuitous.

If an agent has "actual authority" to enter into a contract on behalf of the principal, then the principal is bound by the agent's actions in the same way as if the principal had engaged in those actions himself. As a matter of law, the principal becomes a party to the contract by virtue of the agent's actions, while the agent is not a party. Id. §6.01. The Restatement of Agency provides that an agent can have actual authority in several ways. First, an agent has actual authority to take actions "designated . . . in the principal's manifestations." Id. §2.02(1). Many courts and the former Restatement use the term "express authority" to refer to this form of authorization. Id. §2.01, Comment *b*. Thus, if the Board of Directors of Indian Refining Co. had passed a resolution directing its vice president to send the letters in question to the plaintiffs, those letters would in law have been sent by the company itself.

Second, an agent has actual authority to take actions "implied in the principal's manifestations." Id. §2.02(1). For example, suppose the board of directors had directed the vice president to develop a plan to reduce the company's work force to a level sufficient to maintain the company's operations despite the economic conditions then prevailing (a national depression) with appropriate provision for payment of partial salary to any long-term employees who were laid off as part of this plan. In this case the board would not have expressly authorized the sending of these particular letters, but authority to do so might fairly have been implied from the vice president's general mandate.

Third, an agent has actual authority to perform "acts necessary or incidental to achieving the principal's objectives." Id. §2.02(1). Thus, if the board had passed a resolution authorizing the vice president to enter into contracts with long-term employees on the terms discussed in the case, the vice president would have had actual authority to sign the contracts and other documents necessary or incidental to carrying out the resolution.

Suppose, on the other hand, that the board had passed a resolution authorizing the vice president to develop a plan to reduce the company's work force to a level sufficient to maintain the company's operations despite the economic conditions then prevailing. However, suppose that in this situation the board did not specify that the vice president had authority to pay reduced salaries to workers who were laid off without any corresponding obligation by these workers to the company. In this example, the vice president might well lack actual authority to enter into the contracts involved in the case because the arrangement would probably amount to a gift by the corporation to its long-term employees. Generally, the authorization of an agent to make a gift of the principal's property must be quite specific. Id. §2.02, Comment *h*.

Even in the absence of any actual authority, however, a principal may be legally bound by the actions of its agent if the principal has done or said something that leads the other party reasonably to believe that the agent does indeed have actual authority to do the act in question. Suppose that Indian Refining's Board of Directors had ordered that a letter be sent to all employees, advising them that "Vice President Anglin will shortly be communicating with you about the way in which our company will respond to the drastic change in economic conditions, in order to assure its survival and the continued well-being of its employees." Even if the board had made it plain to the vice president that his actual authority merely extended to the reshuffling of work shifts and the discharge of some employees, such a letter might be held to have created in the minds of the employees a reasonable belief that he also had the authority to promise pension payments. In that case he would have had "apparent authority" to make the promises in the letters. Id. §2.03. See also §3.03, Comment *e* (discussing the apparent authority of organizational executives and corporate officers).

Finally, even where an agent has no authority at all — either actual or apparent — to enter into a particular contract on behalf of the principal, a principal that later learns of its agent's action and approves of it will be liable on that contract by virtue of such "ratification." Id. §4.01. This sort of after-the-fact approval was at issue in *Plowman*. The plaintiffs argued that the board of directors had ratified the vice president's promises to them by continuing to make salary payments after the plaintiffs stopped work. The judge rejected that argument on the ground that effective ratification requires knowledge of all material facts; the board, he declared, could not have known merely from payroll records that the employees were no longer working or were receiving lifetime pensions. See Id. §4.06.

The court also referred to the notion of "estoppel," a concept that crops up in a variety of legal contexts. (In the next chapter we will see another application of the estoppel concept in a contractual context.) Under agency law a principal may be estopped to deny that its agent's actions were unauthorized, where the principal by words or actions caused the other to rely to his detriment on the agent's authority to act. Id. §2.05. This notion is obviously very similar to that of apparent authority. Apparent authority, however, is based on the principal's manifestations, while an estoppel could result from other acts or even inaction by the principal that place the agent in a position to lead the third party to believe that the agent has authority to act for the principal. Id. §2.05, Comment *d*.

Dohrmann v. Swaney

Illinois Appellate Court 14 N.E.3d 605 (2014)

OPINION

Justice FITZGERALD SMITH delivered the judgment of the court, with opinion.

¶ 1 Appellant George J. Dohrmann III appeals from the circuit court's grant of summary judgment to appellee Thomas E. Swaney, independent executor of the estate of Virginia H. Rogers, deceased (the Estate), as to the two remaining counts of his complaint. These counts relate to an alleged agreement made between Dohrmann and Mrs. Rogers prior to Mrs. Rogers' death in which Mrs. Rogers signed a document (the contract) agreeing to give Dohrmann, in part, her apartment and all of the items contained therein, as well as the sum of $4 million. Dohrmann contends on appeal that the trial court erred in granting summary judgment. For the following reasons, we affirm.

¶ 2 **I. BACKGROUND**

¶ 3 Dohrmann, who was Mrs. Rogers' neighbor, filed a five-count fourth amended complaint against Thomas E. Swaney, as guardian of the Estate of Virginia Rogers, a disabled person, and as successor trustee of the Virginia H. Rogers Trust (Trust),[1] based on a contract dated April 1, 2000. Under the purported contract, in exchange for Dohrmann's "past and future services," including helping to continue the Rogers name by incorporating it into his children's name, Mrs. Rogers agreed to convey to Dohrmann upon her death her apartment and everything within it, as well as the sum of $4 million. The contract states that Mrs. Rogers will carry out this promise through her "Will and Testament or other testamentary substitute." Dohrmann alleged that he legally changed the names of his minor children to add the Rogers name and that he believed he had performed all his duties under the contract. Mrs. Rogers filed a counterclaim alleging that the contract was the product of fraud in the execution.

¶ 4 At the time of the summary judgment disputed herein, only counts I and II remained. By count I, Dohrmann requested a declaratory judgment settling the rights of the parties under the contract and imposing a constructive trust on Mrs. Rogers' apartment and $4 million worth of assets for the benefit of Dohrmann. By count II, Dohrmann requested a declaration that the transfer of Mrs. Rogers' apartment to the Trust is void, the creation of a constructive trust on the apartment for the benefit of Dohrmann, or, in the alternative, a money judgment in the amount equal to the present value of Mrs. Rogers' apartment. Mrs. Rogers' estate then filed a one-count counterclaim, alleging that the contract was a product of fraud in the execution and asking the court to declare the contract invalid and unenforceable and to require Dohrmann to pay compensatory and punitive damages.

¶ 5 Most of the background facts are not in dispute. . . . In this Background section, we consider only the facts properly before this court. . . .

¶ 6 Dohrmann first met Mrs. Rogers in 1984. They lived in the same building, the Drake Tower, a cooperative apartment building, at 179 E. Lake Shore Drive. Mrs. Rogers' apartment was substantially larger than Dohrmann's apartment. The apartment was Mrs. Rogers' primary residence, while Dohrmann's apartment was not his primary residence.

¶ 7 At the time they met, Mrs. Rogers was a 73-year-old widow. She had never had nor adopted any children. Dohrmann was a 40-year-old neurosurgeon, married to Dr. Helen Dohrmann. Eventually, they had two children, George IV and Geoffrey. Dohrmann and his wife are still married.

¶ 8 Dohrmann and Mrs. Rogers began to socialize together more frequently in the early 1990s and served together on the board of the Drake Tower apartments. Mrs. Rogers got to know Dohrmann's wife and children during this time. From the record, it appears Mrs. Rogers initially enjoyed Dohrmann's attention,

1. Mrs. Rogers has since died, and the cause is now captioned "GEORGE J. DOHRMANN III v. THOMAS E. SWANEY, as Independent Executor of the Estate of Virginia H. Rogers, Deceased."

but then became concerned that he was befriending her in order to get her property upon her death.

¶ 9 In 1997 or 1998, Dohrmann approached Mrs. Rogers about adult adoption, suggesting that one of them adopt the other. Dohrmann testified in deposition that Mrs. Rogers often said she regretted not having any children, and Dohrmann wanted to give her the family she never had. To that end, Dohrmann consulted with an attorney, who advised him that adult adoptions could be done in Arkansas and referred him to an Arkansas attorney. In March 1998, Dohrmann traveled to Little Rock, Arkansas, and met with an attorney who specialized in adoption law. Upon learning that residency is a prerequisite for adult adoption in Arkansas, Dohrmann entered into a written lease for an apartment in North Conway, Arkansas. The adoption attorney advised Dohrmann that she needed a signed letter of engagement from Mrs. Rogers in order to proceed. However, Mrs. Rogers never submitted a signed letter of engagement to the attorney and Dohrmann never adopted Mrs. Rogers, nor was he ever adopted by Mrs. Rogers.

¶ 10 In February 2000, Dohrmann met with an estate planning attorney in Chicago, inquiring what one would do if he wished to receive something in exchange for something after a person died. The attorney drafted a skeleton agreement and subsequently discussed the agreement with Dohrmann. The attorney did not, however, participate in the preparation or execution of the contract in question here.

¶ 11 On April 1, 2000, Dohrmann and Mrs. Rogers, who was 89 years old at the time, signed the contract. There were no witnesses present at the signing. Mrs. Rogers did not communicate with her long-time lawyer and advisor, Mr. Swaney, regarding the contract. Mr. Swaney did not, in fact, learn of the contract until just prior to the initiation of the instant lawsuit.

The contract in its entirety reads:

Agreement

Dear George:

In exchange for your past and future services and other good and valuable consideration (including helping the Rogers name to continue after my death by incorporating it into your children's names), I (Virginia H. Rogers) agree to give you (George J. Dohrmann III) upon my death 1) my apartment in the Drake Tower (shares of 11-East, Drake Tower Apartments, Inc. in Chicago) and all furniture, furnishings, personal effects and other property contained within it and the elevator vestibule at the time of my death 2) the sum of four million dollars ($4,000,000.00), and so will provide in my Last Will and Testament or other testamentary substitute that may take effect upon my death (my "testamentary documents"). If my testamentary documents fail to provide you with the above, you or your estate, shall have a valid claim against my estate for such amount.

It is my request that you pay my friend and lawyer, Thomas E. Swaney, the sum of one hundred thousand dollars ($100,000.00) as a surprise gift from me.

This agreement may not be amended, modified or canceled except by written agreement signed by you and me. This agreement sets forth our entire agreement and understanding with respect to the matters covered hereby and

> supersedes all of our prior agreements or understandings with respect to the subject matter hereof. This agreement shall be governed by and construed in accordance with the laws of the State of Illinois applicable to contracts to be performed entirely within such State (determined without regard to choice of law provisions thereof).
>
> If the above correctly sets forth your understanding of our agreement, please indicate your acceptance by signing this agreement in the space provided below.
>
> Understood, accepted and agreed on April 1, 2000:
> s/ George J. Dohrmann III
> Signed on April 1, 2000:
> s/ Virginia H. Rogers

¶ 12 An appraiser estimated that the value of Mrs. Rogers' apartment as of April 1, 2000, was approximately $1,438,000. Another appraiser estimated that the value of the "furniture, furnishings, personal effects and other property contained within it and the elevator vestibule" as of April 1, 2000, was approximately $100,045.

¶ 13 Two months later, on June 22, 2000, Dohrmann's two sons' names were legally changed to include "Rogers" as one of their middle names. Their names are now George John Rogers Dohrmann IV, and Geoffrey Edward David Rogers Dohrmann. At that time, George IV was 13 years old and Geoffrey was 7 years old. In practice, the boys (now young men) use the Rogers name inconsistently. George IV used it on his high school diploma and college applications, but, according to George IV's deposition testimony, he did not use it on his driver's license, his student ID card, his checking account, his credit card, his high school papers, his high school exams, or his Facebook page. Geoffrey testified that he did not have a driver's license or state identification card, but that he used the Rogers name "whenever [he] writes down [his] full name when necessary." He testified that he used the Rogers name on his high school applications, his student ID card, and his ATM card. He did not use it on his Facebook page, but did use his two other middle names.

¶ 14 On April 1, 2000, the date the contract was executed, Mrs. Rogers' estate plan consisted of her will and the Trust. Neither included at that time or any other time a provision for the benefit of Dohrmann or for any member of his family. Rather, her estate plan consisted of bequests to various friends and distant relatives aggregating several million dollars, with the remainder of the estate distributable to seven Chicago-based charities and Mrs. Rogers' alma mater.

¶ 15 In November 2004, Mrs. Rogers transferred legal ownership of her apartment to the Trust, where it remains as an asset. In March 2008, an order was entered in probate court designating Mrs. Rogers a disabled person based on her suffering from moderate dementia and probable Alzheimer's disease. She was adjudicated to be without capacity to manage her estate or financial affairs. Mr. Swaney was appointed as the guardian of her estate.

¶16 Dohrmann filed his original complaint in February 2007, of which only counts I and II remained at the time of summary judgment. The Estate filed its counterclaim as part of its answer. The parties then filed cross-motions for summary judgment as to the claims against them. In its motion for summary judgment, the Estate argued that the contract should be set aside as a matter of law because the consideration was so grossly inadequate as to shock the conscience; the undisputed facts demonstrate that this inadequate consideration was accompanied by circumstances of unfairness; and the contract is unconscionable.

. . .

¶ 18 In 2012, the circuit court, in a memorandum order, found that the contract was not enforceable, granted the Estate's motion for summary judgment on counts I and II, and denied Dohrmann's motion for summary judgment on the Estate's counterclaim. Dohrmann appeals the grant of summary judgment against him on counts I and II.

¶ 19 **II Analysis**

¶ 20 On appeal, Dohrmann contends the trial court erred in granting summary judgment. He argues that summary judgment was improper because: (1) the value of Dohrmann's performance, that is, his sons' name changes, is a disputed issue of fact; (2) Mrs. Rogers' motive for entering into the contract is a disputed issue of fact; (3) the existence of "circumstances of unfairness" in the making of the contract is a disputed issue of fact; and (4) the testimony of Rogers' friends that Rogers believed Dohrmann was trying to get her apartment and her estate was inadmissible hearsay and should not have been considered by the court. For the following reasons, we affirm. . . .

¶ 22 The primary objective in contract construction is to give effect to the intent of the parties. If the contract is clear and unambiguous, the court must determine the parties' intent solely from the ordinary and natural meaning of the language of the contract. *Omnitrus Merging Corp. v. Illinois Tool Works, Inc.,* 256 Ill. App. 3d 31, 34, 195 Ill. Dec. 701, 628 N.E.2d 1165 (1993).

¶ 23 The basic requirements of a contract are an offer, acceptance, and consideration. . . . The determination of whether consideration is sufficient to support a contract is a question of law for the court to decide. Valuable consideration for a contract consists of some right, interest, profit or benefit accruing to one party, or some forbearance, detriment, loss or responsibility given, suffered or undertaken by the other. . . . *Steinberg v. Chicago Medical School,* 69 Ill. 2d 320, 330, 13 Ill. Dec. 699, 371 N.E.2d 634 (1977) (any act or promise that benefits one party or disadvantages the other is sufficient consideration to support the formation of a contract). Whether a contract contains consideration is a question of law, which we review *de novo* . . . . "[W]here the amount of consideration is so grossly inadequate as to shock the conscience of the court, the contract will fail." *Ahern v. Knecht,* 202 Ill. App. 3d 709, 715, 150 Ill. Dec. 660, 563 N.E.2d 787 (1990). This court has considered the issue of gross inadequacy of consideration:

> Evidence of gross inadequacy of consideration has been considered by some Illinois courts as tantamount to fraud, whether actual or constructive. [Citations.] Thus, where there is a substantial failure of consideration for a

> contract, particularly where the inadequacy is accompanied by other inequitable or unconscionable features, a court of equity may rescind or cancel the contract. . . .

Ahern, 202 Ill. App. 3d at 715-16, 150 Ill. Dec. 660, 563 N.E.2d 787.

. . .

Moreover, "[w]here the amount of the consideration which passed is not only so grossly inadequate as to shock the conscience of the court, but also accompanied by circumstances of unfairness, the court is in a position to set aside the transaction. [Citations.] Where the inadequacy is great, the circumstances of unfairness need only be slight to cause this court to set aside the transaction. [Citation.]" *Mimica v. Area Interstate Trucking, Inc.*, 250 Ill. App. 3d 423, 431-32, 190 Ill. Dec. 67, 620 N.E.2d 1328 (1993). . . .

¶ 29 **II THE CONSIDERATION PROVIDED**

¶ 30 Here, our review of the record persuades us that the trial court did not err in granting summary judgment to the Estate where, based on the record before us, there was no genuine issue of material fact. The circumstances existing when the contract was entered into in this case were such that the terms of the contract should be set aside where the Estate sufficiently showed the contract should be considered void due to the grossly inadequate consideration provided Mrs. Rogers from Dohrmann, as well as the unfair circumstances surrounding the contract's creation.

¶ 31 Under the terms of the contract, Mrs. Rogers agreed to transfer, upon her death, to Dohrmann over $5.5 million in assets in exchange for Dohrmann adding Rogers as an additional middle name to his two sons' names, so that their names became George John Rogers Dohrmann, IV, and Geoffrey Edward David Rogers Dohrmann. We note here that, in his answers to interrogatories, Dohrmann described the consideration bargained for under the contract:

> . . . Dr. Dohrmann performed by taking actions to change the names of his two sons and incorporate the Rogers name into their legal names in order to continue the Rogers name after the death of Ms. Rogers. Dr. Dohrmann initiated legal proceedings in the Circuit Court of Cook County to change the names of his sons and incorporate the Rogers name into their legal names. On June 22, 2000, George J. Dohrmann IV became legally known as George J. Rogers Dohrmann IV, and Geoffrey Dohrmann became legally known as Geoffrey E.D. Rogers Dohrmann. . . . There were and are no "future services" to be performed. At no time prior to the execution of the Contract did Ms. Rogers and Dr. Dohrmann discuss any "past" services or "future services" to be performed as part of the Contract. . . .

Accordingly, therefore, the sole consideration Dohrmann agreed to give in exchange for over $5.5 million in assets was to add Rogers as an additional middle name to his sons' names. According to the plain language of the contract, the addition of "Rogers" to the boys' names was of value to Mrs. Rogers because it would help the Rogers name to continue after Mrs. Rogers' death. We address that consideration here.

¶ 32 We agree with the Estate that Mrs. Rogers did not gain much by the addition of the Rogers name to the boys' middle names. The stated purpose of adding the name was to "help[] the Rogers name to continue after [her] death." However, Dohrmann did not change the boys' surnames to Rogers, nor even exchange their middle names for Rogers. Rather, he merely added the name Rogers as one of two middle names for George IV and one of three middle names for Geoffrey. This can hardly be said to perpetuate the Rogers name after Mrs. Rogers' death.

¶ 33 We note here Dohrmann acknowledges it is appropriate for a court to consider whether consideration was provided in a contract, but argues that it is improper for a court to consider the relative value or adequacy of the consideration. He states: "a court may examine the consideration exchanged for several purposes, none of which, however, includes determining and/or weighing the relative value of adequacy of legal consideration exchanged." We disagree, as, in cases like the one at bar where the consideration provided is so grossly inadequate as to shock the conscience, a court may examine the adequacy of the consideration. See, *e.g., Bonner v. Westbound Records, Inc.,* 76 Ill. App. 3d 736, 743, 31 Ill. Dec. 926, 394 N.E.2d 1303 (1979) ("It is not the function of either the circuit court or [the appellate] court to review the amount of the consideration which passed to decide whether either party made a bad bargain [Citations] *unless the amount is so grossly inadequate* as to shock the conscience of the court." (Emphasis added)); see also *Ahern,* 202 Ill. App. 3d at 716, 150 Ill. Dec. 660, 563 N.E.2d 787.

¶ 34 Additionally, the contract is brief and makes no provision for when or even if the boys must actually use the name Rogers. It appears from the record before us that the boys have used the name only intermittently. Moreover, there is nothing in the contract to prevent the boys from legally removing Rogers as a middle name, particularly because they, as minors, were not parties to the contract. Where the consideration for a contract is illusory, the contract will be invalidated for gross inadequacy of consideration. See *Mimica,* 250 Ill. App. 3d at 432, 190 Ill. Dec. 67, 620 N.E.2d 1328. Although the children allegedly took the Rogers name as their own in order to perpetuate the Rogers name after Mrs. Rogers' death, enforcing that obligation is a legal impossibility. Accordingly, the consideration to this contract is illusory.

¶ 35 In total, pursuant to the terms of the contract, Mrs. Rogers, an elderly widow, agreed to give Dohrmann upon her death $5,538,000 in cash and property in exchange for Dohrmann adding Rogers as an additional middle name to the names of his sons in an effort to help perpetuate the Rogers name after Mrs. Rogers' death. The contract does not contain any provision mandating how, when, or whether Dohrmann's sons are to use the Rogers name. The disparity is shocking on its face. We agree with the circuit court, which stated that this consideration "seems to be so minimally beneficial to Mrs. Rogers (particularly in light of the goal stated in the Contract of 'continuing the Rogers name') as to be almost nonexistent, especially when contrasted with the $5.5 million Dr. Dohrmann is to receive under the terms of the Contract."

¶ 36 **III CIRCUMSTANCES OF UNFAIRNESS**

¶ 37 Although the inadequacy of consideration in this situation is sufficient in itself to find this contract void, we also agree with the circuit court and the Estate that there were circumstances of unfairness, that is, the extremely disproportionate bargaining power of the contracting parties, surrounding the execution of the contract to such an extent that the contract could be found void on those grounds, as well. . . . Factors relevant to this analysis include the age and education of the contracting parties. See *Ahern,* 202 Ill. App. 3d at 716, 150 Ill. Dec. 660, 563 N.E.2d 787 ("Courts will also look to such factors as the age and education of the contracting parties, their commercial experience [Citation], and whether the aggrieved party had a meaningful choice when faced with unreasonably unfavorable terms [Citations].").

¶ 38 In reviewing the record before us, we have found many of the uncontested facts clearly demonstrate circumstances of unfairness surrounding the execution of the contract, that is, the parties had vastly different bargaining positions. At the time of the contract's execution in 2000, Mrs. Rogers was an 89 year old widow whose husband had died many years previously. Two years following the execution of this contract, Mrs. Rogers was diagnosed with Alzheimer's disease. She had no children nor any immediate family. She was entering into a contract worth $5.5 million with Dohrmann, a physician. Mrs. Rogers had a long-time attorney and advisor, Mr. Swaney, but she did not consult him regarding the execution of this contract. She also had in place an estate plan for the event of her death.

¶ 39 The other contracting party, Dohrmann, is a highly educated neurosurgeon, married with a family. Under the contract, Dohrmann stood to reap a benefit worth $5.5 million. Prior to entering into the contract, Dohrmann consulted an estate planning attorney. This attorney drafted a "skeleton" agreement for him. These facts clearly show that the creation of this contract involved gross inadequacy of consideration as well as circumstances of unfairness. . . .

¶ 45 In the instant case, the circuit court properly granted summary judgment in favor of the Estate where there was no genuine issue as to any material fact. The circuit court properly found that the contract was unenforceable.

¶ 46 **IV CONCLUSION**

¶ 47 For the foregoing reasons, we affirm the judgment of the circuit court of Cook County.

¶ 48 Affirmed.

Presiding Justice HOWSE and Justice LAVIN concurred in the judgment and opinion.

[The court's discussion of the application of the Dead Man's Statute and the Hearsay Rule has been omitted.—EDS.]

NOTES AND QUESTIONS

1. *General rule that courts will not inquire into the adequacy of consideration.* Closely allied to the view of consideration as reflecting the "exchange" element of a transaction is the well-established rule that, in ascertaining the presence of consideration, the courts will not "weigh" the consideration, or insist on a "fair" or "even" exchange. In his treatise, Williston put it thus: "It is an 'elementary principle that the law will not enter into an inquiry as to the adequacy of the consideration.' This rule is almost as old as the law of consideration itself." Williston on Contracts §115 (1920); see also Restatement (Second) §79 (no requirement of "equivalence in the values exchanged"). This view of consideration fits comfortably with the classical view of contract as being content to leave it to the parties to set the terms of their own exchange, with the court's role being limited to confirming that a bargain had in fact been struck.

2. ***Batsakis v. Demotsis:*** *an example of the general rule.* A leading example of the general rule that courts will not inquire into the adequacy of consideration is Batsakis v. Demotsis, 226 S.W.2d 673 (Tex. Civ. Ct. App. 1949). In that case Ms. Demotsis borrowed 500,000 of Greek currency (drachmae) from Mr. Batsakis, giving in exchange her written promise to repay Mr. Batsakis US$2000 plus 8% interest. Demotsis made the promise to obtain money "for the support of my family during these difficult days and because it is impossible for me to transfer dollars of my own from America." After the war Batsakis sued Demotsis in Texas to collect on the promise; she defended claiming that the 500,000 drachmae were worth only US$25. The Texas Court of Appeals rejected defendant's pleas of "want of consideration," "failure of consideration," and "inadequacy of consideration." The first two pleas did not apply because the defendant received 500,000 drachmae and this was exactly what she bargained for. As to the third plea the court held: "Mere inadequacy of consideration will not void a contract." Thus, the court did not require equivalence in the exchange.

Is the following background relevant to the *Batsakis* case? If so, how? In the spring of 1941, German, Italian, and Bulgarian forces invaded and occupied Greece, taking control of food and medical supplies. The Allies imposed a naval blockade that restricted supplies to Greece throughout the winter of 1941-1942, and the Germans systematically looted the country; the result was a devastating famine that killed many thousands of Greeks during that period, possibly as many as 40,000 in the Athens-Piraeus area alone. Rampant inflation during the same period drove the price of bread from 70 drachmas to 2,350. See generally Mark Mazower, Inside Hitler's Greece 23-41, 65-67 (1993).

3. *Exceptions to the general rule.* Courts, like the Illinois Appellate Court in *Dohrmann*, have on rare occasion refused to enforce agreements by finding either no consideration or grossly inadequate consideration. A well-known older example is Newman & Snell's Bk. v. Hunter, 220 N.W. 665 (Mich. 1928), where the court refused to enforce a widow's promise to pay the debt of her deceased husband in exchange for the bank's surrender of his promissory note when the note would not have been collectible anyway because the estate was insolvent.

An approach that is sounder doctrinally considers the adequacy of consideration along with other factors in determining whether to apply one of several doctrines dealing with defects in the bargaining process, particularly fraud, duress, and unconscionability. The Restatement (Second) points out in Comment *e* to §79 that "gross inadequacy of consideration may be relevant" to the application of other doctrines, such as fraud, mistake, lack of capacity, duress, or undue influence. Could this approach have been used in *Dohrmann*? In *Bataskis v. Demotsis*? In Chapter 7 we will examine when various forms of bargaining misconduct could invalidate a contract.

4. *Hypothetical variation of* ***Dohrmann***. As a departure from the general rule regarding consideration, the result in *Dohrmann* is likely to be highly dependent on the facts of that particular case. Suppose that Dohrmann had in fact been a blood-relative of Mrs. Rogers (a nephew — the son of her late sister), and that when Dohrmann's wife bore their first child, a baby girl, Mrs. Rogers promised the Dohrmanns (in a signed writing — perhaps a letter of congratulations) that if they named the child "Virginia Rogers Dohrmann," Mrs. Rogers would pay for the first year of the child's education at a private school. Suppose further that their child indeed was given the name Virginia Rogers Dohrmann, but when the time came for her to begin her education, Mrs. Rogers declined to make any financial contribution to her $5,000 tuition in a private elementary school. Should the Dohrmanns have a valid claim against Mrs. Rogers? Cf. Schumm v. Berg, 231 P.2d 174, 185 (Cal. 1951) (mother's naming child after its father, prominent movie actor Wallace Beery, sufficient consideration for his promise to provide for child financially).

5. *"Quitclaim deed" as example of the general rule.* Sometimes a party attempting to establish a clear title to real property may promise to pay another person who appears possibly to have some conflicting claim, for the delivery of a "quitclaim" deed — an acknowledgment that the person executing the deed has no ownership interest in the property in question. In such a case, the promisee may in fact have no interest at all, and may not even claim to have one, but the documentation of that fact is potentially valuable to the promisor. E.g., Lindy Lu LLC v. Illinois Central RR. Co., 984 N.E.2d 1171 (Ill. App. Ct. 2013); Restatement (Second) of Contracts §74(2).

6. *Change in the law's concern for fairness?* Some scholars have argued that the movement to a bargain theory of consideration in the 19th century showed a shift from away from an earlier willingness to police the "fairness" of bargains and toward a view of contract particularly adaptable to commercial activity where the parties determine contract price based on their appraisal of market conditions. See Morton Horwitz, The Transformation of American Law, 1780-1860, at 917-927 (1977). Other writers have differed sharply with Horwitz and his colleagues over the extent to which classical contract law did indeed represent a change from earlier law in this respect. See, e.g., Alfred W. B. Simpson, The Horwitz Thesis and the History of Contracts, 46 U. Chi. L. Rev. 533 (1979). Whether the exchange-based view of consideration did indeed make a sharp break with the past, or merely undergo a change in emphasis, it does at least appear to be particularly consistent with a society in which the law fully

supports a "free market" economy, permitting commercial entities (individuals or corporations) to make whatever agreements of exchange they wish, at whatever relative values they can agree to, with the backstop of legal enforceability.

Marshall Durbin Food Corp. v. Baker

Mississippi Court of Appeals 909 So. 2d 1267 (2005)

BARNES, J., FOR THE COURT:

Bill Baker, former president of Marshall Durbin Food Corporation, brought suit against his former employer to enforce an agreement which would provide him with five years of monthly compensation equal to his monthly salary while employed. The Chancery Court of Wayne County, Mississippi, held the contract to be valid and ordered Marshall Durbin Food Corporation to pay Mr. Baker in accordance with the terms of the contract, beginning September 10, 2001. Marshall Durbin Food Corporation appealed. We affirm in part and reverse and render in part.

SUMMARY OF FACTS AND DISPOSITION BELOW

Mr. Baker began working as a management trainee for Marshall Durbin Food Corporation ("the Company") in 1965 and ascended through the ranks until, in October of 1998, Mr. Baker was elected to the Company board of directors; he also held the position of vice president, live production.

The Company was in troubled times. Grain prices had gone through the ceiling, and poultry prices had dropped. The Company experienced a loss of approximately thirty million dollars. Disagreements between Marshall Durbin, Jr. ("Mr. Durbin"), who owned approximately 80% of the Company stock, and his two daughters, Elise and Melissa, who owned or controlled about 18% of the stock, caused a great deal of tension in the Company. The minutes of the October 1998 stockholders meeting reflect that Elise and Melissa Durbin were not re-elected to the board because of "disruptions due to the forcing of employees to take sides and matters having been discussed in meetings with employees that should have been resolved in private between family members." Mr. Durbin announced that he would recommend that the new board not reelect his daughters to their position as co-presidents of the company; in the directors meeting which followed, Elise and Melissa Durbin were not elected as officers of the Company.

In the months which followed, several valuable employees, including Mr. Baker, expressed concern regarding the uncertainty of their future with the Company if anything ever happened to Mr. Durbin. The Company's sole witness, John Perri, described this period as "chaos" and testified that Mr. Baker "kind of was put in the breach to help save the company, because we were spiraling downward. [Baker] spoke to me one time and he said . . . we've got to get everybody back working together and save this company . . . I know there is a risk that, God forbid, that something happens . . . the girls come back with the company, the people could lose their job; and I'm going to go to [Mr. Durbin] and see if these key people . . . can get a year's retirement so in the event they come in and you lose your job, at least you've got a year to look for another job . . . ."

In response to this concern, Mr. Durbin offered an "agreement of termination and/or early retirement" to three high level Company employees, one of whom was Mr. Baker. On November 15, 1999, Mr. Baker and Mr. Durbin executed a contract which provided a number of circumstances that would trigger an "effective date." Once triggered, Mr. Baker would receive a specified amount of compensation for five years. The agreement provides in part:

> **EMPLOYMENT:** The corporation and Employee agree that the employment of Employee will be employee-at-will. This contract is not intended to create contractual employment between the Corporation and Employee.
>
> **EFFECTIVE DATE:** The Employee shall be entitled to the following termination and/or early retirement compensation upon the effective date of any of the following:
>
> A. the establishment of an Effective Date by the Board of Directors or President of the Corporation; or
> B. upon any "change in control", where more than 51% of the stock is not owned by the current stockholder owning more than 51% of the stock, and the current majority stockholder is not active in management of the Company; or
> C. upon change in executive management of the Corporation, including Board of Directors, President or Chief Executive Officer, which creates a substantial change in duties of the Employee, requires the Employee to move from their present place of Employment, creates hostile working conditions, or
> D. upon the death or incapacity of Marshall Durbin, Jr.
>
> **TERMINATION AND/OR EARLY RETIREMENT COMPENSATION:** During the term of this Agreement, upon the occurrence of any of the events listed in Paragraph 3, the Employee shall have and receive, subject to withholding and other applicable employment taxes, a monthly salary, payable on the 10th day of each month, mailed to the Employee's address on record. The salary shall be the base pay of the Employee on the Effective Date of the occurrence listed in paragraph 3. The compensation shall extend for a term of five years from the Effective Date, and shall commence upon the occurrence of any of the events in Paragraph 3.

The board of directors ratified the agreement on November 15, 1999, and the existence of the "deferred compensation" agreement was disclosed in the notes to the consolidated financial statements of the Company and its subsidiaries issued November 16, 2000.

In 2001, Mr. Durbin was diagnosed with malignant lymphoma in the central nervous system and received radiation therapy treatments to the brain. On July 9, 2001, Mr. Baker assumed the responsibilities of Company president during Mr. Durbin's absence for medical purposes. On August 14, 2001, on emergency petition of Elise Durbin, the Probate Court of Jefferson County, Alabama, declared Mr. Durbin incapacitated. The court appointed Mr. Durbin's daughters as temporary co-guardians and Mr. Bainbridge, one of the Company's attorneys, as temporary conservator of Mr. Durbin's estate. The petition estimated the value of Mr. Durbin's shares in the Company to be $40,000,000.

On August 30, 2001, Mr. Baker wrote Mr. Bainbridge notifying him that the agreement had been triggered by Mr. Durbin's incapacity. The letter explained that Mr. Baker would perform his duties as a consultant and no longer as an employee. On September 17, 2001, Mr. Durbin died. Within a day or two, Company employees went to Mr. Baker's residence and picked up his Company car, explaining to Mr. Baker that he had resigned. On September 20, 2001, Mr. Baker filed a complaint for specific performance of the contract in the Chancery Court of Wayne County, Mississippi.

By letter dated October 19, 2001, Mr. Baker was informed by the Company's counsel that a new board of directors had been elected on October 1, 2001, and had "immediately" voted to terminate Mr. Baker's employment with the Company in all capacities. The letter referred to Mr. Baker's August 31st letter[1] as a "letter of resignation" and stated that the termination/early retirement agreement referenced therein was "not valid and, accordingly, the Directors have voted, on behalf of the Company to repudiate such agreement." No basis for the claim of invalidity was provided. In answer to the complaint, however, the Company asserted failure of consideration as an affirmative defense.

[After hearing testimony, the trial court ruled that the contract was valid and that the company was bound to make payments to Baker for five years. The trial judge found that the Company had been "spiraling down" prior to the making of the contract and that Mr. Durbin therefore took steps to retain his top management personnel, including Baker. The trial court further concluded that in reliance upon that contract, Baker did not seek other employment opportunities, continued to work for the Company, and appeared to have been effective in getting the company on "a profitable . . . footing." The trial court ruled that the Company's payment obligation commenced on September 10, 2001, thereby entitling Baker to recover a total of $964,517.95, barring early termination upon the death of Baker and his wife. — EDS.]

STANDARD OF REVIEW

This Court employs a limited standard of review when reviewing a chancellor's decision. *Shirley v. Christian Episcopal Methodist Church, 748 So. 2d 672, 674 (P9) (Miss. 1999)*. We will not interfere with or disturb a chancellor's findings of fact unless those findings are manifestly wrong, clearly erroneous, or an erroneous legal standard was applied. . . .

1. Testimony confirmed that this was an attempted reference to Mr. Baker's August 30, 2001, correspondence with Mr. Bainbridge.

ISSUES AND ANALYSIS

I. Whether the Trial Court Erred as a Matter of Law in Finding the Existence of Bargained for Consideration

We are presented with the issue of whether a valid contract was formed between the Company and Mr. Baker. The Company claims the contract is invalid for lack of consideration. Consideration is, of course, . . . required for the existence of a valid contract. *See Rotenberry v. Hooker, 864 So. 2d 266, 270 (P13) (Miss. 2003).* The Mississippi Supreme Court has defined "consideration for a promise as '(a) an act other than a promise, or (b) a forbearance, or (c) the creation, modification or destruction of a legal relation, or (d) a return promise, bargained for and given in exchange for the promise.' " *City of Starkville v. 4-County Electric Power Assoc., 819 So. 2d 1216, 1220 (P10) (Miss. 2002)* (quoting *Lowndes Coop. Ass'n v. Lipsey, 240 Miss. 71, 126 So. 2d 276, 277 (1961)* (quoting Restatement of Contracts §75 (1932))).

A. What is the Effect of the Contract's Recital of Consideration?

Failure of consideration is an affirmative defense. *Daniel v. Snowdoun Ass'n, 513 So. 2d 946, 950 (Miss. 1987)*; *Miss. R. Civ. Pro. 8(c).* "Where the instrument in controversy contains a statement or recital of consideration, it creates a rebuttable presumption that consideration actually existed." *Daniel, 513 So. 2d at 950*; *Estate of Smith v. Samuels, 822 So. 2d 366, 370 (P13) (Miss. Ct. App. 2002).* While the presumption does not preclude the defendant from putting on proof designed to show that the consideration was not actually paid, his "rebuttal must be made by a clear preponderance of the evidence." The trier of fact resolves any conflicting evidence. *Daniel, 513 So. 2d at 950.*

In the instant case, the contract in controversy expressly recites "consideration of Ten and No/100 Dollars ($10.00) and other good and valuable consideration, the receipt and sufficiency of all of which is acknowledged . . . ." At trial, neither party offered any evidence to confirm or rebut the presumption of consideration which arises from this recitation. . . . While the unrebutted presumption is sufficient to affirm the decision of the chancellor as to the existence of consideration, we will, nevertheless, address the arguments raised by the Company.

B. Were the Promises Made by Mr. Baker and the Company Mutually Illusory?

The Company argues that the contract was not supported by consideration because the promises by both Mr. Baker and the Company were illusory. First, the Company alleges that Baker's promise to refrain from seeking other employment and forbearance from leaving the Company renders the promise illusory and thus cannot provide consideration. Second, the Company argues that its absolute right to terminate Baker's employment with the Company at any time renders the promise illusory because it is conditioned upon something completely within the Company's control. Also, the Company argues that the promises of both Mr. Baker and the Company were illusory because their relationship was unquestionably at-will. Although we find the Company correct in its contention that no valid promise was given by Mr. Baker in exchange for the Company's promise of payment, we reject the contention that the Company's promise was also illusory. Accordingly, Mr. Baker could, and did, supply consideration for the Company's promise by "an act other than a promise." *See City of Starkville, 819 So. 2d at 1220 (P10)*; *Lowndes Coop. Ass'n, 126 So. 2d at 277.*

The Mississippi Supreme Court has relied on Professor Corbin's analysis of illusory promises as consideration, which states:

> By the phrase "illusory promise" is meant words in promissory form that promise nothing; they do not purport to put any limitation on the freedom of the alleged promisor, but leave his future action subject to his own future will, just as it would have been had he said no words at all. . . . A prediction of future willingness is not an expression of present willingness and is not a promise. To see a promise in it is to be under an illusion. We reach the same result if B's reply to A is, "I promise to do as you ask if I please to do so when the time arrives." In form this is a conditional promise, but the condition is the pleasure or future will of the promisor himself. The words used do not purport to effect any limitation upon the promisor's future freedom of choice. They do not lead the promisee to have an expectation of performance because of a present expression of will. He may hope that a future willingness will exist; but he has no more reasonable basis for such a hope than if B had merely made a prediction or had said nothing at all. As a promise, B's words are mere illusion. Such an illusory promise is neither enforceable against the one making it, nor is it operative as a consideration for a return promise.

Krebs ex rel. Krebs v. Strange, 419 So. 2d 178, 182-83 (Miss. 1982) (quoting 1 Corbin, *Contracts,* §145 (1 vol. ed. 1952)). Applying this analysis, we determine that no valid promise was given by Mr. Baker in exchange for the Company's promise of payment, however, we reject the contention that the Company's promise was illusory.

The contract expressly disavows any intent "to create contractual employment" between the Company and Mr. Baker; in fact, the parties agreed that Mr. Baker would be an "employee-at-will." By executing the contract, Mr. Baker did not promise to remain in the Company's employ; at trial, Mr. Baker admitted, "I could have quit at any time." The trial court recognized this fact: "Well, as I review the contract, I don't think he was obligated to continue to be an employee of Marshall Durbin. . . . Probably not. But, as long as he did continue to be an employee of Marshall Durbin, and any of those triggering events occurred while he was an employee of Marshall Durbin, then the contract went into effect." Accordingly, the trial court based its finding of consideration not upon any *promise* by Mr. Baker to continue to work for the Company but upon Mr. Baker's *act* of continuing to work for the Company and the Company's corresponding *receipt of benefit* from Mr. Baker's services. The United States Court of Appeals for the Fifth Circuit has recognized that "the presence of an illusory promise does not destroy the possibility of a contract. Instead, it may create a unilateral contract, and 'the promisor who made the illusory promise can accept [it] by performance.'" *Olander v. Compass Bank, 363 F.3d 560, 565 (5th Cir.*

2004) (quoting *Light v. Centel Cellular Co., 883 S.W.2d 642, 645 n.6, 37 Tex. Sup. Ct. J. 838 (Tex. 1994))*.

The Company did not promise to continue to employ Mr. Baker for any definite period of time; however, it did promise that *if* Mr. Baker continued his employment until the happening of a triggering event, the Company would compensate him as set forth in the contract. The Company's promise was contingent; it was not illusory. Mr. Baker apparently trusted Mr. Durbin and was willing to continue his employment at the will of Mr. Durbin. Had Mr. Durbin terminated Mr. Baker's employment prior to the occurrence of one of the triggering events, Mr. Baker would have had no recourse. The contract was not designed to, and did not, provide for that occurrence. This case comes to us, however, after the contingency (Mr. Baker's employment upon the happening of a triggering event) has been fulfilled; and the Company's promise to pay under these circumstances is not illusory.

Mr. Baker's consideration for the Company's promise was not by a return promise, but by "an act other than a promise." *See Lowndes Coop. Ass'n, 126 So. 2d at 277*. . . . In the instant case, the Company focuses only on the alleged return promise of Mr. Baker and ignores the fact that other consideration, such as Mr. Baker's actual performance, is equally sufficient consideration. . . .

D. Is the Contract Unenforceable if Based on Baker's Forbearance from Seeking Other Employment?

The Company contends that Baker's forbearance from seeking other employment was not a legal detriment and cannot constitute consideration. Legal detriment, as opposed to detriment in fact, is present where the promisee gives up something he was privileged to retain prior to the contract. *See* 1 Williston, *Contracts* §§102A, 382 (3d ed. 1957); *Lowndes Coop. Ass'n, 126 So. 2d at 278*. The Company argues that Mr. Baker had no legal duty to refrain from looking for other employment, and, therefore, did not suffer legal, as opposed to factual, detriment. Further, the Company contends that forbearance from seeking other employment is not legal detriment in the context of at-will employment contracts. Mr. Baker argues that his detriment consisted of his refraining from seeking other employment and his commitment to the Company at a time when the Company was in a volatile environment. We need not decide this issue. The trial court found not only detriment to Mr. Baker in forbearing from seeking or accepting other employment, but also benefit to the Company in retaining Mr. Baker's services.

Again, *Lowndes Coop. Ass'n* is instructive: "A benefit to the promisor *or* detriment to the promisee is sufficient consideration for a contract. This may consist *either* in some interest, right, profit or benefit accruing to the one party, *or* some forbearance, detriment, loss or responsibility given, suffered or undertaken by the other." *126 So. 2d at 278* (emphasis added); *see also Iuka Guar. Bank v. Beard, 658 So. 2d 1367, 1372 (Miss. 1995)* ("consideration is sufficient if there is any benefit to the promisor or any loss, detriment, or inconvenience to the promisee").

After reviewing the record, we find as the trial court did, that the Company benefitted by retaining the services of Mr. Baker. Marshall Durbin intended to maintain a secure work environment for his high level management team during a turbulent time. In his bench opinion, the chancellor found Mr. Durbin's business decision to execute such a contract was wise given the fact that the Company was in trouble and Mr. Durbin's daughters were circulating correspondence that was causing concern among top level employees with respect to job security. Mr. Perri testified that Mr. Baker was "put in the breach to help save the company, because we were spiraling downward." Approximately two years later, Elise Durbin, in petitioning for conservatorship of her father, estimated his stock in the Company to be worth $40,000,000. We find that the trial court's assumption "that they turned things around during that period of time and got the company on a profitable . . . footing" to be supported by the record. The Company has never challenged, and in fact completely ignores, the finding that the Company enjoyed the benefits of retaining a valued employee. The trial court correctly determined there to be consideration for the contract, and we affirm.

II. Whether the Trial Court Erred in Determining August 14, 2001 to be the Effective Date of the Agreement

[The court held that that the Company's five-year payment obligation commenced on July 10, 2001, based on when Baker began serving as president of the corporation, rather than the later date as determined by the trial court. — Eds.]

CONCLUSION

We find that the chancery court properly held the agreement between Mr. Baker and the Company to be enforceable. We affirm the lower court's decision as to the validity of the contract and reverse and render as to the effective date. . . .

King, C.J., Bridges, P.J., Irving, Myers, Chandler, Griffis and Ishee, JJ., concur. Lee, P.J., not participating.

NOTES AND QUESTIONS

1. *Recital of consideration.* The *Marshall Durbin* court notes that the contract contains a recital of consideration, and that under Mississippi law this would create a "rebuttable presumption" of consideration that the opposing party would have to refute. Recall that there was also a recital of consideration in the *Dougherty* case. Ultimately, both courts take a similar approach in ascertaining whether there was actual consideration present. Does it seem correct that courts should not accept an assertion of consideration in the written contract as being conclusive?

2. *Defining consideration.* The *Marshall Durbin* court initially defines consideration as "an act other than a promise, a forbearance, the creation, modification or destruction of a legal relation, or a return promise, bargained for and given in exchange for the promise." The court later searches for either a detriment suffered by Baker or some benefit conferred to the Marshall Durbin Corporation that would make enforceable the promise to pay Baker's salary

for five years. Is the court's approach to consideration consistent with the Restatement (Second) §71 definition? The *Marshall Durbin* court also makes a distinction between a "legal detriment" and "a detriment in fact." Although the phrasing may be unfortunate, do you understand the point the court is making? How would this court classify the detriment suffered by the nephew in *Hamer v. Sidway*? When we study promissory estoppel in Chapter 3, we will note again these different types of "detriment."

3. *The problem of "illusory" promises.* Restatement (Second) §77, Comment *a*, provides that a promise, even if bargained for, will not serve as consideration if it is "illusory" – if it makes performance entirely optional with the promisor. One basis for a promise being deemed illusory is when the agreement is "at will"; i.e., the promisor reserves the right to terminate the agreement with the promisee at any time without any period of notice to the promisee. Note, however, that even a slight restriction on the ability to escape the contract can be enough to avoid illusoriness. See Devine v. Notter, 753 N.W.2d 557 (Wis. Ct. App. 2008) (real estate contract that allowed cancellation by either party based upon attorney disapproval of terms within five-day window was not illusory). In *Marshall Durbin,* the contracting parties made it clear in the written contract that the employment was "at will" and therefore either party could terminate at any time. Yet the court found that while Baker made no commitment to remain with the company, the Marshall Durbin Corporation did make a "contingent" commitment through the offer of a unilateral contract. Were you persuaded by the court's analysis? Is it consistent with our discussion of unilateral contracts earlier in this chapter?

You should be aware, however, that other courts may on similar facts find that an illusory promise by one party does render the return promise unenforceable, unless some other consideration is present. Compare E.I. Du Pont de Nemours & Co. v. Claiborne-Reno Co., 64 F.2d 224 (8th Cir.), *cert. denied,* 290 U.S. 646 (1933) (manufacturer's promise to continue distributorship operation not supported by consideration when distributor was free to terminate arrangement at any time), with Bruzesse v. Chesapeake Exploration, LLC, 998 F. Supp. 2d 663 (S.D. Ohio 2014) (terms of leasing agreement enforceable against lessors; agreement not illusory because although company's obligation to proceed qualified by its satisfaction with title and susceptibility to development "in its sole discretion," implied duty of good faith applied to limit company's exercise of discretion). Cf. Wood v. Lucy, Lady Duff-Gordon, in Chapter 6.

4. *"Mutuality of obligation."* In a similar vein to the illusory promise concept, sometimes courts have subjected contracts to a "mutuality of obligation" test, usually articulated as "both parties must be bound or neither is bound." As a broad generality, that is clearly an overstatement: We already have seen that unilateral contracts lack mutuality; a promisee under a unilateral contract is free to perform or not, while the promisor becomes bound once the promisee tenders a beginning of performance. Recall Note 3 after the *Sateriale* case. As we shall see, other promises are also enforceable by a party who is not herself bound to performance in return. (E.g., as discussed in the next chapter, a promise enforceable because of "detrimental reliance" will protect the relying

promisee even though there is no commitment on her part.) The Restatement (Second) strongly asserts the absence of any "mutuality of obligation" test for contract enforcement; if the consideration requirement is met, it declares, that is enough. Restatement (Second) §79(c). Nevertheless, some courts continue to apply a "mutuality of obligation" test for enforceability. E.g., Pick Kwik Food Stores, Inc. v. Tenser, 407 So. 2d 216 (Fla. Dist. Ct. App. 1981) (gasoline company could not enforce agreement for operation of pump on food store's premises where company had right to remove pump at any time); McCalment v. Eli Lilly & Co., 860 N.E.2d 884 (Ind. Ct. App. 2007) (alleged promise by employer that unfavorable performance review would be removed from employee's file within one year was unenforceable due to lack of mutuality of obligation; employee did not commit to do anything or refrain from anything in return).

C. CONTRACT FORMATION UNDER ARTICLE 2 OF THE UNIFORM COMMERCIAL CODE

In the previous sections of this chapter we explored two of the traditional basic requirements for formation of a contract: mutual assent and consideration. While thus far we have dealt primarily with the common law rules for contract formation, in this section our focus turns to corresponding statutory rules under Article 2 of the Uniform Commercial Code (UCC, or the Code). See the Comment on the History of the UCC that follows.

A fundamental aspect of the UCC is that it is not a traditional "code" in the sense that it displaces all prior law in the area. See John E. Murray, Jr., Murray on Contracts 21 (5th ed. 2011). The UCC provides in §1-103(b) that preexisting principles of law and equity supplement the Code unless they are displaced by particular provisions of the Code. Consistent with that approach, the drafters did not attempt to compose an exhaustive set of contract formation rules in Article 2. Rather, the common law rules provide a backdrop against which the UCC makes only a limited number of changes. For example, the UCC does not redefine the concept of consideration, nor does it contain a definition of an offer. Those elements of contract formation would be dependent on the relevant state's common law rules. The changes to formation rules that the Code does make are largely reflected in §§2-201 through 2-210. The following cases and materials consider a number of the issues that can arise under those sections.

Comment on the History of the Uniform Commercial Code

The Code had its origins in the late nineteenth century, when rapid industrialization and the growth of a national commercial economy first highlighted the expense, inconvenience, and uncertainty occasioned by differences between the states in matters of commercial law. Led by New York, a number of states created a National Conference of Commissioners on Uniform State Laws (NCCUSL) to address these problems. Although it did not have the power to make law, the NCCUSL drafted and recommended to the state legislatures a series of "uniform acts," dealing with various commercial matters, such as sales, negotiable instruments, and bills of lading. These uniform acts assumed the existence of an underlying body of common law governing contract formation in general.

By 1940, it appeared that an updating of a number of uniform acts was in order. As that project proceeded, however, it grew into something rather different. Joining with the American Law Institute (a prestigious and influential organization of lawyers, judges, and law teachers) that had drafted Restatements of the Law, the NCCUSL produced a general revision and consolidation of all the existing uniform commercial laws, the Uniform Commercial Code. Professor Karl Llewellyn was the architect of the UCC and the principal drafter of Article 2, its Sales article. Reflecting his influence, the Code attempted to harmonize commercial law with business practice, so as to effectuate the legitimate expectations of those engaged in business dealings. Although its acceptance by the states was at first slow in coming, all or part of the UCC has been adopted and is now in force in every American state.

The UCC, like contract law in general, has not been static. In 1987, a new Article 2A was adopted, dealing with leases of goods (a topic that many courts deemed to be covered, if at all, only "analogically" by Article 2, Sales). Various articles of the UCC have been comprehensively revised since the Code's widespread adoption in the 1960s, some, such as Article 9, more than once. In 2001, a revised version of Article 1 was promulgated by ALI/NCCUSL and it has been adopted by a clear majority of the states. Efforts to revise Article 2 have been marked by controversy surrounding the development of electronic contractual transactions, and have not been successful. That story is told by one of the Reporters of the proposed revised article, Richard E. Speidel, in Revising Article 2, A View from the Trenches, 52 Hastings L.J. 607 (2002).

1. Mutual Assent Under the Uniform Commercial Code

The following cases provide our first extensive exposure to Article 2 of the Uniform Commercial Code. Before reading the cases below, a brief introduction to Article 2 may be useful. (See also the Editors' Note to the UCC in the supplement.)

One of the first issues you must consider in analyzing a contracts problem is whether the transaction is governed by Article 2 of the UCC. It deals with transactions in "goods." UCC §2-102. Goods are generally defined as "movable" property, such as a car or a computer. UCC §2-105(1). Article 2 does *not* apply to other types of transactions; for example it does not apply to contracts for the sale of real estate, contracts to provide services, or contracts to lease goods. (UCC Article 2A, which has many provisions similar to Article 2, governs contracts for the leasing of goods; like Article 2, it also has been adopted in every state except Louisiana.) Article 2 also does not cover contracts involving patents, trademarks, or other intellectual property; although property of this type may be referred to as "personalty" (i.e., not "realty"), it is not tangible goods. Its provisions are supplemented by the general provisions of UCC Article 1, which (unless otherwise stated) apply to all the articles of the Code.

Despite the UCC's title (a "commercial" code), Article 2 *does* apply to both consumer and commercial sales of goods. Thus, if a consumer buys an automobile from a dealer (a consumer-merchant contract), Article 2 applies. If an airline corporation buys a jet airplane from the manufacturer or a dealer (a merchant-merchant contract), Article 2 applies. If an individual person buys a bicycle from its owner at a yard sale (a consumer-consumer contract), Article 2 definitely applies also, even though in that transaction neither party is a "merchant," as the UCC defines that term. (UCC §2-104(1).) Students often make the mistake of assuming that Article 2 does not apply unless all of the parties to the contract are merchants. Article 2 would govern all three types of contracts described above, absent specific language in a particular section that limits the application of that section to merchants. (There are some UCC sections that are so limited; we will see examples of such "merchant rules" later in these materials.)

Even if Article 2 applies to a particular contract, this does not mean that common law principles are necessarily irrelevant to its enforcement. As we noted earlier, the drafters of Article 2 wrote against a common law background. To the extent that Article 2 specifically deals with a problem, then Article 2 controls. But, as provided in UCC §1-103(b), if Article 2 does not cover an issue, then courts and lawyers will turn to common law principles to resolve the matter.

Sometimes a contract will involve both the sale of goods and the transfer of something other than goods, such as services, intangible rights, or real property. For example, when you take your car to be serviced, the dealer typically will sell you certain goods, such as oil to lubricate the car or replacement parts. In addition, the dealer charges you for the labor to repair the vehicle. Does the UCC apply to such a transaction with a mixture of goods and services? You can probably think of several possible approaches to this issue. We will return to this subject in connection with the cases that follow in this chapter.

Even if Article 2 clearly applies to a transaction, other statutory law may also govern the contract. For example, if a consumer buys an automobile from a dealer, Article 2 applies to the sale, but various consumer protection statutes may also apply. Section 2-102 clearly states that it does not displace consumer protection laws. A lawyer representing a consumer who purchased an automobile that turns out to be a "lemon" would want to be sure to uncover all possible claims the consumer might have under common law as well as any federal and state statutes that may regulate the transaction.

Jannusch v. Naffziger

Illinois Appellate Court 379 Ill. App. 3d 381; 883 N.E.2d 711 (2008)

Justice Cook delivered the opinion of the court:

Plaintiffs, Gene Jannusch and his wife, Martha, brought this action for breach of an oral contract against defendants, Lindsey Naffziger and her mother, Louann Naffziger. Following a bench trial, the trial court found in favor of defendants. Plaintiffs appeal. We reverse and remand with directions.

I. BACKGROUND

Plaintiffs operated a business, Festival Foods, which served concessions to the general public at festivals and events throughout Illinois and Indiana from late April to late October each year. The assets of the business included a truck and servicing trailer and equipment such as refrigerators and freezers, roasters, chairs and tables, fountain service and signs and lighting equipment.

Defendants were interested in purchasing the concession business, met several times with plaintiffs, and observed the business in operation. Gene testified that on August 13, 2005, plaintiffs entered into an oral agreement to sell Festival Foods to defendants for $150,000. For the $150,000, defendants would receive the truck and trailer, all necessary equipment, and the opportunity to work at event locations secured by plaintiffs. Defendants paid $10,000 immediately, with the balance to be paid when defendants received their loan money from the bank. Defendants took possession of Festival Foods the next day and operated Festival Foods for the remainder of the 2005 season. Gene acknowledged that the insurance and titles to the truck and trailer remained in his name because he had not yet received the purchase price from defendants.

Louann acknowledged testifying during a deposition that an oral agreement to purchase Festival Foods for $150,000 existed but later testified she could not recall specifically making an oral agreement on any particular date. Lindsey testified she and Louann met with plaintiffs on August 13, 2005, and paid the $10,000 for the right to continue to purchase the business because plaintiffs had another interested buyer. She also stated that the parties agreed defendants would run Festival Foods as they pursued buying the business. According to Lindsey, Gene suggested the parties sign something and she replied that defendants were "in no position to sign anything" because they had not received any loan money from the bank and did not have an attorney. The following week, Lindsey consulted with an attorney regarding the legal aspects of buying and owning a business. She asked the attorney to prepare a contract for the purchase. Ultimately, the bank approved defendants for a loan. Lindsey admitted taking possession of Festival Foods, receiving the income from the business, purchasing inventory, replacing equipment, paying taxes on the business and paying employees.

Defendants operated six events, three in Indiana and three in Illinois. Gene attended the first two festivals in Valparaiso and Auburn, Indiana, with defendants, who paid him $10 an hour and paid for his lodging. Gene and Louann testified that plaintiffs' minimal involvement with the operations after August 13 was merely as advisors to defendants, who were unfamiliar with this type of business. Two days after the business season ended, defendants returned Festival Foods to the storage facility where it had been stored by Gene. Gene testified he had canceled his lease with the storage facility, telling the owner that he had sold his business. Someone at the storage facility called Gene and reported that Festival Foods had been returned. Thereafter Gene attempted to sell Festival Foods, but was unsuccessful. Lindsey testified one of the reasons defendants returned Festival Foods was because the income from the events they operated was lower than expected. She stated Gene specifically asked defendants to run certain events for him and he ran the events where he was present. She testified Gene asked for the trailer back, stating he needed it "so he could make money on it for the end of the year," and that Gene stated he did not have money to buy back the inventory.

The trial court first held that the Uniform Commercial Code (UCC) . . . governed the issues raised in this case, rejecting defendants' argument that a sale of goods was not involved. The trial court then found that there was a contract formed but that the evidence was insufficient to establish by a preponderance of the evidence that there was a meeting of the minds as to what that agreement was. "If this is an agreement to reach an agreement, I suspect that the action for the price must fail."

II. Analysis

Where there are no questions as to the facts essential to a purported contract, the existence of the contract is a question of law. Magee v. Garreau, 332 Ill. App. 3d 1070, 1076, 774 N.E.2d 441, 446, 266 Ill. Dec. 335 (2002). In general, the construction or interpretation of a contract is a matter to be determined by the court as a question of law. Avery v. State Farm Mutual Automobile Insurance Co., 216 Ill. 2d 100, 129, 835 N.E.2d 801, 821, 296 Ill. Dec. 448 (2005).

A. Application of UCC

Defendants argue the UCC should not apply because this case involves the sale of a business rather than just the sale of goods. The "predominant purpose" test is used to determine whether a contract for both the sale of goods and the rendition of services falls within the scope of article 2 of the UCC. . . . A contract that is primarily for services, with the sale of goods being incidental, will not fall within the scope of *Article 2*. Belleville Toyota, Inc. v. Toyota Motor Sales, U.S.A., Inc., 199 Ill. 2d 325, 352-53, 770 N.E.2d 177, 194-95, 264 Ill. Dec. 283 (2002). . . . Certainly significant tangible assets were involved in this case. Cf. Fink v. DeClassis, 745 F. Supp. 509, 516 (N.D. Ill. 1990) (intangible assets accounted for $1 million of the total purchase price of $1.2 million). The evidence presented in this case was sufficient to support the conclusion that the proposed agreement was predominantly one for the sale of goods.

B. Statute of Frauds

[The court found that the alleged agreement came within the writing requirement of UCC §2-201 as a contract with a price of $500 or more, but that the contract would also come within exceptions in that section based on admissions in legal proceedings that a contract was made and part performance through payment of the price to the seller or acceptance of the goods by the buyer. — Eds.]

C. Formation of Contract

Under the UCC:

> "(1) A contract for sale of goods may be made in any manner sufficient to show agreement, including conduct by both parties which recognizes the existence of such a contract.

(2) An agreement sufficient to constitute a contract for sale may be found even though the moment of its making is undetermined.

(3) Even though one or more terms are left open a contract for sale does not fail for indefiniteness if the parties have intended to make a contract and there is a reasonably certain basis for giving an appropriate remedy." 810 ILCS 5/[UCC§]2-204 (West 2004).

Defendants argue that nothing was said in the contract about allocating a price for good will, a covenant not to compete, allocating a price for the equipment, how to release liens, what would happen if there was no loan approval, and other issues. Defendants argue these are essential terms for the sale of a business and the Internal Revenue Service requires that parties allocate the sales price. "None of these items were even discussed much less agreed to. There is not an enforceable agreement when there are so many essential terms missing."

"A contract may be enforced even though some contract terms may be missing or left to be agreed upon, but if the essential terms are so uncertain that there is no basis for deciding whether the agreement has been kept or broken, there is no contract." Academy Chicago Publishers v. Cheever, 144 Ill. 2d 24, 30, 578 N.E.2d 981, 984, 161 Ill. Dec. 335 (1991). In *Cheever*, the widow of John Cheever signed an agreement to publish a collection of Cheever's short stories. *Cheever*, 144 Ill. 2d at 27, 578 N.E.2d at 982. The Illinois Supreme Court held there was no valid and enforceable contract because there was no agreement as to the length and content of the book, who would decide which stories to include, the criteria used by the publisher in determining whether the manuscript was "satisfactory," or other terms. *Cheever*, 144 Ill. 2d at 29-30, 578 N.E.2d at 984. "[I]n fact, all they had really agreed to was a tentative title (*The Uncollected Stories of John Cheever*)." See also Dawson v. General Motors Corp., 977 F.2d 369, 373 (7th Cir. 1992).

The essential terms were agreed upon in this case. The purchase price was $150,000, and the items to be transferred were specified. No essential terms remained to be agreed upon; the only action remaining was the performance of the contract. Defendants took possession of the items to be transferred and used them as their own. "Rejection of goods must be within a reasonable time after their delivery or tender. It is ineffective unless the buyer seasonably notifies the seller." 810 ILCS 5/[UCC§]2-602(1) (West 2004). Defendants paid $10,000 of the purchase price. The fact that defendants were disappointed in the income from the events they operated is not inconsistent with the existence of a contract.

The trial court noted that "the parties have very very different views about what transpired in the course of the contract[-]formation discussions." It is not necessary that the parties share a subjective understanding as to the terms of the contract; the parties' conduct may indicate an agreement to the terms. Steinberg v. Chicago Medical School, 69 Ill. 2d 320, 330-31, 371 N.E.2d 634, 640, 13 Ill. Dec. 699 (1977). The conduct in this case is clear. Parties discussing the sale of goods do not transfer those goods and allow them to be retained for a substantial period before reaching agreement. Defendants replaced equipment, reported income, paid taxes, and paid Gene for his time and expenses, all of which is inconsistent with the idea that defendants were only "pursuing buying the business." An agreement to make an agreement is not an agreement, but there was clearly more than that here.

The trial court believed it was significant that Lindsey told Gene that defendants were "in no position to sign anything" because they had not received any loan money from the bank and did not have any attorney. "The fact that a formal written document is anticipated does not preclude enforcement of a specific preliminary promise." *Dawson,* 977 F.2d at 374 (1992). Defendants' loan was eventually approved, they did consult with an attorney, and defendants remained in possession of and continued to operate Festival Foods. The parties' agreement could have been fleshed out with additional terms, but the essential terms were agreed upon. Louann admitted there was an agreement to purchase Festival Foods for $150,000 but could not recall specifically making an oral agreement on any particular date. "An agreement sufficient to constitute a contract for sale may be found even though the moment of its making is undetermined." 810 ILCS 5//[UCC§]2-204(2) (West 2004). Returning the goods at the end of the season was not a rejection of plaintiffs' offer to sell, it was a breach of contract.

III. Conclusion

We conclude there was an agreement to sell Festival Foods for the price of $150,000 and that defendants breached that agreement. We reverse the circuit court's judgment and remand for the entry of an order consistent with this opinion.

Reversed and remanded with directions.

MYERSCOUGH and STEIGMANN, JJ., concur.

NOTES AND QUESTIONS

1. *Applicability of common law or UCC Article 2.* The *Jannusch* court must first consider whether the dispute is a type which comes within the scope of Article 2 of the UCC or should be governed by the common law. Although brief, the court's discussion correctly sets forth the "predominant thrust" test that courts have commonly applied to this type of question. Moreover, most case law would support the court's conclusion that the primary purpose of this contract was the sale of goods, rather than transfer of intangible assets related to the sale of the business (e.g., goodwill, booking contracts or training in business procedures). The *Princess Cruises* case in the next section will present a similar question concerning a contract with a mixture of goods and services.

2. *Contract formation under the UCC.* We have seen that under common law principles a contract requires a bargain in which there is a manifestation of mutual assent. UCC Section 2-204(3), however, places a clear emphasis on the question whether the parties had an intent to be bound even if some terms were left open. Under this Article 2 standard, does it appear that the parties

formed a contract based on the facts in the *Jannusch* case? How do these principles compare to the common law principles we examined earlier?

3. *Oral contracts and the statute of frauds.* The buyers in *Jannusch* argued that any alleged contract would not be enforceable because it was not in a signed writing. As we noted in the introductory materials in Chapter 1, virtually every state has enacted "statute of frauds" provisions that require certain contracts to be reduced to writing to be fully enforceable. A contract for the sale of goods for the price of $500 or more must comply with the writing requirement of UCC §2-201 or fall within an exception. The contract in *Jannusch* was not in a signed writing but came within two of those exceptions. Chapter 4 examines the requirements of the UCC statute of frauds in more detail. It is sufficient for you to know at this point that a contract that fails to satisfy the writing requirement in some cases may still be enforceable.

4. *The effect of relaxed rules for contract enforcement under the UCC?* Does the "relaxed" approach to contract formation under the UCC favor sellers or buyers? In *Jannusch* the court found that a contract was formed even though many terms were left open, thus imposing liability on the buyers. A similar case is Lowe v. Smith, 2016 Tenn. App. LEXIS (Tenn. Ct. App.) (finding the buyers liable for breach of an oral agreement to purchase a convenience store even though there was no discussion of the amount of gasoline inventory to be included in the sale or whether the sale also covered the real estate where the store was located). Of course, a flexible approach to contract formation does not mean that a court will always find that a contract was formed. See Sun City Pet Mkt., LLC v. Honest Kitchen, Inc., 2017 U.S. Dist. LEXIS 78278 (D. Ariz.) (dismissing plaintiff's complaint for breach of contract when it alleged that plaintiff had ordered pet products based on "Special" prices defendant had posted online to potential buyers attending a commercial show for sellers of pet products) and the case that follows.

E.C. Styberg Engineering Co. v. Eaton Corp.

United States Court of Appeals 492 F.3d 912 (7th Cir. 2007)

Judges: Before FLAUM, MANION, and ROVNER, Circuit Judges.

FLAUM, Circuit Judge. E.C. Styberg Engineering Co. ("Styberg") sued Eaton Corp. ("Eaton"), claiming that it breached a contract to buy 13,000 transmission components from Styberg. After a bench trial, the district court found that no contract existed and entered judgment for Eaton. Styberg appeals, and, for the following reasons, we affirm.

I. BACKGROUND

Styberg manufactures custom components for other manufacturers, and Eaton manufactures, among other things, motor vehicle parts and accessories, including transmissions. From 1998 to 2000, Styberg manufactured Part No. A-6871, an Inertia Brake Assembly ("I-brake"), for Eaton's six-speed transmissions. In August 1998, Styberg began selling prototype I-brake units to Eaton, and, in

November, Eaton began purchasing limited quantities of I-brakes so it could test the product in the marketplace. Subsequently, Eaton decided to pursue full production of I-brakes, and, in 1999, the parties began negotiating an agreement under which Styberg would produce large quantities of I-brakes for Eaton.

As negotiations proceeded, John Baker, Styberg's Engineering and Quality Assurance Manager, kept in contact with two Eaton employees: Al Davis, an engineer, and Lisa Fletcher, Eaton's buyer.[2] On May 27, 1999, Davis sent Baker an e-mail expressing Eaton's willingness to make a minimum purchase commitment to Styberg. Davis stated,

> I know that Styberg wants a commitment for a minimum number of units that Eaton will buy (to protect Styberg's capital expenditures). I believe Eaton is willing to give Styberg that commitment as well. . . . At the very least, I believe Eaton will guarantee the number of units it takes to pay off your capital investments, however many that is. (like the 13,000 we were discussing before). . . .

Getting a minimum unit commitment from Eaton was important to Styberg because, as Davis' e-mail suggests, Styberg had to expend significant capital to mass-produce the custom-designed parts.

On July 8, 1999, Baker sent Fletcher a proposal for a 60,000 unit order. According to the proposal, the first 13,000 units sold would have an average price of $544.88. The initial price of the units would be $595, but the price would progressively decrease as Styberg tweaked and perfected its manufacturing process. The proposal contained additional conditions, including a re-evaluation of the price and delivery schedule after the first 6,000 units were produced and an additional $31 per unit charge until a certain snap-in coil became available for manufacturing. Furthermore, the proposal requested $343,000 in "tooling money" — money that would assist Styberg in acquiring materials for its customized production. It also stated that Styberg would begin full production of the I-brakes in six months.

In his telephone log from July 16, 1999, Baker wrote, "Lisa Fletcher Quote was received. We have the 13,000 order!" A few days later, on July 22 and 23, Davis was visiting Styberg and met with its Vice President of Manufacturing, Ron Jones. Jones asked Davis for Eaton's commitment to buy at least 60,000 units, or, in the alternative, to buy 20,000 units with an additional capital investment of $1.2 million. Davis did not respond to the request while he was on site. On July 26, he e-mailed Fletcher, noting that Styberg representatives had indicated that they needed "a larger total unit commitment [than 13,000]" before the company would increase its monthly production capacity.

In a letter to Baker dated July 29, 1999, Fletcher wrote:

> Enclosed please find a tooling commitment. . . . [W]ith this $293,000 investment Styberg will be able to produce assembly A-6971 at a rate of up to 1,400 units per month, with an approximate lead time of four months.

2. Fletcher died before trial and was only partially deposed.

> Eaton will purchase a minimum of 13,000 units at an average unit price of $544.88 by July 29th, 2001. Additional requirements will be based on the market competitiveness and product value as the initial 13,000 units are consumed. . . .

On August 9, 1999, Baker and Fletcher spoke on the telephone and Baker told Fletcher, "thank you." According to Baker, he said "thank you" to indicate to Fletcher that Styberg agreed to produce the minimum quantity at the average price. However, Baker's notes from the phone call say, "13,000 units doesn't cover [Styberg's capitalization for the project] . . . 25 to Ron's 30,000." During cross-examination, Baker acknowledged that the notation meant that Styberg's Vice President of Manufacturing wanted a 25,000 to 30,000 unit commitment.

On September 1, 1999, employees from both companies participated in a conference call. Fletcher's notes from the call state, "we commit to 13K units — Styberg sez [sic] not enough to justify their capital investment. Want at least 30K commitment. . . . Styberg will come back w/ capacity + quotes for 13K flat out." According to Baker, the parties to the conference call agreed that, in regard to the 13,000 unit order, Baker would prepare a schedule for Fletcher that detailed the number of units Styberg could produce each month with its present capital.

On September 9, 1999, Baker sent Fletcher a production schedule that included a detailed break-down of Styberg's anticipated monthly production capacity for 13,000 units as well as a quote for an initial unit price of $595 plus $31 per unit until the snap-in coil became available. The quote stated that the estimated delivery date would "be based on a starting date four months after an agreement on casting design, unit price, and delivery schedules." Baker testified that on September 27, 1999, Fletcher told him that the schedule was acceptable. However, Baker's notes from September 27 include the notation "LM," which, according to earlier testimony, meant that he left a message for Fletcher and did not speak with her.

Eaton did not issue a specific purchase order for the 13,000 I-brakes, but Baker contends that Fletcher told him to use an existing purchase order. Styberg did not execute or send Eaton a purchase order acknowledgment for the 13,000 unit order. In April 2000, Eaton notified Styberg that it expected delivery of 240 units. Styberg shipped the units under an existing purchase order, and Eaton paid for the units. On May 8, 2000, Eaton requested another 240 units for shipment, which were to be delivered the following month. Three days later, however, Eaton cancelled the request. After May 11, 2000, Eaton neither ordered nor paid for any I-brakes. In May 2003, after settlement discussions broke down, Styberg sued Eaton in the district court for breach of contract, seeking approximately $3.4 million in damages, which represented Styberg's lost profits and inventory related to the manufacture of 13,000 I-brakes.

After a four-day trial, the district court entered judgment in favor of Eaton, summarizing the case as follows:

> Based on the record, the Court finds that there was not a contract. Styberg could not meet and refused to accept any of the proposed terms. It needed additional money for tooling. It could not meet the monthly production targets

> set in the letter and purchase order. It needed to increase the unit price to cover design changes. It needed a higher total number of unit sales to cover its expenses. Finally, it needed more lead time and needed to extend the timetable by nearly a year. The parties never came to like terms of any kind of agreement. When asked of the Plaintiff to point to what constituted the agreement, Plaintiff was not able to do so in a manner that even came close in a legally satisfactory manner. For a company that did business on the written word of contracts, they were unable to produce one.

The district court characterized the e-mail, telephone, and letter exchanges as evidence of continuing negotiations in which the parties could not agree on key terms like quantity, price, and monthly production volume. Accordingly, it concluded that the parties never formed a contract. Styberg appeals.

II. Discussion

On appeal, Styberg claims that the district court's factual findings and legal conclusions were erroneous, and that this Court should enter judgment in its favor. We review the trial court's determination that no contract existed for clear error. See Thomas v. Gen. Motors Acceptance Corp., 288 F.3d 305, 307 (7th Cir. 2002). . . .

Ohio Revised Code §1302.07(A), the state's codification of UCC §2-204, provides that "a contract for the sale of goods may be made in any manner sufficient to show agreement, including conduct by both parties which recognizes the existence of such a contract." Courts and commentators agree that the UCC takes a liberal view towards what is required to create a contract for the sale of goods. See, e.g., Architectural Metal Sys., Inc. v. Consol. Sys., Inc., 58 F.3d 1227, 1230 (7th Cir. 1995) (recognizing that the UCC tolerates "a good deal of incompleteness and even contradiction in offer and acceptance"); WHITE AND SUMMERS, UNIFORM COMMERCIAL CODE §1-2 at 4-5 (4th Ed. 1995) (noting that Article 2 of the UCC makes contracts easier to form by reducing the required formalities); . . . . Notably, however, nothing in the UCC or Ohio's code eliminates the requirement that, for a contract to be enforceable, it "must . . . be specific as to its essential terms, such as the identity of the parties to be bound, the subject matter of the contract, consideration, a quantity term, and a price term." Alligood v. Procter & Gamble Co., 594 N.E.2d 668, 669 (Ohio Ct. App. 1991).

In this case, Styberg argues that the documentary evidence conclusively established the existence of a contract and that the district court erred in finding that no contract was formed. According to Styberg, the parties agreed that Eaton would purchase 13,000 I-brakes from Styberg at an average unit price of $544.88. Styberg identifies three possible sources for the alleged contract: 1) Lisa Fletcher's July 29, 1999 letter; 2) Baker's September 9, 1999 schedule; and 3) Eaton's request for I-brakes in the Spring of 2000.

First, Styberg argues that Lisa Fletcher's July 29 letter was either an acceptance of Styberg's July 8 offer to supply Eaton with 13,000 I-brakes or an offer to purchase I-brakes that Baker accepted on August 9, 1999 by saying "thank you." Then, according to Styberg, although the parties had a contract with the price and quantity terms firmly in place, they continued to negotiate about larger orders and other open terms. Eaton, on the other hand, characterizes Lisa Fletcher's letter as part of a series of ongoing negotiations, during which Eaton and Styberg could not agree on the essential terms. Eaton claims that Styberg wanted a commitment for some 20,000 to 60,000 I-brakes in order to justify its capital investment, and Eaton did not want to be bound by such a large commitment.

In our view, the district court did not err by concluding that the communications were ongoing negotiations about a contract that never came to fruition rather than an actual contract. Indeed, the court's decision was supported by relevant case law, which states that typically, a price quotation is considered an invitation for an offer, rather than an offer to form a binding contract. See Dyno Constr. Co. v. McWane, Inc., 198 F.3d 567, 572 (6th Cir. 1999) (applying Ohio law). If Styberg's July 8 price quotation was not an offer, then the July 29 letter could not have been an acceptance. Moreover, "it is most often the buyer's purchase order, submitted in response to such a quotation that constitutes the offer." Babcock & Wilcox Co. v. Hitachi Am., Ltd. 406 F. Supp. 2d 819, 827 (N.D. Ohio 2005). The parties agree that Lisa Fletcher did not send Styberg a purchase order for 13,000 I-brakes.

Even assuming that Fletcher's letter was an offer in response to the price quotation, the district court's finding that Styberg rejected the offer and continued to push for a higher minimum-unit commitment was a reasonable interpretation of the evidence. After Baker allegedly manifested his acceptance by saying "thank you" on August 9, the two companies participated in a conference call during which Styberg again indicated that a 13,000 unit commitment was not enough. Baker's own notes from the September 1 call state that September 15 was " 'D' Day agreement," presumably meaning the parties had not yet formed a contract on September 1.

Next, Styberg argues that a contract was formed on September 27, 1999, when Fletcher told Baker that his proposed schedule from September 9 was acceptable. We reject this argument as well. The district court found that Fletcher never made such a comment, and that finding was not clearly erroneous. The court emphasized that Baker's own notes from September 27 indicated only that he left a message for Fletcher, suggesting that he never spoke with her at all. Because the district court's conclusion was supported by its assessment of Baker's credibility as well as the documentary evidence, we are in no position to second-guess it.

Finally, Styberg contends that the parties' conduct clearly demonstrated the existence of a contract. We disagree. The district court found that Eaton's request for two 240-unit orders at the price specified in Styberg's quotes was insufficient to prove an agreement for the sale of 13,000 units, and that conclusion was not clearly erroneous. Although one Ohio court has required a buyer who accepted $5,500 worth of cable to accept all $35,000 worth of it, the buyer in that case had sent the seller a purchase order for the full amount, which the seller accepted by shipping the goods. TLG Elecs, Inc. v. Newcome Corp., 2002 Ohio 882, 2002 WL 338203, at *3 (Ohio Ct. App. 2002). Here, by contrast, Eaton did not submit a purchase order for 13,000 I-brakes, so accepting the 240-unit shipment did not require it to accept 13,000.

Moreover, courts finding contracts based on parties' conduct have typically done so either where there was repeated and ongoing conduct manifesting an agreement or where the parties had an established course of dealing to which they adhered. See, e.g., Central Transp., Inc. v. Cleveland Metallurgical Supply Co., No. 63055, 1993 Ohio App. LEXIS 3513, 1993 WL 266924, at *2-3 (Ohio Ct. App. July 15, 1993) (holding that the parties' conduct manifested an agreement where the buyer submitted a purchase order, the seller shipped coal to the buyer on numerous occasions, the buyer paid for each shipment, and the parties continued to do business even after a dispute arose between them); [American Bronze Corp. v. Streamway Prods., 8 Ohio App. 3d 223, 456 N.E.2d 1295, 1300 (Ohio Ct. App. 1982)] (finding a binding contract was formed where the parties followed their usual procedures for placing and accepting orders). In this case, Eaton's two requests for 240 I-brakes, one of which was cancelled, did not come close to the repeated, ongoing dealing that proved a contract in *Central Transport*, nor did it adhere to the parties' usual course of dealing as in *American Bronze*. In fact, if the parties intended to contract, they deviated from their usual procedure because, historically, Eaton would submit a specific purchase order to Styberg and Styberg would send Eaton a purchase order acknowledgment form. Therefore, the district court properly could have concluded that Eaton placed the orders pursuant to the parties' previous arrangement dating back to 1998 rather than a new contract for 13,000 units.

In short, the district court accepted Eaton's interpretation of ambiguous evidence and its choice between two reasonable interpretations of that evidence was not clearly erroneous. See Anderson v. Bessemer City, 470 U.S. 564, 573, 105 S. Ct. 1504, 84 L. Ed. 2d 518 (1985) (stating that clear error review does not permit an appellate court to reverse merely because it would have decided the case differently).

III. CONCLUSION

For the foregoing reasons, we AFFIRM the judgment of the district court.

NOTES AND QUESTIONS

1. *Offer and acceptance under UCC Article 2.* As indicated in the *E.C. Styberg* case as well as in the *Jannusch* opinion, Section 2-204 liberalizes the rules for contract formation under Article 2. Subsection 2-204(2) states that "a contract for sale may be found even though the moment of its making is undetermined." The official comment to the section further underscores this approach: "Subsection (2) is directed primarily to the situation where the interchanged correspondence does not disclose the exact point at which the deal was closed, but the actions of the parties indicate that a binding obligation has been undertaken." Are you persuaded by the seller's argument in *E.C. Styberg* that the parties reached an agreement for the sale of 13,000 units of the goods

even though they continued to negotiate for a larger quantity? Did the court expect too much in stating that the absence of a written purchase order from the buyer and purchase order acknowledgment from the seller indicated that a contract had not been made?

2. *Same rule, different outcomes?* The courts in two preceding cases rely on the same UCC provisions. Can the finding that a contract was not made in *E.C. Styberg* be reconciled with the decision that a contract was made in *Jannusch*? What are the key factual differences between the two cases?

3. *Acceptance through conduct.* Consistent with Section 2-204, the Code goes on to provide in Section 2-206(1) that unless the offeror "unambiguously" indicates how acceptance should be made, "an offer to make a contract shall be construed as inviting acceptance in any manner and by any medium reasonable in the circumstances." Do you think that the buyer in *E.C. Styberg* ever made an offer that the seller might have accepted?

4. *Agreement despite open terms.* Recall that the court in the *Quake Construction* case earlier in this chapter recognized that parties might have a binding agreement despite the fact that some terms still were subject to negotiation and, alternatively, that the concurring opinion in that case recognized that parties might have a binding agreement to negotiate in good faith even though a contract had not been finalized. Would either of those arguments be relevant to the *E.C. Styberg* case?

Comment: Introduction to the CISG

We have previously referred several times to the Convention on Contracts for the International Sale of Goods (CISG), an international treaty to which the United States is a party. It is useful to think of the CISG as the international equivalent to Article 2 of the UCC. If a contract has international aspects, one of the first issues you must analyze is whether the CISG applies. For further discussion of the CISG see the Editors' Note to the CISG in the supplement.

Scope. Just as the court in the *Jannusch* case had to first address the question whether UCC Article 2 would apply to the transaction at issue, it is inherent in the nature of the CISG as a treaty that it applies only to those transactions that come with the scope of its provisions. The CISG states rather simply in Article 1 that it "applies to contracts for the sale of goods" in phrasing similar to the UCC Article §2-102 provision that it applies to "transactions in goods." Beyond that initial point, however, the CISG scope provisions depart in significant ways from those of Article 2.

An initial difference between the UCC and the CISG is that the latter treaty generally applies to contracts for the sale of goods when the contracting parties have places of business in different countries that are signatories to the CISG. See Article 1(a). For a list of signatory countries, see the Editors' Note to the CISG in the supplement. Most of the United States' major trading partners, with the exception of the United Kingdom, are parties to the CISG. Thus, if a Chinese garment manufacturer sells goods to a New York department store, the contract would be subject to the CISG. Keep in mind, however, that many foreign companies establish U.S. subsidiaries. A contract between a U.S. subsidiary of a Chinese company and a U.S. company would not be subject to the CISG.

A second difference between the two law sources is that the UCC Article 2 applies to sales of goods to consumers, while the CISG excludes consumer transactions. See Article 2(a). This exclusion covers goods that are bought for a "personal, family, or household use." Thus, a U.S. national who travels to a European country to purchase an automobile for family use will not have made a transaction that comes within the scope of the CISG.

It is also significant that parties to an international contract that is otherwise subject to the CISG may by contract agree that the CISG does not apply and that some other source of law governs. See Article 6. Under the UCC the parties may, subject to some limitations, vary the provisions by agreement, but the parties do not have the power to exclude the application of the UCC entirely. UCC §1-302.

Professor John Coyle conducted a study to determine the extent to which large U.S. companies rely on the CISG in their international agreements. After examining actual contracts from U.S. companies and interviewing U.S. lawyers who draft and negotiate contracts with foreign parties, Professor Coyle found that U.S. companies routinely exclude the CISG from their international sales agreements and almost never intentionally select it as the governing law, at least partly due to lack of familiarity with the CISG. He concluded that the CISG has yet to achieve much traction among large U.S. companies doing business internationally. John F. Coyle, The Role of the CISG in U.S. Contract Practice: An Empirical Study, 38 U. Pa. J. Int'l L. 195 (2016). These observations may be read to highlight a need for more study of the CISG by U.S. lawyers.

Contract formation under the CISG. The provisions on formation under the CISG bear many similarities to the UCC and U.S. common law, speaking in terms of offer and acceptance. Article 14 defines an offer as a proposal addressed to one or more specific persons that is sufficiently definite as to the goods involved, the quantity, and the price and that indicates a willingness to be bound if the offeree accepts. In a similar vein to the prevailing U.S. rule on advertisements, Article 14(2) states that a proposal sent to multiple addressees is most likely an invitation to make offers rather than an offer itself. Ultimately, Article 23 provides that a contract is concluded, or formed, when an effective acceptance is made.

There are a number of other provisions under the CISG relevant to contract formation. Throughout the following materials we will address a number of those CISG articles as well as provisions addressing the performance and enforcement of international contracts for the sale of goods.

PROBLEM 2-5

Marsha Boyston is an investor who specializes in acquiring income producing real estate, such as office buildings and apartment projects. In the typical transaction, Boyston does the following: locates desirable property, assembles a group of individuals who will invest in the project (these investors usually put up 20 percent of the purchase price), and obtains bank financing for the remaining 80 percent of the purchase price. For her services Boyston usually receives 10 percent ownership in the project.

Recently, Boyston negotiated a contract with Herbert Smith, the owner of the Village Garden Apartments, to acquire the property for $1.5 million. She paid Smith $25,000 down. The contract contains a standard "financing contingency" clause, which provides that Boyston will not be obligated to purchase the property if she is unable to obtain financing. If she cannot obtain financing, however, she forfeits the $25,000 down payment.

After signing the contract, Boyston went to the National Bank of City and applied for a loan of $1.2 million (80 percent of the purchase price). On September 24, 2018, she received the following loan commitment letter from Andrea Wilson, the loan officer at National:

> September 24, 2018
>
> Ms. Marsha Boyston
> 219 Olive St.
> City, SC 29205
>
> Re: Village Garden Apartments
> Dear Marsha:
>
> National Bank of City is pleased to offer a loan commitment to you for the purpose of financing the acquisition of the Village Garden apartments located at 1919 Downing Street, on the following terms and conditions:
>
> 1. Borrower — Village Garden Limited Partnership. You are the sole general partner. Other investors will be limited partners.
> 2. Amount — $1,200,000.
> 3. Purpose — to purchase the land and buildings known as the Village Garden Apartments.
> 4. Terms — 15-year amortization.
> 5. Interest rate — 6% fixed.
> 6. Commitment fee — none.
> 7. Collateral — first mortgage on the Village Garden apartment project located at 1919 Downing Street.
> 8. Expiration date of this commitment — This commitment is valid for 30 days from the date of this letter.
> 9. The Village Garden Partnership must furnish evidence of its organization and its authority to enter into this transaction.
> 10. Opinion of Counsel — The note and all other documents with regard to this transaction shall be in a form that is satisfactory to counsel for the Bank.
> 11. Closing Expenses — All legal and other expenses incurred by National Bank will be paid by the borrower.
>
> If the terms of this commitment are acceptable to you, please sign and date this letter and return it to me in the enclosed envelope. If you have any questions, please let me know.

Sincerely,
Andrea Wilson
Loan Officer
National Bank of City

Accepted by:

____
(date)

While the bank was evaluating the loan, Boyston had been busy contacting business acquaintances who had invested in her previous projects. By the time she received the commitment letter, she had obtained promises from investors for $200,000 of the $300,000 that she needed. After receiving the above letter, she continued her efforts, and by October 1, she had put together a group of eight investors willing to put up $300,000. She immediately contacted Herbert Smith, the owner of the Village Garden apartments, and informed him that she had obtained financing. They agreed to a closing date of October 28, 2018. She also called Ms. Wilson at the bank to tell her that she wished to accept the terms of the bank's loan. Boyston told Wilson that she would personally deliver the signed commitment letter the next day. Later that afternoon, however, Wilson called Boyston and told her that she had just received word from her boss that the bank was withdrawing its commitment letter. Boyston was shocked. She pointed out that she had already told Wilson that she had agreed to the loan. Wilson was very apologetic. Wilson said that she didn't even know the reason why the bank was withdrawing its commitment. Boyston then contacted Smith to inform him of the problem. She asked Smith if he would be willing to agree to an extension of the closing. Smith said he would, but only for two weeks. During that time Boyston tried to obtain other bank financing, but was unable to do so. She finally had to tell Smith that she was unable to go forward with the sale. As a result she forfeited her $25,000 deposit.

Boyston has asked your advice about whether she has any legal rights against the bank because of its withdrawal of the commitment letter. Be prepared to present your analysis of her legal rights and to outline the advice that you would give.

2. Qualified Acceptance: The "Battle of Forms"

If our experience is any guide, it may be that for law students in general, the notion of a "contract" conjures up the image of a sort of all-purpose document, full of legal jargon — whereases, heretofores, and parties of the first and second part — that experienced lawyers know by heart. In fact, the "legal ritual" part of most contracts is negligible or nil; the heart of a written contract is an accurate description of the particular exchange of performances to which the parties are agreeing, plus an identification of the principal risks entailed for one or both parties, with specification of the parties' rights should any of those risk-events occur.

This is not to say there are not "legal forms" for contract lawyers to employ; models can be found in "form books" in law libraries and many companies publish computer software with forms for various types of transactions. But the suggested forms vary with each type of transaction, and the language used in such forms reflects the practicalities of the business in question as well as the rules of law that govern it. Most lawyers who practice extensively in a particular commercial area develop their own set of forms, or "precedents" – model contracts that are used over and over in substantially the same form. Typically these contain at least some language that is almost always repeated verbatim (often referred to as "boilerplate"); other parts will be varied to suit the particular transaction. Of course, no careful lawyer would use a prior contract as a precedent without reviewing it to see what changes might be required. A cautious reliance on precedents is standard practice, however, and for good reason: It saves the lawyer's time and labor; it thereby helps keep down the cost of legal services to the client; and it provides the attorney with a checklist of things to watch out for in the transaction at hand. The use of computers with word processing programs and other "apps" has made the adaptation of standard forms to the specifics of each transaction much easier.

For many clients, this use of prototype contracts can be carried a step further. Most businesses enter into a large number of substantially similar transactions – sales of goods, for instance, in which the typical variations are the type, number, and price of the items sold, the name of the buyer, the time and place agreed on for delivery, and whether the buyer wishes to purchase a service contract and/or an extended warranty. For such repetitive transactions, use of a series of individually prepared contracts (even if developed with the time-saving help of precedents) would be inefficient. What is needed is a "standard form," a pre-prepared document that gives all the legal protection required in a particular type of transaction, with blanks to be completed either by selling personnel or with information supplied by the purchaser in on-line transactions.

From the lawyer's point of view, such forms are important principally as a means of bringing legal counsel to bear in multiple transactions that would otherwise have to be conducted without it. To the client, however, the forms have additional utility. Because they serve as efficient organizers of information, they facilitate storage and retrieval of the data important to particular transactions. Standard forms also permit relatively error-free dissemination of identical information to the various persons within and without the organization who have responsibility for different aspects of the completed exchange. On the other hand, we all know from experience that the efficiency gained from the use of standardized forms is likely to be purchased at the cost of some depersonalizing of the individual transaction. If the forms do not completely replace personal contact and negotiation, but only supplement it, their use creates an additional potential risk: that the transaction as recorded will differ from the transaction-in-fact, perhaps in important ways.

We noted earlier in this chapter that the traditional rules of contract law were fashioned on the assumption that the parties would deal with each other in the conventional manner: An offer would be made; it would be either accepted or rejected; if the latter, perhaps a counteroffer would be made; that in turn would be accepted or rejected; and so on. Certainly that mode of contracting may still be employed today. But for most businesses, such a leisurely approach to contracting is too expensive and time-consuming to be taken for any but the most important and idiosyncratic of transactions. Most deals will be made — or at least recorded — on forms, either paper or electronic. Courts and legislatures have therefore had to fashion new rules for determining when sufficient agreement has been reached to justify a finding that a contract has been made and for deciding in light of the various communications between the parties what the terms of that contract are.

The materials in this section will be devoted to the situation where the parties are business enterprises utilizing paper forms of the type described above. The first case, *Princess Cruises, Inc. v. General Electric Co.*, although it involves issues of federal law, turns in the end on a pair of common law principles established in the heyday of classical contract law: the "mirror image" and "last shot" rules, as they are often called. The following cases, *Brown Machine* and *Paul Gottlieb*, illustrate the different approach taken by UCC Article 2 to the question of nonmatching forms, as spelled out in UCC §2-207.

Princess Cruises, Inc. v. General Electric Co.

United States Court of Appeals 143 F.3d 828 (4th Cir. 1998)

Before Ervin and Williams, Circuit Judges, and Goodwin, United States District Judge for the Southern District of West Virginia, sitting by designation.

OPINION

GOODWIN, District Judge:

This suit arises out of a maritime contract between General Electric Company (GE) and Princess Cruises, Inc. (Princess) for inspection and repair services relating to Princess's cruise ship, the SS *Sky Princess.* In January 1997, a jury found GE liable for breach of contract and awarded Princess $4,577,743.00 in damages. J.A. at 1876. On appeal, GE contends that the district court erred in denying its renewed motion for judgment as a matter of law, which requested that the court vacate the jury's award of incidental and consequential damages. Specifically, GE argues that the district court erroneously applied Uniform Commercial Code principles, rather than common-law principles, to a contract primarily for services. We agree and hold that when the predominant purpose of a maritime or land-based contract is the rendering of services rather than the furnishing of goods, the U.C.C. is inapplicable, and courts must draw on common-law doctrines when interpreting the contract. Accordingly, we reverse the district court's decision denying GE's renewed motion for judgment as a matter of law and remand for modification of the judgment consistent with this opinion.

I. FACTUAL BACKGROUND

Princess scheduled the SS *Sky Princess* for routine inspection services and repairs in December 1994 and requested that GE, the original manufacturer

The SS Sky Princess docked in Auckland, New Zealand.

of the ship's main turbines, perform services and provide parts incidental to the ship's inspection and repair. Princess issued a Purchase Order in October 1994. The Purchase Order included a proposed contract price of $260,000.00 and contained a brief description of services to be performed by GE. The reverse side of the Purchase Order listed terms and conditions which indicated that Princess intended the Purchase Order to be an offer. These terms and conditions also stated that GE could accept the Purchase Order through acknowledgment or performance; that the terms and conditions could not be changed unilaterally; and that GE would provide a warranty of workmanlike quality and fitness for the use intended. J.A. at 75-76.

On the same day that GE received the Purchase Order, GE faxed a Fixed Price Quotation to Princess. The Fixed Price Quotation provided a more detailed work description than Princess's Purchase Order and included a parts and materials list, an offering price of $201,888.00, and GE's own terms and conditions. When GE reviewed Princess's Purchase Order, it discovered that Princess requested work not contemplated by GE in its Fixed Price Quotation. GE notified Princess of GE's error. On October 28, 1994, GE faxed a Final Price Quotation to Princess. In the Final Price Quotation, GE offered to provide all services, labor, and materials for $231,925.00. Attached to both GE Quotations were GE's terms and conditions, which: (1) rejected the terms and conditions set forth in Princess's Purchase Order; (2) rejected liquidated damages; (3) limited GE's liability to repair or replacement of any defective goods or damaged equipment resulting from defective service, exclusive of all written, oral, implied, or statutory warranties; (4) limited GE's liability on any claims to not more than the greater of either $5000.00 or the contract price; and (5) disclaimed any liability for consequential damages, lost profits, or lost revenue. J.A. at 106-13. During an October 31, 1994 telephone call, Princess gave GE permission to proceed based on the price set forth in GE's Final Price Quotation. J.A. at 825, 1850.

On November 1, 1994, GE sent a confirmatory letter to Princess acknowledging receipt of Princess's Purchase Order and expressing GE's intent to perform the services. J.A. at 115. The letter also restated GE's $231,925.00 offering price from its Final Price Quotation and specified that GE's terms and conditions, attached to the letter, were to govern the contract. Id.

When the SS *Sky Princess* arrived for inspection, GE noted surface rust on the rotor and recommended that it be taken ashore for cleaning and balancing. The parties agree that during the cleaning, good metal was removed from the rotor, rendering the rotor unbalanced. Although GE attempted to correct the imbalance, Princess canceled a ten-day Christmas cruise as a result of delays caused by the repair. At trial, Princess alleged that the continued vibration and high temperatures caused damage to the ship, forcing additional repairs and the cancellation of a ten-day Easter cruise. It was undisputed, however, that Princess paid GE the full amount of the contract: $231,925.00. J.A. at 1008.

On April 22, 1996, Princess filed a four-count complaint against GE, alleging breach of contract, breach of express warranty, breach of implied maritime warranty, and negligence. The district court granted GE's motion for summary judgment as to the negligence claim. Following Princess's presentation of evidence at trial, GE made a motion for judgment as a matter of law, which the district court denied. At the conclusion of the defendant's presentation of evidence, the district court denied GE's second motion for judgment as a matter of law. In instructing the jury, the district court drew on principles set forth in U.C.C. §2-207 and allowed the jury to imply the following terms as part of the contract: (1) the warranty of merchantability; (2) the warranty of fitness for a particular purpose; (3) the warranty of workmanlike performance; (4) Princess's right to recover damages for GE's alleged breach of the contact; and (5) Princess's right to recover incidental and consequential damages, as well as lost profits, proximately caused by GE's alleged breach. On January 24, 1997, the jury returned a $4,577,743.00 verdict in favor of Princess. On February 3, 1997, GE renewed its motion for judgment as a matter of law requesting that the court vacate the jury's award of incidental and consequential damages. The district court heard oral argument on May 6, 1997. Following oral argument, the district court denied GE's renewed motion for judgment as a matter of law and issued an opinion clarifying its ruling.

II. Standard of Review

The Court reviews de novo the district court's denial of GE's renewed motion for judgment as a matter of law. . . . In reviewing the district court's decision, we consider the evidence in the light most favorable to the nonmovant to determine whether the evidence presented at trial was sufficient to allow a reasonable jury to render a verdict in the nonmovant's favor. . . .

III. To Apply U.C.C. Principles to a Maritime Contract for Services Would Hinder Admiralty Law's Goals of Uniformity and Predictability

Although GE contended that the district court was required to determine whether goods or services predominated before applying U.C.C. principles to the GE-Princess contract, the district court found it "unnecessary for the Court to determine whether the contract is primarily one for goods or services. In either case, the UCC is regarded as a source of admiralty law." J.A. at 2024. We respectfully disagree.

One of the primary concerns of admiralty law is uniformity and predictability. See American Dredging Co. v. Miller, 510 U.S. 443, 450-51 (1994). . . . To avoid the creation of multiple and conflicting rules of decision in admiralty, the Fourth Circuit has stated that, "Absent reason to do otherwise, we prefer to adopt rules in admiralty that accord with, rather than diverge from, standard commercial practice." Finora Co. v. Amitie Shipping, Ltd., 54 F.3d 209, 213-14 (4th Cir. 1995). As discussed in more detail below, standard commercial practice requires that a transaction be predominantly for the sale of goods before the U.C.C. applies. See Coakley & Williams, Inc. v. Shatterproof Glass Corp., 706 F.2d 456, 460 (4th Cir. 1983); Bonebrake v. Cox, 499 F.2d 951, 960 (8th Cir. 1974).

In its May 13, 1997 opinion, the district court correctly noted that U.C.C. principles inform admiralty law. See Southworth Mach. Co. v. F/V Corey Pride, 994 F.2d 37, 40 n.3 (1st Cir. 1993); Clem Perrin Marine Towing, Inc. v. Panama Canal Co., 730 F.2d 186, 189 (5th Cir. 1984). However, we are unpersuaded by cases cited to support the district court's legal determination that U.C.C. §2-207 applies to maritime transactions regardless of the nature of the transaction. . . .

Given admiralty law's goals of uniformity and predictability, we find that mixed maritime contracts for goods and services are subject to the same inquiry as land-based mixed contracts. Therefore, a court must first determine whether the predominant purpose of the transaction is the sale of goods. Once this initial analysis has been performed, the court then may properly decide whether the common law, the U.C.C., or other statutory law governs the transaction. Cf. Little Beaver Enters. v. Humphreys Rys., 719 F.2d 75, 79 n.7 (4th Cir. 1983) (noting that maritime contract for services was not covered by U.C.C.); In re American Export Lines, Inc., 620 F. Supp. 490, 515 (S.D.N.Y. 1985). This method accords with standard commercial practice and lends predictability to maritime contracts.

IV. The GE-Princess Contract Was Predominantly for Services

In its order denying GE's renewed motion for judgment as a matter of law, the district court addressed GE's contention that the district court erroneously included U.C.C. principles in its jury instructions. J.A. at 2021. Both by motion and at trial, GE argued that the district court was required to find that the sale of goods predominated in the GE-Princess contract before employing U.C.C. principles in its instructions.

Although the U.C.C. governs the sale of goods, the U.C.C. also applies to certain mixed contracts for goods and services. Whether a particular transaction is governed by the U.C.C., rather than the common law or other statutory law, hinges on the predominant purpose of the transaction, that is, whether the contract primarily concerns the furnishing of goods or the rendering of services. See Coakley & Williams, 706 F.2d at 458 ("Whether the U.C.C. applies turns on a question as to whether the contract . . . involved principally a sale of goods, on the one hand, or a provision of services, on the other."). . . . Thus, before applying the U.C.C., courts generally examine the transaction to determine whether the sale of goods predominates. See Coakley & Williams, 706 F.2d at 458. Because the facts in this case are sufficiently developed and undisputed, it is proper for the Court to determine on appeal whether the GE-Princess transaction was a contract for the sale of goods within the scope of the U.C.C. Cf. Cambridge Plating Co. v. Napco, Inc., 991 F.2d 21, 24 (1st Cir. 1993).

In determining whether goods or services predominate in a particular transaction, we are guided by the seminal case of Bonebrake v. Cox, 499 F.2d 951 (8th Cir. 1974). In holding the U.C.C. applicable, the *Bonebrake* court stated:

> The test for inclusion or exclusion is not whether they are mixed but, granting that they are mixed, whether their predominant factor, their thrust, their purpose, reasonably stated, is the rendition of service, with goods incidentally involved (e.g., contract with artist for painting) or is a transaction of sale, with labor incidentally involved (e.g., installation of a water heater in a bathroom).

Bonebrake, 499 F.2d at 960. The Fourth Circuit has deemed the following factors significant in determining the nature of the contract: (1) the language of the contract, (2) the nature of the business of the supplier, and (3) the intrinsic worth of the materials. See Coakley & Williams, 706 F.2d at 460 (applying Maryland law).

It is plain that the GE-Princess transaction principally concerned the rendering of services, specifically, the routine inspection and repair of the SS *Sky Princess,* with incidental — albeit expensive — parts supplied by GE. Although Princess's standard fine-print terms and conditions mention the sale of goods, J.A. at 76, Princess's actual purchase description requests a GE "service engineer" to perform service functions: the opening of valves for survey and the inspection of the ship's port main turbine. J.A. at 75. GE's Final Price Quotation also contemplates service functions, stating in large print on every page that it is a "Quotation for Services." J.A. at 107-09. The Final Price Quotation's first page notes that GE is offering a quotation for "engineering services." J.A. at 106. GE's Quotation further specifies that the particular type of service offered is "Installation/Repair/Maintenance." J.A. at 107. The Final Price Quotation then lists the scope of the contemplated work — opening, checking, cleaning, inspecting, disassembling — in short, service functions. J.A. at 110; see also J.A. at 1862-68 (listing service tasks actually performed by GE). Although GE's materials list shows that GE planned to manufacture a small number of parts for Princess, Princess appeared to have had most of the needed materials onboard. J.A. at 111. Thus, the language of both the Purchase Order and the Final Price Quotation indicates that although GE planned to supply certain parts, the parts were incidental to the contract's predominant purpose, which was inspection, repair, and maintenance services.

As to the second *Coakley* factor — the nature of the business of the supplier — although GE is known to manufacture goods, GE's correspondence and Quotations came from GE's Installation and Service Engineering Department. J.A. at 97, 106, 115. Evidence at trial showed that GE's Installation and Service Engineering division is comprised of twenty-seven field engineers who perform service functions, such as overhauls and repairs. J.A. at 1076. Finally, the last *Coakley* factor — the intrinsic worth of the materials supplied — cannot be determined because neither Princess's Purchase Order nor GE's Final Price Quotation separately itemized the value of the materials. Instead, both the Purchase Order and the Final Price Quotation blend the cost of the materials into the final price of a services contract, thereby confirming that services rather than materials predominated in the transaction. Although not a *Coakley* factor, it is also telling that, during oral argument, Princess's counsel admitted that the gravamen of Princess's complaint did not arise out of GE's furnishing of deficient parts, but rather out of GE's deficient services. See J.A. at 23-27 (Princess's Complaint stating that Princess's damages arose out of "GE's inspection, supervision . . . recommendation . . . reinstallation and realignment of the turbine unit."). . . . Accordingly, we find as a matter of law that services rather than goods predominated in the GE-Princess contract.

V. Under Common Law, GE's Final Price Quotation Was a Counteroffer Accepted by Princess

The parties do not dispute that a contract was formed by their exchange of documents. J.A. at 2020. And there is no dispute that the GE-Princess contract for ship inspection and repair is maritime in nature and governed by the substantive law of admiralty. . . . However, the issue here — whether courts should draw on U.C.C. principles or on common-law doctrines when assessing the formation of a maritime services contract — is undecided. When no federal statute or well-established rule of admiralty exists, admiralty law may look to the common law or to state law, either statutory or decisional, to supply the rule of decision. Byrd v. Byrd, 657 F.2d 615, 617 (4th Cir. 1981) (admiralty may look to state law to supply rule of decision). . . . Because the majority of states refer to common-law principles when assessing contracts predominantly for services, we choose to do the same.

Under the common law, an acceptance that varies the terms of the offer is a counteroffer which rejects the original offer. RESTATEMENT (SECOND) OF CONTRACTS §59 (1981) ("A reply to an offer which purports to accept it but is conditional on the offeror's assent to terms additional to or different from those offered is not an acceptance but is a counter-offer."). Virginia follows the same rule. See Chang v. First Colonial Savs. Bank, 242 Va. 388, 410 S.E.2d 928, 931 (1991). Here, GE's Final Price Quotation materially altered the terms of Princess's Purchase Order by offering a different price, limiting damages and liability, and excluding warranties. Thus, GE's Final Price Quotation was a counteroffer rejecting Princess's Purchase Order. Although Princess could have rejected GE's counteroffer, Princess accepted the Final Price Quotation by giving GE permission to proceed with the repair and maintenance services, by not objecting to the confirmatory letter sent by GE, and by paying the amount set forth in GE's Final Price Quotation, $231,925.00, rather than the $260,000.00 price term set forth in Princess's Purchase Order. At common law, an offeror who proceeds under a contract after receiving the counteroffer can accept the terms of the counteroffer by performance. See Diamond Fruit Growers, Inc. v. Krack Corp., 794 F.2d 1440, 1443 (9th Cir. 1986) (citing C. Itoh & Co. (America) v. Jordan Intl. Co., 552 F.2d 1228, 1236 (7th Cir. 1977)); Durham v. National Pool Equip. Co. of Va., 205 Va. 441, 138 S.E.2d 55, 58 (1964) ("Assent may be inferred from the acts and conduct of the parties.") (citations omitted). Although GE and Princess never discussed the Purchase Order's and the Final Price Quotation's conflicting terms and conditions, both Princess's actions and inaction gave

GE every reason to believe that Princess assented to the terms and conditions set forth in GE's Final Price Quotation. See RESTATEMENT (SECOND) OF CONTRACTS §19(1) (1981) ("The manifestation of assent may be made wholly or partly by written or spoken words or by other acts or by failure to act."); Wells v. Weston, 229 Va. 72, 326 S.E.2d 672, 676 (1985) ("The mental assent of [contracting] parties is not requisite for the formation of a contract. . . . In evaluating a party's intent . . . we must examine his outward expression rather than his secret, unexpressed intention.") (citations omitted). Accordingly, we find that the terms and conditions of GE's Final Price Quotation control liability and damages in the GE-Princess transaction.

VI. The Verdict Demonstrates That the Jury Impermissibly Relied on a Contract Other Than GE's Final Price Quotation

For the reasons stated above, the jury could only have considered one contract in awarding damages: GE's Final Price Quotation. The Quotation restricted damages to the contract price, $231,925.00, and eliminated liability for incidental or consequential damages and lost profits or revenue. Moreover, GE's Final Price Quotation controlled the warranties available to its customers. Yet the jury awarded $4,577,743.00 in damages to Princess. This verdict demonstrates that the jury relied on Princess's Purchase Order or some other contract when awarding damages. See J.A. at 2025 (district court opinion noting that "the jury either found that Princess'[s] Purchase Order governed or that neither parties' document established the complete contract"). As a matter of law, the jury could only have awarded damages consistent with the terms and conditions of GE's Final Price Quotation and could not have awarded incidental or consequential damages. By requesting that the Court award Princess the maximum amount available under the Final Price Quotation, see Appellant's Brief at 39-40; Appellant's Reply Brief at 20, GE concedes that it breached its contract with Princess and that damages consistent with its Final Price Quotation are appropriate. Accordingly, we find it unnecessary to remand for a new trial on this issue. We reverse the district court's decision denying GE's motion for judgment as a matter of law and remand for entry of judgment against GE in the amount of $231,925.00, interest to accumulate from the date of the original judgment.

Reversed and Remanded.

NOTES AND QUESTIONS

1. *Applicability of common law or UCC Article 2.* The *Princess Cruises* case is first and foremost a dispute governed by federal admiralty law, as the court indicates. Nevertheless, the court still finds it appropriate to determine whether the dispute is of a type which would otherwise be governed by Article 2 of the UCC, or by the common law of contract. The question is similar to the one raised in the *Jannusch* case earlier in this chapter. The *Princess Cruises* court's conclusion that the predominant thrust of the contract would be properly seen as "services" rather than a "sale of goods" seems in line with most of the case

law in this area. Is the conclusion that Article 2 does not apply in *Princess Cruises* consistent with the decision in *Jannusch* that Article 2 would apply to the transaction in that case?

2. *Application of common law — the "mirror-image" rule.* Having concluded that the common law of contract should apply, rather than the UCC (or, more precisely, that the admiralty law applicable to this case should be informed by common law rather than by UCC Article 2 principles), the court proceeds to apply what it views as the common law rules of offer and acceptance. Classical contract law employed the "mirror-image" rule and the "last shot" rule. The first of these gives a "varying" acceptance the effect of only a counter-offer, preventing the contract from being made on the terms of the original offer. In *Princess Cruises,* the court applies the classical mirror-image rule in a contemporary setting. In support, the court cites Restatement (Second) §59, which merely echoes the classical rule of the first Restatement §60. The court fails, however, to quote Comment *a* to Restatement (Second) §59, which provides as follows:

> *a. Qualified acceptance.* A qualified or conditional acceptance proposes an exchange different from that proposed by the original offeror. Such a proposal is a counter-offer and ordinarily terminates the power of acceptance of the original offeree. See §39. The effect of the qualification or condition is to deprive the purported acceptance of effect. But a definite and seasonable expression of acceptance is operative despite the statement of additional or different terms if the acceptance is not made to depend on assent to the additional or different terms. See §61; UCC §2-207(1). The additional or different terms are then to be construed as proposals for modification of the contract. See UCC §2-207(2). Such proposals may sometimes be accepted by the silence of the original offeror. See §69.

The Restatement (Second) on the "varying acceptance" issue thus attempts to steer a course somewhat closer to the UCC than indicated in the court's opinion. In the case that follows, we will compare UCC §2-207 with the common law on this point.

3. *Application of common law — the "last shot" rule.* Classical courts followed the last shot rule to determine when a counter-offer was accepted. Under that rule, a party impliedly assented to and thereby accepted a counter-offer by conduct indicating lack of objection to it. In addition to being based on a questionable notion of implied assent, the last shot rule tended in practice to favor sellers over buyers, because sellers normally "fire the last shot" — i.e., send the last form. Professor John Murray well described the working of the common law rule; as his analysis shows (and as *Princess Cruises* continues to demonstrate), the favored party was typically — though not always — the seller.

> A typical variation of the problem occurs in innumerable contracts between buyers and sellers of goods. The buyer sends its offer through its standardized purchase order form. The seller replies and purportedly accepts the offer through its standardized acknowledgment (acceptance) form. Usually, the only written or typewritten terms on either form set forth the description,

> price and quantity of the goods. The buyer's form which contains the offer may or may not indicate the quality of the goods ordered. If no quality term is contained in the form, the buyer is entitled to goods of fair average quality or merchantable goods. This is an implied warranty of merchantability which is set forth in the U.C.C. Often, the seller's form will contain a disclaimer of that implied warranty of merchantability. The disclaimer will be contained in a printed provision among many others somewhere on the form. The forms are exchanged, the goods are shipped and, perhaps, even paid for by the purchaser. When the buyer attempts to use the goods, he finds them to be of inferior, non-merchantable quality. The buyer brings an action for breach of contract, specifically, breach of the implied warranty of merchantability. The seller argues that since his acknowledgment form did not exactly match the terms of the buyer's offer, the form was not an acceptance of the offer. Rather, it was a counter-offer which created a new power of acceptance in the original offeror. When the goods were accepted and received by the purchaser, the counter-offer was accepted. Therefore, the contract or deal was made on the terms set forth in the seller's form. In effect, the seller had the "last shot" since his form created the last power of acceptance which the buyer exercised presumably by accepting and receiving the goods on the terms set forth in the seller's form. Under the matching acceptance rule, this analysis was clearly correct. Yet, the buyer never read the seller's form, the seller never read the buyer's form and neither read their own forms. The printed forms were simply a convenient means of expressing assent to the "dickered" terms, i.e., the written or typewritten terms which described the goods, their quantity and their price. Quaere: did the parties intend to be bound by the terms on the forms and, even if they did, which terms did they intend as binding? The question scarcely survives its statement. In the typical exchange, the parties manifested no intention whatsoever as to the printed provisions of their forms. Yet, they did physically exchange them and the forms constituted the only written evidence of their deal. The traditional judicial reaction was that the forms could not be ignored and since the terms thereon did not match, the last form had to be a counter-offer permitting the seller to have his "last shot" and to prevail.

John Edward Murray, Jr., Contracts §54, at 112-113 (2d ed. 1974).

The court in *Princess Cruises* applies the classical last shot rule. Having concluded that GE's response should be viewed as a counter-offer under the mirror image rule, the court then goes on to hold that Princess Cruises accepted that counter-offer by conduct: by not objecting to its terms; by accepting the services performed by GE; and by paying the price stated in GE's counter-offer. In support, the court cites Restatement (Second) of Contracts §19(1), along with case law to the same effect. See Sharp Electronics Corp. v. Deutsche Financial Services Corp., 216 F.3d 388 (4th Cir. 2000) (manufacturer effectively accepted financer's revised version of financing arrangement for customer's purchases of inventory by continuing to ship inventory to customer with knowledge of terms of financer's counter-offer).

4. *Contrast with UCC Article 2.* On both points — the effect of a varying or qualified acceptance; the effect of performance on the issue of acceptance — the UCC departs from the common law rules noted above. UCC §2-207

significantly modifies, though it does not reject entirely, the application of both the mirror image rule and the last shot doctrine. The following cases and problem explore the Code's approach. Before you study the next case, read through §2-207 and its comments. (No, it's not easy going; we are well aware of that. Many courts have found this provision difficult to understand and apply.) Note that in Comment 1 to §2-207, the drafters identify two different situations which (somewhat awkwardly) they have attempted to cover in this single section. The first one mentioned in that comment, the use of "written confirmations," involves an oral agreement between the parties (by telephone, typically), followed by written confirmations sent by one or both of the parties. The second situation mentioned in Comment 1 is the "varying acceptance" case where the parties exchange standard forms that disagree in their content. (*Princess Cruises* would fall into this general category, although of course that contract was not regarded as being primarily one for the sale of goods.) The following cases well illustrate the UCC's handling of the "varying acceptance" situation under §2-207.

Brown Machine, Inc. v. Hercules, Inc.

Missouri Court of Appeals 770 S.W.2d 416 (1989)

STEPHAN, Judge.

Hercules Inc. ("Hercules") appeals from the judgment of the trial court awarding respondent Brown Machine $157,911.55 plus interest after a jury verdict in favor of Brown Machine in its action against Hercules for indemnification. We reverse.

In early 1976 Brown Machine had sold appellant Hercules a T-100 trim press. The trim press was a piece of equipment apparently used in manufacturing Cool Whip bowls. The initial sales negotiations between the two companies for the trim press began in October 1975. Bruce Boardman, an engineer at Hercules, asked Jim Ryan, Brown Machine's district sales manager, to send Hercules a quote for a trim press. On November 7, 1975, Brown Machine submitted its original proposal No. 51054 for the model T-100 trim press to Hercules. The proposal set out sixteen numbered paragraphs describing the machine to be sold. Attached to the proposal was a printed form of fifteen paragraphs in boilerplate style captioned "TERMS AND CONDITIONS OF SALE." The eighth paragraph provided as follows:

> 8. LIABILITY: The purchaser agrees to pay in behalf of BROWN all sums which BROWN becomes legally obligated to pay because of bodily injury or property damage caused by or resulting from the use or misuse of the IOS [item of sale], including reasonable attorneys fees and legal expenses. The purchaser agrees to indemnify and hold BROWN harmless from all actions, claims, or demands arising out of or in any way connected with the IOS, its operation, use or misuse, or the design construction or composition of any product made or handled by the IOS, including all such actions, claims, or demands based in whole or in part on the default or negligence of BROWN.

Tim Wilson, Hercules' purchasing agent, reviewed the proposal submitted by Brown Machine. On January 7, 1976, he telephoned Jim Ryan at Brown Machine. Mr. Ryan's call report reflected that Hercules had prepared its purchase order No. 03361 in response to Brown Machine's proposal but that Hercules had objected to the payment term requiring a twenty percent deposit be paid with the order. After talking with Mr. Fassett, Brown Machine's product manager, Mr. Ryan told Mr. Wilson that Brown Machine could not waive the deposit and that an invoice for payment would be forwarded to Hercules.

Mr. Fassett issued a work order that day giving the shop instructions concerning the trim press equipment, followed by a written order the next day. The written order noted that "customer gave verbal P.O. [purchase order] for this stock machine. Will issue revision when formal purchase order received."

On January 19, 1976, Brown Machine received Hercules' written purchase order No. 03361 dated January 6, 1976. The order was for a "Brown T-100 Trimpress in accordance with Brown Machine quote # 51054. All specifications cited within quote except item # 6.1.1 which should read: 'Reverse trim' instead of 'Standard regular forward trim.' " In a blue box on the bottom left of the purchase order form in bold print appeared "THIS ORDER EXPRESSLY LIMITS ACCEPTANCE TO THE TERMS STATED HEREIN INCLUDING THOSE PRINTED ON THE REVERSE SIDE. ANY ADDITIONAL OR DIFFERENT TERMS PROPOSED BY THE SELLER ARE REJECTED UNLESS EXPRESSLY AGREED TO IN WRITING." The reverse side of Hercules' purchase order, captioned "TERMS AND CONDITIONS" contained sixteen boilerplate paragraphs, the last of which provided:

> 16. OTHER TERMS: No oral agreement or other understanding shall in any way modify this order, or the terms or the conditions hereof. Seller's action in (a) accepting this order, (b) delivering material; or (c) performing services called for hereunder shall constitute an acceptance of the above terms and conditions.

The purchase order contained no indemnity provision.

Brown Machine received two copies of the purchase order. One had been stamped "Vendor's Copy" at the bottom; the other was marked "ACKNOWLEDGMENT," with a space labeled "accepted by" for signature by Brown Machine. Brown Machine did not return this prepared acknowledgment to Hercules.

The next day, on January 20, 1976, Mr. Fassett issued his second machine order to the shop revising his description to reflect that Brown Machine had received Hercules' formal purchase order and that the machine was no longer inventoried as a Brown stock item. On January 21, 1976, Brown Machine sent Hercules an invoice requesting payment of $4,882.00, the twenty percent deposit for the trim press.

Rather than returning the acknowledgment of the purchase order prepared by Hercules, Mr. Fassett of Brown Machine sent Hercules an "ORDER ACKNOWLEDGEMENT" dated February 5, 1976. This letter stated as follows:

> Below in detail are the specifications covering the equipment ordered, and the equipment will be manufactured to meet these specifications. If these

> specifications and terms and conditions of Sale are not in accordance with your understanding, please ADVISE US WITHIN SEVEN (7) DAYS OF RECEIPT OF THIS ACKNOWLEDGEMENT. If we do not hear from you within this period of time, we are proceeding with the construction of the equipment as per these specifications and terms as being agreed; and any changes occurring later may result in additional charges.
>
> *ONE T-100 TRIM PRESS AS FOLLOWS . . .*

The paragraphs following set out the same sixteen specifications contained in Brown Machine's original proposal. Paragraph 6.1.1 of the specifications again provided for "Standard-regular forward trim." Page four of the acknowledgment contained the same "TERMS AND CONDITIONS OF SALE" which had accompanied Brown Machine's earlier proposal of November 7, 1975, including paragraph eight on liability and indemnity. Only two minor changes had been penned in on page four, neither of which has any bearing on the issues presented for appeal.

Hercules responded with a letter on February 9, 1976, to Mr. Fassett that "This is to advise you that Provision 6.1 of your order acknowledgment dated 2/5/76 should read 'Reverse Trim' instead of 'Standard-regular forward trim.' All other specifications are correct." On February 16, 1976, Mr. Fassett confirmed the change in provision 6.1.1 and informed the shop that same day of the requested modification to be made.

Hercules never paid the twenty percent deposit. Brown Machine sent Hercules an invoice dated April 14, 1976, requesting final payment of the total purchase price. Brown eventually shipped the trim press to Hercules and Hercules paid the agreed-upon purchase price.

Sometime later, James Miller, an employee of Hercules, and his wife sued Brown Machine because of injuries he sustained while operating the trim press at Hercules' plant in Union, Missouri. Brown Machine demanded that Hercules defend the Miller lawsuit, but Hercules refused. Brown Machine eventually settled the Millers' lawsuit. Brown Machine later initiated this action against Hercules for indemnification of the settlement amount paid the Millers. Brown Machine claimed a condition of the original sales contract for the trim press required Hercules to indemnify Brown Machine for any claims arising from operation or misuse of the trim press.

Hercules' four points on appeal challenge the submissibility of Brown Machine's case, the verdict director given by Brown Machine, admission of certain allegedly prejudicial testimony and, finally, an instructional error. The dispositive issue on appeal is whether the parties had agreed to an indemnification provision in their contract for the sale of the T-100 trim press.

Hercules' first point disputes Brown Machine's contention that its initial proposal on November 7, 1975, constitutes the offer and that Hercules verbally accepted the offer by the telephone call on January 7, 1976, followed by its written purchase order dated January 6, 1976, which Brown Machine received January 19, 1976.

Article 2 of the Uniform Commercial Code governs transactions involving the sale of goods. UCC §2-102 (1977). Because the term "offer" is not defined in the code, the common law definition remains relevant. UCC §1-103. An offer is made when the offer leads the offeree to reasonably believe that an offer has been made. Gilbert & Bennett Manufacturing Co. v. Westinghouse Electric Corp., 445 F. Supp. 537, 545[3] (D. Mass. 1977). Restatement (Second) of Contracts §24 (1981) defines "offer" as "the manifestation of willingness to enter into a bargain, so made as to justify another person in understanding that his assent to that bargain is invited and will conclude it."

The general rule is that a price quotation is not an offer, but rather is an invitation to enter into negotiations or a mere suggestion to induce offers by others. Maurice Electrical Supply Co. v. Anderson Safeway Guard Rail Corp., 632 F. Supp. 1082, 1087[3] (D.D.C. 1986); USEMCO, Inc. v. Marbro Co., 60 Md. App. 351, 483 A.2d 88, 93[1] (1984). However, price quotes, if detailed enough, can amount to an offer creating the power of acceptance; to do so, it must reasonably appear from the price quote that assent to the quote is all that is needed to ripen the offer into a contract. Quaker State Mushroom Co. v. Dominick's Finer Foods, Inc., 635 F. Supp. 1281, 1284[3] (N.D. Ill. 1986); see Boese-Hilburn Co. v. Dean Machinery Co., 616 S.W.2d 520, 524-25 (Mo. App. 1981).

In this case Hercules could not have reasonably believed that Brown Machine's quotation was intended to be an offer, but rather an offer to enter into negotiations for the trim press. The cover letter accompanying the proposal mentioned that Brown Machine's sales representative would contact Hercules "to discuss this quote" and that the quotation was submitted for Hercules [sic] "approval." The sale price as quoted also included the notation "We have included a mechanical ejector (item 9.1.2) because we understand this unit may be used for development of many items that would require this option. However, if you decide this is not necessary $2,575.00 could be deducted from the above price for a total of $21,835.00." Most importantly, paragraph three of the terms and conditions of sale attached to the proposal expressly provided: "No order, sale, agreement for sale, accepted proposal, offer to sell and/or contract of sale shall be binding upon BROWN unless accepted by BROWN . . . on BROWN standard 'Order Acknowlegment'[sic] form." Thus, because the quotation reasonably appeared to be an offer to enter into negotiations for the sale of a trim press with a mechanical ejector for $24,410.00 with acceptance conditioned upon Brown's order acknowledgment form, no firm offer existed. Accord, Quaker State Mushroom, Inc., 635 F. Supp. at 1285. Brown's price quote was merely a proposal, not an offer, because of its provision that Hercules' acceptance was not binding upon Brown until Brown acknowledged the acceptance.

Even if we were to accept Brown Machine's characterization of its proposal as an offer, the quotation by its own terms and conditions expired thirty days after its issuance ("All quoted prices are subject to change without notice except those written proposals which shall expire without notice . . . thirty (30) calendar days from date issued . . ."). Hercules' written purchase order was dated January 6, 1976, and their telephone conversation of January 7, 1976, were both well beyond the expiration of the quote. Thus, even if the quotation were construed as an offer, there was no timely acceptance. See Gilbert & Bennett, 445 F. Supp. at 545[4].

If the acceptance of a price quotation, sufficiently detailed to constitute an offer, is not binding on the seller because the time within which it could have been accepted has lapsed, the purchase order, not the price quotation, is treated as the offer since the purchase order did not create an enforceable contract. McCarty v. Verson Allsteel Press Co., 89 Ill. App. 3d 498, 44 Ill. Dec. 570, 411 N.E.2d at 936, 943[5] (1980). Thus, we believe Hercules' purchase order constitutes the offer. As a general rule, orders are considered as offers to purchase. Aaron E. Levine & Co. v. Calkraft Paper Co., 429 F. Supp. 1039, 1048[15] (E.D. Mich. 1976).

The question then arises whether Brown Machine's acknowledgment containing the indemnity provision constitutes a counter offer or an acceptance of Hercules' offer with additional or different terms. Section 400.2-207, RSMo 1986, which mirrors §2-207 of the Uniform Commercial Code provides the workable rule of law addressing the problem of the discrepancies in the independently drafted documents exchanged between the two parties. . . .

Under subsection (1) an offeree's response to an offer operates as a valid acceptance of the offer even though it contains terms additional to, or different from, the terms of the offer unless the "acceptance is expressly made conditional" on the offeror's assent to the additional or different terms. Where the offeree's acceptance is made "expressly conditional" on the offeror's assent, the response operates not as an acceptance but as a counter offer which must be accepted by the original offeror. Falcon Tankers, Inc. v. Litton Systems, Inc., 355 A.2d 898, 906[7] (Del. Super. 1976). Restatement (Second) of Contracts §59 (1981) expresses it succinctly: "[A]n offeree's reply which purports to accept an offer but makes acceptance conditional on the offeror's assent to terms not contained in the original offer is effective as a counteroffer rather than acceptance."

The general view held by the majority of states is that, to convert an acceptance to a counter offer under UCC §2-207(1), the conditional nature of the acceptance must be clearly expressed in a manner sufficient to notify the offeror that the offeree is unwilling to proceed with the transaction unless the additional or different terms are included in the contract. See Annot., "What Constitutes Acceptance 'Expressly Made Conditional' Converting it to Rejection and Counteroffer under UCC §2-207(1)," 22 A.L.R. 4th 939, 948-49 (1983) and cases cited therein. The conditional assent provision has been construed narrowly to apply only to an acceptance which clearly shows that the offeree is unwilling to proceed absent assent to the additional or different terms. Id.; see Challenge Machinery Co. v. Mattison Machine Works, 138 Mich. App. 15, 359 N.W.2d 232, 235[3] (1984) citing Idaho Power Co. v. Westinghouse Electric Corp., 596 F.2d 924 (9th Cir. 1979); Dorton v. Collins & Aikman Corp., 453 F.2d 1161 (6th Cir. 1972).

We find nothing in Brown Machine's acknowledgment of February 5, 1976, which reflects its unwillingness to proceed unless it obtained Hercules' assent to the additional and different terms in Brown Machine's acknowledgment, that is, page four of the acknowledgment styled "TERMS AND CONDITIONS OF SALE" which contained the indemnity provision. Brown Machine's acknowledgment was not "expressly made conditional" on Hercules' assent to the additional or different terms as provided for under §2-207(1). Acceptance will be considered a counteroffer only if the acceptance is expressly made conditional on assent to the additional terms. Clifford-Jacobs Forging Co. v. Capital Engineering & Mfg. Co., 107 Ill. App. 3d 29, 62 Ill. Dec. 785, 787, 437 N.E.2d 22, 24 (1982). We conclude Brown Machine's acknowledgment did not operate as a counter offer within the scope of §2-207(1).

Having determined that Brown Machine's order acknowledgment is not a counter offer, we believe that Brown Machine's acknowledgment operates as acceptance with additional or different terms from the offer, since the purchase order contained no indemnity provision. Under §2-207(2), additional terms become a part of the contract between merchants unless (a) the offer expressly limits acceptance to the terms of the offer; (b) they materially alter it; or (c) notification of objection to them has already been given or is given within a reasonable time after notice of them is given. Hercules' purchase order here expressly limited acceptance to the terms of its offer. Given such an express limitation, the additional terms, including the indemnification provision, failed to become part of the contract between the parties.

We can conclude Hercules intended the indemnity provision to become a part of the parties' contract only if Hercules, as offeror, expressly assented to the additional terms, and, thus, effectively waived its condition that acceptance be limited to the terms of its offer, the purchase order. While the text of §2-207 does not incorporate such a provision, Official Comment 3 to §2-207 states: "Whether or not additional or different terms will become part of the agreement depends upon the provisions of subsection (2). If they are such as materially to alter the original bargain, they will not be included unless expressly agreed to by the other party." The indemnification provision was clearly a material alteration to the parties' agreement.

The evidence does not establish that Hercules expressly assented to the additional terms contained in Brown Machine's order acknowledgment. Brown Machine's order acknowledgment of February 5, 1976, indicated that "[i]f these specifications and terms and conditions of Sale are not in accordance with your understanding, please ADVISE US WITHIN SEVEN (7) DAYS OF RECEIPT OF THIS ACKNOWLEDGMENT." Hercules replied by letter four days later advising Brown Machine that provision 6.1.1 should provide for reverse trim instead of standard regular forward trim, followed by "all other specifications are correct." Hercules' use of the term "specifications" is unambiguous and clearly refers only to the protocol for the machine's manufacture. Nothing in its response can be construed as express assent to Brown Machine's additional "terms and conditions of sale." Express assent under §2-207(2) cannot be presumed by silence or mere failure to object. N & D Fashions, Inc. v. DHJ Industries, Inc., 548 F.2d 722, 726-27[5] (8th Cir. 1977).

We believe it is clear as a matter of law that the indemnification clause cannot be held to be part of the contract agreed upon by the parties. The judgment of the trial court is reversed. We need not address the remaining points raised by Hercules.

Reversed.

SMITH, P.J., and SATZ, J., concur.

NOTES AND QUESTIONS

1. *The UCC's treatment of the "varying acceptance."* Courts and commentators frequently begin discussion of UCC §2-207 by noting that it appears to have as one of its principal purposes the amelioration of a strict "mirror image" approach to contract formation, by permitting non-matching communications to form a contract if the parties apparently intended that they should. E.g., Stelluti Kerr, L.L.C. v. Mapei Corp., 2017 U.S. App. LEXIS 11804 (5th Cir.); ConocoPhillips Alaska, Inc. v. Williams Alaska Petro., Inc., 322 P.3d 114 (Alaska 2014) (§2-207 abrogates mirror image rule). The UCC's modification of the mirror-image rule is stated in §2-207(1): "A definite and seasonable expression of acceptance . . . operates as an acceptance even though it states terms additional to or different from those offered. . . . " (If this seems to be merely a tautology, it may help to read the first use of the term *acceptance* as meaning, essentially, *assent,* and the second as meaning *legal acceptance.*)

2. *Finding the first offer.* Under UCC §2-207, as in the classical approach to agreement-formation, the first step is to ascertain at what point an "offer" was first made by one party to the other. The court in *Brown Machine* thus begins by examining the communications between the parties and concludes that the first offer was the buyer's purchase order of January 6; the seller's "proposal" (or "quote") of November 7 was not an offer, the court states, but merely an invitation to the buyer to submit an offer. Although a price quotation is often held to be only a preliminary negotiation, it may in some cases amount to an offer. The *Brown Machine* court recognizes this possibility but concludes that in this case the buyer could not have reasonably understood that the seller was making an offer. In reaching that conclusion, however, the court relies in part on the language of the seller's form regarding the need for further acceptance by the seller. This is of course "boilerplate," about which §2-207 might suggest we should be somewhat skeptical. (Do you think the buyer read that language?) If the seller's initial proposal had not contained that provision, would the court's characterization of it as a mere invitation for an offer still be persuasive?

3. *Testing the response.* Having established that the buyer's purchase order was the first operative offer, the court then proceeds to apply the test of UCC §2-207(1) to the seller's reply. If the seller had (as requested) merely signed and returned the buyer's form, then the "battle of forms" would have been over at this point, and the buyer would have won — the terms of its purchase order would constitute the contract. See Michels Corp. v. Resitech Indus., LLC, 2016 U.S. Dist. LEXIS 18466 (E.D. Wis.) (seller's "sales order" in response to buyer's purchase order was a pure acceptance that did not precipitate a battle of the forms because it listed terms in purchase order and did not contain any fine

print terms and conditions). But — as in *Princess Cruises* — each party preferred to use its own forms, so the seller instead responded with a form of its own, an "Order Acknowledgment." Assuming that this form demonstrated sufficient general assent to the buyer's order to be regarded as potentially an "acceptance," the next issue under UCC §2-207(1) is whether the seller's acceptance was "expressly conditional" (in which case, as the court declares, it functions not as an acceptance, but as a "counter-offer").

Courts have differed on when an acceptance should be treated as "expressly conditional" and therefore function as a counter-offer. An early case, Roto-Lith, Ltd. v. F.P. Bartlett & Co., 297 F.2d 497 (1st Cir. 1962), held that an acceptance with terms that were materially different from the offer amounted to an expressly conditional acceptance. Courts and commentators criticized this view because it effectively reestablished the common law mirror image rule, contrary to the intentions of the drafters of UCC §2-207. E.g., White & Summers, Uniform Commercial Code §2-3, at 40 (6th ed. 2010). In Ionics, Inc. v. Elmwood Sensors, Inc., 110 F.3d 184 (1st Cir. 1997), the First Circuit recognized its error in *Roto-Lith* and overruled the decision.

Since *Roto-Lith* has been overruled, it now seems well established that an acceptance does not amount to an expressly conditional acceptance simply because it contains terms that materially differ from the terms of the offer. But when is an acceptance expressly conditional? Most courts focus on the language of the acceptance. If the acceptance uses very clear language indicating that the offeree's assent is expressly conditional on the offeror's agreement to the terms of the offeree's document, then the acceptance will be treated as expressly conditional, even if the language is essentially boilerplate. E.g., Diamond Fruit Growers, Inc. v. Krack Corp., 794 F.2d 1440, 1444 (9th Cir. 1986) (seller's response expressly conditional; its "form tracks the language of the section"). The language, however, must be very clear. If the offeree simply states that its acceptance is "subject to the following terms and conditions" or equivalent conditional language, that is generally held not to be sufficient to treat the acceptance as expressly conditional. See Dorton v. Collins & Aikman Corp., 453 F.2d 1161, 1167 (6th Cir. 1972) ("subject to all of the terms and conditions on the face and reverse side hereof, including arbitration, all of which are accepted by buyer" held not to be an expressly conditional acceptance); Option Wireless, Ltd. v. Openpeak, Inc., 2012 WL 6045936 (S.D. Fla.) (court should interpret "expressly made conditional" language narrowly; provision must either track the language of the statute or express intent to condition acceptance in no uncertain terms). Under this test Brown's order acknowledgment was not an expressly conditional acceptance. How could you redraft Brown's form to turn it into an expressly conditional acceptance?

4. *Have the additional terms been expressly assented to?* If the court concludes that the offeree's response did amount to an "acceptance" but not a "conditional" one, it must in most cases go on to determine whether the additional terms in that acceptance have become part of the parties' agreement under UCC §2-207. At this point, the §2-207 analysis proceeds to §2-207(2), which

declares that the additional terms are to be viewed as "proposals for addition to the contract." The logical first question under UCC §2-207(2) would be, therefore: Has the offeror assented to the offeree's proposed additional terms? In *Brown Machine,* the seller argued that the buyer had in effect accepted the seller's terms by indicating (in writing) that, with one exception, "all other specifications are correct." Was the court right to reject that argument? In another case involving a similar seller-indemnification clause, the seller contended that a "course of dealing" between the parties established that the clause had indeed been assented to by the buyer, the parties having "exchanged the same forms on prior occasions." The court rejected that argument because there was no showing that any employee of the buyer had ever read such a form, or that a previous dispute had called the clause at issue to the buyer's attention. The mere use or even repeated use of forms implies nothing about the parties' awareness of their contents, the court asserted, because such forms are never read. Maxon Corp. v. Tyler Pipe Industries, Inc., 497 N.E.2d 570, 575-576 (Ind. Ct. App. 1986). As the *Brown Machine* opinion puts it, "*express* assent under §2-207(2) cannot be presumed by silence or mere failure to object" (emphasis supplied).

5. *Do the additional terms become part of the contract anyway?* If the additional terms have not been expressly assented to, might they nevertheless in some cases become part of the contract? UCC §2-207(2) provides for this possibility, in a case where the parties are both merchants. This will happen, however, only if the terms in question have not been objected to (either in advance — through language in the offer or otherwise — or thereafter) *and* if the terms in question are not "material." The *Paul Gottlieb* case below and the Notes that follow it address the "material" alteration question.

6. *Has a counter-offer (conditional acceptance) been accepted?* Because it finds the seller's response not to be a conditional acceptance, the court in *Brown Machine* does not have to face the other tough issue frequently raised in §2-207 cases: What constitutes effective assent to a counter-offer expressed in the form of a "conditional acceptance?" When will the additional terms it contains be binding on the other party? It is possible, of course, that the offeror could expressly agree to the terms of the offeree's counter-offer. E.g., In re Mostek Corp., 502 N.Y.S.2d 181 (App. Div. 1986) (seller had signed buyer's purchase order form with arbitration clause). In the absence of such express assent, can agreement be found in the offeror's subsequent conduct? UCC §2-207 itself gives no clear answer to that question. The clear consensus of courts and commentators, however, is that conduct alone should not be sufficient to amount to assent to an expressly conditional acceptance. To find that mere performance equals assent to all the terms of a counter-offer would be to continue in effect the common law's "last shot" approach, which the drafters of UCC §2-207 clearly were attempting to abrogate. See, e.g., Diamond Fruit Growers, Inc. v. Krack Corp., 794 F.2d 1440, 1445 (9th Cir. 1986) (buyer did not agree to terms of conditional acceptance containing disclaimer of warranties and limitation of consequential damages by continuing to receive and pay for goods; policy of Code requires "specific and unequivocal expression of assent"); White

& Summers, Uniform Commercial Code §2-3, at 45-46 (6th ed. 2010). In the absence of real assent to the proposed additional terms, what then? In that case, even if the documents of the parties have not formed a contract, their actions (shipment and receipt of the goods) may at least establish a contractual relationship under UCC §2-207(3), and Comment 7 to §2-207. If the seller in *Brown Machine* had by tracking the statutory language succeeded in making its "acceptance" only a "conditional" one (and thus in effect a counter-offer), would its proposed indemnification clause have become part of the contract under UCC §2-207(3)?

7. *What are "supplementary terms" under UCC §2-207(3)?* If an offeree's response is deemed to be at most an "expressly conditional" acceptance, and thus in effect a counter-offer, but the parties nevertheless did proceed to performance without an express acceptance of the counter-offer's terms, what then? Under UCC §2-207(3), the contract will consist of those terms on which the writings of the parties agree, "together with any supplementary terms incorporated under any other provisions of this act [i.e., the UCC]." Clearly those "supplementary terms" would include such implied terms under Article 2 as the implied warranties of merchantibility and fitness (UCC §§2-314 and 2-315) and the damages provisions, including seller liability for consequential damages (UCC §2-715), along with more innocuous "gap-filler" provisions of Article 2 (UCC §§2-307, 2-308, etc.). They also may include terms that are deemed part of the parties' agreement by virtue of the Code's provisions regarding "course of performance," "course of dealing," and "usage of trade" (UCC §1-303). See SFEG Corp. v. Blendtec, Inc., 2017 U.S. Dist. LEXIS 12413 (M.D. Tenn.). But mere receipt of forms without objection may not be held to constitute a course of dealing or course of performance sufficient to establish assent to the terms of those forms, under UCC §2-207, even where forms are repeatedly sent over time:

> . . . [A] course of dealing may become part of an agreement, via a type of estoppel, when one party fails to object to the manner in which the other party performs under the agreement. Terms and conditions contained in a form continually sent by one party do not constitute performance and cannot become binding as a course of dealing. . . . The reason for this distinction between (a) a repeated manner of performance and (b) the repeated sending of forms is pragmatic. A party will certainly be cognizant of the manner in which the other side continually performs under the agreement, and if there is no objection to that performance by the first party, over a sufficient period of time, the first party is assumed to have acquiesced to the second party's manner of performance. The same cannot be said of forms continually sent by one party to the other, which are often not read until a dispute arises.

Premix-Marbletite Mfg. Corp. v. SKW Chemicals, Inc., 145 F. Supp. 2d 1348, 1356 (S.D. Fla. 2001), citing and quoting Step-Saver Data Systems, Inc. v. Wyse Tech., 939 F.3d 91 (3d Cir. 1991). In later sections we will return to a closer examination of the concepts of course of performance, course of dealing, and usage of trade.

Paul Gottlieb & Co., Inc. v. Alps South Corp.

District Court of Appeal of Florida 985 So.2d 1 (2007)

CASANUEVA, Judge.

Paul Gottlieb & Co., Inc. (Gottlieb) appeals a final judgment awarding damages to Alps South Corp. (Alps) on its claim for breach of warranty. Gottlieb contends that the trial court erred by awarding consequential damages because the contract between the parties included a limitation of liability clause or, alternatively, because consequential damages were inappropriate in this case and were not sufficiently established by competent proof. We agree with Gottlieb in part and therefore reverse and remand with directions to the trial court. We conclude that the trial court erred in its analysis that the limitation of liability clause materially altered the contract. However, we also conclude Gottlieb's undisputed breach of contract entitles Alps to seek certain benefit-of-the-bargain damages that flow directly and incidentally from Gottlieb's breach under provisions of the Florida Uniform Commercial Code (U.C.C.). Accordingly, we remand the case to the circuit court to hold a new hearing on the limited question of the amount of damages only.

I. FACTUAL BACKGROUND

Gottlieb is a fabric converter based in New York City. Gottlieb supplies its customers specialty knitted fabrics that are shipped directly from third-party knitting and finishing mills. Alps is a manufacturer of medical devices located in St. Petersburg, Florida. Alps produces various types of liners that amputees use to attach prosthetic devices. In January 2000, Alps used liners that consisted of a specially designed gel material covered in spandex fabric that stretched to allow the liner to be placed over the appendage and then compressed to provide stability.

Alps began testing a number of new fabrics in February 2000 hoping to develop a new product possessed of enhanced durability and stability. Gottlieb was a source of the new fabrics. After some initial testing, Alps settled on a specialty fabric provided by Gottlieb identified as TL2646 Coolmax[1] fabric which outperformed the other fabrics. Alps began incorporating the new fabric into its liners. Alps received positive feedback from its customers that the new liners had increased comfort. The commercial relationship between Alps and Gottlieb started out in a promising fashion.

Unfortunately, six months later, in August 2000, the relationship began showing signs of a downturn. Alps rejected some fabric samples Gottlieb submitted because of unacceptable inconsistencies in both color and texture. On August 29, 2000, Alps sent a letter promptly notifying Gottlieb of the product deficiencies and stating that any future commercial relationship mandated that Gottlieb

1. The TL2646 Coolmax fabric in question is the sole item of the contract between Gottlieb and Alps. Coolmax is a technologically advanced yarn developed by DuPont that is often used in athletic performance clothing because of its unique dimensions, shape, and wicking properties.

provide a more consistent product. However, the letter did not inform Gottlieb of the possibility that Alps could incur substantial additional costs as a result of using a different fabric. Also Alps did not disclose the specialized use of the fabric to Gottlieb.[2] Gottlieb agreed to rework the fabric before delivering it to Alps.

Later events resulted in a worsening of the situation. Gottlieb exhausted its supply of the yarn used to produce the specialized high-tech fabric. It substituted a similar, but not identical, yarn without notifying Alps of the substitution. The trial court found this substitution caused a defect that was not easily discoverable by Alps. The new fabric did not stretch nearly as well as the original fabric that had been designated, tested, and approved by Alps. In early December of that same year, Alps began receiving complaints from customers that the fabric in the liners was less comfortable. The problems were so severe that Alps recalled the liners it had placed on the market and destroyed the devices in its inventory.

When Alps and Gottlieb discovered that the cause of the defective products was the undisclosed substitute yarn, the parties' business relationship further deteriorated. The business relationship ended when Gottlieb failed to receive payment for a submitted bill. Gottlieb then brought an action to collect damages due to the nonpayment. In turn, Alps counterclaimed for damages it asserted were caused by Gottlieb's breach of warranty. Of importance to the damage claim is the language set forth on the back of Gottlieb's finished goods contract which purports to limit its liability. The trial court ultimately considered this language to be an affirmative defense to the counterclaim.

Following a nonjury trial, the trial court awarded damages to Gottlieb on its claim totaling $28,846.29; awarded damages to Alps on its counterclaim of $694,640.04; and determined that under Florida's U.C.C. provisions, the limitation of liability clause was a material alteration of the parties' contract. The trial court declined to enforce the provision concluding that by operation of law, it was not a part of the contract.

II. LIMITATION OF LIABILITY CLAUSE

This dispute arises from the common, but risky, commercial practice where the seller and buyer negotiate a contract involving goods by exchanging each others' standardized forms. The transactions of this type involved here are governed by section 2-207 of the U.C.C., codified in section 672.207, Florida Statutes (2000).

Here, Gottlieb first contends that the trial court erred by failing to enforce the limitation of liabilities clause found on the back of its finished goods contract. The clause in contention reads:

> BUYER SHALL NOT IN ANY EVENT BE ENTITLED TO, AND SELLER SHALL NOT BE LIABLE FOR INDIRECT OR CONSEQUENTIAL DAMAGES OF ANY

2. The record reflects Gottlieb was not aware of Alps' specific use of the fabric in a prosthetic device. However, this letter and additional communications between the parties indicates that Gottlieb knew the fabric needed to conform to the original sample.

NATURE, INCLUDING, WITHOUT BEING LIMITED TO, LOSS OF PROFIT, PROMOTIONAL OR MANUFACTURING EXPENSES, INJURY TO REPUTATION OR LOSS OF CUSTOMER.

In its analysis, the trial court determined the clause constituted a material alteration under section 672.207(2) and as such it did not become part of the contract. In reaching this conclusion, the trial court determined that were it given effect, the limitation of liability "would allow Gottlieb to substitute a product without notice to Alps that would affect the final marketability of the final product." We do not apply the same reasoning as the trial court. The fact that Gottlieb altered a yarn type that resulted in a breach of contract is separate and distinct from the legal analysis of how the language of the contract is construed. In other words, the cause of the breach, the substituted yarn, is a question of fact which the parties did not dispute. Therefore, the trial court only needed to determine whether the clause, as a matter of law, materially altered the contract. Since this is a pure question of law, we review the trial court's conclusion de novo. Am. Strategic Ins. Co. v. Lucas-Soloman, 927 So. 2d 184 (Fla. 2d DCA 2006).

A. Preservation

[The court held that Gottlieb failed to plead the limitation of liability clause as an affirmative defense to an amended complaint, but that the issue was still preserved because the parties argued it and the trial court ruled on it without objection by Alps. — Eds.]

B. The Battle of the Forms

We next determine whether the trial court erred by failing to enforce the limitation of liability clause. For the following reasons, we conclude the trial court erred.

"[T]he rules of engagement for the 'battle of the forms' are set out in the Uniform Commercial Code ('U.C.C') §2-207." Bayway Ref. Co. v. Oxygenated Mktg. & Trading, 215 F.3d 219, 223 (2d Cir. 2000). . . .

[S]ection 672.207(1) provides that, between merchants, where a "definite and seasonable expression of acceptance or a written confirmation is sent within a reasonable time," it operates as "an acceptance even though it states terms additional to or different from those offered or agreed upon, unless acceptance is expressly made conditional on assent to the additional or different terms."

. . . Subsection 672.207(2) provides:

> The additional terms are to be construed as proposals for addition to the contract. Between merchants such terms become part of the contract *unless:*
>
> (a) The offer expressly limits acceptance to the terms of the offer;
> (b) They materially alter it; or
> (c) Notification of objection to them has already been given or is given within a reasonable time after notice of them is received.

(Emphasis provided.)

. . . Within the context of section 672.207(2), the parties do not dispute that they are merchants, that Gottlieb's [sic; Alps's?] offer did not expressly limit acceptance to its terms, and that Alps did not object to the additional terms within a reasonable amount of time. The remaining issue is whether the limitation of damages clause, as an additional term, materially altered the contract. If the additional term materially alters the contract, it is excluded.

Procedurally, in determining whether a term constitutes a material alteration, other courts have placed the burden of proof upon the party seeking the term's exclusion. See Bayway, 215 F.3d at 223-24; JOM, Inc. v. Adell Plastics, Inc., 193 F.3d 47 (1st Cir. 1999); Avedon Eng'g, Inc. v. Seatex, 126 F.3d 1279 (10th Cir. 1997); . . . . We conclude that this rule is appropriate and hold that a party seeking the exclusion of a contractual term or provision pursuant to section 672.207(2), as constituting a material alteration, has the burden of proof. In doing so, we align this court with the great majority of this nation's courts. . . .

C. Surprise or Hardship

Having determined which party appropriately bears the burden of proof, we next address the nature of proof that a party must offer to meet its burden. Unfortunately, the law in this area is not yet clearly developed. For example, Official Comment 4 to U.C.C. §2-207 offers examples of "typical clauses which would normally 'materially alter' the contract" and that would "result in surprise or hardship if incorporated without express awareness by the other party." For other examples, see Marvin Lumber & Cedar Co. v. PPG Indus., Inc., 401 F.3d 901 (8th Cir. 2005); . . . Dale R. Horning Co. v. Falconer Glass Indus., Inc., 730 F. Supp. 962 (S.D. Ind. 1990).

In contrast, Official Comment 5 to U.C.C. §2-207 offers "[e]xamples of clauses which involve no element of *unreasonable surprise* and which therefore are to be incorporated in the contract unless notice of objection is seasonably given." (Emphasis added.) Relying on this language and common law principles, some courts have removed hardship from the analysis and look solely for surprise. See Union Carbide Corp. v. Oscar Mayer Foods Corp., 947 F.2d 1333 (7th Cir. 1991); Suzy Phillips Originals, Inc. v. Coville, Inc., 939 F. Supp. 1012 (E.D.N.Y. 1996). Previously, this court considered whether a term was a material alteration under section 672.207 in Advanced Mobilehome Systems of Tampa, Inc. v. Alumax Fabricated Products, Inc., 666 So. 2d 166 (Fla. 2d DCA 1995), and approved of the rationale of *Union Carbide* to reach its decision (observing that a change is material if agreement to it cannot be presumed). There, Judge Posner explained:

> What is expectable, hence unsurprising, is okay; what is unexpected, hence surprising, is not. Not infrequently the test is said to be "surprise or hardship," but this appears to be a misreading of Official Comment 4 to UCC §2-207. The comment offers examples of "typical clauses which would normally 'materially alter' the contract *and so result in surprise or hardship* if incorporated without express awareness by the other party" (emphasis added). Hardship is a consequence,

> not a criterion. (Surprise can be either.) You cannot walk away from a contract that you can fairly be deemed to have agreed to, merely because performance turns out to be a hardship for you, unless you can squeeze yourself into the impossibility defense or some related doctrine of excuse.

Union Carbide, 947 F.2d at 1336 (citations omitted). Today, we continue to follow this rationale.

Turning first to the surprise prong, Alps must prove "that, under the circumstances, it cannot be presumed that a reasonable merchant would have consented to the additional term." See *Bayway Refining,* 215 F.3d at 224. The finished goods contract at issue was the sixth in a series between the two parties and each contract included the limitation of liability term. Each proposed contract contained the terms which were visible on its face. The sole evidence presented at trial to establish surprise was that Alps had not read the contract before the dispute arose. Florida law has never excused a party from a contract simply because it failed to read the contract terms. See Allied Van Lines, Inc. v. Bratton, 351 So. 2d 344 (Fla. 1977); . . . . Additionally, Official Comment 5 to UCC §2-207 includes clauses which limit remedies in a reasonable manner among the examples of terms which do not involve unreasonable surprise. The record in this case does not allow a conclusion that Gottlieb's limitation of liability clause was an unreasonable surprise to Alps.

The record is similarly lacking with respect to hardship as a result of surprise. Courts that consider hardship look to whether the term would "impose substantial economic hardship on the non-assenting party." *Horning,* 730 F. Supp. at 962 . . . . The *Horning* court reviewed a clause that provided "the buyer's exclusive and sole remedy for defective goods shall be to secure replacement." Id. at 963. In that case, the supplier was aware that the buyer could incur substantial liability if a breach occurred. Id. at 967. Further, the supplier's actions, in offering to work with the buyer, caused the buyer to believe that its costs would be reimbursed because of the breach. Id. at 963-64. The *Horning* court concluded that "[i]n this situation, where [the supplier] knew or had reason to know that [the buyer] could incur substantial liability for delays in finishing its subcontract, there can be no doubt that a limitation of consequential damages would work a hardship on the buyer." Id. at 963.

Here, the facts do not permit a result identical to that of *Horning.* Gottlieb never represented that, in the event of a breach, it would reimburse Alps for any or all consequential damages it sustained resulting from the breach. Instead, the evidence showed that Alps previously had returned a sample of nonconforming fabric to Gottlieb with a letter insisting on conforming goods. This letter did not mention or make claim for additional costs or damages resulting from Gottlieb's prior breach of performance. The evidence shows that Alps never informed Gottlieb of any consequences other than discontinuing their relationship. Alps did not inform Gottlieb of the specific manner in which the subject fabric would be used or what product would be crafted. Thus, Gottlieb could not foresee the *greater extent* of its potential liability, should a subsequent breach occur. Because Alps neglected to inform Gottlieb of the larger consequences of the breach, we conclude that Alps cannot maintain that incorporating the limitation of liability clause would result in a severe economic hardship. Thus, Alps failed to carry the burden of proof on hardship.

For these reasons, we conclude that the trial court erred by not enforcing the limitation of consequential damages clause. The award of consequential damages must be stricken.

Finally, we note that enforcing of the clause at issue only bars consequential damages. The limitation in this clause does not exclude other damages available under the law. See §672.719; Council Bros., Inc. v. Ray Burner Co., 473 F.2d 400 (5th Cir. 1973) (interpreting Florida law). We observe that section 671.106(1), Florida Statutes (2000), suggests that an injured party should not be worse off because the other party breached:

> The remedies provided by this code shall be liberally administered to the end that the aggrieved party may be put in as good as a position as if the other party had fully performed but neither consequential or special nor penal damages may be had except as specifically provided in this Act or by other rule of law.

Thus, Alps is still able to recover some of its direct and incidental damages, although it is precluded from receiving consequential damages. See §672.714-.715. Comment (a) of the Restatement of Contracts (Second) section 347 echoes this sentiment in that expectation damages are intended to give the injured party "the benefit of his bargain by putting him in as good as a position as he would have been had the contract been performed." The code also provides for incidental damages arising from the breach. These "include expenses reasonably incurred in inspection, receipt, transportation and care and custody of goods rightfully rejected, any commercially reasonable charges, expenses or commissions in connection with effecting cover and any other reasonable expense incident to the delay or other breach." §672.715(1). Therefore, the trial court may award Alps its direct and incidental damages. See Adam Metal Supply, Inc. v. Electrodex, Inc., 386 So. 2d 1316 (Fla. 2d DCA 1980) (holding a buyer's expenses incurred before discovering a defect are recoverable as incidental damages).

III. LOST PROFITS

Although our holding enforces the limitation of liability clause which barred lost profits, we alternatively hold it was also error to award Alps damages for lost profits because Alps failed to prove them with reasonable certainty. Florida law allows for the award of consequential damages. See §§672.714-.715; Twyman v. Roell, 123 Fla. 2, 166 So. 215 (1936). However, lost profits "must be proven with a reasonable degree of certainty before [the loss] is recoverable." Shadow Lakes, Inc. v. Cudlipp Constr. & Dev. Co., 658 So. 2d 116, 117 (Fla. 2d DCA 1995). . . .

IV. INSTRUCTIONS ON REMAND

Although we find that Alps did not prove lost profits with reasonable certainty, we do recognize that Alps' damages under the UCC came into existence at the moment Gottlieb delivered the fabric containing the unapproved yarn. This deficiency was neither obvious nor discoverable until after Alps had incorporated the fabric into its product line investing time, labor, and materials in the finished products. As a merchant, Gottlieb is expected to know that direct and incidental damages could flow from a delivery of unapproved goods. Due to the limitation of liability clause, Gottlieb properly insulated itself from consequential damages, but it cannot shield itself from the direct and incidental damages naturally arising from the undisputed breach. We note again that the contract between the parties dealt only with supplying a specific and highly technical fabric made of a particular yarn combination. Gottlieb should have consulted with Alps prior to making a change in the yarn. However, Gottlieb did not notify Alps that it substituted an unapproved yarn for the earlier specified yarn. A clear nexus between the breach by Gottlieb and the injury to Alps exists. Accordingly, we leave open the possibility of more specific findings by the trial court as it revisits the issue of damages, including Gottlieb's familiarity with Alps' product requirements, the common trade practices and course of dealings in the fabric industry, the nature of Alps' inventory and its cost to recover the defective items, and any other indicia of Alps' loss or Alps' ability to mitigate such loss that the trial court may find helpful. . . .

Reversed and remanded with instructions.

NORTHCUTT and SALCINES, JJ., concur.

NOTES AND QUESTIONS

1. *Does the additional term materially alter the contract?* Although the *Paul Gottlieb* opinion does not expressly address all of the steps, remember that the court necessarily had to resolve several other questions before getting to the issue of material alteration under UCC §2-207(2). First, the court had to find either that Alps made an offer that Paul Gottlieb accepted with a document that was "not expressly conditioned" on the buyer's assent to the different or additional term, or that the parties had reached agreement and that Paul Gottlieb sent a written contract in confirmation. Either way, the exchange between the parties would have resulted in a contract, and the additional term excluding seller liability for consequential damages would have become a "proposal for addition." Since both parties were merchants, the proposal to limit liability would become part of the contract unless excluded under UCC §2-207(2). There was no evidence that Alps objected in its offer to future changes, or that it objected after receiving the seller's acceptance. Thus, Paul Gottlieb's term would become part of the contract unless it would result in material alteration.

As noted by the *Paul Gottlieb* court, the comments to UCC §2-207 provide examples of clauses that typically do or do not amount to a material alteration of the contract. Comment 5 offers examples of terms that would not materially alter, including one that limits remedies "in a reasonable manner." In addition, as the opinion indicates, many courts have used the test whether a term would result in "surprise or hardship" to determine material alternation. In concluding that the term excluding consequential damages would not result in material alteration, the *Paul Gottlieb* court notes that the parties had a series of contracts with the same limiting language and that there was not any evidence that the seller knew much about possible financial hardship to the buyer if the fabric was defective. Are you persuaded by the court's reasoning on this issue? Recall that the authority cited in Note 4 after the *Brown Machine* case rejected the argument that repeated use of a standard document was evidence that anyone had ever read it. Courts differ widely in their approach to determining materiality under UCC §2-207(2). See, e.g., C.A.I., Inc. v. Vitex Packaging Group, Inc., 2015 WL 4396266 (D. Mass.) (provision limiting damages to cost of product and excluding consequential damages held to be not material, but provision excluding all express and implied warranties was material).

2. *Additional vs. different terms.* Note that UCC §2-207(1) mentions both "additional" and "different" terms, while UCC §2-207(2) addresses only "additional" terms as possibly becoming part of the contract. Many, if not most, courts have read the omission of "different" terms from UCC §2-207(2) to mean that "different" terms in the acceptance or confirmation drop out altogether and cannot become part of the contract. See John E. Murray, Jr., Murray on Contracts 185-186 (5th ed. 2011). On the other hand, Official Comment 3 begins by stating, "[w]hether or not additional or different terms will become part of the agreement depends upon the provisions of subsection (2)." That language supports the view that the omission of different terms from the text of UCC §2-207(2) was merely an oversight by the drafters. This latter construction is also supported by the difficulty of distinguishing whether a particular change in terms by the offeree is an "additional" or a "different" term. How would you classify the limitation on liability in *Paul Gottlieb* and *Princess Cruises* or the indemnification clause in *Brown Machine*? As an additional term? Or a different one?

3. *The "knockout" rule.* As the foregoing cases and notes demonstrate, UCC §2-207 is very complicated, and difficult to interpret and apply. Another problem with the section is that some courts have developed a "knockout approach" to deal with situations where the standard form offer has a term, such as a seller's limitation of warranty protection to 90 days, and the standard form acceptance by the buyer provides for a warranty of unlimited duration. Under the "knockout" approach, both terms would drop out and the duration of the warranty would be determined by application of Article 2. The underlying rationale for the knockout rule is that it favors neither the offer nor the acceptance where the terms disagree. See Northrop Corp. v. Litronic Industries, 29 F.3d 1173 (7th Cir. 1994); Operating Tech. Elecs., Inc. v. Generac Power Sys., 2014 U.S. Dist. LEXIS 199100 (N.D. Tex.) (discussing and recognizing that the "knockout" rule is the majority view but predicting that the Texas Supreme Court would not follow that approach). Do you see anything in the section or comments that would support the knockout rule?

4. *Approach of the CISG to Battle of the Forms.* Unlike UCC Article 2, the Convention on Contracts for the International Sale of Goods (CISG) appears to follow essentially the common law approach. Article 19 of the CISG starts by providing that an acceptance with changes is a "counter-offer," but goes on to state that a reply with "additional or different terms" which do not materially alter the terms is still effective. Finally, Article 19 defines a "material" term as one affecting things such as price, payment, quality and quantity, place and time of delivery, party liability for breach, and the settlement of disputes. Professor Dodge's assessment is that ultimately the CISG does not deviate much from the American common law:

> The CISG . . . adopts what is essentially a mirror-image rule. Article 19(1) provides: "A reply to an offer which purports to be an acceptance but contains additions, limitations or other modifications is a rejection of the offer and constitutes a counter-offer." Article 19(2) attempts to soften this rule a little by providing that if the additional or different terms are not material *and* the offeror does not object to them, then the purported acceptance is an acceptance and the additional or different terms become part of the contract. But Article 19(3) defines materiality so broadly that it is hard to imagine a change that the CISG would not consider material. This means that, in almost every case, an acceptance that varies the terms of the offer will be a counteroffer which will be accepted by the other party's conduct.

William S. Dodge, Teaching the CISG in Contracts, 50 J. Leg. Ed. 72, 82-83 (2000). See Chateau Des Charmes Wines Ltd. v. Sabate USA Inc., 328 F.3d 528 (9th Cir. 2003) (addition of forum selection clause in a written confirmation would be a material alteration under CISG Article 19); VLM Food Trading Int'l, Inc. v. Illinois Trading Co., 748 F.3d 780, 785 (7th Cir. 2014) (because CISG applied and not UCC Article 2, provisions in seller's form for interest and attorney's fees became part of contract).

5. *Remedial issues.* The extended discussion of remedies in this book will not come until later chapters. However, the *Princess Cruises* and *Paul Gottlieb* cases both provide a look ahead to some remedies issues we will consider. The *Paul Gottlieb* court correctly distinguishes between direct or immediate damages that flow from the breach, and less direct damages that still are caused by the breach but are classified as "consequential" damages. Finally, UCC §§2-710 and 2-715 allow to both buyers and sellers incidental damages for administrative costs resulting from the other party's breach. Based on the information available, what evidence of direct and incidental damages would you present to the trial court on remand? Apart from that question, does it appear that the loss of consequential damages in *Paul Gottlieb* or *Princess Cruises* would be significant?

6. *Lawyering issues — the effect of "additional" and "different" terms.* As many commentators have pointed out, the structure of UCC §2-207 makes it likely that the "well-counseled" buyer will include in its "order" (offer) form a provision requiring the seller's acceptance of all of the buyer's terms and objecting in advance to any and all different and additional terms in the seller's response, while an equally well-counseled seller will respond with an "acknowledgment"

(acceptance) form that is expressly conditional on the buyer's assent to all the seller's terms. Suppose that both buyer and seller adopt such a strategy, and then proceed to performance without stopping to iron out the differences between their forms. What would be the result?

PROBLEM 2-6

How would the following dispute be resolved under UCC §2-207?

Mendoza Construction Company is a general contractor that handles major commercial construction projects. Mendoza is the general contractor for the construction of several buildings on the "campus" of Wintel, Inc., a major communications company that is consolidating its operations outside of Columbus. G&P Industries is a supplier of various industrial products, including roofing materials and compounds.

On September 15, Margaret Novak, the Mendoza supervisor for the Wintel project, called Frank Park at G&P to determine the price, availability, and delivery schedule for various roofing materials and compounds for the Wintel project. Park provided Novak with the information she requested and told her that if she wished to place an order she should do so as soon as possible because demand for the company's products was very brisk. On the afternoon of October 1, Novak sent an email to Park. The email stated that Mendoza wished to place an order for various roofing products and compounds. The price and delivery schedule stated in Novak's note were as quoted by Park in the conversation on September 15, which provided that delivery of all materials was to be made by November 15.

On the morning of October 2, Park sent a fax back to Novak confirming receipt of Novak's order. In addition to confirming the basic terms of Novak's order, the fax also stated:

Acceptance of Your Order Is Subject to the Following Terms and Conditions

1. 10% payment due in 10 days. Payment in full of balance due 7 days after completion of delivery.
2. Any unpaid amounts accrue interest at the rate of 1% per month.
3. Purchaser agrees to pay seller's reasonable attorneys' fees and costs of collection should that be necessary.
4. All disputes under this order shall be submitted to arbitration under the Commercial Arbitration Rules of the American Arbitration Association.
5. G&P will supply purchaser with the manufacturer's warranty on all materials sold to purchaser.
6. G&P will notify purchaser of any delays in delivery. If for any reason delivery cannot be made within 60 days of scheduled date, purchaser shall have the right to cancel this contract. G&P will not otherwise be liable for delays in delivery that are beyond its control.

On October 7, Mendoza sent G&P a check for $35,643.20, which represented 10 percent of the price of its order.

On November 4, Park sent an email to Novak informing her that he had just learned from the manufacturer that supplied G&P with roofing materials that the manufacturer's next delivery would be delayed; Park told Novak that G&P anticipated that the materials would be delivered in 30-45 days. Novak immediately called Park to complain about the delay, but Park informed her that there was simply nothing he could do. Novak told Park that the delay would subject Mendoza to damages to Wintel under a liquidated damages provision of the contract between Wintel and Mendoza, and that Mendoza would hold G&P responsible for the damages. Park replied that G&P was not responsible for any delays beyond its control. Park also said that if Mendoza refused to honor the contract, G&P would retain the deposit and seek other damages. The telephone conversation ended without resolution of the issue.

Novak then contacted other suppliers of roofing materials and learned that another company could in fact supply Mendoza's needs in a timely fashion. Novak attempted to negotiate cancellation of the contract with G&P, but Park stubbornly refused to make any concessions.

(a) Novak contacts you seeking advice as to whether Mendoza has the legal right to cancel its contract with G&P and enter into a substitute contract with another seller. Later in the course we will examine various legal doctrines, such as "impossibility" or "impracticability," that might excuse a party such as G&P from performance even in the absence of a contractual provision providing some form of excuse. It is likely, however, that none of these doctrines would apply to a situation like this one, and that the seller's failure to make timely delivery would be a breach. It would also ordinarily be the case, under the general rules of Article 2, that a seller's delay in delivery would entitle the buyer to cancel and potentially to seek damages for delay. Paragraph 6 of the seller's Terms and Conditions appears intended to change the application of those "default" rules to this transaction. In light of all this, what advice would you give to Novak?

(b) Assume that Novak decided to cancel the contract with G&P; she sent written notice to that effect, which G&P promptly objected to in writing. G&P has now filed a demand for arbitration seeking damages from Mendoza for breach of contract. You are an associate with a law firm representing Mendoza. The senior attorney responsible for the case has asked you to research and analyze the issues of Mendoza's contractual liability to G&P. Be prepared for a meeting with him to discuss these issues and any additional factual information that you think is necessary to analyze the issues involved in the case.

(c) How would your analysis in (a) or (b) above be affected if either or both of the following provisions had been included in the documents:

1. Novak's email of October 1 on behalf of Mendoza contained the following provision: "Supplier shall be responsible for any penalties or damages incurred by Mendoza as a result of any delays in delivery by Supplier."
2. G&P's October 2 response to Novak's order contained the following provision: "Acceptance of your order is expressly conditional on your assent to the terms of this document pursuant to UCC §2-207(1)."

D. ELECTRONIC AND "LAYERED" CONTRACTING

As we have seen, the classical model of contract formation was based on two major assumptions: The contracting parties had relatively equal bargaining power, and they actually engaged in the process of bargaining — perhaps by mail, but often in person. For more than a century the assumptions upon which the classical model were based have been breaking down. Although many significant commercial contracts still conform to the classical model, most modern contracts do not. The vast majority of present-day contracts involve parties with radically unequal bargaining power; their contracts consist of standard forms and involve little, if any, negotiation; and the contracts are often formed through electronic transactions rather than person-to-person communications.

As illustrated by the *Meyer* case in Chapter 1, courts are now confronting issues involving contracts made over the Internet or by other electronic means. Naturally and as a matter of necessity, courts have attempted to adapt existing legal sources to deal with these issues. At the same time, courts and commentators have developed a new terminology to describe the various transactions the courts are encountering. The case law and literature involving electronic contracts refer to various types of terms, including "shrinkwrap," "clickwrap" or "clickthrough," and "browsewrap." (We have used the word "terms" here rather than "contracts" or "agreements" because the principal legal issue is whether these terms do in fact have contractual significance.)

In a transaction involving *shrinkwrap terms*, the purchaser orders a product (for example, a computer, a home appliance, or software). The order could be placed by telephone or over the Internet, or the product might be purchased at a "brick-and-mortar" store. When the purchaser receives physical possession of the product, it is boxed and wrapped in plastic. Often (but not always) a warning on the outside of the box informs the purchaser that the package contains the seller's contract terms and that the purchaser's use of the product will constitute agreement with those terms. After removing the wrapping, the purchaser has an opportunity to inspect the product and review the contract terms. These typically (but again, not in every situation) state that if the purchaser is dissatisfied with the product or with the contract terms, the purchaser may return the product to the seller within a certain number of days. The contract terms also state that if the purchaser does not return the product within that period of time, the purchaser agrees to the seller's terms. These could involve both "substantive" terms (disclaimers of warranty, limitations on liability, exclusions of consequential damages, etc.) and "procedural" ones (choice of law or forum provisions, arbitration clauses, etc.). The seller may, but will not necessarily, agree to pay for the cost of shipment back to the seller if the product is returned by the buyer. Transactions involving shrinkwrap terms are sometimes referred to as "rolling contracts," "layered contracts," or "money now, terms later" contracts.

In the typical transaction involving *clickwrap terms*, before completing the purchase of the product, the purchaser must click a button labeled "I agree," "submit," or some equivalent phrase. Often the purchaser must scroll through the seller's terms of sale before clicking the agreement button. In the typical transaction involving *clickwrap terms*, before completing the purchase of the product, the purchaser must scroll through the seller's terms of sale and click a button labeled "I agree," "submit," or some equivalent phrase. Some sellers may go further and require the purchaser to put his or her initials in a box to signify agreement with the seller's terms of sale. If the purchaser refuses to do so, the seller will not complete the sale. Clickwrap transactions over the Internet can involve software, services, or tangible products. If the purchaser buys software or a tangible product at a store in a box, the box will typically have a shrinkwrap contract, and any software will be subject also to a clickwrap contract to which the purchaser must agree before being able to use the software.

Finally, transactions with *browsewrap terms* typically involve information made available by Internet providers on their websites, often (but not necessarily) free of charge, and often (although again, not necessarily) involving information that the user accesses but does not always download. In the typical browsewrap transaction, the Internet provider has posted the terms of use on its website. The terms of use state that by using the site the user agrees to the provider's terms of use. As noted in the *Meyer* case, the browsewrap and the clickwrap transactions have a fundamental difference. In the clickwrap transaction the terms are available for review, and the purchaser must click an agreement button in order to complete the transaction. In a browsewrap transaction the terms of use are normally accessible from the provider's home page by clicking a button, but the user is not required (or even encouraged) to scroll through the terms of use, and is not required to click any agreement button. The user's purported agreement to the provider's terms of use comes simply from the user's actions in browsing the site. For example, this language appears on the website of FindLaw, a legal research firm:

> This website is a service made available by FindLaw, a Thomson Reuters business, and its affiliates (collectively referred to in this document as "FindLaw"). All use of this website, including all content, information and services provided on this website, is subject to the following terms of use ("Terms"), which constitute a legal agreement between you and FindLaw. By accessing, browsing or using this website, you acknowledge that you have read, understood and agree to be bound by these Terms. We may update these Terms at any time, without notice to you. Each time you access this website, you agree to be bound by the Terms then in effect. If you have any questions about these Terms, or about the content, information or services on this website, you may contact us via our contact us page. - See more at: http://company.findlaw.com/findlaw-terms-of-service.html.

http://company.findlaw.com/findlaw-terms-of-service.html (visited October 7, 2018). With this background in mind, consider the following cases.

DeFontes v. Dell, Inc.

Supreme Court of Rhode Island 984 A.2d 1061 (2009)

Present: GOLDBERG, FLAHERTY, JJ., and WILLIAMS, C.J. (ret.).

Chief Justice WILLIAMS (ret.), for the Court.

The defendants, Dell, Inc. f/k/a Dell Computer Corp. (Dell), Dell Catalog Sales LP (Dell Catalog), Dell Marketing LP (Dell Marketing), QualxServ, LLC (QualxServ), and BancTec, Inc. (BancTec), collectively (defendants), appeal from a Superior Court order denying their motion to stay proceedings and compel arbitration. This case is the first of two companion cases now before this Court. See Long v. Dell, Inc., No. 2007-346-M.P., 984 A.2d 1074, 2009 R.I. LEXIS 141 (R.I., filed Dec. 14, 2009). It arises out of a long-frustrated putative class-action suit brought against the defendants. For the reasons set forth below, we affirm the judgment of the Superior Court.

I. FACTS AND TRAVEL

This litigation began on May 16, 2003, when Mary E. DeFontes, individually and on behalf of a class of similarly situated persons, brought suit against Dell, alleging that its collection of taxes from them on the purchase of Dell optional service contracts violated the Deceptive Trade Practices Act, G.L. 1956 chapter 13.1 of title 6. Ms. DeFontes asserted that service contracts, such as the option service contract offered by Dell, were not taxable within the State of Rhode Island. Nicholas Long joined the suit as a plaintiff, and an amended complaint was filed on July 16, 2003, that also added Dell subsidiaries Dell Catalog and Dell Marketing, and two service providers, QualxServ and BancTec as defendants.

Dell is an international computer hardware and software corporation. Within the Dell corporate umbrella, Dell Catalog and Dell Marketing primarily are responsible for selling computers via the internet, mail-order catalogs, and other means to individual and business consumers. Dell ships these orders throughout all fifty states from warehouses located in Texas and Tennessee. As part of these purchases, Dell offers consumers an optional service contract for on-site repair of its products, with Dell often acting as an agent for third-party service providers, including BancTec and QualxServ. Parties opting to purchase a service contract are charged a "tax," which is either paid to the State of Rhode Island directly or collected by the third-party service provider and then remitted to the state.

The two initial plaintiffs, Ms. DeFontes and Mr. Long, engaged in slightly different transactions. Ms. DeFontes purchased her computer through Dell Catalog and selected a service contract with BancTec. She paid a total of $950.51, of which $13.51 was characterized as tax on the service contract. Mr. Long purchased his computer through Dell Marketing and opted for a service contract managed by Dell. In total, he paid $3,037.73, out of which $198.73 was designated as tax paid on the service contract. There is no allegation that Dell improperly retained any of the collected tax. Several months after plaintiffs filed their amended complaint, defendants filed a motion to stay proceedings and compel arbitration, citing an arbitration provision within the parties' purported agreements.[2] The defendants argued that the arbitration provision was part of a "Terms and Conditions Agreement," which they contended plaintiffs had accepted by accepting delivery of the goods. Specifically, they averred that plaintiffs had three separate opportunities to review the terms and conditions agreement, to wit, by selecting a hyperlink on the Dell website, by reading the terms that were included in the acknowledgment/invoice that was sent to plaintiffs sometime after they placed their orders, or by reviewing the copy of the terms Dell included in the packaging of its computer products.

The hearing justice issued a written decision on January 29, 2004. He . . . found that although plaintiffs had three opportunities to review the terms, none was sufficient to give rise to a contractual obligation. First, he noted that plaintiffs could have reviewed the terms and conditions agreement had they clicked a hyperlink that appeared on Dell's website. The hearing justice found, however, that this link was "inconspicuously located at the bottom of the webpage" and insufficient to place customers on notice of the terms and conditions.[3] Nevertheless, the hearing justice noted that the terms and conditions agreement also appeared both in the acknowledgment that Dell sent to plaintiffs when they placed their orders and later within the packaging when the computers were delivered.

The hearing justice noted that "courts generally recognize that shrinkwrap agreements, paper agreements enclosed within the packaging of an item, are sufficient to put consumers on inquiry notice of the terms and conditions of a transaction." He also observed, however, that shrinkwrap agreements generally contain an express disclaimer that explains to consumers that they can reject the proposed terms and conditions by returning the product. The crucial test, according to the hearing justice, was "whether a reasonable person would have known that return of the product would serve as rejection of those terms." He looked to the introductory language of the terms and conditions agreement, which he quoted as follows,

---

2. The arbitration clause in Ms. DeFontes' "Terms and Conditions Agreement," quoted by the hearing justice in his decision, provided,

> "ANY CLAIM, DISPUTE, OR CONTROVERSY (WHETHER IN CONTRACT, TORT, OR OTHERWISE, WHETHER PREEXISTING, PRESENT OR FUTURE, AND INCLUDING STATUTORY, COMMON LAW, INTENTIONAL TORT AND EQUITABLE CLAIMS) AGAINST DELL, its agents, employees, successors, assigns or affiliates * * * arising from or relating to this Agreement, its interpretation, or the breach, termination or validity thereof, the relationships which result from this Agreement (including, to the full extent permitted by applicable law, relationships with third parties who are not signatories to this Agreement), Dell's advertising, or any related purchase SHALL BE RESOLVED EXCLUSIVELY AND FINALLY BY BINDING ARBITRATION ADMINISTERED BY THE NATIONAL ARBITRATION FORUM (NAF) under its Code of Procedure then in effect * * *. The arbitration * * * will be limited solely to the dispute or controversy between Customer and Dell * * *. Any award of the arbitrator(s) shall be final and binding on each of the parties, and may be entered as a judgment in any court of competent jurisdiction."

The arbitration provision in the terms and conditions agreement sent to Mr. Long contained substantially similar language.

3. We also note that Mr. Long appears to have purchased his computer over the telephone and it is unclear from the record whether he viewed the Dell website in relation to his purchase.

> *"PLEASE READ THIS DOCUMENT CAREFULLY! IT CONTAINS VERY IMPORTANT INFORMATION ABOUT YOUR RIGHTS AND OBLIGATIONS, AS WELL AS LIMITATIONS AND EXCLUSIONS THAT MAY APPLY TO YOU. THIS DOCUMENT CONTAINS A DISPUTE RESOLUTION CLAUSE.*
>
> "This Agreement contains the terms and conditions that apply to purchases by Home, Home Office, and Small Business customers from the Dell entity named on the invoice ('Dell'). By accepting delivery of the computer systems, related products, and/or services and support, and/or other products described on that invoice. [*sic*] You ('Customer') agrees [*sic*] to be bound by and accepts [*sic*] these terms and conditions * * * These terms and conditions are subject to change without prior written notice at any time, in Dell's sole discretion."

The hearing justice found that this language was insufficient to give a reasonable consumer notice of the method of rejection. He found that defendants' failure to include an express disclaimer meant that they could not prove that plaintiffs "knowingly consent[ed]" to the terms and conditions of the agreement. Accordingly, the hearing justice found that Plaintiffs could not be compelled to enter arbitration.

Although the hearing justice noted that it was unnecessary to address plaintiffs' alternative arguments that the contract was both illusory and unconscionable, he discussed them in his decision "for the sake of completeness." First, he rejected plaintiffs' argument that the agreement was unconscionable because it prevented them from asserting rights as a class. He found that there was no right under Texas law to proceed as a class action litigant. See Autonation U.S.A. Corp. v. Leroy, 105 S.W.3d 190, 199-200 (Tex. App. 2003).

Second, the hearing justice addressed whether the agreement was illusory. He found that the arbitration agreement was not illusory merely because it required plaintiffs to submit to arbitration while allowing defendants to litigate any of its claims in court. He noted the well-settled principle that "although mutuality of obligation is necessary to create a valid contract, 'equivalency of obligation' is not." The hearing justice went on, however, to find that the terms and conditions agreement was illusory because it included the language "[t]hese terms and conditions are subject to change without prior written notice, at any time, in Dell's sole discretion." He rejected defendants' contention that this language applied only to future transactions and found that it failed to bind defendants to the terms and conditions agreement.

. . . On June 13, 2005, upon discovery that Ms. DeFontes was an employee of plaintiffs' counsel, plaintiffs filed an assented to motion to substitute a proposed class representative that replaced Ms. DeFontes with Julianne Ricci. . . .

II. Discussion

[The parties acknowledged that the transactions involved interstate commerce and came under the Federal Arbitration Act (FAA), 9 U.S.C. §§1 through 16. The FAA requires enforcement of privately negotiated arbitration agreements "save upon such grounds as exist at law or in equity for the revocation of any contract." 9 U.S.C. §2. . . . The parties did not contest the hearing justice's application of the Uniform Commercial Code and Texas law. — Eds.]

We therefore evaluate whether plaintiffs are bound by the terms and conditions agreement by resorting to a careful review of the provisions of the U.C.C. Under U.C.C. §2-204, contracts for the sale of goods may be formed "in any manner sufficient to show agreement, including conduct by both parties which recognizes the existence of such a contract." . . . The U.C.C. creates the assumption that, unless circumstances unambiguously demonstrate otherwise, the buyer is the offeror and the seller is the offeree. See Klocek v. Gateway, Inc., 104 F. Supp. 2d 1332, 1340 (D. Kan. 2000). Moreover, U.C.C. §2-206 provides in relevant part,

> "(a) Unless otherwise unambiguously indicated by the language or circumstances,
>
> "(1) an offer to make a contract shall be construed as inviting acceptance in any manner and by any medium reasonable in the circumstances;
>
> "(2) an order or other offer to buy goods for prompt or current shipment shall be construed as inviting acceptance either by a prompt promise to ship or by the prompt or current shipment of conforming or nonconforming goods * * *." . . .

If contract formation occurred at the moment Dell's sales agents processed the customer's credit card payment and agreed to ship the goods, as plaintiffs argue, then any additional terms would necessarily be treated as "[a]dditional [t]erms in [a]cceptance or [c]onfirmation" under U.C.C. §2-207 or offers to modify the existing contract under U.C.C. §2-209. Yet, the modern trend seems to favor placing the power of acceptance in the hands of the buyer after he or she receives goods containing a standard form statement of additional terms and conditions, provided the buyer retains the power to "accept or return" the product.

The eminent Judge Frank Easterbrook has authored what are widely considered to be the two leading cases on so-called "shrinkwrap" agreements. In ProCD, Inc. v. Zeidenberg, 86 F.3d 1447, 1452-53 (7th Cir. 1996), the court challenged the traditional understanding of offer and acceptance in consumer transactions by holding that a buyer of software was bound by an agreement that was included within the packaging and later appeared when the buyer first used the software.[11] Id. The court first held that U.C.C. §2-207 was inapplicable because in cases involving only one form, the "battle-of-the-forms" provision was irrelevant. *ProCD, Inc.*, 86 F.3d at 1452. It then proceeded to evaluate the agreement under U.C.C. §2-204 and reasoned that "[a] vendor, as master of the offer, may invite acceptance by conduct, and may propose limitations on the kind of conduct that constitutes acceptance. A buyer may accept by performing the acts the vendor proposes to treat as acceptance." *ProCD, Inc.*, 86 F.3d at

11. Although not discussed in the appellate decision, the trial court indicated that the agreement included the language,

"By using the discs and the listings licensed to you, you agree to be bound by the terms of this License. If you do not agree to the terms of this License, promptly return all copies of the software, listings that may have been exported, the discs and the User Guide to the place where you obtained it." ProCD, Inc. v. Zeidenberg, 908 F. Supp. 640, 644 (W.D. Wis. 1996).

1452. In Hill v. Gateway 2000, Inc., 105 F.3d 1147, 1148-49 (7th Cir. 1997), the court expanded its earlier holding in *ProCD* beyond transactions involving software where the consumer is prompted to accept or decline the terms when he first uses the program. It determined that when a merchant delivers a product that includes additional terms and conditions, but expressly provides the consumer the right to either accept those terms or return the product for a refund within a reasonable time, a consumer who retains the goods beyond that period may be bound by the contract. Id. Judge Easterbrook explained,

> "Practical considerations support allowing vendors to enclose the full legal terms with their products. Cashiers cannot be expected to read legal documents to customers before ringing up sales. If the staff at the other end of the phone for direct-sales operations such as Gateway's had to read the four-page statement of terms before taking the buyer's credit card number, the droning voice would anesthetize rather than enlighten many potential buyers. Others would hang up in a rage over the waste of their time. And oral recitation would not avoid customers' assertions (whether true or feigned) that the clerk did not read term X to them, or that they did not remember or understand it."

Id. at 1149.

The defendants argue that *ProCD* represents the majority view and we have found considerable support for their contention. See, e.g., O'Quin v. Verizon Wireless, 256 F. Supp. 2d 512, 515-16 (M.D. La. 2003) ("Terms and Conditions Pamphlet" binding where acceptance expressed by activation and use of wireless services as long as "opportunity to return"); . . . Brower v. Gateway 2000, Inc., 246 A.D.2d 246, 676 N.Y.S.2d 569, 572 (N.Y. App. Div. 1998) (arbitration clause of standard terms and conditions agreement valid where consumer informed that by keeping product beyond thirty days after delivery he was accepting terms); M.A. Mortenson Co., v. Timberline Software Corp., 140 Wn. 2d 568, 998 P.2d 305, 308 (Wash. 2000) (adopting *ProCD* analysis but noting shrinkwrap agreement explicitly instructed consumers "IF YOU DO NOT AGREE TO THESE TERMS AND CONDITIONS, PROMPTLY RETURN * * * TO THE PLACE OF PURCHASE AND YOUR PURCHASE PRICE WILL BE REFUNDED"). Moreover, as plaintiffs' counsel has initiated nationwide litigation, a number of sister jurisdictions have decided more or less the precise issue put before us in defendants' favor. For instance, in Stenzel v. Dell, Inc., 2005 ME 37, 870 A.2d 133 (Me. 2005), the Maine Supreme Judicial Court reviewed a similar terms and conditions agreement sent to Dell customers that included the language,

> "By accepting delivery of the computer systems, related products, and/or services and support, and/or other products described on that invoice [, the customer] agrees to be bound by and accepts these terms and conditions. If for any reason Customer is not satisfied with a Dell-branded hardware system, Customer may return the system under the terms and conditions of Dell's Total Satisfaction Return Policy * * *." Id. at 140.

The court held that by "accepting delivery of the computers, and then failing to exercise their right to return the computers as provided by the agreement, [the plaintiffs] expressly manifested their assent to be bound by the agreement * * *."

Id.; see also Carideo v. Dell, Inc., 520 F. Supp. 2d 1241, 1244 (W.D. Wash. 2007); . . . .

Courts have not been universal in embracing the reasoning of *ProCD* and its progeny, however. In Step-Saver Data Systems, Inc. v. Wyse Technology, 939 F.2d 91, 98 (3d Cir. 1991), the court determined that when parties exchange the shipment of goods for remuneration the existence of a contract is not in doubt; rather, any dispute relates solely to the nature of its terms. After deciding that U.C.C. §2-207 applies to situations in which a party sends a confirmatory document that claims to establish additional terms of the contract, the court held that U.C.C. §2-207 "establishes a legal rule that proceeding with a contract after receiving a writing that purports to define the terms of the parties's contract is not sufficient to establish the party's consent to the terms of the writing to the extent that the terms of the writing either add to, or differ from, the terms detailed in the parties's earlier writings or discussions." Id. at 99. The court therefore held that a licensing agreement affixed to the packaging constituted a proposal for additional terms that was not binding unless expressly agreed to by the purchaser. Id. at 100; see also *Klocek,* 104 F. Supp. 2d at 1339, 1341 (finding buyer's "act of keeping the computer past five days was not sufficient to demonstrate that plaintiff expressly agreed to the Standard Terms" and criticizing the *Hill* court's summary dismissal of U.C.C. §2-207 by stating "nothing in its language precludes application in a case which involves only one form"); Licitra v. Gateway, Inc., 189 Misc. 2d 721, 734 N.Y.S.2d 389, 396 (N.Y. Civ. Ct. 2001) (construing arbitration clause of a shrinkwrap agreement as a proposal for additional terms under U.C.C. §2-207 because it materially altered the existing agreement).

The Supreme Court of Oklahoma, which has also been drawn into this nationwide class-action suit against defendants, has rejected *Hill*'s reasoning as well. See Rogers[v. Dell Computer Corp., 2005 OK 51, 138 P.3d 826, 833 (Okla. 2005)]. Although remanding the case to determine whether the arbitration provision was included in the parties' agreement, it noted,

> The plaintiffs' accepting the computers and not returning them is consistent with a contract being formed at the time that the orders were placed and cannot be construed as acquiescing in the "Terms and Conditions of Sale" document whether included with the invoice or acknowledgment or with the computer packaging. If the contracts were formed at the time the orders were placed, see U.C.C. §2-206(1), the "Terms and Conditions of Sale" document, including the arbitration provision, would be an additional term of the contracts under section 2-207. The arbitration provision would not be part of the contracts but proposals to add it as a term to the contracts. *Rogers,* 138 P.3d at 833 (citing U.C.C. §2-207).[13]

---

13. It appears that the drafters of the Uniform Commercial Code were themselves flummoxed by this issue. Amended U.C.C. §2-207, which, although not adopted, could provide some insight into any evolving consensus among commercial law scholars and practitioners, states in Official Comment 5,

After reviewing the case law pertaining to so-called "shrinkwrap" agreements, we are satisfied that the *ProCD* line of cases is better reasoned and more consistent with contemporary consumer transactions. It is simply unreasonable to expect a seller to apprise a consumer of every term and condition at the moment he or she makes a purchase. A modern consumer neither expects nor desires to wade through such minutia, particularly when making a purchase over the phone, where full disclosure of the terms would border on the sadistic. Nor do we believe that, after placing a telephone order for a computer, a reasonable consumer would believe that he or she has entered into a fully consummated agreement. See Axelson, Inc. v. McEvoy-Willis, a Division of Smith International (North Sea), Ltd., 7 F.3d 1230, 1232-33 (5th Cir. 1993) ("An offer is an act that leads the offeree reasonably to believe that assent (i.e., acceptance) will conclude the deal."). Rather, he or she is aware that with delivery comes a multitude of standard terms attendant to nearly every consumer transaction.

We therefore decline to adopt the minority view, as urged by plaintiffs, that a contract is fully formed when a buyer orders a product and the seller accepts payment and either ships or promises to ship. Instead, formation occurs when the consumer accepts the full terms after receiving a reasonable opportunity to refuse them. Yet in adopting the so-called "layered contracting"[14] theory of formation, we reiterate that the burden falls squarely on the seller to show that the buyer has accepted the seller's terms after delivery. Thus, the crucial question in this case is whether defendants reasonably invited acceptance by making clear in the terms and conditions agreement that (1) by accepting defendants' product the consumer was accepting the terms and conditions contained within and (2) the consumer could reject the terms and conditions by returning the product.

On the first question, defendants notified plaintiffs that "[b]y accepting delivery of the computer systems, related products, and/or services and support, and/or other products described on that invoice[,] You ('Customer') agrees to be bound by and accepts those terms and conditions." This language certainly informed plaintiffs that defendants intended to bind them to heretofore undisclosed terms and conditions, but it did not advise them of the period beyond which they will have indicated their assent to those terms. The defendants argue that the meaning of the term "accepting delivery" is apparent to a reasonable consumer. We are not so sure. . . . "Acceptance of goods" has a technical

---

"The section omits any specific treatment of terms attached to the goods, or in or on the container in which the goods are delivered. This article takes no position on whether a court should follow the reasoning in Step-Saver Data Systems, Inc. v. Wyse Technology, 939 F.2d 91 (3d Cir. 1991) and Klocek v. Gateway, Inc., 104 F. Supp. 2d 1332 (D. Kan. 2000) (original 2-207 governs) or the contrary reasoning of Hill v. Gateway 2000, 105 F.3d 1147 (7th Cir. 1997) (original 2-207 inapplicable)." Amended §2-207, Comment 5 (2003).

14. This phrase is taken from the Supreme Court of Washington and is meant to denote that "while some contracts are formed and their terms fully defined at a single point in time, many transactions involve a rolling or layered process." M.A. Mortenson Co. v. Timberline Software Corp., 140 Wn.2d 568, 998 P.2d 305, 313 n.10 (Wash. 2000) (quoting the Uniform Computer Information Transactions Act §208 cmt. 3 (Approved Official Draft)).

meaning not easily discernable to the average consumer. A consumer may believe that simply by opening the package he or she has agreed to be bound by the terms and conditions contained therein. Indeed, many of the courts that have enforced so-called "approve-or-return" agreements cite language informing the consumer of a specific period after which he or she will have accepted the terms. See, e.g., *Hill,* 105 F.3d at 1148 (terms govern if consumer retains beyond thirty days); *Brower,* 676 N.Y.S.2d at 570 ("By keeping your Gateway 2000 computer system beyond thirty (30) days after the date of delivery, you accept the Terms and Conditions."). The more problematic issue, however, is whether plaintiffs were aware of their power to reject by returning the goods.

Significantly, the agreement sent to Ms. DeFontes, who is no longer a plaintiff in this case, contained additional language advising her of the method of rejection. The introductory provision of the terms and conditions agreement that defendants sent to her stated, "[i]f for any reason Customer is not satisfied with a Dell-branded hardware system, Customer may return the system under the terms and conditions of Dell's Total Satisfaction Return Policy * * *." In doing so, defendants explicitly contrasted acceptance of the terms with rejection of the goods, albeit while retaining some ambiguity whether rejection of defendants' proposed terms could reasonably be construed as dissatisfaction with "Dell-branded hardware." Many of the cases upholding shrinkwrap agreements cite explicit disclaimers advising consumers of their right to reject the terms. See, e.g., ProCD, Inc. v. Zeidenberg, 908 F. Supp. 640, 644 (W.D. Wis. 1996) ("If you do not agree to the terms of this License, promptly return all copies of the software, listings that may have been exported, the discs and the User Guide to the place where you obtained it."); . . . *M.A. Mortenson Co.,* 998 P.2d at 308 ("IF YOU DO NOT AGREE TO THESE TERMS AND CONDITIONS, PROMPTLY RETURN * * * TO THE PLACE OF PURCHASE AND YOUR PURCHASE PRICE WILL BE REFUNDED"). . . . Although the above language is significantly clearer, the terms and conditions agreement sent to Ms. DeFontes nevertheless made the important connection between acceptance of the terms by accepting delivery and rejection by returning the goods.

That this language is absent in the documents sent to current plaintiffs Mr. Long and Ms. Ricci is troubling and raises the specter that they were unaware of both their power to reject and the method with which to do so. The introductory provision that purportedly bound plaintiffs does not mention either the "Total Satisfaction Return Policy" or the thirty-day period in which a consumer may exercise his or her right to return the product. Rather, this policy is explained, if at all, in a distinct section of the terms and conditions agreement, which confusingly informed plaintiffs that "Dell Branded Hardware systems and parts that are purchased directly from Dell by an end-user Customer may be returned by Customer in accordance with Dell's 'Total Satisfaction Return Policy' in effect on the date of the invoice." . . . We believe the hearing justice rightly concluded that although "Dell does provide a 'total satisfaction policy' whereby a customer may return the computer, this return policy does not mention the customer's ability to return based on their unwillingness to comply with the terms."

In reviewing the language of the terms and conditions agreement it cannot be said that it was reasonably apparent to the plaintiffs that they could reject the terms simply by returning the goods. We believe that too many inferential steps were required of the plaintiffs and too many of the relevant provisions were left ambiguous. We are not persuaded that a reasonably prudent offeree would understand that by keeping the Dell computer he or she was agreeing to be bound by the terms and conditions agreement and retained, for a specified time, the power to reject the terms by returning the product. Because we hold that the hearing justice properly denied the defendants' motion to compel arbitration on the ground that the plaintiffs did not agree to be bound by the terms and conditions agreement, we need not discuss any of the alternative grounds the hearing justice offered for denying the defendants' motion to compel arbitration. . . .

III. Conclusion

For the reasons set out above, the judgment of the Superior Court is affirmed. The papers of the case are returned to the Superior Court.

Chief Justice Suttell and Justice Robinson did not participate.

NOTES AND QUESTIONS

1. *Offer and acceptance under **ProCD** and **Hill**.* The *DeFontes* court decided to follow the majority rule reflected in the *ProCD* and *Hill* opinions, both authored by Judge Frank Easterbrook of the United States Court of Appeals for the Seventh Circuit. ProCD, Inc. v. Zeidenberg, 86 F.3d 1447 (7th Cir. 1996); Hill v. Gateway, Inc., 105 F.3d 1147 (7th Cir. 1997). Those decisions are based on two propositions about offer and acceptance. First, when a purchaser places an order in person, by telephone or over the Internet, the purchaser has *not* made an offer. Instead, the vendor makes the offer by shipping the product to the purchaser with the vendor's terms of sale included. Second, the vendor is the "master of the offer." If the vendor's offer states that the purchaser accepts the offer by retaining the product beyond the period of time set forth in the vendor's terms of sale, the purchaser is bound by the vendor's terms if he does not return the product within that period. Judge Easterbrook stated in *ProCD*:

> What then does the current version of the UCC have to say? We think that the place to start is §2-204(1): "A contract for sale of goods may be made in any manner sufficient to show agreement, including conduct by both parties which recognizes the existence of such a contract." A vendor, as master of the offer, may invite acceptance by conduct, and may propose limitations on the kind of conduct that constitutes acceptance. A buyer may accept by performing the acts the vendor proposes to treat as acceptance. And that is what happened. ProCD proposed a contract that a buyer would accept by using the software after having an opportunity to read the license at leisure. This Zeidenberg did. He had no choice, because the software splashed the license on the screen and would not let him proceed without indicating acceptance. So although the

> district judge was right to say that a contract can be, and often is, formed simply by paying the price and walking out of the store, the UCC permits contracts to be formed in other ways. ProCD proposed such a different way, and without protest Zeidenberg agreed. Ours is not a case in which a consumer opens a package to find an insert saying "you owe us an extra $10,000" and the seller files suit to collect. Any buyer finding such a demand can prevent formation of the contract by returning the package, as can any consumer who concludes that the terms of the license make the software worth less than the purchase price. Nothing in the UCC requires a seller to maximize the buyer's net gains.

ProCD, 86 F.3d at 1452.

As the *DeFontes* court asserts, many other courts have accepted this reasoning. However, many scholarly commentators have been highly critical of Judge Easterbrook's reasoning. See William H. Lawrence, Rolling Contracts Rolling over Contract Law, 41 San Diego L. Rev. 1099, 1109 n.51 (2004) (citing authorities). Among other criticisms, they have pointed out that Judge Easterbrook failed to explain why the vendor rather than the purchaser should be considered to be the offeror, especially when the natural understanding of the transaction is that the purchaser is offering to buy the product and the vendor accepts by charging the purchaser for the product and by shipping the goods. This latter view of the transaction finds support in UCC §2-206, which provides that an offer may be accepted by prompt shipment of goods. For a detailed criticism of Judge Easterbrook's reasoning in *ProCD* and *Hill,* see the article by Professor John E. Murray, Jr., The Dubious Status of the Rolling Contract Formation Theory, 50 Duq. L. Rev. 35 (2012). In this article Professor Murray, who at the time of his death in 2015 was one of the most senior and respected of American contracts scholars, subjects the developing case law in this area to extensive critical analysis, before concluding as follows:

> To assure a buyer a reasonable opportunity to become aware of a vendor's otherwise invisible terms, the confusion, doubt, and controversy attending the rolling contract theory clearly requires its rejection. The theory is not only unnecessary to assure efficiency; at a minimum, its failure to alert the buyer to expect later contract terms undermines the buyer's opportunity to become aware of such terms. There is no need to continue the deliberate misconstructions of statutes or precedent that the theory requires. Nor is it simply a matter of the number of major flaws in the theory. It is systemically incapable of providing reasonably clear and effective guidelines. An effective response to the question of the operative effect of boilerplate terms that accompany the goods or appear only after the goods have been received should not require a discussion of several theories. The irrationality and attendant confusion of the rolling theory will continue to preclude its effective assimilation. A confusing legal reaction to the felt needs of society has no redeeming virtue.

Id. at 80-81. For more favorable analyses, see, e.g., Randy E. Barnett, Consenting to Form Contracts, 71 Fordham L. Rev. 627 (2002) (defending the *ProCD/Hill* approach to formation, provided the buyer has notice that more terms are forthcoming); Colin P. Marks, Not What, but When is an Offer: Rehabilitating the Rolling Contract, 46 Conn. L. Rev. 73, 118 (2013) (courts should resist "mechanical applications in either direction"; should take realistic approach that balances context and expectations, and employs such protections as unconscionability to protect reasonable expectations of buyers).

2. *Offer and acceptance under Klocek v. Gateway, Inc.* Perhaps the leading case rejecting Judge Easterbrook's reasoning in *ProCD* and *Hill*, is Klocek v. Gateway, Inc., 104 F. Supp. 2d 1332 (D. Kan. 2000), also cited and quoted in the *DeFontes* opinion. In that case, the court held that it was the purchaser rather than the vendor who made the offer:

> . . . [T]he Seventh Circuit provided no explanation for its conclusion that "the vendor is the master of the offer." See *ProCD*, 86 F.3d at 1452 (citing nothing in support of proposition); *Hill*, 105 F.3d at 1149 (citing *ProCD*). In typical consumer transactions, the purchaser is the offeror, and the vendor is the offeree. See Brown Mach., Div. of John Brown, Inc. v. Hercules, Inc., 770 S.W.2d 416, 419 (Mo. App. 1989) (as general rule orders are considered offers to purchase). . . . While it is possible for the vendor to be the offeror, see *Brown Machine*, 770 S.W.2d at 419 (price quote can amount to offer if it reasonably appears from quote that assent to quote is all that is needed to ripen offer into contract), Gateway provides no factual evidence which would support such a finding in this case. The Court therefore assumes for purposes of the motion to dismiss that plaintiff offered to purchase the computer (either in person or through catalog order) and that Gateway accepted plaintiff's offer (either by completing the sales transaction in person or by agreeing to ship and/or shipping the computer to plaintiff).

104 F. Supp. 2d at 1340. Under this reasoning, shrinkwrap terms found in the box containing the vendor's product are merely proposals for additions to an already-formed contract, governed by UCC §2-207(2). In a transaction involving a consumer purchaser and a merchant seller, the merchant's terms would not become part of the contract unless agreed to by the consumer. If the transaction were between two merchants, the terms might become part of the contract, but would not do so if any of the three situations set forth in §2-207(2) applied, as discussed earlier in the *Paul Gottlieb* case and notes. In particular, any terms proposed by the vendor that materially altered the contract would *not* automatically become part of the contract, even between merchants.

3. *Policy considerations.* Judge Easterbrook based his legal analysis on the policy argument that contracting through standard forms is efficient and socially desirable, and should be facilitated by the law. In characterizing the vendor as the offeror and the purchaser's conduct as an acceptance, he relied on the fact that in the modern market place it is common for payment to precede the delivery of contract terms, citing contracts for air transportation and insurance as examples. *Hill,* 105 F.3d at 1149. But important policy considerations also support the approach in cases such as *Klocek*. Contract law is traditionally said to be based on mutual consent. To claim that a purchaser who receives a product and only thereafter is informed of the terms of sale has "consented" to those terms simply by failing to return the product strains the concept of consent — some would argue, to the breaking point. In addition, Judge Easterbrook's approach enables vendors to dictate the terms of

the transaction. It is interesting to note that when referring to a concededly unreasonable term that a vendor might include — payment of an additional $10,000 for the product — Judge Easterbrook appears to require the purchaser to return the product in order to avoid being bound even by this term of sale. (See his language quoted in Note 1, above.) Finally, even if the reasoning used in *Klocek* were to prevail, vendors could respond to avoid the consequences of the decision and still bind purchasers to their terms. Indeed, the court in *Klocek* expressly recognized this fact:

> The Court is mindful of the practical considerations which are involved in commercial transactions, but it is not unreasonable for a vendor to clearly communicate to a buyer — at the time of sale — either the complete terms of the sale or the fact that the vendor will propose additional terms as a condition of sale, if that be the case.

104 F. Supp. 2d at 1341, n.14.

4. *Is **Klocek** or **Hill** better for consumers?* While the decision in *Klocek* may appear to give purchasers, particularly consumer purchasers, greater rights than the decisions in *Hill* and *ProCD*, that might not always be the case. Under the *Hill/ProCD* approach, purchasers are not bound contractually until they receive both the product and the seller's terms of sale, inspect them (if they choose to do so) for a period of time, and decide whether to keep the product or return it. Under *Klocek*, both parties are bound when the vendor accepts payment. If *Klocek* were to be the controlling rule, purchasers might lose the right to cancel the sale within the period of time specified by the vendor for return of the product. On the other hand, if the seller's additional terms did not apply because the *Klocek* analysis was used, even if the consumer did not have a contractual right to simply avoid the contract, she might under the general provisions of the UCC have the right to return it in certain circumstances or to seek damages for defective performance. See generally UCC §§2-601 through 2-608; §§2-714 and 2-715. Which would you prefer: (1) a contract in which the seller dictates the terms, subject to some limitations discussed below, but in which you have the ability to cancel the sale within a specified period after receiving the product (assuming you are aware that you do have that right, that is); or (2) a contract that consists of the terms on which you actually agree with the vendor plus the implied-in-law terms that apply in the absence of agreement, but under which you do not necessarily have the right to cancel within a designated period after receiving the product? As the preceding analysis indicates, contract formation in the rolling-contract situation involves competing legal and policy arguments over which reasonable people could disagree.

5. *Regulation of unfair terms.* In a number of the cases cited in *DeFontes*, you can find examples of vendors overreaching to include in standard form documents terms that are unreasonable and effectively deny purchasers the opportunity for a hearing before even an arbitration tribunal. We examine legal doctrines in later chapters that can be used by courts to invalidate extremely unreasonable terms found in vendors' terms of sale, even if those

terms of sale generally govern the transaction. See Robert A. Hillman & Jeffrey J. Rachlinski, Standard-Form Contracting in the Electronic Age, 77 N.Y.U. L. Rev. 429 (2002) (arguing that existing law regarding standard form contracts provides sufficient protection for purchasers). It is interesting to note that other countries have adopted a more regulatory approach to standard form contracts than the United States. For example, in the European Union, standard form contracts are subject to several directives issued by the European Commission that invalidate particularly oppressive provisions. See Robert L. Oakley, Fairness in Electronic Contracting: Minimum Standards for Non-Negotiated Contracts, 42 Hous. L. Rev. 1041 (2005); Jane K. Winn & Brian H. Bix, Diverging Perspectives on Electronic Contracting in the U.S. and E.U., 54 Clev. St. L. Rev. 175 (2006). Recent full treatments of this area include Margaret Jane Radin, Boilerplate: The Fine Print, Vanishing Rights, and the Rule of Law (Princeton Univ. Press 2012), and Nancy S. Kim, Wrap Contracts: Foundations and Ramifications (Oxford Univ. Press 2013). A good general discussion of the state of contract law in the present technological age can be found in an article by Prof. William J. Woodward, Jr., "Contraps," 66 Hastings L.J. 915 (2015).

6. *Does the UCC apply?* Contracts for the sale of consumer durables, such as refrigerators or washing machines, that come with shrinkwrap terms are clearly subject to the UCC because such products are "goods" under the Code. UCC §2-105(1) ("all things . . . movable at the time of identification to the contract for sale"). The status of software, on the other hand, is unclear. For many years software was sold on disks; the disks were goods, but the disk itself was not the product and its value was an inconsequential portion of the overall value of the transaction. Today, most software is downloaded over the Internet, so even a disk may not be present. Computers constitute goods under Article 2 because they are tangible moveable things, but computers typically come loaded with software, producing uncertainty regarding the application of the UCC. Most courts that have dealt with the issue have either applied the UCC to all of these transactions or have indicated that the result would be the same even if common law principles applied. See, e.g. Specht v. Netscape Communication Corp., 306 F.3d 17, 29 n.13 (2nd Cir. 2002).

Long v. Provide Commerce, Inc.

California Court of Appeal 200 Cal. Rptr. 3d 117 (2016)

OPINION

JONES, J.

INTRODUCTION

Defendant Provide Commerce, Inc. (Provide), appeals from an order denying its petition to compel arbitration of certain consumer fraud claims brought by plaintiff Brett Long (Plaintiff) on behalf of himself and a putative class of

California consumers who purchased flower arrangements through Provide's Web site, ProFlowers.com. Provide sought to compel arbitration based on a provision contained in the company's "Terms of Use," which were viewable via a hyperlink displayed at the bottom of each page on the ProFlowers.com Web site.

The Terms of Use on ProFlowers.com fall into a category of Internet contracts commonly referred to as "browsewrap" agreements. Unlike the other common form of Internet contract—known as "clickwrap" agreements—browsewrap agreements do not require users to affirmatively click a button to confirm their assent to the agreement's terms; instead, a user's assent is inferred from his or her use of the Web site. Because assent must be inferred, the determination of whether a binding browsewrap agreement has been formed depends on whether the user had actual or constructive knowledge of the Web site's terms and conditions.

Plaintiff opposed the petition to compel arbitration on the ground that he was never prompted to assent to the Terms of Use, nor did he actually read them, prior to placing his order on ProFlowers.com. The trial court concluded the Terms of Use hyperlinks were too inconspicuous to impose constructive knowledge on Plaintiff, and denied the petition as such. We likewise find the hyperlinks and the overall design of the ProFlowers.com Web site would not have put a reasonably prudent Internet user on notice of Provide's Terms of] Use, and Plaintiff therefore did not unambiguously assent to the subject arbitration provision simply by placing an order on ProFlowers.com. We affirm.

Facts And Procedural Background

There is no material dispute about the underlying facts. Provide is an online retailer that owns and operates several Web sites, including ProFlowers.com. Through ProFlowers.com, Provide advertises and sells a variety of floral products, which are shipped to order from the grower to the online customer.

Plaintiff alleges he purchased a floral arrangement on ProFlowers.com, which had been depicted and advertised on the Web site as a "completed assembled product," but which was delivered as a "do-it yourself kit in a box requiring assembly by the recipient."[2] Based on this allegation, Plaintiff sued Provide in the superior court, asserting claims for violations of the Consumers Legal Remedies Act (Civ. Code, § 1750 et seq.) and unfair competition law (Bus. & Prof. Code, § 17200 et seq.) on behalf of himself and a putative class of California consumers who purchased similarly advertised floral arrangements on ProFlowers.com.

Provide moved to compel arbitration pursuant to the Federal Arbitration Act (9 U.S.C. § 1 et seq.), arguing Plaintiff was bound by the Terms of Use for ProFlowers.com, including the dispute resolution provision contained therein. Provide's evidence, consisting of a series of screenshots from the ProFlowers.

2. The evidence shows Plaintiff purchased a Mother's Day card and floral arrangement from ProFlowers.com for delivery to his mother in Kansas on the day before Mother's Day in 2013.

com Web site, showed that at the time Plaintiff placed his order, the Terms of Use were available via a capitalized and underlined hyperlink titled "TERMS OF USE" located at the bottom of each Web page. The hyperlink was displayed in what appears to have been a light green typeface on the Web site's lime green background, and was situated among 14 other capitalized and underlined hyperlinks of the same color, font and size.

Provide's evidence also showed that, to complete his order, Plaintiff was required to input information and click through a multi-Web-page "checkout flow." The checkout flow screenshots show the customer information fields and click-through buttons displayed in a bright white box set against the Web site's lime green background. At the bottom of the white box was a notice indicating, "**Your order is safe and secure**," displayed next to a "VeriSign Secured" logo. Below the white box was a dark green bar with a hyperlink titled "SITE FEEDBACK" displayed in light green typeface. Finally, below the dark green bar, at the bottom of each checkout flow page, were two hyperlinks titled "PRIVACY POLICY" and "TERMS OF USE," displayed in the same light green typeface on the Web site's lime green background.

After Plaintiff placed his order on ProFlowers.com, Provide sent him an e-mail confirming the order. The e-mail, beginning from the top, displayed the ProFlowers logo alongside the title "order confirmation." This was followed by a dark green bar with several hyperlinks to apparent product offerings titled "Birthday," "Anniversary," "Get Well," "Roses," "Plants," and "Gourmet Gifts." Next, the e-mail displayed a light green bar thanking Plaintiff for his order, followed by order summary information, including the order number, shipping address, delivery date, the product ordered, and a billing breakdown for the product, delivery charge, tax, and total charge. The order details were followed by two banner advertisements, then a notification regarding online account management services, with four hyperlinks to account management pages on ProFlowers.com. Another dark green bar with the text "Our Family of Brands" followed the account management hyperlinks, then six brand logos for "ProFlowers," "*red*ENVELOPE," "ProPlants," "Shari's Berries," "CHERRY MOON FARMS," and "personalcreations. com." Next, the e-mail included a paragraph listing customer service contact information in small grey typeface. Then, in the same grey typeface, were two hyperlinks titled "Privacy Policy" and "Terms." Finally, the e-mail listed Provide's corporate address, again in the same grey typeface.

According to Plaintiff's declaration in opposition to Provide's petition to compel arbitration, Plaintiff "did not notice a reference of any kind to ProFlowers 'Terms and Conditions' nor a hyperlink to ProFlowers 'Terms of Use'" when he purchased flowers for delivery on ProFlowers.com. Had Plaintiff noticed the hyperlink and clicked on it, he would have been taken to a page containing the full text of the Terms of Use, which began with the following notice: "**By using any one of our Sites, you ... acknowledge that you have read, understand, and expressly agree to be legally bound by these Terms and Conditions**."[3]

3. ProFlowers.com is among the "Sites" listed in Provide's Terms of Use.

Later, under the heading "Dispute Resolution," Plaintiff would have found the following arbitration provision: "***Agreement to Arbitrate Disputes***: BY ACCESSING OR USING THE SITES, YOU EXPRESSLY AGREE THAT ANY LEGAL CLAIM, DISPUTE OR OTHER CONTROVERSY BETWEEN YOU AND PROVIDE COMMERCE ARISING OUT OF OR OTHERWISE RELATING IN ANY WAY TO THE SITES ... SHALL BE RESOLVED IN CONFIDENTIAL BINDING ARBITRATION CONDUCTED BEFORE ONE COMMERCIAL ARBITRATOR FROM THE AMERICAN ARBITRATION ASSOCIATION ('AAA'), RATHER THAN IN A COURT, AS DESCRIBED HEREIN. ... YOU SPECIFICIALLY AGREE THAT YOU ARE BOUND TO RESOLVE ALL DISPUTES IN ARBITRATION, AND YOU ACKNOWLEDGE THAT YOU ARE VOLUNTARILY AND KNOWINGLY FORFEITING YOUR RIGHT TO A TRIAL BY JURY AND TO OTHERWISE PROCEED IN A LAWSUIT IN STATE OR FEDERAL COURT."

Plaintiff argued he was not bound by the foregoing arbitration provision because he neither had notice of nor assented to the Terms of Use. In response, Provide argued the placement of the Terms of Use hyperlinks, particularly within the checkout flow, coupled with the hyperlink to "Terms" in the subsequent order confirmation e-mail, was sufficiently conspicuous to put Plaintiff on inquiry notice as to the contents of the agreement. Accordingly, Provide maintained Plaintiff's decision to continue with the order, whether he took the time to review the Terms of Use or not, was sufficient to establish his assent to be bound by the arbitration and venue provisions contained therein. The trial court agreed with Plaintiff, concluding the hyperlinks were too inconspicuous to put a reasonably prudent Internet consumer on inquiry notice. Provide now appeals this order.

Discussion

A. Legal Principles; Arbitration and Browsewrap Agreements

. . . As our Supreme Court has observed, "[t]here is indeed a strong policy in favor of enforcing agreements to arbitrate, but there is no policy compelling persons to accept arbitration of controversies which they have not agreed to arbitrate. . . ." (*Freeman v. State Farm Mut. Auto. Ins. Co.* (1975) 14 Cal.3d 473, 481 [121 Cal. Rptr. 477, 535 P.2d 341].)

(2) This requirement applies with equal force to arbitration provisions contained in contracts purportedly formed over the Internet. While Internet commerce has exposed courts to many new situations, it has not fundamentally changed the requirement that "[m]utual manifestation of assent, whether by written or spoken word or by conduct, is the touchstone of contract." (*Nguyen v. Barnes & Noble Inc.* (9th Cir. 2014) 763 F.3d 1171, 1175 (*Nguyen*).) "Mutual assent is determined under an objective standard applied to the outward manifestations or expressions of the parties, i.e., the reasonable meaning of their words and acts, and not their unexpressed intentions or understandings." (*HM DG, Inc. v. Amini* (2013) 219 Cal. App. 4th 1100, 1109 [162 Cal. Rptr. 3d 412] (*HM DG*).) In applying this objective standard, outward manifestations of a party's supposed assent are to be judged with due regard for the context in which they arise. California law is clear—"an offeree, regardless of apparent manifestation of his consent, is not bound by inconspicuous contractual provisions of which he was unaware, contained in a document whose contractual nature is not obvious." (*Windsor Mills, Inc. v. Collins & Aikman Corp.* (1972) 25 Cal. App. 3d 987, 993 [101 Cal. Rptr. 347]; see *Specht v. Netscape Communications Corp.* (2d Cir. 2002) 306 F.3d 17, 30 (*Specht*) [applying California law to commercial Internet transaction].) [Double quotation marks eliminated — EDS.]

"Contracts formed on the Internet come primarily in two flavors: 'clickwrap' (or 'click-through') agreements, in which website users are required to click on an 'I agree' box after being presented with a list of terms and conditions of use; and 'browsewrap' agreements, where a website's terms and conditions of use are generally posted on the website via a hyperlink at the bottom of the screen." (*Nguyen, supra,* 763 F.3d at pp. 1175-1176.) The parties agree that the subject Terms of Use for the ProFlowers.com Web site fall into the browsewrap category.

" 'Unlike a clickwrap agreement, a browsewrap agreement does not require the user to manifest assent to the terms and conditions expressly ... [a] party instead gives his assent simply by using the website.' [Citation.] Indeed, 'in a pure-form browsewrap agreement, "the website will contain a notice that—by merely using the services of, obtaining information from, or initiating applications within the website—the user is agreeing to and is bound by the site's terms of service." ' Thus, 'by visiting the website—something that the user has already done—the user agrees to the Terms of Use not listed on the site itself but available only by clicking a hyperlink.' 'The defining feature of browsewrap agreements is that the user can continue to use the website or its services without visiting the page hosting the browsewrap agreement or even knowing that such a webpage exists.' 'Because no affirmative action is required by the website user to agree to the terms of a contract other than his or her use of the website, the determination of the validity of the browsewrap contract depends on whether the user has actual or constructive knowledge of a website's terms and conditions.' " (*Nguyen, supra,* 763 F.3d at p. 1176.) More to the point here, absent actual notice, "the validity of [a] browsewrap agreement turns on whether the website puts a reasonably prudent user on inquiry notice of the terms of the contract." (*Id.* at p. 1177.)

With these foundational legal principles in place, we turn our focus to the specifics of the browsewrap agreement in the instant case, and whether the design of Provide's Web site and order confirmation e-mail were sufficient to conclude Plaintiff agreed to be bound by the Terms of Use and arbitration provision contained therein simply by placing his order on ProFlowers.com.

B. The "Terms of Use" Hyperlinks Are Not Sufficiently Conspicuous to Put a Reasonably Prudent Internet Consumer on Inquiry Notice; Plaintiff Did Not Manifest His Unambiguous Assent to Be Bound by the Terms of Use

Provide does not dispute Plaintiff's testimony that he had no actual knowledge of the Terms of Use when he placed his order on ProFlowers.com. Accordingly, we must decide whether the design of the ProFlowers.com Web site and/or the conspicuousness of the hyperlinks to the Terms of Use were sufficient to put a reasonably prudent Internet consumer on inquiry notice of the browsewrap agreement's existence and contents. (See *Nguyen, supra*, 763 F.3d at p. 1177.) Because the material evidence consists exclusively of screenshots from the Web site and order confirmation e-mail, and the authenticity of these screenshots is not subject to factual dispute, we review the issue de novo as a pure question of law. (See *HM DG, supra*, 219 Cal. App. 4th at p. 1109 [" 'if the material facts are certain or undisputed, the existence of a contract is a question for the court to decide' "].)

It appears that no California appellate court has yet addressed what sort of Web site design elements would be necessary or sufficient to deem a browsewrap agreement valid in the absence of actual notice. Accordingly, in addition to the general contract principles discussed above, our analysis is largely guided by two federal cases from the Second and Ninth Circuit Courts of Appeals, each of which considered the enforceability of a browsewrap agreement applying the objective manifestation of assent analysis dictated by California law. (See *Specht, supra*, 306 F.3d at p. 30, fn. 13; *Nguyen, supra*, 763 F.3d at p. 1175.) In keeping with the principles articulated in these authorities, we conclude the design of the ProFlowers.com Web site, even when coupled with the hyperlink contained in the confirmation e-mail, was insufficient to put Plaintiff on inquiry notice of the subject Terms of Use.

In *Specht*, the Second Circuit declined to enforce an arbitration provision contained in a software licensing browsewrap agreement where the hyperlink to the agreement appeared on "a submerged screen" below the " 'Download' " button that the plaintiffs clicked to initiate the software download. (*Specht, supra*, 306 F.3d at pp. 30–32.) After reviewing California contract law, the *Specht* court acknowledged that a user's act of clicking a download button, combined with " 'circumstances sufficient to put a prudent man upon inquiry' " as to the existence of licensing terms, would constitute a sufficient manifestation of assent to be bound. (*Id.* at p. 31.) However, the court was quick to point out that the opposite must also be true—that "a consumer's clicking on a download button does not communicate assent to contractual terms if the offer did not make clear to the consumer that clicking on the download button would signify assent to those terms." (*Id.* at pp. 29–30.) The design of the defendant's Web site, the *Specht* court concluded, exemplified the latter circumstance.

Though the Web site advised users to " 'Please review and agree to the terms of the ... software license agreement before downloading and using the software,' " the *Specht* court emphasized that users would have encountered this advisement only if they scrolled down to the screen below the Web site's invitation to download the software by clicking the download button. (*Specht, supra*, 306 F.3d at p. 23, italics omitted.) This meant that when the plaintiffs clicked the download button, they "were responding to an offer that did not carry an immediately visible notice of the existence of license terms or require unambiguous manifestation of assent to those terms." (*Id.* at p. 31.) The fact that users might have noticed from the position of the scroll bar that an unexplored portion of the Web page remained below the download button did not change the reasonableness calculation. Under the circumstances presented, "where consumers [were] urged to download free software at the immediate click of a button," the *Specht* court concluded placing the notice of licensing terms on a submerged page " 'tended to conceal the fact that [downloading the software] was an express acceptance of [the defendant's] rules and regulations.' " (*Id.* at p. 32.) Thus, notwithstanding what the plaintiffs might have found had they taken " 'as much time as they need[ed]' to scroll through multiple screens on a webpage" (*ibid.*), the *Specht* court held that "a reasonably prudent offeree in plaintiffs' position would not have known or learned ... of the reference to [the software's] license terms hidden below the 'Download' button on the next screen" (*id.* at p. 35).

More than a decade after the Second Circuit decided *Specht*, the Ninth Circuit in *Nguyen* considered whether the conspicuous placement of a " 'Terms of Use' " hyperlink, standing alone, would be sufficient to put an Internet consumer on inquiry notice. (*Nguyen, supra*, 763 F.3d at p. 1178.) Unlike in *Specht*, the hyperlink in *Nguyen* was visible "without scrolling" on some of the Web site's pages, while on others "the hyperlink [was] close enough to the 'Proceed with Checkout' button that a user would have to bring the link within his field of vision" to complete an online order. (*Ibid.*) These differences with *Specht* notwithstanding, the *Nguyen* court concluded the plaintiff's act of placing an order did not constitute an unambiguous manifestation of assent to be bound by the browsewrap agreement, holding "proximity or conspicuousness of the hyperlink alone is not enough to give rise to constructive notice." (*Ibid.*) The court reasoned that *Specht* had only identified a circumstance that was *not sufficient* to impart inquiry notice—where the only reference to license terms appeared on a submerged screen. (*Ibid.*) But in cases where courts had "relied on the proximity of the hyperlink *to enforce* a browsewrap agreement," the *Nguyen* court explained, those Web sites had "also included something more to capture the user's attention and secure her assent." (*Id.* at p. 1178, fn. 1, italics added.) Typically that "something more" had taken the form of an explicit textual notice warning users to " 'Review terms' " or admonishing users that by clicking a button to complete the transaction " 'you agree to the terms and conditions in the [agreement].' " (*Id.* at p. 1178 & fn. 1.) From those cases, the *Nguyen* court derived the following bright-line rule for determining the validity of browsewrap agreements: "[W]here a website makes its terms of use available via a conspicuous hyperlink on every page of the website but otherwise provides no notice to users nor prompts them to take any affirmative action to demonstrate assent, even close proximity of the hyperlink to relevant buttons users must click on—without more—is insufficient to give rise to constructive notice." (*Id.* at pp. 1178-1179.)

Provide argues we should disregard *Nguyen* as an outlier case, and follow *Specht* to the extent it suggests a conspicuous hyperlink that provides " 'immediately visible notice' " of a browsewrap agreement is sufficient, standing alone, to put a reasonably prudent Internet consumer on inquiry notice of the agreement's terms. In that regard, Provide observes that "in *Specht*, the *only* reference to license terms appeared *on a submerged screen out of sight to users when they clicked on buttons to download software*." In contrast, Provide argues the Terms of Use hyperlink on ProFlowers.

com "is immediately visible on the checkout flow, is viewable without scrolling, and located next to several fields that the website user is required to fill out and the buttons he must click to complete an order." Given this distinction, Provide argues the hyperlink was sufficiently conspicuous to "put a reasonable user on notice of the Terms of Use." We disagree.

(4) Though it may be that an especially observant Internet consumer could spot the Terms of Use hyperlinks on some checkout flow pages without scrolling, that quality alone cannot be all that is required to establish the existence of an enforceable browsewrap agreement. Rather, as the *Specht* court observed, "[r]easonably conspicuous notice of the existence of contract terms and unambiguous manifestation of assent to those terms by consumers are essential if electronic bargaining is to have integrity and credibility." (*Specht, supra*, 306 F.3d at p. 35.) Here, the Terms of Use hyperlinks—their placement, color, size and other qualities relative to the ProFlowers.com Web site's overall design—are simply too inconspicuous to meet that standard.

(5) Indeed, our review of the screenshots reveals how difficult it is to find the Terms of Use hyperlinks in the checkout flow *even when one is looking for them*.[4] This of course is to say nothing of how observant an Internet consumer must be to discover the hyperlinks in the usual circumstance of using ProFlowers.com *to purchase flowers*, without any forewarning that he or she should also be on the lookout for a reference to Terms of Use somewhere on the Web site's various pages. Contrary to Provide's characterization, the subject hyperlinks in the checkout flow are not "located next to" the fields and buttons a consumer must interact with to complete his order. Those fields and buttons are contained in a separate bright white box in the center of the page that contrasts sharply with the Web site's lime green background. To find a Terms of Use hyperlink in the checkout flow, a consumer placing an order must (1) remove attention from the fields in which he or she is asked to enter his information; (2) look below the buttons he must click to proceed with the order; (3) look even further below a "VeriSign Secured" logo and notification advising that his or her "**order is safe and secure**," which itself includes a hyperlink to "**Click here** for more details"; (4) look still further below a thick dark green bar with a hyperlink for "SITE FEEDBACK"; and (5) finally find the "TERMS OF USE" hyperlink situated to the right of another hyperlink for the Web site's "PRIVACY POLICY," both of which appear in the same font and light green typeface that, to the unwary flower purchaser, could blend in with the Web site's lime green background. True, on a handful of these pages no scrolling is required to complete the hunt. But that, in our assessment, does not change the practical reality that the checkout flow is laid out " 'in such a manner that it tended to conceal the fact that [placing an order] was an express acceptance of [Provide's] rules and regulations.' " (*Specht, supra*, 306 F.3d at p. 32.)

As for Provide's contention that the subsequent order confirmation e-mail somehow provides the notice that was missing from the checkout flow, again,

4. We focus our analysis on the checkout flow as Provide concedes the placement of Terms of Use hyperlink on the product Web page is "less conspicuous."

we disagree. Unlike the hyperlink on some checkout flow pages, the screenshots suggest the hyperlink in the e-mail is located on a submerged page, requiring the customer to scroll below layers of order summary details, advertisement banners, hyperlinks to "convenient account management services," several logos for Provide's "Family of Brands," and customer service contact information to finally find a reference to "Terms" printed in grey typeface on a white background. This is not the sort of conspicuous alert that can be expected to put a reasonably prudent Internet consumer on notice to investigate whether disputes related to his or her order will be subject to binding arbitration.

(6) While the lack of conspicuousness resolves the instant matter, we agree with the *Nguyen* court that, to establish the enforceability of a browsewrap agreement, a textual notice should be required to advise consumers that continued use of a Web site will constitute the consumer's agreement to be bound by the Web site's terms of use. (See *Nguyen, supra,* 763 F.3d at pp. 1178–1179.) In our view, the problem with merely displaying a hyperlink in a prominent or conspicuous place is that, without notifying consumers that the linked page contains binding contractual terms, the phrase "terms of use" may have no meaning or a different meaning to a large segment of the Internet-using public. In other words, a conspicuous "terms of use" hyperlink may not be enough to alert a reasonably prudent Internet consumer to click the hyperlink.[5] As the *Nguyen* court observed, "[w]hile failure to read a contract before agreeing to its terms does not relieve a party of its obligations under the contract, [citation], the onus must be on website owners to put users on notice of the terms to which they wish to bind consumers. Given the *breadth of the range of technological savvy of online purchasers*, consumers cannot be expected to ferret out hyperlinks to terms and conditions to which they have no reason to suspect they will be bound." (*Nguyen*, at p. 1179, italics added.) Though we need not resolve the issue here given the inconspicuousness of the Terms of Use hyperlinks on the ProFlowers.com Web site, in our view the bright-line rule established by *Nguyen* is necessary to ensure that Internet consumers are on inquiry notice of a browsewrap agreement's terms, regardless of each consumer's degree of technological savvy. Online retailers would be well-advised to include a conspicuous textual notice with their terms of use hyperlinks going forward.

C. Plaintiff Did Not Agree to the Venue Provision Either

In the alternative, Provide argues the trial court erred by denying its request to transfer venue to San Diego pursuant to a forum selection clause in the Terms of Use. That clause, which is itself presented as an alternative to a class arbitration waiver, provides: "[I]f an arbitrator deems your Waiver of Class Arbitration to be invalid or unenforceable, then ... you expressly acknowledge and agree that: (ii) all Disputes shall be resolved by a state or federal court located in the county of San Diego, California." The trial court denied the request to transfer venue for the same reason it denied the petition to compel arbitration—namely,

5. Notably, this was not a problem in *Specht* because, although the hyperlink to the subject license agreement was displayed on a submerged portion of the download page, the hyperlink

because Plaintiff did not agree to the Terms of Use, he did not agree to the forum selection clause contained therein.

Provide argues the trial court's reasoning was flawed, because forum selection clauses are presumptively valid. Thus, Provide maintains, though it had the burden to establish an enforceable arbitration agreement, "the presumption in favor of [forum selection clause] enforcement shift[ed] the burden to [Plaintiff] ... to show why the provision should not be enforced." Insofar as Plaintiff "fail[ed] to establish the unenforceability of the venue provision" in his opposition papers, Provide argues the trial court was required to enforce the provision and transfer the action to San Diego. We disagree.

Provide's reliance on the presumptive validity of forum selection clauses *in otherwise enforceable contracts* proves too much. Contrary to Provide's implicit premise, the presumption of validity is not a substitute for proof of the resisting party's objective manifestation of assent to the larger contract. If it were, a party would establish the existence of a binding contract simply by showing that the contract contained a presumptively valid forum selection clause—an obviously absurd result. The trial court was correct; because Plaintiff was not bound by Provide's Terms of Use, he also could not have been bound by the forum selection clause contained therein.

DISPOSITION

The order is affirmed. Plaintiff Brett Long is entitled to his costs.

Aldrich, Acting P. J., and Lavin, J., concurred.

NOTES AND QUESTIONS

1. *Comparing **Long** and **Meyer**.* The court in the *Meyer* case in Chapter 1 held that a customer had assented to and was contractually bound by the terms of Uber's Terms and Conditions, which included a clause requiring arbitration of disputes. In contrast, the court in *Long* concluded that the customer was not bound by the terms and conditions on the Provide Commerce website. Are the two decisions consistent with one another?

2. *Bright line rules in browsewrap cases.* Both *Long* and *Meyer* engage in an extensive analysis of the websites to determine if consumers were reasonably on notice that they were bound by the terms and conditions of the sellers. Should courts instead use bright line rules to decide cases? Would you agree with the following propositions?

   (a) Browsewrap terms are not contractually binding unless the user clicks "I agree" or similar button.

---

included a notice to "'Please review and agree to the terms of the Netscape SmartDownload software license agreement before downloading and using the software.'" (*Specht, supra*, 306 F.3d at p. 23, italics omitted.)

(b) A prominent hyperlink to terms and conditions alone is never sufficient to amount to agreement, even if the link is conspicuous.

Consider the following remarks about bright line rules by District Judge Jack B. Weinstein:

> It is desirable to have hard-edged rules of adhesion that apply no matter what the consumer's background. Such rules reduce substantial litigation costs. But, until useful consumer studies demonstrate that average consumers using the computer understand what contract terms are being accepted when a purchase is made, preemptive rules in favor of vendors who do not forcefully draw purchasers' attention to terms disadvantageous to them should be rejected. . . . The burden of showing agreement to details of a contract on a website's contract of adhesion is on the vendors. It is the vendor who designs the website and puts into it terms favoring itself.
>
> Proof of special know-how based on the background of the potential buyer or adequate warning of adverse terms by the design of the agreement page or pages should be required before adverse terms, such as compelled arbitration or forced venue, are enforced.

Berkson v. Gogo LLC, 97 F.3d 359, 402-403 (E.D.N.Y. 2015). The case was subsequently settled, 147 F. Supp. 3d 123 (E.D.N.Y. 2015).

3. *Scholarly commentary.* In a survey of case law and policy arguments involving browsewrap agreements, the authors (Christina L. Kunz, John E. Ottaviani, Elaine D. Ziff, Juliet M. Moringiello, Kathleen M. Porter, and Jennifer C. Debrow) contend that browsewrap agreements should be enforceable even if the user has not clicked an agreement button, if four requirements are met:

(i) The user is provided with adequate notice of the existence of the proposed terms.
(ii) The user has a meaningful opportunity to review the terms.
(iii) The user is provided with adequate notice that taking a specified action manifests assent to the terms.
(iv) The user takes the action specified in the latter notice.

Christina L. Kunz et al., Browse-wrap Agreements: Validity of Implied Assent in Electronic Form Agreements, 59 Bus. Law. 279 (2003). On the other hand, in Online Boilerplate: Would Mandatory Website Disclosure of E-standard Terms Backfire? 104 Mich. L. Rev. 837 (2006), Professor Robert Hillman argues that mandatory disclosure of terms of use on websites might backfire "because it may not increase reading or shopping for terms or motivate businesses to draft reasonable ones, but instead, may make heretofore suspect terms more likely enforceable." Id at 839. In particular, mandated disclosure might make it more difficult for consumers to establish unfair surprise. Id. at 840.

PROBLEM 2-7

David Copperfield is a resident of a midwestern city, where he lives in and operates a bed-and-breakfast inn, which he calls "Merlin's Castle." The inn is comfortably and attractively furnished with antique furniture, oil paintings, and oriental rugs. Recently David saw on television an "infomercial" program advertising the "CarpetWizard" (TM), a machine for vacuuming and steam-cleaning carpets and rugs. In that program, the CarpetWizard was advertised for sale at the price of $399.95, for which sum it was stated that the buyer would also receive "absolutely free" a lightweight carpet sweeper and a device for dusting blinds, shades, and ceiling fixtures. Watching the program, David was persuaded that the CarpetWizard and its accompanying devices would be useful in keeping his inn clean and neat.

The program listed a website where David could purchase the CarpetWizard: http://www.morek.com/carpetwizard. When David accessed the CarpetWizard, Inc. (or CWI) website, he saw pictures of various vacuum cleaners and similar devices, with specifications for each of the products. Below the pictures of all the products was the following statement: **MONEY BACK GUARANTEE IF NOT COMPLETELY SATISFIED WITH OUR PRODUCT.** Immediately below the guarantee was a button also in all caps and bold face stating **PLACE AN ORDER**. Several other buttons, in somewhat smaller, nonbold type, were located at the bottom of the page. One of these buttons was labeled "contract terms and product guarantee." David clicked on the button, scrolled part of the way through the document, saw that it was fairly long with some provisions in all caps bold while others were in regular type. Included in the document were the following: (1) Any claim for refund of your purchase price under our money back guarantee must be made within five days of the buyer's receipt of the merchandise, and must be accompanied by all of the merchandise in the original packing case, sent postage prepaid and insured to the seller's factory in Florida (regular nonbold type); (2) a disclaimer of any liability on CWI's part for any consequential damage resulting from the use or misuse of any CWI products (**IN BOLD ALL CAPS**); and (3) a statement that any and all disputes arising out of the buyer's purchase of any CWI product must be submitted to arbitration in Florida (**IN BOLD ALL CAPS**). David clicked the back button, returned to the home page, clicked the button to **PLACE AN ORDER**, and moved to a page that asked for credit card and delivery information. David entered this information and clicked the button at the bottom of the page which stated "complete order." A page appeared confirming David's entry of credit card and delivery information. At the bottom of the page appeared another button which stated: "Confirm order. Your order is not complete until you click here." David clicked this button and a message appeared on the screen with his order confirmation number. He was told that he would receive an email when his order was shipped. He received the confirming email the next day.

Two weeks later, the merchandise he had ordered was delivered. In the packing box, in addition to the CarpetWizard plus the sweeper and duster, was a booklet entitled "CONTRACT TERMS, PRODUCT GUARANTEE, AND INSTRUCTION MANUAL," the contents of which consisted mostly of instructions for operating those products. However, the booklet repeated the three provisions outlined above that were found on the website. Attached to the last page of the Instruction Manual was a tear-off card entitled "WARRANTY REGISTRATION." The card stated: "Please fill out and return so that we may have a record of your purchase, to ensure that you receive updates regarding your product." The card provided a space for the buyer to fill in the place and date of the purchase and the serial number of the CarpetWizard. The card then asked several questions about the buyer's purchasing habits, followed by a space for the buyer's signature, name, and address. David filled out the card, signed it, and mailed it back to CWI.

A week after receiving the CarpetWizard, David got around to trying it out. After reading the instructions in the manual to be sure he was operating the machine correctly, David used the CarpetWizard to clean the rugs in his inn, starting with those in his own personal apartment. When it appeared to work as promised, he went on to use the machine on the rugs in the guest rooms and common areas of the inn. Within a few hours, several of the rugs appeared discolored and worn as a result of its operation. When David attempted to go over the affected areas again, in an effort to improve the result, the CarpetWizard short-circuited and caught fire. The machine itself was damaged beyond repair, as was the rug that David was cleaning at the time.

For the purpose of this question, ignore the application of UCC warranty law, any possible application of tort law, and the possibility that statutes or regulations (federal, state, or local) we have not studied might provide various types of protection for David in this case. Assuming that the damage to David's rugs could be characterized as "consequential damage," answer the following questions on the basis of general contract law and UCC Article 2.

1. Is David entitled to a full refund of the price he paid for the CWI products?
2. Is he entitled to compensation for any injury to his rugs that resulted from his use of the CarpetWizard?
3. If CWI declines to make compensation as David requests, will David have to initiate an arbitration proceeding in Florida to recover any money from CWI?

REVIEW QUESTIONS – CHAPTER TWO

1. Xena (X) is a young woman living in Ohio. Recently she wrote the following email to her cousin Yancey (Y), an Indiana resident:

   Dear Y: After some consideration, I've decided that I need to sell the antique roll-top desk that our grandfather left to me. I need the money, and it takes up a lot of space in my small house. I know you've always admired it, so I thought I would give you a chance to buy it before I put it up for sale on Craigslist. I had it appraised not long ago, and I was told that it's worth at least $15,000. I'd certainly sell it for that, or you could make me an offer. I need to hear from you by the end of the week, if possible.

   – Fondly, your cousin X.

   Has X made an offer to Y?

2. Y responds to X's note the next day, with the following note:

   Dear X: Thanks for thinking of me. I'd certainly love to own Grandpa's desk, but $15K is pretty high for me. I guess I can go up to $12K. Would you take that for it? – Y

   Given the facts of Questions 1 and 2, which of the following statements is/are potentially accurate?

   A. If X's communication was not an offer, Y's response is an offer.
   B. If X's communication was an offer, Y's response is a counter-offer.
   C. If X's communication was an offer, Y's response necessarily acts as a rejection of that offer.

3. After receiving Y's note on Friday, X answers the same day:

   Dear Y: Sorry, but I can't go as low as that. I know it's worth at least $15K, and I might be able to get even more. – X

   After thinking it over for a few days, Y responds to X on Monday with the following note:

   Dear X: It's a stretch for me, but I hate to see Grandpa's desk leave the family. I'll meet your price of $15K. Let me know when I can come to pick it up. – Y

   Assuming the facts of Questions 1, 2 and 3, which of the following statements is/are potentially accurate?

   A. Y's last note to X is an acceptance of X's original offer.
   B. Y's last note to X is not an acceptance of X's original offer, because that was terminated by an earlier rejection.
   C. Y's last note to X is not an effective acceptance of X's original offer, because it was not communicated in time to be effective.
   D. Y's last note to X is an offer which Y is free to accept or reject.

4. During the December pre-holiday sales period, Donaldson's Department Store (DDS) had a prominent sign in its window:

   ENTER NOW TO WIN A NEW MUSTANG!!

   Put your name in the box at the customer service counter on the fourth floor of our store. Drawing to be held Jan 2. Not necessary to be present to win. Don't miss this fabulous once-in-a-lifetime opportunity!!

While doing her holiday shopping at DDS, Ashley Andrews filled out one of the blank cards provided and dropped it in the box in the DDS store. On Jan. 2, one of the store employees pulled Ashley's card from the box. The store notified her of that fact, but when she came to claim her prize of a new Ford Mustang automobile, she was given a plastic model of that car. She promptly complained to the manager, who told her that the holiday sales at DDS had been too disappointing to justify awarding her an automobile.

Does Ashley have a valid claim against DDS for a new Mustang (or its value)?

A. Yes, because the store's promise was supported by consideration and Ashley reasonably expected to receive an automobile if her name was drawn.
B. No, because the store got no consideration for its promise.
C. No, because the store's statement was ambiguous.

5. Three years ago Chuck Carlson agreed to lease from Lily Landon a vacant storefront in which Chuck intended to operate a gourmet food shop, "Chucky's Cheeses." The term of the lease was three years, and the rent provided in the written lease (which was signed by both parties) was $2,000 a month. The lease contained the following provision:

> **Renewal Option.** Tenant is to have the option to renew for an additional three-year period, at the monthly rate of $2,250 or such other amount as the parties may agree to, provided Tenant gives Landlord written notice of intent to renew at least 60 days before the end of the term of this lease.

The shop proved to be successful. When 80 days remained on his lease term, Chuck delivered to Lily a written notice of his intent to renew the lease for three years at the rate of $2,250 per month. Lily stated she would not recognize his right to renew unless he agreed to a monthly rental of $2,500.

Which of the following statements best describes the parties' legal position?

A. Chuck cannot enforce the option to renew because it is only an agreement to agree.
B. Chuck can enforce the option to renew, but only if he can demonstrate reliance on the renewal provision in the lease.
C. Chuck can enforce the option to renew at the monthly rental of $2,250.
D. Chuck cannot enforce the option to renew unless he can show that Lily is acting in bad faith.

6. Your client Bob, a building contractor, makes many purchases through the exchange of emails. He wants to be able to avoid waiving any rights that he ordinarily would have for legal remedies for defective materials, especially if the defects are discovered only after the materials have been incorporated in a building project, because this could prove very costly for him to repair or replace. Typically, he attaches to every email order a set of his own "Terms and Conditions," which his email order refers to as follows:

> By accepting this order you are agreeing to the attached Terms and Conditions, which are part of every purchase contract we make. All inconsistent terms are hereby objected to.

The following language appears in Bob's attached Terms and Conditions form:

> Buyer retains all rights under the Uniform Commercial Code to remedies for breach of contract or of warranty, including consequential damages.

Bob has asked you if this language will protect against a seller's attempt (in "Terms and Conditions" of its own) to disclaim the warranties that would otherwise be implied by law, or to exclude consequential damages as a remedy. What would you tell him?

A. The language will absolutely preserve for Bob his legal remedies under the UCC.

B. The language will protect him generally, but not if he or his agent signs a seller's form that contains terms unfavorable to him.

C. The effect of his language can be defeated if Bob receives and does not expressly object to a seller's form that provides "Seller's Terms and Conditions are part of this contract if Buyer accepts the goods without objecting to them."

D. There is no way the buyer can achieve his objective; a seller's form always has the benefit of being the "last shot" if the buyer accepts the goods.

CHAPTER 3

Liability in the Absence of Bargained-for Exchange: Reliance on Gratuitous Promises, Unaccepted Offers, and the Principle of Restitution

In the preceding chapter, we explored the traditional elements of the basic contract paradigm: assent (offer and acceptance) and consideration. This chapter addresses what may seem on the face of it to be an unrelated collection of different doctrines and rules. They are all connected, however, by a common theme: When can one person enforce against another an obligation of performance that is similar to the obligation imposed by contract law, even though one of the traditional elements of contract-formation is missing? Section A presents the notion of promise-enforcement based on reliance, usually referred to as "promissory estoppel." In Section B, we return to the fundamental contract-law tenet that offers are freely revocable (recall the *Normile* case) to survey a variety of approaches that might protect an offeree against the offeror's attempt to withdraw her offer. And finally in Section C, we take a brief look at the notion of restitution (or relief for "unjust enrichment") both as an independent basis for liability and as an influence on the development of contract law.

A. PROTECTION OF PROMISEE RELIANCE: THE DOCTRINE OF PROMISSORY ESTOPPEL

It is common for legal commentators to regard traditional, or "classical," contract law as a system of abstract, formal rules, self-contained and logically consistent, based on principles enunciated in the first instance by Professor Christopher Langdell and more fully developed by Professor Samuel Williston. And indeed this does pretty well describe the original Restatement of Contracts, officially adopted by the American Law Institute in 1932. During the preparation of the first Restatement, however, Professor Arthur Corbin argued that courts often used reliance as a basis of contractual obligation. Corbin's work led to the inclusion of the reliance principle in §90 of the first Restatement.

Section 90 of the first Restatement was both short and deceptively simple. The section was entitled "Promise Reasonably Inducing Definite and Substantial Action." (Although the principle is commonly called "promissory estoppel," that term was not used in §90.) Its text provided as follows:

> A promise which the promisor should reasonably expect to induce action or forbearance of a definite and substantial character on the part of the promisee and which does induce such action or forbearance is binding if injustice can be avoided only by enforcement of the promise.

When the Restatement (Second) was drafted, the concept of promissory estoppel was preserved, and §90 was retained with only slight modification. The case law has generally accepted this concept, and applied it in a variety of ways to make enforceable what would otherwise be an unenforceable promise, when that promise has been relied on. In this chapter we focus on two of those situations. In this section we address the role of "unbargained-for reliance" generally as a substitute for consideration; in Section B we focus on the application of promissory estoppel to prevent an offeror from revoking her offer. In later chapters, we consider the effect of promisee-reliance on other contract doctrines, such as the statute of frauds.

1. Promises Within the Family

On its face, the system of classical contract law would appear to apply as readily to dealings between two family members as it would to any other transaction. Upon reflection, however, it should be obvious that the nature of the bargain theory of consideration would exclude from the contract sphere most of the dealings between family members. Of course relatives can, and frequently do, enter into formal contracts with each other, but promises in the family context are likely to be actuated mainly by feelings of affection and altruism rather than by the expectation of a quid pro quo in return. In short, they are "gratuitous" – not part of a bargained-for exchange. To the extent that the law does impose legal obligations between persons in the family context, these obligations are for the most part based on the relationship of the parties – the parental duty of support, for example – rather than on contract. (We will see in the last section of this chapter, however, that some contemporary courts have also used the doctrine of restitution to create legal obligations in the family context when justice seems to demand it.) As the following materials demonstrate, promissory estoppel provides an important tool for courts to reach what they consider to be equitable resolutions for intra-family disputes. The first case below, Kirksey v. Kirksey, illustrates the doctrinal approaches available under the earlier common law of contract to resolve intra-family disputes stemming from promises made but not kept. The second case, Harvey v. Dow, and the Notes which follow it, demonstrate some of the ways in which courts have employed promissory estoppel in such situations to provide protection to promisees when justice seemed to require that.

Kirksey v. Kirksey

Alabama Supreme Court 8 Ala. 131 (1845)

Assumpsit by the defendant, against the plaintiff in error. The question is presented in this Court, upon a case agreed, which shows the following facts:

The plaintiff was the wife of defendant's brother, but had for some time been a widow, and had several children. In 1840, the plaintiff resided on public land, under a contract of lease, she had held over, and was comfortably settled, and would have attempted to secure the land she lived on. The defendant resided in Talladega county, some sixty, or seventy miles off. On the 10th October, 1840, he wrote to her the following letter:

> Dear sister Antillico—Much to my mortification, I heard, that brother Henry was dead, and one of his children. I know that your situation is one of grief, and difficulty. You had a bad chance before, but a great deal worse now. I should like to come and see you, but cannot with convenience at present. . . . I do not know whether you have a preference on the place you live on, or not. If you had, I would advise you to obtain your preference, and sell the land and quit the country, as I understand it is very unhealthy, and I know society is very bad. If you will come down and see me, I will let you have a place to raise your family, and I have more open land than I can tend; and on the account of your situation, and that of your family, I feel like I want you and the children to do well.

Within a month or two after the receipt of this letter, the plaintiff abandoned her possession, without disposing of it, and removed with her family, to the residence of the defendant, who put her in comfortable houses, and gave her land to cultivate for two years, at the end of which time he notified her to remove, and put her in a house, not comfortable, in the woods, which he afterwards required her to leave.

A verdict being found for the plaintiff, for two hundred dollars, the above facts were agreed, and if they will sustain the action, the judgment is to be affirmed, otherwise it is to be reversed.

ORMOND, J.—The inclination of my mind, is, that the loss and inconvenience, which the plaintiff sustained in breaking up, and moving to the defendant's, a distance of sixty miles, is a sufficient consideration to support the promise, to furnish her with a house, and land to cultivate, until she could raise her family. My brothers, however think, that the promise on the part of the defendant, was a mere gratuity, and that an action will not lie for its breach. The judgment of the Court below must therefore be reversed, pursuant to the agreement of the parties.

NOTES AND QUESTIONS

1. *Analyzing* ***Kirksey***. In light of cases like Hamer v. Sidway, does it appear that the plaintiff in *Kirksey* suffered a "legal detriment?" Is it also

possible that her brother-in-law, the defendant, received from her actions a "benefit" —at least a legal one, and possibly a real one as well? If either of these questions should be answered affirmatively, could the court have held that the defendant's promise was supported by consideration? Perhaps, because he disagrees with the majority, the writer of the opinion does not shed much light on the question of why the court refused to find that the defendant's promise was supported by consideration. (If nothing else, *Kirksey* demonstrates the wisdom of the more usual practice of having a proponent of the decision write the opinion explaining it.) Recall Professor Williston's discussion of the "tramp hypothetical," quoted in the *Pennsy Supply* case in Chapter 2. Could Professor Williston's reasoning provide a rationale for the decision in *Kirksey*?

2. *Questions about* ***Kirksey.*** *Kirksey* raises a number of questions. Why did plaintiff's brother-in-law invite her to move to his part of the state? Was his promise to her altruistic or did he expect something in return? Why did the defendant evict plaintiff from the property? Since there were good arguments for both sides of the case, why did the court decide for what appears to be the less sympathetic party? Was there perhaps gender bias on their part? See Debora L. Threedy, Dancing Around Gender: Lessons from Arthur Murray on Gender and Contracts, 45 Wake Forest L. Rev. 749, 751 n.16 (2010) (comparing *Kirksey* and *Hamer v. Sidway*, and suggesting that gender may be one explanation of the different results in the cases). What happened to the parties after the case was over? For the answers to these and many more questions, see William R. Casto & Val D. Ricks, "Dear Sister Antillico . . . ": The Story of *Kirksey v. Kirksey,* 94 Geo. L.J. 321 (2006). See also Gerald Caplan, Legal Autopsies: Assessing the Performance of Judges and Lawyers Through the Window of Leading Contract Cases, 73 Albany L. Rev. 1, 40-45 (2009) (citing *Kirksey* as an example of a case in which the record did not reveal the real "deal" between the parties, making it difficult for appellate judges to properly decide the case).

Harvey v. Dow

Maine Supreme Judicial Court 962 A.2d. 322 (2008)

MEAD, J.

Teresa L. Harvey appeals from a judgment entered by the Superior Court (Penobscot County, *Hjelm, J.*) in favor of Jeffrey B. Dow Sr. and Kathryn L. Dow on Harvey's complaint seeking to compel the Dows to convey to her the land on which she built a house, or for damages based on the value of the house. Harvey contends that she is entitled to a judgment on theories of promissory estoppel or the existence of a confidential relationship. We note that the findings of the Superior Court do not address the actions of the Dows beyond their generalized statements of intent and the possible application of section 90 of the Restatement of Contracts thereto. We vacate the judgment and remand for further proceedings.

I. Facts and Procedure

Jeffrey Dow Sr. and Kathryn Dow are the parents of Teresa Harvey. The Dows own 125 acres of land in Corinth in two adjoining parcels, one fifty acres and the other seventy-five acres. They, their daughter Teresa, and their son Jeffrey Dow Jr. each have homes on the property. From the time they were young, Teresa and her brother talked about the houses they would eventually like to build on the homestead; Teresa said she wanted her home to be located near a spring, close to where it now sits. For their part, the Dows saw the land as their children's heritage that would be left to them or given to them when they were older. Jeffrey Sr. testified that when the children were teenagers, he believed that his wife had promised them some land in the future, and the subject of the children living on the homestead was commonly discussed within the family.

The Superior Court found that the Dows had a general, non-specific plan to transfer land to the children at some undetermined time. In the court's words, the "evidence at most reveals that Jeffrey Sr. expressed an intention to enter into an agreement to convey property sometime in the future," and "Kathryn had made it clear that eventually, both Teresa and Jeffrey Jr. would end up with all or part of the two parcels."

In 1999, Teresa and her future husband, Jarrod Harvey, installed a mobile home on her parents' land with their permission at the location where her brother's mobile home is now located. She did not pay rent and did not ask her parents for a deed. Later, she and Jarrod built a garage near the mobile home, again with the Dows' permission.

Around January 2003, Teresa and Jarrod, by then married, decided to build a house on the lot where their mobile home then stood. At the Harveys' request, the Dows agreed to use their home equity line of credit to initially finance the house. At trial, Teresa testified that part of the plan for repaying her parents included having them convey the building site to her by deed once the house was completed. Jeffrey Sr. denied any discussion of a deed at that time. In March 2003, Jarrod Harvey died in a motorcycle accident. Following his death, Teresa decided to finance the house with life insurance proceeds rather than use her parents' home equity line.

When it came time to do site preparation work for the new house, Teresa, her father, and her grandfather determined that it would cost no more to build further back on the property where Teresa had always wanted her house to be. Jeffrey Sr. agreed that she could build the house at its current site. Before construction began, Teresa and Jeffrey Sr. went to obtain a building permit from the town. There was no discussion of Teresa obtaining a deed at that point; she testified at trial that she did not ask her father for one directly because she did not need it then. The town initially denied Teresa a permit because she would not have the requisite amount of road frontage. A permit was eventually issued to Jeffrey Sr. for him to build another house on his property. Teresa testified that her father told her he would execute a deed to her for the property after the house was built; Jeffrey Sr. said there was no discussion about a deed.

Construction of the new house began in the summer of 2003 and was completed in May 2004 at a cost to Teresa of about $200,000. Jeffrey Sr. did a substantial amount of the construction himself, including much of the foundation work, and the carpentry, and helped to get underground electrical lines installed. In January 2004, while construction of the house was underway, Teresa lent $25,000 to her brother, Jeffrey Dow Jr. The record indicates that by the spring of 2004, around the time the house was completed, the relationship between Teresa and her parents and brother began to deteriorate over when and how the loan from Teresa to Jeffrey was to be repaid, and over the Dows' dissatisfaction with Teresa's partner, who lived with her. Eventually Teresa sued Jeffrey Jr. for the money, and the Dows filed a grandparents' rights action to see Teresa's children.

At some point after moving into her new house, Teresa began to ask Jeffrey Sr. for a deed so that she could obtain a mortgage to finance other projects. After a period of discussion, it became clear that the Dows were not going to execute a deed. At the time of trial, Teresa was paying the taxes on the house itself, but she was not paying the property taxes or any rent. Both Kathryn Dow and Jeffrey Jr. testified that they had no knowledge of Jeffrey Sr. ever offering or agreeing to deed any land to Teresa.

In March 2006, Teresa filed a seven-count complaint in the Superior Court, primarily seeking a judgment compelling the Dows to convey unspecified real property to her, or for damages on her claims of breach of contract, breach of fiduciary duty, and fraud. The Dows counterclaimed, seeking a judgment declaring that Teresa had no rights in their property. Following a two-day bench trial, the court found for the Dows on the real property claims and on their request for a declaratory judgment. Based on her assertion that the court failed to address whether she was entitled to a judgment on a theory of promissory estoppel, Teresa filed motions for further findings, to amend the judgment, and for a new trial. In a written decision, the court recognized that Teresa's argument was properly raised and then rejected it, finding that "[the Dows'] statements were not promises that could be enforced even if they were the subject of detrimental reliance," and concluding that "the plaintiffs have not established that Harvey received an offer or promise that can be enforced in this action." This appeal followed.

II. Discussion

A. Existence of an Enforceable Promise

Teresa contends that the Dows, having made general promises to convey land to her at some point and then assenting to her building a $200,000 house on their property in reliance on those promises, are now estopped from asserting that she has no rights to the land the house is located on. The Superior Court agreed that the Dows made general promises to convey land to Teresa, but concluded that they were too indefinite to enforce because there was no agreement on basic elements such as the boundaries or size of the property involved. We review the court's factual findings for clear error, and its legal conclusion that those facts do not make out a claim of promissory estoppel de novo. *Daigle Commercial Group, Inc. v. St. Laurent*, 1999 ME 107, ¶13, 734 A.2d 667, 672.

The doctrine of promissory estoppel "applies to promises that are otherwise unenforceable," and is "invoked to enforce [such] promises . . . so as to avoid injustice." Id. ¶14, 734 A.2d at 672 (quotation marks omitted). . . . It is an accepted doctrine in Maine. *June Roberts Agency, Inc. v. Venture Props., Inc.*, 676 A.2d 46, 49 (Me. 1996). We have adopted the definition of promissory estoppel set out in the Restatement (Second) of Contracts, which states:

> A promise which the promisor should reasonably expect to induce action or forbearance on the part of the promisee or a third person and which does induce such action or forbearance is binding if injustice can be avoided only by enforcement of the promise. The remedy granted for breach may be limited as justice requires.

Restatement (Second) of Contracts §90(1) (1981); *Bracale v. Gibbs*, 2007 ME 7, ¶14, 914 A.2d 1112, 1115.

Here, the record supports the trial court's finding that although they made general promises to Teresa that she would at some time receive some of their land as a gift or inheritance, the Dows did not make an express promise to convey a parcel of land of any specified size, or with any defined boundaries, at any time certain. The court was correct in finding that the existence of a promise to convey property was an essential element of Teresa's claim, and in holding that if there was no promise on which Teresa could rely, then her claim of promissory estoppel failed. . . .

If the evidence consisted only of the Dows' general promises to convey land as a gift or inheritance, we would agree that Teresa's claim of promissory estoppel should be denied. However, the evidence included an important second component: the Dows' acquiescence, support, and encouragement of Teresa's construction of a house upon the property and the application of section 90 of the Restatement of Contracts to those facts. Neither the initial decision and judgment nor the order on Teresa's motion for findings of fact addressed these critical points.

Against the backdrop of the parties' general understanding that Teresa would one day receive property as a gift or inheritance from her parents, she decided to build a new house on their land. Jeffrey Dow Sr. agreed to the location, obtained a building permit to allow construction at that site, and not only acquiesced in the house being built, but built a large portion of it himself. In a promissory estoppel analysis, "[t]he promise relied on by the promisee need not be express but may be implied from a party's conduct." *June Roberts Agency, Inc.*, 676 A.2d at 50; *see Nappi v. Nappi Distribs.*, 1997 ME 54, ¶9, 691 A.2d 1198, 1200 (stating that promise may be implied from a party's conduct).

At least as to the land on which Teresa's house now sits, a promise by Jeffrey Dow Sr. to convey that specific parcel could be implied from his conduct, and if that implication is made, given that Teresa now has an immobile $200,000 asset on that parcel, "[t]he circumstances [are] such that the refusal to enforce the promise to make a gift would work a fraud upon the donee." *Tozier v. Tozier,* 437 A.2d 645, 648-49 (Me. 1981); *see Nappi,* 1997 ME 54, ¶9, 691 A.2d at 1200 (stating that when applying the doctrine of promissory estoppel "[i]n the context of the transfer of land, when the donee has made substantial improvements to the land in reliance upon the promise to convey the land, courts will enforce the promise to convey." (quotation marks omitted)). Under these circumstances, a promise is enforceable notwithstanding a lack of consideration. *See Nappi,* 1997 ME 54, ¶9, 691 A.2d at 1200.

In *Tozier,* a father told his son that he could have a parcel of land to live on. 437 A.2d at 646. The son moved from where he had been living and built a house on the parcel with his father's help. Id. Years after the father's death, the son's brother made a claim to the property and eventually filed an action for possession. Id. at 646-47.

Analyzing the father's original parol promise to give his son a parcel of land, we said:

> [T]he enforceability of a promise *to make a gift* of land depends not upon contract principles, but upon principles of fraud. A mere showing that a donee incurred some detriment at the instance of the donor is insufficient to enforce a parol gift. When the donee, however, has made substantial improvements to the land, and the donee has made the improvements in reliance upon the promise to convey the land, courts will enforce the promise to convey.

Id. at 648 (emphasis in original). We then held that building a house constituted a "valuable and permanent improvement[]" such that "[t]o deny the [son] his rights in the property . . . would be both unjust and inequitable." Id. at 649. The same equities are applicable in this case.

The Restatement (Second) of Contracts also lends support to the inference that the Dows might have made an enforceable promise to convey the site of Teresa's house to her. It defines a "promise" as "a manifestation of intention to act or refrain from acting in a specified way, so made as to justify a promisee in understanding that a commitment has been made." Restatement (Second) of Contracts §2(1) (1981); *see* §90, reporters' note cmt. a (stating that "[o]n the meaning of 'promise,' see §2"). Jeffrey Dow Sr.'s actions in approving the site of Teresa's house, obtaining a building permit for it, and then building a substantial part of it himself at that location would seem to be "manifestation[s] of [his] intention to act . . . in a specified way"—namely a manifestation of his intent to confirm his general promise to convey land to Teresa and to direct it to that specific parcel.

In addition to giving a general definition of the term "promise," section 90 specifically discusses promises to make a gift. It explains that "[s]uch a promise is ordinarily enforced by virtue of the promisee's reliance only if his conduct is foreseeable and reasonable and involves a definite and substantial change of position which would not have occurred if the promise had not been made." Restatement (Second) of Contracts §90 cmt. f. An illustration to that discussion describes a scenario analogous to the one presented here:

> A orally promises to give her son B a tract of land to live on. As A intended, B gives up a homestead elsewhere, takes possession of the land, lives there for a year and makes substantial improvements. A's promise is binding.

Restatement (Second) of Contracts §90 cmt. f, illus. 16.

In sum, on the facts found by the Superior Court, Teresa's reliance on the Dows' general promise to give her land at some time, when coupled with their affirmative actions in allowing her to build a substantial house on a particular piece of their land, would seem to be eminently foreseeable and reasonable. From those actions, a promise by the Dows to convey that specific site could be fairly implied. Neither the absence of an explicitly articulated promise, nor the absence of consideration is a bar to enforcing that promise. The Superior Court erred in failing to consider the Dows' actions, in conjunction with their generalized statements, in determining whether the existence of a promissory estoppel is established on these facts. Accordingly, we vacate the judgment and remand the matter to the Superior Court for consideration of the issues identified herein. . . .

NOTES AND QUESTIONS

1. *Later history of* ***Harvey v. Dow****.* After the decision reported above, the *Harvey* case was returned to the Maine Superior Court, which then ruled that the plaintiff was not entitled to relief because it was not clear when the promised performance was to have been rendered by the defendants. On appeal from that decision, the Supreme Judicial Court held that it was clear from the facts that the defendants had implicitly promised the plaintiff a present conveyance of the land. This time the court remanded the case with directions to the court below to enter judgment for the plaintiff, and to determine the proper remedy for defendant's breach in light of the text of Restatement (Second) §90 and its Comment *d.* Harvey v. Dow, 11A.3d 303 (Me. 2011).

2. *The evolution of promissory estoppel.* While the rule of Restatement (Second) §90 is usually referred to as "promissory estoppel," you will note that the text of the section does not use that term. In addition to providing a convenient label, the term "promissory estoppel" is useful in distinguishing promissory estoppel from its doctrinal forerunner, "equitable estoppel." The doctrine of equitable estoppel (sometimes called "estoppel in pais") is generally said to apply where one party has made a misstatement of fact, rather than a promise. In its traditional form, equitable estoppel can be seen at work in cases like Hetchler v. American Life Insurance Co., 254 N.W. 221 (Mich. 1934) (insurance company estopped to assert true expiration date of life insurance policy where the insured relied on company's statement of later date by failing to extend term of policy before his death). The doctrine is still recognized today, although it is normally applied defensively. See Ford Motor Credit Co. v. Ryan, 939 N.E.2d 891, 921 (Ohio Ct. App. 2010) (holding that equitable estoppel is an affirmative defense rather than the basis of a claim for damages). Prior to the solidification

of promissory estoppel as a doctrine in the 1930s, some courts employed the doctrine of equitable estoppel to enforce promises made between family members, in circumstances where today promissory estoppel would probably apply. E.g., Ricketts v. Scothorn, 77 N.W. 365 (Neb. 1898) (promissory note given by grandfather to induce granddaughter to stop work enforced under doctrine of equitable estoppel).

3. *Promissory estoppel in the family context.* Harvey v. Dow is a recent case, but promissory estoppel has been used as a basis for enforcement of a promise in the absence of a contract in a family setting since the inception of promissory estoppel. One such early case was Greiner v. Greiner, 293 P. 759 (Kan. 1930), in which a Kansas court held the defendant had made an enforceable promise to give her son an 80-acre tract of land, inducing him to move from another part of the state.

Both *Harvey* and *Greiner* involved claimed promises to convey land, but the application of promissory estoppel in the family context is not limited to this fact pattern. One example is Wright v. Newman, 467 S.E.2d 533 (Ga. 1996). In *Wright* the plaintiff Newman sought child support for her son and daughter from Wright. Wright admitted paternity of the daughter, but not of the son, and DNA testing established that he was not the father of the boy. The Georgia Supreme Court held that a legally enforceable obligation to provide child support was not limited to principles of family law but could be based on contract doctrine, including promissory estoppel. The court found that Wright had listed himself on the child's birth certificate as his father and had given the child his name, even though he knew at that time that he was not the child's father. In addition, for more than ten years he allegedly held himself out to others as the child's father. These actions were sufficient to amount to a promise to provide child support, the court held, because he knew that parents had a legal obligation to do so.

4. *Necessity of an express promise.* In *Harvey* the Dows did not make an express promise to convey to Teresa the land on which she had built her house, but the court was willing to imply such a promise because Mr. Dow's actions in approving the site for the house, obtaining a building permit, and then building a portion of the house himself were a "manifestation of intention" sufficient to amount to a promise. Similarly, in Wright v. Newman, Note 3 above, the defendant did not make an express promise to support the child, but the court implied a promise from Wright's actions. Courts seem to have generally recognized that an estoppel, whether promissory or equitable, can be based on conduct as well as an express promise. E.g., Nappi v. Nappi Distributors, 691 A.2d 1198 (Me. 1997) (promise may be implied from conduct). The court in *Harvey* cited *Nappi* with approval. However, some courts may require a clear express promise. See Simpson v. Murkowski, 129 P.3d 435 (Alaska 2006) (promissory estoppel requires actual promise that is very clear). Do you agree with the view that promissory estoppel can be based on an implied promise?

5. *When is reliance reasonable?* In its discussion of the plaintiff's claim of promissory estoppel, the *Harvey* court spends most of its time on the issue of "promise" – whether the defendant had expressly or implicitly made a

commitment to the plaintiff sufficient to justify her claim of compensable detrimental reliance. Restatement (Second) §90, quoted by the court, provides (as did its predecessor in the first Restatement) that the promisee's reliance be "foreseeable," but does not specifically require that it be "reasonable." However, the section is captioned "Promise Reasonably Inducing Action or Forbearance," and Comment *b* to that section states that the requirement that enforcement be necessary to avoid "injustice" may depend in part on whether the promisee's change of position in reliance on the promise was reasonable. This may involve two possibly distinguishable issues: Whether it was reasonable for the plaintiff to rely at all, and whether the manner and degree of her reliance was reasonable. Does the plaintiff's reliance in the *Harvey* case pass that two-pronged test?

When a claim of reliance stems from an intra-family transaction, it is natural to assume that the promisee was justified in expecting the promisor to perform his promise, because of the familial relationship between them. E.g., both *Harvey* and the *Greiner* case discussed in Note 3, above. But in cases like these, it often appears that the plaintiff promisee did not seek legal counsel until after she had substantially relied on the promisor's apparent commitment to perform. Suppose that at the time she relied on the defendant's promise, the plaintiff had actually possessed sufficient knowledge of the rules of contract law to know that the promise made to her would not be enforceable under ordinary contract principles — because of lack of consideration, failure to satisfy the statute of frauds (discussed in the next chapter), or some other legal rule. Would that knowledge render her reliance on the promisor's apparent commitment "unreasonable"? In Bouton v. Byers, 321 P.3d 780 (Kan. Ct. App. 2014), the plaintiff alleged that she was induced by her father to leave her job as a law professor and come to work for him on his cattle ranch, by promises that he would bequeath to her land worth over $1 million. He later disinherited her, after several years of reliance on her part. In granting summary judgment for the father in the daughter's suit for reliance damages, the trial court gave as one of its reasons for dismissing her claim the plaintiff's "education and the circumstances as a whole." The Appellate Court responded to that finding as follows:

> We pause over the district court's reference to Bouton's education. The district court no doubt meant Bouton's legal training and her abilities as a capable and respected law professor. The district court apparently presumed that someone with that background would insist on a legally enforceable written agreement or contract memorializing a promise to transfer land. Most lawyers and law professors — and business executives, for that matter — surely recognize the benefits of written agreements to order their professional and financial affairs. And they would agree with the abstract proposition that oral promises may be difficult to enforce. But none of that translates into a rule depriving members of those groups of claims based on promissory estoppel as a matter of law. The district court's ruling, however, would have it that way.
>
> Reasonableness of reliance is quintessentially a fact question. Bouton's training and expertise do not change it to one that can be decided as a matter of law on this record. The district court's willingness to fashion that sort of a

> bar seems particularly inappropriate given the familial aspects of the dispute. The parties are father and daughter, not disembodied corporations undertaking a joint venture purely for business advantage. The land promised arguably appeared to be the family ranch rather than some portion of Byers' other real estate holdings. Leading up to the disputed promise, Bouton sought to help Byers at least partly out of a sense of fealty and devotion resting on their blood relationship. In turn, that relationship arguably caused Bouton to leave her sharper legal instincts in the classroom. All of those circumstances ought to be for the factfinder assessing reasonableness in a trial setting rather than on the inanimate summary judgment record of affidavits and deposition excerpts.

Id. at 798. See also Charles L. Knapp, Rescuing Reliance: The Perils of Promissory Estoppel, 49 Hastings L.J. 1191, 1286-1296 (1998) (arguing that reasonableness of reliance should depend on reasonableness of promisee's expectation that promisor will voluntarily perform, not the belief that promisor could be legally compelled to do so).

6. *Detrimental reliance.* Although the text of Restatement (Second) §90 speaks only of enforcement in order to avoid "injustice," the section is routinely referred to as protecting "detrimental reliance." In fact, the degree of detrimental reliance may be the most significant element in judicial determination that promissory estoppel should be invoked. In both *Harvey* and *Greiner*, while the existence of a promise was contested, the reliance was substantial: building of the home on parents' land in *Harvey* and moving from another part of the state in *Greiner*. When detrimental reliance is not so clear, a court may be less willing to apply promissory estoppel. In Wright v. Newman the Georgia Supreme Court found that the mother had detrimentally relied on Wright's implied promise to provide child support by refraining from seeking support from the child's natural father. According to the majority opinion, had she done so she might have had a source of financial support and the child might have received emotional support from the actual father. In dissent the Chief Justice argued that Newman had presented no evidence that she could have obtained child support from the actual father or that she was unable to do so at the time of the suit.

2. Charitable Subscriptions

If the bargain theory of consideration has as a principal function distinguishing exchanges from gifts (with enforcement to be accorded only to the former), then obviously charitable gifts will generally fall on the nonenforcement side of the line. In scores of charitable cases, courts have found consideration for the subscriber's promise, but the consensus of legal commentators appears to be that such analyses are often unconvincing, reflecting more a desire to uphold the gift than a genuine finding that a true bargain has been made. In an early study of the roots of promissory estoppel, Professor Boyer discussed at length the charitable subscription cases, suggesting that the use of promissory estoppel in this area has afforded courts a measure of relief from the vexing problem of whether and how promises of charitable contributions should be legally enforced. Benjamin F. Boyer, Promissory Estoppel: Principle from Precedents (Pt. 1), 50 Mich. L. Rev. 639, 644-653 (1952). The following case is a recent example.

King v. Trustees of Boston University

Supreme Judicial Court of Massachusetts 420 Mass. 52, 647 N.E.2d 1196 (1995)

ABRAMS, Justice.

A jury determined that Dr. Martin Luther King, Jr., made a charitable pledge to Boston University (BU) of certain papers he had deposited with BU. The plaintiff, Coretta Scott King, in her capacity as administratrix of the estate of her late husband, and in her individual capacity, appeals from that judgment. The plaintiff sued BU for conversion, alleging that the estate and not BU held title to Dr. King's papers, which have been housed in BU's library's special collection since they were delivered to BU at Dr. King's request in July, 1964.

The case was submitted to the jury on theories of contract, charitable pledge, statute of limitations, and laches. In response to special questions the jury determined that Dr. King made a promise to give absolute title to his papers to BU in a letter signed by him and dated July 16, 1964, and that the promise to give the papers was enforceable as a charitable pledge supported by consideration or reliance. The jury also determined that the letter promising the papers was not a contract. The jury accordingly did not reach BU's additional statute of limitations and laches defenses. The trial judge denied the plaintiff's motion for judgment notwithstanding the verdict or for a new trial. The plaintiff appealed. We granted the plaintiff's application for direct appellate review. We affirm.

Dr. Martin Luther King, Jr. and Coretta Scott King in 1964.

I. *Facts.* In reviewing the judge's denial of the plaintiff's motion for directed verdict on the affirmative defense of charitable pledge, we summarize the evidence in a light favorable to the nonmoving party, BU. . . . In 1963, BU commenced plans to expand its library's special collections. Once plans for construction of a library to house new holdings were firm, the newly appointed director of special collections, Dr. Howard Gotlieb, began his efforts to obtain Dr. King's papers. Dr. King, an alumnus of BU's graduate school program, was one of the first individuals BU officials sought to induce to deposit documents in the archives.

Around the same time, Dr. King was approached regarding his papers by other universities, including his undergraduate alma mater, Morehouse College. Mrs. King testified that, although her late husband thought "Boston seemed to be the only place, the best place, for safety," he was concerned that depositing his papers with BU would evoke criticism that he was "taking them away from a black institution in the South." However, the volatile circumstances during the 1960s in the South led Dr. King to deposit some of his papers with BU pursuant to a letter, which is the centerpiece of this litigation and is set forth herewith:

> 563 Johnson Ave. NE
> Atlanta, Georgia
> July 16, 1964
>
> Boston University Library
> 725 Commonwealth Ave.
> Boston 15, Massachusetts
>
> Dear Sirs:
>
> On this 16th day of July, 1964, I name the Boston University Library the Repository of my correspondence, manuscripts and other papers, along with a few of my awards and other materials which may come to be of interest in historical or other research.
>
> In accordance with this action I have authorized the removal of most of the above-mentioned papers and other objects to Boston University, including most correspondence through 1961, at once. It is my intention that after the end of each calendar year, similar files of materials for an additional year should be sent to Boston University.
>
> All papers and other objects which thus pass into the custody of Boston University remain my legal property until otherwise indicated, according to the statements below. However, if, despite scrupulous care, any such materials are damaged or lost while in custody of Boston University, I absolve Boston University of responsibility to me for such damage or loss.
>
> I intend each year to indicate a portion of the materials deposited with Boston University to become the absolute property of Boston University as an outright gift from me, until all shall have been thus given to the University. In the event of my death, all such materials deposited with the University shall become from that date the absolute property of Boston University.
>
> Sincerely yours,
> Martin Luther King, Jr. /s/

At issue is whether the evidence at trial was sufficient to submit the question of charitable pledge to the jury. BU asserts that the evidence was sufficient to raise a question of fact for the jury as to whether there was a promise by Dr. King to transfer title to his papers to BU and whether any such promise was supported by consideration or reliance by BU. We agree.

II. *Evidence of an enforceable charitable pledge.*[3] Because the jury found that BU had acquired rightful ownership of the papers via a charitable pledge, but not a contract, we review the case on that basis. We note at the outset that there is scant Massachusetts case law in the area of charitable pledges and subscriptions.

A charitable subscription is "an oral or written promise to do certain acts or to give real or personal property to a charity or for a charitable purpose." See generally E.L. Fisch, D.J. Freed, & E.R. Schacter, Charities and Charitable Foundations §63, at 77 (1974). To enforce a charitable subscription or a charitable pledge in Massachusetts, a party must establish that there was a promise to give some property to a charitable institution and that the promise was supported by consideration or reliance. Congregation Kadimah Toras-Moshe v. DeLeo, 405 Mass. 365, 367 & n.3, 540 N.E.2d 691 (1989), and cases cited therein.[4] See In re Morton 1200 Shoe Co., 40 B.R. 948 (Bankr. D. Mass. 1984) (discussing Massachusetts law of charitable subscriptions).

The jurors were asked two special questions regarding BU's affirmative defense of rightful ownership by way of a charitable pledge: (1) "Does the letter, dated July 16, 1964, from Martin Luther King, Jr., to [BU], set forth a promise by

---

3. The term "subscription" and "pledge" are frequently used interchangeably. . . . See generally Annot., Lack of Consideration as Barring Enforcement of Promise to Make Charitable Contribution or Subscription-Modern Cases, 86 A.L.R.4th 241 (1991). We note that, because of the bailor-bailee relationship between the donor and charitable institution, the transaction here technically is a charitable pledge. See R.A. Brown, Personal Property §15.1, at 469 (3d ed. 1975) (defining a pledge as "a bailment of personal property to secure an obligation of the bailor").

4. In Congregation Kadimah Toras-Moshe v. DeLeo, 405 Mass. 365, 540 N.E.2d 691 (1989), the Congregation sued the estate of a decedent who had made an oral gratuitous promise to give $25,000 to the synagogue. The Congregation planned to spend the $25,000 on renovation of a storage room in the synagogue into a library. The oral promise was never memorialized in a writing or consummated by delivery before the decedent died intestate. Noting that "[a] hope or expectation, even though well founded, is not equivalent to either legal detriment or reliance," id. at 366-367, 540 N.E.2d 691, we affirmed the judgment of the trial court that the oral charitable subscription was not enforceable because it was oral, not supported by consideration, and without evidence of reliance.

By requiring that a promise to make a charitable subscription be supported by consideration or reliance, we declined to adopt the standard for enforceable charitable subscriptions set forth in the Restatement (Second) of Contracts §90 (1981). See id. at 368, 540 N.E.2d 691. Section 90(1), as modified for charitable subscriptions by subsection (2), provides that, "[a] promise which the promisor should reasonably expect to induce action or forbearance on the part of the promisee or a third person . . . is binding if injustice can be avoided only by enforcement of the promise. . . ." We noted that, although §90 thus dispenses with a strict requirement of consideration or reasonable reliance for a charitable subscription to be enforceable, the official comments to the Restatement make clear that consideration and reliance remain relevant to whether the promise must be enforced to avoid injustice. Id. See Arrowsmith v. Mercantile-Safe Deposit & Trust Co., supra 313 Md. at 353-354, 545 A.2d 674 (rejecting argument that court should adopt Restatement [Second] of Contracts §90[2]); Jordan v. Mount Sinai Hosp. of Greater Miami, Inc., 276 So. 2d 102, at 108 ("Courts should act with restraint in respect to the public policy arguments endeavoring to sustain a mere charitable subscription. To ascribe consideration where there is none, or to adopt any other theory which affords charities a different legal rationale than other entities, is to approve fiction").

Dr. King to transfer ownership of his papers to [BU]?"; and (2) "Did [BU] take action in reliance on that promise or was that promise supported by consideration?" In determining whether the case properly was submitted to the jury, we consider first, whether the evidence was sufficient to sustain a conclusion that the letter contained a promise to make a gift and second, whether the evidence was sufficient to support a determination that any promise found was supported by consideration or reliance.

III(A). *Evidence of a promise to make a gift.* The plaintiff argues that the terms of the letter promising "to indicate a portion of the materials deposited with [BU] to become the absolute property of [BU] as an outright gift . . . until all shall have been thus given to [BU]," could not as a matter of basic contract law constitute a promise sufficient to establish an inter vivos charitable pledge because there is no indication of a bargained for exchange which would have bound Dr. King to his promise. The plaintiff asserts that the above-quoted excerpt (hereinafter "first statement") from the letter merely described an unenforceable "unilateral and gratuitous mechanism by which he might" make a gift of the papers in the future but by which he was not bound. In support of her position that Dr. King did not intend to bind himself to his statement of intent to make a gift of the papers he deposited with BU, the plaintiff points to the language which appears above the promise to make gifts of the deposited papers that "[a]ll papers and other objects which thus pass into the custody of [BU] remain my legal property until otherwise indicated, according to the statements below." According to the plaintiff, because of Dr. King's initial retention of legal ownership, BU could not reasonably rely on the letter's statements of intent to make a gift of the papers. We do not agree.

The letter contains two sentences which might reasonably be construed as a promise to give personal property to a charity or for a charitable purpose. The first statement, quoted above, is that Dr. King intended in subsequent installments to transfer title to portions of the papers in BU's custody until all the papers in its custody became its property. The second statement immediately follows the first, expressing an intent that "[i]n the event of [Dr. King's] death, all . . . materials deposited with [BU] shall become from that date the absolute property of [BU]" (hereinafter "second statement"). BU claims that these two sentences should be read together as a promise to make a gift of all of the papers deposited with it at some point between the first day of deposit and at the very latest, on Dr. King's death.

Before analyzing the first and second statements, we note the considerations governing our review. A primary concern in enforcing charitable subscriptions, as with enforcement of other gratuitous transfers such as gifts and trusts, is ascertaining the intention of the donor. . . . If donative intent is sufficiently clear, we shall give effect to that intent to the extent possible without abandoning basic contractual principles, such as specificity of the donor's promise, consideration, and reasonableness of the charity's reliance. *DeLeo,* supra 405 Mass. at 368 n.5, 540 N.E.2d 691. In determining the intention of Dr. King as expressed in the letter and the understanding BU had of that letter, we look first to the language of the letter, in its entirety, but also consider the circumstances and relationship of the parties with respect to the papers.

III(A)(1). *First statement.* Regarding the first statement, the plaintiff contends that it is not a promise but a mere statement of intent to do something in the future. . . . However, our interpretation of that first statement is strongly influenced by the bailor-bailee relationship the letter unequivocally establishes between Dr. King and BU.

A bailment is established by "delivery of personalty for some particular purpose, or on mere deposit, upon a contract, express or implied, that after the purpose has been fulfilled it shall be redelivered to the person who delivered it, or otherwise dealt with according to his directions, or kept until he reclaims it, as the case may be." 9 S. Williston, Contracts §1030 (3d ed. 1967), quoting State v. Warwick, 48 Del. 568, 576, 108 A.2d 85 (1954). . . . The terms of the letter establish a bailment in which certain "correspondence, manuscripts and other papers, along with a few of [Dr. King's] awards" were placed in "the custody of [BU]." The bailed papers were to "remain [Dr. King's] legal property until otherwise indicated." By accepting delivery of the papers, BU assumed the duty of care as bailee set forth in the letter, that of "scrupulous care." . . .

Generally there will be a case for the jury as to donative intent if property allegedly promised to a charity or other eleemosynary institution is placed by the donor in the custody of the donee.[5] The bailor-bailee relationship established in the letter could be viewed by a rational factfinder as a security for the promise to give a gift in the future of the bailed property, and thus as evidence in addition to the statement in the letter of an intent of the donor to be bound. Furthermore, while we have been unwilling to abandon fundamental principles of contract law in determining the enforceability of charitable subscriptions, see *DeLeo,* supra 405 Mass. at 368 n.4, 540 N.E.2d 691, second par. (declining to adopt Restatement [Second] of Contracts rule that charitable subscriptions enforceable without consideration or reliance where justice so requires), we do recognize that the "meeting of minds" between a donor and a charitable institution differs from the understanding we require in the context of enforceable arm's-length commercial agreements. Charities depend on donations for their existence, whereas their donors may give personal property on conditions they choose, with or without imposing conditions or demanding consideration. In re Field's Will, 15 Misc. 2d 950, 951, 181 N.Y.S.2d 922 (1959), modified, 11 A.D.2d 774, 204 N.Y.S.2d 947 (1960) ("Charitable subscription agreements can rarely be regarded as part of a bargaining agreement that provide for a quid pro quo"). In combination with the letter and in the context of a disputed pledge to a charity, the bailment of Dr. King's letters provided sufficient evidence of donative intent to submit to the jury the questions whether there was a promise to

5. We do not suggest that bailment of property allegedly promised to a bailee-charity creates an irrebuttable presumption of donative intent on the part of the bailor. Nor do we suggest that we would weigh bailment more heavily than evidence that the parties agreed to conditions or terms of a bailment that express a lack of donative intent.

Intent is our primary concern and a bailment may be evidence of donative intent. However, a bailor and a bailee-charity may agree to a contractual bailment in terms that make clear that the bailed property is not being pledged as a future gift or that the bailed property may remain in the custody of the charity or become the charity's property only if certain conditions are met. . . .

transfer ownership of the bailed property and whether there was consideration or reliance on that promise.[6]

III(A)(2). *Second statement.* [The second statement in Dr. King's letter — "In the event of my death, all such materials deposited with the University shall become from that date the absolute property of Boston University" — posed an additional legal issue because it did not take effect until his death. The plaintiff argued that this statement amounted to a will and that it was therefore unenforceable because it failed to comply with the statutory formalities for a will, including the requirement of at least two subscribing witnesses. The court rejected this argument. It found that the statute of wills did not prevent a person from making a contract or a promise to take effect at his death, and that was what Dr. King had done. — EDS.]

III(B). *Evidence of consideration or reliance.* The judge did not err in submitting the second question on charitable pledge, regarding whether there was consideration for or reliance on the promise, to the jury. "It may be found somewhat difficult to reconcile all the views which have been taken, in the various cases that have arisen upon the validity of promises, where the ground of defence has been that they were gratuitous and without consideration." Ives v. Sterling, 6 Met. 310, 315 (1843). There was evidence that BU undertook indexing of the papers, made the papers available to researchers, and provided trained staff to care for the papers and assist researchers. BU held a convocation to commemorate receipt of the papers. Dr. King spoke at the convocation. In a speech at that time, he explained why he chose BU as the repository for his papers.

As we explained above, the letter established that so long as BU, as bailee, attended the papers with "scrupulous care," Dr. King, as bailor, would release them from liability for "any such materials . . . damaged or lost while in [its] custody." The jury could conclude that certain actions of BU, including indexing of the papers, went beyond the obligations BU assumed as a bailee to attend the papers with "scrupulous care" and constituted reliance or consideration for the promises Dr. King included in the letter to transfer ownership of all bailed papers to BU at some future date or at his death. Trustees of Amherst Academy v. Cowls, 6 Pick. 427, 431 (1828) ("It seems that an actual benefit to the promisor, or an actual loss or disadvantage to the promisee, will be a sufficient consideration to uphold a promise deliberately made. Whether the consideration received is equal in value to the sum promised to be paid, seems not to be

---

6. The jury could have found on that evidence alone that the first statement in the letter expressing an intent to give all papers in BU's custody to it at some future date was not a mere statement of future intent when the bailment relationship is considered. However, there was evidence in addition to the bailor-bailee relationship which justified submission of the special questions on whether there was a charitable pledge to the jury. First, there was evidence the papers would be appraised for (Dr. King's) tax purposes. Second, as promised in the letter, Dr. King delivered additional papers after the initial boxes of papers were delivered. This evidence could be considered by a jury in determining whether Dr. King intended to be bound by his promise. Thus, the trial judge did not err in submitting to the jury the first special question on charitable pledge. There was evidence which the jury could weigh in determining whether the statement of intent to give a gift of portions of the papers was an expression of an intent to be bound.

material to the validity of a note . . . "); *Ives*, supra at 317-319; Ladies' Collegiate Inst. v. French, 16 Gray 196, 202 (1860).

The issue before us is not whether we agree with the jury's verdict but whether the case was properly submitted to the jury. We conclude that the letter could have been read to contain a promise supported by consideration or reliance; "[t]he issue [of whether transfer of ownership to BU was transferred by way of a charitable pledge by Dr. King] was, therefore, properly submitted to the jury, and their verdicts, unless otherwise untenable, must stand." Carr v. Arthur D. Little, Inc., 348 Mass. 469, 474, 204 N.E.2d 466 (1965) (evidence sufficient as matter of contract law to raise question of fact for jury as to existence of common employment). . . .

Judgment affirmed.

NOTES AND QUESTIONS

1. *Analyzing the **King** case.* Dr. King's letter had two statements expressing his intention regarding his papers. Was it necessary for the court to find both statements legally enforceable? Why? Note that the *King* case was brought in Massachusetts and decided by a Massachusetts jury. Do you think a Georgia jury would have been more sympathetic to the claim of Dr. King's estate? Why? Why was the case brought in Massachusetts rather than Georgia? What happens to Dr. King's papers that were not on deposit with BU at his death?

2. *The Restatement's proposed rule for charitable subscriptions.* As finally adopted by the American Law Institute, Restatement (Second) §90(2) provides, "A charitable subscription or a marriage settlement is binding under Subsection (1) without proof that the promise induced action or forbearance." A handful of courts have considered whether to adopt the approach of §90(2), jettisoning entirely the requirement of either consideration or reliance for enforcement of charitable subscriptions. See Salsbury v. Northwestern Bell Telephone Co., 221 N.W.2d 609 (Iowa 1974); In re Schmidt, 723 N.W. 2d 454 (Table), 2006 W.L. 2561231 (Iowa Ct. App.) (*Salsbury* holding not limited to written promise; oral pledge to church for building projects enforceable against estate). The *Salsbury* court offered the following rationale for its decision: "Charitable subscriptions often serve the public interest by making possible projects which otherwise could never come about. . . . [In addition,] where a subscription is unequivocal the pledgor should be made to keep his word." 221 N.W. 2d at 613.

In *King* the Supreme Judicial Court of Massachusetts joins several other courts that have rejected §90(2), but it does not offer any reasons for refusing to accept the Restatement recommendation. In Maryland National Bank v. United Jewish Appeal Federation, 407 A.2d 1130 (Md. 1979), the Maryland court justified its rejection of §90(2) on the following grounds:

> UJA would have us "view traditional contract law requirements of consideration liberally" in order to maintain what it believes to be a judicial policy of favoring charities. We deeply appreciate the fact that private philanthropy serves a highly important function in our society. . . . But we are not persuaded

> that we should, by judicial fiat, adopt a policy of favoring charities at the expense of the law of contracts which has been long established in this state. We do not think that this law should be disregarded or modified so as to bestow a preferred status upon charitable organizations and institutions. It may be that there are cases in which judgments according to the law do not appear to subserve the purposes of justice, but this, ordinarily, the courts may not remedy. "It is safer that a private right should fail, or a wrong go unredressed, than that settled principles should be disregarded in order to meet the equity of a particular case." . . . If change is to be made it should be by legislative enactment, as in the matter of the tax status of charitable organizations.

Id. at 1135-1136. Would a shift in the law to the approach set forth in Restatement (Second) §90(2) be desirable? What effect do you think it would have on charitable organizations and their potential financial supporters? The common law of contracts and the federal income tax treatment of charitable gifts are discussed and compared in William A. Drennan, Conspicuous Philanthropy: Reconciling Contract and Tax Laws, 66 Am. U. L. Rev. 1323 (2017).

3. *Other case examples.* Of course, even the adoption of Restatement (Second) §90(2) would not necessarily mean that every charitable subscription is enforceable. See, e.g., In re Bashas' Inc., 468 B.R. 381 (D. Ariz. 2012). In this bankruptcy proceeding a charitable medical organization sought to hold the bankruptcy estate of the debtors (apparently related business corporations) liable for promises of annual charitable gifts to be used toward construction of a medical facility. The bankruptcy court disallowed the claim, finding that the debtors' promises were made without consideration, and that promissory estoppel did not apply. On appeal, after finding that no consideration was given for the defendants' pledge, the U.S. District Court went on to affirm dismissal of the claim of promissory estoppel:

> Arizona has adopted the definition of promissory estoppel found in the Restatement (Second) of Contracts § 90(1) (1981). . . . The bankruptcy court found the appellants' claimed reliance "not credible," noting that the Barrow Tower was completed despite debtors' contribution of only a fraction of their pledged amount. Memorandum Decision at 3. We agree. There was no detrimental reliance here. Nor is there any injustice. Enforcement of the promise to the detriment of creditors who gave true consideration would be an injustice.
>
> The court then considered subsection 2 of § 90, which provides that "[a] charitable subscription or a marriage settlement is binding under Subsection (1) without proof that the promise induced action or forbearance." Although Arizona has not adopted subsection 2, appellants urged the bankruptcy court to apply this provision. It declined, preferring to "tread the more conventional path" by requiring consideration or reliance to make a charitable pledge enforceable. Memorandum Decision at 2. As of 2005, only two states, Iowa and New Jersey, appeared to have adopted subsection 2 of § 90. Evelyn Brody, *The Charity in Bankruptcy and Ghosts of Donors Past, Present, and Future,* 29 Seton Hall Legis. J. 471, 514 n.133 (2005). *See also* E. Allan Farnsworth, *Promises and Paternalism,* 41 Wm. & Mary L. Rev. 385, 404-05 (2000) ("The exception for charitable subscriptions has played to mixed reviews.").

> We doubt whether Arizona would or should adopt § 90(2). But even if it did, the promise is still not enforceable. While subsection 2 dispenses with subsection 1's requirement of reliance, the element of injustice still must be satisfied. Appellants have not shown that injustice can only be avoided by enforcement of this promise. Debtors experienced an extreme negative change in their economic situation after making the pledge. Appellants finished construction of Barrow Tower without the promised donations. Their existence was not threatened because the pledge was not paid, nor did they enter into binding contracts or suffer liabilities in reliance on the pledge. There is no evidence that other donors made pledges in consideration of the debtors' promise.

Id. at 383-384. How does Boston University's claim of reliance in *King* compare to the charity's in the *Bashas'* case?

While courts have generally refused to adopt Restatement (Second) §90(2), they have on the whole been sympathetic to the claims of charitable organizations to enforce pledges. In the leading case of Allegheny College v. National Chautauqua County Bank, 159 N.E.173 (1927), Judge Cardozo of the New York Court of Appeals held that a pledge to the plaintiff college by a donor, later deceased, was binding contractually on the ground that the college made an "implied promise" to memorialize the donor's name, thus creating an enforceable bilateral contract. In "dictum" (statements by a court not necessary to the decision of the case) Cardozo also indicated that the doctrine of promissory estoppel could be used to enforce donative promises that had been relied on by charities. Cardozo suggested that the willingness of courts to find liability on the basis of either a contract or promissory estoppel rested on public policy. In a later New York case, Woodmere Academy v. Steinberg, 363 N.E.2d 1169 (N.Y. 1977), the New York Court of Appeals enforced Mr. Steinberg's pledge in the unpaid amount of $200,000. Steinberg decided not to honor the pledge because he had moved from the community, his children were no longer attending the Academy, and he had decided to redirect the funds to support the State of Israel. The Court rejected Steinberg's argument that the Academy had failed to honor various conditions to the pledge, noting that "as a matter of public policy, pledge agreements calculated to enforce eleemosynary enterprises are enforceable." Id. at 1172. On the facts of the case, Steinberg's pledge was probably enforceable either on the basis of consideration or promissory estoppel because the Academy had renamed its library in honor of Steinberg's wife. For a more recent case similar to *Steinberg*, see The Paul & Irene Bogoni Foundation v. St. Bonaventure University, 913 N.Y.S.2d 154 (App. Div. 2010) (trial court order dismissing complaint by donor foundation seeking to impose additional conditions on its pledge affirmed; university allowed to collect balance of $900,000 on pledge of $2.5 million). But cf. In re Kramer, N.Y.L.J., Apr. 21, 2014 (Sur. Ct.) (charitable pledge would not be enforced where neither consideration nor substantial detrimental reliance were shown).

4. *Practical and legal constraints.* Comment *b* to Restatement (Second) §90 suggests generally that whether a promise should be enforced may depend in part on "the extent to which the evidentiary, cautionary, deterrent and channeling functions of form are met." In In re Payson, N.Y.L.J., July 26, 1978, at 14,

a New York Surrogate's Court enforced a promise to donate nearly $1.5 million (the unpaid balance of a $5 million gift promised during the decedent's lifetime) to the Metropolitan Museum of Art. Although there was substantial evidence that the promise was in fact made and adhered to by the decedent during her lifetime, the original promise was oral and informally made. While upholding the enforceability of the gift, the court cautioned both donors and charities against treating such gifts casually. Urging charities to adhere to "prudent business methods," the court noted that informality exposes donors (or their estates) to the risk of unforeseen tax problems. And, the court observed, even charities that are successful in obtaining court enforcement of casually made pledges may suffer harm: Potential donors could become more reticent about making gifts. In connection with the court's admonition about the dangers of informal practices by charities, consider the problem below.

5. *American Law Institute proposed solution.* As these materials indicate the circumstances under which a charitable pledge will be enforceable remain unclear. The America Law Institute is sponsoring a project attempting to clarify principles governing nonprofit corporations. Section 490 of the 2009 tentative draft proposes the following:

> (a) A charity may seek to recover from a donor who fails to fulfill a material pledge that the parties intended to be binding, but the decision to sue or to compromise is governed by the general fiduciary duties of §300.
>
> (b) The court will enforce a binding pledge to the extent enforcement would be fair under the circumstances.
>
> (c) Except as the governing board may otherwise specify in a policy covering the enforceability of pledges, a donor to a charity is presumed to intend that an oral promise or an ambiguous written instrument is binding in any of the following circumstances —
>
> (1) The donor has partially performed the pledge;
>
> (2) At the time of the pledge or as a result thereof, the donor served on the governing board or as an officer of the charity;
>
> (3) The charity reasonably relied to its detriment on the donor's promise; or
>
> (4) The promise induced one or more others to give to the charity, or counted towards a matching gift.

ALI, Principles of the Law of NonProfit Organizations, Donor's Failure To Perform A Pledge, Principles of the Law of Nonprofit Organizations §490 (T.D. #2, March 18, 2009) (on Westlaw). What is your opinion of the ALI proposal? How does it compare to Restatement (Second) §90(2)? Consider the solution proposed in the following problem.

PROBLEM 3-1

You are a legislative aide to a member of your state legislature. Another member of the legislature has introduced the following act dealing with charitable subscriptions:

Charitable Subscription Act

Section 1. Preamble. The legislature finds that uncertainty exists in this state as to the binding effect of charitable subscriptions or pledges. To protect the interests of charities and donors, and to reduce litigation, the legislature hereby adopts the following act, which shall be known as the "Charitable Subscription Act."

Section 2. Binding Charitable Subscription. A donor may make a charitable subscription or pledge that is legally binding against the donor or his estate, even though not supported by consideration, and not otherwise enforceable as a completed gift or contract, if it satisfies either of the following requirements:

(a) If the subscription is on a written form supplied by the charity, it must contain in bold face type, at least 10 point in size, on the front of the form, the following statement: **Legally Binding Pledge**.
(b) If the subscription is not on a form supplied by the charity, it must be in writing, signed by the donor, and contain clear language showing that the donor intends to make a legally binding subscription or pledge.

An oral pledge, not evidenced by a writing, shall be conclusively presumed to be nonbinding and may be revoked by the donor at any time until the gift is completed. Partial payments are completed gifts and may not be revoked. In construing this act, in case of doubt, a court shall construe a pledge or subscription as nonbinding.

Section 3. Effective Date. This Act shall take effect for all charitable pledges or subscriptions made after ___________________.

Your boss has asked you the following questions:

(a) What changes in the law would be made by the adoption of this act?
(b) As a matter of policy, would adoption of the act be wise?

Prepare a memorandum that addresses these questions.

3. Promises in a Commercial Context

Although significant amounts of money or property were often at stake, the cases examined earlier in this section did not involve transactions of the sort one ordinarily thinks of as commercial. Of course, one might view the operation of modern charitable organizations as commercial in every sense other than profitmaking; many of them receive and pay millions of dollars each year and in the course of their activities enter into all kinds of contracts for goods and services. (Cf. the suggestion in UCC §2-104, Comment 2 that for some purposes a university — and, presumably, other nonprofit entities such as a hospital or even a church — should be considered a "merchant," as that term is used in the Code.) But the promises of contributions made to charities have generally been viewed by donor and donee alike as essentially gratuitous, made from altruistic motives rather than for the purpose of reciprocal financial gain.

In its early days, the principle of promissory estoppel was often viewed as appropriately confined to the noncommercial sphere, with one significant exception: employee benefit or pension cases. You will recall from the *Plowman* case that an employer's promise to pay a pension or other benefit at or after retirement might not satisfy the requirement of bargained-for exchange. Professor Boyer's history of promissory estoppel showed that employee bonus and pension plan cases made an important contribution to the genesis of §90. In fact, one of the few illustrations to the original Restatement §90 presented such a case:

> 2. *A* promises *B* to pay him an annuity during *B's* life. *B* thereupon resigns a profitable employment, as *A* expected that he might. *B* receives the annuity for some years, in the meantime becoming disqualified from again obtaining good employment. *A's* promise is binding.

In his 1960 survey of the case law under §90, however, Professor Stanley Henderson concluded that promissory estoppel had outgrown any earlier limitations and that protection of unbargained-for reliance on commercial promises had become its principal application. Stanley D. Henderson, Promissory Estoppel and Traditional Contract Doctrine, 78 Yale L.J. 343, 343-344 (1960). In this section we examine a few situations in which courts have employed the doctrine to enforce commercial promises even in the absence of consideration.

Katz v. Danny Dare, Inc.

Missouri Court of Appeals 610 S.W.2d 121 (1980)

TURNAGE, Presiding Judge.

I. G. Katz filed three suits in the Associate Division of the Circuit Court seeking pension payments for three separate time periods alleged to be due from Danny Dare, Inc. Two suits resulted in judgment in favor of Katz, but a request for a trial de novo was filed and those cases were assigned to a circuit judge for trial. The other suit pending in the Associate Division was transferred to the same circuit judge and all the cases were consolidated for trial without a jury. Judgment was entered in favor of Dare in all cases. On this appeal Katz contends the promise of pension payments made to him by Dare is binding under the Doctrine of Promissory Estoppel. Reversed and remanded.

There is little or no dispute as to the facts in this case. Katz began work for Dare in 1950 and continued in that employ until his retirement on June 1, 1975. The president of Dare was Harry Shopmaker, who was also the brother of Katz's wife. Katz worked in a variety of positions including executive vice president, sales manager, and a member of the board of directors, although he was not a member of the board at the time of his retirement. In February 1973, Katz was opening a store, operated by Dare, for business and placed a bag of money on the counter next to the cash register. A man walked in, picked up the bag of money and left. When Katz followed him and attempted to retrieve the money, Katz was struck in the head. He was hospitalized and even though he returned to work he conceded he had some difficulties. His walk was impaired and he suffered some memory loss and was not able to function as he had before. Shopmaker and others testified to many mistakes which Katz made after his return at considerable cost to Dare. Shopmaker reached the decision that he would have to work out some agreeable pension to induce Katz to retire because he did not feel he could carry Katz as an employee. At that time Katz's earnings were about $23,000 per year.

Shopmaker began discussions with Katz concerning retirement but Katz insisted that he did not want to retire but wanted to continue working. Katz was 65 at the time of his injury and felt he could continue performing useful work for Dare to justify his remaining as an employee. However, Shopmaker persisted in his assessment that Katz was more of a liability than an asset as an employee and continued negotiating with Katz over a period of about 13 months in an effort to reach an agreement by which Katz would retire with a pension from Dare. Shopmaker first offered Katz $10,500 per year as a pension but Katz refused. Thereafter, while Katz was on vacation, Shopmaker sent Katz a letter to demonstrate how Katz could actually wind up with more take-home pay by retiring than he could by continuing as an employee. In the letter Shopmaker proposed an annual pension payable by Dare of $13,000, added the Social Security benefit which Katz and his wife would receive after retirement, and added $2,520 per year which Katz could earn for part-time employment, but not necessarily from Dare, to demonstrate that Katz would actually realize about $1,000 per year more in income by retiring with the Dare pension over what he would realize if he continued his employment. Shopmaker testified that he sent this letter in an effort to persuade Katz to retire.

Katz acceded to the offer of a pension of $13,000 per year for life, and on May 22, 1975, the board of directors of Dare unanimously approved the following resolution:

> WHEREAS, I. G. Katz has been a loyal employee of Danny Dare, Inc. and its predecessor companies for more than 25 years; and,
>
> WHEREAS, the said I. G. Katz has requested retirement because of failing health; and,
>
> WHEREAS, it has been the custom in the past for the company to retire all executives having loyally served the company for many years with a remuneration in keeping with the sum received during their last five years of employment;
>
> NOW THEN BE IT RESOLVED, that Danny Dare, Inc. pay to I. G. Katz the sum of $500.00 bi-weekly, or a total of $13,000.00 per year, so long as he shall live.

Katz retired on June 1, 1975, at age 67, and Dare began payment of the pension at the rate of $500 every other week. Katz testified that he would not have retired without the pension and relied on the promise of Dare to pay the pension when he made his decision to retire. Shopmaker testified that at the time the board resolution was passed, the board intended for Katz to rely on the resolution and to retire, but he said Katz would have been fired had he not elected to retire.

In the Fall of 1975, Katz began working for another company on 3 to 4 half-days per week. At the end of that year Shopmaker asked Katz if he could do part-time work for Dare and Katz told him he could work one-half day on

Wednesdays. For the next two and one-half years Katz continued to work for Dare one-half day per week.

In July, 1978, Dare sent a semi-monthly check for $250 instead of $500. Katz sent the check back and stated he was entitled to the full $500. Thereafter Dare stopped sending any checks. Shopmaker testified that he cut off the checks to Katz because he felt Katz's health had improved to the point that he could work, as demonstrated by the part-time job he held. Katz testified the decrease was made after Shopmaker told him he would have to work one-half day for five days a week for Dare or his pension would be cut in half. Katz testified, without challenge, that he was not able to work 40 hours per week in 1978 at age 70.

The trial court entered a judgment in which some findings of fact were made. The court found that Katz based his claim on the Doctrine of Promissory Estoppel as applied in Feinberg v. Pfeiffer Company, 322 S.W.2d 163 (Mo. App. 1959). The court found that Katz was not in the same situation as Feinberg had been because Katz faced the prospect of being fired if he did not accept the pension offer whereas there was no such evidence in the *Feinberg* case. The court found the pension from Dare did not require Katz to do anything and he was in fact free to work for another company. The court found Katz did not give up anything to which he was legally entitled when he elected to retire. The court found that since Katz had the choice of accepting retirement and a pension or being fired, that it could not be said that he suffered any detriment or significant change of position when he elected to retire. The court further found that it could not find any injustice resulting to Katz because by the time payments had been terminated, he had received about $40,000 plus a paid vacation for his wife and himself to Hawaii. The court found these were benefits he would not have received had he been fired.

Katz contends he falls within the holding in *Feinberg* and Dare contends that because Katz faced the alternative of accepting the pension or being fired that he falls without the holding in *Feinberg*.

At the outset it is interesting to note in view of the argument made by Dare that the court in *Feinberg* stated at p. 165:

> It is clear from the evidence that there was no contract, oral or written, as to plaintiff's length of employment, and that she was free to quit, and the defendant to discharge her, at any time.

In *Feinberg* the board of directors passed a resolution offering Feinberg the opportunity to retire at any time she would elect with retirement pay of $200 per month for life. Feinberg retired about two and one-half years after the resolution was passed and began to receive the retirement pay. The pay continued for about seven years when the company sent a check for $100 per month, which Feinberg refused and thereafter payments were discontinued.

The court observed that Section 90 of the Restatement of the Law of Contracts had been adopted by the Supreme Court in In Re Jamison's Estate, 202 S.W.2d 879 (Mo. 1947). The court noted that one of the illustrations under

§90 was strikingly similar to the facts in *Feinberg*. The court applied the Doctrine of Promissory Estoppel, as articulated in §90, and held that Feinberg had relied upon the promise of the pension when she resigned a paying position and elected to accept a lesser amount in pension. The court held it was immaterial as to whether Feinberg became unable to obtain other employment before or after the company discontinued the pension payment. The court held the reliance by Feinberg was in giving up her job in reliance on the promise of a pension. Her subsequent disability went to the prevention of injustice which is part of the Doctrine of Promissory Estoppel.

There are three elements to be satisfied to invoke the Doctrine of Promissory Estoppel. These are: (1) a promise; (2) a detrimental reliance on such promise; and (3) injustice can be avoided only by enforcement of the promise.

This court is not convinced that the alternative Shopmaker gave to Katz of either accepting the pension and retiring or be fired takes this case out of the operation of Promissory Estoppel. The fact remains that Katz was not fired, but instead did voluntarily retire, but only after the board of directors had adopted the resolution promising to pay Katz a pension of $13,000 per year for life. Thus, the same facts are present in this case as were present in *Feinberg*. When Katz elected to retire and give up earnings of about $23,000 per year to accept a pension of $13,000 per year, he did so as a result of a promise made by Dare and to his detriment by the loss of $10,000 per year in earnings. It is conceded Dare intended that Katz rely on its promise of a pension and Dare does not contend Katz did not in fact rely on such promise. The fact that the payments continued for about three years and that Katz at age 70 could not work full-time was unquestioned. Thus, the element that injustice can be avoided only by enforcement of the promise is present, because Katz cannot now engage in a full-time job to return to the earnings which he gave up in reliance on the pension.

Dare's argument that the threat of being fired removes this case from the operation of Promissory Estoppel is similar to an argument advanced in Trexler's Estate, 27 Pa. Dist. & Co. Rep. 4 (1936), cited with approval in Fried v. Fisher, 328 Pa. 497, 196 A. 39 (1938). In *Trexler* the depression had forced General Trexler to decide whether to fire several employees who had been with him for many years or place them on a pension. The General decided to promise them a pension of $50 per month and at his death, the employees filed a claim against his estate for the continuation of the payments. The court observed that the General could have summarily discharged the employees, but was loath to do this without making some provision for their old age. This was shown by the numerous conferences which the General had with his executives in considering each employee's financial situation, age and general status. The court said it was clear that the General wanted to reduce overhead and at the same time wanted to give these faithful employees some protection. The court stated it as an open question of what the General would have done if the men had not accepted his offer of a lifetime pension. The court said it would not speculate on that point but it was sufficient to observe that the men accepted the offer and received the pension. The court applied §90 of the Restatement and held that under the Doctrine of Promissory Estoppel the estate was bound to continue the payments.

The facts in this case are strikingly similar to *Trexler.* Shopmaker undoubtedly wanted to reduce his overhead by reducing the amount being paid to Katz and it is true that Katz could have been summarily discharged. However, it is also true that Shopmaker refused to fire Katz, but instead patiently negotiated for about 13 months to work out a pension which Katz did agree to accept and voluntarily retired.

While Dare strenuously urges that the threat of firing effectively removed any legitimate choice on the part of Katz, the facts do not bear this out. The fact is that Katz continued in his employment with Dare until he retired and such retirement was voluntary on the part of Katz. Had Shopmaker desired to terminate Katz without any promise of a pension he could have done so and Katz would have had no recourse. However, the fact is that Shopmaker did not discharge Katz but actually made every effort to induce Katz to retire voluntarily on the promise of a pension of $13,000 per year.

Dare appears to have led the trial court into error by relying on Pitts v. McGraw-Edison Co., 329 F.2d 412 (6th Cir. 1964). Pitts was informed that the company had retired him and would pay him a certain percentage of sales thereafter. Thus, the main distinction between this case and *Pitts* is that Pitts did not elect to retire on the promise of any payment, but was simply informed that he had been retired by the company and the company would make payment to him. There was no promise made to Pitts on which he acted to his detriment. In addition, the court was applying the law of Tennessee and the court stated that Tennessee had not adopted §90 of the Restatement. The court in *Pitts* found that Pitts had not given up anything to which he was legally entitled and was not restricted in any way in his activities after being placed in retirement by his company.

The facts in *Pitts* would not enable Pitts to recover under Promissory Estoppel in Missouri because there was no action taken by Pitts in reliance on a promise. The test to be applied in this case is not whether Katz gave up something to which he was legally entitled, but rather whether Dare made a promise to him on which he acted to his detriment. The legally entitled test could never be met by an employee such as Katz or Feinberg because neither could show any legal obligation on the company to promise a pension. The Doctrine of Promissory Estoppel is designed to protect those to whom a promise is made which is not legally enforcible until the requirements of the doctrine are met. *Pitts* is not applicable either on the facts or the law.

The trial court misapplied the law when it held that Katz was required to show that he gave up something to which he was legally entitled before he could enforce the promise of a pension made by Dare. The elements of Promissory Estoppel are present: a promise of a pension to Katz, his detrimental reliance thereon, and injustice can only be avoided by enforcing that promise. The judgment is reversed and the case is remanded with directions to enter judgment in all suits in favor of Katz for the amount of unpaid pension.

All concur.

NOTES AND QUESTIONS

1. *Analyzing the **Katz** case.* The trial court in *Katz* found that Katz "did not give up anything to which he was legally entitled when he elected to retire." Was the trial court simply (and mistakenly) applying the test for consideration? Or did it have something else in mind? In the Court of Appeals' opinion, Judge Turnage states, "The legally entitled test could never be met by an employee such as Katz or Feinberg because neither could show any legal obligation on the company to promise a pension." Of course, if Danny Dare had already been obligated to pay Katz a pension, then Katz wouldn't have needed to rely on the doctrine of promissory estoppel to enforce the company's promise. Can the trial court really have meant something that obvious? Or is the Court of Appeals unfairly representing the trial court's position? What do you think the trial court probably meant by the "not legally entitled" explanation of its decision? Is its position persuasive?

2. *When is reliance detrimental?* Although Restatement §90 does not use the term "detrimental reliance," that phrase is commonly used to refer to the section's requirement that the promise induce "action or forbearance" by the promisee. In many actions in which promissory estoppel is involved, the plaintiff will have made actual expenditures in reliance on the promise. Such conduct not only satisfies the requirement of "action or forbearance" in reliance on the promise but also constitutes reliance that is detrimental to the plaintiff. As the *Katz* case indicates, however, a change of position will often be sufficient to invoke promissory estoppel even if the conduct does not involve an expenditure of funds. E.g., Romano v. Site Acquisitions, LLC, 2017 WL 2634643 at *7 (D.N.H.) (evidence that defendant's promise of bonus induced plaintiffs to "hustle more and work harder," to "become more efficient," and finish work sooner, could support finding of sufficient detrimental reliance to satisfy §90). Further, in some cases a change of position that might be viewed as financially beneficial can nonetheless support an action for promissory estoppel. A case illustrative of such a situation is Vastoler v. American Can Co., 700 F.2d 916 (3d Cir. 1983). Vastoler accepted a promotion to a supervisory position in part because of the employer's promise of certain pension benefits. When the employer subsequently denied making the promise, Vastoler brought suit on the basis of promissory estoppel. The trial court granted summary judgment for the employer on the ground that Vastoler did not suffer financial loss because he was better off economically having accepted the supervisory position. In reversing that decision, the Court of Appeals made the following remarks on the issue of detrimental reliance:

> The second error in the district court's reasoning involves an even more fundamental deficiency. It failed to consider the human dynamics and anxieties inherent in supervisory positions. All jobs are not the same, and work involves more than one's "daily bread" and the weekly paycheck. Certain jobs have higher levels of stress and anxiety. Often, increased responsibilities torture the mind as well as the body. The different levels of stress associated with different jobs explains why some qualified people do not want to be President of Fortune

> 500 corporations, nominee for the Presidency of the United States, or foreman of their plants. Some privates do not want the decision-making burdens of majors and generals. . . .
>
> A jury could certainly find that when Vastoler changed his position from an hourly worker responsible for his individual tasks to a salaried supervisor responsible for approximately fifty subordinate employees he was forced to absorb additional stress and emotional trauma. As a supervisor, he would have had the additional responsibility for assigning jobs to workers, disciplining workers, and perhaps recommending that some be fired or laid off. The stress and emotional trauma inherent in such a supervisory position cannot be measured in purely financial terms. Therefore, the presence of detrimental reliance in this case is a sufficiently disputed issue for the trier of fact that summary judgment cannot be granted to American Can Company.

Id. at 919.

3. ***Katz** compared with **Hayes**.* Not all employees have been as successful as Mr. Katz. In Hayes v. Plantations Steel Co., 438 A.2d 1091 (R.I. 1982), the plaintiff Hayes, after 25 years of employment, announced his decision to retire, effective in six months. One week before his actual date of retirement, Hayes met with an officer of the defendant company, who promised him that the company "would take care" of him. After Hayes's retirement, the company paid him a pension for four years but stopped doing so because of financial conditions and a change of ownership. The trial court ruled that the company was contractually bound to pay Hayes his pension, but the Supreme Court reversed. The Court first held that even if the company had made a promise, the promise was not supported by consideration. Citing the classical requirement of consideration as bargained-for exchange, the Court concluded that Hayes's retirement could not constitute consideration because he announced his decision before the company made its promise. For similar reasons the court rejected Hayes's promissory estoppel theory. Under that theory Hayes was required to show that the promise induced detrimental reliance, and he could not do so because his decision to retire preceded the promise. Do you think the factual differences between *Katz* and *Hayes* warrant different legal results? For further discussion and comparison of *Katz* and *Hayes,* see Charles L. Knapp, Rescuing Reliance: The Perils of Promissory Estoppel, 49 Hastings L.J. 1191, 1254-1261 (1998).

4. *Promissory estoppel's role in avoiding "injustice."* In the *Katz* case, both the trial and appellate courts focused primarily on the issue of detrimental reliance in assessing Katz's ability to invoke promissory estoppel to enforce Danny Dare's promises to him. Besides the issues of foreseeable and detrimental reliance, §90 provides that the court should enforce a promise based on the promisee's reliance only where this action is needed to "prevent injustice." It appears from the facts recited by the court in *Katz* that the defendant's desire to induce Katz to retire was based at least in part on his physical and mental impairment, and that these may have been attributable to the injury he sustained in attempting to retrieve defendant's property from a thief. If these assumptions are correct, should those facts be relevant to Katz's ability

to enforce the defendant's promises to him? Should it matter whether Katz's attempt to retrieve the defendant's money was successful? Lamenting the courts' tendency to ignore the element of "injustice" when deciding whether to apply promissory estoppel, Professor Orit Gan has argued that the issue of injustice should play a larger role in the jurisprudence of promissory estoppel, and that this could well extend beyond "corrective" to "distributive" justice as well. Reviewing cases in a variety of areas such as employment, lending, insurance and franchising, Professor Gan argues that, particularly where there are imbalances of power between parties, a robust application of the "injustice" prong of promissory estoppel could promote both types of justice. She concludes:

> A significant justice element will . . . make promissory estoppel a more meaningful doctrine of contract formation. This will result in a more flexible, egalitarian, and conscionable contracting process. And more generally, this will result in a more inclusive and pluralist contract law. This will benefit first and foremost the underprivileged parties. But this is desirable also to parties generally, including dominant parties. It might be that in the short run, privileged parties profit from denying their promises after benefiting from the promisee's behavior. However, in the long term, all parties, including privileged parties, will benefit from promoting trust and cooperation between the parties, from protecting the reliance interest, and from including in contract law parties who have been excluded from it in the past.

Orit Gan, The Justice Element of Promissory Estoppel, 89 St. John's L. Rev. 55, 99 (2015).

Aceves v. U.S. Bank, N.A.

California Court of Appeals 120 Cal. Rptr. 3d 507 (2011)

MALLANO, P.J.

. . .

I. BACKGROUND

The facts of this case are taken from the allegations of the operative complaint, which we accept as true. (See *Hensler v. City of Glendale* (1994) 8 Cal. 4th 1, 8, fn. 3, 32 Cal. Rptr. 2d 244, 876 P.2d 1043.)

A. Complaint

. . . Plaintiff Claudia Aceves, a married woman, obtained a loan from Option One Mortgage Corporation (Option One) on April 20, 2006. The loan was evidenced by a note secured by a deed of trust on Aceves's residence. Aceves borrowed $845,000 at an initial rate of 6.35 percent. After two years, the rate became adjustable. The term of the loan was 30 years. Aceves's initial monthly payments were $4,857.09.

On March 25, 2008, Option One, the mortgagee, transferred its entire interest under the deed of trust to defendant U.S. Bank, National Association, as the "Trustee for the Certificateholders of Asset Backed Securities Corporation Home Equity Loan Trust, Series OOMC 2006-HE5" (U.S. Bank). . . . U.S. Bank, by way of a "Substitution of Trustee," designated Quality Loan Service Corporation (Quality Loan Service) as the trustee under the deed of trust. . . .

In January 2008, Aceves could no longer afford the monthly payments on the loan. On March 26, 2008, Quality Loan Service recorded a "Notice of Default and Election to Sell Under Deed of Trust." (See Civ. Code, §2924.) Shortly thereafter, Aceves filed for bankruptcy protection under chapter 7 of the Bankruptcy Code (11 U.S.C. §§701-784), imposing an automatic stay on the foreclosure proceedings (see 11 U.S.C. §362(a)). Aceves contacted U.S. Bank and was told that, once her loan was out of bankruptcy, the bank "would work with her on a mortgage reinstatement and loan modification." She was asked to submit documents to U.S. Bank for its consideration.

Aceves intended to convert her chapter 7 bankruptcy case to a chapter 13 case (see 11 U.S.C. §§1301-1330) and to rely on the financial resources of her husband "to save her home" under chapter 13. In general, chapter 7, entitled "Liquidation," permits a debtor to discharge unpaid debts, but a debtor who discharges an unpaid home loan cannot keep the home; chapter 13, entitled "Adjustment of Debts of an Individual with Regular Income," allows a homeowner in default to reinstate the original loan payments, pay the arrearages over time, avoid foreclosure, and retain the home. . . .

U.S. Bank filed a motion in the bankruptcy court to lift the stay so it could proceed with a nonjudicial foreclosure.

On or about November 12, 2008, Aceves's bankruptcy attorney received a letter from counsel for the company servicing the loan, American Home Mortgage Servicing, Inc. (American Home). The letter requested that Aceves's attorney agree in writing to allow American Home to contact Aceves directly to "explore Loss Mitigation possibilities." Thereafter, Aceves contacted American Home's counsel and was told they could not speak to her before the motion to lift the bankruptcy stay had been granted.

In reliance on U.S. Bank's promise to work with her to reinstate and modify the loan, Aceves did not oppose the motion to lift the bankruptcy stay and decided not to seek bankruptcy relief under chapter 13. On December 4, 2008, the bankruptcy court lifted the stay. On December 9, 2008, although neither U.S. Bank nor American Home had contacted Aceves to discuss the reinstatement and modification of the loan, U.S. Bank scheduled Aceves's home for public auction on January 9, 2009.

On December 10, 2008, Aceves sent documents to American Home related to reinstating and modifying the loan. On December 23, 2008, American Home informed Aceves that a "negotiator" would contact her on or before January 13, 2009 — four days *after* the auction of her residence. On December 29, 2008, Aceves received a telephone call from "Samantha," a negotiator from American Home. Samantha said to forget about any assistance in avoiding foreclosure because the "file" had been "discharged" in bankruptcy. On January 2, 2009, Samantha contacted Aceves again, saying that American Home had mistakenly decided not to offer her any assistance: American Home incorrectly thought

Aceves's loan had been *discharged* in bankruptcy; instead, Aceves had merely *filed* for bankruptcy. Samantha said that, as a result of American Home's mistake, it would reconsider a loss mitigation proposal. On January 8, 2009, the day before the auction, Samantha called Aceves's bankruptcy attorney and stated that the new balance on the loan was $965,926.22; the new monthly payment would be more than $7,200; and a $6,500 deposit was due immediately via Western Union. Samantha refused to put any of those terms in writing. Aceves did not accept the offer.

On January 9, 2009, Aceves's home was sold at a trustee's sale to U.S. Bank. On February 11, 2009, U.S. Bank served Aceves with a three-day notice to vacate the premises and, a month later, filed an unlawful detainer action against her and her husband (*U.S. Bank, N.A. v. Aceves* (Super. Ct. L.A. County, 2009, No. 09H00857)). Apparently, Aceves and her husband vacated the premises during the eviction proceedings.

U.S. Bank never intended to work with Aceves to reinstate and modify the loan. The bank so promised only to convince Aceves to forgo further bankruptcy proceedings, thereby permitting the bank to lift the automatic stay and foreclose on the property.

The complaint alleged causes of action against U.S. Bank for quiet title, slander of title, fraud, promissory estoppel, and declaratory relief. It also sought to set aside the trustee's sale and to void the trustee's deed upon the sale of the home.

B. Demurrer

U.S. Bank filed a demurrer separately attacking each cause of action and the requested remedies. Aceves filed opposition.

At the hearing on the demurrer, Aceves's attorney argued that Aceves and her husband "could have saved their house through bankruptcy," but "due to the promises of the bank, they didn't go those routes to save their house. [¶] . . . [¶] . . . [T]hat's the whole essence of promissory estoppel. [¶] . . . [¶] Prior to [American Home's November 12, 2008] letter, there's numerous phone contacts and conversations with [American Home], which was the agent for U.S. Bank, regarding, 'Yes, once we get leave, we will work with you, . . . and they did not work with her at all.' "The trial court replied: "The foreclosure took place. There's no promissory fraud or anything that deluded [Aceves] under the circumstances."

On October 29, 2009, the trial court entered an order sustaining the demurrer without leave to amend and a judgment in favor of U.S. Bank. Aceves filed this appeal.

II. Discussion

Aceves focuses primarily on her claim for promissory estoppel, arguing it is adequately pleaded. She also contends her other claims should have survived the demurrer. U.S. Bank counters that the trial court properly dismissed the case.

We conclude Aceves stated a claim for promissory estoppel. As alleged, in reliance on a promise by U.S. Bank to work with her in reinstating and modifying the loan, Aceves did not attempt to save her home under chapter 13. Yet U.S. Bank then went forward with the foreclosure and did not commence negotiations toward a possible loan solution. As demonstrated in its brief on appeal, U.S. Bank fails to appreciate that chapter 13 may be used legitimately to assist a borrower in reinstating a home loan and avoiding foreclosure after a default. . . .

A. Promissory Estoppel

" 'The elements of a promissory estoppel claim are "(1) a promise clear and unambiguous in its terms; (2) reliance by the party to whom the promise is made; (3) [the] reliance must be both reasonable and foreseeable; and (4) the party asserting the estoppel must be injured by his reliance." . . . ' " (*Advanced Choices, Inc. v. State Dept. of Health Services* (2010) 182 Cal. App. 4th 1661, 1672, 107 Cal. Rptr. 3d 470.)

1. *Clear and Unambiguous Promise*

" '[A] promise is an indispensable element of the doctrine of promissory estoppel. The cases are uniform in holding that this doctrine cannot be invoked and must be held inapplicable in the absence of a showing that a promise had been made upon which the complaining party relied to his prejudice. . . .' . . . The promise must, in addition, be 'clear and unambiguous in its terms.' " (*Garcia v. World Savings, FSB* (2010) 183 Cal. App. 4th 1031, 1044, 107 Cal. Rptr. 3d 683, citation omitted.) To be enforceable, a promise need only be ' "definite enough that a court can determine the scope of the duty[,] and the limits of performance must be sufficiently defined to provide a rational basis for the assessment of damages." ' . . . It is only where ' "a supposed 'contract' does not provide a basis for determining what obligations the parties have agreed to, and hence does not make possible a determination of whether those agreed obligations have been breached, [that] there is no contract." ' (*Id.* at p. 1045, 107 Cal. Rptr. 3d 683, citation omitted.) "[T]hat a promise is conditional does not render it unenforceable or ambiguous." (*Ibid.*)

U.S. Bank agreed to "work with [Aceves] on a mortgage reinstatement and loan modification" if she no longer pursued relief in the bankruptcy court. This is a clear and unambiguous promise. It indicates that U.S. Bank would not foreclose on Aceves's home without first engaging in negotiations with her to reinstate and modify the loan on mutually agreeable terms.

U.S. Bank's discussion of *Laks v. Coast Fed. Sav. & Loan Assn.* (1976) 60 Cal. App. 3d 885, 131 Cal. Rptr. 836 misses the mark. There, the plaintiffs applied for a loan and relied on promissory estoppel in arguing that the lender was bound to make the loan. The Court of Appeal affirmed the dismissal of the case on demurrer, explaining that the alleged promise to make a loan was unclear and ambiguous because it did not include all of the essential terms of a loan, including the identity of the borrower and the security for the loan. In contrast, Aceves contends U.S. Bank promised but failed to engage in negotiations toward a solution of her loan problems. Thus, the question here is simply whether U.S. Bank made and kept a promise to *negotiate* with Aceves, not whether, as in *Laks,* the bank promised to make a loan or, more precisely, to modify a loan. Aceves does not, and could not, assert she relied on the terms of a *modified loan agreement* in forgoing bankruptcy relief. She acknowledges that the parties never got that far because U.S. Bank broke its promise to negotiate with her in an attempt to reach a mutually agreeable modification. While *Laks* turned on the sufficiency of the terms of a loan, Aceves's claim rests on whether U.S. Bank engaged in the promised negotiations. The bank either did or did not negotiate.

Further, U.S. Bank asserts that it *offered* Aceves a loan modification, referring to the offer it made the day before the auction. That assertion, however, is of no avail. Aceves's promissory estoppel claim is not based on a promise to make a *unilateral offer* but on a promise to *negotiate* in an attempt to reach a mutually agreeable loan modification. And, even assuming this case involved a mere promise to make a unilateral offer, we cannot say the bank's offer satisfied such a promise in light of the offer's terms and the circumstances under which it was made.

2. Reliance on the Promise

Aceves relied on U.S. Bank's promise by declining to convert her chapter 7 bankruptcy proceeding to a chapter 13 proceeding, by not relying on her husband's financial assistance in developing a chapter 13 plan, and by not opposing U.S. Bank's motion to lift the bankruptcy stay.

3. Reasonable and Foreseeable Reliance

" 'Promissory estoppel applies whenever a "promise *which the promissor should reasonably expect* to induce action or forbearance on the part of the promisee or a third person and which does induce such action or forbearance" would result in an "injustice" if the promise were not enforced. . . . ' " (*Advanced Choices, Inc. v. State Dept. of Health Services, supra,* 182 Cal. App. 4th at pp. 1671-1672, 107 Cal. Rptr. 3d 470, citation omitted, italics added.)

"[A] party plaintiff's misguided belief or guileless action in relying on a statement on which no reasonable person would rely is not justifiable reliance. . . . 'If the conduct of the plaintiff in the light of his own intelligence and information was manifestly unreasonable, . . . he will be denied a recovery.' " (*Kruse v. Bank of America* (1988) 202 Cal. App. 3d 38, 54, 248 Cal. Rptr. 217, citation omitted.) A mere "hopeful expectation [] cannot be equated with the necessary justifiable reliance." (*Id.* at p. 55, 248 Cal. Rptr. 217.)

We conclude Aceves reasonably relied on U.S. Bank's promise; U.S. Bank reasonably expected her to so rely; and it was foreseeable she would do so. U.S. Bank promised to work with Aceves to reinstate and *modify* the loan. That would have been more beneficial to Aceves than the relief she could have obtained under chapter 13. The bankruptcy court could have reinstated the loan — permitted Aceves to cure the default, pay the arrearages, and resume regular loan payments — but it could not have *modified* the terms of the loan, for example, by reducing the amount of the regular monthly payments or extending the life of the loan. (See 11 U.S.C. §1322(b)(2), (3), (5), (c)(1); . . . By promising to work with Aceves to *modify* the loan in addition to reinstating it, U.S. Bank presented Aceves with a compelling reason to opt for negotiations with the bank instead of seeking bankruptcy relief. (See *Garcia v. World Savings, FSB, supra,* 183 Cal. App. 4th at pp. 1041-1042, 107 Cal. Rptr. 3d 683 [discussing justifiable reliance].) . . .

4. Detriment

U.S. Bank makes no attempt to hide its disdain for the protections offered homeowners by chapter 13, referring disparagingly to Aceves's bankruptcy case as "bad faith." But "Chapter 13's greatest significance for debtors is its use as a weapon to avoid foreclosure on their homes. Restricting initial . . . access to Chapter 13 protection will increase foreclosure rates for financially distressed homeowners. Loss of homes hurts not only the individual homeowner but also the family, the neighborhood and the community at large. Preserving access to Chapter 13 will reduce this harm.

"Chapter 13 bankruptcies do not result in destruction of the interests of traditional mortgage lenders. Under Chapter 13, a debtor cannot discharge a mortgage debt and keep her home. Rather, a Chapter 13 bankruptcy offers the debtor an opportunity to cure a mortgage delinquency over time — in essence it is a statutorily mandated payment plan — but one that requires the debtor to pay precisely the amount she would have to pay to the lender outside of bankruptcy. Under Chapter 13, the plan must provide the amount necessary to cure the mortgage default, which includes the fees and costs allowed by the mortgage agreement and by state law. Mortgage lenders who are secured only by an interest in the debtor's residence enjoy even greater protection under 11 U.S.C. §1322(b)(2). . . . Known as the 'anti-modification provision,' [section] 1322(b)(2) bars a debtor from modifying any rights of such a lender — including the payment schedule provided for under the loan contract. . . .

"Even though a debtor must, through reinstatement of her delinquent mortgage by a Chapter 13 repayment plan . . . , pay her full obligation to the lender, Chapter 13 remains the only viable way for most mortgage debtors to cure defaults and save their homes. Mortgage lenders are extraordinarily unwilling to accept repayment schedules outside of bankruptcy. . . . There is no history to support any claim that lenders will accommodate the need for extended workouts without the pressure of bankruptcy as an option for consumer debtors. Reducing the availability of [C]hapter 13 protection to mortgage debtors is most likely to result in higher foreclosure rates, not in greater flexibility by lenders." (DeJarnatt, *Once Is Not Enough: Preserving Consumers' Rights To Bankruptcy Protection* (Spring 1999) Ind. L.J. 455, 495-496, fn. omitted.)

"It is unrealistic to think mortgage companies will do workouts without the threat of the debtor's access to Chapter 13 protection. The bankruptcy process is still very protective of the mortgage industry. To the extent that the existence of Chapter 13 protections increases the costs of mortgage financing to all consumers, it can and should be viewed as an essential form of consumer insurance. . . ." (DeJarnatt, *Once Is Not Enough: Preserving Consumers' Rights To Bankruptcy Protection, supra,* Ind. L.J. at p. 499, fn. omitted.)

We mention just a few of the rights Aceves sacrificed by deciding to forgo a chapter 13 proceeding. First, although Aceves initially filed a chapter 7 proceeding, "a chapter 7 debtor may convert to a case[] under chapter []13 *at any time* without court approval, so long as the debtor is eligible for relief under the new chapter." (1 Collier on Bankruptcy, *supra*, ¶1.06, p. 24, italics added; . . . In addition, Aceves could have "cured" the default, reinstating the loan to predefault conditions. . . . She also would have had a "reasonable time" — a maximum of five years — to make up the arrearages. (See 11 U.S.C. §1322(b)(5), (d); . . . And, by complying with a bankruptcy plan, Aceves could have prevented U.S. Bank from foreclosing on the property. . . .

U.S. Bank maintains that even if Aceves had pursued relief under chapter 13, she could not have afforded the payments under a bankruptcy plan. But the complaint alleged that, with the financial assistance of her husband, Aceves could have saved her home under chapter 13. We accept the truth of Aceves's allegations over U.S. Bank's speculation. . . .

5. *Absence of Consideration*

U.S. Bank argues that an oral promise to postpone either a loan payment or a foreclosure is unenforceable. We have previously addressed that argument.

[The court then discussed prior cases holding that a written contract could be altered by an oral agreement and Civil Code §1698, which was modified in 1976, to provide as follows:

> A contract in writing may be modified by a contract in writing [or] by an oral agreement to the extent that the oral agreement is executed by the parties . . . . *Nothing in this section precludes in an appropriate case the application of rules of law concerning estoppel.* . . . (emphasis added by the court) — EDS.]

Finally, a promissory estoppel claim generally entitles a plaintiff to the damages available on a breach of contract claim. . . . Because this is not a case where the homeowner paid the funds needed to reinstate the loan before the foreclosure, promissory estoppel does not provide a basis for voiding the deed of sale or otherwise invalidating the foreclosure. . . .

B. Remaining Claims

The elements of fraud are similar to the elements of promissory estoppel, with the additional requirements that a false promise be made and that the promisor know of the falsity when making the promise. (See *McClain v. Octagon Plaza, LLC* (2008) 159 Cal. App. 4th 784, 792-794, 71 Cal. Rptr. 3d 885 [discussing elements of fraud].) Aceves has adequately alleged those facts. . . .

III. DISPOSITION

The order and the judgment are reversed to the extent they dismissed the claims for promissory estoppel and fraud. In all other respects, the order and judgment are affirmed. Appellant is entitled to costs on appeal.

We concur : ROTHSCHILD, and JOHNSON, J.J.

NOTES AND QUESTIONS

1. *The economic crisis, home foreclosures, and the impact on contract law.* *Aceves* is one of millions of foreclosure cases that have arisen because of the economic crisis that began in 2008. Another example is Dixon v. Wells Fargo Bank, N.A., 798 F. Supp. 2d 336 (D. Mass. 2011), which allegedly involved conduct perhaps even more egregious than that of the bank in *Aceves*. In *Dixon,* the court found that the plaintiff mortgagors stated a cause of action under the doctrine of promissory estoppel sufficient to enjoin the defendant bank from proceeding with a foreclosure sale. When the Dixons had sought to renegotiate their loan, the defendant bank told them they would have to stop making payments on their existing loan, which was current, and provide financial information before it would engage in negotiations. The Dixons did so, but the bank proceeded to initiate foreclosure proceedings anyway. Some courts in cases with similar facts have permitted the plaintiffs to proceed with their claims of promissory estoppel. Other courts have been less receptive. E.g., Rosen v. Bank of Amer., N.A., 2012 WL 6722060 (Cal. Ct. App.) (claim dismissed; *Aceves* distinguished); MacKenzie v. Flagstar Bank, FSB, 738 F.3d 486 (1st Cir. 2013) (pleadings did not adequately allege reliance; *Dixon* distinguished). The economic crisis has also raised a number of other difficult issues dealing with the enforceability of contracts when dramatically changed circumstances occur. We explore these topics in more detail in Chapter 8. See Nathan M. Crystal & Francesca Giannoni-Crystal, Contract Enforceability During Economic Crisis: Legal Principles and Drafting Solutions, *Global Jurist*: Vol. 10: Iss. 3 (Advances), Article 3 (2010).

2. *Will the plaintiff's case ultimately succeed?* It should be remembered that in many of the cases we study, including *Aceves*, the plaintiff has succeeded in convincing the court that her pleadings sufficiently stated a cause of action, and will withstand a demurrer or similar motion to dismiss. In many situations, that degree of success on the plaintiff's part will persuade the defendant to settle the case rather than carry on with (and pay attorney fees for) further litigation. This may not be the case, however, and the defendant may ultimately prevail in a trial on the merits. This apparently happened in Aceves's case. Aceves v. U.S. Bank, N.A., 2015 WL 6515185 (Cal. Ct. App.).

3. *Promissory fraud.* The *Aceves* court also stated that the plaintiff's allegations against the bank were legally sufficient to establish fraud. While a breach of promise may be actionable under either a contract or promissory estoppel theory, it is not normally actionable in tort as fraud because a claim of fraud requires a misrepresentation of a present fact rather than a promise to do something in the future. In some cases, however, a breach of promise may be fraudulent — if the promisor did not intend to perform the promise at the time the promise was made. In such a case, the promisor has misrepresented a present fact, namely the promisor's intention to perform the promise. Restatement (Second) of Torts §530 provides as follows: "A representation of the maker's own intention to do or not to do a particular thing is fraudulent if he does not have that intention." We will encounter more examples of promissory fraud in later chapters.

4. *Other commercial cases.* Since its promulgation in the 1930s, §90 has been applied to enforce a wide variety of promises in commercial situations. See, e.g., Cohen v. Cowles Media Co., 479 N.W.2d 387 (Minn. 1992) (news source allowed to recover on promissory estoppel theory from newspaper that breached promise of confidentiality); Chesus v. Watts, 967 S.W.2d 97 (Mo. Ct. App. 1998) (homeowners association had standing to bring promissory estoppel claim against developers to enforce promise to turn over common areas in good repair); The Superlative Group, Inc. v. WIHO, L.L.C., 2014 WL 1385533 (D. Kan.) (plaintiff asserted claim of promissory estoppel based on defendant's alleged promise to pay commissions to plaintiff for sales of season tickets to games of defendant's hockey team; defendant's motion for summary judgment denied).

On the other hand, courts have denied recovery when the defendant *failed to make a promise* on which liability could be based or when the plaintiff *failed to establish detrimental reliance.* See, e.g., Creative Demos, Inc. v. Wal-Mart Stores, Inc., 142 F.3d 367 (7th Cir. 1998) (food demonstration contractor failed to establish detrimental reliance element of promissory estoppel claim against grocery store chain for refusal to honor promise to retain contractor's services through specific date when contractor continued to earn substantial profit after promise was made); Jones v. Best, 950 P.2d 1 (Wash. 1998) (en banc) (vendor's promissory estoppel defense against real estate agent failed because evidence showed that real estate agent did not make promise to accept reduced commission).

5. *The Restatement (Second) view of promissory estoppel.* In light of the widespread acceptance of promissory estoppel as enunciated in §90 of the first Restatement, it is not surprising that the drafters of the Restatement (Second) chose to retain and expand the doctrine. As we noted earlier, the revised §90 has an additional subsection providing for enforcement of charitable subscriptions even without a showing of detrimental reliance. In addition, the drafters revised the text of §90 by adding a reference to the possibility of third-party reliance, by indicating that the remedy to be awarded "may be limited as justice requires," and by deleting the requirement that in order for reliance to be protectable it must be "definite and substantial." Various aspects of the Restatement (Second) approach to promissory estoppel are considered in Charles L. Knapp, Reliance in the Revised *Restatement:* The Proliferation of Promissory Estoppel, 81 Colum. L. Rev. 52 (1981).

6. *The CISG and promissory estoppel.* In Geneva Pharm. Technology Corp. v. Barr Laboratories, 201 F. Supp. 2d 236 (S.D.N.Y. 2002), plaintiff pharmaceutical manufacturer asserted a variety of claims against defendant competitor and raw material supplier, including antitrust, breach of contract, and tort. Because the plaintiff was an American corporation and the defendant Canadian, the CISG governed their contractual relations, and preempted the plaintiff's state law contract claims. The plaintiff's tort claims, on the other hand, were clearly not preempted. The plaintiff also asserted a promissory estoppel claim, however, and the court had to decide whether that was preempted along with the contract claim. Noting that the CISG in Article

16(2)(b) recognizes reliance, the court indicated that perhaps a reliance claim intended to establish a "firm offer" would be preempted by that provision. Here, however, the plaintiff's claim of promissory estoppel was a more general one asserted to make a promise binding, and the court held such a claim not to be preempted by the CISG. Accord Caterpillar, Inc. v. Usinor Industeel, 393 F. Supp. 2d 659, 675-676 (N.D. Ill. 2005).

7. *Bankruptcy and contracts.* Article I, §8, clause 4 of the U.S. Constitution authorizes Congress to enact "uniform Laws on the subject of Bankruptcies throughout the United States." Bankruptcy law is based on the policy that debtors sometimes need a fresh start to overcome a burden of debt that the debtor would otherwise be unable to pay. Without bankruptcy relief, those debtors would be unable to function as part of the economic life of the society. At the same time, the bankruptcy process can be misused by debtors, and the law contains a number of provisions to protect creditors from bad faith use of the bankruptcy process. Of course, as *Aceves* points out, a creditor may feel that the debtor is abusing the bankruptcy process, but if the debtor is asserting a right granted by law, that is not abuse.

The basic form of bankruptcy is a liquidation of the debtor's assets under chapter 7 of the United States Code, 11 U.S.C. ch. 7. In a liquidation, a court-appointed trustee assembles and sells the assets of the debtor to pay the claims of the creditors. In a chapter 7 bankruptcy, the debtor will not keep any assets, except those that are exempt from bankruptcy. If a debtor wishes to maintain its assets, it must seek court approval of some form of reorganization. For individuals with regular income, chapter 13 is a vehicle for such a reorganization. In a chapter 13 case, a bankrupt individual may be able to avoid foreclosure. Thus, it would have been to defendant's advantage to deter Aceves's shift from a chapter 7 liquidation to a chapter 13 reorganization.

Comment: The Status and Future of Promissory Estoppel

As this doctrine developed over the years, it came to have an independent significance, to be viewed not just as a subcategory of "contract," but as a distinct theory of action — one not necessarily grounded in the principles of contract or circumscribed by its limitations. See Kevin M. Teeven, A History of Promissory Estoppel: Growth in the Face of Doctrinal Resistance, 72 Tenn. L. Rev. 1111 (2005).

The remarkable growth and expansion of promissory estoppel since its incorporation in the first Restatement led Professor Knapp to suggest in 1981 that promissory estoppel had become "perhaps the most radical and expansive development of this century in the law of promissory liability." Charles L. Knapp, Reliance in the Revised *Restatement:* The Proliferation of Promissory Estoppel, 81 Colum. L. Rev. 52, 53 (1981). In a comprehensive review of the status of promissory estoppel almost two decades later, however, Professor Knapp suggested that a "reassessment appears to be in order," and that "1980 may have been the high-water mark for promissory estoppel." Charles L. Knapp, Rescuing Reliance: The Perils of Promissory Estoppel, 49 Hastings L.J. 1191, 1192 (1998). See also E. Allan Farnsworth, Developments in Contract Law

During the 1980's: The Top Ten, 41 Case W. Res. L. Rev. 203, 219-220 (1990) (failure of promissory estoppel to make headway in overcoming formal barriers to contract enforcement included as one of top ten developments).

One factor contributing to this more cautious appraisal of promissory estoppel was scholarly commentary critical of the doctrine. Since the early 1980s many scholars have questioned the intellectual foundations of promissory estoppel. Some writers have been directly critical of the doctrine. E.g., Jay M. Feinman, The Last Promissory Estoppel Article, 61 Fordham L. Rev. 303 (1992). In addition to outright criticism, a number of scholars have argued for "assent-based" theories of liability, less focused on reliance. E.g., Daniel A. Farber & John H. Matheson, Beyond Promissory Estoppel: Contract Law and the "Invisible Handshake," 52 U. Chi. L. Rev. 903, 945 (1985); Edward Yorio & Steve Thel, The Promissory Basis of Section 90, 101 Yale L.J. 111 (1991).

In assessing the status and future of promissory estoppel, however, scholarly commentary is less important than the extent to which the doctrine has been applied by courts. Virtually every jurisdiction has accepted the doctrine, see Eric Mills Holmes, Restatement of Promissory Estoppel, 32 Willamette L. Rev. 263 (1996), but the evidence is conflicting about the extent to which courts have used the doctrine favorably. See, e.g., Robert A. Hillman, Questioning the "New Consensus" on Promissory Estoppel: An Empirical and Theoretical Study, 98 Colum. L. Rev. 580, 589 (1998) (generally unsuccessful); but see Juliet P. Kostritsky, The Rise and Fall of Promissory Estoppel or Is Promissory Estoppel Really as Unsuccessful as Scholars Say It Is: A New Look at the Data, 37 Wake Forest L. Rev. 531 (2002); Marco J. Jimenez, The Many Faces of Promissory Estoppel: An Empirical Analysis Under the Restatement (Second) of Contracts, 57 UCLA L. Rev. 669 (2010). See also two articles by Professor Orit Gan: The Justice Element of Promissory Estoppel, 89 St. John's L. Rev. 55 (2015), and Promissory Estoppel: A Call for a More Inclusive Contract Law, 16 J. Gender, Race & Just. 47 (2013).

B. LIABILITY IN THE ABSENCE OF ACCEPTANCE: OPTION CONTRACTS, OFFEREE RELIANCE, AND STATUTORY LIMITATIONS ON REVOCATION

Having surveyed in the preceding section some instances of promise-enforcement despite the absence of consideration for the promise, we turn now to an issue that has proven to be problematic to the common law of contract for over a century: The principle of free revocability of an offer. What, if anything, can limit the power that an offeror possesses under traditional rules of contract law to freely revoke her offer at any time, without any requirement that she have a good reason for doing so — and even if she has in fact promised to keep her offer open?

In Chapter 2, we saw that the traditional method of mutual assent was through the process of offer and acceptance. We also encountered the fundamental Anglo-American common law rule that an offer is revocable unless and until it is accepted by the offeree, even if the offer itself expressly states that it cannot and will not be revoked. (Recall the *Normile* case.) This principle of free revocability, however logical it may have seemed as part of the structure of classical contract law, is certainly no manifestation of a necessary "natural law" of contract. For example, Article 16 of the CISG provides as follows:

> (1) Until a contract is concluded an offer may be revoked if the revocation reaches the offeree before he has dispatched an acceptance.
>
> (2) However, an offer cannot be revoked:
>
> (a) If it indicates, whether by stating a fixed time for acceptance or otherwise, that it is irrevocable; or
>
> (b) If it was reasonable for the offeree to rely on the offer as being irrevocable and the offeree has acted in reliance on the offer.

In this section of Chapter 3, we consider three possibilities: the offeree may have the benefit of an option contract; the offeree may have relied on the offer's continuing to remain available for acceptance; and statutory provisions may in some cases change what would otherwise be the common law's position on free revocability.

1. Option Contract

The offerees in the *Normile* case apparently believed they had the benefit of an option contract — an offer which (at least for some specified, or perhaps "reasonable," time period) they could delay accepting without losing the power of acceptance, even if the offeror should attempt to revoke it in the meantime. They turned out to be wrong, however, in part because the court in that case found that the seller had never expressly promised not to revoke her counter-offer to them. In the following case, the would-be buyer claims that the potential seller did in fact promise not to revoke his offer, and that he (the buyer) therefore retained the power to accept it, even in the teeth of the seller's attempt at revocation.

Berryman v. Kmoch

Supreme Court of Kansas 221 Kan. 304, 559 P.2d 790 (1977)

FROMME, Justice:

Wade Berryman, a landowner, filed this declaratory judgment action to have an option contract declared null and void. Norbert H. Kmoch, the optionee, answered and counter-claimed seeking damages for Berryman's failure to convey the land. After depositions were taken and discovery proceedings completed both parties filed separate motions for summary judgment. The trial court entered a summary judgment for plaintiff and held the option was granted without consideration, was in effect an offer to sell subject to withdrawal at any time prior to acceptance and was withdrawn in July, 1973, prior to its being exercised by Kmoch. Kmoch has appealed.

The option agreement dated June 19, 1973, was signed by Wade Berryman of Meade, Kansas, and was addressed to Mr. Norbert H. Kmoch, 1155 Ash Street, Denver, Colorado. The granting clause provided:

> For $10.00 and other valuable consideration, I hereby grant unto you or your assigns an option for 120 days after date to purchase the following described real estate: [Then followed the legal description of 960 acres of land located in Stanton County, Kansas.]

The balance of the option agreement sets forth the terms of purchase including the price for the land and the growing crops, the water rights and irrigation equipment included in the sale, the time possession was to be delivered to the purchaser, and other provisions not pertinent to the questions presented here on appeal.

Before examining the questions raised on appeal it will be helpful to set forth a few of the facts admitted and on which there is no dispute. Berryman was the owner of the land. Kmoch was a Colorado real estate broker. A third person, Samuel M. Goertz, was a Nebraska agricultural consultant. Goertz learned that Berryman was interested in selling the land and talked to Berryman about obtaining an option on the land for Kmoch. Goertz talked to Kmoch and Kmoch prepared the option contract dated June 19, 1973. Goertz and Kmoch flew to Johnson, Kansas, where a meeting with Berryman had been arranged. At this meeting the option agreement was signed by Berryman. Although the agreement recited the option was granted "for $10.00 and other valuable consideration," the $10.00 was not paid.

The next conversation between Berryman and Kmoch occurred during the latter part of July, 1973. Berryman called Kmoch by telephone and asked to be released from the option agreement. Nothing definite was worked out between them. Berryman sold the land to another person. In August, Kmoch decided to exercise the option and went to the Federal Land Bank representative in Garden City, Kansas, to make arrangements to purchase the land. He was then informed by the bank representative that the land had been sold by Berryman. Kmoch then recorded the option agreement in Stanton County. After a telephone conversation with Berryman was unproductive, Kmoch sent a letter to Berryman in October, 1973, attempting to exercise his option on the land. Berryman responded by bringing the present action to have the option declared null and void.

Appellant, Kmoch, acknowledges that the $10.00 cash consideration recited in the option agreement was never paid. However, he points out the agreement included a provision for "other valuable consideration" and that he should have been permitted to introduce evidence to establish time spent and expenses incurred in an effort to interest others in joining him in acquiring the land. He points to the deposition testimony of Goertz and another man by the name of Robert Harris, who had examined the land under option. Their services were sought by Kmoch to obtain a farm report on the land which might interest other investors. In addition appellant argues that promissory estoppel should have been applied by the trial court as a substitute for consideration.

An option contract to purchase land to be binding must be supported by consideration the same as any other contract. If no consideration was given in the present case the trial court correctly found there was no more than a continuing offer to sell. An option contract which is not supported by consideration is a mere offer to sell which may be withdrawn at any time prior to acceptance. . . .

We turn next to appellant's contention that the option contract should have been enforceable under the doctrine of promissory estoppel. This doctrine has been discussed in Marker v. Preferred Fire Ins. Co., 211 Kan. 427, 506 P.2d 1163. . . . In *Marker* it is held:

> In order for the doctrine of promissory estoppel to be invoked the evidence must show that the promise was made under circumstances where the promisor intended and reasonably expected that the promise would be relied upon by the promisee and further that the promisee acted reasonably in relying upon the promise. Furthermore promissory estoppel should be applied only if a refusal to enforce it would be virtually to sanction the perpetration of fraud or would result in other injustice.

211 Kan. 427, Syl. 4, 506 P.2d 1163. . . .

In order for the doctrine of promissory estoppel to be invoked as a substitute for consideration the evidence must show (1) the promise was made under such circumstances that the promisor reasonably expected the promisee to act in reliance on the promise, (2) the promisee acted as could reasonably be expected in relying on the promise, and (3) a refusal by the court to enforce the promise must be virtually to sanction the perpetration of fraud or must result in other injustice.

The requirements are not met here. This was an option contract promising to sell the land to appellant. It was not a contract listing the real estate with Kmoch for sale to others. Kmoch was familiar with real estate contracts and personally drew up the present option. He knew no consideration was paid for the same and that it had the effect of a continuing offer subject to withdrawal at any time before acceptance. The acts which appellant urges as consideration conferred no special benefit on the promisor or on his land. The evidence which appellant desires to introduce in support of promissory estoppel does not relate to acts which could reasonably be expected as a result of extending the option promise. It relates to time, effort, and expense incurred in an attempt to interest other investors in this particular land. The appellant chose the form of the contract. It was not a contract listing the land for sale with one entrusted with duties and obligations to produce a buyer. The appellant was not obligated to do anything and no basis for promissory estoppel could be shown by the evidence proposed.

An option contract can be made binding and irrevocable by subsequent action in reliance upon it even though such action is neither requested nor given in exchange for the option promise. An option promise is no different from other promises in this respect but cases are rare in which an option holder will be reasonably induced to change his position in reliance upon an option promise that is neither under seal nor made binding by a consideration, or in which the option promisor has reason to expect such change of position. (1A Corbin on Contracts, §263, pp. 502-504.)

When an option is conditioned upon a performance of certain acts, the performance of the acts may constitute a consideration to uphold a contract for option; but there is no such condition imposed if the acts were not intended to benefit nor were they incurred on behalf of the optionor.

The appellant argues that to assume Berryman gave the option without expecting something from him in return is to avoid the realities of the business world and that consideration was encompassed by a promise for a promise. The difficulty with that argument is apparent. Appellant did not promise to purchase the land. He was required to do nothing and any assertion that Berryman expected him to raise and pay money for the land as consideration for the option confuses motive with consideration.

In 17 Am. Jur. 2d, Contracts, §93, pp. 436, 437, it is said:

> The motive which prompts one to enter into a contract and the consideration for the contract are distinct and different things. . . . These inducements are not . . . either legal or equitable consideration, and actually compose no part of the contract. . . .

In 1 Williston on Contracts, 3d ed., §111, p. 439, it is stated:

> Though desire to obtain the consideration for a promise may be, and ordinarily is, the motive inducing the promisor to enter into a contract, yet this is not essential nor, on the other hand, can any motive serve in itself as consideration. . . .

Appellant here confuses Berryman's possible motives — to sell the land — with consideration given. The fact Berryman expected appellant to expend time and money to find a buyer is really irrelevant because he was not bound to do so. He made no promise legally enforceable by Berryman to that effect. To be sufficient consideration, a promise must impose a legal obligation on the promisor. (17 Am. Jur. 2d, Contracts, §105, pp. 450-451.) As stated in 1A Corbin on Contracts, §263, p. 505: ". . . So, if the only consideration is an illusory promise, there is no contract and no binding option, although there may still be an operative offer and a power of acceptance."

Time and money spent by a party in trying to sell property for which he holds an option cannot be construed as a consideration to the party from whom he has secured the option. . . .

Two cases relied on by appellant to support his position are Talbott v. Nibert, supra, and Steel v. Eagle, 207 Kan. 146, 483 P.2d 1063. They are not persuasive and are readily distinguishable on the facts.

In *Talbott* the plaintiff had acquired an option to purchase majority stock interests in an oil drilling company from another stockholder. In reliance on the option plaintiff personally obtained valuable drilling contracts for the company, paid off a $23,000.00 mortgage on a drilling rig and pulled the company out of financial straits. During this time the stock had increased in value from

$90.00 per share to $250.00 per share, largely as a result of plaintiff's efforts. It was plaintiff's intention to acquire a controlling interest in the company by exercising the option, this the optionor knew. The court found the option-offer was duly accepted and the purchase price was tendered before revocation. In our present case the option-offer was withdrawn before acceptance. We will discuss the withdrawal of the option later in this opinion.

In *Steel* the option was for the sale of a milling company. The option agreement stated that the optionee promised to place $5,000.00 with an escrow agent no later than a specified time in the future and that if the option was not exercised according to its terms the $5,000.00 would be forfeited. It was held that the option was adequately supported by consideration, a promise for a promise. The optionor granted the option and promised to transfer title to the company. The optionee promised to pay $5,000.00 as evidence of good faith, said sum to be forfeited in event the option was not exercised. This is not the case here. Our present option recited a completed payment of $10.00, even though it had not been paid. Payment during the option period was not contemplated by either party and the tender of the $10.00 was not made by defendant-appellant in his counter-claim when that pleading was filed.

Now we turn to the question of revocation or withdrawal of the option-promise before acceptance.

Where an offer is for the sale of an interest in land or in other things, if the offeror, after making the offer, sells or contracts to sell the interest to another person, and the offeree acquires reliable information of that fact, before he has exercised his power of creating a contract by acceptance of the offer, the offer is revoked.

In Restatement of the Law, Second, Contracts, §42, p. 96, it is said:

> An offeree's power of acceptance is terminated when the offeror takes definite action inconsistent with an intention to enter into the proposed contract and the offeree acquires reliable information to that effect.

The appellant in his deposition admitted that he was advised in July, 1973, by telephone that Berryman no longer wanted to be obligated by the option. Appellant further admitted that he was advised in August, 1973, by a representative of the Federal Land Bank, which held a substantial mortgage on the land, that Berryman had disposed of this land. The appellant's power of acceptance was terminated thereby and any attempted exercise of the option in October came too late when you consider the appellant's own admissions.

Summary judgment was therefore proper and the judgment is affirmed.

NOTES AND QUESTIONS

1. *Option as consideration-supported contract.* In Chapter 2, we encountered the fundamental common law rule that an offer generally is freely revocable unless and until it is accepted by the offeree, even if the offer itself expressly states that it will not be revoked. See Restatement (Second) §42, Comment *a*.

As the court in *Berryman* recognizes, however, the offeror's power of revocation may be bargained away in exchange for return consideration. Such a contract restricting the power to revoke an offer is usually referred to as an "option contract." But like contracts generally, it must be made for consideration to be enforceable. See, e.g., Polk v. BHRGU Avon Properties, LLC, 946 So. 2d 1120 (Fla. Dist. Ct. App. 2006) (purported option contract without consideration is merely continuing offer, may be revoked any time before acceptance, and will be terminated by the offeree's rejection or counter-offer). In contrast with *Normile* and *Berryman*, examples of enforceable option contracts are plentiful. See, e.g., Harley v. Indian Spring Land Co., 3 A.3d 992 (Conn. App. Ct. 2010) (payment of refundable $10,000 "good faith deposit" was consideration to bind option contract to purchase land for $1.2 million; detriment suffered by losing use of deposited money was sufficient consideration); Terraces of Sunset Park, LLC v. Chamberlin, 929 N.E.2d 1161 (Ill. App. Ct. 2010) (payment of nonrefundable $100,000 fee provided consideration for two-year option to purchase land for price of $1,750,000). To hold seller Berryman to a contract with plaintiff Kmoch, the court would — among other things — have to find that the seller had made a promise not to revoke his offer for the stated time period. Does the court so interpret the writing signed by *Berryman*? Would you?

Option contracts serve a useful purpose in commercial relations, by permitting one who is considering a contractual transaction to delay committing herself to the contemplated exchange without fearing that such delay will cost her the ability to enter into that contract, should she eventually decide to accept it. The optionee thus has some time to consider the deal before committing to the actual contract to purchase, giving her a chance perhaps to investigate its feasibility or desirability or to make related arrangements. On the other hand, the optionee is also free simply to allow the option to lapse and not exercise the right to enter the principal contract. In that case the consideration paid for the option is presumably retained by the offeror, unless the parties have agreed otherwise. There are a number of issues that can arise in connection with option contracts, as discussed below.

2. *Nominal consideration.* Apart from the possible payment of substantial consideration, as illustrated in the cases noted above, option contracts will often recite the payment of what is traditionally called "nominal" consideration, such as $10, $5, or perhaps even as little as $1. The question thus arises whether the payment of such nominal consideration will make the option contract enforceable, since it appears not to have been the actual inducement for granting the option. (Do you think it was the actual inducement in *Berryman*?) The cases generally appear to hold that even a very small amount of money can serve as effective consideration to make an option contract irrevocable. See Board of Control of Eastern Michigan Univ. v. Burgess, 206 N.W.2d 256 (Mich. Ct. App. 1973) ($1, if paid or at least tendered, could be sufficient consideration for 60-day option to buy house for $14,000); Keaster v. Bozik, 623 P.2d 1376 (Mont. 1981) ($5 could be sufficient consideration to bind one-year option to purchase land for $200,000). Some courts have even found consideration in an implied promise on the part of the option holder to pay the nominal

consideration at some later time. See, e.g., Smith v. Wheeler, 210 S.E.2d 702 (Ga. 1974) (recital of consideration "gives rise to an implied promise to pay which can be enforced by the other party"). Note that this minimalist approach to consideration appears to some extent to be inconsistent with the Restatement (Second) position that "nominal consideration" generally is not effective. See Restatement (Second) §79, Comment *d* ("sham or 'nominal' consideration does not satisfy the requirement of §71").

3. *Services as consideration.* Consistent with the definition of consideration in Restatement (Second) §71, the offeree in an option contract may give services or some other form of consideration instead of the payment of money. The services could be acts such as conducting engineering studies of the land, engaging in efforts to obtain a loan to finance the purchase, or searching for investors, if that performance was bargained for as the price of the option. See, e.g., Mack v. Coker, 523 P.2d 1342 (Ariz. Ct. App. 1974) (purchaser promised to make efforts to obtain a loan); In re Estate of Jorstad, 447 N.W.2d 283 (N. D. 1989) (son's promise to stay and work on parents' farm was sufficient consideration to enforce their promise to sell farm to him for $70,000). Does the *Berryman* court convincingly reject the plaintiff's argument that he had performed services sufficient to serve as consideration for the defendant's promise to keep his offer open?

4. *Should use of a "formality" be effective to create an option contract?* In Restatement (Second) §87(1)(a), the drafters suggested an additional rule for option contracts, making an option enforceable if it is stated in a writing signed by the offeror which "recites a purported consideration" for its making and "proposes an exchange on fair terms within a reasonable time." If the payment of a sum as small as $5 or $10 can be enough consideration to bind an option contract, should such a contract be enforced even if the recited payment was not actually made, but only "purported"? Although traditionally most courts would (like the *Berryman* court) require that the nominal consideration actually be paid, the Restatement (Second) §87(1)(a) adopts a different approach. Comment *c* to §87 frankly refers to this rule as one that calls for enforcement on the basis of a "false recital of nominal consideration." The comment explains that the rule is based on form rather than on the implication of a promise: The signed writing has "vital significance as a formality," and therefore its recital of consideration should not be open to invalidation by "oral testimony which is easily fabricated." After an extensive review of the issue, the Texas Supreme Court in 1464-Eight, Ltd. v. Joppich, 154 S.W.3d 101 (Tex. 2004), adopted the position of Restatement (Second) §87(1)(a); the option contract was in a writing signed by the respondent, acknowledged the receipt of ten dollars as consideration, and proposed the sale of land on fair terms within a reasonable time. The court recognized, however, that its new rule was the minority position. See also Knott v. Racicot, 812 N.E.2d 1207 (Mass. 2004) (adopting the Restatement (Second) §87(1)(a) approach). No one involved in the *Berryman* case appears to have been aware of this possibility. If the plaintiff in *Berryman* had persuaded the court to adopt in general the rule of Restatement (Second) §87(1)(a), would it necessarily follow that the writing

in that case would have satisfied that rule, making the seller's offer irrevocable until its stated deadline?

5. *Other formality rules as grounds for enforcing an option contract.* Recall that the plaintiffs in *Normile* argued (unsuccessfully) that an option contract made under seal would be enforceable on that basis alone. While the seal has lost most of its vitality, the *Normile* opinion correctly indicates that the area of option contracts is one where a seal may still have legal significance. Cf. Knott v. Racicot, 812 N.E.2d 1207 (Mass. 2004) (discussing the history and declining importance of the seal; abolishing the common law rule that option contracts under seal import consideration). Note that the approach stated in Restatement (Second) §87(1)(a) is a modern formality rule somewhat akin to having a contract under seal. Moreover, UCC §2-205, the Code's "firm offer" rule, adopts a formality standard that may render an option contract for the sale of goods enforceable without consideration. That rule is discussed in the next section of this chapter.

6. *Application of the "mailbox rule" to option contracts.* Should an option contract be an exception to the deposited-acceptance rule, so that even if use of the mail is contemplated, an acceptance to be effective must be *received* by the offeror within the time limit specified? The Restatement (Second) takes this position in §63(b); Comment *f* explains "the usual understanding is that the notification that the option has been exercised must be received by the offeror" before the stated time limit. Not all courts agree, however. In Worms v. Burgess, 620 P.2d 455 (Okla. Ct. App. 1980), the court rejected the Restatement position, on the ground that the "mailbox rule" is so widely known that the parties to an option contract should be presumed to have contracted with reference to that rule unless they have expressly provided otherwise. Accord Pennsylvania Academy of Fine Arts v. Grant, 590 A.2d 9 (Pa. Super. Ct. 1991).

7. *Effectiveness of revocation.* At the risk of stating the obvious, it should be recalled here that even if the offer is held to have been revocable, acceptance of that offer will ordinarily still bind the offeror to a contract unless a valid revocation was received by the offeree before acceptance. See, e.g., I. R. Kirk Farms, Inc. v. Pointer, 897 S.W.2d 183 (Mo. Ct. App. 1995) (even if option is unenforceable due to lack of consideration, offer reflected in option may be accepted prior to revocation). In *Berryman,* the court found that the offer was revocable; did the offeror effectively revoke it in his phone conversation with Kmoch in late July? If not, then it was apparently terminated in August, when he learned from a bank representative that the seller had sold the land to someone else. This rule of indirect communication of revocation, currently expressed in Restatement (Second) §43, was established by the English case of Dickinson v. Dodds, 2 Ch. Div. 463 (1876). You may recall that we first encountered the *Dickinson* rule in Normile v. Miller early in Chapter 2, when the broker told Normile that "you snooze, you lose."

8. *Termination of an option.* As reflected in the Notes following the *Normile* case, Restatement (Second) §36 states a variety of ways in which an ordinary

offer may normally be terminated: rejection, counter-offer, revocation, death of the offeror or offeree, etc. An option contract, however, is in fact a "contract" itself, not a mere offer subject to the rules stated in §36. Restatement (Second) §37 provides that "the power of acceptance under an option contract is *not* terminated by rejection or counter-offer, by revocation, or by death or incapacity of the offeror . . . ." (Emphasis added.) To discharge an option, the parties would need to make another binding agreement, ostensibly with new consideration on both sides, or establish other grounds for termination of the power of acceptance, pursuant to doctrines that will be discussed later in these materials.

2. Offeree's Reliance on an Unaccepted Offer as Limitation on Revocability

If an offeree wants to be certain that an offer will remain open for her to accept while she explores the desirability of the deal it proposes, she might enter into an option contract with the offeror, and provide some consideration (typically money) for his promise to keep the offer open. But in many cases, for a variety of reasons, this does not happen. Suppose the offeree nevertheless does delay accepting, in the belief that the offeror will not revoke his offer, and in the meantime takes various actions in reliance on her expectation that the offer will remain open. If the offeror does attempt to revoke before the offeree has actually made an acceptance, can the offeree claim that her reliance provides a sufficient reason to hold the offeror to his offer? In the *Berryman* case, the court briefly considers that possibility, but rejects it. The cases that follow demonstrate a variety of judicial responses to this same question.

James Baird Co. v. Gimbel Bros., Inc.

United States Court of Appeals 64 F.2d 344 (2d Cir. 1933)

L. HAND, Circuit Judge.

The plaintiff sued the defendant for breach of a contract to deliver linoleum under a contract of sale; the defendant denied the making of the contract; the parties tried the case to the judge under a written stipulation and he directed judgment for the defendant. The facts as found, bearing on the making of the contract, the only issue necessary to discuss, were as follows: The defendant, a New York merchant, knew that the Department of Highways in Pennsylvania had asked for bids for the construction of a public building. It sent an employee to the office of a contractor in Philadelphia, who had possession of the specifications, and the employee there computed the amount of the linoleum which would be required on the job, underestimating the total yardage by about one-half the proper amount. In ignorance of this mistake, on December twenty-fourth the defendant sent to some twenty or thirty contractors, likely to bid on the job, an offer to supply all the linoleum required by the specifications at two different lump sums, depending upon the quality used. These offers concluded as follows: "If successful in being awarded this contract, it will be absolutely guaranteed, . . . and . . . we are offering these prices for reasonable" (sic), "prompt acceptance after the general contract has been awarded." The plaintiff, a contractor in Washington, got one of these on the twenty-eighth, and on the same day the defendant learned its mistake and telegraphed all the contractors to whom it had sent the offer, that it withdrew it and would substitute a new one at about double the amount of the old. This withdrawal reached the plaintiff at Washington on the afternoon of the same day, but not until after it had put in a bid at Harrisburg at a lump sum, based as to linoleum upon the prices quoted by the defendant. The public authorities accepted the plaintiff's bid on December thirtieth, the defendant having meanwhile written a letter of confirmation of its withdrawal, received on the thirty-first. The plaintiff formally accepted the offer on January second, and, as the defendant persisted in declining to recognize the existence of a contract, sued it for damages on a breach.

Unless there are circumstances to take it out of the ordinary doctrine, since the offer was withdrawn before it was accepted, the acceptance was too late. Restatement of Contracts, §35. To meet this the plaintiff argues as follows: It was a reasonable implication from the defendant's offer that it should be irrevocable in case the plaintiff acted upon it, that is to say, used the prices quoted in making its bid, thus putting itself in a position from which it could not withdraw without great loss. While it might have withdrawn its bid after receiving the revocation, the time had passed to submit another, and as the item of linoleum was a very trifling part of the cost of the whole building, it would have been an unreasonable hardship to expect it to lose the contract on that account, and probably forfeit its deposit. While it is true that the plaintiff might in advance have secured a contract conditional upon the success of its bid, this was not what the defendant suggested. It understood that the contractors would use its offer in their bids, and would thus in fact commit themselves to supplying the linoleum at the proposed prices. The inevitable implication from all this was that when the contractors acted upon it, they accepted the offer and promised to pay for the linoleum, in case their bid were accepted.

It was of course possible for the parties to make such a contract, and the question is merely as to what they meant; that is, what is to be imputed to the words they used. Whatever plausibility there is in the argument, is in the fact that the defendant must have known the predicament in which the contractors would be put if it withdrew its offer after the bids went in. However, it seems entirely clear that the contractors did not suppose that they accepted the offer merely by putting in their bids. If, for example, the successful one had repudiated the contract with the public authorities after it had been awarded to him, certainly the defendant could not have sued him for a breach. If he had become bankrupt, the defendant could not prove against his estate. It seems plain therefore that there was no contract between them. And if there be any doubt as to this, the language of the offer sets it at rest. The phrase, "if successful in being awarded this contract," is scarcely met by the mere use of the prices in the bids. Surely such a use was not an "award" of the contract to the defendant. Again, the phrase, "we are offering these prices for . . . prompt acceptance after the general contract has been awarded," looks to the usual communication of an acceptance, and precludes the idea that the use of the offer in the bidding shall be the equivalent. It may indeed be argued that this last language contemplated no more than an early notice that the offer had been accepted, the actual acceptance being the bid, but that would wrench its natural meaning too far, especially in the light of the preceding phrase. The contractors had a ready escape from their difficulty by insisting upon a contract before they used the figures; and in commercial transactions it does not in the end promote justice to seek strained interpretations in aid of those who do not protect themselves.

But the plaintiff says that even though no bilateral contract was made, the defendant should be held under the doctrine of "promissory estoppel." This is to be chiefly found in those cases where persons subscribe to a venture, usually charitable, and are held to their promises after it has been completed. It has been applied much more broadly, however, and has now been generalized in section 90, of the Restatement of Contracts. We may arguendo accept it as it there reads, for it does not apply to the case at bar. Offers are ordinarily made in exchange for a consideration, either a counter-promise or some other act which the promisor wishes to secure. In such cases they propose bargains; they presuppose that each promise or performance is an inducement to the other. Wisconsin, etc., Ry. v. Powers, 191 U.S. 379, 386, 387, 24 S. Ct. 107, 48 L. Ed. 229; Banning Co. v. California, 240 U.S. 142, 152, 153, 36 S. Ct. 338, 60 L. Ed. 569. But a man may make a promise without expecting an equivalent; a donative promise, conditional or absolute. The common law provided for such by sealed instruments, and it is unfortunate that these are no longer generally available. The doctrine of "promissory estoppel" is to avoid the harsh results of allowing the promisor in such a case to repudiate, when the promisee has acted in reliance upon the promise. Siegel v. Spear & Co., 234 N.Y. 479, 138 N.E. 414, 26 A.L.R. 1205. Cf. Allegheny College v. National Bank, 246 N.Y. 369, 159 N.E. 173, 57 L.R.A. 980. But an offer for an exchange is not meant to become a promise until a consideration has been received, either a counter-promise or whatever else is stipulated. To extend it would be to hold the offeror regardless of the stipulated condition of his offer. In the case at bar the defendant offered to deliver the linoleum in exchange for the plaintiff's acceptance, not for its bid, which was a matter of indifference to it. That offer could become a promise to deliver only when the equivalent was received; that is, when the plaintiff promised to take and pay for it. There is no room in such a situation for the doctrine of "promissory estoppel."

Nor can the offer be regarded as of an option, giving the plaintiff the right seasonably to accept the linoleum at the quoted prices if its bid was accepted, but not binding it to take and pay, if it could get a better bargain elsewhere. There is not the least reason to suppose that the defendant meant to subject itself to such a one-sided obligation. True, if so construed, the doctrine of "promissory estoppel" might apply, the plaintiff having acted in reliance upon it, though, so far as we have found, the decisions are otherwise. Ganss v. Guffey Petroleum Co., 125 App. Div. 760, 110 N.Y.S. 176; Comstock v. North, 88 Miss. 754, 41 So. 374. As to that, however, we need not declare ourselves.

Judgment affirmed.

NOTES AND QUESTIONS

1. *Bilateral contract analysis.* Judge Hand admits that if the plaintiff had become bound to the defendant by virtue of its use of defendant's bid, then the plaintiff might have a case; he rejects that possibility, however, stating that "it seems entirely clear that the contractors did not suppose that they accepted the [defendant's] offer merely by putting in their bids." Most courts that have considered similar cases have on this point agreed with Judge Hand: Mere use by a general contractor of one particular subcontractor's bid does not constitute acceptance of that bid, forming a bilateral contract binding both parties. See, e.g., Electrical Construction & Maintenance Co. v. Maeda Pacific Corp., 764 F.2d 619 (9th Cir. 1985); Electro-Lab of Aiken, Inc. v. Sharp Constr. Co. of Sumter, Inc., 593 S.E.2d 170 (S.C. Ct. App. 2004). If in the *Baird* case such a bilateral contract had been formed and then the general contract had been awarded to someone else, would Baird have been stuck with a building full of Gimbel Bros. linoleum?

2. *Option contract.* We have seen that an offeree can be protected against the effect of a surprise revocation of an offer by an option contract. In *Baird*, Judge Hand rejects the argument that the plaintiff was protected by an option contract. Why? Is his analysis persuasive?

3. *Effect of mistake.* The trial court in *Baird* apparently found as a fact that the defendant had made a serious mistake in computing the amount of square yardage required by the contract on which plaintiff was bidding. Was this mistake material to the outcome of the case? Should it have been? We will return in Chapter 8 to the general problem of mistake.

Drennan v. Star Paving Co.

California Supreme Court 51 Cal. 2d 409, 333 P.2d 757 (1958)

TRAYNOR, Justice.

Defendant appeals from a judgment for plaintiff in an action to recover damages caused by defendant's refusal to perform certain paving work according to a bid it submitted to plaintiff.

On July 28, 1955, plaintiff, a licensed general contractor, was preparing a bid on the "Monte Vista School Job" in the Lancaster school district. Bids had to be submitted before 8:00 P.M. Plaintiff testified that it was customary in that area for general contractors to receive the bids of subcontractors by telephone on the day set for bidding and to rely on them in computing their own bids. Thus on that day plaintiff's secretary, Mrs. Johnson, received by telephone between fifty and seventy-five subcontractors' bids for various parts of the school job. As each bid came in, she wrote it on a special form, which she brought into plaintiff's office. He then posted it on a master cost sheet setting forth the names and bids of all subcontractors. His own bid had to include the names of subcontractors who were to perform one-half of one per cent or more of the construction work, and he had also to provide a bidder's bond of ten per cent of his total bid of $317,385 as a guarantee that he would enter the contract if awarded the work.

Later in the afternoon, Mrs. Johnson had a telephone conversation with Kenneth R. Hoon, an estimator for defendant. He gave his name and telephone number and stated that he was bidding for defendant for the paving work at the Monte Vista School according to plans and specifications and that his bid was $7,131.60. At Mrs. Johnson's request he repeated his bid. Plaintiff listened to the bid over an extension telephone in his office and posted it on the master sheet after receiving the bid form from Mrs. Johnson. Defendant's was the lowest bid for the paving. Plaintiff computed his own bid accordingly and submitted it with the name of defendant as the subcontractor for the paving. When the bids were opened on July 28th, plaintiff's proved to be the lowest, and he was awarded the contract.

On his way to Los Angeles the next morning plaintiff stopped at defendant's office. The first person he met was defendant's construction engineer, Mr. Oppenheimer. Plaintiff testified: "I introduced myself and he immediately told me that they had made a mistake in their bid to me the night before, they couldn't do it for the price they had bid, and I told him I would expect him to carry through with their original bid because I had used it in compiling my bid and the job was being awarded them. And I would have to go and do the job according to my bid and I would expect them to do the same."

Defendant refused to do the paving work for less than $15,000. Plaintiff testified that he "got figures from other people" and after trying for several months to get as low a bid as possible engaged L & H Paving Company, a firm in Lancaster, to do the work for $10,948.60.

The trial court found on substantial evidence that defendant made a definite offer to do the paving on the Monte Vista job according to the plans and specifications for $7,131.60, and that plaintiff relied on defendant's bid in computing his own bid for the school job and naming defendant therein as the subcontractor for the paving work. Accordingly, it entered judgment for plaintiff in the amount of $3,817.00 (the difference between defendant's bid and the cost of the paving to plaintiff) plus costs.

Defendant contends that there was no enforceable contract between the parties on the ground that it made a revocable offer and revoked it before plaintiff communicated his acceptance to defendant.

There is no evidence that defendant offered to make its bid irrevocable in exchange for plaintiff's use of its figures in computing his bid. Nor is there evidence that would warrant interpreting plaintiff's use of defendant's bid as the acceptance thereof, binding plaintiff, on condition he received the main contract, to award the subcontract to defendant. In sum, there was neither an option supported by consideration nor a bilateral contract binding on both parties.

Plaintiff contends, however, that he relied to his detriment on defendant's offer and that defendant must therefore answer in damages for its refusal to perform. Thus the question is squarely presented: Did plaintiff's reliance make defendant's offer irrevocable?

Section 90 of the Restatement of Contracts states: "A promise which the promisor should reasonably expect to induce action or forbearance of a definite and substantial character on the part of the promisee and which does induce such action or forbearance is binding if injustice can be avoided only by enforcement of the promise." This rule applies in this state. . . .

Defendant's offer constituted a promise to perform on such conditions as were stated expressly or by implication therein or annexed thereto by operation of law. (See 1 Williston, Contracts [3d ed.], §24A, p. 56, §61, p. 196.) Defendant had reason to expect that if its bid proved the lowest it would be used by plaintiff. It induced "action . . . of a definite and substantial character on the part of the promisee."

Had defendant's bid expressly stated or clearly implied that it was revocable at any time before acceptance we would treat it accordingly. It was silent on revocation, however, and we must therefore determine whether there are conditions to the right of revocation imposed by law or reasonably inferable in fact. In the analogous problem of an offer for a unilateral contract, the theory is now obsolete that the offer is revocable at any time before complete performance. Thus section 45 of the Restatement of Contracts provides: "If an offer for a unilateral contract is made, and part of the consideration requested in the offer is given or tendered by the offeree in response thereto, the offeror is bound by a contract, the duty of immediate performance of which is conditional on the full consideration being given or tendered within the time stated in the offer, or, if no time is stated therein, within a reasonable time." In explanation, Comment *b* states that the "main offer includes as a subsidiary promise, necessarily implied, that if part of the requested performance is given, the offeror will not revoke his offer, and that if tender is made it will be accepted. Part performance or tender may thus furnish consideration for the subsidiary promise. Moreover, merely acting in justifiable reliance on an offer may in some cases serve as sufficient reason for making a promise binding (see §90)."

Whether implied in fact or law, the subsidiary promise serves to preclude the injustice that would result if the offer could be revoked after the offeree had acted in detrimental reliance thereon. Reasonable reliance resulting in a foreseeable prejudicial change in position affords a compelling basis also for implying a subsidiary promise not to revoke an offer for a bilateral contract.

The absence of consideration is not fatal to the enforcement of such a promise. It is true that in the case of unilateral contracts the Restatement finds consideration for the implied subsidiary promise in the part performance of the bargained-for exchange, but its reference to section 90 makes clear that consideration for such a promise is not always necessary. The very purpose of section 90 is to make a promise binding even though there was no consideration "in the sense of something that is bargained for and given in exchange." (See 1 Corbin, Contracts 634 et seq.) Reasonable reliance serves to hold the offeror in lieu of the consideration ordinarily required to make the offer binding. In a case involving similar facts the Supreme Court of South Dakota stated that

> we believe that reason and justice demand that the doctrine [of section 90] be applied to the present facts. We cannot believe that by accepting this doctrine as controlling in the state of facts before us we will abolish the requirement of a consideration in contract cases, in any different sense than an ordinary estoppel abolishes some legal requirement in its application. We are of the opinion, therefore, that the defendants in executing the agreement [which was not supported by consideration] made a promise which they should have reasonably expected would induce the plaintiff to submit a bid based thereon to the Government, that such promise did induce this action, and that injustice can be avoided only by enforcement of the promise.

Northwestern Engineering Co. v. Ellerman, 69 S.D. 397, 408, 10 N.W.2d 879, 884; see also, Robert Gordon, Inc., v. Ingersoll-Rand Co., 7 Cir., 117 F.2d 654, 661; cf. James Baird Co. v. Gimbel Bros., 2 Cir., 64 F.2d 344.

When plaintiff used defendant's offer in computing his own bid, he bound himself to perform in reliance on defendant's terms. Though defendant did not bargain for this use of its bid neither did defendant make it idly, indifferent to whether it would be used or not. On the contrary it is reasonable to suppose that defendant submitted its bid to obtain the subcontract. It was bound to realize the substantial possibility that its bid would be the lowest, and that it would be included by plaintiff in his bid. It was to its own interest that the contractor be awarded the general contract; the lower the subcontract bid, the lower the general contractor's bid was likely to be and the greater its chance of acceptance and hence the greater defendant's chance of getting the paving subcontract. Defendant had reason not only to expect plaintiff to rely on its bid but to want him to. Clearly defendant had a stake in plaintiff's reliance on its bid. Given this interest and the fact that plaintiff is bound by his own bid, it is only fair that plaintiff should have at least an opportunity to accept defendant's bid after the general contract has been awarded to him.

It bears noting that a general contractor is not free to delay acceptance after he has been awarded the general contract in the hope of getting a better price. Nor can he reopen bargaining with the subcontractor and at the same time claim a continuing right to accept the original offer. See, R. J. Daum Const. Co. v. Child, Utah, 247 P.2d 817, 823. In the present case plaintiff promptly informed defendant that plaintiff was being awarded the job and that the subcontract was being awarded to defendant.

Defendant contends, however, that its bid was the result of mistake and that it was therefore entitled to revoke it. It relies on the rescission cases of M. F. Kemper Const. Co. v. City of Los Angeles, 37 Cal. 2d 696, 235 P.2d 7, and Brunzell Const. Co. v. G. J. Weisbrod, Inc., 134 Cal. App. 2d 278,

285 P.2d 989. See also, Lemoge Electric v. San Mateo County, 46 Cal. 2d 659, 662, 297 P.2d 638. In those cases, however, the bidder's mistake was known or should have been known to the offeree, and the offeree could be placed in status quo. Of course, if plaintiff had reason to believe that defendant's bid was in error, he could not justifiably rely on it, and section 90 would afford no basis for enforcing it. Robert Gordon, Inc. v. Ingersoll-Rand, Inc., 7 Cir., 117 F.2d 654, 660. Plaintiff, however, had no reason to know that defendant had made a mistake in submitting its bid, since there was usually a variance of 160 per cent between the highest and lowest bids for paving in the desert around Lancaster. He committed himself to performing the main contract in reliance on defendant's figures. Under these circumstances defendant's mistake, far from relieving it of its obligation, constitutes an additional reason for enforcing it, for it misled plaintiff as to the cost of doing the paving. Even had it been clearly understood that defendant's offer was revocable until accepted, it would not necessarily follow that defendant had no duty to exercise reasonable care in preparing its bid. It presented its bid with knowledge of the substantial possibility that it would be used by plaintiff; it could foresee the harm that would ensue from an erroneous underestimate of the cost. Moreover, it was motivated by its own business interest. Whether or not these considerations alone would justify recovery for negligence had the case been tried on that theory (see Biakanja v. Irving, 49 Cal. 2d 647, 650, 320 P.2d 16), they are persuasive that defendant's mistake should not defeat recovery under the rule of section 90 of the Restatement of Contracts. As between the subcontractor who made the bid and the general contractor who reasonably relied on it, the loss resulting from the mistake should fall on the party who caused it.

Leo F. Piazza Paving Co. v. Bebek & Brkich, 141 Cal. App. 2d 226, 296 P.2d 368, 371, and Bard v. Kent, 19 Cal. 2d 449, 122 P.2d 8, 139 A.L.R. 1032, are not to the contrary. In the *Piazza* case the court sustained a finding that defendants intended, not to make a firm bid, but only to give the plaintiff "some kind of an idea to use" in making its bid; there was evidence that the defendants had told plaintiff they were unsure of the significance of the specifications. There was thus no offer, promise, or representation on which the defendants should reasonably have expected the plaintiff to rely. The *Bard* case held that an option not supported by consideration was revoked by the death of the optionor. The issue of recovery under the rule of section 90 was not pleaded at the trial, and it does not appear that the offeree's reliance was "of a definite and substantial character" so that injustice could be avoided "only by the enforcement of the promise."

There is no merit in defendant's contention that plaintiff failed to state a cause of action, on the ground that the complaint failed to allege that plaintiff attempted to mitigate the damages or that they could not have been mitigated. Plaintiff alleged that after defendant's default, "plaintiff had to procure the services of the L & H Co. to perform said asphaltic paving for the sum of $10,948.60." Plaintiff's uncontradicted evidence showed that he spent several months trying to get bids from other subcontractors and that he took the lowest bid. Clearly he acted reasonably to mitigate damages. In any event any uncertainty in plaintiff's allegation as to damages could have been raised by special demurrer. Code Civ. Proc. §430, subd. 9. It was not so raised and was therefore waived. Code Civ. Proc. §434.

The judgment is affirmed.

GIBSON C. J., and SHENK, SCHAUER, SPENCE and MCCOMB, JJ., concur.

NOTES AND QUESTIONS

1. *Reasonable reliance on an offer.* In his opinion Justice Traynor first discusses Restatement of Contracts §45, which provides protection to the offeree against revocation of an offer to enter into a unilateral contract when the offeree has relied on the offer by beginning the requested performance. We previously discussed §45 in connection with Cook v. Coldwell Banker in Chapter 2. While *Drennan* involves an offer to enter into a bilateral contract, Justice Traynor concludes that protection against revocation of an offer should also apply in that situation when the offeree has reasonably relied resulting in foreseeable prejudice. Justice Traynor bases his analysis on the first Restatement of Contracts §90.

The *Drennan* case was decided in 1958, some 25 years after the *James Baird* decision, but well before the promulgation of the Restatement (Second) of Contracts. When the revised Restatement was prepared, its drafters endorsed the *Drennan* result, but put forth a new corollary to §90, to reflect the fact that — as Judge Hand had earlier maintained — the legal term "offer" is not quite synonymous with "promise." In the new §87(2), the Restatement (Second) agrees with the proposition that an offeree may in some cases reasonably and detrimentally rely on an offer that she has not yet accepted. Much of Justice Traynor's discussion in *Drennan* is devoted to explaining why in that case the plaintiff offeree's reliance was reasonable, and deserving of protection. Do you understand his argument? Do you agree with him? So far, relatively few cases have applied §87(2) outside of the construction-bidding situation exemplified by *Drennan* itself. Compare First National Bankshares of Beloit, Inc. v. Geisel, 853 F. Supp. 1344 (D. Kan. 1994) (under Kansas law as established by *Berryman*, promissory estoppel available to enforce option to sell stock in bank, but summary judgment granted for defendants because plaintiffs failed to establish detrimental reliance) with Strata Prod. Co. v. Mercury Exploration Co., 916 P.2d 822 (N.M. 1996) (promissory estoppel applied to make oil and gas "farmout" agreement irrevocable for period of time stated in option plus extension; §87(2) cited with approval).

2. ***Drennan vs. Baird.*** Despite the coyness of the "cf." signal used by Justice Traynor to introduce his reference to the *James Baird* case, most commentators have viewed the *James Baird* and *Drennan* decisions as being squarely in conflict. If so, *Drennan* has clearly prevailed. Since that case was decided, the

overwhelming majority of courts that have considered this type of case have accepted Justice Traynor's analysis. Examples include APAC-Southeast, Inc. v. Coastal Caisson Corp., 514 F. Supp. 2d 1373 (N.D. Ga. 2007); Weitz Co. v. Hands, Inc., 882 N.W.2d 659 (Neb. 2016); contra Home Electric Co. v. Hall & Underdown Heating & Air Cond. Co., 358 S.E.2d 539 (N.C. Ct. App. 1987), *aff'd,* 366 S.E.2d 441 (1988) (*per curiam*). See also Hottinger Excavating & Ready Mix, LLC, v. R.E. Crawford Constr., LLC, 2016 WL 9735771 (D. Colo.) (applying principle of *Drennan* to suit by general contractor against subcontractor). Although the essence of promissory estoppel might seem to be a case-by-case examination of all the factors that could cause the court's sense of injustice to be aroused, in practice the *Drennan* line of cases appears to have matured to the point where establishment of the basic facts will entitle the plaintiff general contractor to judgment more or less automatically, unless the defendant subcontractor can take the case out of the ordinary run by demonstrating some additional factor in its favor. E.g., Crook v. Mortenson-Neal, 727 P.2d 297 (Alaska 1986) (despite some post-award bargaining over terms of proposed subcontract, defendant subcontractor's defense properly characterized by trial court as so "weak" and "incredible" as to be "bordering on bad faith," justifying award of attorney fees to plaintiff general contractor).

3. *Limitations on the* ***Drennan*** *rule.* In *Drennan* the court indicated in dictum several situations in which the general contractor would not be allowed to invoke the protections of promissory estoppel. If the defendant's bid had "expressly stated or clearly implied that it was revocable at any time before acceptance," the court would have "treat[ed] it accordingly." Even such language might not be sufficient to preserve for the offeror the power of free revocability, however. In Lyon Metal Products, Inc. v. Hagerman Construction Corp., 391 N.E.2d 1152 (Ind. Ct. App. 1979), the defendant subcontractor's offer was in response to specifications that required (with respect to the general contract) that all bids submitted by general contractors remain open for 120 days. Defendant's bid was on a quotation form that stated (on the reverse side, in small print), "This quotation may be withdrawn and is subject to change without notice after 15 days from the date of quotation." Judgment in favor of the plaintiff general contractor on the basis of promissory estoppel was affirmed by the Indiana Court of Appeals. In response to the defendant's argument based on the above language, the court held that the trial court could have inferred that Lyon did not intend the 15-day clause to be the controlling time period but rather the 120-day period found in the specifications. But cf. Jackman Construction, Inc. v. Rock Springs Winnelson Co., 385 P.3d 311 (Wyo. 2016) (*Lyon* distinguished; subcontractor's clearly stated bid expiration date enforced).

In addition, inequitable conduct by the general contractor may preclude the use of promissory estoppel. Two such situations involve "bid shopping," the practice of trying to find another subcontractor who will do the work more cheaply while continuing to claim that the original bidder is bound, and "bid chopping," the attempt to renegotiate with the bidder to reduce the price. See Lahr Construction Corp. v. J. Kozel & Son, Inc., 640 N.Y.S.2d 957 (Sup. Ct.

1996). For a discussion of the various exceptions to the general contractor's right to recover from the subcontractor on the basis of promissory estoppel, particularly the exception for bid shopping, see Complete General Const. Co. v. Kard Welding, Inc., 911 N.E.2d 959 (Ohio Ct. App. 2009) and Donald W. Gregory & Eric B. Travers, Ethical Challenges of Bid Shopping, 30-SUM Construction Law 29 (2010).

4. *Bidding statutes.* Some states have enacted statutes to protect subcontractors from bid shopping by general contractors in connection with government contracts. See Gregory & Travers, Ethical Challenges of Bid Shopping, note 3 above, at 33, n.30. Such statutes commonly restrict the general contractor's freedom to substitute other subcontractors for those listed by it in the bid on the general contract without the approval of the granting authority. E.g., Cal. Pub. Contract Code §4107. The statute provides a list of circumstances under which a general contractor may seek the consent of the public agency to substitution of a subcontractor.

5. *Scholarly commentary. James Baird* and *Drennan* have received considerable scholarly commentary. For an in-depth examination and comparison of the cases that includes insights gathered from trial records, the appellate briefs, and the preconference memoranda circulated among the judges in the cases, see Alfred S. Konefsky, Freedom and Interdependence in Twentieth-Century Contract Law: Traynor and Hand and Promissory Estoppel, 65 U. Cin. L. Rev. 1169 (1997). Other scholarship has approached the cases from the perspective of economic analysis. See Richard Craswell, Offer, Acceptance, and Efficient Reliance, 48 Stan. L. Rev. 481 (1996); Avery Katz, When Should an Offer Stick? The Economics of Promissory Estoppel in Preliminary Negotiations, 105 Yale L.J. 1249 (1996). See also Carl J. Circo, The Evolving Role of Relational Contract in Construction Law, 32-FALL Construction Law. 16, 17 (2012) (describing *Drennan* result as consistent with relational contract theory in its stress on industry practice and reasonable expectations of parties in context); Victor P. Goldberg, Traynor (Drennan) versus Hand (Baird): Much Ado about (Almost) Nothing, 3 J. Legal Analysis 539, 578-584 (2011) ("only a few cases outside the construction bidding context even consider §87(2)").

In the area of construction-bidding law, some academic writers have been skeptical of the *Drennan* rule, as unduly favoring the general contractor, typically a more powerful economic party. For a description of the construction industry and a call for reform of the applicable rules, see Thomas J. Stipanowich, Reconstructing Construction Law: Reality and Reform in a Transactional System, 1998 Wis. L. Rev. 463. Despite arguments advanced in favor of a symmetrical, "both-parties-are-bound-or-neither-is-bound" approach, however, the decisions have continued to follow the *Drennan* approach, invoking promissory estoppel to protect the general contractor against the subcontractor's withdrawal while declining to find the general contractor bound to a particular sub-merely because its sub-bid was used. E.g. Holman Erection Co. v. Orville E. Madsen & Sons, Inc., 330 N.W.2d 693 (Minn. 1983).

Pop's Cones, Inc. v. Resorts International Hotel, Inc.

Superior Court of New Jersey, Appellate Division 307 N.J. Super. 461, 704 A.2d 1321 (1998)

KLEINER, J.A.D.

Plaintiff, Pop's Cones, Inc., t/a TCBY Yogurt, ("Pop's"), appeals from an order of the Law Division granting defendant, Resorts International, Inc. ("Resorts"), summary judgment and dismissing its complaint seeking damages predicated on a theory of promissory estoppel. . . . In reversing summary judgment, we rely upon principles of promissory estoppel enunciated in Section 90 of the Restatement (Second) of Contracts, and recent cases which, in order to avoid injustice, seemingly relax the strict requirement of "a clear and definite promise" in making a prima facie case of promissory estoppel.

Pop's is an authorized franchisee of TCBY Systems, Inc. ("TCBY"), a national franchisor of frozen yogurt products. Resorts is a casino hotel in Atlantic City that leases retail space along "prime Boardwalk frontage," among other business ventures.

From June of 1991 to September 1994, Pop's operated a TCBY franchise in Margate, New Jersey. Sometime during the months of May or June 1994, Brenda Taube ("Taube"), President of Pop's, had "a number of discussions" with Marlon Phoenix ("Phoenix"), the Executive Director of Business Development and Sales for Resorts, about the possible relocation of Pop's business to space owned by Resorts. During these discussions, Phoenix showed Taube one location for a TCBY vending cart within Resorts Hotel and "three specific locations for the operation of a full service TCBY store."

A TCBY Yogurt franchise store.

The Resorts Hotel in Atlantic City, NJ.

According to Taube, she and Phoenix specifically discussed the boardwalk property occupied at that time by a business trading as "The Players Club." These discussions included Taube's concerns with the then-current rental fees and Phoenix's indication that Resorts management and Merv Griffin personally[2] were "very anxious to have Pop's as a tenant" and that "financial issues . . . could easily be resolved, such as through a percentage of gross revenue." In order to allay both Taube's and Phoenix's concerns about whether a TCBY franchise at The Players Club location would be successful, Phoenix offered to permit Pop's to operate a vending cart within Resorts free of charge during the summer of 1994 so as to "test the traffic flow." This offer was considered and approved by Paul Ryan, Vice President for Hotel Operations at Resorts.

These discussions led to further meetings with Phoenix about the Players Club location, and Taube contacted TCBY's corporate headquarters about a possible franchise site change. During the weekend of July 4, 1994, Pop's opened the TCBY cart for business at Resorts pursuant to the above stated offer. On July 6, 1994, TCBY gave Taube initial approval for Pop's change in franchise site. In late July or early August of 1994, representatives of TCBY personally visited the Players Club location, with Taube and Phoenix present.

Based on Pop's marketing assessment of the Resorts location, Taube drafted a written proposal dated August 18, 1994, addressing the leasing of Resorts' Players Club location and hand-delivered it to Phoenix. Taube's proposal offered Resorts "7% of net monthly sales (gross less sales tax) for the duration of the

2. Merv Griffin was the Chief Executive Officer and a large shareholder of Resorts.

[Player's Club] lease . . . [and][i]f this proposal is acceptable, I'd need a 6 year lease, and a renewable option for another 6 years."

In mid-September 1994, Taube spoke with Phoenix about the status of Pop's lease proposal and "pressed [him] to advise [her] of Resorts' position. [Taube] specifically advised [Phoenix] that Pop's had an option to renew the lease for its Margate location and then needed to give notice to its landlord of whether it would be staying at that location no later than October 1, 1994." Another conversation about this topic occurred in late September when Taube "asked Phoenix if [Pop's] proposal was in the ballpark of what Resorts was looking for." He responded that it was and that "we are 95% there, we just need Belisle's[3] signature on the deal." Taube admits to having been advised that Belisle had "ultimate responsibility for signing off on the deal" but that Phoenix "assured [her] that Mr. Belisle would follow his recommendation, which was to approve the deal, and that [Phoenix] did not anticipate any difficulties." During this conversation, Taube again mentioned to Phoenix that she had to inform her landlord by October 1, 1994, about whether or not Pop's would renew its lease with them. Taube stated: "Mr. Phoenix assured me that we would have little difficulty in concluding an agreement and advised [Taube] to give notice that [Pop's] would not be extending [its] Margate lease and 'to pack up the Margate store and plan on moving.' "

Relying upon Phoenix's "advice and assurances," Taube notified Pop's landlord in late-September 1994 that it would not be renewing the lease for the Margate location.

In early October, Pop's moved its equipment out of the Margate location and placed it in temporary storage. Taube then commenced a number of new site preparations including: (1) sending designs for the new store to TCBY in October 1994; and (2) retaining an attorney to represent Pop's in finalizing the terms of the lease with Resorts.

By letter dated November 1, 1994, General Counsel for Resorts forwarded a proposed form of lease for The Players Club location to Pop's attorney. The letter provided:

> Per our conversation, enclosed please find the form of lease utilized for retail outlets leasing space in Resorts Hotel. You will note that there are a number of alternative sections depending upon the terms of the deal.
>
> As I advised, I will contact you . . . to inform you of our decision regarding TCBY. . . .

By letter dated December 1, 1994, General Counsel for Resorts forwarded to Pop's attorney a written offer of the terms upon which Resorts was proposing to lease the Players Club space to Pop's. The terms provided:

> [Resorts is] willing to offer the space for an initial three (3) year term with a rent calculated at the greater of 7% of gross revenues or: $50,000 in year one; $60,000 in year two; and $70,000 in year three . . . [with] a three (3) year option to renew after the initial term . . .

3. The reference to Belisle is John Belisle, then-Chief Operating Officer of Resorts.

The letter also addressed a "boilerplate lease agreement" provision and a proposed addition to the form lease. The letter concluded by stating:

> *This letter is not intended to be binding upon Resorts.* It is intended to set forth the basic terms and conditions upon which Resorts would be willing to negotiate a lease and is subject to those negotiations and the execution of a definitive agreement.
>
> . . . [W]e think TCBY will be successful at the Boardwalk location based upon the terms we propose. We look forward to having your client as part of . . . Resorts family of customer service providers and believe TCBY will benefit greatly from some of the dynamic changes we plan.
>
> . . . [W]e would be pleased . . . to discuss this proposal in greater detail. (Emphasis added.)

In early-December 1994, Taube and her attorney met with William Murtha, General Counsel of Resorts, and Paul Ryan to finalize the proposed lease. After a number of discussions about the lease, Murtha and Ryan informed Taube that they desired to reschedule the meeting to finalize the lease until after the first of the year because of a public announcement they intended to make about another unrelated business venture that Resorts was about to commence. Ryan again assured Taube that rent for the Players Club space was not an issue and that the lease terms would be worked out. "He also assured [Taube] that Resorts wanted TCBY . . . on the boardwalk for the following season."

Several attempts were made in January 1995 to contact Resorts' representatives and confirm that matters were proceeding. On January 30, 1995, Taube's attorney received a letter stating: "This letter is to confirm our conversation of this date wherein I advised that Resorts is withdrawing its December 1, 1994 offer to lease space to your client, TCBY."[4]

According to Taube's certification, "As soon as [Pop's] heard that Resorts was withdrawing its offer, we undertook extensive efforts to reopen [the] franchise at a different location. Because the Margate location had been re-let, it was not available." Ultimately, Pop's found a suitable location but did not reopen for business until July 5, 1996.

On July 17, 1995, Pop's filed a complaint against Resorts seeking damages. The complaint alleged that Pop's "reasonably relied to its detriment on the promises and assurances of Resorts that it would be permitted to relocate its operation to [Resorts'] Boardwalk location. . . ."

After substantial pre-trial discovery, defendant moved for summary judgment. After oral argument, the motion judge, citing Malaker Corp. Stockholders Protective Comm. v. First Jersey Nat. Bank, 163 N.J. Super. 463, 395 A.2d 222 (App. Div. 1978), certif. denied, 79 N.J. 488, 401 A.2d 243 (1979) [granted the defendant's motion — Eds.].

. . .

4. Apparently, in late January 1995, Resorts spoke with another TCBY franchise, Host Marriott, regarding the Players Club's space. Those discussions eventually led to an agreement to have Host Marriott operate a TCBY franchise at the Players Club location. That lease was executed in late May 1995, and TCBY opened shortly thereafter.

The doctrine of promissory estoppel is well-established in New Jersey. *Malaker,* supra, 163 N.J. Super. at 479, 395 A.2d 222 ("Suffice it to say that given an appropriate case, the doctrine [of promissory estoppel] will be enforced."). A promissory estoppel claim will be justified if the plaintiff satisfies its burden of demonstrating the existence of, or for purposes of summary judgment, a dispute as to a material fact with regard to, four separate elements which include:

> (1) a clear and definite promise by the promisor; (2) the promise must be made with the expectation that the promisee will rely thereon; (3) the promisee must in fact reasonably rely on the promise, and (4) detriment of a definite and substantial nature must be incurred in reliance on the promise.

The essential justification for the promissory estoppel doctrine is to avoid the substantial hardship or injustice which would result if such a promise were not enforced. Id. at 484, 395 A.2d 222.

In *Malaker,* the court determined that an implied promise to lend an unspecified amount of money was not "a clear and definite promise" justifying application of the promissory estoppel doctrine. Id. at 478-81, 395 A.2d 222. Specifically, the court concluded that the promisor-bank's oral promise in October 1970 to lend $150,000 for January, February and March of 1971 was not "clear and definite promise" because it did not describe a promise of "sufficient definition." Id. at 479, 395 A.2d 222.

It should be noted that the court in *Malaker* seems to have heightened the amount of proof required to establish a "clear and definite promise" by searching for "*an express promise* of a 'clear and definite' nature." Id. at 484, 395 A.2d 222 (emphasis added). This sort of language might suggest that New Jersey Courts expect proof of most, if not all, of the essential legal elements of a promise before finding it to be "clear and definite."

Although earlier New Jersey decisions discussing promissory estoppel seem to greatly scrutinize a party's proofs regarding an alleged "clear and definite promise by the promisor," see, e.g., id. at 479, 484, 395 A.2d 222, as a prelude to considering the remaining three elements of a promissory estoppel claim, more recent decisions have tended to relax the strict adherence to the *Malaker* formula for determining whether a prima facie case of promissory estoppel exists. This is particularly true where, as here, a plaintiff does not seek to enforce a contract not fully negotiated, but instead seeks damages resulting from its detrimental reliance upon promises made during contract negotiations despite the ultimate failure of those negotiations.

. . .

Further, the Restatement (Second) of Contracts §90 (1979), "Promise Reasonably Inducing Action or Forbearance," provides, in pertinent part:

> (1) A promise which the promisor should reasonably expect to induce action or forbearance on the part of the promisee or a third person and which does induce such action or forbearance is binding *if injustice can be avoided only by enforcement of the promise.* The remedy granted for breach may be limited as justice requires.

[Ibid. (emphasis added).]

The Restatement approach is best explained by illustration 10 contained within the comments to Section 90, and based upon Hoffman v. Red Owl Stores, Inc., 26 Wis. 2d 683, 133 N.W.2d 267 (1965):

> 10. A, who owns and operates a bakery, desires to go into the grocery business. He approaches B, a franchisor of supermarkets. B states to A that for $18,000 B will establish A in a store. B also advises A to move to another town and buy a small grocery to gain experience. A does so. Later B advises A to sell the grocery, which A does, taking a capital loss and foregoing expected profits from the summer tourist trade. B also advises A to sell his bakery to raise capital for the supermarket franchise, saying "Everything is ready to go. Get your money together and we are set." A sells the bakery taking a capital loss on this sale as well. Still later, B tells A that considerably more than an $18,000 investment will be needed, and the negotiations between the parties collapse. At the point of collapse many details of the proposed agreement between the parties are unresolved. The assurances from B to A are promises on which B reasonably should have expected A to rely, and A is entitled to his actual losses on the sales of the bakery and grocery and for his moving and temporary living expenses. Since the proposed agreement was never made, however, A is not entitled to lost profits from the sale of the grocery or to his expectation interest in the proposed franchise from B.

[Restatement (Second) of Contracts §90 cmt. *d,* illus. 10 (1979).]

. . .

As we read the Restatement, the strict adherence to proof of a "clear and definite promise" as discussed in *Malaker* is being eroded by a more equitable analysis designed to avoid injustice. . . .

The facts as presented by plaintiff by way of its pleadings and certifications filed by Taube, which were not refuted or contradicted by defendant before the motion judge or on appeal, clearly show that when Taube informed Phoenix that Pop's option to renew its lease at its Margate location had to be exercised by October 1, 1994, Phoenix instructed Taube to give notice that it would not be extending the lease. According to Phoenix, virtually nothing remained to be resolved between the parties. Phoenix indicated that the parties were "95% there" and that all that was required for completion of the deal was the signature of John Belisle. Phoenix assured Taube that he had recommended the deal to Belisle, and that Belisle would follow the recommendation. Phoenix also advised Pop's to "pack up the Margate store and plan on moving."

It is also uncontradicted that based upon those representations that Pop's, in fact, did not renew its lease. It vacated its Margate location, placed its equipment and personalty into temporary storage, retained the services of an attorney to finalize the lease with defendant, and engaged in planning the relocation to defendant's property. Ultimately, it incurred the expense of relocating to its present location. That plaintiff . . . relied to its detriment on defendant's assurances seems unquestionable; the facts clearly at least raise a jury question. Additionally, whether plaintiff's reliance upon defendant's assurances was reasonable is also a question for the jury.

Conversely, following the Section 90 approach, a jury could conclude that Phoenix, as promisor, should reasonably have expected to induce action or forbearance on the part of plaintiff to his precise instruction "not to renew the lease" and to "pack up the Margate store and plan on moving." In discussing the "character of reliance protected" under Section 90, comment *b* states:

> The principle of this Section is flexible. The promisor is affected only by reliance which he does or should foresee, and enforcement must be necessary to avoid injustice. Satisfaction of the latter requirement may depend on the reasonableness of the promisee's reliance, on its definite and substantial character in relation to the remedy sought, on the formality with which the promise is made, on the extent to which evidentiary, cautionary, deterrent and channeling functions of form are met by the commercial setting or otherwise, and on the extent to which such other policies as the enforcement of bargains and the prevention of unjust enrichment are relevant. . . .

[Restatement (Second) of Contracts §90 cmt. *b* (1979) (citations omitted).]

Plaintiff's complaint neither seeks enforcement of the lease nor speculative lost profits which it might have earned had the lease been fully and successfully negotiated. Plaintiff merely seeks to recoup damages it incurred, including the loss of its Margate leasehold, in reasonably relying to its detriment upon defendant's promise. Affording plaintiff all favorable inferences, its equitable claim raised a jury question. . . . Plaintiff's complaint, therefore, should not have been summarily dismissed.

Reversed and remanded for further appropriate proceedings.

NOTES AND QUESTIONS

1. *Requirement of a promise.* In *Pop's Cones* the court dispensed with the requirement indicated by some prior New Jersey decisions that promissory estoppel must be based on a "clear and definite promise." Sections 90 and 87(2) of the Restatement are in accord that a promise or offer will be sufficient without any heightened requirements of proof. Some courts, however, continue to adhere to this increased standard. See Jensen v. Taco John's International, Inc., 110 F.3d 525 (8th Cir. 1997). Would Resorts's promise have met even the greater standard of a "clear and definite promise"?

Even if a court rejects the standard of a clear and definite promise, not every assurance will be sufficient to invoke promissory estoppel. Compare Security Bank & Trust Co. v. Bogard, 494 N.E.2d 965 (Ind. Ct. App. 1986) (assurances by defendant bank's branch manager that plaintiff's application would go to loan committee and "within two or three days, we ought to have something here, ready for you to go with" held to be merely an "expression of intention" coupled with a "prediction" which were not sufficient to invoke promissory estoppel) with Twin City Fire Insurance Co. v. Philadelphia Life Insurance Co., 795 F.2d 1417 (9th Cir. 1986) (quote by defendant insurance broker of cost of annuity that plaintiff relied on in settlement of personal injury claim amounted to sufficient commitment to invoke promissory estoppel). In BH 329 NB LLC v. CBRE, Inc., 2017 WL 3641566 (D.N.J.), defendant seller's assurances to plaintiff would-be buyer of real property that defendant would not attempt to market property to others while negotiations continued, coupled with plaintiff's reliance in making expenditures and forgoing other opportunities, were held to potentially justify liability on promissory estoppel basis; *Pop's Cones* was cited and relied on.

2. *The* ***Hoffman*** *case.* The court cites with approval Hoffman v. Red Owl Stores, Inc., 133 N.W.2d 267 (Wis. 1967), a leading decision holding that assurances made during negotiations that a contract will be forthcoming amount to a promise sufficient to invoke promissory estoppel, when the promisee has relied to its detriment by giving up another business location and by incurring out-of-pocket expenses in preparation for the new location. As the court notes, the facts of *Hoffman* form the basis of Illustration 10 to Restatement (Second) §90, quoted in full by the court. See generally William C. Whitford & Stewart Macaulay, Hoffman v. Red Owl Stores: The Rest of the Story, 61 Hastings L.J. 801 (2010).

We earlier saw that in the construction bidding cases most courts and the Restatement have adopted the holding of Drennan v. Star Paving, allowing a general contractor to recover on the basis of promissory estoppel against a subcontractor who attempts to revoke a bid. Does the fact pattern presented by *Pop's Cones* and *Hoffman* present a stronger or weaker basis for invoking promissory estoppel than the type of situation illustrated by *Drennan*?

3. *Nature of the parties.* To what extent do cases like *Pop's Cones* and *Hoffman* turn on the plaintiffs' relative lack of business sophistication, as compared to the agents of the defendants? In Gruen Industries, Inc. v. Biller, 608 F.2d 274 (7th Cir. 1979), the court considered a claim for breach of an asserted promise to sell to plaintiff a controlling block of stock in a business corporation. Since Wisconsin law applied, the principles of Hoffman v. Red Owl governed the case. After finding that the agreement between the parties was not intended to be binding until negotiations were complete, the court went on to hold also that promissory estoppel did not apply. The court distinguished *Hoffman* on a number of points: Any promises were conditional; plaintiffs were represented by sophisticated agents (banker and attorney); both parties had made expenditures in reliance on the likelihood of agreement; the defendants were not in any way enriched by plaintiffs' reliance. It then concluded as follows:

> In summary, the plaintiffs' promissory estoppel argument seeks to transform these complex negotiations into a "no lose" situation. Every business man faces the risk that the substantial transaction costs necessary to bring about a mutually beneficial contract will be lost if the negotiations fail to yield a satisfactory agreement. It is difficult to find the degree of injustice necessary for recovery in estoppel when the promises incorporate so many contingencies and complexities and as a matter of sound business practice are to be formalized before the parties carry them out. We conclude on this basis that the losses are best left where they have fallen, because it is clear that no injustice will result from not enforcing the alleged promise.

Id. at 282. Compare 1861 Group, L.L.C. v. Wild Oats Markets, Inc., 728 F. Supp. 2d 1052, 1064 (E.D. Mo. 2010) (denying promissory estoppel claim by landlord against tenant on the ground that "it was unreasonable as a matter of law for a sophisticated landlord to rely on such promises from a tenant") with United Parcel Service Co. v. Rickert, 996 S.W.2d 464 (Ky. 1999) (plaintiff pilot permitted to recover both in fraud and in promissory estoppel against defendant, on the basis that he had been assured continuing employment with defendant if he remained for the time being in the employ of a contract air carrier with which defendant had maintained an ongoing relationship).

On the issue of sophistication, see Meredith R. Miller, Contract Law, Party Sophistication and the New Formalism, 75 Mo. L. Rev. 493 (2010). Professor Miller argues that "sophistication" is a vague concept. She proposes a standard in which a court "assesses whether a party, relative to the other parties to the contract, has sufficient experience and access to information and resources that the person or entity understands or should understand the intricacies, risks and consequences of the transaction." Id. at 497.

4. *Plaintiff's damages.* Pop's Cones sought to recover what are usually referred to as "reliance" damages: the loss of income from the Margate location that it gave up in reliance on receiving a lease for the Resorts location coupled with its out-of-pocket expenses preparing for the Resorts lease. Pop's could have attempted to recover "expectation" damages, the loss in income that it would have received from the Resorts location during the life of the lease. We will see in Chapter 11 that courts are divided on the question whether a plaintiff in a promissory estoppel case should be limited to its reliance damages or may recover its expectation damages, which are usually greater in amount.

5. *Scholarly commentary.* A number of scholars have addressed the question of whether and the extent to which legal obligations should flow from assurances made during preliminary negotiations. In one of the earliest treatments of this subject, Professor Knapp suggested that assurances of a deal made during negotiations should in some cases give rise to a duty to bargain in good faith in an effort to conclude the negotiations. Charles L. Knapp, Enforcing the Contract to Bargain, 44 N.Y.U. L. Rev. 673, 686-689 (1969). See Quake Construction, Inc. v. American Airlines, Inc., in Chapter 2, and its accompanying Notes. See also Juliet Kostritsky, Bargaining with Uncertainty, Moral Hazard, and Sunk Costs: A Default Rule for Precontractual Negotiations, 44 Hastings L.J. 621 (1993) (arguing for a duty to notify of change in intentions); Alan Schwartz & Robert E. Scott, Precontractual Liability and Preliminary Agreements, 120 Harv. L. Rev. 661, 672 (2007) (courts look for intention to be bound before protecting reliance).

PROBLEM 3-2

Selma Simpson is a wealthy local resident, vice president of the local bank, and owner of much property in and around your town of Springfield. She is also a faithful attender of a local church, the First Church of Springfield. The church has for some time been thinking of moving to a new location, closer to the residential center of the community, which has shifted substantially northward over the past several decades. Selma has been discussing with Reverend Lovejoy, the church's minister, the possibility of selling to the church several acres of land she owns on the edge of town, to be the site of a new church building. Several months ago, on March 15, she wrote, signed, and delivered the following letter to Rev. Lovejoy:

> Dear Rev. Lovejoy:
>
> As a long-time member of First Church, I would be willing to sell to the church my 15-acre property on the north side of Springfield, on the road to Shelbyville. I believe this land is worth at least $800,000, but I would be willing to sell it to the church for $500,000, because I believe in your mission and have received much spiritual benefit from the church over the years. I know that this is a major step for your congregation, so I will leave this offer open for your consideration until the end of the year, to give you time to fully weigh this purchase. I look forward to hearing from you when your governing body has done so.
>
> Faithfully yours, Selma Simpson

Over the next several months, the church's officers investigated the pros and cons of acquiring Selma's property and building a new church on that land. They hired a local architect to draw plans for a potential new building on that site, and employed a professional fund-raising firm to evaluate the church's potential for raising a capital investment of this size. At the same time, they considered the possibility of acquiring an alternate site on Evergreen Terrace in another part of town. Finally, in late September, they notified the owner of the Evergreen Terrace property that they were no longer interested, and prepared to contact Selma to communicate their intention to proceed with purchasing her land. Before they did so, however, they received the following handwritten note from Selma:

> Dear friends of First Church:
>
> Some time ago I suggested to you the possibility of selling my property on Shelbyville Road to the church. However, I have now received from Montgomery Burns an offer to buy that property for a much larger sum than we had discussed. As much as I would like to help the church out, I cannot afford to pass up such an opportunity. I must therefore regretfully withdraw my offer to you. I wish the church and its members good fortune in the years ahead.
>
> Your friend, Selma Simpson

You have been consulted by Reverend Lovejoy and the governing body of First Church. They tell you the above story, and ask you whether the church has a legal right to enforce against Selma Simpson a contract to sell her 15-acre property to the church. What would you tell them, and how would you counsel them to proceed?

3. Statutory Limits on the Power of Revocation

Restatement (Second) §87(1)(b) notes that an offer may be "made irrevocable by statute" and its comments refer to the fact that the Uniform Commercial Code has such provisions. The most important of those UCC sections for our purposes is the following provision in Article 2:

§2-205 Firm Offer

> An offer by a merchant to buy or sell goods in a signed writing which by its terms gives assurance that it will be held open is not revocable, for lack of consideration, during the time stated or if no time is stated for a reasonable time, but in no event may such period of irrevocability exceed three months; but any such term of assurance on a form supplied by the offeree must be separately signed by the offeror.

In §2-205, the drafters of Article 2 made a fundamental shift from traditional common law doctrine by providing that at least some offers will be irrevocable despite the absence of any consideration. Notably, the CISG takes an even more expansive attitude toward the possibility of "firm offers," by giving legal effect to the apparent intention to make an offer binding, without the restrictions imposed by §2-205. CISG Art. 16(2)(a) (an offer cannot be revoked if it indicates "that it is irrevocable" by stating a fixed time for acceptance or by other means).

UCC §2-205 applies to "offers," a term which the Code does not define; accordingly, on this point general common law principles apply. See I & R Mechanical, Inc. v. Hazelton Mfg. Co., 817 N.E.2d 799 (Mass. Ct. App. 2004) (price quotation not an offer under UCC §2-205). But note that many of the other terms employed in UCC §2-205, even those with everyday meanings, have specialized definitions in the Code. E.g., "merchant," UCC §2-104(1); "goods," UCC §2-105(1); "signed," UCC §1-201(b)(37), and "writing," UCC §1-201(b)(43). Observe also that UCC §2-205 applies to offers made by buyers as well as by sellers. E.g., City University of New York v. Finalco, Inc., 514 N.Y.S.2d 244 (App. Div. 1987) (buyer's offer to purchase used computers from university not revocable during period stated). And of course the section only applies to an offer that is "firm" — i.e., that "gives assurance that it will be held open."

Two other aspects of UCC §2-205 may be important in applying it to a given situation. One is the length of the period of irrevocability that it creates. Clearly if an offer merely states that it is "firm," but without saying for how long, the "reasonable" period of irrevocability created might be less than three months, but in any event under §2-205 would not *exceed* that time. If the offer does specify a period of firmness that is greater than three months, the period of irrevocability will be limited to three months unless consideration has been given or the firm offer is extended through a renewal. In re Wheeling-Pittsburgh Steel Corp., 360 B.R. 632, 639 (N.D. Ohio 2006); UCC §2-205 Comment 3. (On this point, compare CISG Art. 16(2)(a), which contains no similar time limitation.) The other point to be noted is UCC §2-205's requirement that any "term of assurance [i.e., of 'firmness'] on a form supplied by the offeree must be separately signed by the offeror." What abuse were the drafters seeking here to avoid? Comment 4 indicates this provision offers protection "against the inadvertent signing of a firm offer." Comment 2 elaborates on the requirement of a "signed writing," and notes that a "signature" for this purpose would typically consist at a minimum of an "initialing of the clause involved." If a given "offeror" would indeed "inadvertently" sign a firm offer, might she be likely also to "inadvertently" initial a "firmness" clause? (Have you ever signed or initialed something without reading it?) Comment 4 suggests that in such cases UCC §2-302 might possibly be applied to prevent an "unconscionable result."

PROBLEM 3-3

After retiring from the practice of law in Chicago, Wallace Branch purchased a tract of land in Kentucky and began to buy and breed thoroughbred racehorses. Although at first this was merely a hobby for Branch, many of his horses did very well on the track, and it has turned into a profitable business for him. In June of this year, Dorothy Gale comes to Branch's property to have a look at Branch's racehorse, "Tinman," which she has heard might be for sale. Branch tells Gale that Tinman can be purchased for $500,000. After watching the horse in action over a two-day period, Gale tells Branch that she is indeed interested in buying the animal, but will not be in a position to do so unless and until she can assemble a group of investors to go in with her on the purchase, which will take some time. Branch asks her how long she would need, and Gale replies that four months should be ample. At Gale's request, Branch signs the following:

> Dear Ms. Gale:
>
> For valuable consideration, I hereby grant unto you or your assigns an option for 120 days after date to purchase my horse "Tinman" for the price of $500,000. If this offer is accepted, the horse will be warranted sound as of the date of delivery but no warranty will be made as to his performance on the track or at stud.
>
> Dated: June 19, 2018 *(signed) Wallace Branch*

Gale takes the above writing (leaving a copy with Branch) to her home in Greensboro, NC, where she proceeds to attempt to interest investors in joining her in the purchase. By mid-September, she has enough commitments from investors to enable her to accept Branch's offer. She is about to do so when she receives the following email message:

> Dear Ms. Gale: Not having heard anything from you, I have decided to sell Tinman to another buyer. Thank you for your interest. — All best wishes, Wallace Branch

As of the time when she receives the above letter, what if any rights does Gale have against Branch? If you represented her, what course of action would you advise her to take, and why? Would your answers to these questions (or the reasoning behind your answers) be any different if Gale's home were not in North Carolina, but in Ontario, Canada?

C. LIABILITY FOR BENEFITS RECEIVED: THE PRINCIPLE OF RESTITUTION

The material in this section introduces you to a body of law now known as "restitution." In its inception, the law of restitution had contractual roots. Beginning in the latter part of the eighteenth century, however, judges and scholars began to think of restitutionary actions as distinct from contract law. During the twentieth century, restitution broke away from its contractual origins and became a separate body of law. (This process is described in the Comment that follows the *Pelo* case, below.) Although restitution has achieved independence from contract law, the institution of contract is still extremely important to the law of restitution because restitutionary actions often arise out of contractual relationships. The Restatement (Third) of Restitution §1 succinctly states the basis of liability as follows: "A person who is unjustly enriched at the expense of another is subject to liability in restitution." This formula identifies two elements that are central to restitutionary recovery: *enrichment* of one person under circumstances where the retention of benefits would be *unjust* to another person. But what is "enrichment"? And when is enrichment "unjust"? The materials that follow address these questions.

1. Restitution in the Absence of a Promise

In all the preceding materials, we have focused primarily on the various reasons why the law might choose to enforce an apparently seriously intended promise. Suppose, however, that one party has received a benefit from another, but made no promise to pay for that benefit. Ordinarily, classical contract law would find no basis for imposing a promissory obligation in those circumstances. Might there still be some other form of legal obligation, based on principles of restitution? The following cases explore that possibility.

Credit Bureau Enterprises, Inc. v. Pelo

Supreme Court of Iowa 608 N.W.2d 20 (2000)

Considered en banc.

McGiverin, Chief Justice.

In this appeal of a small claims decision, defendant Russell N. Pelo contends the district court erred by entering judgment against him for payment of a hospital bill.

Upon our review, we agree with the district court's conclusion and judgment that defendant Pelo is personally liable for the hospital bill.

I. Background Facts and Proceedings.

On Sunday January 8, 1995, at 3:00 A.M., the Hardin County Magistrate was contacted by Dr. Gude from the Ellsworth Municipal Hospital in Iowa Falls in regard to a patient, Russell N. Pelo. The record indicates that Pelo left his marital residence, after having an argument with his wife, and checked into a motel in Iowa Falls. Pelo later telephoned his wife "making threats of self harm" and purchased a shotgun. While the record is silent regarding the subsequent events, Pelo was apparently taken to the Ellsworth Municipal Hospital by the police, who had been advised of his threats.

Pursuant to the emergency hospitalization procedures set forth in Iowa Code section 229.22(3) and (4) (1995), the magistrate found probable cause that Pelo was seriously mentally impaired and likely to physically injure himself. The magistrate thus entered an emergency hospitalization order on January 8, requiring that Pelo be detained in custody at the hospital's psychiatric unit for examination and care for a period not to exceed forty-eight hours.

During admission to the hospital, Pelo was given a hospital release form to sign which would have made either Pelo or his insurance company responsible for the hospital bill. Pelo refused to sign the form. According to Pelo, at approximately five o'clock that morning, a nurse awakened him and demanded that he sign the hospital release form or the hospital could not insure the safety or return of his personal items. Pelo eventually read and signed the form. The form stated that Pelo understood he remained liable for any charges not covered by insurance.

Thereafter, Pelo's wife filed an application for involuntary hospitalization of Pelo pursuant to Iowa Code section 229.6 and apparently an order for immediate hospitalization was entered by a hospitalization referee under Iowa Code section 229.11.

An evidentiary hearing was held before the judicial hospitalization referee on January 13, concerning Pelo's commitment status. Medical reports and testimony were received by the referee. Pursuant to a written order, the hospitalization referee found that Pelo suffers from mental illness described as bipolar disorder, an illness from which Pelo has suffered for many years. In addition, the referee concluded "that although the Respondent [Pelo] clearly is in need of and would benefit from treatment for a serious mental illness, the required elements for involuntary hospitalization are lacking," and that further involuntary hospitalization was not authorized. Pelo was released from the hospital and court jurisdiction as of January 13, 1995.

The hospital later sought compensation from Pelo in the amount of $2,775.79 for medical services provided to him from January 8 to January 13, 1995. Pelo refused to pay the bill or authorize his health insurance carrier to do so. The hospital later assigned its claim against Pelo concerning the hospital bill to plaintiff Credit Bureau Enterprises, Inc., for collection. Plaintiff Credit Bureau filed a petition against Pelo on the small claims docket in district court, seeking judgment on the hospital bill. Credit Bureau later also named Cerro Gordo county as a defendant, based on the theory that the county, Pelo's county of legal settlement, would be liable for mental health services provided to Pelo. See Iowa Code §§230.1, 230.2.

At a hearing concerning plaintiff's small claims petition, Pelo admitted that he was hospitalized from January 8 through January 13, 1995, but argued that he made no agreement to pay for services provided to him. Pelo explained that upon being admitted to the hospital, he refused to complete the hospital release form so that his health insurance carrier could be contacted for payment because he believed that he did not need evaluation or treatment. Pelo argued he later signed the release form under duress and that he did not agree to pay for medical services provided. Pelo stated he had health insurance and was not indigent at the time he was hospitalized.

The district associate judge concluded that there was no statutory requirement that Cerro Gordo county pay for medical services provided to Pelo during his hospitalization because Pelo was hospitalized at a private hospital and not a state hospital. See Iowa Code §230.1. The court further concluded, however, that as a matter of public policy and under a reasonable interpretation of the involuntary commitment and mentally ill support statutes in Iowa Code chapters 229 and 230, Pelo could not be permitted to receive court-ordered services and then choose to ignore his responsibility to pay for those services. The court therefore entered judgment in favor of plaintiff Credit Bureau and against Pelo in the amount of $2,775.79, plus interest. The court also dismissed Credit Bureau's claim against Cerro Gordo county.

Under Iowa Code section 631.13, Pelo appealed to a district court judge the district associate court's decision that he was personally liable for the hospital bill. However, neither Pelo nor the plaintiff appealed that portion of the decision dismissing plaintiff's claim against Cerro Gordo county. The county is therefore not involved in this appeal and is out of the case.

On Pelo's appeal, the district court judge affirmed. The court concluded that by signing the hospital form, Pelo had entered into a valid, enforceable contract to be financially responsible for the hospital bill. In doing so, the court rejected Pelo's contention that the agreement was not enforceable because he allegedly signed the form under duress. In the alternative, the court concluded that Pelo was liable for payment of the hospital bill under a theory of contract implied in law or quasi-contract, based on the court's conclusion that Pelo benefited from his hospitalization for which he should pay.

We granted Pelo's application for discretionary review. See Iowa Code §631.16.

II. Standard of Review.

On discretionary review of a small claims action, see Iowa Code §631.16, our standard of review depends on the nature of the case. Hyde v. Anania, 578 N.W.2d 647, 648 (Iowa 1998). If the action is a law case, we review the district judge's ruling on error. Id. This small claims case began as an action to collect on account, which is a law action. In such cases, we review the judgment of the district court for correction of errors at law. Iowa R. App. P.4; Meier v. Sac & Fox Indian Tribe, 476 N.W.2d 61, 62 (Iowa 1991).

III. Defendant's Liability.

The issue we must decide is who pays for mental health medical services provided to a patient who is involuntarily committed to a private hospital. To answer this question, we first examine the applicable statutes governing involuntary hospitalization procedures for persons with mental illness. [The court concludes that under statutory law, there is no clear requirement that the county of a patient's residence pay for the cost of treatment at a private, as opposed to a public, hospital. Later statutory changes addressed the problem revealed in this case. — Eds.]

B. Liability Under Implied Contract Theory.

The district court judge concluded that Pelo was liable for payment of the private hospital bill under a contract implied in law or quasicontract theory.

1. *Applicable law.*

"A contract implied in law is an obligation imposed by the law without regard to either party's expressions of assent either by words or acts." Irons v. Community State Bank, 461 N.W.2d 849, 855 (Iowa App. 1990) (citing Corbin on Contracts §19 (1952)). Such contracts do not arise from the traditional bargaining process, but rather "rest on a legal fiction arising from considerations of justice and the equitable principles of unjust enrichment." Hunter v. Union State Bank, 505 N.W.2d 172, 177 (Iowa 1993). As such, they are not real contracts and the general rules of contracts therefore do not apply to them. Id.; accord 1 Samuel Williston, A Treatise on the Law of Contracts §1:6, at 27 (Richard A. Lord ed., 4th ed. 1990) (hereinafter "Williston"). More specifically, the contracts clause of article I, section 10 of the United States Constitution does not apply to quasi-contracts. Williston, §1:6, at 27.

"Restitution and unjust enrichment are modern designations for the older doctrine of quasi contracts or contracts implied in law, sometimes called constructive contracts." Robert's River Rides v. Steamboat Dev. Corp., 520 N.W.2d 294, 302 (Iowa 1994) (citations omitted). The term " 'unjust enrichment is an equitable principle mandating that one shall not be permitted to unjustly enrich oneself at the expense of another or to receive property or benefits without making compensation for them.' " Id. (quoting West Branch State Bank v. Gates, 477 N.W.2d 848, 851-52 (Iowa 1991)). Under these principles, where a person acts to confer benefits on another in a setting in which the actor is not acting officiously, the benefited party may be required to make restitution to the actor. Okoboji Camp Owners Coop. v. Carlson, 578 N.W.2d 652, 654 (Iowa 1998) (citing Restatement of Restitution §§1, 2 (1936)). Thus, where a person performs services for another which are known to and accepted by the latter, the law implies a promise to pay for those services. Patterson v. Patterson's Estate, 189 N.W.2d 601, 604 (Iowa 1971); Snyder v. Nixon, 188 Iowa 779, 781, 176 N.W. 808, 809 (1920) ("The general rule is that where one renders services of value to another with his knowledge and consent, the presumption is that the one rendering the services expects to be compensated, and that the one to whom the services are rendered intends to pay for the same, and so the law implies a promise to pay.").

The Restatement of Restitution states that "[a] person who officiously[2] confers a benefit upon another is not entitled to restitution therefor." Restatement of Restitution §2. Under this rule, recovery is denied so that one will not have to pay for a benefit forced upon one against one's will, see 1 E. Allan Farnsworth, Farnsworth on Contracts §2.20, at 173 (2d ed. 1998), or for which one did not request or knowingly accept. See Nursing Care Servs. v. Dobos, 380 So. 2d 516, 518 (Fla. Dist. Ct. App. 1980) (referring to rule as the "officious intermeddler doctrine").

In certain circumstances, however, restitution for services performed will be required even though the recipient did not request or voluntarily consent to receive such services. For example, section 116 of the Restatement of Restitution provides:

---

2. "Officiousness means interference in the affairs of others not justified by the circumstances under which the interference takes place." Restatement of Restitution §2 cmt. a.

> A person who has supplied things or services to another, although acting without the other's knowledge or consent, is entitled to restitution therefor from the other if
>
> (a) he acted unofficiously and with intent to charge therefor, and
> (b) the things or services were necessary to prevent the other from suffering serious bodily harm or pain, and
> (c) the person supplying them had no reason to know that the other would not consent to receiving them, if mentally competent; and
> (d) *it was impossible for the other to give consent or,* because of extreme youth or *mental impairment, the other's consent would have been immaterial.*

(Emphasis added.) Comment b to section 116 states:

> Knowledge of dissent. There can be no restitution for services or things rendered to a person who *refuses to accept the services and who is of sufficient mental capacity to understand the necessity of receiving them. . . . If, however, the person is insane, or if he is otherwise not fully mentally competent,* . . . a person rendering necessaries or professional services is entitled to recover from such person under the conditions stated in this Section, *although the person expresses an unwillingness to accept the things or services.*[3]

(Emphasis added.)

In addition to the principles set forth in the Restatement of Restitution discussed above, cases from other jurisdictions have concluded that a patient is liable for the reasonable value of medical services rendered by a hospital based on an implied in law contract theory. See *Nursing Care Servs.*, 380 So. 2d at 518 (concluding that provider of nursing care services was entitled to value of services provided to patient based on emergency aid quasicontract theory); Galloway v. Methodist Hosps., Inc., 658 N.E.2d 611, 614 (Ind. Ct. App. 1995) (holding that equity demanded that patients pay for medical services rendered by hospital in birth of child to prevent unjust enrichment); Heartland Health Sys. v. Chamberlin, 871 S.W.2d 8, 11 (Mo. Ct. App. 1993) (affirming on appeal judgment entered in favor of hospital against patient for payment of medical services under quantum meruit theory). . . .

2. *Application of law to facts.*

The district court concluded that Pelo benefitted by his hospitalization and that Pelo was liable for medical services rendered to him. Upon our review, we agree with the district court's decision.

We first point out that Pelo does not challenge the factual basis for his hospitalization. Nor is it likely that such a challenge would be successful given the fact that the necessary probable cause findings concerning emergency

---

3. Another illustration explains:

> A is seriously hurt in an accident. Becoming hysterical with pain, he fights his rescuers and refuses to permit anyone to touch him. Over his protests, B, a surgeon, renders first aid services in stopping a hemorrhage which soon would have caused A's death. B is entitled to compensation from A.

Restatement of Restitution §116 cmt. b, illus. 4.

hospitalization by the magistrate, see Iowa Code §229.22(3), and involuntary commitment procedures by the hospitalization referee, see Iowa Code §229.11, were made. These factfinding requirements are in place to guarantee a patient's liberty and due process interests when the state exercises its authority through emergency hospitalization and involuntary commitment proceedings. This authority is based on the standard for commitment, "serious mental impairment" as defined in section 229.1(14), which "melds the important elements of the police power and parens patriae doctrine." B.A.A. v. University of Iowa Hosps., 421 N.W.2d 118, 122-23 (Iowa 1988) (discussing historical background of state's authority in involuntary commitment proceedings).

Pelo also does not challenge the hospitalization referee's finding that he suffers from mental illness described as bipolar disorder. Nor does Pelo challenge the district court's finding that $2,775.79 was the reasonable cost of services provided to him during his hospitalization. Pelo contends, however, that he has no duty to pay for those services because he did not ask to be hospitalized and derived no benefit from his hospitalization. Pelo bases his argument, in part, on the hospitalization referee's finding made after the commitment hearing that further hospitalization was not authorized (based on a finding that there was not clear and convincing evidence that Pelo was seriously mentally impaired, see Iowa Code §229.13). Pelo apparently interprets the referee's decision to mean that he should not have been hospitalized in the first place and that he therefore derived no benefit from his hospitalization.

We find no merit in these contentions. First, the hospitalization referee's final decision is not relevant to Pelo's duty to pay for services previously rendered to him by the hospital. The referee's decision only addressed the propriety of any *future* hospitalization, not whether there was an adequate basis for hospitalization of Pelo in the first place or whether he medically benefited from his hospitalization.

Second, Pelo's opinion as to whether he needed or consented to medical services provided to him during his hospitalization is essentially irrelevant. This is because the emergency hospitalization order, which was based on the magistrate's probable cause finding that Pelo was seriously mentally impaired, see Iowa Code §229.22(3), establishes that Pelo lacked sufficient judgment to make responsible decisions concerning hospitalization and lacked the ability to consent to treatment. See Iowa Code §229.1(14) (defining "seriously mentally impaired").

Additionally, like the district court, we find that Pelo's hospitalization was indeed of medical benefit to him. The hospital provided services to Pelo from January 8 to 13, 1995, in good faith and not gratuitously. Such services were provided for Pelo's benefit, pursuant to court orders based on probable cause findings that Pelo was seriously mentally impaired and likely to injure himself or others if not immediately detained in the hospital. Based on the later reports of the physicians who examined and evaluated Pelo during his hospitalization, the referee found that Pelo "clearly is in need of and would benefit from treatment for a serious mental illness." This finding, we believe, would at a minimum alert Pelo to the seriousness of his mental illness and the need for further treatment, a fact that would surely be of medical benefit to him. The fact that Pelo was involuntarily hospitalized in order that this evaluation and finding could be made, and the fact that he may disagree with whether this finding is of medical benefit to him, does not eliminate the medical benefit he received from such hospitalization.

We conclude that plaintiff is entitled to recover the value of those medical services provided to Pelo. See Restatement of Restitution §116 cmt. b (if a person is otherwise not fully mentally competent, a person rendering necessaries or professional services is entitled to recover from such person although the person expresses an unwillingness to accept the services). The district court therefore properly determined that Pelo was legally obligated to pay for those services based on an implied in law contract theory. See Heartland Health Sys., 871 S.W.2d at 11 (affirming on appeal judgment entered in favor of hospital against patient for payment of medical services under quantum meruit theory).

Because we conclude that Pelo is legally obligated to pay for medical services provided to him under an implied contract in law or quasicontract theory, we need not consider whether an express contract was formed based on Pelo's later signature on the hospital admission form. See Johnson v. Dodgen, 451 N.W.2d 168, 175 (Iowa 1990) (the existence of a contract generally precludes the application of the doctrine of unjust enrichment); Chariton Feed & Grain, Inc. v. Harder, 369 N.W.2d 777, 791 (Iowa 1985) (an express and an implied contract cannot be found to exist on the same subject matter).

C. Constitutional Claims.

Pelo further contends that to require him to pay for medical services he did not want or ask for violates either his constitutional right to due process under article I, section 9 of the Iowa Constitution, or his right to contract under article I, section 21 of the Iowa Constitution. These contentions have no merit. First, quasi-contracts are not true contracts and therefore the general rules of contract, including the constitutional provisions concerning the right to contract, do not apply to them. See Williston, §1:6, at 27.

Additionally, we point out that Pelo does not assert that the emergency hospitalization or involuntary commitment proceedings are constitutionally invalid. Based on this fact, and the preliminary factual probable cause findings of the magistrate and hospitalization referee that Pelo was seriously mentally impaired, we assume that Pelo's involuntary hospitalization complied with the requisite procedural due process safeguards. Having established these facts, holding Pelo liable for payment of the medical services provided to him during his hospitalization does not violate his constitutional right to due process or his right to contract under the Iowa Constitution.

IV. DISPOSITION.

We conclude that the district court properly determined that defendant Pelo was liable for payment of mental health medical services provided to him during his hospitalization at Ellsworth Municipal Hospital under a quasi-contract theory. The court therefore properly entered judgment in favor of plaintiff Credit Bureau against defendant Pelo for the amount of the hospital bill.

We affirm the judgment of the district court.
AFFIRMED.

All justices concur except CARTER, J., who takes no part.

NOTES AND QUESTIONS

1. *Analyzing* ***Pelo***. Because the court is satisfied that Pelo's apparent need for care was clear and the procedural protections afforded him were adequate, it never has to reach the issue of whether true contractual liability could have been imposed on the basis of the form he signed while under the hospital's care. Do you think that other claim should have succeeded? Consider Restatement (Second) of Contract §§174-177, "Duress and Undue Influence"; consider also §15, "Mental Illness or Defect." We will consider those topics in Chapter 7, but at this point note that *Pelo* might well have had one or more effective defenses to contractual liability, given his apparent mental condition at the time he signed the form. In particular, regardless of whether the hospital is seen as having applied an "improper" threat to obtain his assent, the mere fact that the hospital was clearly aware of his mental state might well prevent its enforcement of any contractual obligation on his part.

2. *Restitutionary liability for emergency services rendered.* As the court in *Pelo* points out, the Restatement (First) of Restitution §116 provided for restitution in favor of one furnishing emergency services in a situation where serious bodily harm or pain will otherwise result, provided the plaintiff acted "unofficiously." Sometimes, as in In re Estate of Crisan, 107 N.W.2d 907 (Mich. 1961), the patient is unconscious when the care is rendered, and dies without ever regaining consciousness. Even more than in *Pelo*, there can be no question of "real" assent in such a case; to talk of an "implied contract" is clearly a legal fiction. Moreover, since in *Crisan* the patient did not recover, it is possible that the services ultimately did not "benefit" her. The restitutionary obligation will presumably lie anyway, however, based on the "reasonable value" of the services received. Cf. Doe v. HCA Health Services of Tennessee, Inc., 46 S.W.3d 191, 198-199 (Tenn. 2001) (even if price term in agreement between patient and hospital too indefinite for contract to be enforceable, patient can be liable for the reasonable value of services rendered, based on the costs of the hospital's operation and the prices charged for similar services by other hospitals in the area). In other cases, however, the patient was conscious and could have entered into an agreement, and perhaps the issue of payment was even discussed, but no definite agreement was reached. In such a case, the provider will be able to recover the reasonable value of the care furnished, not under the rubric of Restatement (First) of Restitution §116, but on the more general restitutionary principle that one who receives services, with the knowledge that the person furnishing them reasonably expects to be paid, will be liable for the reasonable value of those services. See, e.g., the *Doe* case cited above, and Galloway v. Methodist Hospitals, Inc., cited by the court in *Pelo*. Section 20 of the Restatement (Third) of Restitution now provides:

§20. Protection Of Another's Life Or Health

(1) A person who performs, supplies, or obtains professional services required for the protection of another's life or health is entitled to restitution from the other as necessary to prevent unjust enrichment, if the circumstances justify the decision to intervene without request.

(2) Unjust enrichment under this section is measured by a reasonable charge for the services in question.

What changes if any would this section make from §116 of the First Restatement? Would application of this revised section have affected the result in *Pelo*?

3. *Contrast between contract and "pure" restitution (or "quasi-contract").* The court in *Pelo* is at pains to make clear that the liability of the defendant is based in restitution, not pursuant to a contract, and that these are two quite separate bases of obligation. Contracts "implied in law" are "not real contracts," the court declares; they "do not arise from the traditional bargaining process," and "general rules of contracts . . . do not apply to them." Despite the theoretical separation between "true" contract and "quasi" contract, they do have some potential overlap, as the Restatement (Third) of Restitution recognizes in the following provision:

§107. Effect of Existence of Bargain upon Right to Restitution

(1) A person of full capacity who, pursuant to a contract with another, has performed services or transferred property to the other or otherwise has conferred a benefit upon him, is not entitled to compensation therefor other than in accordance with the terms of such bargain, unless the transaction is rescinded for fraud, mistake, duress, undue influence or illegality, or unless the other has failed to perform his part of the bargain.

(2) In the absence of circumstances indicating otherwise, it is inferred that a person who requests another to perform services for him or to transfer property to him thereby bargains to pay therefor.

As Restatement (Third) of Restitution §107(2) states, when a person "requests another to perform services for him or to transfer property to him," the law will infer a bargain to pay. Such cases are usually referred to as "implied-in-fact" contracts. Implied-in-fact contracts, like express contracts, are "true" contracts. While the distinction between implied-in-fact contracts and restitution claims may be hazy, the crucial factor will often be whether the party receiving the benefit of services or property had "requested" it. See Candace S. Kovacic, A Proposal to Simplify Quantum Meruit Litigation, 35 Am. U.L. Rev. 547, 550-551 (1986). If so, a claim based on implied-in-fact contract will lie. The distinction between implied-in-fact and implied-in-law contracts is discussed in more detail in the two cases that follow *Pelo.*

Frequently the distinction between express contract, implied-in-fact contract, and restitution will be immaterial. See Restatement (Third) of Restitution §107, cmt. *b.* However, sometimes the distinction will be important. In *Pelo,* for example, the court states that constitutional claims regarding the right to contract do not apply to restitutionary claims. Many procedural or evidentiary rules applicable to contracts will also not apply when restitution is the basis for recovery. See In re Estate of Etherton, 671 N.E.2d 364 (Ill. App. Ct. 1996) (holding that an evidentiary rule, the "Dead Man's Act," which prevents proof of an express contract between plaintiff and the decedent, did not apply to a claim for restitution).

4. *Protection of another's property.* The Restatement (Third) of Restitution also recognizes a right to restitution when a person acts to protect the property of another, rather than his life or health.

> **§21. Protection Of Another's Property**
>
> (1) A person who takes effective action to protect another's property from threatened harm is entitled to restitution from the other as necessary to prevent unjust enrichment, if the circumstances justify the decision to intervene without request. Unrequested intervention is justified only when it is reasonable to assume the owner would wish the action performed.
>
> (2) Unjust enrichment under this section is measured by the loss avoided or by a reasonable charge for the services provided, whichever is less.

The Restatement provides a number of illustrations applying this section, including the following:

> 1. Owner's car is stolen, damaged, and abandoned by the thief. The car is later found by the police, who direct Garage to tow and store it. Despite appropriate efforts, 10 months pass before Owner is identified by the police. In the interim, Insurer pays Owner's claim for theft loss and takes an assignment of title. Discovering the whereabouts of the car, Insurer reclaims possession. Absent a statute defining Garage's rights in these circumstances, Garage has a claim in restitution against Insurer for its reasonable and customary charges for towing and 10 months' storage, not exceeding the car's value.

Restatement (Third) of Restitution §21, Illus. 1.

5. *Economic analysis of restitutionary claims.* Professor (now Judge) Richard Posner, the leading advocate for the application of economic analysis to legal problems, has offered the following economic justification for the modern rule allowing restitutionary recovery for benefits conferred to preserve life, health, or property:

> A doctor chances on a stranger lying unconscious on the street, treats him, and later demands a fee. Has he a legal claim? The law answer is yes. . . .
>
> In the case of the doctor, the costs of a voluntary transaction would be prohibitive. The reason is incapacity. In other cases it might be time (for example, the stranger is conscious but bleeding profusely, and there is no time to discuss terms). In such cases, the law considers whether, had transaction costs not been prohibitive, the parties would have come to terms, and if so, what (approximately) the terms would have been. If a court is reasonably confident both that there would have been a transaction and what its essential terms would have been (that the doctor use his best efforts and that the patient pay the doctor's normal fee for treatment of the sort rendered), it does not hesitate to write a contract between the parties after the fact. . . .
>
> But now suppose that a man stands under my window, playing the violin beautifully, and when he has finished, knocks on my door and demands a fee

> for his efforts. Though I enjoyed his playing, I nonetheless refuse to pay anything for it. The court would deny the violinist's claim for a fee — however reasonable the fee might appear to be — on the ground that, although the violinist conferred a benefit on me (and not with the intent that it be gratuitous), he did so officiously. Translated from legal into economic terminology, this means he conferred an unbargained-for benefit in circumstances where the costs of a voluntary bargain would have been low. In such cases the law insists that the voluntary route be followed — and is on firm economic grounds in doing so.

Richard A. Posner, Economic Analysis of Law 150-151 (9th ed. 2014). What does Posner mean by "transaction costs"? When transaction costs are low, why should the law insist that obligations be dependent on an actual bargain rather than being imposed by law? According to Posner, when is it permissible for a court to impose an obligation to pay for benefits received even in the absence of an actual bargain?

Comment: Development of the Law of Restitution

One of the most perplexing problems that students face in trying to understand the concept of restitution is a confusing array of terms: *implied contract, implied-in-fact contract, implied-in-law contract, quasi contract, common counts, quantum meruit,* and *quantum valebat,* to mention a few. The text that follows attempts to clarify this muddle by focusing on the historical development of the right to restitution. (Even if the textual material helps to clarify your understanding of these terms, do not be surprised if judges confuse the terms or use them loosely.)

Before Slade's Case, 76 Eng. Rep. 1074 (1602), the common law courts drew the boundary between the action of assumpsit and the action of debt on the basis of whether an express promise was made. If a person sold goods or provided services to another on request, the action of debt would lie against the recipient. If the recipient, in addition, expressly promised to pay for the goods or services after they were received, assumpsit was available. In Slade's Case, the Exchequer Chamber held that every executory contract implied a promise. As a result, assumpsit would lie even in the absence of an express promise. Because it was more favorable procedurally than debt, assumpsit soon replaced debt as the action to recover the price of goods or services.

After Slade's Case, standardized forms of pleading, called "common counts," were developed for use in typical cases arising under assumpsit, such as actions to recover the promised price of goods sold, services performed, or money loaned. At about the same time, common counts were also developed for recovery of the reasonable value of goods delivered ("quantum valebat") or services performed ("quantum meruit"). Technically, these actions were separate from assumpsit because the claim was for an unliquidated sum rather than a sum certain. Eventually, however, these new forms of action were absorbed into the general action of assumpsit. In all of these actions, liability was originally based on a consensual transaction. Soon, however, the courts expanded liability to nonconsensual situations by making use of the concept of an "implied promise." Thus, by the end of the seventeenth century, an action in assumpsit was also available in many nonconsensual situations. For example, if a bank or other commercial party made an overpayment by mistake, the amount of the overpayment could be recovered in an action of assumpsit. See A.W.B. Simpson, A History of the Common Law of Contract 489-505 (1987); James B. Ames, The History of Assumpsit (Pt. II), 2 Harv. L. Rev. 53, 63-69 (1888) (history of common law developments).

Ultimately, the nonconsensual basis of some of the situations in which assumpsit was available was recognized and expressed. In 1760, in Moses v. Macferlan, 97 Eng. Rep. 676, Lord Mansfield faced the question of whether assumpsit could be used in an action for money had and received when no express agreement had been made and it was impossible under the facts to imply an agreement. Mansfield stated,

> If the defendant be under an obligation, from the ties of natural justice, to refund; the law implies a debt, and gives this action, founded in the equity of the plaintiff's case, as it were upon a contract ("quasi ex contractu," as the Roman law expresses it).

97 Eng. Rep. at 678. After that time, it became common to speak of two types of implied contracts that were actionable in assumpsit, one being "implied-in-fact" and the other "implied-in-law" (quasi contract).

In the United States, the concept of quasi-contractual liability founded on unjust enrichment was widely accepted, but the scope of liability remained unclear. In 1937, the American Law Institute (ALI) published its first Restatement of Restitution, a major attempt at systematic treatment of the field. The reporters for the Restatement consciously rejected the term *quasi contract*, selecting instead the label *restitution*, which was broader in at least two ways. First, while the term *quasi contract* implies a relationship to contract law, the modern law of restitution is based on unjust enrichment and has no particular relationship to contract. Although some restitutionary situations arise in a contractual context, many do not. For example, restitution is available when a person has wrongfully obtained property from another tortiously, by fraud or conversion. Second, at common law, the remedy in a quasi-contractual action was damages. In restitutionary actions, however, modern courts can fashion equitable remedies such as a "constructive trust" or "accounting." Warren A. Seavey & Austin W. Scott, Restitution, 54 L.Q. Rev. 29, 38-39 (1938) (discussing relationship between restitution and common law quasi-contractual actions).

In more recent years, scholarship regarding restitution has continued to develop. See George E. Palmer, Law of Restitution (1978); Andrew Kull, Rationalizing Restitution, 83 Cal. L. Rev. 1191 (1995); Symposium: Restitution and Unjust Enrichment, 79 Tex. L. Rev. 1763 (2001). In 2011, the ALI adopted the Restatement (Third) of Restitution and Unjust Enrichment (cited in the following materials as the "Restatement (Third) of Restitution"), with Professor Andrew Kull as chief reporter. For an examination of various aspects of the revised Restatement, see Symposium, Restitution Rollout: The Restatement (Third) of Restitution and Unjust Enrichment, 68 Wash. & Lee L. Rev. 899 (2011).

Commerce Partnership 8098 Limited Partnership v. Equity Contracting Co.

Florida District Court of Appeal, En Banc 695 So. 2d 383 (1997)

GROSS, Judge.

Equity Contracting Company, Inc. ("Equity") filed a one-count complaint against Commerce Partnership 8098 Limited Partnership ("Commerce"). The count was set forth under the heading "Quantum Meruit." The complaint contained the following allegations:

> Commerce was the owner of an office building. Commerce contracted with a general contractor, World Properties, Inc., to perform improvements on its property. Equity was the stucco and surfacing subcontractor for the job, having contracted with the general contractor to perform the work. Because it inspected the job on a weekly basis, Commerce was aware of Equity's work. Equity completely performed its subcontract and the reasonable value of its work was $17,100. Commerce failed to pay the general contractor the full amounts due for the job. The general contractor did not pay Equity. Commerce was unjustly enriched because it had accepted Equity's services without paying any entity for them.

In its answer, Commerce asserted that it had paid the general contractor in full.

At the non-jury trial, Equity presented its direct case in under 30 minutes. Equity's president testified that his company had contracted with the general contractor to stucco Commerce's property for $17,100. He indicated that at the start of the job he expected payment only from the general contractor and not from Commerce. Both the general contractor and a representative from Commerce inspected the work as it progressed. After the work was completed, Commerce gave Equity a punch list of remedial work. When Equity's president asked for at least partial payment from Commerce, the latter's representative indicated that "he couldn't do it." Having received no payment, Equity did not complete the punch list. Equity brought suit against the general contractor, who later declared bankruptcy. Equity adduced no evidence regarding Commerce's payments to the general contractor under the construction contract or to any other party for work covered by the contract.

After Equity rested, Commerce moved for an involuntary dismissal, arguing that the evidence did not establish a contract implied in fact. Commerce's attorney contended that the term "quantum meruit" was synonymous with a contract implied in fact. The trial court denied the motion. During closing argument, Equity asserted that it had established a claim for quantum meruit, which it interpreted to mean unjust enrichment. Arguing that a quasi contract claim had first been injected into the case during closing argument, Commerce's attorney obtained permission to reopen his case. By this point in the trial, there was no agreement as to the cause of action at issue or the requirements of proof. The trial judge observed, "[w]e are in equity and I have some difficulty with wondering what the issues are and who is going to prove what."

Commerce's witness testified that the contract price it had negotiated with the general contractor for the improvements was $256,894. He identified three payments totalling $223,065.04 that Commerce made to the general contractor — $173,088.07 in progress payments, $24,976.97 in response to application for payment number 8, and $25,000 in final settlement of the general contractor's lawsuit against Commerce. Commerce also sought to introduce evidence that it had paid $64,097 directly to three subcontractors who had performed work on the building, who were not paid by the general contractor, and who had perfected mechanics' liens. The trial court sustained Equity's objection to this testimony on the ground of relevance.

Relying on Zaleznik v. Gulf Coast Roofing Co., Inc., 576 So. 2d 776 (Fla. 2d DCA 1991), the trial court entered judgment in favor of Equity for $17,100.

Contract Implied in Fact and Quasi Contract

This case is a paradigm for the confusion that often surrounds the litigation of implied contracts.

A contract implied in fact is one form of an enforceable contract; it is based on a tacit promise, one that is inferred in whole or in part from the parties' conduct, not solely from their words. 17 Am. Jur. 2d "Contracts" §3 (1964); 1 Arthur Linton Corbin, Corbin on Contracts §§1.18-1.20 (Joseph M. Perillo ed. 1993). Where an agreement is arrived at by words, oral or written, the contract is said to be "express." 17 Am. Jur. 2d "Contracts" at §3. A contract implied in fact is not put into promissory words with sufficient clarity, so a fact finder must examine and interpret the parties' conduct to give definition to their unspoken agreement. Id.; 3 Corbin on Contracts §562 (1960). . . .

Common examples of contracts implied in fact are where a person performs services at another's request, or "where services are rendered by one person for another without his expressed request, but with his knowledge, and under circumstances" fairly raising the presumption that the parties understood and intended that compensation was to be paid. . . . In these circumstances, the law implies the promise to pay a reasonable amount for the services. . . .

A contract implied in law, or quasi contract, is not based upon the finding, by a process of implication from the facts, of an agreement between the parties. A contract implied in law is a legal fiction, an obligation created by the law without regard to the parties' expression of assent by their words or conduct. 1 Corbin on Contracts §1.20; . . . . The fiction was adopted to provide a remedy where one party was unjustly enriched, where that party received a benefit under circumstances that made it unjust to retain it without giving compensation. . . .

The elements of a cause of action for a quasi contract are that: (1) the plaintiff has conferred a benefit on the defendant; (2) the defendant has knowledge of the benefit; (3) the defendant has accepted or retained the benefit conferred and (4) the circumstances are such that it would be inequitable for the defendant to retain the benefit without paying fair value for it. Hillman Const. Corp. v. Wainer, 636 So. 2d 576, 577 (Fla. 4th DCA 1994); Henry M. Butler, Inc. v. Trizec Properties, Inc., 524 So. 2d 710, 711-12 (Fla. 2d DCA 1988). Because the basis for recovery does not turn on the finding of an enforceable agreement, there may be recovery under a contract implied in law even where the parties had no dealings at all with each other. . . . This is unlike a contract implied in fact which must arise from the interaction of the parties or their agents.

To describe the cause of action encompassed by a contract implied in law, Florida courts have synonymously used a number of different terms — "quasi contract," "unjust enrichment," "restitution," "constructive contract," and "quantum meruit." This profusion of terminology has its roots in legal history. Concerned about the confusion between contracts implied in law and fact, two legal scholars sought to "extirpate the term 'contract implied in law' from legal usage and to substitute for it the term "quasi contract." 1 Corbin on Contracts §1.20. As Corbin explains, although the term "quasi contract" took hold, "the older term successfully resisted extirpation to the further confusion of law students and lawyers." Id. . . .

At trial in this case, Commerce's attorney understood "quantum meruit" to mean a contract implied in fact. Equity and the trial court were proceeding under a theory of quasi contract. This confusion over "quantum meruit" is understandable, since there are cases to support both positions. . . .

The blurring of the distinction between contract implied in fact and quasi contract has been exacerbated by the potential for both theories to apply to the same factual setting. For example, a common form of contract implied in fact is where one party has performed services at the request of another without discussion of compensation. These circumstances justify the inference of a promise to pay a reasonable amount for the service. The enforceability of this obligation turns on the implied promise, not on whether the defendant has received something of value. A contract implied in fact can be enforced even where a defendant has received nothing of value.

However, where there is no enforceable express or implied in fact contract but where the defendant has received something of value, or has otherwise benefitted from the service supplied, recovery under a quasi contractual theory may be appropriate. See Lamborn v. Slack, 107 So. 2d 277 (Fla. 2d DCA 1958) (in which the court found a contract implied in fact but discussed the issue using quasi contractual principles). When properly raised in the pleadings, this overlapping of theories may require a fact finder to view the facts as they might apply to both. 3 Corbin on Contracts §561(1960).

Contrary to Commerce's belief at trial, Equity was asserting a quasi contract claim against it, not a contract implied in fact.

A Subcontractor's Quasi Contract Action Against an Owner

In [Maloney v. Therm Alum Industries Corp., 636 So. 2d 767 (Fla. Dist. Ct. App. 1994)], this court considered the availability of a quasi contract theory to a construction subcontractor seeking recovery against an owner of property, where there had been no dealings between the owner and the subcontractor. Pursuant to a contract with the general contractor, the subcontractor in *Maloney* furnished glass walls, windows and doors for the construction of an office building. The subcontractor was not paid in full for its work. The general contractor and subcontractor submitted their claims against each other to arbitration. In the circuit court action, the subcontractor sought to recover damages against the owner on a quasi contract theory. Id. at 768. Relying on two out-of-state cases, this court held that a subcontractor could maintain a quasi contract action against an owner, provided that it pled and proved two elements to establish that the enrichment of the owner was unjust — that the subcontractor had exhausted all remedies against the general contractor and still remained unpaid and that the owner had not given consideration to any person for the improvements furnished by the subcontractor. Id. at 769-70. We quoted the following passage from Paschall's Inc. v. Dozier, 219 Tenn. 45, 407 S.W.2d 150, 155 (1966):

> The most significant requirement for a recovery on quasi contract is that the enrichment to the defendant be unjust. Consequently, if the landowner has given any consideration to any person for the improvements, it would not be unjust for him to retain the benefit without paying the furnisher. Also, we think that before recovery can be had against the landowner on an unjust enrichment theory, the furnisher of the materials and labor must have exhausted his remedies against the person with whom he had contracted, and still has not received the reasonable value of his services.

Id. 636 So. 2d at 770. *Maloney* reversed the judgment for the contractor based upon quasi contract because the status of the subcontractor's arbitration claim with the general contractor was not established at trial. Under these circumstances, we held that it was "premature and therefore improper to permit the subcontractor to pursue" a quasi contract claim against the owner. Id. at 769.

In *Gene B. Glick Co.,* 651 So. 2d at 190, we affirmed a judgment in favor of a property owner who had been sued by a subcontractor on a quasi contract theory. We held that an unjust enrichment cannot exist "where payment has been made for the benefit conferred." The payment to which we referred was the owner's payment to the general contractor on the construction contract. . . .

There is language in *Maloney* which can be read to suggest that we imposed a third limitation on the ability of a subcontractor to maintain a quasi contract claim against an owner. *Maloney* quotes two paragraphs from Construction and Design Law §8.8C.1(1989), which include the following sentence:

> First, the subcontractor may not recover an equitable remedy if he has failed his legal remedies, such as a statutory mechanic's lien.

636 So. 2d at 770. We expressly recede from this statement in *Maloney* because it is without support in Florida law.

Florida's construction lien statute does not purport to be the exclusive remedy for a lienor, such as a subcontractor, against an owner. Section 713.30, Florida Statutes (1995), provides that the construction lien part of Chapter 713 "shall be cumulative to other existing remedies." The plain language of the statute does not supersede any remedies available to a party seeking payment. St. Regis Paper Co. v. Quality Pipeline, Inc., 469 So. 2d 820, 822-23 (Fla. 2d DCA 1985). Applying section 713.30, the third district rejected the argument that a materialman's failure to perfect a statutory lien left it without any remedy to recover for materials which it had furnished to a construction project. Peninsular Supply Co. v. C.B. Day Realty of Florida, Inc., 423 So. 2d 500, 501-502 (Fla. 3d DCA 1982). As the *Peninsular Supply* court observed:

> The purpose of the Mechanics' Lien Law is to prevent an owner from being obligated to pay for an improvement more than once. It was not intended, nor shall we interpret it to permit an unjust enrichment.

Id. at 503 (citations omitted).

. . .

. . . [T]wo requirements that *Maloney* imposes on a subcontractor's quasi contract action against an owner — exhaustion of remedies against the contractor and the owner's receipt of the benefit conferred without paying consideration to anyone — limit the cause of action to those situations where the enrichment of the owner is truly unjust when compared to the uncompensated subcontractor. The contractor with whom the subcontractor is in privity is always the pocket of first resort. Moreover, the owner can be liable only where it received a windfall benefit, something for nothing.

. . .

Reversal Is Required Under The Facts Of This Case

In this case, Equity did not prove at trial that Commerce had not made payment to any party for the benefits conferred on the property by Equity. This was not an affirmative defense, but an essential element of a quasi contract claim by a subcontractor against an owner. . . . Had Commerce moved for an involuntary dismissal on this ground, the motion should have been granted. Contrary to the trial court's evidentiary ruling, Commerce's attempt to prove that it had paid $64,097 directly to subcontractors for work on the building was relevant to issues in this case. What Commerce expended on this project was central to Equity's cause of action. Commerce contended that these payments were for work covered under the construction contract for which the subcontractors had not been paid by the general contractor. If the $64,097 is added to the $256,894 [sic; $223,065.04?] that Commerce paid to the general contractor, then the total amount Commerce spent on the project exceeded the contract price for the improvements. As we have observed, where an owner has given consideration for the subcontractor's work by paying out the contract price for the work, an unpaid subcontractor's claim that the owner has been unjustly enriched must fail.

The trial court's reliance on *Zaleznik* was misplaced. In that case it was undisputed that the owner received over $70,000 in construction work for which it paid no one. What Commerce paid out on this project was not fully litigated below, so whether its "enrichment" was "unjust" is an open question.

The judgment appealed is reversed, and the cause is remanded to the trial court to take additional evidence from the parties on whether Commerce made payment to or on behalf of its general contractor covering the benefits Equity conferred on the subject property. Equity shall have the burden of proving its claim of a contract implied in law that Commerce has failed to make such payment by the greater weight of the evidence. If the court shall determine that Commerce has not paid anyone for the benefits conferred by Equity, then it shall enter judgment for Equity; correspondingly, if the court shall determine that Equity has failed to prove that Commerce did not make such payment, then the court shall enter judgment for Commerce.

GUNTHER, C.J., and GLICKSTEIN, DELL, STONE, WARNER, POLEN, FARMER, KLEIN, PARIENTE, STEVENSON and SHAHOOD, JJ., concur.

NOTES AND QUESTIONS

1. *Owner's liability in restitution.* The court in *Commerce Partnership* holds that a subcontractor may recover in restitution from an owner when the owner has not paid the general contractor for the work performed and the subcontractor has exhausted its remedies against the general contractor. Accord, Maintenance Enterp., LLC v. Orascom E & C USA, Inc., 2016 WL 9450684 (S.D. Iowa). The principle of *Commerce Partnership* has also been extended to suits against a general contractor by a sub-subcontractor that has not been paid by the subcontractor. E.g., Hottinger Excav. & Ready Mix, LLC, v. R.E. Crawford Constr., LLC, 2016 WL 9735771 (D. Colo.); C. Szabo Contracting, Inc. v. Lorig Constr. Co., 19 N.E.3d 638 (Ill. App. Ct. 2014). Not all courts accept the restitutionary principle applied in *Commerce Partnership,* however. E.g., Bennett Heating & Air Conditioning, Inc. v. NationsBank of Maryland, 674 A.2d 534, 540-541 (Md. 1996). The question is discussed in detail and the various policy arguments pro and con are weighed in Doug Rendleman, Quantum Meruit for the Subcontractor: Has Restitution Jumped Off Dawson's Dock? 79 Tex. L. Rev. 2055 (2001).

2. *Restitutionary liability of lessors.* Restitutionary claims have also been brought by contractors against lessors of property when the lessee has contracted but has not paid for improvements to the leased property. Courts have commonly denied recovery for such claims, on the ground that the owner has not been unjustly enriched, where there has been no showing that the owner needed or wanted the improvements contracted for by the tenant. E.g., Graves v. Berkowitz, 15 S.W.3d 59 (Mo. Ct. App. 2000) (not inequitable for defendant owner to retain benefit of construction work without paying for it; landlord knew of work but was only "passive beneficiary"); Puttkammer v. Minth, 266 N.W.2d 361 (Wis. 1978) (contractor does not state cause of action for unjust enrichment when complaint alleges only that owner knew that improvements were being made). Some courts, however, will allow restitutionary recovery if such a showing can be made. E.g., Idaho Lumber, Inc. v. Buck, 710 P.2d 647 (Idaho Ct. App. 1985) (contractor allowed to recover from landlord on restitutionary basis for remodeling work done for tenant). See generally 2 George E. Palmer, Law of Restitution §10.7, at 422-425 (1978).

3. *The mechanic's lien.* The statutory law of virtually every jurisdiction includes provisions for "mechanic's liens." A mechanic's lien is a statutory encumbrance (as opposed to a contractual encumbrance like a mortgage) on

real property for the value of improvements made to the property by a laborer or supplier of materials pursuant to contract. Typically, the lien must be filed in the public records and suit must be brought to enforce the lien within a set period. Failure to meet these requirements results in loss of the lien. Owners of property on which improvements are being made (along with banks and other institutions that finance construction) typically protect themselves from mechanic's liens by releasing funds only when all subcontractors have signed "lien waivers." If an owner has released funds based on a lien waiver by a subcontractor, the subcontractor will almost certainly be unable to maintain a claim for restitution. See George M. Morris Construction Co. v. Four Seasons Motor Inn, Inc., 567 P.2d 965 (N.M. 1977) (lien waivers precluded action by laborers against owner who had made payments in reliance on waivers).

Watts v. Watts

Supreme Court of Wisconsin 137 Wis. 2d 506, 405 N.W.2d 303 (1987)

Shirley S. ABRAHAMSON, Justice.

This is an appeal from a judgment of the circuit court for Dane County, William D. Byrne, Judge, dismissing Sue Ann Watts' amended complaint, pursuant to sec. 802.06(2)(f), Stats. 1985-86, for failure to state a claim upon which relief may be granted. This court took jurisdiction of the appeal upon certification by the court of appeals under sec. (Rule) 809.61, Stats. 1985-86. For the reasons set forth, we hold that the complaint states a claim upon which relief may be granted. Accordingly, we reverse the judgment of the circuit court and remand the cause to the circuit court for further proceedings consistent with this opinion.

The case involves a dispute between Sue Ann Evans Watts, the plaintiff, and James Watts, the defendant, over their respective interests in property accumulated during their nonmarital cohabitation relationship which spanned 12 years and produced two children. The case presents an issue of first impression and comes to this court at the pleading stage of the case, before trial and before the facts have been determined.

The plaintiff asked the circuit court to order an accounting of the defendant's personal and business assets accumulated between June 1969 through December 1981 (the duration of the parties' cohabitation) and to determine plaintiff's share of this property. The circuit court's dismissal of plaintiff's amended complaint is the subject of this appeal. The plaintiff rests her claim for an accounting and a share in the accumulated property on the following legal theories: (1) she is entitled to an equitable division of property under sec. 767.255, Stats. 1985-86; (2) the defendant is estopped to assert as a defense to plaintiff's claim under sec. 767.255, that the parties are not married; (3) the plaintiff is entitled to damages for defendant's breach of an express contract or an implied-in-fact contract between the parties; (4) the defendant holds the accumulated property under a constructive trust based upon unjust enrichment; and (5) the plaintiff is entitled to partition of the parties' real and personal property pursuant to the partition statutes, secs. 820.01 and 842.02(1), 1985-86, and common law principles of partition.

The circuit court dismissed the amended complaint, concluding that sec. 767.255, Stats. 1985-86, authorizing a court to divide property, does not apply to the division of property between unmarried persons. Without analyzing the four other legal theories upon which the plaintiff rests her claim, the circuit court simply concluded that the legislature, not the court, should provide relief to parties who have accumulated property in non-marital cohabitation relationships. The circuit court gave no further explanation for its decision.

We agree with the circuit court that the legislature did not intend sec. 767.255 to apply to an unmarried couple. We disagree with the circuit court's implicit conclusion that courts cannot or should not, without express authorization from the legislature, divide property between persons who have engaged in nonmarital cohabitation. Courts traditionally have settled contract and property disputes between unmarried persons, some of whom have cohabited. Nonmarital cohabitation does not render every agreement between the cohabiting parties illegal and does not automatically preclude one of the parties from seeking judicial relief, such as statutory or common law partition, damages for breach of express or implied contract, constructive trust and quantum meruit where the party alleges, and later proves, facts supporting the legal theory. The issue for the court in each case is whether the complaining party has set forth any legally cognizable claim. . . .

We test the sufficiency of the plaintiff's amended complaint by first setting forth the facts asserted in the complaint and then analyzing each of the five legal theories upon which the plaintiff rests her claim for relief.

I.

The plaintiff commenced this action in 1982. The plaintiff's amended complaint alleges the following facts, which for purposes of this appeal must be accepted as true. The plaintiff and the defendant met in 1967, when she was 19 years old, was living with her parents and was working full time as a nurse's aide in preparation for a nursing career. Shortly after the parties met, the defendant persuaded the plaintiff to move into an apartment paid for by him and to quit her job. According to the amended complaint, the defendant "indicated" to the plaintiff that he would provide for her.

Early in 1969, the parties began living together in a "marriage-like" relationship, holding themselves out to the public as husband and wife. The plaintiff assumed the defendant's surname as her own. Subsequently, she gave birth to two children who were also given the defendant's surname. The parties filed joint income tax returns and maintained joint bank accounts asserting that they were husband and wife. The defendant insured the plaintiff as his wife on his medical insurance policy. He also took out a life insurance policy on her as his wife, naming himself as the beneficiary. The parties purchased real and personal property as husband and wife. The plaintiff executed documents and obligated herself on promissory notes to lending institutions as the defendant's wife.

During their relationship, the plaintiff contributed childcare and home making services, including cleaning, cooking, laundering, shopping, running errands, and maintaining the grounds surrounding the parties' home. Additionally, the plaintiff contributed personal property to the relationship which she owned at the beginning of the relationship or acquired through gifts or purchases during the relationship. She served as hostess for the defendant for social and business-related events. The amended complaint further asserts that periodically, between 1969 and 1975, the plaintiff cooked and cleaned for the defendant and his employees while his business, a landscaping service, was building and landscaping a golf course.

From 1973 to 1976, the plaintiff worked 20-25 hours per week at the defendant's office, performing duties as a receptionist, typist, and assistant bookkeeper. From 1976 to 1981, the plaintiff worked 40-60 hours per week at a business she started with the defendant's sister-in-law, then continued and managed the business herself after the dissolution of that partnership. The plaintiff further alleges that in 1981 the defendant made their relationship so intolerable that she was forced to move from their home and their relationship was irretrievably broken. Subsequently, the defendant barred the plaintiff from returning to her business.

The plaintiff alleges that during the parties' relationship, and because of her domestic and business contributions, the business and personal wealth of the couple increased. Furthermore, the plaintiff alleges that she never received any compensation for these contributions to the relationship and that the defendant indicated to the plaintiff both orally and through his conduct that he considered her to be his wife and that she would share equally in the increased wealth.

The plaintiff asserts that since the breakdown of the relationship the defendant has refused to share equally with her the wealth accumulated through their joint efforts or to compensate her in any way for her contributions to the relationship.

II.

The plaintiff's first legal theory to support her claim against the property accumulated during the cohabitation is that the plaintiff, defendant, and their children constitute a "family," thus entitling the plaintiff to bring an action for property division under sec. 767.02(1)(h), Stats. 1985-86, and to have the court "divide the property of the parties and divest and transfer the title of any such property" pursuant to sec. 767.255, 1985-86.

The plaintiff asserts that the legislature intended secs. 767.02(1)(h) and 767.255, which usually govern division of property between married persons in divorce or legal separation proceedings, to govern a property division action between unmarried cohabitants who constitute a family. The plaintiff points out that secs. 767.02(1)(h) and 767.255 are part of chapter 767, which is entitled "Actions Affecting the Family," and that in 1979 the legislature deliberately changed the title of the chapter from "Actions Affecting Marriage" to "Actions Affecting the Family." The legislature has failed to provide any definition for "family" under ch. 767, or for that matter under any chapter of the Family Code.

The plaintiff relies on Warden v. Warden, 36 Wash. App. 693, 676 P.2d 1037 (1984), to support her claim for relief under secs. 767.02(1)(h) and 767.255. In *Warden,* the Washington court of appeals held that the statute providing guidelines for property division upon dissolution of marriage, legal separation, etc., could also be applied to divide property acquired by unmarried cohabitants in what was "tantamount to a marital family except for a legal marriage." *Warden,* 36 Wash. App. at 698, 676 P.2d at 1039. *Warden* is remarkably similar on its facts to the instant case. The parties in *Warden* had lived together for 11 years, had two children, held themselves out as husband and wife, acquired property together, and filed joint tax returns. On those facts, the Washington court of appeals held that the trial court correctly treated the parties as a "family" within the meaning of the Washington marriage dissolution statute. In addition, the trial court had considered such statutory factors as the length and purpose of the parties' relationship, their two children, and the contributions and future prospects of each in determining their respective shares of the property.

Although the *Warden* case provides support for the plaintiff's argument, most courts which have addressed the issue of whether marriage dissolution statutes provide relief to unmarried cohabitants have either rejected or avoided application of a marriage dissolution statute to unmarried cohabitants. See, e.g., Marvin v. Marvin, 18 Cal. 3d 660, 681, 134 Cal. Rptr. 815, 557 P.2d 106 (1976); Metten v. Benge, 366 N.W.2d 577, 579-80 (Iowa 1985); Glasgo v. Glasgo, 410 N.E.2d 1325, 1331 (Ind. Ct. App. 1980); Kozlowski v. Kozlowski, 80 N.J. 378, 383, 403 A.2d 902, 905 (1979).

The purpose of statutory construction is to ascertain the intent of the legislature and give effect to that intent. If the language of the statute is unclear, the court will endeavor to discover the legislature's intent as disclosed by the scope, history, context, subject matter and purpose of the statute. Ball v. District No. 4, Area Bd., 117 Wis. 2d 529, 538, 345 N.W.2d 389 (1984).

While we agree with the plaintiff that some provisions in ch. 767 govern a mother, father, and their children, regardless of marriage,[7] upon our analysis of sec. 767.255 and the Family Code, we conclude that the legislature did not intend sec. 767.255 to extend to unmarried cohabitants.

When the legislature added what is now sec. 767.255 in 1977 as part of the no fault divorce bill, it stated that its "sole purpose" was "to promote an equitable and reasonable adjudication of the economic and custodial issues involved in *marriage* relationships." (emphasis supplied) Moreover, the unambiguous language of sec. 767.255 and the criteria for property division listed in sec. 767.255 plainly contemplate that the parties who are governed by that section are or have been married. Finally, secs. 767.02(1)(h) and 767.255 were both in existence before the 1979 legislature changed the title of ch. 767 from "Marriage" to "Family." A change in the title of the chapter would not change the import of these statutory provisions.

---

7. The plaintiff correctly points out that ch. 767 includes actions for determining paternity, which are not dependent upon the marital status of the parents. See secs. 767.45-767.53, Stats. 1985-86.

Furthermore, the Family Code emphasizes marriage. The entire Family Code, of which ch. 767 is an integral part, is governed generally by the provisions of sec. 765.001(2), which states in part that "[i]t is the intent of chs. 765 to 768 to promote the stability and best interests of *marriage and the family*. . . . *Marriage* is the institution that *is the foundation of family and of society*. Its stability is basic to morality and civilization, and of vital interest to society and the state." (emphasis supplied) Section 765.001(3) further states that "[c]hapters 765 to 768 shall be liberally construed to effect the objectives of sub. (2)." The conclusion is almost inescapable from this language in sec. 765.001(2)(3) that the legislature not only intended chs. 765-768 to protect and promote the "family," but also intended "family" to be within the "marriage" context.[10]

The statutory prohibition of marriages which do not conform to statutory requirements, sec. 765.21, Stats. 1985-86,[11] further suggests that the legislature intended that the Family Code applies, for the most part, to those couples who have been joined in marriage according to law.

On the basis of our analysis of sec. 767.255 and the Family Code which revealed no clear evidence that the legislature intended sec. 767.255 to apply to unmarried persons, we decline the invitation to extend the application of sec. 767.255 to unmarried cohabitants. We therefore hold that the plaintiff has not stated a claim for property division under sec. 767.255.

III.

The plaintiff urges that the defendant, as a result of his own words and conduct, be estopped from asserting the lack of a legal marriage as a defense against the plaintiff's claim for property division under sec. 767.255. . . .

Although the defendant has not discussed this legal theory, we conclude that the doctrine of "marriage by estoppel" should not be applied in this case. We reach this result primarily because we have already concluded that the legislature did not intend sec. 767.255 to govern property division between unmarried cohabitants. We do not think the parties' conduct should place them within the ambit of a statute which the legislature did not intend to govern them.

IV.

The plaintiff's third legal theory on which her claim rests is that she and the defendant had a contract to share equally the property accumulated during their relationship. The essence of the complaint is that the parties had a contract, either an express or implied in fact contract, which the defendant breached.

10. When the legislature abolished criminal sanctions for cohabitation in 1983, it nevertheless added a section to the criminal code stating that while the state does not regulate private sexual activity of consenting adults, the state does not condone or encourage sexual conduct outside the institution of marriage. . . .

11. Common law marriages were abolished in 1917. Laws of 1917, ch. 218, sec. 21. Sec. 765.21, Stats. 1985-86, provides that marriages contracted in violation of specified provisions of ch. 765 are void.

Wisconsin courts have long recognized the importance of freedom of contract and have endeavored to protect the right to contract. A contract will not be enforced, however, if it violates public policy. A declaration that the contract is against public policy should be made only after a careful balancing, in the light of all the circumstances, of the interest in enforcing a particular promise against the policy against enforcement. Courts should be reluctant to frustrate a party's reasonable expectations without a corresponding benefit to be gained in deterring "misconduct" or avoiding inappropriate use of the judicial system. . . .; Restatement (Second) of Contracts Section 178 comments *b* and *e* (1981).

The defendant appears to attack the plaintiff's contract theory on three grounds. First, the defendant apparently asserts that the court's recognition of plaintiff's contract claim for a share of the parties' property contravenes the Wisconsin Family Code. Second, the defendant asserts that the legislature, not the courts, should determine the property and contract rights of unmarried cohabiting parties. Third, the defendant intimates that the parties' relationship was immoral and illegal and that any recognition of a contract between the parties or plaintiff's claim for a share of the property accumulated during the cohabitation contravenes public policy.

The defendant rests his argument that judicial recognition of a contract between unmarried cohabitants for property division violates the Wisconsin Family Code on Hewitt v. Hewitt, 77 Ill. 2d 49, 31 Ill. Dec. 827, 394 N.E.2d 1204, 3 A.L.R.4th 1 (1979). In *Hewitt* the Illinois Supreme Court concluded that judicial recognition of mutual property rights between unmarried cohabitants would violate the policy of the Illinois Marriage and Dissolution Act because enhancing the attractiveness of a private arrangement contravenes the Act's policy of strengthening and preserving the integrity of marriage. The Illinois court concluded that allowing such a contract claim would weaken the sanctity of marriage, put in doubt the rights of inheritance, and open the door to false pretenses of marriage. *Hewitt*, 77 Ill. 2d at 65, 31 Ill. Dec. at 834, 394 N.E.2d at 1211.

We agree with Professor Prince and other commentators that the *Hewitt* court made an unsupportable inferential leap when it found that cohabitation agreements run contrary to statutory policy and that the *Hewitt* court's approach is patently inconsistent with the principle that public policy limits are to be narrowly and exactly applied.[14]

Furthermore, the Illinois statutes upon which the Illinois supreme court rested its decision are distinguishable from the Wisconsin statutes. The Illinois supreme court relied on the fact that Illinois still retained "fault" divorce and that cohabitation was unlawful. By contrast, Wisconsin abolished "fault" in divorce in 1977 and abolished criminal sanctions for nonmarital cohabitation in 1983.

14. Prince, Public Policy Limitations in Cohabitation Agreements: Unruly Horse or Circus Pony, 70 Minn. L. Rev. 163, 189-205 (1985).

The defendant has failed to persuade this court that enforcing an express or implied in fact contract between these parties would in fact violate the Wisconsin Family Code. The Family Code, chs. 765-68, Stats. 1985-86, is intended to promote the institution of marriage and the family. We find no indication, however, that the Wisconsin legislature intended the Family Code to restrict in any way a court's resolution of property or contract disputes between unmarried cohabitants.

The defendant also urges that if the court is not willing to say that the Family Code proscribes contracts between unmarried cohabiting parties, then the court should refuse to resolve the contract and property rights of unmarried cohabitants without legislative guidance. The defendant asserts that this court should conclude, as the *Hewitt* court did, that the task of determining the rights of cohabiting parties is too complex and difficult for the court and should be left to the legislature. We are not persuaded by the defendant's argument. Courts have traditionally developed principles of contract and property law through the case-by-case method of the common law. While ultimately the legislature may resolve the problems raised by unmarried cohabiting parties, we are not persuaded that the court should refrain from resolving such disputes until the legislature gives us direction. Our survey of the cases in other jurisdictions reveals that *Hewitt* is not widely followed.

We turn to the defendant's third point, namely, that any contract between the parties regarding property division contravenes public policy because the contract is based on immoral or illegal sexual activity. . . . [A]t oral argument defendant's attorney indicated that he did not find this argument persuasive in light of the current community mores, the substantial number of unmarried people who cohabit, and the legislature's abolition of criminal sanctions for cohabitation. . . . Because illegal sexual activity has posed a problem for courts in contract actions, we discuss this issue even though the defendant did not emphasize it.

Courts have generally refused to enforce contracts for which the sole consideration is sexual relations, sometimes referred to as "meretricious" relationships. See In Matter of Estate of Steffes, 95 Wis. 2d 490, 514, 290 N.W.2d 697 (1980), citing Restatement of Contracts Section 589 (1932). Courts distinguish, however, between contracts that are explicitly and inseparably founded on sexual services and those that are not. This court, and numerous other courts,[17] have concluded that "a bargain between two people is not illegal merely because there is an illicit relationship between the two so long as the bargain is independent of the illicit relationship and the illicit relationship does not constitute any part of the consideration bargained for and is not a condition of the bargain." *Steffes,* supra, 95 Wis. 2d at 514, 290 N.W.2d 697.

---

17. See, e.g., Glasgo v. Glasgo, 410 N.E.2d 1325, 1331 (Ind. App. 1980); Tyranski v. Piggins, 44 Mich. App. 570, 573-74, 205 N.W.2d 595, 598-99 (1973); Kozlowski v. Kozlowski, 80 N.J. 378, 387, 403 A.2d 902, 907 (1979); Latham v. Latham, 274 Or. 421, 426-27, 547 P.2d 144, 147 (1976); Marvin v. Marvin, 18 Cal. 3d 660, 670-71, 134 Cal. Rptr. 815, 822, 557 P.2d 106, 113 (1976).

While not condoning the illicit sexual relationship of the parties, many courts have recognized that the result of a court's refusal to enforce contract and property rights between unmarried cohabitants is that one party keeps all or most of the assets accumulated during the relationship, while the other party, no more or less "guilty," is deprived of property which he or she has helped to accumulate. . . .

The *Hewitt* decision, which leaves one party to the relationship enriched at the expense of the other party who had contributed to the acquisition of the property, has often been criticized by courts and commentators as being unduly harsh.[18] Moreover, courts recognize that their refusal to enforce what are in other contexts clearly lawful promises will not undo the parties' relationship and may not discourage others from entering into such relationships. Tyranski v. Piggins, 44 Mich. App. 570, 577, 205 N.W.2d 595 (1973). A harsh, per se rule that the contract and property rights of unmarried cohabiting parties will not be recognized might actually encourage a partner with greater income potential to avoid marriage in order to retain all accumulated assets, leaving the other party with nothing. See Marvin v. Marvin, supra, 18 Cal. 3d at 683, 134 Cal. Rptr. at 831, 557 P.2d at 122. . . .

The plaintiff has alleged that she quit her job and abandoned her career training upon the defendant's promise to take care of her. A change in one party's circumstances in performance of the agreement may imply an agreement between the parties. *Steffes,* supra, 95 Wis. 2d at 504, 290 N.W.2d 697; *Tyranski,* supra, 44 Mich. App. at 574, 205 N.W.2d at 597.

In addition, the plaintiff alleges that she performed housekeeping, childbearing, childrearing, and other services related to the maintenance of the parties' home, in addition to various services for the defendant's business and her own business, for which she received no compensation. Courts have recognized that money, property, or services (including housekeeping or childrearing) may constitute adequate consideration independent of the parties' sexual relationship to support an agreement to share or transfer property. . . . *Steffes,* supra 95 Wis. 2d at 501, 290 N.W.2d 697.[19]

According to the plaintiff's complaint, the parties cohabited for more than twelve years, held joint bank accounts, made joint purchases, filed joint income tax returns, and were listed as husband and wife on other legal documents. Courts have held that such a relationship and "joint acts of a financial nature

18. See Prince, Public Policy Limitations on Cohabitation Agreements: Unruly Horse or Circus Pony, 70 Minn. L. Rev. 163, 189-205 (1985); Oldham & Caudill, A Reconnaissance of Public Policy Restrictions upon Enforcement of Contracts between Cohabitants, 18 Fam. L.Q. 93, 132 (Spring 1984); Comment, Marvin v. Marvin: Five Years Later, 65 Marq. L. Rev. 389, 414 (1982).

19. Until recently, the prevailing view was that services performed in the context of a "family or marriage relationship" were presumed gratuitous. However, that presumption was rebuttable. See *Steffes,* 95 Wis. 2d at 501, 290 N.W.2d at 703-704. In *Steffes,* we held the presumption to be irrelevant where the plaintiff can show either an express or implied agreement to pay for those services, even where the plaintiff has rendered them "with a sense of affection, devotion and duty." Id., 95 Wis. 2d at 503, 290 N.W.2d at 703-704. For a discussion of the evolution of thought regarding the economic value of homemaking services by cohabitants, see Bruch, Property Rights of De Facto Spouses Including Thoughts on the Value of Homemakers' Services, 10 Fam. L.Q. 101, 110-14 (Summer 1976).

can give rise to an inference that the parties intended to share equally." Beal v. Beal, 282 Or. 115, 122, 577 P.2d 507, 510 (1978). The joint ownership of property and the filing of joint income tax returns strongly implies that the parties intended their relationship to be in the nature of a joint enterprise, financially as well as personally. See *Beal,* 282 Or. at 122, 577 P.2d at 510; Warden v. Warden, supra, 36 Wash. App. at 696-97, 676 P.2d at 1038.

. . . Accordingly, we conclude that the plaintiff in this case has pleaded the facts necessary to state a claim for damages resulting from the defendant's breach of an express or an implied in fact contract to share with the plaintiff the property accumulated through the efforts of both parties during their relationship. Once again, we do not judge the merits of the plaintiff's claim; we merely hold that she be given her day in court to prove her claim.

V.

The plaintiff's fourth theory of recovery involves unjust enrichment. Essentially, she alleges that the defendant accepted and retained the benefit of services she provided knowing that she expected to share equally in the wealth accumulated during their relationship. She argues that it is unfair for the defendant to retain all the assets they accumulated under these circumstances and that a constructive trust should be imposed on the property as a result of the defendant's unjust enrichment. In his brief, the defendant does not attack specifically either the legal theory or the factual allegations made by the plaintiff.

Unlike claims for breach of an express or implied in fact contract, a claim of unjust enrichment does not arise out of an agreement entered into by the parties. Rather, an action for recovery based upon unjust enrichment is grounded on the moral principle that one who has received a benefit has a duty to make restitution where retaining such a benefit would be unjust. Puttkammer v. Minth, 83 Wis. 2d 686, 689, 266 N.W.2d 361, 363 (1978).

Because no express or implied in fact agreement exists between the parties, recovery based upon unjust enrichment is sometimes referred to as "quasi contract," or contract "implied in law" rather than "implied in fact." Quasi contracts are obligations created by law to prevent injustice. Shulse v. City of Mayville, 223 Wis. 624, 632, 271 N.W. 643 (1937).

In Wisconsin, an action for unjust enrichment, or quasi contract, is based upon proof of three elements: (1) a benefit conferred on the defendant by the plaintiff, (2) appreciation or knowledge by the defendant of the benefit, and (3) acceptance or retention of the benefit by the defendant under circumstances making it inequitable for the defendant to retain the benefit. *Puttkammer,* supra, 83 Wis. 2d at 689, 266 N.W.2d 361; Wis. J.I. Civil No. 3028 (1981).

The plaintiff has cited no cases directly supporting actions in unjust enrichment by unmarried cohabitants, and the defendant provides no authority against it. . . .

The *Steffes* case, however, does provide . . . support for the plaintiff's position. Although *Steffes* involved a claim for recovery in contract by an unmarried cohabitant for the value of services she performed for the decedent, the same equitable principles that governed that case would appear to apply in a case where the plaintiff is seeking recovery based upon unjust enrichment. In *Steffes,* the court cited with approval a statement by the trial judge that "[t]he question I have in mind is why should the estate be enriched when that man was just as much a part of the illicit relationship as she was and not let her have her fair dues. I don't understand that law that would interpret unjust enrichment that way and deprive one and let the other benefit and do it on the basis that there was an illicit relationship but not equally held against the both. . . ." *Steffes,* supra, 95 Wis. 2d at 508, 290 N.W.2d 697.

As part of his general argument, the defendant claims that the court should leave the parties to an illicit relationship such as the one in this case essentially as they are found, providing no relief at all to either party. For support, the defendant relies heavily on Hewitt v. Hewitt, supra, and the dissent in *Steffes,* to argue that courts should provide no relief whatsoever to unmarried cohabitants until the legislature provides specifically for it. See *Steffes,* supra, 95 Wis. 2d at 521-22, 290 N.W.2d 697 (Coffey, J., dissenting).

As we have discussed previously, allowing no relief at all to one party in a so-called "illicit" relationship effectively provides total relief to the other, by leaving that party owner of all the assets acquired through the efforts of both. Yet it cannot seriously be argued that the party retaining all the assets is less "guilty" than the other. Such a result is contrary to the principles of equity. Many courts have held, and we now so hold, that unmarried cohabitants may raise claims based upon unjust enrichment following the termination of their relationships where one of the parties attempts to retain an unreasonable amount of the property acquired through the efforts of both.

In this case, the plaintiff alleges that she contributed both property and services to the parties' relationship. She claims that because of these contributions the parties' assets increased, but that she was never compensated for her contributions. She further alleges that the defendant, knowing that the plaintiff expected to share in the property accumulated, "accepted the services rendered to him by the plaintiff" and that it would be unfair under the circumstances to allow him to retain everything while she receives nothing. We conclude that the facts alleged are sufficient to state a claim for recovery based upon unjust enrichment. . . .

VI.

The plaintiff's last alternative legal theory on which her claim rests is the doctrine of partition. The plaintiff has asserted in her complaint a claim for partition of "all real and personal property accumulated by the couple during their relationship according to the plaintiff's interest therein and pursuant to Chapters 820 and 842, Wis. Stats." . . .

In Wisconsin partition is a remedy under both the statutes and common law. Partition applies generally to all disputes over property held by more than one party. . . .

In this case, the plaintiff has alleged that she and the defendant were engaged in a joint venture or partnership, that they purchased real and personal property as husband and wife, and that they intended to share all the property acquired during their relationship. . . . We do not, of course, presume to judge the merits of the plaintiff's claim. Proof of her allegations must be made to the circuit court. We merely hold that the plaintiff has alleged sufficient facts in her complaint to state a claim for relief statutory or common law partition.

In summary, we hold that the plaintiff's complaint has stated a claim upon which relief may be granted. We conclude that her claim may not rest on sec. 767.255, Stats. 1985-86, or the doctrine of "marriage by estoppel," but that it may rest on contract, unjust enrichment or partition. Accordingly, we reverse the judgment of the circuit court, and remand the cause to the circuit court for further proceedings consistent with this opinion.

The judgment of the circuit court is reversed and the cause remanded.

NOTES AND QUESTIONS

1. *The **Marvin** case; contractual and restitutionary recovery for nonmarried cohabitants.* If parties are legally married, either by a "ceremonial" marriage, or by a "common law" marriage (recognized in a minority of jurisdictions), and subsequently separate or divorce, the spouse who sacrificed income while rendering services to the other may obtain court-ordered awards of support or alimony. In addition, in many jurisdictions courts have the power to order an equitable division of marital assets. Beginning with the leading case of Marvin v. Marvin, 557 P.2d 106 (Cal. 1976) (en banc), a substantial majority of jurisdictions has allowed a party to a nonmarital relationship who makes substantial contributions to the other party to obtain some form of recovery from the other. Such courts have relied on a number of legal theories, including express contract, implied-in-fact contract, and restitution based on unjust enrichment. The court in *Marvin* indicated that the opinion did "not preclude the evolution of additional equitable remedies to protect the expectations of the parties to a nonmarital relationship in cases in which existing remedies prove inadequate. . . ." Id. at 123 n.25. Since its rendition nearly 40 years ago, the *Marvin* case has become the seminal and generally accepted authority for the allowance of claims between unmarried cohabiting partners. See generally Alexander C. Morey & Dixie Grossman, Property Rights of Unmarried Cohabitants — Nothing New under the Sun, 25 J. Am. Acad. Matrim. Law. 87, 88, 100 (2015) ("Although the world has vastly changed since 1976 . . . *Marvin* and its progeny remain the standard-bearers"). Types of claims sustainable under the general umbrella of *Marvin* include quantum meruit, express contract, contract implied-in-fact and implied-in-law, constructive trust, joint venture and partition. Id. See, e.g., In re Estate of Mousel, 869 N.W.2d 169 (Wis. Ct. App. 2015) (court could apply promissory estoppel against estate of claimant's deceased partner to give her the financial equivalent of half-ownership of joint domicile; *Watts* decision cited and relied on as authorizing generally the maintenance of property claims between unmarried cohabitants).

Courts in a few states, however, have continued to find contracts between unmarried cohabitants unenforceable. For example, Hewitt v. Hewitt, 394

N.E.2d 1204 (Ill. 1979), discussed by the court in *Watts*, denied recovery to a plaintiff who had lived with the defendant for 15 years in a nonmarital relationship to which three children were born. Despite vigorous arguments based both on intervening changes in Illinois statutory law and on the virtually unanimous opinions of other courts faced with similar cases, the rule of the *Hewitt* case was recently affirmed by the Illinois Supreme Court. Blumenthal v. Brewer, 69 N.E.3d 834 (Ill. 2016).

Section 28 of the Restatement (Third) of Restitution recognizes the right of one unmarried cohabitant to recover in restitution from another cohabitant:

> **§28 Unmarried Cohabitants**
>
> (1) If two persons have formerly lived together in a relationship resembling marriage, and if one of them owns a specific asset to which the other has made substantial, uncompensated contributions in the form of property or services, the person making such contributions has a claim in restitution against the owner as necessary to prevent unjust enrichment upon the dissolution of the relationship.
>
> (2) The rule of subsection (1) may be displaced, modified, or supplemented by local domestic relations law.

2. *Measure of recovery.* Assuming that a court recognizes a right to quantum meruit recovery on behalf of a cohabitant, how is such recovery to be measured? On trial following remand in *Watts*, a jury awarded the plaintiff $113,000 on her unjust enrichment claim. The evidence showed that the defendant's net worth had increased by $1,113,900.88, during the 11 years the parties cohabited, so the jury's award amounted to about 10 percent of the defendant's increase in net worth. The Wisconsin Court of Appeals affirmed. 448 N.W.2d 292 (Wis. Ct. App. 1989). By contrast, in Waage v. Borer, 525 N.W.2d 96 (Wis. Ct. App. 1994), the court distinguished *Watts* and held that uncompensated services rendered during a cohabitation period of eight years were not sufficient to establish a claim for unjust enrichment because the claimant had failed to show that the defendant's wealth had been increased during the period of cohabitation. The court also ruled that the claimant's forgone employment opportunities were not relevant to her unjust enrichment claim. Accord, Sands v. Menard, 904 N.W.2d 789 (Wis. 2017) (two justices dissenting).

Although the Wisconsin courts appear to focus on the increase in the defendant's net worth in measuring quantum meruit recovery in claims between cohabitants, courts in other jurisdictions will not necessarily agree, particularly in cases in which the increase in the defendant's wealth has been substantial. For example, in Maglica v. Maglica, 78 Cal. Rptr. 2d 101 (Ct. App. 1998), the California Court of Appeals reversed a jury verdict awarding one cohabitant $84 million on a quantum meruit theory. The court ruled that the trial judge had committed reversible error by instructing the jury to measure recovery by the amount by which the defendant had benefited from the plaintiff's services. The court held that the proper measure of recovery was the reasonable value of the plaintiff's services. See also Comment *e* of the Restatement (Third) of Restitution §28, which adopts the approach of *Maglica* with regard to the measure of recovery.

3. *Intra-family claims.* Another common family situation in which restitutionary claims have been asserted involves cases in which one family member has cared for an aged parent or relative and then asserts a restitutionary claim against the estate of the deceased parent or relative. The effect of allowing such claims is to enable the family member asserting the claim to obtain a larger share of the estate than would otherwise be received under either the deceased person's will or the state's intestacy law (if no will is involved). Underlying such claims may be family tensions resulting from feelings that the family member providing services has made a personal sacrifice while the others (often siblings of the claimant) have not done their fair share in caring for the aged parent. The general rule followed in deciding such claims is that services rendered by family members to each other are presumed to be gratuitous, while services rendered between individuals who are not members of the same family are presumed to be for compensation. Whether the parties are part of the same family depends on the facts and circumstances rather than simply kinship. Consider, for example, Adams v. Underwood, 470 S.W.2d 180 (Tenn. 1971), where the Tennessee Supreme Court stated:

> where, as in this case, an adult or emancipated child, by pre-arrangement with a parent, gives up an established home and moves into the home of the parent, not for the purposes of reestablishing a family relationship, but for the purpose of rendering services of an extraordinarily burdensome nature, over a long period of time, the presumption of gratuity need not apply.

Id. at 186. See also In re Estate of Bush (Fuller v. Terrell), 908 S.W.2d 809 (Mo. 1995) (plaintiff allowed to recover for services rendered to sister-in-law without having to overcome presumption that services were rendered gratuitously).

Even if the presumption that the services were rendered gratuitously applies, the presumption can be overcome, but courts differ on what the party seeking recovery must establish. See In re Grossman's Estate, 27 N.W.2d 365 (Wis. 1947) (presumption overcome when adult daughter left her home three times for extended periods to move 100 miles to care for ailing parents). Other courts may require a stronger showing to allow recovery between family members. Some courts demand proof by "clear and convincing evidence," a standard that is more demanding than the normal civil standard of the "preponderance of the evidence." Harrison v. Harrison, 75 So. 2d 620 (Ala. 1954). Which approach would you favor? Why? What factors should a court take into account in deciding whether to allow such a restitutionary claim?

2. Promissory Restitution

In the preceding section we examined situations in which one party sought a restitutionary recovery for benefits conferred on another where the other party never expressly promised to pay for those benefits. Suppose the recipient of services does make an express promise to pay for them, but only after the benefits are received? As we saw in the *Plowman* case in the previous chapter, classical theory would hold that a promise for benefits previously received was not binding because the benefits constituted "past consideration." Even classical theory recognized some exceptions to the past consideration doctrine; as we will see, additional exceptions are being created or explored by contemporary courts and the Restatement (Second). The following cases examine these developments.

Mills v. Wyman

Massachusetts Supreme Judicial Court 20 Mass. (3 Pick.) 207 (1825)

This was an action of assumpsit brought to recover a compensation for the board, nursing, &c., of Levi Wyman, son of the defendant, from the 5th to the 20th of February, 1821. The plaintiff then lived at Hartford, in Connecticut; the defendant, at Shrewsbury, in this county. Levi Wyman, at the time when the services were rendered, was about 25 years of age, and had long ceased to be a member of his father's family. He was on his return from a voyage at sea, and being suddenly taken sick at Hartford, and being poor and in distress, was relieved by the plaintiff in the manner and to the extent above stated. On the 24th of February, after all the expenses had been incurred, the defendant wrote a letter to the plaintiff, promising to pay him such expenses. There was no consideration for this promise, except what grew out of the relation which subsisted between Levi Wyman and the defendant, and Howe J., before whom the cause was tried in the Court of Common Pleas, thinking this not sufficient to support the action, directed a non-suit. To this direction the plaintiff filed exceptions.

PARKER, C.J.

General rules of law established for the protection and security of honest and fair-minded men, who may inconsiderately make promises without any equivalent, will sometimes screen men of a different character from engagements which they are bound in foro conscientiae to perform. This is a defect inherent in all human systems of legislation. This rule that a mere verbal promise, without any consideration, cannot be enforced by action, is universal in its application, and cannot be departed from to suit particular cases in which a refusal to perform such a promise may be disgraceful.

The promise declared on in this case appears to have been made without any legal consideration. The kindness and services towards the sick son of the defendant were not bestowed at his request. The son was in no respect under the care of the defendant. He was twenty-five years old, and had long left his father's family. On his return from a foreign country, he fell sick among strangers, and the plaintiff acted the part of the good Samaritan, giving him shelter and comfort until he died. The defendant, his father, on being informed of this event, influenced by a transient feeling of gratitude, promises in writing to pay the plaintiff for the expenses he had incurred. But he has determined to break this promise, and is willing to have his case appear on record as a strong example of particular injustice sometimes necessarily resulting from the operation of general rules.

It is said a moral obligation is a sufficient consideration to support an express promise; and some authorities lay down the rule thus broadly; but upon examination of the cases we are satisfied that the universality of the rule cannot be supported, and that there must have been some preexisting obligation, which has become inoperative by positive law, to form a basis for an effective promise. The cases of debts barred by the statute of limitations, of debts incurred by infants, of debts of bankrupts, are generally put for illustration of the rule. Express promises founded on such preexisting equitable obligations may be enforced; there is a good consideration for them; they merely remove an impediment created by law to the recovery of debts honestly due, but which public policy protects the debtors from being compelled to pay. In all these cases there was originally a quid pro quo; and according to the principles of natural justice the party receiving ought to pay; but the legislature has said he shall not be coerced; then comes the promise to pay the debt that is barred, the promise of the man to pay the debt of the infant, of the discharged bankrupt to restore to his creditor what by the law he had lost. In all these cases there is a moral obligation founded upon an antecedent valuable consideration. These promises therefore have a sound legal basis. They are not promises to pay something for nothing; not naked pacts; but the voluntary revival or creation of obligation which before existed in natural law, but which had been dispensed with, not for the benefit of the party obliged solely, but principally for the public convenience. If moral obligation, in its fullest sense, is a good substratum for an express promise, it is not easy to perceive why it is not equally good to support an implied promise. What a man ought to do, generally he ought to be made to do, whether he promise or refuse. But the law of society has left most of such obligations to the *interior* forum, as the tribunal of conscience has been aptly called. Is there not a moral obligation upon every son who has become affluent by means of the education and advantages bestowed upon him by his father, to relieve that father from pecuniary embarrassment, to promote his comfort and happiness, and even to share with him his riches, if thereby he will be made happy? And yet such a son may, with impunity, leave such a father in any degree of penury above that which will expose the community in which he dwells, to the danger of being obliged to preserve him from absolute want. Is not a wealthy father under strong moral obligation to advance the interest of an obedient, well disposed son, to furnish him with the means of acquiring and maintaining a becoming rank in life, to rescue him from the horrors of debt incurred by misfortune? Yet the law will uphold him in any degree of parsimony, short of that which would reduce his son to the necessity of seeking public charity.

Without doubt there are great interests of society which justify withholding the coercive arm of the law from these duties of imperfect obligation, as they are called; imperfect, not because they are less binding upon the conscience than those which are called perfect, but because the wisdom of the social law does not impose sanctions upon them.

A deliberate promise, in writing, made freely and without any mistake, one which may lead the party to whom it is made into contracts and expenses, cannot be broken without a violation of moral duty. But if there was nothing paid or promised for it, the law, perhaps wisely, leaves the execution of it to the conscience of him who makes it. It is only when the party making the promise gains something, or he to whom it is made loses something, that the law gives the promise validity. And in the case of the promise of the adult to pay the debt of the infant, of the debtor discharged by the statute of limitations or bankruptcy, the principle is preserved by looking back to the origin of the transaction, where an equivalent is to be found. An exact equivalent is not required by the law; for there being a consideration, the parties are left to estimate its value: though here the courts of equity will step in to relieve from gross inadequacy between the consideration and the promise.

These principles are deduced from the general current of decided cases upon the subject, as well as from the known maxims of the common law. The general position, that moral obligation is a sufficient consideration for an express promise, is to be limited in its application, to cases where at some time or other a good or valuable consideration has existed.

A legal obligation is always a sufficient consideration to support either an express or an implied promise; such as an infant's debt for necessaries, or a father's promise to pay for the support and education of his minor children. But when the child shall have attained to manhood, and shall have become his own agent in the world's business, the debts he incurs, whatever may be their nature, create no obligation upon the father; and it seems to follow, that his promise founded upon such a debt has no legally binding force.

The cases of instruments under seal and certain mercantile contracts, in which considerations need not be proved, do not contradict the principles above suggested. The first import a consideration in themselves, and the second belong to a branch of the mercantile law, which has found it necessary to disregard the point of consideration in respect to instruments negotiable in their nature and essential to the interests of commerce. . . .

It has been attempted to show a legal obligation on the part of the defendant by virtue of our statute, which compels lineal kindred in the ascending or descending line to support such of their poor relations as are likely to become chargeable to the town where they have their settlement. But it is a sufficient answer to this position, that such legal obligation does not exist except in the very cases provided for in the statute, and never until the party charged has been adjudged to be of sufficient ability thereto. We do not know from the report any of the facts which are necessary to create such an obligation. Whether the deceased had a legal settlement in this commonwealth at the time of his death, whether he was likely to become chargeable had he lived, whether the defendant was of sufficient ability, are essential facts to be adjudicated by the court to which is given jurisdiction on this subject. The legal liability does not arise until these facts have all been ascertained by judgment, after hearing the party intended to be charged.

For the foregoing reasons we are all of opinion that the nonsuit directed by the Court of Common Pleas was right, and that judgment be entered thereon for costs for the defendant.

NOTES AND QUESTIONS

1. *Hypothetical variations of **Mills**.* Suppose the plaintiff had written the defendant about his son's illness on February 5 and the defendant had promptly written back promising to pay his son's expenses. Would the result have been different? Suppose instead that Levi Wyman was a 16-year-old boy, living at home with his parents, when he became ill while on a short trip away from home. Would the result have been different? On the latter assumed facts, would it have mattered whether the father had written the letter of February 24, promising to pay for his son's care?

2. *Moral obligation.* Cases like Mills v. Wyman are often referred to as involving enforcement of a "moral obligation." It is useful, however, to refine this point. The court in *Mills* clearly holds that the law will not necessarily enforce every promise, regardless of the morality of failing to honor a promise seriously made. In stating the general rule, the court notes that "there are great interests of society which justify withholding the coercive arm of the law from these duties of imperfect obligation." What interests do you suppose the court had in mind? Charles Fried, a noted philosopher and contract scholar, argues that this view is wrong and that the law should follow morality, enforcing a promise seriously made. Recall the material following the *Plowman* case in Chapter 2.

The court in *Mills* also declares that a moral obligation can give rise to a legal obligation in certain specific situations: If a person was subject to a legal obligation that has become unenforceable (either because of passage of time, such as the statute of limitations, or for some other reason), a subsequent promise to honor or revive the legal obligation will be enforceable at law. Is it accurate to characterize this liability as being based on "moral obligation"?

3. *Debts barred by time.* The court states that promises to pay debts barred by the statute of limitations are enforceable because the debt is a preexisting legal obligation. A modern statement of this rule can be found in Restatement (Second) §82. A promise to pay a debt barred by the statute of limitations can be express or it may be implied from the conduct of the obligor. Id. §82(2). Today, in most jurisdictions, statutes regulate the enforceability of promises to pay debts barred by the statute of limitations. Such statutes often define the type of conduct that constitutes an implied promise to pay the debt. See, e.g., S.C. Code Ann. §15-3-120 (part payment of principal or interest equivalent of written promise).

4. *Debts discharged in bankruptcy.* Promises to pay debts previously discharged in bankruptcy are also legally enforceable. Restatement (Second) §83. Unlike promises to pay debts barred by the statute of limitations, promises to pay debts discharged in bankruptcy will not be judicially implied. Restatement (Second) §83 provides that the promise must be "express." Can this difference in treatment be justified? Consider the following comment from the Restatement: "In modern times discharge in bankruptcy has been thought to reflect a somewhat stronger public policy than the statute of limitations, and a promise implied from acknowledgment or part payment does not revive a debt discharged in bankruptcy." Restatement (Second) §83 Comment *a.*

5. *Statutory restrictions on promises to revive debt.* Some states have enacted statutes requiring promises to revive debts barred by the statute of limitations or bankruptcy to be in writing. See, e.g., N.Y. Gen. Oblig. Law §5-701(a)(5) (promise to pay debt discharged in bankruptcy), §17-101 (promise to pay debt barred by statute of limitations). Sections §524(c), (d) of the U.S. Bankruptcy Code impose a number of limitations on the ability of debtors to reassume by agreement debts discharged in bankruptcy.

6. *Obligations of minors.* The court in *Mills* also refers to "debts incurred by infants" as a situation in which the law will enforce a promise for benefits previously received. The court's statement requires some elaboration. Contracts made by a minor prior to the time the minor reaches the legal age of majority (now 18) are unenforceable unless they are for "necessaries," goods and services needed by the minor. After reaching the age of majority a minor becomes legally liable on any contracts made during minority that the minor elects to "affirm." A minor may affirm a contract either expressly or by failure to "disaffirm" the contract within a reasonable time after reaching the age of majority. We will return in Chapter 7 to the subject of minors' capacity to contract.

7. *Scholarly commentary.* In recent years a number of scholars have conducted extensive historical research into leading contract cases. Professor Geoffrey Watson's inquiry into Mills v. Wyman has led him to reach some surprising conclusions:

> A close reading of the historical record reveals a starkly different version of the facts of Mills v. Wyman. . . . Seth Wyman never made the promise that the court said he made, and . . . young Levi Wyman did not meet the untimely death that the court said he had met. Thus the court rightly absolved Seth Wyman, but for the wrong reasons. . . . [O]ther records from the period, including evidence of Seth Wyman's considerable wealth, . . . raise new questions about the motivations of the parties.

In the Tribunal of Conscience: *Mills v. Wyman* Reconsidered, 71 Tul. L. Rev. 1749, 1751 (1997). In his article Professor Watson goes beyond historical research to propose reform of the moral obligation doctrine. Finding the various explanations of the doctrine unpersuasive, he argues that promises made with an intention to be bound should be enforceable because such a rule would increase "allocational efficiency" and would link "legal liability more closely to moral responsibility." Id. at 1805.

Webb v. McGowin

Alabama Court of Appeals 27 Ala. App. 82, 168 So. 196 (1935), cert. denied, 232 Ala. 374, 168 So. 199 (1936)

BRICKEN, Presiding Judge.

This action is in assumpsit. The complaint as originally filed was amended. The demurrers to the complaint as amended were sustained, and because of this adverse ruling by the court the plaintiff took a nonsuit, and the assignment of errors on this appeal are predicated upon said action or ruling of the court.

A fair statement of the case presenting the questions for decision is set out in appellant's brief, which we adopt.

> On the 3d day of August, 1925, appellant while in the employ of the W. T. Smith Lumber Company, a corporation, and acting within the scope of his employment, was engaged in clearing the upper floor of mill No. 2 of the company. While so engaged he was in the act of dropping a pine block from the upper floor of the mill to the ground below; this being the usual and ordinary way of clearing the floor, and it being the duty of the plaintiff in the course of his employment to so drop it. The block weighed about 75 pounds.
>
> As appellant was in the act of dropping the block to the ground below, he was on the edge of the upper floor of the mill. As he started to turn the block loose so that it would drop to the ground, he saw J. Greeley McGowin, testator of the defendants, on the ground below and directly under where the block would have fallen had appellant turned it loose. Had he turned it loose it would have struck McGowin with such force as to have caused him serious bodily harm or death. Appellant could have remained safely on the upper floor of the mill by turning the block loose and allowing it to drop, but had he done this the block would have fallen on McGowin and caused him serious injuries or death. The only safe and reasonable way to prevent this was for appellant to hold to the block and divert its direction in falling from the place where McGowin was standing and the only safe way to divert it so as to prevent its coming into contact with McGowin was for appellant to fall with it to the ground below. Appellant did this, and by holding to the block and falling with it to the ground below, he diverted the course of its fall in such a way that McGowin was not injured. In thus preventing the injuries to McGowin appellant himself received serious bodily injuries, resulting in his right leg being broken, the heel of his right foot torn off and his right arm broken. He was badly crippled for life and rendered unable to do physical or mental labor.
>
> On September 1, 1925, in consideration of appellant having prevented him from sustaining death or serious bodily harm and in consideration of the

The W.T. Smith Lumber Saw Mill in Chapman, AL, circa 1930.

> injuries appellant had received, McGowin agreed with him to care for and maintain him for the remainder of appellant's life at the rate of $15 every two weeks from the time he sustained his injuries to and during the remainder of appellant's life; it being agreed that McGowin would pay this sum to appellant for his maintenance. Under the agreement McGowin paid or caused to be paid to appellant the sum so agreed on up until McGowin's death on January 1, 1934. After his death the payments were continued to and including January 27, 1934, at which time they were discontinued. Thereupon plaintiff brought suit to recover the unpaid installments accruing up to the time of the bringing of the suit.
>
> The material averments of the different counts of the original complaint and the amended complaint are predicated upon the foregoing statement of facts.

In other words, the complaint as amended averred in substance: (1) That on August 3, 1925, appellant saved J. Greeley McGowin, appellee's testator, from death or grievous bodily harm; (2) that in doing so appellant sustained bodily injury crippling him for life; (3) that in consideration of the services rendered and the injuries received by appellant, McGowin agreed to care for him the remainder of appellant's life, the amount to be paid being $15 every two weeks; (4) that McGowin complied with this agreement until he died on January 1, 1934, and the payments were kept up to January 27, 1934, after which they were discontinued.

The action was for the unpaid installments accruing after January 27, 1934, to the time of the suit.

The principal grounds of demurrer to the original and amended complaint are: (1) It states no cause of action; (2) its averments show the contract was without consideration; (3) it fails to allege that McGowin had, at or before the services were rendered, agreed to pay appellant for them; (4) the contract declared on is void under the statute of frauds.

1. The averments of the complaint show that appellant saved McGowin from death or grievous bodily harm. This was a material benefit to him of infinitely more value than any financial aid he could have received. Receiving this benefit, McGowin became morally bound to compensate appellant for the services rendered. Recognizing his moral obligation, he expressly agreed to pay appellant as alleged in the complaint and complied with this agreement up to the time of his death; a period of more than 8 years.

Had McGowin been accidentally poisoned and a physician, without his knowledge or request, had administered an antidote, thus saving his life, a subsequent promise by McGowin to pay the physician would have been valid. Likewise, McGowin's agreement as disclosed by the complaint to compensate appellant for saving him from death or grievous bodily injury is valid and enforceable.

Where the promisee cares for, improves, and preserves the property of the promisor, though done without his request, it is sufficient consideration for the promisor's subsequent agreement to pay for the service, because of the material benefit received. . . .

In Boothe v. Fitzpatrick, 36 Vt. 681, the court held that a promise by defendant to pay for the past keeping of a bull which had escaped from defendant's premises and been cared for by plaintiff was valid, although there was no previous request, because the subsequent promise obviated that objection; it being equivalent to a previous request. On the same principle, had the promisee saved the promisor's life or his body from grievous harm, his subsequent promise to pay for the services rendered would have been valid. Such service would have been far more material than caring for his bull. Any holding that saving a man from death or grievous bodily harm is not a material benefit sufficient to uphold a subsequent promise to pay for the service, necessarily rests on the assumption that saving life and preservation of the body from harm have only a sentimental value. The converse of this is true. Life and preservation of the body have material, pecuniary values, measurable in dollars and cents. Because of this, physicians practice their profession charging for services rendered in saving life and curing the body of its ills, and surgeons perform operations. The same is true as to the law of negligence, authorizing the assessment of damages in personal injury cases based upon the extent of the injuries, earnings, and life expectancies of those injured.

In the business of life insurance, the value of a man's life is measured in dollars and cents according to his expectancy, the soundness of his body, and his ability to pay premiums. The same is true as to health and accident insurance.

It follows that if, as alleged in the complaint, appellant saved J. Greeley McGowin from death or grievous bodily harm, and McGowin subsequently agreed to pay him for the service rendered, it became a valid and enforceable contract.

2. It is well settled that a moral obligation is a sufficient consideration to support a subsequent promise to pay where the promisor has received a material benefit, although there was no original duty or liability resting on the promisor. . . . State ex rel. Bayer v. Funk, 105 Or. 134, 199 P. 592, 209 P. 113, 25 A.L.R. 625, 634. . . . In the case of State ex rel. Bayer v. Funk, supra, the court held that a moral obligation is a sufficient consideration to support an executory promise where the promisor has received an actual pecuniary or material benefit for which he subsequently expressly promised to pay.

The case at bar is clearly distinguishable from that class of cases where the consideration is a mere moral obligation or conscientious duty unconnected with receipt by promisor of benefits of a material or pecuniary nature. . . . Here the promisor received a material benefit constituting a valid consideration for his promise.

3. Some authorities hold that, for a moral obligation to support a subsequent promise to pay, there must have existed a prior legal or equitable obligation, which for some reason had become unenforceable, but for which the promisor was still morally bound. This rule, however, is subject to qualification in those cases where the promisor, having received a material benefit from the promisee, is morally bound to compensate him for the services rendered and in consideration of this obligation promises to pay. In such cases the subsequent promise to pay is an affirmance or ratification of the services rendered carrying with it the presumption that a previous request for the service was made. . . .

Under the decisions above cited, McGowin's express promise to pay appellant for the services rendered was an affirmance or ratification of what appellant had done raising the presumption that the services had been rendered at McGowin's request.

4. The averments of the complaint show that in saving McGowin from death or grievous bodily harm, appellant was crippled for life. This was part of the consideration of the contract declared on. McGowin was benefited. Appellant was injured. Benefit to the promisor or injury to the promisee is a sufficient legal consideration for the promisor's agreement to pay. Fisher v. Bartlett, 8 Greenl. (Me.) 122, 22 Am. Dec. 225; State ex rel. Bayer v. Funk, supra.

5. Under the averments of the complaint the services rendered by appellant were not gratuitous. The agreement of McGowin to pay and the acceptance of payment by appellant conclusively shows the contrary.

6. The contract declared on was not void under the statute of frauds (Code 1923, §8034). The demurrer on this ground was not well taken. 25 R.C.L. 456, 457 and 470, §49. . . .

From what has been said, we are of the opinion that the court below erred in the ruling complained of; that is to say, in sustaining the demurrer, and for this error the case is reversed and remanded.

Reversed and remanded.

SAMFORD, Judge (concurring).

The questions involved in this case are not free from doubt, and perhaps the strict letter of the rule, as stated by judges, though not always in accord, would bar a recovery by plaintiff, but following the principle announced by Chief Justice Marshall in Hoffman v. Porter, Fed. Cas. No. 6,577, 2 Brock. 156, 159, where he says, "I do not think that law ought to be separated from justice, where it is at most doubtful," I concur in the conclusions reached by the court.

NOTES AND QUESTIONS

1. *Promissory restitution principle.* The above case is often cited as an example of the "material benefit" rule, which holds that if a person receives a material benefit from another, other than gratuitously, a subsequent promise to compensate the person for rendering such benefit is enforceable. For further discussion of the background of Webb v. McGowin, see Richard Danzig & Geoffrey Watson, The Capability Problem in Contract Law: Further Readings on Well-Known Cases ch. V (2d ed. 2004). Restatement (Second) §86 adopts the material benefit rule. Professor Stanley Henderson has referred to §86 as "promissory restitution." Stanley D. Henderson, Promises Grounded in the Past: The Idea of Unjust Enrichment and the Law of Contracts, 57 Va. L. Rev. 1115, 1118 (1971). Is this a proper characterization of the section? If the receipt of material benefit alone is not enough to give rise to a right of recovery, why does the additional fact of the subsequent promise justify imposing an obligation?

Note that promissory restitution cases can be seen as occupying a middle ground between classical contracts and the pure restitution cases discussed in the previous section of this chapter. The promissory restitution cases bear a similarity to classical contract because the obligation rests on the assent of the person subject to liability. On the other hand, the promissory restitution cases involve liability even though no bargained-for exchange has occurred. In addition, as discussed in Note 2 below, the measure of recovery is based on restitutionary principles. For an examination of the application of §86 see Clay B. Tousey III, Exceptional Circumstances: The Material Benefit Rule in Practice and Theory, 28 Campbell L. Rev. 153 (2006). See also Kevin M. Teeven, Moral Obligation Promise for Harm Caused, 39 Gonz. L. Rev. 349 (2004).

Not all courts agree with the material benefit rule. In Harrington v. Taylor, 36 S.E.2d 227 (N.C. 1945), a wife after being assaulted by her husband took refuge in the plaintiff's house. The next day the husband gained entry to the plaintiff's house. In the ensuing struggle, the wife knocked her husband down and was about to strike him with an ax when the plaintiff intervened and was struck by the ax, receiving a severely mutilated hand, but saving the husband's life. Subsequently, the husband orally promised to pay the plaintiff for her damages. When the husband later refused to honor the promise, the plaintiff brought suit. The North Carolina Supreme Court affirmed the lower court's decision to sustain the demurrer to the complaint. The court stated that "however much the defendant should be impelled by common gratitude to alleviate the plaintiff's misfortune, a humanitarian act of this kind, voluntarily performed, is not such consideration as would entitle her to recover at law." Id. at 227. For further discussion of Harrington v. Taylor, see Richard Danzig & Geoffrey Watson, The Capability Problem in Contract Law: Further Readings on Well-Known Cases ch. VI (2d ed. 2004). Are *Webb* and *Harrington* in direct conflict or can the two cases be reconciled?

2. *The Restatement (Second) version of the principle.* Would the promise in Mills v. Wyman be enforceable under Restatement (Second) §86? Consider the following illustration to that section:

> 1. *A* gives emergency care to *B*'s adult son while the son is sick and without funds far from home. *B* subsequently promises to reimburse *A* for his expenses. The promise is not binding under this Section.

Is this illustration consistent with the text of §86?

How would Webb v. McGowin be decided under §86? In particular, how would you respond to an argument that recovery should be denied because Webb rendered his services gratuitously in that he did not expect to receive compensation?

The text, comments, and illustrations to Restatement (Second) §86 recognize other limitations on the availability of promissory restitution. If enforcement of the promise would be disproportionate to the reasonable value of the benefit received, enforcement may be limited to that value. Restatement (Second) §86 comment *i*. The Restatement gives the following illustrations of this principle:

> 12. *A*, a married woman of sixty, has rendered household services without compensation over a period of years for *B*, a man of eighty living alone and having no close relatives. *B* has a net worth of three million dollars and has often assured *A* that she will be well paid for her services, whose reasonable value is not in excess of $6,000. *B* executes and delivers to *A* a written promise to pay *A* $25,000 "to be taken from my estate." The promise is binding.
>
> 13. The facts being otherwise as stated in Illustration 12, *B's* promise is made orally and is to leave *A* his entire estate. *A* cannot recover more than the reasonable value of her services.

In Comment *f* to §86, the Restatement also suggests that a promise to pay an additional sum for benefits received under a preexisting bargain is not enforceable:

> By virtue of the policy of enforcing bargains, the enrichment of one party as a result of an unequal exchange is not regarded as unjust, and this Section has no application to a promise to pay or perform more or to accept less than is called for by a pre-existing bargain between the same parties.

3. *Legislation.* New York has enacted legislation making promises based on moral obligation enforceable provided the promise complies with certain formal requirements:

> A promise in writing and signed by the promisor or by his agent shall not be denied effect as a valid contractual obligation on the ground that consideration for the promise is past or executed, if the consideration is expressed in the writing and is proved to have been given or performed and would be a valid consideration but for the time when it was given or performed.

N.Y. Gen. Oblig. Law §5-1105. New York courts have applied the statute in a number of cases to enforce promises that met the statutory requirements even though a bargained-for exchange had not occurred. See, e.g., Braka v. Travel Assistance Int'l., 807 N.Y.S.2d 372 (App. Div. 2006) (finding that son's written promise to repay father for expenses incurred by father when son was injured while traveling in Fiji was enforceable under statute, thus allowing son to recover from travel insurance company). However, the statute has been criticized as "too broad in scope and too restrictive in formal requirements." Robert Braucher, Freedom of Contract and the Second Restatement, 78 Yale L.J. 598, 605 (1969). What do you think Professor Braucher had in mind?

4. *"Chestnut" cases.* The *Webb* case is a favorite of casebook editors, and has been for years. An online search will quickly reveal, however, that court decisions actually citing and relying on the *Webb* case are few and far between. When periodically revising and updating their casebooks, the editors of these and other collections of contracts materials must face the decision whether to drop or retain cases like this one: old "chestnuts" familiar to generation after generation of law students. These are cases that are remembered more for their facts — often odd, sometimes funny, always in some sense "memorable" — than for their legal content. Another contracts casebook author, Professor Carol Chomsky, addresses this issue with particular attention to *Webb*:

> I'm . . . old-school enough to still believe that to be good lawyers and good public citizens, students need to understand more generally how the law works (or sometimes does not) and how it evolves, and that means teaching them something of the history of settled doctrine and even some obscure corners of the law. For example, one of the doctrines traditionally included in contracts casebooks is enforcement of promises made for benefit received, memorialized in Restatement (Second) of Contracts section 86. Looking for cases to update the presentation of that issue . . . I found virtually none addressing this issue, under the Restatement or otherwise, since the old classic opinions that appear in most of the casebooks (*Mills v. Wyman* and *Webb v. McGowin*). Lawyers do not need to know this doctrine in order to practice contract law; it rarely, if ever, comes up as a mechanism for enforcement in the "real world" of contracts, and certainly not in drafting contracts, because the doctrine fills a gap that exists precisely when there is no agreement, express or implied. We could have decided to remove the topic from the book and therefore the course. But the development and application of the rule in Restatement (Second) of Contracts section 86 is nonetheless a worthwhile story about how judges worked their way to a solution when faced with circumstances that seemed to warrant a remedy, but existing doctrine did not produce one. Considering how and why judges decide that such a development is necessary, how they move the law forward (or sideways), whether the newly crafted rule is a good one, and even why the rule is rarely or maybe never invoked — that is a worthwhile conversation.

Carol L. Chomsky, Casebooks and the Future of Contracts Pedagogy, 66 Hastings L.J. 879, 884 (2015). Obviously the editors of these materials once more opted (like Professor Chomsky) to retain *Webb* as a principal case, despite these qualms. Did reading the opinions in *Webb* help you understand the judicial process better? Consider and contrast the majority opinion written by Judge Bricken and Judge Samford's concurrence. Would the case have been satisfactorily decided by either of those opinions alone? Further discussion of *Webb* and other "chestnut" cases can be found in Charles L. Knapp, Cases and Controversies: Some Things to Do with Contracts Cases, 88 Wash. L. Rev. 1337, 1359-1360 (2013).

5. *Recovery in the absence of a promise.* Suppose McGowin had *not promised* to care for Webb. Could he have still been held liable to Webb on pure restitutionary principles? Recall the *Pelo* case and its discussion of Restatement (First) of Restitution §116. The difficulty facing Webb in such an action would be having to show that the services were not rendered gratuitously (i.e., were rendered with an "intent to charge" under Restatement §116). In cases involving professional providers of services, modern courts have been willing to find an intent to charge and have allowed recovery for the reasonable value of the services rendered. The courts have refused, however, to allow recovery by nonprofessionals even for out-of-pocket losses involved in rescues. In a similar vein, Section 20 of the Restatement (Third) of Restitution (quoted in the notes following *Pelo*) follows this case law by limiting restitutionary recovery to protect the life or health of another to providers of "professional services." However, Comment *b*, after discussing various justifications for this limitation, states that this

restriction is not "logically inevitable. On the contrary, a claim in restitution based on an emergency rescue by a nonprofessional would be entirely consistent with the rule of this Section, in any case in which the court was satisfied *(inter alia)* that the claimant had not acted gratuitously, and that the benefit conferred was capable of valuation."

PROBLEM 3-4

Alliance Aviation, Inc., a large manufacturer of military aircraft, employs a number of pilots to test fly its experimental aircraft. Because of the riskiness of the work, test pilots command substantial salaries, in many cases well over $250,000 per year.

Several years ago one of the pilots employed by Alliance, William "Buck" Rogers, made a test flight of the prototype of Alliance's A-1 bomber. During the flight a fire broke out in the cockpit. While Rogers could have avoided injury to himself by ejecting from the aircraft, had he done so the A-1 would have crashed, possibly into a nearby residential community. Under company policy, which was incorporated into Rogers's employment contract, test pilots were required to use their best efforts to avoid the risk of harm to civilians. Instead of ejecting, Rogers flew the crippled plane back to its base, where he made an emergency crash landing; unfortunately, Rogers suffered serious injuries resulting in partial paralysis and ending his career as a test pilot.

Because of the severity of his injuries, Rogers was hospitalized for several months. While recuperating, he received frequent visits from co-workers at Alliance, including Tom Agnew, the president of the company. During one of the visits, after expressing regret that Rogers had suffered permanent injury, Agnew told Rogers that the company planned to provide for him financially. A few weeks later Rogers received the following letter from Agnew:

> Dear Buck:
>
> Everyone at Alliance is so glad to hear that you are making such fine progress and that you'll be home soon. I know Mary and the kids will be over-joyed to have you home again.
>
> Buck, you have worked for Alliance for almost ten years and if my memory is correct you have test flown every major military plane that the company now manufactures. During this time, your safety record is unblemished. Now, because of your professionalism, your career as a pilot is over. But we at Alliance want you to know that we haven't forgotten your efforts over these last ten years. I am enclosing a check for $7500. You'll receive checks in this amount every month so long as the company's financial condition continues to be solid.
>
> Sincerely,
> *Tom*

Over the next few years, the company regularly sent these monthly checks to Buck. Buck in turn often visited the company; at Agnew's request, he even met on occasion with some of the company's test pilots to discuss their work and give them advice.

During this same period of time, Buck was the subject of an interview and series of newspaper stories by Ruth Tarbell, a reporter for a nationally known daily. As a result of this project, an idea emerged for Buck and Ruth to collaborate on a book about the military aircraft industry. Although Buck began work on the book as a staunch supporter of both the military and private industry, his research first led to surprise and then anger. In the end, Buck and Ruth produced a best-selling exposé of the military aircraft industry: "The Wrong Stuff: The Government and the Military Aircraft Industry."

Although the book contains only a few unfavorable portions about Alliance, Agnew is furious, feeling that Buck betrayed the company. At best, he thinks the book will lead to more government red tape, at worst, loss of government contracts. Agnew has asked you whether the company can legally terminate Rogers's pension. What advice would you give?

PROBLEM 3-5

On November 1, Ronald Chang, a wealthy businessman, died suddenly of a heart attack. Ronald left a will in which he appointed the National Bank of City as his personal representative. Melinda O'Shea is the trust officer at National Bank who is in charge of Ronald's estate. The bank has retained the law firm in which you are an associate to provide legal services in connection with the administration of the estate. Today Ms. O'Shea called Edna Prinkley, the partner with whom you work, to ask for advice. The matter deals with Ronald's sister, Patricia Chang. Patricia has presented to Ms. O'Shea the following handwritten letter to her from her brother:

> December 26
>
> Dear Pat:
>
> It was wonderful spending Christmas with you and mother. I can't believe it's been ten years since we had Christmas dinner together, but it seems like every year something urgent keeps me away. Anyway, I can't tell you how much I enjoyed the few hours we had together.
>
> It's hard for me to believe that it's been 15 years since dad died. You have sacrificed in so many ways living with and taking care of mother. I guess your decision to move back home to live with mother pretty much ended your relationship with James; I know it put any thought of an academic career on hold, at least for the time being. I wish I could have contributed more financially to help you out, but it's only been in the last couple of years that I have really come into my own.
>
> Anyway, this is more than a thank you note for Christmas and an apology for my failings. I have thought about the situation for some time, and I want to compensate you for what you have done and are continuing to do for mother and for me. I am making arrangements to transfer to you 1 million dollars in shares that I have in a mutual fund. I hope this gift will ease any concern you may have about your financial future.
>
> With love,
> *Ron*

Ronald did not transfer the $1 million in mutual fund shares to Patricia Chang before his death. Under his will, his estate, which is valued at approximately $50 million, passes to his wife and his children. The will makes no mention of any bequest to Patricia. Ms. O'Shea wants to know whether the letter from Ronald to Patricia Chang legally obligates the estate to pay Patricia the $1 million mentioned in the letter. What advice would you give? If you think there are additional facts that might affect your answer to Ms. O'Shea's question, indicate what they would be, and why they might be relevant.

REVIEW QUESTIONS – CHAPTER THREE

1. Rebecca Ray is the CEO and chief stockholder of a company which operates a successful on-line dating service, "Dates with Destiny." Two weeks ago, when Rebecca was dining out with friends at a local seafood restaurant, she got a fishbone stuck in her throat. Making the throat-clutching gesture to signal choking, she attracted the attention of Myles Marlin, a real estate salesperson from out of town who was visiting local friends. Being familiar with the Heimlich Maneuver, Myles was able to assist Rebecca in dislodging the bone and breathing normally again. She thanked him profusely for saving her life at a time when her companions and the others around her seemed unable to be of assistance, and asked for his mailing address, so that she might send him a proper note of thanks and a suitable reward. He protested that it was really nothing, anyone would have done the same, but he did give her his business card, with an email and mailing address. Five days later, Myles received in the mail a thank-you greeting card, along with a check from Rebecca, made out to him, in the amount of $10,000. Written on the card was the message "Thank you – I owe you my life!! And here is my reward for you. – Rebecca."

   Myles immediately deposited the check in his bank account, and wrote Rebecca a note of thanks, which he mailed to her address (which was on the check). A few days later he got back from her a brief note, saying merely: "Sorry but my accountant says that was a mistake. But thanks anyway." Around the same time, Myles was advised by his bank that payment on Rebecca's check had been stopped before it cleared.

   Assume that under applicable law the issuance of a check like this one creates a rebuttable presumption of consideration. If Myles attempts to recover $10,000 in a lawsuit against Rebecca, what would be the most likely outcome, and why?

   A. Myles should win, because Rebecca's promise was evidenced by a writing.
   B. Myles should lose, because there was no consideration for Rebecca's promise.
   C. Miles should lose, because Rebecca promptly withdrew her offer.
   D. Myles should win, because public policy should encourage people to assist others who are in need of emergency aid.

2. A year ago, Ashley Anderson was a college senior, making plans to attend college. She was accepted at a community college in her hometown, and also at a large private university, Stepford U. Initially, Ashley planned to attend the local college because of the high cost of attending Stepford, but her Aunt Ivy (her mother's wealthy sister, who had attended Stepford herself) urged Ashley to attend Stepford even if it did mean Ashley would incur a larger burden of student debt. When Ashley hesitated, Aunt Ivy promised Ashley (in a written email note) that she (Aunt Ivy) would pay Ashley's tuition at Stepford for her sophomore year if she finished the first year at Stepford with a grade point average of 3.0 or better. Ashley agreed, and attended Stepford for her first year of college with some financial help from her parents and the benefit of substantial student loans. She finished the year with a 3.4 GPA. When she notified her Aunt Ivy of that achievement, Ashley received the following response:

> Ashley:
>
> I'm delighted to hear of your excellent work at Stepford this past year. I'd like to help with your tuition this coming year, but some of my business ventures require additional attention and investment from me. I'm sure with your outstanding record you'll have no problem getting scholarship aid from Stepford for next year. - Your loving Aunt Ivy

It may be unlikely that Ashley would actually bring a lawsuit against her aunt, but should she decide to do that, is her claim likely to succeed?

- **A.** No, because Aunt Ivy received no consideration for her promise.
- **B.** No, because it was unreasonable for Ashley to rely on her aunt's promise.
- **C.** Yes, because Ashley reasonably and detrimentally relied on her aunt's promise.
- **D.** No, because justice does not require enforcement of her aunt's promise because she can get other scholarship aid.

3. Your local city school board operates a fleet of school buses to serve the students who live far enough from their school to require transportation. The 25 buses it is currently using were all purchased in 1995. Recently, the local newspaper reported that the school board was considering replacing a large part of its fleet of buses with newer, more energy-efficient ones. Hank Hill, the owner and operator of a tourists' sightseeing business, wrote the following email note to Linda Lawrence, the chairman of the school board:

> Dear Linda:
> I understand that your board is considering replacing all or some of its buses with new ones. I would buy five of your old ones, for the price of $20K each. (My son rides one every day and I have a good sense of their condition.) This offer is good for the next two weeks.
> - Your friend, Hank Hill

Three days after receiving this note, the school board entered into a contract with Monarch Motors to purchase ten new school buses, delivery to be in three months. Linda then received another email from Hank:

Dear Linda:

I've had second thoughts about buying the buses. I think I'll go in another direction. Sorry to disappoint you.

– Hank

As of this point, which of the following statements best describes the school board's legal position with respect to the sale of buses to Hank Hill?

A. Hank is free to withdraw his offer without liability because he is not in the business of selling buses.

B. Hank is free to withdraw his offer without liability because it was not a "firm offer."

C. Hank's offer can still be accepted by the school board, so long as two weeks have not gone by since it was made.

D. Hank is free to withdraw his offer because it was not hand-signed by him.

4. Megan Murphy went shopping last Monday at a local bookstore and bought several books for herself and as gifts for her friends, at a total price of $92.58. She paid in cash, with five 20-dollar bills, and received back some bills and coins, which she put in her purse without looking carefully at them. When she got home she found a message on her land-line phone from the clerk in the bookstore (which had her number on file from prior ordering requests) saying that Megan had apparently been accidentally given a $50 bill in change, instead of a five. Megan looked in her purse and found a $50 bill there which had not been there earlier. Megan called the store, spoke to the clerk, confirmed the error, and said she would be in the store later that day to refund the extra amount. Which of the following is the best description of her legal position?

   A. Megan is obligated to pay the store $45 only because she promised to do so.

   B. Megan is obligated to pay the store $45 because otherwise she would be unjustly enriched.

   C. Megan is not obligated to pay the store, because the mistake was not her fault, and she got no consideration for her promise to repay.

CHAPTER 4

The Statute of Frauds

Early in our study, we encountered the rule — now of only limited importance — that a promise might be made enforceable merely by virtue of its expression in a sealed writing. At this point we turn our attention to a different kind of legal "formality": the statute of frauds. Unlike use of the seal (in the few situations where that device is still effective), a promisor's compliance with the formality imposed by the statute of frauds will not by itself make her promise enforceable. If a promise is not supported by consideration (or some substitute), then compliance with the statute of frauds will not be sufficient for enforcement. *Failure* to comply with the statute of frauds, however, has the reverse effect: The promise, even if it is supported by consideration, will be *unenforceable.*

The original statute of frauds (actually titled "An act for prevention of frauds and perjuries") was passed by the English parliament in 1677. It covered a variety of subjects, including some questions of civil procedure and succession to property, but the major part of the statute consisted of provisions requiring *certain types of contracts* to be in writing to be legally effective. "No action shall be brought," the statute declared, to enforce any such agreement, "unless that agreement . . . or some memorandum or note thereof, shall be in writing, and signed by the party to be charged therewith . . ." (i.e., the person against whom enforcement is sought).

The statute of frauds remained a part of English law for nearly three centuries. (Most of its provisions were repealed by Parliament in 1954.) During this time it became, either by legislative imitation or in a few cases by judicial decision, part of the law of every American state. The American statutes vary in their wording and today are likely to apply to other types of contracts beyond those originally covered by the English statute. Today any statute that requires a transaction to be memorialized in writing for legal efficacy is likely to be referred to as a "statute of frauds." In fact, it is a misnomer to refer to the statute of frauds as a single statute. Most states have a general statutory provision referred to as the statute of frauds but also a number of other statutory sections scattered in different parts of the state's code of statutory law requiring various types of contracts to be in writing. In section 110, the Restatement (Second) of Contracts describes the coverage of the typical American statute of frauds:

> **§110. Classes of Contracts Covered**
>
> (1) The following classes of contracts are subject to a statute, commonly called the Statute of Frauds, forbidding enforcement unless there is a written memorandum or an applicable exception:
>
> (a) a contract of an executor or administrator to answer for a duty of his decedent (the executor-administrator provision);
>
> (b) a contract to answer for the duty of another (the suretyship provision);
>
> (c) a contract made upon consideration of marriage (the marriage provision);
>
> (d) a contract for the sale of an interest in land (the land contract provision);
>
> (e) a contract that is not to be performed within one year from the making thereof (the one-year provision).

In addition, the original English statute of frauds applied to contracts for the sale of goods. This aspect of the statute of frauds is now covered by UCC §2-201, which requires contracts for the sale of goods for a price of $500 or more to be evidenced by a writing signed by the party against whom enforcement is sought, unless some exception to the statute applies. The second part of this chapter examines §2-201. Note that the statute of frauds provisions of the Uniform Commercial Code are separate from the general statute of frauds. Note also that the Restatement refers to the possibility of special statutory provisions in each state requiring certain classes of contracts to be in writing. See, e.g., N.Y. Gen. Oblig. Law §5-701(a)(10) (McKinney) (contracts to pay compensation for services rendered in sale or purchase of business opportunities); Tex. Bus. & Com. Code Ann. §26.01(b)(3) (agreement made in consideration of nonmarital conjugal cohabitation). It should also be recalled that statutes commonly require that a testamentary disposition must be in writing to be given legal effect. Additional formalities, such as attestation by witnesses, are also usually required.

Despite their statutory character, the original sections of the English statute have been so commonly reproduced and so frequently given judicial construction that they have acquired a distinct common law flavor. It is therefore possible to generalize in common law fashion about the construction of the statute of frauds — indeed, not merely possible, but *necessary*. The statute of frauds as a living rule of law cannot now be understood from statutory language alone; the body of court decisions applying the statute form an essential part of its substance. (This is why the Restatement (Second) of Contracts, which ordinarily confines itself to restating the rules of common law, devotes a whole chapter (§§110-150) to explicating the application of the various traditional provisions of the statute of frauds, as listed in §110, quoted above.)

The first section of this chapter examines the judicial treatment of contracts subject to the general statute of frauds, while the second section addresses contracts governed by UCC §2-201.

A. GENERAL PRINCIPLES: SCOPE AND APPLICATION

Whenever the statute of frauds is asserted as a defense against the enforcement of an alleged contract, a series of questions is likely to be raised. First, is the contract at issue one of the types to which the statute of frauds applies, so that a signed memorandum will be required for its enforcement? (Or, as courts often put it, is this contract "within" the statute?) If the answer to that question is *No*, then the statute of frauds has no application to the case, and the plaintiff is free to prove her contract by any combination of relevant evidence, written or oral, direct or circumstantial. If, however, the answer to that first question is *Yes*, then a second question must be addressed: Is the statute of frauds "satisfied"? That is, is there some sort of written statement ("some memorandum or note") of its terms, signed by the defendant (the "party to be charged"), that is sufficient to meet the statute's requirements? If the answer to this second question is *Yes*, then the statute again presents no bar to enforcement, and the case may proceed in normal fashion. (Note that the plaintiff will still have the burden of persuading the trier of fact that the agreement was made as she alleges; the existence of a signed writing may help the plaintiff prove that the asserted contract was actually made, but it will not necessarily be conclusive on that issue.) Suppose, however, that the answers to the first two questions are *Yes* and *No*: Yes, the contract sued on is within the statute; no, there is not a writing sufficient to satisfy the statutory requirement. Does this end the case? Not necessarily. A third question must still be answered: Are there other factors in the case, such as performance or reliance by the plaintiff, which might invoke an exception to the statutory bar?

Crabtree v. Elizabeth Arden Sales Corp.

New York Court of Appeals 305 N.Y. 48, 110 N.E.2d 551 (1953)

FULD, Judge.

In September of 1947, Nate Crabtree entered into preliminary negotiations with Elizabeth Arden Sales Corporation, manufacturers and sellers of cosmetics, looking toward his employment as sales manager. Interviewed on September 26th, by Robert P. Johns, executive vice-president and general manager of the corporation, who had apprised him of the possible opening, Crabtree requested a three-year contract at $25,000 a year. Explaining that he would be giving up a secure well-paying job to take a position in an entirely new field

Elizabeth Arden in 1939.

of endeavor — which he believed would take him some years to master — he insisted upon an agreement for a definite term. And he repeated his desire for a contract for three years to Miss Elizabeth Arden, the corporation's president. When Miss Arden finally indicated that she was prepared to offer a two-year contract, based on an annual salary of $20,000 for the first six months, $25,000 for the second six months and $30,000 for the second year, plus expenses of $5,000 a year for each of those years, Crabtree replied that that offer was "interesting." Miss Arden thereupon had her personal secretary make this memorandum on a telephone order blank that happened to be at hand:

EMPLOYMENT AGREEMENT WITH

NATE CRABTREE — Date Sept. 26-1947
At 681 — 5th Ave — 6:PM

Begin 20000.
6 months 25000.
6 months 30000.
5000. — per year
Expense money
[2 years to make good]

Arrangement with Mr. Crabtree
By Miss Arden
Present Miss Arden
Mr. Johns
Mr. Crabtree
Miss O'Leary

A few days later, Crabtree phoned Mr. Johns and telegraphed Miss Arden; he accepted the "invitation to join the Arden organization," and Miss Arden wired back her "welcome." When he reported for work, a "pay-roll change" card was made up and initialed by Mr. Johns, and then forwarded to the payroll department. Reciting that it was prepared on September 30, 1947, and was to be effective as of October 22d, it specified the names of the parties, Crabtree's "Job Classification" and, in addition, contained the notation that:

> This employee is to be paid as follows:
>
> | | |
> |---|---|
> | First six months of employment | $20,000. per annum |
> | Next six months of employment | 25,000. per annum |
> | After one year of employment | 30,000. per annum |
>
> Approved by *RPJ* [initialed]

After six months of employment, Crabtree received the scheduled increase from $20,000 to $25,000, but the further specified increase at the end of the year was not paid. Both Mr. Johns and the comptroller of the corporation, Mr. Carstens, told Crabtree that they would attempt to straighten out the matter with Miss Arden, and, with that in mind, the comptroller prepared another "pay-roll change" card, to which his signature is appended, noting that there was to be a "Salary increase" from $25,000 to $30,000 a year, "per contractual arrangements with Miss Arden." The latter, however, refused to approve the increase and, after further fruitless discussion, plaintiff left defendant's employ and commenced this action for breach of contract.

At the ensuing trial, defendant denied the existence of any agreement to employ plaintiff for two years, and further contended that, even if one had been made, the statute of frauds barred its enforcement. The trial court found against defendant on both issues and awarded plaintiff damages of about $14,000, and the Appellate Division, two justices dissenting, affirmed. Since the contract relied upon was not to be performed within a year, the primary question for decision is whether there was a memorandum of its terms, subscribed by defendant, to satisfy the statute of frauds, Personal Property Law, §31.

Each of the two payroll cards — the one initialed by the defendant's general manager, the other signed by its comptroller — unquestionably constitutes a memorandum under the statute. That they were not prepared or signed with the intention of evidencing the contract, or that they came into existence subsequent to its execution, is of no consequence, see Marks v. Cowdin, 226 N.Y. 138, 145, 123 N.E. 139, 141; Spiegel v. Lowenstein, 162 App. Div. 443, 448-449, 147 N.Y.S. 655, 658; see, also, Restatement, Contracts, §§209, 210, 214; it is enough, to meet the statute's demands, that they were signed with intent to authenticate the information contained therein and that such information does evidence the terms of the contract. See . . . Corbin on Contracts [1951], pp. 732-733, 763-764; 2 Williston on Contracts [Rev. ed., 1936], pp. 1682-1683. Those two writings contain all of the essential terms of the contract — the parties to it, the position that plaintiff was to assume, the salary that he was to receive — except that relating to the duration of plaintiff's employment. Accordingly, we must consider whether that item, the length of the contract, may be supplied by reference to the earlier unsigned office memorandum, and, if so, whether its notation, "2 years to make good," sufficiently designates a period of employment.

The statute of frauds does not require the "memorandum . . . to be in one document. It may be pieced together out of separate writings, connected with one another either expressly or by the internal evidence of subject-matter and occasion." Marks v. Cowdin, supra, 226 N.Y. 138, 145, 123 N.E. 139, 141, see, also, 2 Williston, op. cit., p. 1671; Restatement, Contracts, §208, subd. [a]. Where each of the separate writings has been subscribed by the party to be charged, little if any difficulty is encountered. See, e.g., Marks v. Cowdin, supra, 226 N.Y. 138, 144-145, 123 N.E. 139, 141. Where, however, some writings have been signed, and others have not — as in the case before us — there is basic disagreement as to what constitutes a sufficient connection permitting the unsigned papers to be considered as part of the statutory memorandum. The courts of some jurisdictions insist that there be a reference, of varying degrees of specificity, in the signed writing to that unsigned, and, if there is no such reference, they refuse to permit consideration of the latter in determining whether the memorandum satisfies the statute. . . . That conclusion is based upon a construction of the statute which requires that the connection between the writings and defendant's acknowledgement of the one not subscribed, appear from examination of the papers alone, without the aid of parol evidence. The other position — which has gained increasing support over the years — is that a sufficient connection between the papers is established simply by a reference in them to the same subject matter or transaction. . . . The statute is not pressed "to the extreme of a literal and rigid logic," Marks v. Cowdin, supra, 226 N.Y. 138, 144, 123 N.E. 139, 141, and oral testimony is admitted to show the connection between the documents and to establish the acquiescence, of the party to be charged, to the contents of the one unsigned. See Beckwith v. Talbot, 95 U.S. 289, 24 L. Ed. 496; . . . 2 Corbin, op. cit., §§512-518; cf. Restatement, Contracts, §208, subd. [b], par. [iii].

The view last expressed impresses us as the more sound, and, indeed — although several of our cases appear to have gone the other way . . . — this court has on a number of occasions approved the rule, and we now definitively adopt it, permitting the signed and unsigned writings to be read together, provided that they clearly refer to the same subject matter or transaction. . . .

The language of the statute — "Every agreement . . . is void, unless . . . some note or memorandum thereof be in writing, and subscribed by the party to be charged," Personal Property Law, §31 — does not impose the requirement that the signed acknowledgment of the contract must appear from the writings alone, unaided by oral testimony. The danger of fraud and perjury, generally attendant upon the admission of parol evidence, is at a minimum in a case such as this. None of the terms of the contract are supplied by parol. All of them must be set out in the various writings presented to the court, and at least one writing, the one establishing a contractual relationship between the parties, must bear the signature of the party to be charged, while the unsigned document must on its face refer to the same transaction as that set forth in the one that was signed. Parol evidence — to portray the circumstances surrounding the making of the memorandum — serves only to connect the separate documents and to show that there was assent, by the party to be charged, to the contents of the one unsigned. If that testimony does not convincingly connect the papers, or does not show assent to the unsigned paper, it is within the province of the judge to conclude, as a matter of law, that the statute has not been satisfied. True, the possibility still remains that, by fraud or perjury, an agreement never in fact made may occasionally be enforced under the subject matter or transaction test. It is better to run that risk, though, than to deny enforcement to all agreements, merely because the signed document made no specific mention of the unsigned writing. As the United States Supreme Court declared, in sanctioning the admission of parol evidence to establish the connection between the signed and unsigned writings, "There may be cases in which it would be a violation of reason and common sense to ignore a reference which derives its significance from such [parol] proof. If there is ground for any doubt in the matter, the general rule should be enforced. But where there is no ground for doubt, its enforcement would aid, instead of discouraging, fraud." Beckwith v. Talbot, supra, 95 U.S. 289, 292, 24 L. Ed. 496; see also, . . . 2 Corbin, op. cit. §512, and cases there cited.

Turning to the writings in the case before us — the unsigned office memo, the payroll change form initialed by the general manager Johns, and the paper signed by the comptroller Carstens — it is apparent, and most patently, that all three refer on their face to the same transaction. The parties, the position to be filled by plaintiff, the salary to be paid him, are all identically set forth; it is hardly possible that such detailed information could refer to another or a different agreement. Even more, the card signed by Carstens notes that it was prepared for the purpose of a "Salary increase per contractual arrangements with Miss Arden." That certainly constitutes a reference of sorts to a more comprehensive "arrangement," and parol is permissible to furnish the explanation.

The corroborative evidence of defendant's assent to the contents of the unsigned office memorandum is also convincing. Prepared by defendant's agent, Miss Arden's personal secretary, there is little likelihood that the paper was fraudulently manufactured or that defendant had not assented to its contents. Furthermore, the evidence as to the conduct of the parties at the time it was prepared persuasively demonstrates defendant's assent to its terms. Under such circumstances, the courts below were fully justified in finding that the three papers constituted the "memorandum" of their agreement within the meaning of the statute.

Nor can there be any doubt that the memorandum contains all of the essential terms of the contract. . . . Only one term, the length of the employment, is in dispute. The September 26th office memorandum contains the notation, "2 years to make good." What purpose, other than to denote the length of the contract term, such a notation could have, is hard to imagine. Without it, the employment would be at will, see Martin v. New York Life Ins. Co., 148 N.Y. 117, 121, 42 N.E. 416, 417, and its inclusion may not be treated as meaningless or purposeless. Quite obviously, as the courts below decided, the phrase signifies that the parties agreed to a term, a certain and definite term, of two years, after which, if plaintiff did not "make good," he would be subject to discharge. And examination of other parts of the memorandum supports that construction. Throughout the writings, a scale of wages, increasing plaintiff's salary periodically, is set out; that type of arrangement is hardly consistent with the hypothesis that the employment was meant to be at will. The most that may be argued from defendant's standpoint is that "2 years to make good," is a cryptic and ambiguous statement. But, in such a case, parol evidence is admissible to explain its meaning. See Martocci v. Greater New York Brewery, 301 N.Y. 57, 63, 92 N.E.2d 887, 889; Marks v. Cowdin, supra, 226 N.Y. 138, 143-144, 123 N.E. 139, 140, 141; 2 Williston, op. cit., §576; 2 Corbin, op. cit., §527. Having in mind the relations of the parties, the course of the negotiations and plaintiff's insistence upon security of employment, the purpose of the phrase — or so the trier of the facts was warranted in finding — was to grant plaintiff the tenure he desired.

The judgment should be affirmed, with costs.

LOUGHRAN, C.J., and LEWIS, CONWAY, DESMOND, DYE AND FROESSEL, JJ., concur. Judgment affirmed.

NOTES AND QUESTIONS

1. *The "one year" clause.* The contract in *Crabtree* was governed by the "one year" provision of the statute of frauds, which requires a contract to be in writing if it is "not to be performed within one year" from the date the contract is made. What is the rationale for subjecting contracts of a longer duration to the statute of frauds, while exempting shorter contracts from that provision?

Courts on the whole have been quite lenient in interpreting the one-year provision of the statute of frauds. The standard view is that a contract is not subject to the statutory provision if it is *possible to be performed* within a year, even though the prospect of such performance is remote. Thus, in Freedman v. Chemical Constr. Corp., 372 N.E.2d 12 (N.Y. 1977), the plaintiff alleged that the defendant had orally promised to pay him a commission for procuring a contract for the construction of a chemical plant in Saudi Arabia. The plaintiff's fee was to be payable on completion of the plant. Some nine years passed between the making of the alleged promise and the plant's completion, but the court nevertheless held the contract not to be within the one-year clause; the whole process *could* have taken place within a year, said the court, even if that would have been "unlikely or improbable." Under the prevailing interpretation of the one-year provision, contracts of no duration or indefinite duration are not within the statute of frauds; a contract is within the statute only when by the express terms of the contract it cannot be performed in less than one year.

See Tardy v. Willis, 2009 WL 3286003 (Conn. Super.); Restatement (Second) of Contracts §130, Comment *a*. In *Freedman*, however, the plaintiff's claim was barred by another provision of the New York statute of frauds, which applies to certain claims for brokerage commissions and finder's fees (N.Y. Gen. Oblig. Law §5-701(a)(10) (McKinney)).

In applying the one-year provision, courts typically distinguish between the possibility of *performance* within one year and *termination* within one year. The fact that a contract may be terminated within a year is not sufficient to remove the contract from the requirements of the statute; only performance will do. (Without this distinction, the one-year provision of the statute of frauds would be judicially negated because any contract can be terminated within one year due to breach.) Thus, a contract for a definite duration (like five years) is subject to the statute of frauds even though it might be terminated within one year because of breach by one party or because of some excusing event, such as impossibility of performance. Restatement (Second) §130, Comment *b*.

The distinction between performance and termination is often a fine one, however. Compare D & N Boening, Inc. v. Kirsch Beverages, Inc., 472 N.E.2d 992 (N.Y. 1984) (oral contract for beverage distributorship to continue for as long as products were "satisfactorily distributed" was subject to statute of frauds; contract could only end within one year because of termination on account of breach), with Ohanian v. Avis Rent A Car Systems, Inc., 779 F.2d 101 (2d Cir. 1985) (oral employment agreement interpreted by court as providing for termination by defendant employer only for "just cause"; held not within one-year clause because some events that might have constituted proper basis for termination under that provision would not have amounted to an unexcused breach by plaintiff employee).

2. *Lifetime contracts.* Sometimes an employee will allege that her employer orally agreed to a contract of "permanent" or "lifetime" employment. If the employer asserts the statute of frauds one-year clause as a defense to enforcement, the court is likely to hold it inapplicable, on the basis that contracts measured by a lifetime are inherently capable of termination by full performance in less than a year, if the measuring lifetime should end before a year is up, as of course is always a possibility. Perhaps reacting to the expansion of employee rights in the employment-at-will area, some judges and commentators in recent years have urged reconsideration of this issue, arguing that such an agreement is really a contract for a term of years, and should be regarded as falling within the statute. E.g., McInerney v. Charter Golf, Inc., 680 N.E.2d 1347 (Ill. 1997) (employee who allegedly gave up existing employment in exchange for oral offer of permanent employment from defendant barred from asserting claim by one-year statute of frauds because relationship of more than one year clearly contemplated; strong three-judge dissent argued majority's holding contrary to both the statute and the great weight of authority, and poor policy as well); Sawyer v. Mills, 295 S.W. 3d 79 (Ky. 2009) (one-year statute applies to bonus agreement when the parties did not contemplate performance within a year even though performance was possible). See also Daniel P. O'Gorman, The Statute of Frauds and Oral Promises of Job Security: The Tenuous Distinction

Between Performance and Excusable Nonperformance, 40 Seton Hall L. Rev. 1023 (2010) (arguing that in case of doubt an event that permits early termination of a contract should not be treated as defining "full performance" for statute of frauds purposes).

3. *Promises to answer for the debt of another or "suretyship" contracts.* As reflected in the introduction to this chapter and the preceding notes on the one-year clause, the law of the statute of frauds has been contoured greatly by common law decisions. The courts have often moved toward a more narrow application by imposing limitations not dictated by the statutory language itself. Thus, a promise "to answer for the debt of another person" or a "suretyship" contract is usually held not to be within the statute unless it was made to the creditor to whom that debt is owed (as opposed to being made to the debtor himself or to someone else) (see Restatement (Second) §112); even then the promise will probably not be subject to the statute if the creditor, in return for the making of the new promise, discharged the original debtor from his obligation (a "novation") (§115). The "debt of another" provision also has been held to be inapplicable when the promisor who has guaranteed payment of another's debt did so mainly for his own economic advantage, rather than out of solicitude for the debtor's well-being (§116). See Rosewood Care Center, Inc. v. Caterpillar, Inc., 877 N.E.2d 1091 (Ill. 2007) (holding that a question of fact exists as to whether an oral promise by an employer to pay for nursing care services provided by a facility to an employee was subject to the "main purpose" exception); accord Fitzgerald v. Hutchins, 983 A.2d 382 (Me. 2009).

4. *Contracts made upon consideration of marriage.* Although statutes in many jurisdictions have restricted or abolished it, breach of a promise to marry was once a valid cause of action in most jurisdictions; nevertheless, mutual promises to marry have consistently been held not to constitute a "Contract Made Upon Consideration of Marriage" (Restatement (Second) §124) even though the language of the original statute seemed broad enough to encompass them. Moreover, to come within this class, the promise in question must be an actual "consideration" for the promise to marry and not just made on the "condition" of marriage or in "contemplation" of marriage. See Restatement (Second) §124, Comment *c*. Such judicial constructions obviously have the effect of narrowing the scope of the marriage category, thus widening the potential enforceability of oral agreements. See John E. Murray, Jr., Murray on Contracts, §71, at 347-348 (5th ed. 2011).

5. *Requirements for linking documents.* *Crabtree* allows the memorandum requirement of the statute of frauds to be satisfied by linking several documents through oral testimony even though the documents do not expressly refer to each other. Other issues may arise with regard to linking documents: Is assent to the unsigned writing necessary? In *Crabtree* the court stated: "If that testimony does not convincingly connect the papers, *or does not show assent to the unsigned paper,* it is within the province of the judge to conclude, as a matter of law, that the statute has not been satisfied" (emphasis supplied). The Restatement (Second) is to the same effect, although perhaps somewhat more generous. Section 132 provides that a memorandum may consist of several

writings if one is signed and the others clearly relate to the same transaction. Comment *c* states: "Even if there is no internal reference or physical connection, the documents may be read together if in the circumstances they clearly relate to the same transaction *and the party to be charged has acquiesced in the contents of the unsigned writing*" (emphasis supplied).

It seems likely that the more persuasive the evidence that the plaintiff's story is true, the readier a court will be to combine the writings in *Crabtree* fashion. See, e.g., Gregerson v. Jensen, 617 P.2d 369 (Utah 1980) (check endorsed by defendant vendor of land contained reference to "deed"; held sufficient when taken with later-drafted deed containing sufficient description of property, apparently prepared at direction of defendant but never signed by him). Suppose the memorandum quoted in the *Crabtree* opinion had been made not by Arden's secretary but by Crabtree himself, during his meeting with the Arden executives. Would the contract have been enforced?

Must the signed writing show the existence of a contract? In Horn & Hardart Co. v. Pillsbury Co., 888 F.2d 8 (2d Cir. 1989), the court stated:

> . . . [T]he rule fashioned in *Crabtree* to permit satisfaction of the Statute of Frauds by a series of signed and unsigned writings contains two strict threshold requirements. First, the signed writing must itself establish "a contractual relationship between the parties." . . . Second, the unsigned writing must "on its face refer to the same transaction as that set forth in the one that was signed." . . . Compliance with these two threshold requirements may be decided by the district court as a matter of law, and must be considered without the introduction of parol evidence.

Id. at 11. Here again, the Restatement seems more liberal. As discussed in the next Note, under Restatement (Second) §133 and its illustrations, it is not necessary for the signed writing to establish a contractual relationship; the memorandum may consist of an informal writing (even a letter that is not sent), an offer, or a document that attempts to repudiate contractual liability.

6. *Alternate analysis of* ***Crabtree***. Could the court in *Crabtree* have reached the same outcome on other grounds? Restatement (Second) §133 states that a memorandum sufficient to satisfy the statute of frauds need *not* have been "made as a memorandum of a contract." The comments to that section amplify this rule by suggesting that the memorandum may consist of "an entry in a diary or in the minutes of a meeting," a "communication to or from an agent of the party [to be charged]," or "an informal letter to a third person" (Comment *b*). A memorandum may even be sufficient even though it "repudiates or cancels the contract, or asserts that it is not binding because not in writing" (Comment *c*). Section 133 is accompanied by the following illustrations:

> 1. *A* and *B* enter into an oral contract for the sale of Blackacre. *A* writes and signs a letter to his friend *C* containing an accurate statement of the contract. The letter is a sufficient memorandum to charge *A* even though it is never mailed.

2. *A* writes to *B* the following letter:

> Dear *B:* I will employ you as superintendent of my mill for a term of three years from date, at a salary of $28,000 a year. Let me know if you wish to accept this offer. [Signed]*A*.

B accepts the offer orally. The letter is a sufficient memorandum to charge *A*. . . .

4. *A* and *B* enter into an oral contract by which *A* promises to sell and *B* promises to buy Blackacre for $5,000. *A* writes and signs a letter to *B* in which he states accurately the terms of the bargain, but adds "our agreement was oral. It, therefore, is not binding upon me, and I shall not carry it out." The letter is a sufficient memorandum to charge *A*.

See also Uhar & Co., Inc. v. Jacob, 840 F. Supp. 2d 287 (D.D.C. 2012) (lease with tenant signed by lessor's agent stating promise to pay monthly commission to realtor was sufficient to satisfy statute of frauds even though not formal agreement with realtor). Could any of the principles illustrated above have been applied in *Crabtree*?

7. *The requirement of a "signed writing."* Although the requirements of a writing and a signature are commonly referred to as legal "formalities," it is clear that neither the writing itself nor the signature need be "formal" in order to satisfy the statutory requirement. Both the Restatement and the Uniform Commercial Code take a lenient view of what may constitute a "signature" and a "writing" for purposes of the statute of frauds. Restatement (Second) §§131-137; UCC §1-201(b)(37), (43) and comments thereto. See, e.g., Rosenfeld v. Basquiat, 78 F.3d 84 (2d Cir. 1996) (short memo written and signed by artist in crayon on large piece of paper could be sufficient memo for enforcement of asserted contract for sale of three paintings – eventually worth over $350,000 – for total price of $12,000); Owen v. Kroger Co., 936 F. Supp. 579 (S.D. Ind. 1996) (preprinted wording on memos, showing corporate logo and indicating memos were "from the desk of" named agents of defendant, could serve as signature; jury question whether by using pad writers intended to "authenticate" information stated).

Technological changes during the last few decades have dramatically changed methods of communication. Individuals and companies now transact much of their business electronically. Recognizing these developments Congress in 2000 passed the Electronic Signatures in Global and National Commerce Act (E-Sign Act), requiring states to recognize both electronic communications and signatures in transactions affecting interstate or foreign commerce. See 15 U.S.C. §7001. States may elect to adopt measures of their own in this area, for which the Uniform Electronic Transactions Act (UETA) may serve as a model, so long as those are not inconsistent with the E-Sign Act. The Rules of Contract Law Supplement contains the text of the E-Sign Act, UETA, and an Editor's Note discussing these statutes. See PayoutOne v. Coral Mortg. Bankers, 602 F. Supp. 2d 1219 (D. Colo. 2009) (multiple emails satisfy writing requirement under Colorado's credit agreement statute of frauds, citing cases from other jurisdictions).

Beaver v. Brumlow

Court of Appeals of New Mexico 148 N.M. 172, 231 P.3d 628 (2010)

OPINION

VIGIL, Judge.

This case is about a verbal agreement made by Warren and Betty Beaver (Sellers) to sell land for a home site to Michael and Karen Brumlow (Buyers). Sellers reneged on the agreement after Mr. Brumlow left Sellers' employment and started working for a competitor. The trial court ordered specific performance of the oral agreement, and Sellers appeal. Sellers acknowledge that the evidence was sufficient for the trial court to find that they made the agreement with Buyers. Nevertheless, Sellers contend that specific enforcement of the verbal agreement is barred pursuant to the statute of frauds. We disagree and affirm.

BACKGROUND

Sellers do not challenge the findings of fact made by the trial court. Therefore, the trial court findings of fact are undisputed and are binding on appeal.

Buyer Michael Brumlow worked for Sellers in their race horse transportation business for approximately ten years, beginning in 1994, and ending in 2004. In October 2000, Sellers purchased twenty-four acres of property in the Village of Ruidoso Downs, and in approximately June or July of 2001, Mr. Brumlow asked Seller Warren Beaver if he would sell some of the land to put a home on. Mr. Beaver agreed, and the parties walked the specific boundaries of the property that Sellers would sell to Buyers.

Sellers allowed Buyers to rely on their representations to Buyers that Sellers would sell Buyers the subject property. Buyers went into possession of the land with Sellers' consent. In reliance on Sellers' agreement to sell, Buyer Karen Brumlow cashed in her IRA and 401-K retirement plans, at a substantial penalty, to pay for the home and improvements. Buyers purchased a double-wide home and moved it onto the property. Mr. Beaver signed an application with the Village of Ruidoso Downs for placement of the home on the property he agreed to sell to Buyers. In reliance on the agreement, Buyers also skirted the mobile home, poured concrete footers and a concrete foundation for the home, built a deck and two sets of stairs to access the home, had electricity and a water supply run to the property, had a septic system installed, had a propane system installed, brought a Tuff Shed for storage onto the property, and landscaped the property. Mr. Beaver signed the application/approval required by the Village of Ruidoso Downs for the construction of the septic system. In reliance on the agreement, Buyers spent approximately $85,000.

Sellers sought legal advice as to the manner in which to sell the property to Buyers, and the parties discussed with Sellers' attorney the requirement of a survey, and either a real estate contract or a note and mortgage. A fair inference from the record is that formal documents were not prepared and executed because Sellers discovered that their property was encumbered with a mortgage containing a due on sale clause. Throughout their time on the land, Buyers repeatedly requested that their contract be formalized, and Sellers responded, "We will work it out."

A date certain was never determined for the sale of the property or transfer of title to the property, nor was a price actually determined. However, Mr. Brumlow assumed he would pay whatever the market would bear in that particular neighborhood. He testified he thought the price would be "whatever it was worth."

Sellers drove by Buyers' home location daily during the time Buyers were making improvements to the land and setting up the home without ever expressing an intent not to sell the subject property to Buyers. Sellers never attempted to interrupt Buyers' quiet possession of the property during the years of possession. Sellers allowed Buyers to rely on their representations to Buyers that Sellers would sell Buyers the subject property for years without notifying Buyers they intended to renege on their promise.

In March 2004, Mr. Brumlow gave Mr. Beaver a two-week notice of termination of his employment with Sellers, intending to go to work for a competitor of Sellers in the race horse transportation business. The relationship between the parties rapidly deteriorated, and Sellers changed their mind and decided not to sell the agreed upon tract of land to Buyers because of hurt or anger. Sellers then attempted to restructure the agreement as a "lease" as opposed to a sale, and then attempted to terminate the "lease" and evict Buyers. Sellers prepared and required Buyers to sign an "Agreement." The "Agreement" required Buyers to pay Sellers $400 per month, and Buyers complied, believing it was payment for the land. When Buyers began writing "Land Payment" on the checks, Sellers stopped cashing the checks and alleged that the "Agreement" was for rental, although the "Agreement" did not contain the words "Rent," "Rental," "Lease," or "Leasehold." Buyers attempted to amicably resolve the dispute by offering to pay cash in the amount of the fair market value for the property and to have the property surveyed at their expense. Sellers refused.

Sellers then filed a suit for ejectment against Buyers, seeking to remove them from the property by alleging that Buyers were in violation of a rental agreement. Buyers denied the existence of a rental agreement and affirmatively alleged that their occupancy was pursuant to an agreement to purchase the property. Buyers also filed counterclaims which included claims for breach of contract, fraud, and prima facie tort. Sellers pleaded the statute of frauds as a defense.

The trial court concluded that Sellers entered into a contract with Buyers to sell them a specific portion of their land and that Sellers reneged on their agreement to sell the property to Buyers. The trial court further determined that Sellers changed their mind three years after making the contract, chose not to honor it, and attempted to unilaterally restructure the contract into a lease, which was never intended. In committing these acts, the trial court concluded, Sellers committed a prima facie tort, which they knew would harm Buyers. Addressing the statute of frauds defense, the trial court concluded that while the parties had no written agreement, the verbal agreement was proven by clear, cogent, and convincing evidence and that part performance of the contract by both Buyers and Sellers was sufficient to remove the contract from the statute of frauds. Furthermore, the trial court concluded, requiring a cash payment of the fair market value, as determined by a professional appraiser, was a proper equitable remedy.

The trial court allowed Buyers a choice of remedy: money damages for the prima facie tort or specific performance of the contract. Buyers chose specific performance. The property was appraised at a value of $10,000 by a professional appraiser, and a survey of the property to be sold was prepared. The final judgment directs that Buyers tender to Sellers the amount of $10,000 by depositing that amount into the trust account of Buyers' attorney within thirty days from the entry of the judgment, and that Sellers prepare and execute a good and sufficient warranty deed to Buyers for the property as described in the testimony of Mr. Brumlow and as depicted on the survey of the property. Upon receipt of the warranty deed executed by Sellers, payment of the $10,000 is to be made to Sellers. All other claims and counterclaims were dismissed with prejudice. Sellers appeal.

Sellers contend that specific enforcement of the oral contract is barred pursuant to the statute of frauds because: (1) Buyers' part performance was not "unequivocally referable" to the verbal agreement; and (2) the verbal agreement was not certain as to the purchase price and time of performance. Sellers also argue that specific performance was improper because Buyers had an adequate remedy at law in damages. For the following reasons, we disagree and affirm. . . .

THE STATUTE OF FRAUDS

[The court describes the history of the statute of frauds from the English statute of 1677, to the adoption by the Territory of New Mexico of the statute of frauds as part of the common law of the territory. The court noted that enactment in England was impelled, in part, by the unreliability of the jury system and by limitations in the evidentiary rules at that time. — EDS.]

While [some of] the underlying reasons justifying adoption of the statute of frauds no longer exist, retention of the statute has been justified for three primary reasons: the statute still serves an evidentiary function, and thereby lessens the danger of perjured testimony (the original reason for the statute); the requirement of a writing causes the parties to reflect on the importance of the agreement; and the writing requirement makes it easier to distinguish agreements which are enforceable from those which are not. . . .

This case involves the fourth section of the English statute of frauds, which in pertinent part states,

> No action shall be brought upon any contract or sale of lands, tenements, or hereditaments, or any interest in or concerning them . . . unless the agreement upon which such action shall be brought, or some memorandum or note thereof, shall be in writing, signed by the party to be charged therewith, or by some person thereunto by him lawfully authorized.

[*Childers v. Talbott*, 4 N.M. 336, 340, 16 P. 275, 276 (1888)] (quoting Section 4 of the statute of frauds).

PART PERFORMANCE

Notwithstanding its language, judicial construction of the statute of frauds has resulted in limiting its application in order to overcome the harshness and injustice of a literal and mechanical application of its terms. . . . One well settled exception, recognized in New Mexico, is the doctrine of part performance. Alvarez v. Alvarez, 72 N.M. 336, 341, 383 P.2d 581, 584 (1963).

"Where an oral contract not enforceable under the statute of frauds has been performed to such extent as to make it inequitable to deny effect thereto, equity may consider the contract as removed from operation of the statute of frauds and decree specific performance." Id. In this case, the trial court concluded:

> [T]he evidence is clear, cogent and convincing so as to remove the case from the application of the [s]tatute of [f]rauds and that there is significant partial performance by both parties, [Buyers] in expending so much time, energy and money developing the parcel of property and [Sellers] in applying for permission to have the personal property placed on the land, seeking advice of counsel as to the manner in which to sell the property and allowing [Buyers] to rely on their representations and to reside on the property for years. The [c]ourt finds that applying the [s]tatute of [f]rauds would be unfair and inequitable.

Sellers do not contend that proof of the oral contract is lacking; in fact, they concede that the evidence is sufficient. . . . Sellers' sole argument is that the *character* of Buyers' performance was not sufficiently indicative of an oral agreement to sell land to qualify as partial performance. *See* Burns v. McCormick, 233 N.Y. 230, 135 N.E. 273, 273 (1922) ("Not every act of part performance will move a court of equity, though legal remedies are inadequate, to enforce an oral agreement affecting rights in land. There must be performance 'unequivocally referable' to the agreement, performance which alone and without the aid of words of promise is unintelligible or at least extraordinary unless as an incident of ownership, assured, if not existing."); Woolley v. Stewart, 222 N.Y. 347, 118 N.E. 847, 848 (1918) ("An act which admits of explanation without reference to the alleged oral contract or a contract of the same general nature and purpose is not, in general, admitted to constitute a part performance."), quoted with approval in *Alvarez*, 72 N.M. at 342, 383 P.2d at 585.

> A court of equity [therefore] requires that a part performance relied on to take the case out of the statute [of frauds] should be of a character, not only consistent with the reasonable presumption that what was done was done on the faith of such a contract, but also that it would be unreasonable to presume that it was done on any other theory.

Alvarez, 72 N.M. at 342, 383 P.2d at 585 (internal quotation marks and citation omitted).

Sellers argue that Buyers' acts are not "unequivocally referable" to their agreement because Buyers' actions could also be consistent with those taken by a person who needs a place to live and who is given an opportunity to reside on another person's property. Sellers argue that if there is an alternative explanation for the actions taken in reliance of the oral contract, those actions are not "unequivocally referable" to the contract, and application of the part performance doctrine is improper. We disagree.

In Nashan v. Nashan, 119 N.M. 625, 630-31, 894 P.2d 402, 407-08 (Ct. App. 1995), we discussed the interrelationship of the factors that may be considered in determining whether a contract to convey land has been proven and whether it would be inequitable to enforce the contract. We said:

> Whatever the purpose of each test, however, the main questions are the same for a court faced with a case such as this one — was there actually an oral agreement such as that alleged by the plaintiff, and if so would it be inequitable to deny enforcement to the agreement? The factors should not be applied mechanically to determine whether the plaintiff's performance has met a particular test. Instead, the case must be viewed as a whole to determine whether specific performance of the agreement is required.

Id. at 631, 894 P.2d at 408. Thus, we reject the suggestion that the "unequivocally referable" concept means that outside of the contract, there can be no other plausible explanation for the part performance. In fact, we described the "unequivocally referable" concept in plain language as "meaning that an outsider, knowing all of the circumstances of a case except for the claimed oral agreement, would naturally and reasonably conclude that a contract existed regarding the land, of the same general nature as that alleged by the claimant." Id. at 630, 894 P.2d at 407 (citing Smith v. Smith, 466 So. 2d 922, 925 (Ala. 1985)). We did not say that the performance must relate exclusively to the oral contract; rather, the performance must lead an outsider to "naturally and reasonably" conclude that the contract alleged actually exists. Two key specific factors, approved by this Court and many other courts, in coming to such a conclusion, are taking possession of the property, and making valuable, permanent, and substantial improvements to the property. Id. at 630-31, 894 P.2d at 407-08. Where these two factors coincide, specific performance usually results. Id.

In this case, Buyers went into possession of the specific land Sellers agreed to convey with Sellers' consent. In reliance on the agreement, Buyers cashed IRA and 401-K retirement plans at a substantial penalty, purchased a double-wide mobile home, and with Sellers' consent, moved it onto the property. Buyers also erected valuable temporary and permanent improvements on the land, and landscaped the property with Sellers' consent. In reliance on the agreement, Buyers spent approximately $85,000 in purchasing the home and making improvements. We hold Buyers' actions were sufficient part performance in reliance on the oral agreement to take the agreement outside of the statute of frauds.

SUFFICIENCY OF THE VERBAL AGREEMENT

The trial court concluded:

> [T]he terms of the contract were that [Sellers] would sell to [Buyers] the piece of property included in the demarcation of the landmarks as testified to by [Mr. Brumlow]. While the purchase price was never agreed upon, the [c]ourt finds that [Buyers] should pay to [Sellers] the fair market value of the property as determined by an objective appraiser, in one lump sum, within sixty days of the [c]ourt's decision. Imposing fair market value and requiring a cash payment is the equitable remedy.

Sellers assert that by ruling that the purchase price would be established by an appraisal and that the terms of the payment would be in cash payable within thirty days, the trial court "formulated an agreement between the parties that never existed" and it "enforced terms and conditions on the parties that they had not had a meeting of the minds upon" which is "exactly" what the court in Bellamah v. Schmider, 68 N.M. 247, 360 P.2d 656 (1961) "said the courts should not do."

[The Court distinguished *Bellamah*. In that case the buyer sought specific performance of a contract to sell land with abatement of the purchase price because the seller did not own all of the land under contract. The court denied relief stating that it would not make an agreement for the parties. In that case the buyer knew at the time the contract was made that the seller did not own all of the land but the contract did not contain a provision for abatement. – EDS.]

This case is more analogous to Colcott v. Sutherland, 36 N.M. 370, 16 P.2d 399 (1932), in which our Supreme Court suggested that a claim for specific performance of a contract involving land will not fail for failure to specify a price where the contract is otherwise complete, and there has been part performance of the contract by a transfer of possession. . . . In *Colcott*, the buyer alleged that the owner agreed to sell the buyer two acres from a parcel he owned for the sum of $150 per acre, provided that the buyer gave the seller an option to buy the land back if the buyer decided to move a gin he was planning on constructing on the land in the future. . . . In reliance on the agreement, the buyer alleged he went into possession of the land and constructed the gin at a cost of $25,000. . . . However, the parties never agreed on a price at which the seller could repurchase the property, nor did they agree on a means for determining the repurchase price. . . . On this basis, the seller asserted that the allegations failed to state a claim for specific performance because there was no contract. . . . Our Supreme Court said:

> The parties having thus agreed, what is the effect of the omission to stipulate the price for a repurchase? [The seller] contends that it results in incompleteness and uncertainty fatal to the remedy of specific performance. [The buyer] says there is no incompleteness or uncertainty, since the law's implication binds the parties to a reasonable price, and equity has means to determine it. *This may be entirely sound.*

Id. at 374-75, 16 P.2d at 401 (emphasis added) (citing John Norton Pomeroy & John C. Mann, *Specific Performance of Contracts* §148, at 380-82 (3d ed. 1926)).

However, the suit was not for specific performance of the seller's option to repurchase; it was to enforce the contract to sell to the buyer. Accordingly, the Court did not decide whether an action would lie for specific performance of the option itself. . . . While our Supreme Court did not decide the issue, its statement that the buyer's position "may be entirely sound" and citation to Pomeroy & Mann is highly suggestive of its answer. . . . [T]he Pomeroy reference states:

> . . . A valid contract of sale may be made without any stipulation as to the price, the law in such case implying that the price is the reasonable value of the thing which is the subject-matter of the agreement. . . .

Pomeroy & Mann, *supra,* §148, at 380-82 (footnotes omitted).

[The court then discussed a California case, O'Keefe v. Aptos Land & Water Co., 134 Cal. App. 2d 772, 286 P.2d 417 (1955), where the court had enforced an oral agreement to buy real estate. The buyer had relied on the agreement by taking possession and making valuable improvements, including building a house. While the parties, who were formerly close business associates, had not agreed on the price, the court concluded that a reasonable price should be implied to prevent an inequitable result. — EDS.]

We adopt the holding of *O'Keefe* in this case. Buyers proved to the satisfaction of the trial court by clear, cogent, and convincing evidence that Sellers entered into a contract to sell specific land to Buyers, as reflected in its conclusions of law quoted above. In addition, there was significant specific part performance by both Buyers and Sellers in reliance on the contract they made. In particular, Buyers cashed their retirement plans, went into possession of the property, moved their home onto the property, and made significant improvements to the land at a total cost of approximately $85,000, all with the knowledge and consent of Sellers for several years. Buyers assumed they would have to pay whatever the property was worth, and Sellers consulted an attorney to draft the sale documents. When Buyers repeatedly asked that the contract be formalized, Sellers' response was, "We will work it out." Thus, it is through no fault of Buyers that formal contract documents were not written with a set price and terms. Under these circumstances, it was within the equitable jurisdiction of the trial court to set the price at the fair market value as determined by an objective appraiser. We take particular note that Sellers do not dispute on appeal the fairness of the price established by the trial court.

Sellers would have us invalidate what was unquestionably a valid contract based on a mechanical application of contract law. We decline to do so. . . . Sellers do not seem to acknowledge that this is a case under the equitable jurisdiction of the trial court. "In the general juristic sense, equity means the power to meet the moral standards of justice in a particular case by a tribunal having discretion to mitigate the rigidity of the application of strict rules of law so as to adapt the relief to the circumstances of the particular case." Henry L. McClintock, *Principles of Equity* §1, at 1 (2d ed. 1948). We hold that there was no error committed by the trial court by decreeing specific performance of the contract for Sellers to sell, and Buyers to buy, the subject property for its fair market value.

Sellers also assert that the trial court erred in decreeing that the sale would close within sixty days of its decision because that term was absent from the agreement. Largely for the reasons already expressed, we reject this argument as well. Moreover, when an agreement does not specify a time for performance, it is implied that it is to be performed within a reasonable time, and what is a reasonable time is a question of fact. . . .

ADEQUACY OF REMEDY AT LAW

. . . Sellers also argue that Buyers' part performance "could have been very easily compensated for with money." However, Buyers did not seek damages for their part performance; they relied on their own part performance, as well as the part performance of Sellers to compel specific performance of the contract to sell them land. Moreover, it is well settled that land is assumed to have special value not replaceable in money. 3 Dan B. Dobbs, *Dobbs Law of Remedies* §12.11(3), at 299 (2d ed. 1993).

> When real property is the subject matter of the agreement, the legal remedy of damages may be assumed to be inadequate, since each parcel of land is unique. Thus, even though the availability of an equitable remedy such as specific performance generally depends on the inadequacy of any remedy at law, where land is the subject matter of the agreement, jurisdiction of equity to grant specific performance does not depend upon the existence of special facts showing that legal remedy is inadequate.

81A C.J.S. Specific Performance §56, at 229-30 (2004) (footnotes omitted). . . .

CONCLUSION

The judgment of the trial court is affirmed.

IT IS SO ORDERED.

We Concur: James J. WECHSLER and Robert E. ROBLES, Judges.

NOTES AND QUESTIONS

1. *Interests in land.* When the statute of frauds was enacted in England in the seventeenth century, land was the basis of the English economy. It is not surprising, therefore, that contracts for the transfer of an interest in land were one of the types of contracts subject to the original English statute of frauds. While land may be of less relative significance in modern times, contracts involving the sale of land do typically involve fairly large sums of money. Note that the land provision of the statute of frauds is not limited to contracts for the sale of land but can apply to the transfer of other interests in land, such as easements, mortgages, and leases. E.g., Presten v. Sailer, 542 A.2d 7 (N.J. Super. Ct. App.

Div. 1988) (purchase of cooperative apartment proprietary lease held subject to the statute of frauds); contra Firth v. Lu, 49 P.3d 117 (Wash. 2002) (sale of stock in corporation that operates housing cooperative, not interest in real property for purpose of statute of frauds; *Presten* discussed and distinguished). In many jurisdictions statutes of frauds are limited to "long-term" leases; for example, ones lasting more than a year. See, e.g., Duck Creek Tire Serv., Inc. v. Goodyear Corners, L.C., 796 N.W.2d 886 (Iowa 2011) (statute of frauds applies to lease or transfer of lease exceeding one year). (It should be noted, however, that the land clause and the one-year clause of the statute of frauds are independent provisions; if an agreement is within either one it will be subject to the statutory requirements.) On the scope of the land contract provision of the statute of frauds, see generally E. Allan Farnsworth, Contracts §6.5 (4th ed. 2004).

2. *The "part performance" doctrine.* After the statute of frauds was enacted in the seventeenth century, the English courts soon encountered cases in which one party claimed to have taken possession of land pursuant to an oral agreement that the other party denied making — hardly surprising during an era in which literacy was not widespread. The English "equity" courts recognized an exception to the statute in the case of "part performance." Butcher v. Stapley, 23 Eng. Rep. 524 (Ch. 1685).

What type of part performance will be sufficient to make an oral promise to transfer an interest in land enforceable? (The terminology that is often used is "to take the contract out of the statute.") The court in *Beaver* uses the "unequivocally referable" test, which is traceable to Cardozo's opinion in Burns v. McCormick, 135 N.E. 273, 273 (N.Y. 1922). The court clarifies and broadens the meaning of this test by deciding that it is unnecessary for the promisee to show that his performance does not have a "plausible explanation" other than the existence of a contract. It is sufficient, the court declares, that "the performance must lead an outsider to 'naturally and reasonably' conclude that the contract alleged actually exists." In deciding whether the promisee's performance is "unequivocally referable" to the contract, two factors are crucial: first, whether the party seeking enforcement has obtained possession of the property; and second, whether that party has made valuable improvements to the property. Most courts agree that the presence of these factors is sufficient to justify application of the part performance exception; mere payment of money, however, is unlikely to be enough. See Zuk v. Zuk, 55 A.3d 102 (Pa. Super. Ct. 2012) (part performance exception established by possession, improvement, and partial payment); E. Allan Farnsworth, Contracts §6.9, at 396-397 (4th ed. 2004).

The Restatement (Second) does not employ the "unequivocally referable" test. Section 129, states:

§129. Action in Reliance; Specific Performance

A contract for the transfer of an interest in land may be specifically enforced notwithstanding failure to comply with the Statute of Frauds if it is established that the party seeking enforcement, in reasonable reliance on the contract and on the continuing assent of the party against whom enforcement is sought, has so changed his position that injustice can be avoided only by specific enforcement.

Comment *a* criticizes the unequivocally-referable test, as well as the "virtual fraud" test that has been applied by a number of other courts:

> A more accurate statement is that courts with equitable powers are vested by tradition with what in substance is a dispensing power based on the promisee's reliance, a discretion to be exercised with caution in the light of all the circumstances.

Suppose that in reliance on the Beavers' promise, the Brumlows had cashed in their IRA and 401(k) plans at substantial penalty and had bought a double-wide mobile home. However, before they had moved on to the property or paid the Beavers anything, the Beavers decided not to go forward with the transaction. What do you think the result would be under the unequivocally-referable test used by the court in *Beaver*? What result under Restatement (Second) §129?

3. *Limitation of the part performance exception to the land contract provision to actions for specific performance rather than damages.* In *Beaver* the buyers were seeking specific performance, a remedy that was traditionally granted by courts of equity. (A brief history of the distinction between law and equity is set forth in the Comment following these Notes.) Could the buyers have used the part performance exception to the statute of frauds to recover damages for their various financial expenses rather than seeking to obtain title to the land? Most courts have limited the part performance exception to claims for specific performance rather than damages. See, e.g., Winternitz v. Summit Hills Joint Venture, 532 A.2d 1089 (Md. Ct. App. 1987) (part performance is equitable doctrine and inapplicable to action by tenant against landlord for money damages). The Restatement agrees with this limitation on the part performance doctrine. See Restatement (Second) of Contracts §129, Comment *c*.

4. *Other forms of part performance.* *Beaver* deals with one type of part performance — part performance of a contract for the sale of land as an exception to the statute of frauds. We will see later in this chapter in connection with the *Buffaloe* case that there is also a part performance exception to the UCC statute of frauds for the sale of goods. In contracts that do not involve the sale of land or goods, part performance may be important in determining whether a court should apply the promissory estoppel exception to the statute of frauds. The next case examines this exception.

Comment: The Historical Development of Law and Equity

The English origins of our modern legal system began in the thirteenth century with the establishment of a centralized court system. 1 William S. Holdsworth, A History of English Law 194-264 (1982). To obtain relief in court a party had to show that his situation fit within one of the well-established "writs" for granting relief. The writ system was, of course, not static; new writs were recognized over time, and old writs were redefined to deal with changing circumstances.

Not every litigant could obtain relief through the writ system, and over the years many subjects petitioned the King for help when they were unable to find a remedy in the law courts. These petitions ultimately became the basis for an independent Court of Chancery, administered by one of the King's assistants, the Chancellor. Id. at 401-402. As time passed tension developed between the law courts and the Court of Chancery, but in the seventeenth century, the power of the Court of Chancery to act became firmly established. Id. at 461. Originally discretionary in its decision making, the Court of Chancery gradually developed a more legalistic, precedent-based method of decision. Id. at 465-469. One principle followed by the Court of Chancery was that equity would act only when the remedy at law (typically damages) was "inadequate" to compensate the plaintiff. Id. at 456-457. Since land was fundamental to the English economy, and each piece of land was deemed "unique," a damage remedy for breach of a contract to transfer an interest in land was necessarily considered inadequate. The equity courts took jurisdiction in such cases and would award a decree of specific performance. (The remedy of specific performance is discussed in more detail in Chapter 11.) The court in *Beaver* refers to the presumption of the uniqueness of land in affirming the trial court's award of specific performance. Thus, disputes involving land typically came before the equity courts rather than the law courts, and it was in the equity courts that the exception to the statute of frauds for part performance developed.

When America achieved its independence, each of the American states in its original constitution adopted or "received" the English common law as the basis for the law of that state. (Americans did not see themselves as revolting against the English system but against its King. Indeed, Americans relied on the fundamental rights of Englishmen as the basis of the revolution. For a history of these developments, see Gordon S. Wood, The Creation of the American Republic 1776-1787 (1972).) In the nineteenth century, under the intellectual influence of David Dudley Field, procedural reform swept the United States. One of the major aspects of this reform was the "merger" of the law and equity courts. Rather than dual court systems as in the original English system, a single court of general jurisdiction was granted the power to provide any form of relief, whether traditionally given at law or in equity. See generally Daun van Ee, David Dudley Field and the Reconstruction of the Law (1986).

Despite this procedural merger, the historical distinction between law and equity continues to have some modern significance. For example, in your course in civil procedure, you will learn that a litigant has a right to a jury trial if the matter was one that historically was decided by the law courts rather than the equity courts. Beacon Theatres, Inc. v. Westover, 359 U.S. 500 (1958). When we discuss remedies later on in this course, we will see that the basic remedy for breach of contract is damages. If a party wishes to obtain in personam relief, such as an injunction or specific performance (remedies that traditionally were awarded by the equity courts), the litigant must show that the damage remedy is "inadequate." The limitation of the part performance exception to the statute of frauds, as discussed in the notes after *Beaver*, is another example of the continued influence of the distinction between law and equity.

In a famous speech, Justice Oliver Wendell Holmes bemoaned the influence of history on the law:

> It is revolting to have no better reason for a rule of law than that so it was laid down in the time of Henry IV. It is still more revolting if the grounds upon which it was laid down have vanished long since, and the rule simply persists from blind imitation of the past.

Oliver Wendell Holmes, The Path of the Law, 10 Harv. L. Rev. 457, 469 (1897). Keep Justice Holmes's observation in mind as your study of the rules of contract law progresses.

Alaska Democratic Party v. Rice

Supreme Court of Alaska 934 P.2d 1313 (1997)

Before COMPTON, C.J., and RABINOWITZ, MATTHEWS, EASTAUGH AND FABE, JJ.

OPINION

RABINOWITZ, Justice.

I. INTRODUCTION

Kathleen Rice (Rice) contended that Greg Wakefield, in his capacity as chair-elect of the Alaska Democratic Party (Party), offered her a two-year position as executive director of the Party. When the job failed to materialize, Rice sued on the alleged oral contract. She was awarded damages after a jury trial. The Party and Wakefield now appeal. We affirm.

II. FACTS AND PROCEEDINGS

Rice worked for the Party in one capacity or another from approximately 1987 to 1991. In 1991, she was fired from her position as executive director by Rhonda Roberts, the then current chair of the Party. In 1991, Rice began working for the Maryland Democratic Party. While she was in Maryland, Greg Wakefield contacted her regarding his potential candidacy for the Party chair and the possibility of Rice serving as his executive director.

In May 1992, Wakefield was in fact elected to chair the Party. His term was set to begin the following February. Rice claims that sometime during the summer after Wakefield had been elected, he "confirmed his decision" to hire her as executive director on the following specific terms: "$36,000.00 a year for at least two years and an additional two years if . . . Wakefield is re-elected; and approximately $4,000.00 a year in fringe benefits."

In August 1992, Nathan Landau, the chair of the Maryland Democratic Party, resigned and asked Rice to come work for him in his new capacity as co-finance chair of the Gore vice-presidential campaign. She accepted this offer. Rice asserts that later, in either September or October, she accepted Wakefield's offer to work for the Party in Alaska. In November, Rice moved to Alaska, resigning her position with Landau, which she claims "could have continued indefinitely

. . . at a pay scale the same as that offered by Wakefield." No written contract was entered into between Rice and Wakefield or between Rice and the Party.

In a closed-door meeting on February 5, 1993, the executive committee of the Party advised Wakefield that he could not hire Rice as executive director. Rice alleges that even after this meeting, Wakefield continued to assure her that she had the job. However, on February 15, Wakefield informed her that she could not have the job. Rice filed suit.

On cross-motions for summary judgment, the superior court dismissed all counts except those based on the theories of promissory estoppel and misrepresentation. After a trial by jury, Rice was awarded $28,864 in damages on her promissory estoppel claim and $1,558 in damages on her misrepresentation claim. The superior court denied the Party's and Wakefield's motions for directed verdicts and judgment N.O.V. This appeal followed.

III. Discussion

A. The Superior Court Did Not Err in Denying the Party's Motion for Summary Judgment on Rice's Promissory Estoppel Claim.

The question of whether the doctrine of promissory estoppel can be invoked to enforce an oral contract that falls within the Statute of Frauds presents a question of first impression. In order to resolve this question, the policy concerns behind both the Statute of Frauds and the doctrine of promissory estoppel must be examined. The purpose of the Statute of Frauds is to prevent fraud by requiring that certain categories of contracts be reduced to writing. However, "it is not intended as an escape route for persons seeking to avoid obligations undertaken by or imposed upon them." Eavenson v. Lewis Means, Inc., 105 N.M. 161, 730 P.2d 464, 465 (1986), overruled on other grounds by Strata Prod. Co. v. Mercury Exploration Co., 121 N.M. 622, 916 P.2d 822 (1996).

In its ruling on cross summary judgment motions in this case, the superior court addressed some of the conflicting case law on this question and ultimately concluded that as between the Statute of Frauds and promissory estoppel, the latter would prevail. It based this conclusion, in large part, on section 139 of the Restatement (Second) of Contracts which provides that

> [a] promise which the promisor should reasonably expect to induce action or forbearance on the part of the promisee or a third person and which does induce the action or forbearance is enforceable *notwithstanding the Statute of Frauds* if injustice can be avoided only by enforcement of the promise. . . .

Restatement (Second) of Contracts §139 (1981) (emphasis added). Section 139(2) then goes on to enumerate factors to consider in making the determination of "whether injustice can be avoided only by enforcement of the promise." Id.

In reaching its decision on this issue, the superior court reasoned:

> The Restatement test referenced herein provides an appropriate balance between the competing considerations supporting strict enforcement of the

> Statute, on the one hand, and prevention of a miscarriage of justice, on the other. Plaintiff's burden in overriding the Statute *is to establish the promise's existence by clear and convincing evidence.* This heightened burden, along with the other criteria imposed by Section 139, insure that the polices which gave rise to the Statute of Frauds will not, in fact, be nullified by application of the Restatement exception.

(Emphasis added.) Commentators have noted that "there is no question that many courts are now prepared to use promissory estoppel to overcome the requirements of the statute of frauds." 2 Arthur L. Corbin, Corbin on Contracts §281A (1950 & Supp. 1996). We join those states which endorse the Restatement approach in employment disputes such as this one.[2]

Concerning the applicability of section 139,[3] the requisites for a claim must be met, as the jury reasonably found they were here. The Party and Wakefield reasonably could have expected to induce Rice's action by their promise. Rice did in fact resign from her job, move from Maryland, and lose money as a result of her reliance on the Party and Wakefield, which amounted to a substantial worsening of her position. In addition, her reliance on the oral representations was reasonable.

---

2. See McIntosh v. Murphy, 52 Haw. 29, 469 P.2d 177 (1970); Eavenson v. Lewis Means, Inc., 105 N.M. 161, 730 P.2d 464 (1986), overruled by Strata Prod. Co. v. Mercury Exploration Co., 121 N.M. 622, 916 P.2d 822, 828 (1996) (recasting elements of promissory estoppel), and Glasscock v. Wilson Constructors, Inc., 627 F.2d 1065 (10th Cir. 1980).

Numerous decisions have rejected the Restatement approach both implicitly and explicitly. See, e.g., Venable v. Hickerson, Phelps, Kirtley & Assoc., Inc., 903 S.W.2d 659 (Mo. App. 1995), Greaves v. Medical Imaging Sys., Inc., 124 Wash. 2d 389, 879 P.2d 276 (1994), Collins v. Allied Pharmacy Management, Inc., 871 S.W.2d 929 (Tex. App. 1994), Dickens v. Quincy College Corp., 245 Ill. App. 3d 1055, 185 Ill. Dec. 822, 615 N.E.2d 381 (1993), Stearns v. Emery-Waterhouse Co., 596 A.2d 72 (Me. 1991), Sales Serv., Inc. v. Daewoo Int'l (America) Corp., 770 S.W.2d 453 (Mo. App. 1989), Whiteco Indus., Inc. v. Kopani, 514 N.E.2d 840 (Ind. App. 1987), Cunnison v. Richardson Greenshields Securities, Inc., 107 A.D.2d 50, 485 N.Y.S.2d 272 (N.Y. App. Div. 1985), Moran v. NAV Servs., 189 Ga. App. 825, 377 S.E.2d 909 (1989), Munoz v. Kaiser Steel Corp., 156 Cal. App. 3d 965, 203 Cal. Rptr. 345 (1984).

3. In reviewing a jury's determination, this court views the evidence in the light most favorable to the judgment. It does not "weigh the evidence or judge the credibility of the witnesses," but instead, "determine[s] whether there is room for diversity of opinion among reasonable people. If so, the question is one for the jury." Levar v. Elkins, 604 P.2d 602, 604 (Alaska 1980).

In denying the Party's and Wakefield's motions for judgment N.O.V., the superior court stated in part:

> Rice, however, testified that Caroline Covington had told her that the Chair makes the decision regarding employment of executive directors. Rice claimed Wakefield told her it was his decision who to hire. He allegedly said that if everyone was mad, he and Kathleen would work together through May and then both quit, suggesting again that the decision would be his, notwithstanding opposition. Plaintiff said that when John Pugh was chair, he had communicated that it was within his discretion to fire executive director Bob Speed. And the Party Plan did not give the executive committee authority over such hiring decisions. This was sufficient evidence for the jury to decide that Rice relied on Wakefield's implicit promise that the executive committee could not derail his selection for executive or finance director. While the Party focuses on the reasonableness of Rice's reliance, that is only one factor for the jury to evaluate in deciding whether injustice could be avoided only by enforcing the contract.

Our review of the record persuades us that there is ample evidence supporting the superior court's analysis.

Nonetheless, the promise is only enforceable where injustice can only be avoided by enforcement of the promise. The following circumstances are relevant to this inquiry:

> a) the availability and adequacy of other remedies, particularly cancellation and restitution;
> b) the definite and substantial character of the action or forbearance in relation to the remedy sought;
> c) the extent to which the action or forbearance corroborates evidence of the making and terms of the promise, *or the making and terms are otherwise established by clear and convincing evidence;*
> d) the reasonableness of the action or forbearance;
> e) the extent to which the action or forbearance was foreseeable by the promisor.

Restatement (Second) of Contracts §139(2). In the context of this factual record, the jury could reasonably find that Rice would be a victim of injustice without an award of damages, considering her induced resignation, her move from Maryland, and her loss of money and position.

The Statute of Frauds represents a traditional contract principle that is largely formalistic and does not generally concern substantive rights. The extent to which a reliance exception would undermine this principle is minimal and the rights that it would protect are significant. The need to satisfy the clear and convincing proof standard with respect to the subsection 139(2)(c) factor also reassures us that promissory estoppel will not render the statute of frauds superfluous in the employment context. Accordingly, we affirm the superior court's treatment of this issue and adopt section 139 as the law of this jurisdiction.[4]

B. The Superior Court did Not Commit an Error by Not Incorporating the Phrase "Definite And Substantial" into Jury Instruction Number 12.

In regard to Rice's section 139 claim, one aspect ofJury Instruction 12 directed the jury to decide whether Rice "took action in reliance upon the promise. . . ." The Party and Wakefield claim that section 139 of the Restatement (Second) of Contracts requires more than that "action" be taken; they contend that the action must be of a "definite and substantial" character. As such, they argue that "instruction 12 omitted a crucial component of the section 139 factors."

The Restatement lists "the definite and substantial character of the action or forbearance in relation to the remedy sought" as a significant "circumstance

4. The Party and Wakefield present further arguments as to why they should prevail on the promissory estoppel claim. They argue first that "[t]here was no substantial change of position, no reliance, and no foreseeability of reliance." And second, that " '[t]he interests of justice' do not require enforcement of the alleged 'promise.' "

These arguments were not included in the points on appeal submitted at filing, nor were they presented anywhere in the body of the opening brief; they are only argued in the reply brief. As such, they will not be considered by this court. Alaska Rule of Appellate Procedure 204(e). See also Swick v. Seward School Bd., 379 P.2d 97 (Alaska 1963). The arguments are, in any event, without merit. They involve issues that were appropriately resolved against the Party and Wakefield by the jury. . . .

[]" to consider when applying the doctrine of promissory estoppel. Restatement (Second) of Contracts §139. The Party and Wakefield are wrong to characterize this language as creating a "requirement[]." Further, the "definite and substantial" language was given to the jury in Instruction 13.[6]

When read as a whole, the instructions clearly direct the jury to consider the definite and substantial character of Rice's action before concluding that an injustice could be avoided only by enforcing the promise. As such, the instructions are compatible with the Restatement, and it was not error to omit this modifier from the text of Instruction 12.

C. The Evidentiary Record Supports the Jury's Verdict

1. Agency

The Party argues that Wakefield, as chair-elect, had neither implied nor apparent authority to contract on behalf of the party. Consequently, they conclude that "the Party is not vicariously liable to Rice under the law of agency." The jury, after being properly instructed on the law of agency, apparently concluded that Wakefield was acting as an agent for the Party when he allegedly offered Rice the job.

The superior court declined to reverse the jury's implied determination of this issue. In denying the Party's motion for a judgment N.O.V. on this issue, the superior court concluded that it would have been reasonable for the jury to find that Wakefield had implied authority, apparent authority, or both. In this respect, the superior court observed that "[t]he Party elected Greg Wakefield as its new Chair. In so doing, the Party arguably cloaked Wakefield with apparent authority to conduct business on behalf of his incoming administration." The superior court also concluded, after discussing the Party Plan and comments allegedly made by Party officials, that the "evidence provides a sufficient basis for a finding of the Chair's implied general authority to make hiring decisions regarding executive personnel."

In addition to its more general complaints on this topic, the Party specifically claims that "even if Wakefield, as chair-elect, had the implied or apparent authority to hire someone, he lacked the authority to hire Rice at all, and most especially for a set term employment contract of two or more years, as opposed to an employment contract at will." The superior court properly refuted both branches of this argument. In response to the first branch, the superior court concluded that "[b]ecause the evidence supported a finding of general authority, there was no need to adduce evidence of a specific intention to authorize

---

6. Instruction 13 reads in full as follows:

In determining whether injustice can be avoided only by enforcement of a promise, you may consider, among others, the following circumstances:

(a) the definite and substantial character of the plaintiff's action in relation to the remedy sought;

(b) the extent to which plaintiff's action corroborates evidence of the making and terms of the promise, or the making and terms are otherwise established by clear and convincing evidence;

(c) the reasonableness of plaintiff's action;

(d) the extent to which plaintiff's action was foreseeable by the promisor.

Rice's hiring in particular." With respect to whether Wakefield had the authority to hire someone for a term of years, the superior court held that since the question had not been raised at trial or on motion for directed verdict, it was accordingly waived.

The question of whether Wakefield had implied or apparent authority to retain an executive director during the term of his chairmanship was properly submitted to the jury for resolution.

2. Misrepresentation

The Party and Wakefield do not, in this appeal, dispute the fact that the jury instructions covering Rice's misrepresentation claim accurately set forth the correct legal standards. The only legal contention that they raise with this claim is that since at the time that the alleged representations were made "Wakefield was a volunteer, not speaking in his business or professional capacity," his representations cannot provide a basis for recovery. This argument is derived from the text of subsection 552(1) of the Restatement (Second) of Torts (1977). That section would allow recovery against "[o]ne who, in the course of his business, profession or employment, or in any other transaction in which he has a pecuniary interest, supplies false information. . . ." Id.

The Party and Wakefield argue that this language constitutes a "prerequisite for claiming negligent misrepresentation." However, the comment to Subsection 552(1) explains that it is designed primarily to distinguish cases where "the information is given purely gratuitously. . . ." That is not this case. Wakefield had a significant stake in Rice's acceptance of his alleged offer; he apparently wanted her to serve as his executive director. Despite the fact that his term had not yet commenced when the representations were made, they were clearly made in the course of the business of running a political party. As such, even if the Restatement (Second) of Torts does create a prerequisite, that prerequisite was functionally met in this case. . . .

Both legal and factual support for the jury's verdict on the misrepresentation claim are found in this record. The Party's and Wakefield's arguments to the contrary are without merit.

D. The Damage Amount Was not Excessive in Light of the Evidence.

1. Section 139 claim

According to the special verdict form, Rice was awarded $28,864.00 in damages for lost earnings and benefits on her section 139 claim. The salary that Rice claims to have been offered was $36,000.00 per year plus $4,200.00 in employee benefits. The Party and Wakefield do not seem to dispute the fact that the $28,864.00 amount is a fair measure of Rice's lost wages based upon the salary figures she alleges. The gist of their argument on the promissory estoppel claim is rather that the full "benefit of the bargain [was] not necessary to avoid injustice."

As discussed in section III.A., supra, a proven section 139 claim has the effect of rendering the oral contract, which would have been invalid under the

Statute of Frauds, legally enforceable on the terms established by Rice. The superior court correctly instructed the jury as to the proper method of calculating damages.

Further, since this jury was specifically instructed not to find for Rice on this claim unless "[i]njustice can be avoided only be enforcement of the promise," it can be inferred that the jury concluded that the damages award was "necessary to avoid injustice." This question was properly reserved for the jury, and there is nothing unreasonable or outrageous about their award. The Party's and Wakefield's contentions to the contrary are without merit.

2. *Misrepresentation*

The special verdict forms indicate that the jury awarded Rice $1,558.00 on her misrepresentation claim. This amount represents what Rice claims to have spent on moving expenses. As a result of this award, the Party and Wakefield complain that "under the judgment, [Rice] gets both her travel costs . . . and damages calculated with reference to the terms of the promise," giving her more than she would have received even if the alleged contract had been honored.

This argument would have been valid if the superior court had actually awarded this damage item to Rice. It did not. The final judgment order reduced the total award of the jury, which would have been $30,422.00 with the misrepresentation award, to the $28,864.00 amount that represents only lost wages and benefits.[12] Consequently, we reject the Party and Wakefield's contention that the damage award is excessive on this ground.

IV. CONCLUSION

We affirm the judgment of the superior court.

NOTES AND QUESTIONS

1. *Reliance on the promise of a writing, under the first Restatement.* The first Restatement envisioned two distinct situations in which enforcement of an oral contract could be based on an estoppel to assert the statute of frauds. In the first situation, the plaintiff detrimentally relied on the defendant's misrepresentation that a writing had been created that would comply with the statute. In the second, the plaintiff similarly relied on a promise by the defendant to create such a memorandum. Restatement (First) of Contracts §178, Comment *f.* Numerous courts have applied promissory estoppel to overcome the statute of frauds in cases where the defendant was shown to have promised the plaintiff a signed memorandum of their agreement, as suggested by Comment *f.* See, e.g., Alaska Airlines, Inc. v. Stephenson, 217 F.2d 295 (9th Cir. 1954) (plaintiff quit a job in California and moved to Alaska on strength of defendant's

12. In its jury instructions on the misrepresentation claim, the superior court explicitly noted its intention to "make any adjustments that may be necessary to insure that there is no double recovery."

promise to employ him as general manager; written contract repeatedly promised but never delivered); Klinke v. Famous Recipe Fried Chicken, Inc., 616 P.2d 644 (Wash. 1980) (plaintiff quit his job and moved to Washington on strength of defendant's promise to enter into written ten-year franchise contract). What is there in such cases that would justify overriding the principle of requiring a writing signed by the defendant? Is the evidentiary function of the statute sufficiently protected?

2. *Reliance on oral promises of performance, under Restatement (Second).* In adopting the rule of §139, the drafters of the revised Restatement have moved a considerable distance (at least in theory) beyond the estoppel applications suggested in Comment *f* to §178. As the court in the above case indicates, a number of courts have expressed their approval of §139 and applied it to permit enforcement of asserted oral contracts within the statute of frauds. See, e.g., Kolkman v. Roth, 656 N.W.2d 148 (Iowa 2003) (recognizing promissory estoppel exception to statute of frauds to enforce oral agreement for lease of farmland in excess of one year) and the cases cited by the court in *Alaska Democratic Party* in the first paragraph of footnote 2. On the other hand, some courts still refuse to recognize a promissory estoppel exception to the statute of frauds. E.g., DK Arena, Inc. v. EB Acquisitions I, LLC, 112 So. 3d 85 (Fla. 2013) (court noting split among jurisdictions before reaffirming its position that promissory estoppel is not an exception to the statute of frauds); Fast Ball Sports v. Metropolitan Entm't & Convention Auth., 835 N.W.2d 782, 794 (Neb. 2013) (promissory estoppel cannot be used to "circumvent" statute of frauds) and the cases cited by the court in *Alaska Democratic Party* in the second paragraph of footnote 2. Some courts, while refusing to recognize as broad an exception to the statute of frauds as §139 contemplates, will use the doctrine of promissory estoppel to avoid application of the statute of frauds to prevent "unjust and unconscionable injury and loss." See Coca-Cola Co. v. Babyback's Intern., Inc., 841 N.E.2d 557, 569 (Ind. 2006). Finally, still other courts have expressed the view that any estoppel exception to the statute of frauds should be limited to the two situations described in Comment *f* to former §178. See the *Klinke* case, cited in Note 1 above; Diaz-Amador v. Wells Fargo Home Mortg., 856 F. Supp. 2d 1074, 1080 (D. Ariz. 2012) (under Arizona law promissory estoppel bars application of statute of frauds only when there has been: (1) a misrepresentation that statute's requirements have been met, or (2) a promise to put agreement in writing). Which approach seems preferable to you: §139 of the revised Restatement (promissory estoppel generally available to overcome statute of frauds), Comment *f* of the original Restatement (promissory estoppel available only where defendant has promised to create a sufficient writing), or rejection of any promissory estoppel exception to the statute of frauds? Why?

3. *Application of §139.* Even if a deciding court accepts the principle of §139, enforcement of the oral contract will not necessarily follow. See Nieto v. Litton Loan Servicing, LP, 2011 WL 797496 (D. Nev.) (promissory estoppel under §139 may apply to land transactions but Nevada statute of frauds is strict and reliance must be objectively reasonable; plaintiffs did not reasonably rely on unspecific promise to modify loan). Besides listing several factors commonly

associated with claims based on reliance, §139 directs the court also to consider whether other remedies, such as restitution, might be available and adequate in the circumstances. Where the plaintiff has rendered partial performance to the defendant pursuant to a contract unenforceable because of the statute of frauds, the court will ordinarily grant the plaintiff a remedy in restitution for the reasonable value of that partial performance. Such an award is not viewed as contravening the statute, since the theory of recovery is not enforcement of the contract but prevention of unjust enrichment. See, e.g., Montanaro Brothers Builders, Inc. v. Snow, 460 A.2d 1297 (Conn. 1983) (recognizing right to restitution of payment for real estate option that was unenforceable due to the statute of frauds) and Restatement (Second) §139, Illustration 4, based on Chevalier v. Lane's, Inc., 213 S.W.2d 530 (Tex. 1948) (employee entitled to payment for services performed, but not to damages for wrongful discharge). As Restatement (Second) §375 points out, sometimes even a restitutionary recovery will not be available, because the relevant statute of frauds specifically forbids it. See, e.g., N.Y. Gen. Oblig. Law §5-701(a)(10) (McKinney) (broker's commissions; statute also applies to contract "implied in fact or in law to pay reasonable compensation" for such services).

For the plaintiff to obtain enforcement of the oral contract under §139, it may thus be necessary for him to demonstrate that by virtue of his reliance he suffered injury that will not be compensable on any other basis. In Munoz v. Kaiser Steel Corp., 203 Cal. Rptr. 345 (Ct. App. 1984), the plaintiff employee alleged that he had left Texas and moved to California in reliance on the defendant's promise to employ him as a plant foreman for at least three years. The plaintiff asserted that to make the move he sold his house in Texas (albeit at a substantial profit over the original purchase price) and bought a house in California for an even higher price, which he subsequently "lost" because he could not keep up the mortgage payments after being fired by the defendant. The California appellate court upheld the trial court's grant of summary judgment for the defendant on the plaintiff's claim for breach of contract. Citing numerous cases, the court held that estoppel to overcome the statute of frauds could only rest on either unjust enrichment of the defendant or unconscionable injury to the plaintiff. The former did not apply, the court found, because the plaintiff had been adequately compensated for all his services to the defendant. As for unconscionable injury, the court noted that the plaintiff had wished to return to California (his childhood home) and had been unemployed at the time he accepted the defendant's offer of work. Without expressly adopting or rejecting Restatement (Second) §139, the court merely observed that the outcome would have been the same in any event, because that section's standard of "injustice" appeared to be substantially the same as the rule of decision employed by the court.

4. *Tort claim.* As indicated by the success of the fraud claim in the *Alaska Democratic Party* case, the borderline between promissory estoppel and claims for fraud or misrepresentation may be a thin one. Although we ordinarily think of actionable misrepresentation as involving a misstatement of fact, the making of a promise with the intention not to keep it has also traditionally

been regarded as a species of "fraud" in Anglo-American law. Should such a tort claim be barred if the fraudulent promise was made as part of an oral agreement that would have been unenforceable as a contract because of the statute of frauds principles? See, e.g., Hurwitz v. Bocian, 670 N.E.2d 408 (Mass. Ct. App. 1996). Plaintiff Hurwitz claimed that defendant Bocian had promised to marry her when his divorce became final, and had also promised to make her a partner in his advertising agency if she would remain at her job with his company and help him see it through "hard times." Her story was supported by credible evidence that he had not intended to keep those promises when he made them (for one thing, he had never applied for a divorce). In affirming a lower court judgment for the plaintiff on her fraud claim, the appellate court considered authority from other jurisdictions denying such an action unless the statute of frauds is complied with, but nevertheless held that the action could be allowed on an estoppel basis. See also Irish Oil and Gas, Inc. v. Riemer, 794 N.W.2d 715 (N.D. 2011) (noting split among courts on the issue but concluding better position is that statute of frauds cannot be used as a defense in a tort action for deceit, even when the statute serves as a valid defense to a breach of contract action).

PROBLEM 4-1

You are a judge of the General Trial Court of Madison County, in the southern state of Madison. An action was recently commenced in your court by Elizabeth Ross against Aaron Burr School of Law, a private law school located in Colonial City, in the state of Madison. The plaintiff's complaint in that action alleges the following facts:

1. Plaintiff is a June 2015 magna cum laude graduate of Hamilton Law School, in Franklin City, capital city of the eastern state of Franklin. From August 2015 through July 2016, plaintiff served as clerk to Judge Brandex of the United States Court of Appeals for the Twelfth Circuit. From August 2016 through July 2017, plaintiff served as clerk to Justice Marshall Law of the United States Supreme Court in Washington, D.C.

2. On or about December 14, 2016, plaintiff was interviewed for employment by defendant. Defendant at that time offered to employ plaintiff as an assistant professor of law, a tenure-track position, at an annual salary starting at $96,000 per year, to commence in August 2017.

3. At the time defendant made the offer referred to in paragraph 2 above, plaintiff asked defendant for some assurance that her employment would continue for a substantial period of time, stating that if she were to accept his offer she would have to move herself and her belongings to Colonial City, leaving behind friends and family in Washington, D.C., and would be embarking on a career in teaching without having prior experience in teaching at the university level. Defendant responded that because faculty members were sometimes requested to assist students in the school's clinical programs with certain legal responsibilities, plaintiff's continued employment past the first year would be contingent on her taking and passing the Madison State Bar Examination

during that time. Except for that contingency, however, defendant asserted that its practice was to evaluate entry-level faculty hires (such as plaintiff would be) for promotion during their third year of teaching, so her position with defendant would be secure for at least a three-year period, through July of 2020.

4. On January 5, 2017, plaintiff received the following signed letter, dated January 2, 2017, from Arnold Benedict, dean of defendant law school:

> **Dear Elizabeth:**
>
> I hope you have had time since our conversation of two weeks ago to consider further our offer of a teaching position commencing with the coming academic year. As we discussed, your salary for the academic year 2017-2018 would be $96,000 per year, to be adjusted in subsequent years, plus the health and retirement benefits enjoyed by our faculty members generally. Your teaching load would be worked out between you and our associate dean for academic affairs. All of us here are looking forward to welcoming you as a colleague, and I hope you will see fit to accept this offer.
>
> All best wishes,
> [signed]*Arnold Benedict*
> Dean, Aaron Burr School of Law

5. On January 10, 2017, plaintiff sent the following signed letter to Dean Benedict:

> **Dear Dean Benedict:**
>
> Thank you for your letter of January 2. Although it will be difficult for me to leave my friends and family here in Washington, I am strongly attracted by your offer to join the Aaron Burr faculty. I have therefore decided to accept your offer of a position as an assistant professor on your faculty. I understand that my starting salary in this position will be $96,000 per year upon commencement of work in August 2017, with possible adjustment upward in the second and third year. I also understand that my employment will be for at least a three-year period, provided I take and pass the Madison State Bar Exam, with my retention beyond that period being dependent on your evaluation of my performance during that period.
>
> Thank you again for your offer. I am excited at the prospect of joining you and your colleagues at Aaron Burr, and I hope that I can justify your faith in my ability.
>
> Sincerely,
> [signed]*Elizabeth Ross*

6. Plaintiff moved to Colonial City in July of 2017, and in August she commenced her work as a member of defendant's faculty. In July 2017 she took the Madison State Bar Examination, and was notified in November 2017 that she had passed that exam.

7. On March 15, 2018, plaintiff was told by Dean Benedict that her appointment would be terminated as of the end of the current academic year. Plaintiff completed her teaching and other responsibilities over the remainder of the spring semester and was paid her salary through the end of July 2018.

8. At the time plaintiff was discharged, she asked defendant for a statement of the reasons for her discharge, and was informed that defendant's budgetary problems made it necessary to reduce expenses. Plaintiff did at all times between August 1, 2017, and July 31, 2018, satisfactorily perform her services as an assistant professor on defendant's faculty, to the best of her knowledge and belief.

9. After her discharge by defendant, plaintiff was unable to find employment as a law professor for the academic year 2018-2019. On February 1, 2019, she accepted a job as an associate attorney with the Colonial City law firm of Dewey, Wyndham & Howe, at an annual salary of $60,000, where she continues to be employed at the present time.

Plaintiff's complaint goes on to ask for damages in the amount of lost wages at the rate of $8,000 per month from August 1, 2018 through January 31, 2019, and at the rate of $3,000 per month for the eighteen-month period thereafter, plus interest.

In its answer to plaintiff's complaint, defendant admits the truth of plaintiff's allegations numbered 1, 2, 4, 5, 6, 7, and 8, above, and of the first and second sentences of the plaintiff's allegation numbered 3. With respect to the third paragraph of plaintiff's complaint, defendant admits that Dean Benedict did tell plaintiff that tenure-track faculty assistant professors were evaluated for promotion during their third year of teaching, but denies that Dean Benedict or any other representative of defendant ever assured plaintiff that she would have three years of employment with defendant, or that her employment by defendant during that period would be "secure." Defendant asserts that all of its untenured faculty members are hired on a one-year contract basis, renewable at the pleasure of the defendant, and that plaintiff was or should have been aware of that fact. Defendant's answer also denies any knowledge of the truth or falsity of plaintiff's allegation numbered 9.

As an affirmative defense, the answer alleges that if there was any contract for three years' employment of plaintiff by defendant, as alleged in plaintiff's complaint, such contract is not evidenced by any note or memorandum signed by the defendant and thus is unenforceable because of the statute of frauds. Defendant also moves that summary judgment be entered for it on plaintiff's complaint on the ground that plaintiff's action is barred by the statute of frauds.

The statutes of your state include a modern version of the old English statute of frauds, providing as follows:

> No contract which . . . by its terms is not to be performed within one year from the date of making thereof . . . shall be enforceable unless the contract or some note or memorandum thereof shall be in writing and signed by the party to be charged.

The statutes of the state of Franklin contain a substantially similar provision.

How will you rule on defendant's motion? What reasons will you give for that ruling?

PROBLEM 4-2

Nora Nance graduated from high school in June 2013. Being unsure about college or career plans, Nora began work for her aunt, Fay Farmer, on Fay's almond farm as a temporary job. Nora received a modest salary of $500 per week and commuted from her family home in Smallville to Fay's farm ten miles outside of town. Nora found that she liked the farm work and proved to be a valuable asset in the almond farming business. Thus, Nora stayed much longer than she or Fay expected.

In June 2018, Nora told Fay that she was considering leaving the job at the almond farm to take a higher paying job in town so that she could move out of her family home. Fay told Nora that she would be willing to sell Nora an unused cabin on the almond farm and the acre of land on which it sat for a price of $15,000. Although the cabin had an appraised value of at least $40,000, Fay said she would sell the cabin to Nora for only $15,000 to make it easier for Nora to continue to work on the almond farm as long as possible and because Nora had been working for such a modest salary for five years. Fay said Nora could pay her $1,000 per year until the full price was paid. Nora immediately agreed to buy the cabin for $15,000. Nora and Fay shook hands to conclude the deal but did not prepare a written contract.

Later that same day, June 26, 2018, Nora completed an electronic funds transfer of $1000 to Fay's bank account. After getting notice of the deposit into her account, Fay sent Nora an email message which read, "Dear Nora: Thanks for the initial payment of $1000 for the cabin. Only fourteen more to go. I am so happy that you are staying on the farm. Love, Aunt Fay."

Nora moved into the cabin in July 2018, promptly repaired the roof, and soon built a fence around the backyard for her pet dog. In June 2019, Nora sent to Fay a second payment of $1,000 for the cabin, but Fay promptly returned the funds. Fay met with Nora and explained that she was planning to sell a part of the almond farm including the acre with the cabin to raise some badly needed funds. Fay told Nora she had to move out of the cabin by September 2019. Is Nora likely to be able to enforce the contract to purchase the cabin from Fay?

B. THE SALE OF GOODS STATUTE OF FRAUDS: UCC §2-201

By the time the Uniform Commercial Code was drafted, it was obvious that not everyone viewed the statute of frauds as an unmixed blessing. Courts often regarded it as an obstacle to the doing of justice, rather than an aid. Some commentators flatly advocated its abolition on the ground that changes in the law of procedure and evidence since the statute's adoption had mooted its original purpose, with the result that the statute was not only unpredictable and exception-riddled, but also unnecessary. See, e.g., Hugh E. Willis, The Statute of Frauds — A Legal Anachronism, 3 Ind. L.J. 427 (1928). As we have already noted, Parliament substantially repealed the English statute of frauds in 1954.

Nevertheless, instead of eliminating the formal writing requirement, the UCC recodified the notion of a sale of goods statute of frauds in §2-201.

This renewed fealty to the concept of a writing requirement may have stemmed in part from the views of Professor Karl Llewellyn, principal author of UCC Article 2, who had earlier in his career declared the statute of frauds to be "an amazing product . . . after two centuries and a half . . . better adapted to our needs than when it first was passed." Karl N. Llewellyn, What Price Contract? — An Essay in Perspective, 40 Yale L.J. 704, 747 (1931). And much of the Code is devoted to business documents of various types, which by their very nature entail at least a writing and typically an authenticating signature as well. See, e.g., UCC §§3-104 (negotiable instruments), 5-104 (letters of credit), 7-202 (warehouse receipts), and 9-203 (security interests). When it came to the sale of goods, however, the drafters of the Code took a fresh look at the statute of frauds. In some minor respects they slightly tightened up its requirements. While proposals for revision have been considered by the drafters since its adoption, the section has remained unchanged with: (1) a fairly low threshold for application (price of $500 or more), (2) a minimal set of requirements to have a sufficient writing, and (3) a number of exceptions to the writing requirement. These aspects of UCC §2-201 are explored in the following case and notes.

Given the debate over its usefulness, it is perhaps not surprising that the Convention for the International Sale of Goods (CISG) contains no provision similar to the statute of frauds. Instead, in Article 11, the CISG expressly negates any requirement of a writing or other formality, and provides that a contract for sale may be proved by witnesses. It should be further noted, however, that the CISG provides in Articles 12 and 96 that a state may "declare" that its statutory writing requirements will apply when any party to a contract has its place of business in that state.

Buffaloe v. Hart

North Carolina Court of Appeals 114 N.C. App. 52, 441 S.E.2d 172 (1994)

GREENE, Judge.

Patricia Hart and Lowell Thomas Hart (defendants) appeal from the trial court's denial of their motions for directed verdict and judgment notwithstanding the verdict in this action brought by Homer Buffaloe (plaintiff) for breach of contract.

Plaintiff filed a complaint for breach of contract and damages in Franklin County Superior Court on 13 November 1989. Defendants, in their answers, denied the existence of the contract and contended the alleged contract was unenforceable because it violated the statute of frauds. The case was tried with a jury during the 28 September 1992 term of Franklin County Superior Court. Plaintiff presented evidence that tended to show that he is a tobacco farmer in Franklin County, North Carolina, has known defendants for about ten years and rented tobacco from them in 1988 and 1989. Plaintiff rented from defendants, pursuant to an oral agreement, five "roanoke box [tobacco] barns" (the barns) located on their farm for use in his tobacco farming operations during the 1988 farming year. The agreement with defendants for rental of the tobacco and the barns was not reduced to writing and was based on a "handshake, oral" agreement. Plaintiff stated, "I had bought some equipment prior to then, and we always done it on a handshake agreement, cash basis. That's the way it was." Defendants agreed to provide insurance coverage for the barns in 1988. On 20 October 1988, plaintiff paid the $2,000.00 rent owed for the barns and the $992.64 owed to Patricia Hart (Mrs. Hart) for the tobacco rent.

Tobacco barns in Dunn, NC.

Plaintiff began negotiating with defendants several days later about purchasing the barns. Plaintiff offered to pay $20,000.00 for the five barns in annual installments of $5,000.00 over a four year period, but did not offer any interest payments. The offer was made in Mrs. Hart's front yard with only defendants and plaintiff present. Defendants accepted the offer, and both parties shook hands. Plaintiff already had possession of the barns under the rental agreement. Plaintiff did not remove the barns from defendants' land because he agreed to farm their land in 1989 with tobacco he rented from defendants.

On 3 January 1989, plaintiff applied for a loan with Production Credit Association in order to pay for the barns. He informed Lowell Thomas Hart (Mr. Hart) that he would pay for all the barns if the loan came through. Mr. Hart responded that it "would be fine with us." On the financial statement portion of the application, he listed the barns, but his loan was denied. Plaintiff and Mr. Hart then reconfirmed that plaintiff was to pay four yearly installments of $5,000.00 for the barns. Because he was unsuccessful in obtaining insurance coverage for the barns, defendants agreed to provide insurance for the five barns for 1989 if plaintiff would reimburse them for the cost. On 20 October 1989, plaintiff promptly reimbursed defendants in full for the insurance coverage.

Plaintiff testified that "[a]fter I bought the barns was the only time I agreed to pay insurance" and when he rented the barns in 1988, Mrs. Hart "was supposed to pay" the insurance.

During the 1989 tobacco farming season, plaintiff decided to sell the barns and placed a "for sale" ad which expired 23 October 1989 under farm equipment saying "five roanoke box barns, gas, [plaintiff's] phone number" in The News and Observer. The ad ran two lines for four days and resulted in several calls, including contact with Ashley P. Mohorn (Mr. Mohorn), Ronald E. Stainback (Mr. Stainback), and Lawrence Elliot (Mr. Elliot). Plaintiff received a $500.00 check dated 22 October 1989 as a down payment from Mr. Mohorn for two of the barns after quoting a price of $8,000.00 each. Mr. Stainback met with plaintiff, informed him that he would take two barns, and Mr. Elliot would take one. Mr. Stainback wrote plaintiff a check for $1,000.00 dated 25 October 1989, representing a deposit on the three barns.

Mrs. Hart called plaintiff in the fall of 1989 and asked if he could "straighten up with her," and he "told her it would be in the next two or three days" and that he was going to sell the barns. She responded that would "be fine with her." On the morning of 22 or 23 October 1989, plaintiff delivered a check in person to her for the first $5,000.00 due defendants. The payment was in the form of plaintiff's personal check number 1468, dated 23 October 1989, payable to Patricia Hart, signed by plaintiff, and with written words on the "for" line indicating the check was for payment for the five barns. When plaintiff gave her the check, she asked him if he wanted a receipt, but he said "no, the check would be the receipt." The next night after plaintiff delivered the check, she called him and told him "she didn't want to sell [him] the barns; she'd already sold them" to somebody else. Plaintiff received a letter, postmarked 26 October 1989, with the check in it. "She had torn . . . [the check] so bad you couldn't hardly put it back together," and "had tore off [plaintiff's] name — tore off her name, the 'for' line, and the date." Plaintiff was able to piece the check back together to see his signature and the five thousand dollars. He later discovered that defendants sold the five barns to "the same guys" plaintiff had agreed to sell them to.

Randy Baker (Baker) testified that plaintiff told him he had bought the barns and had him repair boxes on the barns. Plaintiff paid Baker for this work. J.R. Fowler, Jr. testified that plaintiff told him he had bought the five barns in 1989, was going to pay five thousand dollars a year until they were paid for, was going to sell them, and had run an ad in the paper. Jack Stone (Stone), an auctioneer for the State of North Carolina, testified that "[plaintiff] approached me and said that he had some bulk barns," "said that he had purchased the barns," and "asked if [Stone] could sell them." Stone received a $41,000.00 check for the five barns and held it in escrow until he could inform plaintiff; however, plaintiff told Stone "he thought he already had them sold." After Stone informed plaintiff to let him know if he had already sold the barns, "[plaintiff] calls back and said that the lady had backed out on him and he couldn't sell the barns to nobody 'til he got this straight." At the close of plaintiff's evidence, defendants moved for a directed verdict which was denied.

Defendants presented evidence tending to show that "[plaintiff] agreed to pay [Mr. Hart] twenty thousand dollars for the five barns, and he agreed to pay it over a four year period of time"; however, plaintiff later called Mr. Hart and wished to make a new arrangement in that plaintiff would secure a loan and pay for the barns all at one time. When the loan was not approved, plaintiff contacted Mr. Hart and "wanted to know if he could continue the rental agreement that he had had the previous year." When Mr. Hart's wife told him that plaintiff "had come over and brought the rent check, and left the five thousand dollars as an enticement to buy the barns, [he] told her that it just wasn't sufficient considering the fact that there had been a tremendous acreage increase in the tobacco poundage." He instructed Mrs. Hart to call plaintiff and "tell him we weren't interested." His wife tore up the check, put it in an envelope, and mailed it to plaintiff. At the close of all the evidence, defendants moved for a directed verdict which was denied.

The jury answered the questions submitted to them as follows:

> WAS THERE A CONTRACT BETWEEN THE PLAINTIFF, HOMER BUFFALOE, AND THE DEFENDANTS, LOWELL THOMAS HART AND PATRICIA HART?
>
> ANSWER: YES
>
> . . .
>
> IF SO, DID HOMER BUFFALOE ACCEPT THE TOBACCO BARNS UNDER THE TERMS AND CONDITIONS OF THE CONTRACT?
>
> ANSWER: YES
>
> . . .
>
> IF THERE WAS A CONTRACT, DID PATRICIA HART AND LOWELL THOMAS HART ACCEPT A PAYMENT FOR THE TOBACCO BARNS UNDER THE TERMS AND CONDITIONS OF THE CONTRACT?
>
> ANSWER: YES
>
> . . .
>
> IF THERE WAS A CONTRACT, DID LOWELL THOMAS HART AND PATRICIA HART BREACH THIS CONTRACT?
>
> ANSWER: YES
>
> . . .
>
> WAS THERE A RENTAL CONTRACT FOR THE TOBACCO BARNS FOR THE YEAR 1989 BETWEEN THE PLAINTIFF, HOMER BUFFALOE, AND THE DEFENDANTS, LOWELL THOMAS HART AND PATRICIA HART?
>
> ANSWER: NO

The jury awarded plaintiff damages of $21,000.00. Defendants filed a motion for judgment notwithstanding the verdict which was denied.

The issues presented are whether (I) a personal check signed by plaintiff, describing the property involved and containing an amount representing partial payment is sufficient to constitute a writing under the statute of frauds; and (II) there is substantial relevant evidence that plaintiff "accepted" the barns and defendants "accepted" plaintiff's check, taking the contract out of the statute of frauds.

Because the barns, the subject of this dispute, are "goods" within the meaning of the Uniform Commercial Code, N.C.G.S. §25-2-105 (1986), and because the price for the barns is at least $500.00, the provisions of N.C. Gen. Stat. §25-2-201 apply. . . .

I

Defendants argue in their brief that the check delivered by plaintiff to Mrs. Hart fails to meet the requirements of N.C. Gen. Stat. §25-2-201(1), commonly referred to as a statute of frauds, because the check "was not negotiated or endorsed by the Defendants and therefore the signature of the Defendants did not appear on the check." A check may constitute a writing sufficient to satisfy the requirements of Section 25-2-201(1) provided it (1) contains a writing sufficient to indicate a contract of sale between the parties; (2) is signed by the party or his authorized agent against whom enforcement is sought; and (3) states a quantity. See N.C.G.S. §25-2-201 official cmt.; Harper v. Battle, 180 N.C. 375, 376, 104 S.E. 658, 659 (1920) (check collected by defendant with her written endorsement thereon, in which property is described as "Watts Street House" is sufficient writing within statute of frauds); Burriss v. Starr, 165 N.C. 657, 661, 81 S.E. 929, 931 (1914) (note drawn up by defendant, signed by plaintiff, not sufficient to satisfy statute of frauds because it did not obligate defendant to perform); Arthur Linton Corbin, Corbin on Contracts §508, at 734 (1950).

The only writing in this case is a personal check which, although specifying the quantity of "five barns" on the "for" line, addressed to Patricia Hart, signed by plaintiff, and containing an amount of $5,000.00, is not sufficient to satisfy Section 25-2-201. Defendants, the parties "against whom enforcement is sought," did not endorse the check, and therefore, their handwriting does not appear anywhere on the check. In fact, the name of defendant, Mr. Hart, is totally absent from the check. Therefore, because the requirement of Section 25-2-201(1) that the writing be "signed by the party against whom enforcement is sought or by his authorized agent or broker" is absent from the check, the alleged oral contract between plaintiff and defendants is unenforceable under that section. See Manyon v. Graser, 66 A.D.2d 1012, 411 N.Y.S.2d 746 (1978) (check for $100 on which was stated "deposit on purchase of nine-foot strip" which was not endorsed and letter stating "not feasible to sell property" were not sufficient memoranda to take oral agreement to sell land out of statute of frauds).

II

Defendants further argue that the part performance exception in Section 25-2-201(3)(c) does not apply because "there was no overt action by the plaintiff, purported buyer, in fact no change from the rental period and therefore no basis for a finding of part performance," "[t]here is no overt action of the Defendants in giving up possession of the tobacco barns," and "the delivery of the check by the Plaintiff to the Defendant, Patricia Hart, did not constitute partial payment of the contract because the check was never accepted legally by the Defendants." We disagree.

To qualify under Section 25-2-201(3)(c), the seller must deliver the goods and have them accepted by the buyer. "Acceptance must be voluntary and unconditional" and may "be inferred from the buyer's conduct in taking physical possession of the goods or some part of them." Howse v. Crumb, 143 Colo. 90, 352 P.2d 285, 288 (Colo. 1960). The official comment to Section 25-2-201 explains that for the buyer, he is required to deliver "something . . . that is accepted by the seller as such performance. Thus, part payment may be made by money or check, accepted by the seller." N.C.G.S. §25-2-201 official cmt. Under this standard, Section 25-2-201(3)(c) presents questions of fact, which are questions for the jury, on the issue of acceptance. See Sass v. Thomas, 90 N.C. App. 719, 724, 370 S.E.2d 73, 76 (1988); Coffman v. Fleming, 226 S.W. 67 (Mo. App. 1920), *aff'd,* 301 Mo. 313, 256 S.W. 731 (1923) (question of whether plaintiff accepted check as part payment one of fact to be determined by jury).

In this case, the evidence, in the light most favorable to plaintiff, establishes that plaintiff told several people about purchasing the barns, reimbursed defendants for insurance on the barns, paid for improvements, took possession, enlisted the aid of an auctioneer and the paper to sell the barns, and received deposits from three buyers on the barns. The evidence, in the light most favorable to plaintiff, also establishes that plaintiff delivered a check for $5,000.00 on 22 October 1989 to defendants, and the check was not returned to plaintiff until 26 October 1989. Under the standards for deciding motions for directed verdict and judgment notwithstanding the verdict, Guyther v. Nationwide Mut. Fire Ins. Co., 109 N.C. App. 506, 513-14, 428 S.E.2d 238, 242 (1993), this evidence represents substantial relevant evidence that a reasonable mind might accept as adequate to support the conclusions reached by the jury that there was a "contract between the plaintiff, Homer Buffaloe, and the defendants," plaintiff "accept[ed] the tobacco barns under the terms and conditions of the contract," and defendants "accept[ed] a payment for the tobacco barns under the terms and conditions of the contract." See Kaufman v. Solomon, 524 F.2d 501 (3d Cir. 1975) (whether possession by seller of check from buyer for 30 days is "acceptance" poses issue for resolution by fact finder); Fournier v. Burby, 121 Vt. 88, 148 A.2d 362 (1959) (enforceable contract where plaintiff delivered check to defendant on 21 July 1957 and defendant returned it unendorsed by letter postmarked 6 August 1957); Maryatt v. Hubbard, 33 Wash. 2d 325, 205 P.2d 623 (1949) (enforceable contract where plaintiff delivered check to defendant on 23 December 1946 and defendant marked through her endorsement on check and returned it to plaintiff on 17 January 1947); Miller v. Wooters, 131 Ill. App. 3d 682, 86 Ill. Dec. 835, 476 N.E.2d 11 (1985) (oral contract within exception to statute of frauds where buyer gave check to seller in payment for truck even though buyer stopped payment on check the next day). Therefore, the trial court did not err in denying defendants' motions for directed verdict or motion for judgment notwithstanding the verdict.

No error.

COZORT and ORR, JJ., concur.

NOTES AND QUESTIONS

1. *Application of UCC §2-201.* As you should recall from the discussion in Chapter 2, a contract must involve the sale of goods (at least primarily) to come within the scope of UCC Article 2. Classification as "goods" depends on movability of the items. See UCC §2-105(1). While the issue was not expressly addressed by the court, the parties clearly did not dispute that the "roanoke box tobacco barns" were movable items of goods and that §2-201 provided the relevant statute of frauds. Would the case have been decided differently if the barns were deemed to be immovable real property and thus governed by other statute of frauds provisions?

2. *UCC writing requirements.* By reducing the required contents of the writing, §2-201(1) makes enforcement possible on the basis of very fragmentary notations of terms that meet three minimal requirements:

- the writing must be signed or authenticated, though perhaps by only initials or even a printed letterhead (see UCC §1-201(b)(37) and Comment);
- the court must be persuaded that the writing does "indicate a contract for sale has been made" (or that "the offered oral evidence rests on a real transaction," in the words of Comment 1 to UCC §2-201); and
- the writing must contain a quantity term.

The drafters have stated in UCC §2-201(1) that "a term agreed upon" may be omitted from the memorandum, thereby implicitly allowing enforcement even in the absence of a writing stating the price term. Comment 1 to §2-201 makes this explicit, observing that parties often contract on the basis of a published price list or a market price, which provides a safeguard against fraud. Section 2-201 also states, however, that enforcement will be limited to the quantity "shown" in the writing.

The court in Buffaloe v. Hart considered the possibility that the buyer's check could constitute a memorandum sufficient to satisfy the statute, but rejected that possibility because the sellers never signed it. If Mr. Buffaloe had delivered his check to the Harts, then changed his mind and immediately stopped payment on it, could the Harts have enforced against him the agreement to purchase the barns?

3. *Partial performance.* In permitting enforcement on the basis of "payment . . . made and accepted" or "goods . . . which have been received and accepted," the Code might appear simply to be repeating the original statute's provision regarding partial performance of a sale of goods contract. However, as amplified by Comment 2, UCC §2-201(3)(c) appears not to go quite so far as the English statute, which validated the *entire* contract on the basis of only partial performance. After some initial authority to the contrary, the courts have generally taken the view that where the asserted contract is for one unit of the goods in question, even a payment of only part of the price will be sufficient under UCC §2-201(3)(c) to validate the entire contract (since the goods cannot be apportioned). See, e.g., Sedmak v. Charlie's Chevrolet, Inc., 622 S.W.2d 694 (Mo. Ct. App. 1981) ($500 payment sufficient for enforcement of purchase of

one Corvette auto). In its opinion, the court in *Buffaloe* never directly addresses the issue of whether Buffaloe's partial payment might be insufficient to enable him to enforce the agreement for all five barns. In light of the discussion above, should that factor have prevented the plaintiff from prevailing? Or can the decision be explained consistently with that aspect of UCC §2-201(3)(c)?

4. *The "admissions" exception.* In the early days of the English statute of frauds, it appears that the defendant was not permitted to assert the statutory defense if in fact he admitted making the agreement; later, however, the rule developed that even oral admissions in court would not preclude the defendant's raising the statutory bar. Similarly, prior to the UCC, the prevailing view of courts in the United States was that not even an admission of the contract would defeat the statute of frauds. See John E. Murray, Jr., Murray on Contracts, §86, at 385 (5th ed. 2011). Thus, the "admissions" exception adopted in UCC §2-201(3)(b) was not generally reflected in pre-Code law. The UCC exception, however, is based on a compelling "common-sense" argument that a party should not be able to admit the making of a contract in legal proceedings and yet avoid liability because of the lack of a writing. DF Activities Corp. v. Brown, 851 F.2d 920, 923 (7th Cir. 1988). Indeed, it appears that the law in non-UCC cases has now moved toward adoption of the judicial admissions exception. See Gibson v. Arnold, 288 F.3d. 1242 (10th Cir. 2002) (surveying decisions and observing that the growing weight of authority is to recognize the admissions exception in non-UCC cases). Moreover, if a party denies that he made a contract, but admits facts that in the court's view establish that such a contract was indeed made, the statute of frauds defense will be lost. See, e.g., Wehry v. Daniels, 784 N.E.2d 532 (Ind. Ct. App. 2003) (defendant's testimony as to facts sufficient to form contract constitutes admission even if defendant denies that contract was created).

5. *The "special manufacture" exception.* UCC §2-201(3)(a) establishes an exception to the statute of frauds for "specially manufactured goods." Under this subsection, the goods must be specially manufactured for the buyer and "not suitable for sale to others in the ordinary course of the seller's business." Compare ReMapp Int'l Corp. v. Comfort Keyboard Co., 560 F.3d 628 (7th Cir. 2009) (oral agreement for sale of computer circuit boards made with buyer's specific, proprietary design that could not be sold to others came under special manufacture exception) with Packgen v. BP Exploration, Inc., 754 F.3d 61 (1st Cir. 2014) (oil containment boom allegedly made for BP after major oil spill did not come within specially manufactured goods exception because it was sold to another buyer without alteration).

6. *Confirmation between merchants.* Section 2-201(2) creates another exception to the UCC statute of frauds that applies only if the transaction is "between merchants." (The term "merchant" is defined in UCC §2-104(1), essentially, as someone who regularly deals in goods of a kind or holds herself out as having particular skills or knowledge involved in a transaction.) Under this exception, one of the merchants must send a written "confirmation of the contract" within a reasonable period of time after the contract was formed. The confirmation must be received by the other party who must have reason

to know its contents and then fail to object within ten days. Importantly, the confirmation must be "sufficient against the sender" through satisfying the requirements of UCC §2-201(1) by: (1) giving evidence of the existence of a contract, (2) being "signed" by the sender, and (3) having a quantity term. See, e.g., Brooks Peanut Co., Inc. v. Great Southern Peanut, LLC, 746 S.E.2d 272 (Ga. Ct. App. 2013) (seller not entitled to summary judgment when peanut broker sent written confirmation of sales terms to both buyer and seller and neither party objected; broker allegedly signed "sufficient" writing as agent for buyer).

Comment 3 to UCC §2-201 makes the explicit point that compliance with the merchant confirmation exception does not necessarily mean that a contract has been formed. The comment states: "The only effect, however, is to take away from the party who fails to answer the defense of the Statute of Frauds; the burden of persuading the trier of fact that a contract was in fact made orally prior to the record confirmation is unaffected." It is also important to remember that the statute of frauds "confirmation exception" is different from the concept of a "confirmation" under UCC §2-207 (the "battle of the forms" section) which deals with contract formation and whether terms become part of a contract. See the discussion of UCC §2-207 in Chapter 2.7.

7. *The requirement of a signed writing in a world of electronic transactions.* We noted earlier in this chapter that both the general law of contract and the UCC have taken a rather lenient approach to the requirement of a "signed writing." UCC §1-201(b)(37) defines "signed" to include "any symbol executed or adopted with present intention to adopt or accept a writing." UCC §1-201(b)(43) defines "writing" to include "printing, typewriting, or any other intentional reduction to tangible form." In addition, UCC §1-201(b)(31) recognizes the existence of electronic transactions by creating the concept of a record, which is defined as "information that is inscribed on a tangible medium or that is stored in an electronic or other medium and is retrievable in perceivable form."

8. *Promissory estoppel.* As we have seen, many courts are disposed to accept the suggestion of Restatement (Second) §139 that the principle of promissory estoppel may justify enforcement of an oral contract despite the one-year clause of the statute of frauds. Suppose an oral agreement subject to UCC §2-201 has not been memorialized but has been substantially relied on by the plaintiff — perhaps by performance, preparation for performance, or in other ways. Should the principle of Restatement (Second) §139 be applicable to such a case? The majority view is that promissory estoppel can operate as an exception to UCC §2-201 by virtue of UCC §1-103(b), but a substantial minority of decisions have concluded that the exceptions specifically listed in UCC §2-201 "displace" any common law exceptions, including estoppel. See East River Energy, Inc. v. Gaylord Hosp., Inc., 2011 WL 3198251 (Conn. Super. Ct.) (surveying split among courts but concluding that the more persuasive approach interprets UCC §1-103(b) to allow promissory estoppel as exception to the Article 2 statute of frauds when necessary to prevent fraud or injustice).

9. *The CISG.* We have earlier mentioned that CISG Article 11 rejects the statute of frauds as a general rule, though a state may opt to retain writing

requirements from its state law under Article 96. As Professor William Dodge has observed, American lawyers need to be knowledgeable about the CISG or risk making costly errors for their clients. See William S. Dodge, Teaching the CISG in Contracts, 50 J. Leg. Ed. 72, 74-77 (2000) (recommending that contracts teachers and casebook editors make greater efforts to acquaint students with the applicability and effect of the CISG). As an example of the possible effect of such ignorance, he cites GPL Treatment, Ltd. v. Louisiana-Pacific Corp., 894 P.2d 470 (Or. Ct. App. 1995), *aff'd*, 914 P.2d 682 (Or. 1996) (en banc). In that case, the plaintiff, with considerable effort, was able to overcome the defendant's statute of frauds defense by invoking the merchant's exception in UCC §2-201(2); the case was decided for the plaintiff at both the intermediate appellate and Supreme Court levels by sharply divided courts. But, as Professor Dodge points out:

> There was an easier way. Because the plaintiffs had their places of business in Canada and the defendant had its in the United States, and because both Canada and the United States have ratified the CISG, the CISG rather than the UCC was applicable to this transaction. . . . [T]he CISG does not have a statute of frauds and would have allowed the plaintiffs to submit their evidence of an oral contract for the sale of cedar shakes to the jury without the need to produce a writing of any sort. Apparently the plaintiffs raised [that] argument, but . . . so late that the trial judge ruled the argument had been waived. The result was that the plaintiffs gave up an argument that was a sure winner, . . . presumably costing the plaintiffs a good deal more in attorney's fees.

50 J. Leg. Ed. at 75.

PROBLEM 4-3

Machine Tools, Inc. manufactures a variety of tools for businesses and consumers. The company is owned equally by three individuals: Ellen Gilchrist, Sue Miller, and Tom Wolfe. In late February 2018, Gilchrist, Miller, and Wolfe were approached by the representatives of a large tobacco company, which has been engaged in a program of diversification through acquisitions. After some negotiations, the parties agreed in principle to the sale of the assets of Machine Tools. The parties also agreed that their lawyers would prepare a formal, written contract reflecting the terms of their agreement. On March 2, 2018, Helen Franklin, an attorney for the tobacco company, wrote the following letter to the owners of Machine Tools:

> **Dear Ms. Gilchrist, Ms. Miller, and Mr. Wolfe:**
>
> This letter will confirm the agreement that was reached last week between my client, Tobacco National, Inc., and the three of you, who are the only shareholders of Machine Tools, Inc. of New City.
>
> 1. *Agreement of Sale.* You agree to sell and Tobacco National agrees to purchase all of the assets of Machine Tools, Inc. on the terms set forth below. These assets consist of the company's land and building located in New City, the equipment used in the company's operations, and all inventory of raw

materials and finished tools. Accounts receivable shall be retained by you. All debt including accounts payable shall be paid by you at or before closing.

2. *Purchase Price.* The purchase price is ten million dollars ($10,000,000), subject to adjustment as follows: An inventory of raw materials and finished tools shall be made as of the date of closing. The purchase price shall be adjusted up or down to the extent the cost of the inventory, based on your current accounting practices, exceeds or is less than $1,000,000. The purchase price shall be payable at closing $1 million in cash and $9 million in the common stock of Tobacco National. Sale or other disposition of your common stock shall be subject to regulations and restrictions of the Securities & Exchange Commission and applicable state law.

3. *Closing.* The closing will be held no sooner than January 2, 2019, and no later than January 31, 2019, the exact time and place to be agreed by the parties.

4. *Other Documents; Arbitration.* A formal, written contract containing customary warranties and representations of the seller will be prepared by Tobacco National and submitted for review by you and your counsel. You agree to execute any documents necessary to effect the transfer of assets from Machine Tools, Inc. to Tobacco National. It is the intention of the parties that a final binding agreement has already been reached and that execution of any other documents is a mere formality. The parties agree to negotiate in good faith to resolve any disputes over the provisions of these documents and to submit to arbitration any dispute that cannot be resolved by negotiation. Arbitration shall be governed by the rules of the American Arbitration Association.

Each of you should sign the original of this letter, and return it to me, retaining a copy for your files. I look forward to meeting you as this transaction proceeds.

Sincerely,
Helen Franklin, Esq.

Gilchrist, Miller, and Wolfe received the letter on March 3 and immediately consulted with their attorney to discuss the details of the transaction. During the next week they began to have "cold feet" about the sale, principally because so much of the purchase price was payable in restricted stock of Tobacco National, and ultimately decided that they did not want to go forward with the transaction. On March 8, they asked their lawyer whether they were legally bound to the sale, and how they should proceed. If you were their lawyer, what advice would you give?

REVIEW QUESTIONS – CHAPTER FOUR

1. Bill Bendix was a popular, thirty-year old singer in local clubs in a small, Midwestern city. In June 2017, Bill decided that he wanted to perform nationally and he contacted Anne Adams, a talent agent with business connections in New York, Los Angeles, and other major cities. Anne agreed to help Bill with bookings but only if he would agree that she would be his exclusive agent for as long as he performed professionally and that she would receive a 10 percent fee for all bookings. Bill orally agreed. Anne then

sent Bill her standard representation contract, but he never read or signed it. Nevertheless, Anne arranged an average of three bookings per month for Bill in major cities during the next two years and she received her 10 percent fee for each. In July 2019, Bill sang the national anthem on a televised baseball game to great acclaim and he was soon approached by Mega Artists, the top ranked talent agency in the country, which offered him an exclusive contract. Today, Bill comes to your law office and wants your opinion on whether the lack of a signed writing would give him a good defense to any lawsuit Anne might bring for breach of contract if he signs with Mega Artists. Assuming that there is no applicable writing requirement specifically for agency contracts, would Anne be able to enforce the oral agreement if Bill raises the statute of frauds as a defense?

A. Yes, Anne can enforce the oral agreement because it is not subject to the writing requirement under the typical statute of frauds.
B. Yes, Anne can enforce the oral agreement because Bill's conduct would amount to authentication of the written contract.
C. No, Anne cannot enforce the oral agreement because Bill's career has already lasted for more than a year after the contract was made.
D. No, Anne cannot enforce the oral agreement because she has been fully compensated for her past services.

2. Carl decided to sell his classic car, a 1963 Chevy Corvette. He advertised in the newspaper and received a call from Donna. Donna went to Carl's house on Monday to look at the car and decided to offer Carl $20,000 for the Corvette, stating that she could pay $1,000 at that moment and that she would return with the balance on Tuesday and take possession of the car at that time. Carl agreed to that arrangement. Donna then wrote out and signed a personal check for $1,000, noting on the memo line "Deposit on 1963 Chevy Corvette." The next morning Donna called to say that she had changed her mind and would not be buying the car. On what basis is Carl likely to be able to enforce the contract against Donna without a written sales agreement?

A. Carl can enforce the contract only if Donna admits in court that she agreed to buy the car.
B. Carl can enforce the contract only if he promptly cashes the check.
C. Carl can enforce the contract because the check is a sufficient writing.
D. Carl can enforce the contract because the car is relatively unique.

3. Dina Drew decided in May 2019 to leave her job as an accountant and to pursue a long-time goal by opening a children's day care center in Oaktown. Dina had saved $500,000, all of which she used to purchase a commercial building and buy furniture and supplies. Upon inspection by the Oaktown City Building Department in July 2019, it was discovered that the building needed two more emergency exits to meet city safety code requirements. Dina contacted Carl Cruz, a contractor who had often done work for her mother, Megan Drew. Carl offered to do the renovations within a week at

a price of $25,000. Dina did not have cash funds to pay Carl and was having trouble getting a loan from a bank. Upon hearing about the problem, Megan called Carl and spoke with him over the telephone. Megan told Carl, "If you will go ahead and do the work for my daughter, Dina, I will pay you the $25,000 in two months if Dina cannot borrow the money from a bank by then." After that conversation, Carl agreed with Dina to do the work, and they both signed a brief one-page contract. In the margin Carl had added this sentence: "Payment in two months guaranteed by Megan Drew." If Carl completes the work and after two months Dina cannot borrow the money to pay him, is Carl likely to be able to enforce Megan's oral promise to pay him the $25,000?

A. Yes, Carl can probably enforce the promise because Megan's performance would be completed in less than one year.
B. Yes, Carl can probably enforce the promise because Megan made it directly to him and Dina signed the writing confirming it.
C. No, Carl probably cannot enforce Megan's promise because his performance affected an interest in real property.
D. No, Carl probably cannot enforce the promise because Megan did not sign the written contract.

4. Ed Evans graduated from State College in May 2019 with a master's degree in computer science. On June 1, 2019, Ed participated in a job fair where he met Gina Givens, the owner of the Givens Greeting Card Company. Gina was very impressed by Ed and said she wanted to offer Ed a position in her company's technology department. Gina pulled from her brief case a blank piece of Givens stationery with the company logo and letterhead, and wrote on it, "Two-year position in IT, $75,000 per year salary, start date August 1, plus $5,000 moving allowance." Gina told Ed, "You will also get standard benefits." She gave the piece of paper to Ed who said he would think about the offer. Two days later, Ed called Gina and told her that he accepted the job offer and would see her August 1. Gina replied, "Great. See you in August." Ed stopped looking for work and took a month long vacation in Europe and Asia. On July 30, 2019, Gina sent an email message to Ed which said, "Due to some financial reversals here at the company, I am imposing a hiring freeze and backing out of our agreement for the two-year position. Maybe you can work for us at some other time. Best wishes, Gina." Which of the following statements would likely be true regarding possible application of the statute of frauds?

   A. Ed can enforce the contract because it might come to an end in less than one year if he were to be terminated for breaching company policy.
   B. Ed can enforce the contract because Gina wrote the details of the offer on company stationery and the email referenced those same terms.
   C. Ed cannot enforce the contract because neither the piece of stationery nor the email message contains all the details of the alleged employment contract.

D. Ed cannot enforce the contract because neither the piece of stationery nor the email message contains a personal signature by Gina or someone serving as her agent.

5. In June 2019, Sam Seller, a high school teacher, decided to sell a unique chair that had been designed in 1920 by world renowned architect, Fred L. Bright, to go into a house he had also designed. The "Bright" chair had been passed down through Sam's family for four generations. He advertised the chair for sale online and received a call from Ben Buyer, a wealthy art collector. Ben went to Sam's house on June 20 to look at the chair and decided to offer $150,000 for it. Sam orally agreed to sell the chair for that price. The next day, June 21, Ben obtained from his bank a cashier's check payable to Sam Seller, for $150,000. Ben sent the check in a letter to Sam by messenger, along with a signed note that accurately described the agreement. The following day, June 22, Sam returned the check to Ben with the letter unopened. Ben immediately called Sam to ask why the check was returned. Sam stated, "I never really agreed to sell the chair. I merely agreed to consider your offer and I have decided that I cannot part with it." Ben promptly filed a lawsuit for breach of contract, but Sam filed a motion to dismiss with a sworn affidavit that he never agreed to sell the chair. Would Ben be likely to succeed in his lawsuit to enforce the oral agreement?

A. Yes, because the chair was an item of specially manufactured goods.
B. Yes, because the note he sent would satisfy the statute of frauds against Ben and it was received by Sam.
C. No, because the part performance exception to the statute of frauds would require both payment by the buyer and delivery of goods by the seller.
D. No, because Sam did not sign a writing, promptly denied making a contract, and did not accept the payment.

CHAPTER 5

The Meaning of the Agreement: Principles of Interpretation and the Parol Evidence Rule

At this point in our studies, we have seen enough to realize that issues affecting the outcome of contractual disputes can be divided roughly into questions of "substance" and "form." To the extent that contract law is concerned with the actual assent of the parties to an asserted contract, one might characterize this as concern with the "substance" of their agreement. Questions such as "Was an offer truly made?" or "Was an acceptance manifested?" would seem to fall into this category. By contrast, the various "statutes of frauds" discussed in the preceding chapter seem to be requirements not of substance, but only of "form" — the expression of an agreement in a particular medium and with a particular indicium of assent. Of course, this distinction between substance and form tends (like many others) to blur somewhat on closer examination: The requirement of "definiteness," for instance, seems (for some courts at least) to be an issue of form as well as substance; thoughtful application of the statute of frauds is likely to be concerned not merely with the minimum requirements of form but also with the issue of real agreement. And commentators have debated whether the requirement of consideration is truly one of form or of substance (or both). Nevertheless, the distinction between form and substance has appeared to many to be a useful one. See, e.g., Lon Fuller, Consideration and Form, 41 Colum. L. Rev. 799 (1941); P.S. Atiyah & Robert S. Summers, Form and Substance in Anglo-American Law (1987).

Chapter 5 continues this parallel and to some extent overlapping examination of form and substance in contract law. The first section of this chapter is devoted to the methods employed by courts to interpret the parties' expressions of assent. Even where the parties have initially agreed on particular words and phrases to describe their contemplated exchange of performances, they may disagree later about the meaning that should be attached to those manifestations of agreement. In the second section of this chapter we examine the particular problems of interpretation that arise when the parties have chosen to memorialize their agreement in a written document. As we have seen, the law does not require all types of contracts to be in writing in order to be enforceable, and even those that are within the scope of a statute of frauds usually do not have to be written out in complete and exhaustive detail. Where the parties have prepared a written agreement, one of them may later contend that this writing does not accurately or completely express their "true" agreement — that there were additional agreements made between them not contained in the writing, or even that the writing in some respect describes their agreement in an inaccurate or misleading fashion. Courts over the years have worked out a method of screening evidence of such "extrinsic" matters, through the application of the so-called "parol evidence rule." The meaning and application of that rule is examined in the latter part of this chapter.

A. PRINCIPLES OF INTERPRETATION

Language is a system of symbols by which we express ideas. But, as we all know, language as a medium for expression of ideas is far from perfect. The words a person uses may not fully express the ideas that the person was trying to convey. Even when people appear to be using the same words, they may attribute different meaning to those words. Contracts, like other linguistic expressions, suffer from these problems of meaning. In these materials we use the term *interpretation* to refer to the process by which a court gives meaning to contractual language when the parties attach materially different meanings to that language. Some courts and writers have drawn a distinction between *interpretation* — the process of determining the meaning that the parties attributed to contractual language — and *construction*, which is the judicial role in determining the legal effect of that language. These materials will ordinarily use the term *interpretation* to include construction, a usage favored by modern contract theorists because the distinction between interpretation and construction is both cumbersome and usually unnecessary. See E. Allan Farnsworth, Contracts §7.7 (4th ed. 2004).

Over the first three-quarters of the nineteenth century, English and American courts adopted a "subjective" approach to problems of interpretation. Under the subjectivist view, if the parties attributed materially different meanings to contractual language, no contract was formed. Courts reasoned that the formation of a contract required a "meeting of the minds."

The prime example of the subjectivist approach to contractual interpretation is the case of Raffles v. Wichelhaus, 159 Eng. Rep. 375 (1864), often referred to as the "Peerless Case." In *Raffles*, two merchants entered into a contract for the sale of cotton to arrive "ex Peerless from Bombay." In fact there were two ships named Peerless that were sailing from Bombay, one leaving in October, the other in December. The seller contemplated making delivery by the December Peerless, while the buyer expected the cotton to be shipped on the October Peerless. When the buyer refused to take delivery in December, the seller brought suit for breach of contract. The Court of Exchequer held for the buyer, accepting his plea that because "the defendant meant one Peerless and the plaintiff another . . . there was no consensus ad idem, and therefore no binding contract." Id. at 376.

In his lectures on the common law, given in 1881, Holmes criticized the subjective theory, arguing that courts should instead adopt an "external" approach to contractual interpretation. In a later article Holmes defended his theory of interpretation on two grounds: (1) The subjective approach made enforcement of contracts too difficult; (2) The external method was fair because a speaker should always expect his words to be understood in accordance with their normal usage. Oliver Wendell Holmes, The Theory of Legal Interpretation, 12 Harv. L. Rev. 417, 419 (1899). Professor Williston, both in his treatise and in the original Restatement, presented a systematic, "objective" theory of contractual interpretation. Under this theory, words and conduct should be interpreted in accordance with the standard of a reasonable person familiar with the circumstances, rather than in accordance with the subjective intention of either of the parties. Restatement §§230, 233. This objective approach, however, led to the striking conclusion that contractual language could be given a meaning that *neither* of the parties intended. Restatement §230, Comment *b.* Consider Illustration 1 to §230 of the first Restatement:

> 1. In an integrated agreement *A* promises to sell, and *B* promises to buy certain patents. *A* intends to sell only English patents on a certain invention. *B* understands that *A* promises to sell the English, French, and American patents on the invention. If a reasonably intelligent person . . . would understand the agreement to state a promise to sell the English and American patents, but not the French patents, there is a contract and *A* and *B* are bound by that meaning.

Modern contract law has departed from the extreme objectivist approach, adopting instead what could be characterized as a modified objective approach. Professor Corbin laid the foundation of the modern approach in his treatise. According to Corbin, in interpreting a contract, a court should answer two questions: (1) Whose meaning controls the interpretation of the contract? (2) What was that party's meaning? 3 Corbin on Contracts §536 (1960), at 31-32. Corbin thought that it would be absurd for a court to give a contract a meaning that neither of the parties intended.

> If a court says that parties are bound by this meaning even though neither one of them held it, it is very probable that the court believes, either that both of them did in fact hold it, or that one of them did and the other had reason to know that he did. But to hold that, although *A* intends to sell Blackacre and *B* intends to buy Whiteacre, *A* must convey and *B* must accept Greenacre because their "integration" would so be understood by *C* or by a large community of third persons, is to hold justice up to ridicule.

3 Corbin on Contracts §539 (1960), at 81. The updated version of the Corbin treatise continues to embrace the modified objective approach which "would never enable a court to impose an interpretation on the parties that was reasonably held by a third party but that differed from what the contracting parties understood or had reason to understand." Margaret N. Kniffin, 5 Corbin on Contracts §24.6 (Joseph M. Perillo ed., 1998).

The Restatement (Second) follows Corbin's view. Section 200 states that the purpose of interpretation is the determination of meaning of contractual language. Under §201(1), if both parties do in fact attach the same meaning to a provision, that meaning will govern. Thus, the mutual understanding of the parties controls, even if it is different from the interpretation that would be given to the contract by a reasonable person. Restatement (Second) §203, Comment *c*. As the Seventh Circuit Court of Appeals said:

> [P]arties, like Humpty Dumpty, may use words as they please. If they wish the symbols "one Caterpillar D9G tractor" to mean "500 railroad cars full of watermelons," that's fine — provided [the] parties share this weird meaning.

TKO Equipment Co. v. C & G Coal Co., 863 F.2d 541, 545 (7th Cir. 1988). As Professor Lawrence Solan has noted, the law's willingness to enforce a meaning which both parties actually intended, even where this diverges from the "plain" or "reasonable" meaning of the words, represents not a true "objective" standard, but one based on mutual assent. Lawrence M. Solan, Contract as Agreement, 83 Notre Dame L. Rev. 353, 358-364 (2007). If the parties attach different meanings to their contractual language, however, the agreement is to be interpreted in accordance with the meaning of one party if the other party either knew or had reason to know of the meaning attached by the former. Restatement (Second) §201(2).

In many cases, therefore, the crucial issue in interpreting a contract is whether one party knew (or had reason to know) of the meaning attached to the contract by the other. If so, the party having knowledge or reason to know is bound by the meaning of the other. Restatement (Second) §201(2)(b); Margaret N. Kniffin, 5 Corbin on Contracts §24.5 (Joseph M. Perillo ed., 1998).

What if a court should conclude that the parties did indeed attach different meanings to a material term of the contract, but neither party knew or had reason to know the meaning of the other? Then, even under the modern approach of the Restatement (Second), the result in *Raffles* would still follow: No contract exists because of the absence of mutual assent. Restatement (Second) §201(3) and Comment *d;* see also Hill-Shafer P'ship v. Chilson Family Trust, 799 P.2d 810 (Ariz. 1990) (en banc) (no contract formed for sale of real estate when buyer and seller had different reasonable understandings of property being sold); Stitch Ranch v. Double B.J. Farms, 21 Neb. App. 328, 837 N.W.2d 870 (2013) (where contract required seller of farm land to obtain "feedlot permit" but each party acted inconsistently as to whether that meant an "operating permit" or "pollution permit" or both, the parties did not attach a consistent meaning, let alone the same meaning, and contract was properly rescinded).

Joyner v. Adams

North Carolina Court of Appeals 87 N.C. App. 570, 361 S.E.2d 902 (1987)

This is an action for rents allegedly due under the terms of a lease. Plaintiff, Marguerite B. Joyner, owns real property known as Waters Edge Office Park. To develop the property into an office park, plaintiff and her husband, William T. Joyner, Jr., contracted with Brown Investment Company (Brown) in 1972. Brown agreed, under the "Base Lease," to lease the property from plaintiff at an annual rent, increased each year to correspond with the increase in the Wholesale Price Index, published by the United States Department of Labor. The parties contemplated that Brown would remove all existing buildings, regrade the property, prepare an appropriate land plan, and subdivide the area into individual lots. When each lot was subdivided, the lease called for the execution of individual "Lot Leases" to take the place of the Base Lease. The rent due under the Lot Leases was based, in part, on the occupancy of buildings planned for each lot.

Due to financial difficulties suffered by Brown, the lease was amended in 1975 to substitute defendant, J. R. Adams, as the lessee/developer. The amendment also suspended the annual rent increases. Instead, defendant agreed to pay a fixed rate until 30 September 1980, at which time he was obligated to have subdivided "all of the undeveloped land . . . whereby all portions are deemed lots and eligible for the execution of a [Lot Lease]." If defendant failed to comply with that provision, the amendment required him to pay, retroactively, the amount of rent which would have been due under the terms of the Base Lease. As of 30 September 1980, defendant had executed separate lot leases and had built buildings on all lots except one. Defendant had, however, subdivided the remaining lot, graded it, installed water and sewer lines on it, and built all planned roads and driveways leading to the lot. A building was not built on the lot and a Lot Lease was not executed until late 1982.

Plaintiff filed this action on 27 September 1983, claiming that defendant failed to comply with the requirements of the lease for developing the property and seeking to recover the difference between the actual, fixed rent paid by defendant and the rent recomputed under the terms of the Base Lease. On 5 July 1985, summary judgment was granted for defendant. In an unpublished opinion, 80 N.C. App. 166, 341 S.E.2d 619, this court reversed, holding that the provision of the 1975 amendment relating to the conditions upon which the retroactive rent escalation would occur was ambiguous. Consequently, the case was remanded for a factual determination of the parties' intent.

On remand, the trial court, sitting without a jury, found that plaintiff intended the escalation clause to require defendant to complete, or at least be ready to begin, construction of all buildings planned for the lot. It also found, however, that defendant intended the clause to require only the subdivision of all lots or, at most, whatever development was necessary to prepare the lot for building construction. The court concluded there was "no meeting of the minds" on the question of what conditions would trigger the rent escalation.

The court also concluded that, although the parties had different intentions, the ambiguity should be resolved against defendant, who was "the party that drafted the 1975 amended lease." Accordingly, the court awarded plaintiff damages in the stipulated amount of $93,695.75. Defendant appeals. . . .

EAGLES, Judge.

I

Both parties argue that the trial court erred in concluding that there was no "meeting of the minds" on the rent escalation provision. Each contends that there is no evidentiary basis for finding the other party had a contrary intention. A trial court's findings of fact, however, are conclusive on appeal if supported by competent evidence, Hill v. Town of Hillsborough, 48 N.C. App. 553, 269 S.E.2d 303 (1980), and there is evidence here to support the trial court's findings.

Plaintiff introduced three memoranda written during the negotiation process. One, written to Mr. Joyner by Mr. Mark Lynch, an accountant negotiating on behalf of the Joyners, stated that defendant "would agree" that completion of all buildings within five years would be required to avoid retroactive recomputation of the rent under the Base Lease. The other two memoranda, one written by defendant's negotiator, Mr. Ed Clark, referred to the "completed development" of the property as a possible condition to avoiding rent escalation. Mr. Lynch testified that he and Mr. Joyner interpreted "completed development" to mean the construction of all buildings. In addition, plaintiff testified that she expressed to defendant her wish that the contract contain a more specific provision regarding the construction of buildings on the lots. This evidence is sufficient to support the trial court's finding that plaintiff intended the provision in question to require defendant at least to have begun construction of all buildings on the lots.

Defendant argues that, when read in conjunction with the terms of the Base Lease, his interpretation is the only reasonable interpretation of the rent escalation provision. That argument was rejected in this court's previous decision in this case. The law of the case is that the language in the amendment is ambiguous and susceptible to more than one reasonable meaning, even when considered with the terms of the Base Lease.

Contrary to plaintiff's contention, there is also evidence that defendant attributed a different meaning to the disputed provision. The evidence indisputably shows that both parties intended the rent escalation clause to require defendant to develop all the property by 30 September 1980. Defendant's evidence showed that, in the local real estate market, a lot is considered "developed" when water and sewer lines are installed and the lot is otherwise ready for the construction of a building. Defendant also established that he was an experienced commercial real estate developer and that Mr. Joyner had personal experience in the real estate business. There is, therefore, competent evidence to support the trial court's finding that defendant intended the provision to require, at most, what he actually accomplished by 30 September 1980.

In arguing that her meaning was the only one intended by the parties, plaintiff specifically cites evidence of her purpose in entering the lease with defendant as well as evidence of the conduct of the parties after the lease was executed. Evidence of the parties' purposes in entering a contract and their conduct after the agreement is some evidence of their intent. See Century Communications v. Housing Authority of City of Wilson, 313 N.C. 143, 326 S.E.2d 261 (1985). However, much of the evidence relied on by plaintiff, as well as other evidence in the record, can support more than one inference. Which among those possible inferences should be deemed credible and worthy of belief is a decision for the trial court. See Williams v. Insurance Co., 288 N.C. 338, 218 S.E.2d 368 (1975). The evidence here does not show, as a matter of law, what effect the parties intended the language in the rent escalation provision to have. Therefore, while the evidence and applicable rules of interpretation would have permitted the trial court to find plaintiff's meaning was intended by both parties, they clearly did not compel that finding. It is not the province of this court to reweigh the evidence. . . .

II

It is axiomatic that where parties have attributed different meanings to a term within a contract, there is no "meeting of the minds" on that provision and a court will not enforce either party's meaning. See O'Grady v. Bank, 296 N.C. 212, 250 S.E.2d 587 (1978); Elliott v. Duke University, 66 N.C. App. 590, 311 S.E.2d 632, *disc. rev. denied,* 311 N.C. 754, 321 S.E.2d 132 (1984); Restatement (Second) of Contracts, sections 20, 201 (1979) (difference must be "material"); Frigaliment Importing Co. v. B.N.S. International Sales Corp., 190 F. Supp. 116 (S.D.N.Y. 1960). Consequently, having found divergent meanings between the parties, the trial court did not err in concluding there was no meeting of the minds on the question of what conditions would trigger the retroactive rent escalation.

It is also well-established, although not often enunciated in North Carolina cases, that, where one party knows or has reason to know what the other party means by certain language and the other party does not know or have reason to know of the meaning attached to the disputed language by the first party, the court will enforce the contract in accordance with the innocent party's meaning. See Insurance Agency v. Leasing Corp., 31 N.C. App. 490, 229 S.E.2d 697 (1976); Restatement (Second) of Contracts, sections 20, 201(2) (1979); 3 Corbin, Contracts, section 537 (1960 and Supp. 1984). In fact, it seems that a determination of whether either or both parties knew or had reason to know of a different meaning attributed by the other is essential in almost every case where the court finds a lack of mutual assent. Id. Here, much of the evidence of the negotiations reflects directly on each party's knowledge of what the other party intended the provision to require. Since the trial court failed to make findings of fact on that crucial question, this case must be remanded.

. . . In this case, whether the parties knew or had reason to know of the other's meaning of the disputed language is essential to the proper determination of the contract's enforceability. Accordingly, we remand for findings of fact on that issue.

In remanding, we necessarily find that the trial court erred in awarding judgment for plaintiff based on the rule that ambiguity in contract terms must be construed most strongly against the party which drafted the contract. See Root v. Insurance Co., supra; Restatement (Second) of Contracts, section 206 (1979). The rule is essentially one of legal effect, of "construction" rather than "interpretation," since "it can scarcely be said to be designed to ascertain the meanings attached by the parties." Farnsworth, Contracts, section 7.11, page 500 (1982). The rule's application rests on a public policy theory that the party who chose the word is more likely to have provided more carefully for the protection of his own interests, is more likely to have had reason to know of uncertainties, and may have even left the meaning deliberately obscure. Id.; Restatement (Second) Contracts, section 206, comment a (1979); 3 Corbin supra, section 559. Consequently, the rule is usually applied in cases involving an adhesion contract or where one party is in a stronger bargaining position, although it is not necessarily limited to those situations. Id. In this case, where the parties were at arms length and were equally sophisticated, we believe the rule was improvidently invoked.

Before this rule of construction should be applied, the record should affirmatively show that "the form of expression in words was actually chosen by one [party] rather than by the other." 3 Corbin supra, section 559 at 266. The only evidence admitted regarding who drafted the 1975 amendment is Mr. Joyner's testimony that no one in his law firm had anything to do with it. Even assuming this is sufficient to support an inference that defendant or his agent wrote the provision, it does not establish that defendant can be charged with having chosen its language.

The record reveals that both parties are experienced in the real estate business and that they bargained from essentially equal positions of power. The record also shows the parties engaged in a fairly protracted negotiation process, with the provision in question undergoing particular scrutiny. Nothing in the record shows that it was defendant, rather than plaintiff, who "drafted" the provision. Instead, it appears that the language was assented to by parties who had both the knowledge to understand its import and the bargaining power to alter it. Therefore, the policy behind the rule is not served in its application here and the trial court erred in using the rule to award judgment for plaintiff. . . .

If, on remand, the trial court finds that defendant knew or had reason to know what meaning plaintiff attached to the disputed terminology and that plaintiff did not know or have reason to know of the meaning attached to the disputed language by defendant, the trial court should conclude that there is a contract as to the plaintiff's meaning. Otherwise, plaintiff's claim does not prevail.

Affirmed in part, reversed and remanded in part.

WELLS and MARTIN, JJ., concur.

NOTES AND QUESTIONS

1. *Whose meaning prevails?* In remanding the *Joyner* case for findings of fact, the court declares that the plaintiff can prevail only if the trial court concludes that the defendant knew or at least had reason to know of the meaning

she intended while she did *not* know (or have reason to know) of the meaning he intended. Why is this particular combination of findings necessary to the plaintiff's case? Suppose the court were to find that *neither* party knew or had reason to know of the meaning intended by the other: Who would prevail, and why? Suppose instead that the lower court on remand was to find that the defendant actually did know of the meaning intended by the plaintiff, but also that the plaintiff, although she did not actually know of defendant's meaning, did at least have "reason to know" of that meaning. What then?

The rule of Restatement (Second) §201(2)(b) generally has been approved by the courts. E.g., Centron DPL Co. v. Tilden Fin. Corp., 965 F.2d 673 (8th Cir. 1992) (in dispute between lender and borrower about meaning of prepayment term of note, case remanded for factual determination of whether lender knew or had reason to know of borrower's meaning); Ragen v. Hancor, Inc., 920 F. Supp. 2d 810 (N.D. Ohio 2013) (sales representative who worked under multiple contracts over 20-year period had reason to know that manufacturer did not view contracts as granting him exclusive territorial rights because of detailed information given with regular commission payments).

2. ***Subsequent proceedings in Joyner.*** When the *Joyner* case was heard again on remand, the trial court found that the defendant neither knew nor had reason to know of the plaintiff's meaning, and therefore it held for the defendant. In affirming this decision, the court of appeals referred to the following evidence to support the trial court's finding of fact regarding the defendant's lack of knowledge or reason to know of the plaintiff's meaning:

> We determine that at least four instances of competent evidence exist to support the trial court's finding. First, plaintiff's testimony reveals two versions of her meaning of the conditions triggering the recomputation agreement. Her initial testimony was that "completed building" was the condition for avoiding recomputation. However, her subsequent testimony was that the condition meant "completed buildings" *and* tenant occupation of the buildings. Plaintiff also testified about her inexperience and unfamiliarity with commercial real estate transactions.
>
> Second, even if plaintiff did not have more than one meaning, plaintiff's lack of direct communication with defendant during negotiations was insufficient to give defendant reason to know that either version of plaintiff's meaning of the conditions triggering the recomputation provision differed from defendant's meaning. In negotiations, plaintiff did not meet with defendant; she was represented by her husband-attorney and several accountants. Nowhere does the record show that plaintiff's negotiators conveyed either version of plaintiff's meaning to defendant.
>
> The third instance is the lack of evidence that defendant assented to the contract in reliance on a "completed building" meaning of the recomputation conditions. The record shows that plaintiff's negotiators recommended a "completed building" clause for the recomputation provision without stating whether it was plaintiff who requested the recommendation. The record also shows that defendant flatly rejected plaintiff's negotiators' recommendation that the agreement recomputation provision include "completed building" language. Subsequent to defendant's rejection, the record shows that none of

> plaintiff's negotiators informed defendant that plaintiff knew of defendant's rejection, that plaintiff disagreed with defendant's rejection, or that defendant's rejection was to have no effect.
>
> The fourth instance is defendant's evidence showing that his previous extensive business knowledge and experience with commercial real estate transactions led him to attribute meanings to the recomputation terms "subdivision," "development," and "construction" different from plaintiff's meanings. Defendant offered this evidence to show that he did not have reason to know that the recomputation provision should have been understood to include "completed buildings."
>
> Based on the record before us, we determine that a reasonable lessee in defendant's position would not have been reasonably induced to believe that he must complete all buildings by the recomputation provision deadline. Thus, the trial court properly found that defendant had no knowledge or reason to know plaintiff's meaning that would allow plaintiff to prevail.

Joyner v. Adams, 387 S.E.2d 235, 239 (N.C. Ct. App. 1990).

3. *Construction against drafter.* In the trial court's second decision in the *Joyner* case (the one reversed by the above-reproduced appellate decision), the trial court broke the tie resulting from its finding that no "meeting of the minds" had occurred and found for plaintiff Joyner by invoking the principle that a contractual ambiguity should generally be resolved against the party who drafted the language in question (sometimes known as the maxim of interpretation *contra proferentem* — see item 5 in the Comment below). As the court indicates, this maxim is frequently employed in cases involving "adhesion contracts" but is by no means limited to such cases. See St. Charles Foods, Inc. v. America's Favorite Chicken Co., 198 F.3d 815 (11th Cir. 1999) (letter agreement with franchisee that was ambiguous about right of first refusal construed against franchisor that drafted language); Guerrant v. Roth, 777 N.E.2d 499 (Ill. App. Ct. 2002) (ambiguity in contingency fee agreement written by attorney particularly subject to rule requiring construction against drafter). Does the appellate court adequately justify its refusal to apply this maxim in *Joyner*? Other courts have agreed that the maxim should be limited in its application to cases where one party can fairly be regarded as solely responsible for the language in question. Compare Western Sling & Cable Co. v. Hamilton, 545 So. 2d 29, 32 (Ala. 1989) ("[w]here both parties to a contract are sophisticated business persons advised by counsel and the contract is a product of negotiations at arm's length between the parties, . . . no reason to automatically construe ambiguities in the contract against the drafter"), with Speedway Motorsports Int'l Ltd. v. Bronwen Energy Trading, Ltd., 707 S.E.2d 385 (N.C. Ct. App. 2011) (sophisticated parties, but language chosen by one; maxim applied, citing *Joyner*). See generally Meredith R. Miller, Contract Law, Party Autonomy and the New Formalism, 75 Mo. L. Rev. 493 (2010) (suggesting caution in characterizing parties as "sophisticated," to avoid exacerbating imbalances of bargaining power). Court decisions also emphasize that the rule should be used only when other means of

interpretation cannot resolve an ambiguity. E.g., Cruz v. Visual Perceptions, LLC, 84 A.3d 828 (Conn. 2014) (*contra proferentem* applicable only as a last resort).

Comment: Interpretive Principles

Over the years, courts have developed a number of principles of interpretation to aid them in giving meaning to expressions of contractual agreement. The following useful list was compiled by Professor Edwin Patterson:

> In this brief treatment we can only quote a list of standard maxims, which may not be complete. The ones most often phrased in Latin are given first:
>
> 1. *Noscitur a sociis.* The meaning of a word in a series is affected by others in the same series; or, a word may be affected by its immediate context. The example for the next maxim may be taken to illustrate this one.
>
> 2. *Ejusdem generis.* A general term joined with a specific one will be deemed to include only things that are like (of the same genus as) the specific one. This one if applied usually leads to a restrictive interpretation. E.g., *S* contracts to sell *B* his farm together with the "cattle, hogs, and other animals." This would probably not include *S*'s favorite house-dog, but might include a few sheep that *S* was raising for the market.
>
> 3. *Expressio unius exclusio alterius.* If one or more specific items are listed, without any more general or inclusive terms, other items although similar in kind are excluded. E.g., *S* contracts to sell *B* his farm together with "the cattle and hogs on the farm." This language would be interpreted to exclude the sheep and *S*'s favorite house-dog.
>
> 4. *Ut magis valeat quam pereat.* By this maxim an interpretation that makes the contract valid is preferred to one that makes it invalid.
>
> 5. *Omnia praesumuntur contra proferentem.* This maxim states that if a written contract contains a word or phrase which is capable of two reasonable meanings, one of which favors one party and the other of which favors the other, that interpretation will be preferred which is less favorable to the one by whom the contract was drafted. This maxim favors the party of lesser bargaining power, who has little or no opportunity to choose the terms of the contract, and perforce accepts one drawn by the stronger party. . . . However, the maxim is commonly invoked in cases that do not reveal any disparity of bargaining power between the parties.
>
> 6. *Interpret contract as a whole.* A writing or writings that form part of the same transaction should be interpreted together as a whole, that is, every term should be interpreted as a part of the whole and not as if isolated from it. This maxim expresses the contextual theory of meaning, which is, perhaps, a truism.
>
> 7. *"Purpose of the parties."* "The principal apparent purpose of the parties is given great weight in determining the meaning to be given to manifestations of intention or to any part thereof." This maxim must be used with caution. In fact, the two parties to a (bargain) contract necessarily have different purposes, and if these are apparent, then the court can construe a principal or common purpose from the two as a guide to the interpretation of language or the filling of gaps. Thus a contract to sell, buy, and export scrap copper was construed

to make the buyer's obtaining of an export license a condition of the seller's promise to deliver. However, if the purposes of the parties are obscure the court may well fall back upon "plain meaning."

8. *Specific provision is exception to a general one.* If two provisions of a contract are inconsistent with each other and if one is "general" enough to include the specific situation to which the other is confined, the specific provision will be deemed to qualify the more general one, that is, to state an exception to it. A lease of a truck-trailer provided that the lessee should be absolutely liable for loss or damage to the vehicle, yet another clause stated that no party's liability should be increased by this contract. It was held that the former was more specific and therefore controlled the general provision, hence the lessee was liable. A careful draftsman would have stated the former as an exception to the latter, and the court in effect does it for him.

9. *Handwritten or typed provisions control printed provisions.* Where a written contract contains both printed provisions and handwritten or typed provisions, and the two are inconsistent, the handwritten or typed provisions are preferred. This maxim is based on the inference that the language inserted by handwriting or by typewriter for this particular contract is a more recent and more reliable expression of their intentions than is the language of a printed form. While this maxim is used in interpreting insurance contracts and other contracts of adhesion, it is also applicable to all contracts drawn up on a printed form.

10. *Public interest preferred.* If a public interest is affected by a contract, that interpretation or construction is preferred which favors the public interest. The proper scope of application of this rule seems doubtful. It may have some appropriate uses in construing contracts between private parties. However, as applied to government contracts it would, if applied, be used to save the taxpayers' money as against those contracting with the government. But this is not, it is believed, a standard of interpretation or construction uniformly applied to government contracts.

This battery of maxims is never fired all together. The judge or other interpreter-construer of a contract may, by making prudent choices, possibly obtain some useful guides for his reasoning and justifications for his conclusion.

Edwin W. Patterson, The Interpretation and Construction of Contracts, 64 Colum. L. Rev. 833, 853-855 (1964).

Rational reading of terms. One maxim omitted from Professor Patterson's list is reflected in Restatement (Second) §203(a). The section provides that in interpreting an agreement, a court should prefer an interpretation that makes an agreement reasonable, lawful, and effective to one that produces an unreasonable or unlawful result or that renders the agreement ineffective. The Restatement gives the following example:

1. *A* licenses *B* to manufacture pipes under *A*'s patents, and *B* agrees to pay "a royalty of 50 cents per 1,000 feet for an output of 5,000,000 or less feet per year, and for an output of over 5,000,000 per year at the rate of 30 cents per thousand feet." The 50 cent rate is payable on the first 5,000,000 feet, the 30 cent

> rate only on the excess. The more literal reading is unreasonable, since it would involve a smaller payment for 6,000,000 feet than for 4,000,000 feet.

Restatement (Second) §203, Illustration 1. See also Fishman v. LaSalle Nat'l Bank, 247 F.3d 300 (1st Cir. 2001) (loan agreement term setting amount of prepayment premium would be interpreted to produce rational result rather than apply implausible meaning that would come from literal reading); Cadle Co. v. Vargas, 771 N.E.2d 179 (Mass. App. Ct. 2002) (loan guarantee agreement would not be interpreted to lead to absurd result; "common sense is as much a part of contract interpretation as . . . the arsenal of canons"). Judge Richard A. Posner has cited the *Fishman* case as an example of a judicial technique he calls the "Best Guess" rule, in which a court combines common sense and some practical knowledge of the ways of the business world to reach results that are both commercially efficient and generally within the realm of what either party could reasonably have expected the contract to mean. Richard A. Posner, The Law and Economics of Contract Interpretation, 83 Tex. L. Rev. 1581, 1603 (2005).

Supplying an omitted term. The possibility exists that even after applying the array of interpretive principles, a court may conclude that the parties failed to agree upon a material term. Depending on the posture of the case, it may be appropriate for a court to conclude that the parties did not make an enforceable agreement. See Restatement (Second) §33, Comment *a.* In other cases, however, the evidence of intent to be bound or the degree of performance already rendered may cause rescission to be inappropriate. Restatement (Second) §204 recommends that in those situations the courts should supply a term that is reasonable under the circumstances. Professor Prince has addressed the topic of omitted terms and noted that gaps in the contract may result from lack of foresight, incomplete bargaining, or excessive initial optimism about performance of the contract. Harry G. Prince, Contract Interpretation in California: Plain Meaning, Parol Evidence and Use of the "Just Result" Principle, 31 Loy. L.A. L. Rev. 557, 619-620 (1998). Professor Prince argues that in such cases, courts should not strain to apply principles of interpretation to fill the gap, but should instead strive to achieve a just outcome:

> A tremendously better approach would be to simply recognize that, in such cases of *lacunae* within the contract terms, the courts are empowered to weigh a number of equitable factors and attempt to reach a just result. Those equitable factors would include addressing public interests and public good, allowing for sharing of unanticipated losses and gains, avoiding the award of a windfall to one party at the cost of denying recovery to the other side, and considering the parties' good or bad faith behavior.

Id. at 650. See Weston Investments, Inc. v. Domtar Indus., Inc., 2002 W.L. 31011141 (Del. Super. Ct.) (relying on §204 in supplying omitted term where parties consciously failed to agree on provision with large tax consequences but still intended to be bound; in rare circumstances courts will provide terms consistent with good faith and reasonable expectations).

Frigaliment Importing Co. v. B.N.S. International Sales Corp.

United States District Court 190 F. Supp. 116 (S.D.N.Y. 1960)

FRIENDLY, Circuit Judge.

The issue is, what is chicken? Plaintiff says "chicken" means a young chicken, suitable for broiling and frying. Defendant says "chicken" means any bird of that genus that meets contract specifications on weight and quality, including what it calls "stewing chicken" and plaintiff pejoratively terms "fowl." Dictionaries give both meanings, as well as some others not relevant here. To support its [interpretation], plaintiff sends a number of volleys over the net; defendant essays to return them and adds a few serves of its own. Assuming that both parties were acting in good faith, the case nicely illustrates Holmes' remark "that the making of a contract depends not on the agreement of two minds in one intention, but on the agreement of two sets of external signs — not on the parties' having *meant* the same thing but on their having *said* the same thing." The Path of the Law, in Collected Legal Papers, p. 178. I have concluded that plaintiff has not sustained its burden of persuasion that the contract used "chicken" in the narrower sense.

The action is for breach of the warranty that goods sold shall correspond to the description, New York Personal Property Law, McKinney's Consol. Laws, c.41, §95. Two contracts are in suit. In the first, dated May 2, 1957, defendant, a New York sales corporation, confirmed the sale to plaintiff, a Swiss corporation, of

> U.S. Fresh Frozen Chicken, Grade A, Government Inspected, Eviscerated
>
> 2½-3 lbs. and 1½-2 lbs. each
> all chicken individually wrapped in cryovac, packed in secured fiber cartons or wooden boxes, suitable for export
>
> | | |
> |---|---|
> | 75,000 lbs. 2½-3 lbs. | @$33.00 |
> | 25,000 lbs. 1½-2 lbs. | @$36.50 |
>
> per 100 lbs. FAS New York
>
> scheduled May 10, 1957 pursuant to instructions from Penson & Co., New York.

The second contract, also dated May 2, 1957, was identical save that only 50,000 lbs. of the heavier "chicken" were called for, the price of the smaller birds was $37 per 100 lbs., and shipment was scheduled for May 30. The initial shipment under the first contract was short but the balance was shipped on May 17. When the initial shipment arrived in Switzerland, plaintiff found, on May 28, that the 2½-3 lbs. birds were not young chicken suitable for broiling and frying but stewing chicken or "fowl"; indeed, many of the cartons and bags plainly so indicated. Protests ensued. Nevertheless, shipment under the second contract was made on May 29, the 2½-3 lbs. birds again being stewing chicken. Defendant stopped the transportation of these at Rotterdam.

This action followed. Plaintiff says that, notwithstanding that its acceptance was in Switzerland, New York law controls under the principle of Rubin v. Irving

Trust Co., 1953, 305 N.Y. 288, 305, 113 N.E.2d 424, 431; defendant does not dispute this, and relies on New York decisions. I shall follow the apparent agreement of the parties as to the applicable law.

Since the word "chicken" standing alone is ambiguous, I turn first to see whether the contract itself offers any aid to its interpretation. Plaintiff says the 1½-2 lbs. birds necessarily had to be young chicken since the older birds do not come in that size, hence the 2½-3 lbs. birds must likewise be young. This is unpersuasive — a contract for "apples" of two different sizes could be filled with different kinds of apples even though only one species come in both sizes. Defendant notes that the contract called not simply for chicken but for "U.S. Fresh Frozen Chicken, Grade A, Government Inspected." It says the contract thereby incorporated by reference the Department of Agriculture's regulations, which favor its interpretation; I shall return to this after reviewing plaintiff's other contentions.

The first hinges on an exchange of cablegrams which preceded execution of the formal contracts. The negotiations leading up to the contracts were conducted in New York between defendant's secretary, Ernest R. Bauer, and a Mr. Stovicek, who was in New York for the Czechoslovak government at the World Trade Fair. A few days after meeting Bauer at the fair, Stovicek telephoned and inquired whether defendant would be interested in exporting poultry to Switzerland. Bauer then met with Stovicek, who showed him a cable from plaintiff dated April 26, 1957, announcing that they "are buyer" of 25,000 lbs. of chicken 2½-3 lbs. weight, Cryovac packed, grade A Government inspected, at a price up to 33¢ per pound, for shipment on May 10, to be confirmed by the following morning, and were interested in further offerings. After testing the market for price, Bauer accepted, and Stovicek sent a confirmation that evening. Plaintiff stresses that, although these and subsequent cables between plaintiff and defendant, which laid the basis for the additional quantities under the first and for all of the second contract, were predominantly in German, they used the English word "chicken"; it claims this was done because it understood "chicken" meant young chicken whereas the German word, "Huhn," included both "Brathuhn" (broilers) and "Suppenhuhn" (stewing chicken), and that defendant, whose officers were thoroughly conversant with German, should have realized this. Whatever force this argument might otherwise have is largely drained away by Bauer's testimony that he asked Stovicek what kind of chickens were wanted, received the answer "any kind of chickens," and then, in German, asked whether the cable meant "Huhn" and received an affirmative response. . . .

Plaintiff's next contention is that there was a definite trade usage that "chicken" meant "young chicken." Defendant showed that it was only beginning in the poultry trade in 1957, thereby bringing itself within the principle that "when one of the parties is not a member of the trade or other circle, his acceptance of the standard must be made to appear" by proving either that he had actual knowledge of the usage or that the usage is "so generally known in the community that his actual individual knowledge of it may be inferred." 9 Wigmore, Evidence (3d ed. 1940) §2464. Here there was no proof of actual knowledge of the alleged usage; indeed, it is quite plain that defendant's belief was to the contrary. In order to meet the alternative requirement, the law of New York demands a showing that "the usage is of so long continuance, so well established, so notorious, so universal and so reasonable in itself, as that the presumption is violent that the parties contracted with reference to it, and made it a part of their agreement." Walls v. Bailey, 1872, 49 N.Y. 464, 472-473.

Plaintiff endeavored to establish such a usage by the testimony of three witnesses and certain other evidence. Strasser, resident buyer in New York for a large chain of Swiss cooperatives, testified that "on chicken I would definitely understand a broiler." However, the force of this testimony was considerably weakened by the fact that in his own transactions the witness, a careful businessman, protected himself by using "broiler" when that was what he wanted and "fowl" when he wished older birds. Indeed, there are some indications, dating back to a remark of Lord Mansfield, Edie v. East India Co., 2 Burr. 1216, 1222 (1761), that no credit should be given "witnesses to usage, who could not adduce instances in verification." 7 Wigmore, Evidence (3d ed. 1940), §1954; see McDonald v. Acker, Merrall & Condit Co., 2d Dept. 1920, 192 App. Div. 123, 126, 182 N.Y.S. 607. While Wigmore thinks this goes too far, a witness' consistent failure to rely on the alleged usage deprives his opinion testimony of much of its effect. Niesielowski, an officer of one of the companies that had furnished the stewing chicken to defendant, testified that "chicken" meant "the male species of the poultry industry. That could be a broiler, a fryer or a roaster," but not a stewing chicken; however, he also testified that upon receiving defendant's inquiry for "chickens," he asked whether the desire was for "fowl or frying chickens" and, in fact, supplied fowl, although taking the precaution of asking defendant, a day or two after plaintiff's acceptance of the contracts in suit, to change its confirmation of its order from "chickens," as defendant had originally prepared it, to "stewing chickens." Dates, an employee of Urner-Barry Company, which publishes a daily market report on the poultry trade, gave it as his view that the trade meaning of "chicken" was "broilers and fryers." In addition to this opinion testimony, plaintiff relied on the fact that the Urner-Barry service, the Journal of Commerce, and Weinberg Bros. & Co. of Chicago, a large supplier of poultry, published quotations in a manner which, in one way or another, distinguish between "chicken," comprising broilers, fryers and certain other categories, and "fowl," which, Bauer acknowledged, included stewing chickens. This material would be impressive if there were nothing to the contrary. However, there was, as will now be seen.

Defendant's witness Weininger, who operates a chicken eviscerating plant in New Jersey, testified "Chicken is everything except a goose, a duck, and a turkey. Everything is a chicken, but then you have to say, you have to specify which category you want or that you are talking about." Its witness Fox said that in the trade "chicken" would encompass all the various classifications. Sadina, who conducts a food inspection service, testified that he would consider any bird coming within the classes of "chicken" in the Department of Agriculture's regulations to be a chicken. The specifications approved by the General Services Administration include fowl as well as broilers and fryers under the classification "chickens." Statistics of the Institute of American Poultry Industries use the phrases "Young chickens" and "Mature chickens," under the general heading "Total chickens," and the Department of Agriculture's daily and weekly price reports avoid use of the word "chicken" without specification.

Defendant advances several other points which it claims affirmatively support its construction. Primary among these is the regulation of the Department of Agriculture, 7 C.F.R. §70.300-70.370, entitled, "Grading and Inspection of Poultry and Edible Products Thereof," and in particular §70.301 which recited:

> *Chickens.* The following are the various classes of chickens:
>
> (a) Broiler or fryer . . .
> (b) Roaster . . .
> (c) Capon . . .
> (d) Stag . . .
> (e) Hen or stewing chicken or fowl . . .
> (f) Cock or old rooster . . .

Defendant argues, as previously noted, that the contract incorporated these regulations by reference. Plaintiff answers that the contract provision related simply to grade and Government inspection and did not incorporate the Government definition of "chicken," and also that the definition in the Regulations is ignored in the trade. However, the latter contention was contradicted by Weininger and Sadina; and there is force in defendant's argument that the contract made the regulations a dictionary, particularly since the reference to Government grading was already in plaintiff's initial cable to Stovicek.

Defendant makes a further argument based on the impossibility of its obtaining broilers and fryers at the 33¢ price offered by plaintiff for the 2½-3 lbs. birds. There is no substantial dispute that, in late April, 1957, the price for 2½-3 lbs. broilers was between 35 and 37¢ per pound, and that when defendant entered into the contracts, it was well aware of this and intended to fill them, by supplying fowl in these weights. It claims that plaintiff must likewise have known the market since plaintiff had reserved shipping space on April 23, three days before plaintiff's cable to Stovicek, or, at least, that Stovicek was chargeable with such knowledge. It is scarcely an answer to say, as plaintiff does in its brief, that the 33¢ price offered by the 2½-3 lbs. "chickens" was closer to the prevailing 35¢ price for broilers than to the 30¢ at which defendant procured fowl. Plaintiff must have expected defendant to make some profit — certainly it could not have expected defendant deliberately to incur a loss.

Finally, defendant relies on conduct by the plaintiff after the first shipment had been received. On May 28 plaintiff sent two cables complaining that the larger birds in the first shipment constituted "fowl." Defendant answered with a cable refusing to recognize plaintiff's objection and announcing "We have today ready for shipment 50,000 lbs. chicken 2½-3 lbs. 25,000 lbs. broilers 1½-2 lbs.," these being the goods procured for shipment under the second contract, and asked immediate answer "whether we are to ship this merchandise to you and whether you will accept the merchandise." After several other cable exchanges, plaintiff replied on May 29 "Confirm again that merchandise is to be shipped since resold by us if not enough pursuant to contract chickens are shipped the missing quantity is to be shipped within ten days stop we resold to our customers pursuant to your contract chickens grade A you have to deliver us said merchandise we again state that we shall make you fully responsible for all resulting costs."[2] Defendant argues that if plaintiff was sincere in thinking it was entitled to young chickens, plaintiff would not have allowed the shipment under the second contract to go forward, since the distinction between broilers and chickens drawn in defendant's cablegram must have made it clear that the larger birds would not be broilers. However, plaintiff answers that the cables show plaintiff was insisting on delivery of young chickens and that defendant shipped old ones at its peril. Defendant's point would be highly relevant on another disputed issue — whether if liability were established, the measure of damages should be the difference in market value of broilers and stewing chicken in New York or the larger difference in Europe, but I cannot give it weight on the issue of interpretation. Defendant points out also that plaintiff proceeded to deliver some of the larger birds in Europe, describing them as "poulets"; defendant argues that it was only when plaintiff's customers complained about this that plaintiff developed the idea that "chicken" meant "young chicken." There is little force in this in view of plaintiff's immediate and consistent protests.

When all the evidence is reviewed, it is clear that defendant believed it could comply with the contracts by delivering stewing chicken in the 2½-3 lbs. size. Defendant's subjective intent would not be significant if this did not coincide with an objective meaning of "chicken." Here it did coincide with one of the dictionary meanings, with the definition in the Department of Agriculture Regulations to which the contract made at least oblique reference, with at least some usage in the trade, with the realities of the market, and with what plaintiff's spokesman had said. Plaintiff asserts it to be equally plain that plaintiff's own subjective intent was to obtain broilers and fryers; the only evidence against this is the material as to market prices and this may not have been sufficiently brought home. In any event it is unnecessary to determine that issue. For plaintiff has the burden of showing that "chicken" was used in the narrower rather than in the broader sense, and this it has not sustained.

This opinion constitutes the Court's findings of fact and conclusions of law. Judgment shall be entered dismissing the complaint with costs.

NOTES AND QUESTIONS

1. *Whose meaning prevails?* *Joyner* illustrated the application of the principles of the modified objective theory of contract interpretation: A party is bound by the other party's meaning if the first party either knew or had reason to know of the second party's meaning while the second party did not know or

---

2. These cables were in German; "chicken," "broilers" and, on some occasions, "fowl," were in English.

have reason to know of the first party's interpretation. Consider the effect of these principles in *Frigaliment.* Does the court hold that a contract was formed and that the word *chicken* is to be interpreted in accordance with the defendant's meaning, or does the court hold that no contract was formed because there was no reasonable basis for choosing between the conflicting meanings of the word *chicken*? Does it make any difference to the result in the case? Would the choice between these theories have made a difference if Frigaliment had refused to accept the "chickens" and B.N.S. had brought suit for breach of contract?

2. *Ambiguity and "plain meaning."* More extensively than *Joyner*, *Frigaliment* examines the various types of evidence that each party can introduce to convince the trier of fact that its meaning should prevail. Before proceeding to an examination of the circumstances surrounding the making of the contract, the court notes that the word *chicken* is ambiguous. Is it necessary for a court to make a preliminary determination that the contract is ambiguous before receiving evidence of surrounding circumstances? Courts often state that the "plain meaning" of the language of a contract should govern and that extrinsic evidence is admissible only if the court concludes that the contract is ambiguous. E.g., Abdelrhman v. Ackerman, 76 A.3d 883 (D.C. 2013) (plain meaning rule required exclusion of extrinsic evidence where tenant agreed in writing that new purchaser of building would have option to terminate his lease, even though inclusion of that term was inexplicable in light of parties' negotiating history).

Contract scholars (including both objectivists and advocates of a more flexible, modern approach to interpretation) have consistently rejected the idea that words can have only one precise meaning. As Holmes said, "It is not true that in practice (and I know no reason why theory should disagree with the facts) a given word or even a given collocation of words has one meaning and no other. A word generally has several meanings, even in a dictionary." Oliver Wendell Holmes, The Theory of Legal Interpretation, 12 Harv. L. Rev. 417 (1899). Professor Corbin argued that a court should admit all relevant evidence in order to determine the intention of the parties, including evidence of subjective intent. 3 Corbin on Contracts §538 (1960), at 73. See also Margaret N. Kniffin, 5 Corbin on Contracts §24.7 (Joseph M. Perillo ed., 1998). The Restatement adopts Corbin's view on the admissibility of extrinsic evidence. Restatement (Second) §202.

Although contract theorists have been practically unanimous in their rejection of the plain meaning rule, many (perhaps most) courts will nonetheless rely on the rule and refuse to receive extrinsic evidence of meaning unless the court first concludes that the agreement is ambiguous. Joseph M. Perillo, Contracts §3-10, at 136-137 (7th ed. 2014).

3. *Patent and latent ambiguity.* Assuming a court requires the contract to be ambiguous before admitting extrinsic evidence, when is an agreement ambiguous? Courts and scholars have identified two types of ambiguity: patent or intrinsic ambiguity and latent or extrinsic ambiguity. In Bohler-Uddeholm Am., Inc. v. Ellwood Group, Inc., 247 F.3d 79 (3d Cir. 2001), the defendant

appealed after a jury returned a verdict against it for $4.1 million, asserting that the contract had a plain meaning that favored its position and that the trial court had erred in admitting extrinsic evidence to uncover a latent ambiguity. The Third Circuit Court of Appeals, faced with apparently conflicting Pennsylvania precedents, first noted that the state's courts have often held that where a written contract is facially clear a court should not look for its meaning beyond its "four corners." Nevertheless, Pennsylvania decisions also permit the court to receive and consider extrinsic evidence to determine whether there may be in the agreement a "latent ambiguity," one not apparent from the words alone (at least in their common meanings) but visible in the light of surrounding circumstances. Such evidence should consist of more than the parties' own declarations of their "intentions" at the time of contracting, however, and it should not seek to impose on the writing a meaning beyond any reasonable understanding of its terms. The cases thus resolve the apparent tension between "plain meaning" and "latent ambiguity" analyses, the court concluded,

> . . . by allowing only extrinsic evidence of a certain nature to establish latent ambiguity in a contract; a court should determine whether the type of extrinsic evidence offered could be used to support a reasonable alternative interpretation under the precepts of Pennsylvania law on contract interpretation. . . . Once the court determines that a party has offered extrinsic evidence capable of establishing latent ambiguity, a decision as to which of the competing interpretations of the contract is the correct one is reserved for the factfinder, who would examine the content of the extrinsic evidence (along with all the other evidence) in order to make this determination. . . .

247 F.3d at 92-94. The Third Circuit Court thus upheld the trial court finding of a latent ambiguity based on permissible extrinsic evidence, but remanded the case on other grounds.

In a similar approach, the Seventh Circuit Court of Appeals has made a distinction between objective and subjective extrinsic evidence. *Objective evidence*, testimony of disinterested third parties or trade usage or the like, is deemed permissible to establish latent ambiguity because such evidence cannot be easily fabricated. *Subjective evidence*, testimony about what the parties believed the contract meant, is not acceptable for that purpose because it tends to be self-serving. AM International, Inc. v. Graphic Mgmt. Associates, Inc., 44 F.3d 572, 574-576 (7th Cir. 1995). Would you classify the term "chicken" as involving patent or latent ambiguity? If the *Frigaliment* court had applied the Pennsylvania approach, would extrinsic evidence of the meaning of the word "chicken" have been admitted? Why?

4. *Effect of relevant statute.* What effect does the court give to the Department of Agriculture regulation defining the classes of chickens? The modern view is that definitions of terms contained in statutes or administrative regulations are not determinative of the meaning of such terms in contracts. Restatement (Second) §201, Comment *c*; Margaret N. Kniffin, 5 Corbin on Contracts §24.26 (Joseph M. Perillo ed., 1998). E.g., Bull Motor Co.

v. Murphy, 270 S.W.3d 350 (Ark. Ct. App. 2008) (where car purchased as "new" had been previously driven 40 miles by a thief, question whether car was "new" as provided by contract was not governed by statutory definition of "new" vehicle). What is the justification for this approach?

5. *Relevance of trade usage.* The plaintiff buyer in *Frigaliment* attempted to show the existence of a trade usage by which the term "chicken" would be understood to mean a young chicken. While ultimately rejecting that contention as not sufficiently established by the testimony of the plaintiff's witnesses, the court appears to have regarded evidence of this type as admissible and relevant to the disputed issue of interpretation. Indeed, the existence of a relevant trade usage can overcome even the apparently unambiguous, "plain meaning" of contract language. See Galardi v. Naples Polaris, LLC, 301 P.3d 364, 367 (Nev. 2013) (modern view is that trade usage can be used both to interpret an ambiguous term and "also to determine whether a contract provision is ambiguous in the first place," citing Restatement (Second) §220, Comment *d*). But cf. White City Shopping Ctr., LP, v. PR Restaurants, LLC, 2006 WL 3292641 (Mass. Super. Ct.) (holding that shopping center lease precluding landlord from renting space to new tenants who would sell "sandwiches" did not apply to sale of "burritos" because "sandwich" is unambiguous and not commonly understood to include burritos, notwithstanding any commercial definition to contrary). For a skeptical view of the *White City* decision, see Marjorie Florestal, Is a Burrito a Sandwich? Exploring Race, Class and Culture in Contracts, 14 Mich. J. Race & L. 1 (2008).

In §1-303, the Uniform Commercial Code defines "usage of trade" and generally provides that evidence of trade usage should be relevant to the interpretation of the parties' agreement. Section 1-303 also defines two other concepts relevant to issues of interpretation: "course of performance" (actions of the parties in carrying out the contract at issue) and "course of dealing" (actions taken by the parties in performing previous contracts between them). ("Course of performance" is also defined in §2-208; prior to the revision of Article 1, "usage of trade" and "course of dealing" were defined in §1-205.) Of course, under the Code (as in *Frigaliment,* decided under the common law) the court may receive evidence of an asserted trade usage and yet ultimately find that the contended usage has not been sufficiently established as a fact. E.g., Williams v. Curtin, 807 F.2d 1046 (D.C. Cir. 1986) (evidence failed to establish trade usage that "slaw cabbage" referred to cabbage of a certain minimum size). Later in this chapter we examine more closely the role of trade usage and related concepts under the UCC, particularly in light of the Code's version of the parol evidence rule (§2-202).

6. *Scholarly commentary.* Professor Lisa Bernstein is skeptical about the weight that decision makers should give to general standards, such as trade usage. Professor Bernstein has drawn a distinction between cases in which the parties wish to preserve their relationship and "end game" situations in which the relationship has collapsed and the parties are attempting to maximize their gains or minimize their losses. She argues that norms such as trade usage, course of dealing, and course of performance are relationship preserving, but

parties to a dispute do not usually want a dispute-resolution body to apply these norms, preferring that relationship-preserving norms be left to the non-legal realm. Lisa Bernstein, Merchant Law in a Merchant Court: Rethinking the Code's Search for Immanent Business Norms, 144 U. Pa. L. Rev. 1765, 1770-1771 (1996).

Other commentators have considered issues of contract interpretation from an economic perspective. Professors Alan Schwartz and Robert Scott have argued that courts, in interpreting written contracts between firms, should adopt a strict formalist approach rather than a contextual one because this is what firms themselves prefer. Alan Schwartz & Robert E. Scott, Contract Theory and the Limits of Contract Law, 113 Yale L. J. 541 (2003). Further discussion of this proposition can be found in James W. Bowers, Murphy's Law and the Elementary Theory of Contract Interpretation: A Response to Schwartz and Scott, 57 Rutgers L. Rev. 587 (2005); Juliet P. Kostritsky, Plain Meaning v. Broad Interpretation: How the Risk of Opportunism Defeats a Unitary Default Rule for Interpretation, 96 Ky. L.J. 43 (2008); Steven J. Burton, A Lesson on Some Limits of Economic Analysis: Schwartz and Scott on Contract Interpretation, 88 Ind. L.J. 339 (2013).

C & J Fertilizer, Inc. v. Allied Mutual Insurance Co.

Supreme Court of Iowa 227 N.W.2d 169 (1975)

REYNOLDSON, Justice.

This action to recover for burglary loss under two separate insurance policies was tried to the court, resulting in a finding plaintiff had failed to establish a burglary within the policy definitions. Plaintiff appeals from judgment entered for defendant. We reverse and remand.

Trial court made certain findings of fact in support of its conclusion reached. Plaintiff operated a fertilizer plant in Olds, Iowa. At time of loss, plaintiff was insured under policies issued by defendant and titled "BROAD FORM STOREKEEPERS POLICY" and "MERCANTILE BURGLARY AND ROBBERY POLICY." Each policy defined "burglary" as meaning,

> . . . the felonious abstraction of insured property (1) from within the premises by a person making felonious entry therein by actual force and violence, of which force and violence there are visible marks made by tools, explosives, electricity or chemicals upon, or physical damage to, the exterior of the premises at the place of such entry. . . .

On Saturday, April 18, 1970, all exterior doors to the building were locked when plaintiff's employees left the premises at the end of the business day. The following day, Sunday, April 19, 1970, one of plaintiff's employees was at the plant and found all doors locked and secure. On Monday, April 20, 1970, when the employees reported for work, the exterior doors were locked, but the front office door was unlocked.

There were truck tire tread marks visible in the mud in the driveway leading to and from the plexiglas door entrance to the warehouse. It was demonstrated this door could be forced open without leaving visible marks or physical damage.

There were no visible marks on the exterior of the building made by tools, explosives, electricity or chemicals, and there was no physical damage to the exterior of the building to evidence felonious entry into the building by force and violence.

Chemicals had been stored in an interior room of the warehouse. The door to this room, which had been locked, was physically damaged and carried visible marks made by tools. Chemicals had been taken at a net loss to plaintiff in the sum of $9,582. Office and shop equipment valued at $400.30 was also taken from the building.

Trial court held the policy definition of "burglary" was unambiguous, there was nothing in the record "upon which to base a finding that the door to plaintiff's place of business was entered feloniously, by actual force and violence," and, applying the policy language, found for defendant.

Certain other facts in the record were apparently deemed irrelevant by trial court because of its view the applicable law required it to enforce the policy provision. Because we conclude different rules of law apply, we also consider those facts.

The "BROAD FORM STOREKEEPERS POLICY" was issued April 14, 1969; the "MERCANTILE BURGLARY AND ROBBERY POLICY" on April 14, 1970. Those policies are in evidence. Prior policies apparently were first purchased in 1968. The agent, who had power to bind insurance coverage for defendant, was told plaintiff would be handling farm chemicals. After inspecting the building then used by plaintiff for storage he made certain suggestions regarding security. There ensued a conversation in which he pointed out there had to be visible evidence of burglary. There was no testimony by anyone that plaintiff was then or thereafter informed the policy to be delivered would define burglary to require "visible marks made by tools, explosives, electricity or chemicals upon, or physical damage to, the exterior of the premises at the place of . . . entry."

The import of this conversation with defendant's agent when the coverage was sold is best confirmed by the agent's complete and vocally-expressed surprise when defendant denied coverage. From what the agent saw (tire tracks and marks on the interior of the building) and his contacts with the investigating officers ". . . the thought didn't enter my mind that it wasn't covered. . . ." From the trial testimony it was obvious the only understanding was that there should be some hard evidence of a third-party burglary vis-à-vis an "inside job." The latter was in this instance effectively ruled out when the thief was required to break an interior door lock to gain access to the chemicals.

The agent testified the insurance was purchased and "the policy was sent out afterwards." The president of plaintiff corporation, a 37-year-old farmer with a high school education, looked at that portion of the policy setting out coverages, including coverage for burglary loss, the amounts of insurance, and the "location and description." He could not recall reading the fine print defining "burglary" on page three of the policy. . . .

I. Revolution in Formation of Contractual Relationships

Many of our principles for resolving conflicts relating to written contracts were formulated at an early time when parties of equal strength negotiated in the historical sequence of offer, acceptance, and reduction to writing. The concept that both parties assented to the resulting document had solid footing in fact.

Only recently has the sweeping change in the inception of the document received widespread recognition:

> Standard form contracts probably account for more than ninety-nine percent of all contracts now made. Most persons have difficulty remembering the last time they contracted other than by standard form; except for casual oral agreements, they probably never have. But if they are active, they contract by standard form several times a day. Parking lot and theater tickets, package receipts, department store charge slips, and gas station credit card purchase slips are all standard form contracts. . . .
>
> The contracting still imagined by courts and law teachers as typical, in which both parties participate in choosing the language of their entire agreement, is no longer of much more than historical importance.
>
> — W. Slawson, Standard Form Contracts and Democratic Control of Lawmaking Power, 84 Harv. L. Rev. 529 (1971).

With respect to those interested in buying insurance, it has been observed that:

> His chances of successfully negotiating with the company for any substantial change in the proposed contract are just about zero. The insurance company tenders the insurance upon a "take it or leave it" basis. . . .
>
> Few persons solicited to take policies understand the subject of insurance or the rules of law governing the negotiations, and they have no voice in dictating the terms of what is called the contract. They are clear upon two or three points which the agent promises to protect, and for everything else they must sign ready-made applications and accept ready-made policies carefully concocted to conserve the interests of the company. . . . The subject, therefore, is *sui generis*, and the rules of a legal system devised to govern the formation of ordinary contracts between man and man cannot be mechanically applied to it.
>
> — 7 Williston on Contracts §900, pp. 29-30 (3d ed. 1963).

See also 3 Corbin on Contracts §559, p. 266 (1960); 6A Corbin on Contracts §1376, p. 21; Grismore on Contracts §294, pp. 505-507 (rev. ed. J. E. Murray, Jr. 1965); R. Keeton, Insurance Law Rights At Variance With Policy Provisions, 83 Harv. L. Rev. 961, 966-967 (1970); F. Kessler, Contracts of Adhesion — Some Thoughts About Freedom of Contract, 43 Colum. L. Rev. 629 (1943); C. Oldfather, Toward a Usable Method of Judicial Review of the Adhesion Contractor's Lawmaking, 16 Kansas L. Rev. 303 (1968).

It is generally recognized the insured will not read the detailed, cross-referenced, standardized, mass-produced insurance form, nor understand it if he does. 7 Williston on Contracts §906B, p. 300 ("But where the document thus delivered to him is a contract of insurance the majority rule is that the insured is not bound to know its contents"); 3 Corbin on Contracts §559, pp. 265-266 ("One who applies for an insurance policy . . . may not even read the policy, the number of its terms and the fineness of its print being such as to discourage him"); Note, Unconscionable Contracts: The Uniform Commercial Code, 45 Iowa L. Rev. 843, 844 (1960) ("It is probably a safe assertion that most involved standardized form contracts are never read by the party who 'adheres' to them. In such situations, the proponent of the form is free to dictate terms most advantageous to himself"). . . .

The concept that persons must obey public laws enacted by their own representatives does not offend a fundamental sense of justice: an inherent element of assent pervades the process.

But the inevitable result of enforcing all provisions of the adhesion contract, frequently, as here, delivered subsequent to the transaction and containing provisions never assented to, would be an abdication of judicial responsibility in the face of basic unfairness and a recognition that persons' rights shall be controlled by private lawmakers without the consent, express or implied, of those affected. See Grismore, supra §294 at p. 506; K. Llewellyn, What Price Contract? — An Essay in Perspective, 40 Yale L.J. 704, 731 (1931); Meyer, Contracts of Adhesion and the Doctrine of Fundamental Breach, 50 Va. L. Rev. 1178, 1179 (1964); C. Oldfather, supra at 303-304. A question is also raised whether a court may constitutionally allow that power to exist in private hands except where appropriate safeguards are present, including a right to meaningful judicial review. See W. Slawson, supra at 553.

The statutory requirement that the form of policies be approved by the commissioner of insurance, §515.109, The Code, neither resolves the issue whether the fineprint provisions nullify the insurance bargained for in a given case nor ousts the court from necessary jurisdiction. . . . In this connection it has been pertinently stated:

> Insurance contracts continue to be contracts of adhesion, under which the insured is left little choice beyond electing among standardized provisions offered to him, even when the standard forms are prescribed by public officials rather than insurers. Moreover, although statutory and administrative regulations have made increasing inroads on the insurer's autonomy by prescribing some kinds of provisions and proscribing others, most insurance policy provisions are still drafted by insurers. Regulation is relatively weak in most instances, and even the provisions prescribed or approved by legislative or administrative action ordinarily are in essence adoptions, outright or slightly modified, of proposals made by insurers' draftsmen.
>
> Under such circumstances as these, judicial regulation of contracts of adhesion, whether concerning insurance or some other kind of transaction, remains appropriate.
>
> — R. Keeton, supra at 966-967.

See also 3 Corbin on Contracts §559, p. 267.

The mass-produced boiler-plate "contracts," necessitated and spawned by the explosive growth of complex business transactions in a burgeoning population left courts frequently frustrated in attempting to arrive at just results by applying many of the traditional contract-construing stratagems. As long as fifteen years ago Professor Llewellyn, reflecting on this situation in his book "The Common Law Tradition — Deciding Appeals," pp. 362-371 wrote,

> What the story shows thus far is first, scholars persistently off-base while judges grope over well-nigh a century in irregular but dogged fashion for escape from a recurring discomfort of imbalance that rests on what is in fact substantial *non*agreement despite perfect semblance of agreement. (pp. 367-368). . . .
>
> The answer, I suggest, is this: Instead of thinking about "assent" to boilerplate clauses, we can recognize that so far as concerns the specific, there is no assent at all. What has in fact been assented to, specifically, are the few dickered terms, and the broad type of transaction, and but one thing more. That one thing more is a blanket assent (not a specific assent) to any not unreasonable or indecent terms the seller may have on his form, which do not alter or eviscerate the reasonable meaning of the dickered terms. The fine print which has not been read has no business to cut under the reasonable meaning of those dickered terms which constitute the dominant and only real expression of agreement, but much of it commonly belongs in. (p. 370)

In fairness to the often-discerned ability of the common law to develop solutions for changing demands, it should be noted appellate courts take cases as they come, constrained by issues the litigants formulated in trial court — a point not infrequently overlooked by academicians. Nor can a lawyer in the ordinary case be faulted for not risking a client's cause on an uncharted course when there is a reasonable prospect of reaching a fair result through familiar channels of long-accepted legal principles, for example, those grounded on ambiguity in language, the duty to define limitations or exclusions in clear and explicit terms, and interpretation of language from the viewpoint of an ordinary person, not a specialist or expert.

. . .

Plaintiff's claim it should be granted relief under the legal doctrines of reasonable expectations, implied warranty and unconscionability should be viewed against the above backdrop.

II. Reasonable Expectations

This court adopted the doctrine of reasonable expectations in Rodman v. State Farm Mutual Ins. Co., 208 N.W.2d 903, 905-908 (Iowa 1973). The *Rodman* court approved the following articulation of that concept:

> The objectively reasonable expectations of applicants and intended beneficiaries regarding the terms of insurance contracts will be honored even though painstaking study of the policy provisions would have negated those expectations.

208 N.W.2d at 906.

See Gray v. Zurich Insurance Company, 65 Cal. 2d 263, 54 Cal. Rptr. 104, 107-108, 419 P.2d 168, 171-172 (1966); Allen v. Metropolitan Life Ins. Co., 44 N.J. 294, 305, 208 A.2d 638, 644 (1965); Restatement (Second) of Contracts, [§237, Comments *e* and *f*, pp. 540-541 (Tentative Draft, 1973)]; 1 Corbin on Contracts §1, p. 2 ("That portion of the field of law that is classified and described as the law of contracts attempts the realization of reasonable expectations that have been induced by the making of a promise"); 7 Williston on Contracts §900, pp. 33-34 ("Some courts, recognizing that very few insureds even try to read and understand the policy or application, have declared that the insured is justified in assuming that the policy which is delivered to him has been faithfully prepared by the company to provide the protection against the risk which he had asked for. . . . Obviously this judicial attitude is a far cry from the old motto 'caveat emptor.' ").

At comment *f* to §237 of Restatement (Second) of Contracts, supra pp. 540-541 [Tentative Draft, 1973], we find the following analysis of the reasonable expectations doctrine:

> Although customers typically adhere to standardized agreements and are bound by them without even appearing to know the standard terms in detail, they are not bound to unknown terms which are beyond the range of reasonable expectation. A debtor who delivers a check to his creditor with the amount blank does not authorize the insertion of an infinite figure. Similarly, a party who adheres to the other party's standard terms does not assent to a term if the other party has reason to believe that the adhering party would not have accepted the agreement if he had known that the agreement contained the particular term. Such a belief or assumption may be shown by the prior negotiations or inferred from the circumstances. Reason to believe may be inferred from the fact that the term is bizarre or oppressive, from the fact that it eviscerates the non-standard terms explicitly agreed to, or from the fact that it eliminates the dominant purpose of the transaction. The inference is reinforced if the adhering party never had an opportunity to read the term, or if it is illegible or otherwise hidden from view. This rule is closely related to the policy against unconscionable terms and the rule of interpretation against the draftsman.

Nor can it be asserted the above doctrine does not apply here because plaintiff knew the policy contained the provision now complained of and cannot be heard to say it reasonably expected what it knew was not there. A search of the record discloses no such knowledge.

The evidence does show, as above noted, a "dicker" for burglary insurance coverage on chemicals and equipment. The negotiation was for what was actually expressed in the policies' "Insuring Agreements": the insurer's promise "To pay for loss by burglary or by robbery of a watchman, while the premises are not open for business, of merchandise, furniture, fixtures and equipment within the premises. . . ."

In addition, the conversation included statements from which the plaintiff should have understood defendant's obligation to pay would not arise where the burglary was an "inside job." Thus the following exclusion should have been reasonably anticipated:

> Exclusions
>
> This policy does not apply: . . .
>
> (b) to loss due to any fraudulent, dishonest or criminal act by any Insured, a partner therein, or an officer, employee, director, trustee or authorized representative thereof. . . .

But there was nothing relating to the negotiations with defendant's agent which would have led plaintiff to reasonably anticipate defendant would bury within the definition of "burglary" another exclusion denying coverage when, no matter how extensive the proof of a third-party burglary, no marks were left on the exterior of the premises. This escape clause, here triggered by the burglar's talent (an investigating law officer, apparently acquainted with the current modus operandi, gained access to the steel building without leaving any marks by leaning on the overhead plexiglas door while simultaneously turning the locked handle), was never read to or by plaintiff's personnel, nor was the substance explained by defendant's agent.

Moreover, the burglary "definition" which crept into this policy comports neither with the concept a layman might have of that crime, nor with a legal interpretation. See State v. Murray, 222 Iowa 925, 931, 270 N.W. 355, 358 (1936) ("We have held that even though the door was partially open, by opening it farther, in order to enter the building, this is a sufficient breaking to comply with the demands of the statute"); State v. Ferguson, 149 Iowa 476, 478-479, 128 N.W. 840, 841-842 (1910) ("It need not appear that this office was an independent building, for it is well known that it is burglary for one to break and enter an inner door or window, although the culprit entered through an open outer door. . . ."); see State v. Hougland, 197 N.W.2d 364, 365 (Iowa 1972).

The most plaintiff might have reasonably anticipated was a policy requirement of visual evidence (abundant here) indicating the burglary was an "outside" not an "inside" job. The exclusion in issue, masking as a definition, makes insurer's obligation to pay turn on the skill of the burglar, not on the event the parties bargained for: a bona-fide third party burglary resulting in loss of plaintiff's chemicals and equipment.

The "reasonable expectations" attention to the basic agreement, to the concept of substance over form, was appropriately applied by this court for the insurer's benefit in Central Bearings Co. v. Wolverine Insurance Company, 179 N.W.2d 443 (Iowa 1970), a case antedating *Rodman.* We there reversed a judgment for the insured which trial court apparently grounded on a claimed ambiguity in the policy. In denying coverage on what was essentially a products liability claim where the insured purchased only a "Premises-Operations" policy (without any misrepresentation, misunderstanding or overreaching) we said at page 449 of 179 N.W.2d:

> In summation we think the insured as a reasonable person would understand the policy coverage purchased meant the insured was not covered for loss if the "accident" with concomitant damage to a victim occurred away from the premises and after the operation or sale was complete.

The same rationale of reasonable expectations should be applied when it would operate to the advantage of the insured. Appropriately applied to this case, the doctrine demands reversal and judgment for plaintiff. . . .

Reversed and remanded.

HARRIS and MCCORMICK, JJ., concur.

MASON and RAWLINGS, JJ., concur in Divisions I, II and IV and the result.

LEGRAND, J., MOORE, C.J., and REES AND UHLENHOPP, JJ., dissent.

LEGRAND, Justice (dissenting).

I dissent from the result reached by the majority because it ignores virtually every rule by which we have heretofore adjudicated such cases and affords plaintiff ex post facto insurance coverage which it not only did not buy but which it *knew* it did not buy. . . .

While it may be very well to talk in grand terms about "mass advertising" by insurance companies and "incessant" assurances as to coverage which mislead the "unwary," particularly about "fine-print" provisions, such discussion should somehow be related to the case under review. Our primary duty, after all, is to resolve *this* dispute for *these* litigants under *this* record.

There is total silence in this case concerning any of the practices the majority finds offensive; nor is there any claim plaintiff was beguiled by such conduct into believing it had more protection than it actually did.

The record is even stronger against the majority's fine-print argument, the stereotype accusation which serves as a coup de grace in all insurance cases. Except for larger type on the face sheet and black (but not larger) print to designate divisions and sub-headings, the entire policies are of one size and style of print. To compare the *face* sheet with the body of the policy is like comparing a book's jacket cover with the narrative content; and the use of black type or other means of emphasis to separate one part of an instrument from another is an approved editorial expedient which serves to *assist,* not *hinder,* readability. In fact many of our opinions, including that of the majority in the instant case, resort to that device.

Tested by any objective standard, the size and style of type used cannot be fairly described as "fine print." The majority's description, right or wrong, of the plight of consumers generally should not be the basis for resolving the case now before us.

Like all other appeals, this one should be decided on what the record discloses — a fact which the majority concedes but promptly disregards.

Crucial to a correct determination of this appeal is the disputed provision of each policy defining burglary as "the felonious abstraction of insured property . . . by a person making felonious entry . . . by actual force and violence, of which force and violence there are visible marks made by tools, explosives, electricity or chemicals upon, or physical damage to, the exterior of the premises at the place of such entry. . . ." The starting point of any consideration of that definition is a determination whether it is ambiguous. Yet the majority does not even mention ambiguity.

The purpose of such a provision, of course, is to omit from coverage "inside jobs" or those resulting from fraud or complicity by the assured. The overwhelming weight of authority upholds such provisions as legitimate in purpose and unambiguous in application. Annot. 99 A.L.R.2d 129, 134 (1965); 44 Am. Jur. 2d Insurance §1400, §1401 (1969); 10 Couch Cyclopedia of Insurance Law (2d ed.) 42:128-42:130 (1962); 5 Appleman Insurance Law and Practice §3176, §3177. . . .

Once this indisputable fact is recognized, plaintiff's arguments virtually collapse. We may not — at least we *should* not — by any accepted standard of construction meddle with contracts which clearly and plainly state their meaning simply because we dislike that meaning, even in the case of insurance policies. . . .

. . . Here we have affirmative and unequivocal testimony from an officer and director of the plaintiff corporation that he knew the disputed provision was in the policies because "it was just like the insurance policy I have on my farm."

I cannot agree plaintiff may now assert it reasonably expected from these policies something it knew was not there. . . .

NOTES AND QUESTIONS

1. *Reasonable expectation of coverage in C & J Fertilizer case.* Does the court in *C & J Fertilizer* adequately justify its determination that the "reasonable expectations" of the insured included coverage on the facts of that case? In Atwater Creamery Co. v. Western Nat'l Mut. Ins. Co., 366 N.W.2d 271 (Minn. 1985), the insured sought a declaratory judgment that the loss from a burglary from its chemical storage building was covered by its policy with the defendant, despite the absence of visible marks of physical damage to the exterior of the plaintiff's building. The policy language on this point was identical to that employed in the *C & J Fertilizer* case, and the Minnesota Supreme Court upheld a trial court determination that the doctrine of reasonable expectations applied to permit recovery on the policy. Investigators including local, county, and state police personnel had determined that none of the plaintiff's employees were involved in the burglary. Calling this definition of "burglary" a "classic example of a policy provision that should be, and has been, interpreted according to the reasonable expectations of the insured" (id. at 277), the appellate court went on to observe as follows:

> There are, of course, fidelity bonds which cover employee theft. The creamery had such a policy covering director and manager theft. The fidelity company, however, does not undertake to insure against the risk of third-party burglaries. A business that requests and purchases burglary insurance reasonably is seeking coverage for loss from third-party burglaries whether a break-in is accomplished by an inept burglar or by a highly skilled burglar. . . . [Plaintiff] could reasonably have expected the burglary policy to cover this burglary where the police, as well as the trial court, found that it was an "outside job."

Id. at 278. The Minnesota Supreme Court clarified in a later decision that the reasonable expectations doctrine "has a very narrow application" and that the essential problem in the *Atwater Creamery* case was that the policy exclusion was "hidden" in a definitional provision. See Midwest Family Mut. Ins. Co. v. Wolters, 831 N.W.2d 628, 638-639 n.4 (Minn. 2013).

2. *Development of reasonable expectations doctrine.* The doctrine of reasonable expectations as applied to insurance policies has been adopted by a majority of states. See Eugene R. Anderson & James J. Fournier, Why Courts Enforce Insurance Policyholder's Objectively Reasonable Expectations of Insurance

Coverage, 5 Conn. Ins. L.J. 335, 356 n.57 (1998) (listing 34 jurisdictions that had accepted the doctrine in some form) and Dudi Schwartz, Interpretation and Disclosure in Insurance Contexts, 21 Loy. Consumer L. Rev. 105, 124-28 (2008) (describing development of doctrine over period from 1970 through turn of century). In his 1970 article, which appears to have played a key part in the burgeoning interest in this doctrine, Professor Robert Keeton stated the principle thus:

> The objectively reasonable expectations of applicants and intended beneficiaries regarding the terms of insurance contracts will be honored even though painstaking study of the policy provisions would have negated those expectations.

Robert E. Keeton, Insurance Law Rights at Variance with Policy Provisions, 83 Harv. L. Rev. 961, 967 (1970). In its strongest form, the doctrine may involve the court's refusing to apply an exclusion unambiguously stated in the policy or negating some other clearly phrased term.

However, many jurisdictions substantially limit the reasonable expectations doctrine by requiring the presence of ambiguity or a hidden or inconspicuous term, or have otherwise displayed a reluctance to adopt it as a broad rule. See Arthur J. Park, What to Reasonably Expect in the Coming Years From the Reasonable Expectations of the Insured Doctrine, 49 Willamette L. Rev. 165 (2012) (noting a number of variations of the doctrine and that many states require an ambiguity or hidden term before it will apply).

Some courts resist application of the doctrine even in modified form. The Florida Supreme Court declined to adopt the reasonable expectations doctrine in a case involving a question whether ammonia fumes came within an exclusion from insurance coverage for harm resulting from "escape of pollutants." Deni Associates of Florida, Inc. v. State Farm Fire & Cas. Ins. Co., 711 So. 2d 1135 (Fla. 1998). After noting that some jurisdictions apply the reasonable expectations doctrine only when the contract term is ambiguous and other courts apply the doctrine even when the meaning of the term is clear and unambiguous, the Florida court declined to apply the concept in either situation. The court stated:

> We decline to adopt the doctrine of reasonable expectations. There is no need for it if the policy provisions are ambiguous because in Florida ambiguities are construed against the insurer. To apply the doctrine to an unambiguous provision would be to rewrite the contract and the basis upon which the premiums are charged. . . .
>
> Constructing insurance policies upon a determination as to whether the insured's subjective expectations are reasonable can only lead to uncertainty and unnecessary litigation.

711 So. 2d at 1140.

3. ***Restatement approach to reasonable expectations.*** The court in *C & J Fertilizer* quotes with approval Restatement (Second) of Contracts §211, Comment *f* (cited in the court opinion as §237 in a tentative draft). Professor

Roger Henderson notes, however, that §211 is narrower than a full-fledged version of the doctrine of reasonable expectations:

> The "black letter" formulation of the Restatement reflects the American Law Institute's conservative approach in its recognition of an exception to the rule that standardized agreements will be enforced as written. The exception was narrowly drawn so as to assess the situation from the drafter's perspective: "Where the other party has reason to believe that the party manifesting such assent would not do so if he knew that the writing contained a particular term, the term is not part of the agreement." Only where a party has "reason to believe" that the other party, one who understands that a typical form contract is being used, would not have assented to a particular term is that term to be ignored. . . . [A]pplication of the exception requires taking the perspective of the insurer. As it is almost always the insured who will want to avoid a term of the policy or form contract, the decision maker asked to apply the exception must focus on information that was available to the insurer, i.e., what the insurer had reason to believe. If adhered to faithfully, this approach could disclose a significantly different "reasonable belief" from that derived by application of the Keeton formulation — the objectively determinable reasonable expectations of the insured.

Roger C. Henderson, The Doctrine of Reasonable Expectations in Insurance Law After Two Decades, 51 Ohio St. L.J. 823, 846-847 (1990). See Sutton v. Banner Life Ins. Co., 686 A.2d 1045 (D.C. 1996) (§211(3) applied to insurer's defense of suicide to claim under life insurance policy; question of fact exists as to whether insurer should have known that insured would not have agreed to running of new two-year suicide period when insured applied for increase in coverage).

4. *Defining "adhesion contract."* Although developed in the case law as a doctrine relating specifically to insurance contracts, the doctrine of reasonable expectations appears potentially applicable to adhesion contracts generally. The Restatement formulation, although it narrows the doctrine by focusing on the expectations of the drafter, broadens the principle to cover all standardized contracts, not just insurance agreements. The court in *C & J Fertilizer* cites and quotes from a number of the leading articles discussing contracts of adhesion, including Professor Kessler's classic 1943 essay. Attempts to define the adhesion contract usually include references to the employment of a standardized form and some degree of imbalance of bargaining power, involving a "take-it-or-leave-it" approach, that is to say: "a standardized contract, which, imposed and drafted by the party of superior bargaining strength, relegates to the subscribing party only the opportunity to adhere to the contract or reject it." Neal v. State Farm Ins. Cos., 10 Cal. Rptr. 781, 784 (Ct. App. 1961) (Tobriner, J.).

Professor Todd Rakoff offered a similar analysis of what constitutes a contract of adhesion, but also noted that the contracts normally involve a drafting party who participates in numerous such transactions, while the adhering party enters into few of them, and that the adhering party's principal obligation is usually the payment of money. Todd D. Rakoff, Contracts of

Adhesion: An Essay in Reconstruction, 96 Harv. L. Rev. 1173, 1176-1177 (1983). Professor Rakoff argued that underlying the issue of enforceability of contracts of adhesion is the allocation of power and freedom between commercial organizations and individuals. Viewed from this perspective, Rakoff concluded that contracts of adhesion should be presumptively unenforceable. Rakoff went on to propose a specific framework by which judges could implement the general principles he advocated, including imposition of the burden of proof on the drafter of an adhesion contract to show the reasonableness of the provision in question. Id. at 1248-1261.

5. *Relationship to unconscionability doctrine.* As we shall see in Chapter 7, the employment of standardized forms and the absence of bargaining over terms may also be the first step toward application of the doctrine of unconscionability. Unconscionability goes beyond interpretation, however, and involves either judicial invalidation of provisions of a written contract or imposition of terms different from those stated in the contract, without requiring ambiguity or departure from reasonable expectations.

B. THE PAROL EVIDENCE RULE

We saw in Chapter 2 that from a very early time the common law established a link between the enforceability of a promise and compliance by the promisor with certain formalities when the promise was made. (Recall the action of covenant, which was used to enforce written promises made under seal.) Over time the seal has declined in importance, but contract law continues in a number of ways to attach significance to the execution of an agreement in writing. One of these is the preference for agreement expressed in a formal writing, over various other modes of expression, both oral and written. This preference is implemented by a rule of contract law commonly referred to as the "parol evidence rule." (Note: *parol*, not *parole*, which is a different legal term.) As use of the word "parol" suggests, this rule is usually thought of as involving the admissibility of evidence of oral agreements, but it may apply as well to various types of written evidence.

Unless the parties to a legal dispute are able to reduce their differences to ones solely of law rather than fact, resolution of that dispute by the litigation process will require a trial on the merits, at which the disputed issues of fact can be considered and decided by the trier of fact (which may be a jury or a judge). In the course of that trial, the parties are likely to offer a wide variety of evidence on those issues. Some of this evidence will be in the form of oral testimony by persons who have firsthand knowledge of the facts at issue, while some of it will be evidence in written form — letters or memoranda, perhaps, or business records. Under the rules of evidence commonly applied in American courts, any evidence to be prima facie admissible into court must be "relevant" — rationally probative of some fact material to the parties' dispute. (Thus, in a contract dispute, the plaintiff's testimony that she had a conversation with the defendant in which they mutually agreed to an exchange of performances would ordinarily be relevant and admissible in a case where the plaintiff sought to enforce that agreement while the defendant denied making it.) Relevant evidence may, however, be excluded by some other rule of evidence based on the likelihood that evidence of a given type will be misleading or otherwise untrustworthy. The rules of evidence are of considerable theoretical difficulty and immense practical importance, and even a nodding acquaintance with them involves considerable study, as you will probably discover later in your law school career.

Despite its commonly employed appellation, the "parol evidence rule" is considered by authorities on evidence and contracts alike to be not a rule of evidence, but a rule of "substantive" law. E. Allan Farnsworth, Contracts §7.2 (4th ed. 2004). This distinction is for our purposes not very important, although it does have some practical consequences. For example, under ordinary rules of evidence, the right to object to inadmissible evidence is lost if not asserted at the time when the evidence is offered. This is not necessarily the case with evidence admitted in violation of the parol evidence rule, however. See Estate of Parker v. Dorchak, 673 So. 2d 1379 (Miss. 1996) (since parol evidence rule is matter of substantive law, evidence admitted in violation of that rule, even though without objection, should be disregarded if objection is made before case is submitted to trier of fact).

The parol evidence rule can be found in various sources, and the wordings may differ somewhat. E.g., Restatement (Second) of Contracts §§209-218; Uniform Commercial Code §2-202. The gist of it can be stated thus: When the parties to a contract have mutually agreed to incorporate (or "integrate") a final version of their entire agreement in a writing, neither party will be permitted to contradict or supplement that written agreement with "extrinsic" evidence (written or oral) of prior agreements or negotiations between them. When the writing is intended to be final only with respect to a part of their agreement, the writing may not be contradicted, but it may be supplemented by such extrinsic evidence. Excellent discussions of the parol evidence rule can be found in E. Allan Farnsworth, Contracts §§7.2-7.6 (4th ed. 2004), and in Joseph M. Perillo, Contracts §§3.2-3.8 (7th ed. 2014). An interesting account of the historical origins of the rule, as well as a provocative exploration of its implications for present-day contract law, can be found in Hila Keren, Textual Harassment: A New Historicist Reappraisal of the Parol Evidence Rule with Gender in Mind, 13 Am. U. J. Gender Soc. Pol'y & L. 251 (2005).

In order to understand the working of the parol evidence rule, it is necessary first to apprehend its basic function: The rule does not define what evidence is affirmatively admissible, it only operates to *exclude* evidence — evidence that would otherwise be admissible as rationally probative of some fact at issue. If the parol evidence rule applies at all in a given situation, it has the effect of preventing one party from introducing into court extrinsic (or "collateral") evidence of matters not contained in the written agreement between the parties (hence, "extrinsic" to it), where that evidence is offered to supplement or contradict the written agreement.

To begin our examination of the parol evidence rule in action, let us first envision the procedural setting in which a parol evidence issue arises. Suppose the owner of an apartment building enters into a written contract with a painting contractor calling for the painting of the "interior of the building, including walls, ceilings, and trim." Later, a dispute develops about whether the contract requires the contractor to paint the common areas (hallways, etc.). When the parties are unable to resolve the dispute through negotiation, the owner discharges the contractor, who then brings suit against the owner claiming that the discharge constitutes a breach of contract. At trial the contractor offers to introduce evidence (either oral testimony or correspondence) that the owner was informed (at or before the time of contracting) that the contractor's bid for the work did not include common areas, and the owner agreed to that. The owner objects to such evidence being considered by the fact finder because of the parol evidence rule. If the matter were being tried before a jury, the judge would hold an "in camera" hearing, that is, out of the presence of the jury, in which the party offering parol evidence would outline what the evidence would show, both parties would make legal arguments about the application of the parol evidence rule, and the judge would decide if the evidence were admissible under the rule. (Such in camera hearings are not unique to contract law; they are employed whenever evidence of doubtful admissibility is being offered by one of the parties. Another common example is the determination of the admissibility of an alleged confession by a defendant in a criminal case.) If the matter were being tried by a judge sitting without a jury, the in camera hearing would be unnecessary, but the judge would still be required to rule on the admissibility of the evidence.

We will see that both courts and commentators differ widely over the scope and application of the parol evidence rule. The following case illustrates the classical approach.

Thompson v. Libby

Minnesota Supreme Court 34 Minn. 374, 26 N.W. 1 (1885)

MITCHELL, J. The plaintiff being the owner of a quantity of logs marked "H. C. A.," cut in the winters of 1882 and 1883, and lying in the Mississippi river, or on its banks, above Minneapolis, defendant and the plaintiff, through his agent, D. S. Mooers, having fully agreed on the terms of a sale and purchase of the logs referred to, executed the following written agreement:

AGREEMENT.

Hastings, Minn., June 1, 1883.

I have this day sold to R. C. Libby, of Hastings, Minn., all my logs marked "H. C. A.," cut in the winters of 1882 and 1883, for ten dollars a thousand feet, boom scale at Minneapolis, Minnesota. Payments cash as fast as scale bills are produced.

[Signed] *J. H. Thompson,*
Per *D. S. Mooers.*
R. C. Libby

This action having been brought for the purchase-money, the defendant — having pleaded a warranty of the quality of the logs, alleged to have been made at the time of the sale, and a breach of it — offered on the trial oral testimony to prove the warranty, which was admitted, over the objection of plaintiff that it was incompetent to prove a verbal warranty, the contract of sale being in writing. This raises the only point in the case.

No ground was laid for the reformation of the written contract, and any charge of fraud on part of plaintiff or his agent in making the sale was on the trial expressly disclaimed. No rule is more familiar than that "parol contemporaneous evidence is inadmissible to contradict or vary the terms of a valid written instrument," and yet none has given rise to more misapprehension as to its application. It is a rule founded on the obvious inconvenience and injustice that would result if matters in writing, made with consideration and deliberation, and intended to embody the entire agreement of the parties, were liable to be controlled by what Lord Coke expressively calls "the uncertain testimony of slippery memory." Hence, where the parties have deliberately put their engagements into writing in such terms as to import a legal obligation, without any uncertainty as to the object or extent of such engagement, it is conclusively presumed that the whole engagement of the parties, and the manner and extent of their undertaking, was reduced to writing. 1 Greenl. Ev. §275. Of course, the rule presupposes that the parties intended to have the terms of their complete agreement embraced in the writing, and hence it does not apply where the writing is incomplete on its face and does not purport to contain the whole agreement, as in the case of mere bills of parcels, and the like.

But in what manner shall it be ascertained whether the parties intended to express the whole of their agreement in writing? It is sometimes loosely stated that where the whole contract be not reduced to writing, parol evidence may be admitted to prove the part omitted. But to allow a party to lay the foundation for such parol evidence by oral testimony that only part of the agreement was reduced to writing, and then prove by parol the part omitted, would be to work in a circle, and to permit the very evil which the rule was designed to prevent. The only criterion of the completeness of the written contract as a full expression of the agreement of the parties is the writing itself. If it imports on its face to be a complete expression of the whole agreement, — that is, contains such language as imports a complete legal obligation, — it is to be presumed that the parties have introduced into it every material item and term; and parol evidence cannot be admitted to add another term to the agreement, although the writing contains nothing on the particular one to which the parol evidence is directed. The rule forbids to add by parol where the writing is silent, as well as to vary where it speaks, — 2 Phil. Evidence, (Cow. & H. Notes,) 669; Naumberg v. Young, 44 N.J. Law, 331; Hei v. Heller, 53 Wis. 415, — and the law controlling the operation of a written contract becomes a part of it, and cannot be varied by parol any more than what is written. 2 Phil. Ev. (Cow. & H. Notes,) 668; La Farge v. Rickert, 5 Wend. 187; Creery v. Holly, 14 Wend. 26; Stone v. Harmon, 31 Minn. 512.

The written agreement in the case at bar, as it appears on its face, in connection with the law controlling its construction and operation, purports to be a complete expression of the whole agreement of the parties as to the sale and purchase of these logs, solemnly executed by both parties. There is nothing on its face (and this is a question of law for the court) to indicate that it is a mere informal and incomplete memorandum. Parol evidence of extrinsic facts and circumstances would, if necessary, be admissible, as it always is, to apply the contract to its subject-matter, or in order to a more perfect understanding of its language. But in that case such evidence is used, not to contradict or vary the written instrument, but to aid, uphold, and enforce it as it stands. The language of this contract "imports a legal obligation, without any uncertainty as to its object or the extent of the engagement," and therefore "it must be conclusively presumed that the whole engagement of the parties, and the manner and extent of the undertaking, was reduced to writing." No new term, forming a mere incident to or part of the contract of sale, can be added by parol. . . .

. . . [W]e are referred to a few cases which seem to hold that parol evidence of a warranty is admissible on the ground that a warranty is collateral to the contract of sale, and that the rule does not exclude parol evidence of matters collateral to the subject of the written agreement. It seems to us that this is based upon a misapprehension as to the sense in which the term "collateral" is used in the rule invoked. There are a great many matters that, in a general sense, may be considered collateral to the contract; for example, in the case of leases, covenants for repairs, improvements, payment of taxes, etc., are, in a sense, collateral to a demise of the premises. But parol evidence of these would not be admissible to add to the terms of a written lease. So, in a sense, a warranty is collateral to a contract of sale, for the title would pass without a warranty. It is also collateral in the sense that its breach is no ground for a rescission of the contract by the vendor [*sic*; vendee?], but that he must resort to his action on the warranty for damages. But, when made, a warranty is a part of the contract of sale. The common sense of men would say, and correctly so, that when, on a sale of personal property, a warranty is given, it is one of the terms of the sale, and not a separate and independent contract. To justify the admission of a parol promise by one of the parties to a written contract, on the ground that it is collateral, the promise must relate to a subject distinct from that to which the writing relates. Dutton v. Gerrish, 9 Cush. 89; Naumberg v. Young, supra; 2 Taylor, Ev. §1038. See Lindley v. Lacey, 34 Law J., C. P., 7.

We have carefully examined all the cases cited in the quite exhaustive brief of counsel for defendant, and find but very few that are at all in conflict with the views already expressed, and these few do not commend themselves to our judgment. Our conclusion therefore is that the court erred in admitting parol evidence of a warranty, and therefore the order refusing a new trial must be reversed.

NOTES AND QUESTIONS

1. *Rationale for parol evidence rule.* The court states that the parol evidence rule is "founded on the obvious inconvenience and injustice" that would result if extrinsic evidence were admissible to contradict or vary the terms of a written agreement. What specific "inconvenience" and "injustice" can result from the introduction of extrinsic evidence?

2. *Meaning of "integration."* As the *Thompson* court indicates, at the core of the parol evidence rule is the concept that parties typically arrive at contract terms through a process of preliminary negotiations and then produce a writing containing the final terms that have been mutually adopted. (As you are well aware, however, adhesion contracts do not fit this pattern.) The final writing is then considered the best evidence of the contract and displaces any earlier agreement or proposals, whether oral or written. See E. Allan Farnsworth, Contracts §7.2, at 418 (4th ed. 2004) (the useful function of the parol evidence rule is to replace negotiations and superseded understandings with a final authoritative statement of the agreement). Both classical and modern contract law use the term *complete integration* to refer to a writing that is intended to be a final and exclusive expression of the agreement of the parties. First Restatement §228; Restatement (Second) §210. Both classical and modern contract law also recognize the possibility of a *partial integration*, a writing that is intended to be final but not complete because it deals with some but not all aspects of a transaction between the parties. The correct application of the parol evidence rule thus requires that the court first determine whether the writing in question is intended to be a final expression of the parties agreement and, if so, whether it is a complete or partial statement of the contract terms. How would you assess the writing in *Thompson* in light of these standards?

3. *Determining integration.* The *Thompson* court states that the written contract does not appear on its face to be either an "informal or incomplete" memorandum, and therefore the court concludes that the writing is a completely integrated agreement. The court's determination is based on an approach often identified with Professor Williston, who argued that the question of integration must be determined from the "four corners" of the writing without resort to extrinsic evidence. 4 Williston on Contracts §633, at 1015. Moreover, Williston asserted that the inclusion in the writing of a "merger clause" would conclusively establish that the writing was integrated. Id. at 1014. A merger clause states that the writing is intended to be final and complete; all prior understandings are deemed to have been "merged" into or superseded by the final writing. The following is an example of a typical merger clause:

> *Entire Agreement.* This document constitutes the entire agreement of the parties and there are no representations, warranties, or agreements other than those contained in this document.

A substantial number of jurisdictions still generally adhere to the "four corners" approach to determining integration and accord conclusive or nearly conclusive weight to the presence of a merger clause. See, e.g., RBS Citizens Bank, N.A. v. Purther, 22 F. Supp. 3d 747 (E.D. Mich. 2014) (under Michigan law, written integration clause is conclusive evidence that the parties intended the document to be the final and complete expression of their agreement unless agreement is obviously incomplete on its face); Fontbank, Inc. v. CompuServe, Inc., 742 N.E.2d 674 (Ohio Ct. App. 2000) (contract which appears complete and unambiguous on its face will be presumed final and complete expression of agreement; presumption is strongest where writing contains merger or integration clause). What policy considerations could be used to justify the "four corners" approach to the parol evidence rule?

Not surprisingly, perhaps, many other courts have adopted an alternative method to determining integration which more readily looks beyond the contents of the writing. The central precept for this contextual approach is reflected in Restatement (Second) §210, Comment *b*: "[A] writing cannot of itself prove its own completeness, and wide latitude must be allowed for inquiry into circumstances bearing on the intention of the parties." This approach is also frequently identified with Professor Corbin. A finding of integration should always depend on the actual intent of the parties, according to Corbin, and a court should consider evidence of all the facts and circumstances surrounding the execution of the contract, as well as the writing, in uncovering that intent. 3 Corbin on Contracts §§578, 582, at 411-412, 448-450 (1960). In this approach, a merger clause will not be solely determinative of the issue of integration. See, e.g., St. James Mut. Homes v. Andrade, 951 A.2d 766 (D.C. Ct. App. 2008) (agreement between cooperative association and one of its members not fully integrated despite presence of merger clause; silence on material point requires court to look outside the writing); Morgan Bldgs. and Spas, Inc. v. Humane Soc'y of Southeast Texas, 249 S.W.3d 480 (Tex. Ct. App. 2008) (written agreement between customer and building manufacturer was only partially integrated, despite merger clause, permitting plaintiff to recover for defects in completed building). See also Restatement (Second) §216, Comment *e* (merger clause does not control question of integration); UCC §2-202, Comment 1(a) (rejects any assumption that writing that is final on some terms is necessarily exclusive). Professor Farnsworth reported that the trend among courts favors the Corbin-Restatement (Second) approach to determining integration. E. Allan Farnsworth, Contracts §7.3, at 419 (4th ed. 2004). Professor Linzer, however, more recently expressed doubts about the accuracy of that assessment. See Peter Linzer, 6 Corbin on Contracts § 25.7 (Joseph M. Perillo ed., 2010).

The court in Thompson v. Libby indicated that not all extrinsic evidence would be excluded by the parol evidence rule, even in the case of a fully integrated written agreement. Such evidence would be admissible, the court indicated, "if necessary . . . to apply the contract to its subject-matter, or in order to a more perfect understanding of its language." In addition, the *Thompson* court alluded in passing to the existence of certain exceptions to that rule. "No ground was laid for the reformation of the written contract, and any charge of fraud on part of plaintiff or his agent in making the sale was . . . expressly disclaimed." Although the various exceptions have not yet reached the point where they "swallow up" the rule, they at least are so numerous and collectively so broad that the parol evidence rule has become — even more than the statute of frauds — a rule that can be understood only in light of its exceptions.

The parol evidence rule does not apply to exclude evidence offered to interpret or explain the meaning of the agreement. The parol evidence rule, as we have seen, applies only to written agreements that are in some sense intended by the parties to be a final expression of their agreement, or "integrated," either "partially" or "completely." If found to be a partial integration, the writing may not be contradicted by extrinsic evidence, but it may be supplemented by additional *consistent* terms. If the writing is a complete integration, then not only may it not be contradicted, it may not even be supplemented. Restatement (Second) §§210, 213; UCC §2-202. Whatever the degree of integration, however — partial, complete, or not at all — a written agreement may, as the *Thompson* court suggested, always be *explained* by extrinsic evidence for purposes of interpretation. Restatement (Second) §214(c), and Comment *b*.

To illustrate these principles in application, let us return to the facts of Thompson v. Libby. Given the written agreement which existed in that case, extrinsic evidence would not have been admissible to prove that the agreed-on price for the wood was $8 a thousand feet, rather than $10, for this would have been regarded as a "contradictory" term. Nor would it have been permissible to show by extrinsic evidence that the seller was obliged not only to deliver the logs but also to mill them into planks; even if this were seen as a "consistent additional term," rather than a contradictory one, the Thompson-Libby agreement was apparently regarded by the court as fully integrated, thus precluding the showing of additional terms (whether contradictory or not). It should, however, have been permissible to show by extrinsic evidence of the parties' agreement what periods of time were intended to be included in the phrase "winters of 1882 and 1883," or what was meant by the term "boom scale," because such evidence would have served merely to "explain" the agreement. (On those points, evidence of trade usage might have been relevant as well.) Classical and modern courts might differ, however, on the scope of this latter exception. Classical courts generally admitted parol evidence for explanatory purposes only if the writing appeared on its face to be ambiguous, while modern courts are more likely to admit parol evidence to show that the language used in the agreement has a special meaning, even if that language does not appear unclear merely from an inspection of the writing. Restatement (Second) §214, Comment *b*. (Recall our discussion of patent and latent ambiguity after the *Frigaliment* case above.)

Explanation or interpretation of the agreement may be in practice the most important of the reasons why extrinsic evidence may be admitted despite the parol evidence rule, but it only begins the catalog of that rule's exceptions. The following are some of the other commonly accepted ones:

The parol evidence rule does not apply to agreements, whether oral or written, made after the execution of the writing. Litman v. Massachusetts Mut. Life Ins. Co., 739 F.2d 1549, 1558 (11th Cir. 1984) (evidence of subsequent oral modification of plaintiff's written employment contract not barred by parol evidence rule; later written amendments not fully integrated so as to exclude proof of asserted oral agreement); John E. Murray, Jr., Murray on Contracts §85[A], at 424 (5th ed. 2011) (noting that "innumerable cases" support principle that parol evidence rule has no application to subsequent agreements or modifications). Suppose Thompson and Libby, having made the initial contract in June 1883, had orally agreed in August 1883 that payment for the logs would be made partly in cash and partly by promissory notes. In the event of subsequent litigation between them, the parol evidence rule would not bar testimony as to this later oral agreement.

The parol evidence rule does not apply to evidence offered to show that effectiveness of the agreement was subject to an oral condition precedent. Brown Dev. Corp. v. Hemond, 956 A.2d 104 (Me. 2008) (summary judgment for buyer reversed where seller alleged that buyer's acquisition of an additional lot from a third party was oral condition precedent to seller's obligation to transfer land; contract was not fully integrated, alleged oral condition did not contradict written terms, and thus evidence of oral condition was not barred by parol evidence rule); Restatement (Second) §217. But cf. Torres v. D'Alesso, 910 N.Y.S.2d 1 (N.Y. App. Div. 2010) (oral condition precedent exception will not be applied where agreement contains broad merger clause and asserted condition would contradict language of written agreement). Suppose Libby had told Thompson (or his agent) when the contract was signed that the agreement was contingent upon the local bank's approval of a loan for which Libby had applied, and about which he would hear within a week. If the bank had denied the loan, the parol evidence rule would not bar evidence of Libby's oral statement, even though the writing was absolute on its face, because the evidence would establish an oral condition to the effectiveness of the agreement.

The parol evidence rule does not apply to evidence offered to show that the agreement is invalid for any reason, such as fraud, duress, undue influence, incapacity, mistake, or illegality. Restatement (Second) §214(d). This exception can be justified theoretically on the basis that such invalidating factors result in what is apparently a contract being in legal contemplation not a "contract" at all and thus not entitled to the benefit of the parol evidence rule. It also can be justified on the practical ground that while a written agreement may in fact be "a forgery, a joke, a sham, or an agreement without consideration, or it may be voidable for fraud, duress, mistake, or the like, or it may be illegal," none of these things is likely to appear on the face of the document. Restatement (Second) §214, Comment *c*. To apply the parol evidence rule to exclude such evidence would in effect create a roadblock to the application of many important policies of the law. To continue our series of illustrations, suppose that when Thompson and Libby entered into their contract, they both believed that 20,000 feet of logs had been cut, when in fact the true number was closer to 5,000. In that case, evidence of their discussions about the quantity to be sold should be admissible as bearing on the possible defense of mutual mistake of fact.

The case of fraud is a little more problematic, however. Some courts would limit the fraud exception to cases of "fraud in the execution" (sometimes referred to as "fraud in the factum"). For example, suppose Thompson asks Libby to sign what he says is a receipt for logs delivered, but it's really a "contract" for the sale of more logs. See DeArmitt v. New York Life Ins. Co., 73 A.3d 578 (Pa. Super. Ct. 2013) (under fraud in the execution exception to parol evidence rule plaintiffs could offer evidence that agent misrepresented that product being purchased was an investment annuity when it actually was a standard life insurance policy; plaintiffs had stated they did not want a life insurance policy). Most courts, however, will extend the fraud exception also to instances of "fraud in the inducement" — misrepresentations of fact that induce the other party to enter into the contract. Poeppel v. Lester, 827 N.W.2d 580 (S.D. 2013) (substantial majority of jurisdictions follow the traditional view that parol evidence rule is inapplicable in cases of fraudulent inducement even when writing is completely integrated or contains a merger clause). However, some courts will prohibit the introduction of parol evidence to support a claim of fraud in the inducement if the alleged misrepresentation directly contradicts a term in the writing. This limitation is discussed in the *Sherrodd* case later in this chapter and also in the section on misrepresentation in Chapter 7. Suppose Libby sought to show that in order to induce him to sign the contract, Thompson had represented that to his own personal knowledge at least half of the cut logs were good quality hardwood, while it later appeared that only a quarter or less met that description. Many courts would view evidence of that statement by Thompson as admissible under the fraud exception, even though as you can see it comes very close to the claim that Libby tried unsuccessfully to make in the actual case.

The parol evidence rule does not apply to evidence that is offered to establish a right to an "equitable" remedy, such as "reformation" of the contract. Restatement (Second) §214(e). If one party can establish that a part of the agreement was inadvertently omitted from the writing due to some mistake (perhaps the error of a "scrivener," a secretary, or even a computer printer), that party may seek judicial reformation of the agreement — a court order declaring that the mistakenly omitted provision will be treated in law as part of the agreement. Generally, however, a writing may be reformed in this fashion only if it is shown by "clear and convincing evidence" that the parties really did intend their written agreement to contain the term in question. Kimmel & Silverman, P.C. v. Porro, 53 F. Supp. 3d 325 (D. Mass. 2014) (parol evidence rule allows extrinsic evidence to prove parties did not intend terms in settlement agreement to release claim against former attorneys, but mutual mistake in drafting must be shown by clear and convincing evidence). In

Thompson, the defendant Libby might have sought to have the agreement reformed to include the warranty of quality, on grounds that it was accidentally omitted, but he probably would have been unable to meet this higher standard of proof — indeed, the court's opinion suggests he did not even attempt to do so.

The parol evidence rule does not apply to evidence introduced to establish a "collateral" agreement between the parties. In *Thompson*, the court held that evidence of an oral warranty as to quality was not admissible under the collateral agreement exception because that exception only applied to an agreement about a "subject distinct from that to which the writing relates." By the time the first Restatement was drafted in the 1930s, a growing number of courts were adopting a more flexible approach to the parol evidence rule than that illustrated by the court in *Thompson*. Frequently, these courts relied on the collateral agreement exception to justify the admission of parol evidence, even when the evidence did not relate to a separate or distinct transaction. See Peter Linzer, 6 Corbin on Contracts §25.9 (Joseph M. Perillo ed., 2010). The Restatement (Second) continues the collateral agreement exception in §216(2), which provides that an agreement will not be regarded as fully integrated if the parties have made a consistent additional agreement which is either agreed to for separate consideration or is "such a term as in the circumstances might naturally be omitted from the writing." As Professor Linzer has noted, if there is separate consideration for the oral "collateral agreement," then it is a separate contract and the parol evidence rule should be irrelevant. On the other hand, if there is not separate consideration from that in the written contract, then the "collateral agreement" notion is indistinguishable from the question whether the contract was intended to be a complete integration. Id.

The Uniform Commercial Code Comments express a somewhat similar approach regarding admissibility: Comment 3 to §2-202 indicates that "consistent additional terms" should be excluded under §2-202(b) only where the parties intend the writing to be a complete and exclusive statement of all terms (a complete integration) or the court concludes that if such terms had actually been agreed upon they would "certainly have been included in the document." If the Thompson-Libby contract were made today, it would as a sale of goods be subject to Article 2 of the UCC; on the facts of *Thompson*, would buyer Libby have fared better under §2-202? Suppose that Libby were also to allege that Thompson had promised at the time their written agreement was signed that if Libby would buy the logs, Thompson would mill them into planks for Libby at Thompson's sawmill for a discounted price (two-thirds of Thompson's usual charge for that service), and that Thompson had later refused to honor that promise. Would evidence of the oral milling agreement be barred by the parol evidence rule? See §2-202 Comment 3.

Taylor v. State Farm Mutual Automobile Insurance Co.

Supreme Court of Arizona, en banc 175 Ariz. 148, 854 P.2d 1134 (1993)

FELDMAN, Chief Justice.

Bobby Sid Taylor petitions us to review a decision reversing a jury verdict in his favor in a bad faith claim against State Farm Mutual Automobile Insurance Co. He argues that the court of appeals erroneously held that his bad faith claim was barred by a release he signed in 1981. We granted review because the case raises important issues in the area of contract and insurance law. . . .

FACTS AND PROCEDURAL HISTORY

This insurance bad faith action arises out of an accident that occurred approximately sixteen years ago. Many of the facts are undisputed. The accident involved three vehicles — one occupied by Anne Ring and passenger James Rivers, the second by Douglas Wistrom, and the third by Bobby Sid Taylor. Ring, Rivers, and Taylor all were injured. The facts surrounding the accident are set forth in Ring v. Taylor, 141 Ariz. 56, 59, 685 P.2d 121, 124 (Ct. App. 1984). Ring, her husband, and Rivers filed actions against Taylor and Wistrom. These actions were consolidated before trial. Taylor's insurer, State Farm, retained attorney Leroy W. Hofmann to defend Taylor. Taylor also personally retained attorney Norman Bruce Randall, who filed a counterclaim against Ring for Taylor's damages. Taylor, therefore, was represented by both Randall and Hofmann in the matter. Because the Rings and Rivers agreed with Wistrom to a stipulated judgment and covenant not to execute, Taylor was the only party vulnerable to the Ring/Rivers claims. At trial, the Rings and Rivers obtained combined verdicts against Taylor for approximately $2.5 million in excess of his insurance policy limits. The court of appeals affirmed these judgments. *Taylor,* 141 Ariz. at 59, 71, 685 P.2d at 124, 136.

The Rings eventually settled with State Farm. Taylor, however, sued State Farm for bad faith seeking damages for the excess Rivers judgment, claiming, among other things, that State Farm improperly failed to settle the Rivers matter within policy limits. State Farm moved for summary judgment, asserting that Taylor relinquished his bad faith claim when, in 1981, he signed a release drafted by attorney Randall in exchange for State Farm's payment of $15,000 in uninsured motorist benefits.[1] Taylor also moved for partial summary judgment, seeking a ruling that, as a matter of law, the release did not preclude his bad faith claim. The judge denied both motions, finding that the release was ambiguous and that therefore parol evidence was admissible at trial to aid in interpreting the release. A second judge, who presided at trial, also denied State Farm's motion for directed verdict based on the release. Having been instructed

1. Because Wistrom was uninsured, Randall believed that Taylor might be entitled to recover for his injuries under the uninsured motorist provisions of Taylor's policy. State Farm, however, disputes Taylor's entitlement to these benefits. In any event, Randall prepared a release as part of the transaction. It is this release that is at issue. The extent of State Farm's participation in its drafting is disputed.

on the interpretation of the release, the jury returned a verdict in favor of Taylor for compensatory damages of $2.1 million. The court also awarded Taylor $300,000 in attorney fees.

The court of appeals reversed, holding that the release agreement was not ambiguous and therefore the judge erred by admitting parol evidence to vary its terms. Taylor v. State Farm Mut. Auto. Ins. Co., No. 1 CA-CV 9908 (Sep. 17, 1991) (mem. dec.). Based on the agreement's "four corners," the court held that "it clearly release[d] all policy contract rights, claims, and causes of action that Taylor has or may have against State Farm." Id. at 20. According to the court, because the release should have been strictly enforced, there was no basis for Taylor's bad faith claim. Id. We believe the court's decision both incorrectly applies settled legal principles and raises unsettled issues of contract interpretation.

DISCUSSION

Much of the dispute in this case centers on the events that surround the drafting of the release and the inferences that can be drawn from those events. As noted, the trial court found that the release was ambiguous and admitted extrinsic evidence to aid in its interpretation. The court of appeals found no ambiguity. *Taylor,* mem. dec. at 20, 23. In resolving this issue, we must address the scope and application of the parol evidence rule in Arizona and decide whether, under these facts, the trial court properly admitted extrinsic evidence to interpret the release.

A. Legal Principles

The application of the parol evidence rule has been the subject of much controversy and scholarly debate. . . . "When two parties have made a contract and have expressed it in a writing to which they have both assented as the complete and accurate integration of that contract, evidence, whether parol or otherwise, of antecedent understandings and negotiations will not be admitted for the purpose of varying or contradicting the writing." 3 Arthur L. Corbin, Corbin on Contracts §573, at 357 (1960) ("Corbin"). . . . Antecedent understandings and negotiations may be admissible, however, for purposes other than varying or contradicting a final agreement. 3 Corbin §576, at 384. Interpretation is one such purpose. 3 Corbin §579, at 412-13; Restatement (Second) of Contracts §214(c) & cmt. b (1979) ("Restatement").

Interpretation is the process by which we determine the meaning of words in a contract. See Restatement §200. Generally, and in Arizona, a court will attempt to enforce a contract according to the parties' intent. . . . "The primary and ultimate purpose of interpretation" is to discover that intent and to make it effective. 3 Corbin §572B, at 421 (1992 Supp.). The court must decide what evidence, other than the writing, is admissible in the interpretation process, bearing in mind that the parol evidence rule prohibits extrinsic evidence to vary or contradict, but not to interpret, the agreement. See 3 Corbin §543, at 130-34. These substantive principles are clear, but their application has been troublesome.

1. Restrictive View

Under the restrictive "plain meaning" view of the parol evidence rule, evidence of prior negotiations may be used for interpretation only upon a finding that some language in the contract is unclear, ambiguous, or vague. E. Allan Farnsworth, Farnsworth on Contracts §7.12, at 270 (1990) ("Farnsworth"). Under this approach, "if a writing, or the term in question, appears to be plain and unambiguous on its face, its meaning must be determined from the four corners of the instrument without resort to extrinsic evidence of any nature." Calamari & Perillo, supra §3-10, at 166-67. . . . Thus, if the judge finds from the face of a document that it conveys only one meaning, parol evidence is neither considered nor admitted for any purpose. The danger here, of course, is that what appears plain and clear to one judge may not be so plain to another (as in this case), and the judge's decision, uninformed by context, may not reflect the intent of the parties.

2. Corbin View

Under the view embraced by Professor Corbin and the Second Restatement, there is no need to make a preliminary finding of ambiguity before the *judge considers* extrinsic evidence. 3 Corbin §542, at 100-05 (1992 Supp.); Restatement §212 cmt. b; Farnsworth §7.12, at 272. . . . Instead, the court considers all of the proffered evidence to determine its relevance to the parties' intent and then applies the parol evidence rule to exclude from the fact finder's consideration only the evidence that contradicts or varies the meaning of the agreement. 3 Corbin §542, at 100-01 (1992 Supp.). According to Corbin, the court cannot apply the parol evidence rule without first understanding the meaning the parties intended to give the agreement. Id. To understand the agreement, the judge cannot be restricted to the four corners of the document. Again, even under the Corbin view, the court can admit evidence for *interpretation* but must stop short of *contradiction*. See 3 Corbin §574, at 371-72. . . .

3. Arizona View

Writing for a unanimous court in Smith v. Melson, Inc., 135 Ariz. 119, 121-22, 659 P.2d 1264, 1266-67 (1983), Chief Justice Holohan expressly committed Arizona to the Corbin view of contract interpretation. . . . We have held that a court may consider surrounding circumstances, including negotiation, prior understandings, and subsequent conduct, but have not elaborated much further. . . .

According to Corbin, the proper analysis has two steps. First, the court *considers* the evidence that is alleged to determine the extent of integration, illuminate the meaning of the contract language, or demonstrate the parties' intent. See 3 Corbin §542, at 100-01 (1992 Supp.). The court's function at this stage is to eliminate the evidence that has no probative value in determining the parties' intent. Id. The second step involves "finalizing" the court's understanding of the contract. Id. at 100. Here, the parol evidence rule applies and *precludes admission* of the extrinsic evidence that would vary or contradict the meaning of the written words. Id.

Even during the first step, the judge may properly decide not to consider certain offered evidence because it does not aid in interpretation but, instead, varies or contradicts the written words. See id. at 101. This might occur when the court decides that the asserted meaning of the contract language is so unreasonable or extraordinary that it is improbable that the parties actually subscribed to the interpretation asserted by the proponent of the extrinsic evidence. See id. "The more bizarre and unusual an asserted interpretation is, the more convincing must be the testimony that supports it." 3 Corbin §579, at 420. At what point a judge stops "listening to testimony that white is black and that a dollar is fifty cents is a matter for sound judicial discretion and common sense." Id.

When interpreting a contract, nevertheless, it is fundamental that a court attempt to "ascertain and give effect to the intention of the parties at the time the contract was made if at all possible." . . . If, for example, parties use language that is mutually intended to have a special meaning, and that meaning is proved by credible evidence, a court is obligated to enforce the agreement according to the parties' intent, even if the language ordinarily might mean something different. See Restatement §212 cmt. b, illus. 3 & 4. The judge, therefore, must avoid the often irresistible temptation to automatically interpret contract language as he or she would understand the words. This natural tendency is sometimes disguised in the judge's ruling that contract language is "unambiguous." See 3 Corbin §543A, at 159 (1992 Supp.). Words, however, are seldom so clear that they "apply themselves to the subject matter." Restatement §214 cmt. b. On occasion, exposition of the evidence regarding the intention of the parties will illuminate plausible interpretations other than the one that is facially obvious to the judge. See id. Thus, ambiguity determined by the judge's view of "clear meaning" is a troublesome concept that often obstructs the court's proper and primary function in this area — to enforce the meaning intended by the contracting parties. See 3 Corbin §542, at 122-24. . . .

Recognizing these problems, we are hesitant to endorse, without explanation, the often repeated and usually over-simplified construct that ambiguity must exist before parol evidence is admissible. We have previously criticized the ambiguity prerequisite in the context of non-negotiated agreements. See State Farm Mut. Auto. Ins. Co. v. Wilson, 162 Ariz. 251, 257, 782 P.2d 727, 733 (1989) (recognizing the lack of logic in requiring ambiguity, which may be fortuitous, to prove the true terms of an agreement). . . . Moreover, a contract may be susceptible to multiple interpretations and therefore truly ambiguous yet, given the context in which it was negotiated, not susceptible to a clearly contradicting and wholly unpersuasive interpretation asserted by the proponent of extrinsic evidence. In such a case, it seems clear that a court should exclude that evidence as violating the parol evidence rule despite the presence of some contract ambiguity. Finally, and most important, the ambiguity determination distracts the court from its primary objective — to enforce the contract as intended by the parties. Consequently, although relevant, contract ambiguity is not the only linchpin of a court's decision to admit parol evidence.

The better rule is that the judge first considers the offered evidence and, if he or she finds that the contract language is "reasonably susceptible" to the interpretation asserted by its proponent, the evidence is admissible to determine the meaning intended by the parties. See Restatement §215 cmt. b; see also Pacific Gas & Elec. Co. v. G.W. Thomas Dray. & Rigging Co., 69 Cal. 2d 33, 69 Cal. Rptr. 561, 564, 566, 567-68, 442 P.2d 641, 644, 645-46 (1968). . . . The meaning that appears plain and unambiguous on the first reading of a document may not appear nearly so plain once the judge considers the evidence. In such a case, the parol evidence rule is not violated because the evidence is not being offered to contradict or vary the meaning of the agreement. To the contrary, it is being offered to explain what the parties truly may have intended. We believe that this rule embodies the concepts endorsed by Corbin and adopted by this court ten years ago in *Melson*. Other courts more recently have expressed approval of the position taken by Corbin and the Restatement (Second) of Contracts. See, e.g., C.R. Anthony Co. v. Loretto Mall Partners, 817 P.2d 238, 241-44 & n.3 (N.M. 1991); Isbrandtsen v. North Branch Corp., 150 Vt. 575, 556 A.2d 81, 83-85 (1988); Berg v. Hudesman, 115 Wash.2d 657, 801 P.2d 222, 227-30 (1990); see also 3 Corbin §542, at 105-112 (Supp. 1992) (citing cases).

A judge may not always be in a position to rule on a parol evidence objection at first blush, having not yet heard enough relevant evidence on the issue. If this occurs, the judge might, for example, admit the extrinsic evidence conditionally, reserve ruling on the issue until enough relevant evidence is presented, or, if the case is being tried to a jury, consider the evidence outside the jury's presence. See, e.g., Ariz. R. Evid. 103(c), 104(b), 104(c), 105. Because the judge is in the best position to decide how to proceed, we leave this decision to his or her sound discretion. As noted also, the judge need not waste much time if the asserted interpretation is unreasonable or the offered evidence is not persuasive. A proffered interpretation that is highly improbable would necessarily require very convincing evidence. In such a case, the judge might quickly decide that the contract language is not reasonably susceptible to the asserted meaning, stop listening to evidence supporting it, and rule that its admission would violate the parol evidence rule. See 3 Corbin §542, at 112; §579, at 420.

We now apply these principles to the facts of this case.

B. Was the Release so Clear That the Trial Judge Erred in Admitting Extrinsic Evidence to Interpret It?

Taylor released "all *contractual* rights, claims, and causes of action he ha[d] or may have against STATE FARM under the policy of insurance . . . in connection with the collision . . . *and all subsequent matters.*" See Appendix (emphasis added). Taylor argued that the bad faith claim sounds in tort and was therefore neither covered nor intended to be covered by the language releasing "all contractual" claims. The trial court found that

> [p]arts of the document suggest that the parties contemplated the question of the insurer's settlement of claims within policy limits. Yet on page 2 of the document, the release satisfies "all contractual rights, claims, and causes of action." As a matter of statutory or contract construction, the word "contractual" modifies the words "rights," "claims," and the words "causes of action." Although the breach of the duty of good faith and fair dealing arises out of contract, the action itself is a tort claim. Thus, there is ambiguity here. Where there is an ambiguity, parol evidence will be admitted on this issue.

Minute Entry, Jan. 12, 1987 at 1-2 (citations omitted). The court of appeals held that Taylor's bad faith action was purely contractual and therefore, unlike the trial judge, found no ambiguity in the release language. *Taylor,* mem. dec. at 16.[3] We must decide whether the release language is reasonably susceptible to Taylor's proffered interpretation in light of the evidence relevant to the parties' intent. If it is, admission of extrinsic evidence supporting his interpretation did not violate the parol evidence rule.

1. *Was the Release Language Reasonably Susceptible to Differing Interpretations, Including that the Bad Faith Claim was not Released Despite the Contractual Quality of Such a Claim?*

First, we address the court of appeals' holding that Taylor's bad faith claim was only contractual and that the trial court erred by finding that the release language, which indisputably covered contractual matters, was unclear, requiring extrinsic evidence for interpretation. *Taylor,* mem. dec. at 16, 23.

. . .

It is true that bad faith has its genesis in contract. . . . Our cases show, however, that the precise legal character of a bad faith claim may depend on the context of the discussion. . . .

Because the legal character of bad faith was and is not universally established, the release reasonably could be interpreted as Taylor asserts. The trial court, therefore, did not err in concluding that the text of the release did not necessarily cover claims for bad faith.

2. *Was there Extrinsic Evidence to Support the Conclusion that the Release Language was Reasonably Susceptible to Taylor's Interpretation?*

At the time the parties made the agreement, it was obvious that Taylor had a sizable potential claim for bad faith. The release was agreed to months after the jury returned verdicts against Taylor and less than six months after this court recognized the tort of bad faith in *Noble.* Most of the alleged

3. These conflicting rulings illustrate the problems inherent in finding ambiguity. Two trial judges found the agreement ambiguous, that is, "doubtful or uncertain . . . [or] capable of being understood in two or more possible senses or ways." Webster's Ninth New Collegiate Dictionary 77 (1989). Three court of appeals judges, reading the same agreement, found the meaning clear beyond all question. At one time, this court held that if one court found a contract ambiguous and another found it clear, it must be ambiguous. See Federal Ins. Co. v. P.A.T. Homes, Inc., 113 Ariz. 136, 138-39, 547 P.2d 1050, 1052-53 (1976). For obvious reasons, we should discard such doctrine and have done so. See *Wilson,* 162 Ariz. at 256-58, 782 P.2d at 732-34.

conduct that is the basis for Taylor's bad faith claim had already occurred. In fact, although occurring later, the Rings garnished State Farm seeking to satisfy their entire judgment, including the excess above the policy limits, based on State Farm's liability to Taylor for alleged bad faith. Ring v. State Farm Mut. Auto. Ins., 147 Ariz. 32, 33, 708 P.2d 457, 458 (Ct. App. 1985). There was some evidence that Hofmann, on behalf of State Farm, directed that "general release language" be used in the agreement without expressly mentioning "bad faith." The document's cryptic language supports this. Such a direction, in light of the obvious nature of the claim, supports Taylor's interpretation.

Also, State Farm internally designated the $15,000 payment to Taylor as being for uninsured motorist ("UM") coverage. Although State Farm denies its importance, its ultimate significance was for the fact finder to determine. State Farm's subsequent conduct may shed light on its understanding of what was covered by the agreement. See *Darner,* 140 Ariz. at 393, 682 P.2d at 398. This, too, supports the idea that the release is reasonably susceptible to Taylor's interpretation.

The potential size of the bad faith claim also cannot be ignored. At the time the parties entered into the release agreement, a jury had already rendered verdicts against Taylor far exceeding his insurance policy limits. Thus, the potential size of Taylor's bad faith claim was obvious. We recognize that, with few exceptions, parties are free to structure a deal in any way they wish. Nevertheless, it is arguably reasonable to conclude that Taylor and his counsel would seek something more than just the payment of a potentially bona fide $15,000 UM claim to release a bad faith claim possibly worth millions of dollars.

Finally, and perhaps most telling, is the fact that the parties used limiting language in the release. It is reasonable to believe that if the parties had agreed to release the bad faith claim, they would not have drawn the release so narrowly — confining it to "contractual" and "subsequent" matters, with *no* mention of tort claims or bad faith. Surely, State Farm knew what language would effectively release it from Taylor's potential bad faith claim. It can be inferred that sophisticated parties in the business of settling insurance claims, faced with the task of releasing a claim as large as Taylor's, would have used more specific or at least broader[7] language if that was their agreement. This is especially true in light of the conspicuous nature of the claim, the parties' obvious knowledge of its existence, and the very recent supreme court authority characterizing the claim as a tort. . . . For these reasons, we hold that extrinsic evidence produces support for Taylor's contention that the release language was not intended to release his bad faith claim.

This is *not* to say, however, that the release language excluded bad faith as a matter of law. Substantial evidence supports State Farm's interpretation as well. The release language is broad enough to release something more than just the

7. State Farm apparently did not insist that the release contain the broad language usually found in insurance company forms — releasing all claims of whatever nature, known or unknown.

contractual UM claim.[8] Also, the recitals refer to matters that may not pertain to UM coverage but are relevant to Taylor's bad faith claim.[9] Finally, there was credible evidence that both parties contemplated that bad faith would be covered by the release. All of the evidence, however, does not render the release language impervious to Taylor's interpretation. Instead, it demonstrates that there were three reasonable, but conflicting, interpretations of the language used in the agreement: (1) the parties agreed to release the bad faith claim; (2) the parties agreed to exclude the bad faith claim; and (3) the parties did not reach any agreement regarding release of the bad faith claim (in which case, of course, the claim would not be released). In light of this, the trial judge correctly concluded that the release could not as a matter of law be interpreted to include or exclude Taylor's bad faith claim.

C. Was the Parol Evidence for the Jury?

Whether contract language is reasonably susceptible to more than one interpretation so that extrinsic evidence is admissible is a question of law for the court. See Leo Eisenberg & Co., Inc. v. Payson, 162 Ariz. 529, 532-33, 785 P.2d 49, 52-53 (1989). We have concluded in the preceding section that the language of the agreement, illuminated by the surrounding circumstances, indicates that either of the interpretations offered was reasonable. Because interpretation was needed and because the extrinsic evidence established controversy over what occurred and what inferences to draw from the events, the matter was properly submitted to the jury. See *Burkons,* 168 Ariz. at 351, 813 P.2d at 716; *Leo Eisenberg,* 162 Ariz. at 533, 785 P.2d at 53. The trial judge, therefore, instructed the jury as follows:

> . . . [State Farm] has alleged the affirmative defense of release. In this regard, [State Farm] contends that the agreement . . . was intended by the parties thereto to, among other things, release [State Farm] from all bad faith claims.
>
> . . . Whether the parties intended the bad faith claims to be released is for you to determine. If you find that the parties to said agreement intended thereby that [State Farm] be released from bad faith claims, then your verdict must be for [State Farm].
>
> . . .
>
> A release is to be construed according to the intent of the parties to it. This intention is to be determined by what was within the contemplation of the

8. There was evidence that Randall believed that at least one claim other than UM and bad faith remained — a medical payment claim — that was released by the agreement. At oral argument, it was conceded that any medical payment claim would have been released by the agreement. Whether or not that claim was valid, Randall's belief dispels the notion that bad faith was the only claim other than UM that could have been contemplated by the breadth of the release language.

9. We recognize, as did the court of appeals, that a contract should be interpreted, if at all possible, in a way that does not render parts of it superfluous. *Taylor,* mem. dec. at 18. State Farm, however, strenuously argued this very point to the jury, which nevertheless remained unconvinced — a permissible result. Cf. Restatement §203 cmts. a & b. Also, State Farm argues that any uncertainty in the language should be construed against the drafter. This rule, however, is subordinate to the rule that the intent of the parties should govern. *Polk,* 111 Ariz. at 495, 533 P.2d at 662. In any event, it is the *missing* language of "bad faith" that makes this agreement unclear. Although Randall drafted the agreement, he alleges that State Farm is responsible for the omission. Thus, it is unclear who, if anyone, the rule should be applied against.

> parties when the release was executed, which, in turn, is to be resolved in the light of all of the surrounding facts and circumstances under which the parties acted.

Reporter's Transcript, Mar. 12, 1987, at 184-85. The instruction states the issue quite clearly. So instructed, the jury resolved the release issue in Taylor's favor. We leave that resolution undisturbed.

CONCLUSION

The trial court properly considered and then admitted extrinsic evidence to interpret the release and determine whether it included Taylor's bad faith claim. That question, in this case, was appropriately left to the trier of fact. There remain other issues not resolved by the court of appeals. We are aware of the frustration that additional delay imposes on all involved, especially in a case as old as this. Nevertheless, because the other issues were initially and fully presented to the court of appeals, prudence dictates that the court of appeals complete its review of this case as expeditiously as possible. The decision of the court of appeals pertaining to the release is vacated and the matter is remanded to the court of appeals for resolution of the remaining issues.

MOELLER, V.C.J., ZLAKET, J., and JAMES D. HATHAWAY, Judge, concur.

Justice FREDERICK J. MARTONE did not participate in this matter; pursuant to Ariz. Const. art. VI, §3, Judge JAMES D. HATHAWAY of the Court of Appeals, Division Two, was designated to sit in his stead.

CORCORAN, Justice, specially concurring:

I concur with the opinion — but without enthusiasm. It is certainly true that wavering and overlapping lines of interpretation, rather than bright straight borders prevail in this area of contract interpretation. I don't know whether our opinion helps.

The canon of interpretation which we propound today is amorphous. The problem with an amorphous rule is that in the end, only *this* court can make a *final* determination in construing any contract. Our interpretation will be based upon which parol evidence impresses us the most. That ultimately means that this court *must* decide every contract dispute subject to this analysis. As the history of this case shows, the trial court may go one way and the court of appeals another and this court yet another.

I fear that this opinion makes this court the supreme court of arguments "that white is black and that a dollar is fifty cents" — to use the colorful words of Professor Corbin.

APPENDIX

Full Text of Release:

AGREEMENT

> This Agreement made and entered into this 4th day of August, 1981, by and between BOBBY SID TAYLOR and the STATE FARM MUTUAL AUTOMOBILE INSURANCE COMPANY, (hereinafter referred to as STATE FARM), by and through its agent undersigned.

WHEREAS, BOBBY SID TAYLOR was covered by an automobile insurance policy issued by STATE FARM, which was in effect on the 9th day of April, 1977, providing liability and uninsured motorist coverage to him, and

WHEREAS, an automobile collision occurred on April 9, 1977 between vehicles operated by BOBBY SID TAYLOR, DOUGLAS ALAN WISTROM and ANNE L. RING, and

WHEREAS, a trial took place in the Superior Court of Maricopa County, State of Arizona in consolidated causes C-382960 and C-383090, resulting in a jury verdict against BOBBY SID TAYLOR in the total amount of $2,621,000, and judgments having been entered against BOBBY SID TAYLOR in accordance with said jury verdicts, and

WHEREAS, having been fully apprised of all settlement offers made by the plaintiffs in the consolidated cases referred to above, during the discovery process, prior to trial, during the trial, and subsequently, BOBBY SID TAYLOR maintained and does now maintain that the operation of his motor vehicle on April 9, 1977 did not contribute to the injuries sustained by the plaintiffs, and at no time has he insisted, demanded, or even encouraged his insurer to settle the plaintiffs' claims within his policy limits, and

WHEREAS, one of the drivers of an automobile involved in the collision on April 9, 1977, to wit: DOUGLAS ALAN WISTROM, was uninsured on the date of said collision, and BOBBY SID TAYLOR having a bona fide belief that the negligence of DOUGLAS ALAN WISTROM contributed to his bodily injuries sustained in that collision, and

WHEREAS, BOBBY SID TAYLOR has demanded compensation from STATE FARM under the uninsured motorist coverage afforded to him, and

WHEREAS, BOBBY SID TAYLOR desires to settle the uninsured motorist claim, and to relieve STATE FARM of any and all other contractual claims, interests, or causes of action he has or may have against STATE FARM, and

WHEREAS, STATE FARM has agreed that uninsured motorist coverage is available to BOBBY SID TAYLOR and appropriate under the facts surrounding the collision on April 9, 1977, and STATE FARM having been fully apprised in the premises,

THEREFORE, in consideration of the mutual [cov]enants contained herein, STATE FARM agrees to pay the sum of $15,000 to BOBBY SID TAYLOR in full satisfaction of all contractual rights, claims, and causes of action he has or may have against STATE FARM under the policy of insurance referred to herein, in connection with the collision on April 9, 1977, and all subsequent matters, and BOBBY SID TAYLOR hereby accepts that sum pursuant to the recitals contained herein.

[SIGNATURES]

NOTES AND QUESTIONS

1. *Contrasting* ***Thompson*** *with* ***Taylor.*** *Thompson* dealt with what is sometimes referred to as "supplementation" of the written agreement. In a case of

supplementation, one party offers extrinsic evidence to show that the contracting parties entered into an agreement that was not expressed in the final writing. Recall that in *Thompson* the defendant claimed that the plaintiff's agent had made an oral warranty about the quality of the logs. By contrast, *Taylor* involved a case of interpretation rather than supplementation. The extrinsic evidence offered in *Taylor* did not show a separate agreement, but rather conduct and other background circumstances that Taylor claimed were relevant to the issue of whether the release should be interpreted to cover a claim in tort against State Farm for bad faith refusal to settle. For discussions of the distinction between supplementation and interpretation, see Harry G. Prince, Contract Interpretation in California: Plain Meaning, Parol Evidence and Use of the "Just Result" Principle, 31 Loy. L.A. L. Rev. 557, 605-613 (1998); Margaret N. Kniffin, Conflating and Confusing Contract Interpretation and The Parol Evidence Rule: Is The Emperor Wearing Someone Else's Clothes? 62 Rutgers L. Rev. 75 (2009). What was the extrinsic evidence that Taylor offered to interpret the agreement?

2. *Claims of insurer bad faith.* The *Taylor* opinion raises several significant points about insurance law and practice. The court indicates that Arizona recognizes a cause of action in tort against an insurance company for bad faith refusal to settle a policy claim. The issue of tort liability of insurers and other contracting parties for breach of contract is explored in a comment in Chapter 10 on the availability of punitive damages. For now it is probably sufficient for you to know that throughout the country courts have generally recognized that insurance companies can be liable when they refuse in bad faith to defend or settle claims brought under their policies. See generally Douglas R. Richmond, An Overview of Insurance Bad Faith Law and Litigation, 25 Seton Hall L. Rev. 74 (1994). Cases of bad faith refusal to defend or settle fall into two broad categories: third-party and first-party claims. In a third-party claim, the insured seeks to recover damages from her insurer because the insurer failed in bad faith to defend or settle a claim brought by a third party against the insured (for example, a claim covered by an automobile insurance policy). The significance of a bad faith claim is that the insurer can be held liable even for amounts in excess of the policy limit because of its bad faith conduct. In a first-party claim, the insured seeks to recover damages because the insurance company refused in bad faith a claim brought by the insured rather than a third party (for example, under a health or fire insurance policy). Courts have been somewhat more resistant to first-party than to third-party claims perhaps because damage to the insured in a third-party claim is clear and substantial (the amount in excess of the policy limit), while damage in a first-party claim (often emotional distress and punitive damages) may be more problematic. Nonetheless, a growing number of jurisdictions have recognized first-party bad faith tort claims. See generally, Sharon Tennyson & William J. Warfel, The Law and Economics of First-Party Insurance Bad Faith Liability, 16 Conn. Ins. L.J. 203 (2009).

Note also that Taylor was represented by two lawyers. This situation can arise when the interests of the insured differ from those of the insurer. For a general discussion of the many difficult conflict of interest problems facing insurance defense counsel, see Nathan M. Crystal, Professional Responsibility: Problems of Practice and the Profession 233-317 (6th ed. 2017).

3. *Plain meaning, ambiguity, and the parol evidence rule.* The facts in *Taylor* point to the relationship between the "four corners" approach to determining integration of a writing under the parol evidence rule (as in *Thompson*) and the "plain meaning" approach to interpreting written terms (as used by the intermediate appellate court in *Taylor*). Courts that rely on the facial completeness of a written contract to conclude that it is fully integrated are likely to rely on the apparent plain meaning of words to bar use of extrinsic evidence to aid interpretation, and the presence of a merger clause may further impel such courts to assign a plain meaning to words. This tendency continues even though the usual formulation of the parol evidence rule, as reflected in both *Thompson* and *Taylor*, explicitly states that the parol evidence rule does not bar the use of extrinsic evidence to explain or interpret a writing.

While all courts will allow use of extrinsic evidence to interpret a contract with a patent or facial ambiguity, the point of difference is that "plain meaning" adherents will not allow use of extrinsic evidence to uncover a latent ambiguity. (Recall the discussion in the notes after the *Frigaliment* case on patent and latent ambiguity.) By contrast, the modern approach used by the Arizona Supreme Court in *Taylor* allows use of extrinsic evidence if the disputed language of the contract is "reasonably susceptible" to the different proffered meanings advanced by the parties. In making the determination of whether the language is susceptible of more than one meaning, the court will consider at least preliminarily the extrinsic evidence and need not find the agreement to be patently ambiguous. As the *Taylor* opinion states, the Restatement (Second) adopts generally the Corbin or modern approach. See particularly Restatement (Second) §214(c) and Comment *b* thereto ("[e]ven though words seem on their face to have only a single possible meaning, other meanings often appear when the circumstances are disclosed").

4. *Continuing debate on use of parol evidence.* While the *Taylor* court and many others have adopted the Restatement or Corbin approach to use of extrinsic evidence in the process of interpretation, other judges strongly disagree. In Shay v. Aldrich, 790 N.W.2d 629 (Mich. 2010), the plaintiff alleged that he had been assaulted by a group of police officers, including three from one municipality (who were accused by the plaintiff of actual physical assault) and two from another (who were accused only of gross negligence in failing to intervene). Plaintiff's claims against the latter two officers were settled by agreement between plaintiff and their insurer for an aggregate of $25,000. His claims against the remaining three officers had earlier been independently evaluated as being worth roughly $1.5 million. In plaintiff's suit against those other three officers, their insurer relied on the settlement agreement, arguing that because its language at one point referred to a discharge of the two named defendants "together with all other firms, persons or corporations," it necessarily released

plaintiffs' claims against the other three officers as well, even though there was much evidence that this was *not* the parties' intent, and no evidence that it *was*. Overruling an earlier decision, the Michigan Supreme Court held that in these circumstances parol evidence could be admitted to show that the actual intent of the parties was to discharge plaintiff's claims against only the two named officers. Writing for a four-person majority, Justice Weaver declared:

> Under the facts of this case, if plaintiff were not permitted to present extrinsic evidence in order to ascertain the intent of the settling parties, the settling parties' intent would undoubtedly be perverted. Plaintiff would be deprived of his claim for assault and battery against the Melvindale Officers. . . . Further, the Melvindale Officers would obtain a complete windfall by being released from liability for their acts in exchange for no bargained-for promise and no consideration at all, despite the fact that they do not dispute that this was not the intent of the settling parties. Not only would this be an unjust result, it would be contrary to the cardinal rule of contract interpretation: that the contracting parties' intent should control.

790 N.W.2d 629, at 673-674. Writing for himself and two other dissenting justices, Justice Markman (himself the author of the overruled earlier decision) spent some 28 pages explaining why the majority was wrong on both the law and the facts to rule as it did. At one point, declaring that the Michigan court had "long ago" (citing and quoting an 1858 decision) held that a party to a contract has the duty to read and understand the contract that he signs, Justice Markman continued:

> There are reasons why these fundamental principles have withstood the test of time and have served as the bedrock of contract law in this state from time immemorial. Courts adhere to these fundamental rules — enforcing contracts according to their unambiguous terms, responsibly and diligently executing their judicial duty in determining if a contract is ambiguous, and insisting that parties read their contracts — because doing so respects the freedom of individuals freely to arrange their affairs via contract. . . . [T]he general rule [of contracts] is that competent persons shall have the utmost liberty of contracting and that their agreements voluntarily and fairly made shall be held valid and enforced in the courts. . . . It is precisely because these fundamental principles are so well settled and so essential to a free society, governed by the equal rule of law, that our citizens' reliance on them is so great. Courts rightly adhere to these rules so as not to upend the expectations of the citizenry in an area of the law that touches upon their personal and commercial relations every day in myriad ways.

Id. at 648 (inner quotation marks omitted). Conceding that such a brief quotation cannot do justice to a 28-page argument, do you find this passage sufficiently persuasive to overcome the majority's analysis quoted above?

5. ***Interpretation and the parol evidence rule under the CISG.*** Article 8 of the CISG sets forth general principles of contract interpretation:

> (1) For the purposes of this Convention statements made by and other conduct of a party are to be interpreted according to his intent where the other party knew or could not have been unaware what that intent was.

> (2) If the preceding paragraph is not applicable, statements made by and conduct of a party are to be interpreted according to the understanding a reasonable person of the same kind as the other party would have had in the same circumstances.
>
> (3) In determining the intent of a party or the understanding a reasonable person would have had, due consideration is to be given to all relevant circumstances of the case including the negotiations, any practices which the parties have established between themselves, usages and any subsequent conduct of the parties.

CISG, art. 8. Thus, the CISG takes a modified objective approach to interpretation which focuses on what the parties knew or had reason to know about each other's intent, consistent with the Restatement (Second) §201, and permits use of all relevant extrinsic evidence in arriving at that interpretation, an approach that also appears largely consistent with the Restatement (Second) Contracts §§212, 214, as discussed in *Taylor.* See William S. Dodge, Teaching the CISG in Contracts, 50 J. Leg. Ed. 72, 87-88 (2000) (observing that the CISG approach to interpretation is "barely distinguishable" from the approach of the Restatement (Second)).

Given that the CISG does not have a statute of frauds, it is perhaps not surprising that the CISG also fails to include a parol evidence rule. In MCC-Marble Ceramic Center, Inc. v. Ceramica Nuova d'Agostino, S.p.A., 144 F.3d 1384 (11th Cir. 1998), an American buyer and Italian seller disputed performance of a ceramic tile purchase transaction. The parties differed as to whether their transaction should be governed by their earlier oral agreement or by the terms of a later form contract, written in Italian, which contained terms not previously agreed on orally. The buyer claimed it never intended to be bound by the additional terms in the seller's form, and that the seller knew that at the time. Framing the key question as whether the evidence of the earlier oral contract would be barred under the parol evidence rule since the parties later adopted a writing, the court concluded that the drafters of the CISG intended to reject the parol evidence rule and that Article 8(3) "is a clear instruction to admit and consider parol evidence regarding the negotiations to the extent they reveal the parties' subjective intent." 144 F.3d at 1389. The court thus reversed a grant of summary judgment in favor of the seller and remanded the case.

Sherrodd, Inc. v. Morrison-Knudsen Co.

Supreme Court of Montana 249 Mont. 282, 815 P.2d 1135 (1991)

TURNAGE, Chief Justice.

This action arises out of a construction contract on which plaintiff Sherrodd, Inc., was a subcontractor. Sherrodd, Inc., appeals from a summary judgment entered for defendants by the District Court for the Thirteenth Judicial District, Yellowstone County. We affirm.

The issue is whether the entry of summary judgment for defendants was proper.

Sherrodd, Inc. (Sherrodd), is a family-owned Montana construction corporation. Sherrodd subcontracted with COP Construction (COP) to do certain earth-moving work involved in the construction of fifty family housing units in Forsyth, Montana, for the Army Corps of Engineers. COP itself was a subcontractor to the general contractors Morrison-Knudsen Company, Inc. (Morrison-Knudsen), and Schlekeway Construction, Inc. (Schlekeway). Safeco Insurance Company of America (Safeco) provided COP's payment bond on the job.

Sherrodd contends that while its officer William Sherrodd was examining the building site in preparation for submitting a bid on this project, a representative of Morrison-Knudsen told him that there were 25,000 cubic yards of excavation to be performed on the job. It claims that its bid of $97,500 on the subcontract was made in reliance on that representation, based on $3.90 per cubic yard for 25,000 cubic yards. Morrison-Knudsen denies that its representative made any such statement to William Sherrodd.

Sherrodd's bid, and, in turn, COP's bid including Sherrodd's bid, were submitted and accepted. Sherrodd began work before a written contract was signed. While performing the earthwork, Sherrodd discovered that the quantity of work far exceeded 25,000 cubic yards.

The written contract between Sherrodd and COP provided that Sherrodd would perform earthwork in the quantity "LS" for the consideration of $97,500. The parties agree that the letters "LS" mean lump sum. Sherrodd contends that its officers signed the contract, even though by then they knew that the job involved more than 25,000 cubic yards of earthwork, because a COP officer threatened to withhold payment for work already done unless the contract was signed. Sherrodd further contends that the COP officer verbally represented that a deal would be worked out wherein Sherrodd would be paid more than the sum provided for in the contract. COP's position is that it only agreed to assist Sherrodd in presenting a claim for additional compensation to the Army Corps of Engineers, based on differences in the moisture content of the soil from that stated in the bid proposal. That was done, but the claim was denied.

In its "Standard Subcontract Provisions," the contract entered between Sherrodd and COP also provided that

> the Subcontractor has, by examination, satisfied himself as to the . . . character, quantity and kind of materials to be encountered . . . No verbal agreement with any agent either before or after the execution of this Subcontract shall affect or modify any of the terms or obligations herein contained and this contract shall be conclusively considered as containing and expressing all of the terms and conditions agreed upon by the parties hereto. No changes . . . shall be valid . . . unless reduced to writing and signed by the parties hereto.

Sherrodd was paid the $97,500 provided for in the contract, less approximately $9,750 for work left uncompleted. It brought this suit to set aside the price provisions in the contract and to recover quantum meruit plus tort damages. Its legal theories were fraud, both actual and constructive, and breach of the covenant of good faith and fair dealing. Defendants moved for summary judgment, which was granted based on the parol evidence rule regarding modification of written contracts.

Summary judgment is proper when the pleadings, depositions, answers to interrogatories, and admissions on file, together with the affidavits, if any, show that there are no genuine issues of material fact and that the moving party is entitled to judgment as a matter of law. Rule 56(c), M.R. Civ. P. The District Court held that, under the parol evidence rule, Sherrodd could not introduce evidence of the alleged oral misrepresentations by either the Morrison-Knudsen representative or the COP officer. Therefore, it concluded that even taking the evidence in the light most favorable to Sherrodd, summary judgment for defendants was proper.

The parol evidence rule is codified in Montana statutes. Section 28-2-904, MCA, provides that:

> The execution of a contract in writing, whether the law requires it to be written or not, supersedes all the oral negotiations or stipulations concerning its matter which preceded or accompanied the execution of the instrument.

Section 28-2-905, MCA, provides that when an agreement has been reduced to writing by the parties, there can be no evidence of the terms of the agreement other than the contents of the writing except when a mistake or imperfection of the writing is claimed or when the validity of the agreement is the fact in dispute.

Although it mentions mutual mistake in its brief to this Court, Sherrodd did not rely on that theory in the proceedings below, as evidenced in the pretrial order and in the District Court's memorandum on the summary judgment. We will not consider on appeal a theory not raised at the trial court level. Morse v. Cremer (1982), 200 Mont. 71, 81, 647 P.2d 358, 363.

A further exception is made to the parol evidence rule when fraud is alleged. Section 28-2-905(2), MCA. However, that exception only applies when the alleged fraud does not relate directly to the subject of the contract. Where an alleged oral promise directly contradicts the terms of an express written contract, the parol evidence rule applies. Continental Oil Co. v. Bell (1933), 94 Mont. 123, 133, 21 P.2d 65, 67. Accord, Superior Oil Company v. Vanderhoof (D. Mont. 1969), 297 F. Supp. 1086.

Here, any reliance on the alleged fraudulent statement of the Morrison-Knudsen representative is contradicted by the terms of the written contract that Sherrodd has, "by examination, satisfied himself as to the . . . character, quantity and kind of materials to be encountered." The contention that the $97,500 covered only 25,000 cubic yards of earthwork contradicts the terms of the written agreement that all "negotiations and agreements" prior to the date of the contract are merged in the writing and that the work to be done is "lump sum." We conclude that the parol evidence rule applies. Because the written agreement supersedes all previous oral agreements, the rule prohibits admission of any evidence of the representation by the Morrison-Knudsen representative.

Next we consider Sherrodd's claim that COP officers induced Sherrodd officers to sign the contract with the promise that more money would be paid than the contract provided. Section 28-2-1602, MCA, provides that a written contract may be altered only by a subsequent contract in writing or by an executed oral agreement. Also, Sherrodd's subcontract provided that "No changes . . . shall be valid . . . unless reduced to writing and signed by the parties hereto." As the District Court noted, there is no allegation of a subsequent contract in writing, and if there had been an executed oral agreement to pay additional sums for the work, there would have been no reason for this lawsuit.

Because of the inadmissibility of Sherrodd's evidence as to alleged misrepresentations, the claim of breach of the covenant of good faith and fair dealing also fails. There is no allegation of any violation of the express terms of the written contract, as would be required in this arms-length contract under our opinion in Story v. City of Bozeman (1990), 242 Mont. 436, 791 P.2d 767.

As we have stated,

> Commercial stability requires that parties to a contract may rely upon its express terms without worrying that the law will allow the other party to change the terms of the agreement at a later date.

Baker v. Bailey (1989), 240 Mont. 139, 143, 782 P.2d 1286, 1288.

The parol evidence rule is the public policy of Montana and it is clearly established by statute and the decisions of this Court. If this public policy and rule is not upheld, contracting parties that include lawful provisions in written contracts would be under a cloud of uncertainty as to whether or not their written contracts may be relied upon. The public policy and law does not permit such uncertainty to occur.

We conclude that the compensation of Sherrodd is governed exclusively by the written contract and that Sherrodd's claims are barred under the parol evidence rule. We hold that the District Court did not err in granting summary judgment for defendants.

Affirmed.

HARRISON, GRAY, MCDONOUGH and WEBER, JJ., concur.

TRIEWEILER, Justice, dissenting.

I dissent from the opinion of the majority.

If the facts are as alleged by the plaintiff (and for purposes of this proceeding we must assume that they are), then the result of this case is that no party can be held accountable for its fraudulent conduct so long as it is in a sufficiently superior bargaining position to compel its victim to sign a document relieving it of liability.

The facts, as alleged by the plaintiff, offend any reasonable sense of fairness. No court should be so bound by a 58-year-old precedent that it cannot adapt to circumstances such as those presented in this case.

The plaintiff was informed by Lou Castino, the construction manager for Schlekeway and Associates, that the project he was being asked to bid on involved moving 25,000 cubic yards of dirt. It was based on that information that he submitted his bid. It was based on his bid that he was given an oral request to proceed with the work.

After commencing work on the project, plaintiff realized that the amount of earth that had to be moved greatly exceeded 25,000 cubic yards, and was actually more than twice that amount. He had conversations with representatives of both COP Construction and Schlekeway and Associates, during which it was agreed that the amount of work to be performed would be recalculated, and during which the defendants agreed to compensate plaintiff on the basis of the actual amount of work done, rather than the price which was originally agreed upon.

By May 22, 1985, plaintiff had already been working on the project and had incurred substantial expenses and obligations to his own employees. He had not been paid for his work, and was still operating without a written agreement. It was on that date that he was requested by COP Construction's superintendent to sign the written contract which the defendants now assert as a bar to his cause of action. He was advised that if he did not sign the agreement he would not receive the progress payment in the amount of $70,372.80 which was due. Without the progress payment he would not have been able to pay his current expenses and payroll.

He was further advised that he would not be bound by the terms of the written agreement, but that he would be paid for the actual work done at the rate of $3.90 per cubic yard.

Thereafter, the amount of earth work to be done was recalculated at approximately 50,000 cubic yards. On that basis, plaintiff tried to recover the full amount due, but payment was refused. Instead, the defendants raised the written agreement as a bar to any further payment to the plaintiff.

Because of the defendants' failure to pay the plaintiff the additional $100,000 to $120,000 which they owed him, plaintiff's business lost its ability to borrow money, lost its bonding, and was unable to complete additional contracts because of a lack of operating capital. Plaintiff was unable to bid on contracts that required bonding, and completely lost its ability to carry on business as it had in the past. As a direct result of the defendants' failure to pay the amounts due, plaintiff was unable to continue in business as a construction company, which it had done for the previous 30 years.

If the plaintiff's allegations are true, then defendant COP Construction Company's conduct, at least, satisfies the elements of fraud. See Poulsen, et al. v. Treasure State Industries, 192 Mont. 69, 626 P.2d 822 (1981). COP's employees represented to the plaintiff that he would be paid for the full amount of work done, regardless of the written terms of the contract. That representation was untrue and material, and COP's superintendent either knew it was untrue or had no reason to believe that it was true. COP Construction intended that the plaintiff act in reliance upon that representation. Plaintiff did rely on it, and had no reason to believe that COP's superintendent would mislead him. As a result, plaintiff has sustained the total loss of his business and substantial damages.

The majority has affirmed the dismissal of plaintiff's claim based solely on the parol evidence rule found at §28-2-904, MCA. That rule provides that a written agreement supersedes all oral negotiations which preceded or accompanied the execution of the instrument. Furthermore, §28-2-905, MCA, provides that the terms of a written agreement cannot be proven by evidence other than what is contained in the written document.

However, an important exception is found at §28-2-905(2), MCA, which provides, in relevant part, as follows:

> This section does not exclude other evidence of the circumstances under which the agreement was made or to which it relates . . . or other evidence to explain . . . fraud.

In addition, §28-2-1611, MCA, provides as follows:

> When, through *fraud* or a mutual mistake of the parties or a mistake of one party while the other at the time knew or suspected, a written contract does not truly express the intention of the parties, it may be revised on the application of a party aggrieved so as to express that intention, so far as it can be done without prejudice to rights acquired by third persons in good faith and for value. (Emphasis added.)

In this case, in spite of the exceptions to the parol evidence rule set forth by statute above, the majority has chosen to rely on this Court's 58-year-old decision in Continental Oil v. Bell, 94 Mont. 123, 133, 21 P.2d 65, 68 (1933). In that case, this Court held that parol evidence of fraud was not admissible when the oral promise directly contradicts a provision of the written contract.

I would not follow this Court's previous decision in *Continental Oil* for two reasons:

1. That decision made no specific reference to the statute which is controlling, and yet adds qualifications to the statute which were not included by the legislature. The legislature provided that parol evidence could be offered to establish that a contract was induced by fraud. It made no exception where evidence of the fraudulent oral agreement contradicted a term in the written agreement.

2. To follow the decision in *Continental Oil* creates a terrible injustice, rewards fraudulent parties who are in a superior bargaining position, and totally defeats the purpose for which the fraud exception was provided to the parol evidence rule.

Based on this decision, and our previous decision in *Continental Oil,* all that a fraudulent party needs to do in order to avoid accountability for fraudulent conduct is to obtain the signature of his defrauded victim on a written agreement.

The majority expresses concern that but for this decision general contractors would not be able to rely on written agreements with their subcontractors. However, general contractors who induce subcontractors to enter into a written agreement by fraudulent representations should find no security in the piece of paper which resulted from their culpable conduct. Furthermore, a justice system worth its salt should have equal compassion for Montana's many subcontractors who, while operating without the benefit of legal advice, sign whatever is necessary in order to keep their operations afloat and their crews at work. When what they have signed results from an obvious misrepresentation and causes them the kind of substantial damages and hardship that have resulted in this case, those subcontractors are entitled to the protection of Montana's laws and its courts.

For these reasons, I dissent from the majority opinion. I would reverse the judgment of the District Court and remand for a jury trial to determine the merits of the plaintiff's claim. That is really all the protection that Montana's general contractors need.

HUNT, J., concurs with the foregoing dissent of Justice TRIEWEILER.

NOTES AND QUESTIONS

1. *Fraud and the Parol Evidence Rule.* The parol evidence rule, as typically stated, recognizes a general exception for fraud. See Restatement (Second) §214(d). Many courts agree with the majority in *Sherrodd*, however, that a party cannot base a claim of fraud upon the very type of representation that is expressly disclaimed in the writing. See, e.g., Solymar Investments, Ltd. v. Banco Santander S.A., 672 F.3d 981 (11th Cir. 2012) (under Florida law parol evidence rule bars proof of alleged fraud that would directly contradict express terms in written agreement or when writing purports to be complete agreement of parties). On the other hand, a number of courts would agree with the dissent in *Sherrodd* that not even the combination of a merger clause and a specific disclaimer can shield a party from a claim of fraud. See, e.g., Pancakes of Hawaii, Inc. v. Pomare Properties Corp., 944 P.2d 97 (Haw. Ct. App. 1997) (merger clause with disclaimer of oral representations would not bar parol evidence to support allegation of false statements about occupancy level of new shopping center). In Riverisland Cold Storage, Inc. v. Fresno-Madera Production Credit Ass'n, 291 P. 3d 316 (Cal. 2013), the California Supreme Court held — overruling long-standing California precedent to the contrary — that the traditional fraud exception to application of the parol evidence rule should be available in claims of both fraud in the execution and fraud in the inducement (see the text following the *Thompson* case, supra), even if the asserted fraud appeared to be directly contradicted by the written agreement. The fraud alleged in *Riverisland* was fraud in the inducement, but it was also "promissory fraud." The court clearly intended that evidence of such fraud — although typically difficult to prove, because of the need to show intent — should fall within the fraud exception, and be admissible despite the presence of an integrated writing apparently negating it. See also IIG Wireless, Inc. v. Yi, 231 Cal. Rptr. 3d 771 (Ct. App. 2018) (*Riverisland* should be broadly interpreted to apply both to

claims for rescission and to actions for damages based on fraud). On remand, however, the trial court in *Riverisland* again granted summary judgment for the defendant, ruling that the plaintiff had not been able to show justifiable reliance on the asserted fraudulent promise. That ruling was affirmed on appeal. Riverisland Cold Storage, Inc. v. Fresno-Madera Production Credit Ass'n, 2015 WL 2213195 (Cal. Ct. App.), *Cal. Sup. Ct. review denied (*Aug. 12, 2015).

2. *Policy implications of **Sherrodd**.* The majority and dissenting opinions in *Sherrodd* obviously differ on the application of the fraud exception to the parol evidence rule, but at a deeper level the opinions reflect a fundamental disagreement about values. In his analysis of the role of reliance in modern contract law, Professor Knapp offers the following view of *Sherrodd*:

> Each party has a reliance story to tell, and each story — if true — is compelling. If Sherrodd is telling the truth, he has at least been misled, possibly been consciously lied to, and in any event been bullied and ultimately betrayed by the defendant's agents. In reliance on their assurances, he has completed his performance while at the same time binding himself to the very written document that may prevent him from recovering the full payment that he was promised, which he has honestly earned. To deny him his claim in these circumstances is clearly an injustice.
>
> But what if Sherrodd's story is a lie? Then COP is being asked to pay more than Sherrodd had agreed to accept for his services, even though COP has bound itself in turn to Morrison-Knudsen, relying on Sherrodd's willingness to render his performance at the originally agreed upon figure. And all this in the teeth of Sherrodd's signing of a written contract that expressly binds him to the agreement he now repudiates. If these are indeed the true facts, then surely to allow Sherrodd his claim would also be an injustice. How should this dilemma be resolved?

Professor Knapp goes on to suggest that the judge should hear evidence of these conflicting stories and determine whether Sherrodd's story is sufficiently credible to be considered by the trier of fact. In support of the modern, Corbinian view of the parol evidence rule, Professor Knapp argues that this approach should be used because the stricter view of the parol evidence rule represented by *Sherrodd* embodies a flawed world view:

> Proponents of a strong parol evidence rule may see [the conflict between approaches to the parol evidence rule] simply as the difference between tidiness and sloppiness, or as the difference between prudence and heedlessness, and those factors surely play a part. But at the most basic level, it's the difference between a world that runs on paper, and a world that runs on face-to-face communication — between a world that says "I don't believe it unless I see it in writing, and I won't *do* it unless a writing tells me to," and a world that says, "If you assure me this is so, I will take you at your word, and rely on that, as you well know."
>
> Each one of us lives, simultaneously, in both of those worlds. We have no choice in the matter. If the parol evidence rule forces a court to envision our world as being one where *only* paper matters, or — the slightly weaker version — a world where paper *always* prevails over face-to-face communication, then that rule forces the court (along with the rest of us) to deny something we

> know to be true. And that something is simply this: There are situations where it is, truly, more reasonable to rely on a spoken word of commitment than on a piece of paper, signed or not. And there should be.

Charles L. Knapp, Rescuing Reliance: The Perils of Promissory Estoppel, 49 Hastings L. J. 1191, 1322-1323, 1325 (1998). Other scholars have also expressed concern about the willingness of courts to give great deference to the written contract despite the reality of parties' frequent reliance on oral commitments. See Ralph James Mooney, The New Conceptualism in Contract Law, 74 Or. L. Rev. 1131, 1170-1171 (1995); Jay M. Feinman, Un-Making Law: The Classical Revival in the Common Law, 28 Seattle U. L. Rev. 1, 22-26 (2004).

3. *Other exceptions to the parol evidence rule.* Sherrodd could have asserted legal theories other than fraud in an effort to convince the court to admit parol evidence. The court mentions the possibility of mutual mistake, but rejects this contention because the plaintiff did not raise the issue at the trial court. Another theory not mentioned in the opinion is the possibility that the agreement was unenforceable because of economic duress. Sherrodd claimed that he signed the agreement when the defendant threatened to refuse to make a progress payment for work that was already done, without which Sherrodd could not pay his employees or meet current expenses. We discuss duress further in Chapter 7 and mistake in Chapter 8. Based on your studies thus far, does it seem to you that Sherrodd might have had more success if he had attempted to proceed on either a mistake or a duress theory? Why? At the very least the possible applicability of these doctrines shows how the quality of lawyering may have an impact on the outcome of a case.

4. *Promissory estoppel and the parol evidence rule.* In earlier chapters, we saw the doctrine of promissory estoppel being used by courts in a variety of ways: as a substitute for consideration, permitting recovery for detrimental reliance on a gratuitous promise; as a basis for holding an offer open despite the offeror's attempt to revoke; as a basis for enforcing an oral agreement within the statute of frauds despite the lack of a memorandum signed by the defendant. While there are a handful of cases that appear to hold that the parol evidence rule does not bar a showing of extrinsic evidence that the plaintiff detrimentally relied on promises or assurances not contained in an integrated written contract, most cases have rejected the use of promissory estoppel to avoid the parol evidence rule. Compare Prudential Ins. Co. of Am. v. Clark, 456 F.2d 932 (5th Cir. 1972) (evidence of reliance on insurance agent's oral promise to obtain life insurance without war risk exclusion not barred), with Banbury v. Omnitrition Int'l Inc., 533 N.W.2d 876 (Minn. Ct. App. 1995) (party cannot use the doctrine of promissory estoppel to alter a contract based on evidence barred by the parol evidence rule). The relationship between the parol evidence rule and promissory estoppel is further discussed in Charles L. Knapp, Rescuing Reliance: The Perils of Promissory Estoppel, 49 Hastings L. J. 1191, 1322-1330 (1998); see also David G. Epstein, Melinda Arbuckle & Kelly Flanagan, Contract Law's Two "P.E.'s": Promissory Estoppel and the Parol Evidence Rule, 62 Baylor L. Rev. 397 (2010), which argues that the real issue is not whether the parol evidence rule

should bend to the doctrine of promissory estoppel, but whether the asserted reliance was reasonable in the circumstances.

Nanakuli Paving & Rock Co. v. Shell Oil Co.

United States Court of Appeals 664 F.2d 772 (9th Cir. 1981)

HOFFMAN, District Judge:

Appellant Nanakuli Paving and Rock Company (Nanakuli) initially filed this breach of contract action against appellee Shell Oil Company (Shell) in Hawaiian State Court in February, 1976. Nanakuli, the second largest asphaltic paving contractor in Hawaii, had bought all its asphalt requirements from 1963 to 1974 from Shell under two long-term supply contracts; its suit charged Shell with breach of the later 1969 contract. The jury returned a verdict of $220,800 for Nanakuli on its first claim, which is that Shell breached the 1969 contract in January, 1974, by failing to price protect Nanakuli on 7200 tons of asphalt at the time Shell raised the price for asphalt from $44 to $76. Nanakuli's theory is that price-protection, as a usage of the asphaltic paving trade in Hawaii, was incorporated into the 1969 agreement between the parties, as demonstrated by the routine use of price protection by suppliers to that trade, and reinforced by the way in which Shell actually performed the 1969 contract up until 1974. Price protection, appellant claims, required that Shell hold the price on the tonnage Nanakuli had already committed because Nanakuli had incorporated that price into bids put out to or contracts awarded by general contractors and government agencies. The District Judge set aside the verdict and granted Shell's motion for judgment n.o.v., which decision we vacate. . . .

Nanakuli offers two theories for why Shell's failure to offer price protection in 1974 was a breach of the 1969 contract. First, it argues, all material suppliers to the asphaltic paving trade in Hawaii followed the trade usage of price protection and thus it should be assumed, under the U.C.C., that the parties intended to incorporate price protection into their 1969 agreement. This is so, Nanakuli continues, even though the written contract provided for price to be "Shell's Posted Price at time of delivery," F.O.B. Honolulu. Its proof of a usage that was incorporated into the contract is reinforced by evidence of the commercial context, which under the U.C.C. should form the background for viewing a particular contract. The full agreement must be examined in light of the close, almost symbiotic relations between Shell and Nanakuli on the island of Oahu, whereby the expansion of Shell on the island was intimately connected to the business growth of Nanakuli. The U.C.C. looks to the actual performance of a contract as the best indication of what the parties intended

A highway along the coastline in Hawaii.

those terms to mean. Nanakuli points out that Shell had price protected it on the two occasions of price increases under the 1969 contract other than the 1974 increase. In 1970 and 1971 Shell extended the old price for four and three months, respectively, after an announced increase. This was done, in the words of Shell's agent in Hawaii, in order to permit Nanakuli's to "chew up" tonnage already committed at Shell's old price.[4]

Nanakuli's second theory for price protection is that Shell was obliged to price protect Nanakuli, even if price protection was not incorporated into their contract, because price protection was the commercially reasonable standard for fair dealing in the asphaltic paving trade in Hawaii in 1974. Observance of those standards is part of the good-faith requirement that the Code imposes on merchants in performing a sales contract. Shell was obliged to price protect Nanakuli in order to act in good faith, Nanakuli argues, because such a practice was universal in that trade in that locality.

Shell presents three arguments for upholding the judgment n.o.v. or, on cross appeal, urging that the District Judge erred in admitting certain evidence. First, it says, the District Court should not have denied Shell's motion in limine to define trade, for purposes of trade usage evidence, as the sale and purchase of asphalt in Hawaii, rather than expanding the definition of trade to include other suppliers of materials to the asphaltic paving trade. Asphalt, its argument runs, was the subject matter of the disputed contract and the only product Shell supplied to the asphaltic paving trade. Shell protests that the judge, by expanding the definition of trade to include the other major suppliers to the asphaltic paving trade, allowed the admission of highly prejudicial evidence of routine price protection by all suppliers of aggregate. Asphaltic concrete paving is formed by mixing paving asphalt with crushed rock, or aggregate, in a "hot-mix" plant and then pouring the mixture onto the surface to be paved. Shell's second complaint is that the two prior occasions on which it price protected Nanakuli, although representing the only other instances of price increases under the 1969 contract, constituted mere waivers of the contract's price term, not a course of performance of the contract. A course of performance of the contract, in contrast to a waiver, demonstrates how the parties understand the terms of their agreement. Shell cites two U.C.C. Comments in support of that argument: (1) that, when the meaning of acts is ambiguous, the preference is for the waiver interpretation, and (2) that one act alone does not constitute a relevant course of performance. Shell's final argument is that, even assuming its prior price protection constituted a course of performance and that the broad trade definition was correct and evidence of trade usages by aggregate suppliers was admissible, price protection could not be construed as reasonably consistent with the express price term in the contract, in which case the Code provides that the express term controls. . . .

4. Price protection was practiced in the asphaltic paving trade by either extending the old price for a period of time after a new one went into effect or charging the old price for a specified tonnage, which represented work committed at the old price. In addition, several months' advance notice was given of price increases.

I. History of Nanakuli-Shell Relations Before 1973

[Until 1963, Nanakuli was the smaller of two major paving contractors in Hawaii and was unable to compete with the larger contractor, Hawaiian Bitumuls (H.B.), for government contracts. In 1963, Nanakuli negotiated a five-year contact with Shell, which provided Nanakuli with a guaranteed supply of asphalt at reduced prices. The new agreement enabled Shell to increase its presence as an asphalt supplier in Hawaii and allowed Nanakuli to expand its paving business.

In 1968, Shell and Nanakuli entered into further negotiations. Nanakuli wished to expand its cement plant at a cost of approximately $300,000. Nanakuli and Shell originally discussed Shell's financing of the expansion, but the parties finally agreed on indirect financing through a $2 discount on all sales of asphalt over 5,000 tons. In 1969, Nanakuli borrowed funds from its bank to finance the expansion. At the same time, Nanakuli and Shell executed several agreements, including a long-term supply contract to run until 1976.

Nanakuli offered evidence from its president, Lennox, and its vice president, Smith, that the 1969 contract included a commitment by Shell never to charge Nanakuli more than Chevron charged H.B., but the trial court ruled this evidence inadmissible as parol evidence because the court found that the price term of the 1969 contract was not ambiguous. — Eds.]

II. Trade Usage Before and After 1969

The key to price protection being so prevalent in 1969 that both parties would intend to incorporate it into their contract is found in one reality of the Oahu asphaltic paving market: the largest paving contracts were let by government agencies and none of the three levels of government — local, state, or federal — allowed escalation clauses for paving materials. If a paver bid at one price and another went into effect before the award was made, the paving company would lose a great deal of money, since it could not pass on increases to any government agency or to most general contractors. Extensive evidence was presented that, as a consequence, aggregate suppliers routinely price protected paving contractors in the 1960's and 1970's, as did the largest asphaltic supplier in Oahu, Chevron. . . .

III. Shell's Course of Performance of the 1969 Contract

The Code considers actual performance of a contract as the most relevant evidence of how the parties interpreted the terms of that contract. In 1970 and 1971, the only points at which Shell raised prices between 1969 and 1974, it price protected Nanakuli by holding its old price for four and three months, respectively, after announcing a price increase. . . .

IV. Shell-Nanakuli Relations, 1973-74

Two important factors form the backdrop for the 1974 failure by Shell to price protect Nanakuli: the Arab oil embargo and a complete change of command and policy in Shell's asphalt management. The jury was read a page or so from the World Book about the events and effect of the partial oil embargo, which shortened supplies and increased the price of petroleum, of which asphalt is a byproduct. The federal government imposed direct price controls on petroleum, but not on asphalt. Despite the international importance of those events, the jury may have viewed the second factor as of more direct significance to this case. The structural changes at Shell offered a possible explanation for why Shell in 1974 acted out of step with, not only the trade usage and commercially reasonable practices of all suppliers to the asphaltic paving trade on Oahu, but also with its previous agreement with, or at least treatment of, Nanakuli. . . .

We conclude that the decision to deny Nanakuli price protection was made by new Houston management without a full understanding of Shell's 1969 agreement with Nanakuli or any knowledge of its past pricing practices toward Nanakuli. If Shell did commit itself in 1969 to price protect Nanakuli, the Shell officials who made the decisions affecting Nanakuli in 1974 knew nothing about that commitment. Nor did they make any effective effort to find out. They acted instead solely in reliance on the 1969 contract's express price term, devoid of the commercial context that the Code says is necessary to an understanding of the meaning of the written word. Whatever the legal enforceability of Nanakuli's right, Nanakuli officials seem to have acted in good faith reliance on its right, as they understood it, to price protection and rightfully felt betrayed by Shell's failure to act with any understanding of its past practices toward Nanakuli.

V. Scope of Trade Usage

The validity of the jury verdict in this case depends on four legal questions. First, how broad was the trade to whose usages Shell was bound under its 1969 agreement with Nanakuli: did it extend to the Hawaiian asphaltic paving trade or was it limited merely to the purchase and sale of asphalt, which would only include evidence of practices by Shell and Chevron? Second, were the two instances of price protection of Nanakuli by Shell in 1970 and 1971 waivers of the 1969 contract as a matter of law or was the jury entitled to find that they constituted a course of performance of the contract? Third, could the jury have construed an express contract term of Shell's posted price at delivery as reasonably consistent with a trade usage and Shell's course of performance of the 1969 contract of price protection, which consisted of charging the old price at times of price increases, either for a period of time or for specific tonnage committed at a fixed price in non-escalating contracts? Fourth, could the jury have found that good faith obliged Shell to at least give advance notice of a $32 increase in 1974, that is, could they have found that the commercially reasonable standards of fair dealing in the trade in Hawaii in 1974 were to give some form of price protection?

We approach the first issue in this case mindful that an underlying purpose of the U.C.C. as enacted in Hawaii is to allow for liberal interpretation of commercial usages. The Code provides, "This chapter shall be liberally construed and applied to promote its underlying purposes and policies." Haw. Rev. Stat. §490:1-102(1). Only three purposes are listed, one of which is "[t]o permit the continued expansion of commercial practices through custom, usage and agreement of the parties. . . ." Id. §490:1-102(2)(b). . . .

The Code defines usage of trade as "any practice or method of dealing having such regularity of observance in a *place, vocation or trade* as to justify an expectation that it will be observed with respect to the transaction in question." Id. §490:1-205(2) (emphasis supplied). We understand the use of the word "or" to mean that parties can be bound by a usage common to the *place* they are in business, even if it is not the usage of their particular vocation or trade. That reading is borne out by the repetition of the disjunctive "or" in subsection 3, which provides that usages "in the vocation or trade in which they are engaged *or* of which they are or should be aware give particular meaning to and supplement or qualify terms of an agreement." Id. §490: 1-205(3). The drafters' Comments say that trade usage is to be used to reach the ". . . commercial meaning of the agreement. . . ." by interpreting the language "as meaning what it may fairly be expected to mean to parties involved in the particular transaction *in a given locality or* in a given *vocation or trade.*" Id., Comment 4 (emphasis supplied). The inference of the two subsections and the Comment, read together, is that a usage need not necessarily be one practiced by members of the party's own trade or vocation to be binding *if* it is so commonly practiced in a locality that a party should be aware of it. . . . This language indicates that Shell would be bound not only by usages of sellers of asphalt but by more general usages on Oahu, as long as those usages were so regular in their observance that Shell should have been aware of them. This reading of the Code, in our opinion, achieves an equitable result. A party is always held to conduct generally observed by members of his chosen trade because the other party is justified in so assuming unless he indicates otherwise. He is held to more general business practices to the extent of his actual knowledge of those practices or to the degree his ignorance of those practices is not excusable: they were so generally practiced he should have been aware of them.

[The court then cites two leading treatises — Corbin on Contracts and White & Summers, Uniform Commercial Code — to support its interpretation. — EDS.]. [Thus,] even if Shell did not "regularly deal" with aggregate supplies, it did deal constantly and almost exclusively on Oahu with one asphalt paver. It therefore should have been aware of the usage of Nanakuli and other asphaltic pavers to bid at fixed prices and therefore receive price protection from their materials suppliers due to the refusal by government agencies to accept escalation clauses. Therefore, we do not find the lower court abused its discretion or misread the Code as applied to the peculiar facts of this case in ruling that the applicable trade was the asphaltic paving trade in Hawaii. . . .

Shell argued not only that the definition of trade was too broad, but also that the practice itself was not sufficiently regular to reach the level of a usage and that Nanakuli failed to show with enough precision how the usage was carried out in order for a jury to calculate damages. The extent of a usage is ultimately a jury question. The Code provides, "The existence and scope of such a usage are to be proved as facts." Haw. Rev. Stat. §490:1-205(2). The practice must have "such regularity of observance . . . as to justify an expectation that it will be observed. . . ." Id. The Comment explains:

> The ancient English tests for "custom" are abandoned in this connection. Therefore, it is not required that a usage of trade be "ancient or immemorial," "universal" or the like. . . . [F]ull recognition is thus available for new usages and for usages currently observed by the great majority of decent dealers, even though dissidents ready to cut corners do not agree.

Id., Comment 5. The Comment's demand that "not universality but only the described 'regularity of observance' " is required reinforces the provision only giving "effect to usages of which the parties 'are or should be aware.' . . ." Id., Comment 7. A "regularly observed" practice of protection, of which Shell "should have been aware," was enough to constitute a usage that Nanakuli had reason to believe was incorporated into the agreement.[28]

Nanakuli went beyond proof of a regular observance. It proved and offered to prove that price protection was probably a universal practice by suppliers to the asphaltic paving trade in 1969. It had been practiced by H.C. & D. since at least 1962, by P.C. & A. since well before 1960, and by Chevron routinely for years, with the last specific instance before the contract being March, 1969, as shown by documentary evidence. The only usage evidence missing was the behavior by Shell, the only other asphalt supplier in Hawaii, prior to 1969. That was because its only major customer was Nanakuli and the judge ruled prior course of dealings between Shell and Nanakuli inadmissible. Shell did not point in rebuttal to one instance of failure to price protect by any supplier to an asphalt paver in Hawaii before its own 1974 refusal to price protect Nanakuli. Thus, there clearly was enough proof for a jury to find that the practice of price protection in the asphaltic paving trade existed in Hawaii in 1969 and was regular enough in its observance to rise to the level of a usage that would be binding on Nanakuli and Shell.

Shell next argues that, even if such a usage existed, its outlines were not precise enough to determine whether Shell would have extended the old price for Nanakuli for several months or would have charged the old price on the volume of tonnage committed at that price. The jury awarded Nanakuli damages based on the specific tonnage committed before the price increase of 1974. Shell says the jury could not have ascertained with enough certainty how price protection was carried out to calculate such an award for Nanakuli. The argument is not persuasive. The Code provides, "The remedies provided by this chapter shall be liberally administered to the end that the aggrieved party may be put in as good a position as if the other party had fully performed. . . ." Id. §490:1-106(1). The Comments list as one of three purposes of this section "to reject any doctrine that damages must be calculable with mathematical accuracy. Compensatory damages are often at best approximate: they have to be proved with whatever definiteness and accuracy the facts permit, but no more." Id., Comment

28. White and Summers write that Code requirements for proving a usage are "far less stringent" than the old ones for custom. "A usage of trade need not be *well known*, let alone 'universal.' " It only needs to be regular enough that the parties expect it to be observed. White & Summers, supra §3-3 at 87 (emphasis supplied). "Note particularly [in 1-205(1) & (2)] that it is not necessary for both parties to be consciously aware of the trade usage. It is enough if the trade usage is such as to 'justify an expectation' of its observance." Id. at 84.

1. Nanakuli got advance notices of each but the disputed increase by Shell, as well as an extension of several months at the old price in 1970, 1971, 1977, and 1978. Shell protests that in 1970 and 1971 Nanakuli's protected tonnage only amounted to 3,300 and 1,100 tons, respectively. Chevron's price protection of H.B. in 1969 however, is also part of the trade usage; H.B.'s protection amounted to 12,000 tons. The increase in Nanakuli's tonnage by 1974 is explained by its growth since the 1970 and 1971 increases.

In addition, the scope of protection offered by a particular usage is left to the jury. . . . The manner in which the usage of price protection was carried out was presented with sufficient precision to allow the jury to calculate damages at $220,800.

VI. Waiver or Course of Performance

Course of performance under the Code is the action of the parties in carrying out the contract at issue, whereas course of dealing consists of relations between the parties *prior* to signing that contract. Evidence of the latter was excluded by the District Judge; evidence of the former consisted of Shell's price protection of Nanakuli in 1970 and 1971. Shell protested that the jury could not have found that those two instances of price protection amounted to a course of performance of its 1969 contract, relying on two Code comments. First, one instance does not constitute a course of performance. "A single occasion of conduct does not fall within the language of this section. . . ." Haw. Rev. Stat. §490:2-208, Comment 4. Although the Comment rules out one instance, it does not further delineate how many acts are needed to form a course of performance. The prior occasions here were only two, but they constituted the only occasions before 1974 that would call for such conduct. In addition, the language used by a top asphalt official of Shell in connection with the first price protection of Nanakuli indicated that Shell felt that Nanakuli was entitled to some form of price protection. On that occasion in 1970 Blee, who had negotiated the contract with Nanakuli and was familiar with exactly what terms Shell was bound to by that agreement, wrote of the need to "bargain" with Nanakuli over the extent of price protection to be given, indicating that some price protection was a legal right of Nanakuli's under the 1969 agreement.

Shell's second defense is that the Comment expresses a preference for an interpretation of waiver. . . . Id., Comment 3. The preference for waiver only applies, however, where acts are ambiguous. It was within the province of the jury to determine whether those acts were ambiguous, and if not, whether they constituted waivers or a course of performance of the contract. The jury's interpretation of those acts as a course of performance was bolstered by evidence offered by Shell that it again price protected Nanakuli on the only two occasions of post-1974 price increases, in 1977 and 1978.

VII. Express Terms as Reasonably Consistent with Usage and Course of Performance

Perhaps one of the most fundamental departures of the Code from prior contract law is found in the parol evidence rule and the definition of an agreement between two parties. Under the U.C.C., an agreement goes beyond the written words on a piece of paper. " 'Agreement' means the bargain of the parties in fact as found in their language or by implication from other circumstances including course of dealing or usage of trade or course of performance as provided in this chapter (sections 490:1-205 and 490:2-208)." Id. §490:1-201(3). Express terms, then, do not constitute the entire agreement, which must be sought also in evidence of usages, dealings, and performance of the contract itself. The purpose of evidence of usages, which are defined in the previous section, is to help to understand the entire agreement. . . . Id. §490:1-205, Comment 4. Course of dealing is more important than usages of the trade, being specific usages between the two parties to the contract. "[C]ourse of dealing controls usage of trade." Id. §490:1-205(4). It "is a sequence of previous conduct between the parties to a particular transaction which is fairly to be regarded as establishing a common basis of understanding for interpreting their expressions and other conduct." Id. §490:1-205(1). Much of the evidence of prior dealings between Shell and Nanakuli in negotiating the 1963 contract and in carrying out similar earlier contracts was excluded by the court.

A commercial agreement, then, is broader than the written paper and its meaning is to be determined not just by the language used by them in the written contract but "by their action, read and interpreted in the light of commercial practices and other surrounding circumstances. The measure and background for interpretation are set by the commercial context, which may explain and supplement even the language of a formal or final writing." Id., Comment 1. Performance, usages, and prior dealings are important enough to be admitted always, even for a final and complete agreement; only if they cannot be reasonably reconciled with the express terms of the contract are they not binding on the parties. "The express terms of an agreement and an applicable course of dealing or usage of trade shall be construed wherever reasonable as consistent with each other; but when such construction is unreasonable express terms control both course of dealing and usage of trade and course of dealing controls usage of trade." Id. §490:1-205(4).

Of these three, then, [i.e., course of performance, course of dealing, and usage of trade — EDS.] the most important evidence of the agreement of the parties is their actual performance of the contract. Id. The operative definition of course of performance is as follows: "Where the contract for sale involves repeated occasions for performance by either party with knowledge of the nature of the performance and opportunity for objection to it by the other, any course of performance accepted or acquiesced in without objection shall be relevant to determine the meaning of the agreement." Id. §490:2-208(1). "Course of dealing . . . is restricted, literally, to a sequence of conduct between the parties previous to the agreement. However, the provisions of the Act on course of performance make it clear that a sequence of conduct after or under the agreement may have equivalent meaning (Section 2-208)." Id. 490:1-205, Comment 2. The importance of evidence of course of performance is explained: "The parties themselves know best what they have meant by their words of agreement and their action under that agreement is the best indication of what that meaning was. This section thus rounds out the set of factors which determines the meaning of the 'agreement.' . . ." Id. §490:2-208, Comment 1. "Under this section a course of performance is always relevant to determine the meaning of the agreement." Id., Comment 2.[33]

Our study of the Code provisions and Comments, then, form the first basis of our holding that a trade usage to price protect pavers at times of price increases for work committed on nonescalating contracts could reasonably be construed as consistent with an express term of seller's posted price at delivery. Since the agreement of the parties is broader than the express terms and includes usages, which may even add terms to the agreement,[34] and since the commercial background provided by those usages is vital to an understanding of the agreement, we follow the Code's mandate to proceed on the assumption that the parties have included those usages unless they cannot reasonably be construed as consistent with the express terms. . . .

[The Court then reviews a number of federal and state decisions holding that trade usage, course of dealing, and course of performance should be freely admitted. — EDS.]

Some guidelines can be offered as to how usage evidence can be allowed to modify a contract.[44] First, the court must allow a check on usage evidence by demanding that it be sufficiently definite and widespread to prevent unilateral post-hoc revision of contract terms by one party. The Code's intent is to put usage evidence on an objective basis. J. H. Levie, Trade Usage and Custom Under the Common Law and the Uniform Commercial Code, 40 N.Y.U.L. Rev. 1101 (1965), states:

33. Section 2-208, much like 1-205, provides "[t]he express terms of the agreement and any such course of performance, as well as any course of dealing and usage of trade, shall be construed whenever reasonable as consistent with each other; but when such construction is unreasonable, express terms shall control course of performance and course of performance shall control both course of dealing and usage of trade (section 490:1-205)." Id. §490:2-208(2).

34. "The agreement of the parties includes that part of their bargain found in course of dealing, usage of trade, or course of performance. These sources are relevant not only to the interpretation of express contract terms, but may themselves constitute contract terms." White & Summers, supra, §3-3 at 84.

44. White and Summers write that usage and dealings evidence "may not only supplement or qualify express terms, but in appropriate circumstances may even override express terms." White & Summers, supra, §3-3 at 84. "[T]he provision that express terms control inconsistent course of dealing and [usages and performance evidence] really cannot be taken at face value." Id. at 86. That reading, although at odds with the actual wording of the Code, is a realistic reading of what some of the cases allow. A better formulation of the Code's mandate is offered by R. W. Kirst, Usage of Trade and Course of Dealing: Subversion of the UCC Theory, 1977 [U. Ill.] Law Forum 811:

> The need to determine whether the parties intended a usage . . . to be part of the contract does not end if the court finds that the commercial practice is inconsistent with or contradicts the express language of the writing. If an inconsistency exists, the intention of the parties remains unclear. The parties may have intended either to include or exclude the practice. Determining the intent of the parties requires that the court attempt to construe the written term consistently with the commercial practice, if that is reasonable. If consistent construction is unreasonable the Code directs that the written term be taken as expressing the parties' intent. Before concluding that a jury could not reasonably find a consistent construction, the judge must understand the commercial background of the dispute.

Id. at 824.

> When trade usage adds new terms to cover matters on which the agreement is silent the court is really making a contract for the parties, even though it says it only consulted trade usage to find the parties' probable intent. There is nothing wrong or even unusual about this practice, which really is no different from reading constructive conditions into a contract. Nevertheless the court does create new obligations, and perhaps that is why the courts often say that usage . . . must be proved by clear and convincing evidence. . . .

Id. at 1102. Although the Code abandoned the traditional common law test of nonconsensual custom and views usage as a way of determining the parties' probable intent, id. at 1106-07, thus abolishing the requirement that common law custom be universally practiced, trade usages still must be well settled, id. at 1113. . . .

Evidence of a trade usage does not need to be protected against perjury because, as one commentator has written, "an outside standard does exist to help judge the truth of the assertion that the parties intended the usage to control the particular dispute: the existence and scope of the usage can be determined from other members of the trade." Kirst, supra, at 839. Kirst sets out guards on jury determination of usage evidence:

> Questions of the parties' intentions concerning an asserted trade usage or course of dealing will not always require a jury determination. If the evidence fails to show a practice is regularly observed, the judge can exclude the evidence because it does not show a course of dealing or usage of trade as defined in the Code. If the members of the trade confirm an actual usage but do not support the assertion that the usage applies to the particular facts in litigation, the judge will exclude evidence of the usage as irrelevant. If the parties used new and different language to convey their agreed intention to abandon the past practice, the court will recognize that practice under the old language is irrelevant to the contract containing the new language and, consequently, will exclude the evidence.

. . . That formulation of relevance of the usage evidence seems a fair one to follow in this case. Here the evidence was overwhelming that all suppliers to the asphaltic paving trade price protected customers under the same types of circumstances. Chevron's contract with H.B. was a similar long-term supply contract between a buyer and seller with very close relations, on a form supplied by the seller, covering sales of asphalt, and setting the price at seller's posted price, with no mention of price protection. The same commentator offers a second guideline:

> Because the stock printed forms cannot always reflect the changing methods of business, members of the trade may do business with a standard clause in the forms that they ignore in practice. If the trade consistently ignores obsolete clauses at variance with actual trade practices, a litigant can maintain that it is reasonable that the courts also ignore the clauses. Similarly, members of a trade may handle a particular subset of commercial transactions in a manner consistent [sic: inconsistent?] with written terms because the writing cannot provide for all variations or contingencies. Thus, if the trade regards an express term and a trade usage as consistent because the usage is not a complete contradiction but

> only an occasional but definite exception to a written term, the courts should interpret the contract according to the usage.

Kirst, supra, at 824. Levie, supra, at 1112, writes, "Astonishing as it will seem to most practicing attorneys, under the Code it will be possible in some cases to use custom to contradict the written agreement. . . . Therefore usage may be used to 'qualify' the agreement, which presumably means to 'cut down' express terms although not to negate them entirely." Here, the express price term was "Shell's Posted Price at time of delivery." A total negation of that term would be that the buyer was to set the price. It is a less than complete negation of the term that an unstated exception exists at times of price increases, at which times the old price is to be charged, for a certain period or for a specified tonnage, on work already committed at the lower price on nonescalating contracts. Such a usage forms a broad and important exception to the express term, but does not swallow it entirely. Therefore, we hold that, under these particular facts, a reasonable jury could have found that price protection was incorporated into the 1969 agreement between Nanakuli and Shell and that price protection was reasonably consistent with the express term of seller's posted price at delivery.

VIII. Good Faith in Setting Price

Nanakuli offers an alternative theory why Shell should have offered price protection at the time of the price increases of 1974. Even if price protection was not a term of the agreement, Shell could not have exercised good faith in carrying out its 1969 contract with Nanakuli when it raised its price by $32 effective January 1 in a letter written December 31st and only received on January 4, given the universal practice of advance notice of such an increase in the asphaltic paving trade. The Code provides, "A price to be fixed by the seller or by the buyer means a price for him to fix in good faith," Haw. Rev. Stat. §490:2-305(2). For a merchant good faith means "the observance of reasonable commercial standards of fair dealing in the trade." Id. 490:2-103(1)(b). The comment to Section 2-305 explains, "[I]n the normal case a 'posted price' . . . satisfies the good faith requirement." Id., Comment 3. However, the words "in the normal case" mean that, although a posted price will usually be satisfactory, it will not be so under all circumstances. In addition, the dispute here was not over the amount of the increase — that is, the price that the seller fixed — but over the manner in which that increase was put into effect. It is true that Shell, in order to observe the good faith standards of the trade in 1974, was not bound by the practices of aggregate companies, which did not labor under the same disabilities as did asphalt suppliers in 1974. However, Nanakuli presented evidence that Chevron, in raising its price to $76, gave at least six weeks' advance notice, in accord with the long-time usage of the asphaltic paving trade. Shell, on the other hand, gave absolutely no notice, from which the jury could have concluded that Shell's manner of carrying out the price increase of 1974 did not conform to commercially reasonable standards. In both the timing of the announcement and its refusal to protect work already bid at the old price, Shell could be found to have breached the obligation of good faith imposed by the

Code on all merchants. "Every contract or duty within this chapter imposes an obligation of good faith in its performance or enforcement," id. §490:1-203, which for merchants entails the observance of commercially reasonable standards of fair dealing in the trade. The Comment to 1-203 reads:

> This section sets forth a basic principle running throughout this Act. The principle involved is that in commercial transactions good faith is required in the performance and enforcement of all agreements or duties. Particular applications of this general principle appear in specific provisions of the Act. . . . It is further implemented by Section 1-205 on course of dealing and usage of trade.

Id. §490:1-203, Comment. Chevron's conduct in 1974 offered enough relevant evidence of commercially reasonable standards of fair dealing in the asphalt trade in Hawaii in 1974 for the jury to find that Shell's failure to give sufficient advance notice and price protect Nanakuli after the imposition of the new price did not conform to good faith dealings in Hawaii at that time.

Because the jury could have found for Nanakuli on its price protection claim under either theory, we reverse the judgment of the District Court and reinstate the jury verdict for Nanakuli in the amount of $220,800, plus interest according to law.

Reversed and remanded with directions to enter final judgment.

KENNEDY, Circuit Judge, concurring specially:

The case involves specific pricing practices, not an allegation of unfair dealing generally. Our opinion should not be interpreted to permit juries to import price protection or a similarly specific contract term from a concept of good faith that is not based on well-established custom and usage or other objective standards of which the parties had clear notice. Here, evidence of custom and usage regarding price protection in the asphaltic paving trade was not contradicted in major respects, and the jury could find that the parties knew or should have known of the practice at the time of making the contract. In my view, these are necessary predicates for either theory of the case, namely, interpretation of the contract based on the course of its performance or a finding that good faith required the seller to hold the price. With these observations, I concur.

NOTES AND QUESTIONS

1. *Defining usage of trade and related concepts.* In its opinion the court discusses usage of trade, course of dealing, and course of performance. As we saw earlier (Note 5 following the *Frigaliment* case), the UCC now defines each of those concepts in §1-303. The Restatement contains provisions that are similar to these Code provisions. Restatement (Second) §§222 (trade usage), 223 (course of dealing), and 202(4) (course of performance). How are these concepts different from one another? Which is most important in interpreting a contract? Why?

2. *Establishing a relevant trade usage.* As *Nanakuli* indicates, evidence of trade usage is only admissible if the party offering the evidence establishes that the usage exists. What is the burden of proof necessary to establish the existence of a trade usage? Who makes the determination of whether the usage exists? In Duffey v. Twentieth Century Fox Film Corp., 14 F. Supp. 3d 120, 132-133 (S.D.N.Y. 2014), the court held that the plaintiff actor in the "cult classic" movie "Office Space" did not establish a trade usage based on evidence drawn from a few dated, dissimilar cases that would limit the unambiguous contract language granting the production company all merchandising rights "throughout the universe" based on the film images. Once a trade usage is established by showing that it has sufficient regularity of observance in a place or market to justify the expectation that it will be followed, a party in that trade is presumed to be bound by it. See Joseph M. Perillo, Contracts §3.17, at 152 (7th ed. 2014); but see Flower City Painting Contractors, Inc. v. Gumina Constr. Co., 591 F.2d 162 (2d Cir. 1979) (newcomer to painting business not bound by a trade usage that term "units" included not only apartment interiors but exteriors and common buildings as well).

3. *Consistency between trade usage and express terms.* Courts are divided on the issue of when evidence of trade usage, course of dealing, or course of performance is admissible. Some courts adopt a restrictive view, holding that such evidence is inadmissible if it appears to contradict the terms of the written agreement between the parties. See, e.g., Southern Concrete Services, Inc. v. Mableton Contractors, Inc., 407 F. Supp. 581 (N.D. Ga. 1975), *aff'd per curiam,* 569 F.2d 1154 (5th Cir. 1978) (evidence of trade usage showing that quantity term of contract was not binding on either buyer or seller was inadmissible). Other courts have gone to the opposite extreme, holding that such evidence is almost always admissible, even if it appears, as suggested by the *Nanakuli* court, that the trade usage "cuts down" the express terms. See, e.g., Tigg Corp. v. Dow Corning Corp., 822 F.2d 358 (3d Cir. 1987) (evidence of trade usage admissible to show that agreement should be regarded as contract for buyer's requirements, despite stated minimums in writing; no requirement that written contract be found ambiguous before such evidence admitted).

4. *"Careful negation" of trade usage.* Comment 2 to UCC §2-202 provides that terms derived from a course of dealing or a usage of trade are deemed to be part of the agreement unless "carefully negated." Professor Kirst, in an article cited extensively by the court in *Nanakuli*, argued that mere "boilerplate" language generally negating the effect of trade usage or course of dealing should not be conclusive; to give it that effect would elevate form over the actual intent of the parties. Roger W. Kirst, Usage of Trade and Course of Dealing: Subversion of the UCC Theory, 1977 U. Ill. L.F. 811, 863-868. Professor Kirst would agree, however, that a clause that specifically negates a particular trade usage or course of dealing may be given effect. Compare Allapattah Services, Inc. v. Exxon Corp., 61 F. Supp. 2d 1308 (S.D. Fla. 1999) (typical merger clause does not suffice to negate importance of trade usage and course of dealing) with Madison Indus., Inc. v. Eastman Kodak Co., 581 A.2d 85 (N.J. Super. Ct. App. Div. 1990) (evidence of trade usage excluded where contract provided in general language that

no course of dealing, course of performance, or usage of trade should be effective unless in a writing signed by authorized agents of both parties).

5. The Nanakuli case as an exemplar of "modern" contract law. The *Nanakuli* case was decided in 1981, a time that can with hindsight be seen as a high-water mark for the kind of "modern" contract law developed over roughly the middle half of the twentieth century. See generally Charles L. Knapp, An Offer You Can't Revoke, 2004 Wis. L. Rev. 309, 316-319 (listing some characteristics of "modern" contract law). The seeming modern consensus formed by the convergence of UCC Article 2 and the Restatement (Second) of Contracts has since splintered, however, under the dual onslaught of Critical Legal Studies from the left and Law and Economics from the right. Professor DiMatteo has characterized *Nanakuli* as displaying for the most part an embrace of full "contextualism" – the interpretation and enforcement of contracts in light of the commercial setting of the transaction, the aims of the parties and the real-world context of the case, as advocated by Karl Llewellyn and other legal realists. Larry A. DiMatteo, Reason and Context: A Dual Track Theory of Interpretation, 109 Penn. St. L. Rev. 397, 471-474 (2004). Others have seen in the *Nanakuli* case an illustration of the kind of "relational" contract law advocated by Ian Macneil. Peter Linzer, Uncontracts: Context, Contorts and the Relational Approach, 1988 Ann. Surv. of Amer. L. 139, 155-160, 182-185.

PROBLEM 5-1

A & B Tax Preparers, Inc. is a corporation engaged in the nationwide business of preparing state and federal income tax returns. In 2015, Herbert Keynes, a resident of Minneapolis, answered A & B's advertisement seeking a local manager for its Neville, California office. After investigating Keynes's background and interviewing him personally, A & B offered Keynes the position of manager of the Neville office. Keynes signed one of the company's printed forms it uses for hiring managers. (A copy of the contract follows this problem; portions in italic are handwritten.)

After signing the contract, Keynes resigned his job in Minneapolis and moved to Neville. Over the next several years the Neville office became very successful. Keynes's share of profits increased from approximately $75,000 in 2016 to over $100,000 for the year ending January 31, 2018.

In September 2018, Keynes received a letter from A & B in which the company stated that effective February 1, 2019, his percentage of net profits would be reduced from 50 percent to 40 percent. The letter referred to paragraph 6.1 of the policy manual of the company, which provided as follows:

> **6.1 Compensation of Managers**. Profit percentages for managers are guaranteed only for the first two years of employment. The Company reserves the right to adjust percentages in subsequent years based on the profitability of the local branch.

The letter stated that Keynes should sign and return the letter to A & B by October 15, 2018. Keynes telephoned Henry Adams, the president of the company, to complain about this change, saying that he understood that the company would not unilaterally change his profit percentage.

Adams responded that Keynes had received a copy of the policy manual and that he assumed Keynes had read and understood it. Adams also said that considering the growth in profits of the Neville branch, Keynes's income should continue to increase, even though Keynes would be receiving a lower percentage of the profits. Keynes wasn't satisfied with these answers and told Adams that he wouldn't agree to the change. Adams said that Keynes did not have a choice and that if he did not return the letter by October 15, the company would be forced to terminate the agreement.

Keynes ignored Adams's threats and refused to sign the letter. On October 20, 2018, Keynes received a letter from A & B informing him that the company was terminating his contract as manager effective immediately. The company has now brought suit against Keynes seeking an injunction to prevent him from using the company's name and property; Keynes has filed counterclaims for damages and injunctive relief.

During the direct examination of Mr. Keynes at trial the following takes place:

Keynes's lawyer: Mr. Keynes, did you have a telephone conversation with Mr. Adams on December 14, 2015?

A & B's lawyer: Objection, your honor. Parol evidence rule.

Judge: Bailiff, please escort the jury out of the courtroom. [After the jury leaves] All right, counsel, what will the testimony show?

Keynes's lawyer: Your honor, Mr. Keynes will testify that he called Mr. Adams on December 14, 2015 and the parties discussed paragraph 6.1 of the manual. Mr. Keynes will testify that he told Mr. Adams that he did not think that it would be fair for him to resign his job, move to Neville, build up the business, and then have the company arbitrarily increase its share of the profits. Mr. Keynes will also testify that Adams told him that if he did a good job he didn't need to worry about the company increasing its share of profits. He said that the company had only increased its percentage of profits in the past when a manager had not met company projections of profitability. Mr. Keynes will also testify that he asked Adams to put that in writing but that Adams refused because he said the company's lawyers had told him not to have any side agreements.

Judge: [Speaking to counsel for A & B] I'll hear you now, counsel.

As counsel for A & B, what arguments would you make against admissibility of the evidence? As counsel for Keynes, what arguments would you make to admit the evidence? As judge, how would you rule on A & B's objection?

MANAGER'S CONTRACT

Agreement made and entered into this *17th* day of *December, 2015*, by and between *Herbert Keynes* (hereinafter referred to as "Manager") and A & B Tax Preparers, Inc. (hereinafter referred to as "Company").

In consideration of the mutual covenants contained in this document, the parties hereby agree as follows:

1. **Employment and Duties.** Company hereby employs Manager to manage its office at *Neville, California.* Manager agrees to operate the office in accordance with the provisions of the Company's policy manual, a copy of which has previously been given to Manager. Company reserves the right to change the provisions of the manual at any time. The provisions of the manual, as modified from time to time, are incorporated by reference as part of this contract.

2. **Compensation.** As compensation for his services, Manager shall be entitled to 50% of the net profits of the office, after deduction of all expenses of the office.

3. **Accounting and Inspection of Records.** Manager shall remit to the Company on the fifteenth and last days of each month the Company's share of profits of the office, along with an income statement for such period certified by the Manager to be correct. The Company reserves the right to audit the books and records of the office at any time.

4. **Termination.** This agreement shall continue for a two-year period from *January 31, 2016* until *January 31, 2018*. The agreement shall automatically renew for additional two-year periods until either party gives written notice of termination at least ninety days prior to the end of any such two-year period. The Company reserves the right to terminate this agreement at any time for cause.

5. **Entire Agreement.** This document constitutes the entire agreement of the parties. The Company makes no representations, warranties, or guarantees of any kind whatsoever.

6. **Additional Provisions.**

The Company agrees to pay Keynes's moving expenses to Neville, California in an amount not to exceed $7,000.

In witness whereof, the parties have executed this agreement on the day and year first above written.

A & B Tax Preparers, Inc.

By: */s/ Henry Adams*

Henry Adams, Pres.

By: */s/ Herbert Keynes*

Signature of Manager

PROBLEM 5-2

Pursuant to an urban redevelopment plan, the city of Northeast "condemned" property located at 1416 F Street for $2.5 million, the fair market value of the property at the time of the condemnation. (In condemnation proceedings, either a government agency or someone acting pursuant to governmental authority acquires privately owned property to be used for a public purpose. The owner is entitled to receive fair market value for her property. Although the condemnor and owner frequently reach agreement for a voluntary transfer of the property, the property may be taken against the owner's will.

Condemnation proceedings are controlled by statutory provisions which vary from state to state.)

At the time of the taking, the property was owned by Janice N. Owens, a local real estate developer, and was under a 30-year lease (expiring October 31, 2030) to Metropolitan Parking, Inc., which used the property for a parking garage.

Owens claims that the entire condemnation award properly belongs to her as owner of the property, while Metropolitan claims that it is entitled to a portion of the award measured by the fair market value of its leasehold interest. Because of the dispute between Owens and Metropolitan, the city has paid the condemnation award into court for a judicial determination of the distribution of the condemnation award.

The lease between Owens and Metropolitan does not specifically mention condemnation; it contains the following clauses:

ARTICLE I

Definitions

For the purposes hereof, unless the context otherwise requires: . . .

Section 1.04. Any reference herein to the termination of this lease shall be deemed to include any termination hereof by expiration, default, or otherwise. . . .

ARTICLE XX

Section 20.01. Upon termination of this lease by default, lapse of time, or for any reason, all of the right, title, and interest of Lessee in and to the premises and the leasehold estate created hereby shall automatically vest in Lessor without the execution of any further instrument.

(1) Assume you are a lawyer representing Metropolitan. What fact investigation would you undertake in preparing your case? Be prepared to explain why the factual questions you would investigate would be significant.

(2) Assume you know no facts other than those stated above. What arguments would you make in support of Metropolitan's claim to a share of the condemnation award?

(3) Assume you represent Owens. What arguments would you make in support of her claim to the entire condemnation award?

(4) Assume you represent a tenant who is negotiating a lease of property. Draft a clause to include in the agreement that would protect the tenant against the risk of loss resulting from condemnation.

REVIEW QUESTIONS – CHAPTER FIVE

1. In February 2019, Jim, the owner of a janitorial company, contacted Ann, the owner of an accounting business, about Ann taking over the billing process for Jim. After negotiating for a month in person and by email, Jim

and Ann both signed a two-page contract on March 24 that provided Anne would "receive billing invoices on Friday of each week for customers served by Jim's Janitorial Service that week and will mail bills to customers on Wednesdays." The contract was to last for one year from April 1, 2019. The contract also included a statement that "this writing contains the entire agreement of the parties." In August, Jim discovered that Ann was not sending out bills to customers each week, but instead was sending out bills every two weeks. Jim asked Ann about this practice. Ann responded she was only required to send out bills by Wednesday during weeks that she did mailings, but she was not required to send bills every week. She stated her staff had calculated that it was more efficient to do mailings every other week. Jim has an email from Ann on March 3, 2019, in which she stated, "I will collect your service invoices each Friday and send bills the following week." Would Jim be likely to succeed in action against Ann for breach of the contract due to her mailing practice?

A. Yes, because the email from Ann is relevant negotiating history that would explain the parties' agreement.
B. Yes, because the terms in the written contract have only one plain meaning which requires a mailing every week.
C. No, because the email from Ann would be barred from consideration due to the merger clause.
D. No, because Ann offered a compelling business reason for deviating from the parties' contract terms.

2. Clara, a home improvement contractor, and Hannah, a home-owner, both signed a brief one-page "work bill" form which simply stated, "$4,000 – a new fence for backyard – redwood five-foot high – pay in full on completion." The writing did not contain a merger clause. Hannah alleges that there was also an oral understanding that Clara would receive an additional $500 for removing debris from the old fence and disposing of it at a waste facility. Clara dismantled the old fence and placed it in the center of Hannah's backyard. When Clara completed the new fence and asked for payment, Hannah asked about removal of the old fence debris. Clara replied that she never committed to the $500 price to remove the old fence and that she is only willing to do so for $1,000. Hannah then refused to pay the $4,000 for the new fence. If a lawsuit ensues, would Hannah be able to offer evidence of the alleged oral agreement to have the old fence removed for $500?

A. No, because the alleged oral agreement would contradict the written agreement.
B. No, because there is no ambiguity in the written agreement.
C. Yes, because the alleged oral agreement would be a separate contract with separate consideration from the written agreement.
D. Yes, because the absence of a merger clause would make the written agreement a partial integration.

3. Lucy Lee, an art collector, writes the following email to Grant Gilmore, a prominent art dealer:

> Dear Grant:
>
> As you know, I own four oil paintings by Warren Wyatt, entitled "Spring," "Summer," "Autumn," and "Winter." Because I am temporarily in need of immediate funds for another project, I'm offering to sell all my Wyatts to you for a total of $280,000, delivery and payment to be made within one month. As you know, the paintings were recently appraised at $300,000. Please let me know if you accept my offer. - Lucy Lee

Grant immediately writes back to Lucy:

> Lucy: That's great news! I accept gladly. I'll be in touch shortly to work out the details. - Grant

In the discussions that follow, Grant tells Lucy that for his $280,000 he expects to receive not only the four oil paintings mentioned in her email but also a set of six small water-color sketches by Wyatt that Lucy owns. Lucy denies that she intended to include those in her offer and correctly states that the six sketches themselves have been valued at more than $500,000. Would Grant be likely to succeed in an action to obtain the oil paintings and the sketches for $280,000?

A. Yes, because Lucy's written offer clearly stated "all my Wyatts" for $280,000.
B. Yes, because any ambiguity in the agreement would be due to Lucy's drafting error.
C. No, because Lucy's note refers to the four oil paintings by name, and only to them.
D. No, because interpreting the contract to include the paintings and the sketches would be unreasonable.
E. No, because there was no meeting of the minds.

4. Olga was the owner of two homes, a primary home in the capital city and a lakeside cabin on the other side of the state of Adams. Olga owned a car in each location. Olga's daughter, Enid, graduated from college in June 2018 and decided to live in the cabin for the following year with her college friend, Fay, while the two of them collaborated on a writing project. Olga contacted her automobile insurance company, Acme Insurance, to renew her auto insurance policy for the coming year and to make sure that both Enid and Fay would be fully covered while driving her second car. The Acme agent said that the policy covered friends who were not listed on the policy when driving with Olga's permission. Olga paid her annual premium on June 10, 2018, and received a new copy of the policy one week later. On April 15, 2019, Fay was involved in an accident while driving Olga's car. The driver of the other car promptly brought a lawsuit against Olga and Fay for physical injuries and property damage. Olga filed a claim with Acme under her auto policy but Acme denied coverage based on language on page 7 of the 20-page policy which defined a "permissive driver" as "someone other

than a listed driver who does not regularly drive the auto for more than 30 consecutive days." Because Fay had driven the car regularly for more than nine months, Acme said that she was not a permissive driver and was not covered. Olga had never read the policy and was not aware of the definition of a "permissive driver." If the state of Adams has adopted a broad version of the reasonable expectations doctrine, would Olga be likely to succeed in a lawsuit to assert coverage under the policy for Fay's accident?

A. Yes, because Olga did not receive her copy of the policy until after she had paid her renewal premium.
B. Yes, because the limitation in the policy was fundamentally at odds with the contract terms as represented by the agent to Olga.
C. No, because Olga has admitted that she never read the full insurance policy.
D. No, because there was not any patent ambiguity in the insurance policy.

5. Bob Byer entered into negotiations to purchase a house from Sam Seller during April 2019. On April 15, while touring the house with his realtor, Bob noticed some water stains on the ceiling in an upstairs bedroom. Bob asked Sam, who happened to be present, about the condition of the roof. Sam stated that there had been a leak in the roof but said it was repaired during March 2019. Sam went on to say, "Rest assured that the roof is in good shape." In fact, the roof actually had not been repaired. On April 21, 2019, Bob signed a five-page, standardized purchase contract for the house which contained a provision which read, "Seller makes no representations concerning the condition of the roof, plumbing, or electrical wiring in the house. Buyer may conduct any inspections of the house that may be desired." Another paragraph read, "This writing contains the entire agreement of the parties." Bob took possession of the house on June 2, 2016, and the next day he discovered that the roof was still leaking in the upstairs bedroom when a rainstorm occurred. Would Bob be likely to succeed in an action to rescind the home sales contract?

A. Yes, because the oral commitment about the roof would modify the written contract.
B. Yes, because a merger clause would not bar evidence of a claim for fraud in the inducement.
C. No, because the writing would supersede Sam's earlier oral statement about the roof.
D. No, because a buyer cannot reasonably rely on any oral statements from a seller.

CHAPTER 6

Supplementing the Agreement: Implied Terms, the Obligation of Good Faith, and Warranties

Up to this point, we have generally concentrated on the problem of discovering and applying the agreement of the parties. As Chapter 5 demonstrated, the parties' true "agreement" may involve more than their formal written expressions of agreement; it may be found as well in their informal writings and in their conversations, or even in their actions. And all of these may be interpreted in the light of the parties' own dealings, past and present, and of the customs and mores of the community in which they were acting. In this chapter we widen our field of vision still further, to take in the possibility that the "contract" (meaning, here, a set of legal obligations) that the court enforces in a given case will include not merely those terms on which the parties have thus "agreed," but also other terms, which the court finds to be "implied" in that agreement.

A. THE RATIONALE FOR IMPLIED TERMS

The phrase *implied term* is itself ambiguous, of course. In one sense, any term that the court finds to be "implicit" in the parties' words or conduct even though not literally expressed by them is an implied term – implied, in fact, by the parties themselves. In this chapter, we will be using the notion of an implied term to refer also to a term that the court does not find in the parties' agreement, even as broadly viewed, but that the court holds should be "implied by law" – made a part of that agreement by operation of the rules of law rather than by the agreement of the parties themselves. Sometimes a term will be implied (in this latter sense) because a statute so provides; sometimes because common law precedents dictate, or because the court concludes that in the particular case its implication is appropriate.

By the time our survey of this area has been completed, you may well conclude that the borderline between terms that are implied-in-fact (i.e., agreed to in some meaningful sense by the parties themselves) and implied-in-law (imposed by the court) is not an easy one to draw. Certainly one of the reasons militating in favor of an implied-by-law term may be its apparent consistency with the intention of the parties, as evinced by those terms to which they did agree. Nevertheless, the process of implication is somewhat more complicated than this, and the goals this area of contract law may serve are more varied than merely an effectuating of the parties' own intent, as the following materials will demonstrate.

Wood v. Lucy, Lady Duff-Gordon

New York Court of Appeals 222 N.Y. 88, 118 N.E. 214 (1917)

Appeal from a judgment entered April 24, 1917, upon an order of the Appellate Division of the Supreme Court . . . which reversed an order of Special Term denying a motion by defendant for judgment in her favor upon the pleadings and granted said motion. . . .

CARDOZO, J.

The defendant styles herself "a creator of fashions." Her favor helps a sale. Manufacturers of dresses, millinery and like articles are glad to pay for a certificate of her approval. The things which she designs, fabrics, parasols and what not, have a new value in the public mind when issued in her name. She employed the plaintiff to help her to turn this vogue into money. He was to have the exclusive right, subject always to her approval, to place her indorsements on the designs of others. He was also to have the exclusive right to place her own designs on sale, or to license others to market them. In return, she was to have one-half of "all profits and revenues" derived from any contracts he might make. The exclusive right was to last at least one year from April 1, 1915, and thereafter from year to year unless terminated by notice of ninety days. The plaintiff says that he kept the contract on his part, and that the defendant broke it. She placed her indorsement on fabrics, dresses and millinery without his knowledge, and withheld the profits. He sues her for the damages, and the case comes here on demurrer.

Lady Duff-Gordon, date unknown.

The agreement of employment is signed by both parties. It has a wealth of recitals. The defendant insists, however, that it lacks the elements of a contract. She says that the plaintiff does not bind himself to anything. It is true that he does not promise in so many words that he will use reasonable efforts to place the defendant's indorsements and market her designs. We think, however, that such a promise is fairly to be implied. The law has outgrown its primitive stage of formalism when the precise word was the sovereign talisman, and every slip was fatal. It takes a broader view today. A promise may be lacking, and yet the whole writing may be "instinct with an obligation," imperfectly expressed (Scott, J., in McCall Co. v. Wright, 133 App. Div. 62; Moran v. Standard Oil Co., 211 N.Y. 187, 198). If that is so, there is a contract.

The implication of a promise here finds support in many circumstances. The defendant gave an *exclusive* privilege. She was to have no right for at least a year to place her own indorsements or market her own designs except through the agency of the plaintiff. The acceptance of the exclusive agency was an assumption of its duties (Phoenix Hermetic Co. v. Filtrine Mfg. Co., 164 App. Div. 424; W.G. Taylor Co. v. Bannerman, 120 Wis. 189; Mueller v. Bethesda Mineral Spring Co., 88 Mich. 390). We are not to suppose that one party was to be placed at the mercy of the other (Hearn v. Stevens & Bro., 111 App. Div. 101, 106; Russell v. Allerton, 108 N.Y. 288). Many other terms of the agreement point the same way. We are told at the outset by way of recital that "the said Otis F. Wood possesses a business organization adapted to the placing of such indorsements as the said Lucy, Lady Duff-Gordon has approved."

The implication is that the plaintiff's business organization will be used for the purpose for which it is adapted. But the terms of the defendant's compensation are even more significant. Her sole compensation for the grant of an exclusive agency is to be one-half of all the profits resulting from the plaintiff's efforts. Unless he gave his efforts, she could never get anything. Without an implied promise, the transaction cannot have such business "efficacy as both parties must have intended that at all events it should have" (Bowen, L.J., in The Moorcock, 14 P.D. 64, 68). But the contract does not stop there. The plaintiff goes on to promise that he will account monthly for all moneys received by him, and that he will take out all such patents and copyrights and trademarks as may in his judgment be necessary to protect the rights and articles affected by the agreement. It is true, of course, as the Appellate Division has said, that if he was under no duty to try to market designs or to place certificates of indorsement, his promise to account for profits or take out copyrights would be valueless. But in determining the intention of the parties, the promise *has* a value. It helps to enforce the conclusion that the plaintiff *had* some duties. His promise to pay the defendant one-half of the profits and revenues resulting from the exclusive agency and to render accounts monthly, was a promise to use reasonable efforts to bring profits and revenues into existence. For this conclusion, the authorities are ample. . . .

The judgment of the Appellate Division should be reversed, and the order of the Special Term affirmed, with costs in the Appellate Division and in this court.

CUDDEBACK, MCLAUGHLIN and ANDREWS, JJ., concur; HISCOCK, Ch. J., CHASE and CRANE, JJ., dissent.

Judgment reversed, etc.

NOTES AND QUESTIONS

1. *Factual context.* The historical and economic context of the Wood case is discussed by Professor Walter F. Pratt, Jr., in his article, American Contract Law at the Turn of the Century, 39 S.C. L. Rev. 415 (1988). Professor Pratt explains that Lady Duff-Gordon rose from a meager start in business to become one of the preeminent designers of her time and that she breached her exclusive marketing contract with Wood by directly entering into a very "innovative" arrangement to sell her designer dresses through the Sears, Roebuck and Company mail order catalogue. Id. at 429-430, 438-439. Professor Pratt identifies a number of other imaginative business measures taken by Lady Duff-Gordon and observes that she is also remembered for having survived the sinking of the Titanic. Id. at 419 n.14, 429-432. In 2007, in honor of the 90th anniversary of the decision, Pace University held a symposium on the case. See Symposium, The Enduring Legacy of Wood v. Lucy, Lady Duff-Gordon, 28 Pace U. L. Rev. 162 (2008).

2. *Implied terms and illusory promises.* In the course of his opinion for the court in *Wood*, Judge Cardozo declares that the implication of a promise on Wood's part is necessary to give the parties' agreement "business efficacy." "We are not to suppose," he declares, "that one party was to be placed at the mercy of the other." Do you agree? Is it conceivable that Lady Duff-Gordon might have regarded even an agreement that did *not* impose such obligations on Wood as having sufficient "business efficacy" from her point of view to make it worth entering into? Suppose the agreement between them had generally been as described in the above case, but that it had in addition expressly provided that while Wood was free to make efforts on her behalf (from which, if successful, he and she would both profit), he was not *obligated* to do so. Would such an agreement have been enforceable by Lady Duff-Gordon? By Wood? In an article discussing generally the requirement of consideration, Professor Melvin Eisenberg takes the position that agreements in which one party makes only a nonbinding, "illusory" promise frequently reflect a rational bargain and ought to be enforceable according to their terms. The party making the *non*illusory promise, he asserts, has in effect bargained for a "chance": the chance to show that his performance is attractive. (As an analogy, Eisenberg cites the "money-back" guarantee, by which the seller demonstrates his own confidence in his product by promising to refund the buyer's money if she is not satisfied for any reason. See UCC §2-326, defining the "sale on approval.") Melvin A. Eisenberg, The Principles of Consideration, 67 Cornell L. Rev. 640, 649-651 (1982).

Recent decisions continue to follow the principle recognized in *Wood* that an implied obligation to use reasonable efforts will prevent a somewhat indefinite promise from being illusory. See TMG Kreations, LLC v. Seltzer, 771 F.3d 1006 (7th Cir. 2014) (citing *Wood* as accepted, uniform law that exclusive distributorship contract includes implied promise to use best efforts); A.J. Amer Agency, Inc. v. Astonish Results, LLC, 2014 WL 3496964 (D.R.I.) (describing holding in *Wood* on implied terms as "iconic").

3. *When should a promise to use "reasonable" or "best efforts" be implied?* In *Wood*, the defendant claimed that although their agreement obligated her to

market her designs only through Wood, it left him apparently free to do nothing on her behalf, while at the same time representing whomever else he pleased. Such an arrangement would have lacked "business efficacy," according to Judge Cardozo, because it would have effectively placed one party (Lucy) at the mercy of another (Wood), and therefore the court implied a duty on Wood's part to use reasonable efforts on Lucy's behalf. The *Wood* case is generally regarded as the genesis of the provision in UCC §2-306(2) that imposes a "best efforts" obligation in cases where the contract for sale calls for "exclusive dealing." See MDC Corp. v. John H. Harland Co., 228 F. Supp. 2d 387, 393 n.3 (S.D.N.Y. 2002). Cases under the Code have explored the extent to which an arrangement must be "exclusive" to trigger the best efforts obligation of §2-306(2). In *MDC*, the contract permitted a requirements seller to maintain certain other existing relationships with particular customers; the parties' relationship was nevertheless held to be sufficiently "exclusive" to obligate the requirements buyer to use its best efforts to generate a market for the seller's goods. MDC Corp, 228 F. Supp. 2d at 394; see also Tigg Corp. v. Dow Corning Corp., 962 F.2d 1119, 1125 (3d Cir. 1992) (contract permitting supplier to sell to others if buyer failed to buy stated minimum amounts nevertheless held to be "exclusive dealing arrangement" invoking UCC §2-306(2); once minimum was reached seller could sell only to buyer under their contract). Other aspects of the law's treatment of requirements contracts are discussed in the Comment that follows Seidenberg v. Summit Bank in the next section of this chapter.

4. *Assessing best or reasonable efforts.* Suppose that the plaintiff in this case had instead been Lady Duff-Gordon, asserting that defendant Wood should respond in damages because allegedly he had failed to use reasonable efforts to promote the sale of her designs and endorsements. In that case, would the implied obligation assumed by Wood under their agreement have been sufficient to enable her complaint to survive defendant Wood's demurrer? If so, what obstacle would she still have faced before achieving her goal of recovering a judgment?

Parties frequently define an express obligation in terms of "best efforts" or "reasonable efforts." The court in *Wood* found an implied promise to use "reasonable efforts," while UCC §2-306(2) implies a duty to use "best efforts." Do the two different wordings suggest different levels of obligation? Courts have adopted widely differing approaches to the meaning of "best efforts" clauses. A minority of courts refuse to enforce such clauses on the ground of vagueness; some courts treat the clauses as the equivalent of "good faith"; for others the clauses impose fiduciary obligations on the performing party. See Zachary Miller, Comment, Best Efforts?: Differing Judicial Interpretations of a Familiar Term, 48 Ariz. L. Rev. 615 (2006). Most courts, however, seem to define "best efforts" in terms of reasonableness or diligence. See Samica Enterprises, LLC v. Mail Boxes Etc. USA, Inc., 637 F. Supp. 2d 712 (C.D. Cal. 2008) (under California law "best efforts" requires a party to make such efforts as are reasonable based on the abilities of the party, the means available to it, and the expectations of the other party); Maestro West Chelsea SPE LLC v. Pradera Realty Inc., 954 N.Y.S.2d 819 (Sup. Ct. 2012) (duty of best efforts imposes obligation to act in good faith in light of one's capabilities and to pursue all reasonable methods, usually a question of fact); E. Allan Farnsworth, On Trying to Keep One's Promises: The Duty of Best Efforts in Contract Law, 46 U. Pitt. L. Rev. 1, 8 (1984) (distinguishing good faith, which has honesty and fairness at its core, and best efforts, a more exacting standard, the essence of which is diligence).

5. *Implied-in-fact or implied-in-law?* Would you characterize the promise to use reasonable efforts in *Wood* as implied-in-law or implied-in-fact? Both? Does it make any difference? Cf. Alta Vista Properties, LLC v. Mauer Vision Ctr., PC, 855 N.W.2d 722 (Iowa 2014) (holding that explicit right of landlord to sell property during lease would also require implied right to show property at reasonable times to prospective purchasers, based on express terms and applicable legal principles). The connection between implication from facts and implication by law is further illustrated by the following cases.

Leibel v. Raynor Manufacturing Co.

Kentucky Court of Appeals 571 S.W.2d 640 (1978)

HOWERTON, Judge.

This is an appeal from a summary judgment dismissing Count I of appellant's three-count complaint. The dismissal of Count I was deemed to be a final, appealable judgment. With this we agree and accept jurisdiction.

The essential facts are that the parties entered into an oral agreement whereby appellant was to have an exclusive dealer-distributorship for appellee's garage doors in a territory extending for a 50-mile radius from Lexington, Kentucky. The agreement was entered into on or about March 1, 1974. The appellee agreed to sell and deliver to the appellant its garage doors, operators and parts at the factory distributor price, and the appellant agreed to sell, install and service Raynor products exclusively, thereby establishing a relationship of dealer-distributor and manufacturer-supplier. There is no real dispute concerning the nature of the relationship.

As a result of the agreement, the appellant borrowed substantial sums of money in order to make certain capital expenditures, purchase an inventory, and to provide working capital for starting the business, including the rental of storage and office space, employment of personnel, and the purchase of a service truck, tools and equipment.

After two years of what appears to have been decreasing sales of Raynor products in the Lexington area, appellee notified the appellant on or about June 30, 1976, that as of that date the relationship was terminated. Appellant was also notified that Helton Overhead Door Sales had been established by the appellee as the new dealer-distributor for the area, and that the appellant would be required to order all future doors, operators and parts from the new dealer-distributor.

Appellee's motion for a summary judgment was based on the ground that the agreement was for an indefinite duration, and that it could be terminated at will by either party. The appellant resisted the motion on the theory that he was entitled to reasonable notice of appellee's intention to terminate the agreement.

On April 20, 1977, the circuit court granted the summary judgment and entered its memorandum opinion, setting forth its . . . reasons for the judgment. . . .

We disagree with the conclusions of the trial court and hold that reasonable notification is required in order to terminate an on-going oral agreement for the sale of goods in a relationship of manufacturer-supplier and dealer-distributor or franchisee. The summary judgment must therefore be set aside and a determination must be made on the factual issue of whether or not the notification of termination given in this case was reasonable under the circumstances.

Appellant argues that this contract is now controlled by Article II of the Uniform Commercial Code. The opinion of the trial court provided only that, "It is the opinion of the court that the Uniform Commercial Code applies to the sale of goods and is not intended to apply to the type of situation we have in this case." The rule for application of Article II in Kentucky was stated in Buttorff v. United Electronic Laboratories, Inc., Ky., 459 S.W.2d 581 (1970). According to the opinion in *Buttorff*, supra, we are to look to the real nature of the agreement, the real purpose, and what the parties really intended. It appears that the case sub judice can be distinguished from *Buttorff*, supra, on its facts. The relationship in *Buttorff*, supra, was found to be a contract for personal services, not for the sale of goods or merchandise. Buttorff was actually a commissioned salesman for United Electronics Laboratories' cameras and related equipment.

We must now consider the provisions of the Uniform Commercial Code in order to determine whether or not the article on sales is applicable to the situation at bar. This question has not yet been decided by a Kentucky court.

Article II of the Uniform Commercial Code applies to transactions involving goods and merchandise. "A contract between an automobile manufacturer and an automobile dealer is a contract of sale since it is apparent that its over all purpose and object is to effect the sale of the automobiles manufactured by the manufacturer, and the fact that it may speak in terms of franchises does not change its true character." 1 Anderson, UCC §2-101:5, p. 201 (2d ed.) "When a manufacturer sells its product to the public through a local dealer, the transaction is a sale, and the application of the Code is not avoided by describing the relationship as a 'sales distribution' plan." Id., at 202. In relation to the same section of the Code, Anderson also cites a Pennsylvania case which held that, "A dealership contract for the sale of automobile parts is a contract for the sale of goods, even though the contract declares that it is a personal service contract." Cum. Supp., Anderson, UCC, p. 174 (2d ed.) Anderson also cites a California case holding that, "Where a supplier of milk agreed with a distributor that the latter would resell milk purchased from the supplier to wholesalers, the relationship between the supplier and the distributor was a sale of goods, and not a contract for services." Id.

In the case at bar, we have a clear situation where the dealer-distributor was to sell the "goods" of the manufacturer-supplier. Appellant was not a commissioned salesman, and the agreement appears to be for the sale of goods.

We conclude that the time has come to recognize that a distributorship agreement must be recognized as an agreement for the sale of goods and subject to the provisions of Article II of the Uniform Commercial Code, which has been adopted by Kentucky in Chapter 355 of the Kentucky Revised Statutes. The amount of money being invested pursuant to distributorship agreements is ever increasing. Often there are no formal written agreements, and it may be that the manufacturer's policy is to have no written agreements. By not establishing a length of time for the contract to exist, either party may terminate the relationship at will, but without a requirement for good faith and fair play, either party may be severely damaged. When sales are the primary essence of the distributorship agreement, the dealer is compelled to keep a large inventory on hand. If the distributorship is terminated without allowing the dealer sufficient time to sell his remaining inventory, substantial damages may result, even if the manufacturer agrees to repurchase the inventory. Reasonable notification should be the minimum amount of protection afforded to either party upon the termination of an ongoing sales agreement. When such reasonable notice is not given, a cause of action for damages may exist.

Having concluded that the Code is applicable to the relationship between the appellant and appellee, we must look at the specific requirements of KRS 355.2-309, "Absence of Specific Time Provisions — Notice of Termination." Subsection (2) reads, "Where the contract provides for successive performances, but is indefinite in duration, it is valid for a reasonable time but unless otherwise agreed may be terminated at any time by either party." Subsection (3) goes on to provide, "Termination of a contract by one (1) party except on the happening of an agreed event requires that reasonable notification be received by the other party and an agreement dispensing with notification is invalid if its operation would be unconscionable." There can be no doubt that reasonable notice is now required. . . . Today, in Kentucky, if the provisions of Article II of the Uniform Commercial Code apply to the relationship, reasonable notice of the intention to terminate the agreement must be given. In some cases, it would be required even if a written agreement provided for dispensing with notification. We therefore find additional error in the trial court's opinion when it concluded that even if the provisions of the Code were applicable, only actual notice of termination would be required.

Comment 8 to §2-309 in 1 Anderson, supra, at p. 445 reads:

> Subsection (3) recognizes that the application of principles of good faith and sound commercial practice normally call for such notification of the termination of a going contract relationship as will give the other party reasonable time to seek a substitute arrangement. An agreement dispensing with notification, or limiting the time for the seeking of a substitute arrangement, is of course valid under this subsection unless the results of putting it into operation would be the creation of an unconscionable state of affairs.

It is also quite clear that the requirement of a reasonable notification does not relate to the method of giving notice, but to the circumstances under which the notice is given and the extent of advanced warning of termination that the notification gives.

Anderson, supra, in the cumulative supplement volume at p. 282, cites two Minnesota cases relating to the time which might be needed for recoupment of investment. McGinnis Piano and Organ Co. v. Yamaha International Corporation, 480 F.2d 474 (8th Cir. 1973) is cited for the proposition that "in some states, it is implied that a dealership contract which may be terminated upon notice must be allowed to continue for a sufficient period to enable the franchisee to recoup his investment." The case of O.M. Droney Beverage Co. v. Miller Brewing Co., 365 F. Supp. 1067 (D. Minn. 1973), is cited for the proposition that "under Minnesota law 'a reasonable duration will be implied in franchise agreements where a dealer has made substantial investments in reliance on the agreement.' "

The distributorship agreement existing between appellant and appellee is one in which the essence was the sale of goods. Appellant was certainly not an employee or commissioned salesman of appellee. Appellant purchased the products of the appellee at wholesale prices, and marketed them in the Lexington area. The appellant does not dispute the fact that the agreement was terminable at will, but he contends, and the law so holds, that the appellee was required to give reasonable notification of intent to terminate the contract. What length of time constitutes reasonable notice is a question of material fact which remains to be decided. We cannot say that the written notice given in this case was "reasonable" as a matter of law.

The summary judgment granted by the trial court must therefore be vacated, and the case remanded for further proceedings.

All concur.

NOTES AND QUESTIONS

1. *"Gap-Filling" provisions of UCC Article 2.* Article 2 of the Code provides many terms — like those stated in §2-309 — that will as a matter of law be implied in contracts for the sale of goods unless otherwise agreed by the parties. (Other examples are UCC §§2-308 (place of delivery), 2-310 (time of payment), 2-509 (risk of loss), and 2-513 (buyer's right of inspection).) Rules of law that supply implied terms for the parties may be supported on the basis that the terms they provide are "fair" or "just." Indeed, some of the implied-by-law obligations imposed by the UCC are mandatory and may not be varied even if the parties expressly agree otherwise. (See, e.g., UCC §§2-309(3), 2-719(3); see generally UCC §1-302.) For the most part, however, such rules are regarded merely as "gap-fillers," subject to preemption by the parties' express agreement. (Sometimes the form of an agreement varying the Code rule is itself prescribed by a Code provision; see, e.g., UCC §2-316, regulating disclaimers of implied warranties.)

The Code's system of implied terms can be justified not only on grounds of fairness, but also because such terms represent the probable intention of the parties if they had bargained over the particular issue. Under this rationale, implied terms are validated on the ground of economic efficiency: If the terms that the law would supply are indeed those most parties would voluntarily choose for themselves, then the process of agreement-making will in general be less costly because contracting parties will have fewer terms to bargain out. We have seen that parties may employ standardized forms for this reason; implied terms that are standardized by law can serve the same purpose. "Off-the-rack" terms, like ready-made suits, are less costly than custom-tailored ones. See Selcke v. New England Ins. Co., 995 F.2d 688, 690 (7th Cir. 1993) (noting that the law could require that parties specify every right or duty, "but then contracts would be very long"). Additionally, it would be extremely inefficient for parties to bargain over terms to address situations that are not likely to occur. David Charny, Hypothetical Bargains: The Normative Structure of Contract Interpretation, 89 Mich. L. Rev. 1815 (1991).

2. *Implied terms as default rules.* The general approach of the courts has been to devise implied terms, often called "default rules," that reflect a "hypothetical bargain," the agreement that the parties probably would have made had they bargained over the issue. Lisa Bernstein, Social Norms and Default Rules Analysis, 3 S. Cal. Interdisc. L.J. 59, 62-63 (1993). Many writers have suggested other bases for supplying default rules. Some observers assert that default rules should be premised on relational aspects of repeated or long-term transactions between the same parties. See, e.g., Jay M. Feinman, Relational Contract and Default Rules, 3 S. Cal. Interdisc. L.J. 43 (1993). Professors Ayres and Gertner argue that in determining the proper default rule it is important to understand the reason for contractual incompleteness. Some contracts are incomplete because one of the parties has more information than the other and engages in strategic behavior. In such cases, Ayres and Gertner argue that efficiency-minded courts should consider adopting what they refer to as "penalty default rules," ones that penalize parties for strategic behavior and thereby create incentives for knowledgeable parties to reveal information in the course of bargaining with the other side. Ian Ayres & Robert Gertner, Filling Gaps in Incomplete Contracts: An Economic Theory of Default Rules, 99 Yale L.J. 87, 94 (1989).

In light of the *Leibel* decision and the foregoing discussion, consider what the appropriate repayment terms should be for a loan made without an agreed due date. See Barnes v. Michalski, 925 N.E.2d 323 (Ill. App. Ct. 2010) (apparent majority view is that loan without repayment terms is due in reasonable time, relying partly on the Restatement (Second) §204 provision on supplying an omitted term).

3. *Enforcing distributorship agreements.* The enforceability of exclusive distributorship agreements was problematic under the common law. If the agreement failed to impose definite obligations on the dealer, or if it was of indefinite duration (so that either party was free to terminate the agreement at any time), the agreement could be held unenforceable for lack of consideration or lack of mutuality of obligation. A classic example is Du Pont v. Claiborne-Reno Co., 64 F.2d 224 (8th Cir. 1933). Although Reno served from 1924 to 1930 as

the exclusive distributor in Iowa of certain Du Pont products, the contract did not expressly provide that Reno was committed for a specific period of time. Applying the same presumption used in employment contracts of indefinite duration, the court deemed Reno free to terminate at will. Moreover, because Reno was deemed not bound, the court held that the contract could not be enforced against Du Pont. Id. at 232-233.

As *Leibel* demonstrates, distributorship agreements today are likely to fall within the general scope of Article 2, as "transactions in goods." If so, the implied obligations found in UCC §§2-306 and 2-309 should eliminate most problems of lack of consideration or lack of mutuality. E.g., Thermal Systems of Alabama, Inc. v. Sigafoose, 533 So. 2d 567 (Ala. 1988) (rejecting arguments of lack of mutuality and indefiniteness against enforceability of a distributorship agreement, based on UCC §§2-306 and 2-309). A distributorship contract of indefinite duration, however, will still be subject to termination at-will upon reasonable notice. See, e.g., Fitzpatrick v. Teleflex, Inc., 763 F. Supp. 2d 224 (D. Maine 2011) (applying Maine law).

4. *Assessing reasonable notice.* Discussing whether Raynor had given Leibel "reasonable notification" of its intention to terminate their arrangement, the *Leibel* opinion refers to some possibly relevant factors: the distributor's need to sell off its remaining inventory and the question whether it still has substantial unrecouped investment made in reliance on the agreement. See, e.g., Sofa Gallery, Inc. v. Stratford Co., 872 F.2d 259 (8th Cir. 1989) (reasonable notice of termination without cause takes into account time needed to recoup reasonable initial or continuing investment, close out product line, and minimize losses). Some courts have made a distinction between cases involving an investment by a distributor and those without startup or similar costs. See Italian & French Wine Co. v. Negociants USA, Inc. 842 F. Supp. 693 (W.D.N.Y. 1993) (distributorship agreements without an investment may be merely a type of employment or personal services contract that is properly terminable at will). Comment 8 to UCC §2-309 refers to a related factor: whether there has been sufficient or "reasonable time" to find a "substitute arrangement."

The determination whether notice is reasonable may also be affected by the terms contained in the parties' present or prior agreement and by industry standards. See Retail Associates, Inc. v. Macy's East, Inc., 245 F.3d 694 (8th Cir. 2001) (90 days' notice for termination of consignment contract to place maternity clothes in department stores was reasonable given that consignor had virtually no capital investment, that inventory would turn over in six-month seasons, and that consignor had other outlets to sell any remaining inventory).

5. *Effect of express termination provisions.* Unlike *Leibel*, most modern commercial contracts will specify events of termination. Suppose Leibel and Raynor had entered into a written agreement that provided for immediate termination on written notice by Raynor. What result? Suppose the written agreement provided that Raynor could terminate the agreement on written notice to Leibel if its sales declined for two consecutive years. Compare Delta

Services & Equip., Inc. v. Ryko Mfg. Co., 908 F.2d 7 (5th Cir. 1990) (distributorship contract that specified various grounds for termination, including minimum sales provision, was not thereby terminable only on the occurrence of one of those agreed-upon events; instead, contract was for indefinite duration, terminable either on reasonable notice under UCC §2-309(3) or on happening of one of agreed events), with Viking Supply v. National Cart Co., Inc., 310 F.3d 1092 (8th Cir. 2002) (agreement that provided for termination by manufacturer of shopping cart corrals if distributor lost key sales contract with Target stores was not at-will and was terminable upon the occurrence of the specified event).

B. THE IMPLIED OBLIGATION OF GOOD FAITH

We saw in Chapter 2 that occasionally parties will be held to a duty to bargain in good faith when negotiating toward a contract. Once a contract has been concluded, however, the authorities are unanimous in declaring that its terms will be deemed to include an obligation of good faith that is binding on both parties. The Uniform Commercial Code declares in §1-304 (formerly §1-203) that "every contract or duty" within its scope "imposes an obligation of good faith in its performance and enforcement." Restatement (Second) §205 echoes the above UCC provision, extending the "duty of good faith and fair dealing" to "every contract." To say that generally an obligation of good faith will be implied does not, of course, answer the harder question of what that obligation requires of each party in the context of their particular agreement.

The UCC meaning of good faith. The UCC provides in Article 1 (revised 2001) that good faith "means honesty in fact and the observance of reasonable commercial standards of fair dealing." See UCC §1-201(b)(20). With the exception of a narrower provision in Article 5, the UCC would now generally apply to all parties (both merchant and nonmerchant) the complementary concepts of "subjective honesty" and "objective reasonableness" in determining good faith. See Official Comment to UCC §1-201(b)(20). Revised Article 1 has now been adopted in a clear majority of states, but not all jurisdictions have acquiesced in its expanded definition of "good faith." While most states have adopted the revised, single definition, a number of states have chosen to retain the more minimal standard of "honesty in fact," at least for parties who are not Article 2 merchants.

The "fruit of the contract" concept of good faith. In a 1933 decision, the New York Court of Appeals declared,

> In every contract there is an implied covenant that neither party shall do anything which will have the effect of destroying or injuring the right of the other party to receive the fruits of the contract, which means that in every contract there is an implied obligation of good faith and fair dealing.

Kirke La Shelle Co. v. Paul Armstrong Co., 188 N.E. 163, 167 (N.Y. 1933). Courts continue to embrace this concept. E.g., Dick Broad. Co., Inc. of Tennessee v. Oak Ridge FM, Inc., 395 S.W.3d 653 (Tenn. 2013) (noting accepted principle in American courts that every contract includes the implied covenant of good faith to protect receipt of the fruits of the contract).

A number of commentators have also pursued this "fruits of the contract" approach. Thus, Professor Steven Burton has suggested that bad faith consists of attempts by one party to recapture "forgone opportunities" – occasions for the realization of gain that (in light of any applicable business practices or the course of dealing between the parties) he should have understood to be precluded by the contract at issue. Steven J. Burton, Breach of Contract and the Common Law Duty to Perform in Good Faith, 94 Harv. L. Rev. 369 (1980); Steven J. Burton & Eric G. Andersen, Contractual Good Faith (1995). See also Dennis M. Patterson, Good Faith and Lender Liability 7 (1990) (arguing that good faith should be seen as protecting the "reasonable expectations" of the contracting parties considered in light of the background practices and customs in which the agreement arose).

Judicial application of the doctrine of "good faith." Professor Michael Van Alstine reported that beginning in the 1990s courts moved toward "a new textualist approach," giving a near absolute priority to express terms and rendering the implied duty of good faith irrelevant in many situations. Michael P. Van Alstine, Of Textualism, Party Autonomy, and Good Faith, 40 Wm. & Mary L. Rev. 1223 (1999). Professor Van Alstine's study gives evidence that while nearly all courts recognize the implied duty of good faith, at least in principle, not all will give that concept a broad application. See Max N. Helveston, Judicial Deregulation of Consumer Markets, 36 Cardozo L. Rev. 1739 (2015); Emily M.S. Houh, The Doctrine of Good Faith in Contract Law: A (Nearly) Empty Vessel? 2005 Utah L. Rev. 1 (2005).

Perhaps reflecting this more recent tendency to approach "good faith" with caution, the drafters of the revised UCC Article 1 have stated in the Comment to revised §1-304 that the "section does not support an independent cause of action for failure to perform or enforce in good faith. . . . [T]he doctrine of good faith merely directs a court towards interpreting contracts within the commercial context in which they are created, performed, and enforced, and does not create a separate duty of fairness and reasonableness which can be independently breached."

In one way or another, most courts and writers who have spoken of an obligation of good faith do appear at least to share the view that this concept should be employed in cases where one party's actions were such as to undermine the "spirit" of the contract – either by enabling that party to realize gains that in making that contract he had implicitly agreed to surrender, or by unfairly denying to the other party the fruits of the contract that she reasonably expected to receive. The following cases illustrate the process by which the abstract obligation of good faith may be given concrete application.

Seidenberg v. Summit Bank

Superior Court of New Jersey, Appellate Division. 348 N.J. Super. 243, 791 A.2d 1068 (2002)

Before Judges KING, WINKELSTEIN and CLARKSON S. FISHER, Jr.

The opinion of the court was delivered by

CLARKSON S. FISHER, Jr., J.S.C. (temporarily assigned).

After settling all their disputes concerning the express terms of their commercial transaction, plaintiffs filed a second amended complaint alleging a breach of the implied covenant of good faith and fair dealing. The Law Division dismissed the action, finding that plaintiffs failed to state a claim upon which relief may be granted. Because we conclude the assessment of the validity of the claim was both erroneous and premature, we reverse.

. . .

II

Plaintiffs Richard Seidenberg and Eric Raymond formed two Pennsylvania corporations — Corporate Dynamics and Philadelphia Benefits Corporation — in 1971 and 1985, respectively. These entities marketed, provided consultation services and sold health insurance benefit plans to employers. Plaintiffs were the sole shareholders of the two entities.

In 1997, plaintiffs sold their stock in Corporate Dynamics and Philadelphia Benefits Corporation (hereafter collectively referred to as "the brokerage firms") to defendant Summit Bank ("Summit") in exchange for 445,000 shares of the common stock of Bancorp Corporation, Summit's parent corporation;[1] in addition, plaintiffs agreed to place 49,500 shares of Bancorp Corporation into escrow until December 12, 2001, as security for any existing but unknown or undisclosed liabilities. As part of the transaction, plaintiffs retained their positions as executives of the brokerage firms and also were to be placed in charge of the daily operations of any other employee benefits insurance business which might be acquired by Summit.

Plaintiffs' employment agreements with Summit acknowledged the parties' joint obligation to work together with respect to the future performance of the brokerage firms:

> Summit and [plaintiffs] shall work together to formulate joint marketing programs which will give [the brokerage firms] access to the market resources of Summit to the extent permitted by applicable laws, regulations and administrative policies and guidelines, including but not limited to those relating to customer privacy, issued by Federal or state regulatory authorities or agencies or self-regulatory organizations or financial industry trade groups.

In the second amended complaint, plaintiffs contend, among other things, that Summit (a) failed to allow for the creation of a close working relationship between the entities, (b) failed to create an effective cross-selling structure to

1. As of the date of closing, the stock had a value of $43.50 per share.

generate leads, (c) failed to introduce the brokerage firms to vendors doing business with Summit as a way of increasing their potential customer base, (d) failed to develop existing relationships (referred to in the pleadings as "low hanging fruit") which could easily be picked and turned into clients for the brokerage firms, (e) failed to provide plaintiffs with information necessary to provide full advice concerning health and other employee benefits, thereby precluding plaintiffs from quoting coverage to Summit, (f) unreasonably delayed a direct mail campaign, (g) thwarted an agreed-upon joint marketing campaign, and (h) failed to advise of Summit's pursuit of the acquisition of another entity which plaintiffs claim would fall within their ambit and right to operate.

Plaintiffs claimed that Summit's lack of performance in these areas impacted their reasonable expectations of compensation and future involvement. For example, plaintiffs' salaries were reduced in exchange for a bonus to which they would be entitled based on the growth of the brokerage firms. They claim this was agreeable due to the anticipation of a substantial bonus upon the growth of the business. Accordingly, the allegations contained in the second amended complaint, briefly outlined above, are linked to plaintiffs' compensation. In addition, plaintiffs claim there was an expectation of continued employment since their employment agreements contained a minimum term of five years and provided also that, in the absence of termination by Summit, employment would continue until each reached the age of 70.

Plaintiffs assert that these allegations give rise to an inference of bad faith. They claim that these circumstances demonstrate that Summit "never had any intention to perform to begin with," and that Summit "from the start, . . . never [was] committed to developing the business with [plaintiffs], but rather simply wanted to acquire the business and seek out their own broker to run it or grow it." In December 1999, Summit terminated plaintiffs from their positions, triggering this lawsuit.

III

On February 10, 2000, plaintiffs filed a complaint in the Chancery Division. After the joinder of issue, the parties reached a partial settlement of their disputes and, on July 25, 2000, a consent order was entered which eliminated all claims except plaintiffs' claim of a breach of the implied covenant of good faith and fair dealing. With the resolution of the equity claims, the Chancery judge, as was his prerogative, transferred the matter to the Law Division. On August 16, 2000, plaintiffs filed a second amended complaint and defendants quickly filed a motion to dismiss for failure to state a claim upon which relief may be granted. . . .

The motion was granted. In essence, the Law Division judge held that plaintiffs were not claiming a breach of the implied covenant of good faith and fair dealing but were seeking to prove the existence (and obtain enforcement) of an oral agreement allegedly made beyond the four corners of the written agreements in violation of the parol evidence rule:

> I am satisfied that the facts as pled do not allege as a matter of law and cannot allege as a matter of law a breach of the covenant of good faith and fair dealing. Because in fact what the complaint is alleging is that there were agreements made orally outside of the written agreements that the bank would do certain things. And, that because the bank didn't do certain things, the plaintiffs were deprived of certain income.

The ruling under review also placed emphasis on the bargaining power of the parties:

> We are not dealing with unsophisticated people. [Plaintiffs], from the record it would appear, are very sophisticated businessmen, developed very successful businesses. And, with the assistance of very able counsel entered into certain contracts with the bank that set out the framework for the way they would act as president and vice-president of [the brokerage firms]. . . . [They] leaned back in reliance on things that were said to them during the course of the negotiations by the people from the bank, then they certainly had the opportunity to have those representations and considerations put into the written agreement and they weren't done — that just simply wasn't done.

Based upon these observations as to the meaning of plaintiffs' allegations, the motion to dismiss was granted. We find the Law Division judge's conclusions misapprehend the nature of the cause of action and represent an erroneous interpretation of the evolving implied covenant of good faith and fair dealing.

IV

We start with the premise that in New Jersey the covenant of good faith and fair dealing is contained in all contracts and mandates that "neither party shall do anything which will have the effect of destroying or injuring the right of the other party to receive the fruits of the contract." Sons of Thunder v. Borden, Inc., 148 N.J. 396, 420, 690 A.2d 575 (1997); Palisades Properties, Inc. v. Brunetti, 44 N.J. 117, 130, 207 A.2d 522 (1965). While this general statement represents the guiding principle in such matters, determining whether the present action may be maintained requires closer examination.

The implied covenant of good faith and fair dealing has evolved to the point where it permits the adjustment of the obligations of contracting parties in a number of different ways. Some cases have focused on a plaintiff's inadequate bargaining power or financial vulnerability in order to avoid an inequitable result otherwise permitted by a contract's express terms. See e.g., *Sons of Thunder.* Other decisions have revolved around the expectations of the parties, generating a need to contrast those expectations with the absence of any express terms. See e.g., Onderdonk v. Presbyterian Homes, 85 N.J. 171, 425 A.2d 1057 (1981). And still others have emphasized the defendant's bad faith or outright dishonesty. See e.g., Pickett v. Lloyd's, 131 N.J. 457, 621 A.2d 445 (1993). Yet, as the implied covenant of good faith and fair dealing continues to develop, and in light of the covenant's essential factors as discerned from the existing case law, we cannot say, in examining the unadorned record in this case, that an actionable claim cannot be found in plaintiffs' allegations.

In granting defendant's motion to dismiss, we understand the Law Division to have relied on two points: the parties' equal strength at the time the contract was formed and plaintiffs' assertion of oral discussions unreflected by the written contract. We find erroneous both the undue emphasis placed on the absence of plaintiffs' financial vulnerability and the misperceived importance of the parol evidence rule, particularly when viewed at the pleading stage.

A

Sons of Thunder — often viewed as a watershed event in the course of the implied covenant of good faith and fair dealing — is, perhaps, the best example of how a plaintiff's unequal bargaining power will bring the implied covenant to the forefront even if defendant acted in conformity with the express terms of the contract. In the wake of *Sons of Thunder,* it certainly would have been fair to conclude that bargaining power is a critical aspect of any application of the implied covenant to a contractual dispute.

In *Sons of Thunder,* the Court emphasized the parties' unequal bargaining power as one factor in finding a breach of the implied covenant of good faith and fair dealing. *Sons of Thunder* involved an operator of a vessel which contracted to supply clams to Borden. Even though the contract's term was for one year and was also terminable on 90 days' notice, the Court found that Borden could still be found to have violated the implied covenant because it had preyed on Sons of Thunder's lack of sophistication and desperate financial straits. The Court stressed the importance of protecting and vindicating plaintiff's expectations particularly in light of the significant investments made by Sons of Thunder in anticipation of Borden's good faith performance. The Court also emphasized this feature in the earlier case of Bak-A-Lum Corp. v. Alcoa Bldg. Prods., Inc., 69 N.J. 123, 130, 351 A.2d 349 (1976). That these two seminal cases in the growth of the implied covenant stressed economic dependency and financial strength understandably suggests the importance of this factor. Nevertheless, while disparate strength may sometimes be a prominent feature, it is not the *sine qua non* of such a cause of action. It is merely one factor among many to be considered. . . .

In this case, it is undisputed that the parties are all sophisticated and financially strong; it appears undisputed that plaintiffs possessed sufficient bargaining power during the formation of their agreement with Summit. According to their own contentions, plaintiffs have been in the insurance industry for several years and built two very successful brokerage firms. Furthermore, the record reflects that both parties were assisted by able counsel in negotiating their agreement. But equal bargaining power and the advice of competent counsel at the formation of the contract are not determinative. Rather, we conclude that while the bargaining power and sophistication of the parties must be viewed as significant, and should be considered in the analysis of any such dispute, it is not the sole criterion by which this claim must be resolved.

B

We also discern from her oral opinion that the Law Division judge believed plaintiffs would be unable to substantiate their claim because, in reality, they seek to prove some oral agreement dehors the written contract. In short, the Law Division judge appears to have found the parol evidence rule an insurmountable obstacle to plaintiffs' claim. We find this erroneous.

The parol evidence rule prohibits the introduction of oral promises which tend to alter or vary an integrated written instrument. . . . Parol evidence may, however, be admitted in order to provide understanding into the parties' intentions. . . .

Put in the present context, it must first be observed that the parol evidence rule does not even come into play "until it is first determined what the true agreement of the parties is." *Ibid.* Accordingly, the rule cannot inhibit the application of the implied covenant of good faith and fair dealing because that covenant is contained in all contracts made in New Jersey by operation of law. Sons of Thunder, 148 N.J. at 420, 690 A.2d 575. Moreover, the central premise of the implied covenant is the enhanced status of the parties' reasonable expectations. If the parol evidence rule is vigorously applied in such situations, the opportunity to pursue such a claim would be extremely limited. The manner in which our courts have defined the scope of the covenant demonstrates the fallacy of such a broad application of the parol evidence rule.

The implied covenant of good faith and fair dealing has been applied in three general ways, each largely unaffected by the parol evidence rule. First, the covenant permits the inclusion of terms and conditions which have not been expressly set forth in the written contract. The earlier cases, such as *Bak-A-Lum* . . . and *Onderdonk* . . . provide examples of the imposition of absent terms and conditions. The covenant acts in such instances to include terms "the parties must have intended . . . because they are necessary to give business efficacy" to the contract. New Jersey Bank v. Palladino, 77 N.J. 33, 46, 389 A.2d 454 (1978). . . . Second, the covenant has been utilized to allow redress for the bad faith performance of an agreement even when the defendant has not breached any express term, as in *Sons of Thunder.* And third, the covenant has been held, in more recent cases, to permit inquiry into a party's exercise of discretion expressly granted by a contract's terms. See Wilson v. Amerada Hess Corporation, 168 N.J. 236, 250, 773 A.2d 1121 (2001); R.J. Gaydos Ins. Agency, Inc. v. National Consumer Ins. Co., 168 N.J. 255, 281, 773 A.2d 1132 (2001); Emerson Radio, 253 F.3d at 170-172.

The second aspect, exemplified by *Sons of Thunder,* and the third, represented by cases such as *Wilson,* are implicated in this case. In both these situations, the parol evidence rule has a potential for coming into play. For, while the implied covenant has gone far in altering the way in which contractual performance will be weighed, our Supreme Court has consistently held that the "implied covenant of good faith and fair dealing cannot override an express term in a contract." *Wilson*, 168 N.J. at 244, 773 A.2d 1121; *Sons of Thunder*, 148 N.J. at 419, 690 A.2d 575. But, instead of altering or overriding an express term, the implied covenant requires that a contracting party act in good faith when exercising either discretion in performing its contractual obligations . . . or its right to terminate. . . . Accordingly, it may occur that a party will be found to have breached the implied covenant even if the action complained of does not violate a "pertinent express term." *Wilson,* 168 N.J. at 244, 773 A.2d 1121. By staying within those parameters, the implied covenant — while necessarily "vague and amorphous" . . . — remains faithful to the purposes of the parol evidence rule.

Accordingly, it can readily be seen that the parol evidence rule appears to have no present application in the case at hand. By concluding that plaintiffs seek to prove an oral agreement outside the bounds of a fully integrated written contract, the Law Division judge misapprehended the scope of the implied covenant of good faith and fair dealing and overly-expanded the importance of the parol evidence rule. The parol evidence rule is not impacted because the obligation to act with good faith and fair dealing is, by its very nature, "implied." The prohibition on parol evidence to alter or vary a written contract relates, in the present context, only to the creation of the contract. Because the covenant of good faith and fair dealing is implied by operation of law, the view that the parol evidence rule somehow inhibits plaintiffs' claim is erroneous. And, because plaintiffs do not seek to contradict or alter any express term in their written contract, but rather question Summit's *bona fides* in both its performance and termination of the contract, there presently appears to be no concern that the particular manner in which plaintiffs would have the implied covenant applied would run afoul of the parol evidence rule.

To determine what is considered a good faith performance, the court must consider the expectations of the parties and the purposes for which the contract was made. It would be difficult, if not impossible, to make that determination without considering evidence outside the written memorialization of the parties' agreement. Therefore, in determining whether a breach of the covenant has occurred, a court must allow for parol evidence and the Law Division's determination that the need for parol evidence is fatal to the second amended complaint is erroneous.

C

The guiding principle in the application of the implied covenant of good faith and fair dealing emanates from the fundamental notion that a party to a contract may not unreasonably frustrate its purpose:

> [W]here a party alleges frustration of its expectation or fundamental purpose in entering the contract, the question of what interest will be protected by the implied duty answers itself; the plaintiff's interest is internal to the understanding of the parties and good faith requires the defendant not exercise such discretion as it may have under the literal terms of the contract to thwart plaintiff's expectation or purpose.

[Emerson Radio Corp. v. Orion Sales Inc., 80 F. Supp. 2d 307, 314 (D.N.J. 2000), *rev'd in part on other grounds,* 253 F.3d 159 (3d Cir. 2001), cited with approval in *Wilson,* 168 N.J. at 250, 773 A.2d 1121.]

See also . . . Restatement (Second) of Contracts, §205, comment *a* (1979) ("Good faith performance . . . emphasizes faithfulness to an agreed common purpose and consistency with the justified expectations of the other party").

As discussed earlier, the application of the implied covenant of good faith and fair dealing has addressed three distinct type of situations: (1) when the contract does not provide a term necessary to fulfill the parties' expectations, . . . (2) when bad faith served as a pretext for the exercise of a contractual right to terminate, . . . and (3) when the contract expressly provides a party with discretion regarding its performance, *see e.g., Wilson,* 168 N.J. 236, 773 A.2d 1121. . . .

Here, plaintiffs appear to urge an application of both the second and third facets of the implied covenant. The Law Division judge's decision to dismiss the second amended complaint constituted a mistaken understanding of the covenant in these areas.

Faced with a motion to dismiss pursuant to R. 4:6-2(e), the court below was required to determine only whether the second amended complaint sufficiently outlined a cause of action consistent with any of these categories. In this case, the second amended complaint alleges circumstances which, if proven, might support a claim based upon Summit's termination of their relationship. To some extent, plaintiffs alleged there was an expectation — despite the express contractual right of Summit to terminate — that the relationship would last until they reached retirement age. This contention would, on its face, fall within that type of implied covenant claim prohibiting a party from terminating a contractual relationship in bad faith notwithstanding the expressed right to do so.

The second amended complaint also alleges that Summit used insufficient energy in discretionary areas. That is, plaintiffs allege that Summit failed to pursue or create leads, frustrated or delayed marketing efforts, and deprived plaintiffs of information which might improve their benefits under the contract, thus sufficiently alleging a cause of action under the discretionary tranche of the multi-faceted implied covenant of good faith and fair dealing.

D

The last element of a maintainable cause of action based upon the implied covenant of good faith and fair dealing is bad faith or ill motive. Courts have described this element in various ways. Most importantly, our Supreme Court has recently emphasized the level of bad faith and improper motive which will be required in a party's exercise of the discretion permitted by the contract:

> [A]party exercising its right to use discretion in setting price under a contract breaches the duty of good faith and fair dealing if that party exercises its discretionary authority arbitrarily, unreasonably, or capriciously, with the objective of preventing the other party from receiving its reasonably expected fruits under the contract.
>
> . . . In that setting, an allegation of bad faith or unfair dealing should not be permitted to be advanced in the abstract and absent improper motive. Without

> bad motive or intention, discretionary decisions that happen to result in economic disadvantage to the other party are of no legal significance.

[*Wilson,* 168 N.J. at 251, 773 A.2d 1121 (citations omitted).]

While *Wilson*'s description of good faith relates to price setting, we fail to see why it would not be similarly applied in examining the type of performance (or lack thereof) as alleged by plaintiffs.

Before finding a breach of the implied covenant, care must be taken that the bad faith element is fully realized. Recognizing a concern for an overly ambitious application of the implied covenant, the Court in *Wilson* — in defining the level of bad faith required in such matters — charted a careful course between implying a promise to avoid an apparent unjust result and requiring parties to adhere to the bargain they freely and voluntarily made. Referencing one federal court of appeal's holdings that the covenant is not intended to supplant the prohibition on judicial rewriting of contracts or provide undue protection to contracting parties who can protect themselves,[4] the *Wilson* decision represents an increased emphasis on the importance of this factor:

> [A]n allegation of bad faith or unfair dealing should not be permitted to be advanced in the abstract and absent improper motive.
>
> Because the implied covenant of good faith and fair dealing applies to the parties' performance under the contract notwithstanding [a] provision in the contract permitting [the exercise of discretion in setting prices] . . . the issue is whether . . . [the defendant] acted in bad faith or violated any commercially reasonable standard thereby depriving plaintiffs of their right to make a reasonable profit.

[168 N.J. at 251, 253, 773 A.2d 1121.]

Providing a more precise definition of bad faith in the context of this, or any other similar case, is unrealistic. *See e.g.,* Wade v. Kessler Institute, 343 N.J. Super. 338, 346-348, 778 A.2d 580 (App. Div. 2001). We recognize that expressions such as "bad faith," "improper motive," and other similar words and phrases used to describe this requisite state of mind provide little guidance. While the particular defining words chosen will inherently be of "little assistance to the trial judge who must distinguish bad faith from mere sharp commercial practice," *Emerson Radio,* 80 F. Supp. 2d at 311, it is best to entrust the drawing of such a line to trial judges and juries with the admonition that an unduly expansive version of bad faith, as Judge Greenberg cautioned in *Northview Motors,* "could become an all-embracing statement of the parties' obligations under contract law, imposing unintended obligations upon parties and destroying the mutual benefits created by legally binding agreements." 227 F.3d at 92. In the final analysis, bad faith must be judged not only in light

4. "Contract law does not require parties to behave altruistically toward each other; it does not proceed on the philosophy that I am my brother's keeper." Original Great Am. Chocolate Chip Cookie Co. v. River Valley Cookies, Ltd., 970 F.2d 273, 280 (7th Cir. 1992) (quoted with approval in *Wilson,* 168 N.J. at 251-252, 773 A.2d 1121). *See also,* Kham & Nate's Shoes No. 2, Inc. v. First Bank of Whiting, 908 F.2d 1351, 1357 (7th Cir. 1990) (the covenant of good faith and fair dealing "does not imply a general duty of 'kindness' in performance").

of the proofs regarding the defendant's state of mind but also in the context from which the claim arose. The Court in *Wilson* coupled the element of bad faith with a requirement that the plaintiff demonstrate a violation of "any commercially reasonable standard." 168 N.J. at 253, 773 A.2d 1121. Accordingly, this element may be determined, at least in part, by the nature of the parties' undertaking and the standards applicable to the business or industry in which they have engaged. Ultimately, however, the presence of bad faith is to be found in the eye of the beholder or, more to the point, in the eye of the trier of fact. Any attempt to provide greater definition is to expect some "delusive exactness" which, as Justice Holmes said, is "a source of fallacy throughout the law." Truax v. Corrigan, 257 U.S. 312, 342, 42 S. Ct. 124, 133, 66 L. Ed. 254, 267 (1921) (dissenting opinion).

Even though the order of dismissal was not based upon some insufficiency in regard to its allegations of bad faith, we lastly pause, in providing guidance for future proceedings in this case, to observe that the second amended complaint was adequate in this regard, alleging that plaintiffs "suffered as a result of . . . Summit's bad faith" and that Summit's actions were "wanton and willful and without privilege or right." Whether plaintiffs' proofs will meet the bad faith standard defined in *Wilson,* or even survive summary judgment, remains to be seen. This question, however, certainly cannot be resolved until the parties are at least given a full and fair opportunity for further investigation and discovery.

V

To summarize, plaintiffs' claim of a breach of the implied covenant of good faith and fair dealing is not precluded merely because the parties possessed equal bargaining power, or because plaintiffs were not financially vulnerable during the contract's formation, or even if the plaintiffs negotiated the contract with the assistance of highly competent counsel. These are factors which the trier of fact may consider in weighing the sufficiency of plaintiffs' claim but they are not the only factors. Also, we conclude that the parol evidence rule presently appears to have no impact upon the ability of plaintiffs to substantiate either their claim that they had a reasonable expectation of a continued relationship (notwithstanding the expressed right of Summit to terminate), or their claim that Summit failed to perform its contractual obligations in good faith. And lastly, while the appropriate level of bad faith may be difficult to define and may also vary depending upon the nature of the alleged breach and the type of business engaged in by the parties, we find plaintiffs' allegations of bad faith and ill motives are sufficient to survive dismissal.

. . . Whether those allegations can be substantiated remains to be seen after the parties have been afforded a full and fair opportunity for further investigation and discovery.

The order of dismissal is reversed and the matter remanded for further proceedings in conformity herewith. We do not retain jurisdiction.

NOTES AND QUESTIONS

1. *Applications of the good faith principle.* In the course of its discussion, the *Seidenberg* court gives us an overview of the ways in which the doctrine of good faith may come into play in the course of adjudicating a contract dispute. First, a court may be persuaded that in order for the contract between the parties to have "business efficacy," it is necessary to imply terms not expressly incorporated in the agreement. The court is careful to add, as have many other courts and commentators, that it will not imply any term that conflicts with the express terms of the parties' agreement. Second, the court in *Seidenberg* indicates that the covenant of good faith may permit a finding of breach even where no express term of the agreement has been violated. *Seidenberg* itself appears to be, potentially, an example of such as a case; so also are the *Sons of Thunder* and *Mathis* cases, discussed in the following notes. (*Nanakuli* could also be so described.) And finally, the notion of good faith has often been applied to judge the appropriateness of a party's exercise of some type of discretion expressly granted to it by the terms of a contract. The next two principal cases, Morin Bldg. Products Co. v. Baystone Constr. Inc., and Locke v. Warner Bros. Inc., exemplify this latter type of analysis in two very different settings.

2. *Application of the parol evidence rule.* In light of the recent tendency of some courts toward a higher regard for the "formalism" reflected in the parol evidence rule, note the *Seidenberg* court's treatment of that issue. While conceding that the parol evidence rule might apply in a case where the offered evidence appears to directly contradict an express term in the contract, the appellate court asserts that because the obligation of good faith is an implied term rather than an express one, the parol evidence rule will ordinarily be irrelevant to the issue of its existence and application. Do you agree that the parol evidence rule should not be relevant to resolution of the plaintiff's claims in *Seidenberg*?

3. *Express terms versus duty of good faith.* The court in *Seidenberg* describes Sons of Thunder v. Borden, Inc., 690 A.2d 575 (N.J. 1997), as a case that is "often viewed as a watershed event in the course of the implied covenant of good faith and fair dealing," demonstrating as it does a situation where, in light of all the circumstances, the court may apply the covenant of good faith and fair dealing even where the defendant has apparently "acted in conformity with the express terms of the contract." In that case, the plaintiffs invested large amounts of funds in clam-fishing vessels, based on assurances of purchases to be made by the defendant Borden. Borden, however, consistently failed to make these purchases and eventually exercised an express right to terminate the contracts with 60 and 90 days' notice. The New Jersey Supreme Court agreed with the defendant that the implied covenant of good faith could not override the express right to terminate, but also held that Borden could have breached the implied covenant of good faith in its *performance* before exercising the right to terminate. The court stated that Borden "destroyed Sons of Thunder's reasonable expectations and right to receive the fruits of the contract" by never buying the required amount of clams. 690 A.2d at 589.

Resolving the tension between express terms in a contract and the implied duty of good faith continues to be a significant challenge for the courts. As stated by the Wisconsin Supreme Court, a party may breach the implied duty of good faith by defeating the purpose of the contract even without technically violating an express provision, but, on the other hand, the implied covenant cannot be used to "undo express terms of an agreement." Beidel v. Sideline Software, Inc., 842 N.W.2d 240, 250-251 (Wis. 2013) (holding that on remand court would need to decide whether employer's financially advantageous timing of decision to repurchase stock from minority shareholder was permitted by plain language of contract). Similarly, a federal judge noted the absence of consistency among the courts, with ardent and persuasive decisions on both sides of the debate, before concluding that the express term in the particular case allowing each party discretion to approve assignment of a contract would not be restricted by an implied duty of good faith. Humantech, Inc. v. Caterpillar, Inc., 2012 WL 6214371 (E.D. Mich.).

4. *Need to show bad faith or ill motive.* The *Seidenberg* court also held that establishing a breach of the covenant of good faith would require a showing of bad faith or ill motive. The effect of that approach is that merely arbitrary, capricious, or unreasonable conduct is not a breach of the implied duty. The requisite ill motive could be found in the intentional exercise of discretion to deprive a contracting partner of the reasonable expectations under the contract, as alleged in the cited New Jersey case, Wilson v. Amerada Hess Corp. (involving the seller's discretion in setting gasoline prices) and illustrated by cases in the following note. See also Deom v. Walgreen Co., 591 Fed. Appx. 313 (6th Cir. 2014) (court holds that Illinois law requires improper motive intended to prevent other party from receiving "fruits of the bargain" and not just negligent, arbitrary, or unreasonable behavior, in dismissing seller's claim that buyer breached covenant by failing to promote pharmacy business sales upon which seller's bonus depended).

5. *Good faith and open price terms.* As we have noted earlier, the definition of good faith incorporated in UCC §1-201(b)(20) recognizes the obligations of both subjective honesty in fact and objective commercially reasonable behavior. The distinction between those two standards was highlighted in Mathis v. Exxon Corp., 302 F.3d 448 (5th Cir. 2002). A group of 54 plaintiff franchisees alleged that Exxon breached the duty of good faith in setting gasoline prices for the purpose of driving the franchisees out of business and then replacing them with stores owned directly by Exxon. The Fifth Circuit noted that the contract expressly allowed Exxon to set the prices at which it would sell gasoline to the franchisees, that Comment 3 to UCC §2-305 suggested that a "posted price" set by a merchant would "normally" meet the requirements of good faith, and that the prices charged by Exxon were comparable to its competitors. Id. at 453-454. Nevertheless, the court upheld a jury verdict against Exxon for $5.7 million on the strength of substantial evidence that Exxon set its prices to the franchisees at a level that was intended to make the franchises unprofitable and drive them out of business. Thus, a breach of the duty of good faith could be shown through the improper motive even though the prices set might

appear to be objectively reasonable. Id. at 458-459. Accord Marcoux v. Shell Oil Products Co., LLC, 524 F.3d 33 (1st Cir. 2008) (finding that a situation in which a merchant is raising its prices to drive its customer out of business is "hardly the 'normal case' "); contra Shell Oil Co. v. HRN, Inc., 144 S.W.3d 429 (Tex. 2004) (holding that subjective bad faith by refiner in attempt to force dealers out of business is irrelevant as long as the refiner is charging "commercially reasonable" prices and is not discriminating among its purchasers).

6. *The duty of good faith in loan agreements.* "Lender liability" is a term that refers to claims asserted by borrowers against lenders for alleged misconduct by the lender in connection with a loan transaction. The claim may be based on various legal theories. See Michelle Z. McDonald, The Complicated World of Lender Liability, 40 Colo. Law. 13 (Apr. 2011). Loan agreements sometimes provide that the lender may call the loan "on demand." One type of lender liability case involves a claim by the borrower that the lender exercised this right in bad faith. Courts have been divided on the effect of the duty of good faith in these situations. In K.M.C. Co., Inc. v. Irving Trust Co., 757 F.2d 752 (6th Cir. 1985), the court held that the duty of good faith limited a lender's express right to terminate a financing agreement with and demand repayment from a grocery business, especially since the lender also had control of the grocery business's bank account with its operating funds. In contrast, however, many subsequent decisions have been critical of *K.M.C.* on the ground that the court effectively overrode the express terms of the contract. See Reger Dev., LLC v. National City Bank, 592 F.3d 759 (7th Cir. 2010) (holding that the implied covenant of good faith cannot limit express contract rights). The courts giving priority to the express provisions in loan agreements find support in the official comment to UCC §1-309, which states that the obligation of good faith "has no application to demand instruments . . . whose very nature permits call at any time with or without reason."

In another line of cases involving discretionary conduct by lenders, home loan borrowers (or mortgagors) have alleged that the lenders (or mortgagees) have abused their express contract right to obtain hazard insurance for the home, if the borrower fails to provide the insurance herself, and add the costs to the loan balance. The borrowers typically allege that the lenders purchase such "force-placed" insurance at highly inflated prices in collusion with certain insurers and in return for "kickbacks," and thereby breach the implied covenant of good faith. See, e.g., Hamilton v. Suntrust Mortg. Inc., 6 F. Supp. 3d 1300 (S.D. Fla. 2014) (denying lender's motion to dismiss and finding that plaintiff had stated a claim for breach of implied covenant of good faith); Gallo v. PHH Mortg. Corp., 916 F. Supp. 2d 537 (D.N.J. 2012) (finding that plaintiff stated a claim for lender breach of implied covenant of good faith by exercising discretion in unreasonable and bad faith manner designed to reap improper financial benefit).

Comment: Requirements and Output Contracts

Although a contract to buy and sell goods, even a long-term one, may be very precise in stating the quantity of goods to be delivered, often the parties choose instead to leave that term flexible. Sometimes the parties will agree that the seller undertakes to supply all goods of a given type that the buyer may "require" during the term of their contract; in other cases, the buyer will be obligated to buy all the seller's "output" of a given commodity. Such arrangements, likely to stretch over a period of months or even years, may be commercially advantageous to both parties. On the one hand, they provide the output seller with a guaranteed market for its goods, and the requirements buyer with an assured source for its needs. They do involve some risk for the other party, to be sure, but if the output buyer is confident that it can use as much as the seller is likely to produce, the risk may appear small; conversely, the requirements seller may see little chance that the buyer's requirements will exceed its capacity to supply. Those risks may of course be further controlled by contractual provisions imposing some maximum on the output buyer's obligation to buy, or the requirements seller's obligation to supply.

Initially, "requirements" contracts got a cold reception from American courts. They were frequently held invalid on various grounds: as lacking in consideration (the buyer was felt to have made only an illusory promise to buy); as lacking in mutuality (the seller was bound, but the buyer in effect was not); as too vague or indefinite for enforcement (the quantity that buyer was bound to purchase could not be precisely ascertained). Such agreements continued to be made, however, and answers to the objections described above were developed. The theoretical problem of lack of consideration was effectively met by Professor Corbin, who asserted that consideration existed because of the commitment by the buyer to either buy goods from the designated seller or *not buy at all.* See 1A Corbin on Contracts §156 (1960); Restatement (Second) §77. The buyer's performance of such an agreement does therefore entail sufficient legal "detriment" to constitute consideration because each alternative would have been sufficient consideration if bargained for separately. See Restatement (Second) §77, Comment *b.*

The second objection to enforcement of requirements contracts, their lack of mutuality, was met by a growing willingness (which we have already noted in Chapter 2) on the part of courts and commentators to demote mutuality of obligation to the status of a mere corollary of the consideration rule, with no independent force of its own. And the indefiniteness problem in many cases was overcome by the fact that sufficient information to allow for enforcement can often be gleaned from the buyer's past history, estimates by the parties, a prior course of dealing between them, or their course of performance under the agreement at issue. See, e.g., Eastern Air Lines, Inc. v. Gulf Oil Corp., 415 F. Supp. 429, 436-437 (S.D. Fla. 1975) (obligation of Eastern to purchase fuel exclusively from Gulf, but only at certain cities, was enforceable and would be construed in light of extensive past dealings between the parties and industry practices).

Thus, by the time the Uniform Commercial Code was drafted, the requirements contract had a long legal history. In §2-306, the drafters of the Code apparently attempted to continue the trend toward validation of such agreements in general, and also to provide assistance to any court that must decide whether a particular "requirements buyer" or "output seller" has failed to perform its obligation. See generally Elliot Axelrod, The Requirements Contract — What Is Required?, 31 Drake L. Rev. 83 (1981). Even today, however, an agreement that does not to some appreciable degree bind the buyer to buy *only* from the particular seller is likely to be viewed as invalid and unenforceable, because lacking in consideration or mutuality of obligation. See, e.g., Brooklyn Bagel Boys, Inc. v. Earthgrains Refrigerated Dough Products, Inc., 212 F.3d 373 (7th Cir. 2000) (contract which contained price structure and required buyer's "non-binding" forecast of needs every three months held not to be requirements contract because buyer was not required to buy all of its bagels or any specified quantity from seller). Sometimes, however, courts will find an implied promise of exclusivity that renders the contract binding. See, e.g., Essco Geometric v. Harvard Indus., 46 F.3d 718 (8th Cir. 1995) (extrinsic evidence established that both buyer and seller understood arrangement to be exclusive even though not expressly stated in letter agreement); Pepsi-Cola Co. v. Steak 'N Shake, Inc., 981 F. Supp. 1149 (S.D. Ind. 1997) (contract must be read as a whole to determine parties' intent; exclusivity may be implied).

The Comments to UCC §2-306 include further suggestions on the operation of requirements and output contracts, including the possibility (Comment 3) that the agreement may contain a "maximum or minimum." Comment 2 indicates that the seller in a requirements contract is to be protected against increases in demand that exceed the bounds of "good faith." A "ballooning" of demand by a requirements buyer has often been held to be in bad faith, both at common law and under the Code. See, e.g., A&A Mechanical, Inc. v. Thermal Equip. Sales, Inc., 998 S.W. 2d 505 (Ky. Ct. App. 1999) (assuming contract for duct work came under UCC §2-306, 29% increase in quantity would be unreasonable deviation from estimate). The Code also protects the requirements seller against a bad faith reduction in the buyer's demand, but this has proven somewhat more problematic for the courts. Generally courts have held that a requirements buyer may reduce its level of purchases even to zero, so long as it acts in good faith. See Empire Gas Corp. v. American Bakeries, Inc., 840 F.2d 1333 (7th Cir. 1988) (holding that requirements buyer may reduce its level of demand even to zero so long as it acts in good faith); but see Simcala, Inc. v. American Coal Trade, Inc., 821 So. 2d 197 (Ala. 2001) (holding that principles of statutory interpretation require that decreases not be disproportionate to any estimate under plain meaning of UCC §2-306(1); buyer's decrease in purchases from estimate of 17,500 tons of coal to 7,200 tons would be a breach even if buyer acted in good faith).

Assuming that a court applies the test of good faith to a substantial reduction in purchases by a requirements buyer, how is breach established? The cases in this area are not altogether clear, but the reduction will probably be in good faith if resulting directly from reasons beyond the buyer's control. E.g., R. A. Weaver & Associates, Inc. v. Asphalt Constr., Inc., 587 F.2d 1315 (D.C. Cir. 1978) (defendant buyer not liable for breach after construction project was altered to eliminate use of limestone that plaintiff had contracted to supply). In contrast, a buyer that attempts to procure its requirements more cheaply elsewhere or with intent to harm the seller is clearly acting in bad faith. See Chemical Distributors, Inc. v. Exxon Corp., 1 F.3d 1478 (5th Cir. 1993) (jury finding of bad faith justified by evidence that buyer bypassed seller to purchase requirements directly and more inexpensively from manufacturer and in effort to eliminate seller as competitor in related market). Likewise, termination of an output contract by a seller is likely to be judged by a standard very similar to that generally applied in evaluating reduction of requirements by a buyer. See Feld v. Henry S. Levy & Sons, Inc., 335 N.E.2d 320 (N.Y. 1975) (while bankruptcy or imperilment of the company's existence would justify termination of bread crumb production, mere yield of less profit would not be a good faith reason).

Morin Building Products Co. v. Baystone Construction, Inc.

United States Court of Appeals 717 F.2d 413 (7th Cir. 1983)

POSNER, Circuit Judge.

This appeal from a judgment for the plaintiff in a diversity suit requires us to interpret Indiana's common law of contracts. General Motors, which is not a party to this case, hired Baystone Construction, Inc., the defendant, to build an addition to a Chevrolet plant in Muncie, Indiana. Baystone hired Morin Building Products Company, the plaintiff, to supply and erect the aluminum walls for the addition. The contract required that the exterior siding of the walls be of "aluminum type 3003, not less than 18 B & S gauge, with a mill finish and stucco embossed surface texture to match finish and texture of existing metal siding." The contract also provided "that all work shall be done subject to the final approval of the Architect or Owner's [General Motors'] authorized agent, and his decision in matters relating to artistic effect shall be final, if within the terms of the Contract Documents"; and that "should any dispute arise as to the quality or fitness of materials or workmanship, the decision as to acceptability shall rest strictly with the Owner, based on the requirement that all work done or materials furnished shall be first class in every respect. What is usual or customary in erecting other buildings shall in no wise enter into any consideration or decision."

Morin put up the walls. But viewed in bright sunlight from an acute angle the exterior siding did not give the impression of having a uniform finish, and General Motors' representative rejected it. Baystone removed Morin's siding and hired another subcontractor to replace it. General Motors approved the replacement siding. Baystone refused to pay Morin the balance of the contract price ($23,000) and Morin brought this suit for the balance, and won.

The only issue on appeal is the correctness of a jury instruction which, after quoting the contractual provisions requiring that the owner (General Motors) be satisfied with the contractor's (Morin's) work, states: "Notwithstanding the apparent finality of the foregoing language, however, the general rule applying to satisfaction in the case of contracts for the construction of commercial buildings is that the satisfaction clause must be determined by objective criteria. Under this standard, the question is not whether the owner was satisfied in fact, but whether the owner, as a reasonable person, should have been satisfied with the materials and workmanship in question." There was much evidence that General Motors' rejection of Morin's exterior siding had been totally unreasonable. Not only was the lack of absolute uniformity in the finish of the walls a seemingly trivial defect given the strictly utilitarian purpose of the building that they enclosed, but it may have been inevitable; "mill finish sheet" is defined in the trade as "sheet having a nonuniform finish which may vary from sheet to sheet and within a sheet, and may not be entirely free from stains or oil." If the instruction was correct, so was the judgment. But if the instruction was incorrect — if the proper standard is not whether a reasonable man would have been satisfied with Morin's exterior siding but whether General Motors' authorized representative in fact was — then there must be a new trial to determine whether he really was dissatisfied, or whether he was not and the rejection therefore was in bad faith.

Some cases hold that if the contract provides that the seller's performance must be to the buyer's satisfaction, his rejection — however unreasonable — of the seller's performance is not a breach of the contract unless the rejection is in bad faith. See, e.g., Stone Mountain Properties, Ltd. v. Helmer, 139 Ga. App. 865, 869, 229 S.E.2d 779, 783 (1976). But most cases conform to the position stated in section 228 of the Restatement (Second) of Contracts (1979): if "it is practicable to determine whether a reasonable person in the position of the obligor would be satisfied, an interpretation is preferred under which the condition [that the obligor be satisfied with the obligee's performance] occurs if such a reasonable person in the position of the obligor would be satisfied." See Farnsworth, Contracts 556-559 (1982); Annot., 44 A.L.R.2d 1114, 1117, 1119-1120 (1955). Indiana Tri-City Plaza Bowl, Inc. v. Estate of Glueck, 422 N.E.2d 670, 675 (Ind. App. 1981) . . . adopts the majority position as the law of Indiana.

We do not understand the majority position to be paternalistic; and paternalism would be out of place in a case such as this, where the subcontractor is a substantial multistate enterprise. The requirement of reasonableness is read into a contract not to protect the weaker party but to approximate what the parties would have expressly provided with respect to a contingency that they did not foresee, if they had foreseen it. Therefore the requirement is not read into every contract, because it is not always a reliable guide to the parties' intentions. In particular, the presumption that the performing party would not have wanted to put himself at the mercy of the paying party's whim is overcome when the nature of the performance contracted for is such that there are no objective standards to guide the court. It cannot be assumed in such a case that the parties would have wanted a court to second-guess the buyer's rejection. So "the reasonable person standard is employed when the contract involves commercial quality, operative fitness, or mechanical utility which other knowledgeable persons can judge. . . . The standard of good faith is employed when the contract involves personal aesthetics or fancy." Indiana Tri-City Plaza Bowl, Inc. v. Estate of Glueck, supra, 422 N.E.2d at 675; see also Action Engineering v. Martin Marietta Aluminum, 670 F.2d 456, 460-461 (3d Cir. 1982).

We have to decide which category the contract between Baystone and Morin belongs in. The particular in which Morin's aluminum siding was found wanting was its appearance, which may seem quintessentially a matter of "personal aesthetics," or as the contract put it, "artistic effect." But it is easy to imagine situations where this would not be so. Suppose the manager of a steel plant rejected a shipment of pig iron because he did not think the pigs had a pretty shape. The reasonable-man standard would be applied even if the contract had an "acceptability shall rest strictly with the Owner" clause, for it would be fantastic to think that the iron supplier would have subjected his contract rights to the whimsy of the buyer's agent. At the other extreme would be a contract to paint a portrait, the buyer having reserved the right to reject the portrait if it did not satisfy him. Such a buyer wants a portrait that will please him rather than a jury, even a jury of connoisseurs, so the only question would be his good faith in rejecting the portrait, Gibson v. Cranage, 39 Mich. 49 (1878).

This case is closer to the first example than to the second. The building for which the aluminum siding was intended was a factory — not usually intended to be a thing of beauty. That aesthetic considerations were decidedly secondary to considerations of function and cost is suggested by the fact that the contract specified mill-finish aluminum, which is unpainted. There is much debate in the record over whether it is even possible to ensure a uniform finish within and among sheets, but it is at least clear that mill finish usually is not uniform. If General Motors and Baystone had wanted a uniform finish they would in all likelihood have ordered a painted siding. Whether Morin's siding achieved a reasonable uniformity amounting to satisfactory commercial quality was susceptible of objective judgment; in the language of the Restatement, a reasonableness standard was "practicable."

But this means only that a requirement of reasonableness would be read into this contract if it contained a standard owner's satisfaction clause, which it did not; and since the ultimate touchstone of decision must be the intent of the parties to the contract we must consider the actual language they used. The contract refers explicitly to "artistic effect," a choice of words that may seem deliberately designed to put the contract in the "personal aesthetics" category whatever an outside observer might think. But the reference appears as number 17 in a list of conditions in a general purpose form contract. And the words "artistic effect" are immediately followed by the qualifying phrase, "if within the terms of the Contract Documents," which suggests that the "artistic effect" clause is limited to contracts in which artistic effect is one of the things the buyer is aiming for; it is not clear that he was here. The other clause on which Baystone relies, relating to the quality or fitness of workmanship and materials, may seem all-encompassing, but it is qualified by the phrase, "based on the requirement that all work done or materials furnished shall be first class in every respect" — and it is not clear that Morin's were not. This clause also was not drafted for this contract; it was incorporated by reference to another form contract (the Chevrolet Division's "Contract General Conditions"), of which it is paragraph 35. We do not disparage form contracts, without which the commercial life of the nation would grind to a halt. But we are left with more than a suspicion that the artistic-effect and quality-fitness clauses in the form contract used here were not intended to cover the aesthetics of a mill-finish aluminum factory wall.

If we are right, Morin might prevail even under the minority position, which makes good faith the only standard but presupposes that the contract conditioned acceptance of performance on the buyer's satisfaction in the particular respect in which he was dissatisfied. Maybe this contract was not intended to allow General Motors to reject the aluminum siding on the basis of artistic effect. It would not follow that the contract put Morin under no obligations whatsoever with regard to uniformity of finish. The contract expressly required it to use aluminum having "a mill finish . . . to match finish . . . of existing metal siding." The jury was asked to decide whether a reasonable man would have found that Morin had used aluminum sufficiently uniform to satisfy the matching requirement. This was the right standard if, as we believe, the parties would have adopted it had they foreseen this dispute. It is unlikely that Morin intended to bind itself to a higher and perhaps unattainable standard of achieving whatever perfection of matching that General Motors' agent insisted on, or that General Motors would have required Baystone to submit to such a standard. Because it is difficult — maybe impossible — to achieve a uniform finish with mill-finish aluminum, Morin would have been running a considerable risk of rejection if it had agreed to such a condition, and it therefore could have been expected to demand a compensating increase in the contract price. This would have required General Motors to pay a premium to obtain a freedom of action that it could not have thought terribly important, since its objective was not aesthetic. If a uniform finish was important to it, it could have gotten such a finish by specifying painted siding.

All this is conjecture; we do not know how important the aesthetics were to General Motors when the contract was signed or how difficult it really would have been to obtain the uniformity of finish it desired. The fact that General Motors accepted the replacement siding proves little, for there is evidence that the replacement siding produced the same striped effect, when viewed from an acute angle in bright sunlight, that Morin's had. When in doubt on a difficult issue of state law it is only prudent to defer to the view of the district judge, Murphy v. White Hen Pantry Co., 691 F.2d 350, 354 (7th Cir. 1982), here an experienced Indiana lawyer who thought this the type of contract where the buyer cannot unreasonably withhold approval of the seller's performance.

Lest this conclusion be thought to strike at the foundations of freedom of contract, we repeat that if it appeared from the language or circumstances of the contract that the parties really intended General Motors to have the right to reject Morin's work for failure to satisfy the private aesthetic taste of General Motors' representative, the rejection would have been proper even if unreasonable. But the contract is ambiguous because of the qualifications with which the terms "artistic effect" and "decision as to acceptability" are hedged about, and the circumstances suggest that the parties probably did not intend to subject Morin's rights to aesthetic whim.

Affirmed.

NOTES AND QUESTIONS

1. *Interpretation of conditions of satisfactory performance.* Contracts frequently contain express terms that obligate one party to perform to the "satisfaction" of the other, or condition one party's duty of performance on his "satisfaction" with the performance of the other party. As Judge Posner's opinion in *Morin* illustrates, such provisions are unlikely to be interpreted as conferring on the party whose satisfaction is at issue an unlimited power to determine and declare his own dissatisfaction, without external check. Indeed, if pure unbridled discretion were the test, the party whose performance was so conditioned might be held to have made only an "illusory" promise, defeating the contract as a whole. Instead, one of the two approaches described in *Morin* will ordinarily be used: Either the obligor's declaration of dissatisfaction will be judged by a standard of reasonableness; or at minimum he will be held to the standard of "honest" dissatisfaction. As Judge Posner states, the "objective" standard has been traditionally employed in cases where "commercial quality, operative fitness, or mechanical utility" are in question, while the "subjective" standard is likely to be employed where "personal aesthetics or fancy" are at issue.

In an extensive survey of the "satisfaction" cases, Conditions of Personal Satisfaction in the Law of Contract, 27 N.Y.L. Sch. L. Rev. 103 (1981), Professor James Brook pointed out that early decisions did not make the objective/subjective distinction; all cases, whether involving "mechanical utility" or not, were judged by the same, subjective standard of the promisee's honest dissatisfaction. Following later case law, Restatement (Second) §228 declares that the objective test should be preferred when it is "practicable to determine whether a reasonable person in the position of the obligor would be satisfied." Comment *a* to §228 indicates that the subjective standard should be used only where "the agreement leaves no doubt that it is only honest dissatisfaction that is meant and no more." See Sky Angel U.S., LLC v. Discovery Communications, LLC, 95 F. Supp. 3d 860 (D. Md. 2015) (condition of satisfaction in video distribution services contract would be judged by preferred objective standard of reasonableness); FEI Enterprises, Inc. v. Kee Man Yoon, 124 Cal. Rptr. 3d 64 (Ct. App. 2011) (holding that generally the law prefers an objective standard). Where personal services are involved, the court may be more likely to approve the use of a subjective test. E.g., Silvestri v. Optus Software, Inc., 814 A.2d 602 (N.J. 2003) (subjective standard would apply to condition of satisfaction in employment contract for high-level business manager; employer entitled to be highly personal and idiosyncratic in judging performance of employee sharing responsibility for success of business).

Where the contract conditions performance by one party on the other's performance to the satisfaction of some independent third party, such as an architect or engineer, the Restatement (Second) indicates a greater tolerance for the application of a subjective test, on the assumption that a third party is less likely to be affected by the "selfish interests" of the obligor. See Restatement (Second) of Contracts §227, Comment *b*, Illustration 3, and §228, Comment *b*. Accord Hanscom v. Gregorie, 562 A.2d 1232 (Me. 1989) (defendants freed from purchase obligation where their building inspector determined that plaintiff's building was not free from "defects of a substantial nature," even though trial court concluded that defects in question, though expensive to remedy, were not "substantial"; contract left that question to honest judgment of defendant's expert).

2. *Judge Posner's analysis.* Does Judge Posner adequately justify the court's choice of an objective standard in *Morin*? Comment *b* to Restatement (Second) §228 indicates that a preference for the objective test may be justified in part by the desire to avoid "forfeiture," which the Restatement defines elsewhere (Comment *b* to §229) as "the denial of compensation that results when the obligee loses his right to the agreed exchange after he has relied substantially, as by preparation or performance on the expectation of that exchange." Was this factor at work in *Morin*? (You will recall, incidentally, that Judge Posner as an academic was the leader of the so-called Chicago School of "efficiency" theorists. In that light, it is interesting to note in the *Morin* opinion his careful disclaimer of "paternalism" and his expression of solicitude for the "foundations of freedom of contract.")

3. *Effect of standard of interpretation.* Even where the court does agree with the defendant that only the subjective test of "honest dissatisfaction" should be employed, one ought not to assume that the defendant will therefore ultimately prevail. Although the plaintiff's burden of establishing that defendant was not honestly dissatisfied may be a difficult one, it is not necessarily impossible. E.g., Forman v. Benson, 446 N.E.2d 535 (Ill. App. Ct. 1983) (seller's rejection of buyer's credit report held pretextual, an attempt to renegotiate price and interest rate). Conversely, application of the objective, reasonableness standard will not necessarily produce a victory for the plaintiff. See, e.g., Kennedy Associates, Inc. v. Fischer, 667 P.2d 174 (Alaska 1983) (even under objective test, mortgage lender could reasonably disapprove property in question after conducting agreed inspection).

Locke v. Warner Bros., Inc.

California Court of Appeal 57 Cal. App. 4th 354, 66 Cal. Rptr. 2d 921 (1997), review denied (Nov. 19, 1997)

KLEIN, Presiding Judge.

Plaintiffs and appellants Sondra Locke (Locke) and Caritas Films, a California corporation (Caritas) (sometimes collectively referred to as Locke) appeal a judgment following a grant of summary judgment in favor of defendant and respondent Warner Bros., Inc. (Warner).

The essential issue presented is whether triable issues of material fact are present which would preclude summary judgment.

We conclude triable issues are present with respect to whether Warner breached its development deal with Locke by categorically refusing to work with her, and whether Warner fraudulently entered into said agreement without the intention to work with Locke. The judgment therefore is reversed as to the second and fourth causes of action and otherwise is affirmed.

FACTUAL AND PROCEDURAL BACKGROUND

1. Locke's Dispute with Eastwood

In 1975, Locke came to Warner to appear with Clint Eastwood in *The Outlaw Josey Wales* (Warner Bros. 1976). During the filming of the movie, Locke and Eastwood began a personal and romantic relationship. For the next dozen years, they lived in Eastwood's Los Angeles and Northern California homes. Locke also appeared in a number of Eastwood's films. In 1986, Locke made her directorial debut in *Ratboy* (Warner Bros. 1986).

In 1988, the relationship deteriorated, and in 1989 Eastwood terminated it. Locke then brought suit against Eastwood, alleging numerous causes of action. That action was resolved by a November 21, 1990, settlement agreement and mutual general release. Under said agreement, Eastwood agreed to pay Locke additional compensation in the sum of $450,000 "on account of past employment and Locke's contentions" and to convey certain real property to her.

Clint Eastwood and Sandra Locke during the filming of The Outlaw Josey Wales.

2. Locke's Development Deal with Warner

According to Locke, Eastwood secured a development deal for Locke with Warner in exchange for Locke's dropping her case against him. Contemporaneously with the Locke/Eastwood settlement agreement, Locke entered into a written agreement with Warner, dated November 27, 1990. It is the Locke/Warner agreement which is the subject of the instant controversy.

The Locke/Warner agreement had two basic components. The first element states Locke would receive $250,000 per year for three years for a "non-exclusive first look deal." It required Locke to submit to Warner any picture she was interested in developing before submitting it to any other studio. Warner then had 30 days either to approve or reject a submission.

The second element of the contract was a $750,000 "pay or play" directing deal. The provision is called "pay or play" because it gives the studio a choice: It can either "play" the director by using the director's services, or pay the director his or her fee.

Unbeknownst to Locke at the time, Eastwood had agreed to reimburse Warner for the cost of her contract if she did not succeed in getting projects produced and developed. Early in the second year of the three-year contract, Warner charged $975,000 to an Eastwood film, *Unforgiven* (Warner Bros. 1992).

Warner paid Locke the guaranteed compensation of $1.5 million under the agreement. In accordance with the agreement, Warner also provided Locke with an office on the studio lot and an administrative assistant. However, Warner did not develop any of Locke's proposed projects or hire her to direct any films. Locke contends the development deal was a sham, that Warner never intended to make any films with her, and that Warner's sole motivation in entering into the agreement was to assist Eastwood in settling his litigation with Locke.

3. Locke's Action Against Warner

On March 10, 1994, Locke filed suit against Warner, alleging four causes of action.

The first cause of action alleged sex discrimination in violation of public policy. Locke alleged Warner denied her the benefit of the bargain of the development deal on account of her gender.

The third cause of action, captioned "Tortious Breach of the Implied Covenant of Good Faith and Fair Dealing in Violation of Public Policy," alleged a similar claim. Locke pled that in denying her the benefits of the Warner/Locke agreement, Warner was "motivated by [its] discriminatory bias against women in violation of . . . public policy."

The second cause of action alleged that Warner breached the contract by refusing to consider Locke's proposed projects and thereby deprived her of the benefit of the bargain of the Warner/Locke agreement.

Lastly, the fourth cause of action alleged fraud. Locke pled that at the time Warner entered into the agreement with her, it concealed and failed to disclose it had no intention of honoring the agreement.

Warner answered, denied each and every allegation and asserted various affirmative defenses.

4. Warner's Motion for Summary Judgment and Opposition Thereto

On January 6, 1995, Warner filed a motion for summary judgment. Warner contended it did not breach its contract with Locke because it did consider all the projects she presented, and the studio's decision not to put any of those projects into active development or "hand" Locke a script which it already owned was not a breach of any express or implied contractual duty. Warner asserted the odds are slim a producer can get a project into development and even slimmer a director will be hired to direct a film. During the term of Locke's deal, Warner had similar deals with numerous other producers and directors, who fared no better than Locke.

As for Locke's sex discrimination claims, Warner averred there was no evidence it ignored Locke's projects or otherwise discriminated against her on account of her gender. Finally, Warner urged the fraud claim was meritless because Locke had no evidence that when Warner signed the contract, it did not intend to honor the deal, and moreover, Warner had fulfilled its contractual obligations to Locke.

In opposing summary judgment, Locke contended Warner breached the agreement in that it had no intention of accepting any project regardless of its merits. Locke also asserted Warner committed fraud by entering into the agreement without any intention of approving any project with Locke or allowing Locke to direct another film.

Locke's opposition papers cited the deposition testimony of Joseph Terry, who recounted a conversation he had with Bob Brassel, a Warner executive, regarding Locke's projects. Terry had stated to Brassel: " 'Well, Bob, this woman has a deal on the lot. She's a director that you want to work with. You have a deal with her. . . . I've got five here that she's interested in.' And then I would get nothing. . . . I was told [by Brassel], 'Joe, we're not going to work with her,' and then, 'That's Clint's deal.' And that's something I just completely did not understand."

Similarly, the declaration of Mary Wellnitz stated: She worked with Locke to set up projects at Warner, without success. Shortly after she began her association with Locke, Wellnitz submitted a script to Lance Young, who at the time was a senior vice-president of production at Warner. After discussing the script, Young told Wellnitz, "Mary, I want you to know that I think Sondra is a wonderful woman and very talented, but, if you think I can go down the hall and tell Bob Daly that I have a movie I want to make with her he would tell me to forget it. They are not going to make a movie with her here."

5. Trial Court's Ruling

On February 17, 1995, the trial court granted summary judgment in favor of Warner. Thereafter, the trial court signed an extensive order granting summary judgment. The order stated:

> Under the contract, Warner had no obligation either to put into development any of the projects submitted to the studio for its consideration, or to "hand off" to Locke any scripts for her to direct that it previously had acquired from someone else. The implied covenant of good faith and fair dealing cannot be imposed to create a contract different from the one the parties negotiated for themselves. Warner had the option to pass on each project Locke submitted. Warner was not required to have a "good faith" or "fair" basis for declining to exercise its right to develop her material. Such a requirement would be improper and unworkable. A judge or jury cannot and should not substitute its judgment for a film studio's when the studio is making the creative decision of whether to develop or produce a proposed motion picture. Such highly subjective artistic and business decisions are not proper subjects for judicial review. Moreover, Warner had legitimate commercial and artistic reasons for declining to develop the projects Locke submitted.

With respect to Locke's claim she was defrauded by Warner when it entered into the agreement with the undisclosed intention not to honor its contractual obligations, the trial court ruled that because Warner did not breach its contractual obligations to Locke, the fraud claim was meritless. Also, it could not be inferred from the statements by Young and Brassel that two years earlier, when Warner entered into agreement, it had no intention of working with Locke.

As for the two causes of action alleging sex discrimination, the trial court found no evidence Warner declined to develop the projects Locke submitted, and declined to use her directing services, on account of her gender.

Locke filed a timely notice of appeal from the judgment.

CONTENTIONS

Locke contends: The trial court erred by granting Warner's motion for summary judgment based on its conclusion there were no disputed issues of material fact; the trial court erred in weighing the evidence, resolving doubts against Locke, the nonmoving party, and adopting only those inferences favorable to Warner where the evidence supported contrary inferences; and the trial court committed reversible error first by failing to make any findings or evidentiary rulings and then by adopting Warner's defective ruling.

DISCUSSION

1. Standard of Appellate Review

. . .

2. A Triable Issue Exists as to Whether Warner Breached its Contract with Locke by Failing to Evaluate Locke's Proposals on Their Merits

As indicated, the second cause of action alleged Warner breached the contract by "refusing to consider the projects prepared by [Locke] and depriving [Locke] of the benefit of the bargain of the Warner-Locke agreement."

In granting summary judgment on this claim, the trial court ruled "[a] judge or jury cannot and should not substitute its own judgment for a film studio's when the studio is making the creative decision of whether to develop or produce a proposed motion picture. Such highly-subjective artistic and business decisions are not proper subjects for judicial review."

The trial court's ruling missed the mark by failing to distinguish between Warner's right to make a subjective creative decision, which is not reviewable for reasonableness, and the requirement the dissatisfaction be bona fide or genuine.

a. General principles.

" '[W]here a contract confers on one party a discretionary power affecting the rights of the other, a duty is imposed to exercise that discretion in good faith and in accordance with fair dealing.'[Citations.]" (Perdue v. Crocker National Bank (1985) 38 Cal. 3d 913, 923 [216 Cal. Rptr. 345, 702 P.2d 503]; accord, Kendall v. Ernest Pestana, Inc. (1985) 40 Cal. 3d 488, 500 [220 Cal. Rptr. 818, 709 P.2d 837].) It is settled that in " 'every contract there is an implied covenant that neither party shall do anything which will have the effect of destroying or injuring the right of the other party to receive the fruits of the contract. . . .' " (*Kendall,* supra, at p. 500; accord, Waller v. Truck Ins. Exchange, Inc., supra, 11 Cal. 4th at p. 36.)

Therefore, when it is a condition of an obligor's duty that he or she be subjectively satisfied with respect to the obligee's performance, the subjective standard of *honest satisfaction* is applicable. (1 Witkin, Summary of Cal. Law (9th ed. 1987) Contracts, §729, p. 659; Rest. 2d Contracts, §228, coms. a, b, pp.182-183.) "Where the contract involves matters of fancy, taste or judgment, the promisor is the sole judge of his satisfaction. If he asserts *in good faith* that he is not satisfied, there can be no inquiry into the reasonableness of his attitude. [Citations.] Traditional examples are employment contracts . . . and agreements to paint a portrait, write a literary or scientific article, or produce a play or vaudeville act. [Citations.]" (1 Witkin, Summary of Cal. Law, supra, §730, p. 660; accord, Schuyler v. Pantages (1921) 54 Cal. App. 83, 85-87 [201 P. 137].) In such cases, "the promisor's determination that he is not satisfied, *when made in good faith,* has been held to be a defense to an action on the contract. [Citations.]" (Mattei v. Hopper (1958) 51 Cal. 2d 119, 123 [330 P.2d 625], italics added.)

Therefore, the trial court erred in deferring entirely to what it characterized as Warner's "creative decision" in the handling of the development deal. If Warner acted in bad faith by categorically rejecting Locke's work and refusing to work with her, irrespective of the merits of her proposals, such conduct is not beyond the reach of the law.

b. Locke presented evidence from which a trier of fact reasonably could infer Warner breached the agreement by refusing to consider her proposals in good faith.

Merely because Warner paid Locke the guaranteed compensation under the agreement does not establish Warner fulfilled its contractual obligation. As pointed out by Locke, the value in the subject development deal was not merely the guaranteed payments under the agreement, but also the opportunity to direct and produce films and earn additional sums, and most importantly, the opportunity to promote and enhance a career.

Unquestionably, Warner was entitled to reject Locke's work based on its subjective judgment, and its creative decision in that regard is not subject to being second-guessed by a court. However, bearing in mind the requirement that subjective dissatisfaction must be an honestly held dissatisfaction, the evidence raises a triable issue as to whether Warner breached its agreement with Locke by not considering her proposals on their merits.

As indicated, the deposition testimony of Joseph Terry recounted a conversation he had with Bob Brassel, a Warner executive, regarding Locke's projects. In that conversation, Brassel stated " 'Joe, we're not going to work with her,' and then, 'That's Clint's deal.' "

Similarly, the declaration of Mary Wellnitz recalled a conversation she had with Lance Young, a senior vice-president of production at Warner. After discussing the script with Wellnitz, Young told her: "Mary, I want you to know that I think Sondra is a wonderful woman and very talented, but, if you think I can go down the hall and tell Bob Daly that I have a movie I want to make with her he would tell me to forget it. They are not going to make a movie with her here."

The above evidence raises a triable issue of material fact as to whether Warner breached its contract with Locke by categorically refusing to work with her, irrespective of the merits of her proposals. While Warner was entitled to reject Locke's proposals based on its subjective dissatisfaction, the evidence calls into question whether Warner had an honest or good faith dissatisfaction with Locke's proposals, or whether it merely went through the motions of purporting to "consider" her projects.

c. No merit to Warner's contention Locke seeks to rewrite the instant agreement to limit Warner's discretionary power.

Warner argues that while the implied covenant of good faith and fair dealing is implied in all contracts, it is limited to assuring compliance with the express terms of the contract and cannot be extended to create obligations not contemplated in the contract. (Racine & Laramie, Ltd. v. Department of Parks & Recreation (1992) 11 Cal. App. 4th 1026, 1032 [14 Cal. Rptr. 2d 335].)

This principle is illustrated in Carma Developers (Cal.), Inc. v. Marathon Development California, Inc. (1992) 2 Cal. 4th 342, 351-352 [6 Cal. Rptr. 2d 467, 826 P.2d 710], wherein the parties entered into a lease agreement which stated that if the tenant procured a potential sublessee and asked the landlord for consent to sublease, the landlord had the right to terminate the lease, enter into negotiations with the prospective sublessee, and appropriate for itself all profits from the new arrangement. *Carma* recognized "[t]he covenant of good faith finds particular application in situations where one party is invested with a discretionary power affecting the rights of another." (Id., at p. 372.) The court expressed the view that "[s]uch power must be exercised in good faith." (Ibid.) At the same time, *Carma* upheld the right of the landlord under the express terms of the lease to freely exercise its discretion to terminate the lease in order to claim for itself — and deprive the tenant of — the appreciated rental value of the premises. (Id., at p. 376.)

In this regard, *Carma* stated: "We are aware of no reported case in which a court has held the covenant of good faith may be read to prohibit a party from doing that which is expressly permitted by an agreement. On the contrary, as a general matter, implied terms should never be read to vary express terms. 'The general rule [regarding the covenant of good faith] is plainly subject to the exception that the parties may, by express provisions of the contract, grant the right to engage in the very acts and conduct which would otherwise have been forbidden by an implied covenant of good faith and fair dealing. . . . This is in accord with the general principle that, in interpreting a contract "an implication . . . should not be made when the contrary is indicated in clear and express words." 3 Corbin, Contracts, §564, p. 298 (1960). . . . *As to acts and conduct authorized by the express provisions of the contract,* no covenant of good faith and fair dealing can be implied which forbids such acts and conduct. And if defendants were given the right to do what they did by the express provisions of the contract there can be no breach.'[Citation.]" (Carma Developers (Cal.), Inc. v. Marathon Development California, Inc., supra, 2 Cal. 4th at p. 374, italics added.)

In Third Story Music, Inc. v. Waits (1995) 41 Cal. App. 4th 798, 801 [48 Cal. Rptr. 2d 747], the issue presented was "whether a promise to market music, or to refrain from doing so, at the election of the promisor is subject to the implied covenant of good faith and fair dealing where substantial consideration has been paid by the promisor."

In that case, Warner Communications obtained from Third Story Music (TSM) the worldwide right to manufacture, sell, distribute and advertise the musical output of singer/songwriter Tom Waits. (Third Story Music, Inc. v. Waits, supra, 41 Cal. App. 4th at pp. 800-801.) The agreement also specifically stated that Warner Communications " 'may at our election refrain from any or all of the foregoing.' " (Id., at p. 801.) TSM sued Warner Communications for contract damages based on breach of the implied covenant of good faith and fair dealing, claiming Warner Communications had impeded TSM's receiving the benefit of the agreement. (Id., at p. 802.) Warner Communications demurred to the complaint, alleging the clause in the agreement permitting it to " 'at [its] election refrain' from doing anything to profitably exploit the music is controlling and precludes application of any implied covenant." (Ibid.) The demurrer was sustained on those grounds. (Ibid.)

The reviewing court affirmed, holding the implied covenant was unavailing to the plaintiff. (Third Story Music, Inc. v. Waits, supra, 41 Cal. App. 4th at pp. 808-809.) Because the agreement expressly provided Warner Communications had the right to refrain from marketing the Waits recordings, the implied covenant of good faith and fair dealing did not limit the discretion given to Warner Communications in that regard. (Ibid.; Carma Developers (Cal.), Inc. v. Marathon Development California, Inc., supra, 2 Cal. 4th at p. 374.)

Warner's reliance herein on *Third Story Music, Inc.*, is misplaced. The Locke/Warner agreement did not give Warner the express right to refrain from working with Locke. Rather, the agreement gave Warner *discretion* with respect to developing Locke's projects. The implied covenant of good faith and fair dealing obligated Warner to exercise that discretion honestly and in good faith.

In sum, the Warner/Locke agreement contained an implied covenant of good faith and fair dealing, that neither party would frustrate the other party's right to receive the benefits of the contract. (Comunale v. Traders & General Ins. Co., supra, 50 Cal. 2d at p. 658; Waller v. Truck Ins. Exchange, Inc., supra, 11 Cal. 4th at p. 36.) Whether Warner violated the implied covenant and breached the contract by categorically refusing to work with Locke is a question for the trier of fact.

3. A Triable Issue Exists as to Whether Warner Made a Fraudulent Promise

In the fourth cause of action, Locke pled at the time Warner entered into the agreement with her, it concealed and failed to disclose it had no intention of honoring the agreement.

The trial court held that because Warner did not breach any express or implied obligations owed to Locke, she could not prevail on the fraud claim. However, as explained above, a triable issue exists as to whether Warner breached the agreement with Locke. Therefore, the trial court's rationale for disposing of the fraud claim is undermined.

The trial court also ruled Locke could not prevail on the fraud claim because there was no evidence Warner had a fraudulent intent at the time the parties entered into the contract. The trial court acknowledged Locke "filed a declaration of her development assistant, Mary Wellnitz, in which Ms. Wellnitz states that a Warner Bros. executive, Lance Young, remarked in late 1992 that Warner Bros. was 'not going to make a movie' with Ms. Locke. [Locke] also offered the deposition testimony of a third party, Joe Terry, in which he recalled a 1993 conversation with another Warner Bros. production executive, Bob Brassel, in which Mr. Brassel said that the studio was not going to work with Ms. Locke.

However, the Court does not believe that these statements would permit a jury to infer that two years earlier, when plaintiffs and the defendant entered into their contract, Warner Bros. intended to breach its obligations."

We disagree. Fraudulent intent must often be established by circumstantial evidence, and may be "inferred from such circumstances as defendant's . . . failure even to attempt performance, . . ." (Tenzer v. Superscope, Inc., supra, 39 Cal. 3d at p. 30.) Based on the above evidence that Warner had expressed an absolute unwillingness to work with Locke, a trier of fact reasonably could infer Warner never intended to give Locke's proposals a good faith evaluation and that Warner entered into the agreement with Locke solely as an accommodation to Eastwood, who had promised to reimburse Warner for any losses under the agreement. The trial court erred in concluding such an inference could not be drawn from the evidence. We conclude the issue of fraudulent intent is one for the trier of fact.

4. Locke Waived any Error in the Trial Court's Ruling with Respect to her Causes of Action Alleging Gender Bias

Locke's opening brief does not assert any error in the trial court's disposition of her two causes of action alleging sex discrimination. Accordingly, this court may treat the claims as having been waived.

Belatedly, Locke's reply brief contends she presented evidence which raised the inference she was discriminated against because of her gender. "Ordinarily, [appellants'] failure to raise an issue in their opening brief waives the issue on appeal. [Citation.]" (Tisher v. California Horse Racing Bd. (1991) 231 Cal. App. 3d 349, 361 [282 Cal. Rptr. 330]; accord, 1119 Delaware v. Continental Land Title Co. (1993) 16 Cal. App. 4th 992, 1004 [20 Cal. Rptr. 2d 438]; Regency Outdoor Advertising, Inc. v. Carolina Lanes, Inc. (1995) 31 Cal. App. 4th 1323, 1333 [37 Cal. Rptr. 2d 552].) Locke has not shown good cause for the untimely contention. Therefore, we disregard Locke's argument the trial court erred in granting summary judgment on the first and third causes of action.

5. Remaining Issues not Reached

Because we find triable issues are present with respect to the second and fourth causes of action, it is unnecessary to address Locke's remaining contentions.

DISPOSITION

The judgment is reversed with respect to the second and fourth causes of action and is otherwise affirmed. Locke to recover costs on appeal.

KITCHING, J., and ALDRICH, J., concurred.

NOTES AND QUESTIONS

1. *Standards for the exercise of discretion.* In *Morin*, we saw the court choosing between an "objective" and a "subjective" standard for the good faith exercise of discretion – between a "reasonable person" standard and one of mere "honesty in fact." In the *Locke* case, it appears that defendant Warner Brothers argued that the contract with Locke gave it an absolute right to refrain from

developing any of Locke's proposals, so long as it paid her the minimum amounts required by their agreement. Locke on the other hand took the position, accepted by the appellate court, that while their contract gave Warner discretion in deciding whether to proceed with any of her projects, the implied obligation of good faith required at a minimum that it exercise that discretion honestly — that it judge her various proposals on their merits, not simply refuse "categorically" to work with her. Do you agree with the court's view? What other evidence should Locke be required to produce at trial to establish bad faith on the part of Warner Brothers? Should Warner be required to produce evidence of objective, rational bases for rejecting all of Locke's proposals? Cf. Dick Broadcasting Co., Inc. of Tennessee v. Oak Ridge FM, Inc., 395 S.W.3d 653 (Tenn. 2013) (holding that the implied covenant of good faith would require that party having right to approve assignment of an asset purchase contract exercise the right in commercially reasonable manner; approving party would not have arbitrary or unfettered discretion absent explicit term to that effect).

2. *Factual context for Locke.* As the court indicated, the *Locke* case had its beginning in the intimate and professional relationship between actors Sondra Locke and Clint Eastwood. News accounts indicate that the relationship came to an abrupt end when Eastwood had locks changed on the shared home and packed Locke's belongings while she was away. See generally Ann W. O'Neill, Locke Feels Vindicated After Lawsuit, L.A. Times, Sept. 29, 1996, at A1. Locke originally brought suit against Eastwood in 1989 for a share in the real property and on other theories in what is commonly called a "palimony" lawsuit, similar to that in the *Watts* case in Chapter 3. As part of a 1990 settlement of the 1989 lawsuit, Eastwood facilitated the $1.5 million three-year development contract between Locke and Warner. In 1994, Locke sued Warner for breach after all her proposals were rejected under the development contract. While pursuing the case against Warner, Locke discovered evidence of the "side-deal" between Warner and Eastwood that required Eastwood to reimburse Warner for its payments to Locke. Locke then initiated a second lawsuit against Eastwood for fraud relating to the Warner contract, seeking recovery for the damage allegedly done to her career. The second Locke-Eastwood lawsuit was settled in 1996 for an undisclosed amount after the jury in the case had begun deliberations. Id. Thus, this action by Locke against Warner constituted the remaining part of the litigation. Note that Restatement (Second) §205, Comment *d* states that "[s]ubterfuges and evasions violate the obligation of good faith even though the actor believes his conduct to be justified." Suppose the court had accepted Warner's contention that the contract (and perhaps industry practice as well) gave it a completely unfettered right to accept or reject Locke's proposals for whatever reason it chose — indeed, to act for "a good reason, a bad reason, or no reason at all," as the freedom to be completely arbitrary is often described. Would it necessarily follow that Locke's suit should fail?

3. *Gender or racial discrimination as breach of duty of good faith.* Locke's complaint also alleged that Warner denied her the benefits of the contract because of gender bias against women, but Locke's appellate briefs failed to make a timely challenge to the trial court's grant of summary judgment on this issue. If Locke had been able to prove that Warner rejected her proposals because of her gender, would that constitute a breach of the implied covenant of good faith? What sort

of evidence might Locke have been able to produce to prove gender discrimination? Similar questions could be raised whether discrimination in contract performance on the basis of race, ethnicity, sexual orientation, or disability would amount to a breach of the duty of good faith, apart from perhaps violating federal or state antidiscrimination statutes. Cf. Doe v. Kohn Nast & Graf, 862 F. Supp. 1310 (E.D. Pa. 1994) (plaintiff alleged discrimination covered by Americans with Disabilities Act on the basis of HIV-infected status and separate claim for breach of implied duty of good faith after being barred from his office; court refused to dismiss good faith issue); Ricci v. Key Bancshares of Maine, Inc., 662 F. Supp. 1132 (1987) (court upheld jury finding of discrimination based on national origin under federal statute and separate claim for breach of implied covenant of good faith in abrupt termination of credit agreement); Rizzitiello v. McDonald's Corp., 868 A.2d 825 (Del. 2005) (white employee who claimed breach of implied good faith covenant through racial discrimination by black supervisor would need to show disparate treatment on basis of her race; trial court found no evidence of racial animosity).

Professor Steven Burton has taken the position that, while other contract law doctrine may prevent race discrimination in performance of contracts, the implied duty of good faith cannot be used to rule out racially discriminatory conduct. Burton bases this conclusion on the theory that implied terms should rest on the agreement of the parties and, realistically, parties in an "unjust society" might not rule out racial discrimination. Steven J. Burton, Racial Discrimination in Contract Performance: *Patterson* and a State Law Alternative, 25 Harv. C.R.-C.L. L. Rev. 431, 464 n.116 (1990). In response, Professor Neil Williams asserted that society has reached a consensus, reflected in a number of civil rights laws, that racial discrimination is wrong. In Williams' view, construing the implied duty of good faith to prohibit racial discrimination would give "effect to the reasonable expectations of the parties that they will not be treated in a manner offensive to prevailing community norms." Neil G. Williams, Offer, Acceptance, and Improper Considerations: A Common Law Model for the Prohibition of Racial Discrimination in the Contracting Process, 62 Geo. Wash. L. Rev. 183, 214 (1994). In a similar vein, Professor Emily Houh has argued that the concept of good faith could be productively applied in the employment context to reach certain types of invidious discriminatory treatment based on factors such as race or gender but not cognizable under existing statutory law. Emily M.S. Houh, Critical Race Realism: Re-Claiming the Antidiscrimination Principle through the Doctrine of Good Faith in Contract Law, 66 U. Pitt. L. Rev. 455 (2005). Would it be consistent with the express terms and implicit understanding of the parties in *Locke* to imply a term that Warner would not reject Locke's movie proposals based on her gender?

Geysen v. Securitas Security Services, USA, Inc.

Supreme Court of Connecticut 322 Conn. 385, 142 A.3d 227 (2016)

ROGERS, C.J. This consolidated appeal presents the question of whether an at-will employment agreement, providing that an employee's commissions will not be paid unless the employer has invoiced commissionable amounts to the client prior to the employee's termination, is contrary to public policy and a violation of General Statutes (Supp. 2016) §31-72.[2] The defendant, Securitas Security Services, USA, Inc., appeals from the stipulated judgment of the trial court in favor of the plaintiff, Kevin Geysen, on his wage statute claim and the trial court's underlying ruling holding that this commission provision was contrary to public policy. . . . We agree with the defendant that the trial court improperly determined that the commission provision violated public policy and constituted a violation of §31-72. With regard to the plaintiff's cross appeal, we hold that count two of the plaintiff's complaint alleging breach of the implied covenant of good faith and fair dealing should not have been stricken but that count three alleging wrongful discharge was properly stricken. Accordingly, we reverse in part the judgment of the trial court.

The following procedural history and facts are relevant to this appeal. The defendant is a security services company that provides various protection services to industrial and commercial clients. These services are marketed through employees hired as business development managers (managers) who solicit new business from prospective and existing customers. In August, 2005, the defendant offered the plaintiff an at-will position as a manager. The defendant's offer letter, which the plaintiff signed in September, 2005, provided that the plaintiff's compensation was a weekly base salary and commissions on contracts he procured. The offer letter referenced and mirrored the defendant's 2003 sales incentive plan, which was in effect at the time the plaintiff commenced his employment.

The defendant subsequently amended its sales incentive plan effective December 23, 2006, and revised the commission provision at issue. Section II, part C of the 2006 sales incentive plan regarding sales eligibility requirements provides that "*[c]ommission is only paid once work has been performed and invoiced to the client.* Upon termination of services to the client all commissions cease, except that commission will be paid up through and including the final invoice. *Upon the [manager's] termination of employment, all commissions cease, except that any commissionable amounts that have been invoiced [to the client] prior to the [manager's] [t]ermination [d]ate, as defined in* [s]ection *IV.D, will still be paid commission as part of final pay to the [manager].*" (Emphasis added.)

2. General Statutes (Supp. 2016) §31-72 provides in relevant part: "When any employer fails to pay an employee wages in accordance with the provisions of sections 31-71a to 31-71i, inclusive, or fails to compensate an employee in accordance with section 31-76k or where an employee or a labor organization representing an employee institutes an action to enforce an arbitration award which requires an employer to make an employee whole or to make payments to an employee welfare fund, such employee or labor organization shall recover, in a civil action, (1) twice the full amount of such wages, with costs and such reasonable attorney's fees as may be allowed by the court, or (2) if the employer establishes that the employer had a good faith belief that the underpayment of wages was in compliance with law, the full amount of such wages or compensation, with costs and such reasonable attorney's fees as may be allowed by the court. Any agreement between an employee and his or her employer for payment of wages other than as specified in said sections shall be no defense to such action. . . ."

The definition of "wages" under §31-72 includes commissions. . . .

From 2005 to 2008, the plaintiff worked as a manager, on behalf of the defendant, marketing new and supplemental security services to new and existing customers. Based on the applicable sales incentive plan, once the contract was executed and the sales eligibility requirements were satisfied, including invoicing to the client, the plaintiff was entitled to commission payments without having to perform any other work.

On May 22, 2008, Thomas R. Fagan, the defendant's regional vice president for human resources, hand delivered a memorandum to the plaintiff terminating his employment. The memorandum explained that the defendant had conducted an investigation into improper business activities that had resulted in significant risk exposure to the defendant and, as a result of the investigation findings, the defendant was terminating the plaintiff's employment effective May 22, 2008.

On August 18, 2009, the plaintiff filed a complaint alleging that the defendant violated §31-72, breached his employment contract by violating the implied covenant of good faith and fair dealing, and wrongfully discharged him in violation of public policy. The plaintiff alleged that the defendant's reasons for his termination "were false and a pretext for nonpayment of owed commissions." The defendant moved to strike count two, alleging breach of the implied covenant of good faith and fair dealing, and count three, alleging wrongful discharge in violation of public policy. Relying on *Burnham v. Karl & Gelb, P.C.*, 252 Conn. 153, 745 A.2d 178 (2000), the trial court granted the defendant's motion to strike both counts because it believed the plaintiff had an adequate statutory remedy under §31-72. See id., 161-62 (holding that even if plaintiff's termination violated public policy embodied in statute, plaintiff's wrongful discharge claim would be precluded due to existence of statutory remedy under that statute). The trial court then rendered a partial judgment for the defendant on the two stricken counts.

Before trial, the parties agreed that "the plaintiff's claim hinges on whether or not the language in the defendant's sales incentive plan, which provides that the right to commissions ceases upon the plaintiff's termination of employment, is enforceable." Therefore, the trial court agreed to decide the enforceability question and, in order to facilitate the trial court's determination, the parties entered into a stipulation of facts dated March 1, 2012.[6]

The trial court determined that, because the plaintiff's right to commissions was not contingent upon his providing any further services to the defendant's customers, he had fully earned his commissions when his employment was terminated. Thus, the trial court found that since the provision in the sales incentive plan deprived him of those earned commissions, resulted in forfeiture of wages, and applied even to an employee who is terminated for no cause, the provision was unenforceable because it "violate[d] two public policies: the first,

6. In the parties' stipulation, the plaintiff conceded that he understood the provision in the 2006 sales incentive plan, which provides that "[u]pon the [manager's] termination of employment, all commissions cease," to mean that he was not entitled to commissions on invoices executed after his termination date.

which strongly favors the payment of wages, and the second, which disfavors forfeitures."

On October 16, 2014, the parties stipulated to a judgment in favor of the plaintiff for unpaid commissions pursuant to §31-72, but preserved their respective rights to appeal. The defendant appealed from the stipulated judgment and the plaintiff cross appealed. We now turn to the merits of those appeals.

I

We first address the defendant's claim that the commission provision was not void on public policy grounds and, therefore, the failure to pay the plaintiff's commissions was not a violation of §31-72. We begin by setting out the applicable standard of review and relevant legal principles. "Although it is well established that parties are free to contract for whatever terms on which they may agree . . . it is equally well established that contracts that violate public policy are unenforceable. . . . [T]he question [of] whether a contract is against public policy is [a] question of law dependent on the circumstances of the particular case, over which an appellate court has unlimited review." (Citations omitted; internal quotation marks omitted.) . . .

. . . If a contract violates public policy, this would be a ground to not enforce the contract. . . . A contract . . . however, does not violate public policy just because the contract was made unwisely. . . . [C]ourts do not unmake bargains unwisely made. . . .

If the commission provision at issue acts to negate the wage statutes, however, the provision violates public policy. See *Parente v. Pirozzoli*, 87 Conn. App. 235, 246, 866 A.2d 629 (2005) "Generally, agreements contrary to public policy, that is those that negate laws enacted for the common good, are illegal and therefore unenforceable. . . . Agreements that are legal on their face, yet which are designed to evade statutory requirements, are routinely held unenforceable." [Citation omitted; internal quotation marks omitted.]). We must initially determine, therefore, whether the commission provision violates the wage statutes.

We have held that §31-72 "does not embody substantive standards to determine the amount of wages that are payable but provides penalties in order to deter employers from deferring wage payments once they have accrued. Section 31-72 is, therefore, a remedial statute rather than one creating independent substantive rights. . . ." (Citation omitted; emphasis in original; internal quotation marks omitted.) *Mytych v. May Dept. Stores Co.*, 260 Conn. 152, 162, 793 A.2d 1068 (2002). . . .

In *Mytych* [v. *May Dept. Stores Co.*, supra, 260 Conn. 156], [the court] considered the question of whether the defendant employer's practice of calculating the plaintiff employees' sales commissions by deducting from their respective gross sales figures a pro rata share of unidentified returns . . . violated a statutory provision disallowing unauthorized deductions from wages.[7] . . .

7. See General Statutes §31-71e (permitting partial withholding of wages under certain circumstances).

The court held that it did not, as the Connecticut wage statutes left the substantive standards for the determination of wages to the agreement between the employer and the employee. Id. Specifically, the court held that "the formula by which an employee's wage is calculated is determined by the agreement between the employer and the employee"; *Mytych v. May Dept. Stores Co.*, supra, 160; because the definition of wages "expressly [left] the determination of the wage to the employer-employee agreement, assuming some specific conditions, such as a minimum hourly wage, are met." Id., 163.

The court in *Mytych* then explicitly rejected the plaintiffs' reasoning that their wages accrued at the time they rendered their services by making sales because, while the California case cited by the plaintiffs relied "on a long history of California case law and regulatory opinions establishing that an employee's right to a commission accrues or vests at the time of the actual sale . . . [i]n Connecticut, there [was] no such settled doctrine regarding the time at which an employee's rights to his wages vests and, in fact, we [had] concluded [t]herein that *our wage payment statutes expressly leave the timing of accrual to the determination of the wage agreement between the employer and [the] employee*." (Emphasis added.) Id., 164-65. . . .

With these applicable legal principles in mind, we now address whether the commission provision in the present case violates public policy and the wage statutes. The court in *Mytych* clearly addressed the timing of wage accrual and left the determination of this matter to the employment agreement. See *Mytych v. May Dept. Stores Co.*, supra, 260 Conn. 164-65. Additionally, in *Mytych*, this court specifically rejected the doctrine that an employee's right to wages necessarily accrued at the time of sale. In the present case, on the basis of the clear language of the commission provision, invoicing prior to the plaintiff's termination is a condition precedent to earning the commission. . . . Thus, we agree with the defendant that the commissions were not "due" within the meaning of General Statutes 31-71b(a) because there was a condition precedent to their accrual that had not been satisfied. Nevertheless, the plaintiff contends that the commission provision should not be enforceable because he did not have to provide any further services to the defendant's customers and, therefore, he had fully earned his commissions under the wage statutes.[10]

In *Mytych v. May Dept. Stores Co.*, supra, 260 Conn. 163-64 and n.7, however, the employees did not have to provide any additional services and this court still held that their wages had not accrued at the time of sale. . . see also *Mullowney v. Data General Corp.*, 143 F.3d 1081, 1083 (7th Cir. 1998) (applying Massachusetts law and finding that, although there was certainly risk that employee could lose commissions on some sales for which he was primarily responsible based on at-will agreement where employee would be entitled to commissions only on those sales invoiced or shipped before his termination became effective, "[t]his was

10. Although the plaintiff claims that the commission provision causes an unacceptable forfeiture of wages earned, we agree with the defendant that the trial court's reliance on our forfeiture jurisprudence in *Aetna Casualty & Surety Co. v. Murphy*, 206 Conn. 409, 414-15, 538 A.2d 219 (1988), overruled on other grounds by *Arrowood Indemnity Co. v. King*, 304 Conn. 179, 201, 39 A.3d 712 (2012), is inapplicable to the current situation because we have determined that the plaintiff had not earned the commissions under the employment agreement.

the bargain he made . . . he cannot now . . . be heard to complain because [the employer] adhered to this arrangement") . . . .

On the basis of our review of Connecticut law and the public policy of freedom of contract reflected in our common law, we do not believe that this commission provision on its face "negate[s] laws enacted for the common good" or is "designed to evade statutory requirements. . . ." (Internal quotation marks omitted.) *Parente v. Pirozzoli*, supra, 87 Conn. App. 246. We conclude, therefore, that the contract provision providing that commissions will be paid only if the work had been invoiced prior to termination of the employee does not violate public policy and is enforceable. Because the plaintiff was not due his commissions under the express and enforceable terms of his agreement with the defendant, and the agreement does not violate public policy, we hold that there was no violation of the wage statutes.

II

We now turn to the plaintiff's cross appeal from the trial court's grant of the defendant's motion to strike two counts of the complaint. ". . . Because a motion to strike challenges the legal sufficiency of a pleading and, consequently, requires no factual findings by the trial court, our review of the court's ruling . . . is plenary. . . . We take the facts to be those alleged in the complaint that has been stricken and we construe the complaint in the manner most favorable to sustaining its legal sufficiency. . . ."

A

We analyze first the plaintiff's cross appeal seeking reinstatement of the breach of the implied covenant of good faith and fair dealing count. "[I]t is axiomatic that the . . . duty of good faith and fair dealing is a covenant implied into a contract or a contractual relationship. . . . In other words, every contract carries an implied duty requiring that neither party do anything that will injure the right of the other to receive the benefits of the agreement. . . . The covenant of good faith and fair dealing presupposes that the terms and purpose of the contract are agreed upon by the parties and that what is in dispute is a party's discretionary application or interpretation of a contract term."[11] (Citations omitted; internal quotation marks omitted.) *De La Concha of Hartford, Inc. v. Aetna Life Ins. Co.*, 269 Conn. 424, 432-33, 849 A.2d 382 (2004); *Landry v. Spitz*, 102 Conn. App. 34, 47, 925 A.2d 334 (2007) . . .

"To constitute a breach of [the implied covenant of good faith and fair dealing], the acts by which a defendant allegedly impedes the plaintiff's right to receive benefits that he or she reasonably expected to receive under the contract must have been taken in bad faith. . . . Bad faith in general implies . . . actual

11. "Essentially [the implied covenant of good faith and fair dealing] is a rule of construction designed to fulfill the reasonable expectations of the contracting parties as they presumably intended. The principle, therefore, cannot be applied to achieve a result contrary to the clearly expressed terms of a contract, unless, possibly, those terms are contrary to public policy." *Magnan v. Anaconda Industries, Inc.*, 193 Conn. 558, 567, 479 A.2d 781 (1984).

or constructive fraud, or a design to mislead or deceive another, or a neglect or refusal to fulfill some duty or some contractual obligation, not prompted by an honest mistake as to one's rights or duties, but by some interested or sinister motive. . . . Bad faith means more than mere negligence; it involves a dishonest purpose." (Citation omitted; internal quotation marks omitted.) *De La Concha of Hartford, Inc. v. Aetna Life Ins. Co.*, supra, 269 Conn. 433. "[B]ad faith may be overt or may consist of inaction, and it may include evasion of the spirit of the bargain. . . ." *Elm Street Builders, Inc. v. Enterprise Park Condominium Assn., Inc.*, 63 Conn. App. 657, 667, 778 A.2d 237 (2001), quoting 2 Restatement (Second), Contracts §205, comment (d) (1981) . . . .

In *Magnan v. Anaconda Industries, Inc.*, 193 Conn. 558, 479 A.2d 781 (1984), this court addressed the implied covenant of good faith and fair dealing in employment contracts. The plaintiff in that case contended that the good faith principle was applicable and subjected the employer to liability whenever an employee is discharged without just cause. Id., 567. For guidance, the court looked to Massachusetts cases applying the implied covenant of good faith and fair dealing in the employment context. Id., 569-71. While the court recognized the applicability of the covenant of good faith to employment contracts, it concluded that a breach of such an implied covenant cannot be predicated simply upon the absence of good cause for discharge. Id., 571-72. The court specifically declined the plaintiff's invitation "to transform the requirement of good faith into an implied condition that an employee may be dismissed only for good cause." Id., 571; see also . . . *Morris v. Hartford Courant Co.*, 200 Conn. 676, 679 n.2, 513 A.2d 66 (1986). In *Magnan*, the court left for another day the determination of the applicability of the covenant of good faith and fair dealing to a discharge that was motivated by an intent to deprive an employee of clearly identifiable compensation related to past services. See *Magnan v. Anaconda Industries, Inc.*, supra, 573. As such, the court acknowledged, but did not fully consider, the Massachusetts case of *Fortune v. National Cash Register Co.*, 373 Mass. 96, 364 N.E.2d 1251 (1977). See *Magnan v. Anaconda Industries, Inc.*, supra, 570 n.20, 571.

Fortune is particularly illustrative in our present case. In *Fortune*, under the express terms of an at-will employment contract, the plaintiff employee had received all the bonus commissions to which he was entitled when his employment with the defendant was terminated. *Fortune v. National Cash Register Co.*, supra, 373 Mass. 101. The court acknowledged that "an employer is entitled to be motivated by and to serve its own legitimate business interests; that an employer must have wide latitude in deciding whom it will employ in the face of the uncertainties of the business world; and that an employer needs flexibility in the face of changing circumstances." Id., 101-102. Nevertheless, the Massachusetts Supreme Judicial Court held that the employer's written contract contained an implied covenant of good faith and fair dealing and that, in a situation where commissions are to be paid for work performed by the employee, a bad faith termination constituted a breach of that contract.[12] Id.

---

12. The court in *Fortune v. National Cash Register Co.*, supra, 373 Mass. 102, noted that while some other courts had fashioned a remedy in tort to avoid the rigidity of the "at will" rule, it believed

The court in *Fortune* further stated that "[w]here the principal seeks to deprive the agent of all compensation by terminating the contractual relationship when the agent is on the brink of successfully completing the sale, the principal has acted in bad faith and the ensuing transaction between the principal and the buyer is to be regarded as having been accomplished by the agent. . . . The same result obtains where the principal attempts to deprive the agent of any portion of a commission due the agent. Courts have often applied this rule to prevent overreaching by employers and the forfeiture by employees of benefits almost earned by the rendering of substantial services." (Citation omitted.) Id., 104-105.

Thus, although an employer may terminate the employee at will; see *Magnan v. Anaconda Industries, Inc.*, supra, 193 Conn. 572; the employer may not act in bad faith to prevent paying the employee commissions he reasonably expected to receive for services rendered under the contract. See id., 571, 572 . . . see also *Cochran v. Quest Software, Inc.*, 328 F.3d 1, 8 (1st Cir. 2003) ("[t]he rationale behind [the Massachusetts] exception is that every contract contains a covenant of good faith and fair dealing, and an employer breaches that covenant when it dismisses an at-will employee in order to deprive him of compensation fairly earned and legitimately expected for services already rendered") citing *Mullowney v. Data General Corp.*, supra, 143 F.3d 1083-84; *Wakefield v. Northern Telecom, Inc.*, 769 F.2d 109, 112 (2d Cir. ("[w]here . . . a covenant of good faith is necessary to enable one party to receive the benefits promised for performance, it is implied by the law as necessary to effectuate the intent of the parties").

To be clear, an employer does not act in bad faith solely by refusing to pay commissions on sales invoiced after an employee's termination if that obligation is an express contract term. See *Magnan v. Anaconda Industries, Inc.*, supra, 193 Conn. 567, 572 . . . . An employer's action or inaction that attempts to avoid the spirit of the bargain or which evinces a dishonest purpose, however, would violate the implied covenant of good faith and fair dealing as it relates to the contractual provision for payment of commissions. . . .

In the present case, the trial court considered the plaintiff's claim that the covenant was breached to be essentially the same as a wrongful discharge claim. A breach of the implied covenant of good faith and fair dealing contract claim, however, is different than a wrongful termination claim because the former focuses on the fulfillment of the parties' reasonable expectations rather than on a violation of public policy.[13] As articulated in *Wakefield v. Northern Telecom, Inc.*,

---

that there was a remedy based on the contract. . . . The Massachusetts Supreme Judicial Court subsequently stated that the employer's predatory motivation in *Fortune* could be classified as a reason contrary to public policy. See *Cort v. Bristol-Myers Co.*, 385 Mass. 300, 303, 431 N.E.2d 908 (1982); *Magnan v. Anaconda Industries, Inc.*, supra, 193 Conn. 570 n.20 (identifying that in Massachusetts there was wrongful termination cause of action based on contractual implied covenant of good faith and fair dealing where employer's predatory motivation was in violation of public policy). . . .

13. Under such a claim, termination is incidental, or a means, to accomplish the breach of the implied covenant of good faith and fair dealing. Cf., e.g., *Empower Health, LLC v. Providence Health Solutions, LLC*, supra, 2011 U.S. Dist. LEXIS 60142, 2011 WL 2194071, (plaintiff limited liability company alleged that defendant deliberately prevented plaintiff from closing on sales it initiated by assuming control over relationships with plaintiff's sales leads, removing plaintiff's access to sales system, and terminating plaintiff's e-mail account).

supra, 769 F.2d 112, while an at-will employee may not be able to "recover for his termination per se . . . the contract for payment of commissions creates rights distinct from the employment relation, and . . . obligations derived from the covenant of good faith implicit in the commission contract may survive the termination of the employment relationship. Implied contractual obligations may coexist with express provisions which seemingly negate them where common expectations or the relationship of the parties as structured by the contract so dictate. . . . A covenant of good faith should not be implied as a modification of an employer's right to terminate an at-will employee because even a whimsical termination does not deprive the employee of benefits expected in return for the employee's performance. This is so because performance and the distribution of benefits occur simultaneously, and neither party is left high and dry by the termination.

"Where, however, a covenant of good faith is necessary to enable one party to receive the benefits promised for performance, it is implied by the law as necessary to effectuate the intent of the parties. . . . *[A contract] cannot be read to enable the defendant to terminate an employee for the purpose of avoiding the payment of commissions which are otherwise owed.* Such an interpretation would make the performance by one party the cause of the other party's [nonperformance]." (Emphasis added; citations omitted.) Accord *Arbeeny v. Kennedy Executive Search, Inc.*, 71 App. Div. 3d 177, 184, 893 N.Y.S.2d 39 (2010) ("[a]lthough an at-will employee such as [the] plaintiff would not be able to sue for wrongful termination of the contract [under New York law], he should nonetheless be able to state a claim that the employer's termination action was specifically designed to cut off commissions that were coming due to the employee").[14]

We find the reasoning in *Fortune, Wakefield* and *Arbeeny* persuasive, and therefore, recognize the availability of a breach of the implied covenant of good faith and fair dealing contract claim when the termination of an employee was done with the intent to avoid the payment of commissions.

Turning to the allegations of the plaintiff's complaint in the present case, the plaintiff claims in relevant part that the defendant had "failed to pay commissions due to [the] [p]laintiff on certain sales made" and as such, the "[d]efendant's aforementioned conduct violated the implied covenant of good faith and fair dealing by failing to comply with [the] [p]laintiff's reasonable expectation that the [d]efendant would pay commissions earned by the [p]laintiff." These allegations focus on damages suffered due to the violation of the plaintiff's reasonable expectation regarding the payment of commissions.[15] If an employer

14. In *Wakefield v. Northern Telecom, Inc.*, supra, 769 F.2d 111-13, in analyzing New Jersey and New York law, the Second Circuit Court of Appeals held that the jury could have awarded damages if it found that the employer discharged the employee in order to avoid paying him commissions earned on sales that were completed but for formalities. In *Arbeeny v. Kennedy Executive Search, Inc.*, supra, 71 App. Div. 3d 183-84, the court held that an at-will employee could state a claim for breach of contract to recover unpaid earned commissions.

15. The defendant claims that "the plaintiff did not allege that [he was fired] in order to deprive him of commissions that he might have earned at some unknown time in the future" due to the plaintiff's numerous assertions that the alleged commissions were "earned" and "due to him." Reading the complaint broadly, as we must, we find this argument unpersuasive. We believe that,

can be shown to have interfered in bad faith with an employee's ability to secure his commissions, this would violate the reasonable expectation that his employer would not inhibit his ability to earn commissions he worked for under the contract. . . . Accordingly, on the basis of the allegations in the complaint, the plaintiff has stated a legally sufficient claim for breach of the implied covenant of good faith and fair dealing.

B

As to the plaintiff's wrongful discharge against public policy count, we agree with the trial court that it should have been stricken. "In *Sheets v. Teddy's Frosted Foods, Inc.*, [179 Conn. 471, 475, 427 A.2d 385 (1980)] . . . we recognized . . . a common law cause of action in tort for discharges if the former employee can prove a demonstrably *improper* reason for dismissal, a reason whose impropriety is derived from some important violation of public policy. . . . This public policy exception to the employment [at-will] rule carved out in *Sheets* attempts to balance the competing interests of [the] employer and [the] employee. Under the exception, the employee has the burden of pleading and proving that his dismissal occurred for a reason violating public policy. The employer is allowed, in ordinary circumstances, to make personnel decisions without fear of incurring civil liability. Employee job security, however, is protected against employer actions that contravene public policy." (Citations omitted; emphasis omitted; internal quotation marks omitted.) *Morris v. Hartford Courant Co.*, supra, 200 Conn. 678-79.

"The question of whether a challenged discharge violates public policy . . . is a question of law to be decided by the court . . . ." *Faulkner v. United Technologies Corp.*, 240 Conn. 576, 588, 693 A.2d 293 (1997). [*408] "In *Morris v. Hartford Courant Co.*, supra, [200 Conn. 680], we recognized the inherent vagueness of the concept of public policy and the difficulty encountered when attempting to define precisely the contour of the public policy exception. In evaluating claims, [w]e look to see whether the plaintiff has . . . alleged that his discharge violated any explicit statutory or constitutional provision . . . or whether he alleged that his dismissal contravened any judicially conceived notion of public policy. . . . *Faulkner v. United Technologies Corp.*, [supra, 580-81]." (Internal quotation marks omitted.) . . .

"[W]e repeatedly have underscored our adherence to the principle that the public policy exception to the general rule allowing unfettered termination of an at-will employment relationship is a narrow one . . . . Consequently, we have rejected claims of wrongful discharge that have not been predicated upon an employer's violation of an important and clearly articulated public policy." (Citations omitted; internal quotation marks omitted.) Id., 701.

---

although the plaintiff had not "earned" the commissions under the wage statutes, he may yet be able to demonstrate that he was nevertheless "owed" them because he was prevented from earning them due to the employer's breach of the implied covenant of good faith and fair dealing. In the present case, the plaintiff did allege that the defendant's "reasons for [his] termination were false and a pretext for nonpayment of *owed* commissions." (Emphasis added.)

In his reply brief, the plaintiff points us to the wage statutes and suggests that they espouse the important public policy in favor of the payment of wages, which the defendant contravened with his termination. Consistent with our conclusion in part I of this opinion, however, the wage statutes promote a public policy favoring the payment of *earned* wages. They should not be read to provide a broader public policy mandate than that which is represented. . . . In other words, while the wage statutes provide a remedy for unpaid earned wages, they do not provide one for unearned wages that were not due. *Mytych v. May Dept. Stores Co.*, supra, 260 Conn. 162.

As we have determined in this case that the commission provision provided is enforceable and does not violate the public policy embodied in §31-72, the exercise of the defendant's at-will right to terminate the plaintiff does not violate statutorily based public policy.[16]

We acknowledge that the plaintiff goes beyond statutorily based public policy in his complaint. The plaintiff alleges that his employment was terminated "as a pretext to deprive him of the just fruits of his labor" and that this violates "the public policy of justly compensating employees for their work." We believe, however, that the parameters of the public policy of this state with regard to the payment of wages is reflected in the wage statutes and that an employee cannot use the nonpayment of wages that have not accrued as the basis for a wrongful discharge claim. . . .We leave it to the legislature to decide if it wishes to expand this public policy to include unearned wages in this context. Consequently, we agree with the judgment of the trial court striking this count.

The judgment is reversed only with respect to the trial court's determination that the agreement violated public policy and §31-72, and with respect to that court's granting of the motion to strike the count of the complaint alleging breach of the implied covenant of good faith and fair dealing, and the case is remanded with direction to deny the motion to strike that count of the complaint and for further proceedings according to law.

In this opinion the other justices concurred.

NOTES AND QUESTIONS

1. *Presumption of employment at-will and its limitations.* The "at-will" doctrine is a concept that we have encountered before. You should recall from the *Leibel* case earlier in this chapter that a franchise contract of indefinite duration is presumed to be at-will, meaning that either party is free to terminate the contract at any time and without a requirement of good or just cause. Application of the at-will doctrine to employment contracts in the United States has been traced back to the nineteenth century and is the prevailing rule throughout

16. Based on our discussion in part II A of this opinion, if an employer exercises the right to terminate in order to interfere in bad faith with an employee's ability to secure commissions, however, the employee's reasonable expectations would be violated and he or she can recover in contract.

the country. See Restatement of Employment Law §2.01, Comment *b* (2015) (noting that 49 states and District of Columbia recognize at-will employment as presumptive rule; sole exception is Montana, which has a "good cause" rule by statute).

By definition, the at-will doctrine does not apply to a contract with a specified duration, e.g., a one-year or five-year contract. A contract that includes a specified duration is construed to mean that the employee may be terminated only for just or good cause. See, e.g., Mart v. Forest River, Inc., 854 F. Supp. 2d 577 (N.D. Ind. 2012) (discussing two types of employment contracts under Indiana law—definite term in which the employee may only be fired for cause and at-will in which the employee may be fired regardless of reason). The presumption of at-will employment, however, cannot be easily overcome and therefore an agreement for a term must be specific. See Bernard v. IMI Systems, Inc., 618 A.2d 338 (N.J. 1993) (overruling judicial precedent that salary stated in annual terms would implicitly create a year-long contract; more required to overcome at-will presumption). But see Rooney v. Tyson, 697 N.E.2d 571 (N.Y. 1998) (agreement to employ fight trainer "for as long as [defendant] fought professionally" established legally cognizable duration and was not contract subject to termination at-will).

Moreover, if the contract is for "permanent employment" or similar language, courts steeped in the traditional approach to at-will employment contracts have routinely held that permanent employment does not mean employment "for life," merely that the employee's position will be of indefinite duration. See Reddington v. Staten Island Univ. Hosp., 511 F.3d 126 (2d Cir. 2007) (finding that statements made to hospital employee that new position would "always" be available did not overcome presumption that employment was at-will). Even if interpreted literally, promises of "permanent" employment have customarily been held to be unenforceable unless supported by some additional consideration beyond the employee's performance of her duties on the job. See, e.g., Worley v. Wyoming Bottling Co., 1 P.3d 615 (Wyo. 2000). On the other hand, if the employee truly provides additional consideration for the employment, such additional consideration may be sufficient to require the employer to have good cause for termination. See NRG Solutions v. Neurogistics Corp., 2011 WL 1118838 (N.D. Ill.) (plaintiff adequately pled additional consideration to overcome at-will presumption in that she agreed to transfer assets of business she owned, including client database, to new employer and became full-time employee). For such courts, the role of extra consideration is to indicate the parties' intent to have a more lasting relationship than a presumed at-will contract. See, e.g., Ciardi v. Laurel Media Inc., 2012 WL 70656 (W.D. Pa.).

2. *The implied duty of good faith and at-will employment.* The *Geysen* court recognizes, as have the other cases in this section, that the implied covenant of good faith and fair dealing applies to every contract and prevents a contracting party from engaging in conduct that defeats the reasonable expectations of the other party or undermines the spirit of the bargain. The court relies on a line of cases in which employers have been held liable to employees for breach of the implied duty of good faith by intentionally discharging the employee

for the purpose of depriving the employee of compensation that the employee had already earned or was on the verge of doing so. The leading case is Fortune v. National Cash Register Co., 364 N.E.2d 1251 (Mass. 1977) (discharge motivated by desire to deny plaintiff the benefit of a sales commission that had been earned in full would be breach of duty of good faith). See also Wilson v. Career Educ. Corp., 729 F.3d 665 (7th Cir. 2013) (employer may breach covenant of good faith by using its discretion to terminate bonus plan with intent to deprive employee commission already earned).

The duty of good faith might also apply to the manner in which an at-will employee is terminated. See E. I. DuPont de Nemours & Co. v. Pressman, 679 A.2d 436 (Del. 1996) (breach of the implied covenant of good faith would be established by proving that employer created false grounds and fictitious basis for termination of at-will employee but not by the termination itself).

However, as the *Geysen* court holds the implied covenant of good faith will not transform an at-will employment relationship into one that requires good cause for discharge. See also Bollinger v. Fall River Rural Elec. Co-op., Inc., 272 P.3d 1263 (Idaho 2012). Furthermore, some jurisdictions take the position that the implied duty of good faith simply does not apply in at-will employment relationships. See Campeggi v. Arche Inc., 2016 U.S. Dist. LEXIS 124814 at *17 (S.D.N.Y.) ("well-settled New York law holds that no implied covenant of good faith and fair dealing attaches to at-will employment contracts").

The Geysen court clearly holds that the implied duty of good faith would not prevent the employer from discharging the at-will employee, but would place some limit on the timing and purpose of termination. Are you persuaded, however, that the court made a meaningful distinction between wages "earned," as permissibly defined by the contract under the statute, and wages "owed" which would be protected from a bad faith termination, as suggested by footnote 15 in the opinion?

3. ***Public policy exception to at-will doctrine.*** The *Geysen* court along with a clear majority of jurisdictions recognize a public policy exception to the at-will employment doctrine and often treat such claims as sounding in tort. See Wholey v. Sears, Roebuck & Co., 803 A.2d 482, 488-489 (Md. 2002) (citing 30 jurisdictions recognizing public policy exception in nonexhaustive listing). The decision usually regarded as the leading case applying the public policy limitation is Petermann v. International Brotherhood of Teamsters, 344 P.2d 25 (Cal. Ct. App. 1959), which held that an at-will employee would be entitled to relief for wrongful discharge if he were fired because he refused to commit perjury at the request of his employer. See also Thompson v. St. Regis Paper Co., 685 P.2d 1081 (Wash. 1984) (employee's discharge would be tortious if based on steps taken to comply with anti-bribery measures in Foreign Corrupt Practices Act).

As indicated by *Geysen*, however, courts generally restrict this theory to circumstances involving a "clear mandate" of public policy founded on constitutional, legislative, administrative, or established judicial authority. Courts will, of course, differ on when a "clear mandate" exists. Compare Moore v. Warr Acres Nursing Ctr., LLC, 376 P.3d 894 (Oklahoma 2016) (given state and federal health codes prohibiting nurses from working while infected with influenza, it would violate public policy to terminate a licensed practical nurse for missing work in a nursing center based on vomiting on the job and a doctor's note stating that the employee should not work) with Dukowitz v. Hannon Sec. Servs., 841 N.W.2d 147 (Minn. 2014) (because Minnesota recognizes a common-law cause of action for wrongful discharge only as to discharges resulting from an employee's good-faith refusal to violate the law, the public-policy exception to the employment-at-will rule did not apply to a termination alleged to have been in retaliation for an employee's application for unemployment benefits when a temporary assignment ended). Further, some jurisdictions have rejected the public policy limitation altogether. See, e.g., De Petris v. Union Settlement Ass'n, Inc., 657 N.E.2d 269 (N.Y. 1995) (confirming that New York does not recognize a tort of wrongful discharge in at-will employment).

4. *Other exceptions to the employment-at-will doctrine: employee handbooks and promissory estoppel.* Yet another exception to the at-will presumption is found in cases recognizing a cause of action for breach of contract when the defendant employer had committed itself, by public statements in personnel manuals or otherwise, to refrain from terminating employees except for good cause. A leading decision in this area is Toussaint v. Blue Cross & Blue Shield, 292 N.W.2d 880 (Mich. 1980), in which the employee received assurance of job security before accepting employment and the company manual stated there would be dismissal only for cause. The court deemed the company's statement to create an "implied-in-fact" term that the employee would be discharged only for cause. Id. at 894. Not all courts agree, however, that statements of job security made in policy manuals are contractually binding. See, e.g., Fleming v. AT&T Info. Services, Inc., 878 F.2d 1472, 1474 (D.C. Cir. 1989) (company's written policies of treating employees fairly and of providing post-termination counseling are "irrelevant" in determining whether the employee is hired at-will). It should be noted that most large employers who are well-counseled by their employment lawyers will typically have strong disclaimer language in their employment manuals and handbooks, and courts have generally held that such disclaimers constitute a defense against liability based on a claim arising from the employee handbook. See Collins v. City of Newton, 240 So. 3d 1211, 1217-1220 (Miss. 2018). But see Silchia v. MCI Telcoms. Corp., 942 F. Supp. 1369, 1375 (D. Colo. 1996) ("Even if there is a valid employment-at-will disclaimer in an employment handbook, an employer may nevertheless be found to have manifested an intent to be bound by its terms if the handbook contains mandatory termination procedures or requires 'just cause' for termination.").

Some courts have also held that detrimental reliance by a discharged employee may serve as a basis for relief. See Sheppard v. Morgan-Keegan, 266 Cal. Rptr. 784 (Ct. App. 1990) (employee who resigned a position and moved across country would not expect to be terminated before he had a chance to perform in job; summary judgment for employer reversed, citing promissory estoppel as well as the implied covenant of good faith); Nelson v. Town of Johnsbury Selectboard, 115 A.3d 423 (Vt. 2015) (promissory estoppel may modify at-will relationship, but promise must be definite and specific in nature and not just vague assurance); Restatement of Employment Law §2.02(b). On the other hand, a number of jurisdictions have held that a promissory estoppel claim by an employee is fundamentally inconsistent with at-will status. See, e.g., Krueger v. Home Depot USA, Inc., 2015 WL 4763653 (W.D. Ky.) (at-will status precludes promissory estoppel claim under Kentucky law).

5. *At-will doctrine and personnel actions other than discharge.* If a court recognizes restrictions on an employer's right to discharge an at-will employee, will such limitations also apply to demotions or other changes in employment conditions? Compare Scott v. Pacific Gas & Electric Co., 904 P.2d 834 (Cal. 1995) (extending policy manual exception to demotions), with White v. State of Washington, 929 P.2d 396 (Wash. 1997) (refusing to extend public policy exception to employer's personnel actions that are less than discharge).

6. *At-will employment and ethical duties of lawyers.* Termination of at-will employees may raise additional questions when the party terminated is an attorney. In Wieder v. Skala, 609 N.E.2d 105 (N.Y. 1992), the New York Court of Appeals ruled that an associate attorney's employment contract with a law firm should be read to implicitly incorporate certain ethical standards of the profession, such as the duty to report suspected unfitness of other attorneys. Thus, the court found a termination wrongful when the plaintiff associate was discharged for reporting another attorney's misconduct. But see Bohatch v. Butler & Binion, 977 S.W.2d 543 (Tex. 1998) (law firm could not be held liable in damages for wrongful expulsion of partner who alleged in good faith that another partner engaged in unethical conduct). *Wieder* and *Bohatch* both involved lawyers in private firms who were discharged because they reported misconduct by other attorneys. Lawyers employed by private corporations rather than law firms have also brought wrongful discharge claims. Compare General Dynamics Corp. v. Superior Court, 876 P.2d 487 (Cal. 1994) (recognizing right of in-house counsel to bring claim for wrongful discharge based on public policy and implied contract theories), with Balla v. Gambro, Inc., 584 N.E.2d 104 (Ill. 1991) (in-house counsel did not have cause of action against employer for wrongful discharge when employer fired him after he threatened to take whatever action was necessary to prevent company from selling defective kidney dialysis machines).

7. *Scholarly analysis.* What interests are at stake in cases involving the employment-at-will rule? Many legal scholars have advocated a change in the at-will doctrine to benefit employees based on the individual's interest in freedom from unjust discharge, along with the public's interest in a securely employed labor force. See, e.g., Cynthia L. Estlund, Wrongful Discharge Protections in an At-Will World, 74 Tex. L. Rev. 1655 (1996). Professor Matthew Bodie has proposed that courts recognize a new exception to the at-will rule, the "personal-autonomy" exception, meaning that an implied term of every employment contract should be that employers agree not to take any action

against an employee based on the employee's personal autonomy, so long as that autonomy does not interfere with the employer's business or reputation. Employee personal autonomy includes political affiliations, religious observance, and recreational activities. Matthew T. Bodie, The Best Way Out is Always Through: Changing The Employment At-Will Default Rule to Protect Personal Autonomy, 2017 U. Ill. L. Rev. 223.

Other writers have argued in favor of the employment at-will rule on grounds of efficiency. Limitations on an employer's right of discharge increase litigation costs and may harm employees as a class by making employers more reluctant to hire risky employees. See Richard A. Epstein, In Defense of the Contract At Will, 51 U. Chi. L. Rev. 947 (1984). See also John P. Frantz, Market Ordering Versus Statutory Control of Termination Decisions: A Case for the Inefficiency of Just Cause Dismissal Requirements, 20 Harv. J.L. & Pub. Poly. 555 (1997); Andrew P. Morriss, Bad Data, Bad Economics, and Bad Policy: Time to Fire the Wrongful Discharge Law, 74 Tex. L. Rev. 1901 (1996).

A rebuttal to the efficiency arguments can be found in Peter Linzer, The Decline of Assent: At-Will Employment as a Case Study of the Breakdown of Private Law Theory, 20 Ga. L. Rev. 323, 409-415 (1986). Professor Linzer asserts that many attempts by the courts to ground relief against wrongful discharge on one of the traditional common law bases — contract or tort — are not entirely convincing and that the traditional subject-area divisions should not be controlling. Id. at 335-369. Relying on a variety of strands of theory (including modern notions of "the firm" and the "relational contract" theories of Professor Ian Macneil), Linzer argues that relief from improper discharge in many cases is appropriate and, moreover, that the courts, and not merely the legislatures, are appropriate organs for creating such rules of relief.

> I think it can even be argued that courts are institutionally at least as capable as legislatures to apply community values to problems of private law. Courts — at least Anglo-American courts — have done this as long as there have been courts. Certainly they can easily get out of touch, and in any event we are not speaking of a Gallup Poll. But judges seeking a policy basis will be affected by the attitudes of the time, as well as by their own ethical, economic, social and political biases. Legislators hear from constituents and lobbyists, but with many private law matters they are likely to be importuned more loudly, and to hear more clearly, after the courts have acted rather than while the issue is "abstract" and unresolved.

Id. at 423. Noting that "inaction" is action that preserves the employer-dominant power regime, Linzer concludes by calling on courts to return to "common law creativity" by discerning and applying community values in this and other areas where traditional common law rules appear inadequate. Id. at 424. Linzer also urges courts to recognize that "all contributors to an enterprise deserve some security and some share of the enterprise itself." Id. at 425. For an empirical survey aimed at measuring the reactions of employees to various discharge scenarios, see Larry A. DiMatteo et al., Justice, Employment, and the Psychological Contract, 90 Or. L. Rev. 449 (2011).

PROBLEM 6-1

Ed Evers owned an accounting company in Santa Carlita, your city. Last January, Ed was approached by Fran Farmer of Acme Accountants, a large accounting firm with a number of branch offices in Santa Carlita and neighboring communities. Fran suggested that Ed come to work for Acme as a manager. "You'll be paid a salary plus commissions," Fran told Ed, "and I'm sure you'll make more money than you're making now." "That's tempting," Ed responded, "I plan to retire in five years or so, and it sure would be nice to get rid of the headache of running my own business in the meantime. But I averaged $10,000 per month in profits over the last five years. Can you match that?" Fran said, "Come with us and you should do even better than that, no question about it."

Ed then notified his clients that he was closing his business and would start work for Acme on February 1. On his first day at Acme, Ed completed a one-page employment form that stated that he would be on "probation status" for three months and then would become a "permanent employee." Just above the signature block was a clause that read, "This form is the entire employment agreement of the parties." The personnel officer told Ed the form was mandatory and was used only to initiate the company benefit programs.

Ed was assigned to manage the largest Acme branch office in downtown Santa Carlita. Business at the branch grew steadily as Ed's old clients brought their work to that location. Ed was paid a base salary of $10,000 and commissions of about $3,000 each month during the first three months. Although pleased with his income, Ed also became concerned because Acme charged a 20 percent fee to customers who took "instant payment" of their income tax refunds. Ed told Fran on April 30 that this fee was too high, as the market rate was only 10 percent for that service; clients might be put off, he argued, and go elsewhere. Fran said she would reconsider the fee.

Shortly after joining Acme, Ed also began to have lunch on a regular basis and go out on dates after hours with a coworker, Andy Lee. On May 1, Fran stopped Ed as he returned from lunch with Andy and told Ed that intra-office romantic relationships were strictly forbidden. Ed responded that he had meticulously avoided socializing with Andy during business hours and would continue to do so, but that he intended to continue to see Andy for lunch and on his own time. One week later, Ed received Acme's "Manager of the Month" award for April. On May 15, Fran gave notice to Ed that he was being reassigned to a small Acme branch in the suburbs as a tax preparer, and would receive a $6,000 monthly base salary plus commissions.

Ed comes to your office today very upset. He believes Fran reassigned him either because of his complaint about the "instant payment" fee or because of his relationship with Andy. Ed tells you that although he is a new Acme employee, he is familiar with Acme practices over the past ten years, and that over that time period only two managers have been demoted or terminated, both of whom were found to have inflated their monthly commissions with false numbers. Ed wants to know whether he has any claim against Fran or Acme, and what issues would likely arise in an action against them. Besides your knowledge of basic contract law, you know that your state's constitution has an article that protects "freedom of association" in language similar to the First Amendment of the U.S. Constitution. What is your assessment?

PROBLEM 6-2

Reallybike.com is a startup bicycle sharing company. In 2016 reallybike hired Ken Tanaka as assistant director of technology development. The parties did not have a formal employment agreement, but the company sent Tanaka an email as follows:

> Ken – We are very excited to have you on board at reallybike and are confident that you will work well in our dynamic environment.
>
> By this email we want to confirm the terms of your employment. We understand that you have many opportunities that have been offered to you, and we are appreciative of your willingness to devote time to developing reallybike. You have agreed that you will stay with us through a contemplated public offering of our common stock. While it is impossible to fix a time for that, we estimate two years.
>
> In exchange for your commitment to the company you will receive a fixed salary of $10,000 per month, subject to normal deductions for taxes, health insurance, etc. plus an equity interest of 1% of the company, which will vest on the public offering.
>
> As is the case with other equity owners in the company, the company has the right to buy back your stock at any time at a price determined by the board of directors of the company in its sole discretion, taking into account relevant factors, including buy-back prices of the shares of other equity owners of the company.
>
> Please let me know if you have any questions.

Tanaka worked for the company from November 2016 until August 2018 when to his surprise he received both a letter by registered mail and an email message from the company terminating his services effective immediately. The communications stated that while the company did not have an obligation to purchase his non-vested equity interest, the company would pay him two months' salary of $20,000 as the value of his equity interest, as determined by the Board of Directors. Tanaka's surprise turned to anger when the company soon announced a public offering of its common stock scheduled for December 2018. The company did in fact go public, with a market capitalization of $50 million. Based on the public offering of its stock, Tanaka's 1% equity interest would be worth $500,000.

Tanaka has come to you for advice about his legal rights against the company. Analyze the claims that he might have.

PROBLEM 6-3

You are an attorney in Center City, a small Midwestern town. One of your long-time clients is Marjorie Glazier, the owner of a local gift shop and a lifelong resident of Center City. Ms. Glazier's sister, Ruth, was married several years ago to Francis Fallon; Ruth and her husband have recently returned to Center City to live, following his retirement from the United States Navy. Although Mr. Fallon retired with full pension rights, he is still a relatively young man (48), with two children aged 13 and 16, and wants to establish himself in some business enterprise in order to meet the expenses (which he foresees as substantial) of his children's education and also to hedge against inflation and consequent devaluation in the purchasing power of his pension payments. He has saved a substantial sum from his Navy pay over the years and is willing to invest all or most of it in a promising opportunity.

Recently Mr. Fallon purchased, at a favorable price, a corner lot on Maple Avenue, near the city limits, with a small building on it in which the previous owner had operated a food market. Believing this location to be ideal for the operation of a small luncheonette/bakery shop, Fallon has been discussing with representatives of Captain Donut, Inc. (a nationwide franchisor of doughnut shops) the possibility of opening a Captain Donut shop in the building on his Maple Avenue lot. He has, he tells you, been assured by them that his store building can be converted to the standard Captain Donut format with remodeling and equipment costs of probably no more than $80,000, and that (based on figures from comparable locations in your state) a shop at that location should — after an initial period of operation, and with efficient management — earn for its owner a net profit of $85,000 a year, or more. In his purchase of the Maple Avenue lot, Fallon was not represented by a lawyer. At the urging of Ms. Glazier, however, he has now consulted you about his proposed entry into a franchise agreement with Captain Donut, Inc. He submits for your examination and advice the following form, which — he has been assured — is the standard agreement between Captain Donut, Inc. and its franchisees:

FRANCHISE AGREEMENT

AGREEMENT dated, ______________, between CAPTAIN DONUT, INC., a Delaware corporation with its principal offices at 493 E. Martindale Rd., Pittsburgh, Pennsylvania (herein called "Franchisor") and ________________ ("Franchisee").

WHEREAS, Franchisor has originated and developed a plan for operating retail establishments for the preparation and sale of doughnuts, pastry, cakes, pies, and related food items; and

The distinguishing characteristics of Franchisor's above-mentioned plan (herein called the "Captain Donut system") include the trade name "Captain Donut" and the registered trademark of a cartoon figure bearing the name "Captain Donut," a unique and standardized color scheme and layout for the place where such retail business is conducted (herein called a "Captain Donut shop"), and the recipes and secret formulas from which Franchisor's unique types of doughnuts and other pastry foods can be prepared (herein called "the secret formulas"), together with such other trademarks, trade names, design and layout schemes, and secret formulas as may from time to time be developed by Franchisor and incorporated into the Captain Donut system; and

Franchisor's Captain Donut shops have an established national reputation for high-quality and distinctive doughnuts and pastry products, prepared and sold in conditions of convenience, cleanliness, and attractiveness, all of which Franchisor has fostered through advertising in various national media and through its enforcement of the contractual obligations of Captain Donut franchisees to operate their Captain Donut shops according to the quality standards set forth in Franchisor's Manual of Operations; and

Franchisor has developed a course for training qualified persons to operate a Captain Donut shop according to the Captain Donut system, and is willing to train franchisees in such methods of operation, and to assist them in the establishment and initial operation of their Captain Donut shops; and

Franchisee has applied to be granted a franchise for operation of a Captain Donut shop at the following premises: ____________________________ ___, and Franchisor is willing to grant such a franchise upon the terms and conditions set forth below.

Now, Therefore, the parties hereby agree as follows:

1. *Franchise.* Franchisor hereby grants to Franchisee, upon the terms and conditions herein set forth, a franchise to operate a Captain Donut shop upon the above-specified premises (herein called "the Premises"), and in connection therewith a license to use in the operation of Franchisee's shop (herein called "the Shop") the trade name "Captain Donut," the trademark figure of Captain Donut, and such other trade name, trademarks, layout and color schemes, secret formulas, and other information as shall now or during the term of this Agreement constitute a part of the Captain Donut system, as communicated to Franchisee by Franchisor.

2. *Term.* Except as provided in Paragraph 11 hereof, the term of Franchisee's license hereunder shall be ten years from the date of this Agreement, but may be renewed thereafter for such period or periods, and upon such terms, as Franchisor and Franchisee shall then find mutually agreeable.

3. *Exclusive License.* Franchisor agrees that it will not, while Franchisee's license hereunder is in force, grant to any other person the right to open or operate a Captain Donut shop within five miles of the Premises. Except as stated in the preceding sentence, Franchisor's right to use and/or license the trade name and trademark of Captain Donut and the other components of the Captain Donut system during the term of this Agreement is acknowledged by Franchisee to be unimpaired hereby.

4. *Training.* Before the opening of the Shop, Franchisor will make available to one representative of Franchisee, at the Franchisor's headquarters in Pittsburgh, Pa., a five-day training course in the operation of a Captain Donut shop. There shall be no charge to Franchisee for such training other than the fees specified in Paragraphs 7 and 8 hereof, but Franchisee shall bear the cost of all such representative's traveling and living expenses in connection with the training course.

5. *Uniformity of Operations.* Franchisee agrees that in order to preserve the distinctive value of the Captain Donut system to the parties hereto and to all other franchisees thereunder, the Franchisor must establish and maintain uniform standards of quality, cleanliness, appearance, and efficiency

of operation. In furtherance thereof, Franchisor shall furnish to Franchisee hereunder one or more copies of its Manual of Operations, together with such supplements and amendments thereto as may be issued by it from time to time (herein called collectively "the Manual"). Franchisee agrees that it shall forthwith erect upon the Premises such distinctive signs bearing the trademarks or other emblems of the Captain Donut system as shall be therein specified, and shall decorate the exterior and interior of the Shop in accordance therewith, shall acquire such bakery and kitchen equipment as shall be required thereby in order to produce doughnuts and other pastry of sufficient quantity and quality, shall prepare the doughnuts and other foods to be sold in the Shop according to the secret formulas of Franchisor as contained therein, using only approved ingredients as specified in Paragraph 6, below, and shall in all respects conform its operation of the Shop to the system as outlined in the Manual, all to the satisfaction of Franchisor. Franchisor shall have the right to inspect the Premises and the Shop from time to time hereunder, at any time during regular business hours, to assure itself that the provisions of this Agreement and of this Paragraph 5 are being observed. In connection with the initial public opening of the Shop, Franchisor shall conduct such advertising and promotional activities as may appear to it advisable, and will furnish to Franchisee for one week, at Franchisor's expense, one or more of Franchisor's advisory personnel to assist in such campaign and in the opening and initial operation of the Shop. Franchisee acknowledges that the Manual contains much secret and confidential information, the continued confidentiality of which is necessary for the continued success of the Captain Donut system, and agrees not to divulge such information to any person other than its own authorized employees, agrees not to copy or permit any other person to copy the Manual or any portion thereof, and agrees that the Manual delivered to it hereunder shall be and remain the sole and exclusive property of Franchisor, and shall be redelivered to Franchisor upon the termination of Franchisee's license hereunder.

6. *Purchases.* In order further to assure the uniform quality of the items to be sold at the Shop, Franchisee agrees that it will purchase all food products sold or used in the Shop from Franchisor or from suppliers listed in the Manual or otherwise approved in writing by Franchisor as authorized suppliers of products meeting its specifications; provided, further, that Franchisor will upon Franchisee's request approve for purchases by Franchisee hereunder any supplier whose products in Franchisor's judgment conform to the specifications and standards of Franchisor for use in the Captain Donut system; provided, however, that all doughnuts sold by Franchisee during the entire period of this Agreement shall be made from Franchisor's own secret-formula mix, and Franchisee shall purchase all of its requirements of such mix from Franchisor itself, at such prices as shall be set from time to time by Franchisor.

7. *Initial Franchise Fee.* In consideration of the rights acquired by it hereunder, including without limitation the franchise granted herein, the license of rights, the training course provided, and the communication to it of the Manual and other information necessary for the operation of the Shop, Franchisee hereby agrees to pay to Franchisor upon the execution of this

Agreement an initial nonrefundable franchise fee of Twenty-five Thousand ($25,000) Dollars.

8. *Weekly Franchise Fee.* During the entire term of this Agreement, as further consideration for the rights acquired hereunder, Franchisee shall pay to Franchisor a weekly franchise fee of Five (5%) Percent of Franchisee's gross sales in the Shop. Such fees shall be payable on Tuesday of each week with respect to the gross sales of the preceding week, and shall be accompanied by weekly financial reports in such form as Franchisor shall prescribe. Franchisee shall maintain financial records in such form as Franchisor shall require (which records shall be available for inspection and copy by Franchisor at any time during regular business hours), and shall furnish Franchisor on or before the 15th day of April in each year with a certified profit and loss statement for the preceding year and balance sheet as of the end of such year.

9. *Competition with Franchisor.* Franchisee shall during the term of this Agreement devote substantially its full time to the operation of the Shop. Franchisee shall not, directly or indirectly, own, engage in, be interested in, or be associated with any doughnut shop, pastry shop, "convenient" market, or other food shop within a ten-mile radius of the Premises, both for the duration of the rights granted to the Franchisee hereunder (except for Franchisee's operation of the Shop itself) and for a period of five years after their termination for any reason whatsoever.

10. *Insurance.* Franchisee shall at its own expense maintain liability insurance with personal injury coverage of not less than $200,000 per person and $500,000 per accident, and property damage coverage of not less than $50,000. Such insurance policies shall name Franchisor as an additional insured, and shall be in form and with insurers satisfactory to Franchisor; Franchisor shall receive copies of all such policies, together with satisfactory evidence of premium payment. Franchisee shall indemnify Franchisor and save it harmless from all loss, liability, and expense (including attorneys' fees) arising from any occurrence in or in connection with Franchisee's operation of the Shop.

11. *Termination for Cause.* If Franchisee shall fail to pay Franchisor any monies owed it hereunder when due, or fail to operate the Shop to the satisfaction of Franchisor as required by Paragraph 5 hereof, or in any other respect whatsoever fail to comply with the terms and provisions of this Agreement, or cease to do business at the Premises, or make an assignment for the benefit of creditors, or be the subject of a receivership, bankruptcy, or insolvency proceeding, then unless Franchisee shall cure such default within ten (10) days after written notice thereof is sent to it by Franchisor, Franchisor shall have the right forthwith to terminate this Agreement and all of Franchisee's rights hereunder. In the event of such termination, Franchisee shall remain liable to Franchisor for any sums then owed and for any damages incurred by Franchisor by reason of such termination, and the provisions of this Agreement relating to termination shall apply.

12. *Events upon Termination.* Upon the expiration or termination of its license hereunder for any reason, Franchisee shall immediately discontinue use of the trade name and trademark licenses hereunder, and the secret formulas and other information contained in the Manual, and all signs, emblems, advertising matter, distinctive layout, color scheme, or other materials indicative of

or identified with the Captain Donut system, and shall thereafter do nothing to indicate that it or any food products sold by it have any connection with the Captain Donut system, and shall return to Franchisor all copies of the Manual theretofore furnished hereunder. Franchisee will immediately refrain from selling any doughnuts prepared from Franchisor's mix (Paragraph 6); provided, that Franchisor will upon such termination repurchase any unopened bags of such mix at the price previously paid to it by Franchisee therefor. The provisions of Paragraph 9 shall continue to be applicable to Franchisee in the event of such termination, and Franchisor shall be entitled to specific enforcement, by injunctive relief, of the provisions of this Paragraph 12 and of Paragraph 9, above.

13. *Relationship of Parties.* In all respects the relation of the parties hereto shall be that of independent contractors. Nothing herein shall be deemed to create a partnership, joint venture, or agency between them, and no employee of one shall be deemed an employee of the other.

14. *Transfer of Rights.* Neither this Agreement nor any of Franchisee's rights or privileges hereunder shall be assigned or transferred, by operation of law or otherwise in any manner, by Franchisee without the prior written consent of Franchisor. Without limitation of the foregoing sentence, the words "Franchisor" and "Franchisee" as used herein shall wherever appropriate refer to the parties hereto and their respective heirs, executors, administrators, successors, and assigns.

15. *Notices.* Any notice to be given hereunder shall be deemed given when sent by registered or certified mail, return receipt requested, to Franchisor at its address first above given and to Franchisee at the following address: ______

__________________________.

16. *Miscellaneous Provisions.* This Agreement contains the entire agreement between the parties, and may not be modified except by a writing signed by both parties. Franchisee acknowledges that in entering into this Agreement it is relying on no promises, representations, or warranties made by Franchisor other than those stated herein. No waiver by Franchisor of any breach or default by Franchisee in any of its obligations hereunder shall be deemed a waiver of any subsequent breach by Franchisee of the same or any other provision of this Agreement. The invalidity or unenforceability of any term or provision of this Agreement shall not affect the remaining terms and provisions, which shall remain in full force and effect, and any court which finds that any provision hereto would be unenforceable because overly broad is hereby authorized and requested to reform such provision to the extent necessary to reduce it to the point where it would be enforceable, and to enforce such provision as reformed.

IN WITNESS WHEREOF, the parties have executed this Agreement on the day and year first above written.

Franchisor: CAPTAIN DONUT, INC.
By:__________________
Franchisee:__________________

1. Answer the following questions based on the agreement:

   A. What rights would Mr. Fallon have under the agreement if he is unable to remodel and equip his shop for the $80,000 projected by the company?

B. Suppose Mr. Fallon's wife decides to open a restaurant in Center City. Would that cause any problem for Mr. Fallon under the franchise agreement?

C. Suppose Mr. Fallon negotiates an agreement to supply local hotels with doughnuts for their restaurants. These doughnuts will be sold under each hotel's label, without use of Captain Donut's name or trademark. Is Mr. Fallon permitted to do this under the agreement? If so, would such sales be subject to the weekly franchise fee?

2. Review the agreement and prepare a list of issues that you would raise for discussion with Mr. Fallon.

C. WARRANTIES

This section examines "warranties." In common usage a warranty is a guarantee of quality of a product or service for a specified period of time. As we will see warranties can arise by statute, by contract, and by common law decision.

The Uniform Commercial Code recognizes several forms of warranties. UCC §2-313 deals with creation of "express warranties." Notably, the section does not require that the seller have the intent to create an express warranty, and this represents a substantial change from the common law approach to warranties. See the Comment on the History of Warranty Law following the *Bayliner* case. The most common application of this section is the written or oral express warranty given by a seller or manufacturer of a consumer product (an automobile or a washing machine, for example), concerning the quality or nature of the goods (for example, "the car will get at least 25 miles per gallon of gas" or "this tractor is a 1999 model").

UCC §2-314 sets forth a second type of warranty — the "implied warranty of merchantability." Under this warranty a "merchant" (see UCC §2-104) who regularly sells goods of a particular kind impliedly warrants to the buyer that the goods are of good quality and are fit for the ordinary purposes for which they are used.

UCC §2-315 defines a third type of warranty, the "implied warranty of fitness for a particular purpose." This warranty differs from the implied warranty of merchantability in several respects. To begin with, the warranty is created only when the buyer relies on the seller's skill or judgment to select suitable goods and the seller has reason to know of this reliance. Further, breach of the warranty does not require a showing that the goods are defective in any way — merely that the goods are not fit for the buyer's particular purpose.

Claims of implied warranty, however, are often made in non-UCC transactions. For example, in the leading case of Javins v. First National Realty Corp., 428 F.2d 1071 (D.C. Cir.), *cert. denied,* 400 U.S. 925 (1970), the United States Court of Appeals for the District of Columbia held that a warranty of habitability would be implied into leases of urban dwelling units. In his opinion, Judge J. Skelly Wright observed that the common law rule absolving the lessor of all obligation to repair had developed during the early Middle Ages in an era when the land was more important than the simple structure that might be included in the leasehold, and at a time when tenants were deemed fully capable of making repairs. Judge Wright then asserted that in more modern times, with more complex structures, tenants are primarily interested in having a dwelling that is suitable for occupation and are more dependent on landlords to maintain the condition of a building. Finally, he noted that there exists a well-documented inequality in bargaining power between landlord and tenant that tends to leave tenants with "little leverage" in negotiating for better housing. Id. at 1077-1080.

The overwhelming majority of states now recognizes an implied warranty of habitability in residential leases, by virtue of legislative or judicial action. See Barbara Jo Smith, Note: Tenants in Search of Parity with Consumers: Creating a Reasonable Expectations Warranty, 72 Wash. U. L.Q. 475 (1994). Many of the statutory provisions have been influenced by the Uniform Residential Landlord Tenant Act adopted by the American Law Institute in 1972. Section 2.104 of that Act accepts the concept of the warranty of habitability and defines the landlord's obligation as follows:

> (a) A landlord shall
>
> (1) comply with the requirements of applicable building and housing codes materially affecting health and safety;
>
> (2) make all repairs and do whatever is necessary to put and keep the premises in a fit and habitable condition;
>
> (3) keep all common areas of the premises in a clean and safe condition;
>
> (4) maintain in good and safe working order and condition all electrical, plumbing, sanitary, heating, ventilating, air-conditioning, and other facilities and appliances, including elevators, supplied or required to be supplied by him;
>
> (5) provide and maintain appropriate receptacles and conveniences for the removal of ashes, garbage, rubbish, and other waste incidental to the occupancy of the dwelling unit and arrange for their removal; and
>
> (6) supply running water and reasonable amounts of hot water at all times and reasonable heat [between [October 1] and [May 1]] except where the building that includes the dwelling unit is not required by law to be equipped for that purpose, or the dwelling unit is so constructed that heat or hot water is generated by an installation within the exclusive control of the tenant and supplied by a direct public utility connection.

As you read the following cases and notes, consider and analyze the policy reasons for judicial and legislative action imposing express and implied warranty liability.

Bayliner Marine Corp. v. Crow

Supreme Court of Virginia 257 Va. 121, 509 S.E.2d 499 (1999)

Present: All the Justices.

KEENAN, Justice.

In this appeal, the dispositive issue is whether there was sufficient evidence to support the trial court's ruling that the manufacturer of a sport fishing boat breached an express warranty and implied warranties of merchantability and fitness for a particular purpose.

In the summer of 1989, John R. Crow was invited by John Atherton, then a sales representative for Tidewater Yacht Agency, Inc. (Tidewater), to ride on a new model sport fishing boat known as a 3486 Trophy Convertible, manufactured by Bayliner Marine Corporation (Bayliner). At that time, Tidewater was the exclusive authorized dealer in southeastern Virginia for this model Bayliner boat. During an excursion lasting about 20 minutes, Crow piloted the boat for a short period of time but was not able to determine its speed because there was no equipment on board for such testing.

When Crow asked Atherton about the maximum speed of the boat, Atherton explained that he had no personal experience with the boat or information from other customers concerning the boat's performance. Therefore, Atherton consulted two documents described as "prop matrixes," which were included by Bayliner in its dealer's manual.

Atherton gave Crow copies of the "prop matrixes," which listed the boat models offered by Bayliner and stated the recommended propeller sizes, gear ratios, and engine sizes for each model. The "prop matrixes" also listed the maximum speed for each model. The 3486 Trophy Convertible was listed as having a maximum speed of 30 miles per hour when equipped with a size "20 × 20" or "20[×]19" propeller. The boat Crow purchased did not have either size propeller but, instead, had a size "20 × 17" propeller.

At the bottom of one of the "prop matrixes" was the following disclaimer: "This data is intended for comparative purposes only, and is available without reference to weather conditions or other variables. All testing was done at or near sea level, with full fuel and water tanks, and approximately 600 lb. passenger and gear weight."

Atherton also showed Crow a Bayliner brochure describing the 1989 boat models, including the 3486 Trophy Convertible. The brochure included a picture of that model fully rigged for offshore fishing, accompanied by the statement that this model "delivers the kind of performance you need to get to the prime offshore fishing grounds."

A 1989 Bayliner 3486 Trophy Convertible.

In August 1989, Crow entered into a written contract for the purchase of the 3486 Trophy Convertible in which he had ridden. The purchase price was $120,000, exclusive of taxes. The purchase price included various equipment to be installed by Tidewater including a generator, a cockpit cover, a "Bimini top," a winch, a spotlight, radar, a navigation system, an icemaker, fishing outriggers, an automatic pilot system, extra fuel gauges, a second radio, and air conditioning and heating units. The total weight of the added equipment was about 2,000 pounds. Crow did not test drive the boat after the additional equipment was installed or at any other time prior to taking delivery.

When Crow took delivery of the boat in September 1989, he piloted it onto the Elizabeth River. He noticed that the boat's speed measuring equipment, which was installed in accordance with the contract terms, indicated that the boat's maximum speed was 13 miles per hour. Crow immediately returned to Tidewater and reported the problem.

During the next 12 to 14 months, while Crow retained ownership and possession of the boat, Tidewater made numerous repairs and adjustments to the boat in an attempt to increase its speed capability. Despite these efforts, the boat consistently achieved a maximum speed of only 17 miles per hour, except for one period following an engine modification when it temporarily reached a speed of about 24 miles per hour. In July 1990, a representative from Bayliner wrote Crow a letter stating that the performance representations made at the time of purchase were incorrect, and that 23 to 25 miles per hour was the maximum speed the boat could achieve.

In 1992, Crow filed a motion for judgment against Tidewater, Bayliner, and Brunswick Corporation, the manufacturer of the boat's diesel engines.[1] Crow alleged, among other things, that Bayliner breached express warranties, and implied warranties of merchantability and fitness for a particular purpose.

At a bench trial in 1994, Crow, Atherton, and Gordon W. Shelton, III, Tidewater's owner, testified that speed is a critical quality in boats used for offshore sport fishing in the Tidewater area of Virginia because of the distance between the coast and the offshore fishing grounds. According to these witnesses, a typical offshore fishing site in that area is 90 miles from the coast. Therefore, the speed at which the boat can travel to and from fishing sites has a major impact on the amount of time left in a day for fishing.

Crow testified that because of the boat's slow speed, he could not use the boat for offshore fishing, that he had no other use for it, and that he would not have purchased the boat if he had known that its maximum speed was 23 to 25 miles per hour. Crow testified that he had not used the boat for fishing since 1991 or 1992. He admitted, however, that between September 1989, and September 1994, the boat's engines had registered about 850 hours of use. Bob Schey, Bayliner's manager of yacht testing, testified that a pleasure boat in a climate such as Virginia's typically would register 150 engine hours per year.

The trial court entered judgment in favor of Crow against Bayliner on the counts of breach of express warranty and breach of implied warranties of

1. Crow nonsuited his claim against Tidewater prior to trial. The negligence claim against Brunswick was dismissed in the trial court's final judgment order.

merchantability and fitness for a particular purpose. The court awarded Crow damages of $135,000, plus prejudgment interest from June 1993. The court explained that the $135,000 award represented the purchase price of the boat, and about $15,000 in "damages" for a portion of the expenses Crow claimed in storing, maintaining, insuring, and financing the boat.

On appeal, we review the evidence in the light most favorable to Crow, the prevailing party at trial. Tuomala v. Regent University, 252 Va. 368, 375, 477 S.E.2d 501, 505 (1996); W.S. Carnes, Inc. v. Board of Supervisors of Chesterfield County, 252 Va. 377, 385, 478 S.E.2d 295, 301 (1996). We will uphold the trial court's judgment unless it is plainly wrong or without evidence to support it. Code §8.01-680; Horton v. Horton, 254 Va. 111, 115, 487 S.E.2d 200, 203 (1997).

Crow argues that the "prop matrixes" he received created an express warranty by Bayliner that the boat he purchased was capable of a maximum speed of 30 miles per hour. We disagree.

Code §8.2-313 provides, in relevant part:

> Express warranties by the seller are created as follows:
>
> (a) Any affirmation of fact or promise made by the seller to the buyer which relates to the goods and becomes part of the basis of the bargain creates an express warranty that the goods shall conform to the affirmation or promise.
>
> (b) Any description of the goods which is made a part of the basis of the bargain creates an express warranty that the goods shall conform to the description.

The issue whether a particular affirmation of fact made by the seller constitutes an express warranty is generally a question of fact. See id., Official Comment 3; Daughtrey v. Ashe, 243 Va. 73, 78, 413 S.E.2d 336, 339 (1992). In *Daughtrey,* we examined whether a jeweler's statement on an appraisal form constituted an express warranty. We held that the jeweler's description of the particular diamonds being purchased as "v.v.s. quality" constituted an express warranty that the diamonds were, in fact, of that grade. Id. at 77, 413 S.E.2d at 338.

Unlike the representation in *Daughtrey,* however, the statements in the "prop matrixes" provided by Bayliner did not relate to the particular boat purchased by Crow, or to one having substantially similar characteristics. By their plain terms, the figures stated in the "prop matrixes" referred to a boat with different sized propellers that carried equipment weighing substantially less than the equipment on Crow's boat. Therefore, we conclude that the statements contained in the "prop matrixes" did not constitute an express warranty by Bayliner about the performance capabilities of the particular boat purchased by Crow.

Crow also contends that Bayliner made an express warranty regarding the boat's maximum speed in the statement in Bayliner's sales brochure that this model boat "delivers the kind of performance you need to get to the prime offshore fishing grounds." While the general rule is that a description of the goods that forms a basis of the bargain constitutes an express warranty, Code

§8.2-313(2) directs that "a statement purporting to be merely the seller's opinion or commendation of the goods does not create a warranty."

The statement made by Bayliner in its sales brochure is merely a commendation of the boat's performance and does not describe a specific characteristic or feature of the boat. The statement simply expressed the manufacturer's opinion concerning the quality of the boat's performance and did not create an express warranty that the boat was capable of attaining a speed of 30 miles per hour. Therefore, we conclude that the evidence does not support the trial court's finding that Bayliner breached an express warranty made to Crow.

We next consider whether the evidence supports the trial court's conclusion that Bayliner breached an implied warranty of merchantability. Crow asserts that because his boat was not capable of achieving a maximum speed of 30 miles per hour, it was not fit for its ordinary purpose as an offshore sport fishing boat. Bayliner contends in response that, although the boat did not meet the needs of this particular sport fisherman, there was no evidence from which the trial court could conclude that the boat generally was not merchantable as an offshore fishing boat. We agree with Bayliner's argument.

Code §8.2-314 provides that, in all contracts for the sale of goods by a merchant, a warranty is implied that the goods will be merchantable. To be merchantable, the goods must be such as would "pass without objection in the trade" and as "are fit for the ordinary purposes for which such goods are used." Code §8.2-314(2)(a), (c). The first phrase concerns whether a "significant segment of the buying public" would object to buying the goods, while the second phrase concerns whether the goods are "reasonably capable of performing their ordinary functions." Federal Signal Corp. v. Safety Factors, Inc., 125 Wash. 2d 413, 886 P.2d 172, 180 (Wash. 1994). In order to prove that a product is not merchantable, the complaining party must first establish the standard of merchantability in the trade. Laird v. Scribner Coop, Inc., 237 Neb. 532, 466 N.W.2d 798, 804 (Neb. 1991). Bayliner correctly notes that the record contains no evidence of the standard of merchantability in the offshore fishing boat trade. Nor does the record contain any evidence supporting a conclusion that a significant portion of the boat-buying public would object to purchasing an offshore fishing boat with the speed capability of the 3486 Trophy Convertible.

Crow, nevertheless, relies on his own testimony that the boat's speed was inadequate for his intended use, and Atherton's opinion testimony that the boat took "a long time" to reach certain fishing grounds in the Gulf Stream off the coast of Virginia. However, this evidence did not address the standard of merchantability in the trade or whether Crow's boat failed to meet that standard. Thus, we hold that Crow failed to prove that the boat would not "pass without objection in the trade" as required by Code §8.2-314(2)(a).

We next consider whether the record supports a conclusion that Crow's boat was not fit for its ordinary purpose as an offshore sport fishing boat. Generally, the issue whether goods are fit for the ordinary purposes for which they are used is a factual question. See Federal Ins. Co. v. Village of Westmont, 271 Ill. App. 3d 892, 649 N.E.2d 986, 990, 208 Ill. Dec. 626 (App. Ct. Ill. 1995); Tallmadge v. Aurora Chrysler Plymouth, Inc., 25 Wash. App. 90, 605 P.2d 1275,

1278 (Wash. Ct. App. 1979). Here, the evidence is uncontroverted that Crow used the boat for offshore fishing, at least during the first few years after purchasing it, and that the boat's engines were used for 850 hours. While Crow stated that many of those hours were incurred during various repair or modification attempts and that the boat was of little value to him, this testimony does not support a conclusion that a boat with this speed capability is generally unacceptable as an offshore fishing boat. Thus, considered in the light most favorable to Crow, the evidence fails to establish that the boat was not fit for the ordinary purpose for which it was intended.

We next address Crow's claim that Bayliner breached an implied warranty of fitness for a particular purpose. Code §8.2-315 provides that when a seller "has reason to know any particular purpose for which the goods are required and that the buyer is relying on the seller's skill or judgment to select or furnish suitable goods, there is . . . an implied warranty that the goods shall be fit for such purpose." See also Medcom, Inc. v. C. Arthur Weaver Co., Inc., 232 Va. 80, 84-85, 348 S.E.2d 243, 246 (1986). This statute embodies a long-standing common law rule in Virginia. Layne-Atlantic Co. v. Koppers Co., 214 Va. 467, 471, 201 S.E.2d 609, 613 (1974). The question whether there was an implied warranty of fitness for a particular purpose in a sale of goods is ordinarily a question of fact based on the circumstances surrounding the transaction. Stones v. Sears, Roebuck & Co., 251 Neb. 560, 558 N.W.2d 540, 547 (Neb. 1997).

Crow contends that the "particular purpose" for which the boat was intended was use as an offshore fishing boat capable of traveling at a maximum speed of 30 miles per hour. However, to establish an implied warranty of fitness for a particular purpose, the buyer must prove as a threshold matter that he made known to the seller the particular purpose for which the goods were required. See *Medcom,* 232 Va. at 84, 348 S.E.2d at 246. The record before us does not support a conclusion that Crow informed Atherton of this precise requirement. Although Crow informed Atherton that he intended to use the boat for offshore fishing and discussed the boat's speed in this context, these facts did not establish that Atherton knew on the date of sale that a boat incapable of travelling at 30 miles per hour was unacceptable to Crow. Thus, we conclude that the evidence fails to support the trial court's ruling that Bayliner breached an implied warranty of fitness for a particular purpose.

For these reasons, we will reverse the trial court's judgment and enter final judgment in favor of Bayliner.

Reversed and final judgment.

NOTES AND QUESTIONS

1. *Elements of an express warranty.* Under UCC §2-313, a seller may provide the basis for an express warranty in several ways: making a representation about the goods, giving a description, or displaying a sample or model. The *Bayliner Marine* court cited the earlier case of Daughtrey v. Ashe, 413 S.E.2d

336 (Va. 1992), as providing an example of an affirmation of fact about goods (the statement about the quality of diamonds) that served as basis for an express warranty. See also Avola v. Louisiana-Pacific Corp., 991 F. Supp. 2d 381 (E.D.N.Y. 2014) (plaintiff sufficiently pled claim for breach of express warranty based on statement that composite siding would "take a nail just like wood"; during installation a nail ricocheted off siding and lodged in plaintiff's eye); Goodwin v. Durant Bank & Trust Co., 952 P.2d 41 (Okla. 1998) (description of backhoe equipment as 1990 model amounted to express warranty; equipment actually was 1987 model). The *Bayliner Marine* court also noted, however, the need to distinguish between a type of factual representation about the quality of goods that may give rise to an express warranty and "mere puffery" or sales talk that will not serve as a basis for a binding commitment. See Boud v. SDNCO, Inc., 54 P.3d 1131 (Utah 2002) (affirmation of fact must be objective and capable of being proven true or false; statement that boat was "best in class" or "superb" would be puffery but statement that boat was "fastest in class" could be verified). How would you assess the seller's statements or conduct in *Bayliner Marine* with regard to this aspect of an express warranty?

As a second element, pre-Code law required that a buyer prove reliance on a representation about the quality of the goods to establish that an express warranty had been created. See Uniform Sales Act §12. Whether reliance is required under the Code is unclear. The text of UCC §2-313 provides that an affirmation, promise, description, sample, or model will amount to an express warranty if it is part of the "basis of the bargain," but does not define that concept. However, Comment 3 to UCC §2-313 provides that once a seller has made an affirmation of fact about the goods, "no particular reliance on such statements need be shown in order to weave them into the fabric of the agreement. Rather, any fact which is to take such affirmations, once made, out of the agreement requires clear affirmative proof." The courts are divided on the issue of whether reliance is an element of an express warranty claim. Three approaches can be found in the case law. Some courts have dispensed with the reliance requirement completely if the claimed warranty reflects the reasonable expectations of the buyer. At the opposite extreme, some jurisdictions require the plaintiff to prove reliance as an element of the cause of action. Finally, other courts take an intermediate approach holding that any affirmations by the seller relating to the goods create a rebuttable presumption that the statements are part of the basis of the bargain. However, the seller can rebut this presumption by clear proof that the buyer did not rely on the statements. See generally Katie McLaughlin, Another Argument "Pops Up" Against Reliance in Express Warranty Law, 28 J.L. & Com. 95 (2009) (surveying various positions on meaning of "basis of bargain" before concluding that increasingly popular view and preferable rule is that proof of reliance is not required once seller makes representation to buyer; seller may state affirmative defense by clearly showing that buyer did not rely).

2. *Implied warranty of merchantability.* The buyer in *Bayliner Marine* also sought recovery based on the implied warranty of merchantability in UCC §2-314. For this warranty to arise, the buyer must establish that the seller is

a "merchant" with respect to the goods sold. A merchant is defined in the Code as a party who regularly deals in goods of the kind or holds itself out as having particular knowledge about the kind of goods. UCC §2-104(1). If the seller is a merchant, UCC §2-314(2) includes several alternative bases for assessing the merchantability of goods, including the two most frequently applied tests: whether the goods would "pass without objection in the trade" and "are fit for the ordinary purposes for which such goods are used." The range of cases involving the implied warranty of merchantability is vast, from the sale of very expensive equipment to the purchase of a hamburger. See, e.g., T & M Solar and Air Conditioning, Inc. v. Lennox Int'l Inc., 83 F. Supp. 3d 855 (N.D. Cal. 2015) (plaintiffs stated claim for breach of implied warranty of merchantability in alleging that solar panels could not operate in solar electrical system as delivered); Mitchell v. BBB Services Co., Inc., 582 S.E.2d 470 (Ga. Ct. App. 2003) (bone in hamburger would constitute breach of implied warranty of merchantability if it would not be reasonably expected by consumer). Do you think the buyer in *Bayliner Marine* could have made a better case for the proposition that the boat was not merchantable? What evidence should the buyer have offered?

3. ***Implied warranty of fitness for a particular purpose.*** The implied warranty of fitness for a particular purpose under §2-315 differs from the implied warranty of merchantability in several respects. First, liability under this warranty is not limited to merchant sellers. Second, the warranty is created only when the buyer relies on the seller's skill or judgment to select suitable goods for the buyer's particular purpose and the seller has reason to know of this reliance. Third, breach of the warranty does not require a showing that the goods are defective in any way — merely that the goods are not fit for the buyer's particular purpose. See, e.g., Neilson Bus. Equip. Ctr., Inc. v. Monteleone, 524 A.2d 1172 (Del. 1987) (computer equipment did not meet needs of buyer who relied on seller to select goods and customize software). Most courts also hold that the buyer's particular purpose must be one other than the ordinary use of the goods. Compare Tamayo v. CGS Tires US, Inc., 2012 WL 2129353 (D. Neb.) (tractor tire which exploded could not give rise to claim for breach of fitness warranty because buyer's use was ordinary use), with In re Atlas Roofing Corp. Chalet Shingle Products Liab. Litig., 22 F. Supp. 3d 1322 (N.D. Ga. 2014) (in class action case involving quality of shingles, South Carolina law allows fitness warranty to apply even if particular use is also ordinary use).

4. ***Disclaimers of express warranties.*** Warranty obligations arise as a matter of contract, and the Code also allows sellers to eliminate or modify the Code's warranties by agreement. The validity of disclaimers of warranties is governed by UCC §2-316. Under §2-316(1), a disclaimer of an express warranty is inoperative if the disclaimer cannot be construed as "consistent" with terms in the contract that would create the express warranty. UCC §2-316(1), Comment 1. See, e.g., Consolidated Data Terminals v. Applied Digital Data Systems, Inc., 708 F.2d 385 (9th Cir. 1983) (manufacturer's specifications about speed of computer constituted express warranty and were not disclaimed by language in contract providing that the manufacturer "makes no warranty, express or implied"). Since express warranties may be created orally or by one of several

writings, the existence of an express warranty may turn on the application of the parol evidence rule. Indeed, UCC §2-316(1) states that it is "subject to" the provisions of UCC §2-202, the parol evidence rule. See, e.g., Hoover Universal, Inc. v. Brockway Imco, Inc., 809 F.2d 1039 (4th Cir. 1987) (evidence regarding seller's earlier representations about machine's capacity was inadmissible since subsequent written contract was intended by parties to be final expression of their agreement). Some courts, however, have found grounds to permit evidence of express warranties despite the parol evidence rule. See, e.g., La Trace v. Webster, 17 So. 3d 1210 (Ala. Civ. App. 2008) (statement at auctions that items sold to buyer were Tiffany lamps went to "core description" and could not be disclaimed despite multiple "as is" disclaimers contained in auction terms and conditions and sales receipt; moreover, description was given during auction after terms and conditions were received by buyer).

5. ***Disclaimers and implied warranties.*** The implied warranties of merchantability and fitness for a particular purpose can be disclaimed in several ways under UCC §2-316(2) and (3). To disclaim the implied warranty of *merchantability* under §2-316(2), "the language must mention merchantability and in the case of a writing must be conspicuous." In contrast, the Code provides that a disclaimer of the implied warranty of *fitness* for a particular purpose must be in a conspicuous writing and will be effective if it states that "[t]here are no warranties which extend beyond the description on the face hereof." UCC §2-316(2). Thus, the disclaiming language for the fitness warranty can be less specific than that required for the implied warranty of merchantability, but it must be in a writing. Moreover, additional methods of excluding the implied warranties are found in §2-316(3), probably the most common of which is the "as is" disclaimer. Section 2-316(3), unlike §2-316(2), does not include a conspicuousness requirement, but most courts agree that one should be implied to carry out the section's purpose of avoiding surprise to buyers. See, e.g., Lumber Mut. Ins. Co. v. Clarklift of Detroit, Inc., 569 N.W.2d 681 (Mich. Ct. App. 1997) ("as is" disclaimer must be conspicuous to be effective); but see DeKalb Agresearch, Inc. v. Abbott, 391 F. Supp. 152 (N.D. Ala. 1974) (applying the statutory language literally and holding that "as is" disclaimer need not be conspicuous), *aff'd,* 511 F.2d 1162 (5th Cir. 1975). Notably, some states have enacted nonuniform versions of §2-316, making all disclaimers of the implied warranty of merchantability ineffective in consumer transactions. See, e.g., Wolfe v. Welton, 558 S.E.2d 363 (W. Va. 2001). In addition, the Magnuson Moss Warranty Act, 15 U.S.C. §2301 et seq., a federal statute that regulates warranties in consumer transactions, prohibits a warrantor who makes a "written warranty" as defined in the act from disclaiming any implied warranties. See Semitekol v. Monaco Coach Corp., 582 F. Supp. 2d 1009 (N.D. Ill. 2008).

6. ***Distinguishing tort and contract claims — the "economic loss" rule.*** If goods are defective, plaintiffs may attempt to bring claims for damages either in tort — typically negligence or strict liability — or in contract for breach of warranty. Tort claims usually offer advantages to plaintiffs because various defenses that apply to contract claims, such as disclaimers, privity of contract, and notice, generally do not apply to tort claims. However, sometimes a contract claim may be beneficial to the plaintiff because the statute of limitations for contract claims in most jurisdictions is longer than the tort statute. But see UCC §2-725(1) (providing for a four-year statute of limitations, but the parties may by contract reduce the statutory period to one year). If the plaintiff has suffered personal injury damages, the plaintiff may be able to sue in either contract for breach of warranty or in tort. However, if the plaintiff has suffered only "economic loss," typically a decline in value of the product or lost profits, courts have generally limited the plaintiff to a contract action. When the plaintiff's claim involves damage to the product itself, some jurisdictions will allow tort law to govern if the damage is the result of a "calamitous event"; however, most courts will treat claims for damage to the product as governed by contract law regardless of the cause. See, e.g., Giddings & Lewis, Inc. v. Industrial Risk Insurer, 348 S.W.3d 729 (Ky. 2011).

Comment on the History of Warranty Law

In the seventeenth century the English courts first adopted what has since come to be known as the principle of "caveat emptor": "let the buyer beware." This doctrine meant that the seller bore no responsibility at all for the quality of the product he was selling unless he expressly guaranteed it or gave a "warranty" to the buyer. The leading case for this doctrine was Chandelor v. Lopus, 79 Eng. Rep. 3, decided by the Court of Exchequer-Chamber in 1603. In *Chandelor* the defendant, a goldsmith, sold a stone to the plaintiff. Although the defendant had "affirmed" that the stone was a "bezar-stone," this representation turned out to be false, and the plaintiff brought suit. The court held for the defendant because "the bare affirmation that it was a bezar-stone, without warranting it to be so, is no cause of action. . . ." Moreover, the court held that the declaration did not state a cause of action even if the defendant knew that his statements were false, because "every one in selling his wares will affirm that his wares are good, or the horse which he sells is sound; yet if he does not warrant them to be so, it is no cause of action. . . ." (A "bezar-stone" was not a precious jewel but instead "an object somewhat similar to a gall stone, but formed in the intestines of goats, and was thought at the time to possess medicinal value." Alfred W. B. Simpson, A History of the Common Law of Contract 536 (1975). Does this fact affect your view of the holding in *Chandelor*?)

American courts embraced the doctrine of caveat emptor in the nineteenth century. For example, in Seixas v. Woods, 2 Caine R. 48 (N.Y. 1804), the defendant, a middleman, sold certain wood, advertised as "brazilletto," to the plaintiff. Unknown to either the buyer or the seller, the wood was "peachum," a much less valuable type of wood. In an action by the buyer seeking a refund of the price, the New York Court of Errors held for the seller because no warranty was made. See generally Walton H. Hamilton, The Ancient Maxim Caveat Emptor, 40 Yale L.J. 1133 (1931).

In the last quarter of the nineteenth century, American courts, responding to changing market conditions, gradually reversed the rule of caveat emptor by imposing obligations on the seller as to the quality of goods sold. These obligations, or "implied warranties," were not based on actual agreement of the parties but were instead imposed by law on the seller. By 1906, the arguments for imposing warranty obligations on sellers had become generally accepted, and enough particular instances had been sanctioned by case law that the National Conference of Commissioners on Uniform State Laws felt justified in including in its newly promulgated Uniform Sales Act several provisions for implied warranties in the sale of goods. See, e.g., §§14 (implied warranty in sale by description); 15 (implied warranties of quality); 16 (implied warranties in sale by sample). See generally Karl N. Llewellyn, On Warranty of Quality, and Society (Pts. I, II), 36 Colum. L. Rev. 699 (1936), 37 Colum. L. Rev. 341 (1937); Timothy J. Sullivan, Innovation in the Law of Warranty: The Burden of Reform, 32 Hastings L.J. 341 (1980).

PROBLEM 6-4

In February 2018, Frank McCarty began a business that involved the home delivery of pet food and supplies at prices substantially lower than those in grocery and pet stores. The business prospered immediately, and by April, Frank was making a profit of $2,000 per week.

Beginning in March 2018, and for several months thereafter, Firebrand Tire Company engaged in an extensive national advertising campaign for its new "Roadsafe Steel Belted X-10 Tire." The typical advertisement contained the following:

> Concerned about tire safety? The new steel belted X-10 from Firebrand has been designed and tested especially for protection against road hazards. No tire on the market is more reliable than the X-10. When you think of safety, think of Firebrand.

In June 2018, McCarty went to an independent local tire dealer to purchase tires for the van that he used in his business. When a salesman asked McCarty if he could be of help, McCarty told him that he wished to buy a reliable, heavy-duty tire for his van. The salesman recommended the X-10. After some discussion McCarty agreed to purchase the tires. The salesman gave him a brochure that described the tires and asked McCarty to sign it. While McCarty was waiting for his tires to be installed, he thumbed through the brochure, which contained the following warranty provision:

> **Limited One-Year Warranty**
>
> Firebrand warrants to the purchaser that the tires which he has purchased will be free from defects in materials and workmanship for a period of one year from the date of purchase. This warranty will be honored by any authorized Firebrand dealer. Firebrand will repair or replace any such defective tire. In no event, however, will Firebrand be liable for actual or consequential damages, purchaser's sole remedy being limited to repair or replacement of any defective tire.
>
> There are no express warranties, whether oral or written, other than in this document. The IMPLIED WARRANTIES OF MERCHANTABILITY AND

> FITNESS FOR A PARTICULAR PURPOSE are hereby LIMITED to a period of ONE YEAR from the date of purchase.

In March 2019, McCarty's van swerved off the road when the left front tire blew out. Evidence indicates that the tire failed when pierced by a large piece of metal lying in the road. The van, which had a value of $25,000, was totally destroyed. McCarty was injured and required hospitalization for several weeks. His total medical and hospital bills were approximately $100,000. Because of McCarty's absence, the business could not continue and subsequently it failed. An expert is prepared to testify that his business had a fair market value of $150,000. McCarty has brought suit against Firebrand and the retailer. Analyze McCarty's rights against Firebrand and the dealer based on both breach of warranty and tort theories.

Speight v. Walters Development Co.

Supreme Court of Iowa 744 N.W.2d 108 (2008)

LARSON, Justice.

The plaintiffs, Robert and Beverly Speight, appeal from a summary judgment entered against them in their suit for breach of implied warranty of workmanlike construction against the builder of their home. The court of appeals affirmed. Both the district court and the court of appeals expressly declined to recognize an implied-warranty claim in favor of third-party purchasers, deferring for such a decision to this court. We now extend our common law of implied warranty to cover such parties and therefore vacate the decision of the court of appeals, reverse the judgment of the district court, and remand for further proceedings.

I. FACTS AND PRIOR PROCEEDINGS

The Speights are the present owners of a home in Clive, Iowa, which was custom-built in 1995 by the defendant, Walters Development Company, Ltd. It was built for use by the original buyers, named Roche. The Roches sold the home to people named Rogers, who in turn sold it to the Speights on August 1, 2000. Sometime after purchasing the home, the Speights noticed water damage and mold. A building inspector determined that the damage was the result of a defectively constructed roof and defective rain gutters. Nothing in the record indicates that any of the owners between the original builder and the Speights had actual or imputed knowledge of these defects.

The Speights filed suit against Walters on May 23, 2005, alleging a breach of implied warranty of workmanlike construction and general negligence in construction of the home. Both the Speights and Walters moved for summary judgment, raising the issue of whether the Speights, as remote purchasers, could pursue a claim for breach of an implied warranty of workmanlike construction. Walters also raised the issue of whether the plaintiffs' claim for breach of implied warranty was barred by Iowa Code section 614.1(4) (2005), the applicable statute of limitations. The district court concluded that, under the present state of the law, the Speights could not maintain an implied-warranty claim, and in any event, such claim would be barred by the statute of limitations. The district court also concluded that the Speights could not bring a general negligence claim because they did not assert an accompanying claim for personal injury—a ruling the plaintiffs do not challenge on appeal.

II. The Implied–Warranty Claim

The implied warranty of workmanlike construction is a judicially created doctrine implemented to protect an innocent home buyer by holding the experienced builder accountable for the quality of construction. *See* 17 Richard A. Lord, Williston on Contracts §50:30 (4th ed. 2007) [hereinafter Lord]. Home buyers are generally in an inferior position when purchasing a home from a builder-vendor because of the buyer's lack of expertise in quality home construction and the fact that many defects in construction are latent. These defects, even if the home were inspected by a professional, would not be discoverable. *See* Sean M. O'Brien, Note, Caveat Venditor: A Case for Granting Subsequent Purchasers a Cause of Action Against Builder–Vendors for Latent Defects in the Home, 20 J. Corp. L. 525, 529 (Spring 1995).

The implied warranty of workmanlike construction addresses the inequities between the buyer and the builder-vendor by requiring that a building be constructed "in a reasonably good and workmanlike manner and . . . be reasonably fit for the intended purpose." Kirk v. Ridgway, 373 N.W.2d 491, 492 (Iowa 1985). In *Kirk* this court applied the doctrine of implied warranty of workmanlike construction to the sale of a home by the builder to the first owner. 373 N.W.2d at 496. In doing so, we noted that interest in consumer protection had increased, and the complexity of homes had increased, making it difficult for a buyer to discover defects in the construction. *Id.* at 493–94. In *Kirk* we rejected the application of the doctrine of *caveat emptor* under which "it has been observed, courts considered purchasing as a game of chance." *Id.* at 493 (citing Roberts, The Case of the Unwary Home Buyer: The Housing Merchant Did It, 52 Cornell L.Q. 835, 836 (1967)). We noted that home buyers are ill-equipped to discover defects in homes, which are increasingly complex, and therefore must rely on the skill and judgment of the vendor. *Id.* at 494.

In *Kirk* we held that, in order to sustain a claim that a builder-vendor has breached the implied warranty of workmanlike construction, the buyer must show:

> (1) [t]hat the house was constructed to be occupied by the [buyer] as a home;
> (2) that the house was purchased from a builder-vendor, who had constructed it for the purpose of sale;
> (3) that when sold, the house was not reasonably fit for its intended purpose or had not been constructed in a good and workmanlike manner;
> (4) that, at the time of purchase, the buyer was unaware of the defect and had no reasonable means of discovering it; and
> (5) that by reason of the defective condition the buyer suffered damages.

Id. at 496; see also Flom v. Stahly, 569 N.W.2d 135, 142 (Iowa 1997).

In *Kirk* we defined a "builder" as:

> a general building contractor who controls and directs the construction of a building, has ultimate responsibility for completion of the whole contract and for putting the structure into permanent form thus, necessarily excluding merchants, material men, artisans, laborers, subcontractors, and employees of a general contractor.

373 N.W.2d at 496 (quoting Jeanguneat v. Jackie Hames Constr. Co., 576 P.2d 761, 762 (Okla. 1978)).

The plaintiffs ask this court to take the cause of action recognized in *Kirk* one step further by applying it to the case of a subsequent purchaser. Jurisdictions outside of Iowa are split on this issue.

Many jurisdictions do not permit subsequent purchasers to recover for a breach of the implied warranty of workmanlike construction.[1] This holding stems from the lack of a contractual relationship between the subsequent purchaser and the builder-vendor. Michael A. DiSabatino, J.D., Annotation, Liability of Builder of Residence for Latent Defects Therein as Running to Subsequent Purchasers from Original Vendee, 10 A.L.R.4th 385, 388 (1981) [hereinafter DiSabatino]. The implied warranty of workmanlike construction is contractual in nature, and because privity is traditionally required in order to maintain a contract action, some courts have concluded that the lack of privity between the subsequent purchaser and the builder-vendor prevents the subsequent purchaser's implied-warranty claim. O'Brien, 20 J. Corp. L. at 537; see also Mary Dee Pridgen, Consumer Protection and the Law §18:19 (2006) [hereinafter Pridgen] (discussing the holding in Crowder v. Vandendeale, 564 S.W.2d 879, 881 (Mo. 1978)); 2 James Acret, Construction Law Digests §14:12 (2007) [hereinafter Acret] . . . . Further, because there is a lack of privity between the subsequent purchaser and the builder-vendor, there is no reliance by the subsequent purchaser on any representations made by the builder-vendor regarding the quality of construction. See Pridgen, §18:19. Finally, some courts have concluded that the justifications for eliminating the privity requirement in products liability cases do not exist in the sale of real estate. See DiSabatino, 10 A.L.R.4th at 397–98 ("The court reasoned that a house which is not the product of a mass marketing scheme or which is not designed as a temporary dwelling differs from the usual item to which the principles of strict liability have generally been applied, in that it is not an item which generally changes owners or occupants frequently." (discussing Coburn v. Lenox Homes, Inc., 173 Conn. 567, 378 A.2d 599 (1977))).

Other jurisdictions do permit subsequent purchasers to recover for a breach of the implied warranty of workmanlike construction.[2] The purpose of the

1. See, e.g., Lee v. Clark & Assocs. Real Estate, Inc., 512 So. 2d 42 (Ala. 1987); Aas v. Super. Ct., 24 Cal. 4th 627, 101 Cal. Rptr. 2d 718, 12 P.3d 1125 (2000) (superseded by statute on other grounds); Cosmopolitan Homes, Inc. v. Weller, 663 P.2d 1041 (Colo. 1983); Coburn v. Lenox Homes, Inc., 173 Conn. 567, 378 A.2d 599 (1977); . . .

2. See, e.g., Richards v. Powercraft Homes, Inc., 139 Ariz. 242, 678 P.2d 427 (1984); Blagg v. Fred Hunt Co., 272 Ark. 185, 612 S.W.2d 321 (1981); Tusch Enters. v. Coffin, 113 Idaho 37, 740 P.2d 1022 (1987); Redarowicz v. Ohlendorf, 92 Ill. 2d 171, 65 Ill. Dec. 411, 441 N.E.2d 324 (1982); . . . .

implied warranty of workmanlike construction is to ensure that innocent home buyers are protected from latent defects. This principle is " 'equally applicable to subsequent purchasers' " who are in no better position to discover those defects than the original purchaser. Acret, §14:12 (discussing and quoting the holding in Lempke v. Dagenais, 130 N.H. 782, 547 A.2d 290 (1988)); see also Pridgen, §18:19 (" 'The purpose of a warranty is to protect innocent purchasers and hold builders accountable for their work. With that object in mind, any reasoning which would arbitrarily interpose a first buyer as an obstruction to someone equally as deserving of recovery is incomprehensible.' " (quoting Moxley v. Laramie Builders, Inc., 600 P.2d 733, 736 (Wyo. 1979))). Thus, the public policy justifications for eliminating the doctrine of *caveat emptor* for original purchasers of new homes similarly support allowing subsequent purchasers to recover on a theory of a breach of the implied warranty of workmanlike construction. . . . Further, the purpose of the implied warranty of workmanlike construction is to ensure the home " 'will be fit for habitation,' a matter that 'depends upon the quality of the dwelling delivered' not the status of the buyer." Pridgen, §18:19 (quoting Tusch Enters. v. Coffin, 113 Idaho 37, 740 P.2d 1022 (1987)).

The lack of privity between the subsequent purchaser and the builder-vendor is not an impediment, in these jurisdictions, to allowing a subsequent purchaser to recover on an implied-warranty claim. Though the implied warranty of workmanlike construction " 'has roots in the execution of the contract for sale,' " it exists independently of the contract by its very nature. O'Brien, 20 J. Corp. L. at 538 (citations omitted). Additionally, requiring privity to sue for a breach of an implied warranty has been disfavored in products liability cases in some jurisdictions. Many jurisdictions find similar justifications for extinguishing the privity requirement in the purchase of a home. See O'Brien, §50:30 ("[T]he builder was in the same position as a manufacturer who sells an article which, if defective, will be imminently dangerous to persons who come in contact with it, 'and liability is not limited to those with whom the manufacturer contracts.' " (quoting Leigh v. Wadsworth, 361 P.2d 849 (Okla. 1961))). From a practical perspective, these jurisdictions note that many latent defects "are often not discoverable for some time after completion of the house. By the time the defects come to light, the original purchasers may have sold the home. For that reason, subsequent purchasers need protection for faulty construction." Pridgen, §18:19. Additionally, the reality is that our society is increasingly mobile, and as a result, a home's ownership is likely to change hands a number of times. *See* O'Brien, 20 J. Corp. L. at 526 (noting that, at the time the note was written, "[n]early four million single-family used homes [were] sold in the United States every year"). A blanket rule prohibiting subsequent purchasers from recovering for a breach of the implied warranty of workmanlike construction would do injustice to those who purchase a home from a previous buyer shortly after the home was constructed when the subsequent purchaser later discovers that the home was defectively constructed. See id. at 538. Finally, one author posits that the doctrine of assignment allows for the transfer to the subsequent purchaser of the original purchaser's right to sue for breach of the implied warranty of workmanlike construction. *Id.* at 538-40.

We believe that Iowa law should follow the modern trend allowing a subsequent purchaser to recover against a builder-vendor for a breach of the implied warranty of workmanlike construction. As in many jurisdictions, this court has eliminated the privity requirement in products liability cases raising a breach-of-implied-warranty claim. See State Farm Mut. Auto. Ins. Co. v. Anderson-Weber, Inc., 252 Iowa 1289, 110 N.W.2d 449, 456 (Iowa 1961). As the court discussed in *State Farm,* the privity requirement was eliminated in other jurisdictions to " 'ameliorate the harsh doctrine of *caveat emptor,*' " and because " 'the [implied warranty] obligations on the part of the seller were imposed by operation of law, and did not depend for their existence upon express agreement of the parties,' " privity was not necessary. *Id.* at 454 (quoting Henningsen v. Bloomfield Motors, Inc., 32 N.J. 358, 161 A.2d 69 (1960)). The same is true in a case such as the present one in which a home buyer raises an implied-warranty claim. Further, the implied warranty of workmanlike construction is a judicial creation and does not, in itself, arise from the language of any contract between the builder-vendor and the original purchaser. Thus, it is not extinguished upon the original purchaser's sale of the home to a subsequent purchaser. The builder-vendor warrants that the home was constructed in a workmanlike manner, not that it is fit for any particular purpose the original owner intended. As such, there is no contractual justification for limiting recovery to the original purchaser.

Additionally, the public policy justifications supporting our decision to recede from the doctrine of *caveat emptor* in the sale of new homes by builder-vendors equally apply to the sale of used homes to subsequent purchasers. As discussed above, latent defects are, by definition, undiscoverable by reasonable inspection. Thus, the subsequent purchaser is in no better position to discover those defects than the original purchaser. It is inequitable to allow an original purchaser to recover while, simultaneously, prohibiting a subsequent purchaser from recovering for latent defects in homes that are the same age.

Walters contends that allowing the recovery the Speights seek would lead to increased costs for builders, increased claims, and increased home prices. However, builder-vendors are currently required to build a home in a good and workmanlike manner. The implied warranty of workmanlike construction reasonably puts the risk of shoddy construction on the builder-vendor. The builder-vendor's risk is not increased by allowing subsequent purchasers to recover for the same latent defects for which an original purchaser could recover. As discussed more fully below, the statute of limitations and statute of repose are the same for original purchasers and subsequent purchasers, thus eliminating any increased time period within which a builder-vendor is subject to suit.

Walters argues that allowing subsequent purchasers to recover for a breach of the implied warranty of workmanlike construction would subject builder-vendors to unlimited liability; however, we are not persuaded. Iowa Code section 614.1(11) provides a safety net—a statute of repose for potential plaintiffs seeking to recover for breach of an implied warranty on an improvement to real property. A statute of repose works to " 'terminate[] any right of action after a specified time has elapsed, regardless of whether or not there has as yet been an injury.' " Bob McKiness Excavating & Grading, Inc. v. Morton, 507 N.W.2d 405, 408 (Iowa 1993) (quoting

Hanson v. Williams County, 389 N.W.2d 319, 321 (N.D. 1986)). Section 614.1(11) applies to an action for breach of the implied warranty of workmanlike construction in the purchase of a building. *See id.* at 409. That section provides:

> an action arising out of the unsafe or defective condition of an improvement to real property based on tort and implied warranty . . . and founded on injury to property, real or personal, or injury to the person or wrongful death, shall not be brought more than fifteen years after the date on which occurred the act or omission of the defendant alleged in the action to have been the cause of the injury or death.

Iowa Code §614.1(11). Pursuant to section 614.1(11), the period of repose begins to run on the date of the act or omission causing the injury. In cases involving the construction of a building, such as this home, that period begins upon completion of the construction of the building. See Bob McKiness Excavating & Grading, Inc., 507 N.W.2d at 409. As a result, builder-vendors are not liable on an implied-warranty claim after the statute of repose has run, regardless of who owns the home. . . .

III. The Statute of Limitations

The defendant contends that, even if we recognize a cause of action under these circumstances, it would be barred by the statute of limitations under Iowa Code section 614.1(4). The district court and the court of appeals agreed and concluded that this suit was time-barred. We disagree.

Under Iowa Code section 614.1,

> [a]ctions may be brought within the times herein limited, respectively, *after their causes accrue,* and not afterwards, except when otherwise specially declared:
>
> . . . .
>
> 4. *Unwritten contracts—injuries to property—fraud—other actions.* Those founded on unwritten contracts, those brought for injuries to property, or for relief on the ground of fraud in cases heretofore solely cognizable in a court of chancery, and all other actions not otherwise provided for in this respect, within five years
>
> . . . .

(Emphasis added.)

The question in this case is when the plaintiffs' cause of action accrued. [The defendant argued that the cause of action arose upon completion of the house in 1995, relying on the provision in UCC §2-725 that a cause of action for breach of warranty in the sale of goods accrues at the time goods are delivered and not when the damage is discovered. The court rejected that argument and held that a "discovery" rule would apply to actions for breach of the implied warranty of workmanlike construction. Thus, the cause of action would not accrue until the plaintiffs had actual or imputed knowledge of the facts that would support a cause of action. Such discovery could not have occurred before the plaintiffs bought the house in August 2000. — Eds.]

We adopt and apply the doctrine of implied warranty of workmanlike construction to subsequent, as well as initial, purchasers. We conclude as a matter of law that the plaintiffs could not have gained actual or imputed knowledge of the defect in their home more than five years prior to commencing this action, and their suit is therefore not time-barred under Iowa Code section 614.1(4). We vacate the decision of the court of appeals, reverse the judgment of the district court, and remand for further proceedings.

All justices concur except APPEL, J., who takes no part.

NOTES AND QUESTIONS

1. *Implied warranties of quality in new home sales.* A clear majority of jurisdictions has recognized an implied warranty of quality in the sale of a new home by a builder-vendor. See Alisa M. Levin, Condo Developers and Fiduciary Duties: An Unlikely Pairing? 24 Loy. Consumer L. Rev. 197, 236 n.134 (2011). The warranty may be called an implied warranty of workmanlike construction, as in *Speight*, or by a variety of other names including warranty of habitability, skillful construction, or merchantability. For example, the New Jersey Supreme Court held that an implied warranty of "reasonable workmanship and habitability" attaches to the sale of a new home by the builder-vendor in McDonald v. Mianecki, 398 A.2d 1283, 1292-1293 (N.J. 1979). The *McDonald* court observed that "[c]learly every builder-vendor holds himself out, expressly or impliedly, as having the expertise necessary to construct a livable dwelling. It is equally as obvious that almost every buyer acts upon these representations and expects that the new house he is buying, whether already constructed or not yet built, will be suitable for use as a home. Otherwise, there would be no sale." Id. Courts adopting the implied warranty of quality for new housing have frequently analogized to the implied warranties under the UCC in the sale of goods and observed that the justifications for such implied terms apply even more compellingly to the purchase of a home, the single largest economic investment for most consumers. Maronda Homes, Inc. of Florida v. Lakeview Reserve Homeowners Ass'n, Inc., 127 So. 3d 1258, 1264 (Fla. 2013).

2. *Habitability versus workmanlike or skillful construction.* The *Speight* court states that the builder-vendor must construct a house "in a reasonably good and workmanlike manner" and that it must "be reasonably fit for the intended purpose." As suggested by the formulation in the *Speight* case, the implied housing warranty may have two separable components — a warranty of habitability and a warranty of workmanlike or skillful construction — though the courts have not been consistent or clear in recognizing the distinction. See Albrecht v. Clifford, 767 N.E.2d 42 (Mass. 2002). First, the implied warranty of workmanlike or skillful construction requires that the quality of work and materials meet average or reasonable standards for the trade. Second, and in contrast, the implied warranty of habitability requires that the home be suitable for occupation and provide inhabitants with a reasonably safe place to live without fear of injury to person, health, safety or property. Id. at 45. In Aronsohn v. Mandara, 484 A.2d 675 (N.J. 1984), the New Jersey Supreme Court

held that a poorly constructed patio added to a preexisting home would not come within the implied warranty of habitability because it did not fall within the scope of necessities to make a home suitable for living; however, the court did hold that a builder could be held liable for breach of an implied warranty that the patio would be constructed in a good quality manner. Do you agree that courts should imply a warranty of skillful construction in addition to a warranty of habitability?

3. *Extended application of the implied warranty.* After recognizing the existence of an implied warranty of quality in a new home sale between the builder-vendor and the initial buyer, courts have considered in subsequent cases whether the warranty should be extended in a substantial number of ways. The *Speight* court decided, of course, that the warranty should extend to subsequent purchasers beyond the initial buyers from the builder-vendor. The builder-vendor's potential liability would be limited by the relevant statute of limitations, but it could not defend against subsequent owners merely because of lack of "privity." As reflected by footnote 1 in *Speight*, however, other jurisdictions have rejected similar claims. The Pennsylvania Supreme Court recently denied standing for subsequent purchasers to bring suit against the builder-vendor, declining to follow the *Speight* court reasoning and instead concluding that the question of extending the implied warranty to subsequent purchasers was a matter "predominantly grounded in policy considerations that necessitate judgments reserved to the legislature after fact-finding and weighing of the ramifications of any decision." Conway v. Cutler Group, Inc., 99 A.3d 67, 72 (Pa. 2014). Nevertheless, the *Conway* case did favorably cite a lower court decision that allowed standing to second purchasers of a new home who were the intended *first users*, having bought a condominium from a developer who was not the builder-vendor. Id. at 70-71 (citing Spivack v. Berks Ridge Corp., 586 A.2d 402 (Pa. Super. Ct. 1990)).

Beyond the subsequent purchaser question, courts have addressed a variety of other possible applications of the implied warranty in home construction. The Iowa Supreme Court that decided *Speight* later refused to extend the implied warranty of quality to a developer who bought a vacant lot intended for residential construction that was improperly graded, filled, and compacted by the vendor. Rosauer Corp. v. Sapp Dev., L.L.C., 856 N.W.2d 906 (Iowa 2014). In *Rosauer*, the court noted the significant difference between the ability of a consumer to protect against latent defects in a completed home and the ability of a developer to inspect and guard against problems with land that did not yet have a structure. Id. at 912-913. The Iowa Supreme Court also declined to extend the implied warranty protection to a bank that acquired a shoddily built, mold-infested apartment complex in lieu of foreclosure, on similar grounds that the bank could protect itself better than a consumer buying a single family residence. Luana Sav. Bank v. Pro-Build Holdings, Inc., 856 N.W.2d 892 (Iowa 2014).

In contrast, the Illinois courts have extended the implied warranty of habitability in a number of ways, including by allowing consumers to bring suit against a subcontractor responsible for the latent defect when the builder-vendor is insolvent. See 1324 W. Pratt Condominium Ass'n v. Platt Constr. Group, Inc., 997 N.E.2d 246 (Ill. App. Ct. 2013) (noting the strong public policy in favor of protecting the innocent purchaser who is unable to guard against latent defects and placing the cost of repair on the contractor who is responsible for the defect). Similarly, the Florida Supreme Court decided to allow standing for a homeowners association asserting breach of an implied warranty of merchantability related to defective construction of storm drainage systems that severely undermined the habitability of homes in the development, even though the infrastructure was not a part of any single house itself. Maronda Homes, Inc. of Florida v. Lakeview Reserve Homeowners Ass'n, Inc., 127 So. 3d 1258 (Fla. 2013). Notably, the Florida state legislature enacted a law while the case was pending that severely limited the application of the *Maronda Homes* decision. Id. at 1270-1272.

4. *Legislative action.* Several states have enacted legislation providing for implied warranties of quality in the sale of new homes. See Wendy B. Davis, Corrosion by Codification: The Deficiencies in the Statutory Versions of the Implied Warranty of Workmanlike Construction, 39 Creighton L. Rev. 103, 108 (2006) (listing states that have adopted statutes providing an implied warranty of quality for new homes). For example, the New York Court of Appeals recognized an implied warranty that a builder-vendor will construct a house in a skillful manner and free from material defect in Caceci v. DiCanio Construction Corp., 526 N.E.2d 266 (N.Y. 1988) and within weeks after the decision was rendered, the New York legislature enacted a housing merchant warranty law. See New York Gen. Bus. §§777-777b. See also Amy L. McDaniel, Note, The New York Housing Merchant Warranty Statute: Analysis and Proposals, 75 Cornell L. Rev. 754 (1990). The New York law creates three types of warranties: a one-year warranty of skillful construction; a two-year warranty on major systems such as plumbing, electrical, and heating and cooling; and a six-year warranty on latent, material defects. The statute also eliminates any "privity" requirement that would limit the warranty to initial purchasers. Notably, however, the law also has the effect of protecting the builder by narrowing the scope of the implied warranty through its definition of the terms "skillful" and "material defect," and by excluding from its scope any obvious defects. Id. at 767-774.

5. *Effectiveness of disclaimers.* Can the builder-vendor contractually modify or "disclaim" the implied warranty of habitability? The prevailing view is that the implied warranty of habitability may be modified or disclaimed. Many courts, however, view disclaimers with great suspicion and will refuse to enforce a disclaimer unless it is conspicuous, clearly states its effect, and reflects both parties' expectations. E.g., McGuire v. Ryland Group, Inc., 497 F. Supp. 2d 1356 (M.D. Fla. 2007); Fattah v. Bim, 31 N.E.3d 922 (Ill. App. Ct. 2015). But see Albrecht v. Clifford, 767 N.E.2d 42, 47 (Mass. 2002) (holding that warranty cannot be waived or disclaimed "because to permit the disclaimer of a warranty protecting a purchaser from the consequences of latent defects would defeat the very purpose of the warranty"). The New York legislation cited above

permits exclusion or modification of the implied warranty if the seller provides a written warranty that complies with certain requirements as to form, but it also provides that a disclaimer is void as against public policy if it attempts to disclaim compliance with applicable building codes or if it permits the home to be unsafe. Should builder-vendors be able to disclaim the implied warranty of habitability? Is the sale of a new home analogous to the sale of goods, where sellers are allowed to disclaim implied warranties under UCC §2-316? Can you imagine circumstances in which both buyer and seller might wish to have an effective disclaimer?

6. *Implied warranties and commercial buildings.* Should the courts imply a warranty of habitability in the sale of real estate that is commercial rather than residential? The courts are divided. Compare, e.g., Conklin v. Hurley, 428 So. 2d 654 (Fla. 1983) (developer of waterfront building lots not liable to investors for breach of implied warranty of habitability), with Tusch Enterprises v. Coffin, 740 P.2d 1022 (Idaho 1987) (investor could recover from vendor of three duplexes for breach of the implied warranty of habitability). See Frona M. Powell & Jane P. Mallor, The Case for an Implied Warranty of Quality in Sales of Commercial Real Estate, 68 Wash. U. L.Q. 305 (1990). Do you think the implied warranty of habitability should apply to sale of commercial property? Why? Could a useful distinction be drawn between residential property held for investment purposes and purely commercial property, such as an office building, implying a warranty in the first situation but not the second?

REVIEW QUESTIONS – CHAPTER SIX

1. Beth Buyer wanted a new sports watch that she could use while participating in water sports. She had frequently noticed ads for a Windsor brand watch in Sports Illuminated magazine which stated that the watch had a "rugged design that is water-resistant to a depth of 50 meters." In May, Beth went to a Windsor Company retail store to look at the Windsor watch. Sam, the store manager, said to Beth, "Windsor makes a wonderful sports watch. They do a good job for all my customers." Beth purchased a Windsor watch for $1,000. Sam had misplaced the original box for the watch and thus Beth did not get a copy of the Windsor written instructions or warranty. Beth took the watch with her on a trip to Hawaii the next month. While in Hawaii, the watch stopped working when some water got inside the watch when Beth was swimming laps in the hotel pool. Does Beth have grounds to assert a claim for breach of an express warranty against Windsor?
   A. Yes, Beth has grounds for an express warranty claim because of Sam's comments about the watch.
   B. Yes, Beth has grounds for an express warranty claim because of Windsor's statements about the watch in the magazine ads.

C. No, Beth does not have grounds for an express warranty claim because Sam's comments and the statements in the magazine ad were mere commendation of the watch.
D. No, Beth does not have grounds for an express warranty claim because neither Sam's statements nor the magazine ad were contained in a signed writing.

2. Regal Roofing Supply was a major seller of wholesale roofing material in Megatown, a large city. Regal sold roofing supplies to contractors and hardware stores. In August 2016, Regal was contacted by Empire Roofing Corp., a fairly new maker of environmentally friendly roofing material. Empire was interested in finding a distributor for its product in the Megatown area. After some negotiations, Regal and Empire signed an exclusive distributorship contract that stated: "Empire hereby grants Regal the exclusive rights to sell Empire roofing products in the Megatown area for five years, beginning September 1, 2016. Regal will use best efforts to promote Empire product sales." Regal promptly began promoting and selling Empire products, and sales were very good. During summer 2018, Regal discovered that some contractors who had previously purchased Empire roofing material from Regal were now buying the Empire products from Suburban Roofing Co., located just outside the Megatown city limits. Moreover, it became clear to Regal that Suburban was buying Empire products at a lower price than the published wholesale price that Regal was paying. When Regal asked Empire about these sales, Empire responded that it had the legal right to sell to Suburban. Would Regal be likely to succeed in a lawsuit against Empire for breach of contract?
   A. No, because the contract did not expressly ban sales outside the Megatown city limits.
   B. No, because the contract would not be enforceable since it contained only an illusory promise by Regal to use best efforts to promote sales.
   C. Yes, because sales by Empire to a competitor just outside the Megatown city limits at a reduced price would frustrate Regal's reasonable expectations under the contract.
   D. Yes, because Empire would be equitably estopped from selling its products to Suburban without the consent of Regal.

3. Edna lost her job in June 2018 after a reduction in staff by her employer. Edna soon applied for two job openings – one as an accounting assistant at Acme Manufacturing Co. and a second as a sales clerk at Best Box Store. Edna interviewed for both jobs and was offered both positons. She decided to accept the position with Acme, effective July 1, 2018. The personnel manager gave Edna a document entitled, "Acme Employee Retention Policy." Part of the document stated that, "all employees are probationary for 90 days and then become permanent employees, eligible to participate in the employee retirement plan." Edna began work and received "excellent" ratings from her supervisor, Sally, for each of her first three quarterly evaluations. On April 7, 2019, Edna had a heated argument with Sally during

lunch about the upcoming presidential election. Edna was suddenly terminated one week later by Sally with the only stated reason being "unsatisfactory performance." If Edna can establish that she was terminated because of the argument, would she be likely to prevail in a lawsuit about her firing?

A. Yes, because Edna's status as a "permanent" employee would mean that she could be let go only for just cause.
B. Yes, because Edna's termination for exercising her right to freedom of speech would be a wrongful discharge in violation of public policy.
C. Yes, because Edna detrimentally relied on the job offer from Acme in turning down the job offer from Best Box Store.
D. No, because Edna would be an at-will employee, subject to termination without just cause.

4. Vern Vendor owned a road paving construction business. He had a used road grader that he no longer needed and decided to offer for sale. Vern advertised the road grader for sale through a listing service for industrial equipment. In August 2018, Bob Buyer contracted Vern about buying the road grader. After some negotiations, Bob agreed to buy the road grader for $325,000. On August 15, 2018, Vern and Bob both signed a brief standard form sales agreement which accurately described the road grader and stated the purchase price. In a space designated, "Date for performance," Bob wrote in, "payment and delivery after Buyer obtains financing." On October 15, 2018, Vern called Bob and asked if the financing had been arranged. Bob responded that he had decided to delay buying the road grader until June 2019 and would let Vern know when he was ready to take delivery. Would Vern have a viable legal claim that Bob was in breach of the contract by delaying performance until June 2019?

A. Yes, because the law would imply a reasonable time to obtain financing since the contract did not specify a date and nine months would be too long in this context.
B. Yes, because the absence of a specific payment and delivery date would give Vern, as seller, the unilateral option of setting a date for performance.
C. No, because the failure to include a date for payment and delivery would render Bob's promise to purchase illusory.
D. No, because the failure to include a deadline for obtaining financing would make the contract an option agreement for Bob.

5. Hugh owned a hotel in Maintown and wanted to make major renovations of the facility. On July 2, 2018, First Bank agreed to make a short-term construction loan of $1 million that would be repayable in six months or at the end of construction, whichever came earlier. Hugh applied to Second Bank for long-term financing of $1 million, repayable over 15 years, to be provided upon completion of work. Second Bank agreed to make the long-term loan at an interest rate of 4 percent but insisted on including an addendum to the loan agreement that read, "Second Bank's obligation to fund the loan is conditioned upon satisfactory monthly progress reports and final certificate of approval issued by an architect named by Second Bank verifying

that all work is of adequate quality." From August through December 2018, the architect issued monthly reports verifying that construction on the hotel met the required quality standards. In early January 2019, Second Bank announced that it was reducing its commercial loan portfolio because residential lending was more profitable. Shortly thereafter, the architect issued a final report on Hugh's hotel which stated that the renovations were not of adequate quality but stated no specific problems that could be corrected. Hugh has read reliable news reports that Second Bank is attempting to withdraw from all pending construction loan agreements. Would Hugh be likely to prevail in an action against Second Bank for breach of the loan agreement?

A. Yes, because Second Bank drafted the addendum and thus it would be construed to require objective dissatisfaction by the architect.
B. Yes, because of the strong evidence that the architect did not act independently and in good faith in refusing the final certificate of approval.
C. No, because the condition of satisfaction would be construed to grant to the architect completely unfettered discretion to approve or disapprove the work.
D. No, because the inclusion of the condition of satisfaction would render the loan agreement too uncertain to be enforceable.

CHAPTER 7

Avoiding Enforcement: Incapacity, Bargaining Misconduct, Unconscionability, and Public Policy

In Chapter 4 we saw that, under the statute of frauds, the failure of the parties to execute a writing may render an agreement unenforceable unless some exception to the statute is applicable. The requirement of *form* expressed by the statute of frauds (and by such other formalities as the parol evidence rule) reflects certain policies. (Recall the evidentiary, cautionary, and channelling functions of formalities discussed by Professor Fuller, reprinted after the *Pennsy Supply* case in Chapter 2.) In this chapter we turn our attention to other grounds for avoiding enforcement of an agreement. The doctrines examined in this chapter reflect policies somewhat different from those on which the statute of frauds is based: a concern with the *competency* of parties to make an agreement, with the *bargaining process* by which an agreement is reached, and with the *substance* of any resulting agreement.

We have seen that modern courts have shown an increasing willingness to expand the scope of contractual obligation, both to rectify unjust enrichment and to redress injury resulting from detrimental reliance. Similarly, courts have broadened their role in interpreting agreements and in implying contractual provisions, to produce what the courts consider to be just outcomes. We will see a similar trend in the following materials, a widening of the grounds for avoiding enforcement of an agreement from those that existed during the classical period. As you study these materials, consider whether this expansion is desirable, or whether, as some critics contend, it is likely to produce arbitrary results that threaten the efficiency of the market system.

A. MINORITY AND MENTAL INCAPACITY

PROBLEM 7-1

You have an appointment with new clients, James and Mary Swan, owners of Swan's Used Auto Sales. The Swans told you over the telephone that they have a problem with a young man, Bob Byers, to whom they sold a car 12 months ago. They tell you that Bob is trying to cancel the deal because he was only 17 at the time that he purchased the car in August 2018. The Swans tell you that they have checked their records and Bob completed a portion of the purchase agreement by indicating that his date of birth was March 1, 2000. Bob is now stating that his date of birth is March 1, 2001, and he is demanding return of the sales price of $6,000. At the same time, Bob has told the Swans that the car is no longer operable and that the Swans should have the car towed from the street in front of Bob's home. Read the following case and accompanying notes and identify the factual questions and legal issues that you will need to pursue in advising the Swans. Your professor may elect to provide you with further instructions.

Dodson v. Shrader

Supreme Court of Tennessee 824 S.W.2d 545 (1992)

O'BRIEN, Justice.

This is an action to disaffirm the contract of a minor for the purchase of a pick-up truck and for a refund of the purchase price. The issue is whether the minor is entitled to a full refund of the money he paid or whether the seller is entitled to a setoff for the decrease in value of the pick-up truck while it was in the possession of the minor.

In early April of 1987, Joseph Eugene Dodson, then 16 years of age, purchased a used 1984 pick-up truck from Burns and Mary Shrader. The Shraders owned and operated Shrader's Auto Sales in Columbia, Tennessee. Dodson paid $4,900 in cash for the truck, using money he borrowed from his girlfriend's grandmother. At the time of the purchase there was no inquiry by the Shraders, and no misrepresentation by Mr. Dodson, concerning his minority. However, Mr. Shrader did testify that at the time he believed Mr. Dodson to be 18 or 19 years of age.

In December 1987, nine (9) months after the date of purchase, the truck began to develop mechanical problems. A mechanic diagnosed the problem as a burnt valve, but could not be certain without inspecting the valves inside the engine. Mr. Dodson did not want, or did not have the money, to effect these repairs. He continued to drive the truck despite the mechanical problems. One month later, in January, the truck's engine "blew up" and the truck became inoperable.

Mr. Dodson parked the vehicle in the front yard at his parents' home where he lived. He contacted the Shraders to rescind the purchase of the truck and requested a full refund. The Shraders refused to accept the tender of the truck or to give Mr. Dodson the refund requested.

Mr. Dodson then filed an action in general sessions court seeking to rescind the contract and recover the amount paid for the truck. The general sessions court dismissed the warrant and Mr. Dodson perfected a de novo appeal to the circuit court. At the time the appeal was filed in the circuit court Mr. Shrader, through counsel, declined to accept the tender of the truck without compensation for its depreciation. Before the circuit court could hear the case, the truck, while parked in Dodson's front yard, was struck on the left front fender by a hit-and-run driver. At the time of the circuit court trial, according to Shrader, the truck was worth only $500 due to the damage to the engine and the left front fender.

The case was heard in the circuit court in November 1988. The trial judge, based on previous common-law decisions and, under the doctrine of stare decisis reluctantly granted the rescission. The Shraders were ordered, upon tender and delivery of the truck, to reimburse the $4,900 purchase price to Mr. Dodson. The Shraders appealed.

The Court of Appeals, per TODD, J., affirmed; CANTRELL, J., concurring separately, KOCH, J., dissenting.

The earliest recorded case in this State, on the issue involved, appears to be in Wheaton v. East, 13 Tenn. 35 (5 Yeager 41) (1833). In pronouncing the rule to apply governing infant's contracts, the court [quoted]:

> . . . "that when the court can pronounce the contract to be to the infant's prejudice, it is void, and when to his benefit, as for necessaries, it is good; and when the contract is of any uncertain nature, as to benefit or prejudice, it is voidable only, at the election of the infant."

The law on the subject of the protection of infant's rights has been slow to evolve. However, in Human v. Hartsell, 24 Tenn. App. 678, 148 S.W.2d 634, 636 (1940) the Court of Appeals noted:

> . . . In Tuck v. Payne, 159 Tenn. 192, 17 S.W.2d 8, in an opinion by Mr. Justice McKinney, the modern rule that contracts of infants are not void but only voidable and subject to be disaffirmed by the minor either before or after attaining majority appears to have been favored.
>
> Under this rule the efforts of early authorities to classify contracts as beneficial or harmful and determine whether they are void or only voidable upon the basis of such classification are abandoned in favor of permitting the infant himself when he has become of age to determine what contracts are and what are not to his interest and liking. He is thus permitted to assume the burden of a contract, clearly disadvantageous to him, if he deems himself under a moral obligation to do so.
>
> The adoption of this rule does not lead to any retrenchment of the infant's rights but gives him the option of invoking contracts found to be advantageous but which, if held void, could not be enforced against the other party to the contract. Thus the minor can secure the advantage of contracts advantageous to himself and be relieved of the effect of an injudicious contract.
>
> . . .

As noted by the Court of Appeals, the rule in Tennessee, as modified, is in accord with the majority rule on the issue among our sister states. This rule is based upon the underlying purpose of the "infancy doctrine" which is to protect minors from their lack of judgment and "from squandering their wealth through improvident contracts with crafty adults who would take advantage of them in the marketplace." Halbman v. Lemke, 99 Wis. 2d 241, 245, 298 N.W.2d 562, 564 (1980).

There is, however, a modern trend among the states, either by judicial action or by statute, in the approach to the problem of balancing the rights of minors against those of innocent merchants. As a result, two (2) minority rules have developed which allow the other party to a contract with a minor to refund less than the full consideration paid in the event of rescission.

The first of these minority rules is called the "Benefit Rule." E.g., Hall v. Butterfield, 59 N.H. 354 (1879); Johnson v. Northwestern Mut. Life Insurance Co., 56 Minn. 365, 59 N.W. 992 (1894); Berglund v. American Multigraph Sales Co., 135 Minn. 67, 160 N.W. 191 (1916); Porter v. Wilson, 106 N.H. 270, 209 A.2d 730 (1965); Valencia v. White, 134 Ariz. 139, 654 P.2d 287 (Ariz. App. 1982). The rule holds that, upon rescission, recovery of the full purchase price is subject to a deduction for the minor's use of the merchandise. This rule recognizes that the traditional rule in regard to necessaries has been extended so far as to hold an infant bound by his contracts, where he failed to restore what he has received under them to the extent of the benefit actually derived by him from what he has received from the other party to the transaction. . . .

The other minority rule holds that the minor's recovery of the full purchase price is subject to a deduction for the minor's "use" of the consideration he or she received under the contract, or for the "depreciation" or "deterioration" of the consideration in his or her possession. See . . . Pettit v. Liston, 97 Or. 464, 191 P. 660 (1920).

We are impressed by the statement made by the Arizona Appeals Court in Valencia v. White, supra, citing the Court of Appeals of Ohio in Haydocy Pontiac Inc. v. Lee, 19 Ohio App. 2d 217, 250 N.E.2d 898 (1969):

> At a time when we see young persons between 18 and 21 years of age demanding and assuming more responsibilities in their daily lives; when we see such persons emancipated, married, and raising families; when we see such persons charged with the responsibility for committing crimes; when we see such persons being sued in tort claims for acts of negligence; when we see such persons subject to military service; when we see such persons engaged in business and acting in almost all other respects as an adult, it seems timely to re-examine the case law pertaining to contractual rights and responsibilities of infants to see if the law as pronounced and applied by the courts should be redefined.

. . . Upon serious reflection we are convinced that a modified form of the Oregon rule should be adopted in this State concerning the rights and responsibilities of minors in their business dealings. . . .

We state the rule to be followed hereafter, in reference to a contract of a minor, to be where the minor has not been overreached in any way, and there has been no undue influence, and the contract is a fair and reasonable one, and the minor has actually paid money on the purchase price, and taken and used the article purchased, that he ought not to be permitted to recover the amount actually paid, without allowing the vendor of the goods reasonable compensation for the use of, depreciation, and willful or negligent damage to the article purchased, while in his hands. If there has been any fraud or imposition on the part of the seller or if the contract is unfair, or any unfair advantage has been taken of the minor inducing him to make the purchase, then the rule does not apply. Whether there has been such an overreaching on the part of the seller, and the fair market value of the property returned, would always, in any case, be a question for the trier of fact. This rule will fully and fairly protect the minor against injustice or imposition, and at the same time it will be fair to a business person who has dealt with such minor in good faith.

This rule is best adapted to modern conditions under which minors are permitted to, and do in fact, transact a great deal of business for themselves, long before they have reached the age of legal majority. Many young people work and earn money and collect it and spend it oftentimes without any oversight or restriction. The law does not question their right to buy if they have the money to pay for their purchases. It seems intolerably burdensome for everyone concerned if merchants and business people cannot deal with them safely, in a fair and reasonable way. Further, it does not appear consistent with practice of proper moral influence upon young people, tend to encourage honesty and integrity, or lead them to a good and useful business future, if they are taught that they can make purchases with their own money, for their own benefit, and after paying for them, and using them until they are worn out and destroyed, go back and compel the vendor to return to them what they have paid upon the purchase price. Such a doctrine can only lead to the corruption of principles and encourage young people in habits of trickery and dishonesty. . . .

We note that in this case, some nine (9) months after the date of purchase, the truck purchased by the plaintiff began to develop mechanical problems. Plaintiff was informed of the probable nature of the difficulty which apparently involved internal problems in the engine. He continued to drive the vehicle until the engine "blew up" and the truck became inoperable. Whether or not this involved gross negligence or intentional conduct on his part is a matter for determination at the trial level. It is not possible to determine from this record whether a counterclaim for tortious damage to the vehicle was asserted. After the first tender of the vehicle was made by plaintiff, and refused by the defendant, the truck was damaged by a hit-and-run driver while parked on plaintiff's property. The amount of that damage and the liability for that amount between the purchaser and the vendor, as well as the fair market value of the vehicle at the time of tender, is also an issue for the trier of fact.

The case is remanded to the trial court for further proceedings in accordance with this judgment. The costs on appellate review are assessed equally between the parties.

REID, C.J. and DROWOTA, DAUGHTREY and ANDERSON, JJ., concur.

NOTES AND QUESTIONS

1. *Traditional infancy or minority doctrine.* The *Dodson* court begins its analysis by recognizing the traditional rule that allows a minor to disaffirm or avoid a contract, even if there has been full performance and the minor cannot return to the adult what was received in the exchange. See E. Allan Farnsworth, Contracts §§4.4-4.5, at 222-227 (4th ed. 2004). Thus, if the minor received services that cannot be returned or the minor received goods that have since lost value, courts have allowed disaffirmance and required the minor to return only what the minor still possesses or any identifiable proceeds. The court in Halbman v. Lemke, 298 N.W.2d 562 (Wis. 1980), cited by the *Dodson* court, applied the traditional rule in holding that a minor who disaffirmed a contract for the purchase of an automobile was not required to make restitution to the seller for the substantial diminution in value of the vehicle, absent a showing that the minor misrepresented his age or willfully destroyed the property. The Court stated: "[W]e believe that to require a disaffirming minor to make restitution for diminished value is, in effect, to bind the minor to a part of the obligation which by law he is privileged to avoid." Id. at 567.

The *Dodson* court, however, departs from the traditional rule and adopts an approach that requires a disaffirming minor to pay "reasonable compensation for the use of, depreciation, and willful or negligent damage to the article purchased, while in his hands," at least when the minor is seeking return of the payment. Are you persuaded that the traditional rule has become outdated and that a disaffirming minor should be obligated to pay for any benefit received?

2. *The minority doctrine in the Internet world.* E.K.D. v. Facebook, Inc., 885 F. Supp. 2d 894 (S.D. Ill. 2012), involved a class action by minor plaintiffs claiming that Facebook's terms and conditions, which allowed Facebook to use a subscriber's name, profile picture, and "likes" for advertising, violated state privacy laws. The plaintiffs claimed that the forum selection provision designating Santa Clara, California, as exclusive judicial venue was unenforceable because they were minors when they clicked the "agreed" button and began using Facebook. Similar to the holding in *Dodson*, the *E.K.D.* court stated that a minor must accept or repudiate the entire contract; a minor cannot keep the benefits of the contract by continuing to use Facebook while rejecting a provision (in this case the forum selection clause) that the minor finds burdensome. Under the traditional minority doctrine, however, the fact that the minor has benefited from the service in the past is not grounds to deny the minor the right to avoid the contract. See T. K. v. Adobe Systems Inc., 2018 WL 1812200 (N.D. Cal.) (under California law minor could disaffirm entire contract with arbitration clause after using Internet service for fourteen months without making restitution for benefit received); Cheryl B. Preston, CyberInfants, 39 Pepp. L. Rev. 225, 232-233 (2012).

Notably, after the *E.K.D.* court rejected the plaintiffs' minority argument, it found that Facebook's forum selection clause was reasonable and enforceable, relying on the Supreme Court's decision in Carnival Cruise Lines, Inc. v. Shute, 499 U.S. 585 (1991), where the Court held that a forum selection clause in a cruise ticket that purported to bind the passenger to exclusive jurisdiction in Florida was enforceable against the plaintiff, a resident of the state of Washington, who was injured during a cruise from Los Angeles to Mexico. For criticism of the case see Charles L. Knapp, Contract Law Walks the Plank: Carnival Cruise Lines, Inc. v. Shute, 12 Nev. L.J. 553 (2012).

3. *Liability for "necessaries" and tortious conduct.* Even under the traditional rule, the right of a minor to avoid a contract has been subject to an important limitation: The minor is liable for the reasonable value of "necessaries." The recovery for the adult allowed in these cases, however, is based on restitution rather than enforcement of the contract. See Garay v. Overholtzer, 631 A.2d 429 (Md. 1993); Restatement (Second) §12, Comment *f.* Necessaries usually have been limited to items that one needs to live, such as food, clothing, and shelter. Some courts have been willing to construe the concept more broadly. See Zelnick v. Adams, 561 S.E.2d 711 (Va. 2002) (contract for legal services may be a necessary if needed to protect rights of minor; legal services to protect inheritance rights could be a necessary depending on facts).

As suggested by the materials in Note 1, the minor's ability to disaffirm may also be restricted if the minor engages in tortious conduct such as misrepresentation of age or willful destruction of goods. Some courts deny a minor's claim for disaffirmance after the minor has misrepresented his age, others will allow disaffirmance despite misrepresentation of age, while a third group allows disaffirmance with potential tort liability. See Cheryl B. Preston & Brandon T. Crowther, Infancy Doctrine Inquiries, 52 Santa Clara L. Rev. 47, 59-62 (2012).

4. *Ratification after reaching majority.* Even if a minor enters into a contract that does not involve necessaries, the contract is not void but only "voidable" at the election of the minor. Restatement (Second) §14. Once the minor reaches the age of majority, she has the power to affirm or ratify the contract, in which event the minor is bound. Moreover, on reaching the age of majority, the minor must act within a reasonable period of time to disaffirm the contract or she will be deemed to have affirmed the transaction. Compare Lopez v. Kmart Corporation, 2015 WL 2062606 (N.D. Cal.) (minor disaffirmed employment contract by filing lawsuit within one month of reaching majority, a reasonable time "by any measure"), with In re The Score Board, Inc., 238 B.R. 585 (Bankr. D.N.J. 1999) (professional basketball player Kobe Bryant, who signed contract while a minor but accepted payment and performed autograph signing duties for more than 18 months after reaching majority, held to have ratified contract).

5. *Statutory limits on the minority doctrine.* Legislative reduction of the age of majority from 21 to 18 in many states has, of course, curtailed the amount of litigation involving minors' contracts. Some statutory provisions may apply to validate specific types of contracts made by a person even before reaching the age of majority. See, e.g., Sharon v. City of Newton, 769 N.E.2d 738 (Mass. 2002) (detailing Massachusetts state laws allowing minors to contract for education financing, life insurance, motor vehicle liability insurance, drug dependency treatment, and medical or dental care). On the other hand, some

statutory provisions may declare certain contracts by minors to be void (rather than voidable). For example, in California a minor cannot give a delegation of power, make a contract relating to real estate or any interest therein, or make a contract relating to personal property not in the immediate possession or control of the minor. See Cal. Fam. Code §6701.

6. *Avoidance of employment contract provisions.* In a number of cases raising issues similar to those in *Dodson*, courts have been divided on the question whether a minor should be allowed to disaffirm an employment agreement after the minor has received benefits derived from being employed. Compare Robinson v. Food Service, 415 F. Supp. 2d 1227 (D. Kan. 2005) (holding Kansas state courts would not allow minors to disaffirm employment contracts that on the whole had been beneficial) with PAK Foods Houston, LLC v. Garcia, 433 S.W.3d 171 (Tex. Ct. App. 2014) (minor employee allowed to rescind employment contract and avoid arbitration provision by disaffirmance in connection with filing of lawsuit against employer while still a minor). You should note that a minor may allege that an arbitration agreement is unenforceable for other reasons that will be discussed further in section D of this chapter on the unconscionability doctrine.

7. *Pre- and postinjury release agreements.* Sponsors of youth recreational activities such as soccer, little league baseball, gymnastics, or skiing, frequently require releases from liability for personal injury as a precondition to children being permitted to participate. Many courts have held that minors are able to disaffirm such preinjury exculpatory agreements signed by the parent. See, e.g., Galloway v. State of Iowa, 790 N.W.2d 252 (Iowa 2010) (public policy precludes parent's pre-injury waiver of child's claim for negligence while on field trip). On the other hand, the court in Zivich v. Mentor Soccer Club, Inc., 696 N.E.2d 201 (Ohio 1998), held that the minor could not disaffirm a release agreement signed by his parent before engaging in soccer play. In deciding to allow the parent to bind the minor to a preinjury release, the Ohio Supreme Court asserted that enforcement of the release supports two policy concerns: encouraging volunteer programs that promote organized recreational activities for children and recognition of the liberty interest of parents in making life choices for children. Id. at 205-206.

Postinjury settlement agreements on behalf of minors will typically involve the execution of a release of the minor's claims. In most jurisdictions, settlements by minors must be approved by a court and may not be later disaffirmed. See, e.g., Wreglesworth v. Arctco, Inc., 738 N.E.2d 964 (Ill. App. Ct. 2000).

8. *Emancipation.* Minors who are emancipated are generally treated as adults for contracting purposes. In most states, the bases for emancipation are established by statute, but they typically include permanent abandonment of the parents' home, military service, or marriage. See Cheryl B. Preston & Brandon T. Crowther, Infancy Doctrine Inquiries, 52 Santa Clara L. Rev. 47, 55-58 (2012); but see Mitchell v. Mitchell, 963 S.W.2d 222 (Ky. Ct. App. 1998) (emancipation through marriage does not confer capacity to contract; minor's marriage frequently may indicate lack of wisdom and maturity).

Sparrow v. Demonico

Supreme Judicial Court of Massachusetts 461 Mass. 322, 960 N.E.2d 296 (2012)

Opinion by: DUFFLY

A family dispute over ownership of what had been the family home in Woburn prompted Frances M. Sparrow to file a complaint in the Superior Court against her sister, Susan A. Demonico, and Susan's husband, David D. Demonico. Prior to trial, the parties resolved their differences by a settlement agreement reached during voluntary mediation. When Sparrow sought an order enforcing the agreement, a Superior Court judge denied her motion, concluding in essence that, due to mental impairment, Susan lacked the capacity to contract at the time of agreement. . . .

We granted . . . appellate review to consider whether a party can establish that she lacked the capacity to contract, thus making the contract voidable by her, in the absence of evidence that she suffered from a medically diagnosed, long-standing mental illness or defect. We conclude that our evolving standard of contractual incapacity does not in all cases require proof that a party's claimed mental illness or defect was of some significant duration or that it is permanent, progressive, or degenerative; but, without medical evidence or expert testimony that the mental condition interfered with the party's understanding of the transaction, or her ability to act reasonably in relation to it, the evidence will not be sufficient to support a conclusion of incapacity. Because the evidence was insufficient to support a determination of incapacity in this case, we vacate the motion judge's order and remand for entry of an order enforcing the settlement agreement.

BACKGROUND

Sparrow's complaint, filed initially in July, 2003, and later amended, alleged that Sparrow was entitled to a one-half interest in the Woburn property, consistent with the wishes of her (and Susan's) now-deceased mother, under theories of constructive and resulting trusts. Susan, who resided in the Woburn property at the time of the mediation, and David, who had been separated from Susan for several years and was no longer residing with her, asserted that they were the sole owners of the property, as reflected in a deed, and denied that Sparrow had any interest in it. Shortly before what was scheduled to be a final pretrial conference, the parties sought to achieve a settlement through voluntary mediation and the matter was removed from the trial list.

The parties and the attorneys who were representing them in the Superior Court proceeding participated in mediation on October 19, 2006. Sparrow contends that the case was settled during this mediation by an agreement that the Demonicos would sell the property and pay Sparrow $100,000 from the sale proceeds. When Sparrow sought an order enforcing the agreement, alleging that the Demonicos "reneged on their obligations under it," the Demonicos claimed that the agreement was unenforceable because Susan had, in their view, experienced a mental breakdown during the mediation and thus lacked the capacity to authorize settlement. At an evidentiary hearing on the motion, David and Susan were the only witnesses and no exhibits were admitted, although they were marked for identification. The motion judge denied Sparrow's motion on the basis that "the purported agreement may have been the product of an emotionally overwrought state of mind on the part of Susan Demonico."[6] The case proceeded to trial by jury before a different judge, who, at the close of evidence, allowed the Demonicos's motion for a directed verdict on all counts. Sparrow appealed from the judgment and the denial of her motion to enforce the mediated settlement agreement.

Findings of Fact

We summarize the motion judge's subsidiary findings of fact, which we accept as not clearly erroneous . . . and include additional details from evidence that the judge implicitly credited. . . .

On the date of the scheduled mediation, Susan drove from her home to David's residence. From there, David drove them to the location of the mediation session because, in David's view, Susan was not capable of driving to the mediation. The mediation began at approximately 9 A.M. and ended at 3 P.M. The judge, crediting David's testimony, found:

> Susan was having a breakdown that day, according to David, and was slurring her words, although she had not had any alcoholic beverages on that day. She became less coherent throughout the day, was crying and out of control. . . . They left the mediation before it was over as Susan could not handle it.

The judge noted Susan's testimony that she had been taking a medication, Zoloft, prior to the mediation, but that she had stopped taking the medication at some point before the mediation, and that she cried much of the day; he specifically credited Susan's testimony that she "was out of control emotionally during the mediation" and found also that "she was not thinking rationally" on that day.

As noted, both sides were represented by counsel throughout the mediation. At some point before they departed from the mediation session, the Demonicos authorized their attorney to execute a settlement agreement on their behalf.[8] According to the terms of a written agreement titled, "Memorandum of Settlement," which was signed by Sparrow, her attorney, and the Demonicos's attorney, and witnessed by the mediator, the Demonicos agreed to pay Sparrow

---

6. No party has raised any question as to the effect of the order on David. David has made no claim that he suffered from any incapacity or that the terms of the agreement are unreasonable. It is not at all clear from the evidence that an agreement void as to Susan because of her incapacity would also be void as to David. The practical consequences of such an order might depend on the nature of the title in which the property is held or whether Susan and David obtain a judgment of divorce. Deciding as we do, these questions need not detain us.

8. The Demonicos have at no time raised any defenses regarding their attorney's authorization to sign the mediated settlement agreement on their behalf. See *Colley v. Benson, Young & Downs Ins. Agency, Inc.* 42 Mass. App. Ct. 527, 534-535, 678 N.E.2d 440 (1997) (describing affirmative burden to demonstrate that counsel not authorized to act on party's behalf). See also *Carey v. New England Organ Bank,* 446 Mass. 270, 285, 843 N.E.2d 1070 (2006) (alternate defenses not raised before trial judge are waived).

"the settlement amount of $100,000.00" from the proceeds of the sale of the property, which would occur "as soon as practicable," and in any event within a specified timeframe. The agreement also set forth other affirmative requirements regarding the marketing and sale of the property.

Discussion

A settlement agreement is a contract and its enforceability is determined by applying general contract law. *Warner Ins. Co. v. Commissioner of Ins.,* 406 Mass. 354, 360 n.7, 548 N.E.2d 188 (1990). It has been long established that a contract is voidable by a person who, due to mental illness or defect, lacked the capacity to contract at the time of entering into the agreement[9]. . . . The burden is on the party seeking to void the contract to establish that the person was incapacitated at the time of the transaction. . . . See *Wright v. Wright,* 139 Mass. 177, 182, 29 N.E. 380 (1885).

a. Standard for Determining Contractual Incapacity

As Justice Holmes observed, it is a question of fact whether a person was competent to enter into a transaction — that is, whether the person suffered from "insanity" or "was of unsound mind, and incapable of understanding and deciding upon the terms of the contract." Id. at 182-183. In *Reed v. Mattapan Deposit & Trust Co.,* 198 Mass. 306, 314, 84 N.E. 469 (1908), we described this inquiry as the "true test" of mental incapacity:

> But while great mental weakness of the individual may exist without being accompanied by an entire loss of reason, and mental incapacity in one case is not necessarily so in another, in such an inquiry the true test is, was the party whose contract it is sought to avoid in such a state of insanity at the time as to render him incapable of transacting the business. When this fact is established the contract is voidable by the lunatic or his representatives, and it is no defense under our decisions that the other party acted fairly and without knowledge of his unsoundness or of any circumstances which ought to have put him upon inquiry.

We applied this test, also known as the "cognitive test," see *Ortelere v. Teachers' Retirement Bd. of the City of N.Y.,* 25 N.Y.2d 196, 202, 250 N.E.2d 460, 303 N.Y.S.2d 362 (1969) *(Ortelere),* without significant modification for fifty years thereafter. See . . . *Adams v. Whitmore,* 245 Mass. 65, 68, 139 N.E. 831 (1923) (incapacity requires proof that person "was too weak in mind to execute the deed with

---

9. The capacity to contract is distinct from testamentary capacity, in which different considerations control the analysis. See *Krasner v. Berk,* 366 Mass. 464, 468, 319 N.E.2d 897 (1974) (upholding finding of incapacity to contract, while noting that the evidence would support a finding of testamentary capacity); *Maimonides Sch. v. Coles,* 71 Mass. App. Ct. 240, 251, 881 N.E.2d 778 (2008), quoting *Palmer v. Palmer,* 23 Mass. App. Ct. 245, 250, 500 N.E.2d 1354 (1986) (in contrast to more demanding test for contractual capacity, standard for testamentary capacity requires ability at time of execution of alleged will to comprehend nature of act of making will); *Farnum v. Silvano,* 27 Mass. App. Ct. 536, 538, 540 N.E.2d 202 (1989) (acting during lucid interval can be basis for executing will but "competence to enter into a contract presupposes something more than a transient surge of lucidity").

understanding of its meaning, effect and consequences"); *Sutcliffe v. Heatley,* 232 Mass. 231, 232, 122 N.E. 317 (1919) (test is whether person "could not understand the nature and quality of the transaction or grasp its significance").

Over time, however, the traditional test for contractual incapacity, both in Massachusetts, see *Krasner v. Berk,* 366 Mass. 464, 467-468, 319 N.E.2d 897 (1974), and in other jurisdictions, see, e.g., *Ortelere, supra,* evolved to incorporate an increased understanding of the nature of mental illness in its various forms. See *Matter of the Marriage of Davis,* 193 Ore. App. 279, 285-287, 89 P.3d 1206 (2004) (Deits, C.J., concurring) (discussing evolution of incapacity standards); 5 R.A. Lord, Williston on Contracts §10:8 at 341-343 (4th ed. 2009) (historically, little distinction made between different kinds of mental incompetency or illness; "[t]he law now recognizes a wide variety of types and degrees of mental incompetency and distinctions among the various types of mental illness"). Based on this understanding, we adopted a second, alternative test for incapacity.

In *Krasner v. Berk, supra,* we recognized that there may be circumstances when, although a party claiming incapacity has some, or sufficient, understanding of the nature and consequences of the transaction, the contract would still be voidable where, "by reason of mental illness or defect, [the person] is unable to act in a reasonable manner in relation to the transaction and the other party has reason to know of his condition." Id. at 468, citing *Ortelere, supra* at 204-205.[11] This modern test — also described as an "affective" or "volitional" test — recognizes that competence can be lost, not only through cognitive disorders, but through affective disorders that encompass motivation or exercise of will. See *Ortelere, supra* at 204-205, . . . See also *Gore v. Gadd,* 268 Ore. 527, 528-529, 522 P.2d 212 (1974) (under affective test, person such as one who is manic-depressive psychotic, although aware of nature and consequences of conduct, may still be considered incompetent because mental illness "impel[s person] to act irrationally" and such person is "incapable of making a rational judgment in the execution of the transaction").

Under this modern, affective test, "[w]here a person has some understanding of a particular transaction which is affected by mental illness or defect, the controlling consideration is whether the transaction in its result is one which a reasonably competent person might have made." *Krasner v. Berk, supra* at 469, . . . Also relevant to the inquiry in these circumstances is whether the party claiming mental incapacity was represented by independent, competent counsel. See *Willett v. Webster,* 337 Mass. 98, 103, 148 N.E.2d 267 (1958). Contrast *Farnum v. Silvano,* 27 Mass. App. Ct. 536, 537, 540, 540 N.E.2d 202 (1989) (plaintiff's mental competence had begun to fail several years before she delivered deed to

11. In *Ortelere v. Teachers' Retirement Bd. of the City of N.Y.,* 25 N.Y.2d 196, 199, 250 N.E.2d 460, 303 N.Y.S.2d 362 (1969) *(Ortelere),* although the decedent's psychosis was undisputed, it was not seriously disputed that "she had complete cognitive judgment or awareness when" she entered into the transaction. The court held that the contract was nonetheless voidable because "[a] modern understanding of mental illness . . . suggests that incapacity to contract or exercise contractual rights may exist, because of volitional and affective impediments or disruptions in the personality, despite the intellectual or cognitive ability to understand."

defendant; she was represented in transfer of real estate by lawyer selected and paid for by defendant, whose mission "was to effect the transaction," rather than to protect plaintiff's interests).[12]

b. Evidence of Contractual Incapacity

We begin by observing that the evidence required to support a finding of incapacity to contract, whether considered under the traditional or modern standard, need not in all cases demonstrate that a party suffers from a mental illness or defect that is permanent, degenerative, progressive, or of significant duration. Although such incapacity has historically been established by evidence of a long-standing mental illness, nothing in our jurisprudence requires such evidence. The inquiry as to the capacity to contract focuses on a party's understanding or conduct only at the time of the disputed transaction. See *Krasner v. Berk, supra* at 468; *Meserve v. Jordan Marsh Co.*, 340 Mass. 660, 662, 165 N.E.2d 905 (1960). Based on the evolving understanding of mental illness, we do not preclude the possibility that a party could establish an incapacity to contract without proof of a mental condition that is permanent, degenerative, progressive, or long standing.

The Demonicos contend that this is such a case; that the evidence established Susan's incapacity without showing a permanent, degenerative, progressive, or long-standing mental illness. They point to evidence that Susan's asserted mental impairment arose and was limited to the period of the mediation session, and argue that this evidence was sufficient to support a conclusion of incapacity, despite the lack of medical evidence or expert testimony as to the nature of Susan's mental impairment and its effect on her decision-making ability.

We have not previously addressed whether medical evidence is required to establish an incapacity to contract, and the Demonicos have not directed our attention to case law in other jurisdictions that would support their contention. In our prior decisions concerning the issue of incapacity to contract, however, evidence of mental illness or defect has been presented consistently through medical evidence, including the testimony of physicians and mental health providers or experts, in addition to lay testimony." Moreover, in other contexts, we have held that a lay witness is not competent to give an opinion as to mental condition. See *Commonwealth v. McDermott*, 393 Mass. 451, 454, 471 N.E.2d 1302 (1984). . . . Expanding on this analysis, we conclude that medical evidence is necessary to establish that a person lacked the capacity to contract due to the existence of a mental condition.

---

12. Additionally, we note that even where evidence of a weakened mental condition is not enough to support a conclusion that the party was "too weak in mind to execute the deed with understanding of its meaning, effect and consequences," this weakened mental condition has nevertheless been a factor "in determining whether advantage was taken of [the party] by misrepresentation, imposition or undue influence." *Adams v. Whitmore*, 245 Mass. 65, 68, 139 N.E. 831 (1923). Cf. *Meserve v. Jordan Marsh Co.*, 340 Mass. 660, 668, 165 N.E.2d 905 (1960) (noting that judge justified in concluding that "there was no undue influence, imposition, or misrepresentation"); [Green, Proof of Mental Incompetency and the Unexpressed Major Premise, 53 Yale L.J. 271, 307 (1944)] (noting "extremely intimate relationship between the concepts of fraud, undue influence, and mental incompetency. They are in a sense complementary and aid each other . . ."). No claim of undue influence, imposition, or misrepresentation has been made in this case, nor would such a claim have been supported by the evidence.

In other contexts, the reliance on medical and expert evidence is routine when addressing issues of mental illness, capacity, and competence. See, e.g., *Commonwealth v. DiPadova,* 460 Mass. 424, 426-428, 951 N.E.2d 891 (2011) (criminal responsibility); *O'Rourke v. Hunter,* 446 Mass. 814, 822, 848 N.E.2d 382 (2006) (testamentary capacity). See also *Vitek v. Jones,* 445 U.S. 480, 495, 100 S. Ct. 1254, 63 L. Ed. 2d 552 (1980), quoting *Addington v. Texas,* 441 U.S. 418, 429, 99 S. Ct. 1804, 60 L. Ed. 2d 323 (1979) (question of mental illness in civil commitment context is "essentially medical," which "turns on the meaning of facts which must be interpreted by expert psychiatrists and psychologists").

Where the issue is the capacity to contract, we have looked to medical providers or experts to explain whether, and to what extent, a person's mental condition has affected the ability to understand the nature of the transaction and its consequences, or to explain why, despite the intellectual and cognitive ability to understand, the person is unable to act reasonably in making the decision. See, e.g., *Krasner v. Berk, supra* at 466; *Meserve v. Jordan Marsh Co., supra* at 663-664. . . .

The inquiry in this area is in contrast to other areas of the law, such as tort claims of emotional distress or mental anguish, where the inquiry is whether the evidence supports a plaintiff's claim to have experienced emotional distress or mental anguish, rather than on the impact of that state on the ability to comprehend. See *Sullivan v. Boston Gas Co.,* 414 Mass. 129, 138, 605 N.E.2d 805 (1993). Yet even in the context of an action sounding in tort, we have often considered medical corroboration to be a highly probative, if not essential, component of a plaintiff's case. See id. at 137-138; . . . See also *Bresnahan v. McAuliffe,* 47 Mass. App. Ct. 278, 285, 712 N.E.2d 1173 (1999) (more difficult, but not impossible, for plaintiff to meet burden in absence of medical evidence). Such corroboration not only guards against feigned or fraudulent claims of mental distress, but also alleviates the concern "that even honest plaintiffs erroneously might convince themselves that they suffer from emotional distress . . . thereby compounding the problem of fraudulent lawsuits." *Sullivan v. Boston Gas Co., supra* at 133, citing *Payton v. Abbott Labs, supra* at 547. These concerns apply with at least equal force where the question is the capacity to contract due to mental impairment. See *Ortelere, supra* at 206 ("nothing less serious than medically classified psychosis should suffice or else few contracts would be invulnerable to some kind of psychological attack").

Here, there was lay evidence, credited by the judge, that Susan's speech was "slurr[ed]," that she was in a state of uncontrollable crying, and that she had experienced an inability to focus or "think rationally" throughout the day of the mediation. Susan testified also that she had recently discontinued taking the prescribed medication Zoloft. However, she presented no medical evidence regarding a diagnosis that would have required her to take the medication, or the effect, if any, that ceasing to take the medication would have had on her medical or mental condition. There was also no evidence that Susan's condition at the mediation was related to or caused by her discontinuing the medication.[14]

14. At the evidentiary hearing, defense counsel argued that Susan "testified to all of the classic symptoms" of discontinuing Zoloft: "anxiety, confusion, the inability to focus, crying, and loss of

"A non-expert is competent to testify to the physical appearance and condition and acts of a person both for their probative value for the jury and for the purpose of furnishing facts as the basis of hypothetical questions for experts." *Cox v. United States,* 103 F.2d 133, 135 (7th Cir. 1939). See *Brown v. United States Fid. & Guar. Co.* 336 Mass. 609, 614, 147 N.E.2d 160 (1958) (wife's testimony about nervous condition of husband prior to his death, although admissible as matter of common observation by lay person, not sufficient to prove whether disease was proximate or contributing cause of death). However, there was no expert or medical testimony to explain the effect of Susan's experiences or behavior on her ability to understand the agreement, to appreciate what was happening, or to comprehend the reasonableness of the settlement terms or the consequences to her of authorizing the settlement. Without such medical evidence, there was no basis to conclude that Susan lacked the capacity to contract. See *Farnum v. Silvano, supra* at 539-540 (plaintiff, who "suffered mental disease which had manifested itself in erratic and irrational conduct and was confirmed by diagnostic test," did not possess "requisite contextual understanding" of transaction). Contrast *Grindlinger v. Grindlinger,* 10 Mass. App. Ct. 823, 823, 406 N.E.2d 424 (1980) ("fatigue and anxiety" not sufficient to invalidate separation agreement).

The evidence did not support a conclusion that, under the traditional test for incapacity, Susan was incapable of understanding the nature and quality of the transaction, or of grasping its significance. Indeed, based on Susan's testimony, she understood at the time that she was participating in a mediation to discuss settlement of the lawsuit; she was aware that the subject of the mediation was to resolve the dispute regarding the family home in Woburn; she participated in the mediation and listened to the arguments of counsel; and she "couldn't believe how things [were] turning out."

It is apparent from Susan's testimony that, even if she suffered from a transient mental defect, or "breakdown" as the judge concluded, she had at least some understanding of the nature of the transaction and was aware of its consequences. Under the modern test to establish Susan's incapacity, the evidence was similarly insufficient. There was no evidence that the settlement agreement was unreasonable, or that a reasonably competent person would not have entered into it.[15]

---

memory." Not only was there no evidence presented to support the proposition that these are indeed "classic symptoms" associated with the cessation of Zoloft, but the Demonicos also failed to present any evidence linking such generalities to Susan's mental capacity. Contrary to the Demonicos's argument, it would not have been reasonable for the judge to infer that Susan was experiencing "possible withdrawal effects" based on the evidence presented.

15. . . . [T]here was no evidence as to the current market value of the property or whether any mortgages or other encumbrances would affect the reasonableness of the $100,000 settlement amount, . . . nor was there evidence that otherwise reasonable settlement terms were unreasonable in light of Susan's particular circumstances. Contrast *Farnum v. Silvano*, 27 Mass. App. Ct. 536, 540, 540 N.E.2d 202 (1989). There was also no evidence that Sparrow was, or should have been, aware of Susan's condition. Finally, there is no indication that Susan was not represented by independent, competent counsel in connection with the settlement agreement. Compare *M. DeMatteo Constr. Co. v. Daggett*, 341 Mass. 252, 260-261, 168 N.E.2d 276 (1960), with *Farnum v. Silvano*, supra.

Conclusion

Because the evidence does not support a conclusion that Susan lacked the mental capacity to authorize settlement on the day of the mediation, it was error to deny Sparrow's motion to enforce the agreement. The order denying the motion to enforce the mediated settlement agreement is vacated. The case is remanded to the Superior Court for entry of an order that the settlement agreement be enforced.

So ordered.

NOTES AND QUESTIONS

1. *Cognitive and volitional tests for incapacity and the requirement of medical testimony.* Even without a formal adjudication of incompetency, contract law provides that a person may lack contractual capacity, as recognized by the court in *Sparrow.* As the court discusses, the traditional test for incapacity was the "cognitive" test under which a person lacks capacity to enter into a contract if the person is unable to understand the nature of the transaction or its consequences. The more modern "volitional" test looks to whether the person is unable to act reasonably in the transaction and the other party has reason to know of the condition. The court relies on the *Ortelere* case decided by the New York Court of Appeals in 1969 for its adoption of the volitional test. The Restatement (Second) in §15 also follows the volitional test and includes the following illustration based on *Ortelere*:

> *A*, a school teacher, is a member of a retirement plan and has elected a lower monthly benefit in order to provide a benefit to her husband if she dies first. At age 60 she suffers a "nervous breakdown," takes a leave of absence, and is treated for cerebral arteriosclerosis. When the leave expires she applies for retirement, revokes her previous election, and elects a larger annuity with no death benefit. In view of her reduced life expectancy, the change is foolhardy, and there are no other circumstances to explain the change. She fully understands the plan, but by reason of mental illness is unable to make a decision based on the prospect of her dying before her husband. The officers of the plan have reason to know of her condition. Two months after the changed election she dies. The change of election is voidable.

Restatement (Second) §15, Illustration 1. Further understanding of the *Ortelere* case can be gained from Richard Danzig & Geoffrey R. Watson, The Capability Problem in Contract Law 242-306 (2d ed. 2004), which includes excerpts from the *Ortelere* trial transcript.

A dissenting judge in *Ortelere* expressed concern that any benefit gained by use of the volitional test would be "outweighed by frivolous claims which will burden our courts and undermine the security of contracts." Ortelere v. Teachers' Retirement Bd., 250 N.E.2d 460, 468 (N.Y. 1969) (Jasen, J., dissenting). The court's decision in *Sparrow* to require medical evidence or expert testimony to establish a claim of contractual incapacity is responsive to this concern. On the other hand, it could be argued that a strict requirement of medical evidence may be too expensive and burdensome, particularly when the case is relatively small. Moreover, the court's effort to distinguish tort claims of mental distress damages, which are not subject to a requirement of medical testimony, could be viewed as unpersuasive. Do you agree with the court's requirement of medical evidence or expert testimony to establish contractual incapacity? But see Whitlock v. Burke, 2018 WL 3482003 (Mass. Land Ct.) (interpreting *Sparrow* to require *medical evidence,* but not necessarily from a *medical doctor,* in assessing testimony from a clinical psychologist).

2. *Mental incapacity contrasted with minority doctrine.* The law concerning mental incapacity has a great deal in common with the minority doctrine concerning matters such as liability for necessaries and the possibility of disaffirmance or ratification. Regarding the obligation to make restoration of consideration upon disaffirmance, however, an important distinction between the traditional rules on minority doctrine and mental incapacity exists: the minor generally can disaffirm even if restoration cannot be made, but the mentally incompetent person is required to make restoration to the other party unless special circumstances are present. See Restatement (Second) §15(2). Are you persuaded that there is good justification for the different approaches to restitution in minority and mental incapacity cases?

3. *Effect of court-decreed guardianship.* Statutory law in each state establishes procedures by which a court on petition of a family member or other interested party can declare a person legally incompetent and appoint a guardian or conservator to care for the incompetent's person or property. E.g., Unif. Prob. Code, §§5-301 (guardian of person of incompetent), 5-401 (conservator of property of incompetent). The general rule is that a person does not have capacity to enter into contracts if the person's property is under conservatorship. Restatement (Second) §13. See Sun Trust Bank v. Harper, 551 S.E.2d 419 (Ga. Ct. App. 2002) (after being placed under guardianship by court, decedent lacked capacity to modify terms of retirement account notwithstanding alleged lucid moments); Huntington National Bank v. Toland, 594 N.E.2d 1103 (Ohio Ct. App. 1991) (though decedent maintained "sparkling" record in dealings with bank for four-year period before death, adjudication of mental incompetency 35 years earlier still rendered contract voidable unless ratified by guardian). While cases involving court-appointed guardians and/or conservators do arise, they are typically extreme situations.

4. *Vulnerability to misconduct by other parties.* In another type of case a party asserts not only lack of capacity but also a claim that the other party engaged in overreaching or other improper conduct. In such cases claims of incapacity are often combined with allegations of fraud, duress, or undue influence. An example is Farnum v. Silvano, 540 N.E.2d 202 (Mass. App. Ct. 1989), cited by the court in *Sparrow*, which involved a sale by an elderly plaintiff, Viola Farnum, of her home to the defendant for a price of $65,000 when the home had a fair market value of $115,000 and at a time when she had a growing need

for income. The defendant, who did yard work for the plaintiff, knew of the plaintiff's unstable mental condition, which manifested itself in a variety of ways, including the following:

> She would lament not hearing from sisters who were dead. She would wonder where the people upstairs in her house had gone, but there was no upstairs to her house. . . . She became abnormally forgetful. Frequently, she locked herself out of her house and broke into it, rather than calling on a neighbor with whom she had left a key. . . . She hid her cat to protect it from "the cops . . . looking for my cat." She would express a desire to return to Cape Cod although she was on Cape Cod. . . .

Id. at 203. Finding that the plaintiff lacked the mental capacity to enter into the contract and that the defendant was aware of this condition, the Court of Appeals ordered rescission of the contract. In light of this conclusion, the court found it unnecessary to consider the claims of fraud, undue influence, and constructive trust that Farnum had also advanced. See also footnote 12 in *Sparrow* where the court states that even when the evidence is insufficient to establish incapacity, evidence of a weakened mental state may be relevant to other legal theories seeking to show that advantage was taken of the weaker party.

5. *Burden of proof and relevant time for determining capacity.* As stated in *Sparrow*, the burden of proof is on the party seeking to avoid a contract. This burden may be difficult to carry. See In re Estate of Obermeier, 540 N.Y.S.2d 613 (App. Div. 1989) (fact that decedent resided in nursing home, was often confused, suffered from dementia, and was on sedatives did not prove lack of capacity at time of signing contract to sell real property); Rawlings v. John Hancock Mutual Life Ins. Co., 78 S.W.3d 291 (Tenn. Ct. App. 2001) (evidence that decedent was an alcoholic and suffered from depression and dementia was insufficient to prove that she did not have capacity to understand consequences or act in reasonable manner at particular time transaction was made).

6. *Mental incapacity in other areas of law.* The court states that incapacity to contract is subject to a more demanding standard of proof than lack of testamentary capacity. Why should this be so? In criminal cases, the traditional standard for mental capacity has been the M'Naghten test. M'Naghten's Case, 8 Eng. Rep. 718 (1843). Under this test a defendant lacks mental capacity to commit a crime if the defendant is unable to distinguish right from wrong. Rollin M. Perkins & Ronald Boyce, Criminal Law 958-963 (1982). The Model Penal Code recognizes incapacity as consisting of inability to either "appreciate the criminality" of conduct or "conform his conduct to the requirements of law." Model Penal Code §4.01 (1962). How do these standards compare to the standard for contractual capacity as expressed in §15 of the Restatement (Second)? Should it be easier or more difficult to establish incapacity in criminal prosecutions or breach of contract cases? Why?

7. *Incapacity resulting from intoxication.* The Restatement (Second) §16 provides that a contract is voidable if a party has reason to know that because of intoxication the other person is unable to either understand the transaction

or act in a reasonable manner. Comment *a* to the section states that "compulsive alcoholism" may be a form of mental illness but also recognizes that intoxication may be "voluntary." Should intoxication that is a temporary, self-induced condition affect a person's ability to disaffirm a contract? See Adamar of N.J., Inc. v. Luber, 2011 WL 1325978 (D.N.J.) (triable issue of fact whether defendant's $220,000 gambling debt was incurred while his judgment was so impaired by intoxication, to plaintiff's knowledge, as to render him incapable of consent); Miller v. Rhode Island Hospital, 625 A.2d 778 (R.I. 1993) (reversing trial court and holding intoxication can render a patient incompetent to give consent to treatment).

8. *Mediation in the practice of law.* You are probably already aware that many modern contracts contain provisions requiring any dispute related to the contract be resolved by binding arbitration. We consider such provisions in more detail later in this chapter, particularly on the issue of when they may be so one-sided as to be considered "unconscionable." However, *Sparrow* involves a different form of alternative dispute resolution that is probably even more common than arbitration – mediation. In fact, mediation has become so widespread that many lawyers devote a substantial portion of their practice to serving as mediators. Compared to litigation and arbitration, mediation is the least formal and least binding of the three. In mediation a neutral third party assists the parties in attempting to reach an agreement to resolve their dispute. Unlike a judge or an arbitrator, a mediator does not have the power to render a decision. Instead, the mediator is a facilitator. In the typical mediation after a joint session, where the parties make presentations to the mediator and each other, the mediator meets separately with the parties in a series of private meetings that can last for hours in small cases and weeks or longer in more complex ones. Skilled mediators can help the parties understand the other side's position, see weaknesses in their own positions, evaluate alternatives for compromise that they may not have considered, and make concessions to bridge the gaps between the parties. Mediation comes in two varieties: court ordered and voluntary. Many court systems require the parties to mediate any dispute before the case can proceed to trial. However, in court-ordered mediation parties are only required to bargain in good faith; they are not required to reach agreement. Even if the rules of court do not require mediation, parties may choose to do so in an attempt to avoid the time and expense of trial if possible. If a mediation results in an agreement, it will be reduced to writing and amounts to a contract, subject to the same requirements of other contracts. Thus, in *Sparrow* Susan Demonico claimed that the contract that resulted from the mediation in the case was unenforceable because of her incapacity at the time of the mediation.

Comment: Historical Development of the Law of Contractual Capacity

Quite early, the common law declared that certain classes of persons lacked "capacity" to contract. Alfred W. B. Simpson, A History of the Common Law of Contract 539-557 (1987). In the case of minors (also commonly referred to as "infants"), this restriction could be justified on the ground that they did not have the judgment to protect themselves in the marketplace. The same justification was not applicable to married women, however, who were also denied the right to contract at common law. Instead, the theory behind this restriction was that marriage resulted in the union of husband and wife into a single legal personality, that of the husband. As Professor Lawrence Friedman has put it, "husband and wife were one flesh; but the man was the owner of that flesh." Lawrence M. Friedman, A History of American Law (3d ed. 2005). During the nineteenth century, this legal disability was removed by the passage of the Married Women's Property Acts. See Richard H. Chused, Married Women's Property Law: 1800-1850, 71 Geo. L.J. 1359 (1983).

Statutory restrictions have also been imposed on the capacity of other persons to make contracts. During the period of legalized slavery in this country, many states enacted "Slave Codes," which denied enslaved persons legal capacity to contract for themselves. See Anthony R. Chase, Race, Culture, and Contract Law: From the Cottonfield to the Courtroom, 28 Conn. L. Rev. 1 (1995). During the same period, some states restricted the ability of free African-Americans to enter into certain types of contracts and exercise other civil rights. See John Hope Franklin and Alfred A. Moss, Jr., From Slavery to Freedom 141(8th ed. 2000); Steven A. Siegel, The Federal Government's Power to Enact Color-Conscious Laws: An Originalist Inquiry, 92 Nw. U. L. Rev. 477 (1998). Even after the Civil War and the end of legalized slavery, many states enacted "Black Codes," which continued to restrict the ability of African-Americans to make and enforce contracts. See John Hope Franklin and Alfred A. Moss, Jr., From Slavery to Freedom 250-251 (8th ed. 2000). Restrictions on contract and property rights have also been placed on other people of color, including Asian-Americans. See Angelo N. Ancheta, Race, Rights and the Asian American Experience (2d ed. 2006); Natsu Taylor Saito, Alien and Non-Alien Alike: Citizenship, "Foreignness," and Racial Hierarchy in American Law, 76 Or. L. Rev. 261 (1997). Some writers have discussed such restrictions on contract and property rights as part of a broader denial of "economic personality." See Adrienne D. Davis, The Private Law of Race and Sex: An Antebellum Perspective, 51 Stan. L. Rev. 221 (1999); Thomas W. Joo, New "Conspiracy Theory" of the Fourteenth Amendment: Nineteenth Century Chinese Civil Rights Cases and the Development of Substantive Due Process Jurisprudence, 29 U.S.F. L. Rev. 353 (1995). While such formal legal restrictions on the capacity to contract were largely removed with the enactment of federal and state civil rights laws, informal cultural and social barriers have been much more difficult to overcome. See Keith Aoki, Direct Democracy, Racial Group Agency, Local Government Law and Residential Racial Segregation: Some Reflections on Radical and Plural Democracy, 33 Cal. W. L. Rev. 185 (1997); Neil G. Williams, Offer, Acceptance, and Improper Consideration: A Common Law Model for the Prohibition of Racial Discrimination in the Contracting Process, 62 Geo. Wash. L. Rev. 183 (1994). The removal of race- and gender-based restrictions on the ability to contract reflected a new societal consensus that such laws were designed to oppress, rather than protect, the affected groups.

B. DURESS AND UNDUE INFLUENCE

At a very early time the common law recognized that some agreements should not be legally enforceable because of the process by which they were made. In the thirteenth century, agreements made while one party was under physical imprisonment or threat of physical harm were unenforceable at law because made under "duress." While such relief at law was limited to cases involving actual or threatened physical harm, over time the courts of equity recognized a right to relief against other types of coercion, under the doctrine of "undue influence." The equitable doctrine of undue influence, however, was not unlimited in its application. Generally, a court of equity would not act unless the undue influence arose between family members or in some other confidential or "fiduciary" relationship, such as between lawyer and client or between trustee and beneficiary.

Since these early days, the doctrines of duress and undue influence have undergone a dramatic expansion. Courts have gradually broadened the types of threats that are considered improper under the defense of duress, first to threats to a person's property (known as "duress of goods") and later to "economic duress." Similarly, the defense of undue influence has been extended to situations that do not involve a confidential relationship. The history of these developments is traced in John P. Dawson, Economic Duress — An Essay in Perspective, 45 Mich. L. Rev. 253 (1947). The materials that follow illustrate this more modern approach.

Totem Marine Tug & Barge, Inc. v. Alyeska Pipeline Service Co.

Supreme Court of Alaska 584 P.2d 15 (1978)

BURKE, Justice.

This appeal arises from the superior court's granting of summary judgment in favor of defendants-appellees Alyeska Pipeline Services, et al., in a contract action brought by plaintiffs-appellants Totem Marine Tug & Barge, Inc., Pacific, Inc., and Richard Stair.

The N. Joseph Guidry tugboat (renamed the Vinton Crosby in 2012).

The following summary of events is derived from the materials submitted in the summary judgment proceedings below.

Totem is a closely held Alaska corporation which began operations in March of 1975. Richard Stair, at all times relevant to this case, was vice-president of Totem. In

June of 1975, Totem entered into a contract with Alyeska under which Totem was to transport pipeline construction materials from Houston, Texas, to a designated port in southern Alaska, with the possibility of one or two cargo stops along the way. In order to carry out this contract, which was Totem's first, Totem chartered a barge (the "Marine Flasher") and an ocean-going tug (the "Kirt Chouest"). These charters and other initial operations costs were made possible by loans to Totem from Richard Stair individually and Pacific, Inc., a corporation of which Stair was principal stockholder and officer, as well as by guarantees by Stair and Pacific.

By the terms of the contract, Totem was to have completed performance by approximately August 15, 1975. From the start, however, there were numerous problems which impeded Totem's performance of the contract. For example, according to Totem, Alyeska represented that approximately 1,800 to 2,100 tons of regular uncoated pipe were to be loaded in Houston, and that perhaps another 6,000 or 7,000 tons of materials would be put on the barge at later stops along the west coast. Upon the arrival of the tug and barge in Houston, however, Totem found that about 6,700 to 7,200 tons of coated pipe, steel beams and valves, haphazardly and improperly piled, were in the yard to be loaded. This situation called for remodeling of the barge and extra cranes and stevedores, and resulted in the loading taking thirty days rather than the three days which Totem had anticipated it would take to load 2,000 tons. The lengthy loading period was also caused in part by Alyeska's delay in assuring Totem that it would pay for the additional expenses, bad weather and other administrative problems.

The difficulties continued after the tug and barge left Houston. It soon became apparent that the vessels were travelling more slowly than anticipated because of the extra load. In response to Alyeska's complaints and with its verbal consent, on August 13, 1975, Totem chartered a second tug, the "N. Joseph Guidry." When the "Guidry" reached the Panama Canal, however, Alyeska had not yet furnished the written amendment to the parties' contract. Afraid that Alyeska would not agree to cover the cost of the second tug, Stair notified the "Guidry" not to go through the Canal. After some discussions in which Alyeska complained of the delays and accused Totem of lying about the horsepower of the first tug, Alyeska executed the amendment on August 21, 1975.

By this time the "Guidry" had lost its preferred passage through the Canal and had to wait two or three additional days before it could go through. Upon finally meeting, the three vessels encountered the tail of a hurricane which lasted for about eight or nine days and which substantially impeded their progress.

The three vessels finally arrived in the vicinity of San Pedro, California, where Totem planned to change crews and refuel. On Alyeska's orders, however, the vessels instead pulled into port at Long Beach, California. At this point, Alyeska's agents commenced off-loading the barge, without Totem's consent, without the necessary load survey, and without a marine survey, the absence of which voided Totem's insurance. After much wrangling and some concessions by Alyeska, the freight was off-loaded. Thereafter, on or about September 14,

1975, Alyeska terminated the contract. Although there was talk by an Alyeska official of reinstating the contract, the termination was affirmed a few days later at a meeting at which Alyeska officials refused to give a reason for the termination.

Following termination of the contract, Totem submitted termination invoices to Alyeska and began pressing the latter for payment. The invoices came to something between $260,000 and $300,000. An official from Alyeska told Totem that they would look over the invoices but that they were not sure when payment would be made—perhaps in a day or perhaps in six to eight months. Totem was in urgent need of cash as the invoices represented debts which the company had incurred on 10-30 day payment schedules. Totem's creditors were demanding payment and according to Stair, without immediate cash, Totem would go bankrupt. Totem then turned over the collection to its attorney, Roy Bell, directing him to advise Alyeska of Totem's financial straits. Thereafter, Bell met with Alyeska officials in Seattle, and after some negotiations, Totem received a settlement offer from Alyeska for $97,500. On November 6, 1975, Totem, through its president Stair, signed an agreement releasing Alyeska from all claims by Totem in exchange for $97,500.

On March 26, 1976, Totem, Richard Stair, and Pacific filed a complaint against Alyeska, which was subsequently amended. In the amended complaint, the plaintiffs sought to rescind the settlement and release on the ground of economic duress and to recover the balance allegedly due on the original contract. In addition, they alleged that Alyeska had wrongfully terminated the contract and sought miscellaneous other compensatory and punitive damages.

Before filing an answer, Alyeska moved for summary judgment against the plaintiffs on the ground that Totem had executed a binding release of all claims against Alyeska and that as a matter of law, Totem could not prevail on its claim of economic duress. In opposition, plaintiffs contended that the purported release was executed under duress in that Alyeska wrongfully terminated the contract; that Alyeska knew that Totem was faced with large debts and impending bankruptcy; that Alyeska withheld funds admittedly owed knowing the effect this would have on plaintiffs and that plaintiffs had no alternative but to involuntarily accept the $97,500 in order to avoid bankruptcy. Plaintiffs maintained that they had thus raised genuine issues of material fact such that trial was necessary, and that Alyeska was not entitled to judgment as a matter of law. Alyeska disputed the plaintiffs' assertions.

On November 30, 1976, the superior court granted the defendant's motion for summary judgment. This appeal followed. . . .

II

As was noted above, a court's initial task in deciding motions for summary judgment is to determine whether there exist genuine issues of material fact. In order to decide whether such issues exist in this case, we must examine the doctrine allowing avoidance of a release on grounds of economic duress.

This court has not yet decided a case involving a claim of economic duress or what is also called business compulsion. At early common law, a contract could be avoided on the ground of duress only if a party could show that the agreement was entered into for fear of loss of life or limb, mayhem or imprisonment. 13 Williston on Contracts, §1601 at 649 (3d ed. Jaeger 1970). The threat had to be such as to overcome the will of a person of ordinary firmness and courage. Id., §1602 at 656. Subsequently, however, the concept has been broadened to include myriad forms of economic coercion which force a person to involuntarily enter into a particular transaction. The test has come to be whether the will of the person induced by the threat was overcome rather than that of a reasonably firm person. Id., §1602 at 657.

At the outset it is helpful to acknowledge the various policy considerations which are involved in cases involving economic duress. Typically, those claiming such coercion are attempting to avoid the consequences of a modification of an original contract or of a settlement and release agreement. On the one hand, courts are reluctant to set aside agreements because of the notion of freedom of contract and because of the desirability of having private dispute resolutions be final. On the other hand, there is an increasing recognition of the law's role in correcting inequitable or unequal exchanges between parties of disproportionate bargaining power and a greater willingness to not enforce agreements which were entered into under coercive circumstances.

There are various statements of what constitutes economic duress, but as noted by one commentator, "The history of generalization in this field offers no great encouragement for those who seek to summarize results in any single formula." Dawson, Economic Duress—An Essay in Perspective, 45 Mich. L. Rev. 253, 289 (1947). Section 492(b) of the Restatement of Contracts defines duress as:

> any wrongful threat of one person by words or other conduct that induces another to enter into a transaction under the influence of such fear as precludes him from exercising free will and judgment, if the threat was intended or should reasonably have been expected to operate as an inducement.

Professor Williston states the basic elements of economic duress in the following manner:

> 1. The party alleging economic duress must show that he has been the victim of a wrongful or unlawful act or threat, and
>
> 2. Such act or threat must be one which deprives the victim of his unfettered will.

13 Williston on Contracts, §1617 at 704 [footnotes omitted].

Many courts state the test somewhat differently, eliminating use of the vague term "free will," but retaining the same basic idea. Under this standard, duress exists where: (1) one party involuntarily accepted the terms of another, (2) circumstances permitted no other alternative, and (3) such circumstances were the result of coercive acts of the other party. . . . W. R. Grimshaw Co. v. Nevil C. Withrow Co., 248 F.2d 896, 904 (8th Cir. 1957). . . . The third element is further explained as follows:

> In order to substantiate the allegation of economic duress or business compulsion, the plaintiff must go beyond the mere showing of reluctance to accept and of financial embarrassment. There must be a showing of acts on the part of the defendant which produced these two factors. The assertion of duress must be proven by evidence that the duress resulted from defendant's wrongful and oppressive conduct and not by the plaintiff's necessities.

W. R. Grimshaw Co., supra, 248 F.2d at 904.

As the above indicates, one essential element of economic duress is that the plaintiff show that the other party by wrongful acts or threats, intentionally caused him to involuntarily enter into a particular transaction. Courts have not attempted to define exactly what constitutes a wrongful or coercive act, as wrongfulness depends on the particular facts in each case. This requirement may be satisfied where the alleged wrongdoer's conduct is criminal or tortious but an act or threat may also be considered wrongful if it is wrongful in the moral sense. Restatement of Contracts §492, Comment *g*. . . .

In many cases, a threat to breach a contract or to withhold payment of an admitted debt has constituted a wrongful act. . . . Austin Instrument, Inc. v. Loral Corp., 29 N.Y.2d 124, 324 N.Y.S.2d 22, 25, 272 N.E.2d 533, 535 (1971); . . . see also 13 Williston, supra, §1616A at 701. Implicit in such cases is the additional requirement that the threat to breach the contract or withhold payment be done in bad faith. . . . Restatement (Second) of Contracts §318, Comment *e*.

Economic duress does not exist, however, merely because a person has been the victim of a wrongful act; in addition, the victim must have no choice but to agree to the other party's terms or face serious financial hardship. Thus, in order to avoid a contract, a party must also show that he had no reasonable alternative to agreeing to the other party's terms, or, as it is often stated, that he had no adequate remedy if the threat were to be carried out. First National Bank of Cincinnati v. Pepper, 454 F.2d 626, 632-633 (2d Cir. 1972); *Austin Instrument,* supra, 324 N.Y.S.2d at 25, 272 N.E.2d at 535; . . . Tri-State Roofing Company of Uniontown v. Simon, 187 Pa. Super. 17, 142 A.2d 333, 335-336 (1958). What constitutes a reasonable alternative is a question of fact, depending on the circumstances of each case. An available legal remedy, such as an action for breach of contract, may provide such an alternative. *First National Bank of Cincinnati,* supra; *Austin Instrument,* supra; *Tri-State Roofing,* supra. Where one party wrongfully threatens to withhold goods, services or money from another unless certain demands are met, the availability on the market of similar goods and services or of other sources of funds may also provide an alternative to succumbing to the coercing party's demands. *Austin Instrument,* supra; *Tri-State Roofing,* supra. Generally, it has been said that "[t]he adequacy of the remedy is to be tested by a practical standard which takes into consideration the exigencies of the situation in which the alleged victim finds himself." Ross Systems [v. Linden Dari-Delite, Inc., 35 N.J. 329, 173 A.2d 258, 262 (1961)]. See also *First National Bank of Cincinnati,* supra at 634; Dalzell, Duress By Economic Pressure I, 20 N.C.L. Rev. 237, 240 (1942).

An available alternative or remedy may not be adequate where the delay involved in pursuing that remedy would cause immediate and irreparable loss to one's economic or business interest. For example, in *Austin Instrument,* supra, and Gallagher Switchboard Corp. v. Heckler Electric Co., 36 Misc. 2d 225, 232 N.Y.S.2d 590 (N.Y. Sup. Ct. 1962), duress was found in the following circumstances: A subcontractor threatened to refuse further delivery under a contract unless the contractor agreed to modify the existing contract between the parties. The contractor was unable to obtain the necessary materials elsewhere without delay, and if it did not have the materials promptly, it would have been in default on its main contract with the government. In each case such default would have had grave economic consequences for the contractor and hence it agreed to the modifications. In both, the courts found that the alternatives to agreeing to the modification were inadequate (i.e., suing for breach of contract or obtaining the materials elsewhere) and that modifications therefore were signed under duress and voidable.

Professor Dalzell, in Duress By Economic Pressure II, 20 N.C.L. Rev. 340, 370 (1942), notes the following with regard to the adequacy of legal remedies where one party refuses to pay a contract claim:

> Nowadays, a wait of even a few weeks in collecting on a contract claim is sometimes serious or fatal for an enterprise at a crisis in its history. The business of a creditor in financial straits is at the mercy of an unscrupulous debtor, who need only suggest that if the creditor does not care to settle on the debtor's own hard terms, he can sue. This situation, in which promptness in payment is vastly more important than even approximate justice in the settlement terms, is too common in modern business relations to be ignored by society and the courts.

This view finds support in Capps v. Georgia Pacific Corporation, 253 Or. 248, 453 P.2d 935 (1969). There, the plaintiff was owed $157,000 as a commission for finding a lessee for defendant's property but in exchange for $5,000, the plaintiff signed a release of his claim against defendant. The plaintiff sued for the balance of the commission, alleging that the release had been executed under duress. His complaint, however, was dismissed. On appeal, the court held that the plaintiff had stated a claim where he alleged that he had accepted the grossly inadequate sum because he was in danger of immediately losing his home by mortgage foreclosure and other property by foreclosure and repossession if he did not obtain immediate funds from the defendant. One basis for its holding was found in the following quote by a leading commentator in the area of economic duress:

> The most that can be claimed [regarding the law of economic duress] is that change has been broadly toward acceptance of a general conclusion—that in the absence of specific countervailing factors of policy or administrative feasibility, restitution is required of any excessive gain that results, in a bargain transaction, from impaired bargaining power, whether the impairment consists of economic necessity, mental or physical disability, or a wide disparity in knowledge or experience.

Dawson, Economic Duress—An Essay In Perspective, 45 Mich. L. Rev. 253, 289 (1947).

III

Turning to the instant case, we believe that Totem's allegations, if proved, would support a finding that it executed a release of its contract claims against Alyeska under economic duress. Totem has alleged that Alyeska deliberately withheld payment of an acknowledged debt, knowing that Totem had no choice but to accept an inadequate sum in settlement of that debt; that Totem was faced with impending bankruptcy; that Totem was unable to meet its pressing debts other than by accepting the immediate cash payment offered by Alyeska; and that through necessity, Totem thus involuntarily accepted an inadequate settlement offer from Alyeska and executed a release of all claims under the contract. If the release was in fact executed under these circumstances,[5] we think that under the legal principles discussed above that this would constitute the type of wrongful conduct and lack of alternatives that would render the release voidable by Totem on the ground of economic duress. We would add that although Totem need not necessarily prove its allegation that Alyeska's termination of the contract was wrongful in order to sustain a claim of economic duress, the events leading to the termination would be probative as to whether Alyeska exerted any wrongful pressure on Totem and whether Alyeska wrongfully withheld payment from Totem.[6] . . .

Our examination of the materials presented by Totem in opposition to Alyeska's motion for summary judgment leads us to conclude that Totem has made a sufficient factual showing as to each of the elements of economic duress to withstand that motion. There is no doubt that Alyeska disputes many of the factual allegations made by Totem[7] and drawing all inferences in favor of Totem, we believe that genuine issues of material fact exist in this case such that trial is necessary. Admittedly, Totem's showing was somewhat weak in that, for example, it did not produce the testimony of Roy Bell, the attorney who represented Totem in the negotiations leading to the settlement and release. At trial, it will probably be necessary for Totem to produce this evidence if it is to prevail on its claim of duress. However, a party opposing a motion for summary judgment need not produce all of the evidence it may have at its disposal but need only show that issues of material fact exist. 10 C. Wright and A. Miller, Federal Practice and Procedure: Civil, §2727 at 546 (1973). Therefore, we hold that the

---

5. By way of clarification, we would note that Totem would not have to prove that Alyeska admitted to owing the precise sum Totem claimed it was owed upon termination of the contract but only that Alyeska acknowledged that it owed Totem approximately that amount which Totem sought.

6. We make no comment as to whether Alyeska's termination of the contract was wrongful nor as to the truth of Totem's other allegations.

7. For example, Alyeska has denied that it ever admitted to owing any particular sum to Totem and has disputed the truthfulness of Totem's assertions of impending bankruptcy. Other factual issues which remain unresolved include whether or not Alyeska knew of Totem's financial situation after termination of the contract and whether Alyeska did in fact threaten by words or conduct to withhold payment unless Totem agreed to settle.

superior court erred in granting summary judgment for appellees and remand the case to the superior court for trial in accordance with the legal principles set forth above. . . .

Reversed and remanded.

NOTES AND QUESTIONS

1. *Void vs. voidable contracts.* As noted by the *Totem Marine* court, duress had its origin in cases in which a party manifested assent as a result of a threat to life or limb, mayhem, or imprisonment. The Restatement (Second) recognizes that a contract is *void* if made under physical compulsion, so that a person is compelled by "actual physical force" to appear to sign a contract or otherwise manifest assent. Restatement (Second) §174, Comment *a.* Some courts, however, have recognized more broadly that coercion involving a threat of physical harm may also result in ineffectual assent and a void contract. In Everbank v. Marini, 134 A.3d 189 (Vt. 2015), a husband called his wife and two children to the kitchen table and waved around a large pair of scissors while "berating" the wife about her refusal to sign a mortgage application. The Vermont Supreme Court held that "physical compulsion" sufficient to render a contract void would include "a threat of imminent physical violence" to get a person to sign a document, even though the Restatement (Second) §174 would deem such a contract only voidable. Id. at 200. But see Shultz v. Shultz, 867 So. 2d 745 (La. Ct. App. 2003) (reversing trial court and finding duress was not established in signing child support reduction agreement where claimant feared ex-husband as violent man and wanted to avoid argument but there was no evidence of use of force or threats).

It is presently more common that a party claims to be the victim of economic coercion, as in *Totem Marine*, rather than physical compulsion or a threat of physical harm. Contracts made under economic duress are deemed voidable rather than void. Thus, such contracts will be binding unless disaffirmed and may be expressly or implicitly ratified by the purported victim. See, e.g., Hyman v. Ford Motor Co., 142 F. Supp. 2d 735 (D.S.C. 2001) (contract executed under duress may be ratified by acceptance of benefits, remaining silent after opportunity to disavow, or rendering performance).

2. *Wrongful or improper threat.* Faced with a question of first impression, the *Totem Marine* court cited a number of authorities in arriving at a definition of economic duress. Consistent with the Restatement (Second) §175, the court's test can be viewed as requiring three elements: a wrongful or improper threat, a lack of reasonable alternative, and actual inducement of the contract by the threat. Restatement (Second) §§175 and 176 use the term "improper threat" while courts such as *Totem Marine* will often use the term "wrongful" to describe an actionable threat. More important than the use of either particular term is the fact the threat need not be "illegal" in order to give rise to a claim of duress. See Quigley v. KPMG Peat Marwick, LLP, 749 A.2d 405 (N.J. Super. Ct. App. Div. 2000) (threat that establishes duress may be wrongful in moral or

equitable sense even if not illegal). But see Whirlpool Corp. v. Grigoleit Co., 713 F.3d 316 (6th Cir. 2013) (under Michigan law duress requires showing of illegal compulsion or coercion).

When is a threat wrongful or improper? The Restatement (Second) §176 definition includes threats to commit a crime or tort and threats of criminal prosecution. While threats to engage in litigation or to refuse to honor a contractual obligation are not per se improper, such threats may be improper if the circumstances show that the threat was made in "bad faith." Id. §176(1)(c), (d). See also Kelso v. McGowan, 604 So. 2d 726 (Miss. 1992) (threat to breach enforceable contract can constitute "wrongful" act); but cf. Professional Service Network, Inc. v. American Alliance Holding Co., 238 F.3d 897 (7th Cir. 2001) (not an improper threat for seller of stock to insist on settlement of dispute under the contract before cooperating in tax filing worth $5 million to buyer; seller had "colorable case" and its position was not frivolous). What was the threat in the *Totem Marine* case? How could the plaintiff establish that the threat was made in bad faith?

3. *Economic duress and market change.* Because of market changes, a party might find itself in the position to dictate to the other party conditions that are extremely unfavorable to the weaker party. For example, in a "seller's market" a supplier might impose a dramatic price increase on a buyer for whom a certain product is essential. Cabot Corp. v. AVX Corp., 863 N.E.2d 503 (Mass. 2007), dealt with the enforceability of a long-term supply contract. In 2001, AVX agreed to a long-term supply contract with Cabot when Cabot threatened to refuse to supply AVX with tantalum under letters of intent previously agreed between the parties. AVX subsequently sued to invalidate the contract on the ground of economic duress. The Massachusetts Supreme Judicial Court recognized that Cabot had a superior bargaining position with regard to the 2001 contract, but it rejected the claim that this amounted to economic duress: "[T]he strength of Cabot's bargaining position in negotiating the supply contract, as well as AVX's weakened position, were the result of a worldwide shortage of the rare tantalum product. . . ." Id. at 512. The case stands for the proposition that a party's use of increased bargaining power resulting from dramatic changes in the market does not amount to economic duress. Professor Crystal and Francesca Giannoni-Crystal have analyzed the legal grounds for invalidation of contracts because of dramatic market change under both the common law and international contract principles (the CISG and UNIDROIT Principles). They conclude that the common law is very unlikely to provide relief, but international principles may be somewhat more receptive to such claims. Instead, lawyers should protect their clients from dramatic market change by appropriate contractual provisions. See Nathan M. Crystal & Francesca Giannoni-Crystal, *Contract Enforceability During Economic Crisis: Legal Principles and Drafting Solutions,* Global Jurist: Vol. 10: Iss. 3 (Advances), available at: *http://www.bepress.com/gj/vol10/iss3/art3.*

4. *Threat of criminal proceedings.* A threat by an attorney to institute criminal proceedings in order to aid a client in a civil dispute may not only render any resulting agreement unenforceable because of duress but may also subject

the attorney to discipline because of professional misconduct. Such threats may amount to extortion under state criminal statutes and could also be found to be unethical under general ethical concepts. E.g., ABA Model Rules of Professional Conduct, Rule 1.2(d) (lawyer may not counsel or assist a client in conduct that is criminal or fraudulent); Model Rule 4.4 (respect for rights of third persons). In addition, some states have modified the ABA's Model Rules to prohibit using threats of criminal proceedings to obtain an advantage in a civil matter. E.g., S.C. R. Prof. Cond. 4.5.

5. *Lack of reasonable alternative.* Even if a threat is improper, the resulting agreement is enforceable unless the party who submitted to the agreement had no reasonable alternative but to accept the agreement. Comment *b* to §175 of the Restatement (Second) indicates a number of possible reasonable alternatives: the availability of legal action if, in the circumstances, that course presents a viable option; alternative sources of goods, services, or funds when there is a threat to withhold such things; and toleration if the threat involves only a minor vexation. Compare Uniwill v. City of Los Angeles, 21 Cal. Rptr. 3d 464 (Ct. App. 2004) (developer of shopping mall stated viable claim for economic duress in alleging that city and electric company wrongfully threatened to stop project unless easement was granted and resort to legal proceedings would have led to financial ruin), with Dunes Hospitality, L.L.C. v. Country Kitchen Int'l, Inc., 623 N.W.2d 484 (S.D. 2001) (no duress where claimant company included sophisticated principals, had assistance of counsel, and had reasonable alternative of filing lawsuit rather than signing settlement agreement). In Reliford v. United Parcel Service, 2008 WL 4865987 (N.D. Ill.), the plaintiff employee was held to have sufficiently pled facts showing his release of age discrimination claims for only a $200 payment was procured by economic duress where he feared the loss of health benefits necessary to preserve his wife's life if he chose to litigate the claims.

6. *Inducement of involuntary assent.* The *Totem Marine* court would also require a showing that the wrongful threat "caused" the victim to involuntarily enter into the transaction. Consistently, Comment *c* to Restatement (Second) of Contracts §175 states that "the improper threat must induce the making of the contract," meaning that the threat must "substantially contribute" to the manifestation of assent. (This requirement suggests, at least implicitly, that the victim of the threat might have additional reasons for manifesting assent to the agreement.) Despite earlier standards that required the threat be "such as to overcome the will of a person of ordinary firmness and courage," as stated in *Totem Marine*, the standard is now a subjective one that asks whether the particular victim was induced by the threat. Comment *c* goes on to state that "[a]ll attendant circumstances must be considered, including such matters as the age, background and relationship of the parties." See Holler v. Holler, 612 S.E.2d 469 (S.C. Ct. App. 2005) (immigrant wife who spoke little English, had no means of financial self-support, was pregnant, and had visa that was about to expire stated good claim for duress in signing prenuptial agreement as demanded by husband before marriage). For a feminist critique of the current scope of the duress doctrine, see Orit

Gan, Contractual Duress and Relations of Power, 36 Harv. J.L. Gender 171 (2013).

7. *Must threatening party cause hardship?* A question which frequently arises is the role that an alleged victim's financial difficulty plays in the determination of economic duress. In Selmer Co. v. Blakeslee-Midwest Co., 704 F.2d 924 (7th Cir. 1983), Judge Posner stated that the fact a party agreed to a settlement because of a desperate need for cash could not be the basis for duress unless the other side had caused the financial hardship. The judge further observed that the inability of parties in dire straits to enter into enforceable agreements could cause other parties to refuse to settle even when both sides wanted to do so, thus ultimately working to the detriment of the alleged victim. Id. at 928. Most courts that have faced the issue agree with *Selmer.* Indeed, the Alaska Supreme Court that decided *Totem Marine* later adopted this view. Northern Fabrication Co. v. UNOCAL, 980 P.2d 958 (Alaska 1999) (for economic duress there must be a causal link between coercive acts and circumstances of economic duress).

On the other hand, a few courts have held, sometimes implicitly, that it is enough that one party takes advantage of the other side's dire circumstances without having caused the financial hardship. See, e.g., Advanced Cleanup Technologies, Inc. v. BP America, 2016 WL 67671 (C.D. Cal.) (plaintiff adequately pled economic duress when defendant made "take it or leave it" offer of $1.4 million to settle invoices for $3.2 million in emergency services to clean up massive Deepwater Horizon oil spill, taking "wrongful" advantage of fact that plaintiff was facing financial ruin or bankruptcy); Butitta v. First Mortgage Corp., 578 N.E.2d 116 (Ill. App. Ct. 1991) (duress may consist of taking undue advantage of the business or financial stress of the other party).

Odorizzi v. Bloomfield School District

California District Court of Appeals 246 Cal. App. 2d 123, 54 Cal. Rptr. 533 (1966)

FLEMING, Justice.

Appeal from a judgment dismissing plaintiff's amended complaint on demurrer.

Plaintiff Donald Odorizzi was employed during 1964 as an elementary school teacher by defendant Bloomfield School District and was under contract with the District to continue to teach school the following year as a permanent employee. On June 10 he was arrested on criminal charges of homosexual activity, and on June 11 he signed and delivered to his superiors his written resignation as a teacher, a resignation which the District accepted on June 13. In July the criminal charges against Odorizzi were dismissed under Penal Code, section 995, and in September he sought to resume his employment with the District. On the District's refusal to reinstate him he filed suit for declaratory and other relief.

Odorizzi's amended complaint asserts his resignation was invalid because obtained through duress, fraud, mistake, and undue influence and given at a time when he lacked capacity to make a valid contract. Specifically, Odorizzi declares he was under such severe mental and emotional strain at the time he signed his resignation, having just completed the process of arrest, questioning by the police, booking, and release on bail, and having gone for forty hours without sleep, that he was incapable of rational thought or action. While he was in this condition and unable to think clearly, the superintendent of the District and the principal of his school came to his apartment. They said they were trying to help him and had his best interests at heart, that he should take their advice and immediately resign his position with the District, that there was no time to consult an attorney, that if he did not resign immediately the District would suspend and dismiss him from his position and publicize the proceedings, his "aforedescribed arrest" and cause him "to suffer extreme embarrassment and humiliation"; but that if he resigned at once the incident would not be publicized and would not jeopardize his chances of securing employment as a teacher elsewhere. Odorizzi pleads that because of his faith and confidence in their representations they were able to substitute their will and judgment in place of his own and thus obtain his signature to his purported resignation. A demurrer to his amended complaint was sustained without leave to amend.

By his complaint plaintiff in effect seeks to rescind his resignation pursuant to Civil Code, section 1689, on the ground that his consent had not been real or free within the meaning of Civil Code, section 1567, but had been obtained through duress, menace, fraud, undue influence, or mistake. A pleading under these sections is sufficient if stripped of its conclusions, it sets forth sufficient facts to justify legal relief. . . . In our view the facts in the amended complaint are insufficient to state a cause of action for duress, menace, fraud, or mistake, but they do set out sufficient elements to justify rescission of a consent because of undue influence. We summarize our conclusions on each of these points.

1. No duress or menace has been pleaded. Duress consists in unlawful confinement of another's person, or relatives, or property, which causes him to consent to a transaction through fear. (Civ. Code, §1569.) Duress is often used interchangeably with menace . . . but in California menace is technically a threat of duress or a threat of injury to the person, property, or character of another. (Civ. Code, §1570; Restatement, Contracts, §§492, 493.) We agree with respondent's contention that neither duress nor menace was involved in this case, because the action or threat in duress or menace must be unlawful, and a threat to take legal action is not unlawful unless the party making the threat knows the falsity of his claim. (Leeper v. Beltrami, 53 Cal. 2d 195, 204, 1 Cal. Rptr. 12, 347 P.2d 12, 77 A.L.R.2d 803.) The amended complaint shows in substance that the school representatives announced their intention to initiate suspension and dismissal proceedings under Education Code, sections 13403, 13408 et seq. at a time when the filing of such proceedings was not only their legal right but their positive duty as school officials. (Educ. Code, §13409; Board of Education, etc. v. Weiland, 179 Cal. App. 2d 808, 4 Cal. Rptr. 286.) Although the filing of such proceedings might be extremely damaging to plaintiff's reputation, the injury would remain incidental so long as the school officials acted in good faith in the performance of their duties. (Schumm by Whymer v. Berg,

37 Cal. 2d 174, 185-186, 231 P.2d 39, 21 A.L.R.2d 1051.) Neither duress nor menace was present as a ground for rescission.

2. Nor do we find a cause of action for fraud, either actual or constructive. (Civ. Code, §§1571 to 1574.) Actual fraud involves conscious misrepresentation, or concealment, or non-disclosure of a material fact which induces the innocent party to enter the contract. (Civ. Code, §1572; Pearson v. Norton, 230 Cal. App. 2d 1, 7, 40 Cal. Rptr. 634; Restatement, Contracts, §471.) A complaint for fraud must plead misrepresentation, knowledge of falsity, intent to induce reliance, justifiable reliance, and resulting damage. (Sixta v. Ochsner, 187 Cal. App. 2d 485, 489, 9 Cal. Rptr. 617; Zinn v. Ex-Cell-O Corp., 148 Cal. App. 2d 56, 68, 306 P.2d 1017.) While the amended complaint charged misrepresentation, it failed to assert the elements of knowledge of falsity, intent to induce reliance, and justifiable reliance. A cause of action for actual fraud was therefore not stated. . . .

Constructive fraud arises on a breach of duty by one in a confidential or fiduciary relationship to another which induces justifiable reliance by the latter to his prejudice. (Civ. Code, §1573.) Plaintiff has attempted to bring himself within this category, for the amended complaint asserts the existence of a confidential relationship between the school superintendent and principal as agents of the defendant, and the plaintiff. Such a confidential relationship may exist whenever a person with justification places trust and confidence in the integrity and fidelity of another. . . . Plaintiff, however, sets forth no facts to support his conclusion of a confidential relationship between the representatives of the school district and himself, other than that the parties bore the relationship of employer and employee to each other. Under prevailing judicial opinion no presumption of a confidential relationship arises from the bare fact that parties to a contract are employer and employee; rather, additional ties must be brought out in order to create the presumption of a confidential relationship between the two. . . . The absence of a confidential relationship between employer and employee is especially apparent where, as here, the parties were negotiating to bring about a termination of their relationship. In such a situation each party is expected to look after his own interests, and a lack of confidentiality is implicit in the subject matter of their dealings. We think the allegations of constructive fraud were inadequate.

3. As to mistake, the amended complaint fails to disclose any facts which would suggest that consent had been obtained through a mistake of fact or of law. The material facts of the transaction were known to both parties. Neither party was laboring under any misapprehension of law of which the other took advantage. The discussion between plaintiff and the school district representatives principally attempted to evaluate the probable consequences of plaintiff's predicament and to predict the future course of events. The fact that their speculations did not forecast the exact pattern which events subsequently took does not provide the basis for a claim that they were acting under some sort of mistake. The doctrine of mistake customarily involves such errors as the nature of the transaction, the identity of the parties, the identity of the things to which the contract relates, or the occurrence of collateral happenings. (Restatement,

Contracts §502, Comment *e*.) Errors of this nature were not present in the case at bench.

4. However, the pleading does set out a claim that plaintiff's consent to the transaction had been obtained through the use of undue influence.

Undue influence, in the sense we are concerned with here, is a shorthand legal phrase used to describe persuasion which tends to be coercive in nature, persuasion which overcomes the will without convincing the judgment. (Estate of Ricks, 160 Cal. 467, 480-482, 117 P. 539.) The hallmark of such persuasion is high pressure, a pressure which works on mental, moral, or emotional weakness to such an extent that it approaches the boundaries of coercion. In this sense, undue influence has been called overpersuasion. (Kelly v. McCarthy, 6 Cal. 2d 347, 364, 57 P.2d 118.) Misrepresentations of law or fact are not essential to the charge, for a person's will may be overborne without misrepresentation. By statutory definition undue influence includes "taking an unfair advantage of another's weakness of mind; or . . . taking a grossly oppressive and unfair advantage of another's necessities or distress." (Civ. Code, §1575.) While most reported cases of undue influence involve persons who bear a confidential relationship to one another, a confidential or authoritative relationship between the parties need not be present when the undue influence involves unfair advantage taken of another's weakness or distress. . . .

We paraphrase the summary of undue influence given the jury by Sir James P. Wilde in Hall v. Hall, L.R. 1, P & D 481, 482 (1868): To make a good contract a man must be a free agent. Pressure of whatever sort which overpowers the will without convincing the judgment is a species of restraint under which no valid contract can be made. Importunity or threats, if carried to the degree in which the free play of a man's will is overborne, constitute undue influence, although no force is used or threatened. A party may be led but not driven, and his acts must be the offspring of his own volition and not the record of someone else's.

In essence undue influence involves the use of excessive pressure to persuade one vulnerable to such pressure, pressure applied by a dominant subject to a servient object. In combination, the elements of undue susceptibility in the servient person and excessive pressure by the dominating person make the latter's influence undue, for it results in the apparent will of the servient person being in fact the will of the dominant person.

Undue susceptibility may consist of total weakness of mind which leaves a person entirely without understanding (Civ. Code, §38); or, a lesser weakness which destroys the capacity of a person to make a contract even though he is not totally incapacitated (Civ. Code, §39; Peterson v. Ellebrecht, 205 Cal. App. 2d 718, 721-722, 23 Cal. Rptr. 349); or, the first element in our equation, a still lesser weakness which provides sufficient grounds to rescind a contract for undue influence (Civ. Code, §1575; . . .). Such lesser weakness need not be longlasting nor wholly incapacitating, but may be merely a lack of full vigor due to age, . . . physical condition, . . . emotional anguish, . . . or a combination of such factors. The reported cases have usually involved elderly, sick, senile persons alleged to have executed wills or deeds under pressure. (Malone v. Malone,

155 Cal. App. 2d 161, 317 P.2d 65 [constant importuning of a senile husband]; Stewart v. Marvin, 139 Cal. App. 2d 769, 294 P.2d 114 [persistent nagging of elderly spouse].) In some of its aspects this lesser weakness could perhaps be called weakness of spirit. But whatever name we give it, this first element of undue influence resolves itself into a lessened capacity of the object to make a free contract.

In the present case plaintiff has pleaded that such weakness at the time he signed his resignation prevented him from freely and competently applying his judgment to the problem before him. Plaintiff declares he was under severe mental and emotional strain at the time because he had just completed the process of arrest, questioning, booking, and release on bail and had been without sleep for forty hours. It is possible that exhaustion and emotional turmoil may wholly incapacitate a person from exercising his judgment. As an abstract question of pleading, plaintiff has pleaded that possibility and sufficient allegations to state a case for rescission.

Undue influence in its second aspect involves an application of excessive strength by a dominant subject against a servient object. Judicial consideration of this second element in undue influence has been relatively rare, for there are few cases denying persons who persuade but do not misrepresent the benefit of their bargain. Yet logically, the same legal consequences should apply to the results of excessive strength as to the results of undue weakness. Whether from weakness on one side, or strength on the other, or a combination of the two, undue influence occurs whenever there results "that kind of influence or supremacy of one mind over another by which that other is prevented from acting according to his own wish or judgment, and whereby the will of the person is overborne and he is induced to do or forbear to do an act which he would not do, or would do, if left to act freely." (Webb v. Saunders, 79 Cal. App. 2d 863, 871, 181 P.2d 43, 47.) Undue influence involves a type of mismatch which our statute calls unfair advantage. (Civ. Code, §1575.) Whether a person of subnormal capacities has been subjected to ordinary force or a person of normal capacities subjected to extraordinary force, the match is equally out of balance. If will has been overcome against judgment, consent may be rescinded.

The difficulty, of course, lies in determining when the forces of persuasion have overflowed their normal banks and become oppressive flood waters. There are second thoughts to every bargain, and hindsight is still better than foresight. Undue influence cannot be used as a pretext to avoid bad bargains or escape from bargains which refuse to come up to expectations. A woman who buys a dress on impulse, which on critical inspection by her best friend turns out to be less fashionable than she had thought, is not legally entitled to set aside the sale on the ground that the saleswoman used all her wiles to close the sale. A man who buys a tract of desert land in the expectation that it is in the immediate path of the city's growth and will become another Palm Springs, an expectation cultivated in glowing terms by the seller, cannot rescind his bargain when things turn out differently. If we are temporarily persuaded against our better judgment to do something about which we later have second thoughts, we must abide the consequences of the risks inherent in managing our own affairs. (Estate of Anderson, 185 Cal. 700, 706-707, 198 P. 407.)

However, overpersuasion is generally accompanied by certain characteristics which tend to create a pattern. The pattern usually involves several of the following elements: (1) discussion of the transaction at an unusual or inappropriate time, (2) consummation of the transaction in an unusual place, (3) insistent demand that the business be finished at once, (4) extreme emphasis on untoward consequences of delay, (5) the use of multiple persuaders by the dominant side against a single servient party, (6) absence of third-party advisers to the servient party, (7) statements that there is no time to consult financial advisers or attorneys. If a number of these elements are simultaneously present, the persuasion may be characterized as excessive. The cases are illustrative:

Moore v. Moore, 56 Cal. 89, 93, and 81 Cal. 195, 22 P. 589, 874. The pregnant wife of a man who had been shot to death on October 30 and buried on November 1 was approached by four members of her husband's family on November 2 or 3 and persuaded to deed her entire interest in her husband's estate to his children by a prior marriage. In finding the use of undue influence on Mrs. Moore, the court commented: "It was the second day after her late husband's funeral. It was at a time when she would naturally feel averse to transacting any business, and she might reasonably presume that her late husband's brother would not apply to her at such a time to transact any important business, unless it was of a nature that would admit of no delay. And as it would admit of delay, the only reason which we can discover for their unseemly haste is, that they thought that she would be more likely to comply with their wishes then than at some future time, after she had recovered from the shock which she had then so recently experienced. If for that reason they selected that time for the accomplishment of their purpose, it seems to us that they not only took, but that they designed to take, an unfair advantage of her weakness of mind. If they did not, they probably can explain why they selected that inappropriate time for the transaction of business which might have been delayed for weeks without injury to any one. In the absence of any explanation, it appears to us that the time was selected with reference to just that condition of mind which she alleges that she was then in.

"Taking an unfair advantage of another's weakness of mind is undue influence, and the law will not permit the retention of an advantage thus obtained." (Civ. Code, §1575.)

Weger v. Rocha, 138 Cal. App. 109, 32 P.2d 417. Plaintiff, while confined in a cast in a hospital, gave a release of claims for personal injuries for a relatively small sum to an agent who spent two hours persuading her to sign. At the time of signing plaintiff was in a highly nervous and hysterical condition and suffering much pain, and she signed the release in order to terminate the interview. The court held that the release had been secured by the use of undue influence. . . .

The difference between legitimate persuasion and excessive pressure, like the difference between seduction and rape, rests to a considerable extent in the manner in which the parties go about their business. For example, if a day or two after Odorizzi's release on bail the superintendent of the school district had called him into his office during business hours and directed his attention to those provisions of the Education Code compelling his leave of absence and authorizing his suspension on the filing of written charges, had told him that the District contemplated filing written charges against him, had pointed out the alternative of resignation available to him, had informed him he was free to consult counsel or any adviser he wished and to consider the matter overnight and return with his decision the next day, it is extremely unlikely that any complaint about the use of excessive pressure could ever have been made against the school district.

But, according to the allegations of the complaint, this is not the way it happened, and if it had happened that way, plaintiff would never have resigned. Rather, the representatives of the school board undertook to achieve their objective by overpersuasion and imposition to secure plaintiff's signature but not his consent to his resignation through a high-pressure carrot-and-stick technique—under which they assured plaintiff they were trying to assist him, he should rely on their advice, there wasn't time to consult an attorney, if he didn't resign at once the school district would suspend and dismiss him from his position and publicize the proceedings, but if he did resign the incident wouldn't jeopardize his chances of securing a teaching post elsewhere.

Plaintiff has thus pleaded both subjective and objective elements entering the undue influence equation and stated sufficient facts to put in issue the question whether his free will had been overborne by defendant's agents at a time when he was unable to function in a normal manner. It was sufficient to pose ". . . the ultimate question . . . whether a free and competent judgment was merely influenced, or whether a mind was so dominated as to prevent the exercise of an independent judgment." (Williston on Contracts, §1625 [rev. ed.]; Restatement, Contracts §497, Comment *c*.) The question cannot be resolved by an analysis of pleading but requires a finding of fact.

We express no opinion on the merits of plaintiff's case, or the propriety of his continuing to teach school (Educ. Code, §13403), or the timeliness of his rescission (Civ. Code, §1691). We do hold that his pleading, liberally construed, states a cause of action for rescission of a transaction to which his apparent consent had been obtained through the use of undue influence.

The judgment is reversed.

ROTH, P.J., and HERNDON, J., concur.

NOTES AND QUESTIONS

1. *Defining undue influence.* The *Odorizzi* court identifies the essence of undue influence as involving the use of excessive pressure by a dominant party in overcoming the will of a vulnerable person. Similarly, the Restatement (Second) §177(1) describes undue influence as involving "unfair persuasion of a party who is under the domination of the person exercising the persuasion or who by virtue of the relation between them is justified in assuming that

that person will not act in a manner inconsistent with his welfare." Although neither the *Odorizzi* court nor the Restatement (Second) requires the presence of a special relationship, such a finding will often be a significant factor in a court's assessment of undue influence. See, e.g., In re Estate of Jones, 287 P.3d 610 (Wash. Ct. App. 2012) (existence of fiduciary relationship creates rebuttable presumption of undue influence). The mere fact that parties have a close relationship, however, or that some influence is exerted, will not necessarily prove undue influence. See, e.g., Robertson v. Robertson, 15 S.W.3d 407 (Mo. Ct. App. 2000) (even though defendant held special relationship of confidence and trust as farm manager for elderly grantor and the challenged deed recited price of $100 paid for land worth between $100,000 and $250,000, plaintiffs raised only suspicion of undue influence and presented no actual proof).

2. *Factors indicating undue influence.* As an aid to applying the general concept of undue influence, the *Odorizzi* court identifies seven characteristics that are often found in such cases. Should all of the seven elements be required to find a contract tainted by undue influence? In Keithley v. Civil Service Board, 89 Cal. Rptr. 809 (Ct. App. 1970), a police officer's resignation from the force was held to have been coerced, and therefore unlawful, despite the absence of the factors numbered (4) and (7) in the *Odorizzi* opinion. The officer had been charged with rape by a woman — not his wife — with whom he admitted having intercourse, but with her consent, not by force. The court's opinion observed that the officer had not slept for 24 hours, that he was called to police headquarters for three successive days, and that on the third day was questioned by a superior officer who emphasized that the charges should not be made public. The court concluded that there was substantial evidence of undue influence. Id. at 815. More recently, in Kelly v. Provident Life & Accident Ins. Co., 734 F. Supp. 2d 1085 (S.D. Cal. 2010), a California federal court held that even if none of the *Odorizzi* factors was present, a plaintiff could establish his claim for rescission based on undue influence where he was suffering from mental illness known to the defendant insurer, and defendant conducted an investigation in bad faith and engaged in other harassing activity to pressure him into dropping his disability claim.

3. *Assessing* ***Odorizzi*** *for possible duress.* You will note that duress as defined by the court in *Odorizzi* is substantially narrower than the second Restatement's concept of duress. Subsequent California decisions indicate that the doctrine has evolved under state law to now encompass wrongful threats that leave the victim without reasonable alternatives. See Rich & Whillock v. Ashton Development, Inc., 204 Cal. Rptr. 86, 89 (Ct. App. 1984). Could the plaintiff's resignation in *Odorizzi* have been rescinded under a more contemporary definition of duress? In what respect could undue influence be easier to establish than duress? How might it be more difficult?

4. *Role of bad faith.* Does the decision in *Odorizzi* depend on whether the school officials honestly believed the charges were likely to be upheld? The court's opinion indicates that the charges originally lodged against Odorizzi were dropped the following month, but the court does not state the reasons for that action. Suppose when the school officials urged Odorizzi to resign,

they had proceeded as the court in *Odorizzi* indicates they should have, giving him time to consider their proposition and advising him to seek legal counsel before deciding. If you had been consulted by Odorizzi at that time, what advice would you have given?

5. ***Undue influence and duress in agreements related to marriage.*** In a category of cases that combine economic interests and personal relationships, claims of duress and undue influence have been used to challenge prenuptial as well as marriage dissolution agreements. A notable example is In re Bonds, 5 P.3d 815 (Cal. 2000), in which Sun Bonds, the former wife of professional baseball player Barry Bonds, challenged the validity of their premarital agreement which provided that each party waived any interest in the earnings made by the other party during the marriage. The contract was signed the day before the marriage, only Barry had assistance of counsel, and English was not Sun's first language. Nevertheless, the trial court held that the agreement was enforceable, basing its decision on findings that Sun had not been subject to any threat or coercion, that she had been advised that she could seek counsel, and that there was substantial evidence that she understood the agreement. Id. at 834-36. The California Supreme Court upheld the trial court's decision, noting that the applicable Family Code provisions placed the burden of proof on Sun to demonstrate that the agreement was not voluntarily made and that the absence of counsel was not decisive. Id. at 829. Notably, the California Legislature responded to the *Bonds* decision by amending the statute to provide that a premarital agreement is not voluntary if a party is not represented by counsel when signing the agreement, unless that party waives the right to independent counsel "in a separate writing." See Cal. Fam. Code §1615(c)(1).

Prenuptial agreements continue to be the basis of a significant amount of litigation. See Ellis v. Ellis, 2014 Tenn. Lexis App. 760 (Tenn. Ct. App.) (holding that prenuptial agreement was unenforceable where the husband failed to reveal holdings that were valued at $4,750,000; the wife did not have independent knowledge of the full nature, extent, and value of the husband's property and holdings; and the agreement was presented to the wife three days before the wedding and two days before Christmas, which gave the wife no reasonable opportunity to consult with independent counsel). Similar issues may also arise with regard to "postnuptial" or "marital agreements." See also Golding v. Golding, 581 N.Y.S.2d 4 (App. Div. 1992) (settlement agreement was voidable on basis of duress in light of husband's threat not to grant "Get" or Jewish divorce and wife's fears based on sister's failure to obtain "Get" in earlier divorce).

In 2012, the American Law Institute adopted a Uniform Premarital and Marital Agreements Act. Section 9 of the act deals with the enforceability of premarital and marital agreements:

> A premarital agreement or marital agreement is unenforceable if a party against whom enforcement is sought proves:
>
> (1) the party's consent to the agreement was involuntary or the result of duress;
>
> (2) the party did not have access to independent legal representation . . . ;

> (3) unless the party had independent legal representation at the time the agreement was signed, the agreement did not include a notice of waiver of rights . . . or an explanation in plain language of the marital rights or obligations being modified or waived by the agreement; or
>
> (4) before signing the agreement, the party did not receive adequate financial disclosure. . . .

The act goes on to specify when a party has access to legal representation, the form of a notice of waiver of rights, and the requirements for adequate financial disclosure. The law also provides that some provisions are unenforceable, such as a waiver of a right to child support. See §10(b)(1). For a discussion of the act, see Barbara A. Atwood & Brian H. Bix, A New Uniform Law for Premarital and Marital Agreements, 46 Fam. L.Q. 313 (2012).

C. MISREPRESENTATION AND NONDISCLOSURE

Early in the history of the common law, with rare exceptions, the English courts did not generally recognize fraud as a defense to an action in assumpsit. The courts did provide indirect relief, however, by allowing recovery for damages flowing from fraud in a separate action, which later came to be known as the tort action of "deceit." The modern tort action for misrepresentation is a descendent of this common law remedy.

Although fraud was not recognized as a defense at law, courts of equity allowed a party who had been a victim of fraud to avoid the contract by way of equitable "rescission." Rescission amounted to a judicial return of the parties to the status quo that existed before the contract was formed. In rescission a court of equity ordered both the wrongdoer and the injured party to return to the other any money or property received from the other. Over time the law courts recognized a legal right of rescission, which was similar to the equitable remedy but differed in some technical respects. In particular, at law in order to obtain rescission, a party had to show that she had made a "tender" of any money or property received before instituting the action, while in equity tender was unnecessary. With the procedural merger of law and equity in the nineteenth century, the difference between legal and equitable rescission has become relatively unimportant, although there are still situations in which the difference can be significant. (For example, if a party complies with the requirements of legal rescission, including tender, she is entitled to avoid the contract; a court could refuse to grant the remedy of equitable rescission if the court concludes that fairness does not warrant rescission of the transaction.)

As a result of these historical developments, under modern law a victim of misrepresentation may have a choice between two significant avenues of redress: a tort action for damages or a right to avoid the enforceability of the contract by way of rescission. (This right of rescission could be exercised either by defense to an action to enforce the contract or in an affirmative action seeking restitution of benefits conferred on the other party.) What factors affect the choice between these two remedies, making one or the other more attractive or, possibly, unavailable as a remedy? One such factor is that the remedy of rescission requires the injured party to return any money or property that he has received; thus, if the defrauded party does not want to do so, rescission is not a desirable remedy. Suppose, for example, that the purchaser of a home receives a "termite letter" from the seller stating that the home is free of wood-boring insects. After purchasing the home, the buyer learns that the home is infested with termites. It turns out that the seller fraudulently procured the termite letter by bribing the termite company. If the buyer does not want to give up the home, a tort action for money damages to compensate the buyer for the termite problem is a more attractive remedy than rescission. For a discussion of the election between an action in tort for damages and rescission of the contract seeking restitution, see InterCall, Inc. v. Egenera, Inc., 824 N.W.2d 12 (Neb. 2012).

Sometimes rescission may be unavailable even if the defrauded party would prefer this remedy. If the defrauded party is unable to return the property received from the wrongdoer because it has been transferred to a third person, rescission may not be allowed. Restatement (Third) of Restitution and Unjust Enrichment §66. On the other hand, sometimes a party may be able to obtain rescission even though a tort remedy would be unavailable. A party may rescind a contract for a material misrepresentation even if the misrepresentation was not made with fraudulent intent. Restatement (Second) §164(1) (contract voidable for either fraudulent or material misrepresentation). The law may not recognize a tort action or may limit the scope of the remedy, however, if the misrepresentation was not made with fraudulent intent (often called "scienter"). Compare Restatement (Second) of Torts §549 (damages for fraudulent misrepresentation) with §§552, 552B, and 552C (remedy and damages for negligent and innocent misrepresentation).

The materials that follow address several questions: When is a misrepresentation actionable either by way of rescission or in tort? When does a failure to disclose information amount to misrepresentation? What effect does a contractual disclaimer of representations have on an injured party's right to rescind a contract or recover damages for misrepresentation?

Syester v. Banta

Iowa Supreme Court 257 Iowa 613, 133 N.W.2d 666 (1965)

SNELL, Justice.

This is a law action seeking damages, actual and exemplary, for allegedly false and fraudulent representations in the sale of dancing instruction to plaintiff. From the final judgment entered after a jury verdict for plaintiff in a substantial amount defendants have appealed.

Plaintiff is a lonely and elderly widow who fell for the blandishments and flattery of those who saw some "easy money" available.

Ginger Rogers and Fred Astaire in a dance studio during the filming of Swing Time.

Defendants are the owners of the Des Moines Arthur Murray Dance Studio. They have a legitimate service to sell but when their selling techniques transcend the utmost limits of reason and fairness they must expect courts and juries to frown thereon. In this case the jury has done so.

Since the beginning of recorded history men and women have persisted in selling their birthrights for a mess of pottage and courts cannot protect against the folly of bad judgment. We can, however, insist on honesty in selling. The old doctrine of caveat emptor is no longer the pole star for business.

Much of the testimony was uncontradicted. The testimony as to intentional fraud and misrepresentation as well as the motive and credibility of some witnesses was attacked but these were questions for the jury. It was for the jury to say who should be believed.

It is not for us to say who should have prevailed with the jury. It is for us to determine the sufficiency of the admissible evidence to generate a jury question and the correctness of the instructions given the jury. We will mention only as much of the testimony as is necessary for that purpose.

Plaintiff is a widow living alone. She has no family. Her exact age does not appear but a former employee of defendants and a favorite dancing instructor of plaintiff testified "that during the period from 1957 through the fall of 1960 she was 68 years old."

After her husband's death plaintiff worked at Bishop's as a "coffee girl." She first went to the Arthur Murray Studio in 1954 as a gift from a friend. On the first visit there was no attempt to sell her any lessons but she was invited to return a few days later. When she returned she was interviewed by the manager and sold a small course of dancing lessons. From that time on there appears to have been an astoundingly successful selling campaign.

The testimony of defendants' manager and his written summary of payments, received as Exhibit 1, are not in complete accord, but the variation is not vital. By May 2, 1955 defendants sold plaintiff 3222 hours of dancing instruction for which she paid $21,020.50. In all, according to the testimony of defendants' manager plaintiff paid $33,497.00 for 4057 hours of instruction. Because of some refunds and credits defendants' Exhibit 1 shows plaintiff's cost to be only $29,174.30. Defendants' Exhibit 1 is as follows:

Exhibit 1
Summary of Dance Course Purchased by Agnes Syester

Date	*Sold by*	*Hours in Course*	*Amt Paid*
9-27-54	Brick	206	1709.50
10-15-54	Neidt	300	2490.00
11-4-54	Neidt	16	88.00
1-8-55	Bersch	500	3825.00
1-19-55	Bersch	1000	6800.00
5-2-55	Bersch	1200	6000.00
5-24-55	Brick	100	995.00
6-22-55	Brick	10	79.80
5-25-57	Brick-Ziegler	11	130.00
6-22-57	Brick	10	106.00
6-4-58	Carey	10	106.00
9-8-58	Carey	10	99.00
1-6-59	Erickson	4	25.00
5-27-59	Wolf	10	116.00
6-10-59	Wolf	10	112.50
6-10-59	Wolf	10	112.50
12-2-59	Carey-Kenton	25	290.00
3-2-60	Carey	625	6090.00
		4057	$29174.30

On May 2, 1955 when plaintiff bought 1200 additional hours of instruction for $6,000 she had already bought 2022 hours and had used only 261 hours.

Included in the courses offered were lifetime memberships. With the purchase of 1,000 or 1,200 hours of instruction it was the policy of defendants to give free attendance to weekly dances for life and two hours of instruction or practice a month to keep active on what had been learned. Included in plaintiff's purchases were three lifetime memberships. Plaintiff attended the weekly dances and incidental entertainments and admitted having fun.

Plaintiff testified that defendants' manager sold her the first lifetime membership. She testified "He promised me all the privileges of the studio and I would be a professional dancer." To make such a promise to a lady plaintiff's age was ridiculous. The fact that she was so gullible as to be an easy victim does not justify taking over $29,000 of her money. She may have been willing and easily sold but nevertheless a victim.

The members of defendants' staff were carefully schooled and supervised in the art of high-powered salesmanship. Mr. Carey, a witness for plaintiff, testified at length as to methods and as to his contact with plaintiff. There was evidence that Mr. Carey was a disgruntled former employee and instructor and had expressed hostility toward defendants, but his credibility was for the jury.

Defendants' studio occupies seven rooms consisting of a grand ballroom and six private studios. Each private studio is wired for sound so the manager could monitor conversations between instructor and student and without the student's knowledge correct the instructor's sales technique.

Mr. Carey had received two months training including a course on sales technique taught by the manager. Plaintiff's Exhibit H is a revised edition of defendants' "Eight Good Rules For Interviewing." It is an exhaustive set of instructions, outlines and suggested conversations covering twenty-two typewritten pages. A few pertinent parts are:

> 1. How to prevent a prospect from consulting his banker, lawyer, wife or friend.
> 2. Avoid permitting your prospect to think the matter over.
> 3. Tell the prospect that has never danced before that it is an advantage and tell the prospect that has danced before that it is an advantage.
> 4. To dance with the prospect and then tell the prospect that the rhythm is very good, their animation or self confidence is good, that their natural ability is very good. That they will be an excellent ballroom dancer in much less time and that if they didn't have natural ability it would take twice as long.
> 5. To summarize the prospect's ability to learn as follows: "Did you know that the three most important points on this D.A. are: Rhythm, natural ability and animation? You've been graded Excellent in all three."
> 6. In quoting the price for various courses, the instructor is supposed to say "the trouble with most people is that they dance lifelessly, but as I told you on your analysis, you have animation—vitality in your dancing. No matter what course you decide on you're going to be a really smooth dancer (men would rather be a smooth dancer—women would rather be a beautiful, graceful dancer)."
> 7. To use "emotional selling" and the instructor is tutored as follows: "This is the warm-up period and is a very important part of your interview. You have proved to him by now that he can learn to dance; now you must appeal to his emotions in such a way that he will want lessons regardless of the cost."

Theoretically, for advancing proficiency in dancing (the jury must have thought that $29,000 had something to do with it), plaintiff was awarded a Bronze Medal, then a Silver Medal and then a Gold Medal. These awards were given plaintiff all in the same year although defendants' manager testified that it takes approximately two to four years to qualify for a Bronze Medal, five to seven years for a Silver Medal and anytime after 1200 hours a student could qualify for the Gold Medal. Finally after considerable thought about new incentives for plaintiff to buy something more she was shown a film on Gold Star dancing. This is a difficult professional type of dancing. "The dancers on the film were brought in from Europe by Mr. Murray. The dancing is English quick step and is the type of dancing done by Ginger Rogers and Fred Astaire only about twice as difficult." This film had been studied 15 to 20 times to determine what parts to stress with plaintiff.

Plaintiff was easily sold a Gold Star course of 625 hours for $6,250. A few days later she came into the ballroom, handed Mr. Carey an envelope and said

"Well, it took some doing but here is the money." The money was delivered to the manager.

The Gold Star course was started although even the instructor was "faking it" and had no idea what he was doing.

Mr. Carey testified that from 1957 through the fall of 1960 plaintiff's dancing ability did not improve. "She was 68 years old and had gone as far as she would ever go in dancing, thereon it would be merely repetitious." In his opinion "it would take 200 to 400 hours of instructions to teach her to dance in the manner she was dancing in 1960." He also testified that while he was at the studio none of his students ever failed to qualify for any of the medals. When he questioned plaintiff's ability to do the advanced type of dancing she was being sold he was reminded by defendants' manager that he was an employee and that the manager made the rules.

Mr. Carey testified at length as to the attentions, inducements, promises and lies (he said they were) lavished on plaintiff. He became plaintiff's regular instructor. He was about twenty-five years old and apparently quite charming and fascinating to plaintiff. She gave him a diamond ring for his birthday in 1960.

The testimony is rather fantastic but it would unduly extend this opinion to set it forth in greater detail. It was in our opinion sufficient for the jury to find that plaintiff was the victim of a calculated course of intentional misrepresentations.

The charge for instruction varied somewhat up to $10 per hour. After some refunds, and, according to defendants' computation, plaintiff paid approximately $6.75 per hour for 3425 hours of instruction or about $23,000.

If Mr. Carey's estimate of plaintiff's ability and possibility of progress is accepted plaintiff was knowingly overcharged for 3025 hours or a total sum of $20,418.75.

Mr. Carey was discharged by defendants in the fall of 1960. Plaintiff quit the studio shortly thereafter. She still had 1750 hours of unused time that she had purchased. She testified that she did so because she "was unhappy because things didn't go right and I was through with dancing, and that was the only reason I quit." Defendants' manager testified that plaintiff "became unhappy over the dismissal of Mr. Carey and left the studio." Another witness for defendants said plaintiff complained mostly about losing her instructor, Mr. Carey.

In January 1961 plaintiff employed counsel to represent her in a lawsuit against defendants. Her counsel contacted defendants. Conferences were held. Apparently a divertive campaign was planned by defendants. Mr. Carey testified:

> I next heard from Mr. Theiss in January of 1961 when he called and asked me to come down to the studio to discuss employment. I went to see him and he told me that Mrs. Syester was suing him and wanted to know if I still had any influence over her, to get her to drop the suit. I told him I felt that I still did and I would try to get her to come back in the studio and drop her legal action against him. He said he would reinstate me and pay all of my past due

> commissions. I accepted the position and went to Bishop's Cafeteria where Mrs. Syester was the coffee girl to see what her feelings were toward the studio. She was very cold toward me and I reported this to Mr. Theiss. He said not to concern myself with the studio, that my job was merely to get her to drop the lawsuit, so I went to Bishop's a couple of times a day to try and talk with Mrs. Syester. Finally I succeeded and told her that I was back in the studio and that Mr. Theiss wanted her back. I told her that there would be no hard feelings on our part if she would just drop the suit and come back but she said she did not want to come back to the studio. I continued talking to her and finally got her to accept coming to a party and told her that I would be out to pick her up and escort her to the studio. This was about a week after I first contacted her, in February of 1961. I told her that I was going to the party and I would save her some waltzes. I knew this was her favorite dance. And I felt that if she would pass up this waltz, she was not interested in dancing. She did not come to the studio so the next day I went down to Bishop's and told her she disappointed me very much. Then I started talking about all of the lessons she and I had had and all of the months we had danced and the fun we had together. I told her how wonderful she had done. I painted word pictures and things so she could see this. I asked her if she remembered about when she got the Bronze. She kept saying that was best but all she wanted was her money back. I finally persuaded her to come to the studio and we danced for about 45 minutes. It was at this time that she called the lawsuit off. . . . When I went to Bishop's Cafeteria to see Mrs. Syester I told her she was a good dancer and that she still had the ability to be a professional, excellent dancer. I told her that she did not need an attorney; after all Mrs. Theiss and myself were her only friends and we wanted her back at the studio to continue with her Gold Star and reminded her of all the waltzes we would do together.

During the month of February several people contacted plaintiff at the instigation of defendants' manager, including Mr. Carey. These efforts were fruitful. Plaintiff made what defendants claim was a complete settlement. Defendants' counsel prepared a written release (defendants' Exhibit 2) and was present during one conference of the parties. Defendants' counsel did not instigate, carry on, nor make the "settlement" with plaintiff. He testified that he "did not want to get that implicated." In any event defendants' manager at plaintiff's home persuaded plaintiff to discharge her counsel by phone and agree to settle for the refund of her March 2, 1960 payment of $6,090. This was reported to defendants' counsel, who in behalf of his client, wrote settlement checks. Plaintiff's counsel received his share although there is no evidence that the settlement was ever pursuant to his advice. There is evidence that defendants were attempting to lead plaintiff away from her own counsel. Their efforts were so far beyond the limits of propriety that their own counsel hesitated to participate.

The release signed by plaintiff is a specific release of her claim based on the March 2, 1960 payment and a general release of all claims. If obtained in good faith it is a bar to all plaintiff's claims. The release was witnessed by Estella M. Smith, whose identity does not appear and by defendants' manager. After signing this release on March 6, 1961 plaintiff's then pending lawsuit was dismissed. Plaintiff returned to the studio and participated in the activities for several months.

A second release dated January 28, 1963 was obtained by defendants' manager. It purports to be a contractual release for $4,000. The $4,000 to be paid was to be evidenced by a note. There is no claim that anything has been paid thereon. The note provided for installment payments but instead of being signed by defendants it is signed by plaintiff. Defendants' manager testified that this was all a mistake and that the studio was to pay.

Accepting defendants' explanation that it was a mistake the most charitable thing that can be said is that plaintiff would sign anything requested, even a note wherein she was the payee.

The present action was filed March 12, 1963. It alleged fraud and misrepresentation in the several sales to plaintiff and in obtaining dismissal of the previous lawsuit and the releases signed by plaintiff.

Defendants denied any fraud or misrepresentations and urged the releases as a complete defense. Defendants offered evidence in support of their position. At the close of plaintiff's evidence and again at the close of all the evidence defendants moved for a directed verdict. The motions were overruled. The jury returned a verdict for plaintiff in the sum of $14,300 actual damages and $40,000 punitive damages. Defendants appealed.

I. The court told the jury to first consider the issues involved in the releases signed by plaintiff and placed on plaintiff the burden of proving by clear, satisfactory and convincing evidence that they were not binding on her. This was proper.

In five instructions, separately numbered but in sequence, the court instructed on fraud, expression of opinion as distinguished from a statement of fact, fraudulent misrepresentation, intent to mislead, consideration for releases, presumption of freedom from fraud, need for prudence in signing and failure of consideration.

On appeal defendants challenged the sufficiency of the evidence to generate a jury question but not the accuracy of the instructions.

Defendants argue in the absence of fraud the execution of a valid release bars a future action based on the rights relinquished. The rule is stated in Kilby v. Charles City Western Railway Company, 191 Iowa 926, 928, 183 N.W. 371 as follows:

> Where a settlement has been had between competent parties, and a release has been fairly entered into, without fraud or overreaching, it becomes binding and effectual, and will be upheld and enforced. It is undoubtedly the law that an instrument of this character can be impeached for fraud in procuring the same or where the same was executed by a party who was mentally incompetent to legally execute such an instrument. The burden of proof is on the party seeking to impeach such written instrument.

Mere failure to read an instrument before signing will not avoid its provisions. Crum v. McCollum, 211 Iowa 319, 233 N.W. 678. These propositions are not in dispute and further citation of authority is unnecessary. . . .

. . . The evidence was such that the jury could find that there was such a concerted effort, lacking in propriety, to obtain the releases as to constitute fraudulent overreaching. The jury obviously concluded that there was a predatory play on the vanity and credulity of an old lady. We find no reason for interfering with that conclusion.

II. Defendants argue that "In an action based upon fraud, certain universally recognized elements must be alleged and shown, and the failure to establish any one or more of such elements is fatal to such action." With this statement we agree and so did the trial court. In Instruction No. 10 the jury was told that to recover the burden was on plaintiff to establish by clear, satisfactory and convincing evidence each of the following propositions:

> 1. That the defendants made one or more of the representations claimed by plaintiff. . . .
> 2. That said statements, or one or more of them, were false.
> 3. That said false statements or representations were as to material matters with reference to the entering into the lesson contracts.
> 4. That the defendants knew the said representations, or one or more of them, were false.
> 5. That said representations were made with intent to deceive and defraud the plaintiff.
> 6. That the plaintiff believed and relied upon said false representations and would not have entered into the lesson contracts, except for believing and relying upon said misrepresentations.
> 7. That the plaintiff was damaged in some amount through relying on said representations.
>
> If you find that the plaintiff has established each and every one of the foregoing propositions, numbered 1 to 7 inclusive by evidence which is clear, satisfactory and convincing, then your verdict will be for the plaintiff and against the defendants in such amount as you find plaintiff is justly entitled to receive.
>
> If you find, however, that the plaintiff has failed to establish any one or more of the foregoing propositions, numbered 1 to 7 inclusive, then your verdict will be for the defendants.

The instruction was adequate. Here again the problem was factual. Defendants argue that the representations proved by plaintiff were nothing more than mere expressions of opinion or "puffing" and that the only substantial expression of opinion was in fact accomplished.

In Christy v. Heil, supra, we considered statements of fact as distinguished from opinion or puffing. We said "Ordinarily the question of whether the representations made are opinion or fact is for the jury to determine and depends upon the facts and circumstances in each case." (Citations) loc. cit. 608, 123 N.W.2d loc. cit. 411. "We must review the evidence in the light most favorable to the purchasers." loc. cit. 613, 123 N.W.2d loc. cit. 414.

Defendants' review of the authorities is exhaustive and scholarly but the fact remains that in the case at bar there was evidence, which if believed by the jury, would support a finding of fraud.

III. Defendants argue that there was no proof of damage. Although the court's instructions on measure of damage were closer to the "out of pocket" rule than to the "benefit of bargain" rule to which we are committed (see 37 C.J.S. Fraud §143, page 477) defendants make no complaint. The instruction was not prejudicial to defendants. Defendants say that the rule was properly stated but suggest that the statement of the issues including the amount prayed for may have been misleading. The fact that plaintiff asked for something beyond the correct measure of damage is not reversible error if, as defendants say, the court properly instructed the jury.

Defendants argue that there was no evidence from which the jury could find the fair and reasonable value of the instruction received other than the amount paid by plaintiff. Defendants' manager testified that plaintiff still has 899 hours of unused lessons. Mr. Carey's testimony would support a finding that plaintiff was knowingly overcharged for 3025 hours or the sum of $20,418.75. The jury's verdict for $14,300 actual damages was within the evidence. We have no means of knowing just how the jury computed the damage. It was for more than the charge for the unused time according to defendants, but less than would be due for unproductive instruction. In argument defendants have stressed the value of plaintiff's enjoyment. That may have entered into the jury's computation.

The verdict was not beyond the scope of the evidence or the instructions.

IV. In addition to actual damages plaintiff asked for exemplary or punitive damages. The claim was submitted to the jury and a verdict for $40,000 punitive damages was returned.

Defendants argue that the record will not support an award of punitive damages in any amount and that the issue should not have been submitted, but do not challenge the accuracy of the instructions relative thereto.

. . . The jury award of $40,000 was large. However, the evidence of greed and avariciousness on the part of defendants is shocking to our sense of justice as it obviously was to the jury.

The allowance of exemplary damages is wholly within the discretion of the jury where there is a legal basis for the allowance of such damages. We may interfere only where passion and prejudice appear and then only by reversal. . . .

We think the question of exemplary damages was properly submitted to the jury; that there was evidence to support a verdict; that there is no indication of such passion and prejudice as to require a reversal and that the case should be and hereby is affirmed.

GARFIELD, C.J., and HAYS, LARSON, PETERSON, THORNTON, and MOORE, JJ., concur.

THOMPSON and STUART, JJ., concur in result.

NOTES AND QUESTIONS

1. *Fraudulent or material misrepresentation.* Section 164(1) of the Second Restatement provides that a contract is voidable if a party's "manifestation

of assent is induced by either a fraudulent or a material misrepresentation by the other party upon which the recipient is justified in relying. . . ." See, e.g., Sarvis v. Vermont State Colleges, 772 A.2d 494 (Vt. 2001) (college could rescind employment agreement when employee gave false information on resume to hide record of criminal incarceration). Restatement (Second) §162(1) (b) and (c) define "fraudulent" also to include an assertion made as true but without knowledge or confidence by the maker whether it is true or false, and thus may include statements that are made recklessly or negligently. See, e.g., Jordan v. Knafel, 880 N.E.2d 1061 (Ill. App. Ct. 2007) (professional basketball player granted declaratory judgment avoiding settlement agreement allegedly induced by fraudulent claim that defendant knew plaintiff to be biological father of her child); Waste Management of Massachusetts, Inc. v. Carver, 642 N.E.2d 1058 (Mass. App. Ct. 1994) (rescission granted where seller made misrepresentation about extent of land contamination without obtaining current information from consultants hired to test land; seller could not avoid liability by ignoring available information).

Additionally, as noted by the introduction to this chapter, a contract may be subject to rescission because of an innocent but material misrepresentation, see Restatement (Second) §162(2) and Comment *c*. See also Alfa Life Ins. Corp. v. Lewis, 910 So. 2d 757 (Ala. 2005) (decedent's presumably innocent failure to disclose heart condition would still amount to material misrepresentation and allow rescission under insurance code); Groothand v. Schlueter, 949 S.W.2d 923 (Mo. Ct. App. 1997) (rescission available for buyers of house with structural problems without showing that sellers knew representations to be false). Was there evidence on which the jury could find that the releases in *Syester* were induced by misrepresentation? Can you think of other bases for avoiding a contract that might be applicable to this case?

2. *Contract or tort claim.* Assuming the jury could properly find that the releases were voidable because induced by misrepresentation, Ms. Syester could then assert a tort claim for damages based on the defendants' fraud in inducing her to enter into the series of contracts for dancing instruction. Could Ms. Syester have also attempted to rescind these contracts rather than attempting to recover damages in tort for fraud? As a tactical matter, should she have done so?

3. *Misrepresentation based on false opinion or prediction.* One of the instructions given by the lower court to the jury dealt with the distinction between statements of opinion and representations of fact. The Restatement (Second) defines an opinion as the expression of a belief, without certainty, as to the existence of a fact. Typically, opinions deal with matters such as quality or value of property. Restatement (Second) §168(1). The classical rule was that a statement of opinion could not be fraudulent, an approach based on the view that the morals of the marketplace required a certain degree of leeway for "puffing" in bargaining. Under the Restatement (Second), however, a statement of opinion amounts to a misrepresentation of fact if the person giving the opinion misrepresented his state of mind (i.e., stated that he held a certain opinion when in fact he did not). Restatement (Second) §159, Comment *d*. See also

Bennett v. Coors Brewing Co., 189 F.3d 1221 (10th Cir. 1999) (employees made prima facie case of misrepresentation by showing that employer made false statements about plans to downsize in order to get employees to take severance package). Moreover, under §169 of the Restatement (Second), a statement of opinion may also be actionable if the one giving the opinion (a) stands in a relationship of trust or confidence to the recipient (a "fiduciary relationship"), (b) is an expert on matters covered by the opinion, or (c) renders the opinion to one who, because of age or other factors, is peculiarly susceptible to misrepresentation. Which of these rules could apply to the facts of the *Syester* case?

4. *Reasonable reliance.* Assuming that a misrepresentation occurred in *Syester*, is it clear that all the other elements for misrepresentation are present? Was reliance by the plaintiff reasonable? See Schlaifer Nance & Co. v. Estate of Andy Warhol, 119 F.3d 91 (2d Cir. 1997) (purchaser of license to reproduce Andy Warhol's artwork did not reasonably rely on false statements that estate held all property rights in light of overt evidence to contrary); Mehta v. Mehta, 602 N.Y.S.2d 142 (App. Div. 1993) (reliance by one party on other's misrepresentation of the value of jointly owned assets was not reasonable where both parties had equal access to business records). Notably, the fact that the misrepresentation relates to a matter of public record will not necessarily preclude reasonable reliance. See, e.g., Cao v. Nguyen, 607 N.W.2d 528 (Neb. 2000) (false statement that house was a duplex constituted grounds for rescission even though public records revealed that house was legal only for single occupancy; buyers' reliance was reasonable under circumstances).

If Mrs. Syester was not reasonable in relying on representations that she had the ability to become a professional dancer, then what could justify the jury verdict and appellate decision in her favor? The case may have involved enough instances of clear fraud, such as the selling of the "Gold Star" lessons that the instructor had no qualifications to teach, to warrant the decision in Mrs. Syester's favor. Or perhaps the outcome suggests that the common law is in fact imbued with principles of morality and the need to protect those perceived as vulnerable. See also Bennett v. Bailey, 597 S.W.2d 532 (Tex. Civ. App. 1980) (upholding award of $78,000 in treble damages to widow under state consumer protection law after dance studio engaged in deceptive practices in selling her almost $30,000 in dance lessons). For further discussion of *Syester* and other similar cases, see Charles L. Knapp, Cases and Controversies: Some Things to Do with Contracts Cases, 88 Wash. L. Rev. 1357, 1366-1368 (2013) (suggesting that the best explanation for the result in *Syester* is the doctrine of undue influence); Debora L. Threedy, Dancing around Gender: Lessons from Arthur Murray on Gender and Contracts, 45 Wake Forest L. Rev. 749 (2010).

5. *Ethical limits on attorney's direct contact with opposing party.* In an effort to get Ms. Syester to sign the releases, the defendants persuaded her to discharge her attorney. At the time the defendants were also represented by counsel. Under the Model Rules of Professional Conduct, it is improper for a lawyer to "communicate about the subject of the representation with a person the lawyer knows to be represented by another lawyer in the matter, unless the lawyer has

the consent of the other lawyer or is authorized to do so by law or court order." Model Rules of Professional Conduct, Rule 4.2. What is the purpose of this rule? Did the defendants' lawyer violate the rule?

Hill v. Jones

Arizona Court of Appeals

151 Ariz. 81, 725 P.2d 1115 (1986), review denied (Oct. 1, 1986)

MEYERSON, Judge.

Must the seller of a residence disclose to the buyer facts pertaining to past termite infestation? This is the primary question presented in this appeal. Plaintiffs Warren G. Hill and Gloria R. Hill (buyers) filed suit to rescind an agreement to purchase a residence. Buyers alleged that Ora G. Jones and Barbara R. Jones (sellers) had made misrepresentations concerning termite damage in the residence and had failed to disclose to them the existence of the damage and history of termite infestation in the residence. The trial court dismissed the claim for misrepresentation based upon a so-called integration clause in the parties' agreement.

Sellers then sought summary judgment on the "concealment" claim arguing that they had no duty to disclose information pertaining to termite infestation and that even if they did, the record failed to show all of the elements necessary for fraudulent concealment. The trial court granted summary judgment, finding that there was "no genuinely disputed issue of material fact and that the law favors the . . . defendants." The trial court awarded sellers $1,000.00 in attorney's fees. Buyers have appealed from the judgment and sellers have cross-appealed from the trial court's ruling on attorney's fees.

I. FACTS

In 1982, buyers entered into an agreement to purchase sellers' residence for $72,000. The agreement was entered after buyers made several visits to the home. The purchase agreement provided that sellers were to pay for and place in escrow a termite inspection report stating that the property was free from evidence of termite infestation. Escrow was scheduled to close two months later.

One of the central features of the house is a parquet teak floor covering the sunken living room, the dining room, the entryway and portions of the halls. On a subsequent visit to the house, and when sellers were present, buyers noticed a small "ripple" in the wood floor on the step leading up to the dining room from the sunken living room. Mr. Hill asked if the ripple could be termite damage. Mrs. Jones answered that it was water damage. A few years previously, a broken water heater in the house had in fact caused water damage in the area of the dining room and steps which necessitated that some repairs be made to the floor. No further discussion on the subject, however, took place between the parties at that time or afterwards.

Mr. Hill, through his job as maintenance supervisor at a school district, had seen similar "ripples" in wood which had turned out to be termite damage. Mr.

Hill was not totally satisfied with Mrs. Jones's explanation, but he felt that the termite inspection report would reveal whether the ripple was due to termites or some other cause.

The termite inspection report stated that there was no visible evidence of infestation. The report failed to note the existence of physical damage or evidence of previous treatment. The realtor notified the parties that the property had passed the termite inspection. Apparently, neither party actually saw the report prior to close of escrow.

After moving into the house, buyers found a pamphlet left in one of the drawers entitled "Termites, the Silent Saboteurs." They learned from a neighbor that the house had some termite infestation in the past. Shortly after the close of escrow, Mrs. Hill noticed that the wood on the steps leading down to the sunken living room was crumbling. She called an exterminator who confirmed the existence of termite damage to the floor and steps and to wood columns in the house. The estimated cost of repairing the wood floor alone was approximately $5,000.

Through discovery after their lawsuit was filed, buyers learned the following. When sellers purchased the residence in 1974, they received two termite guarantees that had been given to the previous owner by Truly Nolen, as well as a diagram showing termite treatment at the residence that had taken place in 1963. The guarantees provided for semi-annual inspections and annual termite booster treatments. The accompanying diagram stated that the existing damage had not been repaired. The second guarantee, dated 1965, reinstated the earlier contract for inspection and treatment. Mr. Jones admitted that he read the guarantees when he received them. Sellers renewed the guarantees when they purchased the residence in 1974. They also paid the annual fee each year until they sold the home.

On two occasions during sellers' ownership of the house but while they were at their other residence in Minnesota, a neighbor noticed "streamers" evidencing live termites in the wood tile floor near the entryway. On both occasions, Truly Nolen gave a booster treatment for termites. On the second incident, Truly Nolen drilled through one of the wood tiles to treat for termites. The neighbor showed Mr. Jones the area where the damage and treatment had occurred. Sellers had also seen termites on the back fence and had replaced and treated portions of the fence.

Sellers did not mention any of this information to buyers prior to close of escrow. They did not mention the past termite infestation and treatment to the realtor or to the termite inspector. There was evidence of holes on the patio that had been drilled years previously to treat for termites. The inspector returned to the residence to determine why he had not found evidence of prior treatment and termite damage. He indicated that he had not seen the holes in the patio because of boxes stacked there. It is unclear whether the boxes had been placed there by buyers or sellers. He had not found the damage inside the house because a large plant, which buyers had purchased from sellers, covered the area. After investigating the second time, the inspector found the damage and evidence of past treatment. He acknowledged that this information should have appeared in the report. He complained, however, that he should have been told of any history of termite infestation and treatment before he performed his inspection and that it was customary for the inspector to be given such information.

Other evidence presented to the trial court was that during their numerous visits to the residence before close of escrow, buyers had unrestricted access to view and inspect the entire house. Both Mr. and Mrs. Hill had seen termite damage and were therefore familiar with what it might look like. Mr. Hill had seen termite damage on the fence at this property. Mrs. Hill had noticed the holes on the patio but claimed not to realize at the time what they were for. Buyers asked no questions about termites except when they asked if the "ripple" on the stairs was termite damage. Mrs. Hill admitted she was not "trying" to find problems with the house because she really wanted it.

II. Contract Integration Clause

We first turn to the trial court's ruling that the agreement of the parties did not give buyers the right to rely on the statement made by Mrs. Jones that the "ripple" in the floor was water damage. We find this ruling to be in error. The contract provision upon which the trial court based its ruling reads as follows:

> That the Purchaser has investigated the said premises, and the Broker and the Seller are hereby released from all responsibility regarding the valuation thereof, and neither Purchaser, Seller, nor Broker shall be bound by any understanding, agreement, promise, representation or stipulation expressed or implied, not specified herein.

In Lufty v. R. D. Roper & Sons Motor Co., 57 Ariz. 495, 506, 115 P.2d 161, 166 (1941), the Arizona Supreme Court considered a similar clause in an agreement and concluded that "any provision in a contract making it possible for a party thereto to free himself from the consequences of his own fraud in procuring its execution is invalid and necessarily constitutes no defense." The court went on to hold that "parol evidence is always admissible to show fraud, and this is true, even though it has the effect of varying the terms of a writing between the parties." 57 Ariz. at 506-507, 115 P.2d at 166; Barnes v. Lopez, 25 Ariz. App. 477, 480, 544 P.2d 694, 697 (1976). In this case, the claimed misrepresentation occurred after the parties executed the contract.[1] Assuming, for the purposes of this decision, that the integration clause would extend to statements made subsequent to the execution of the contract, the clause could not shield sellers from liability should buyers be able to prove fraud.

III. Duty to Disclose

The principal legal question presented in this appeal is whether a seller has a duty to disclose to the buyer the existence of termite damage in a residential

1. Buyers' fraud theory is apparently based on the premise that they were not bound under the contract until a satisfactory termite inspection report was submitted.

dwelling known to the seller, but not to the buyer, which materially affects the value of the property. For the reasons stated herein, we hold that such a duty exists.

This is not the place to trace the history of the doctrine of caveat emptor. Suffice it to say that its vitality has waned during the latter half of the 20th century. E.g., Richards v. Powercraft Homes, Inc., 139 Ariz. 242, 678 P.2d 427 (1984) (implied warranty of workmanship and habitability extends to subsequent buyers of homes); see generally Quashnock v. Frost, 299 Pa. Super. 9, 445 A.2d 121 (1982); Ollerman v. O'Rourke Co., 94 Wis. 2d 17, 288 N.W.2d 95 (1980). The modern view is that a vendor has an affirmative duty to disclose material facts where:

1. Disclosure is necessary to prevent a previous assertion from being a misrepresentation or from being fraudulent or material;
2. Disclosure would correct a mistake of the other party as to a basic assumption on which that party is making the contract and if nondisclosure amounts to a failure to act in good faith and in accordance with reasonable standards of fair dealing;
3. Disclosure would correct a mistake of the other party as to the contents or effect of a writing, evidencing or embodying an agreement in whole or in part;
4. The other person is entitled to know the fact because of a relationship of trust and confidence between them.

Restatement (Second) of Contracts §161 (1981) (Restatement); see Restatement (Second) of Torts §551 (1977).

Arizona courts have long recognized that under certain circumstances there may be a "duty to speak." Van Buren v. Pima Community College Dist. Bd., 113 Ariz. 85, 87, 546 P.2d 821, 823 (1976); Batty v. Arizona State Dental Bd., 57 Ariz. 239, 254, 112 P.2d 870, 877 (1941). As the supreme court noted in the context of a confidential relationship, "[s]uppression of a material fact which a party is bound in good faith to disclose is equivalent to a false representation." Leigh v. Loyd, 74 Ariz. 84, 87, 244 P.2d 356, 358 (1952); National Housing Indus. Inc. v. E. L. Jones Dev. Co., 118 Ariz. 374, 379, 576 P.2d 1374, 1379 (1978).

Thus, the important question we must answer is whether under the facts of this case, buyers should have been permitted to present to the jury their claim that sellers were under a duty to disclose their (sellers') knowledge of termite infestation in the residence. This broader question involves two inquiries. First, must a seller of residential property advise the buyer of material facts within his knowledge pertaining to the value of the property? Second, may termite damage and the existence of past infestation constitute such material facts?

The doctrine imposing a duty to disclose is akin to the well-established contractual rules pertaining to relief from contracts based upon mistake. Although the law of contracts supports the finality of transactions, over the years courts have recognized that under certain limited circumstances it is unjust to strictly enforce the policy favoring finality. Thus, for example, even a unilateral mistake of one party to a transaction may justify rescission. Restatement §153.

There is also a judicial policy promoting honesty and fair dealing in business relationships. This policy is expressed in the law of fraudulent and negligent misrepresentations. Where a misrepresentation is fraudulent or where a negligent misrepresentation is one of material fact, the policy of finality rightly gives way to the policy of promoting honest dealings between the parties. See Restatement §164(1).

Under certain circumstances nondisclosure of a fact known to one party may be equivalent to the assertion that the fact does not exist. For example "[w]hen one conveys a false impression by the disclosure of some facts and the concealment of others, such concealment is in effect a false representation that what is disclosed is the whole truth." State v. Coddington, 135 Ariz. 480, 481, 662 P.2d 155, 156 (App. 1983). Thus, nondisclosure may be equated with and given the same legal effect as fraud and misrepresentation. One category of cases where this has been done involves the area of nondisclosure of material facts affecting the value of property, known to the seller but not reasonably capable of being known to the buyer.

Courts have formulated this "duty to disclose" in slightly different ways. For example, the Florida Supreme Court recently declared that "where the seller of a home knows of facts materially affecting the value of the property which are not readily observable and are not known to the buyer, the seller is under a duty to disclose them to the buyer." Johnson v. Davis, 480 So. 2d 625, 629 (Fla. 1985) (defective roof in three-year old home). In California, the rule has been stated this way:

> [W]here the seller knows of facts materially affecting the value or desirability of the property which are known or accessible only to him and also knows that such facts are not known to, or within the reach of the diligent attention and observation of the buyer, the seller is under a duty to disclose them to the buyer.

Lingsch v. Savage, 213 Cal. App. 2d 729, 735, 29 Cal. Rptr. 201, 204 (1963); contra Ray v. Montgomery, 399 So. 2d 230 (Ala. 1980); see generally W. Prosser & W. Keeton, The Law of Torts §106 (5th ed. 1984).[2] We find that the Florida formulation of the disclosure rule properly balances the legitimate interests of the parties in a transaction for the sale of a private residence and accordingly adopt it for such cases.

As can be seen, the rule requiring disclosure is invoked in the case of material facts.[3] Thus, we are led to the second inquiry—whether the existence of termite damage in a residential dwelling is the type of material fact which gives rise to the duty to disclose. The existence of termite damage and past termite

---

2. There are variations on this same theme. For example, Pennsylvania has limited the obligation of disclosure to cases of dangerous defects. Glanski v. Ervine, 269 Pa. Super. 182, 191, 409 A.2d 425, 430 (1979).

3. Arizona has recognized that a duty to disclose may arise where the buyer makes an inquiry of the seller, regardless of whether or not the fact is material. Universal Inv. Co. v. Sahara Motor Inn, Inc., 127 Ariz. 213, 215, 619 P.2d 485, 487 (1980). The inquiry by buyers whether the ripple was termite damage imposed a duty upon sellers to disclose what information they knew concerning the existence of termite infestation in the residence.

infestation has been considered by other courts to be sufficiently material to warrant disclosure. See generally Annotation, 22 A.L.R.3d 972 (1968).

In Lynn v. Taylor, 7 Kan. App. 2d 369, 642 P.2d 131 (1982), the purchaser of a termite-damaged residence brought suit against the seller and realtor for fraud and against the termite inspector for negligence. An initial termite report found evidence of prior termite infestation and recommended treatment. A second report indicated that the house was termite free. The first report was not given to the buyer. The seller contended that because treatment would not have repaired the existing damage, the first report was not material. The buyer testified that he would not have purchased the house had he known of the first report. Under these circumstances, the court concluded that the facts contained in the first report were material. See Hunt v. Walker, 483 S.W.2d 732 (Tenn. App. 1971) (severe damage to the residence by past termite infestation); Mercer v. Woodard, 166 Ga. App. 119, 123, 303 S.E.2d 475, 481-482 (1983) (duty of disclosure extends to fact of past termite damage).

Although sellers have attempted to draw a distinction between live termites[4] and past infestation, the concept of materiality is an elastic one which is not limited by the termites' health. "A matter is material if it is one to which a reasonable person would attach importance in determining his choice of action in the transaction in question." Lynn v. Taylor, 7 Kan. App. 2d at 371, 642 P.2d at 134-135. For example, termite damage substantially affecting the structural soundness of the residence may be material even if there is no evidence of present infestation. Unless reasonable minds could not differ, materiality is a factual matter which must be determined by the trier of fact. The termite damage in this case may or may not be material. Accordingly, we conclude that buyers should be allowed to present their case to a jury.

Sellers argue that even assuming the existence of a duty to disclose, summary judgment was proper because the record shows that their "silence . . . did not induce or influence" the buyers. This is so, sellers contend, because Mr. Hill stated in his deposition that he intended to rely on the termite inspection report. But this argument begs the question. If sellers were fully aware of the extent of termite damage and if such information had been disclosed to buyers, a jury could accept Mr. Hill's testimony that had he known of the termite damage he would not have purchased the house.

Sellers further contend that buyers were put on notice of the possible existence of termite infestation and were therefore "chargeable with the knowledge which [an] inquiry, if made, would have revealed." Godfrey v. Navratil, 3 Ariz. App. 47, 51, 411 P.2d 470 (1966) (quoting Luke v. Smith, 13 Ariz. 155, 162, 108 P. 494, 496 (1910)). It is also true that "a party may . . . reasonably expect the other to take normal steps to inform himself and to draw his own conclusions." Restatement §161, comment *d*. Under the facts of this case, the question

4. Sellers acknowledge that a duty of disclosure would exist if live termites were present. Obde v. Schlemeyer, 56 Wash. 2d 449, 353 P.2d 672 (1960).

of buyers' knowledge of the termite problem (or their diligence in attempting to inform themselves about the termite problem) should be left to the jury.[5]

By virtue of our holding, sellers' cross-appeal is moot. Reversed and remanded.

CONTRERAS, P.J., and YALE MCFATE, J. (Retired), concur.

NOTES AND QUESTIONS

1. *Historical perspective: Laidlaw v. Organ.* The classical view was that a party to a business transaction could not avoid the transaction because of nondisclosure of material information by the other party. Reflecting the ethic of individualism, courts required a party to protect his own interests by requesting information from the other party or by making an adequate investigation before entering into a transaction. Perhaps the leading example of the nineteenth century approach is Laidlaw v. Organ, 15 U.S. (2 Wheat) 178 (1817). In *Laidlaw*, the plaintiff buyer alleged a wrongful refusal by the defendant seller to deliver a quantity of tobacco pursuant to a contract of purchase. The defendant claimed it was privileged to avoid the contract on the ground of fraud by the buyer. The contract was made in New Orleans, at a time when news of the Treaty of Ghent, ending the war with Britain, had not yet reached that city. The buyer's agent was aware of the ending of the war; the seller's agent was not. And when the seller's agent asked if there was any news "calculated to enhance the price or value" of the tobacco, the buyer's agent remained silent, despite the fact that the ending of the war could increase the market value of the tobacco by as much as 50 percent. The judge at trial refused to allow a defense of fraud into the case and directed a verdict for the buyer. On appeal, the Supreme Court reversed and sent the case back for retrial on the issue of whether the buyer had committed actual fraud. The Court, however, agreed with the buyer's argument that liability could not be based on the buyer's failure to disclose any special knowledge it may have had about the end of the war.

> Even if the vendor had been entitled to the disclosure, he waived it by not insisting on an answer to his question; and the silence of the vendee might as well have been interpreted into an affirmative as a negative answer. But, on principle, he was not bound to disclose. . . . There was, in the present case, no circumvention or manoeuvre practiced by the vendee, unless rising earlier in the morning, and obtaining by superior diligence and alertness that intelligence by which the price of commodities was regulated, be such. . . . [I]t would be difficult to circumscribe the contrary doctrine within proper limits, where the means of intelligence are equally accessible to both parties.

---

5. Sellers also contend that they had no knowledge of any existing termite damage in the house. An extended discussion of the facts on this point is unnecessary. Simply stated, the facts are in conflict on this issue.

Id. at 193-195. An article examining the case argues that the facts of *Laidlaw* show that the buyer's knowledge of the treaty did not come from "superior diligence" but because of special access – the buyer's partner was the brother of one of the members of the American delegation that had negotiated the treaty. See Joshua Kaye, Disclosure, Information, the Law of Contracts, and the Mistaken Use of *Laidlaw v. Organ*, 79 Miss. L.J. 577 (2010).

2. *Modern approach to nondisclosure.* The modern view is that in some situations a failure to disclose a known material fact may justify rescission of a contract. Restatement (Second) §161. While Restatement §161(a), (c), and (d) provide for rescission because of nondisclosure only in limited situations, §161(b) states a broader basis for relief: when the nondisclosure amounts to a failure to act in accordance with standards of good faith and fair dealing. When should this provision be applied? Professor Page Keeton suggested several factors that a court should consider in deciding when fairness requires disclosure of material information, including the differences in intelligences of the parties, their relationship, the manner in which the information was acquired (whether by chance or effort), whether the fact that was not disclosed was readily discoverable, whether the person failing to make disclosure was the seller rather than the buyer, the type of contract (insurance or releases, for example, typically require full disclosure), the importance of the fact not disclosed, and whether active concealment occurred. W. Page Keeton et al., Prosser and Keeton on the Law of Torts §106, at 739 (5th ed. 1984), summarizing factors set forth in W. Page Keeton, Fraud—Concealment and Non-disclosure, 15 Tex. L. Rev. 1 (1936). See, e.g., Capson Physicians Insurance Company v. MMIC Insurance Inc., 829 F.3d 951 (8th Cir. 2016) (rescission granted to professional liability insurer based on nondisclosure by insured physician and hospital of lawsuit pending against physician when prior acts coverage was added).

3. *Different types of "fraud."* While students will encounter claims of "fraud" in many cases in this course and others, the term is often used loosely. Analytically it is important to recognize that misrepresentation or nondisclosure of information can be actionable in various ways, sometimes in tort and sometimes in contract. Each theory will have distinct elements, and theories may have different procedural and substantive consequences (for example, differing statutes of limitation and separate remedies). Moreover, courts may use different labels for the theories. The facts in the *Hill* case could give rise to at least three different claims of fraud: "actual fraud" or fraudulent inducement (as in the *Syester* case and addressed by the Restatement (2d) §164); fraudulent nondisclosure (sometimes labeled as "fraud by silence" and addressed by the Restatement (2d) §161); and "fraudulent concealment" based on the seller allegedly placing boxes or a potted plant over water or termite damage – in other words, a "cover up" in both a literal and figurative sense. See Restatement (Second) §160. In addition, a misrepresentation of material facts may be the basis of an action to rescind a contract even if made innocently, under Restatement (Second) §164(1).

Hill involved a claim for rescission of the contract rather than damages in tort. Could the plaintiffs have recovered in a tort action for damages? The

Restatement (Second) of Torts §551 provides that nondisclosure will give rise to liability if the party is "under a duty to the other to exercise reasonable care to disclose the matter in question" and then indicates that the duty arises in a number of situations including when there is a fiduciary or similar relationship, when partial or earlier disclosures would be misleading, and when the other party would reasonably expect disclosure of facts that are basic to the transaction. See, e.g., Bearden v. Honeywell Int'l Inc., 720 F. Supp. 2d 932 (M.D. Tenn. 2010) (under Tennessee law, seller of goods to consumers has duty to disclose dangerous conditions and material facts unknown to buyer and not reasonably discoverable, citing §551); Pearson v. Simmonds Precision Products, Inc., 624 A.2d 1134 (Vt. 1993) (employer liable in tort for negligent failure to disclose that there was a "good chance" that newly recruited employee's position might be terminated).

4. *Real estate disclosure statutes and common law actions.* Since the time that the *Hill* court rendered its decision, a clear majority of states has adopted statutory law that supplements or perhaps displaces common law requirements for disclosure by sellers in residential real estate transactions. See Stephanie Stern, Temporal Dynamics of Disclosure: The Example of Residential Real Estate Conveyancing, 2005 Utah L. Rev. 57, 60-64. These statutes impose on sellers a duty of disclosure of extensive information regarding the condition of the property being sold. If the particular statute creates a cause of action, the buyer may bring suit under the statutory provision. See, e.g., Hammes v. JCLB Props., L.L.C., 764 N.W.2d 552 (Iowa Ct. App. 2008) (common law claim for fraudulent nondisclosure and statutory claim are distinct causes of action with different elements; statute requires plaintiff to show seller's actual knowledge of condition required to be disclosed). The state disclosure law may also specifically exempt some information from the disclosure requirements even if many buyers might deem the matter to be materially important to the purchase. See, e.g., Lerner v. DMB Realty, LLC, 322 P.3d 909 (Ariz. Ct. App. 2014) (statute precluded seller liability for failure to disclose presence of registered sex offender in neighborhood).

5. *Effect of fiduciary relationship.* One of the factors mentioned by Professor Keeton in determining whether a party has a duty of disclosure of material information to the other party is the relationship between the parties (factor 2). The Restatement refers to a "relationship of trust and confidence." Restatement (Second) §161(d). Such an association is often called a "fiduciary" relationship and a greater duty is imposed between two contracting parties. See E. Allan Farnsworth, Contracts §4.27, at 297-298 (4th ed. 2004). When a fiduciary relationship exists, not only does this duty of disclosure apply, but the law also imposes additional obligations on the fiduciary: The terms of the transaction must be fair and must be fully explained to the other party. Restatement (Second) §173. Moreover, the fiduciary has the burden of proving compliance with her legal obligations by clear and convincing evidence. See Miller v. Sears, 636 P.2d 1183 (Alaska 1981) (contract for sale of property subject to rescission by client because attorney failed to establish that he had fully disclosed all material terms to client; attorney has burden of proving compliance with

fiduciary duties by clear and convincing evidence). What is the justification for these stringent requirements?

Historically, certain relationships — lawyer and client, trustee and beneficiary — have been treated as fiduciary in character. The comment that follows these notes discusses some of the important ethical obligations that lawyers as fiduciaries owe to their clients. In addition, a fiduciary relationship can exist when one party reposes trust and confidence in another party who, in turn, accepts and fosters the relationship. Mere friendship standing alone, however, is not sufficient to establish a fiduciary relationship. See Arko v. Cirou, 700 S.E.2d 604 (Ga. Ct. App. 2010) (lender's close personal relationship with borrowers not enough to establish confidential relationship).

6. *Effect of disclaimer or merger clause.* The court in *Hill* ruled that the contract integration clause did not bar the purchasers' action to rescind the contract on the basis of fraud because "any provision in a contract making it possible for a party thereto to free himself from the consequences of his own fraud in procuring its execution is invalid and necessarily constitutes no defense." The maxim that "fraud vitiates every transaction" has long been part of the common law, e.g., Sabo v. Delman, 143 N.E.2d 906 (N.Y. 1957) (clause in patent assignment agreement disclaiming all verbal representations was ineffective to bar claim to rescind contract due to fraud). However, in the landmark case of Danann Realty Corp. v. Harris, 157 N.E.2d 597 (N.Y. 1959), decided just two years after *Sabo*, the New York Court of Appeals held that when a contract contains a "specific" disclaimer of representations (as opposed to a "general and vague merger clause"), a tort action for fraud will not lie because the clause shows a lack of justified reliance on any oral representations. But see Wilson v. McCann, 2014 WL 5326173 (N.J. Super. Ct. App. Div.) (provision that property sold "as is" or in "present condition" is ineffective with regard to concealment or nondisclosure of material defects that were known or should have been known to seller and were not readily apparent to buyer).

Some courts have held that an "as is" clause precludes a claim for nondisclosure but does not bar a cause of action for fraudulent misrepresentation or fraudulent concealment. See Goddard v. Stabile, 924 N.E.2d 868 (Ohio Ct. App. 2009). Moreover, if the misrepresentation was innocent, a disclaimer may be effective. Compare Wilkinson v. Carpenter, 554 P.2d 512 (Or. 1976) (disclaimer would be effective when alleged misrepresentation was innocent and not intentional), with Bank of Montreal v. Signet Bank, 193 F.3d 818 (4th Cir. 1999) (disclaiming language in contract would not bar claim of innocent misrepresentation because misrepresentation of material fact is always ground for rescission or action for damages).

7. *Economic analysis of nondisclosure.* An article by Professor Anthony Kronman presents an economic analysis of the duty of disclosure. Professor Kronman argues that courts should draw a distinction between information that has been casually acquired and information obtained through a deliberate and costly investigation. Disclosure of deliberately acquired information should

not be required, he contends, because it is socially desirable to give parties an incentive to acquire information. Nondisclosure protects a party's investment in the acquisition of such information. (Kronman points out that a rule permitting nondisclosure amounts to a legal recognition of a property right in the information.) Casually acquired information, on the other hand, does not reflect an investment of resources. Kronman argues that disclosure of such information should be required when the holder knows that the other party is without such information, because disclosure is the least costly method of reducing mistaken contracts. Anthony T. Kronman, Mistake, Disclosure, Information and the Law of Contracts, 7 J. Legal Stud. 1, 16-18 (1978). Compare Robert L. Birmingham, The Duty to Disclose and the Prisoner's Dilemma: *Laidlaw v. Organ,* 29 Wm. & Mary L. Rev. 249 (1988) (criticism of Kronman's economic analysis of the duty of disclosure). Would Professor Kronman's analysis justify imposing a duty of disclosure in the *Hill* case?

Comment: Lawyers' Professional Ethics

In each state, the admission of lawyers to the practice of law and the responsibility for their discipline once admitted rest with the highest court of that state. While the rules and procedures vary in different jurisdictions, typically the highest state court (or some board created by the court and acting pursuant to its authority) has promulgated a set of rules of professional conduct. These rules are usually based on Model Rules of Professional Conduct, originally adopted by the American Bar Association in 1983 and revised periodically since then.[1] The American Bar Association, a private association of lawyers, has no legal authority over the practice of law but is extremely influential in the area of professional ethics by virtue of its studies and publications. Rules of professional ethics impose restrictions on the conduct of lawyers principally in three areas: (1) the lawyer-client relationship, (2) the lawyer's obligations to the system of justice, and (3) permissible methods of obtaining legal business.

A number of the most important rules of professional ethics focus on the lawyer-client relationship. Generally, these rules reflect three cardinal principles: loyalty, competence, and confidentiality. The duty of loyalty, of course, extends to the avoidance of any conflict of interest arising from the attorney's representation of clients with interests adverse to each other. Thus, a lawyer must refuse to represent multiple clients if a conflict of interest exists between those clients (a husband and wife in a contested divorce case, for example). Model Rule (MR) 1.7. The duty of loyalty also extends to avoidance of a conflict between the clients' interests and those of the attorney. For this reason, a lawyer must protect and account for any client money or property that comes into the lawyer's possession. Further, the lawyer must maintain any client money in a separate "trust account" and not "commingle" client funds with funds belonging to the lawyer. MR 1.15. A lawyer must not violate his obligations as

1. California currently has a set of professional standards not based on the Model Rules.

a fiduciary to his client by entering into a business transaction with the client unless the transaction meets a number of requirements, including fairness and full disclosure. MR 1.8(a).

In his representation of a client, a lawyer must handle the matter competently. MR 1.1. A failure to act competently may result in tort liability for malpractice as well as professional discipline. See, e.g., Sierra Fria Corp. v. Evans, 127 F.3d 175 (1st Cir. 1997) (attorney must exercise reasonable care and skill in matter for which attorney was retained); Horne v. Peckham, 158 Cal. Rptr. 714 (Ct. App. 1979) (lawyer who is not a specialist in tax law has a duty either to refer tax matters to a specialist or to conform to the standard expected of a specialist). Finally, subject to certain exceptions, a lawyer must not reveal any confidential information received from a client. MR 1.6. Amendments adopted by the ABA to the Model Rules in the last few years require lawyers to keep abreast of developments in technology as they affect the practice of law and impose an obligation on lawyers to take reasonable precautions to protect the confidentiality of client information particularly in internet-related transactions.

While the lawyer's relationship with his client is central to his role, lawyers are also officers of the court and as such have obligations to the system of justice. A lawyer must not engage in fraud, deceit, or misrepresentation in his representation of a client. MR 8.4(c). Lawyers are generally required to report professional misconduct by other lawyers to the appropriate disciplinary authorities. MR 8.3. To protect the impartiality of decision makers, rules of professional ethics prohibit lawyers from having improper contacts with either judges or jurors. MR 3.5. At times the lawyer's duty to the system of justice may even override the lawyer's duty to his client. Thus, sometimes a lawyer must reveal legal authority that is damaging to his client's case, even though opposing counsel has failed to find the authority. MR 3.3(a)(2). In some situations a lawyer may even be required to reveal confidential information received from a client in order to rectify fraud committed by the client or another person. MR 1.6, 3.3. See Nix v. Whiteside, 475 U.S. 157 (1986) (defendant in criminal case not denied constitutional right to effective assistance of counsel when lawyer informed client that he would report client's intention to commit perjury to the court).

Finally, a number of rules of professional ethics impose restrictions on the ways in which lawyers may obtain business. Traditionally, the legal profession has considered professional advertising or solicitation as ethically improper. In 1976 the U.S. Supreme Court ushered in a period of dramatic change in the rules dealing with delivery of legal services when it held that advertising of the price and availability of routine legal services (uncontested divorces, for example) was protected under the first amendment and could not be prohibited by rules of professional conduct. Bates & O'Steen v. State Bar, 433 U.S. 350 (1977). Since then, the Court has decided a number of cases that have expanded the first amendment protection for lawyer advertising. A review of such cases can be found in Florida Bar v. Went For It, Inc., 515 U.S. 618 (1995) (holding by 5-4 decision that state could ban attorneys from sending direct-mail solicitations to disaster victims or relatives for 30 days after incident). Because of these cases, the rules of ethics dealing with advertising have been liberalized, and lawyer advertising on television, through the Internet, and other media has exploded, although restrictions remain in a number of states. MR 7.1, 7.2, 7.3. Regulation of advertising and solicitation by attorneys will undoubtedly remain a subject of debate and litigation for years to come.

Park 100 Investors, Inc. v. Kartes

Indiana Court of Appeals 650 N.E.2d 347 (1995)

Opinion

BARTEAU, Judge.

Park 100 appeals the trial court's finding that James and Nancy Kartes are not liable for unpaid rent under a personal guaranty of lease. We affirm.

Facts

In 1984, James and Nancy Kartes were part-owners of Kartes Video Communications, Inc. (KVC) in Indianapolis. The company was growing rapidly and required larger operating facilities. Robert Scannell, a representative of the Park 100 industrial complex in Indianapolis, contacted the Karteses and marketed facilities in Park 100 that KVC could lease. After discussing the general requirements and terms for the new facilities, James Kartes delegated all of the lease negotiations to David Kaplan, a KVC senior vice-president.

Kaplan and Scannell worked out the details for KVC's lease of Building 107 in Park 100. Park 100 provided a lease agreement form to KVC. The lease did not include any provisions for a personal guaranty of the lease and a personal guaranty was never mentioned during any of the lease negotiations. KVC's attorney approved the lease and Kaplan signed and delivered the lease to Scannell on or before July 27, 1984. KVC made preparations to move its operations into Building 107 over the weekend of July 28-29, 1984.

On Friday, July 27, 1984, the evening before KVC was to move into Building 107, Scannell went to KVC's offices at 5:00 p.m. and found the Karteses getting into their car to leave for the day. Scannell told the Karteses that he had "lease papers" for them to sign. James Kartes explained that they were late for their daughter's wedding rehearsal and asked if the matter could wait until the following Monday. Scannell informed the Karteses that the matter could not wait and that KVC could not move into Building 107 until the papers were signed.

The Karteses and Scannell then went into KVC's building, where Scannell produced a document entitled "Lease Agreement."[1] From the lobby of the

1. The parties dispute the size of the document Scannell presented to the Karteses. Mr. Kartes testified that the document included approximately fifteen pages, while Scannell maintained that he only presented the two-page guaranty of lease to the Kartes. Combined, the lease agreement and guaranty total 17 pages. The trial court specifically found that Mr. Kartes's testimony was clear, complete, and highly credible, whereas Scannell's testimony was sketchy, inconsistent at best, and far less credible than Mr. Kartes's testimony.

building, James Kartes telephoned Kaplan, who was in another part of the building, and asked if the lease agreement had been approved by KVC's lawyer. Scannell remained silent. Upon ending his discussion with Kaplan, James Kartes asked where he was to sign the document. Scannell opened the papers to the signature page and the Karteses both signed the document. The Karteses, being officers of the corporation, did not think it unusual that their signatures would be required on the lease. Scannell never told the Karteses that what they were signing was actually a personal guaranty of lease.

Years later, Park 100 sent the Karteses a "Tenant Agreement" that included an estoppel certificate. At this time the Karteses first learned of the personal guaranty of lease. They immediately disavowed the guaranty and refused to affirm that portion of the "Tenant Agreement."

Eventually, the Kartes sold their interest in KVC to Saffron Associates, which subsequently failed to make rent payments to Park 100. Park 100 brought suit to collect the unpaid rent from the Karteses under the personal guaranty.

Issues

Park 100 raises numerous issues and arguments on appeal. We find that one issue is dispositive of this matter: whether the trial court erred in finding that Park 100 used fraudulent means to procure the signatures of the Karteses on the guaranty of lease.

Discussion

Upon the motion of Park 100, the trial court entered thorough and well-reasoned Findings of Facts and Conclusions of Law. When the trial court enters special Findings of Fact and Conclusions of Law pursuant to a motion by a party, this court employs a two-tiered standard of review. First, we must determine whether the findings support the judgment. The second inquiry is whether the conclusions and judgment are clearly erroneous based on the facts as found by the trial court. American Cyanamid Co. v. Stephen (1993), Ind. App., 623 N.E.2d 1065, 1070.

The trial court found that Park 100 obtained the signatures of the Karteses on the personal guaranty of lease through fraudulent means. Under Indiana law, the elements of actual fraud are as follows:

> (1) A material misrepresentation of past or existing fact by the party to be charged, which
> (2) was false,
> (3) was made with knowledge or in reckless ignorance of the falsity,
> (4) was relied upon by the complaining party, and
> (5) proximately caused the complaining party injury.

Pugh's IGA v. Super Food Services, Inc. (1988), Ind. App., 531 N.E.2d 1194, 1197, reh'g denied, trans. denied. In its findings and conclusions, the trial court found: (1) The statements made by Scannell, Park 100's agent, that the personal guaranty was "lease papers" and that KVC could not move into the building until the papers were signed, were each misrepresentations of material facts;

(2) Scannell knew that the document he presented for the Karteses' signatures was a guaranty and, therefore, knowingly made false misrepresentations; and (3) the Karteses, through the use of ordinary care and diligence, believed that the document they were signing was a lease, and reasonably relied upon Scannell's statements to their detriment.

The evidence and testimony presented at trial supports these findings and conclusions. A guaranty of lease was never discussed during the lease negotiations, and the lease agreement makes no reference to a guaranty. The document that Scannell presented to the Karteses was entitled "Lease Agreement" and Scannell never told the Karteses that they were signing a personal guaranty of lease, even when he overheard the telephone conversation in which Mr. Kartes asked Kaplan if the lease agreement had been approved by KVC's lawyer.[3]

Park 100 argues that the Karteses failed to prove the third element of actual fraud, that of reliance. Park 100 summarily argues that one's reliance upon a material misrepresentation must be justified and, in an arm's-length relationship involving knowledgeable business people such as the Karteses, such reliance is misplaced. Park 100 concludes that the Karteses had a duty to read the document that they signed and cannot avoid their obligations under the agreement by claiming ignorance of its terms.

Generally, parties are obligated to know the terms of the agreement they are signing, and cannot avoid their obligations under the agreement due to a failure to read it. W.T. Rawleigh Co. v. Snider (1935), 207 Ind. 686, 690, 194 N.E. 356, 358; Givan v. Masterson (1898), 152 Ind. 127, 130, 51 N.E. 237, 238. However, where one employs misrepresentation to induce a party's obligation under a contract, one cannot bind the party to the terms of the agreement.

> It has many times been held, and is a well-settled rule of law, that a contract of guaranty cannot be enforced by the guarantee, where the guarantor has been induced to enter into the contract by fraudulent misrepresentations or concealment on the part of the guarantee.

Doerr v. Hibben Hollweg & Co. (1926), 84 Ind. App. 239, 241-242, 150 N.E. 795, 796.

Scannell misrepresented the personal guaranty as "lease papers," and in furtherance of this misrepresentation, the personal guaranty was disguised under the title of "Lease Agreement." We are not persuaded by Park 100's argument that the Karteses cannot prove actual fraud because the Karteses should have known better than to rely on Scannell's representations.

"Whether one has the right to rely depends largely on the facts of the case." Fire Ins. Exchange v. Bell (1994), Ind. App., 634 N.E.2d 517, 522, *aff'd in part, vacated in part,* 643 N.E.2d 310. When Scannell presented the "lease papers," Mr. Kartes telephoned Kaplan. Only upon confirming that KVC's attorney had

3. The trial court also found that Scannell had a duty to inform the Karteses that the document was a guaranty and not a lease, and that his silence was a fraudulent omission of a material fact. Park 100 argues that Scannell had no such duty and that the trial court erred on this point. We need not address this argument because Scannell's express misrepresentations alone support the finding of actual fraud. But see Midwest Commerce Banking Co. v. Elkhart City Centre (7th Cir. 1993), 4 F.3d 521, 524 and cases cited therein.

examined and approved the lease agreement did the Karteses affix their signatures to the document entitled "Lease Agreement." "While a person relying on another's representations must use ordinary care and diligence to guard against fraud, the requirement of reasonable prudence in business transactions is not carried to the extent that the law will ignore an intentional fraud practiced on the unwary." Fire Ins. Exchange, 634 N.E.2d at 521. The evidence supports the trial court's finding that the Karteses acted with ordinary care and diligence.

CONCLUSION

Whether fraud is present in a case is rooted in the surrounding facts and circumstances and is for the trial court to determine. A.G. Edwards & Sons, Inc. v. Hilligoss (1991), Ind. App., 597 N.E.2d 1, 3. We cannot reweigh the evidence and substitute our judgment for that of the trial court, as Park 100 invites us to do. Wolfeld v. Hanika (1932), 95 Ind. App. 44, 179 N.E. 178. The evidence supports the trial court's conclusion that Park 100 obtained the signatures of the Karteses on the personal guaranty of lease through fraudulent means, and the findings support the judgment. The trial court's conclusion and judgment in favor of James and Nancy Kartes are not clearly erroneous.

Affirmed.

RILEY, J. and SHARPNACK, C.J. concur.

NOTES AND QUESTIONS

1. *Fraud in the execution.* The *Park 100* case differs significantly from the two previous cases in this section. In both *Syester* and *Hill* the parties alleging fraud presumably understood the terms of the written contracts that they signed but alleged that they were fraudulently induced to enter the agreements by false statements or material nondisclosures. The Karteses, however, alleged that they were misled regarding the content of the document that they executed or signed. As to the latter type of fraud, Restatement (Second) §163 provides:

> If a misrepresentation as to the character or essential terms of a proposed contract induces conduct that appears to be a manifestation of assent by one who neither knows nor has reasonable opportunity to know of the character or essential terms of the proposed contract, his conduct is not effective as a manifestation of assent.

Comment *a* goes on to state that that section applies when the misrepresentation relates to the very nature of the contract itself and not just one of its nonessential terms. See, e.g., Rosenthal v. Great Western Fin. Securities Corp., 926 P.2d 1061, 1073 (Cal. 1996) (discussing difference between "fraud in the execution" where the party is deceived as to the nature of the writing and "fraud in the inducement" where the party knows what he is signing but does so as the result of misrepresentations). Cf. Restatement (Second) §166 (assenting party may request "reformation" of writing to express actual terms of the agreement when misled about contents).

Recall the Ray v. Eurice Brothers case from Chapter 2. Is the availability of relief for fraud in the execution consistent with the notion of a "duty to read" that traditionally binds parties to signed agreements whether the agreement is read or not? In TufAmerica, Inc. v. Codigo Music LLC, 162 F. Supp. 3d 295 (S.D.N.Y. 2016), the court, applying New York law, stated that fraud in the execution requires a showing of "excusable ignorance of the written terms which may be proven by presenting evidence that someone secretly changed an important term of the contract before the ignorant party signed it, and that the ignorant party lacked a reasonable opportunity to learn of the change before signing." Id., at 326-327. The court found a triable issue of fraud in the execution based on an allegation that four earlier drafts of contracts conveying property rights in music had material terms that were drastically and inexplicably changed in the final written contract to the benefit of the drafting party. Id.

2. *Hypothetical variations of* ***Park 100****.* Consider whether any of the following changes in the facts might have had any effect on the outcome in *Park 100*, either separately or cumulatively:

(a) When Mr. Kartes phoned Kaplan, he was in a phone booth in the corner of the lobby, where his conversation could not be overheard by Scannell;
(b) Scannell did not claim that when he presented the papers to the Karteses for their signature that it was only a two-page document (see footnote 1 to the court's opinion), but asserted rather that the 15-page document he presented did in fact constitute "lease papers," just as he said it did;
(c) When the Karteses met Scannell in the lobby, they were not hurrying off to their daughter's wedding rehearsal but were headed home at the end of a long day to spend a quiet evening eating dinner and watching television;
(d) Scannell testified that in deals such as this one involving a small, closely held corporation, personal shareholder guarantees were so common that he truly regarded the added provision as a "formality."

D. UNCONSCIONABILITY

We have seen in our earlier study of the doctrine of consideration that courts have generally regarded that doctrine as being ill-suited to policing the "fairness" of a contract. So long as a transaction appears to have been a genuine exchange, it will not be regarded as unenforceable "for lack of consideration" unless the values exchanged are so grossly unbalanced as to suggest some bargaining defect, such as one party's lack of mental capacity. (Recall the *Sparrow* case.) And of course various types of bargaining misconduct such as fraud or duress are likely in fact to produce unequal bargains, which the injured party may be able to avoid because of those factors. (She may even be able to recover damages under the law of torts.) But what of the case where various elements — including, but not necessarily limited to, imbalance of bargaining power in one or more senses — have resulted in an agreement which appears to be extremely unfair, and yet none of the "defensive doctrines" seems squarely to apply? Must a court treat this like any ordinary contract, and enforce it according to its terms?

Over the years, various legal systems, including our own, have grappled with that question. (This historical process is described in more detail in the Comment below.) Since the mid-twentieth century, activated in part by the example of Uniform Commercial Code §2-302, our law of contract generally has been willing to entertain the argument that a given exchange agreement may be unenforceable (in whole or in part) because enforcing it would be just too shocking to the conscience of the court — in short, it is an "unconscionable" contract. The UCC, the Restatement (Second) of Contracts (in §208), and many judges have struggled to define or at least give some predictable content to this amorphous concept.

The inherent vagueness of the unconscionability concept has resulted in a number of issues for courts to resolve. How should a court determine when an agreement is unconscionable? To what extent does the doctrine allow a court to refuse to enforce a contract simply because the contract is harsh, even if the bargaining process has not otherwise been defective? Does the doctrine apply to commercial as well as consumer transactions?

Williams v. Walker-Thomas Furniture Co.

United States Court of Appeals 350 F.2d 445 (D.C. Cir. 1965)

Before BAZELON, Chief Judge, and DANAHER and WRIGHT, Circuit Judges.

J. SKELLY WRIGHT, CIRCUIT JUDGE:

Appellee, Walker-Thomas Furniture Company, operates a retail furniture store in the District of Columbia. During the period from 1957 to 1962 each appellant in these cases purchased a number of household items from Walker-Thomas, for which payment was to be made in installments. The terms of each purchase were contained in a printed form contract which set forth the value of the purchased item and purported to lease the item to appellant for a stipulated monthly rent payment. The contract then provided, in substance, that title would remain in Walker-Thomas until the total of all the monthly payments made equaled the stated value of the item, at which time appellants could take title. In the event of a default in the payment of any monthly installment, Walker-Thomas could repossess the item.

The contract further provided that "the amount of each periodical installment payment to be made by [purchaser] to the Company under this present lease shall be inclusive of and not in addition to the amount of each installment payment to be made by [purchaser] under such prior leases, bills or accounts; *and all payments now and hereafter made by [purchaser] shall be credited pro rata on all outstanding leases, bills and accounts* due the Company by [purchaser] at the time each such payment is made." (Emphasis added.) The effect of this rather obscure provision was to keep a balance due on every item purchased until the balance due on all items, whenever purchased, was liquidated. As a result, the debt incurred at the time of

The storefront of Walker-Thomas Furniture in Washington D.C. Although the company no longer exists, the neon sign was refurbished in 2013.

purchase of each item was secured by the right to repossess all the items previously purchased by the same purchaser, and each new item purchased automatically became subject to a security interest arising out of the previous dealings.

On May 12, 1962, appellant Thorne purchased an item described as a Daveno, three tables, and two lamps, having total stated value of $391.10. Shortly thereafter, he defaulted on his monthly payments and appellee sought to replevy all the items purchased since the first transaction in 1958. Similarly, on April 17, 1962, appellant Williams bought a stereo set of stated value of $514.95.[1] She too defaulted shortly thereafter, and appellee sought to replevy all the items purchased since December, 1957. The Court of General Sessions granted judgment for appellee. The District of Columbia Court of Appeals affirmed, and we granted appellants' motion for leave to appeal to this court.

Appellants' principal contention, rejected by both the trial and the appellate courts below, is that these contracts, or at least some of them, are unconscionable and, hence, not enforceable. In its opinion in Williams v. Walker-Thomas Furniture Company, 198 A.2d 914, 916 (1964), the District of Columbia Court of Appeals explained its rejection of this contention as follows:

> Appellant's second argument presents a more serious question. The record reveals that prior to the last purchase appellant had reduced the balance in her account to $164. The last purchase, a stereo set, raised the balance due to $678. Significantly, at the time of this and the preceding purchases, appellee was aware of appellant's financial position. The reverse side of the stereo contract listed the name of appellant's social worker and her $218 monthly stipend from the government. Nevertheless, with full knowledge that appellant had to feed, clothe and support both herself and seven children on this amount, appellee sold her a $514 stereo set.
>
> We cannot condemn too strongly appellee's conduct. It raises serious questions of sharp practice and irresponsible business dealings. A review of the legislation in the District of Columbia affecting retail sales and the pertinent decisions of the highest court in this jurisdiction disclose, however, no ground upon which this court can declare the contracts in question contrary to public policy. We note that were the Maryland Retail Installment Sales Act, Art. 83 §§128-153, or its equivalent, in force in the District of Columbia, we could grant appellant appropriate relief. We think Congress should consider corrective legislation to protect the public from such exploitive contracts as were utilized in the case at bar.

1. At the time of this purchase her account showed a balance of $164 still owing from her prior purchases. The total of all the purchases made over the years in question came to $1,800. The total payments amounted to $1,400.

We do not agree that the court lacked the power to refuse enforcement to contracts found to be unconscionable. In other jurisdictions, it has been held as a matter of common law that unconscionable contracts are not enforceable.[2] While no decision of this court so holding has been found, the notion that an unconscionable bargain should not be given full enforcement is by no means novel. In Scott v. United States, 79 U.S. (12 Wall.) 443, 445, 20 L. Ed. 438 (1870), the Supreme Court stated:

> If a contract be unreasonable and unconscionable, but not void for fraud, a court of law will give to the party who sues for its breach damages, not according to its letter, but only such as he is equitably entitled to. . . .

Since we have never adopted or rejected such a rule, the question here presented is actually one of first impression.

Congress has recently enacted the Uniform Commercial Code, which specifically provides that the court may refuse to enforce a contract which it finds to be unconscionable at the time it was made. 28 D.C. Code §2-302 (Supp. IV 1965). The enactment of this section, which occurred subsequent to the contracts here in suit, does not mean that the common law of the District of Columbia was otherwise at the time of enactment, nor does it preclude the court from adopting a similar rule in the exercise of its powers to develop the common law for the District of Columbia. In fact, in view of the absence of prior authority on the point, we consider the congressional adoption of §2-302 persuasive authority for following the rationale of the cases from which the section is explicitly derived.[5] Accordingly, we hold that where the element of unconscionability is present at the time a contract is made, the contract should not be enforced.

Unconscionability has generally been recognized to include an absence of meaningful choice on the part of one of the parties together with contract terms which are unreasonably favorable to the other party.[6] Whether a meaningful choice is present in a particular case can only be determined by consideration of all the circumstances surrounding the transaction. In many cases the meaningfulness of the choice is negated by a gross inequality of bargaining power.[7] The manner in which the contract was entered is also relevant to this

---

2. Campbell Soup Co. v. Wentz, 3 Cir., 172 F.2d 80 (1948); Indianapolis Morris Plan Corporation v. Sparks, 132 Ind. App. 145, 172 N.E.2d 899 (1961); Henningsen v. Bloomfield Motors, Inc., 32 N.J. 358, 161 A.2d 69, 84-96, 75 A.L.R.2d 1 (1960). Cf. 1 Corbin, Contracts §128 (1963).

5. See Comment, §2-302, Uniform Commercial Code (1962). Compare Note, 45 Va. L. Rev. 583, 590 (1959), where it is predicted that the rule of §2-302 will be followed by analogy in cases which involve contracts not specifically covered by the section. Cf. 1 State of New York Law Revision Commission, Report and Record of Hearings on the Uniform Commercial Code 108-110 (1954) (remarks of Professor Llewellyn).

6. See Henningsen v. Bloomfield Motors, Inc., supra note 2; Campbell Soup Co. v. Wentz, supra note 2.

7. See Henningsen v. Bloomfield Motors, Inc., supra note 2, 161 A.2d at 86, and authorities there cited. Inquiry into the relative bargaining power of the two parties is not an inquiry wholly divorced from the general question of unconscionability, since a one-sided bargain is itself evidence of the inequality of the bargaining parties. This fact was vaguely recognized in the common law doctrine of intrinsic fraud, that is, fraud which can be presumed from the grossly unfair nature of the terms of the contract. See the oft-quoted statement of Lord Hardwicke in Earl of Chesterfield v. Janssen,

consideration. Did each party to the contract, considering his obvious education or lack of it, have a reasonable opportunity to understand the terms of the contract, or were the important terms hidden in a maze of fine print and minimized by deceptive sales practices? Ordinarily, one who signs an agreement without full knowledge of its terms might be held to assume the risk that he has entered a one-sided bargain.[8] But when a party of little bargaining power, and hence little real choice, signs a commercially unreasonable contract with little or no knowledge of its terms, it is hardly likely that his consent, or even an objective manifestation of his consent, was ever given to all the terms. In such a case the usual rule that the terms of the agreement are not to be questioned[9] should be abandoned and the court should consider whether the terms of the contract are so unfair that enforcement should be withheld.[10]

In determining reasonableness or fairness, the primary concern must be with the terms of the contract considered in light of the circumstances existing when the contract was made. The test is not simple, nor can it be mechanically applied. The terms are to be considered "in the light of the general commercial background and the commercial needs of the particular trade or case."[11] Corbin suggests the test as being whether the terms are "so extreme as to appear unconscionable according to the mores and business practices of the time and place." 1 Corbin, op. cit. supra note 2.[12] We think this formulation correctly states the test to be applied in those cases where no meaningful choice was exercised upon entering the contract.

Because the trial court and the appellate court did not feel that enforcement could be refused, no findings were made on the possible unconscionability of the contracts in these cases. Since the record is not sufficient for our deciding the issue as a matter of law, the cases must be remanded to the trial court for further proceedings.

So ordered.

---

28 Eng. Rep. 82, 100 (1751): ". . . [Fraud] may be apparent from the intrinsic nature and subject of the bargain itself; such as no man in his senses and not under delusion would make. . . ." . . .

8. See Restatement, Contracts §70 (1932); Note, 63 Harv. L. Rev. 494 (1950). See also Daley v. People's Building, Loan & Savings Assn., 178 Mass. 13, 59 N.E. 452, 453 (1901), in which Mr. Justice Holmes, while sitting on the Supreme Judicial Court of Massachusetts, made this observation:

> . . . Courts are less and less disposed to interfere with parties making such contracts as they choose, so long as they interfere with no one's welfare but their own. . . . It will be understood that we are speaking of parties standing in an equal position where neither has any oppressive advantage or power. . . .

9. This rule has never been without exception. In cases involving merely the transfer of unequal amounts of the same commodity, the courts have held the bargain unenforceable for the reason that "in such a case, it is clear, that the law cannot indulge in the presumption of equivalence between the consideration and the promise." 1 Williston, Contracts §115 (3d ed. 1957).

10. See the general discussion of "Boiler-Plate Agreements" in Llewellyn, The Common Law Tradition 362-371 (1960).

11. Comment, Uniform Commercial Code §2-307 [sic; should be §2-302].

12. See Henningsen v. Bloomfield Motors, Inc., supra note 2; Mandel v. Liebman, 303 N.Y. 88, 100 N.E.2d 149 (1951). The traditional test as stated in Greer v. Tweed, [N.Y.C.P., 13 Abb. Pr., N.S., 427, 429 (1872),] is "such as no man in his senses and not under delusion would make on the one hand, and as no honest or fair man would accept, on the other."

DANAHER, Circuit Judge (dissenting):

The District of Columbia Court of Appeals obviously was as unhappy about the situation here presented as any of us can possibly be. Its opinion in the *Williams* case, quoted in the majority text, concludes: "We think Congress should consider corrective legislation to protect the public from such exploitive contracts as were utilized in the case at bar."

My view is thus summed up by an able court which made no finding that there had actually been sharp practice. Rather the appellant seems to have known precisely where she stood.

There are many aspects of public policy here involved. What is a luxury to some may seem an outright necessity to others. Is public oversight to be required of the expenditures of relief funds? A washing machine, e.g., in the hands of a relief client might become a fruitful source of income. Many relief clients may well need credit, and certain business establishments will take long chances on the sale of items, expecting their pricing policies will afford a degree of protection commensurate with the risk. Perhaps a remedy when necessary will be found within the provisions of the "Loan Shark" law, D.C. Code §§26-601 et seq. (1961).

I mention such matters only to emphasize the desirability of a cautious approach to any such problem, particularly since the law for so long has allowed parties such great latitude in making their own contracts. I dare say there must annually be thousands upon thousands of installment credit transactions in this jurisdiction, and one can only speculate as to the effect the decision in these cases will have.

I join the District of Columbia Court of Appeals in its disposition of the issues.

NOTES AND QUESTIONS

1. *Procedural and substantive unconscionability.* The *Williams* court states that unconscionability consists of "an absence of meaningful choice on the part of one of the parties together with contract terms which are unreasonably favorable to the other party" and goes on to note that conspicuousness and intelligibility of a clause will also be relevant. In one of the earliest assessments of UCC §2-302, Professor Leff coined the terms *procedural unconscionability* and *substantive unconscionability* to identify what he perceived as two key aspects of the new provision. Arthur Allen Leff, Unconscionability and the Code—The Emperor's New Clause, 115 U. Pa. L. Rev. 485, 487-488 (1967). Read together, the Leff article and the *Williams* case indicate that procedural unconscionability may refer to either lack of choice by one party or some defect in the bargaining process (such as quasi-fraud or quasi-duress) and that substantive unconscionability relates to the fairness of the terms of the resulting bargain. Many courts now use these concepts as a framework for analysis of unconscionability problems, generally requiring a showing of both procedural and substantive elements. See, e.g., FI-Tampa, LLC v. Kelly-Hall, 135 So. 3d 563, 567 (Fla. Dist. Ct. App. 2014) (requiring evidence of both elements); The McCaffrey

Group, Inc. v. Superior Court, 169 Cal. Rptr. 3d 766 (Cal. Ct. App. 2014) (both elements of unconscionability required under "sliding scale"; if more of one element present, less may be required of the other). But see Maxwell v. Fidelity Financial Services, Inc., 907 P.2d 51, 58 (Ariz. 1995) (agreeing with jurisdictions that accept substantive unconscionability alone as sufficient and leaving open the question of whether procedural alone would be enough); Balogh v. Balogh, 332 P.3d 631, 643-644 (Haw. 2014) (under certain circumstances, an "impermissibly one-sided agreement" may be unconscionable even if there is no unfair surprise or procedural unconscionability).

While Professor Leff agreed that the contract in *Williams* was procedurally unconscionable, he criticized the court's analysis of the substantive aspect of the transaction as follows:

> How does that test apply to the *Williams* facts? What is it about Mrs. Williams' contract which is "unconscionable?" Surprisingly, the answer is not clear, even about *what* in the contract is bad. It seems, however, that there are two possibilities. First, it may be that the provision by which each item purchased became security for all items purchased was the objectionable feature of the contract. Or it might be that the furniture company sold this expensive stereo set to this particular party which forms the unconscionability of the contract. If the vice is the add-on clause, then one encounters the now-familiar problem: such a clause is hardly such a moral outrage as by itself meets Judge Wright's standard of being "so extreme as to appear unconscionable according to the mores and business practices of the time and place." . . . Of the thirty-seven jurisdictions which have statutes regulating retail installment sales, only one has a provision making add-on clauses impermissible. In such circumstances it does seem a bit much to find "so extreme as to appear unconscionable according to the mores and business practices of the time and place" an add-on clause in the District of Columbia which is used and statutorily permitted almost everyplace else, including contiguous Maryland. One's gorge can hardly be expected to rise with such nice geographic selectivity.
>
> If one is not convinced that the unconscionability inheres in the add-on provision, it may be argued that it inheres in the contract as a whole, in the act of having sold this expensive item to a poor person knowing of her poverty. This is quite clearly the primary significance of the case to some of the commentators. . . .

Arthur Allen Leff, Unconscionability and the Code — The Emperor's New Clause, 115 U. Pa. L. Rev. 485, 554-556 (1967). Do Professor Leff's stated choices exhaust the alternatives? Or is it possible that unfairness lies in selling "this expensive item" (the stereo) and others as well, "to a poor person, knowing of her poverty," *pursuant to a contract with an add-on clause*? Failing to make add-on clauses illegal per se is not necessarily the same as giving them a vote of thanks; for instance, the Uniform Consumer Credit Code (UCCC or U3C), promulgated by the National Conference of Commissioners on Uniform State Laws after the *Williams* decision, permits the use of add-on clauses in consumer credit sales but requires that moneys paid by the buyer be allocated to the goods purchased in the order of their purchase, rather than pro rata to all goods as yet unpaid for. UCCC §§3.302, 3.303.

2. *Other tests for unconscionability.* In Judge Wright's opinion, in footnotes 7 and 12, he quotes the old English formulation of "intrinsic fraud" as being a bargain that ". . . no man in his senses and not under delusion would make . . . , and no honest or fair man would accept. . . ." Although this language is sometimes quoted by American courts in discussing unconscionability, some have questioned whether it is a useful test. In Cordova v. World Financial Co. of New Mexico, 208 P.3d 901 (N. Mex. 2009), the court had this to say about it:

> While this dramatically expressive characterization concededly has made it into New Mexico case law, . . . if literally applied it would be inconsistent with all the New Mexico cases that have struck down contracts for unconscionability, as well as most of those from other jurisdictions. Our law has never really required that a person seeking relief from an unconscionable contract must first establish that he or she actually had to have been a madman or a fool to sign it. It is sufficient if the provision is grossly unreasonable and against our public policy. . . . The repetition of this unhelpful terminology from a bygone age only serves to confuse the unconscionability issues without serving any constructive purpose. We specifically disapprove of its use as a controlling standard of unconscionability analysis under New Mexico law.

Id. at 909-910.

As an alternative to the procedural/substantive framework for unconscionability analysis, the Uniform Consumer Credit Code §5.108 and some courts have adopted a multifactor balancing approach. UCCC §5.108 calls for assessment of a number of elements including whether the seller believes the consumer is likely to default on the obligation, whether the consumer will receive substantial benefit from the transaction, gross disparity between the contract and market price, and whether the seller has knowingly taken advantage of a consumer's bargaining disadvantage due to mental impairment, lack of education, or similar factors. The Kansas Supreme Court adopted a balancing test in Wille v. Southwestern Bell Telephone Co., 549 P.2d 903 (Kan. 1976), weighing factors such as the use of a standard form contract, limitation on available remedies for breach, use of inconspicuous or incomprehensible terms, overall imbalance in the bargain, exploitation of a party's lack of experience or education, and inequality of bargaining or economic power. Id. at 906-907.

3. *Factual context for* **Williams.** Is it possible that the judges in *Williams*, and perhaps some current readers of the case, are influenced by stereotypes that may come to mind based on the limited facts that are given in the Court of Appeals opinion? While the court does not reveal Williams's race or ethnicity, educational background, or work experience, the majority opinion reports her monthly income of $218 and the dissent indicates that she received "relief funds." What common assumptions about Williams might be made on the basis of that information and how might they affect the resolution of the case? Would it make a difference to the outcome of the case if Williams happened to be an educated person with business experience who suddenly found herself

with seven children to raise as a single parent because of the accidental death of her husband? Professor Muriel Morisey Spence suggests that possible scenario and warns that discussion of the *Williams* case may often reinforce stereotypes concerning gender, race, and class. Muriel Morisey Spence, Teaching Williams v. Walker-Thomas Furniture Co., 3 Temple Pol. & C.R. L. Rev. 89 (1994). Professor Spence highlights the fact that Williams appears to have made timely payments for about five years before defaulting on the account for reasons not revealed. Id. at 96. Moreover, do you think that even a well-educated person would have understood the add-on clause and been able to protect herself against it? (Did you understand the clause the first time you read it?)

Additional background facts about the appellants, Mrs. Williams and the Thornes, can in fact be gathered from the lower court opinions before the cases were consolidated, Williams v. Walker-Thomas Furniture Co., 198 A.2d 914 (D.C. 1964) and Thorne v. Walker-Thomas Furniture Co., 198 A.2d 914 (D.C. 1964). Further information on the case has surfaced over the years. See Eben Colby, What Did the Doctrine of Unconscionability Do to the Walker-Thomas Furniture Company? 34 Conn. L. Rev. 625 (2002). From those collective sources, it becomes clear that the Thornes and Mrs. Williams did pay their respective accounts faithfully for four to five years before eventually defaulting. While the cause for Mrs. Williams's default is not clear, it appears that illness led to the Thornes' default. The lower court reports that Mrs. Williams was a person of limited education and Colby reports that Mr. Thorne had a third-grade education. Colby also reports that Walker-Thomas was known to have a practice of repossessing goods, having filed "approximately one hundred writs of replevin each year for many years preceding Williams's litigation." 34 Conn. L. Rev. at 652. The lower court opinion also reflects that the store sold most of the goods through door-to-door sales, reporting that Mrs. Williams "testified that most of the purchases were made at her home; that the contracts were signed in blank; that she did not read the instruments; and that she was not provided with a copy. She admitted, however, that she did not ask anyone to read or explain the contracts to her." 198 A.2d at 915. Mrs. Williams's purchases included sheets, curtains, toys, rugs, chairs, a chest of drawers, beds, mattresses, a washing machine, and, finally, the stereo set. Id. Do any of these additional facts affect your opinion about the applicability of the unconscionability doctrine to the cases?

4. *Price term unconscionability.* In *Williams* the court considered whether the doctrine of unconscionability should apply to an "add-on" clause, a part of the contract that consumers are unlikely to read or understand. Should the doctrine also apply to provisions of the contract on which consumers usually do focus their attention, such as the price term in a sales contact or the monthly fee in a rental agreement? Whether the drafters of UCC §2-302 intended the section to be used to police the price term of a contract is unclear from its history. Nonetheless, a number of cases have held consumer contracts unconscionable because of excessive price. E.g., Ahern v. Knecht, 563 N.E.2d 787 (Ill. App. Ct. 1990) (plumber had charged plaintiff $762 for services worth at most

$150; plaintiff given judgment for refund); American Home Improvement, Inc. v. MacIver, 201 A.2d 886 (N.H. 1964) (contract for home improvement in the amount of $2,658, which included $809 in interest and $806 for sales commission, was unconscionable); Frostifresh Corp. v. Reynoso, 274 N.Y.S.2d 757 (Dist. Ct. 1966) (sale of refrigerator-freezer costing $348 for price of $1,396.10 held unconscionable where negotiations were conducted in Spanish, contract was written in English, and salesman represented that unit would pay for itself through $25 referral fees when neighbors bought the same item). Moreover, both the Restatement and the Uniform Consumer Credit Code indicate that excessive price may be a basis of unconscionability. Restatement (Second) §208, Comment *c*; UCCC §5.108(4)(c).

5. ***Dohrmann revisited.*** Recall the *Dohrmann* case in Chapter 2 in which the plaintiff sought to enforce a written contract providing for his receipt of $5.5 million in assets in exchange for adding the promisor's family name as a middle name for the plaintiff's two children. The court in that case held that the plaintiff could not recover due to "gross inadequacy" of consideration, but also noted the presence of other factors that militated against enforcement of the decedent's promises to the plaintiff. Now that we have studied incapacity, duress, undue influence, misrepresentation, and unconscionability, would any of those doctrines have been stronger reasons than failure of consideration for the court's refusing to enforce those promises?

6. *Procedural limits.* The court in *Williams* held that the case must be remanded to the trial court for a determination of whether the clause was unconscionable. Section 2-302 provides that the question of unconscionability is a legal issue to be decided by the court, rather than the trier of fact, but only after providing the parties an opportunity to present evidence relevant to the disputed provision. See Vilella v. AT&T, 953 N.Y.S.2d 554 (Sup. Ct. 2012) (where doubt exists about whether contract is unconscionable, the parties must have an opportunity to present evidence at a hearing; however, where significant facts are essentially undisputed court may decide issue without a hearing); Schroeder v. Fageol Motors, Inc., 544 P.2d 20, 24-25 (Wash. 1975) (en banc) (trial court erred in determining unconscionability on summary judgment without giving parties opportunity to present evidence). UCC §2-302 and Restatement (Second) §208 further provide that unconscionability is to be judged as of the time that the contract is made. Accordingly, courts generally emphasize that contracts should not be judged based on developments after the contract was formed. See Boston Helicopter Charter, Inc. v. Augusta Aviation Corp., 767 F. Supp. 363, 375 (D. Mass. 1991); Strand v. U.S. Bank National Association ND, 693 N.W.2d 918, 921 (N.D. 2005).

7. *Scholarly commentary.* Not all commentators agree with the widespread use of the procedural/substantive framework for determining unconscionability. Professor Robert Hillman advocates, in essence, the use of traditional doctrines, such as duress, undue influence, or fraud, whenever applicable, because they are more specific than the unconscionability doctrine and would limit application of the doctrine to extreme cases that truly shock the conscience. Robert A. Hillman, Debunking Some Myths about Unconscionability: A New

Framework for U.C.C. Section 2-302, 67 Cornell L. Rev. 1 (1981). In a similar vein, Professor Prince has taken aim specifically at the "lack of meaningful choice" test adopted in *Williams* and widely used by the courts. Harry G. Prince, Unconscionability in California: A Need for Restraint and Consistency, 46 Hastings L.J. 459 (1995). Prince observes that the quasi-fraud form of procedural unconscionability involves terms that are likely hidden or unintelligible if found, and therefore relates to the common law forms of bargaining misbehavior. Application of the lack of meaningful choice test, Prince suggests, is much more vague and difficult, except in cases of extreme necessity, and results in further obfuscation of an already imprecise concept. Id. at 474-479.

Professor Richard A. Epstein has offered a critique of unconscionability that analyzes the economic consequences of a variety of common contractual provisions such as the add-on clause in *Williams*. He concludes that such clauses normally promote efficiency by reducing transaction costs and benefit both parties. Richard A. Epstein, Unconscionability: A Critical Reappraisal, 18 J.L. & Econ. 293 (1975). Epstein asserts that the add-on clause provides an efficient means for the seller to obtain additional security to make the transaction feasible for both parties and should not be deemed unconscionable. Id. at 307. He does allow, however, that the unconscionability doctrine can serve an economically useful purpose when applied to agreements made under circumstances where coercive behavior (fraud, duress, etc.) was likely but difficult to prove. In such cases, Epstein suggests that the application of the doctrine advances the principle of freedom of contract while reducing judicial costs. Id. at 303-305. See also Russell Korobkin, Bounded Rationality, Standard Form Contracts, and Unconscionability, 70 U. Chi. L. Rev. 1203 (2003) (noting, inter alia, that limited ability of buyers to read and comprehend terms in standard form contracts inhibits operation of market to produce efficient standard terms).

In a symposium honoring Professor Knapp's 50 years in teaching, Professor Hazel Beh surveys the literature on the unconscionability doctrine and analyzes a number of the doctrine's weaknesses. Nonetheless, she agrees with Professor Knapp's view expressed in several articles that the doctrine of unconscionability serves a fundamental role in promoting fairness in contractual relationships. See Charles L. Knapp, Opting Out or Copping Out, 40 Loyola of L.A. L. Rev. 95, 126-135 (2006) and Blowing the Whistle on Mandatory Arbitration: Unconscionability as a Signaling Device, 46 San Diego L. Rev. 609, 610-614 (2009). Professor Beh proposes several modifications and developments to strengthen the concept: recognition of unconscionability as both a cause of action and a defense, reliance on principles established under the doctrine of illegality when dealing with claims of unconscionability, focus on the ethical implications of drafting clauses that have a "stench" of unconscionability, and judicial acceptance of unconscionability as a "standard of essential contracting fairness that has been entrusted to the common law of contracts." See Hazel G. Beh, Curing the Infirmities of the Unconscionability Doctrine, in Contract Law Present and Future: A Symposium to Honor Professor Charles L. Knapp on Fifty Years of Teaching Contract Law, 66 Hastings L.J. 1011, 1044-1045 (2015).

Comment: Historical Development of the Doctrine of Unconscionability

In civil law countries, the idea that a grossly unfair bargain should be unenforceable has a long history. Under Roman law, which greatly influenced the development of the civil law, the doctrine of "laesio enormis" provided that a party could rescind a land sale transaction if the disproportion between the values exchanged was greater than two to one. Modern civil law countries, such as Germany and France, recognize a number of doctrines that allow courts to refuse to enforce grossly unfair bargains. John P. Dawson, Duress and the Fair Exchange in French and German Law, 11 Tul. L. Rev. 345, 12 Tul. L. Rev. 42 (1937); John P. Dawson, Unconscionable Coercion: The German Version, 89 Harv. L. Rev. 1041 (1976). For example, Section 3.2.7 of the Principles of International Commercial Contracts (see the supplement) provides that a party may avoid a contract because of "gross disparity." For further discussion see Joseph M. Perillo, UNIDROIT Principles of International Commercial Contracts: The Black Letter Text and a Review, 63 Fordham L. Rev. 281, 293-294 (1994).

Unlike the civil law, the Anglo-American common law did not develop an explicit doctrine for dealing with unfair bargains, but there were a number of grounds that the common law courts could use to avoid enforcing such agreements. In equity a court could deny specific performance or other equitable relief if the price was inadequate or if the one seeking relief had "unclean hands." See Emily L. Sherwin, Law and Equity in Contract Enforcement, 50 Md. L. Rev. 253 (1991). At law, a court could manipulate doctrines such as consideration, mutual assent, or principles of interpretation to find in favor of a party who was the victim of an unfair bargain. See Joseph M. Perillo, Contracts, §9.38 (7th ed. 2014).

During the first half of the twentieth century, economic and social changes made the problem of enforceability of unfair bargains even more acute. Large commercial enterprises increasingly began using standard form contracts to conduct business transactions. The typical standard form contract contains numerous "boilerplate" provisions that are extremely favorable to the drafting party. Moreover, negotiation of such terms rarely occurs both because the terms are normally not read and also because the form is usually presented on a "take-it-or-leave-it" basis, as exemplified in the *C & J Fertilizer* case in Chapter 5. Thus, the emergence of the standard form brought into question the concept of mutual assent, a pillar of classical contract law. The same period also witnessed a growing public awareness of the problems of the poor and unsophisticated, potential victims for unscrupulous commercial parties.

One judicial tool that emerged for dealing with unfair contracts was the doctrine of "unconscionability," codified in UCC §2-302. Although §2-302 applies strictly only to contracts for the sale of goods, its formulation of the unconscionability standard has been incorporated in the Restatement (Second) §208 and has been regularly applied to all types of contracts. See E. Allan Farnsworth, Contracts §4.28, at 298-299 (4th ed. 2004). The section was drafted to address concerns that the practice of courts' distorting other doctrinal rules to police for unfairness would produce confusion and unpredictability or, as stated by

Professor Karl Llewellyn, concern that "[c]overt tools are never reliable tools." Karl Llewellyn, Book Review, 52 Harv. L. Rev. 700, 703 (1939). Thus, UCC §2-302 was designed to allow courts to examine contracts explicitly for bargaining unfairness.

In a seminal article on the doctrine, Professor Arthur Leff traced the drafting history of UCC §2-302 and demonstrated that in its earliest draft the doctrine was intended to apply only to standard form contracts. In subsequent drafts, the scope and purpose of the section became increasingly vague. As a result, Leff argued, the drafters produced a section that was a pure abstraction, devoid of content. Arthur Allen Leff, Unconscionability and the Code—The Emperor's New Clause, 115 U. Pa. L. Rev. 485 (1967). Leff also predicted, however, that the courts would likely cure the faults in §2-302 by applying a "smoothing nacre of more or less reasonable applications." Id. at 558-559. Subsequent writers have concluded that the courts, in fact, have shown considerable restraint in applying the unconscionability doctrine. See, e.g., E. Allan Farnsworth, Developments in Contract Law During the 1980s: The Top Ten, 41 Case W. Res. L. Rev. 203 (1990) (describing unconscionability and related doctrines as an area of "arrested development"); but see Anne Fleming, The Rise and Fall of Unconscionability as the "Law of the Poor," 102 Geo. L.J. 1383 (2014) and Charles L. Knapp, Blowing the Whistle on Mandatory Arbitration: Unconscionability as a Signaling Device, 436 San Diego L. Rev. 609, 610-614 (2009) (arguing that court decisions applying the concept of unconscionability spurred specific legislative reactions).

Higgins v. Superior Court of Los Angeles County

California Court of Appeal 140 Cal. App. 4th 1238; 45 Cal. Rptr. 3d 293 (2006)

RUBIN, Judge.

In this writ proceeding, five siblings who appeared in an episode of the television program *Extreme Makeover: Home Edition* (*Extreme Makeover*) challenge an order compelling them to arbitrate most of their claims against various entities involved with the production and broadcast of the program. Petitioners claim the arbitration clause contained in a written agreement they executed before the program was broadcast is unconscionable. We agree. Accordingly, we grant the petition for writ of mandate.

FACTUAL AND PROCEDURAL BACKGROUND

Petitioners Charles, Michael, Charis, Joshua, and Jeremiah Higgins are siblings. In February 2005, when they executed the agreement whose arbitration provision is at issue, they were 21, 19, 17, 16, and 14 years old, respectively.

Real parties in interest, to whom we refer collectively as the television defendants, are (1) American Broadcasting Companies, Inc., the network that broadcasts *Extreme Makeover*; (2) Disney/ABC International Television, Inc., which asserts it had no involvement with the *Extreme Makeover* program in which petitioners appeared; (3) Lock and Key Productions, the show's producer;

(4) Endemol USA, Inc., which is also involved in producing the program; and (5) Pardee Homes, which constructed the home featured in the *Extreme Makeover* episode in which petitioners appeared.

Petitioners' parents died in 2004. The eldest sibling, Charles, became the guardian for the then three minor children. (To avoid confusion with his siblings, we refer to Charles Higgins by his first name.) Shortly thereafter, petitioners moved in with church acquaintances, Firipeli and Lokilani Leomiti, a couple with three children of their own. The Leomitis are defendants in the litigation but are not involved in the present writ proceeding.

According to Charles, after moving in with the Leomitis, he was advised by members of his church that producers of *Extreme Makeover* had contacted the church and had asked to speak to him about the production of a show based on the loss of petitioners' parents and that petitioners were now living with the Leomitis.[1] In July or August 2004, Charles called and spoke with an associate producer of Lock and Key about the program and petitioners' living situation.

Over the next several months, there were additional contacts between petitioners and persons affiliated with the production of the program, including in-person interviews and the filming of a casting tape. By early 2005, petitioners and the Leomitis were chosen to participate in the program in which the Leomitis' home would be completely renovated.

On February 1, 2005, a Lock and Key producer sent by Federal Express to each of the petitioners and to the Leomitis an "Agreement and Release" for their signatures.[2] The Agreement and Release contains 24 single-spaced pages and 72 numbered paragraphs. Attached to it were several pages of exhibits, including an authorization for release of medical information, an emergency medical release, and, as exhibit C, a one-page document entitled "Release." To avoid confusion with the one-page exhibit C Release, we refer to the 24-page Agreement and Release simply as the "Agreement," and to exhibit C as the "Release."

At the top of the first page of the Agreement, the following appears in large and underlined print: "NOTE: DO NOT SIGN THIS UNTIL YOU HAVE READ IT COMPLETELY." The second-to-last numbered paragraph also states in pertinent part: "I have been given ample opportunity to read, and I have carefully read, this entire agreement. . . . I certify that I have made such an investigation of the facts pertinent to this Agreement and of all the matters pertaining thereto as I have deemed necessary. . . . I represent and warrant that I have reviewed this document with my own legal counsel prior to signing (or, IN THE

1. Lock and Key's executive producer describes Extreme Makeover as a " 'reality' based television series" whose "premise . . . is to find needy and deserving families who live in a home which does not serve their needs. The Program takes the selected families' existing homes and land and radically improves them by demolishing and rebuilding the home."

2. The version of the agreement intended for the three minor petitioners was slightly different than the one intended for the two adult petitioners and the Leomitis. The slight variations between the two versions are not relevant to the issue before us. In this opinion, we quote from, and cite to, the adult version.

ALTERNATIVE, although I have been given a reasonable opportunity to discuss this Agreement with counsel of my choice, I have voluntarily declined such opportunity)."

The last section of the Agreement, which includes 12 numbered paragraphs, is entitled "MISCELLANEOUS." None of the paragraphs in that section contains a heading or title. Paragraph 69 contains the following arbitration provision:

> 69. I agree that any and all disputes or controversies arising under this Agreement or any of its terms, any effort by any party to enforce, interpret, construe, rescind, terminate or annul this Agreement, or any provision thereof, and any and all disputes or controversies relating to my appearance or participation in the Program, shall be resolved by binding arbitration in accordance with the following procedure. . . . All arbitration proceedings shall be conducted under the auspices of the American Arbitration Association. . . . I agree that the arbitrator's ruling, or arbitrators' ruling, as applicable, shall be final and binding and not subject to appeal or challenge. . . . The parties hereto agree that, notwithstanding the provisions of this paragraph, Producer shall have a right to injunctive or other equitable relief as provided for in California Code of Civil Procedure §1281.8 or other relevant laws.

There is nothing in the Agreement that brings the reader's attention to the arbitration provision. Although a different font is used occasionally to highlight certain terms in the Agreement, that is not the case with the paragraph containing the arbitration provision. Six paragraphs in the Agreement contain a box for the petitioners to initial; initialing is not required for the arbitration provision. . . .

The one-page Release is typed in a smaller font than the Agreement. It consists of four, single-spaced paragraphs, the middle of which contains the following arbitration clause: "I agree that any and all disputes or controversies arising under this Release or any of its terms, any effort by any party to enforce, interpret, construe, rescind, terminate or annul this Release, or any provision thereof, shall be resolved exclusively by binding arbitration before a single, neutral arbitrator, who shall be a retired judge of a state or federal court. All arbitration proceedings shall be conducted under the auspices of the American Arbitration Association, under its Commercial Arbitration Rules, through its Los Angeles, California office. I agree that the arbitration proceedings, testimony, discovery and documents filed in the course of such proceedings, including the fact that the arbitration is being conducted, will be treated as confidential. . . ."

There is no evidence that any discussions took place between petitioners and any representative of the television defendants regarding either the Agreement or the Release, or that any of the television defendants directly imposed any deadline by which petitioners were required to execute the documents.

On February 5, 2005, a field producer from Lock and Key and a location manager for the program went to the Leomitis' home and met with the Leomitis. Although physically present at the house, petitioners did not participate in the meeting. During the meeting, one of the Leomitis asked about the documents they had received, and the producer and location manager advised the Leomitis that they should read the documents carefully, call if they had questions, and then execute and return the documents.

According to Charles, after this meeting, the Leomitis emerged with a packet of documents, which they handed to petitioners. Mrs. Leomiti instructed petitioners to "flip through the pages and sign and initial the document where it contained a signature line or box." Charles stated that from the time Mrs. Leomiti "handed the document to us and the time we signed it, approximately five to ten minutes passed." The document contained complex legal terms that he did not understand. He did not know what an arbitration agreement was and did not understand its significance or the legal consequences that could flow from signing it. He did not specifically state whether or not he saw the arbitration provisions contained either in paragraph 69 or the Release before he signed the documents.

Each of the petitioners executed the Agreement and signed all exhibits, including the Release.

On February 16, 2005, representatives from the show appeared and started to reconstruct the Leomitis' home. When the new home was completed, it had nine bedrooms, including one for each of the five petitioners. The existing mortgage was also paid off.

The program featuring petitioners and the Leomitis was broadcast on Easter Sunday, 2005.

Petitioners allege that, after the show was first broadcast, the Leomitis informed petitioners that the home was theirs (the Leomitis'), and the Leomitis ultimately forced petitioners to leave. Charles contacted Lock and Key's field producer and asked for help. The producer responded that he could not assist petitioners. Sometime thereafter, the *Extreme Makeover* episode was rebroadcast.

In August 2005, petitioners filed this action against the television defendants and the Leomitis. According to the record before us, the complaint includes claims for, among other things, intentional and negligent misrepresentation, breach of contract, unfair competition . . . , and false advertising. . . . With respect to the television defendants, the complaint appears to allege that those defendants breached promises to provide petitioners with a home, exploited petitioners, and portrayed petitioners in a false light (by rebroadcasting the episode when they knew the episode no longer reflected petitioners' living situation).

The television defendants petitioned to compel arbitration pursuant to the Federal Arbitration Act (FAA) (9 U.S.C. §1 et seq.). The television defendants maintained that all claims against both them and the Leomitis should be arbitrated. The Leomitis joined in the petition.[5]

5. The memorandum of points and authorities filed in support of the petition to compel arbitration appears to rely exclusively on the arbitration provision in the Agreement, and not on the arbitration provision in the one-page Release. . . . The fact that two documents contain an arbitration provision does not affect our analysis.

Petitioners opposed the petition, claiming, among other things, that the arbitration provision was unconscionable. . . .

After argument, the trial court issued an order granting the petition in most respects, conditioned on the television defendants paying all arbitration costs. . . . The court . . . cited United States and California Supreme Court decisions holding that under the FAA, where a party seeks to avoid application of an arbitration provision on the ground that the agreement in which the provision is contained is unenforceable, that claim must be considered by the arbitrator, not the court. The trial court also stated that "since defendants have shown that plaintiffs signed the releases having had an opportunity to read them, the arbitration provisions are found by this court to be enforceable." The court did not address petitioners' other specific claims of unconscionability, presumably because it construed petitioners' opposition to the petition to compel arbitration as an attack only on the entire Agreement and one-page Release, not on the arbitration provisions contained in those documents.

Petitioners then filed this writ petition challenging the trial court's ruling. We issued an alternative writ, received additional briefing from the parties, and heard oral argument.

Discussion

A. Unconscionability as a Defense to Enforcement of Arbitration Provisions

The trial court ruled, and petitioners do not dispute, that the enforceability of the arbitration clause is governed by the FAA. Federal law applies to arbitration provisions in contracts involving interstate commerce. (See 9 U.S.C. §2; . . . .) Numerous cases observe that arbitration is generally favored under both the FAA and California law. (E.g., Balandran v. Labor Ready, Inc. (2004) 124 Cal. App. 4th 1522, 1527 [22 Cal. Rptr. 3d 441]; . . . .) At the same time, our Supreme Court has emphasized that "although we have spoken of a 'strong public policy of this state in favor of resolving disputes by arbitration' [citation], Code of Civil Procedure §1281 makes clear that an arbitration agreement is to be rescinded on the same grounds as other contracts or contract terms. In this respect, arbitration agreements are neither favored nor disfavored, but simply placed on an equal footing with other contracts." (Armendariz v. Foundation Health Psychcare Services, Inc. (2000) 24 Cal. 4th 83, 126-127 [99 Cal. Rptr. 2d 745, 6 P.3d 669] (*Armendariz*); see also Buckeye Check Cashing, Inc. v. Cardegna (2006) [546 U.S. 440], 163 L. Ed. 2d 1038, 1042, 126 S. Ct. 1204, 1207 (*Buckeye*). . . .

Thus, under both the FAA and California law, "arbitration agreements are valid, irrevocable, and enforceable, save upon such grounds as exist at law or in equity for the revocation of any contract." (*Armendariz*, supra, 24 Cal. 4th at p. 98, fn. omitted.)

One ground is unconscionability, the basis asserted by petitioners below and in this writ proceeding. (See Flores v. Transamerica HomeFirst, Inc. (2001) 93 Cal. App. 4th 846, 856 [113 Cal. Rptr. 2d 376].) "The ' "strong public policy of this state in favor of resolving disputes by arbitration' " does not extend to an arbitration agreement permeated by unconscionability." (*Ibid.*) As is frequently the case with inquiries into unconscionability, our analysis begins—although it does not end—with whether the Agreement and Release are contracts of adhesion. (See *Armendariz*, supra, 24 Cal. 4th at p. 113.) Petitioners contend that they are and that the arbitration provisions are unconscionable. A contract of adhesion is a standardized contract that is imposed and drafted by the party of superior bargaining strength and relegates to the other party " 'only the opportunity to adhere to the contract or reject it.' " (*Ibid.*, quoting Neal v. State Farm Ins. Cos. (1961) 188 Cal. App. 2d 690, 694 [10 Cal. Rptr. 781].) Adhesion contracts are routine in modern day commerce, and at least one commentator has suggested they are worthy of neither praise nor condemnation, only analysis. (1 Corbin on Contracts (1993) §1.4, p. 14.) If a court finds a contract to be adhesive, it must then determine whether " 'other factors are present which, under established legal rules—legislative or judicial—operate to render it' " unenforceable. (*Armendariz*, at p. 113, citing Graham v. Scissor-Tail, Inc. (1981) 28 Cal. 3d 807, 820 [171 Cal. Rptr. 604, 623 P.2d 165] (*Graham*).)

One "established rule" is that a court need not enforce an adhesion contract that is unconscionable. (*Graham*, supra, 28 Cal. 3d at p. 820.) As our Supreme Court explained in *Armendariz*, the Legislature has now codified the principle, historically developed in case law, that a court may refuse to enforce an unconscionable provision in a contract. (Civ. Code, §1670.5.)[8] . . .

Unconscionability has both a procedural and a substantive element, the former focusing on "oppression" or "surprise" due to unequal bargaining power, the latter on "overly harsh" or "one-sided" results. (*Armendariz*, supra, 24 Cal. 4th at p. 114.) " 'The prevailing view is that [procedural and substantive unconscionability] must *both* be present in order for a court to exercise its discretion to refuse to enforce a contract or clause under the doctrine of unconscionability.' [Citation.] But they need not be present in the same degree. . . . [T]he more substantively oppressive the contract term, the less evidence of procedural unconscionability is required to come to the conclusion that the term is unenforceable, and vice versa." (*Ibid.*)

Under the FAA, a court may not consider a claim that an arbitration provision is unenforceable if it is a subterfuge for a challenge that the entire agreement (in which the arbitration clause is only a part) is unconscionable. That contention must be presented to the arbitrator. . . . Our task, therefore, is two-fold: (1) Does the petition here challenge the enforceability of the Agreement and the Release, in toto, or does it contest only the arbitration provision? (2) If it is the latter, is the arbitration provision unconscionable?

8. Civil Code §1670.5, subdivision (a), provides: "If the court as a matter of law finds the contract or any clause of the contract to have been unconscionable at the time it was made the court may refuse to enforce the contract, or it may enforce the remainder of the contract without the unconscionable clause, or it may so limit the application of any unconscionable clause as to avoid any unconscionable result."

B. The Standard of Review

. . .

C. The Trial Court Incorrectly Concluded Petitioners were Challenging the Enforceability of the Entire Agreement and Release

The trial court offered two reasons for its decision to order arbitration. First, it concluded that petitioners' opposition to arbitration was predicated on a challenge to the Agreement as a whole, not to the arbitration provision in particular. From this premise, the trial court reasoned that, because the enforceability of the entire agreement is to be considered by the arbitrator, not the court . . . , the petition should be granted. The trial court's framing of the issue was seen in its written ruling, where it stated, "Although plaintiffs argue that the 'arbitration agreements' are enforceable, their argument is directed not at the arbitration provisions but at the releases themselves." . . .

Although we agree with the court's legal analysis, its ultimate conclusion was flawed because petitioners' opposition to the petition was that the arbitration clause in particular, not the entire Agreement, was unconscionable. Petitioners devoted considerable attention to paragraph 69 of the Agreement, emphasizing that it "is not set out or made distinguishable in any manner. It is misidentified within the caption as 'miscellaneous.' It is not distinguished in different type font size, bold letters, capital letters, in red, and does not contain any separate waiver notice." The caption of a four-page argument made by petitioners reads: "The Arbitration Agreements Are Procedurally and Substantively Unconscionable Thereby Barring Their Enforcement." And in arguing that the arbitration provision was substantively unconscionable, petitioners quoted from paragraph 69 in an effort to demonstrate that the provision was one-sided, requiring only them, and not the television defendants, to submit to arbitration. The principal thrust of petitioners' oral argument to the trial court was likewise that "the entire arbitration clause was itself one-sided. So only the plaintiffs under that clause have a duty to arbitrate."

. . .

The second justification offered by the trial court for granting the television defendants' petition to compel arbitration was that petitioners had an opportunity to read the Agreement and Release before signing them. While this is factually correct and legally bears on whether the Agreement is procedurally unconscionable, no authority is cited for a supposed rule that if a party reads an agreement he or she is barred from claiming it is unconscionable. Such a rule would seriously undermine the unconscionability defense.

Given the limited scope of the trial court's ruling, we could remand to permit it to decide whether the arbitration provision is unconscionable. Instead, because the case is before us on uncontested facts and our review is de novo, we decide the legal issues in the first instance. . . .

D. The Arbitration Provision is Unconscionable

1. The Adhesive Nature of the Parties' Agreement

We begin with whether the parties' agreement was adhesive. (See *Armendariz*, supra, 24 Cal. 4th at p. 113.) As discussed above, " '[t]he term [contract of adhesion] signifies a standardized contract, which, imposed and drafted by the party of superior bargaining strength, relegates to the subscribing party only the opportunity to adhere to the contract or reject it.' " (*Ibid.*)

In this case, it is undisputed that the lengthy Agreement was drafted by the television defendants. It is a standardized contract; none of the petitioners' names or other identifying information is included in the body of the document. There is no serious doubt that the television defendants had far more bargaining power than petitioners.

The remaining question is whether petitioners were relegated only to signing or rejecting the Agreement. The television defendants note that there is no evidence petitioners were told they could not negotiate any terms of the Agreement or that petitioners made any attempt to do so. Although literally correct, the uncontested evidence was that on the day petitioners signed the Agreement the television defendants initially met with the Leomitis alone. Inferentially, at the television defendants' urging, immediately after the meeting concluded, the Leomitis gave the Agreement and exhibits to petitioners with directions to "flip through the pages and sign." The documents were returned in five to ten minutes. One of the producers testified that he told the Leomitis "that these agreements must be executed as a condition to their further participation in the program."

From these facts, we conclude the Agreement was presented to petitioners on a take-it-or-leave-it basis by the party with the superior bargaining position who was not willing to engage in negotiations. Accordingly, we conclude the Agreement and exhibits constitute a contract of adhesion.

2. Procedural Unconscionability

"Procedural unconscionability focuses on the factors of surprise and oppression [citations], with surprise being a function of the disappointed reasonable expectations of the weaker party." (Harper v. Ultimo, [(2003) 113 Cal. App. 4th 1402, 1406, 7 Cal. Rptr. 3d 418.])

In this case, the arbitration provision appears in one paragraph near the end of a lengthy, single-spaced document. The entire agreement was drafted by the television defendants, who transmitted copies of it to the petitioners. The television defendants knew petitioners were young and unsophisticated, and had recently lost both parents. Indeed, it was petitioners' vulnerability that made them so attractive to the television defendants. The latter made no effort to highlight the presence of the arbitration provision in the Agreement. It was one of 12 numbered paragraphs in a section entitled "MISCELLANEOUS." In contrast to several other paragraphs, no text in the arbitration provision is highlighted. No words are printed in bold letters or larger font; nor are they capitalized. Although petitioners were required to place their initials in boxes adjacent to six other paragraphs, no box appeared next to the arbitration provision.

It is true that the top of the first page advises petitioners to read the entire agreement before signing it and the second-to-last paragraph states that the person signing acknowledges doing so. This language, although relevant to our inquiry, does not defeat the otherwise strong showing of procedural unconscionability.

We now turn to substantive unconscionability, utilizing our Supreme Court's sliding scale approach. (See *Armendariz*, supra, 24 Cal. 4th at p. 114.) Procedural and substantive unconscionability "need not be present in the same degree. . . ." (*Ibid.*)

3. Substantive Unconscionability

"Substantively unconscionable terms may 'generally be described as unfairly one-sided.'[Citation.] For example, an agreement may lack 'a modicum of bilaterality' and therefore be unconscionable if the agreement requires 'arbitration only for the claims of the weaker party but a choice of forums for the claims of the stronger party.' " (Fitz v. NCR Corp. (2004) 118 Cal. App. 4th 702, 713 [13 Cal. Rptr. 3d 88], quoting *Armendariz*, supra, 24 Cal. 4th at p. 119.)

In this case, the arbitration provision requires only petitioners to submit their claims to arbitration. The clause repeatedly includes "I agree" language, with the "I" being a reference to the "applicant" (i.e., each of the petitioners). The only time the phrase "the parties" is used is in the last sentence, where "the parties" agree that, notwithstanding the arbitration provision, the producer has the right to seek injunctive or other equitable relief in a court of law as provided for in Code of Civil Procedure §1281.1 or other relevant laws.

The television defendants claim that the arbitration provision is bilateral, because "all disputes or controversies arising under this Agreement or any of its terms, any effort by any party to enforce . . . this Agreement . . . and any and all disputes or controversies relating to my appearance or participation in the Program, shall be resolved by binding arbitration." (P 69.) Thus, "all disputes" are subject to arbitration, and either side may move to compel. But they miss the point: only one side (petitioners) agreed to that clause.[11]

The television defendants also assert that their contractual right to seek injunctive relief shows that they are required to arbitrate since, ordinarily, a party may seek injunctive relief as a matter of civil law. The provision would be meaningless, they argue, if the television defendants were not required to submit their claims to arbitration. We disagree. Under the arbitration provision, the television defendants (though not petitioners) can *compel* arbitration. The injunction clause is significant because the television defendants can compel

11. Interestingly, petitioners claim the television defendants did not even sign the Agreement until after the motion to compel arbitration was filed, a point not disputed by the television defendants.

arbitration without fearing that doing so would preclude them from seeking injunctive or other equitable relief in a court of record.[12]

Additional elements of substantive unconscionability are found in the provision barring only petitioners from seeking appellate review of the arbitrator's decision and, at least insofar as it could impact petitioners' statutory claims, the provision requiring arbitration in accordance with the rules of the American Arbitration Association, which provide that arbitration costs are to be borne equally by the parties. . . .[13] The harsh, one-sided nature of the arbitration provision, combined with the elements of procedural unconscionability earlier discussed, leads us to conclude that the arbitration provision is unconscionable and, therefore, unenforceable. Accordingly, it was error for the trial court to have granted the petition to compel arbitration.

DISPOSITION

The petition for writ of mandate is granted. The respondent court is directed to vacate that part of its December 1, 2005, order granting the petition of the television defendants to compel arbitration and staying certain claims, and to thereafter enter a new and different order denying the petition to compel arbitration. Petitioners are entitled to recover their costs in this writ proceeding. . . .

COOPER, P. J., and BOLAND, J., concurred.

NOTES AND QUESTIONS

1. ***Subsequent proceedings in Higgins.*** Although the plaintiffs in the *Higgins* case succeeded in keeping their case out of arbitration, they ultimately fared poorly anyway in their suit against Disney/ABC. A California trial court found that plaintiffs were unable to demonstrate that promises were made to them by the defendants that they would ultimately have ownership interests in the house built for the Leomitis, and that although some portions of their contracts with defendants were perhaps unconscionable, these were relatively minor, and severable. An appellate court affirmed summary judgment for the television defendants. Higgins v. Disney/ABC Int'l Television, Inc., 2009 WL 692701 (Cal. Ct. App.). The plaintiffs apparently settled with the Leomiti family for the modest sum of $50,000, plus costs and attorney fees. Higgins v. Disney/ABC Int'l Television, Inc., 2010 WL 7080549 (Cal. Super. Ct.).

---

12. The fact that the injunction provision is one-sided does not necessarily mean that the clause is substantively unconscionable. A "contracting party with superior bargaining strength may provide 'extra protection' for itself within the terms of the arbitration agreement if 'business realities' create a special need for the advantage. [Citation.] The 'business realities,' creating the special need, must be explained in the terms of the contract or factually established." (Fitz v. NCR Corp., supra, 118 Cal. App. 4th at p. 723.) We observe that although the television defendants explained why it was important to deny petitioners injunctive relief, they did not attempt to explain why they needed such remedy.

13. As noted above, the trial court shifted all arbitration costs to the television defendants. (See Gutierrez v. Autowest, Inc. (2003) 114 Cal. App. 4th 77, 92-93 [7 Cal. Rptr. 3d 267] [unconscionable requirement for payment of arbitration costs may be severed].)

2. *"Adhesion contracts" and procedural unconscionability.* The *Higgins* court begins its discussion of procedural unconscionability by noting that the agreement and release are adhesive, as defined by the court. Recall the discussion of adhesion contracts in the notes after the *C & J Fertilizer* case in Chapter 5. Although the *Higgins* court does not do so, a number of California decisions have held that the fact that a contract is adhesive is enough of itself to render a contract procedurally unconscionable. See, e.g., Grand Prospect Partners, L.P. v. Ross Dress for Less, Inc., 182 Cal. Rptr. 3d 235, 248 (Ct. App. 2015) (procedural aspect of unconscionability can be established either by showing that contract was one of adhesion or by totality of the circumstances). Other California decisions, as well as those from other jurisdictions, have held that something more must be shown before an adhesion contract can be found to be procedurally unconscionable. See, e.g., Morris v. Redwood Empire Bancorp, 27 Cal. Rptr. 3d 797, 807-808 (Ct. App. 2005) (noting that some California decisions seem to "reflexively" find adhesion contracts procedurally unconscionable but holding that there must also be a showing of a lack of market alternatives or a showing of "surprise"). The California Supreme Court has more recently stated that the fact that a contract is adhesive calls for close examination of possible substantive unconscionability, but even more scrutiny is warranted when elements of surprise or sharp practices are present. Baltazar v. Forever 21, Inc., 367 P.3d 6, 12 (Cal. 2016).

The *Higgins* court did highlight some aspects of the transaction, beyond the adhesive nature of the contract, to support its finding of procedural unconscionability. The court noted that the arbitration provision was placed inconspicuously within the writing, that the plaintiffs were urged to quickly sign the document, and that the plaintiffs were young, recently orphaned, and lacking business sophistication. Other cases have focused on similar factors in assessing procedural unconscionability. See, e.g., Beltran v. InterExchange, Inc., 2017 WL 4418711 (D. Colo.) (in addition to being adhesive, arbitration agreement between plaintiff au pairs and placement business held procedurally unconscionable based on facts that plaintiffs were youthful, spoke English as second language, and lacked business experience, and terms were "buried" at end of lengthy contract); Carmona v. Lincoln Millennium Car Wash, Inc., 171 Cal. Rptr. 3d 42 (Ct. App. 2014) (in addition to contract being adhesive, surprise element of procedural unconscionability established by failure of employer to provide Spanish translation of key provisions to plaintiffs who could not read English).

3. *Arbitration agreements and substantive unconscionability.* Following the nearly unanimous view on the question, the appellate court holds that the arbitration agreement must also have an element of substantive unconscionability in order to be rendered unenforceable. Both the trial court and the appellate court agreed that the arbitral costs would be prohibitive for the Higgins family. Many other courts have recognized that the arbitration agreement may be substantively unconscionable if excessive costs of arbitration effectively preclude the claimant from pursing relief. See Adkins v. Labor Ready, Inc., 303 F.3d 496, 502 (4th Cir. 2002). Another possible basis for substantive unconscionability

identified by the *Higgins* court is the lack of "bilateral" application of the arbitration agreement. The California Supreme Court in the cited *Armendariz* case concluded that mandatory arbitration agreements must have a "modicum of bilaterality" to avoid substantive unconscionability. The court stated that if the arbitration system is indeed fair, then the party drafting the arbitration agreement should also be willing to submit claims to arbitration. Armendariz v. Foundation Health Psychcare Services, Inc., 6 P.3d 669, 691-692 (Cal. 2000).

One should not overestimate, however, the likelihood of avoiding enforcement of an arbitration agreement based on alleged unconscionability. As explained in more detail in the Comment below, the U.S. Supreme Court has led the way in narrowing the grounds on which an arbitration agreement may be invalidated. Federal and state court decisions denying relief from arbitration are plentiful. In Muriithi v. Shuttle Express, Inc., 712 F.3d 173 (4th Cir. 2013), for example, the Fourth Circuit reversed a district court's decision and rejected substantive unconscionability arguments based on the agreement, including a class action ban, a one-year limitations period for filing a claim, and an arbitration fee-splitting provision, absent a showing with "firm evidence" that the arbitral costs would likely be prohibitive for the plaintiff. Similarly, the California Supreme Court, in a notable decision, disagreed with the trial court and held that an employment arbitration agreement was enforceable, though adhesive in nature, rejecting the employee's argument that there was substantive unconscionability due to unequal ability of the parties to seek relief outside of arbitration. Baltazar v. Forever 21, Inc., 367 P.3d 6 (Cal. 2016).

4. *Questionable proliferation of mandatory arbitration agreements in consumer contracts.* As you read the *Higgins* opinion, you will observe citations to a range of cases involving mandatory arbitration agreements, often in consumer contracts. The ubiquitous spread of mandatory arbitration agreements is not unique to California. See generally Charles L. Knapp, Taking Contracts Private: The Quiet Revolution in Contract Law, 71 Fordham L. Rev. 761, 796, nn. 118-119 (2002) (listing cases, many involving consumers, in which arbitration agreements were found unconscionable by state or federal courts).

In an article criticizing the widespread use of arbitration agreements in consumer contracts, Professor Richard M. Alderman summarized his findings:

> From a philosophical perspective, it is difficult to find fault with the concept of ADR, specifically the use of arbitration as an alternative to litigation in consumer cases. No one can oppose a system of dispute resolution that is less expensive, more efficient, and more flexible. At first glance, arbitration of consumer disputes would appear to offer substantial benefits over formal litigation. Because the rules of arbitration are less formal, and arbitrators have more freedom to "do the right thing," it should be more likely consumers would fare better in arbitration than before a judge, where they are bound by more formal rules and are subject to appellate review. Additionally, the speed and reduced cost of arbitration should provide prompt resolution. Consumers, if given the choice, would surely favor arbitration over litigation.
>
> Upon further review, however, the realities of pre-dispute mandatory arbitration, as currently employed in American consumer transactions, differ sharply

> from the idealized process described above. First, the consumer rarely, if ever, chooses arbitration; pre-dispute arbitration is imposed upon the consumer by a contract of adhesion in which the consumer has no real choice. Second, arbitration often is not as prompt or as inexpensive as alternative courts, especially small claims courts. Third, the informal rules, lack of guidelines, and finality of the decision often favor the business organization, due in large part to its significant role as a "repeat-player." Finally, and perhaps most importantly, imposition of mandatory arbitration generally precludes the consumer's freedom to choose to litigate in a class action and eliminates any favorable precedent or law reform that could arise through litigation.

Professor Richard M. Alderman, Pre-Dispute Mandatory Arbitration in Consumer Contracts: A Call for Reform, 38 Hous. L. Rev. 1237, 1238 (2001). The interplay of consumer protection, the arbitration statutes and the principle of unconscionability is explored further in the following Comment.

Comment: Mandatory Arbitration and Unconscionability

In the early twentieth century, American courts were often hostile to the notion that parties could by contract bind themselves to submit future disputes to private arbitration, rather than resolving them through litigation in the public courts. Judges saw such arrangements as improper encroachments on judicial power, and often declined to enforce contractual arbitration clauses. But contracting parties, particularly commercial enterprises, were increasingly drawn to arbitration as a mechanism for dispute resolution, for a combination of reasons: Arbitration was seen as faster, less expensive, and more private than the public litigation system. In addition, arbitrators selected by the parties were potentially better able to grasp the commercial realities of the business world than judges with possibly little or no real-world experience in commercial affairs. Arbitrators were also generally freer than courts to reach a commercially reasonable resolution of a business dispute without being bound by rigid and possibly "unrealistic" rules of law. Eventually, at both the state and federal levels, American legislatures adopted Arbitration Acts: laws requiring courts to respect and enforce contractual provisions by which parties bound themselves to arbitrate disputes that might in the future arise between them. See Federal Arbitration Act (FAA), 9 U.S.C. §§1-16. Such agreements for "mandatory" (or "compulsory") arbitration — so called because they were designed to be binding even against a party that might in the meantime have changed its mind about using the arbitration process — could thereafter no longer be ignored or overridden by courts on the ground that they somehow usurped the courts' prerogatives.

By the latter part of the twentieth century, the tables had rather completely turned. American courts, led by the U.S. Supreme Court, interpreted and applied the FAA so vigorously that lower courts and state legislatures found it difficult or impossible to impose any sort of regulatory procedures or decisional process that might in any way prevent disputes from being shunted out of the court system and into arbitration whenever a contract so provided, even if that contract was a contract of adhesion or otherwise of dubious validity. See generally Jeffrey W. Stempel, Bootstrapping and Slouching Toward Gomorrah: Arbitral Infatuation and the Decline of Consent, 62 Brook. L. Rev. 1335 (1996). And where the enthusiasm for arbitration clauses had earlier been mostly confined to contracts between commercial enterprises, large-scale businesses began to insert them into contracts with their customers on a massive scale. Banks, credit-card lenders, telecommunications companies, sellers of goods, insurance companies, even health-care providers, turned to mandatory arbitration, as did employers. David S. Schwartz, Enforcing Small Print to Protect Big Business: Employee and Consumer Rights Claims in an Age of Compelled Arbitration, 1997 Wis. L. Rev. 33. Proponents of this development saw in consumer arbitration the same virtues that an earlier generation had seen in its use in commercial disputes. Consumer advocates, however, argued that by drafting their contracts so as to require arbitration of future disputes, business enterprises with the economic power to impose terms on their customers or employees could obtain a variety of practical advantages, and could even use arbitration provisions to effectively deprive consumers and employees of any means of dispute resolution.

Despite its breadth of application, the FAA does have some limitations on its scope: It expressly provides that a written agreement to arbitrate "shall be valid, irrevocable, and enforceable, save upon such grounds as exist at law or in equity for the revocation of any contract." FAA, 9 U.S.C. §2. Unable to challenge directly the Supreme Court's insistence on a strong preference for arbitration, parties desiring to avoid being forced to submit to arbitration increasingly mounted unconscionability attacks on arbitration clauses, and with mounting success.

As a result of these developments, the number of court decisions in which the unconscionability doctrine was applied increased substantially after 1990. Results of a recent study indicated that the number of unconscionability decisions grew rather dramatically over the period between 1990 and 2010, with much (but not all) of that increase being attributable to disputes over contractual provisions calling for mandatory arbitration. Charles L. Knapp, Blowing the Whistle on Mandatory Arbitration: Unconscionability as a Signaling Device, 46 San Diego L. Rev. 609, 619-626 (2009).

However, the Supreme Court has continued to be highly resistant to any claims that arbitration clauses are unenforceable. See Rent-A-Center, West, Inc. v. Jackson, 561 U.S. 63 (2010) (arbitration clause could effectively delegate to arbitrator the power to decide whether the arbitration clause was unconscionable); American Express Co. v. Italian Colors Rest., 133 S. Ct. 2304 (2013) (class action waiver in arbitration provision was enforceable even if cost of individually arbitrating individual claims exceeded potential recovery). In the absence of change in the Supreme Court or legislative action by Congress, both of which seem highly unlikely, the prospects for use of the doctrine of unconscionability to invalidate arbitration clauses appear to be dismal. Adapted from Charles L. Knapp, Unconscionability in American Contract Law:

A Twenty-first Century Survey, in Contract Law: Transatlantic Perspectives, L. DiMatteo, K. Rowley, S. Saintier, & Q. Zou, Cambridge Univ. Press (2014).

McFarland v. Wells Fargo Bank, N.A.

United States Court of Appeals, 810 F.3d 273 (4th Cir. 2016)

PAMELA HARRIS, Circuit Judge:

In 2006, at the height of the housing market, Philip McFarland was informed by a mortgage broker that his home's value had nearly doubled in two years. Acting on that advice, McFarland refinanced his home so that he could pay down other debt. But it soon became apparent that McFarland could not manage the increased interest payments on his new loan, and when housing prices fell, McFarland was faced with an unaffordable mortgage and a looming foreclosure.

McFarland sued, alleging that his mortgage agreement, providing him with a loan far in excess of his home's actual value, was an "unconscionable contract" under the West Virginia Consumer Credit and Protection Act, W.Va. Code § 46A-1-101, *et seq.* (the "Act" or the "WVCCPA"). The district court rejected that claim, holding that a loan exceeding the worth of a home, without more, is not evidence of "substantive unconscionability" under West Virginia law. And because the district court understood a WVCCPA claim always to require a showing of substantive unconscionability, it stopped its analysis there, without considering the fairness of the process by which the agreement was reached.

We agree with the district court that the amount of a mortgage loan, by itself, cannot show substantive unconscionability under West Virginia law, and that McFarland has not otherwise made that showing. But we disagree as to the proper interpretation of the WVCCPA, and find that the Act allows for claims of "unconscionable inducement" even when the substantive terms of a contract are not themselves unfair. Accordingly, we remand so that the district court may consider in the first instance whether McFarland's mortgage agreement was induced by unconscionable conduct.

I.

A.

In 2004, McFarland purchased his Hedgesville, West Virginia home for roughly $110,000. Just two years later, in June 2006, he availed himself of then-favorable debt markets to engage in the refinancing that is the subject of this appeal. Interested in consolidating his approximately $40,000 in combined student and vehicle debt with his mortgage, McFarland entered into discussions with Greentree Mortgage Corporation ("Greentree"), a third-party mortgage lender. Greentree arranged for an appraisal of McFarland's property, and McFarland was informed that the market value of his home had jumped to $202,000 since its acquisition two years earlier.

McFarland then entered into two secured loan agreements. The first, which is the subject of this dispute, was a mortgage agreement with Wells Fargo Bank,

N.A. ("Wells Fargo"), with a principal amount of $181,800 and an adjustable interest rate that started at 7.75 percent and could increase to 13.75 percent (the "Wells Fargo Loan"). The second, not directly at issue here, was with Greentree, for an interest-only home equity line of credit of $20,000. As planned, McFarland used the proceeds of those two loans to consolidate all of his debts.

McFarland paid the Wells Fargo Loan without incident for roughly a year. In late 2007, however, he began to fall behind on his mortgage payments, and contacted Wells Fargo to ask for assistance. After several failed attempts to restructure McFarland's mortgage, Wells Fargo and McFarland entered into a loan modification in May 2010. The revised agreement reduced McFarland's interest rate and extended the term of the loan in exchange for an increase in the principal amount outstanding. But even under the new arrangement, McFarland remained unable to make his payments. In 2012, Wells Fargo initiated foreclosure on McFarland's home.

B.

To stop the pending foreclosure, McFarland brought this action against Greentree and Wells Fargo, as well as U.S. Bank National Association ("U.S. Bank"), the trustee of a securitized loan trust that now includes the Wells Fargo Loan.[1] Relevant to this appeal, McFarland alleged in his complaint that the Wells Fargo Loan was an "unconscionable contract" under the WVCCPA. *See* W.Va. Code § 46A-2-121(1)(a).

McFarland raised two distinct "unconscionable contract" arguments in his complaint and before the district court, either of which, he contended, could support an unconscionability finding under the WVCCPA. The first was a traditional unconscionability claim with its genesis in the common law, focusing on the terms of the Wells Fargo Loan itself and, in particular, the size of the mortgage it provided. Put simply, McFarland argued that Wells Fargo loaned him too much money. Citing a 2012 retroactive appraisal finding that his home was worth only $120,000 in June 2006—considerably less than the $202,000 valuation that preceded the Wells Fargo Loan—McFarland claimed that Wells Fargo's excess loan tied him to an unaffordable mortgage that increased his housing burden by several hundred dollars a month and put his home at risk. That general species of unconscionability claim (if not this particular variant), alleging the unfairness of the terms of an agreement, is well established in West Virginia: In the context of consumer agreements, it is now codified under the WVCCPA, *see* W.Va. Code § 46A-2-121(1)(a) (court may refuse to enforce a consumer agreement that is "unconscionable at the time it was made"), and it has long roots in West Virginia's common law, *see* Brown v. Genesis Healthcare Corp., 229 W.Va. 382, 729 S.E.2d 217, 226-27 (2012).

McFarland's second theory of unconscionability was more novel. West Virginia's traditional unconscionability doctrine, as is customary, requires

1. After originating McFarland's mortgage loan, Wells Fargo sold the mortgage on the secondary market as part of a securitized loan trust. U.S. Bank is the trustee of that trust, which is owned by investors. Wells Fargo continues to service the loans in the trust.

a showing of both substantive unconscionability, or unfairness in the contract itself, and procedural unconscionability, or unfairness in the bargaining process. . . . But McFarland's alternative argument was that even if the Wells Fargo Loan was not unconscionable when made, the district court could invalidate it on the independent ground that it was "unconscionably induced"—in other words, based solely on factors predating acceptance of the contract and relating to the bargaining process. Specifically, McFarland argued that the Wells Fargo Loan was "induced by misrepresentations," focusing on what he alleged to be the vastly inflated appraisal of his home in 2006. And according to McFarland, that kind of unconscionable inducement is, under the text of the WVCCPA, grounds for relief by itself, without regard to the loan agreement's substantive terms. *See* W.Va. Code § 46A-2-121(1)(a) (court may refuse to enforce a consumer agreement that is "unconscionable at the time it was made, or . . . induced by unconscionable conduct [such as affirmative misrepresentations, active deceit or concealment of a material fact]").

After McFarland filed his complaint, he and the defendants engaged in several months of extensive discovery. McFarland eventually reached a settlement with Greentree, but his case against Wells Fargo and U.S. Bank ("the Banks") proceeded. In the decision that is the subject of this appeal, the district court granted the Banks' motion for summary judgment and dismissed McFarland's unconscionable contract claim. *McFarland v. Wells Fargo Bank, N.A.,* 19 F. Supp. 3d 663, 668–73 (S.D.W.Va. 2014).

As to substantive unconscionability, the district court explained that McFarland had identified two allegedly unconscionable features of the Wells Fargo Loan in both his complaint and his opposition to the Banks' motion for summary judgment: that the loan far exceeded the value of the property, and that the loan provided no "net tangible benefit" to McFarland. But neither, the district court held, provided a basis for a finding of substantive unconscionability.

That a refinanced loan exceeds the value of a home, the court ruled, is not evidence of substantive unconscionability under West Virginia law. "It is not 'overly harsh' or 'one-sided' against the plaintiff that he received *more* financing than he was allegedly entitled to receive." *McFarland,* 19 F. Supp. 3d at 670 (emphasis in original). If anything, the court reasoned, an under-secured mortgage disadvantages the lender, not the borrower. Absent unfairness in specific loan terms like the rate of interest charged or the timing of payments, the court concluded, there is nothing substantively unconscionable about a loan simply because of its size.

Nor does West Virginia law require that a contract provide a "net tangible benefit" to either party, the court held. Under West Virginia law, a contract is substantively unconscionable only if it is "one-sided," with an "overly harsh effect on the disadvantaged party." *Id.* at 673 . . . That is a different standard, the court reasoned, and whether the Wells Fargo Loan was of net benefit to McFarland is simply not relevant to the substantive unconscionability inquiry.

Finally, the district court held that in light of its holding as to substantive unconscionability, there was no need even to consider McFarland's allegations regarding the process that led to contract formation. According to the district court, West Virginia law does not allow for a finding of unconscionable contract without some showing of substantive unconscionability. As a result, the court dismissed McFarland's claim—including his allegation of "unconscionable inducement" under the WVCCPA—without further addressing the purported misrepresentations that led to the Wells Fargo Loan.

McFarland timely appealed the dismissal of his unconscionable contract claim.

II.

We review a district court's award of summary judgment de novo, and view the facts and the reasonable inferences that may be drawn from them in the light most favorable to the nonmoving party—here, McFarland. . . . As a federal court sitting in diversity, our role is to apply governing West Virginia contract law, "or, if necessary, predict how the state's highest court would rule on an unsettled issue." Horace Mann Ins. Co. v. Gen. Star Nat'l Ins. Co., 514 F.3d 327, 329 (4th Cir. 2008).

A.

. . .

1.

McFarland's primary argument is that the district court erred when it ruled that a refinanced loan exceeding the value of a home is not evidence of substantive unconscionability under West Virginia law. Because the West Virginia courts have not decided this question,[2] our task is to apply the relevant principles of state contract law as we believe they would be applied by the West Virginia Supreme Court of Appeals in this context. . . .

Fortunately, the West Virginia courts have made very clear the standard for substantive unconscionability under state law: A contract term is substantively unconscionable only if it is both "one-sided" and "overly harsh" as to the disadvantaged party. *See, e.g.,* Dan Ryan Builders, Inc. v. Nelson, 230 W.Va. 281, 737 S.E.2d 550, 558 (2012); . . . . The point is not to disturb the "reasonable allocation of risks or reasonable advantage because of superior bargaining power." Arnold v. United Cos. Lending Corp., 204 W.Va. 229, 511 S.E.2d 854,

2. McFarland relies on two decisions of the West Virginia Supreme Court of Appeals, but in neither of those cases did the court hold that a loan exceeding the value of a home is evidence of substantive unconscionability. In Quicken Loans, Inc. v. Brown, 230 W.Va. 306, 737 S.E.2d 640, 656–59 (2012) ("*Quicken Loans I*"), the court was presented with evidence that a loan was based on an inflated appraisal. But the loan also contained significant fees, a particularly high interest rate, and an undisclosed balloon payment. *See id.* So when the court found the loan to be unconscionable because its "total cost . . . was exorbitant," its holding turned on much more than the principal amount of the loan. *See id.* at 659. And in Herrod v. First Republic Mortgage Corp., 218 W.Va. 611, 625 S.E.2d 373, 379–81 (2005), although the court reversed summary judgment where it found evidence that the "house was worth at least $20,000 less than the amount for which it was mortgaged," its analysis concentrated singularly upon issues of fact relating to *procedural* unconscionability—namely, whether the loan was based on a fraudulent appraisal—and the decision never mentions substantive unconscionability. *See id.*

860 (1998) (quoting Unif. Consumer Credit Code 1974 § 5.108 cmt. 3), *overruled on other grounds by Dan Ryan Builders,* 230 W.Va. 281, 737 S.E.2d 550. Rather, substantive unconscionability screens for cases in which a "gross imbalance, one-sidedness or lop-sidedness in a contract" will justify a court's refusal to enforce the agreement as written. *Genesis Healthcare,* 729 S.E.2d at 220.

We agree with the district court that under this standard, a mortgage agreement would not be deemed substantively unconscionable solely because it provides a borrower with more money than his home is worth. Whatever the pitfalls, receiving too much money from a bank is not what is generally meant by "overly harsh" treatment, and we have no reason to think that the West Virginia Supreme Court of Appeals would apply its standard in such a counterintuitive manner. As the district court noted, it is not the borrower but the bank that typically is disadvantaged by an under-collateralized loan. That is why borrowers may pay a premium for under- or non-collateralized loans . . .; why it is common practice for banks, as many borrowers can attest, to ensure that their real estate loans are for significantly less than property value . . .; and why a generous mortgage loan is usually cause for celebration and not a lawsuit.

McFarland, with the support of multiple amici,[3] rejects that common-sense application of West Virginia's substantive unconscionability law, arguing that it fails to take account of the broader social and economic context. According to McFarland, the Wells Fargo Loan is but one example of a widespread practice of overvaluing homes and lending too much money that has contributed to a national home foreclosure crisis: When a borrower is bound to a mortgage that exceeds the value of his home, he is trapped, unable to refinance to obtain better terms or sell his home to relocate, and foreclosure is the result. It is that harm to borrowers and to public policy, McFarland argues, that renders mortgage loans in excess of home value substantively unconscionable under West Virginia law.

We certainly agree that consumers may be harmed, sometimes grievously, when they take on more mortgage debt than their homes are worth. . . . And we have no reason to doubt that West Virginia's courts would acknowledge that disproportionate debt may be dangerous both for homeowners and for the broader economy. . . . Indeed, we note that West Virginia already has decided to regulate by statute precisely the lending practices of which McFarland complains, with a law aimed squarely at predatory mortgage lending. *See* W.Va. Code § 31-17-8(m)(8) (prohibiting "a primary or subordinate mortgage loan in a principal amount that . . . exceeds the fair market value of the property").

But here is where we disagree with McFarland: The fact that a practice is harmful does not by itself make it substantively unconscionable as a matter of West Virginia contract law. Rather, as noted above, substantive unconscionability is an equitable doctrine reserved for those cases in which a contract is "so one-sided that it has an overly harsh effect on the disadvantaged party." *Dan*

3. McFarland is joined in this argument by amici curiae The National Consumer Law Center, AARP, The National Association of Consumer Advocates, and The Center for Responsible Lending.

Ryan Builders, 737 S.E.2d at 558. And an under-collateralized loan, though it ultimately may cause harm, cannot meet this standard, because it will benefit the borrower in at least some respects and operate to the detriment of the lender in others. Here, for example, the Wells Fargo Loan provided McFarland with the money he needed to pay off approximately $40,000 of student and automobile debt, as he had hoped. And while it undoubtedly exposed McFarland to certain risks, it posed risks for the bank, as well: When a bank writes a mortgage for more money than a borrower's home is worth, it takes the chance that it will forfeit at least some of its capital in the event of a default.[4] So a loan in excess of home value does not accrue entirely to the lender's benefit, and thus lacks the kind of "gross imbalance, one-sidedness or lopsidedness," *id.,* and evident impropriety that West Virginia courts have identified in setting aside contract terms as substantively unconscionable. *See, e.g., id.* at 559–60 (striking down unilateral arbitration clause because it was wholly one-sided and unfair); . . . .

Our belief that the West Virginia Supreme Court of Appeals would not recognize loan size, by itself, as evidence of substantive unconscionability is confirmed when we consider the problems that would arise in fashioning a remedy in such circumstances. In the typical case, when what is challenged is a particular contract term—say, a rate of interest, or a prepayment penalty—courts may sever the unconscionable term or reform it to avoid an "unconscionable result." *See* W.Va. Code § 46A-2-121(1)(b). But here, the only way to avoid what McFarland alleges is the unconscionable feature of having been loaned too much money would be to cancel the loan agreement altogether—which would spare McFarland a foreclosure but also require that he return the loan principal to Wells Fargo, which is of course the very outcome he seeks to avoid. *See Quicken Loans, Inc. v. Brown,* 236 W.Va. 12, 777 S.E.2d 581, 592 (2014) ("*Quicken Loans II*") (requiring return of loan principal as part of remedy for unconscionable loan agreement). The West Virginia Supreme Court of Appeals has been clear that "cancellation of the debt"—relieving McFarland of the obligation to repay his Wells Fargo Loan altogether—"is not a permissible remedy" in circumstances like these. *See Quicken Loans II,* 777 S.E.2d at 591. And with that off the table and no good alternative proposed, we think it unlikely that the West Virginia Supreme Court of Appeals would reach out to create a new variant of substantive unconscionability for which there appears to be no sensible remedy. *Cf.* Mallet v. Pickens, 206 W.Va. 145, 522 S.E.2d 436, 441 n.6 (1999) (interpreting West Virginia common law to avoid an "illogical, counterintuitive outcome").[5]

4. McFarland contends that today this risk is more illusory than real, given that mortgage lenders can sell their loans on the secondary market and remove them from their balance sheets. But as the Banks explain, they remain accountable to the purchasers of their loans, and in some circumstances even may have to repurchase loans that prove "defective." And indeed, many banks experienced a solvency crisis during the recent economic downturn because of the number of "bad loans" they had issued. . . .

5. Like the district court, we acknowledge that some federal courts in West Virginia appear to have reached a different conclusion, holding or assuming, without significant analysis, that a mortgage's size may be evidence of substantive unconscionability. *See, e.g.,* Petty v. Countrywide Home Loans, Inc., . . . 2013 WL 1837932, at *5 (S.D.W.Va. May 1, 2013). . . . [W]e agree with the district court

2.

McFarland also continues to press his alternative theory of substantive unconscionability: that his contract with Wells Fargo is substantively unconscionable under West Virginia law because the Wells Fargo Loan did not provide him a "net tangible benefit." Like the district court, we think it is clear that the "net tangible benefit" inquiry to which McFarland alludes is irrelevant to substantive unconscionability under West Virginia law.

McFarland appears to have borrowed the "net tangible benefit" test he proposes from West Virginia's anti-predatory lending statute, which prohibits mortgage brokers from charging certain fees "unless the new loan has a reasonable, tangible net benefit to the borrower considering all of the circumstances." *See* W.Va. Code § 31-17-8(d). But McFarland has not alleged that the Wells Fargo Loan violated this provision, nor pointed to any West Virginia case law borrowing its language and applying it in the very different context of a § 46A-2-121 "unconscionable contract" claim. Nor can we see any reason why the "tangible net benefit" standard would be transposed to the unconscionability context. . . . [C]ontracts are made all the time that include terms that might not provide either party with a "net tangible benefit" yet remain fair and evenhanded—or at least fair and even-handed enough not to be considered substantively unconscionable under West Virginia's standard. *Cf. Pingley v. Perfection Plus Turbo-Dry, LLC,* 231 W.Va. 553, 746 S.E.2d 544, 551-52 (2013) (contract between homeowner and sewage removal company not substantively unconscionable even though it disclaimed liability for damages caused by mold); *State ex rel. AT&T Mobility, LLC v. Wilson,* 226 W.Va. 572, 703 S.E.2d 543, 550-51 (2010) (arbitration agreement's ban on class actions does not render it substantively unconscionable).[6]

III.

We turn now to McFarland's contention that the district court erred by dismissing his unconscionable contract claim solely on the ground that he could not show substantive unconscionability. According to McFarland, neither of his unconscionable contract claims—that the loan agreement itself was unconscionable when made, or that it was induced by unconscionable means—could be dismissed under West Virginia law without some assessment of the fairness of the process leading up to contract formation.

We agree, but only in part. Like the district court, we think West Virginia law clearly requires a showing of substantive unconscionability to make out

that the cases are unpersuasive on the merits, [19 F. Supp. 3d] at 672, decided without sustained examination of the issue and providing no reason to think that West Virginia would apply its law in this manner.

6. The Banks argue in the alternative that even if the "tangible net benefit" standard were applicable here, it would be satisfied, given that the Wells Fargo Loan allowed McFarland to pay off his student and vehicle debt and thus reduce his total monthly loan payments. Because we find that West Virginia law does not call for an inquiry into "tangible net benefit" in this context, we need not address that contention.

a traditional claim that a contract is itself unconscionable. But we think it is equally plain that the WVCCPA authorizes a stand-alone unconscionable inducement claim which, unlike its common-law antecedents, may be based entirely on evidence going to process and requires no showing of substantive unfairness.

A.

Having found that McFarland could not show substantive unconscionability, the district court granted the Banks summary judgment on McFarland's unconscionable contract claim. No further analysis was required, the district court held, because under West Virginia law, a claimant must prove substantive unconscionability in order to prevail on a claim of unconscionable contract.

. . .

McFarland's contrary argument rests on cases in which the West Virginia Supreme Court of Appeals has instructed state courts against dismissing unconscionable contract claims when there are outstanding issues of fact relating to procedural unconscionability. . . . That policy is driven by a practical concern that unconscionability claims are context-specific, so that evidence of procedural unconscionability may in some cases also inform the substantive unconscionability analysis. *See Quicken Loans I*, 737 S.E.2d at 657;. . . . Because McFarland could not succeed on his claim that his contract with Wells Fargo was unconscionable when entered even accepting as true all of his allegations regarding the bargaining process, the district court properly awarded summary judgment to the Banks.

B.

We reach a different conclusion with respect to McFarland's claim of unconscionable inducement. Though the question is not fully settled under West Virginia law, we believe the West Virginia Supreme Court of Appeals would rule that the WVCCPA authorizes a stand-alone claim for unconscionable inducement, predicated on the process leading up to contract formation and independent of any showing of substantive unconscionability.

The terms of the WVCCPA are plain enough: Section 46A-2-121 authorizes a court to refuse enforcement of an agreement on one of two distinct findings: that the agreement was "unconscionable at the time it was made, *or* [that it was] induced by unconscionable conduct." W.Va. Code § 46A-2-121(1)(a) (emphasis added). What makes the question interesting is the interplay between West Virginia's unconscionability common law and the codification of an unconscionability provision in the WVCCPA. . . . [T]he question is whether the second part of § 46A-2121(1)(a), covering contracts "induced by unconscionable conduct," is to be read as diverging from this traditional understanding and authorizing a claim for unconscionable inducement that does not require a showing of substantive unconscionability. . . .

For several reasons, we think the West Virginia Supreme Court of Appeals would answer this question in the affirmative. First, it has come very close to doing so already. In its 2012 decision in *Quicken Loans I*, the court sustained findings of "unconscionability in the inducement" based entirely on conduct predating acceptance of the contract and allegations going to the fairness of the process, without regard to substantive unconscionability: a "false promise" of refinancing, the sudden introduction of a balloon payment at closing, a negligently conducted appraisal review, and other similar factors. 737 S.E.2d at 657–58. Because the court's analysis of unconscionable inducement was only one portion of its overall unconscionability analysis—which also reflected that the loan agreement included several substantively unconscionable terms, *id.* at 658—we will err on the side of caution and treat it as something less than a clear holding on the question. But at a minimum, it is a strong indication that the West Virginia Supreme Court of Appeals understands the WVCCPA to allow for unconscionable inducement claims separate and apart from substantive unconscionability.

Second, the West Virginia Supreme Court of Appeals takes a plain meaning approach to statutory construction. . . . And the language of the WVCCPA fits the bill. It expressly authorizes courts to refuse to enforce an agreement that they find "to have been unconscionable at the time it was made, *or to have been induced by unconscionable conduct.*" W.Va. Code § 46A-2-121(1)(a) (emphasis added). The word "or" unmistakably signals two distinct causes of action when it comes to consumer loans: one for unconscionability in the loan terms themselves, and one for unconscionable conduct that causes a party to enter into a loan. If the legislature had intended to require both substantive and process-related unconscionability, subjecting creditors to liability only where an agreement itself is unconscionable, then all it had to do was replace the "or" with an "and." . . .

Finally, the West Virginia courts have advised that the comments to the Uniform Consumer Credit Code ("UCCC") are "highly instructive" when it comes to construing § 46A-2-121 because its unconscionability provisions are "identical" to those of the statute. *Quicken Loans I,* 737 S.E.2d at 656–57. And the comments to the UCCC not only indicate that a stand-alone unconscionable inducement claim exists, but also explain its purpose:

> Subsection (1), as does UCC Section 2-302, provides that a court can refuse to enforce or can adjust an agreement or part of an agreement that was unconscionable on its face at the time it was made. However, many agreements are not in and of themselves unconscionable according to their terms, but they would never have been entered into by a consumer if unconscionable means had not been employed to induce the consumer to agree to the contract. It would be a frustration of the policy against unconscionable contracts for a creditor to be able to utilize unconscionable acts or practices to obtain an agreement. Consequently subsection (1) also gives to the court the power to refuse to enforce an agreement if it finds as a matter of law that it was induced by unconscionable conduct.

Unif. Consumer Credit Code 1974 § 5.108 cmt. 1. . . .

Reading § 46A-2-121(1)(a) to allow for a stand-alone unconscionable inducement claim, we should note, is in no way inconsistent with West Virginia precedent holding that procedural unconscionability alone cannot show that a contract was itself unconscionable when made. The kind of procedural unconscionability that is required (in combination with substantive unconscionability) to render a contract or contract term unconscionable in and of itself may turn on such "status" factors as the "relative positions of the parties, the adequacy of the bargaining position, [and] the meaningful alternatives available to the plaintiff." *Quicken Loans I,* 737 S.E.2d at 657. We of course leave to West Virginia law the precise contours of an unconscionable inducement claim, but it appears that it will turn not on status considerations that are outside the control of the defendant, but instead on affirmative misrepresentations or active deceit. *See id.* at 653–55, 657 (unconscionable inducement findings include lender's concealment of balloon payment and false promise to allow refinancing). As McFarland concedes, in other words, the standard for unconscionable inducement is different and higher than that for procedural unconscionability.

Accordingly, we hold that the district court erred in dismissing McFarland's claim of unconscionable inducement on the ground that substantive unconscionability is a necessary predicate of a finding of unconscionability under the WVCCPA. We take no view as to the underlying merits of McFarland's unconscionable inducement claim, and remand to the district court to consider McFarland's evidence that his loan agreement was "induced by misrepresentations" and determine whether it allows him to proceed against the Banks.

IV.

For the foregoing reasons, we affirm the judgment of the district court in part and vacate and remand in part.

NOTES AND QUESTIONS

1. *Excessive loan amounts and substantive unconscionability.* The federal trial and appellate courts in the *McFarland* case both agreed that while there are risks to borrowers from taking loan amounts that exceed the fair market value of the securing real property, the lending of such excessive funds would not result in a substantively unconscionable contract under West Virginia law as they viewed it. Although it appears that the West Virginia Supreme Court of Appeals has not yet spoken to that precise issue, two justices have cited the *McFarland* case favorably while strongly asserting that singular, primary loans which exceed the value of the property should not be illegal, may be knowingly taken for good reasons, and are not likely to be deceptive to consumers. See Quicken Loans, Inc. v. Walters for Walters, 801 S.E.2d 509, 523-524 (W.Va. 2017) (Loughery, C.J., and Ketchum, J., dissenting). (The *Walters* case involved a dispute about the scope of a West Virginia predatory lending statute, W.Va. Code § 31-17-8(m)(8), that was not at issue in *McFarland*.) Do you agree that extending such excessive loans should not be deemed substantively

unconscionable? How does this questionable practice compare with the use of the "add-on" collateral clause in *Williams v. Walker-Thomas* or the arbitration terms in the *Higgins* case?

2. *Interrelationship between fraud and unconscionability.* The *McFarland* court remanded the case so that the plaintiff could have a chance to pursue a claim that his mortgage agreement was "induced by unconscionable conduct" as defined by the West Virginia Consumer Credit and Protection Act. The statute provides that such a finding would depend on factors "such as affirmative misrepresentations, active deceit or concealment of a material fact." W.Va. Code § 46A-2-121(1)(a). There is obviously potential for overlap between the statutory claim of "unconscionable inducement" and a common law claim of fraud. Indeed, the West Virginia Supreme Court of Appeals made exactly such a determination in the *Quicken Loans I* case cited in footnote 2 of the *McFarland* opinion. A natural question is whether the doctrine of unconscionability is redundant and unnecessary given the availability of fraud and other common law theories. Several answers can be given. First, the requirements for fraud and unconscionability are different, and it may not be possible to prove fraud even though the contract is grossly unfair. Fraud typically requires proof of intentional or at least reckless conduct ("scienter") and may be subject to a higher burden of proof. For example, the court in *Quicken Loans I* states that fraud must be proved by clear and convincing evidence. Quicken Loans, Inc. v. Brown, 737 S.E.2d 640, 653 (W.Va. 2012). Note that in *Quicken Loans I*, the court found that the loan was unconscionable not only in its inducement but also that the "loan product, in and of itself, is unconscionable." Id. at 659.

Second, in some cases the misconduct of a party may not be based on misrepresentation. For example, *In re Checking Account Overdraft Litigation*, 694 F. Supp. 2d 1302 (S.D. Fla. 2010), multidistrict litigation (MDL) transferred to Florida, plaintiffs sought to recover

> excessive overdraft fees for charges made to their accounts on debit card transactions. The alleged common nucleus of specific facts pled assert a common practice by Defendants, to enter charges debiting Plaintiffs' accounts from the "largest to the smallest" thus maximizing the overdraft fee revenue for themselves. In addition to the allegations about posting order, the Complaints set forth a number of other alleged agreements, policies and practices, contended by Plaintiffs to unlawfully damage them. Plaintiffs' asserted claims rely upon the legal theories of breach of contract and breach of a covenant of good faith and fair dealing, unconscionability, conversion, unjust enrichment, and violation of the consumer protection statutes of various states.

694 F. Supp. 2d at 1307. Claims of fraud are notably absent from the allegations. The court in that case found that the plaintiffs had stated a cause of action for unconscionability.

3. *Mortgage Loans and the Great Recession.* As indicated by the court in footnote 1, Wells Fargo sold the McFarland loan as part of a securitized trust package. The trusts were assembled by Wall Street investment banks and sold to large corporate investors. The case gives an example of the lending practices

that created inflated mortgage debt, leading to the Great Recession that began in 2008. See Andrew Ross Sorkin, Too Big to Fail (2009) and the movie of the same name (2011). See also Michael Lewis, *The Big Short: Inside the Doomsday Machine* (2010) and the film *The Big Short* (2015).

4. *"Payday loans" and unconscionability limits.* The plaintiff in *McFarland* argued that the home loan was unconscionable because the amount of credit extended exceeded the value of his property. A different type of loan involves smaller, short-term, unsecured loans, commonly known as "payday loans," and allegations that such loans are unconscionable or otherwise unlawful because of exorbitant fees or interest rates. The loans are usually for a few hundred dollars and are targeted toward low-income borrowers. They are typically offered from store-front lenders that have become as numerous as major fast food restaurants. See generally Lowell Ritter, Payday Lending: Friend or Foe?, 20 J. Consumer & Com. L. 146, 147 (2017). Some courts have found such loan agreements unenforceable on statutory and unconscionability grounds. See, e.g., Johnson v. The Cash Store, 68 P.3d 1099 (Wash Ct. App. 2003) (holding that debtor who entered into series of fourteen transactions over seven months could prevail both on unconscionability and statutory violation grounds; plaintiff paid more than $1100 in interest while still owing original loan amount of $500, paying an annual interest rate of more than 600%). The *Johnson* court observed that the lender's operations appeared to violate a statutory prohibition of "roll over" loans in which the debtor borrows more money to repay a prior loan and thereby incurs more fees, described as a "debt treadmill." Id. at 1106. See also Drogorub v. Payday Loan Store of WI, Inc. 826 N.W.2d 123 (Wis. Ct. App. 2012) (finding unconscionable an "auto title loan" in which debtor took $994 to be repaid with $1242 in one month, but after six monthly extensions, debtor had paid $1491 and still owed $1242 for 294% interest rate).

A number of states have adopted regulations over the years to govern payday lending and this trend has fostered adaptions by lenders to avoid those limitations. This practice is reflected in De La Torre v. CashCall Inc., 422 P.3d 1004 (Cal. 2018), in which the loan product at issue required a minimum loan amount of $2600, repayable in 42 months at an annualized interest rate of 96% or 135%. The required minimum loan amount avoided California state usury laws, which capped maximum interest rates but only on consumer loans of less than $2500. The statutory framework, however, also made all consumer loans subject to the state law on unconscionability. See Cal. Fin. Code §22302. The lender argued that the absence of a statutory cap on the larger loans meant the *interest rates* could not be deemed unconscionable. The California Supreme Court rejected that view and held that "[a]n interest rate is the price charged for lending a particular amount of money to a given individual or entity. . . . As with any other price term in an agreement governed by California law, an interest rate may be deemed unconscionable." 422 P.3d at 1009. Thus, while loans of $2500 or more were not subject to a specific interest rate cap, they were subject to the flexible test of unconscionability, requiring both procedural and substantive elements, taking into account the context and any possible justification for the questioned terms. 422 P.3d at 1013-1015. See also James v. National Financial, LLC, 132 A.3d 799 (Del. Ch. 2016) (finding consumer loan agreement unconscionable that provided for a loan of $200 to be repaid in 26, bi-weekly, interest-only payments of $60 followed by a balloon payment of $260 for an interest rate of 838.5%; extreme bargaining imbalance and lack of meaningful choice for debtor also found).

5. *Unconscionability as a basis for affirmative relief.* Over the years, many courts have construed UCC §2-302 as intended only as a defensive concept, not to be used to gain affirmative relief. This construction is based on the section's indication that courts may "refuse to enforce" or may "limit the application of" an unconscionable contract or clause. See, e.g., Arthur v. Microsoft Corp., 676 N.W.2d 29, 38-39 (Neb. 2004) (purchasers could not claim damages based on allegation that price versus cost disparity was unconscionable). A few courts have allowed damages or restitution after finding that the contract or one of its clauses was unconscionable. See Langemeier v. National Oats, Inc., 775 F.2d 975, 977-978 (8th Cir. 1985) (section allows court to enforce contract without unconscionable term, which may lead to affirmative relief). In *In re Checking Account Overdraft Litigation*, cited above in Note 2, the court rejected the argument by the defendant banks that unconscionability could be used only defensively. The banks had allegedly charged the customers' accounts excessive overdraft fees and retained those funds. The court reasoned that if unconscionability could not be the basis of a cause of action to recover the improper fees, the customers would not have a remedy for the banks' unconscionable conduct.

6. *Unconscionability in commercial cases.* Merchants or other commercial parties frequently allege that they are victims of unconscionable bargains, though the courts usually have been disinclined to give relief to those parties. On appropriate facts, however, courts have occasionally found unconscionability in such cases. A leading example is A & M Produce v. FMC Corp., 186 Cal. Rptr. 114 (Ct. App. 1982) in which a contract for sale of faulty agricultural machinery included a warranty disclaimer and an exclusion of consequential damages. The court found procedural unconscionability on two grounds: (1) due to the disparity in size and bargaining power between the buyer, a local though relatively large farming business, and the seller, an international manufacturer; and (2) because the objectionable terms were located on the back side of the contract and were not pointed out by the salesperson. The court also found substantive unconscionability because the clauses shifted to the buyer the risk of lost crops due to failure of the machinery. Id. at 124-126. *See also* Johnson v. Mobil Oil Co., 415 F. Supp. 264 (E.D. Mich. 1976) (retailer had less than eighth grade education, was practically illiterate, signed the contract with clause excluding consequential damages while busily engaged with service station, and did not discuss any term other than amount of rent). *Cf.* Harry G. Prince, Unconscionability in California: A Need for Restraint and Consistency, 46 Hastings L. J. 460 (1995) (criticizing *A & M Produce* and other California decisions finding parties with substantial business experience to be victims of unconscionability, asserting that merchants are more likely to have

resort to counsel, to read and understand contracts, and to have the ability to find alternative bargains).

Comment: Consumer Protection Legislation

The materials in this chapter examine a variety of judicially developed doctrines for dealing with the problems of coercion in the bargaining process or unfairness of the terms of a bargain. A number of commentators have argued, however, that judicial decision-making in individual cases is not the proper way to deal with such problems. To such critics, the judicial process is an inefficient, often ineffective way of attacking contractual abuses. Moreover, because regulation of such conduct involves important and difficult questions of social policy, legislatures rather than courts are said to be the appropriate institutions to determine the need for and scope of any such regulation. See Robert A. Hillman, Debunking Some Myths about Unconscionability: A New Framework for U.C.C. Section 2-302, 67 Cornell L. Rev. 1, 27-29 (1981); Arthur Allen Leff, Unconscionability and the Crowd — Consumers and the Common Law Tradition, 31 U. Pitt. L. Rev. 349, 356-357 (1970).

Since the late 1960s, both Congress and the individual state legislatures have enacted a number of consumer protection statutes. In addition, administrative agencies and regulatory officials at both the federal and state levels have been increasingly active in dealing with consumer protection issues. Because such regulation covers a wide range of activities (such as consumer credit, sales practices, and collection activities), an exhaustive review is impossible. This comment will touch on some of the major statutory and administrative efforts in this area.

In broad terms, consumer protection legislation has aimed at accomplishing three goals. One of these goals has been to require commercial parties to disclose information to consumers in a meaningful fashion. *Disclosure legislation* is based on the theory that increased information gives consumers an opportunity to avoid entering into unfair contracts. Such legislation has undoubtedly improved the functioning of the marketplace to some degree. As a means of controlling unfair contracts, however, disclosure legislation has its limitations because abusive contractual provisions may be found in standard form contracts that are rarely read by consumers and are not subject to negotiation. Thus, some consumer protection legislation has a goal of *substantive regulation* rather than greater disclosure. Under such regulation, particular contractual provisions thought to be unfair are declared unlawful. Finally, since legal changes to protect consumers are meaningful only if enforced, most consumer protection statutes contain provisions designed to *improve enforcement.*

In 1968 Congress enacted the Consumer Credit Protection Act, 15 U.S.C. §1601 et seq., commonly known as the Truth-in-Lending Act. Principally a disclosure statute, the Act requires lenders in consumer credit transactions to disclose by a uniform method the rate of interest on consumer loans (the annual percentage rate or APR) along with various other terms of the loan, such as the scope of any security interest that the creditor would obtain in the debtor's property. To a limited extent, the Act engages in substantive regulation.

Consumers are granted a right to rescind within three business days any loan contract that involves a mortgage on the consumer's principal residence. (First mortgage loans to acquire or construct the consumer's dwelling are excepted from this right of rescission.) 15 U.S.C. §1635. In an effort to increase creditor compliance, the Act contains a private cause of action for violation of its provisions, including authorization of class actions and the recovery of attorney's fees. 15 U.S.C. §1640. (Since 1968 the Act has been amended on a number of occasions to include provisions dealing with credit reporting, discrimination in extensions of credit, and collection practices.)

In the same year that Congress passed the Truth-in-Lending Act, the National Conference of Commissioners on Uniform State Laws adopted the Uniform Consumer Credit Code; six years later the Conference issued a revised version of the UCCC. Although the 1968 version of the UCCC contained disclosure provisions similar to those found in the Truth-in-Lending Act, the 1974 version eliminated those provisions on the theory that the federal legislation had as a practical matter preempted the field of disclosure. 7A U.L.A., Prefatory Note at 12 (1999). The principal thrust of the revised UCCC is substantive regulation rather than disclosure. In an effort to protect consumers from exorbitant interest charges, the UCCC sets maximum interest rates for various types of consumer loans. Within the bounds set by these rates, market forces are to determine the cost of credit. In addition, the UCCC prohibits a number of creditor practices, such as assignments of wages and confession of judgment clauses. UCCC §§3.305, 3.306. Interestingly, the UCCC allows (with some modification) the cross-collateral clause that was involved in Williams v. Walker-Thomas Furniture Co. UCCC §3.302. See Note 1 following the *Williams* case. As we have seen, the UCCC also contains a provision outlining factors a court should consider in deciding whether a clause is unconscionable. UCCC §5.108. As of October 2018, eleven states have adopted the UCCC.

In 1975 Congress enacted the Magnuson-Moss Warranty — Federal Trade Commission Improvement Act, 15 U.S.C. §2301 et seq. The portion of the Act dealing with consumer product warranties contains provisions requiring increased disclosure of warranty terms, regulating to some degree the substance of warranty obligations, and improving consumer remedies for breach of warranty. The other portion of the Act grants increased regulatory power to the Federal Trade Commission (FTC). Created by Congress in 1914, the FTC had been inactive in consumer protection until the 1970s, when several critical studies of its activities, along with a growing consumer movement, combined to produce political pressure on the Commission to become more aggressive. The 1975 legislation increased the Commission's power by granting it authority to promulgate rules defining unfair or deceptive acts or practices in or affecting commerce. One of the most significant rules adopted by the Commission is designed to prevent creditors from relying on the "holder-in-due-course doctrine" to overcome various consumer defenses against debt enforcement. 40 Fed. Reg. 53,506 (1975) (codified in 16 C.F.R. pt. 433). The Commission also adopted a rule declaring unlawful a variety of creditor practices: confession of judgment clauses, wage assignments, security interests in household goods, waivers of exemptions of property from creditor remedies, pyramiding of late charges, and cosigner liability. 49 Fed. Reg. 7740 (1984) (codified in 16 C.F.R. pt. 444). See American Financial Services Assn. v. FTC, 767 F.2d 957 (D.C. Cir. 1985), *cert. denied*, 475 U.S. 1011 (1986) (2-1 decision upholding FTC's authority to promulgate the Credit Practices Rule).

A number of states have enacted consumer protection statutes, many of which are modeled on the FTC Act (such statutes are often referred to as "little FTC" or "consumer fraud" acts). These acts typically give some state governmental agency, such as the office of the attorney general or the department of consumer affairs, regulatory power in consumer matters, usually including the right to bring lawsuits to protect consumers from improper conduct by sellers and creditors. See, e.g., In re National Credit Management Group, L.L.C., 21 F. Supp. 2d 424 D.N.J. 1998) (action by attorney general under New Jersey Consumer Fraud Act to enjoin certain practices in connection with the sale of credit monitoring services); People ex rel. Hartigan v. Knecht Services, Inc., 575 N.E.2d 1378 (Ill. App. Ct. 1991) (unconscionably high prices alone do not constitute an unfair practice under the Illinois Consumer Fraud Act, but the combination of an unconscionably large price, little or no service, and the absence of reasonable alternatives does violate the Act). In 2012, the attorneys general from 49 states participated with the Justice Department in a $25 billion settlement against major banks involved in abusive and fraudulent lending practices in connection with the residential mortgage crisis that began in 2007. See *www.justice.gov/opa/pr/federal-government-and-state-attorneys-general-reach-25-billion-agreement-five-largest*. The statutory provisions frequently give consumers a right to recover double or treble damages for willful violations, along with attorney fees. E.g., Mass. Gen. Laws Ann. ch. 93A, §9; S.C. Code Ann. §39-5-140; Texas Bus. & Com. Code Ann. §17.50. For a discussion of the importance of state unfair trade practices statutes, see Stewart Macaulay, Bambi Meets Godzilla: Reflections on Contracts Scholarship and Teaching vs. State Unfair and Deceptive Trade Practices and Consumer Protection Statutes, 26 Hous. L. Rev. 575 (1989).

During the 1980s and 1990s, a general social trend toward deregulation and emphasis on free-market economics made for a lessened interest in consumer protective laws and administrative oversight of the economy. In the new century, however, this began to change, particularly when the most severe financial crisis in the United States since the Great Depression reached a perilous point beginning in 2007. Home values around the country dropped precipitously and record numbers of homes went into foreclosure; life savings counted on for retirement shrank drastically; a great many people lost their jobs and had trouble finding other employment. There was a widespread feeling that failure and inadequacy of consumer protection laws and abuses by lenders and other parties during the 2000s contributed to the economic calamity. As a response, President Barack Obama proposed the establishment of a new federal consumer protection agency that would consolidate responsibility for supervision and enforcement of laws governing consumer financial products and services. In July 2010, Congress passed and President Obama signed the Dodd-Frank Wall Street Reform and Consumer Protection Act. This Act created the Consumer Financial

Protection Bureau (CFPB), which assumed responsibility for a number of federal consumer protection efforts that had previously rested with the Federal Trade Commission or other agencies, as well as taking on new watchdog efforts. For a brief description of the creation of the CFPB, see Administrative Law — Agency Design — Dodd-Frank Act Creates the Consumer Financial Protection Bureau, 124 Harv. L. Rev. 2123 (2011). Final and proposed rules and regulations of the CFPB can be found at the agency's website, *www.consumerfinance.gov.*

E. PUBLIC POLICY

For the most part, this chapter has focused on situations in which a party may have a defense against enforceability of a contract because of some bargaining misconduct by the other party. In this section, we examine situations in which, although the process of contract formation is untainted, a contract may still be unenforceable because the contract itself either violates or runs directly contrary to some public policy. Such contracts are often said to be unenforceable because of "illegality," but that term is a misnomer because in many situations the contract itself is not, strictly speaking, illegal. See E. Allan Farnsworth, Contracts §5.1, at 315 (4th ed. 2004).

Judicial refusal to enforce a promise because it violates some standard of public policy has early roots in the common law. Fifteenth and sixteenth century courts refused to enforce contracts that involved usury. Similarly, contracts in "restraint of trade" were held invalid. For example, in John Dyer's Case, 2 Hen. V, f. 5, p. 26 (1414), an action on a bond, the defendant pleaded by way of defense that he had satisfied his obligation to refrain from engaging in his profession of dyer in a certain town for one-half a year. Commenting on the pleadings, the judge stated that the defendant could have demurred to the bond because the condition was against the common law and thereby void. See Alfred W. B. Simpson, A History of the Common Law of Contract 506-524 (1987). The materials that follow examine some contemporary aspects of public policy limitations on the enforceability of contractual obligations.

PROBLEM 7-2

Ellen Erickson has been employed as a genetic researcher by Neogenetics, Inc., a corporation that is engaged in genetic research and commercial sale of products developed by such research. For some time Erickson has been considering leaving the company and starting her own business. She is concerned, however, about the following provision in her employment contract:

> 8. *Covenant not to compete.* Employee hereby covenants and agrees that during the period of her employment and for a period of two years thereafter, she will not engage, whether directly or indirectly, nor will she have any interest, whether as shareholder, creditor, or otherwise, in any business that is engaged in genetic research or in the marketing of products that are generated by such research.

Erickson has asked your advice about the enforceability of this clause and its potential impact on her if she starts her own genetic research firm. In light of the case and notes that follow, what advice would you give?

Valley Medical Specialists v. Farber

Supreme Court of Arizona 194 Ariz. 363, 982 P.2d 1277 (1999)

OPINION

FELDMAN, Justice.

We granted review to determine whether the restrictive covenant between Dr. Steven Farber and Valley Medical Specialists is enforceable. We hold that it is not. Public policy concerns in this case outweigh Valley Medical's protectable interests in enforcing the agreement. We thus vacate the court of appeals' opinion, affirm the trial court's judgment, and remand to the court of appeals to resolve any remaining issues. We have jurisdiction pursuant to Arizona Constitution article VI, §5(3) and A.R.S. §12-120.24.

FACTS AND PROCEDURAL HISTORY

In 1985, Valley Medical Specialists ("VMS"), a professional corporation, hired Steven S. Farber, D.O., an internist and pulmonologist who, among other things, treated AIDS and HIV-positive patients and performed brachytherapy—a procedure that radiates the inside of the lung in lung cancer patients. Brachytherapy can only be performed at certain hospitals that have the necessary equipment. A few years after joining VMS, Dr. Farber became a shareholder and subsequently a minority officer and director. In 1991, the three directors, including Dr. Farber, entered into new stock and employment agreements. The employment agreement contained a restrictive covenant, the scope of which was amended over time.

In 1994, Dr. Farber left VMS and began practicing within the area defined by the restrictive covenant, which at that time read as follows:

> The parties recognize that the duties to be rendered under the terms of this Agreement by the Employee are special, unique and of an extraordinary character. The Employee, in consideration of the compensation to be paid to him pursuant to the terms of this Agreement, expressly agrees to the following restrictive covenants:
>
> (a) The Employee shall not, directly or indirectly:
>
> (i) Request any present or future patients of the Employer to curtail or cancel their professional affiliation with the Employer;
>
> (ii) Either separately, jointly, or in association with others, establish, engage in, or become interested in, as an employee, owner, partner, shareholder or otherwise, or furnish any information to, work for, or assist in any manner, anyone competing with, or who may compete with the Employer in the practice of medicine.

> (iii) Disclose the identity of any past, present or future patients of the Employer to any other person, firm or corporation engaged in a medical practice the same as, similar to or in general competition with the medical services provided by the Employer.
>
> (iv) Either separately, jointly or in association with others provide medical care or medical assistance for any person or persons who were patients or [sic] Employer during the period that Employee was in the hire of Employer.
>
> . . .
>
> (d) *The restrictive covenants set forth herein shall continue during the term of this Agreement and for a period of three (3) years after the date of termination, for any reason, of this Agreement. The restrictive covenants set forth herein shall be binding upon the Employee in that geographical area encompassed within the boundaries measured by a five (5) mile radius of any office maintained or utilized by Employer at the time of execution of the Agreement or at any time thereafter.*
>
> (e) The Employee agrees that a violation on his part of any covenant set forth in this Paragraph 17 will cause such damage to the Employer as will be irreparable and for that reason, that Employee further agrees that the Employer shall be entitled, as a matter of right, and upon notice as provided in Paragraph 20 hereof, to an injunction from any court of competent jurisdiction, restraining any further violation of said covenants by Employee, his corporation, employees, partners or agents. Such right to injunctive remedies shall be in addition to and cumulative with any other rights and remedies the Employer may have pursuant to this Agreement or law, including, specifically with regard to the covenants set forth in subparagraph 17(a) above, the recovery of liquidated damages equal to forty percent (40%) of the gross receipts received for medical services provided by the Employee, or any employee, associate, partner, or corporation of the Employee during the term of this Agreement and for a period of three (3) years after the date of termination, for any reason, of this Agreement. The Employee expressly acknowledges and agrees that the covenants and agreement contained in this Paragraph 17 are minimum and reasonable in scope and are necessary to protect the legitimate interest of the Employer and its goodwill.

(Emphasis added.)

VMS filed a complaint against Dr. Farber seeking (1) preliminary and permanent injunctions enjoining Dr. Farber from violating the restrictive covenant, (2) liquidated damages for breach of the employment agreement, and (3) damages for breach of fiduciary duty, conversion of patient files and confidential information, and intentional interference with contractual and/or business relations.

Following six days of testimony and argument, the trial court denied VMS's request for a preliminary injunction, finding that the restrictive covenant violated public policy or, alternatively, was unenforceable because it was too broad. Specifically, the court found that: any covenant over six months would be unreasonable; the five-mile radius from each of the three VMS offices was unreasonable because it covered a total of 235 square miles; and the restriction was unreasonable because it did not provide an exception for emergency medical aid and was not limited to pulmonology.

The court of appeals reversed, concluding that a modified covenant was reasonable. Valley Med. Specialists v. Farber, 190 Ariz. 563, 950 P.2d 1184 (App. 1997). The court noted that there were eight hospitals outside the restricted area where Dr. Farber could practice. Id. at 567, 950 P.2d at 1188. Although the covenant made no exceptions for emergency medicine, the court held that the severability clause permitted the trial court to modify the covenant so Dr. Farber could provide emergency services within the restricted area. Id. (citing Phoenix Orthopaedic Surgeons, Ltd. v. Peairs (*"Peairs"*), 164 Ariz. 54, 61, 790 P.2d 752, 759 (App. 1989)). Moreover, VMS was allowed to stipulate that Dr. Farber could perform brachytherapy and treat AIDS and HIV patients within the restricted area, again even though the covenant contained no such exceptions. *Valley Med. Specialists,* 190 Ariz. at 567, 950 P.2d at 1188.

The court of appeals found the restriction, when so modified, reasonable as to time and place. Although non-emergency patients might be required to travel further to see Dr. Farber, they could continue to see him if they were willing to drive that far. 190 Ariz. at 567-68, 950 P.2d at 1188-89. Three years was reasonable because the record contained testimony that it might take Dr. Farber's replacement three to five years to develop his pulmonary practice referral sources to the level they were when Dr. Farber resigned. Id.

The court found that the restrictive covenant did not violate public policy, believing that courts must not unnecessarily restrict the freedom of contract. Id. at 568, 950 P.2d at 1189. Moreover, the record was void of any evidence that the availability of pulmonologists in the restricted area would be inadequate without Dr. Farber. Id.

Discussion

A. Standard of Review

. . .

B. History of Restrictive Covenants

A brief reference to basic principles is appropriate. Historically, covenants not to compete were viewed as restraints of trade and were invalid at common law. Ohio Urology, Inc. v. Poll, 72 Ohio App. 3d 446, 594 N.E.2d 1027, 1031 (Ohio App. 1991); see generally Harlan M. Blake, Employee Agreements not to Compete, 73 Harv. L. Rev. 625 (1960); Serena L. Kafker, Golden Handcuffs: Enforceability of Noncompetition Clauses in Professional Partnership Agreements of Accountants, Physicians, and Attorneys, 31 Am. Bus. L. J. 31, 33 (1993). Eventually, ancillary restraints, such as those incident to employment or partnership agreements, were enforced under the rule of reason. See Restatement (Second) of Contracts §188 (hereinafter "Restatement"). Given the public interest in doctor-patient relationships, the validity of restrictive covenants between physicians was carefully examined long ago in Mandeville v. Harman:

> The rule is not that a limited restraint is good, but that it may be good. It is valid when the restraint is reasonable; and the restraint is reasonable when it imposes no shackle upon the one party which is not beneficial to the other.

> The authorities are uniform that such contracts are valid when the restraint they impose is reasonable, and the test to be applied, . . . is this: To consider whether the restraint is such only as to afford a fair protection to the interest of the party in favor of whom it is given, and not so large as to interfere with the interest of the public. Whatever restraint is larger than the necessary protection of the party can be of no benefit to either; it can only be oppressive, and, if oppressive, it is, in the eye of the law, unreasonable and void, on the ground of public policy, as being injurious to the interests of the public.

42 N.J. Eq. 185, 7 A. 37, 38-39 (N.J. 1886) (citations omitted); see also Karlin v. Weinberg, 77 N.J. 408, 390 A.2d 1161, 1165 (N.J. 1978). To be enforced, the restriction must do more than simply prohibit fair competition by the employee. Bryceland [v. Northey, 160 Ariz. 213, 216, 772 P.2d 36, 39 (App. 1989)]. In other words, a covenant not to compete is invalid unless it protects some legitimate interest beyond the employer's desire to protect itself from competition. Amex Distrib. Co. v. Mascari, 150 Ariz. 510, 518, 724 P.2d 596, 604 (App. 1986). The legitimate purpose of post-employment restraints is "to prevent competitive use, for a time, of information or relationships which pertain peculiarly to the employer and which the employee acquired in the course of the employment." Blake, supra, 73 Harv. L. Rev., at 647. Despite the freedom to contract, the law does not favor restrictive covenants. *Ohio Urology, Inc.,* 594 N.E.2d at 1031. This disfavor is particularly strong concerning such covenants among physicians because the practice of medicine affects the public to a much greater extent. Id. In fact, "for the past 60 years, the American Medical Association (AMA) has consistently taken the position that noncompetition agreements between physicians impact negatively on patient care." Paula Berg, Judicial Enforcement of Covenants not to Compete Between Physicians: Protecting Doctors' Interests at Patients' Expense, 45 Rutgers L. Rev. 1, 6 (1992).

C. Level of Scrutiny–Public Policy Considerations

We first address the level of scrutiny that should be afforded to this restrictive covenant. Dr. Farber argues that this contract is simply an employer-employee agreement and thus the restrictive covenant should be strictly construed against the employer. See *Amex Distrib. Co.,* 150 Ariz. at 514, 724 P.2d at 600 (noting employer-employee restrictive covenants are disfavored and strictly construed against the employer). This was the approach taken by the trial court. VMS contends that this is more akin to the sale of a business; thus, the noncompete provision should not be strictly construed against it. See id. (courts more lenient in enforcing restrictive covenants connected to sale of business because of need to effectively transfer goodwill). Finding the agreement here not on all fours with either approach, the court of appeals applied a standard "somewhere between" the two. *Valley Med. Specialists,* 190 Ariz. at 566, 950 P.2d at 1187.

Although this agreement is between partners, it is more analogous to an employer-employee agreement than a sale of a business. See Restatement §188 cmt. *h* ("A rule similar to that applicable to an employee or agent applies to a partner who makes a promise not to compete that is ancillary to the partnership agreement or to an agreement by which he disposes of his partnership interest."). Many of the concerns present in the sale of a business are not present or are reduced where, as here, a physician leaves a medical group, even when that physician is a partner. When a business is sold, the value of that business's goodwill usually figures significantly into the purchase price. The buyer therefore deserves some protection from competition from the former owner. See Kafker, supra, 31 Am. Bus. L.J. at 33. A restraint accompanying the sale of a business is necessary for the buyer to get the full goodwill value for which it has paid. Blake, supra, 73 Harv. L. Rev., at 647.

It is true that in this case, unlike typical employer-employee agreements, Dr. Farber may not have been at a bargaining disadvantage, which is one of the reasons such restrictive covenants are strictly construed. See, e.g., Rash v. Toccoa Clinic Med. Assocs., 253 Ga. 322, 320 S.E.2d 170, 172-173 (Ga. 1984). Unequal bargaining power may be a factor to consider when examining the hardship on the departing employee. But in cases involving the professions, public policy concerns may outweigh any protectable interest the remaining firm members may have. Thus, this case does not turn on the hardship to Dr. Farber.

By restricting a physician's practice of medicine, this covenant involves strong public policy implications and must be closely scrutinized. See *Peairs,* 164 Ariz. at 60, 790 P.2d at 758; *Ohio Urology, Inc.,* 594 N.E.2d at 1032 (restrictive covenant in medical context "strictly construed in favor of professional mobility and access to medical care and facilities"). Although stopping short of banning restrictive covenants between physicians, the American Medical Association ("AMA") "discourages" such covenants, finding they are not in the public interest.

> The Council on Ethical and Judicial Affairs discourages any agreement between physicians which restricts the right of a physician to practice medicine for a specified period of time or in a specified area upon termination of employment or a partnership or a corporate agreement. Such restrictive agreements are not in the public interest.

1989 Current Opinions of the Council on Ethical and Judicial Affairs, Section 9.02 (hereinafter "AMA Opinions"). In addition, the AMA recognizes that free choice of doctors is the right of every patient, and free competition among physicians is a prerequisite of optimal care and ethical practice. See AMA Opinions, Section 9.06; *Ohio Urology, Inc.,* 594 N.E.2d at 1030.

For similar reasons, restrictive covenants are prohibited between attorneys. See Dwyer v. Jung, 133 N.J. Super. 343, 336 A.2d 498, 501 (N.J. Super. Ct. Ch. Div.), *aff'd,* 137 N.J. Super. 135, 348 A.2d 208 (N.J. Super. Ct. App. Div. 1975); Cohen v. Lord, Day & Lord, 75 N.Y.2d 95, 550 N.E.2d 410, 410-411, 551 N.Y.S.2d 157 (N.Y. App. 1989). In 1969, the American Bar Association adopted a code of professional conduct that contained a disciplinary rule prohibiting restrictive covenants between attorneys. See Berg, supra, 45 Rutgers L. Rev., at 37. The ethical rules adopted by this court provide:

> A lawyer shall not participate in offering or making:
>
> (a) a partnership or employment agreement that restricts the rights of a lawyer to practice after termination of the relationship except an agreement concerning benefits upon retirement; or

(b) an agreement in which a restriction on the lawyers right to practice is part of the settlement of a controversy between private parties.

Ethical Rule ("ER") 5.6, Arizona Rules of Professional Conduct, Rule 42, Ariz. R. Sup. Ct.

Restrictive covenants between lawyers limit not only their professional autonomy but also the client's freedom to choose a lawyer. See ER 5.6 cmt. We do not, of course, enact ethical rules for the medical profession, but given the view of the AMA to which we have previously alluded, we believe the principle behind prohibiting restrictive covenants in the legal profession is relevant.

> Commercial standards may not be used to evaluate the reasonableness of lawyer restrictive covenants. Strong public policy considerations preclude their applicability. In that sense lawyer restrictions are injurious to the public interest. A client is always entitled to be represented by counsel of his own choosing. The attorney-client relationship is consensual, highly fiduciary on the part of counsel, and he may do nothing which restricts the right of the client to repose confidence in any counsel of his choice. No concept of the practice of law is more deeply rooted.

Dwyer, 336 A.2d at 500.

We therefore conclude that the doctor-patient relationship is special and entitled to unique protection. It cannot be easily or accurately compared to relationships in the commercial context. In light of the great public policy interest involved in covenants not to compete between physicians, each agreement will be strictly construed for reasonableness.[1]

D. Reasonableness of Covenant

Reasonableness is a fact-intensive inquiry that depends on the totality of the circumstances. *Bryceland,* 160 Ariz. at 217, 772 P.2d at 40 ("Each case hinges on its own particular facts."); Olliver/Pilcher Ins. [v. Daniels, 148 Ariz. 530, 532, 715 P.2d 1218, 1220 (1986)]. A restriction is unreasonable and thus will not be enforced: (1) if the restraint is greater than necessary to protect the employer's legitimate interest; or (2) if that interest is outweighed by the hardship to the employee and the likely injury to the public. See Restatement §188 cmt. *a.*; see also Blake, supra, 73 Harv. L. Rev., at 648-649; Ferdinand S. Tinio, Annotation, Validity and Construction of Contractual Restrictions on Right of Medical Practitioner to Practice, Incident to Partnership Agreement, 62 A.L.R.3d 970, 984 (1975). Thus, in the present case, the reasonableness inquiry requires us to examine the interests of the employer, employee, patients, and public in general. See 62 A.L.R.3d at 976; see also *Peairs,* 164 Ariz. at 57, 790 P.2d at 755; *Amex Distrib. Co.,* 150 Ariz. at 514, 724 P.2d at 600 (accommodating right to work, right to contract, and public's right to competition); see generally Blake, supra.

1. Dr. Farber asks us to hold restrictive covenants in the medical profession void per se as against public policy. Finding the present covenant unreasonable and thus unenforceable by injunction, we need not and do not address that contention.

Balancing these competing interests is no easy task and no exact formula can be used. See Restatement §188 cmt. *a*.

In holding this restrictive covenant enforceable, the court of appeals relied heavily on *Peairs,* noting the restriction here was "very similar to the one in *Peairs,* which restricted a doctor from practicing orthopedic medicine and surgery within a five-mile radius of each of three offices for three years." *Valley Med. Specialists,* 190 Ariz. at 567, 950 P.2d at 1188. As noted, however, each case must be decided on its own unique facts. *Bryceland,* 160 Ariz. at 217, 772 P.2d at 40. Here, the facts are sufficiently distinguishable from *Peairs* to warrant different treatment. For instance, in *Peairs* the three offices were "clustered," and the total restricted area was thus much smaller. 164 Ariz. at 60, 790 P.2d at 758. The *Peairs* restrictive covenant prevented the practice of "orthopedic medicine and surgery." Id. at 56, 790 P.2d at 754. Here, however, the covenant prohibited Dr. Farber from providing any and all forms of "medical care," including not only pulmonology, but emergency medicine, brachytherapy treatment, and HIV-positive and AIDS patient care. Finally, the trial court in *Peairs* granted the preliminary injunction, while the trial court here denied it. Because we review the grant or denial of a preliminary injunction for abuse of discretion, the trial judge's ruling after hearing the evidence in both cases is another factor that distinguishes the two cases.

E. Vms's Protectable Interest

VMS contends, and the court of appeals agreed, that it has a protectable interest in its patients and referral sources. In the commercial context, it is clear that employers have a legitimate interest in retaining their customer base. See, e.g., *Bryceland,* 160 Ariz. at 217, 772 P.2d at 40. "The employer's point of view is that the company's clientele is an asset of value which has been acquired by virtue of effort and expenditures over a period of time, and which should be protected as a form of property." Blake, supra, 73 Harv. L. Rev. at 654. In the medical context, however, the personal relationship between doctor and patient as well as the patient's freedom to see a particular doctor, affects the extent of the employer's interest. See *Ohio Urology Inc.,* 594 N.E.2d at 1031-1032. "The practice of a physician is a thing so purely personal, depending so absolutely on the confidence reposed in his personal skill and ability, that when he ceases to exist it necessarily ceases also. . . ." *Mandeville,* 7 A. at 40-41 (holding medical practice's patient base is not protectable interest); see also Berg, supra, 45 Rutgers L. Rev. at 17.

Even in the commercial context, the employer's interest in its customer base is balanced with the employee's right to the customers. Where the employee took an active role and brought customers with him or her to the job, courts are more reluctant to enforce restrictive covenants. Blake, supra, 73 Harv. L. Rev. at 664, 667. Dr. Farber was a pulmonologist. He did not learn his skills from VMS. Restrictive covenants are designed to protect an employer's customer base by preventing "a skilled employee from leaving an employer and, based on his skill acquired from that employment, luring away the employer's clients or business while the employer is vulnerable—that is—before the employer has had a chance to replace the employee with someone qualified to do the job." *Bryceland,* 160

Ariz. at 217, 772 P.2d at 40. These facts support the trial judge's conclusion that VMS's interest in protecting its patient base was outweighed by other factors.

We agree with VMS, however, that it has a protectable interest in its referral sources. See Medical Specialists, Inc. v. Sleweon, 652 N.E.2d 517, 523 (Ind. App. 1995) ("Clearly, the continued success of [a specialty] practice, which is dependent upon patient referrals, is a legitimate interest worthy of protection."); Ballesteros v. Johnson, 812 S.W.2d 217, 223 (Mo. App. 1991).

F. Scope of the Restrictive Covenant

The restriction cannot be greater than necessary to protect VMS's legitimate interests. A restraint's scope is defined by its duration and geographic area. The frequency of contact between doctors and their patients affects the permissible length of the restraint. Blake, supra, 73 Harv. L. Rev. at 659. The idea is to give the employer a reasonable amount of time to overcome the former employee's loss, usually by hiring a replacement and giving that replacement time to establish a working relationship. Id. Even in the commercial context, "[w]hen the restraint is for the purpose of protecting customer relationships, its duration is reasonable only if it is no longer than necessary for the employer to put a new man on the job and for the new employee to have a reasonable opportunity to demonstrate his effectiveness to the customers." *Amex Distrib. Co.,* 150 Ariz. at 518, 724 P.2d at 604 (quoting Blake, supra, 73 Harv. L. Rev. at 677).

In this case, the trial judge found that the three-year period was an unreasonable duration because

> all of the experts agree that the practice of pulmonology entails treating patients with chronic conditions which require more hospital care than office care and which requires regular contact with the treating physician at least once within each six-month period so that any provision over six months is onerous and unnecessary to protect VMS's economic interests where virtually all of Dr. Farber's VMS patients had an opportunity by late 1994 or early 1995 (Farber left September 12, 1994) to decide which pulmonologist . . . they would consult for their ongoing treatment[.]

On this record, we cannot say this factual finding was clearly erroneous. The three-year duration is unreasonable.

The activity prohibited by the restraint also defines the covenant's scope. The restraint must be limited to the particular speciality of the present employment. See Blake, supra, 73 Harv. L. Rev. at 676. On its face, the restriction here is not limited to internal medicine or even pulmonology. It precludes any type of practice, even in fields that do not compete with VMS. Thus, we agree with the trial judge that this restriction is too broad. Compare *Peairs,* 164 Ariz. at 56, 790 P.2d at 754 (upholding injunction that enforced restrictive covenant preventing doctor from practicing only orthopaedic medicine and orthopaedic surgery).

G. Public Policy

The court of appeals held that the restrictive covenant does not violate public policy, pointing out that the record contains nothing to suggest there will be a lack of pulmonologists in the restricted area if Dr. Farber is precluded from practicing there. Even if we assume other pulmonologists will be available to cover Dr. Farber's patients, we disagree with this view. It ignores the significant interests of individual patients within the restricted area. Kafker, supra, 31 Am. Bus. L.J. at 39-40. A court must evaluate the extent to which enforcing the covenant would foreclose patients from seeing the departing physician if they desire to do so. See *Karlin,* 390 A.2d at 1170; see also AMA Opinions, Section 9.06.

Concluding that patients' right to see the doctor of their choice is entitled to substantial protection, VMS's protectable interests here are comparatively minimal. See Berg, supra, 45 Rutgers L. Rev. at 15-36. The geographic scope of this covenant encompasses approximately 235 square miles, making it very difficult for Dr. Farber's existing patients to continue treatment with him if they so desire. After six days of testimony, the trial judge concluded that this restrictive covenant was unreasonably broad and against public policy. Specifically, the judge found:

(1) the three year duration was unreasonable because pulmonology patients typically require contact with the treating physician once every six months. Thus, a restriction over six months is unnecessary to protect VMS's economic interests. Patients would have had opportunity within approximately six months to decide which doctor to see for continuing treatment;
(2) the five mile radius was unreasonable because with the three offices, the restriction covered more than 235 square miles;
(3) the restriction was unreasonable because it did not expressly provide for an exception for emergency medical treatment;
(4) the restriction was overly broad because it is not limited to pulmonology;
(5) the covenant violates public policy because of the sensitive and personal nature of the doctor-patient relationship.

Given the facts and the principles discussed, that finding is well supported factually and legally.

H. Severance—the Blue Pencil Rule

This contract contains a severance clause.[2] The court of appeals accepted a stipulation by VMS that the restriction would not prohibit Dr. Farber from treating HIV-positive and AIDS patients or from performing brachytherapy. On its face, however, the restriction is broader than that, restricting him from providing "medical care or medical assistance for any person or persons who were

2. "Since it is the agreement and desire of the parties hereto that the provisions of this Paragraph 17 be enforced to the fullest extent possible under the laws and public policies applied in each jurisdiction in which enforcement is sought, should any particular provision of this Paragraph 17 be deemed invalid or unenforceable, the same shall be deemed reformed and amended to delete herefrom that portion thus adjudicated invalid, and the deletion shall apply only with respect to the operation of said provision and, to the extent a provision of this Paragraph 17 would be deemed unenforceable by virtue of its scope, but may be made unenforceable by limitation thereof, each party agrees that this Agreement shall be reformed and amended so that the same shall be enforceable to the fullest extent permissible under the laws and public policies applied in the jurisdiction in which enforcement is sought, the parties hereto acknowledging that the covenants contained in this Paragraph 17 are an indispensable part of the transactions contemplated herein."

patients or [sic] Employer during the period that Employee was in the hire of Employer." Arizona courts will "blue pencil" restrictive covenants, eliminating grammatically severable, unreasonable provisions. See *Amex Distrib. Co.,* 150 Ariz. at 514, 724 P.2d at 600; *Olliver/Pilcher Ins.,* 148 Ariz. at 533, 715 P.2d at 1221 ("If it is clear from its terms that a contract was intended to be severable, the court can enforce the lawful part and ignore the unlawful part."). Here, however, the modifications go further than cutting grammatically severable portions. The court of appeals, in essence, rewrote the agreement in an attempt to make it enforceable. This goes too far. "Where the severability of the agreement is not evident from the contract itself, the court cannot create a new agreement for the parties to uphold the contract." *Olliver/Pilcher Ins.,* 148 Ariz. at 533, 715 P.2d at 1221.

Even the blue pencil rule has its critics. For every agreement that makes its way to court, many more do not. Thus, the words of the covenant have an *in terrorem* effect on departing employees. See Blake, supra, 73 Harv. L. Rev. at 682-83. Employers may therefore create ominous covenants, knowing that if the words are challenged, courts will modify the agreement to make it enforceable. Id. Although we will tolerate ignoring severable portions of a covenant to make it more reasonable, we will not permit courts to add terms or rewrite provisions.

In modifying the agreement, the court of appeals cited *Peairs,* which indeed allowed the trial court to alter the restrictive covenant in a contract "between medical professionals whose services are necessary for the welfare of the public." 164 Ariz. at 61, 790 P.2d at 759. We disapprove of the portion of *Peairs* that permits courts to rewrite and create a restrictive covenant significantly different from that created by the parties.

CONCLUSION

We hold that the restrictive covenant between Dr. Farber and VMS cannot be enforced. Valley Medical Specialists' interest in enforcing the restriction is outweighed by the likely injury to patients and the public in general. See Restatement §188. In so holding, we need not reach the question of the hardship imposed on Dr. Farber. The public policy implications here are enough to invalidate this particular agreement. We stop short of holding that restrictive covenants between physicians will never be enforced, but caution that such restrictions will be strictly construed. The burden is on the party wishing to enforce the covenant to demonstrate that the restraint is no greater than necessary to protect the employer's legitimate interest, and that such interest is not outweighed by the hardship to the employee and the likely injury to the public. Here VMS has not met that burden. The restriction fails because its public policy implications outweigh the legitimate interests of VMS.

Dr. Farber listed in his petition for review several issues "presented to, but not decided by, the court of appeals." Valley Medical Specialists' response also contained "additional issues if the court accepts review." None of the issues were briefed in this court. We thus remand to the court of appeals for a determination of those issues that are capable of decision and still need to be decided.

THOMAS A. ZLAKET, Chief Justice, CHARLES E. JONES, Vice Chief Justice, FREDERICK J. MARTONE, Justice, and RUTH V. MCGREGOR, Justice, concur.

NOTES AND QUESTIONS

1. *Public policy limits and freedom of contract.* The Restatement (Second) §179 recognizes a number of categories of contracts that may be unenforceable on grounds of public policy, including agreements in restraint of trade as in *Valley Medical.* The courts often state, however, that there is a strong public interest in freedom of contract and there must be a well-established basis for any public policy that would deny enforcement of a contract. See, e.g., Swavely v. Freeway Ford Truck Sales, 700 N.E.2d 181 (Ill. App. Ct. 1998) (because public policy strongly favors freedom to contract, courts should refuse enforcement only if contract is clearly contrary to public policy found in constitutions, statutes, or court decisions); Beacon Hill Civic Ass'n. v. Ristorante Toscano, Inc., 662 N.E.2d 1015 (Mass. 1996) (freedom of contract is in the public interest; courts should "not go out of their way" to find inconsistency with public policy). Does the court reveal any evidence that the parties in *Valley Medical* did not freely enter into the contract? Would such a finding be relevant to a decision to refuse enforcement of a contract on grounds of public policy?

2. *Ancillary covenants.* Historically, the common law provided that agreements in restraint of trade were unenforceable. The rationale for this prohibition was that such agreements tend to restrain competition and thereby harm the public interest. John E. Murray, Jr., Murray on Contracts 571 (5th ed. 2011). However, the common law also recognized a number of exceptions to this prohibition. In United States v. Addyston Pipe & Steel Co., 85 F. 271 (6th Cir. 1898), *aff'd*, 175 U.S. 211 (1899), Judge (later President and Chief Justice) Taft outlined the common law exceptions as follows:

> [C]ovenants in partial restraint of trade are generally upheld as valid when they are agreements (1) by the seller of property or business not to compete with the buyer in such a way as to derogate from the value of the property or business sold; (2) by a retiring partner not to compete with the firm; (3) by a partner pending the partnership not to do anything to interfere, by competition or otherwise, with the business of the firm; (4) by the buyer of property not to use the same in competition with the business retained by the seller; and (5) by an assistant, servant, or agent not to compete with his master or employer after the expiration of his time of service. Before such agreements are upheld, however, the court must find that the restraints attempted thereby are reasonably necessary (1, 2, and 3) to the enjoyment by the buyer of the property, good will, or interest in the partnership bought; or (4) to the legitimate ends of the existing partnership; or (5) to the prevention of possible injury to the business of the seller from use by the buyer of the thing sold; or (6) to protection from the danger of loss to the employer's business caused by the unjust use on the part of the employee of the confidential knowledge acquired in such business.

85 F. at 281-282. As Judge Taft stated, the rationale for these exceptions was to protect the right of the covenantee to the legitimate fruits of the contract.

The Restatement (Second) preserves the common law rule that a covenant not to compete is unenforceable unless it is "ancillary" to a valid transaction.

Restatement (Second) §187. Section 188 defines restraints that are ancillary to a valid transaction or relationship to include the following: a promise by a seller of a business not to compete with the buyer so as to injure the business sold; a promise by an employee or agent not to compete with his employer or principal; and a promise by a partner not to compete with the partnership. The clearest example of a nonancillary covenant is an agreement between competitors to fix prices.

3. *Reasonableness of covenant.* Consistent with Restatement (Second) Contracts §188, Comments *f* and *g*, the *Valley Medical* court recognized the level of scrutiny used in examining an ancillary covenant not to compete will depend on the type of transaction involved. A covenant related to partnership or sale of business contracts will not be scrutinized as strictly or closely as a covenant related to employment because employees are usually at a greater bargaining disadvantage and therefore need more protection from the court. The court also indicates that the assessment of the enforceability of the covenant would depend on the nature of Valley Medical's valid protectable interest, if any. In assessing the reasonableness of the covenant, the court indicates that the general considerations are its scope, the hardship imposed on the promisor, and the public interest. More specifically, the court examines the scope of the covenant with regard to the time period covered, the geographical reach, and the scope of activities prohibited. (See also Comment *d* to Restatement (Second) §188.) What conclusions does the court reach on these issues? Are you persuaded by the court's analysis?

4. *Covenants restraining medical practice.* Even though the public interest in the practice of medicine is significant, a majority of courts, like the Arizona Supreme Court in *Valley Medical*, have declined to adopt "per se" rules that would invalidate all such covenants. See, e.g., Deutsch v. Barsky, 795 A.2d 669 (D.C. 2002) (stating that court has never held that ancillary covenants between dentists are per se violation of public policy; rule of reason to be applied); Pierson v. Medical Health Centers, P.A., 869 A.2d 901 (N.J. 2005) (rejecting argument that covenants by doctors should be invalid per se). Notwithstanding the majority approach, some state legislatures have enacted statutes that expressly prohibit covenants not to compete among physicians, and courts in other states have construed more general statutory prohibitions on non-compete covenants to apply to physicians. See Murfreesboro Medical Clinic, P.A. v. Udom, 166 S.W.3d 674 (Tenn. 2005) (citing express statutory prohibitions in Colorado, Delaware, and Massachusetts and judicial construction banning covenants not to compete among physicians in six other states; court decided that such covenants are per se unenforceable in Tennessee except as specifically allowed by statute).

As *Valley Medical* illustrates, of course, a covenant restraining medical practice may still be unreasonable even though not unenforceable per se. See, e.g., Nalle Clinic Co. v. Parker, 399 S.E.2d 363 (N.C. Ct. App. 1991) (covenant by doctor not to practice medicine or surgery for two years in particular county was invalid because of harm to public when county had only one other pediatric endocrinologist). See also S. Elizabeth Wilborn Malloy, Physician Restrictive

Covenants: The Neglect of Incumbent Patient Interests, 41 Wake Forest L. Rev. 189 (2006) (recommending a revision of the reasonableness test to take better account of the interests of patients).

5. *Public policy based on statutes.* As the prior note indicates, some states have enacted statutes that govern covenants not to compete among physicians. The Restatement (Second) §179, Comment *b*, states that "the declaration of public policy has now become largely the province of legislators rather than judges" and courts may refuse to enforce contracts that conflict with statutory law. When statutes explicitly declare that certain contracts are unenforceable or void, courts will obey the legislative mandate. Restatement (Second) §178, Comment *a*. See, e.g., K&K Services, Inc. v. City of Irwindale, 54 Cal. Rptr. 2d 836 (Ct. App. 1996) (statute provides contractor may not "bring or maintain any action" to enforce a contract unless "duly licensed" at all times during performance). In the more typical situation, the making of the contract violates or is inconsistent with a statute, but the statute is silent on the question of whether the contract is unenforceable. Generally a distinction is drawn between regulatory statutes, which are designed to protect the public, and revenue-raising measures. Violation of the latter will not generally prevent the enforceability of a contract. Grace McLane Giesel, 15 Corbin on Contracts §88.3 (Joseph M. Perillo ed. 2003). Compare Professional Property Services, Inc. v. Agler Green Townhouses, Inc., 998 F. Supp. 831 (S.D. Ohio 1998) (state requirement of license for property managers rendered contract void because statute was designed for "police or regulatory" purposes), with Benjamin v. Koeppel, 650 N.E.2d 829 (N.Y. 1995) (statute requiring that attorneys admitted to practice also register with court office and pay fee was primarily intended to raise revenue; failure to pay fee would not render attorney's contracts unenforceable).

6. *Covenants restraining legal practice.* As recognized by the *Valley Medical* court, covenants by lawyers not to compete with their firms after their departure are a special case because of restrictions found in the rules of professional ethics. See Model Rules of Professional Conduct, Rule 5.6, quoted in the *Valley Medical* opinion. Courts also tend to disallow provisions which apply a financial penalty to competition without purporting to prohibit practice directly. In Cohen v. Lord, Day & Lord, 550 N.E.2d 410 (N.Y. 1989), the New York Court of Appeals ruled that a partnership agreement that conditioned payment of a departing partner's share of earned but uncollected revenues on noncompetition by the former partner was unenforceable because of the ethical prohibition on restriction of practice by lawyers. The denial of enforcement to lawyers' restrictive covenants usually is based on the strong public interest in allowing clients to retain counsel of their choice. Id. at 411.

By contrast, in Howard v. Babcock, 863 P.2d 150 (Cal. 1994), the California Supreme Court held "that an agreement among law partners imposing a reasonable toll on departing partners who compete with the firm is enforceable." Id. at 151. The court acknowledged that it was going against the weight of authority, but remarked:

> "The traditional view of the law firm as a stable institution with an assured future is now challenged by an awareness that even the largest and most prestigious firms are fragile economic units. . . ." (Hillman, Law Firm Breakups (1990) §1.1, at p. 1.) Not the least of the changes rocking the legal profession is the propensity of withdrawing partners in law firms to "grab" clients of the firm and set up a competing practice. . . . In response, many firms have inserted noncompetition clauses into their partnership agreements. . . . These noncompetition clauses have grown and flourished, despite, or in defiance of, the consistent holding of many courts across the nation that a noncompetition clause violates the rules of professional conduct of the legal profession. It is evident that these agreements address important business interests of law firms that can no longer be ignored.

Id. at 157.

7. *Covenants restraining nonprofessional employment.* Courts have been willing to enforce reasonable covenants not to compete on employees in a variety of contexts that may not raise the special issues that attach to lawyers and doctors, provided that the employer has a protectable interest and the restraints are reasonable in duration, geographic extent, and restricted activities. See CPG Int'l LLC v. Georgelis, 2015 U.S. Dist. Lexis 51712 (M.D. Pa.) (enforcing covenant not to compete by sales manager of manufacturer of building materials against employment by a competitor when manager had access to confidential sales information). See generally Michael J. Garrison & John T. Wendt, The Evolving Law of Employee Noncompete Agreements: Recent Trends and an Alternative Policy Approach, 45 Am. Bus. L.J. 107 (2008) (comprehensive survey of present law and suggestions for change).

8. *"Blue pencil" reduction of objectionable covenant.* The intermediate appellate court in *Valley Medical* held that the covenant not to compete could be enforced after its scope had been reduced. The Arizona Supreme Court strongly disagreed with this approach, disapproving its earlier decision that seemed to permit such modification of a covenant. At the same time, the Arizona Supreme Court endorsed a mechanical approach to possible reduction of a covenant which allows severance or reduction only if the objectionable term can literally be "lined out" and the remainder enforced. For example, in a covenant that prohibited a former employee from working for competitors in "Stephens or Comanche County," the court could "blue pencil" or line out one of the two counties to make the geographical scope reasonable.

The Reporter's Note to Restatement (Second) §184 makes it clear that the section rejects the mechanical approach and endorses a more flexible method which allows reduction of the effect or scope of a clause to make it reasonable. Comment *b* to §184 indicates, however, that the court's discretion to reduce a covenant should be exercised only when there is no evidence of overreaching or bad faith by the promisee. This qualified approach to granting partial enforcement allows the courts to guard against the possibility recognized by the *Valley Medical* court that employers may intentionally write overbroad covenants not to compete in anticipation that few employees will have the inclination or ability to challenge them. Notably, however, some courts refuse to use either the traditional or more modern approach to severance to save a covenant not to compete that is flawed. See Quality Liquid Feeds, Inc. v. Plunkett, 199 S.W.3d 700, 705 (Ark. Ct. App. 2004) (covenant must be valid as written; court will not make new contract for parties); Ceramic & Metal Coatings Corp. v. Hizer, 529 S.E.2d 160, 163 (Ga. Ct. App. 2000) (completely rejecting the "blue pencil theory of severability" with regard to employment contracts even if contract has severability clause).

P.M. v. T.B.

Supreme Court of Iowa 907 N.W.2d 522 (2018)

OPINION

WATERMAN, Justice.

In this appeal, we must decide a question of first impression: whether gestational surrogacy contracts are enforceable under Iowa law. The plaintiffs, the intended parents, are a married couple unable to conceive their own child. They signed a contract with the defendants, the surrogate mother and her husband, who, in exchange for future payments of up to $13,000 and medical expenses, agreed to have the surrogate mother impregnated with embryos fertilized with the plaintiff-father's sperm and the ova (eggs) of an anonymous donor. The defendants agreed to deliver the baby at birth to the intended parents. The surrogate mother became pregnant with twins, but after demanding additional payments, refused to honor the agreement. The babies were born prematurely, and one died. The intended parents sued to enforce the contract and gain custody of the surviving child. The district court, after genetic testing, ruled the contract is enforceable, terminated the presumptive parental rights of the surrogate mother and her husband, established paternity in the biological father, and awarded him permanent legal and physical custody. The defendants appealed, and we retained the case.

For the reasons explained below, we affirm the rulings of the district court. We hold this gestational surrogacy contract is legally enforceable in favor of the intended, biological father against a surrogate mother and her husband who are not the child's genetic parents. The intended parents would not have entrusted their embryos to the surrogate mother, and this child would not have been born, without their reliance on the surrogate's contractual commitment. A contrary holding invalidating surrogacy contracts would deprive infertile couples of the opportunity to raise their own biological children and would limit the personal autonomy of women willing to serve as surrogates to carry and deliver a baby to be raised by other loving parents. The district court properly established paternity in the biological father based on the undisputed DNA evidence and terminated the presumptive parental rights of the surrogate mother and her husband. The district court correctly awarded permanent custody of the child to the biological, intended father.

Background Facts and Proceedings

P.M. and C.M. were high school sweethearts but parted ways when P.M. joined the Navy upon graduation. After marrying and divorcing other spouses, they reconnected and married each other in 2013. They now live in Cedar Rapids. P.M. had two children from his first marriage, and C.M. had four children from hers. The Ms were nearing age fifty and wanted to have a child together. C.M. was no longer able to conceive, so the Ms placed an advertisement on Craigslist in 2015 seeking a woman willing to act as a surrogate mother.

T.B. and D.B. married each other in January 2009 and live in Muscatine. T.B. has four children from a prior marriage; D.B. has no children and had never been married. The Bs want to have children together. In 2010, T.B. had a tubal pregnancy which was life-threatening and incapable of leading to the birth of a viable child, so she surgically terminated the pregnancy. T.B. and D.B. continued to try to conceive without success. The Bs realized they would need the services of a reproductive endocrinologist in order to have a child. T.B. learned that the Bs' insurance would not cover infertility treatment or in vitro fertilization (IVF). They decided they needed to supplement D.B.'s income to pay for assisted reproduction procedures.

T.B. responded to the Ms' Craigslist advertisement. The four met for dinner in Coralville and got along well at first. They agreed that T.B. would gestate two embryos fertilized in vitro with P.M.'s sperm and the eggs of an anonymous donor. The Ms selected Midwest Fertility Clinic (Midwest) in Downers Grove, Illinois, to perform the IVF and embryo transfers. Midwest required a written contract between the parties, so the Ms hired a lawyer to draft the agreement. Its stated purpose was "to enable the Intended Father [P.M.] and the Intended Mother [C.M.] to have a child who is biologically related to one of them." In exchange for the gestational service, the Ms agreed to pay up to $13,000 for an IVF procedure for T.B. to enable her and D.B. to conceive their own child. This payment was conditioned upon T.B. surrendering custody of a live child upon birth.

> The Intended Parents [the Ms] agree that after the Gestational Carrier [T.B.] has delivered a live child pursuant to this contract for the Intended Parents, the Intended Parents will pay for an IVF (Invitro Fertilization) cycle for the Gestational Carrier and her husband up to the amount of $13,000.

The contract also provided that the Ms would pay T.B.'s pregnancy-related medical expenses. At T.B.'s request, an additional term was included stating that "[i]n the event the child is miscarried or stillborn during the pregnancy, the amount of $2,000 will be paid to the Gestational Carrier." The four adults signed the final "Gestational Carrier Agreement" (the Surrogacy Agreement) on January 5, 2016.

The Surrogacy Agreement provided that T.B.

> understands and agrees that in the best interest of the child, she will not form or attempt to form a parent-child relationship with any child or children she may carry to term and give birth to pursuant to this agreement.

T.B. and D.B. "agree[d] to surrender custody of the child to the Intended Parents immediately upon birth" and "agree[d] that the Intended Parents are the parents to be identified on the birth certificate for this child." The Surrogacy Agreement further provided,

> In the event it is required by law, the Gestational Carrier and her husband agree to institute and cooperate in proceedings to terminate their respective parental rights to any child born pursuant to the terms of this agreement. . . .

The Surrogacy Agreement also stated that

> each party has been given the opportunity to consult with an attorney of his or her own choice concerning the terms [and] legal significance of this agreement, and the effect it has upon any and all interests of the parties.

T.B. and D.B. did not exercise their right to consult a lawyer before the Surrogacy Agreement was signed by all four parties. But each person acknowledged in writing

> that he or she has carefully read and understood every word in this agreement and its legal effect, and each party is signing this agreement freely and voluntarily and that neither party has any reason to believe that the other party or parties did not understand fully the terms and effects of this agreement, or that the other party did not freely and voluntarily execute this agreement.

On March 27, Midwest implanted two embryos into T.B.'s uterus. The embryos were the ova of an anonymous donor fertilized with P.M.'s sperm. On April 4, blood testing confirmed T.B.'s pregnancy. The parties' relationship soon began to break down over their disagreement as to payment of medical expenses. All four attended the first ultrasound, which D.B. videotaped. The Ms later objected to his videotaping and to T.B. posting information about the baby on social media.

Their relationship worsened after the women exchanged text messages on April 13 [in a dispute about scheduling a doctor's appointment during which each woman called the other "crazy."] The Bs retained an attorney to speak for them and cut off direct communication with the Ms, who nevertheless persisted in trying to reach them for updates on the pregnancy.

In a May 20 letter from her attorney, T.B. sought more money from the Ms beyond the $13,000 agreed to in their contract so she could use a costlier clinic for her own IVF. T.B. wanted to replace Midwest because it insisted she use her own medical insurance and because C.M. told her Midwest employees said T.B. was crazy. The clinic T.B. wanted to use charged over twice as much—$30,000—for IVF. T.B. insisted that the Ms pay the higher cost for her to continue to serve as a gestational carrier.

On August 19, P.M. sent Facebook messages to D.B.'s sister, using racial slurs and profanity to insult D.B. D.B.'s sister shared the communication with T.B. On August 24, C.M. sent an email to T.B. and T.B.'s attorney, triggering a lengthy exchange, during which C.M. called T.B. the "N" word. That statement, along with the comments P.M. sent to D.B.'s sister, convinced T.B. that the Ms were racist. T.B. then called the Ms' attorney. When T.B. expressed concern that the Ms would not pay her, the Ms' attorney assured T.B. that the money for the Bs had already been set aside. The Ms' attorney attempted to make payment arrangements with T.B. and arrange P.M.'s listing on the birth certificate, but those matters remained unresolved. Later that day, T.B. decided that she would not turn over the babies to the Ms.

Twin babies were born thirteen weeks prematurely on August 31. T.B. did not tell the Ms about the birth. The babies were placed in the neonatal intensive care unit. One died eight days after birth. T.B. did not inform the Ms about the baby's illness or death. The Bs unilaterally arranged for the deceased baby's cremation.

On October 24, the Ms, still unaware of the birth, filed a petition for declaratory judgment and temporary and permanent injunction. On October 31, the Ms filed a motion for an emergency ex parte injunction, alleging their belief that the babies had been born. The same day, the district court entered an order granting a temporary injunction that ordered T.B. and D.B. to surrender custody of "Baby H" to the Ms. The order prohibited T.B. and D.B. from acting inconsistently with the terms of the Surrogacy Agreement. The Ms have had physical custody of Baby H since that date.

After an evidentiary hearing on November 28, the district court entered a ruling on December 7 denying the Bs' application for temporary custody. At the hearing, the GAL [guardian ad litem for the child] expressed hesitation about agreeing to a shared care arrangement based on her inability to learn more about one of T.B.'s children aging out of foster care and the lack of a custodial arrangement with T.B.'s other children. The district court concluded that P.M., as the biological father, has the superior constitutional right to raise the baby. The court awarded sole legal custody to P.M. pending final resolution of the case. The court also determined this was in the best interest of Baby H. . . .

The district court then issued its ruling on the dispositive motions and on Ms' request for an order regarding the babies' birth certificates. The court found that T.B. is *not* the biological or legal mother of the babies and that D.B. is not the legal father. The court found that P.M. has a legal right to a relationship with Baby H and is entitled to permanent custody. The court concluded that the Surrogacy Agreement was enforceable as a matter of law. . . . The court ruled that P.M. is the biological father of the babies and directed the Iowa Department of Public Health (DPH) to amend the babies' birth certificates accordingly.

The Bs appealed, and we retained the case.

II. Standard of Review

. . .

III. Analysis

We must decide whether the district court erred by enforcing the gestational surrogacy contract, terminating the presumptive parental rights of the surrogate mother and her husband, and placing permanent custody of Baby H with the biological father. We begin with an overview of the law governing gestational surrogacy arrangements. We next determine whether this gestational surrogacy contract is enforceable under Iowa law. We then address the respective legal rights of the parties. We conclude the district court correctly enforced the contract.

A. Overview of Gestational Surrogacy Arrangements

"In general terms, surrogacy 'is the process by which a woman makes a choice to become pregnant and then carry to full term and deliver a baby who, she intends, will be raised by someone else.'" *In re Paternity of F.T.R.*, 349 Wis.2d 84, 833 N.W.2d 634, 643 (2013) (quoting Thomas J. Walsh, *Wisconsin's Undeveloped Surrogacy Law*, 85-Mar. Wis. Law. 16, 16 (2012) [hereinafter Walsh]). The woman who carries the child is the "surrogate mother." An "intended parent" is "an individual . . . who manifests the intent . . . to be legally bound as the parent of a child resulting from assisted or collaborative reproduction." *Id.*. . . . Surrogacies are categorized as "traditional" or "gestational." *Id.*

> In a traditional surrogacy, the surrogate is the genetic mother of the child and is artificially inseminated with the sperm of the intended father or a sperm donor. In a gestational surrogacy, the surrogate is not genetically related to the child; instead, "sperm is taken from the father (or from a donor) and an egg is taken from the mother (or from a donor), fertilization happens outside the womb (called *in vitro* fertilization), and the fertilized embryos are then implanted into the surrogate mother's uterus."

Id. (citation omitted) (quoting Walsh, 85-Mar. Wis. Law. at 17). This case involves a gestational surrogacy because T.B. is not genetically related to the child. T.B. is the surrogate mother, while P.M. and C.M. are the intended parents.

The law regarding surrogacy agreements has evolved with advances in medically assisted reproductive science.

> IVF, egg donation, and gestational surrogacy are decidedly modern phenomena. Indeed, not all that long ago, IVF was still (literally) the stuff of science fiction. *See* Aldous Huxley, *Brave New World* 1 (1932) ("'And this,' said the Director opening the door, 'is the Fertilizing Room.'"). The first IVF-assisted human birth didn't occur until 1978, and it wasn't until the mid to late 1980s that doctors began to use gestational surrogates in conjunction with IVF procedures.
>
> To be sure, IVF and other assisted reproductive technologies represent revolutionary biomedical advances; they have enabled countless couples to conceive who otherwise couldn't have had children biologically. But these advances are not without their complexities. IVF-assisted reproduction involving (as it does here) third-party egg donors and gestational surrogates "raise moral and ethical issues" that can affect multiple, and often divergent, interests—among them, those of biological fathers, egg donors, surrogate mothers, and the resulting embryos. Not surprisingly, the States have tackled IVF- and surrogacy-related issues in very different ways.

Morrissey v. United States, 871 F.3d 1260, 1269 (11th Cir. 2017) (citations omitted); . . . . "The ability to create a family using [assisted reproductive technology] has seemingly outpaced legislative responses to the legal questions it presents, especially the determination of parentage." *In re Paternity of F.T.R.*, 833 N.W.2d at 644.

A majority of states lack statutes addressing surrogacy. *Id.* As a result, "cases often involve ad hoc procedures attempting to effectuate the parties' intent by analyzing surrogacy issues under the state's statutes for [termination of parental rights], adoption, custody and placement, and the like." *Id.* Courts adjudicating disputes over the legality of surrogacy agreements in such states "are forced to confront issues of the most difficult nature." *Id.* at 645.

In the minority of states with statutes specifically addressing surrogacy, the enactments generally impose greater restrictions on traditional surrogacies, and most of the statutes can be grouped into three categories:

> First, some states have legislatively prohibited all surrogacy contracts, declaring their terms unenforceable and, in some instances, imposing criminal penalties for those who attempt to enter into or assist in creating such a contract. *See, e.g.*, D.C. Code §§ 16-401(4)(A)-(B),-402(a) (prohibiting all "[s]urrogate parenting contracts" as defined by statute); Mich. Comp. Laws Ann. §§ 722.851-.863 (declaring surrogate parentage contracts, as defined by statute, to be "void and unenforceable" and imposing criminal penalties for participation in a "surrogate parentage contract for compensation" or a surrogacy contract involving a surrogate who is an unemancipated minor or who has "a mental illness or developmental disability"). A second category of states prohibit only certain types of surrogacy contracts—typically those involving a traditional surrogacy. *See, e.g.*, Ky. Rev. Stat. Ann. § 199.590(4) (prohibiting traditional surrogacy contracts, as defined by statute, without addressing gestational surrogacies); N.D. Cent. Code §§ 14-18-05, -08 (declaring traditional surrogacy agreements void but allowing gestational surrogacies by providing that "[a] child born to a gestational carrier is a child of the intended parents for all purposes and is not a child of the gestational carrier and the gestational carrier's husband, if any"). Finally, states in the third category authorize both traditional and gestational surrogacy contracts, subject to regulation and specified limitations. *See, e.g.*, N.H. Rev. Stat. Ann. §§ 168-B:1 to -B:32 (generally permitting traditional and gestational surrogacy agreements subject to certain conditions, including a traditional surrogate's right to revoke the agreement within seventy-two hours of birth); Va. Code Ann. §§ 20-156 to 20-165 (generally permitting surrogacy contracts, as defined by statute, and providing a multi-step process for judicial pre-approval of such contracts); Wash. Rev. Code Ann. §§ 26.26.210-.260 (generally permitting traditional and gestational surrogacy agreements but prohibiting compensation beyond reasonable expenses and agreements involving a surrogate who is "an unemancipated minor female or a female diagnosed as having an intellectual disability, a mental illness, or developmental disability").

In re Baby, 447 S.W.3d 807, 819-20 (Tenn. 2014).[2] "Tennessee has a unique surrogacy statute" that defines surrogacy for adoption purposes but states,

---

2. *See also* Cal. Fam. Code § 7962 . . . (regulating surrogacy contracts); N.Y. Dom. Rel. Law § 122 . . . ("Surrogate parenting contracts are hereby declared contrary to the public policy of this state, and are void and unenforceable."); Douglas NeJaime, *The Nature of Parenthood*, 126 Yale L.J. 2260 app. at 2376 (2017) (cataloging statutes addressing gestational surrogacy).

"Nothing [herein] shall be construed to expressly authorize the surrogate birth process in Tennessee unless otherwise approved by the courts or the [G]eneral [A]ssembly." *Id.* at 820–21 (quoting Tenn. Code Ann. § 36-1-102(48)(C) (2014)). The Tennessee Supreme Court held that the public policy of that state "does not prohibit the enforcement of traditional surrogacy contracts" yet concluded many contract terms were unenforceable, including compensation "contingent upon the termination of the surrogate's parental rights." *Id.* at 840 (adjudicating claim of surrogate birth mother who was the biological, genetic mother). The *In re Baby* court called for the state "General Assembly to follow the lead of other state legislatures that have enacted statutes to address the fundamental questions related to surrogacy." *Id.*

There are two "commonly cited model acts dealing with surrogacy agreements[:] the American Bar Association Model Act Governing Assisted Reproductive Technology (2008) and article 8 of the Uniform Parentage Act (2002), drafted by the National Conference of Commissioners on Uniform State Laws." *Id.* at 820 n.6.

> Both of these model acts fall into the third category of surrogacy statutes, allowing traditional and gestational surrogacy contracts subject to extensive regulation that includes judicial pre-approval, limits on compensation, and provisions concerning the revocation rights of the parties to the agreement.

Id. The 2017 Uniform Parentage Act (UPA) imposes greater restrictions on traditional surrogacy agreements based on the birth mother's status as a genetic parent:

> As was true of UPA (2002), Article 8 of UPA (2017) regulates and permits both genetic (often referred to as "traditional") and gestational surrogacy agreements. But UPA (2017) differs in the way that it regulates these two types of surrogacy agreements. UPA (2002) set forth a single set of requirements that applied equally to genetic and gestational surrogacy agreements. While UPA (2017) continues to permit both types of surrogacy, UPA (2017) imposes additional safeguards or requirements on genetic surrogacy agreements. . . . This differentiation between genetic and gestational surrogacy is intended to reflect both the factual differences between the two types of surrogacy as well as the reality that policy makers view these two forms of surrogacy as being quite different. Of the states that permit surrogacy, most permit *only* gestational surrogacy agreements.

Unif. Parentage Act art. 8 cmt. at 72 (Unif. Law Comm'n 2017).

The Ohio Supreme Court held *gestational* surrogacy contracts are enforceable in the absence of enabling legislation. *J.F. v. D.B.*, 116 Ohio St.3d 363, 879 N.E.2d 740, 741–42 (2007) ("[N]o public policy is violated when a gestational-surrogacy contract is entered into, even when one of the provisions requires the gestational surrogate not to assert parental rights regarding children she bears that are of another woman's artificially inseminated egg."). And the California Supreme Court enforced a gestational surrogacy contract in favor of the biological parents and rejected constitutional challenges by the gestational surrogate before that state enacted legislation regulating surrogacy contracts.

Johnson v. Calvert, 5 Cal. 4th 84, 19 Cal.Rptr.2d 494, 851 P.2d 776, 784 (1993)(en banc). The *Calvert* court concluded,

> It is not the role of the judiciary to inhibit the use of reproductive technology when the Legislature has not seen fit to do so; any such effort would raise serious questions in light of the fundamental nature of the rights of procreation and privacy.

Id., 19 Cal. Rptr. 2d 494, 851 P.2d at 787; . . . . The Wisconsin Supreme Court held that a traditional surrogacy contract was enforceable without enabling legislation "unless enforcement is contrary to the best interests of the child." *In re Paternity of F.T.R.*, 833 N.W.2d at 638. But the New Jersey Supreme Court held that a traditional surrogacy contract was unenforceable without legislative authorization. *In re Baby M*, 109 N.J. 396, 537 A.2d 1227, 1264 (1988).

The only Iowa legislation specifically mentioning surrogacy exempts traditional "surrogacy arrangements" from the criminal statute that prohibits selling babies. *See* Iowa Code § 710.11 (2017). Against this backdrop, we turn to the issue of whether the Surrogacy Agreement at issue is enforceable under Iowa law.

B. Whether the Surrogacy Agreement Is Enforceable Under Iowa Law

T.B. argues the Surrogacy Agreement is unenforceable under Iowa law as inconsistent with statutory provisions and public policy. We first examine whether this contract between consenting adults is "prohibited by statute, condemned by judicial decision, [or] contrary to the public morals." *Dier v. Peters*, 815 N.W.2d 1, 12 (Iowa 2012) (quoting *Claude v. Guar. Nat'l Ins.*, 679 N.W.2d 659, 663 (Iowa 2004)). We find no such statutory or judicial prohibition in our state. To the contrary, the Iowa legislature tacitly approved of surrogacy arrangements by exempting them from potential criminal liability for selling children. "Also, we need to consider the public policy implications of an opposite ruling." *Id.* Banning gestational surrogacy contracts would deprive infertile couples of perhaps the only way to raise their own biological children and would limit the contractual rights of willing surrogates. We join the better-reasoned cases from other jurisdictions rejecting arguments that gestational surrogacy contracts are void against public policy.

1. Whether the Surrogacy Agreement is Inconsistent with Statutory Provisions

Iowa Code section 710.11 expressly exempts surrogacy arrangements from criminal liability for selling children and provides,

> A person commits a class "C" felony when the person purchases or sells or attempts to purchase or sell an individual to another person. This section *does not apply to a surrogate mother arrangement*. For purposes of this section, a "*surrogate mother arrangement*" means an arrangement whereby a female agrees to be artificially inseminated with the semen of a donor, to bear a child, and to relinquish all rights regarding that child to the donor or donor couple.

Iowa Code § 710.11 (first emphasis added). This provision was enacted in 1989, 1989 Iowa Acts ch. 116, § 1, one year after extensive national publicity over the decision of the New Jersey Supreme Court invalidating a surrogacy contract as contrary to that state's adoption statutes, including its "baby selling" prohibition on payment of money to adopt a child. *In re Baby M*, 537 A.2d at 1250 & n.10. Importantly, the *Baby M* court stated, "[O]ur holding today does not preclude the Legislature from altering the current statutory scheme, within constitutional limits, so as to permit surrogacy contracts." *Id.* at 1235. The Iowa legislature did just that for our state in its next session—expressly exempting surrogacy arrangements from the criminal prohibition on selling babies. The Iowa enactment tracked the surrogacy arrangement at issue in *Baby M*.

In *Baby M*, a married couple, William and Elizabeth Stern, wanted to raise a child, but Elizabeth feared her medical condition rendered pregnancy a serious health risk. *Id.* Mr. Stern's family had perished in the Holocaust, and as the "only survivor, he very much wanted to continue his bloodline." *Id.* He responded to the advertisements of a fertility clinic. *Id.* at 1236. So did Mary Beth Whitehead, who was motivated by "her sympathy with family members and others who could have no children (she stated that she wanted to give another couple the 'gift of life'); she also wanted . . . $10,000 to help her family." *Id.* Stern and Whitehead entered into a surrogacy contract. *Id.* "The contract provided that through artificial insemination using Mr. Stern's sperm, Mrs. Whitehead would become pregnant, carry the child to term, . . . [and] deliver it to the Sterns" for $10,000 to be paid after the child's birth. *Id.* at 1235. Whitehead agreed in the contract to "do whatever was necessary to terminate her maternal rights so that Mrs. Stern could thereafter adopt the child." *Id.* The artificial insemination was successful, and Whitehead gave birth to Baby M after an uneventful pregnancy. *Id.* at 1236. Whitehead, however, had developed a strong emotional attachment. *Id.* When the Sterns arrived at the hospital to see the baby, Whitehead "broke into tears and . . . talked about how the baby looked like her other daughter." *Id.* She made clear to the Sterns that she was unsure she could give up the child. *Id.* Three days after the birth, she turned the baby over to the Sterns, who "were thrilled with their new child." *Id.* But their legal battle ensued over custody and contract rights, with the New Jersey Supreme Court ultimately invalidating the surrogacy contract, awarding custody of the child to the Sterns, and allowing Whitehead visitation. *Id.* at 1234, 1263. While concluding that New Jersey's "present laws do not permit the surrogacy contract used in this case[,]" the court held "the Legislature remains free to deal with this most sensitive issue as it sees fit, subject only to constitutional restraints." *Id.* at 1264.

We conclude, based on the timing of the enactment of Iowa Code section 710.11, the very next legislative session, that our state's general assembly chose in 1989 to allow surrogacy arrangements, not prohibit them. Section 710.11 specifically mentions artificial insemination of the birth mother (who is the genetic or biological mother, as in *Baby M*), but we decline to infer the legislature intended to allow only traditional surrogacy when the birth mother is the genetic mother and yet criminalize gestational surrogacy arrangements. IVF, allowing implantation in the surrogate mother of embryos from donor eggs, was then in its infancy and had not been the subject of a court decision of national prominence. As other courts have noted, a gestational surrogacy in which the birth mother lacks a genetic connection to the child raises fewer concerns than the traditional surrogacy expressly mentioned in section 710.11. The legislature's decision to allow traditional surrogacy arrangements can be taken as a signal that it would also allow gestational surrogacy arrangements. We conclude that neither traditional nor gestational surrogacy contracts are prohibited under section 710.11.

Our conclusion is reinforced by the regulations adopted by the DPH that specifically contemplate IVF gestational surrogacy agreements. The regulations are entitled "Establishment of new certificate of live birth following a birth by gestational surrogate arrangement." *See* Iowa Admin. Code r. 641—99.15. These regulations enjoy a presumption of validity with the force of law. *See Brakke v. Iowa Dep't of Nat. Res.*, 897 N.W.2d 522, 533 (Iowa 2017). . . .

Another reason the Surrogacy Agreement does not violate Iowa Code section 710.11 is because the Ms' payment was for T.B.'s gestational services rather than for her sale of a baby. The Surrogacy Agreement states,

> The consideration of this agreement is compensation for services and expenses as limited by law and in no way is to be construed as a fee for termination of parental rights or a payment in exchange for consent to surrender the child for adoption.

The California Supreme Court held under equivalent circumstances that the contractual payment is for gestational services, not for the sale of a baby. *See Calvert*, 19 Cal. Rptr. 2d 494, 851 P.2d at 784 (explaining that the payments to the surrogate mother "were meant to compensate her for her services in gestating the fetus and undergoing labor"). We reach the same conclusion.

T.B. relies on Iowa Code section 600A.4, which requires parents to wait seventy-two hours after a child's birth before signing a release of custody for an adoption. *See* Iowa Code § 600A.4(2)(*g*) . . . . T.B. claims that the safeguards established in section 600A.4 are violated by the Surrogacy Agreement. We disagree because T.B. is not the genetic mother of Baby H, and section 600A.4 is therefore inapplicable. We agree with other courts that recognize the difference between surrogacy arrangements and giving up one's own genetic child for adoption:

> There is no doubt but that [the statute prohibiting baby selling] is intended to keep baby brokers from overwhelming an expectant mother or the parents of a child with financial inducements to part with the child. But the central fact in the surrogate parenting procedure is that the agreement to bear the child is entered into *before* conception. The essential considerations for the surrogate mother when she agrees to the surrogate parenting procedure are *not* avoiding the consequences of an unwanted pregnancy or fear of the financial burden of child rearing. On the contrary, the essential consideration is to assist a person or couple who desperately want a child but are unable to conceive one in the customary manner to achieve a biologically related offspring.

Surrogate Parenting Assocs., Inc. v. Commonwealth ex rel. Armstrong, 704 S.W.2d 209, 211–12 (Ky. 1986), *superseded by statute*, Ky. Rev. Stat. Ann. § 199.590(4) (West,

Westlaw through 2017 Reg. Sess.); *see also Calvert*, 19 Cal.Rptr.2d 494, 851 P.2d at 784. . . .

We hold that the adoption statute is inapplicable and the Surrogacy Agreement is not inconsistent with Iowa statutes on termination of parental rights.

2. Whether the Surrogacy Agreement is against public policy

T.B. also claims enforcement of the Surrogacy Agreement violates Iowa's public policy. We disagree based on the freedom of contract enjoyed by consenting adults. We start with the presumption that under Iowa law a "contractual agreement is binding on the parties." *Water Dev. Co. v. Lankford*, 506 N.W.2d 763, 766 (Iowa 1993). "The power to invalidate a contract on public policy grounds must be used cautiously and exercised only in cases free from doubt." *Thomas v. Progressive Cas. Ins.*, 749 N.W.2d 678, 687 (Iowa 2008). . . . We reiterate that "[t]o strike down a contract on public policy grounds, we must conclude that 'the preservation of the general public welfare . . . outweigh[s] the weighty societal interest in the freedom of contract.' " *In re Marriage of Witten*, 672 N.W.2d 768, 780 (Iowa 2003). . . .

In *Witten*, we addressed the enforceability of a contract executed by a married couple, Trip and Tamera Witten, and the University of Nebraska Medical Center that stored their frozen embryos. *Id.* at 772–73. . . . The couple later divorced, and the contract "did not explicitly deal with the possibility of divorce." *Id.* at 772–73. Tamera sought "custody" of the embryos to have them "implanted in her or a surrogate mother in an effort to bear a genetically linked child." *Id.* at 772. Trip argued the district court should enforce the contract, which required mutual consent of the parties for any use of the embryos. *Id.* at 773. The district court ruled the contract controlled and enjoined both parties from using the embryos without the written approval of the other party. *Id.* Tamera appealed, and we affirmed, holding that neither party could use the embryos without the contemporaneous consent of the other. *Id.* at 773, 783.

Our decision was consistent with the terms of the contract signed by the Wittens. But we stated a broader holding

> that agreements entered into at the time in vitro fertilization is commenced are enforceable and binding on the parties, "subject to the right of either party to change his or her mind about disposition up to the point of use or destruction of any stored embryo."

Id. at 782 . . . . We concluded that "judicial enforcement of an agreement between a couple regarding their future family and reproductive choices would be against the public policy of this state." *Id.* (emphasis omitted). But we concluded the embryo dispositional agreement remains enforceable as between the donors and the medical facility. *Id.* ("Within this context, the medical facility and the donors should be able to rely on the terms of the parties' contract.").

We see important differences between an embryo disposition agreement signed by the egg and sperm donor during their marriage and the gestational surrogacy agreement at issue here. The former addresses disposition of the parties' own genetic material and assumed the marriage will continue. *See id.* . . . We noted the judicial reluctance to compel procreation of a biological son or daughter after one donor changed his mind. *See id.* at 777–78 (surveying authorities). By contrast, the surrogate mother, T.B., is not the genetic or biological mother of Baby H. All parties sought the birth of Baby H. We conclude the public policy limitations in play in that case are inapposite. We turn to cases specifically adjudicating challenges to gestational surrogacy contracts.

T.B. argues a surrogacy agreement violates public policy against the exploitation of women, and contends,

> Surrogacy agreements, if enforced embody deviant societal pressures, the object of which is to use the woman, and destroy her interests as a mother to satisfy the desires of third parties. Surrogacy exploits women by treating the mother as if she is not a whole woman. It assumes she can be used much like a breeding animal and act as though she is not, in fact, a mother.

Yet T.B. entered into the Surrogacy Agreement voluntarily. She had given birth to four children of her own before signing the Surrogacy Agreement and was no stranger to the effects of pregnancy. T.B. does not allege she signed the Surrogacy Agreement under economic duress or that its terms are unconscionable.

The California Supreme Court rejected a similar exploitation argument in *Calvert*:

> Although common sense suggests that women of lesser means serve as surrogate mothers more often than do wealthy women, there has been no proof that surrogacy contracts exploit poor women to any greater degree than economic necessity in general exploits them by inducing them to accept lower-paid or otherwise undesirable employment. We are likewise unpersuaded by the claim that surrogacy will foster the attitude that children are mere commodities; no evidence is offered to support it. . . .
>
> The argument that a woman cannot knowingly and intelligently agree to gestate and deliver a baby for intending parents carries overtones of the reasoning that for centuries prevented women from attaining equal economic rights and professional status under the law. To resurrect this view is both to foreclose a personal and economic choice on the part of the surrogate mother, and to deny intending parents what may be their only means of procreating a child of their own genetic stock. Certainly in the present case it cannot seriously be argued that Anna, a licensed vocational nurse who had done well in school and who had previously borne a child, lacked the intellectual wherewithal or life experience necessary to make an informed decision to enter into the surrogacy contract.

19 Cal. Rptr. 2d 494, 851 P.2d at 785. California courts continue to reject the view that surrogacy agreements unfairly exploit women. *See C.M. v. M.C.*, 7 Cal.App.5th 1188, 213 Cal.Rptr.3d 351, 370 (2017) (relying on *Calvert*, 19 Cal. Rptr.2d 494, 851 P.2d at 785). We reach the same conclusion.

T.B. alternatively argues the Surrogacy Agreement violates the state's public policy favoring families. We have repeatedly acknowledged Iowa's public policy "promoting the sanctity and stability of the family." *Tyler v. Iowa Dep't of Revenue*,

904 N.W.2d 162, 168 (Iowa 2017) . . . . T.B. characterizes surrogacy agreements as deliberately destroying the surrogate mother–child relationship (a relationship, we note, that would not exist but for the Ms' contribution of their embryos in reliance on T.B.'s willingness to serve as a gestational carrier). We conclude that gestational surrogacy agreements *promote* families by enabling infertile couples to raise their own children and help bring new life into this world through willing surrogate mothers. We agree with the Wisconsin Supreme Court that

> [e]nforcement of surrogacy agreements promotes stability and permanence in family relationships because it allows the intended parents to plan for the arrival of their child, reinforces the expectations of all parties to the agreement, and reduces contentious litigation that could drag on for the first several years of the child's life.

In re Paternity of F.T.R., 833 N.W.2d at 649–50. T.B. has failed to show the Surrogacy Agreement violates the public policy of our state.

For these reasons, we hold the Surrogacy Agreement is enforceable under existing Iowa law. We emphasize that T.B.'s legal attack is on surrogacy agreements in general. We do not foreclose the possibility that a surrogacy agreement in a particular case could be subject to specific contract defenses, such as fraud, duress, or unconscionability.

[The court went on to hold that a gestational surrogate does not fall within the statutory definition of a "biological parent" and rejected T.B.'s argument that her emotional bond formed from acting as Baby H's mother for the two months that she had physical custody after birth gave her greater legal rights than Baby H's biological father. The court also rejected constitutional law claims that T.B. asserted based on substantive due process and equal protection grounds. - EDS.]

AFFIRMED.

NOTES AND QUESTIONS

1. *Public policy and surrogacy contracts.* The *P.M. v. T.B.* court emphatically stated that the public policy favoring freedom of contract is very strong and thus courts should be reluctant to deny enforcement of a contract that was properly made by consenting adults. Nevertheless, the *P.M. v. T.B.* decision raised a number of potential public policy concerns that might justify a refusal to enforce a surrogacy contract, including statutory prohibitions against "baby selling," statutorily mandated waiting-periods before a mother can consent to adoption, possible adverse effect on the children, potential exploitation of women, and laws favoring preservation of families and restricting termination of parental rights. On the other hand, the Iowa state legislature specifically exempted traditional or genetic surrogacy contracts from the criminal law prohibiting baby selling and arguably exempted gestational surrogacy as well. The *P.M. v. T.B.* court also underscored the beneficial effects of surrogacy arrangements in allowing parents to have biological children when they

otherwise might not be able to do so. Do you agree with the *P.M. v. T.B.* court's conclusion that gestational surrogacy contracts should not be deemed to violate public policy? What about traditional or genetic surrogacy contracts?

As suggested by the *P.M. v. T.B.* opinion, there is reason to believe that numerous surrogacy contracts are performed by the parties without difficulty. See Julia Dalzell, The Enforcement of Selective Reduction Clauses in Surrogacy Contracts, 27 Widener Commonwealth L. Rev. 83, 83-84 (2018) (reporting estimate of 2,000 gestational surrogacy births in 2014, most of them completed without problem). The development of the extreme animosity between the parties in *P.M. v. T.B.*, however, reveals how much conflict can arise when the surrogacy contract does not go well. Indeed, the cases from other jurisdictions cited in the *P.M. v. T.B.* opinion, such as the *Baby M* case from New Jersey and *Calvert v. Johnson* from California, also involved severe disruptions in relations between the surrogate and the intended parents. Does the occurrence of this type of problem provide another potential policy argument for denying enforcement to surrogacy contracts?

2. *Public policy and family relations.* The courts recognize a general public policy limit on contracts that are deemed to impair or harm family relations. Restatement (Second) §§189, 190 address promises that are unreasonably in restraint of marriage and promises that are detrimental to marital relationships. The Restatement (Second) §191 provides, more specifically, that a contract affecting the custody of a child is unenforceable on grounds of public policy unless it is consistent with the "best interest of the child." Note that the trial court in *P.M. v. T.B.* ruled that granting the intended father custody was in the best interest of the child in addition to holding that the surrogacy contract was enforceable. What should the court have done if it concluded that the intended father was not well-suited to have custody?

3. *Judicial and legislative roles.* The court in *P.M. v. T.B.* cites both legislation and court decisions from other jurisdictions in support of its approach to determining the enforceability of the surrogate-parenting contract. Based on the description of state statutory laws given in *P.M. v. T.B.*, do you favor legislation to govern the validity of surrogacy contracts? If so, what form of legislation would you support? Why? Consider the two model acts referred to by the court in its opinion. The ABA Model Act is discussed and favorably evaluated in Charles P. Kindregan, Jr. & Steven H. Snyder, Clarifying the Law of ART: The New American Bar Association Model Act Governing Assisted Reproductive Technology, 42 Fam. L.Q. 203 (2008).

4. *The **Baby M** case.* The P.M. v. T.B. court refers in some detail to the *Baby M* case, one of the earliest and best known traditional surrogacy contract decisions. In re Baby M., 537 A.2d 1227 (N.J. 1988). The contract in that case called for payment of $10,000 to the surrogate and, as noted by the court in *P.M. v. T.B.*, stipulated that Mrs. Whitehead, the surrogate, would not "form or attempt to form a parent-child relationship" with the baby she had agreed to bear and would permit Mrs. Stern, the biological father's wife, to become the baby's legal mother. After giving birth, the surrogate decided she could not part with the child and engaged in a protracted custody battle. In deciding that the

contract was unenforceable, the New Jersey Supreme Court concluded that the agreement was inconsistent with statutory provisions that prohibit payment of money in connection with adoptions, that require proof of parental unfitness or abandonment before termination of parental rights, and that make consent to private adoptions revocable for a period after birth. Id. at 1240. In addition, however, the court ruled that the contract was fundamentally at odds with public policy. The *Baby M* case and subsequent developments in the area of surrogacy are surveyed and evaluated in J. Herbie Difonzo & Ruth C. Stern, The Children of Baby M., 39 Cap. U. L. Rev. 345 (2011).

5. *Gestational surrogacy and public policy.* The *P.M. v. T.B.* case dealt with a gestational surrogacy contract and the court relied heavily on an earlier California Supreme Court case holding a gestational surrogate parenting agreement to be enforceable. Johnson v. Calvert, 851 P.2d 776, *cert. denied,* 510 U.S. 874, and *cert. dismissed sub nom.* Baby Boy J. v. Johnson, 510 U.S. 938 (1993). Anna Johnson, the surrogate, did not supply the egg for the baby. Rather, the Calverts provided both the sperm and the egg that were used to form an embryo, which was implanted by in vitro fertilization. The California Supreme Court held that state law would recognize only one natural mother and framed the key issue as whether Crispina Calvert, as the egg donor, or Anna Johnson, as the gestational surrogate, was "the mother" of the resulting child. Id. at 781. The case thus presented the challenge of applying traditional policy concepts to advances in assisted reproductive technology.

The *Johnson* court stated that it would use the surrogacy contract to decide who had the better claim as mother of the child. In contrast to the *Baby M* court, the California court rejected a number of public policy arguments against the enforceability of the contract. As noted in the *P.M. v. T.B.* opinion, the California court reasoned that gestational surrogacy does not involve surrender of parental rights for money because the surrogate is being paid only for gestating services.

Notably, the only woman on the California Supreme Court at that time, Justice Joyce Kennard, filed the lone dissent in the *Johnson* case. Justice Kennard agreed with the majority that both the genetic and the gestational mothers had valid claims to be the legal mother of the child but rejected the idea that the surrogacy contract should be used to break the tie. Justice Kennard reasoned instead that the best interest of the child should be used to determine parental rights. 851 P.2d at 799. Justice Kennard emphasized that children are not "the personal property of anyone, and their delivery cannot be ordered as a contract remedy on the same terms as a court would, for example, order a breaching party to deliver a truckload of nuts and bolts." Id. at 796-797. Justice Kennard agreed with the majority, however, that the legislature should act to provide guidance in this area. Do you think that gender differences between judges are likely to affect how such a case is viewed?

6. *Developments in the law of surrogacy.* The literature on law and assisted reproductive technologies is vast. For a sampling of the academic writing, see Noah Baron & Jennifer Bazzell, eds. Fifteenth Annual Gender and Sexuality Law: Annual Review Article: Assisted Reproductive Technologies, 15 Geo.

J. Gender & L. 57 (2014); Mark Strasser, Traditional Surrogacy Contracts, Partial Enforcement, and The Challenge for Family Law, 18 J. Health Care L. & Pol'y 85 (2015). See generally Nancy Levit, Familial and Matrimonial Agreements: An Annotated Bibliography, 23 J. Am. Acad. Matrim. Law. 453, 467-469 (2010).

7. *Remedial options in public policy cases.* Courts will not necessarily deem void and completely unenforceable a contract that is inconsistent with a statute or other basis of public policy. Rather, the courts may enforce the contract or, more likely yet, may grant restitutionary relief to one of the parties if a benefit has been conferred. The Restatement (Second) adopts an approach that requires the weighing of a number of factors before denying enforcement of a contract or refusing restitutionary relief on public policy grounds, including assessing the nature of the public policy involved, the degree of resulting forfeiture, and whether denial of relief would further the policy. Restatement (Second) of Contracts §§178, 197. See Trees v. Kersey, 56 P.3d 765 (Idaho 2002) (contracts made in violation of public works licensing act were void, but court would not allow party who committed fraud to keep benefit of performance without liability); CitaraManis v. Hallowell, 613 A.2d 964 (Md. 1992) (lease for rental property made without proper license would not necessarily be unenforceable; courts must consider strength of public policy, degree of violation, and whether refund of rent would be disproportionate penalty).

8. *"In pari delicto."* If both parties willfully engage in wrongful conduct, and therefore are "in pari delicto" (equally culpable), the courts usually take the position that the parties should be left where the court finds them and will give no remedy to either party, even if one has received a benefit from the other. See Joseph M. Perillo, Contracts, §§22.1, 22.7 (7th ed. 2014). This rule is applied particularly where the contract involves serious illegal conduct. See, e.g., Al-Ibrahim v. Edde, 897 F. Supp. 620 (D.D.C. 1995) (employee who claimed gambling winnings of employer in plan to avoid federal income tax could not enforce employer's promise of reimbursement of taxes paid; judicial process cannot be used to further illegal acts); but see Maudlin v. Pacific Decision Sciences Corp., 40 Cal. Rptr. 3d 724 (Ct. App. 2006) (former employee who resold stock to company was not in pari delicto where he was aware that employer structured deferred payments to evade taxes but employee derived no benefit from scheme and would have suffered forfeiture of almost $1.7 million if court left the parties where found). See generally Stewart v. Wilmington Trust SP Servs., 112 A.3d 271 (Del. Ch. 2015) (discussing the doctrine and its exceptions).

PROBLEM 7-3

On Monday, September 3, 2018, Marta Owens died from heart disease. At that time Marta was a sixty-year-old widow and mother to three children: Ben, who was thirty years old, Sara, who was twenty-five years old, and Kristin who was twenty years old. Marta's husband, Frank, died in an accident ten years earlier and Marta used the proceeds from his life insurance policy to pay the balance on her mortgage so that she owned the house free of debt. The family home was located at 675 Park Street in the city of Clearview and had a fair market value of about $250,000.

Ben and Sara each left home as soon as they graduated from high school and, due to very strained relations with Marta, they both rarely visited the family home or spoke with their mother. Kristin continued to live in the family home with Marta while she attended college and worked part-time at a coffee shop. Ben attended college for a year before taking a job as a salesperson for a bakery company. Sara completed an Associate's Degree program in business administration and worked as a real estate paralegal.

About two years earlier, in July 2016, Marta suffered a sudden heart attack. Though she recovered well enough to leave the hospital after a week-long stay, her doctor advised Marta that permanent physical damage had been done and that she was at high risk for a recurrence of heart problems. Marta spent most of her savings on medical bills and realized that the only significant asset she owned was the family home. On August 11, 2016, Marta went to see an attorney and executed a deed conveying the family home to her youngest child, Kristin, reserving a life estate for herself. The deed was recorded that day. Neither Marta nor Kristin informed Ben or Sara about the transfer of ownership. Marta did not have a will.

On hearing of Marta's death, Ben and Sara came to the family home on Monday evening to make funeral arrangements. All three agreed that Marta should be interred next to Frank in the local cemetery after funeral services the following Friday, September 7. The funeral parlor quoted a total price of $12,000 for all services, including posting an advance notice in the newspaper. The three siblings began to discuss how that cost would be paid. Marta died with only $700 in her bank account. Kristin had only about $3000 that she needed to pay her next tuition bill. Ben and Sara then said they would split the funeral cost and take reimbursement when the family home was sold and the proceeds divided into three equal shares.

At that point, Kristin told Ben and Sara that Marta had given the house to Kristin, alone, and that she did not plan to sell it. Kristin said she could work extra hours to get the money to pay Ben and Sara back for her share of the funeral expenses, but it would take several months. Ben and Sara were outraged to hear that they had been excluded from ownership of the family home. Sara said heatedly, "I work with lawyers who can undo the deed and you will end up with nothing." Ben added, "Kristin, you need to do the right thing and share the value of the house." Ben and Sara came back to see Kristin the next two evenings and they restated their objections to Kristin keeping the family home for herself. Kristin's response was always the same, "I need time to think about it."

On Thursday evening, the night before the scheduled funeral services, Ben and Sara came back to the family home once again to speak with Kristin about selling the house. This time Sara came with a typewritten document which read,

> I, Kristin Owens, hereby agree to sell the Owens family home at 675 Park Street in the city of Clearview within 90 days from this date, September 6, 2018, and to divide the net proceeds, after expenses of the sale, in three equal shares with Ben Owens and Sara Owens, my brother and sister, in exchange for a loan of $4000 and other valuable consideration.

Sara told Kristin, "If you do not sign this contract, I will call the funeral home this evening and cancel the funeral services and burial. All of the guests will arrive and find a note on the door that the funeral has been canceled. I will have our mother cremated and scatter her ashes at Clearview Lake. And I will still have the deed voided." Kristin asked Ben if he agreed with Sara. Ben replied, "It is only right for you to share the value of the house with us." Kristin then signed the document. The funeral services and burial were held the next day as scheduled.

Assume that two months have passed and Kristin now seeks your legal advice about the enforceability of the contract that she signed. What is your assessment?

PROBLEM 7-4

Arturo Guillen is president and the majority stockholder in Hydrazone Systems, Inc., a small company that manufactures and installs patented equipment designed to simulate ocean waves. Hydrazone is incorporated in the state of New London and is a duly licensed contractor in that state. Mirage Waterpark Company owns and operates a water-oriented amusement park in the neighboring state of Ada. On January 15, 2019, Guillen contracted on behalf of Hydrazone with Mirage to design and manufacture for the park a 29,000-square-foot "surfing pool" using Hydrazone wave equipment. Mirage was represented by its president, Anna Patton. The contract provided for a price of "$750,000 for equipment" and "a maximum of $250,000 in fees for services as necessary to assist in installation." The contract provided that Hydrazone would charge an agreed hourly rate for the services of its employees in assisting with installation. The contract stated that delivery was to be completed in time to allow for installation by May 15, 2019. Patton said that Mirage would primarily use its staff in installation and use a local contractor, if necessary. Mirage was entitled to hold back "10% of total charges as retainage," pending satisfactory completion and operation of the pool.

After signing the contract with Mirage, Guillen became concerned about Ada's contractor licensing statute, which he understood would apply to the new installation. Guillen wrote to Patton on February 1, 2019, stating that Hydrazone wished only to sell and deliver its equipment and to avoid involvement in installation or construction of the pool because of the licensing law. In a letter dated February 9, 2019, Patton responded that "Hydrazone's expertise is essential to proper installation of the equipment" and that Mirage would "hold Hydrazone to its commitment to assist in construction." Patton also promised that she would arrange for a friend who was an Ada licensed contractor "to sign any necessary paperwork and accept any formal liability for the work." After this exchange of correspondence, Hydrazone started delivery of the equipment and began assisting Mirage staff in initial layout on March 1, 2019.

By March 15, Guillen became concerned again that no state licensed contractor was involved in the installation. Upon inquiry by Guillen, Patton stated that her friend was tied up but would start assisting later. Guillen then stated that Hydrazone would cease any work until a licensed contractor was brought on board. Patton responded by stating that Mirage would refuse further payment, even for the $250,000 of equipment that had been delivered, and would hold Hydrazone liable for any lost profits if the wave pool was not operational by the beginning of the 2019 summer season. Because his company was fully extended financially due to three concurrent projects, Guillen needed prompt payment from Mirage to meet his regular operating expenses. Thus, although he continued to complain regularly, Guillen directed Hydrazone employees to continue with the installation. By May 15, the pool was completely installed, primarily by Hydrazone employees. Guillen had charged the full $1,000,000 for equipment and services, and had been paid $800,000. Patton never arranged for an Ada contractor to work with Hydrazone.

The wave pool performed as specified in the contract during the 2019 summer season. After requesting payment of the $200,000 balance, Guillen received on August 1, 2019, a check for $100,000, which he had his financial manager deposit. Patton, however, refused to release the final $100,000 in retainage that had not been paid to Hydrazone. When Guillen complained to Patton, she told him that his last progress payment of $100,000 had been accompanied by a letter that stated it was final payment in full discharge of the contract. Guillen checked his files and discovered in fact that a form letter with a great deal of fine print had been enclosed with the check and that it had included such language. Neither Guillen nor his financial officer had read the form letter before negotiating the check. Hydrazone then filed suit against Mirage to collect the final $100,000.

Assume that you are a law clerk for the magistrate who will be supervising a settlement conference to be held with the parties. The magistrate would like your assessment of the legal issues that are likely to arise if the case goes to trial and the arguments that may be presented to each side to encourage settlement. The state licensing law is given below. What is your assessment?

BUSINESS & PROFESSIONS CODE §7031:

(1) No individual person, partnership or corporate entity engaged in the business or acting in the capacity of a contractor, may bring or maintain any action in an Ada court to recover compensation for the performance of any act or contract for which a contractor's license is required without alleging and proving the maintenance of status as a duly licensed contractor at all times during the performance of act or contract.

(a) A license is required for any erection, construction, or renovation of a fixed structure upon real property.

(b) A license may be obtained by satisfactory completion of the contractor's competency examination and payment of a fee of $500 for individuals and $1000 for partnerships or corporate persons.

(2) The penalty for noncompliance with this provision shall be a fine equal to double the fees that should have been properly paid.

PROBLEM 7-5

You are an attorney with the local legal services program, where you handle a general caseload comprising consumer, welfare, and domestic matters. A 17-year-old girl, Samantha Brown, has come into your office and tells you the following story.

About 18 months ago, Samantha became pregnant. When her mother learned about this, she was furious. Her boyfriend offered to get her an abortion, but Samantha refused, saying that it was wrong. Her pregnancy was extremely difficult, and she was hospitalized for two weeks before giving birth to a daughter, named DeAnna. Because of Samantha's difficult pregnancy, her doctor said that she would need to take it easy for several weeks and that she must have someone to take care of the baby. Unfortunately, Samantha did not have anyone who could help her. (Samantha's mother, who works full time, was unable to do so.)

The next few weeks were almost a total disaster for Samantha. The baby seemed to cry nonstop. Samantha couldn't sleep at night and was constantly exhausted during the day. Samantha lost weight. The baby wouldn't eat properly and hardly gained any weight at all. About a month after the baby was born, a Mrs. Wallace, who said she was from the welfare department, came with Samantha's mother to visit her. Her mother said that Mrs. Wallace had come to take care of the baby because Samantha couldn't do so and the baby was getting sick. Samantha agreed she needed help. Mrs. Wallace told Samantha that Samantha needed to sign a paper to allow Mrs. Wallace to take care of the baby, which Samantha did. Mrs. Wallace left, taking DeAnna with her.

A few weeks of rest did wonders for Samantha. When she felt better, she told her mother that she was going to see DeAnna. On the paper that Mrs. Wallace left with her was the name of an agency where she was able to reach Mrs. Wallace on the telephone. When Samantha said that she would like to visit DeAnna, Mrs. Wallace said that was not possible because once a baby was placed for adoption, the natural mother was not allowed to visit the baby. Samantha cried out that she had not given her baby for adoption. Mrs. Wallace explained that the paper she signed gave up her parental rights and authorized the agency to place the baby for adoption. Confused, Samantha turned to her mother, who said that she had contacted the agency because Samantha was too young to have a child, that she couldn't take care of the baby, and that being a single mother would ruin her life. Samantha said she wanted her baby back, that she could take care of her. Her mother asked her to wait, and think about it for a while.

That was about six months ago. Samantha says she didn't do anything about the baby during that time. For a while she didn't know what to do. Then she returned to high school and found a part-time job that took up a lot of her time. Now she really wants the baby back, she says. She wants to know whether you can help her regain custody of DeAnna.

At this point, of course, you as an attorney could not yet give an opinion; fact investigation and legal research would be necessary before doing so. Suppose you begin by contacting Mrs. Wallace; she gives you a copy of the paper that Samantha signed, which is entitled "Consent to Adoption." The document states that by signing the paper the mother is authorizing the agency to place the child for adoption and that the mother is releasing all parental rights, including any right to visit the child or know the name of the parents. Mrs. Wallace tells you that she explained the adoption to Samantha, who fully understood what she was doing. Mrs. Wallace says that it is not unusual for the mother in such cases to change her mind later. She also informs you that the adoptive parents have begun judicial proceedings, as required by local law, to adopt DeAnna legally.

You then research the state statute governing adoption by consent. Its provisions include the following:

> An adoption of a child may be decreed when there have been filed written consents to adoption executed by:
>
> (a) . . .
>
> (b) the mother, regardless of age, if the child is born out of wedlock, and by the child's natural father if he has consistently on a continuing basis exercised rights and performed duties as a parent. . . .

State law also provides that after entry of a final decree of adoption, any consent is irrevocable. Prior to entry of a final decree, however, a consent may be declared to be ineffective for any reason that would be sufficient to avoid an ordinary contract.

Based on this investigation and research, what advice would you give your client about her right to regain custody of DeAnna? Would further investigation or research be necessary? If so, what would you do?

REVIEW QUESTIONS – CHAPTER SEVEN

1. Adam, age 16, recently lost his parents in an automobile accident. Adam moved into the home of his aunt and uncle, but he has a job, is able to support himself financially, and pays rent to his aunt and uncle. Adam purchased a motorcycle from Sam Seller for a cash payment of $5,000, the market price, and Adam registered the motorcycle in his name with the Department of Motor Vehicles. After keeping the motorcycle for three months and driving it for 2,500 miles, Adam decided he wanted to return it to Sam and get his

money back so that he could buy a car instead. What argument would best support Sam's argument that the contract is binding on Adam?

A. Adam cannot disaffirm the contract because the motorcycle has suffered from depreciation through his use.
B. The motorcycle would be a necessary since he uses it to get to work and support himself financially.
C. The contract is enforceable because the price was fair and there is no evidence that the motorcycle is defective.
D. The contract is enforceable because it has been fully performed by both Adam and Sam for a substantial period of time.

2. Elaine Rosen has consulted with a lawyer about the behavior of her mother, Natalie Schwartz. Elaine tells the lawyer that her mother has started to engage in behavior that Elaine finds strange and financially risky. Recently, her mother has started to go on "buying sprees" in which she spends literally thousands of dollars acquiring new clothes, jewelry, shoes, etc. She has talked with her mother about the situation, and her mother says that sometimes she gets very depressed and lonely, and going shopping makes her feel better. She realizes that she doesn't need a lot of the items that she is buying, but that doesn't seem to stop her behavior. Elaine states that other than the overspending her mother seems perfectly normal. A recent doctor visit resulted in a diagnosis of bi-polar disorder which causes Natalie to be unable to make rational decisions at times. Many of the items that Natalie has purchased are unused. In addition, most of the items were purchased from a large department store, Northrop's. Elaine has talked with the store about return of the items, but they have refused to take them back because the return dates in the sales slips have passed. She wants to know whether her mother has the legal right to return these items to the stores and get her money back. Does her mother have that right?

A. Yes, because Natalie may rescind her contract with Northrop's since she lacks cognitive capacity.
B. Yes, because Natalie may rescind her contract with Northrop's since she lacks volitional capacity, provided that Northrop's either knew or had reason to know of her incapacity.
C. No, because the return period specified in Northrop's contract of sale has expired.
D. No, because it is too difficult for a retail store to determine the capacity of a customer to enter into a contract.

3. The owner of a small electrical company (SEC) has come to you for advice. SEC did a major project for a company that owns residential apartment buildings (RAB) at a contract price of $90,000. RAB expressed dissatisfaction with SEC's work and refused to pay it anything unless SEC reduced its invoice by 50 percent. RAB told SEC to carefully consider its settlement offer because SEC would "flood the Internet with negative reviews if you refuse." Your client reluctantly agreed, received payment from RAB, but now

has regrets about the decision. You are considering a lawsuit against RAB based on claims of duress, undue influence, and breach of fiduciary duty. Which one of the following is most correct?

A. SEC is unlikely to succeed on a claim of duress unless it was in desperate need of the money.

B. If RAB's threat to flood the Internet with negative comments was not illegal, it would not amount to an improper threat.

C. Because SEC was under the domination of RAB, it will be able to rescind the contract on the ground of undue influence.

D. RAB breached a duty of fairness to SEC because the contract created a fiduciary relationship.

4. True or false? Art dealer agrees to sell a painting to Buyer. Dealer represents to Buyer that the painting is an "original painting by Alexander Caldo." Unknown to either Dealer or Buyer, the painting is in fact a Caldo reproduction. In order to rescind the sale it will be necessary for the Buyer to show that the Dealer either knew or should have known that the painting was a reproduction rather than an original. Explain your answer.

5. On a brutally hot day Andre Massati's home air conditioning fails. He calls AAAA Heating & Air, and the company sends out a repairman that afternoon. The repairman arrives late and Andre tells him that he must go to work that evening. The repairman says that he cannot begin the repair without credit card authorization and estimates that the cost would be $200 to $300. Because Andre must go to work, he leaves the repairman at home with his credit card information. When he returns late that evening, he sees a credit card receipt for $1,500 and the air conditioning is still not working well. Andre is furious, calls the company to complain, but gets no response. Andre goes to a consumer lawyer for advice. One of the theories that the lawyer is evaluating is unconscionability. Is a claim by Andre for return of his $1,500 on the ground of unconscionability likely to be successful? Choose the best answer:

A. No, because unconscionability is a defense, not the basis of affirmative relief.

B. No, because excessive price cannot be the basis of a claim of unconscionability.

C. Yes, if Andre can establish that he did not have a reasonable choice with regard to payment and that the price charged was grossly excessive.

D. Yes, if the repairman knowingly made a false prediction about what the total charges would likely be.

6. A law firm is considering hiring a "lateral," i.e., a lawyer who works for another firm and brings with him a book of business. The lateral handles securities fraud litigation, which is highly lucrative to the law firm. The law firm will pay the lateral a "signing bonus" of $1 million. May the

contract between the lateral and the law firm provide that if the lateral leaves the law firm, the lateral agrees not to work for a competing firm in the field of securities litigation for a period of one year? Choose the best answer:

A. Yes, if the one-year period is considered to be reasonable.
B. Yes, because the law firm has a legitimate interest in protecting its investment in the lateral.
C. No, because a covenant not to compete by a lawyer is unenforceable.
D. No, because the agreement interferes with the judicial process.

7. A salesman for a chemical company is considering leaving his employment to work for a competitor of his employer. The salesman's employment agreement has a covenant not to compete. Which of the following would probably *not be relevant* to a determination of the reasonableness of the covenant?
   A. The extent to which the salesman has confidential information about the company's customers.
   B. The duration of the salesman's covenant not to compete.
   C. The geographical area in which the covenant operates.
   D. The salesman's current salary.

8. Which statement about surrogacy contracts is probably *not correct*?
   A. It is against public policy for a surrogate mother to be paid anything in connection with the contract.
   B. In a traditional surrogacy contract, it is against public policy for the contract to provide that the surrogate mother has no parental rights.
   C. In a traditional surrogacy contract the court must determine what is in the best interest of the child with regard to custody.
   D. In a gestational surrogacy contract, the courts are likely to conclude that the surrogate mother has no parental rights.

CHAPTER 8

Justification for Nonperformance: Mistake, Changed Circumstances, and Contractual Modifications

Many of the various defenses surveyed in Chapter 7 have a common basis in the asserted misconduct of one party — misconduct resulting in the bargain being either surprisingly different from what the other party believed it to be or oppressively unfair to that party (perhaps both). Although suggestions of such misconduct may also be found in some of the cases in this chapter, the kinds of excuses from performance here at issue are those arising not from overreaching or deception by either party, but from changes in circumstance that have either occurred or come to light since the original agreement was made.

It is clear from our study thus far that executory contracts are frequently entered into for the purpose of protecting against various risks. Indeed, an insurance contract has (at least for the insured party) no other purpose. Even contracts that have as their main purpose the definition of some mutually beneficial exchange of performances (the sale of goods for money, for instance) may have as a subsidiary function the protection of one or both parties against the risk that certain unfavorable events may occur before the time when performance is to take place (a rise in the market price of the goods, for instance, which in the absence of an existing fixed-price contract would require the buyer to pay more than the presently available price, or a fall in the market, which could similarly force the seller to sell his goods at less profit, or even at a loss). In light of this risk-shifting function that contracts perform, it would not be surprising to find contract law generally resistant to the suggestion that a contractual obligation might be avoided just because unforeseen or unprovided-for circumstances made it less favorable to one of the parties than had been originally contemplated. And indeed it is resistant to such excuses, as we shall see. Nevertheless, there are a variety of established legal categories that hold out the possibility of such an excuse from performance, in appropriate cases.

These categories grow from different strands of case law and have different labels, such as "mistake," "impossibility," "impracticability," or "frustration." Modern contract theory, however, is inclined to stress their similarities rather than their differences, since in most cases the underlying question is the same: If for one of the parties a circumstance not expressly provided for in the contract has adversely affected either performance itself or the value thereof, should that party be permitted as a result to escape the obligation of performance the contract would otherwise impose?

A. MISTAKE

Like most words, *mistake* can be used to describe a variety of things. It may refer simply to a decision that with hindsight turns out to have been clearly wrong. (It was a mistake, for instance, for Napoleon to invade Russia; it was a mistake to have that fourth piece of pizza at bedtime.) Or it may describe a decision that, although not clearly disastrous, has nevertheless turned out to be at least arguably not the best choice that could have been made. Even if not always "20/20," as popular wisdom would have it, hindsight is at least apt to be clearer than foresight, and many a contracting party has later regretted her choice to enter into a particular deal, wishing that she had insisted on better terms, expressly protected herself against some contingency, or even forgone the deal entirely.

We have seen already that contract law sometimes has to deal with the parties' mistaken belief that they were using language with the same intention when in fact they attached different meanings to the terms they employed (recall the *Frigaliment* case in Chapter 5). Occasionally such a misunderstanding will cause the court to hold that no binding contract exists, although as we have seen the more usual judicial response is to choose one of the intended meanings and apply it in enforcing the contract. Should the law permit one party to escape a contractual obligation merely because she later regrets the deal she has made – views it, in effect, as a mistake? Ordinarily, the answer would be "No," for the reason suggested in the introduction to this chapter: Parties make contracts with the aim of binding each other *despite* the myriad changes of circumstance that may occur before the time for performance arrives. Sometimes, however, the court finds that a more particular type of mistake has been made, which lifts the case above the ordinary run. The materials that follow explore various situations in which this extraordinary type of relief has been sought and, sometimes, awarded.

Lenawee County Board of Health v. Messerly

Michigan Supreme Court 417 Mich. 17, 331 N.W.2d 203 (1982)

RYAN, Justice.

In March of 1977, Carl and Nancy Pickles, appellees, purchased from appellants, William and Martha Messerly, a 600-square-foot tract of land upon which is located a three-unit apartment building. Shortly after the transaction was closed, the Lenawee County Board of Health condemned the property and obtained a permanent injunction which prohibits human habitation on the premises until the defective sewage system is brought into conformance with the Lenawee County sanitation code.

We are required to determine whether appellees should prevail in their attempt to avoid this land contract on the basis of mutual mistake and failure of consideration. We conclude that the parties did entertain a mutual misapprehension of fact, but that the circumstances of this case do not warrant rescission.

I

The facts of the case are not seriously in dispute. In 1971, the Messerlys acquired approximately one acre plus 600 square feet of land. A three-unit apartment building was situated upon the 600-square-foot portion. The trial court found that, prior to this transfer, the Messerlys' predecessor in title, Mr. Bloom, had installed a septic tank on the property without a permit and in violation of the applicable health code. The Messerlys used the building as an income investment property until 1973 when they sold it, upon land contract, to James Barnes who likewise used it primarily as an income-producing investment.[1]

Mr. and Mrs. Barnes, with the permission of the Messerlys, sold approximately one acre of the property in 1976, and the remaining 600 square feet and building were offered for sale soon thereafter when Mr. and Mrs. Barnes defaulted on their land contract. Mr. and Mrs. Pickles evidenced an interest in the property, but were dissatisfied with the terms of the Barnes-Messerly land contract. Consequently, to accommodate the Pickleses' preference to enter into a land contract directly with the Messerlys, Mr. and Mrs. Barnes executed a quit-claim deed which conveyed their interest in the property back to the Messerlys. After inspecting the property, Mr. and Mrs. Pickles executed a new land contract with the Messerlys on March 21, 1977. It provided for a purchase price of $25,500. A clause was added to the end of the land contract form which provides:

> 17. Purchaser has examined this property and agrees to accept same in its present condition. There are no other or additional written or oral understandings.

Five or six days later, when the Pickleses went to introduce themselves to the tenants, they discovered raw sewage seeping out of the ground. Tests conducted by a sanitation expert indicated the inadequacy of the sewage system. The Lenawee County Board of Health subsequently condemned the property and initiated this lawsuit in the Lenawee Circuit Court against the Messerlys as land contract vendors, and the Pickleses, as vendees, to obtain a permanent injunction proscribing human habitation of the premises until the property was brought into conformance with the Lenawee County sanitation code. The

1. James Barnes was married shortly after he purchased the property. Mr. and Mrs. Barnes lived in one of the apartments on the property for three months and, after they moved, Mrs. Barnes continued to aid in the management of the property.

injunction was granted, and the Lenawee County Board of Health was permitted to withdraw from the lawsuit by stipulation of the parties.

When no payments were made on the land contract, the Messerlys filed a cross-complaint against the Pickleses seeking foreclosure, sale of the property, and a deficiency judgment. Mr. and Mrs. Pickles then counterclaimed for rescission against the Messerlys, and filed a third-party complaint against the Barneses, which incorporated, by reference, the allegations of the counterclaim against the Messerlys. In count one, Mr. and Mrs. Pickles alleged failure of consideration. Count two charged Mr. and Mrs. Barnes with willful concealment and misrepresentation as a result of their failure to disclose the condition of the sanitation system. Additionally, Mr. and Mrs. Pickles sought to hold the Messerlys liable in equity for the Barneses' alleged misrepresentation. The Pickleses prayed that the land contract be rescinded.

After a bench trial, the court concluded that the Pickleses had no cause of action against either the Messerlys or the Barneses as there was no fraud or misrepresentation. This ruling was predicated on the trial judge's conclusion that none of the parties knew of Mr. Bloom's earlier transgression or of the resultant problem with the septic system until it was discovered by the Pickleses, and that the sanitation problem was not caused by any of the parties. The trial court held that the property was purchased "as is," after inspection and, accordingly, its "negative . . . value cannot be blamed upon an innocent seller." Foreclosure was ordered against the Pickleses, together with a judgment against them in the amount of $25,943.09.

Mr. and Mrs. Pickles appealed from the adverse judgment. The Court of Appeals unanimously affirmed the trial court's ruling with respect to Mr. and Mrs. Barnes but, in a two-to-one decision, reversed the finding of no cause of action on the Pickleses' claims against the Messerlys. Lenawee County Board of Health v. Messerly, 98 Mich. App. 478, 295 N.W.2d 903 (1980). It concluded that the mutual mistake between the Messerlys and the Pickleses went to a basic, as opposed to a collateral, element of the contract,[6] and that the parties intended to transfer income-producing rental property but, in actuality, the vendees paid $25,500 for an asset without value.[7]

We granted the Messerlys' application for leave to appeal. 411 Mich. 900 (1981).

II

We must decide initially whether there was a mistaken belief entertained by one or both parties to the contract in dispute and, if so, the resultant legal significance.

---

6. Mr. and Mrs. Pickles did not appeal the trial court's finding that there was no fraud or misrepresentation by the Messerlys or Mr. and Mrs. Barnes. Likewise, the propriety of that ruling is not before this Court today.

7. The trial court found that the only way that the property could be put to residential use would be to pump and haul the sewage, a method which is economically unfeasible, as the cost of such a disposal system amounts to double the income generated by the property. There was speculation by the trial court that the adjoining land might be utilized to make the property suitable for residential use, but, in the absence of testimony directed at that point, the court refused to draw any conclusions. The trial court and the Court of Appeals both found that the property was valueless, or had a negative value.

A contractual mistake "is a belief that is not in accord with the facts." 1 Restatement Contracts, 2d, §151, p. 383. The erroneous belief of one or both of the parties must relate to a fact in existence at the time the contract is executed. Richardson Lumber Co. v. Hoey, 219 Mich. 643, 189 N.W. 923 (1922); Sherwood v. Walker, 66 Mich. 568, 580, 33 N.W. 919 (1887) (Sherwood, J., dissenting). That is to say, the belief which is found to be in error may not be, in substance, a prediction as to a future occurrence or non-occurrence. . . .

The Court of Appeals concluded, after a de novo review of the record, that the parties were mistaken as to the income-producing capacity of the property in question. 98 Mich. App. 487-488, 295 N.W.2d 903. We agree. The vendors and the vendees each believed that the property transferred could be utilized as income-generating rental property. All of the parties subsequently learned that, in fact, the property was unsuitable for any residential use.

Appellants assert that there was no mistake in the contractual sense because the defect in the sewage system did not arise until after the contract was executed. The appellees respond that the Messerlys are confusing the date of the inception of the defect with the date upon which the defect was discovered.

This is essentially a factual dispute which the trial court failed to resolve directly. Nevertheless, we are empowered to draw factual inferences from the facts found by the trial court. GCR 1963, 865.1(6).

An examination of the record reveals that the septic system was defective prior to the date on which the land contract was executed. The Messerlys' grantor installed a nonconforming septic system without a permit prior to the transfer of the property to the Messerlys in 1971. Moreover, virtually undisputed testimony indicates that, assuming ideal soil conditions, 2,500 square feet of property is necessary to support a sewage system adequate to serve a three-family dwelling. Likewise, 750 square feet is mandated for a one-family home. Thus, the division of the parcel and sale of one acre of the property by Mr. and Mrs. Barnes in 1976 made it impossible to remedy the already illegal septic system within the confines of the 600-square-foot parcel.[10]

Appellants do not dispute these underlying facts which give rise to an inference contrary to their contentions.

Having determined that when these parties entered into the land contract they were laboring under a mutual mistake of fact, we now direct our attention to a determination of the legal significance of that finding.

A contract may be rescinded because of a mutual misapprehension of the parties, but this remedy is granted only in the sound discretion of the court. Harris v. Axline, 323 Mich. 585, 36 N.W.2d 154 (1949). Appellants argue that

---

10. It is crucial to distinguish between the date on which a belief relating to a particular fact or set of facts becomes erroneous due to a change in the fact, and the date on which the mistaken nature of the belief is discovered. By definition, a mistake cannot be discovered until after the contract is executed. If the parties were aware, prior to the execution of a contract, that they were in error concerning a particular fact, there would be no misapprehension in signing the contract. Thus stated, it becomes obvious that the date on which a mistaken fact manifests itself is irrelevant to the determination whether or not there was a mistake.

the parties' mistake relates only to the quality or value of the real estate transferred, and that such mistakes are collateral to the agreement and do not justify rescission, citing A & M Land Development Co. v. Miller, 354 Mich. 681, 94 N.W.2d 197 (1959).

In that case, the plaintiff was the purchaser of 91 lots of real property. It sought partial rescission of the land contract when it was frustrated in its attempts to develop 42 of the lots because it could not obtain permits from the county health department to install septic tanks on these lots. This Court refused to allow rescission because the mistake, whether mutual or unilateral, related only to the value of the property.

> There was here no mistake as to the form or substance of the contract between the parties, or the description of the property constituting the subject matter. The situation involved is not at all analogous to that presented in Scott v. Grow, 301 Mich. 226; 3 N.W.2d 254; 141 A.L.R. 819 (1942). There the plaintiff sought relief by way of reformation of a deed on the ground that the instrument of conveyance had not been drawn in accordance with the intention and agreement of the parties. It was held that the bill of complaint stated a case for the granting of equitable relief by way of reformation. In the case at bar plaintiff received the property for which it contracted. The fact that it may be of less value than the purchaser expected at the time of the transaction is not a sufficient basis for the granting of equitable relief, neither fraud nor reliance on misrepresentation of material facts having been established.

354 Mich. 693-694, 94 N.W.2d 197.

Appellees contend, on the other hand, that in this case the parties were mistaken as to the very nature of the character of the consideration and claim that the pervasive and essential quality of this mistake renders rescission appropriate. They cite in support of that view Sherwood v. Walker, 66 Mich. 568, 33 N.W. 919 (1887), the famous "barren cow" case. In that case, the parties agreed to the sale and purchase of a cow which was thought to be barren, but which was, in reality, with calf. When the seller discovered the fertile condition of his cow, he refused to deliver her. In permitting rescission, the Court stated:

> It seems to me, however, in the case made by this record, that the mistake or misapprehension of the parties went to the whole substance of the agreement. If the cow was a breeder, she was worth at least $750; if barren, she was worth not over $80. The parties would not have made the contract of sale except upon the understanding and belief that she was incapable of breeding, and of no use as a cow. It is true she is now the identical animal that they thought her to be when the contract was made; there is no mistake as to the identity of the creature. Yet the mistake was not of the mere quality of the animal, but went to the very nature of the thing. A barren cow is substantially a different creature than a breeding one. There is as much difference between them for all purposes of use as there is between an ox and a cow that is capable of breeding and giving milk. If the mutual mistake had simply related to the fact whether she was with calf or not for one season, then it might have been a good sale; but the mistake affected the character of the animal for all time, and for her present and

> ultimate use. She was not in fact the animal, or the kind of animal, the defendants intended to sell or the plaintiff to buy. She was not a barren cow, and, if this fact had been known, there would have been no contract. The mistake affected the substance of the whole consideration, and it must be considered that there was no contract to sell or sale of the cow as she actually was. The thing sold and bought had in fact no existence. She was sold as a beef-creature would be sold; she is in fact a breeding cow, and a valuable one.
>
> The court should have instructed the jury that if they found that the cow was sold, or contracted to be sold, upon the understanding of both parties that she was barren, and useless for the purpose of breeding, and that in fact she was not barren, but capable of breeding, then the defendants had a right to rescind, and to refuse to deliver, and the verdict should be in their favor.

66 Mich. 577-578, 33 N.W. 919.

As the parties suggest, the foregoing precedent arguably distinguishes mistakes affecting the essence of the consideration from those which go to its quality or value, affording relief on a per se basis for the former but not the latter. See, e.g., Lenawee County Board of Health v. Messerly, 98 Mich. App. 478, 492, 295 N.W.2d 903 (1980) (Mackenzie, J., concurring in part).

However, the distinctions which may be drawn from *Sherwood* and *A & M Land Development Co.* do not provide a satisfactory analysis of the nature of a mistake sufficient to invalidate a contract. Often, a mistake relates to an underlying factual assumption which, when discovered, directly affects value, but simultaneously and materially affects the essence of the contractual consideration. It is disingenuous to label such a mistake collateral. McKay v. Coleman, 85 Mich. 60, 48 N.W. 203 (1891). Corbin, Contracts (one vol. ed.), §605, p. 551.

Appellant and appellee both mistakenly believed that the property which was the subject of their land contract would generate income as rental property. The fact that it could not be used for human habitation deprived the property of its income-earning potential and rendered it less valuable. However, this mistake, while directly and dramatically affecting the property's value, cannot accurately be characterized as collateral because it also affects the very essence of the consideration. "The thing sold and bought [income generating rental property] had in fact no existence." Sherwood v. Walker, 66 Mich. 578, 33 N.W. 919.

We find that the inexact and confusing distinction between contractual mistakes running to value and those touching the substance of the consideration serves only as an impediment to a clear and helpful analysis for the equitable resolution of cases in which mistake is alleged and proven. Accordingly, the holdings of *A & M Land Development Co.* and *Sherwood* with respect to the material or collateral nature of a mistake are limited to the facts of those cases.

Instead, we think the better-reasoned approach is a case-by-case analysis whereby rescission is indicated when the mistaken belief relates to a basic assumption of the parties upon which the contract is made, and which materially affects the agreed performances of the parties. . . . 1 Restatement Contracts,

2d, §152, pp. 385-386.[11] Rescission is not available, however, to relieve a party who has assumed the risk of loss in connection with the mistake. . . . Corbin, Contracts (one vol. ed.), §605, p. 552; 1 Restatement Contracts, 2d, §§152, 154, pp. 385-386, 402-406.[12]

All of the parties to this contract erroneously assumed that the property transferred by the vendors to the vendees was suitable for human habitation and could be utilized to generate rental income. The fundamental nature of these assumptions is indicated by the fact that their invalidity changed the character of the property transferred, thereby frustrating, indeed precluding, Mr. and Mrs. Pickles' intended use of the real estate. Although the Pickleses are disadvantaged by enforcement of the contract, performance is advantageous to the Messerlys, as the property at issue is less valuable absent its income-earning potential. Nothing short of rescission can remedy the mistake. Thus, the parties' mistake as to a basic assumption materially affects the agreed performances of the parties.

Despite the significance of the mistake made by the parties, we reverse the Court of Appeals because we conclude that equity does not justify the remedy sought by Mr. and Mrs. Pickles.

Rescission is an equitable remedy which is granted only in the sound discretion of the court. . . . A court need not grant rescission in every case in which the mutual mistake relates to a basic assumption and materially affects the agreed performance of the parties.

In cases of mistake by two equally innocent parties, we are required, in the exercise of our equitable powers, to determine which blameless party should assume the loss resulting from the misapprehension they shared.[13] Normally

---

11. The parties have invited our attention to the first edition of the Restatement of Contracts in their briefs, and the Court of Appeals cites to that edition in its opinion. However, the second edition was published subsequent to the issuance of the lower court opinion and the filing of the briefs with this Court. Thus, we take it upon ourselves to refer to the latest edition to aid us in our resolution of this case.

Section 152 delineates the legal significance of a mistake.

§152. When Mistake of Both Parties Makes a Contract Voidable

(1) Where a mistake of both parties at the time a contract was made as to a basic assumption on which the contract was made has a material effect on the agreed exchange of performances, the contract is voidable by the adversely affected party unless he bears the risk of the mistake under the rule stated in §154.

(2) In determining whether the mistake has a material effect on the agreed exchange of performances, account is taken of any relief by way of reformation, restitution, or otherwise.

12. **§154. When a Party Bears the Risk of a Mistake**

A party bears the risk of a mistake when

(a) the risk is allocated to him by agreement of the parties, or

(b) he is aware, at the time the contract is made, that he has only limited knowledge with respect to the facts to which the mistake relates but treats his limited knowledge as sufficient, or

(c) the risk is allocated to him by the court on the ground that it is reasonable in the circumstances to do so.

13. This risk-of-loss analysis is absent in both *A & M Land Development Co.* and *Sherwood,* and this omission helps to explain, in part, the disparate treatment in the two cases. Had such an inquiry been undertaken in *Sherwood,* we believe that the result might have been different.

that can only be done by drawing upon our "own notions of what is reasonable and just under all the surrounding circumstances."

Equity suggests that, in this case, the risk should be allocated to the purchasers. We are guided to that conclusion, in part, by the standards announced in §154 of the Restatement of Contracts 2d, for determining when a party bears the risk of mistake. See footnote 12. Section 154(a) suggests that the court should look first to whether the parties have agreed to the allocation of the risk between themselves. While there is no express assumption in the contract by either party of the risk of the property becoming uninhabitable, there was indeed some agreed allocation of the risk to the vendees by the incorporation of an "as is" clause into the contract which, we repeat, provided:

> Purchaser has examined this property and agrees to accept same in its present condition. There are no other or additional written or oral understandings.

That is a persuasive indication that the parties considered that, as between them, such risk as related to the "present condition" of the property should lie with the purchaser. If the "as is" clause is to have any meaning at all, it must be interpreted to refer to those defects which were unknown at the time that the contract was executed. Thus, the parties themselves assigned the risk of loss to Mr. and Mrs. Pickles.

We conclude that Mr. and Mrs. Pickles are not entitled to the equitable remedy of rescission and, accordingly, reverse the decision the Court of Appeals.

WILLIAMS, C.J., and COLEMAN, FITZGERALD, KAVANAGH and LEVIN, JJ., concur.
RILEY, J., not participating.

NOTES AND QUESTIONS

1. *Factual Context.* Additional facts in the *Lenawee* case can be found in the intermediate appellate court opinion. Testimony at trial established that when the Messerlys initially purchased the property in June 1971, Bloom, the previous owner, made an affirmative statement that there had never been a problem with the sanitation system. Bloom failed to disclose, however, that he had replaced the prior septic tank with a relatively small 500-gallon septic tank and had failed to obtain a required permit from the county agency. Lenawee County Board of Health v. Messerly, 295 N.W.2d 903, 904 (Mich. Ct. App. 1980). County health officials testified that the five-bedroom property did not have the minimum of 2,000 square feet for a drain field that would be needed for a normal septic system and that two septic tanks of at least 1,000

Moreover, a determination as to which party assumed the risk in *A & M Land Development Co.* would have alleviated the need to characterize the mistake as collateral so as to justify the result denying rescission. Despite the absence of any inquiry as to the assumption of risk in those two leading cases, we find that there exists sufficient precedent to warrant such an analysis in future cases of mistake.

gallons would be needed for a costly "pump and haul" system. 295 N.W.2d at 907. The Messerlys never lived at the property, rarely visited there, had the septic tank cleaned once without incident, and never received any complaints or noticed any problems. Prior to executing the land contract, Mr. Pickles did ask the Barneses about the septic tank. Mr. and Mrs. Barnes responded that they had lived in an apartment for three months in early 1974, had visited the property only occasionally after that, had the septic tank cleaned once without notice of irregularity other than some odor in one bathroom, and received no complaints from tenants. 295 N.W.2d at 905, n.3. Do these additional facts affect your impression of the case?

2. *Lack of consistency in mutual mistake cases.* In Gartner v. Eikill, 319 N.W.2d 397 (Minn. 1982), a purchaser of land sought rescission on the ground of mutual mistake, claiming that unknown to him the land had in the past been subjected to a special zoning restriction making it unuseable for the purpose for which he had purchased it. The contract of purchase stated that the seller would convey marketable title subject to, inter alia, "Building and zoning laws, ordinances, State and Federal regulations. . . ." Neither party at the time of the sale was aware of the restriction. Relying on prior Minnesota cases as well as Sherwood v. Walker (discussed in the principal case), the court in *Gartner* allowed rescission on the basis of "mutual mistake of fact." *Gartner* and *Lenawee* obviously reach opposing outcomes; are they necessarily inconsistent decisions? Can they be harmonized so that both cases may be regarded as rightly decided? Or was one of them wrongly decided? Is it possible that *both* were wrongly decided? Additional examples of cases with similar facts reaching apparently contrary results in this area can be found: Compare Nichols v. City of Evansdale, 687 N.W.2d 562 (Iowa 2004) (rescission would be available to both parties where neither knew that sewer lines ran beneath transferred property and the error had a material effect on the agreed exchange), with Maloney v. Sargisson, 465 N.E.2d 296 (Mass. App. Ct. 1984) (rescission denied where purchasers discovered that concrete drain line ran under street fronting their land, precluding building because it made installation of septic tank impossible).

3. *Limiting earlier court decisions.* In analyzing the character of the "mistake" made by the buyers in *Lenawee*, the Michigan Supreme Court discusses and quotes at length from two earlier Michigan decisions, A & M Land Development Co. v. Miller and the "famous 'barren cow' case," Sherwood v. Walker. The *Lenawee* court does not expressly overrule either *Sherwood* or *A & M Land Development Co.*, but it limits the holding of each to its facts, effectively destroying their value as precedent, at least in Michigan. Why did the court so hold? Is the mode of analysis applied by the court in *Lenawee* preferable to that employed in those cases?

4. *Effect of "as is" clause.* Like the Michigan Supreme Court in *Lenawee*, a number of other courts have denied relief on mutual mistake and other grounds when the contract contained an "as is" or similar clause. See Thomas J. Duggan, LLC v. Peacock Point, LLC, 89 So. 3d 283 (Fla. Dist. Ct. App. 2012) (denying rescission to buyer who claimed, among other theories, that parties

made a mutual mistake regarding whether property was ready for residential construction when property was sold "as is"); Firstmerit Bank, N.A. v. Vision Fin. Group, Inc., 2006 U.S. Dist. LEXIS 70507 (W.D. Pa.) (denying claim by assignee to rescind assignment of equipment lease even though equipment did not exist because mistake was the result of misrepresentation by a third party and under language of assignment assignee bore risk of any mistake). There are other decisions, however, which deny such conclusive effect to "as is" provisions. See Shore Builders, Inc. v. Dogwood, Inc., 616 F. Supp. 1004 (D. Del. 1985) (since mutual mistake arises in situations beyond contemplation of contracting parties, all-purpose boilerplate "as is" clauses should be regarded as ineffective because parties lack adequate notice of what is being bargained for); Lesher v. Strid, 996 P.2d 988 (Or. Ct. App. 2000) (claim of mutual mistake not barred by "as is" clause where seller's representation of water rights was incorporated into contract for sale of land).

5. *Conscious ignorance.* Another form of assumption of risk is based on a party's conscious ignorance of all relevant facts before entering an agreement, as suggested by the Restatement (Second) of Contracts §154(b) quoted in *Lenawee.* An example is Estate of Nelson v. Rice, 12 P.3d 238 (Ariz. Ct. App. 2000), in which the representatives of an estate sold two paintings for $60 without having them appraised by an appropriate expert and the paintings later proved to be worth more than $1 million. Relying on §154(b), the court rejected the estate's claim of mutual mistake because the representatives were aware of the possibility that the estate might include fine art but failed to employ a qualified expert before making the sale. See also Land Baron Inv. v. Bonnie Springs Family LP, 356 P.3d 511 (Nev. 2015) (experienced developer assumed risk of conscious uncertainty in making contract to purchase property for $17 million without verifying that access roads could be built or water rights obtained for anticipated residential subdivision; summary judgment denying rescission for mutual mistake affirmed).

6. *Mistake in written expression.* When the mutual mistake consists of the failure of the written contract to state accurately the actual agreement of the parties, reformation of the contract to express the parties' mutual intent is the normal remedy. Compare United Bank v. Ashland Development Corp., 792 P.2d 775 (Ariz. Ct. App. 1990) (property line descriptions in deeds reformed for mutual mistake), with R & B Farms, Inc. v. Cedar Valley Acres, Inc., 798 N.W.2d 121 (Neb. 2011) (denying reformation because record did not contain clear and convincing evidence that description in agreement was the result of mutual mistake).

7. *Equitable relief.* The relief available for mutual mistake other than a mistake in the writing is ordinarily rescission, along with any restitution that may appear appropriate. E.g., O'Connor v. Harger Constr., Inc., 188 P.3d 846 (Idaho 2008) (rescission granted when parties were mutually mistaken that access to property could be granted by easement through private driveway; contractor ordered to make restitution of buyer's deposit less the value of building materials in buyer's possession). As relief for mutual mistake is an equitable remedy, traditionally an area of greater judicial discretion, courts occasionally exercise

creative ingenuity in fashioning a remedy to fit the nature of the mistake. For example, in Donohue v. Picinich, 852 F. Supp. 144 (D. Conn. 1994), both parties to a land purchase contract were mistaken about something — the buyers thought they were getting a tract of land including a pond, although the pond was really on an adjoining lot not intended by the seller to be included in their purchase; on the other hand, the seller's attorney had mistakenly drafted the contract to include all of that additional lot, and both parties had signed it. The court reformed the contract so as to give the purchasers the pond on the adjoining tract, but leaving the rest of that tract as the property of the seller.

8. *Personal injury settlement cases.* Claims of mutual mistake are also frequently made by litigants seeking to overturn releases or settlement agreements. A common fact pattern involves settlement of a personal injury claim that the plaintiff later regrets because the injuries turn out to be worse than they were thought to be at the time of the settlement. Such cases involve tension between the social policies of finality of litigation and fair compensation for injury. Not surprisingly, courts differ in the degree to which they will allow such releases to be set aside. Compare Kendrick v. Barker, 15 P.3d 734 (Wyo. 2001) (rescission based on mutual mistake not available to injured party who settled claim with knowledge that extent of closed head injury was uncertain and with assistance of counsel), with Gibli v. Kadosh, 717 N.Y.S.2d 553 (App. Div. 2000) (to "avoid grave injustice," relief for mutual mistake would be available if plaintiff could demonstrate that injury was of different nature than both parties believed it to be at the time of release).

BMW Financial Services NA, LLC v. Deloach

California Court of Appeal 2017 WL 1832250 (2017)

OPINION

BEDSWORTH, J.

INTRODUCTION

BMW Financial Services NA, LLC (BMW Financial) appeals from an order granting a motion to compel acknowledgment of satisfaction of judgment entered in favor of Frank Deloach. BMW Financial obtained a large default judgment against Deloach relating to a leased car that had been repossessed with an altered odometer. Owing to BMW Financial's mistake in sending the Deloach account to a collection agency, the agency and Deloach's father settled the matter for considerably less than the amount of the default judgment. BMW Financial tried to rescind the settlement, but Deloach filed a motion for satisfaction of judgment, which the trial court granted.

We affirm the order. BMW Financial did not qualify for rescission of the settlement agreement based on mistake. Substantial evidence supported the trial court's determination that BMW Financial bore the risk of the mistake and that enforcing the settlement agreement would not be unconscionable.

FACTS

The facts are not disputed. Deloach leased a 2013 BMW from Shelly BMW in Buena Park.[1] At the time of the lease, the BMW's odometer displayed 4,293 miles. Deloach did not make his payments, and the car was repossessed. At that time, the odometer displayed 94 miles, and inspection revealed that the odometer had been tampered with, in violation of state and federal laws.[2]

BMW Financial sued Deloach for breaching the lease and for tampering with the odometer. He did not respond, and BMW Financial took his default on April 20, 2015. The BMW was sold at auction for $25,000. Because of the odometer tampering, the vehicle had to be sold with a TMU (true mileage unknown) designation, which impaired its value.

The account was sent to a collection agency, Firstsource Advantage, LLC. Firstsource contacted Deloach in August 2015 to collect the balance of the account, which, according to the information sent to the agency, stood at approximately $24,000. At this point, David Deloach, Deloach's father, became involved. David Deloach negotiated a settlement with Firstsource for a complete release in exchange for $14,000. Firstsource confirmed the settlement in writing on August 17, 2015, and thereafter confirmed, not only the receipt of the $14,000, but also "that our client has agreed to accept less than the full balance due as settlement on the above mentioned account."

On August 13, 2015, the trial court entered a default judgment in favor of BMW Financial and against Deloach for $114,677. Most of the judgment, $81,296, was for treble damages for the odometer tampering. (See 49 U.S.C. §32710, subd. (a).) Counsel for BMW Financial contacted Deloach on September 15, 2015, asserting that the August settlement was entered into by mistake and purporting to rescind it by returning the $14,000. Deloach countered with a motion to compel acknowledgement of satisfaction of judgment.

BMW Financial opposed the motion on grounds of mistake. A company representative explained how the mistake occurred. After the BMW was sold at auction, the purchase price was posted to Deloach's account. If the balance on an account exceeds $5,500, it is turned over to a collection agency. If the account is in litigation, however, it is not given to a collection agency. The error occurred because Deloach's account was not flagged as being involved in litigation. It was therefore mistakenly sent to Firstsource for collection.

According to the information sent to Firstsource, the balance on Deloach's account was $24,442. Firstsource sent a letter dated August 10, 2015, to Deloach informing him of the balance and urging him to contact it, as he

1. The lease identifies Shelly BMW as the lessor. The lease was allegedly assigned to BMW Financial. The plaintiff in the subsequent breach of contract action was "Financial Services Vehicle Trust by and through its servicer, BMW Financial Services NA, LLC." For simplicity's sake we refer to the appellant as BMW Financial.

2. BMW Financial's complaint alleged a cause of action only for violation of federal odometer tampering law, 49 U.S.C. sections 32701 et seq. 49 U.S.C. section 32710 allows a private party to bring a civil action for violation of the law in state court and prescribes liability for treble damages in cases of tampering with intent to defraud.

"may be eligible for payment options that were not available to you before." David Deloach sent an email to Firstsource dated August 17 requesting confirmation of an agreement that Firstsource would accept $14,000 in full settlement of the debt and cause BMW Financial to execute a dismissal with prejudice or satisfaction of judgment. Firstsource responded on the same day, in writing, stating "Upon receipt and clearance of your payment as agreed, we will notify our client to update its records accordingly regarding this settlement." The next day, Firstsource sent Deloach a letter stating, "This letter serves as confirmation that our client has agreed to accept less than the full balance due as settlement on the above mentioned account." Firstsource had a preauthorized settlement authority range, and the ultimate settlement of $14,000 was within that range.

The court issued the default judgment for $118,296 on August 13, but BMW Financial did not learn about it until after the settlement had been concluded.[3] It appears that BMW Financial found out about the mistake in mid-September when one of the Deloaches called its counsel about the settlement agreement.[4] BMW Financial's counsel sent Deloach a letter dated September 15 repudiating the settlement.

The court granted Deloach's motion to compel satisfaction of judgment after an unreported hearing on November 23, 2015. It awarded him $2,455 in costs and the statutory penalty of $100. The court ordered Deloach's counsel to prepare a satisfaction of judgment order for its signature. The order was entered on December 21, 2015.

Evidently BMW Financial's counsel submitted proposed orders to the court, only one of which is in the record, purporting to give details of what happened at the hearing. This effort prompted the judge to issue what was in effect a statement of decision on January 7, 2016, explaining his reasoning. The court determined that BMW Financial's "authorized representative made exactly the deal that he wanted to make. He acted within the scope of his negotiating authority and followed those instructions precisely and without error." The court concluded the deal was reasonable, given that settlement amounts are routinely less than the actual debt. The court also concluded that rescinding the settlement agreement would be unconscionable, because there was no evidence of sharp dealing by either Deloach or an overly harsh outcome. The court distinguished the case BMW Financial relied on, noting that the error in that case was made by someone unrelated to the party seeking rescission for mistake, while in this case BMW Financial itself made the error.

---

3. BMW Financial's counsel stated that she mailed the conformed default judgment to her client on August 16, a Sunday, and the earliest the client could have seen it was the next day. Firstsource settled with David Deloach on August 17.

4. In her declaration, counsel identifies the person who called her as "[Frank] Deloach's father, Frank Deloach." Frank Deloach's father is David Deloach. BMW Financial's representative stated in her declaration that the phone calls occurred on August 17, a date before the settlement was even confirmed. We assume the latter is another mistake.

DISCUSSION

Code of Civil Procedure section 724.010, subdivision (a), provides: "A money judgment may be satisfied by payment of the full amount required to satisfy the judgment or by acceptance by the judgment creditor of a lesser sum in full satisfaction of the judgment."[5] Section 724.030 requires a judgment creditor to file an acknowledgement of satisfaction of judgment with the court immediately after a money judgment has been satisfied. If it does not do so, the judgment debtor may demand an acknowledgment, and if the judgment creditor still will not cooperate, the judgment debtor may move the court for an order requiring compliance with the demand. (§724.050, subds. (a), (d).) A judgment creditor may be liable for damages and a $100 penalty for failing to comply with the demand. (§724.050, subd. (e).)

. . .

We first observe that the subject of this dispute is a settlement agreement, and not a commercial contract or a construction bid. Settlement agreements are highly favored under California law. (See, e.g.., City of Orange v. San Diego County Employees Retirement Assn. (2002) 103 Cal.App.4th 45, 55; . . . .) Although ordinary contract principles, including the availability of rescission for mistake (see, e.g., Harris v. Rudin, Richman & Appel (2002) 95 Cal.App.4th 1332), govern settlement agreements, the favored position of these agreements factors into the assessment of the unconscionability of enforcement.

Our Supreme Court's decision in Donovan v. RRL Corp. (2001) 26 Cal.4th 261 (*Donovan*) deals with rescission for mistake of fact.[6] In *Donovan*, a mistake made by a local newspaper caused an error in a car dealer's advertisement regarding the price of a used car. (Id. at pp. 268-269.) The dealer was unaware of the mistake until a customer came in with the advertisement and offered to buy the car for the incorrect price. (Id. at p. 269.) The customer was immediately told that the advertisement was a mistake by both the salesman to whom he made the offer and the sales manager. (Id. at p. 268.) Nevertheless, the customer sued the dealer for breach of contract, fraud, and negligence. (Ibid.)

Adopting the test set forth in the Restatement Second of Contracts, the court held that the following facts must be established to qualify for rescission based on mistake of fact: "(1) the defendant made a mistake regarding a basic assumption upon which the defendant made the contract; (2) the mistake has a material effect upon the agreed exchange of performances that is adverse to the defendant; (3) the defendant does not bear the risk of the mistake; and (4) the effect of the mistake is such that enforcement of the contract would be unconscionable."[7] (*Donovan,* supra, 26 Cal.4th at p. 282.)

---

5. All further statutory references are to the Code of Civil Procedure unless otherwise indicated.

6. Deloach argued that BMW Financial had to file a complaint for rescission rather than oppose his motion under section 724.050. If mistake is a ground for vacating a satisfaction of judgement (see *Remillard Brick Co. v. Dandini* (1950) 98 Cal.App.2d 617, 622), we think it can also be a defense to a motion to compel entry of a satisfaction of judgment.

7. Restatement Second of Contracts, section 153 states: "Where a mistake of one party at the time a contract was made as to a basic assumption on which he made the contract has a material effect on the agreed exchange of performances that is adverse to him, the contract is voidable by him

In this case, the first two parts of the test are undisputed. BMW Financial made a material mistake that led to the Deloach settlement agreement for significantly less money than the default judgment. So who bears the risk of that mistake, and does the effect of the mistake make the enforcement of the settlement agreement unconscionable?

I. ALLOCATION OF RISK

Restatement Second of Contracts, section 154 states: "A party bears the risk of a mistake when [¶] (a) the risk is allocated to him by agreement of the parties, or [¶] (b) he is aware, at the time the contract is made, that he has only limited knowledge with respect to the facts to which the mistake relates but treats his limited knowledge as sufficient, or [¶] (c) the risk is allocated to him by the court on the ground that it is reasonable in the circumstances to do so." The *Donovan* court held that the third alternative applied in that case. (*Donovan,* supra, 26 Cal.4th at p. 283.)

The court then observed that the risk of mistake must be allocated to a party when the mistake results from that party's "neglect of a legal duty." (*Donovan,* supra, 26 Cal.4th at p. 283.) That is, it is reasonable under the circumstances to allocate the risk to the party who had neglected a legal duty. But what constitutes neglect of a legal duty? The *Donovan* case chiefly concentrates on what it is not. It is not, for instance, ordinary carelessness or negligence, but it could be extreme negligence. (Id. at pp. 283-284.) It is not necessarily the violation of a statute. (Id. at pp. 284-285.)

BMW Financial argues that the risk of the mistake can be assigned to it only if it neglected a legal duty. Failing to tag the Deloach account as being in litigation was not neglect of a legal duty, so BMW Financial should not have to bear the risk.

Neglect of a legal duty is not, however, the only circumstance under which a court may allocate risk. The Restatement stresses reasonableness and observes that "the court will consider the purposes of the parties and will have recourse to its own general knowledge of human behavior in bargain transactions [.]" (Rest.2d Contracts, §154, com. d.) The illustrations bear out this observation.

One of the Restatement illustrations to this section posits the sale of farmland that is later discovered to contain valuable mineral deposits unknown to both parties. "In some instances it is reasonably clear that a party should bear the risk of a mistake for reasons other than those stated in Subparagraphs (a) and (b). In such instances, under the rule stated in Subparagraph (c), the court will allocate the risk to that party on the ground that it is reasonable to do so. A court will generally do this, for example, where the seller of farm land seeks to avoid the contract of sale on the ground that valuable mineral rights have newly been found." (Rest.2d Contracts, §154, com. d.) It would be hard to accuse the seller in this illustration of neglecting a legal duty in failing to

---

if he does not bear the risk of the mistake under the rule stated in §154, and [¶] (a) the effect of the mistake is such that enforcement of the contract would be unconscionable, or [¶] (b) the other party had reason to know of the mistake or his fault caused the mistake."

discover that the land contained valuable mineral deposits. Drawing on general knowledge of human behavior in bargain transactions, however, a court could reasonably allocate the risk to the seller on the ground that he was in a better position to know the composition of the property than the buyer was.

Likewise, in another illustration, a landowner and a builder make a contract about removing gravel from the property at a stated rate per cubic yard. Unbeknownst to both of them, part of the gravel is under water and is thus more expensive to remove. The court will allocate the risk to the builder, not because the builder has neglected a legal duty, but because it is reasonable under the circumstances to expect the builder to have looked over the property before entering into the contract. (Rest.2d Contracts, §154, com. d, illus. 4.)

Here, the trial court found it was reasonable under the circumstances to allocate the risk to BMW Financial, and substantial evidence supports this conclusion. The error was attributable solely to BMW Financial's failure to tag Deloach's account as being in litigation. BMW Financial presented no evidence that Firstsource or either Deloach knew about the default judgment when Firstsource and David Deloach entered into negotiations to settle the case. As the court noted, a crucial difference between the circumstances of this case and those of *Donovan* was that in *Donovan* an unrelated third party—a newspaper—had made the mistake by printing the wrong sale price of a car. (*Donovan,* supra, 26 Cal.4th at pp. 289-290 ["The uncontradicted evidence established that the [newspaper] made the proofreading error resulting in [the car dealer's] mistake."].) In this case, however, the mistake was BMW Financial's and no one else's.

There is another significant difference between this case and *Donovan*. In *Donovan* the customer was immediately told when he produced the erroneous advertisement that the price was a mistake, and the sales manager offered to compensate the customer for his expenses. (Id. at p. 268.) In this case, BMW Financial waited nearly a month to inform Deloach that it wanted to rescind.

The hard fact is that someone has to bear the risk of the mistake. Should it be the person who negotiated a reasonable settlement for actual damages with the agent for the other party and received confirmation that the settlement was a done deal, only to be told a month later that the settlement was off? Or should it be the party whose error caused the problem and who is nevertheless coming out roughly even?

II. GOOD FAITH AND FAIR DEALING

The Restatement also observes that "[e]ven though a mistaken party does not bear the risk of a mistake, he may be barred from avoidance if the mistake was the result of his failure to act in good faith and in accordance with reasonable standards of fair dealing." (Rest.2d Contracts, §154, com. a.) It then cites to section 157 of the Restatement, which provides, "A mistaken party's fault in failing to know or discover the facts before making the contract does not bar him from avoidance . . . under the rules stated in this Chapter, unless his fault amounts to a failure to act in good faith and in accordance with reasonable standards of fair dealing." (Rest.2d Contracts, §157.) BMW Financial argues that it acted with good faith and fair dealing, so it should be entitled to rescind.

Although "a failure to act in good faith and in accordance with reasonable standards of fair dealing during pre-contractual negotiations does not amount to a breach[, [n]evertheless, under the rule stated in this Section, the failure bars a mistaken party from relief based on a mistake that otherwise would not have been made. During the negotiation stage each party is held to a degree of responsibility appropriate to the justifiable expectations of the other." (Rest.2d Contracts, §157, com. a.)[8]

Good faith and reasonable standards of fair dealing in this context are not limited to an absence of cheating or of fraud. They include not disappointing the justifiable expectations of the other party. (See *Donovan,* supra, 26 Cal.4th at p. 290.) Deloach was certainly justified in expecting that Firstsource could settle his debt with BMW Financial, especially after receiving a letter from Firstsource stating, "[O]ur client [i.e., BMW Financial] has agreed to accept less than the full balance due as settlement of the above mentioned account." The recipient of this letter could reasonably infer that Firstsource had consulted BMW Financial as to this particular settlement and received its particular approval. BMW Financial therefore had another opportunity to discover that the account was in litigation. Moreover, there is no evidence that David Deloach was pressing Firstsource to settle immediately. There was time to check the records.

III. Unconscionability

In discussing unconscionability, the *Donovan* court focused on the difference between the correct price and the mistaken price. It discussed not only the loss the dealer would sustain by selling the disputed car at the mistaken price, but also other cases involving substantial differences between the two prices. The court concluded that forcing a sale at such a loss would be unconscionable. (*Donovan,* supra, 26 Cal.4th at pp. 292–293.)

In this case, the trial court found that enforcing the settlement agreement would not be unconscionable, and once again substantial evidence supports this conclusion. BMW Financial received $39,000 for the leased BMW—$25,000 from its sale at auction and $14,000 from the settlement. The balance on the Deloach account when it was sent to Firstsource was $24,442. BMW Financial's actual loss was a little over $10,000. On the plus side, as is so often true of settlements, BMW Financial had a $14,000 bird in the hand and did not have to spend money chasing after $24,000 it might never collect. Its recognition of this benefit is reflected in the fact that Firstsource was authorized to accept $14,000 to settle a $24,000 debt. As the court observed, "Judgements are routinely satisfied by a payment of less than its face amount, and the circumstances of this case made such a deal very likely." An additional factor, as discussed above, is the favored position that settlements occupy in California law.

8. As the Restatement acknowledges, the duty of good faith and fair dealing implied in every contract does not apply to pre-contract negotiations. (Rest.2d Contract, §157, com. a; see Racine & Laramie, Ltd. v. Department of Parks & Recreation (1992)11 Cal.App.4th 1026, 1935 and fn. 4.)

The large discrepancy between the amount of the settlement and the amount of the default judgment in this case was, for the most part, the penalty awarded for odometer tampering. BMW Financial considers this the final pivot point of the analysis of the case. At oral argument, its counsel was astonished that we did not realize we were dismantling the entire federal statutory scheme preventing odometer fraud if we did not consider the punitive damages award. This astonishment reflects a fundamental misunderstanding of punitive damages. This amount did not reflect an actual loss to BMW Financial, as was true of the cases cited in *Donovan*. (Cf. Conservatorship of O'Connor (1996) 48 Cal. App.4th 1076, 1098 [contract voidable for mistake only if enforcement more onerous to party seeking avoidance than would it would have been without mistake].) "The purpose of punitive damages is to punish wrongdoers and thereby deter the commission of wrongful acts." (Neal v. Farmers Ins. Exchange (1978) 21 Cal.3d 910, 928, fn. 13; . . . Civ. Code, §3345, subd. (b).) Penalties and punitive damage awards are not intended to compensate plaintiffs or make them whole. Moreover, the loss of this extra cash—assuming it was collectable from a person who could not make his car lease payments—may have the salutary effect of making BMW Financial more vigilant in its bookkeeping. We hope his escape in this case has a similarly salutary effect on the younger Deloach. A lifetime rarely includes two instances of such unconscionable luck.

DISPOSITION

The order granting respondent's motion to compel satisfaction of judgment is affirmed. Respondent is to recover his costs on appeal.
WE CONCUR: O'LEARY, P.J., FYBEL, J.

NOTES AND QUESTIONS

1. *"Palpable" nature or unconscionable effect of mistake.* The *BMW Financial* court relied on a test for unilateral mistake based on the Restatement (Second) §153, quoted in footnote 7. It should be noted, however, that the Restatement (Second) and various courts have recognized a few different bases for unilateral mistake. Early cases granting relief required that the unilateral mistake be *"palpable"* — so obvious that the other party in the circumstances either knew or should have known that a mistake had been made. See Restatement (Second) §153(b). In such cases, the mistake is truly "unilateral" (i.e., the other party knows or has reason to know that there is a mistake). E.g., Belk v. Martin, 39 P.3d 592 (Idaho 2001) (lease agreement reformed on grounds of unilateral mistake where lessee knew that written lease amount should have been $14,768 instead of $1,476.80). Sometimes it is said that one party may not "snap up" an offer that is "too good to be true." The court in *BMW Financial* concluded, however, that the Deloaches had no reason to know that BMW Financial had made a mistake when they agreed to settle the dispute. Cf. Sumerel v. Goodyear Tire & Rubber Co., 232 P.3d 128 (Colo. Ct. App. 2009) (alleged settlement agreement

for $2.7 million that included overpayment of $550,000 would be unenforceable due to obvious mistake by defendant's counsel and inequitable conduct by plaintiffs' attorneys in effort to gain windfall).

The *BMW Financial* court applied an alternative test for unilateral mistake, as stated in Restatement (Second) §153(a) and adopted in the earlier *Donovan* case, that focused largely on the *"unconscionable effect of mistake"* on the adversely affected party if the contract is enforced. This variation of the unilateral mistake excuse, of course, has additional requirements: The mistake must involve a basic assumption of the contract, it must have a material effect on the exchange, and the mistaken party must not bear the risk of the mistake. The court also considered the possibility of harm to the other party if excuse is granted. Although, as we have seen, "unconscionability" in the context of Restatement (Second) §208 or UCC §2-302 is a complex and somewhat amorphous concept, "unconscionable" in the context of §153(a) seems to mean merely severe enough to cause substantial loss. See the *Donovan* and *Wil-Fred's* cases discussed in the following notes. The *BMW Financial* court held that the loss of more than $80,000 in punitive damages did not result in unconscionable harm to the plaintiff because it did not amount to an out-of-pocket loss, but instead was more in the nature of an unrealized gain of "extra cash." In reaching its decision, the *BMW Financial* court also factored in the nature of the plaintiff's mistake, the delay in discovering the mistake, and the defendant's reasonable reliance on the collection agency's authority to settle the dispute.

2. *Requirement that benefitting party cause or induce the mistake.* Apart from palpability and unconscionable effect, the Restatement (Second) §153(b) incorporates a third alternative basis for unilateral mistake when "the other party . . . caused the mistake." Indeed, a few courts have gone further and held that the unilateral mistake *must be caused* by the other party to warrant relief. See, e.g., Environmental Servs., Inc. v. Hull Forest Prods., 2013 WL 1408629 (Conn. Super. Ct.) (claimant for rescission based on unilateral mistake must establish fraud or inequitable conduct by other party that caused mistake). Notably, a Florida District Appellate Court, on its third review of the same case, recently abandoned its interpretation that state law required inducement by the party seeking to benefit from the unilateral mistake. *DePrince v. Starboard Cruise Services,* 2018 WL 3636849 (Fla. Dist. Ct. App.). The *DePrince* case involved a contract made on a cruise ship by the onboard jewelry shop to sell a twenty carat diamond for $235,000 (the per carat price) when the total price should have been nearly $5 million. The mistake resulted entirely from messages between the ship sales staff and its mainland diamond supplier. Based on information from a knowledgeable family member, DePrince clearly had reason to know there was a mistake in the price. The more challenging question for the Florida courts, however, was whether DePrince could be deemed to have "induced" the mistake by merely failing to disclose the pricing error. The answer to that difficult question became irrelevant when the appellate court, after carefully reviewing precedent, concluded that inducement by the other party should not

be a required element of Florida law on unilateral mistake. The appellate court upheld the rescission of the sales contract.

3. *Mistake of fact vs. mistake of judgment.* In addressing claims of unilateral mistake, some courts granted relief for "clerical errors" or other "mistakes of fact," but not for "mistakes in judgment." What policy underlies this distinction? Many of the cases have indeed involved clerical, or "mechanical," errors. See, e.g., First Baptist Church of Moultrie v. Barber Contracting Co., 377 S.E.2d 717 (Ga. Ct. App. 1989) (rescission granted when contractor made $118,776 error in adding cost of materials on its work sheets). See also Belk v. Martin, note 1 above. More recent cases have, like *BMW Financial,* been less disposed to focus on the fact-judgment distinction and more inclined to concentrate on the strength of the proof that a genuine and identifiable mistake was made as to a basic assumption of the contract. The Restatement does not use the fact-judgment distinction although it might be relevant to the question of "risk allocation."

4. *Effect of negligence.* Must a unilateral mistake be "non-negligent" in order to form a basis for relief? Relying on the *Donovan* case, the *BMW Financial* court clearly acknowledged that "ordinary carelessness or negligence" will not amount to the kind of neglect of a legal duty that will preclude relief for unilateral mistake. Thus, the courts tend to recognize there will often be a degree of negligence in a unilateral mistake case. See E. Allan Farnsworth, Contracts §9.3, at 613 (4th ed. 2004). In §157, the Restatement (Second) expressly negates any requirement that the mistaken party be non-negligent, requiring only that its conduct not fall below the level of good faith and fair dealing. But see ATS-1 Corp. v. Rodriguez, 67 N.Y.S.3d 60 (App. Div. 2017) (rescission not available when unilateral mistake resulted from negligence or failure to exercise ordinary care).

5. *Unilateral mistake in construction bidding cases.* A common situation in which claims of unilateral mistake may be raised are construction contracts in which a contractor claims to have made a mistake in submitting its bid. For example, in Wil-Fred's, Inc. v. Metropolitan Sanitary Dist., 372 N.E.2d 946 (Ill. App. Ct. 1978), the defendant Sanitary District solicited bids for rehabilitation work at one of its water reclamation plants. Wil-Fred's submitted a bid and made a $100,000 deposit. The bidding documents stated that Wil-Fred's certified that it had examined the contract documents, that it had made the examination and investigation necessary to submit its bid, that the bid could not be cancelled or withdrawn, and that the Sanitary District would retain a $100,000 deposit as liquidated damages if Wil-Fred's failed to perform after being awarded the contract. However, Wil-Fred's sought to avoid the contract on the ground that its bid price of $882,600 was based in material part on the bid of an excavating subcontractor who had made a $150,000 mistake in bidding based on a misunderstanding of the specifications. While recognizing the importance of maintaining the competitive bidding system, the court granted relief because the mistake related to a material part of the contract, Wil-Fred's had exercised reasonable care (it had dealt with the subcontractor over a period of years without problem), the consequences of denial of relief would be great

because Wil-Fred's forfeiture of the deposit would reduce its bonding capacity for other projects by two to three million dollars, and the Sanitary District had not changed its position in reliance on Wil-Fred's bid and could be returned to status quo. Moreover, the court noted that the difference of $235,775 between Wil-Fred's bid and the next lowest bid should have put the Sanitary District on notice that the bid contained a material mistake. But see Handle Constr. Co. v. Norcon, Inc., 264 P.3d 367 (Alaska 2011) (denying relief to subcontractor on theory of unilateral mistake because subcontractor who underbid by about $140,000 knew that it submitted its bid based on incomplete information and 35 percent differential with next lowest bid was insufficient to place contractor on notice of mistake).

Recall the *Baird* and *Drennan* cases in Chapter 3, involving the enforcement of subcontract bids after attempted revocation. On the basis of the principles illustrated in *Wil-Fred's*, should the subcontractors in those cases have been able to obtain relief from enforcement on the theory of unilateral mistake? If it had chosen to do so, could plaintiff Wil-Fred's have held the subcontractor to its subcontract bid? If the subcontractor had been capable of responding to a judgment for damages in a breach of contract action, should Wil-Fred's have been denied rescission against the defendant sanitary district, on the ground that enforcement against Wil-Fred's would not in the circumstances have been unconscionable?

6. *Effect of unilateral mistake in an advertisement.* The *BMW Financial* court relied heavily on the California Supreme Court decision in Donovan v. RRL Corp., 27 P.3d 702 (Cal. 2001), even though in that earlier case relief for unilateral mistake was granted. In *Donovan* a car dealer offered a used Jaguar for sale in a newspaper ad for about $12,000 less than the intended price of $38,000 due to proofreading errors made by the newspaper's staff in composing the ad. Although the *Donovan* court acknowledged that newspaper ads usually constitute invitations to negotiate rather than offers, the court decided that the ad in this case would constitute an offer, at least when viewed in light of a California consumer protection statute, which requires that a dealer have available for sale any car, that is advertised at a specific price and on specific terms. The plaintiff could thus accept the offer by tendering the full advertised price. The court ruled, however, that the resulting contract was subject to rescission on grounds of unilateral mistake. The erroneous price related to a basic assumption of the contract and had a material adverse effect on the mistaken party. The court further held that the dealer's failure to discover the mistake did not amount to a "neglect of legal duty" that would bar rescission when the other party suffers no loss. Id. at 717-719. Are you persuaded that the ultimate decision in the *BMW Financial* case denying relief on grounds of unilateral mistake can be reconciled with the outcome in the *Donovan* case, which granted rescission?

7. *Unilateral mistake as to content of writing.* In Chapter 2, we first encountered the "objective theory" of contracts, and its corollary, the "duty to read," which generally binds those who manifest agreement to what they know is intended to be a contract, even if they are ignorant of its contents (recall the Ray v. Eurice

Bros. case). But the duty to read is not a principle that always carries the day, as we have since learned; it may be overcome by a variety of other protective doctrines, such as lack of capacity, fraud (recall the *Park 100* case in Chapter 7), or unconscionability. Where the parties are both equally mistaken about the accuracy of the agreement (it contains a typographical error, or a provision has been mistakenly omitted), the remedy of reformation may be available, as discussed in the notes following the *Lenawee County* case, above. But what if only one party is mistaken, because the agreement says just what the other party meant it to say? Can unilateral mistake provide an avenue of escape for the party who failed to read (or to understand) what he or she signed?

In Nauga, Inc. v. Westel Milwaukee Co., 576 N.W.2d 573 (Wis. Ct. App. 1998), Nauga was a selling agent for Westel, a cellular phone company. The parties were involved in two lawsuits and had disputes about their relationship. The existence of these disputes had not, however, resulted in a severance of the agency relationship between Nauga and Westel. While both of those suits were still in litigation, Westel submitted to Nauga and its other Wisconsin agents a proposed new agency agreement, to replace existing contracts. One clause of the proposed agreement was a release of any claims that the agent might have against Westel under their prior agreements or relationship. Believing that its agreement to this clause would result in Nauga's surrender of its pending claims against Westel, Nauga's attorney added to the proposed agency agreement a clause providing for the payment by Westel to Nauga of $250,000 for the settlement of all existing claims. The revised agreement was ultimately signed by Westel, assertedly without either its lawyers or its officers having noticed the existence and effect of the payment clause. (Nauga apparently conceded the truth of Westel's assertion that Westel never intended to assent to the payment term and was surprised to learn later of its existence.) Westel refused to make the $250,000 payment, and Nauga moved to enforce the settlement agreement. The trial court held that although Nauga was not guilty of fraud, the two parties' minds had not met, and the contract was not enforceable. A divided appellate court reversed, and gave judgment for plaintiff Nauga. In the absence of ambiguity, fraud, or mutual mistake, enforcement might "seem harsh," the court conceded, but nevertheless was "based on sound principles." Id. at 578. A strong dissent argued that the trial court should have been upheld in its conclusion that no enforceable agreement existed, because of Nauga's violations of good faith, fair dealing, and the duty to cooperate.

B. CHANGED CIRCUMSTANCES: IMPOSSIBILITY, IMPRACTICABILITY, AND FRUSTRATION

As we have seen, the defense of mistake is commonly characterized as resting on a mistake by one or both parties as to a fact existing at the time their contract was made. The three doctrines considered in this section — "impossibility," "impracticability," and "frustration of purpose" – are usually thought of as involving changes in circumstance that occur between the making of the contract and the time set for performance (although there are cases in which the circumstance in question already existed at the time of contracting, not being discovered until later). Of the three, the earliest to evolve was the notion of "impossibility of performance."

In order to consider why and when impossibility should constitute a defense to a duty of performance, it may be appropriate first to consider why it should *not.* To a nonlawyer, it might appear that the duty to perform a contractual obligation would naturally be excused whenever it should appear that the performance itself was literally impossible. To understand why that has not been the case, it is necessary to recall that contractual liability is historically a form of "strict" liability: Nonperformance is actionable simply because the defendant has failed to perform what he or she promised, not because that nonperformance is also "culpable" in any sense. So any failure to perform a contractual obligation – whether willful, negligent, or innocent – should in theory give the aggrieved party a cause of action. If that obligation was in fact impossible to perform, then the remedy for breach obviously could not be specific performance; however, the court still could and presumably would award damages to compensate the plaintiff for the lost value of the defendant's expected performance.

The English courts first recognized this principle of strict contractual liability in Paradine v. Jane, 82 Eng. Rep. 897 (K.B. 1647). The case arose during the English Civil War. Jane had leased land from Paradine for a term of years but was dispossessed by a certain Prince Rupert and his army. Jane did not regain possession of the land for almost three years, during which time he paid no rent. When Paradine sued for the unpaid rent, Jane's defense was that he should be excused from his obligation to pay rent during the period of dispossession. The court held, however, that the plea was insufficient:

> [W]hen the party by his own contract creates a duty or charge upon himself, he is bound to make it good, if he may, notwithstanding any accident or inevitable necessity, because he might have provided against it by his contract.

Id. at 897-898.

The first notable line of exceptions to this rule of strict liability is generally traced to a much later English case, Taylor v. Caldwell, 122 Eng. Rep. 309 (K.B. 1863). There are indications that earlier decisions gave relief from liability for nonperformance where this was occasioned by an Act of God. See Alfred W.B. Simpson, A History of the Common Law of Contract 525-526 (1987). However, Taylor v. Caldwell is generally regarded as the "fountainhead of the modern law of impossibility." E. Allan Farnsworth, Contracts §9.5, at 621 (4th ed. 2004). In *Taylor,* the defendant Caldwell had agreed to rent a music hall to plaintiff Taylor for several days, so that Taylor might present musical performances there. The hall burned down shortly before the first performance was to take place, and Taylor sued for breach of contract. The court absolved Caldwell of liability, holding that because the hall itself was "essential" to the performance of the contract, and the parties had contracted "on the basis of [its] continued existence," Caldwell's duty of performance should be excused by its accidental destruction.

The principle of Taylor v. Caldwell has been applied to contracts for personal service or for the sale of specific goods: When a person or thing "necessary for performance" of the agreement dies or is incapacitated, is destroyed or damaged, the duty of performance is accordingly excused. See Restatement (Second) §§262, 263; UCC §2-613 ("casualty" to goods "identified when the contract is made" which contract "requires for its performance"). The principle is ordinarily easy to apply to destruction of unique goods (such as a racehorse); its application may be more dubious in cases involving specific goods of a fungible type, because the party seeking excuse will have to convince the court that the contract required for its performance the particular goods that were destroyed. See, e.g., Bende & Sons, Inc. v. Crown Recreation, Inc., 548 F. Supp. 1018 (E.D.N.Y. 1982), *aff'd*, 722 F.2d 727 (2d Cir. 1983) (seller not excused from duty to deliver combat boots by destruction of boots in train wreck; no showing that contract required those particular boots for its performance). Another situation commonly characterized as a form of "impossibility" (although not involving impossibility in any literal sense) is the prohibition of performance by governmental action. See Restatement (Second) §264; UCC §2-615(a) and Comment 10.

As suggested above, the doctrine of excuse for impossibility required for its application a showing of *literal* impossibility — the thing promised simply could not be performed at all. Such a requirement is often referred to as "objective" impossibility — "no one could do it" — as opposed to "subjective" impossibility — "*I* cannot do it." See first Restatement §455. This rule therefore would not serve to excuse a party merely because performance had come to be more difficult or expensive or because the contract itself had lost its value to that party. Another English case, decided 40 years after Taylor v. Caldwell, presented the latter situation. In Krell v. Henry, [1903] 2 K.B. 740 (C.A.), the defendant had agreed to pay the plaintiff for the use of a room overlooking the route that the coronation procession of King Edward VII would travel. The sudden illness of the king forced the cancellation of his coronation, however, making the plaintiff's room useless to the defendant for that purpose on that day. The court held that the defendant was excused from his duty of payment.

Although the court in *Krell* cited and relied on Taylor v. Caldwell and other "impossibility" cases, the result in *Krell* is generally not viewed as involving any true impossibility ("objective" or otherwise), because the promises of each party could literally have been performed. *Krell* is explained rather as a case of "frustration of purpose"; the exchange called for by the contract had lost all value to the defendant, because of a supervening change in extrinsic circumstances. (Note here the overlap of doctrines; if, unknown to Krell and Henry, the king's illness had already occurred at the time the contract was made, the case could also have been analyzed as one of "mutual mistake.") The doctrine of frustration was endorsed by the first Restatement in §288 ("frustration of object or effect"). The case law actually applying the doctrine remained sparse, however.

See Nicholas R. Weiskopf, Frustration of Contractual Purpose — Doctrine or Myth? 70 St. John's L. Rev. 239, 265 (1996) (noting "lack of widespread decisional support").

The third of this trilogy of excuses from performance is — like a number of other innovations in contract law — generally attributed to a decision of the California Supreme Court. In Mineral Park Land Co. v. Howard, 156 P. 458 (Cal. 1916), the defendant contractor had agreed to purchase and extract from plaintiff's land, at fixed prices (varying with the amounts taken), all the gravel required for the construction of a concrete bridge. The defendant procured some of the gravel used in the bridge from another source and was thereupon sued for its failure to take all of its gravel requirements from plaintiff's land. The defendant showed that it had removed from plaintiff's land all the gravel that was above water level, and that removal of that which lay below water level would have entailed not only a different means of extraction, but 10 to 12 times as great a cost. The court held that the extreme increase in the cost of extraction justified the defendant's nonperformance. Even though performance clearly was not literally impossible (indeed, it was not even "subjectively" impossible), it was sufficiently different from what the parties had both contemplated at the time of contracting as to be "impracticable."

As did the first Restatement, the Restatement (Second) incorporates the doctrines of impossibility (§§262, 263, 264), impracticability (§§261, 266), and frustration (§§265, 266). As we have already noted, the Uniform Commercial Code also has a rule covering traditional impossibility (§2-613); it also provides in §§2-615 and 2-616 for complete or partial excuse from the duty of performance in cases of impracticability. The ambit of UCC §2-615 is apparently broad enough to encompass instances of both traditional impossibility and impracticability, as well as frustration of purpose.

For a discussion of these three doctrines of excuse, see Melvin A. Eisenberg, Impossibility, Impracticability, and Frustration, 1 J. Legal Analysis 207 (2009).

Hemlock Semiconductor Operations, LLC v. Solarworld Industries Sachsen GmbH

United States Court of Appeals 867 F.3d 692 (6th Cir. 2017)

Before: MOORE, GILMAN, and COOK, Circuit Judges.

OPINION

RONALD LEE GILMAN, Circuit Judge.

Hemlock Semiconductor Operations, LLC (Hemlock) and SolarWorld Industries Sachsen GmbH (Sachsen) are both involved in manufacturing components of solar-power products. They entered into a series of long-term supply agreements (LTAs), by which Hemlock in Michigan would supply Sachsen in Germany with set quantities of polycrystalline silicon (polysilicon) at fixed prices between the years 2006 and 2019. The market price of polysilicon was initially well above the LTA price, but the market price plummeted several years later after the Chinese government began subsidizing its national production of polysilicon. The parties reached a temporary agreement to lower the LTA price in 2011. When that agreement expired in 2012, however, the price reverted to the original amount. Hemlock then demanded that Sachsen pay the original LTA price for the specified quantity of polysilicon for the year 2012. Sachsen refused.

This caused Hemlock to sue Sachsen for breach of contract in the United States District Court for the Eastern District of Michigan. Based on Hemlock's motion for summary judgment, which the district court granted, Hemlock was awarded nearly $800 million in damages and prejudgment interest. For the reasons set forth below, we **AFFIRM** the judgment of the district court.

I. BACKGROUND

A. Factual Background

Hemlock and Sachsen negotiated a series of four LTAs. The first LTA (LTA I) was executed in 2005 and was to remain in force through 2015. Subsequent LTAs (LTAs II–IV) extended the parties' relationship to the end of 2019. The first three LTAs are nearly identical. LTA IV is structured differently than the others, but the text of the provisions at issue is essentially the same as in LTAs I–III.

Two provisions of the LTAs are particularly relevant to the present case. First, a "take-or-pay" provision required that Sachsen purchase a specified quantity of polysilicon each year at a fixed price. The take-or-pay provision obligated Sachsen to pay this yearly amount even if it declined to take delivery of the polysilicon. Second, in the event that Sachsen failed to pay the specified amount for a given year, Hemlock had the right to terminate the LTAs. Sachsen would then owe Hemlock the full remaining balance of the LTA price, including amounts due for future years. We will refer to this second provision as "the liquidated-damages provision."

After entering into the LTAs, Hemlock began a massive expansion of its manufacturing facilities in the United States at a cost of over $4 billion. The LTAs acknowledged the planned expansion several times. Sachsen was required to make significant advance payments to Hemlock under the LTAs, which were then credited against the purchase price of the polysilicon. Although the LTAs do not explicitly describe the reason for the advance payments, Sachsen acknowledges that the purpose of the payments was to help fund Hemlock's expansion.

For the first few years of the LTAs' existence, Sachsen obtained polysilicon from Hemlock at a price far below the then-current market value. This began to change in 2009, however, when the Chinese government started subsidizing its national production of polysilicon. The result was that the market price of polysilicon eventually dropped below the LTA price.

In response, Hemlock and Sachsen negotiated a temporary adjustment to the LTA price in 2011. After that agreement expired the following year, the parties attempted to negotiate further amendments but were unable to reach an agreement. The district court's order granting summary judgment describes the negotiations in detail, which we find no need to repeat.

In March 2013, Hemlock sent Sachsen a "Shortfall Notice" that set forth the quantities of polysilicon that Sachsen had failed to purchase under the LTAs in 2012 and that demanded payment pursuant to the take-or-pay provision. Sachsen responded by insisting that it "did not fall short of any purchase obligations," that the parties had permanently amended the LTAs, and that Hemlock had waived the ability to enforce the LTAs. Two days later, Hemlock sued, seeking the full amount due under the liquidated-damages provision.

B. Procedural Background

Hemlock filed its complaint in the district court against Sachsen in March 2013. In its answer, Sachsen asserted 17 affirmative defenses, including illegality, commercial impracticability, and frustration of purpose. Hemlock moved to strike several of the affirmative defenses under Rule 12(f) of the Federal Rules of Civil Procedure. The court granted the motion in part, striking Sachsen's argument that the LTAs were illegal under European Union (E.U.) and German antitrust laws. Sachsen filed a motion for reconsideration of that decision, arguing that the court erroneously ignored one of Sachsen's arguments and misinterpreted the burden of proof under the E.U. antitrust laws at issue. The court denied the motion, concluding that despite these alleged errors, Sachsen's illegality defenses still lacked merit.

Hemlock subsequently filed a motion for summary judgment in its favor on its breach-of-contract claim. The district court granted the motion, concluding that all of Sachsen's remaining affirmative defenses were unavailing and that Hemlock was entitled to recover under the liquidated-damages provision. Judgment for the full amount of damages requested by Hemlock, as well as for prejudgment and post-judgment interest, was entered against Sachsen. In a separate order, the district court granted in part Hemlock's motion for attorney fees and costs.

Before us on this appeal are the district court's decisions to strike the illegality defense, to deny reconsideration of the decision to strike that defense, and to grant summary judgment to Hemlock. Sachsen has filed a separate appeal challenging the attorney-fee award.

II. Analysis

A. Standard of Review

Sachsen first argues that the district court improperly granted Hemlock's motion to strike Sachsen's affirmative defense of illegality, and that the district court subsequently erred in denying Sachsen's motion for reconsideration of that decision. Although "[m]otions to strike are viewed with disfavor," such motions are properly granted when "plaintiffs would succeed despite any state of the facts which could be proved in support of the defense." Operating Eng'rs Local 324 Health Care Plan, 783 F.3d 1045, 1050 (6th Cir. 2015). . . .

Sachsen next challenges the district court's grant of summary judgment to Hemlock. We review de novo the district court's grant of summary judgment.

Williams v. AT&T Mobility Servs., 847 F.3d 384, 391 (6th Cir. 2017). Summary judgment is proper when there is no genuine dispute of material fact and the moving party is entitled to judgment as a matter of law. Fed. R. Civ. P. 56(a). . . .

B. The District Court Did Not Abuse its Discretion in Striking Sachsen's Illegality Defense or in Denying Sachsen's Motion to Reconsider that Decision

Sachsen argues that the district court improperly struck its defense that the LTAs were illegal under E.U. and German antitrust law. According to Sachsen, the LTAs were illegal for two reasons. It first argues that the take-or-pay provision and a separate prohibition on resale are inextricably linked, and that the combination of the two is facially illegal under E.U. and German antitrust law. Second, Sachsen argues that the LTAs violated E.U. antitrust law by tying Sachsen's predominant demand for polysilicon to a single seller — Hemlock.

[The court noted that plaintiff Hemlock sought to enforce only the take-or-pay provision, not the prohibition on resale, and held that the former promise standing alone would not violate U.S. antitrust law. U.S. Supreme Court precedent dictated that the court should review for illegality only the particular promise that the plaintiff sought to enforce. The court also found that enforcing the take-or-pay provision alone was consistent with E.U. and German antitrust law. Similarly, the court concluded that defendant Sachsen failed to prove that the LTAs violated E.U. regulations that prohibited long-term "tying" contracts. The court thus found no error in the district court's decision to strike Sachsen's illegality defense. — EDS.]

C. The District Court Did Not Err in Concluding that Sachsen's Affirmative Defenses of Commercial Impracticability and Frustration of Purpose Lack Merit

Sachsen next argues that the district court erred in concluding that the doctrines of commercial impracticability and frustration of purpose do not excuse Sachsen's breach of contract. The theory underlying both defenses is that the Chinese government (1) illegally subsidized its national production of polysilicon and dumped massive quantities of the product onto the market, causing the price of polysilicon to fall; and (2) committed acts of "criminal industrial espionage" against Sachsen's U.S.-based sister company, SWIA. As a result of these illegal actions, Sachsen argues, the price of polysilicon plummeted, rendering Sachsen's performance impracticable and frustrating the purpose of entering into the LTAs.

We will assume without deciding that the alleged illegal actions by the Chinese government actually occurred. Hemlock does not in fact dispute Sachsen's evidence that these actions were deemed illegal by both U.S. and E.U. authorities. Rather, Hemlock argues that the district court properly rejected Sachsen's affirmative defenses because the drop in the price of polysilicon, regardless of cause, was simply a change in market conditions that does not excuse contract performance.

1. Sachsen's Commercial Impracticability Defense Lacks Merit

Sachsen asserts the affirmative defenses of commercial impracticability and impossibility. Both parties and the district court discuss these defenses interchangeably. We will therefore refer to these defenses collectively as "commercial impracticability."

Under Michigan law, a party charged with breaching a contract can assert as an affirmative defense that its performance was rendered impracticable. Capital One Bank USA N.A. v. Ponte, 2013 WL 6692511, at *10 (Mich. Ct. App. Dec. 19, 2013). Performance need not be impossible, but "there must be a showing of impracticability because of extreme and unreasonable difficulty, expense, injury or loss involved." Roberts v. Farmers Ins. Exch., 275 Mich.App. 58, 737 N.W.2d 332, 342 (2007). . . . The impracticability defense applies only if "an unanticipated circumstance has made performance of the promise vitally different from what should reasonably have been within the contemplation of both parties when they entered into the contract." *Capital One Bank*, 2013 WL 6692511, at *10. . . . In other words, the defense is viable only if an unforeseen event occurs and "the non-occurrence of that event [was] . . . a basic assumption on which both parties made the contract." Karl Wendt Farm Equip. Co. v. Int'l Harvester Co., 931 F.2d 1112, 1117 (6th Cir. 1991) (citing Restatement 2d of Contracts §261 cmt. b) (applying Michigan law).

The expectation that current market conditions will continue for the life of the contract is not such a basic assumption, so shifts in market prices ordinarily do not constitute impracticability. Id. Likewise, the simple fact that a contract has become unprofitable for one of the parties is generally insufficient to establish impracticability. Id. (citing Restatement 2d of Contracts §261 cmt. d). This is especially true when the parties have entered into a contract for the sale of goods at fixed prices because such contracts are made for the very purpose of establishing a stable price despite a fluctuating market. Chainworks, Inc. v. Webco Indus., Inc., 2006 WL 461251, at *10 (W.D. Mich. Feb. 24, 2006) (citing Mich. Comp. Laws §440.2615 cmt. 4 ("Neither is a rise or a collapse in the market itself a justification [for asserting the impracticability defense], for that is exactly the type of business risk which business contracts made at fixed prices are intended to cover.")).

Even relatively drastic changes in the market have been held insufficient to trigger the impracticability defense. In Karl Wendt Farm Equipment Co. v. International Harvester Co., 931 F.2d 1112, 1117 (6th Cir. 1991), for example, this court concluded that the Michigan Supreme Court would not apply the impracticability defense when International Harvester (IH) "experienced a dramatic downturn in the farm equipment market," decided to go out of business, and breached a dealership agreement by unilaterally terminating it. Id. The court rejected IH's argument that impracticability excused its contractual duties under circumstances where IH was losing over two million dollars per day. Id. Although the market shift was drastic, it did not alter the parties' basic assumptions underlying the contract. Id. at 1117–18. The court also noted that applying the doctrine of impracticability would contravene the parties' intentions regarding assumption of the risk. Id. at 1118. Because the contract provided for termination procedures in the event that certain conditions occurred, the court concluded that IH had to bear the risk of financial loss until those procedures were completed; excusing IH's performance would therefore have unfairly burdened the plaintiff dealer. See id. at 1114, 1118.

Similarly, a district court applying Michigan law concluded that a defendant could not assert an impracticability defense based on the economic downturn of 2008. See Flathead-Michigan I, LLC v. Penninsula Dev., LLC, 2011 WL 940048, at *3–4 (E.D. Mich. Mar. 16, 2011). The fact that the 2008 market collapse and the ensuing recession were unusually disastrous economic shifts did not excuse the defendant's performance, the court reasoned, because "[t]he state of the market is one of the things on which the parties are gambling when the contract . . . is made." Id. at *4 (quoting Seaboard Lumber Co. v. United States, 41 Fed. Cl. 401, 417 (Fed. Cl. 1998)).

Sachsen, however, argues that the impracticability defense should apply because the illegal actions of the Chinese government caused an out-of-the-ordinary drop in the market price for polysilicon. According to Sachsen, the fact that a third party's illegal actions allegedly caused this market shift differentiates the present case from *Karl Wendt* and other cases finding that changes in market conditions are not a basis for the impracticability defense.

The district court disagreed, reasoning that the allegedly illegal actions of the Chinese government were irrelevant because they had "simply caused a market shift in pricing, making it unprofitable for [Sachsen] to perform as promised." In so ruling, the court incorporated its reasoning from the court's decision in Hemlock's case against another company, Kyocera, under a nearly identical LTA. See Hemlock Semiconductor Corp. v. Kyocera Corp., 2016 WL 67596, at *4 (E.D. Mich. Jan. 6, 2016). Because Sachsen's argument "amount[ed] only to claims of 'economic unprofitableness,'" the court concluded that the impracticability defense did not apply for the reasons stated in *Karl Wendt*. See id. at *4.

We find the district court's reasoning persuasive. Our research has not revealed any caselaw from either this court or the Michigan courts supporting the proposition that a third party's illegal actions can render the performance of a contract impracticable. Hemlock and Sachsen presumably would not have specifically foreseen the allegedly illegal actions of the Chinese government when the parties entered into the LTAs. But the possibility that the market price for polysilicon could skyrocket or plummet for a myriad of reasons would have been well within their contemplation. The fact that the LTAs provided a fixed price for polysilicon suggests that the parties anticipated that the market price could change and that they wanted to establish a stable price that would operate independently of the market. See *Chainworks*, 2006 WL 461251, at *10. Allowing Sachsen to escape its obligation to pay that price simply because the purported illegal actions contributed to the price drop would be unfair to Hemlock.

Applying the impracticability defense here could also open up a flood of similar arguments based on allegedly illegal actions of third parties. In the context of global market fluctuations, which can be affected by the actions of many businesses from different countries, defendants in breach-of-contract cases could easily claim that a violation of the law by a third-party actor contributed to a market shift. Allowing parties to litigate the causes of market shifts would swallow the general rule that a contract's unprofitability does not warrant application of the impracticality defense.

We also note that Sachsen could have protected itself against a large drop in the market price of polysilicon during the 14-year term of the LTAs by requiring a renegotiation if the market price dropped a certain percentage or dollar amount below the contract price. But no such condition was included in the LTAs despite the sophistication of both the parties and their lawyers. Sachsen thus knowingly assumed the unfiltered risk of a drop in price for a high-tech product during a long-term, fixed-price contract.

2. Sachsen's Frustration-of-Purpose Defense Also Lacks Merit

Sachsen makes the related argument that the Chinese government's illegal actions frustrated Sachsen's purpose in entering into the LTAs. Frustration of purpose and impracticability are "overlapping defenses." *Flathead-Michigan I*, 2011 WL 940048, at *4. Both defenses require proof that an unforeseen event altered "a basic assumption on which the contract was made." Liggett Rest. Grp., Inc. v. City of Pontiac, 260 Mich. App. 127, 676 N.W.2d 633, 637 (2003) (quoting Restatement 2d of Contracts §265, cmt. a). The frustration-of-purpose defense also requires that the unforeseen event thwart the parties' purpose in making the contract to such a degree that "one party's performance [becomes] virtually worthless to the other." Id. Like the impracticability defense, the frustration-of-purpose defense generally cannot be based on an argument that the continuation of existing market conditions was a "basic assumption" on which the contract was made. Karl Wendt Farm Equip. Co. v. Int'l Harvester Co., 931 F.2d 1112, 1119–20 (6th Cir. 1991). And courts usually will not assume that "mutual profitability" was the primary purpose of a contract. Id.

The frustration-of-purpose defense is inapplicable to the present case for the same reasons that the impracticability defense is inapplicable. Sachsen points to no evidence that the "primary purpose" of the LTAs was anything other than what the district court found it to be—"for Hemlock to provide [Sachsen] with a stable supply of polysilicon at a predictable price." The court incorporated its reasoning from the court's earlier decision in *Kyocera*. See 2016 WL 67596, at *5. Sachsen's frustration-of-purpose argument essentially amounts to a claim that "mutual profitability" was the purpose of the LTAs. But this argument is unconvincing in light of the fact that the LTAs establish a fixed price under which either party could suffer depending on the relationship of the market price to the LTA price.

3. Sachsen's Attempts to Distinguish Kyocera and to Rely on an Out-of-State Case Are Unavailing

Sachsen next argues that the present case is distinguishable from the decision in *Kyocera*, which the district court incorporated into its decision granting summary judgment to Hemlock. This case is different, Sachsen insists, because (1) *Kyocera* was decided at the motion-to-dismiss stage, not at the summary-judgment stage, so there was less evidence in the record; and (2) the Chinese government's industrial espionage specifically targeted Sachsen's sister company, whereas the only illegal actions affecting the *Kyocera* defendant were the subsidization and dumping of polysilicon. The difference in procedural stages, however, is unhelpful to Sachsen because its defenses fail as a matter of law for the same reasons that the court in *Kyocera* dismissed the defendant's counterclaims. And Sachsen has pointed to no evidence that the industrial espionage aimed at its sister company caused it to suffer anything more than the same drop in market prices that was at issue in *Kyocera*.

Sachsen also relies on Chang v. Pacificorp, 212 Or. App. 14, 157 P.3d 243 (2007), an Oregon Court of Appeals decision concluding that the defendant had established a genuine issue of material fact on its impracticability and frustration-of-purpose defenses. In *Chang*, the defendant asserted these defenses based on a third party's illegal manipulation of the Dow COB index, an index of market prices for electricity in the relevant geographic area. Id. at 246. The contract at issue in *Chang* relied on the index in setting prices. Id.

Hemlock convincingly points out that *Chang* is distinguishable because (1) the parties' very purpose in adopting the contract provision in that case was to use the index to allocate risks, and (2) that purpose was frustrated when the index ceased to accurately reflect the true market price for electricity in the relevant geographic area. Here, the contract price was fixed specifically to avoid market fluctuations, just the opposite of the pricing mechanism in *Chang*. We thus agree that *Chang* is readily distinguishable. In sum, the district court did not err in rejecting Sachsen's impracticability and frustration-of-purpose defenses.

D. The District Court Did Not Err in Awarding Hemlock the Full Amount of the Remaining Contract Price as Liquidated Damages, Despite Sachsen's Argument that the Award Was an Unreasonable Penalty

Sections 5 and 10(b) of LTAs I–III and section 11(c)(iii)(C) of LTA IV provide that, in the event of a breach by Sachsen and termination by Hemlock, the full balance of the contract price for the entire remaining term of the LTAs will be awarded to Hemlock as liquidated damages. Accordingly, after granting summary judgment to Hemlock on its breach-of-contract claim, the district court awarded Hemlock damages in the total amount of $793,467,822.91. This amount included the entire outstanding balance due Hemlock for the full term of each of the LTAs—$585,361,500—plus prejudgment interest. The district court also awarded Hemlock post-judgment interest on the principal amount at the contractually mandated interest rate.

Sachsen does not dispute that the judgment accurately reflects the outstanding balance or the interest thereon. Instead, Sachsen argues that the LTAs' provision for the award of the full outstanding balance constitutes an unenforceable penalty rather than permissible liquidated damages.

[The court first noted that under Michigan law, liquidated damages provisions are enforceable if the agreed amount is reasonably intended to compensate for injury suffered and it is not unconscionable or excessive. Additionally, liquidated damages are deemed especially appropriate where the potential damages from breach are uncertain and difficult to anticipate when the contract is made. Finally, the court found that the contract language expressly contemplated that Hemlock would invest substantial amounts of capital in expanding its manufacturing facilities to fulfill the contract and the liquidated damages provision would address those costs in the event of breach by Sachsen. Thus, the court concluded that the liquidated damages provision was not an unenforceable penalty. — EDS.]

III. CONCLUSION

For all of the reasons set forth above, we **AFFIRM** the judgment of the district court.

NOTES AND QUESTIONS

1. *Comparison of impracticability and frustration doctrines.* While the doctrines of impracticability of performance and frustration of purpose are separate grounds for relief from a contract, the elements of the doctrines are nearly identical. In fact, Professor Farnsworth refers to the Restatement synthesis of the two doctrines as "strikingly similar." E. Allan Farnsworth, Contracts §9.7, at 635 (4th ed. 2004). The doctrines require the disadvantaged party to show: (1) either an extreme change in the nature of performance ("performance is made impracticable") or an extreme reduction in the value of the other party's performance so as to render it nearly worthless ("a party's principal purpose is frustrated"); (2) the occurrence of an event, the nonoccurrence of which was a basic assumption of the contract; (3) without the party's fault; and (4) the party seeking relief does not bear the risk of that event's occurrence either under the language of the contract or the surrounding circumstances. Compare Restatement (Second) §§261 (impracticability) and 265 (frustration of purpose). UCC §2-615 is similar and would apply to the sale of goods contract in *Hemlock*.

The *Hemlock* court found the defendant's claim of impracticability to be unavailing for a number of reasons, including a lack of proof that the nature of the party's performance had drastically changed due to the drop in the market price for the goods. The court also noted that there was not a basic assumption that market price would not change. Rather, in setting a fixed price for a long-term contract, the parties specifically contemplated that there might be fluctuations in the market and allocated the risks that prices might go up or down.

In a more succinct discussion, the *Hemlock* court found that the primary purpose of the contract was a stable supply of goods at a predictable price and that there was no frustration of that purpose. The *Mel Frank* case which follows below further illustrates application of the frustration doctrine.

2. *Performance is made impracticable.* As the *Hemlock* court discusses, for performance to be impracticable, it must involve "extreme and unreasonable difficulty" that renders performance of the promise "vitally different" from what the parties contemplated at the time the contract was made. The court cites a number of cases in which a substantial change in circumstances has been held insufficient to establish impracticability. See also John E. Murray, Jr., Murray

on Contracts, §113, at 712-713 (5th ed. 2011) (noting that it is very difficult to convince a court to excuse a contract due to a significant increase in the cost of performance, even if unforeseeable and caused by factors beyond the promisor's control). The notes below also underscore the difficulty of satisfying this element of the impracticability defense.

As noted in the text before the *Hemlock* case, however, the seminal impracticability case, Mineral Park Land Co. v. Howard, did grant relief due to a tremendous increase in cost of performance (10 to 12 times greater than anticipated) resulting from unexpected developments. Other courts occasionally find impracticability resulting from an unexpected event that causes an overwhelming increase in the cost of performance. See, e.g., Cape-France Enterprises v. Estate of Peed, 29 P.3d 1011 (Mont. 2001) (impracticability excuse granted after notice from government that underground water pollution plume had spread near seller's land and that the drilling of a test well required by land sale contract could exacerbate groundwater contamination and expose seller to liability for "unquantifiable" amount of clean-up costs); Iannuccillo v. Material Sand & Stone Corp., 713 A.2d 1234 (R.I. 1998) (excuse granted for impracticability after discovery of unanticipated rock in area designated for excavation would have effectively increased cost of performance from $5,000 to about $65,000). Successful impracticability cases remain rare.

3. *Failure of basic assumption of contract — market failure.* To obtain relief under the doctrine of impracticability, the obligor must show that a basic assumption of the contract proved to be wrong due to a change in circumstances. As the *Hemlock* court indicates, relying primarily on its earlier decision in the *Karl Wendt* case, continuation of market conditions is generally not such an assumption because parties should know that markets often change dramatically. See, e.g., CRS Proppants LLC v. Preferred Resin Holding Co., LLC, 2016 WL 6094167 (Del. Super. Ct.) (contract requiring buyer to purchase stated quantities of fracking sand not excused by alleged 50% drop in market demand and 40% drop in price that would result in buyer loss of $6 million per quarter; downturn in oil and gas market was foreseeable and buyer assumed risk); Brewer v. J-Six Farms, L.P., 350 P.3d 420 (Okla. Civ. App. 2015) (depression in hog market did not excuse payment of less than contract price under doctrine of impracticability in UCC §2-615). The *Hemlock* court rejected the defendant's argument that the alleged conduct of a foreign government that affected the market price was the relevant change in circumstances. Instead, the court held that the change in market price itself was the pertinent factor, regardless of the cause. Are you persuaded that the court properly identified the correct change in circumstances?

4. *Natural disaster or war as a basis for relief.* Natural disaster or war has been the basis for claims of relief from a contract under the doctrines of impracticability and frustration, but here also the courts have been generally unwilling to grant relief. E.g., American Trading & Production Corp. v. Shell International Marine, Ltd., 453 F.2d 939 (2d Cir. 1972) (shipowners denied relief for increased expense under doctrine of impracticability when Suez Canal was closed due to

war; while parties contemplated use of Suez Canal, that route was not basic assumption of contract and shippers were required to use alternative means when contemplated route became impracticable); Thrifty Rent-A-Car Systems, Inc. v. South Florida Transport, Inc., 2005 U.S. Dist. Lexis 38489 (N.D. Okla.) (nonoccurrence of hurricanes was not a basic assumption of rental car licensing agreement for business located in Florida; contract not excused by multiple storms). But see Opera Company of Boston, Inc. v. Wolf Trap Foundation for the Performing Arts, 817 F.2d 1094 (4th Cir. 1987) (impracticability established when electrical storm caused power outage and safety concerns that led to cancellation of outdoor performance; dissenting judge would have denied relief because Wolf Trap failed to provide for auxiliary power equipment and neglected to include contractual provision providing for relief due to power outage).

5. *Impracticability based on terrorism.* A variation of an impracticability claim based on war or hostilities can be found in a case related to the September 11, 2001, terrorist attack on the World Trade Center in New York City. In Bush v. ProTravel International, Inc., 746 N.Y.S. 2d 790 (Civ. Ct. 2002), the plaintiff sought refund of a $1,500 deposit on a planned honeymoon safari trip scheduled for November 2001 even though the contract provided for refund of the deposit only if cancellation notice was received by September 14, 2001, and the plaintiff's cancellation was not received until September 27, at the earliest. The plaintiff sought to excuse the late cancellation notice on grounds of impracticability due to travel and communication difficulties in New York City in the aftermath of September 11. In denying the defendants' motion for summary judgment, the court noted that in addition to New York City being under a government-imposed state of emergency in the days immediately following September 11, the plaintiff alleged that damage to telephone systems made it almost physically impossible to place a telephone call from Staten Island, where the plaintiff had retreated, to the travel agent's office in Manhattan. The court thus decided that the plaintiff should have the opportunity to prove temporary impossibility that would have suspended the cancellation date. Id. at 797. (See Restatement (Second) §269 on temporary impracticability and frustration.)

In *Bush*, the defendant travel companies asserted that the plaintiff was simply "skiddish [sic] to travel after September 11," and that such concerns were an insufficient basis to excuse performance under the contract. Id. at 794. Should fears for personal safety after a terrorist attack constitute a valid basis for a claim of impracticability? See Restatement (Second) Contracts §261, Comment *d* (performance may be impracticable because it will involve a risk of injury to person or property); but see 7200 Scottsdale Road General Partners v. Kuhn Farm Machinery, 909 P.2d 408 (Ariz. Ct. App. 1995) (conference organizer's good faith apprehension of terrorism danger to attendees traveling by domestic airlines because of 1991 United States involvement in hostilities in Iraq was not substantial enough to rise to the level of impracticability or frustration and excuse late cancellation of hotel; perception of danger must be "objectively reasonable").

6. *Destruction of thing or death of person necessary for performance.* Where the difficulty in performance stems not merely from unprofitability of the enterprise, however, but from the physical impossibility or difficulty of performance, there is somewhat more likelihood of excuse. If a particular person or thing is necessary for performance, the death or incapacity of the person, or the destruction of the thing, will excuse performance. Restatement (Second) §262 (death or incapacity of person); Restatement (Second) §263 (destruction of thing); UCC §2-613 (casualty to identified goods). See, e.g., CNA International Reinsurance Co. v. Phoenix, 678 So. 2d 378 (Fla. Dist. Ct. App. 1996) (whether or not drug usage contributed to death of actor River Phoenix, rule that death constitutes excusing impossibility of personal service contract would be applied); Hilton Oil Transport v. Oil Transport Co., 659 So. 2d 1141 (Fla. Dist. Ct. App. 1995) (tug charter contract would not be discharged by seizure of both tug and charterer's barge in a commercial dispute, but would be discharged by subsequent destruction of barge during storm). Cf. Warner v. Kaplan, 892 N.Y.S.2d 311 (App. Div. 2009) (death of buyer before close of escrow would not discharge contract to purchase cooperative apartment).

7. *Role of foreseeability.* What part should the element of "foreseeability" play in the court's application of the doctrines of frustration or impracticability, as reflected in either the common law or the Uniform Commercial Code? Some courts have tended to require a showing that the event complained of was at least unforeseen — perhaps even unforeseeable — at the time the parties made their contract. Reflecting the traditional preference for self-protection over paternalism (it should be recalled that the parties seeking excuse in these cases tend to be significant commercial enterprises, not consumers or "Mom and Pop" stores), some courts have felt that any party who can foresee an adverse event has the burden of contracting for protection against it. See, e.g., Sunshine Imp & Exp Corp. v. Luxury Car Concierge, Inc., 2015 U.S. Dist. LEXIS 60034 (N.D. Ill.) (frustration of purpose, like impossibility, hinges on the foreseeability of the event that is the claimed basis of excuse). Most courts, however, have held that relief under the doctrines of impracticability or frustration of purpose should not be denied simply because the event may have been foreseeable. As one court explained:

> Foreseeability or even recognition of a risk does not necessarily prove its allocation. Parties to a contract are not always able to provide for all the possibilities of which they are aware, sometimes because they cannot agree, often simply because they are too busy. Moreover, that some abnormal risk was contemplated is probative but does not necessarily establish an allocation of the risk of the contingency which actually occurs.

Transatlantic Financing Corp. v. United States, 363 F.2d 312, 318 (D.C. Cir. 1966). See also Ner Tamid Congregation v. Krivoruchko, 638 F. Supp. 2d 913 (N.D. Ill. 2009) (noting that "unforeseeability" is question of degree and whether parties could have guarded against contingency; court rejects argument that housing market downturn of 2007 and its impact on real estate financing was unforeseeable); Comment *c* to Restatement (Second) §261 (other factors may explain failure to expressly contract against foreseeable risk). The UCC does not in §2-615 expressly impose an "unforeseeability" requirement, although Comment 1 to §2-615 does refer to "unforeseen supervening events."

8. ***Hemlock*** *and the CISG.* Given that the seller (Hemlock) was a U.S. corporation and that the buyer (Sachsen) was a German company, and that both of those countries are parties to the CISG, the question would logically arise whether the CISG should have provided the applicable law for the sale of goods contracts dispute. While both the appellate court and the trial court clearly applied Michigan substantive law, neither court expressly addressed the choice of law question. See Hemlock Semiconductor Corp. v. Deutsche Solar GmbH, 116 F. Supp. 3d 818 (E.D. Mich. 2015) (trial court opinion). You may recall from the discussion of the CISG in Chapter 2 that parties can elect to exclude its application under Article 6. Indeed, inquiry with counsel for Hemlock confirmed that the contracts included a choice-of-law provision designating Michigan state law as governing and specifically disclaiming the CISG.

Would the case have come out differently under the CISG? The relevant provision would have been Article 79(1) which reads:

> A party is not liable for a failure to perform any of his obligations if he proves that the failure was due to an impediment beyond his control and that he could not reasonably be expected to have taken the impediment into account at the time of the conclusion of the contract or to have avoided or overcome it or its consequences.

While there are some obvious similarities between Article 79(1) and U.S. domestic law, there may be room for distinctions as well. See Larry A. DiMatteo, Contractual Excuse Under the CISG: Impediment, Hardship, and the Excuse Doctrines, 27 Pace Int'l L. Rev. 261, 277-278, 298-299 (2015) (noting that Article 79 drafting history reflects an intention to differentiate excuse of "impediment" from very restrictive domestic excuse doctrines, but that case law to date has tended not to recognize severe increases in production costs or market prices as excuses for nonperformance under the CISG).

9. *Economic analysis of impracticability.* In an important article applying principles of economic analysis to the doctrines of impracticability and frustration of purpose, Professors Posner and Rosenfeld argued that the doctrines should be applied to assign the risk of the event to the "superior risk bearer." When the contract specifically allocates the risk to a party, that party is the superior risk bearer. In the absence of a contractual provision, the risk should be assigned to the party who is in the best position to prevent the event from occurring, or if prevention is not possible, to minimize its consequences at the lowest cost, typically by purchasing insurance. Richard A. Posner & Andrew M. Rosenfeld, Impossibility and Related Doctrines in Contract Law: An Economic Analysis, 6 J. Legal Stud. 83 (1977). Judge Posner applied this approach in Northern Indiana Public Service Co. v. Carbon County Coal Co., 799 F.2d 265 (7th Cir. 1986), to deny relief to a power company that sought to avoid a fixed-price contract for the purchase of coal due to escalating market prices. He held that

a fixed-price contract is "an explicit assignment of the risk of market price increases to the seller and the risk of market price decreases to the buyer." Id. at 278. Judge Posner contrasted the case before him with ones involving the destruction of crops:

> Suppose a grower agrees before the growing season to sell his crop to a grain elevator, and the crop is destroyed by blight and the grain elevator sues. Discharge is ordinarily allowed in such cases. The grower has every incentive to avoid the blight; so if it occurs, it probably could not have been prevented; and the grain elevator, which buys from a variety of growers not all of whom will be hit by blight in the same growing season, is in the better position to buffer the risk of blight than the grower is.

Id. Do you agree with this approach? Why? How would it apply to *Hemlock*?

It might be noted, incidentally, that despite the above-stated assumption by Judge Posner that excuse is (and should be, according to his analysis) "ordinarily allowed" in cases of crop destruction, some courts have been surprisingly stingy with excuse in such cases. E.g., Clark v. Wallace County Cooperative Equity Exchange, 986 P.2d 391 (Kan. Ct. App. 1999) (farmer not excused from contract to sell quantity of corn based on freeze which severely damaged his crop; corn to be delivered under contract was not specified to come from his land). The UCC in Comment 9 to §2-615 suggests that crop failure may be regarded as excusing either under that section or under §2-613 ("Casualty to Identified Goods") where a farmer has contracted to sell "crops to be grown on designated land."

10. *Decision by judge or jury.* The Restatement takes the position that a defense such as mistake, impracticability, or frustration of purpose should be decided by the court as a question of law, rather than being submitted to a jury for a finding of fact. The Restatement explains that treating the doctrines as a question of law will contribute to "stability and predictability of contractual relations." Restatement (Second) of Contracts, §212, Comment *d.* Do you think having the courts assess claims of impracticability contributes, rightly or wrongly, to the frequent lack of success for the claimants on the grounds noted above?

Mel Frank Tool & Supply, Inc. v. Di-Chem Co.

Supreme Court of Iowa 580 N.W.2d 802 (1998)

Considered by McGiverin, C.J., and Harris, Lavorato, Snell, and Andreasen, JJ.

Lavorato, Justice.

City authorities informed a lessee, a chemical distributor, that it could no longer use its leased premises to store its hazardous chemicals because of a recently enacted ordinance. The lessee vacated the premises, and the lessor sued for breach of the lease and for damages to the premises. The district court awarded the lessor judgment for unpaid rent and for damages to the premises. The lessee appeals, contending that the district court should have found that the city's actions constituted extraordinary circumstances rendering the performance of the lease impossible. The lessee also contends that language in the lease releases it from liability. In addition, the lessee challenges a district court finding that a real estate agent represented the lessee and prepared the lease on its behalf. We affirm.

I. Facts

Di-Chem Company is a chemical distributor. In May 1994, Di-Chem began negotiating with Mel Frank Tool & Supply, Inc. to lease a storage and distribution facility in Council Bluffs, Iowa. Mel Frank's real estate agent handled the negotiations so there were no actual face-to-face negotiations between the parties. However, a day before the lease was executed, Mel Frank's owner, Dennis Frank, talked with Di-Chem representatives who were touring the premises. Frank asked them what Di-Chem was going to be selling and was told chemicals. The agent brought the lease to Frank for his signature.

The lease appears to be an Iowa State Bar Association form. See Iowa State Bar Association Official Form No. 164. The lease was to start June 1, 1994 and end May 31, 1997. The lease limited Di-Chem's use of the premises to "storage and distribution."

Some of the chemicals Di-Chem distributes are considered "hazardous material." There was no testimony that Dennis Frank was aware of this at the time the lease was executed. A Di-Chem representative, who was present during the earlier-mentioned conversation with Dennis Frank, testified that hazardous materials did not come up in the conversation.

The lease contained several provisions that bear on the issues in this appeal. One requires Di-Chem to "make no unlawful use of the premises and . . . to comply with all . . . City Ordinances." There is also a destruction-of-premises provision that allows either party to terminate the lease under certain circumstances.

On July 21, 1995, the city's fire chief and several other city authorities inspected the premises. Following the inspection, the city's fire marshal wrote Di-Chem, stating:

> At the time of the inspection the building was occupied as Hazardous Materials Storage. I have given you a copy of 1994 Uniform Fire Code, which the City has adopted, covering Hazardous Material Storage. As you can see the building does not comply with the Code requirements which creates Health and Life Safety Hazards. The Hazardous Materials must be removed within seven (7) days to eliminate the hazard.

The letter also informed Di-Chem of the following code deficiencies: complete fire sprinkler system, mechanical exhaust system, spill control, and drainage control. Both Frank and Di-Chem representatives testified they understood the letter to mean that if these deficiencies were eliminated, Di-Chem could continue to store hazardous material. There was testimony that the changes in the code occurred after Di-Chem took occupancy of the premises.

On August 2 Di-Chem informed Mel Frank by letter of the city's action and enclosed a copy of the city's July 25 letter to Di-Chem. In its August 2 letter Di-Chem informed Mel Frank of its intention to re-locate "as soon as possible to avoid civil and criminal proceedings at the hands of the city." Di-Chem also stated

> we believe the city has overreacted and probably has no authority to order us to remove our materials from the property. . . . Nevertheless, we are not willing to contest the city's position, and we feel compelled to remove our operation beyond the city limits.

Di-Chem also stated it intended to pay the rental for the month of August and vacate the premises by September 1.

Thereafter Dennis Frank and Di-Chem representatives met with city officials about what it would take to correct the various code deficiencies to allow Di-Chem to continue storing hazardous materials. Di-Chem representatives and Dennis Frank briefly considered bringing the building up to code. There was talk about the possibility of Di-Chem splitting the costs with Mel Frank, but Dennis Frank felt the cost was prohibitive.

On October 23 Di-Chem notified Mel Frank by letter of its intention to vacate the premises by the end of October. The letter in part stated: "The city's position that we cannot legally store all of our inventory at this site prior to extensive alteration of the building makes the structure useless to us as a chemical warehouse." True to its word, Di-Chem vacated the premises.

II. Proceedings

Later, Mel Frank sued for breach of the lease and for damages to the property. Di-Chem asserted several affirmative defenses: mutual mistake, illegal contract, failure to mitigate damages, fraud in the inducement, and impossibility.

The parties tried the case to the court. In its ruling the court stated the issue this way:

> The principal issue to be determined is whether the defendant may voluntarily terminate the lease agreement based upon defendant's position that the warehouse could not be used for storing hazardous materials [resulting from] the inspection of various departments of the City of Council Bluffs. The conclusion of this issue must be based upon the intention of the litigating parties as well as the terms and conditions of the written lease agreement.

The court found for Mel Frank. The court found that Mel Frank had "no reason to believe or [know] that chemicals classified as hazardous would be stored in the warehouse." The court relied on the testimony of Norm Wirtala, an officer of Di-Chem:

> Mr. Wirtala testified he would be in a "superior position of knowledge" concerning the items to be stored in the building and that he had a general understanding of fire code requirements for the storage of hazardous materials due to his experience in the business although [neither] he nor his agents claimed to have examined the Council Bluffs' fire codes as they may have related to

> hazardous materials and building specifications for storage of hazardous materials.

With this the court concluded that there was

> clear and conclusive [evidence] that the plaintiff made no representations to the defendant that the warehouse was suitable for any specific purpose, nor were any discussions or representations made concerning the character of the products to be stored by the defendant. Consequently, this Court concludes the lease was breached by the defendants for vacating the premises and failing to pay the balance of the lease term as required by its terms and conditions and the defendants owe the sum of $55,913.77 for rent [and $2,357.00 for damage to the property].

III. Scope of Review

The action here was one at law. Our review is therefore for correction of errors. Iowa R. App. P. 4. The district court's findings of fact have the force of a special jury verdict and are binding if supported by substantial evidence. See Iowa R. App. P. 14(f)(1). Evidence is substantial if a reasonable mind could find it adequate to reach the same finding. Pierce v. Farm Bureau Mut. Ins. Co., 548 N.W.2d 551, 553 (Iowa 1996). We are not, however, bound by the district court's application of legal principles or the court's conclusions of law. Hagan v. Val-Hi, Inc., 484 N.W.2d 173, 175 (Iowa 1992).

IV. Impossibility of Performance

A. The Law

The introduction to the Restatement (Second) of Contracts covers impossibility of performance but with a different title: impracticability of performance and frustration of purpose. See Restatement (Second) of Contracts ch. 11, at 309 (1981) [hereinafter Restatement]. According to the Restatement,

> [c]ontract liability is strict liability. . . . The obligor is therefore liable in damages for breach of contract even if he is without fault and even if circumstances have made the contract more burdensome or less desirable than he had anticipated. . . . The obligor who does not wish to undertake so extensive an obligation may contract for a lesser one by using one of a variety of common clauses: . . . he may reserve a right to cancel the contract. . . . The extent of his obligation then depends on the application of the rules of interpretation. . . .

Id.

Even though the obligor has not restricted his or her obligation by agreement, a court may still grant relief: "An extraordinary circumstance may make performance so vitally different from what was reasonably to be expected as to alter the essential nature of that performance." Id. In these circumstances, "the court must determine whether justice requires a departure from the general rule that the obligor bear the risk that the contract may become more burdensome or less desirable." Id. at 310. Whether extraordinary circumstances exist justifying discharge is a question of law for the court. Id.

The Restatement recognizes three distinct grounds for the discharge of the obligor's contractual duty:

> First, the obligor may claim that some circumstance has made his own performance impracticable. . . . Second, the obligor may claim that some circumstance has so destroyed the value to him of the other party's performance as to frustrate his own purpose in making the contract. . . . Third, the obligor may claim that he will not receive the agreed exchange for the obligee's duty to render that agreed exchange, on the ground of either impracticability or frustration.

Id.

The rationale behind the doctrines of impracticability and frustration is whether the nonoccurrence of the circumstance was a basic assumption on which the contract was made. Restatement (Second) of Contracts ch. 11, at 310-311 (1981). The parties need not have been conscious of alternatives for them to have had a "basic assumption." Restatement (Second) of Contracts ch. 11, at 311 (1981). The Restatement gives an example: Where an artist contracts to paint a painting and dies, the artist's death is an "event the nonoccurrence of which was a basic assumption on which the contract was made, even though the parties never consciously addressed themselves to that possibility." Id.

Under the Restatement's rationale,

> the obligor is relieved of his duty because the contract, having been made on a different "basic assumption," is regarded as not covering the case that has arisen. It is an omitted case, falling within a "gap" in the contract. Ordinarily, the just way to deal with the omitted case is to hold that the obligor's duty is discharged, in the case of changed circumstances, or has never arisen, in the case of existing circumstances, and to shift the risk to the obligee.

Id.

B. Discharge by Supervening Frustration

For reasons that follow, we think the facts of this case fall within the parameters of section 265 of the Restatement. Section 265 provides:

> Where, after a contract is made, a party's principal purpose is substantially frustrated without his fault by the occurrence of an event the nonoccurrence of which was a basic assumption on which the contract was made, his remaining duties to render performance are discharged, *unless the language or the circumstances indicate the contrary.*

(Emphasis added.) . . .

The rule deals with the problem that arises when a change in circumstances makes one party's performance virtually worthless to the other, frustrating the purpose in making the contract. Id. §265 cmt. a, at 335. The obligor's contractual obligation is discharged only if three conditions are met:

> First, the purpose that is frustrated must have been a principal purpose of that party in making the contract. It is not enough that he had in mind some specific object without which he would not have made the contract. The object must be so completely the basis of the contract that, as both parties understand,

> without it the transaction would make little sense. *Second, the frustration must be substantial. It is not enough that the transaction has become less profitable for the affected party or even that he will sustain a loss. The frustration must be so severe that it is not fairly to be regarded as within the risks that he assumed under the contract.* Third, the non-occurrence of the frustrating event must have been a basic assumption on which the contract was made. . . . The foreseeability of the event is . . . a factor in that determination, but the mere fact that the event was foreseeable does not compel the conclusion that its non-occurrence was not such a basic assumption.

Id. (emphasis added).

Under this Restatement section, the following pertinent illustration appears:

> A leases a gasoline station to B. A change in traffic regulations so reduces B's business that he is unable to operate the station except at a substantial loss. B refuses to make further payments of rent. If B can still operate the station, even though at such a loss, his principal purpose of operating a gasoline station is not substantially frustrated. B's duty to pay rent is not discharged, and B is liable to A for breach of contract. The result would be the same if substantial loss were caused instead by a government regulation rationing gasoline or a termination of the franchise under which B obtained gasoline.

Id. §265 cmt. a, illus. 6, at 336.

Iowa case law is in accord with Restatement section 265. See Conklin v. Silver, 187 Iowa 819, 822-823, 174 N.W. 573, 574 (1919). The facts in *Conklin* parallel those in illustration 6 set out above.

In *Conklin,* the lease provided that the lessees were "to only use the premises for iron, metal, and rag business." Id. at 820, 174 N.W. at 573. The lease also prohibited the lessees from "engaging in or permitting any unlawful business on the premises, nor to permit the premises to be occupied for any business deemed extra hazardous on account of fire." Id.

About a month into the lease, the Iowa legislature passed a statute declaring as a nuisance the storage of rags "within the fire limits of any city, unless it be in a building of fireproof construction." Id. at 821, 174 N.W. at 573. The statute applied to the lessees because the premises were within the fire limits of the city and were not of fireproof construction. Id. For this reason, the lessees claimed the statute made its business unlawful, exposed them to criminal prosecution, and deprived them of any substantial or beneficial use of the property thereby releasing them from further obligation to pay rent. Id.

This court rejected the lessees' contention and affirmed a directed verdict in favor of the plaintiff-lessor for the unpaid rent. There was evidence that the lessee also dealt in junk metal. For this reason the court concluded:

> Altogether, we are satisfied that, while the operation of the statute mentioned served to narrow or restrict, to some extent, the scope of the business of the lessees, we think the evidence is insufficient to sustain a finding that it deprives them of the beneficial use of the leased property; and, as the defense is an affirmative one, the burden of establishing which is upon the party pleading it, the trial court did not err in refusing to submit it to the verdict of the jury.

Id. at 822, 174 N.W. at 574. The court continued:

> The right to buy, sell, store, and ship junk metals of all kinds, not only in the building but upon the entire lot, is not, in any sense, a mere incident of the rag business, and that a loss of the privilege of using the building for the handling of rags does not deprive the lessees of the beneficial enjoyment of the property for the other specified uses. It may possibly render the use less valuable or less profitable, but there is no rule or principle of law which makes that fact a matter of defense or of counterclaim in an action upon the lease.

187 Iowa at 822-23, 174 N.W. at 574.

The Restatement and *Conklin* represent the prevailing view:

> The parties to a lease may lawfully agree or stipulate that if by reason of a subsequent prohibitory or restrictive statute, ordinance, or administrative ruling, the tenant is prevented from legally using the premises for the purpose for which it was contemplated, the tenant may surrender or terminate the lease for which it was contemplated and be relieved from further liability for rent. In the absence of such a provision for termination, however, there is some uncertainty as to the effect of subsequent legal prohibition or restriction on the use of the premises. *It may generally be said that in the absence of any such stipulation, a valid police regulation which forbids the use of rented property for certain purposes, but leaves the tenant free to devote the property to other legal uses not forbidden or restricted by the terms of the lease, does not invalidate the lease or affect the rights and liabilities of the parties to the lease. And, even though the lease by its terms restricts the tenant's use of the premises to certain specified purposes, but not to a single purpose, the prevailing view is that the subsequent enactment of the legislation prohibiting the use of the premises for one, or less than all, of the several purposes specified does not invalidate the lease or justify the tenant in abandoning the property, even though the legislation may render its use less valuable. If there is a serviceable use for which the property is still available consistent with the limitations of the demise, the tenant is not in a position to assert that it is totally deprived of the benefit of the tenancy.*

49 Am. Jur. 2d Landlord & Tenant §531, at 442-443 (1995) (emphasis added).

Based on the foregoing authorities, we reach the following conclusions. A subsequent governmental regulation like a statute or ordinance may prohibit a tenant from legally using the premises for its originally intended purpose. In these circumstances, the tenant's purpose is substantially frustrated thereby relieving the tenant from any further obligation to pay rent. The tenant is not relieved from the obligation to pay rent if there is a serviceable use still available consistent with the use provision in the lease. The fact that the use is less valuable or less profitable or even unprofitable does not mean the tenant's use has been substantially frustrated.

C. The Merits

It is clear from the pleadings and testimony that Di-Chem was asserting a defense of frustration of purpose. Di-Chem had the burden of persuasion to prove that defense. See *Conklin,* 187 Iowa at 822, 174 N.W. at 574. The district court's decision in favor of Mel Frank is a determination that Di-Chem did not carry its burden on this defense.

Di-Chem produced no evidence that *all* of its inventory of chemicals consisted of hazardous material. In fact, its own correspondence to Mel Frank indicates otherwise. For example, Di-Chem's October 23 letter to Mel Frank stated: "The city's position that we cannot legally store *all* of our inventory at this site prior to extensive alteration of the building makes the structure useless to us as a chemical warehouse." (Emphasis added.) A reasonable inference from this statement is that not all of Di-Chem's inventory consisted of hazardous material.

Testimony from one of Di-Chem's representatives corroborates this inference:

> Q. Were you involved at all in the discussions with the City of Council Bluffs relative to the various code deficiencies that existed at the building? A. My involvement was that the city had pointed out that there was some deficiencies with the building and asked us to remove *what* chemicals they found objective [sic; objectionable?].

(Emphasis added.) Another Di-Chem representative testified that Di-Chem's product line included industrial chemicals and *food additives*. Presumably, food additives are not hazardous materials.

Given the posture of this appeal, Di-Chem has to establish as a matter of law that its principal purpose for leasing the facility — storing and distributing chemicals — was substantially frustrated by the city's actions. Di-Chem presented no evidence as to the nature of its inventory and what percentage of the inventory consisted of hazardous chemicals. The company also failed to show what its lost profits, if any, would be without the hazardous chemicals. Thus, there is no evidence from which the district court could have found the city's actions substantially frustrated Di-Chem's principal purpose of storing and distributing chemicals. Put another way, there is insufficient evidence that the city's action deprived Di-Chem of the beneficial enjoyment of the property for other uses, i.e., storing and distributing nonhazardous chemicals.

Simply put, Di-Chem failed to establish its affirmative defense of what it has termed impossibility. We must therefore affirm the district court's decision as to this issue.

V. LEASE LANGUAGE

Di-Chem also relies on language in the lease which it claims releases it from further obligation to pay rent. The language is found in clause 13 of the lease, which is entitled "Fire and Casualty, Partial Destruction of Premises," and provides:

> (a) In the event of a partial destruction or damage of the leased premises, which is a business interference, that is, which prevents the conducting of a normal business operation and which damage is reasonably repairable within sixty (60) days after its occurrence, this lease shall not terminate but the rent for the leased premises shall abate during the time of such business interference. In the event of partial destruction, Landlord shall repair such damages within 60 days of its occurrence unless prevented from so doing by acts of God, the elements . . . or other causes beyond Landlord's reasonable control.

(b) **Zoning**. Should the zoning ordinance of the city . . . make it impossible for Landlord, using diligent and timely effort to obtain necessary permits and to repair and/or rebuild so that Tenant is not able to conduct its business on these premises, then such partial destruction shall be treated as a total destruction as in the next paragraph provided.

(c) **Total Destruction of Business Use**. In the event of a destruction or damage of the leased premises . . . so that Tenant is not able to conduct its business on the premises or the then current legal use for which the premises are being used and which damages cannot be repaired within sixty (60) days this lease may be terminated at the option of either the Landlord or Tenant. Such termination in such event shall be effected by written notice of one party to the other, within twenty (20) days after such destruction. Tenant shall surrender possession within ten (10) days after such notice issues, and each party shall be released from all future obligations hereunder. . . .

Di-Chem contends that because it was not able to store and distribute the hazardous chemicals, it was "not able to conduct its business on the premises," as specified in clause 13(b). Di-Chem concludes, therefore, that a "total destruction of business use" occurred in accordance with clause 13(c) and for that reason each party was released from all future obligations under the lease.

There is not even a hint of recognition of clause 13 in the district court's ruling. The reason is obvious: clause 13 simply does not apply to the facts of this case. Clause 13 must be read in its entirety and construed in context.

As the title in clause 13 suggests, the clause's language covers the situation where there has been a temporary interruption of the tenant's business because of a partial destruction of the premises. In these circumstances, the lease gives the landlord a period of time to repair or rebuild. During this period the tenant's rent abates but the lease continues in force.

Clause 13 also covers the situation where the landlord cannot rebuild or repair the premises because of some zoning prohibition. A common example involves a nonconforming use. Typically, zoning ordinances prohibit an owner from rebuilding if, for example, fifty percent of the building has been destroyed. In these circumstances, the tenant cannot legally continue in business on the premises and for this reason the lease considers the tenant's business use has been totally destroyed. In this situation, both the landlord and the tenant have the option to terminate the lease with no further obligation on either's part.

One cannot reasonably interpret clause 13 to cover the situation where a subsequent governmental regulation prohibits the use of the premises for one of several purposes specified in the lease. The district court was correct in ignoring clause 13.

VI. District Court Finding That Real Estate Agent Represented Di-Chem

We agree with Di-Chem that the district court erroneously found that the real estate agent represented Di-Chem and prepared the lease on its behalf. There is no evidence to support such a finding; in fact, the evidence is the other way. Nevertheless, we find the error harmless, because Di-Chem has not established any ambiguity in the terms of the lease that affect the outcome of this case. Thus, there was simply nothing to construe against Mel Frank. See Iowa Fuel & Minerals, Inc. v. Board of Regents, 471 N.W.2d 859, 862-863 (Iowa 1991) (holding that ambiguities in a contract are construed against the drafter).

VII. Disposition

In sum, we conclude Di-Chem has failed to establish — as a matter of law — that it is entitled to relief via its impossibility defense or the terms of the lease. The district court's erroneous finding that the real estate agent represented Di-Chem was harmless. We affirm.

AFFIRMED.

NOTES AND QUESTIONS

1. *Governmental regulation as basis for excuse.* Although the lessee in *Mel Frank* did not succeed, the courts have been much more willing to grant relief when the event on which the claim of impracticability or frustration rests is some form of supervening governmental regulation rather than cases in which the event is war, natural disaster, or market change. Indeed, the UCC in §2-615 makes specific mention of "compliance in good faith with any applicable foreign or domestic governmental regulation or order" as a basis for relief. See also Restatement (Second) of Contracts §264 (recognizing compliance with foreign or domestic governmental order as a basis for excuse under the doctrine of impracticability). Examples include Harriscom Svenska, AB v. Harris Corp., 3 F.3d 576 (2d Cir. 1993) (seller of radio equipment excused on grounds of impracticability after government regulations on transfer of military equipment to Iran led to compromise with U.S. government that required discontinuation of sales to plaintiff distributor; not necessary that the law indisputably required or prohibited conduct, as long as party seeking relief acted in good faith compliance with government's clear determination to prohibit the sales); M.J. Paquet, Inc. v. N.J. DOT, 794 A.2d 141 (N.J. 2002) (contract excused for impracticability because revised OSHA regulations governing refurbishment of bridges painted with lead-based paint would have resulted in substantial, unanticipated increase in cost of performance).

Despite a receptiveness to claims of excuse where performance is prevented by supervening governmental action, courts will still impose stringent limits on such relief in that category of frustration cases as well as any other, as demonstrated by the *Mel Frank* decision. Those limits include the requirement that frustration be quite substantial. The *Mel Frank* court stated that the performance must be rendered "virtually worthless" and other courts have similarly stated that the principal purpose of the contract must be substantially undermined. See, e.g., Wheelabrator Environmental Systems v. Galante, 136 F. Supp. 2d 21 (D. Conn. 2001) (contract for "waste-to-energy resource recovery" was made less profitable by court decision invalidating mandatory municipal waste disposal ordinances but not excused because principal purpose was not "utterly defeated"). Additionally, courts may also deny relief on the basis of frustration if the supervening event was foreseeable and the complaining party did not guard against the occurrence or otherwise assumed the risk. See City of Starkville v. 4-County Electric Power Ass'n, 819 So. 2d 1216 (Miss. 2002) (frustration excuse not available because possible change in eminent domain laws that rendered contract less profitable was foreseeable at the time contract was made).

2. *Relief under the UCC.* As noted in the introduction to this section of Chapter 8, UCC §2-615 is broad enough to encompass impracticability as well as frustration. The Code section expressly addresses excuse of performance by a seller on the ground of impracticability but does not mention relief to a buyer. Nonetheless, the courts have been willing to grant relief to buyers as well as sellers. See Comment 9 to §2-615, suggesting the section could properly be applied to buyers in appropriate circumstances. See Power Engineering & Manufacturing, Ltd. v. Krug Int'l, 501 N.W.2d 490 (Iowa 1993) (although Code section expressly mentions only sellers, impracticability defense is equally available to buyers; however, inability of buyer to make planned shipments to Iraq did not establish impracticability). But see Sudamax Industria E Comercio De Cigaros, LTDA v. Buttes & Ashes, Inc., 2007 U.S. Dist. LEXIS 23265 (W.D. Ky.) (impracticability is a seller's excuse not available to buyers).

3. *Force majeure clauses.* The lessee in *Mel Frank* also sought to escape the contract based on a portion of the contract which addressed the possibilities of partial or total destruction of the leased facility or a change in zoning law. Such "force majeure" clauses typically provide for excuse where performance is prevented or delayed by circumstances "beyond the control" of the party seeking excuse. Besides governmental regulation, force majeure clauses are likely to enumerate other particular types of excusing events, such as natural events (windstorm, fire, flood, etc. — often called "acts of God"), prevention by outside forces (war, riot, civil commotion, etc.), and strikes and labor disputes. To a large extent, force majeure clauses merely track ground now covered by UCC §2-615 and corresponding provisions of the Restatement. They may attempt to go further, however, to provide an excuse where the law would not do so. The few cases that have considered the issue have concluded that this is permissible. See PPG Indus., Inc. v. Shell Oil Co., 919 F.2d 17 (5th Cir. 1990) (court rejected buyer's argument that §2-615 imposes limitations on force majeure clauses but recognized that the doctrine of good faith applied to prohibit term that would be manifestly unreasonable). Of course, force majeure clauses, like other contractual provisions, will be subject to doctrines of interpretation, including the maxim of *contra proferentem.* See also Route 6 Outparcels, LLC v. Ruby Tuesday, Inc., 931 N.Y.S.2d 436 (App. Div. 2011) (parties' "fairly broad" force majeure clause would not include 2008 global financial crisis as legal excuse for failure to construct new restaurant as required by contract).

4. *Economic downturn and real estate finance.* Beginning in 2006, as part of a global economic downturn, the United States experienced the most drastic drop in home values since the Great Depression. See Arthur E. Wilmarth, Jr., The Dark Side of Universal Banking: Financial Conglomerates and the Origins

of the Subprime Financial Crisis, 41 Conn. L. Rev. 963, 967 (2009) (estimating the total decline in U.S. home values between mid-2006 and the end of 2008 at $6 trillion). This crisis led to the inability of borrowers to repay mortgage loans and to widespread default. Should borrowers be able to claim excuse based on frustration of purpose or impracticability? What would be the implications of judicial acceptance of those theories? See Bean v. BAC Home Loans Servicing, L.P., 2012 WL 10349 (D. Ariz.) (rejecting impracticability and frustration arguments where home's value dropped to only half the amount of mortgage). Cf. Tri-Town Const. Co., Inc. v. Commerce Park Associates 12, LLC, 139 A.3d 467 (R.I. 2016) (promissory note held enforceable against buyer of land for condo development even after "Great Recession" allegedly made financing unavailable; no evidence of shared basic assumption that financing would remain available nor proof that building condos was impossible).

PROBLEM 8-1

You are an attorney in Garrett's Landing, a small city in one of the southern states. You have just been consulted by Arthur Barlow, proprietor of a florist shop in your city, who tells you the following story:

"Several years ago I went to work for Sam and Martha Stewart as a clerk in their florist shop, over by Good Samaritan Hospital, on Mackenzie Street. I'd only been out of high school a few years, had a few jobs, none of which seemed likely to go anywhere much; this seemed like a chance to learn a business from the inside, and from people who were getting on in years and might be willing to take me in as a partner eventually. Well, the business did well enough, and they paid me a decent salary, so I stayed on, and just when I was getting up enough nerve to ask whether they might be willing to take me in as a partner, Martha died very unexpectedly. Naturally, this threw Sam pretty badly, and for a while there I pretty much ran the business single-handed.

"When Sam got on his feet again I was about to make him an offer when he surprised me by making *me* one. He said he'd decided to retire, said he thought he might sell his house, go and live with his daughter over in Marshallsburg, and did I want to buy the business? I said I sure did, if the price was right. We talked it over, and he said there were eight years to go on his lease, and he was sure Mrs. Duval, the owner of the building, would agree to his assigning the lease to me, and that he'd sell me the business for $100,000 – that is, $80,000 for the fixtures, office equipment, and inventory and $20,000 for good will. That struck me as a real good price, knowing what I did about the earnings of the shop. I said the figure was all right with me, provided I could pay him $20,000 now and $20,000 a year over the next four years; that way I could pay him out of the earnings of the business. He said that was acceptable to him, and he showed me the bill of sale that Jonah Cartwright's lawyer had drawn up nearly 30 years ago when old Cartwright sold the business to Sam. (It was called Good Samaritan Florist Shop then, just like it is now.) I read it through and said it sounded okay to me and told Sam to draw up one just like it, and that would be our contract. I raised the $20,000 by borrowing from my uncle, and I took over the shop.

"Well, all that happened last March, and since then I've been running the shop myself, with one helper. So far it's gone pretty good. This week, though, I got a real shock. The Board of Trustees of Good Samaritan Hospital announced — maybe you saw the story in the paper? — that the hospital was merging with Mercy Hospital, over on the other side of town, that a new wing would be built on Mercy, and the old Good Samaritan Building would be torn down. I don't have to tell you, I guess, what a bad piece of news that is for me. My shop is in an old part of town, and the best part of my business is from people who come to visit sick folks at the hospital; both the new shopping centers in town have florists, and I can't compete with them for the suburban trade. Without the hospital, I'm dead. It's been there for 80 years; I never dreamed it wouldn't be there forever. What really gravels me, though, is old Sam Stewart. I can see now why he made me such a good price for the business. I'm sure he knew the hospital was planning to close. A decision like that, it isn't made overnight, they must have been considering it as long ago as last March. And Sam's cousin, Maureen Leonard, she's a doctor at Good Samaritan, and she's on the governing board there. Sam saw the handwriting on the wall and unloaded on me, I know he did. And what I want to know is, what can I do about it?"

Before attempting to answer his question, you ask Barlow to show you the "Bill of Sale," signed by Stewart and Barlow as Seller and Buyer. It recites that Stewart is selling to Barlow "all the assets, stock in trade, fixtures, and good will of the business presently operated by Seller as 'Good Samaritan Flower Shop,' on Mackenzie Street, in Garrett's Landing." It also contains the following language: "Seller represents and warrants that he is the owner of, and has full power to convey, the property which is the subject of this Bill of Sale. Seller makes no other representations or warranties whatever with respect to this property, and Buyer's acceptance of this Bill of Sale so acknowledges." The document also contains a promise by Barlow to pay Stewart $20,000 on delivery and $20,000 a year for the next four years; the promise is not qualified or conditioned by any reference to the earnings of the business.

What causes of action could Mr. Barlow assert to rescind the agreement with Mr. Stewart? How would you evaluate the likelihood of success of these causes of action?

PROBLEM 8-2

Suppose Mr. Barlow authorizes you to file a lawsuit against Sam Stewart seeking rescission of the contract of sale. Draft a complaint in this action. In doing so, assume that the Federal Rules of Civil Procedure govern.

PROBLEM 8-3

In June 2018, Beth and Bob Byers were looking for a lot near Rustic Lake in Rustic County on which they wished to build a house for their residence. With the assistance of their real estate agent, Don Drew, the Byers looked at a parcel of unimproved property that was available for sale and placed between some existing houses. At the Byers' request, the agent for Sara Seller provided the Byers with a Property Disclosure Statement, outlining the conditions of the real property known to Seller who had owned the property for ten years. On this statement, Seller marked "Yes" in response to the question, "Are you aware of any past or present drainage or flooding problems on the property?" Because of this disclosure, Mr. Drew contacted Sara's real estate agent to inquire further as to the nature of the drainage and flooding issues with the property. Sara responded stating that she marked "Yes" because she was aware the property had flooded during the massive storm of May 2015, which affected many properties in Rustic County.

The Byers then hired Paul Parker, a general contractor and builder, to visit the property and assess whether there were any flooding or drainage problems with the lot that could impede the Byers' ability to build a house on the lot. Mr. Parker inspected the property and reviewed the Federal Emergency Management Agency ("FEMA") flood panel and Flood Insurance Rate Map ("FIRM"), after which he determined that there were no flooding or drainage problems that would hinder Buyers' ability to construct a house on the lot.

On July 1, 2018, the Byers executed a Land Purchase Agreement whereby they agreed to purchase the lot for $100,000, with $10,000 paid at signing and $2500 paid quarterly for the next nine years. The contract contained a Section 6 which provided:

> **6. Inspections and other requirements made a part of this Agreement.** [B]uyer shall have the right and responsibility to enter the property during normal business hours for the purpose of making inspections and/or tests. Buyer shall make such inspections as indicated in this paragraph and either accept the property in its present condition by written notice to Seller or terminate the Agreement as provided for each section marked below.

The Byers "checked" the box immediately preceding the stipulation labeled, "Building Permit," which gave the Byers the option to withdraw from the contract if they were "unable to acquire the necessary licenses and permits to make specific improvements on the Property and notified Sellers of this fact within thirty days of the date of contracting." The Byers did not check a box for the stipulation which read, "No Inspection Contingencies. Buyer accepts the Property in its present condition. All parties acknowledge and agree that the Property is being sold 'AS IS' with any and all faults."

Over the next nine months, Mr. Parker, the contractor retained by Byers, developed building and site plans for the property. In December 2018, Mr. Parker obtained a building permit from the Rustic County Building Department for the Byers' new home on the property. Mr. Parker began work on the property in March 2019. One week after construction commenced, Mr. Parker was informed by Rustic County officials that the property was located in an area of "localized flooding" under a new zoning program that the county had established and that took effect on January 1, 2019. The zoning classification would require special measures to ensure the property would not cause flooding to adjacent property. Mr. Parker immediately stopped construction and notified the Byers of this development.

The Byers then hired a professional engineer, Wesley Warren, to assess the ramifications of the county's determination. Following an extensive study, Mr. Warren concluded that the property generally lies at a lower elevation than the surrounding lots and often receives surface and subsurface rainwater runoff from the adjacent lots. He estimates that property must have flooded at least every other year since the neighborhood was subdivided in 1999. Mr. Warren determined that the "localized flooding" zoning classification by Rustic County was consistent with industry standards given the property's drainage issues. He further determined that the lot would need extensive modifications to prevent flooding; however, these modifications would be extremely costly, an estimated $150,000, and might subject the Byers to future liability due to the displacement of water onto neighboring parcels. Given the unique challenges of this particular parcel, Mr. Warren determined the lot had not been suitable for residential construction since 1999 and it would not be suitable now, even if the county waived the zoning restrictions. As a result, the Byers abandoned the thought of constructing a house on the lot.

The Byers have come to your law office and want your advice about whether they have valid grounds to rescind the Land Purchase Agreement with Sara Seller. What is your assessment?

C. MODIFICATION

We have earlier studied the doctrine of consideration (as a basis for enforcement of a promise), the implied obligation of good faith (both under the UCC and as an element of general contract law), and the concept of duress (as a defense to liability for nonperformance of what would otherwise be an enforceable promise). We have also surveyed a variety of doctrines designed to give relief from the effect of changed circumstances, where those have deprived one of the contracting parties of what may appear to be the benefit fairly to be expected from the originally agreed-to exchange. And we have addressed the statute of frauds, a set of rules requiring writing for enforceability. In this section we will consider a situation in which a number of these doctrines and rules may be brought to bear in deciding the relative rights and duties of the parties: the modification of a preexisting executory contract.

As an introduction, consider the following:

PROBLEM 8-4

You are vice-president and general counsel for Associated Department Stores, Inc., which owns and operates "Schweitzer's," a large department store in your city. Schweitzer's has recently been in the throes of some remodeling, reorganizing, and overall image-upgrading, dropping some lines of goods, adding others, and generally attempting to create a more high-fashion atmosphere in the store. Today you receive a call from Edna Carmody, another Associated executive, who has general responsibility for planning and coordinating the organization and remodeling of the various women's apparel departments. She tells you the following story:

"You probably know that the new women's designer salon on three is scheduled to open at the end of this month; we've had promotions in the papers and on local TV for days about the celebrity fashion show and the charity cocktail party we're throwing for the benefit of the county historical society. Well, virtually everything is done except the laying of the new flooring, which we purposely had left until after the new ceiling tiles and lighting tracks had been installed, and the wallpaper hung, so it wouldn't get the wear of several sets of workmen over it right away. Waller Brothers agreed to do the floor for us — to provide the labor and flooring material and to have the whole job done by next Thursday at the latest. They are the local distributors for EverWare floor tile, which is probably the best product for our needs, and they contracted to install EverWare in the 'Starship' pattern, which we picked to complement the wallpaper and lighting fixtures we had selected.

"Just now I had a call from Jack Waller, who told me that the EverWare Company has notified them that every shipment of EverWare tile from now on — including the lot for our store, which is on its way to the Wallers' now — will be billed to them at a 30 percent increase over the previous prices, due to a settlement EverWare had to make with its employees to prevent a strike, they said. Jack told me that the increase was more than he and Ralph could absorb, and that they had talked it over and agreed that they would have to charge us at least 20 percent more per foot for the Starship tile we ordered. I told him I certainly sympathized with their problem, but I didn't feel they had any right to ask us to agree to a price increase at this point, since for five weeks we had had a firm written contract with them for an agreed price. Jack didn't exactly quarrel with that, but he said he was surely sorry we didn't see things their way, and then he went on to say that these rising costs really had them in a bind, and they thought they'd probably have to lay off some of their help, and it might be pretty difficult to get their work done on schedule under those conditions. Then he said why didn't I think it over for a while, and talk it over with some of the other people here at Schweitzer's; he said he felt sure then I'd see things his way, and that he'd expect me to call him back in a few hours.

"Even if he's telling me the truth about their being hit with a surprise price increase, it seems to me they're way out of line in expecting us to absorb it. Do we have to? And if we say no, what happens if they pull a slowdown on us? Lots of faces are going to be red around here, mine in particular, if all that promotion effort for the new women's shop goes out the window because the redecorating isn't done. I haven't tried yet, of course, but I'm sure we can't get someone else to do the floor on such short notice. Even if we could, no one else stocks the pattern we need to do the job right; the Wallers are exclusive distributors for EverWare in this town. Do they have us over a barrel?"

Obviously, before attempting to advise Ms. Carmody how she might proceed in this situation, you will want to consider the effect of the original agreement with Waller Brothers. You know that there is indeed a "firm written contract . . . for an agreed price" between Associated Department Stores, Inc., and Waller Brothers, because at your direction all agreements with contractors for the renovation were made on purchasing order forms used by Associated. You know that this form contains a standard "force majeure" clause, and also that it contains the following language: "This is the entire agreement of the parties, superseding all prior agreements. No additions or modifications to, or any waivers of provisions contained in, this agreement shall be binding unless in writing and signed by both parties."

Before deciding on the course of action Associated should pursue, you will need to consider the following questions (and perhaps others as well): (1) Can Waller Brothers rely on changes in circumstance occurring since the agreement was made to justify nonperformance on its part? (2) If Associated should (for whatever combination of legal and/or practical reasons) agree to pay Waller Brothers a higher price for the tile work, could it later refuse to pay the amount of the increase, on the ground that its agreement to that increase either was void for lack of consideration, or was entered into as a product of bad faith or duress on Waller Brothers' part? (3) Even if an agreement to pay the increased price would otherwise be enforceable, if you can avoid putting it in writing, can Associated later refuse to pay on the basis of the contractual language quoted above?

On the basis of what we have seen so far, and the materials that follow, how would you answer those questions? Based on your answers, how would you advise Ms. Carmody?

Alaska Packers' Association v. Domenico

United States Court of Appeals 117 F. 99 (9th Cir. 1902)

ROSS, Circuit Judge. The libel in this case was based upon a contract alleged to have been entered into between the libelants and the appellant corporation on the 22d day of May, 1900, at Pyramid Harbor, Alaska, by which it is claimed the appellant promised to pay each of the libelants, among other things, the sum of $100 for services rendered and to be rendered. In its answer the respondent denied the execution, on its part, of the contract sued upon, averred that it was without consideration, and for a third defense alleged that the work performed by the libelants for it was performed under other and different contracts than that sued on, and that, prior to the filing of the libel, each of the libelants was paid by the respondent the full amount due him thereunder, in consideration of which each of them executed a full release of all his claims and demands against the respondent.

The evidence shows without conflict that on March 26, 1900, at the city and county of San Francisco, the libelants entered into a written contract with the appellant, whereby they agreed to go from San Francisco to Pyramid Harbor,

Salmon cannery in Pyramid Harbor, 1912.

Alaska, and return, on board such vessel as might be designated by the appellant, and to work for the appellant during the fishing season of 1900, at Pyramid Harbor, as sailors and fishermen, agreeing to do "regular ship's duty, both up and down, discharging and loading; and to do any other work whatsoever when requested to do so by the captain or agent of the Alaska Packers' Association." By the terms of this agreement, the appellant was to pay each of the libelants $50 for the season, and two cents for each red salmon in the catching of which he took part.

On the 15th day of April, 1900, 21 of the libelants signed shipping articles by which they shipped as seamen on the Two Brothers, a vessel chartered by the appellant for the voyage between San Francisco and Pyramid Harbor, and also bound themselves to perform the same work for the appellant provided for by the previous contract of March 26th; the appellant agreeing to pay them therefor the sum of $60 for the season, and two cents each for each red salmon in the catching of which they should respectively take part. Under these contracts, the libelants sailed on board the Two Brothers for Pyramid Harbor, where the appellant had about $150,000 invested in a salmon cannery. The libelants arrived there early in April of the year mentioned, and began to unload the vessel and fit up the cannery. A few days thereafter, to wit, May 19th, they stopped work in a body, and demanded of the company's superintendent there in charge $100 for services in operating the vessel to and from Pyramid Harbor, instead of the sums stipulated for in and by the contracts; stating that unless they were paid this additional wage they would stop work entirely, and return to San Francisco. The evidence showed, and the court below found, that it was impossible for the appellant to get other men to take the places of the libelants, the place being remote, the season short and just opening; so that, after endeavoring for several days without success to induce the libelants to proceed with their work in accordance with their contracts, the company's superintendent, on the 22d day of May, so far yielded to their demands as to instruct his clerk to copy the contracts executed in San Francisco, including the words "Alaska Packers' Association" at the end, substituting, for the $50 and $60 payments, respectively, of those contracts, the sum of $100, which document, so prepared, was signed by the libelants before a shipping commissioner whom they had requested to be brought from Northeast Point; the superintendent, however, testifying that he at the time told the libelants that he was without authority to enter into any such contract, or to in any way alter the contracts made between them and the company in San Francisco. Upon the return of the libelants to San Francisco at the close of the fishing season, they demanded pay in accordance with the terms of the alleged contract of May 22d, when the company denied its validity, and refused to pay other than as provided for by the contracts of March 26th and April 5th, respectively. Some of the libelants, at least, consulted counsel, and, after receiving his advice, those of them who had signed the shipping articles before the shipping commissioner at San Francisco went before that officer, and received the amount due them thereunder, executing in consideration thereof a release in full, and the others being paid at the office of the company, also receipting in full for their demands.

On the trial in the court below, the libelants undertook to show that the fishing nets provided by the respondent were defective, and that it was on that account that they demanded increased wages. On that point, the evidence was substantially conflicting, and the finding of the court was against the libelants, the court saying:

> The contention of libelants that the nets provided them were rotten and unserviceable is not sustained by the evidence. The defendant's interest required that libelants should be provided with every facility necessary to their success as fishermen, for on such success depended the profits defendant would be able to realize that season from its packing plant, and the large capital invested therein. In view of this self-evident fact, it is highly improbable that the defendant gave libelants rotten and unserviceable nets with which to fish. It follows from this finding that libelants were not justified in refusing performance of their original contract. [112 Fed. 554.]

The evidence being sharply conflicting in respect to these facts, the conclusions of the court, who heard and saw the witnesses, will not be disturbed. . . .

The real questions in the case as brought here are questions of law, and, in the view that we take of the case, it will be necessary to consider but one of those. Assuming that the appellant's superintendent at Pyramid Harbor was authorized to make the alleged contract of May 22d, and that he executed it on behalf of the appellant, was it supported by a sufficient consideration? From the foregoing statement of the case, it will have been seen that the libelants agreed in writing, for certain stated compensation, to render their services to the appellant in remote waters where the season for conducting fishing operations is extremely short, and in which enterprise the appellant had a large amount of money invested; and, after having entered upon the discharge of their contract, and at a time when it was impossible for the appellant to secure other men in their places, the libelants, without any valid cause, absolutely refused to continue the services they were under contract to perform unless the appellant would consent to pay them more money. Consent to such a demand, under such circumstances, if given, was, in our opinion, without consideration, for the reason that it was based solely upon the libelants' agreement to render the exact services, and none other, that they were already under contract to render. The case shows that they willfully and arbitrarily broke that obligation. As a matter of course, they were liable to the appellant in damages, and it is quite probable, as suggested by the court below in its opinion, that they may have been unable to respond in damages. But we are unable to agree with the conclusions there drawn, from these facts, in these words:

> Under such circumstances, it would be strange, indeed, if the law would not permit the defendant to waive the damages caused by the libelants' breach, and enter into the contract sued upon, — a contract mutually beneficial to all the parties thereto, in that it gave to the libelants reasonable compensation for their labor, and enabled the defendant to employ to advantage the large capital it had invested in its canning and fishing plant.

Certainly, it cannot be justly held, upon the record in this case, that there was any voluntary waiver on the part of the appellant of the breach of the original contract. The company itself knew nothing of such breach until the expedition returned to San Francisco, and the testimony is uncontradicted that its superintendent at Pyramid Harbor, who, it is claimed, made on its behalf the contract sued on, distinctly informed the libelants that he had no power to alter the original or to make a new contract; and it would, of course, follow that, if he had no power to change the original, he would have no authority to waive any rights thereunder. The circumstances of the present case bring it, we think, directly within the sound and just observations of the supreme court of Minnesota in the case of King v. Railway Co., 61 Minn. 482, 63 N.W. 1105:

> No astute reasoning can change the plain fact that the party who refuses to perform, and thereby coerces a promise from the other party to the contract to pay him an increased compensation for doing that which he is legally bound to do, takes an unjustifiable advantage of the necessities of the other party. Surely it would be a travesty on justice to hold that the party so making the promise for extra pay was estopped from asserting that the promise was without consideration. A party cannot lay the foundation of an estoppel by his own wrong, where the promise is simply a repetition of a subsisting legal promise. There can be no consideration for the promise of the other party, and there is no warrant for inferring that the parties have voluntarily rescinded or modified their contract. The promise cannot be legally enforced, although the other party has completed his contract in reliance upon it.

In Lingenfelder v. Brewing Co., 103 Mo. 578, 15 S.W. 844, the court, in holding void a contract by which the owner of a building agreed to pay its architect an additional sum because of his refusal to otherwise proceed with the contract, said:

> It is urged upon us by respondents that this was a new contract. New in what? Jungenfeld was bound by his contract to design and supervise this building. Under the new promise, he was not to do anything more or anything different. What benefit was to accrue to Wainwright? He was to receive the same service from Jungenfeld under the new, that Jungenfeld was bound to tender under the original contract. What loss, trouble, or inconvenience could result to Jungenfeld that he had not already assumed? No amount of metaphysical reasoning can change the plain fact that Jungenfeld took advantage of Wainwright's necessities, and extorted the promise of five per cent, on the refrigerator plant as the condition of his complying with his contract already entered into. Nor had he even the flimsy pretext that Wainwright had violated any of the conditions of the contract on his part. Jungenfeld himself put it upon the simple proposition that "if he, as an architect, put up the brewery, and another company put up the refrigerating machinery, it would be a detriment to the Empire Refrigerating Company," of which Jungenfeld was president. To permit plaintiff to recover under such circumstances would be to offer a premium upon bad faith, and invite men to violate their most sacred contracts that they may profit by their own wrong. That a promise to pay a man for doing that which he is already under contract to do is without consideration is conceded by respondents. The rule has been so long imbedded in the common law and decisions of the highest courts of the various states that nothing but the most cogent reasons ought to shake it. [Citing a long list of authorities.] But it is "carrying coals to Newcastle" to add authorities on a proposition so universally accepted, and so inherently just and right in itself.
>
> . . . What we hold is that, when a party merely does what he has already obligated himself to do, he cannot demand an additional compensation therefor; and although, by taking advantage of the necessities of his adversary, he obtains a promise for more, the law will regard it as nudum pactum, and will not lend its process to aid in the wrong.

. . . It results from the views above expressed that the judgment must be reversed, and the cause remanded, with directions to the court below to enter judgment for the respondent, with costs. It is so ordered.

NOTES AND QUESTIONS

1. *Identifying the parties.* The terminology of *Alaska Packers' Assn* is apt to be a bit confusing, since the same party — the Packers' Association — is at different places referred to as the "appellant" and the "respondent." The explanation lies in the nature of the case as an admiralty claim, or "libel"; the plaintiffs are referred to as "libelants," and the defendant, responding to the libel, is the "respondent." The defendant/respondent is also the "appellant," because the petitioners prevailed below.

2. *Pre-existing duty rule.* The *Alaska Packers'* decision reflects the fundamental tenet that merely promising to perform an existing obligation will not serve as valid consideration for additional return compensation from the other

party. This rule continues to be applied, at least as a starting point, even though courts accept even a small or modest addition to or alteration of performance as enough to satisfy the rule. Compare Aerel, S.R.L. v. PCC Airfoils, L.L.C., 448 F.3d 899 (6th Cir. 2006) (alleged promise to pay additional commissions for services already required by contract would constitute unenforceable, one-sided modification), with Oscar v. Simeonidis, 800 A.2d 271 (N.J. Super. Ct. App. Div. 2002) (even insignificant or slight new consideration in modification of lease agreement, such as paying rent one day in advance, would be valid to support modification). If the plaintiffs in *Alaska Packers' Assn* had by good fortune had a lawyer among their number, could they with his counsel have formulated a wage-increase agreement with their employer that would have satisfied the consideration test applied by the court in the above opinion? How? If so, who would have won the case? Could the defendant's other arguments have been foreseen and forestalled by informed lawyering?

3. *Policing coercive behavior.* In discussing the pre-existing duty rule as a barrier to enforcement of a contract modification, Professor Farnsworth referred to *Alaska Packers'* (along with the *Lingenfelder* case, quoted and discussed in *Alaska Packers'*) as a case where "particularly outrageous threats" were made to coerce a one-sided modifying agreement. E. Allan Farnsworth, Contracts §4.22, at 273 n.15 (4th 2004). In Selmer Co. v. Blakeslee-Midwest Co., 704 F.2d 924, 927 (7th Cir. 1983), Judge Posner offered his own approbation of *Alaska Packers'*:

> It undermines the institution of contract to allow a contract party to use the threat of breach to get the contract modified in his favor not because anything has happened to require modification in the mutual interest of the parties but simply because the other party, unless he knuckles under to the threat, will incur costs for which he will have no adequate legal remedy. If contractual protections are illusory, people will be reluctant to make contracts. Allowing contract modifications to be voided in circumstances such as those in *Alaska Packers' Assn.* assures prospective contract parties that signing a contract is not stepping into a trap, and by thus encouraging people to make contracts promotes the efficient allocation of resources.

The Farnsworth and Posner view of this case is more likely to seem appropriate the more strongly one is persuaded that the plaintiffs there were actually lying about their working conditions. Although the evidence on that point was "sharply conflicting," the trial court found on this issue for the defendants, apparently in large measure because plaintiffs' testimony that the defendant had not provided them with serviceable nets was "highly improbable," the defendant's interest requiring that the plaintiffs be supplied with "every facility necessary to their success as fishermen." Do you agree? To the extent that the pre-existing duty rule serves essentially as a guard against coercive behavior, would it be better to police that conduct directly and otherwise to enforce all consensual modifications? For a study suggesting such an approach would be desirable, see Kevin M. Teeven, Consensual Path to Abolition of Preexisting Duty Rule, 34 Val. U. L. Rev. 43 (1999) (advocating enforcement of modifications without requirement of new consideration but subject to policing mechanisms of economic duress, unconscionability, and good faith).

4. *Historical context.* The *Alaska Packers' Assn* courts, as well as the commentators discussed above, discounted the possibility that a rational, profit-seeking enterprise would choose not to replace badly depreciated nets, but a careful examination of the case suggests reasons why that might well have happened. In her article, A Fish Story: Alaska Packers' Association v. Domenico, 2000 Utah L. Rev. 185, Professor Debora L. Threedy reviewed not only the opinions in the *Alaska Packers' Assn* trial and appellate decisions, but also explored the salmon fishing and canning industry at the time of the dispute. Among Professor Threedy's key revelations are the facts that the Pyramid Harbor location was only one of 18 canneries operated by the Association, the canneries purchased fish caught by local native tribes in addition to the catch of the crew, the Association's crew received lower pay than those at nearby competitors, and that the nets at Pyramid Harbor were in fact partially reused while the other Association canneries purchased new nets each year. Most of her findings supporting the claims of the fishing crew about the substandard nets are capsulated in a critique of the crew's lawyer. Professor Threedy writes:

> Hindsight, of course, has perfect vision, but if Banning [the crew's lawyer] had focused on the cannery's capacity and had been able to establish that the 1900 catch met or exceeded the cannery's capacity, then he would have established a motive for the cannery to limit the fishermen's catch. Similarly, if he had been able to bring out the disparities between Pyramid Harbor and other canneries in cost per case and expenditures for fishing gear, along with the extent to which Pyramid Harbor relied on the local tribes, he could have suggested a motive to cut corners on the nets. Either strategy would have bolstered the credibility of the fishermen who testified that the nets were substandard. Moreover, if Banning had been able to bring out the extent to which local tribal fishermen contributed to the cannery's operation, he would have been able to argue that the cannery could have operated even if the fishermen had refused to work during the season.

Id. at 214. Without reaching a firm conclusion on the issue, Professor Threedy questions whether the Association in fact might have decided to supply defective or inefficient nets even if that meant its workers had to expend much greater effort in the performance of their duties. It is also notable that in 1902, when *Alaska Packers'* was decided, the temper of the times (and of the courts) was generally friendly to capital and management, and hostile to labor and collective bargaining. Does the additional information offered by Professor Threedy suggest only that the facts may have been wrongly determined or do they raise concerns about the legal principles applied by the courts?

5. *Modification of employment contracts. Alaska Packers' Assn* can be examined from more than one perspective. If *Alaska Packers'* is regarded as a "labor" case, that does not mean contract principles could not play their part in resolving the dispute. The prospect of an employee union engaging in a strike to obtain a promise of higher pay played out in Contempo Design v. Chicago

& Northeast Illinois Dist. Council of Carpenters, 226 F.3d 535 (7th Cir. 2000). Notwithstanding an applicable "no strike" provision within the current contract, the unionized employees struck at a time when the employer was pursuing a multi-year, multi-million-dollar contract with a major new client, Bank of America, and was facing pressure from an overdue loan. The employer agreed to a pay raise and other benefits but reserved its right to sue the union. Relying heavily on *Alaska Packers' Assn* to develop federal common law, the court's majority held that the modified agreement was unenforceable for lack of consideration and noted that the pre-existing duty rule served to "prevent coercive modifications." Id. at 549-550. The four dissenting judges conceded that the union had the employer "over a barrel" but would have enforced the modified contract because of the view that the union had a good faith, though erroneous, belief that it was not bound by the no strike clause. Id. at 555-557.

Another, more frequent scenario requiring the courts to review the enforceability of a contract modification occurs within the context of non-unionized at-will employment, as typified by the Geysen v. Securitas Security Services case and the following notes in Chapter 6. Frequently these cases will involve an employer's promises of job security or fair treatment contained in a personnel manual that are deemed to become binding through the unilateral-contract formation process. E.g., Doyle v. Holy Cross Hospital, 708 N.E.2d 1140 (Ill. 1999). If the employer later promulgates a new version of its manual, abrogating those earlier promises, should that revision be viewed as a "one-sided" modification of an existing contract, requiring fresh consideration to be effective? And if so, what could constitute the requisite consideration? Some courts have held that such an attempt by an employer to modify its personnel handbook was ineffective because unsupported by any consideration. E.g., Demasse v. ITT Corp., 984 P.2d 1138 (Ariz. 1999). However, other courts have held that the employee's continued employment constitutes consideration for the modification. See Pine River State Bank v. Mettille, 333 N.W.2d 622, 626-627 (Minn. 1983). Finally, some courts adopt an intermediate position, allowing modification without any additional consideration but with some restrictions. See Asmus v. Pacific Bell, 999 P.2d 71 (Cal. 2000) (employer may unilaterally terminate announced policy of indefinite duration, if employer makes the change after a reasonable time, on reasonable notice, and without interfering with employees' vested benefits; given those limitations, no additional consideration is required). See also Bankey v. Storer Broad., 443 N.W.2d 112 (Mich. 1989) (employer may unilaterally replace previous for-cause termination policy with employment at-will with reasonable notice; issue is not one of contract formation but of employment policy).

6. *Other exceptions to the pre-existing duty rule.* As discussed in Note 2, courts generally require that a modification be supported by new consideration on both sides, even if very minimal or slight. Court decisions reveal, however, a number of exceptions to the requirement of new consideration. The first exception is that of "unforeseen circumstances." This concept is included in Restatement (Second) §89(a) which states that a promise of modification is binding if "fair and equitable in view of circumstances not anticipated by the

parties when the contract was made." The concept may be applicable even if the unforeseen circumstances would not fully qualify for excuse based on the impracticability doctrine as discussed in Section B of this chapter. See §89, Illustration 1 (when solid rock unexpectedly encountered making removal nine times more expensive, owner's promise to pay increased amount for excavation is binding); see also Roussalis v. Wyoming Medical Center, Inc., 4 P.3d 209 (Wyo. 2001) (modification that increased the size of promised medical building would be enforceable without additional consideration in light of need to resolve unforeseen safety concerns not addressed by original architect plans).

Second, Restatement (Second) §89(c) recognizes "reliance" on a promised modification as another basis for enforcing a modifying agreement despite the absence of fresh consideration. This is one of several Restatement (Second) provisions in which the principle of §90 is given a more focused application in the context of a particular problem. See generally Charles L. Knapp, Reliance in the Revised Restatement: The Proliferation of Promissory Estoppel, 81 Colum. L. Rev. 52 (1981). What kind of reliance will serve this purpose? Should it be sufficient to make a modification binding that the party seeking enforcement of the modification has "relied" by performing its duties as promised under the original agreement? Neither the comments nor illustrations to §89 are particularly helpful on this issue. The cited article suggests that in light of the apparent intention of §89 to liberalize the consideration requirement for such modifying agreements, the answer may be that simply to perform as originally promised might constitute such reliance as would satisfy §89(c). It seems possible that the drafters of Restatement (Second) §89 would have really preferred to take the approach of UCC §2-209(1) in largely dismissing the pre-existing duty rule, as discussed in the case and notes which follow, but felt unable to make such a complete break with the common law tradition on this point.

Third, many courts also recognize the concept of "mutual release" as another exception to the pre-existing duty rule. In Schwartzreich v. Bauman-Basch, Inc., 131 N.E. 887 (N.Y. 1921), an employee, originally hired as a coat designer for a fixed period at a stated salary, was promised an increase in pay when he reported to his employer that another firm had offered him a higher salary to come with it. The parties tore up their old contract and replaced it with a new one, providing for the promised increase. The employee was later discharged and sued to recover damages based on the increased salary rate. The New York Court of Appeals held that the new contract could be upheld as being the product of a mutual rescission, followed by a new and valid contract. But as the Restatement (Second) points out, in Comment *b* to §89, such a rationale is "fictitious" when the "rescission" and new contract are simultaneous (as they were in *Schwartzreich*). Despite the legal sleight-of-hand involved in its decision, *Schwartzreich* might nevertheless be justified as a case in which the element of coercion was absent and circumstances had changed unexpectedly (the employee later discovered his services were worth more on the market than he had originally anticipated), and the employee had justifiably relied on the promise of a raise (at least by remaining instead of choosing to breach, and possibly also by increased devotion to his efforts on his employer's behalf). See also Margeson v. Artis, 776 N.W. 2d 652, 656 n.4 (Iowa 2009) (parties are free to rescind contract and then form new contract with same consideration being given by one side).

Kelsey-Hayes Co. v. Galtaco Redlaw Castings Corp.

United States District Court 749 F. Supp. 794 (E.D. Mich 1990)

Opinion And Order

COHN, District Judge.

I.

This is a breach of contract case. Plaintiff, Kelsey-Hayes Company (Kelsey-Hayes), alleges defendant, Galtaco Redlaw Castings Corporation (Galtaco), breached a three-year agreement (the 1987 contract) for the purchase of castings. In addition to the damages allegedly suffered as a result of the breach of the 1987 contract, Kelsey-Hayes seeks a declaratory judgment that it does not have to pay Galtaco price increases to which it agreed in 1989. Kelsey-Hayes asserts the 1989 contract modifications (1989 agreements) containing the price increases (1) were agreed to by Kelsey-Hayes under duress, (2) were unconscionable, (3) were demanded by Galtaco in bad faith and (4) constitute unjust enrichment to Galtaco. Galtaco says in response that Kelsey-Hayes waived its breach of contract claims and, in addition, argues that the defenses Kelsey-Hayes raises regarding the validity of the 1989 agreements have no merit. Galtaco also counterclaims for the monies owed under the 1989 agreements. Also before the Court is Kelsey-Hayes' motion for leave to file a second amended complaint. Fed. R. Civ. P. 15(a).

Galtaco has moved for summary judgment, Fed. R. Civ. P. 56, on Kelsey-Hayes' claims and its counterclaim. For the reasons which follow, Galtaco's motion will be denied. In addition, the Court will grant Kelsey-Hayes' motion for leave to file a second amended complaint.

II.

The following facts as gleaned from the affidavits, deposition testimony and documents in the record are not in dispute.

Kelsey-Hayes makes brake assemblies that it sells to auto manufacturers, including Chrysler and Ford. For several years prior to 1987, Galtaco supplied castings to Kelsey-Hayes which incorporated them into the brake assemblies. In 1987, Galtaco and Kelsey-Hayes signed a three-year "requirements" contract. Under the contract, Galtaco was to be the sole source to Kelsey-Hayes of certain types of castings through April 1990. In return, Galtaco was to charge fixed prices for 1987, and scheduled price reductions for 1988 and 1989, respectively. . . .

A.

By the spring of 1989, Galtaco had been experiencing continued monetary losses for several years. Kelsey-Hayes was aware of Galtaco's financial condition. For the seven months ending in April 1989, Galtaco's foundry operations had losses totalling $2,410,000. As a result, on May 10, 1989, Galtaco's Board of Directors made final a decision to discontinue its foundry operations and cease production of castings. Galtaco recognized that an immediate shut down of its foundry operations would seriously inconvenience its customers, because they would need additional castings before they could cover from other sources. Therefore, Galtaco offered all of its customers, including Kelsey-Hayes, an agreement to keep its foundries operating for "several months" in exchange for price increase of 30 percent effective with shipments of May 15, 1989.

If Galtaco were to have immediately terminated its foundry operations, Kelsey-Hayes concluded that it would not have been able to obtain a sufficient supply of castings from alternative sources for 18-24 weeks. As a result, Kelsey-Hayes determined that declining to accept Galtaco's offer would have the effect of shutting down the assembly plants of two of its major clients, Chrysler and Ford. Kelsey-Hayes was Ford's sole source of certain brake assemblies, and Ford had no significant bank of those parts. Any interruption of the supply of brake assemblies longer than five to ten days would likely have resulted in the halting of Ford production of a vehicle line. On May 12, 1989, Kelsey-Hayes accepted Galtaco's offer to continue supplying castings for a time, at a 30 percent price increase for all castings delivered to all plants. Before entering into the 1989 agreements, Kelsey-Hayes did not reserve any rights under the 1987 contract when it accepted Galtaco's offer.

On June 9, 1989, Galtaco informed Kelsey-Hayes it required an additional 30 percent price increase in order to keep its foundry operations going. By this time, Galtaco's other customers had found alternative sources of castings. The additional price increase was asked for to offset the rising fixed costs Galtaco would continue to incur if it were to remain in operation for Kelsey-Hayes' sole benefit. Since Kelsey-Hayes had not yet found another source for castings, it accepted Galtaco's offer to continue providing castings for an additional 30 percent price increase. Again, Kelsey-Hayes did not reserve any rights under the 1987 contract when it entered into the June 1989 agreement.

B.

Between May 15 and August 30, 1989, Galtaco made 282 shipments to Kelsey-Hayes. Galtaco's foundries closed down after the final shipment to Kelsey-Hayes.

Kelsey-Hayes accepted all of the shipments, and it timely paid for the first 197 deliveries according to the terms of the 1989 agreements. However, Kelsey-Hayes failed to pay Galtaco for 84 of the remaining 85 casting shipments. The price for the 84 shipments for which Kelsey-Hayes has not paid approximates the $2 million price increase to which Kelsey-Hayes agreed under the 1989 agreements.

At no time did Kelsey-Hayes explicitly state that it would sue Galtaco; however, Kelsey-Hayes did strenuously protest Galtaco's actions as a breach of the 1987 contract.

III.

As stated, supra, Kelsey-Hayes' claim is based on several alternative theories of liability. However, in order to dispose of the pending motion, the Court must only decide whether Kelsey-Hayes has presented enough evidence to allow a reasonable finder of the facts to conclude the 1989 agreements were executed under duress.[4]

A.

Galtaco says Kelsey-Hayes cannot sue for breach of the 1987 contract, because it entered into the superseding 1989 agreements. It is true that under Michigan law, entering a superseding, inconsistent agreement covering the same subject matter rescinds an earlier contract and operates as a waiver of any claim for breach of the earlier contract not expressly reserved. Joseph v. Rottschafer, 248 Mich. 606, 610-611, 227 N.W. 784 (1929); Culver v. Castro, 126 Mich. App. 824, 827-828, 338 N.W.2d 232 (1983). However, a subsequent contract or modification is invalid and therefore does not supersede an earlier contract when the subsequent contract was entered into under duress. Lafayette Dramatic Production v. Ferentz, 305 Mich. 193, 217-219, 9 N.W.2d 57 (1943). There is sufficient evidence to allow a reasonable finder of the facts to determine that Kelsey-Hayes was under duress when it executed the 1989 agreements. Thus, Galtaco's motion for summary judgment will be denied.

B.

Courts in Michigan have recognized the doctrine of economic duress or "business compulsion" for more than a century. Hackley v. Headley, 45 Mich. 569, 8 N.W. 511 (1881). Galtaco relies on early statutory and judicial general expressions of the doctrine stating that in order to make a claim of duress, a person must be subjected to the threat of an unlawful act in the nature of a tort or a crime. See Burke v. Gould, 105 Cal. 277, 281-283, 38 P. 733 (1894). However, the doctrine of duress has been greatly expanded since its common-law origin.[5] Now, a contract is voidable if a party's manifestation of assent is induced by an improper threat by another party that leaves the victim no reasonable alternative. Rich & Whillock v. Ashton Development, 157 Cal. App. 3d 1154, 204 Cal. Rptr. 86, 89 (1984); Systems Technology Associates, Inc. v. United States, 699 F.2d 1383, 1387 (Fed. Cir. 1983); Restatement (Second) of Contracts, §175(1) (1982). In other words, economic duress can exist in the absence of an illegal threat; the threat must merely be wrongful. Even acts lawful and non-tortious may be wrongful depending on the

---

4. As to the claim of unconscionability, as distinguished from duress, it appears to lack merit. See Northwest Acceptance Corp. v. Almont Gravel, Inc., 162 Mich. App. 294, 412 N.W.2d 719 (1987). The claim of bad faith likewise appears to lack merit, see Genesee Merchants Bank & Trust Co. v. Tucker Motor Sales, 143 Mich. App. 339, 372 N.W.2d 546 (1985), as does the claim of unjust enrichment, see Hollowell v. Career Decisions, Inc., 100 Mich. App. 561, 570, 298 N.W.2d 915 (1980).

5. A survey of Michigan cases involving duress reveals that there has never been a decision that explicitly adopts the modern formulation of duress. . . .

Nevertheless, the Court is satisfied that if the Michigan Supreme Court looked at the issue today, it would rule that economic duress need not stem from an "illegal" threat. . . . See Dunbar v. United States Insurance Co. of America, 557 F. Supp. 228 (E.D. Mich. 1983) (in diversity cases, federal court must make educated guess what state Supreme Court would decide if question was presented to it, and decisions of state trial and appellate courts, while they may be considered, cannot serve as precedent).

circumstances. S. Williston & W. Jaeger, Williston on Contracts §1606 (3rd ed. 1972); Fowler v. Mumford, 48 Del. 282, 102 A.2d 535 (Del. Super. 1954).

C.

1

Kelsey-Hayes has alleged wrongful acts of Galtaco in its complaint and has offered proof of them in affidavits. Specifically, Kelsey-Hayes says Galtaco threatened to breach its contract and go out of business, stopping production and delivery of castings, unless Kelsey-Hayes agreed to significant price hikes. Austin Instrument, Inc. v. Loral Corp., 29 N.Y.2d 124, 324 N.Y.S.2d 22, 272 N.E.2d 533 (1971) (threat by one party to breach contract by not delivering required items is wrongful).

2

Kelsey-Hayes has also presented a triable issue of fact that it had no reasonable alternative other than acquiescing to Galtaco's demand for a contract modification. Affidavits and deposition testimony in the record show Kelsey-Hayes contacted six other casting manufacturers, but none were able to immediately provide an alternate source of castings to meet Kelsey-Hayes' delivery requirements.[6] As a result, Kelsey-Hayes might reasonably have believed a brief interruption in casting shipments would force at least one of its major customers, Ford, to halt production of a vehicle line. Such an occurrence, Kelsey-Hayes could reasonably fear, would injure its business reputation and subject it to large monetary damages.[7] The facts in this case parallel *Austin Instrument,* supra, in which a government contractor faced a genuine possibility of substantial liquidated damages as a result of a subcontractor's threat to stop deliveries unless prices were increased. In *Austin Instrument,* 324 N.Y.S.2d at 26-27, 272 N.E.2d at 537-538, the court held that a company in this position was deprived of its free will and had no alternative other than acquiescing to the demands of the party threatening to breach its contract. Similarly, faced with the imminent shutdown of its major customer's plants, Kelsey-Hayes may have had no alternative other than agreeing to Galtaco's "requests" for price increases.[8] See also Pittsburgh

6. By the time Galtaco demanded the second 30 percent price increase, most of its other customers other than Kelsey-Hayes were able to acquire alternate supplies of castings. Galtaco says this suggests Kelsey-Hayes also could have obtained another source of supply, and thus it was not under economic duress when it assented to the latter 1989 agreement. But this merely presents an issue to be resolved by the trier of fact. Moreover, when seeking alternate supplies of castings, Kelsey-Hayes may have faced more difficulty than Galtaco's other customers. Kelsey-Hayes had to source 30 different safety related castings representing perhaps 45%-50% of the total output of the Galtaco foundries.

7. Given the changing nature of the automobile industry, Galtaco's actions are more likely to constitute duress. It is well known that in an effort to promote efficiency, car manufacturers are reducing the size of their reserve banks of parts. As a result, component parts are often incorporated into a finished product within a few hours of their delivery. A supplier's failure to make scheduled shipments may have immediate and dramatic consequences. Aware of this, companies in the position of Kelsey-Hayes will face more pressure to agree to the extortionate demands of suppliers who breach their contractual obligations. Thus, a breach of contract in the automotive industry may be more coercive than in other industries.

8. The facts here also mirror an example of economic duress cited in Restatement (Second) of Contracts, §175 comment b, illustration 5 (1982):

> A, who has contracted to sell goods to B, makes an improper threat to refuse to deliver the goods to B unless B modifies the contract to increase the price. B attempts to buy substitute goods elsewhere but is unable to do so. Being in urgent need of the goods, he makes the modification. See Uniform Commercial Code §2-209(1). B has no reasonable alternative, A's threat amounts to duress, and the modification is voidable by B.

Steel Co. v. Hollingshead & Blei, 202 Ill. App. 177 (1916); Ross System v. Linden Dari-Delite, 35 N.J. 329, 173 A.2d 258 (1961); Rose v. Vulcan Materials Co., 282 N.C. 643, 194 S.E.2d 521 (1973); King Construction Co. v. W.M. Smith Electric Co., 350 S.W.2d 940 (Tex. Civ. App. 1961).

It is hardly necessary to add that Kelsey-Hayes' normal legal remedy of accepting Galtaco's breach of the contract and then suing for damages would have been inadequate under the circumstances. Kelsey-Hayes might reasonably have feared that if it shunned the 1989 agreements and instead sued for breach of the 1987 contract then Galtaco would have stopped supplying it with castings.[9] As stated, supra, evidence in the record strongly suggests Kelsey-Hayes would not have been able to locate an alternate supply of castings. As a result, Kelsey-Hayes' business reputation may have suffered and its major customers may have been forced to shut down its automobile production lines.

3

In order to state a claim of economic duress a buyer coerced into executing a modification to an existing agreement must "at least display some protest against the higher price in order to put the seller on notice that the modification is not freely entered into." United States v. Progressive Enterprises, 418 F. Supp. 662, 665 (E.D. Va. 1976) (in contract modification situations, the parties must be able to rely on objective, unequivocal manifestations of assent). Galtaco says Kelsey-Hayes executed the 1989 agreements with the secret intention to never pay the higher prices. However, it is undisputed Kelsey-Hayes vigorously objected to Galtaco's breach of the 1987 contract and its demand for price increases. While Kelsey-Hayes did not expressly reserve the right to sue under the 1987 contract, a reasonable trier of the facts could determine its protests effectively put Galtaco on notice that the 1989 agreements were agreed to under duress.

D.

Galtaco argues, in effect, that the common law doctrine of economic duress no longer applies to cases like the one at bar. Instead, Galtaco says, the doctrine has been subsumed by the Uniform Commercial Code's "good faith" test, M.C.L. §440.2209, for determining the enforceability of agreements modifying contracts for the sale of goods. This contention is frivolous. Galtaco relies on a single case, Roth Steel Products v. Sharon Steel Corp., 705 F.2d 134 (6th Cir. 1983), to support its contention that a well-established tenet of law has been abandoned. Moreover, the Court of Appeals for the Sixth Circuit in *Roth Steel* never even held that a person can no longer rely on the doctrine of economic duress to invalidate a contract modification. Finally, M.C.L. §440.1103 states that, absent explicit language to the contrary, the Uniform Commercial Code merely supplements the common law of duress and coercion. M.C.L. §440.2209 contains no such language. . . .

---

9. Galtaco's chief operating officer, T. Cook, testified as follows:

We had conveyed to all of our customers that we needed a written acceptance of the 30 percent price increase or we would not make shipments on May 15th, which was a Monday. The Monday shipments were prepared on Friday night and were shipped out Sunday night. Our shipping supervisors had instructions that those shipments were not to be made unless they had been given approval by me or through someone designated by me that we had, in fact, received those written approvals. Late on Friday we still had not received those from anyone in Kelsey-Hayes. And Ron Olweean called me to find out what he had and how to do it.

V.

Galtaco's motion for summary judgment is denied. Kelsey-Hayes' motion to amend is granted.
So ordered.

NOTES AND QUESTIONS

1. *Modification without consideration under Article 2.* The judge writing the opinion in *Kelsey-Hayes* never raises the pre-existing duty rule as a possible reason for denying effect to the modification. The judge's discussion at the beginning of section IIIA. may be read to suggest that this case is an example of mutual rescission followed by a new agreement, as discussed in Note 6 after the *Alaska Packers'* case. In any event, the court's citation to Michigan's version of the Uniform Commercial Code indicates that this case falls under UCC §2-209(1), which states that a modification "needs no consideration to be binding." The drafters of the UCC appear to be expressing the view that parties regularly modify agreements without having new consideration on both sides, and that such "one-sided" modifications should be routinely enforced except in the presence of special circumstances. Do people in business indeed routinely agree to such one-sided modifications, and if so, why? Consider Comment 1 to §2-209: "This section seeks to . . . make effective all necessary and desirable modifications of sales contracts without regard to the technicalities which at present hamper such adjustments." A comprehensive survey of the Code's approach to contract modification can be found in two studies by Professor Robert Hillman: Policing Contract Modifications under the UCC: Good Faith and the Doctrine of Economic Duress, 64 Iowa L. Rev. 849 (1979); A Study of Uniform Commercial Code Methodology: Contract Modification under Article Two, 59 N.C. L. Rev. 335 (1981). Professor Irma S. Russell also provided a critique of §2-209 in her article, Reinventing the Deal: A Sequential Approach to Analyzing Claims for Enforcement of Modified Sales Contracts, 53 Fla. L. Rev. 49 (2001).

2. *Good faith as a limitation on modification under Article 2.* Assuming that the drafters of the UCC were right to take the position that one-sided contract modifications are by and large an everyday affair, there remains the question of how the law can "police" against the possibility that one party will exploit developing circumstances to coerce the other party's agreement to a modification. While §2-209(1) itself does not directly address that issue, Comment 2 provides that the obligation of good faith serves as a bar to "extortion" of a modifying agreement "without legitimate commercial reason." In a case discussed briefly at the end of the *Kelsey-Hayes* opinion, the Court of Appeals in Roth Steel Products v. Sharon Steel Corp., 705 F.2d 134 (6th Cir. 1983), upheld a district court's determination that a price-increase modification was unenforceable because it had been procured by bad faith. The *Roth* court applied a two-part test. First, it declared that a party may in good faith seek a modification when "unforeseen economic exigencies existed which would prompt an ordinary merchant to seek a modification in order to avoid a loss on the contract." Second, it held that even where circumstances do justify asking for a modification, it is nevertheless bad faith

conduct to attempt to *coerce* one, by threatening a breach. On this point, the court conceded that the inference of bad faith arising when a breach is threatened may be rebutted by a showing that the party threatening not to perform did honestly believe it had a legal defense to the duty of performance. In *Roth*, however, the court held that the inference of bad faith had not been rebutted, principally because it appeared that the legal justification for nonperformance was not offered at the time the modification was sought but only as an afterthought in the context of litigation. This, the court held, was not the "honesty in fact" that the UCC good faith obligation requires. 705 F.2d 145-148.

In Man Indus. (India), Ltd. v. Midcontinent Express Pipeline, LLC, 407 S.W.3d 342 (Tex. App. 2013), the court agreed generally with the *Roth* court's two-part test of objective reasonableness and subjective honesty. However, the court rejected the *Roth* requirement that the change in conditions be unforeseeable, quoting Comment 2 to §2-609, which states: "But such matters as a market shift which makes performance come to involve a loss may provide such a reason *even though there is no such unforeseen difficulty* as would make out a legal excuse from performance under Sections 2-615 and 2-616." (emphasis added). Under the Roth-Man test, should the modification agreement asserted by Galtaco be regarded as the product of bad faith?

3. *Economic duress as a limitation on modification under Article 2.* We have already seen, in connection with the *Totem Marine* case in Chapter 7, that economic duress may generally be grounds under the common law for avoiding an agreement. The *Kelsey-Hayes* court holds that UCC §2-209(1) does not preclude application of the duress doctrine to sales of goods cases, and observes that modern formulations of the duress doctrine no longer require the presence of an "illegal" threat. As also reflected in the *Totem Marine* case, most courts now accept that a "wrongful" threat may leave a party without reasonable alternatives and thereby invoke duress as grounds to excuse enforcement of a contract. Thus, the *Kelsey-Hayes* court anticipated that the Michigan Supreme Court would adopt the modern view of duress if confronted with the question and move away from its early statements which required an illegal threat. The Michigan Supreme Court, however, appears not to have confronted that issue since the time of *Kelsey-Hayes* and the intermediate state appellate opinions still require an illegal threat. See Whirlpool Corp. v. Grigoleit Co., 713 F.3d 316 (6th Cir. 2013) (observing that Michigan law differs from other states and still requires a showing of illegality to establish duress). If the judge in *Kelsey-Hayes* had deemed state law to require an "illegal" threat to establish duress, would that change lead to a different outcome in the case? If so, would you agree with that resolution of the case?

In footnote 4 the *Kelsey-Hayes* opinion summarily held that a claim of bad faith was not supported, while at the same time accepting the argument that the modification may have been the result of economic duress, citing Austin Instrument, Inc. v. Loral Corp., perhaps the leading modern case for this type of duress. While it seems likely that where contract modification is at issue, the law of "duress" and the law of "good faith" will often tend to merge, the two theories may involve somewhat different considerations. See Meredith R. Miller, Revisiting Austin v. Loral: A Study in Economic Duress, Contract Modification and Framing, 2 Hastings Bus. L.J. 357, 411 (2006) (noting that good faith analysis would focus more on a party's reasons for seeking and the fairness of a proposed modification whereas duress analysis looks at alleged threat and lack of choices). Other cases have considered the issues of duress and good faith in the context of an Article 2 case, though claimants seem to succeed only rarely. See, e.g., Sonfast Corp. v. York International Corp., 875 F. Supp. 1099 (M.D. Pa. 1995) (finding neither economic duress nor breach of duty of good faith in making modification; buyer could have insisted on seller honoring existing contract, and had adequate legal remedy if it did not); Gross Valentino Printing Co. v. Clarke, 458 N.E.2d 1027 (Ill. App. Ct. 1983) (claimant failed to establish economic duress; no evidence that alleged threat was sufficient to overcome the will of claimant and failed to show legal redress was inadequate).

4. *Protest of a bad faith modification.* If ties of good faith bind each party to the other under the UCC (and under general contract law as well; see Restatement (Second) §205), they bind not only the party seeking to enforce a modification but also the one who would resist it. In *Kelsey-Hayes*, the buyer at first performed under the modification, but later repudiated it; the seller pointed to this as evidence that the buyer had acted with a "secret intention to never pay the higher prices," suggesting that this might amount to bad faith on the buyer's part. Some courts in similar cases have held that the party agreeing to an assertedly coerced modification has a good faith duty to make plain that it is acting under protest, so that the other party will not be deceived as to its intention eventually to resist enforcement or seek redress. E.g., United States ex rel. Crane Co. v. Progressive Enterprises, Inc., 418 F. Supp. 662 (E.D. Va. 1976) (buyer's secret intention never to pay higher price not in keeping with good faith's requirement of "honesty in fact"); but cf. T & S Brass & Bronze Works, Inc. v. Pic-Air, Inc., 790 F.2d 1098 (4th Cir. 1986) (buyer's failure to make formal protest did not bar later objection to modification; *Crane* distinguished as applying only where other party had acted in good faith in seeking modification). Did the court in *Kelsey-Hayes* appropriately resolve this issue in the buyer's favor?

5. *Revisiting Problem 8-4.* Recall the questions posed in Problem 8-4, above. If Associated Department Stores were now to agree to pay Waller Brothers an increased amount for the installation of tile in its department store, would that agreement be supported by consideration? Does it need to be? Could enforcement of such an agreement be avoided on grounds of bad faith or duress (or any other ground we have studied, such as fraud, mistake, or undue influence)? To answer these questions, do you need more facts? What facts would you need, and how might they be discovered?

Brookside Farms v. Mama Rizzo's, Inc.

United States District Court 873 F. Supp. 1029 (S.D. Tex. 1995)

ORDER

KENT, District Judge.

This is a breach of contract dispute in which Plaintiff Brookside Farms ("Brookside") alleges that Defendant Mama Rizzo's Inc. ("MRI") breached its contract with Brookside to purchase 91,000 pounds of fresh basil leaves.

Before the Court now are Plaintiff's Motion for Partial Summary Judgment and Defendant's Motion for Summary Judgment. For the reasons discussed below, the Court finds that Defendant's Motion is denied and Plaintiff's Motion is granted in part and denied in part.

BACKGROUND

On October 13, 1993, Brookside Farms and MRI entered into a requirements contract for the sale of fresh basil leaves from Brookside to MRI. Under the contract, MRI agreed to buy a minimum of 91,000 pounds of fresh basil leaves for a one-year term. Delivery was to be made daily, five days per week, in lots ranging from a minimum of 350 pounds to a maximum of 800 pounds. MRI agreed to pay for the basil it accepted within fifteen days of delivery date.

The price for the basil leaves under the contract was seasonally based, with one price applicable during the domestic growing season, and a higher price applicable during the non-growing season, when Brookside would look to Mexican growers to supply the basil it would need to fulfill its obligations under the contract. The original price for basil delivered during the domestic growing season — between June 1 and September 30 — was \$3.80 per pound; the original price for basil delivered during the non-growing season — October 1 to May 31 — was \$5.00 per pound.

It is undisputed that Mike Franklin, the vice-president of MRI, requested Wayde Burt, Brookside's general partner, to remove additional parts of the stems of the basil leaves, a task not specifically required under the original contract. Brookside agreed to do this work in exchange for a \$0.50 per pound increase for the remainder of the contract term. The undisputed testimony shows that, because the original contract contained a clause forbidding oral modification, Franklin promised to make a notation of future price changes on MRI's copy of the original contract. The new price terms were also reflected on MRI's internally-generated purchase orders, Brookside's invoices, and MRI's payment checks. Between October 27, 1993, and November 16, 1993, MRI issued twelve separate purchase orders for shipments of basil at \$5.50 per pound, and Brookside filled each order and invoiced MRI at the new price.

Between November 17, 1993, and January 9, 1994, MRI discontinued its order of basil leaves, and Brookside reduced its purchase of basil from its Mexican suppliers as a result. Consequently, Brookside was forced to pay higher prices for its supply of Mexican basil leaves when MRI resumed its orders under the contract. Two price modifications in the contract then followed in close sequence. Initially, Franklin and Burt agreed that MRI would pay \$6.23 [sic] per pound for imported basil. Between January 10 and January 21, 1994, MRI issued fifteen separate purchase orders for shipments of basil at \$6.25 per pound, and Brookside filled each order and invoiced MRI at that price. MRI paid all these invoices at the higher price. In mid-January, MRI agreed to pay \$6.75 per pound for the basil Brookside imported from Mexico and issued sixty-seven separate purchase orders for shipments at that price. Each of these shipments was filled and paid without protest.

Between March 14, 1994, and May 17, 1994, MRI issued twenty-one purchase orders for basil at \$6.75 per pound and issued a check to Brookside for

$10,260 in payment for eight of those invoices. Unfortunately for both parties, this check was dishonored by MRI's bank for insufficient funds. Brookside has brought this suit on the claims that Defendant has breached the executory portion of the contract by refusing to accept the minimum amount of basil it agreed to and that Defendant is also liable to Plaintiff for the 3,041 pounds of basil it accepted but did not pay for. MRI contends that no payment is due because Brookside itself breached the contract by raising prices in violation of the contract's express language that no modification would be binding unless it was reduced to written form. . . .

ANALYSIS

The Price Modification Issue

The parties in this case vigorously dispute the question of whether they entered into a valid modification of the price of fresh basil leaves. Plaintiff has submitted undisputed affidavit testimony that several oral agreements to modify the original contract price for basil occurred. Within one week of the contract's formation, MRI discovered that the stems on the basil leaves would need to be removed before they could be properly used — a task not required by the original contract. As stated above, MRI's vice-president contacted Plaintiff's general partner, and both parties agreed that Plaintiff would remove the basil stems before shipping the leaves and increase the purchase price by $0.50 per pound.

Both parties were aware that the contract contained a clause forbidding oral modifications of the contract's terms. Section 19 of the contract states:

> This Agreement may be modified only by a writing signed by the party against whom or against whose successors and assigns enforcement of the modification is sought.

Consequently, MRI's vice-president agreed to make a notation of the price change on MRI's copy of the original contract. (See Burt Affidavit, Instrument #7, at 2). Several subsequent price hikes were also agreed to by the parties, and MRI accepted and paid for 21,389 pounds of basil at purchase prices ranging from the original price to $6.75 per pound and accepted, but refused to pay for, an additional 3,041 pounds.[1] Plaintiff currently seeks payment on this 3,041 pounds of basil at the purchase price of $6.75 per pound. MRI contends that no payment is due because Plaintiff itself breached the contract by raising prices in violation of the contract's express language that no modification would be binding unless it was reduced to written form. The Court disagrees.

Neither party in this case has properly pointed out that the contract in dispute falls within the Statute of Frauds under §2.201 of the Texas Business and Commerce Code. That statute provides that "a contract for the sale of goods for the price of $500 or more is not enforceable by way of action or defense unless there is some writing sufficient to indicate that a contract for sale has

1. MRI originally tendered payment on this series of shipments, but its bank dishonored the check for insufficient funds.

been made between the parties and signed by the party against whom enforcement is sought." Clearly, the original contract between MRI and Brookside meets these requirements.

It is a general rule of Texas law that oral agreements that materially modify a written agreement within the Statute of Frauds are not enforceable. Tex. Bus. & Comm. Code Ann. §26.01; King v. Texacally Joint Venture, 690 S.W.2d 618, 619 (Tx. App. — Austin, 1985, writ ref'd n.r.e.); Dracopoulas v. Rachal, 411 S.W.2d 719 (Tex. 1967). However, not all modifications are prohibited. If the oral changes do not materially alter the underlying obligations, for example, they are not barred. Horner v. Bourland, 724 F.2d 1142, 1148 (5th Cir. 1984); Group Hospital Services, Inc. v. One and Two Brookriver Center, 704 S.W.2d 886, 890 (Tx. App. — Dallas, 1986, n.w.h.). Second, the Texas Supreme Court has adopted the doctrine of promissory estoppel in some cases to forbid reliance on the Statute of Frauds as a defense to the validity of oral agreements. In specific, the Court has held that where one party reasonably relies on the oral promise of another to reduce an oral agreement to writing, the failure to create such a writing will not prevent the relying party from taking the modification out of the Statute of Frauds.[2] "Moore" Burger, Inc. v. Phillips Petroleum Co., 492 S.W.2d 934, 937 (Tex. 1972); see also, Foster v. Mutual Savings Assoc., 602 S.W.2d 98, 101 (Tx. App. — Ft. Worth, 1980, n.w.h.).

Finally, both parties in this case have also failed to note that Texas has adopted an exception to the Statute of Frauds contained in the Uniform Commercial Code. Sections 2.201(c) & (c)(3) of the Tex. Bus. & Comm. Code state in part that:

> (c) A contract which does not satisfy the requirements of Subsection (a) [the general Statute of Frauds provision] but which is valid in other respects is enforceable
>
> . . .
>
> (3) with respect to goods for which payment has been made and accepted or which have been received and accepted.

Thus, an oral modification that would itself form a binding contract in the absence of Statute of Frauds considerations can be binding on the parties to a sale of goods over $500 insofar as specific goods have been received and accepted. See Tex. Bus. & Comm. Code §2.209.

The Court finds that a valid oral modification of the contract between MRI and Brookside occurred on both estoppel and statutory grounds. As stated above, it is undisputed that the parties agreed to alter the purchase price of the basil leaves. On each occasion, MRI issued separate purchase orders and

---

2. The Court specifically invoked both §§90 and 178, comment F of the Restatement, Contracts. Section 178, comment F reads:

> Though there has been no satisfaction of the Statute, an estoppel may preclude objection on that ground in the same way that objection to the nonexistence of other facts essential for the establishment of a right or a defence may be precluded. A misrepresentation that there has been such satisfaction if substantial action is taken in reliance on the representation, precludes proof by the party who made the representation that it was false.

Brookside filled each order and invoiced MRI on the price. In each case, MRI paid the invoiced price without protest. At the time the first price modification occurred, MRI's vice-president and Brookside's general partner discussed whether or not they needed to redraw the contract to account for the price changes in light of the fact that the contract did not allow for oral modifications. It is undisputed that MRI's vice-president assured Plaintiff that he would make a notation of price changes on MRI's copy of the contract and that this notation would be sufficient. (See Burt Affidavit, at 2).

The Court finds that such behavior clearly brings these parties within the estoppel theory adopted by the Texas Supreme Court in *"Moore" Burger,* 492 S.W.2d at 937. The promised notation would have constituted a valid written modification of the contract's terms. A valid writing under the Statute of Frauds requires only "some writing" signed by the party against whom it is to be enforced, namely, MRI. Tex. Bus. & Comm. Code §2.201(a). In addition, given that the intent of the oral agreement to modify the written form of the contract was clearly designed to bring it within the controlling language of the contract, Plaintiff could have reasonably relied on Defendant's implied promise to initial or sign the price change to indicate its intent to adopt the change; without such an implied promise, MRI's agreement to alter the written price terms would have been a mere fraud on the Plaintiff. Comment 6 to §2.201(a) makes clear that such a writing need not be delivered to any other party; MRI could have made the notation on its signed copy of the contract and retained possession of it. It is also clear that MRI's promise to do so induced Brookside Farms to continue shipping basil leaves at the agreed price changes.[3]

Based on these actions, the Court finds that MRI cannot now invoke the no-oral-modification clause of the contract to bar Plaintiff's claim that a valid modification occurred in this case. To do so would be to reach the inequitable result that thousands of dollars could change hands over an extended period of commercial dealings between the parties, during which the Defendant knowingly and wilfully refrained from acting on the promise that induced the Plaintiff to continue shipments and then object to the course of dealing only when it has issued a bad check. The Court notes that the Uniform Commercial Code, which governs the transaction in question, has codified the contractual duty of good faith and fair dealing in commercial settings like the one presently before the Court. Tex. Bus. & Comm. Code §1.203 [now §1.304] provides that "[e]very contract or duty within this title imposes an obligation of good faith in its performance or enforcement." Where the party is a merchant, its standard of good faith performance requires honesty in fact and the observance of

3. Mr. Burt's affidavit states that MRI promised to make the price change notations in regards to the first $1.50 per pound price increase. The Court notes that Burt does not specifically state that the parties agreed to alter the contract with each subsequent price change. Nevertheless, given the sophistication of the parties involved in this case and their extended course of conduct with one another, it is entirely reasonable to expect that, once having promised to make such changes, and having acted on these changes by shipment and subsequent payment, Plaintiff could have relied on MRI's initial promise to make a written notation to allow their commercial dealings to go forward.

reasonable commercial standards of fair dealing in the trade. Adolph Coors Co. v. Rodriguez, 780 S.W.2d 477, 481 (Tx. App. — Corpus Christi, 1989, writ denied).[4] For the Court to allow Defendant to invoke the no-oral-modification clause after MRI itself induced and participated in the extended course of action it now complains of would be to convert the sale of basil leaves into a "basil sale carcinoma" that would devour all reasonable commercial standards of behavior between merchants.

The Court also finds that a valid modification of the contract's price terms occurred on statutory grounds. As stated above, oral modifications to contracts within the Statute of Frauds are generally forbidden. In addition, the Texas Business and Commerce Code specifically provides that signed contracts that exclude modifications that are not in the form of signed writings are valid in this state. Tex. Bus. & Comm. Code §2.209(b). Nevertheless, comment 4 to §2.209 clearly states that such provisions do not limit the "actual later conduct" of parties that have entered into non-written modifications, despite a contract's provision that all modifications must be in writing. In this case, it is undisputed that the "actual later conduct" of these parties involved the order, shipment, and acceptance of 24,430 pounds of basil leaves, 3,041 pounds of which were paid for by a bad check on MRI's part.

Nevertheless, MRI argues that under the contract's "no waiver" clause, it did not waive its right to insist on the contract's initial terms and that, therefore, it now continues to have the right to demand that all modifications to this contract have been in writing to be valid. The Court disagrees.

Section 21 of the contract in question states:

> The failure of either party to this Agreement to demand full performance of any of its provisions by the other party shall not constitute a waiver of performance unless the party failing to demand performance states in a writing signed by party that the party is waiving that performance. The waiver of any breach of any of the provisions of this Agreement by the parties shall not constitute a continuing waiver or a waiver of any subsequent breach by either party of the same or any other provision of this Agreement.

(Defendant's Motion for Summary Judgment, Instrument # 12, Exhibit A, at 4). The Court agrees with MRI that this "no-waiver" clause protects Defendant from a waiver of the "no-oral-modification" clause of the contract. Indeed, comment 4 of §2.209, quoted above, explicitly relies on the theory that "later conduct" of the parties to a contract "waives" contractual obligations. By agreeing that a failure to demand full performance does not give rise to a waiver, the parties in this case have effectively agreed to their own private Statute of Frauds for modifying the contract. As comment 3 of Tex. Bus. & Comm. Code §2.209 states, agreements to modify a contract's terms only in written form "permits the parties in effect to make their own Statute of Frauds as regards any future

4. The Court realizes, of course, that the duty of good faith and fair dealing under §1.203 does not state an independent cause of action. Rather, it is designed to make an agreement's promises effective and defines other duties which grow out of specific contractual obligations. See id. at 482.

modification of the contract. . . ." Like the general Statute of Frauds, §2.209(b) is designed "to protect against false allegations of oral modifications." Id.

However, this does *not* protect MRI under these facts. Indeed, in one sense it destroys MRI's entire case, for if the failure to object to full performance reserves the right to demand such performance, then Brookside's failure to object to MRI's initial request for de-stemmed leaves reserves Plaintiff's right to demand full performance of the original contract's terms, which apparently allowed basil to be shipped with stems still attached. More importantly, however, the private Statute of Frauds provision of the contract must be analyzed under the rules otherwise applicable to general Statute of Frauds issues, and under this analysis, the Court finds that the parties have entered into an effective agreement for those items Brookside shipped and MRI received and accepted.

Sections 2.201(c) and (c)(3) of the Texas Business and Commerce Code provide:

> (c) A contract which does not satisfy the requirements of Subsection (a) [governing the Statute of Frauds] but which is valid in other respects is enforceable
>
> . . .
>
> (3) with respect to goods for which payment has been made and accepted or which have been received and accepted.

This provision also governs the private Statute of Frauds contained in the contract before the Court. Assuming arguendo that the agreement between MRI and Brookside to modify the contract's terms did not meet the writing requirements of §2.201(a), §2.201(c) operates to bring the oral agreement within the Statute with respect to those goods MRI actually received and accepted, that is, the 24,430 pounds of basil Brookside shipped, including the 3,041 pounds of unpaid-for basil leaves. See Bagby Land and Cattle Co. v. California Livestock Commission Co., 439 F.2d 315, 317 (5th Cir. 1971) ("receipt and acceptance either of goods or of the price constitutes an unambiguous overt admission by both parties that a contract actually exists."). Under the specific language of §2.201(c), the new contractual price terms were not made enforceable as to future shipments of basil by Brookside, but they are enforceable as to the 3,041 pounds shipped under the agreed price of $6.75 per pound.[5]

For all these reasons, the Court finds that Plaintiff's Motion for Partial Summary Judgment is granted on the claim that MRI is liable to Brookside for $20,526.75 in payment for the 3,041 pounds of basil accepted but not paid for.

Plaintiff also claims that MRI's refusal to accept and pay for the minimum amount of basil it agreed to buy in its requirements contract with Plaintiff

5. Because of the general paucity of relevant Texas authority presented in the instant Motions, the Court does not rule on the question of whether sufficient written materials are present in this case to bring the oral agreements out of the Statute of Frauds. The Court notes, however, that purchase orders and invoices were generated for every shipment of basil made and that other courts have found such materials sufficient to satisfy the Statute of Frauds. See Brochsteins, Inc. v. Whittaker Corp., 791 F. Supp. 660, 661 (S.D. Tex. 1992).

constitutes a breach of contract, with the resulting damages to be determined at trial at a later date. In response, MRI claims that it was relieved of any obligation to purchase basil by Brookside's demand for higher prices than provided for in the contract. Having already decided that Plaintiff's price increases were legally justified, the Court now finds that for the same reasons articulated above, Brookside did not breach its contractual obligations and that MRI is liable for a material breach of its obligation to purchase a total of 91,000 pounds of basil from Plaintiff. Consequently, Plaintiff's Motion for Partial Summary Judgment is granted on this point. . . .

CONCLUSION

For all of the reasons stated above, the Court finds that Plaintiff's Motion for Partial Summary Judgment is denied as to any claim for attorney's fees and is granted as to the claims that MRI breached the executory portion of the parties' contract, is liable in the amount of $20,526.75 for the payment of 3,041 pounds of basil accepted but not paid for, and that MRI is liable under the Perishable Agricultural and Commodities Act. For the same reasons, Defendant's Motion for Summary Judgment is denied on all counts, including its counterclaim that MRI is entitled to recover overpayments from Plaintiff for the amounts it paid for basil. Defendant's counterclaim for overpayment is also hereby dismissed with prejudice. All relief not specifically granted herein is also denied. All parties are to bear their own taxable costs incurred in this case to date. It is further ordered that the parties file no further pleadings in the matters determined in this Order, including motions to reconsider and the like. Instead, they are instructed to seek any further relief to which they feel themselves entitled in the United States Court of Appeals for the Fifth Circuit, as may be appropriate in due course.

It is so ordered.

NOTES AND QUESTIONS

1. *Modifications and the statute of frauds.* The first two cases in this section examined primarily the question whether contract modifications must be supported by new consideration and when they will be vulnerable to the defenses of duress or bad faith. In *Brookside Farms*, however, the important question is whether a contract modification must be in writing to be enforceable. Section 2-209(3) of the Code provides that the "requirements of the statute of frauds section of this Article must be satisfied if the contract as modified is within its provisions." Many courts have held not only that a writing is required when the modification brings an oral contract within the statute but also that all modifications must be in writing whenever the contract was within the scope of §2-201 originally and remains within the statute after the change. See Zemco Mfg., Inc. v. Navistar Int'l Transp. Corp., 186 F.3d 815, 819 (7th Cir. 1999) (stating that this is the majority view). However, the opposing view focuses on the point that UCC §2-201(1) requires a memorandum to specify only the quantity;

other terms, such as the price, may be expressed orally. Under this analysis, an oral modification of a written agreement would be enforceable unless the modification would either change the quantity term or increase the price above the $500 UCC threshold. This approach harmonizes the modification section, §2-209, with the basic statute of frauds section, §2-201(1); respects the plain statutory language of §2-209(3); and is consistent with common commercial practice of oral modifications. See Costco v. World Wide, 898 P.2d 347, 351 (Wash. Ct. App. 1995). Commentators support this approach. See Zemco Mfg., Inc. v. Navistar Int'l Transp. Corp., 186 F.3d at 820 n.6. The court in *Brookside Farms* finds a middle ground approach to the question of when modifications must be in writing under §2-209(3). What justifies the court's conclusion? Which approach to defining when modifications are required to be in writing is most persuasive?

2. *No-oral-modification clause.* In *Brookside Farms*, the defendant buyer also relied on a provision of the agreement that any modification must be in writing and signed to be effective — a "no-oral-modification," or "NOM" clause. At common law, such clauses were usually held to be ineffective because parties retained the freedom to later modify their agreement by whatever mode they might choose, written or oral. See Barinaga v. JP Morgan Chase & Co., 749 F. Supp. 2d 1164 (D. Or. 2010) (under Oregon law "no oral modification" clause would not bar evidence of oral promise by bank to alter mortgage payments to avoid foreclosure, but claim failed for lack of consideration and definite terms); Truhe v. Turnac Group, L.L.C., 599 N.W.2d 378 (S.D. 1999) (surveying states and agreeing with majority that "no oral modification" clauses are generally not enforceable under the common law, but noting that California, New York, and Texas have narrowed rule by statutory provision). In §2-209(2), however, the Code authorizes parties to employ a NOM clause to create a "private statute of frauds" governing modifications by providing that a "signed agreement which excludes modification or rescission except by a signed writing cannot be otherwise modified or rescinded. . . ." (Comment 3 indicates that both §§2-209(2) and (3) are "intended to protect against false allegations of oral modifications.") Thus, §2-209(2) departs from the common law by generally making NOM clauses enforceable.

3. *Reliance and oral modifications.* Both §§2-209(2) and (3) must be read in conjunction with §2-209(4), which provides that "[a]lthough an attempt at modification or rescission does not satisfy the requirements of subsection (2) or (3) it can operate as a waiver." In a leading case in this area, Wisconsin Knife Works v. National Metal Crafters, 781 F.2d 1280 (7th Cir. 1986), the parties entered into a written contract containing a "no oral modification" clause. The seller failed to deliver the goods by the dates required in the contract, and the buyer sued for breach. The seller claimed that the parties had orally agreed to modify the delivery schedule. Writing for the majority and remanding for a new trial, Judge Posner ruled that the seller could establish "waiver" of the clause requiring modifications to be in writing if it could show that it detrimentally relied on the buyer's indications that late delivery would be accepted. Dissenting Judge Easterbrook argued that the term "waiver" should

be interpreted traditionally, as a voluntary relinquishment of a known right, not dependent on a showing of reliance. Nevertheless, Judge Easterbrook would arrive at an outcome similar to the majority because he reasoned that a waiver could be retracted under §2-209(5) except if material reliance on the oral modification had occurred and would make a retraction unjust. Ultimately, the cases do generally support the proposition that the NOM clause may be waived, by oral agreement to that effect, or by some combination of words and conduct that in the circumstances evidences the parties' willingness to dispense with its protection, and that reliance will prevent retraction of the waiver. See, e.g., Dynamic Machine Works, Inc. v. Machine & Electrical Consultants, Inc., 831 N.E.2d 875 (Mass. 2005).

In addition to the NOM clause, the contract between Brookside and MRI also contained a "no-waiver" clause, intended to insulate the parties (or at least the drafter) from a claim that any provision in the contract, including the NOM clause, had been orally waived. The *Brookside Farms* court rather ingeniously finds the no-waiver clause to be overcome in the same manner that the statute of frauds may be overcome, by actual performance. It may be useful at this point to see the NOM clause (perhaps in conjunction with its sidekick, the no-waiver clause) as playing in this area the same sort of role that a strong merger clause may play with respect to the parol evidence rule. Hearkening back to formalistic notions of contract law, the combined effect of the merger clause and the NOM clause is to ensure that in the future any dispute between the parties will be resolved on the basis of the writing, and *only* the writing. Arrayed on the other side — in favor of the court's enforcing or at least considering the parties' informal, oral agreements, as evidenced by both words and conduct — are a variety of doctrines characteristic of "modern" contract law: rules proscribing fraud and nondisclosure, the implied obligations of good faith and fair dealing, the concept of estoppel, and perhaps even unconscionability. For a discussion of the reliance issues raised — on both sides — by the parol evidence rule and the NOM clause, see Charles L. Knapp, Rescuing Reliance: The Perils of Promissory Estoppel, 49 Hastings L.J. 1191, 1303-1330 (1998).

4. *Modification through settlement.* A problem with both practical and legal aspects that often arises in the context of settlement negotiations is the "full payment" check question. Suppose that a debtor resists payment of an asserted obligation, claiming that he does not owe as much as the creditor claims. What if at some point the debtor offers the creditor a check for some amount less than she claims, and says, in effect, "Here's a check for what I'm willing to pay, marked 'payment in full.' You can have this now, without a lawsuit, but only if you accept it as a full settlement of your claim." If the creditor accepts and cashes the check, can she later assert a right to payment of the balance of her claim? Pre-Code law was clear on the point: so long as the amount actually owed is either "unliquidated" (generally, not reduced to a dollar amount) or the subject of a good faith dispute, acceptance of a check tendered in full payment will in legal effect amount to an "accord and satisfaction" that discharges any remaining obligation. Agreements to settle a *liquidated, undisputed* claim for

less than the full amount have traditionally not been binding on the creditor, under the rule of the old English case of Foakes v. Beer, L.R. 9 A.C. 605 (H.L. 1884), an extension of the "pre-existing duty" rule, which is itself a corollary of the general doctrine of consideration. The rule of Foakes v. Beer has been the subject of much critical comment, and modern developments have tended to reduce its importance. E.g., UCC §1-306 (claim arising out of breach can be discharged in whole or part without consideration by agreement in authenticated record). See generally E. Allan Farnsworth, Contracts §§4.21-4.25 (4th ed. 2004), for a full discussion of the consideration issues that can arise in connection with settlement and discharge agreements.

Suppose the creditor does not simply cash the debtor's "full payment" check, but instead attempts to do so while at the same time reserving its rights to seek the balance due from the debtor. The creditor might send the debtor a letter to that effect, or might endorse the check "under protest" or "with full reservation of rights." What effect will such steps have? Under the traditional common law rule such an attempted reservation would have no effect; the cashing of the check would still amount to acceptance by the creditor of the debtor's offer of an accord and satisfaction. (See Restatement (Second) §281 on accord and satisfaction as performance of agreement to accept substituted performance in lieu of original duty.) It once appeared that the Code might have changed this result in what is now UCC §1-308(a) [formerly §1-207(1)], which provides for performance of contract under reservation of rights. The subsequent addition of §1-308(b) [formerly §1-207(2)] clarified that cashing a full payment check, even with reservation of rights, still constitutes an accord and satisfaction, barring the creditor from collecting the unpaid balance, unless the creditor can establish a ground for avoiding the accord and satisfaction, such as duress.

5. *Revisting Problem 8-4.* Recall again the facts of Problem 8-4. Based on all the above, how would you counsel Ms. Carmody to proceed in responding to the Waller Brothers' request for an increase in the price of their tile work? Indicate what courses of action you would consider, which you would recommend, and why.

REVIEW QUESTIONS – CHAPTER EIGHT

1. Buyer enters into a contract with Seller to purchase a townhome. Buyer plans to use the first floor of the home as an office for her solo legal practice and the second and third floors as her residence; she informs Seller of her plans. Unknown to Buyer or Seller, zoning restrictions in the area prohibit the use of any part of the townhome for business or commercial purposes. When Buyer learns of this restriction, she wants to rescind the contract with Seller. The contract does not contain an "as is" clause, nor does it make any mention of zoning restrictions. Is it probable that Buyer will be able to rescind the contract on the basis of mutual mistake?

A. No, because rescission based on mutual mistake requires a factual rather than a legal mistake.
B. No, because Buyer probably bears the risk of the mistake.
C. Yes, because both Buyer and Seller were mistaken about the zoning restriction.
D. Yes, because the contract does not contain an "as is" clause.

2. Subcontractor (Sub) submits a bid to the general contractor (GC) for the excavation and foundation work for a new office building for a price of $100,000. During the construction Sub encounters major bedrock problems that require specialized equipment and increased time, both of which together escalated the cost of the work by $35,000. Which of the following statements is most likely to be correct?
   A. If Sub is able to establish the elements of unilateral mistake, it could recover the increased cost of construction from GC.
   B. Sub does not bear the risk of mistake because it did not discover the bedrock problems until after it entered into the contract.
   C. If Sub wishes to avoid the contact on the ground of unilateral mistake, it will need to establish that GC either caused the mistake, knew of the mistake, or that the increased cost would be unconscionable.
   D. Sub cannot avoid the contract because the mistake was not a palpable one.

3. AutoParts, Inc. is a supplier of transmission parts to one of the major automobile manufacturers, Famous Motors, Inc. (FM) under a five-year contract with a fixed price and a monthly minimum amount of goods that must be accepted by FM. FM has been unable to reach an agreement with its labor union, which has now gone on strike. FM has notified AutoParts that it is delaying its purchase of parts until the strike is concluded. Delay by FM of purchases from AutoParts will cause AutoParts difficulties: It will need to lay off workers, and if the strike goes on long enough it could place the company at risk of having to default on its loans. AutoParts wants your advice about whether it can insist on the delivery and payment dates set forth in its contract with FM. Which of the following is the best advice:
   A. The strike does not excuse FM from the delivery dates set forth in its contract because performance by FM is not impossible.
   B. The strike does not excuse FM from the delivery dates set forth in its contract because under the UCC a buyer does not have a right to claim impracticability of performance.
   C. FM's performance of the contract is excused if the contract has a standard force majeure clause.
   D. FM's performance of the contract is excused if taking delivery of the parts will cause FM to incur large storage fees.

4. R2D2 is a singing group from Europe that has contracted with National Artists, LLC for a United States Tour during August and September. R2D2

has applied for and obtained a P-1 Visa for its tour. Unfortunately, two weeks before the tour, the U.S. Immigration and Naturalization Service notified the drummer for the group that he would not be able to enter the country under the P-1 visa. The drummer was not told the reason, but he suspects that it is because of a recent criminal conviction for drug use. R2D2 is prepared to hire a substitute drummer, but National Artists is afraid that the tour will suffer because of the drummer's absence. However, even before the problem with the drummer arose, tickets sales for the group's tour have been surprisingly slow. Is National Artists entitled to cancel the contract because of the unavailability of R2D2's usual drummer?

A. No, because it appears unlikely that the purpose of the contract has been substantially frustrated because of the drummer's absence.
B. No, because the parties could have specified in the contract that all original band members must be on tour.
C. Yes, because the drummer's inability to perform was the result of governmental action.
D. Yes, because R2D2 was at fault.

5. Buyer and Seller entered into a written contract for the sale of 50 desks at a total price of $25,000 with a delivery date of June 1. A few weeks before the delivery date, Seller telephones Buyer to inform it that Seller cannot meet the original delivery date without paying overtime to its workers and to ask for a 30-day extension, to which Buyer agreed. After June 1 but before the Seller ships the goods, Buyer informs Seller that it will not accept the desks because the original delivery date has passed. Seller brings suit against Buyer and offers to prove the oral agreement extending the date for delivery. Is the agreement by the parties to extend the delivery date enforceable?
   A. No, because the Seller did not give any consideration for the Buyer's agreement to extend the delivery date.
   B. No, because the agreement was not reduced to writing.
   C. Yes, because the Seller would have been excused due to impracticability without the oral agreement.
   D. Yes, because the Seller reasonably and materially relied on the oral agreement.

CHAPTER 9

Consequences of Nonperformance: Express Conditions, Material Breach, and Anticipatory Repudiation

While in earlier chapters we have focused on defenses to the contract as a whole, we turn now to a consideration of the performance obligations that a contract imposes. The Restatement (Second) in §235(2) defines "breach" as "any non-performance" of a contractual duty at a time "when performance of [that] duty . . . is due." Comment *b* to that section states that performance is not due if for any reason nonperformance is "justified." In one way or another, the sections of this chapter address those central questions: When is one party's performance due, so that failure to perform will be a breach? When is nonperformance justified?

The first section of this chapter addresses the question whether, by the express terms of the parties' agreement, performance by one party is a presently due obligation. This might involve simply the question of whether the time stated for performance has arrived – the day, perhaps even the hour. Often, however, the express terms of the agreement will state that performance is not due unless and until some specified event has taken place. If the agreement does so provide, then the performance is said to be "conditioned," and the happening of that event is an "express condition" to the duty of performance. The use of express conditions as a drafting device is designed to protect one party (or possibly both parties) against various types of risk, involving the possibility that performance will be less advantageous than hoped for, or will be more difficult or even impossible in ways that might not otherwise offer an excuse from liability for nonperformance. For example, the typical contract for the purchase of residential real estate contains a clause making the buyer's purchase obligation conditional on the buyer's obtaining financing from a lending institution. If the buyer is unable to obtain financing despite a good faith effort, the buyer will not be obligated to purchase the property.

We will see, however, that sometimes a party does have a present duty of performance even though an express condition to that party's duty has not occurred. The nonoccurrence of a condition can be "excused" for a variety of reasons. For instance, if the buyer in our example made no effort whatever to obtain financing, a court might well hold that the buyer was obligated to purchase the property, the financing condition being excused because of his bad faith. When an express condition has simply failed to occur, the conditional duty never arises and the promisor is therefore justified in not performing. When nonoccurrence of the condition is *excused*, however, the conditional duty becomes an *un*conditional one, and the promisor's failure to perform amounts to a breach.

The second situation we will address in this chapter involves the relationship between the parties' performance obligations. As we have seen, although some contracts are "unilateral" in form, the majority are probably "bilateral," mutual exchanges of promises of future performance. In such a case, when the time for performance arrives, one party may fail to render all or some of its promised performance. What effect does that have on the performance obligation of the other? In a construction contract, for instance, the contractor agrees to construct a building according to certain specifications, while in return the owner agrees to pay the contractor, typically in installments of stated amounts payable at the completion of specified portions of the work. Suppose the owner fails to make one of those progress payments when it comes due. What effect does this have on the contractor? Does he simply have to continue construction and hope the owner will eventually make that payment as promised? Can he keep working, but at the same time bring suit for the promised payment? Can the contractor even go so far as to declare the contract at an end, sue the owner for damages, and go on to another job? Similar questions may arise from the other side as well. Suppose the contractor has ostensibly finished the construction as promised and has gone on to another project, but the owner finds the work done to be incomplete or inadequate. Is the owner nevertheless bound to pay the balance of the contract price? Can she simply withhold all payments not yet made until full performance is rendered?

Of course, the answers to questions like these are often found in the terms of the contract itself. If not, they will have to come from the rules of contract law, as applied to the court's understanding of what is often a complicated and highly contested series of events. The law tends to focus on these underlying issues: What is the magnitude of the breach? What is its effect on the other party? What is the likelihood that the breach will be cured? In light of such factors as these, the law determines what responses by the nonbreaching party are or are not permissible.

The final section of this chapter will address a related but distinct situation: where the time for performance has not yet arrived, but the likelihood of nonperformance appears substantial. Sometimes one party to a contract will declare in advance, in no uncertain terms, his unwillingness or inability to perform his duties under that contract. Does the other party have to wait until the time for performance actually arrives before taking any legal action? Or can she treat this "repudiation" as the equivalent of a present breach of contract and act accordingly?

A. EXPRESS CONDITIONS

In this section of Chapter 9, we address the seemingly more clear-cut case where the parties have expressly agreed that the duty of one party (or, perhaps, both of them) should depend on the happening of one or more specified events. The conditioning event might be all or part of one party's performance, but it could just as well be some event completely outside the control of either party. Often it will be an event over which one party has some control, albeit limited.

When an express condition is spelled out in a contract, it will often be a condition to the duty of only one of the parties, because that term has been included in the agreement to protect that party from having to perform in a situation where performance is for some reason less advantageous for her. Thus, for example, a real estate buyer's performance obligation may be conditioned on its ability to obtain a favorable zoning variance, without which the property will be less useful to it. The buyer of a business may condition its duty to complete the purchase on the accuracy of the seller's financial statements at the time of closing. Sometimes one party's duty is conditioned on the other party's giving certain types of notice or providing certain types of information in a particular form, or by a stated time. (This is particularly common in insurance contracts, but it is found in countless other situations as well.) Whatever the motive behind its insistence on a conditioning term, the party whose performance is so conditioned will be referred to in this context as the "obligor," the one whose performance obligation is at issue. The other party will thus be the "obligee" — the one to whom the performance obligation is owed, and the one who is presumably attempting to enforce it.

enXco Development Corp. v. Northern States Power Co.

United States Court of Appeals 758 F.3d 940 (8th Cir. 2014)

Before SMITH, BEAM, and BENTON, Circuit Judges.

SMITH, Circuit Judge.

enXco Development Corp. ("enXco") and Northern States Power Co. (NSP) contracted for the construction of a wind-energy project in North Dakota. enXco did not obtain a permit by a date certain, thus failing to satisfy a condition precedent to the contract. NSP then terminated the contract. enXco suffered several million dollars in losses.

enXco sued NSP for breach of contract. The district court granted NSP's motion for summary judgment. On appeal, enXco contends that the district court erred in granting NSP's motion for summary judgment because the doctrines of temporary impracticability and disproportionate forfeiture prevent the district court from strictly enforcing the relevant condition precedent. We affirm.

I. Background

enXco develops renewable energy projects throughout the United States, especially solar and wind projects. NSP is an electric and gas company that provides energy to customers throughout Minnesota and the Dakotas.

enXco and NSP entered into two contracts in October 2008. The contracts involved a wind-energy-generation project in North Dakota known as the Merricourt Project ("Project"). The parties termed the first contract the Developed Wind Project Purchase and Sale Agreement (PSA). Under the PSA, enXco agreed to develop the Project site, which included obtaining the requisite permits. During this initial phase of the Project, enXco owned the Project's real estate and assets. Upon closing of the PSA, NSP would essentially purchase the Project's real estate and assets for $15 million.

The second, much larger contract was the Engineering, Procurement, and Construction Agreement (EPCA). Pursuant to the EPCA, NSP agreed to pay enXco over $350 million for engineering, procurement of infrastructure, construction, commissioning, start-up, and testing of the Project. The parties agree that one of the principal benefits of this two-contract structure was that neither party had an obligation to proceed with the EPCA until the parties closed the PSA, which would not occur unless the Project developed according to their expectations.

The PSA included various conditions precedent that each party had to satisfy prior to the "Long-Stop Date" set for March 31, 2011. According to enXco, the Long-Stop Date was not a point of contention during contract negotiations. In fact, enXco selected the actual date without argument from NSP. enXco contends that "[t]he purpose of a long-stop date is to serve as a milestone against which to measure whether a project is 'buildable' . . . and such dates are regularly extended." In fact, in two of the parties' previous wind-farm projects, the parties agreed to modify their contracts to postpone the applicable long-stop date.

The PSA also provided that "[t]he obligation of [NSP] to consummate the transactions contemplated by this [PSA] shall be subject to fulfillment at or prior to the Closing of each of the following conditions." One condition precedent required enXco to obtain a Certificate of Site Compatibility (CSC). The CSC is a permit that the North Dakota Public Service Commission (NDPSC) issues that must be obtained before the parties could begin construction on the Project. *See* N.D. Cent. Code §49-22-02. The PSA also included a provision that stated "that in no event shall the Closing occur later than the Long-Stop Date." It also included the following termination clause:

> This Agreement may be terminated prior to the Closing: (i) by either [NSP], on the one side, or [enXco], on the other side, upon written notice to the other

> Party of such termination, in the event the Closing has not occurred or the conditions precedent to Closing in favor of the terminating Party have not been fulfilled or waived on or before the Long-Stop Date. . . .

It also provided that termination could occur without any liability accruing to the terminating party. Finally, the EPCA provided that the parties could terminate the EPCA should they fail to close the PSA.

enXco had approximately 29 months after the execution of the contracts until the Long-Stop Date to obtain the CSC. Under North Dakota law, a party must submit a letter to the NDPSC, stating that it intends to construct an energy conversion facility. *See* N.D. Admin. Code 69-06-03-01. After an applicant like NSP submits this letter, it must wait one year before submitting its CSC application. *See* N.D. Admin. Code 69-06-03-01 (2011) (amended in 2013 to omit the one-year wait period). enXco requested and received from the NDPSC a waiver of the one-year requirement in January 2009; thus, enXco could have submitted its application as early as January 2009.

A CSC application must demonstrate that the project would have a limited impact on endangered species. *See* N.D. Cent. Code §49-22-09(10). Unfortunately for enXco, the United States Fish and Wildlife Service (USFWS) warned enXco that the Project could have a deleterious effect on two species of birds because of the proposed physical locations of the wind turbines. Chris Sternhagen, enXco's Project Development Manager, testified that this problem delayed its submission of the CSC application. He would later testify, however, that the turbine layout actually "played very little impact as to the schedule."

In any event, almost two years expired before enXco submitted the CSC application in October 2010. Thus, enXco had less than six months to obtain the CSC by the Long-Stop Date. North Dakota law, however, allowed the NDPSC to consider the completed CSC application for up to six months after its receipt. *See* N.D. Cent. Code §49-22-08(5). Nonetheless, Sternhagen testified that a NDPSC staff member informed him that a decision would be reached in two-to-four months.

The NDPSC scheduled a statutorily mandated public hearing on the permit for December 21, 2010. Unfortunately, the hearing was postponed due to a snowstorm. The NDPSC conducted the hearing on February 10, 2011, but on March 17, 2011, the NDPSC discovered that the hearing occurred in the wrong county contrary to North Dakota law. *See* N.D. Cent. Code §49-22-13(1). As a result, a new hearing had to be scheduled, but North Dakota law also required a 20-day public notice. *See* N.D. Cent. Code §49-22-13(4). Thus, the hearing was not rescheduled to occur until after the Long-Stop Date. enXco petitioned the NDPSC to waive the 20-day notice requirement. In support of this petition, Sternhagen informed the NDPSC that, unless the NDPSC waived the 20-day requirement, "NSP can terminate the [PSA] between the parties, effectively terminating this Project." At the resulting NDPSC meeting on the petition, enXco's counsel informed the NDPSC that "NSP would have the contractual ability to terminate April 1 and there's nothing that we can do as enXco to prevent that" if enXco did not obtain the CSC prior to the Long-Stop Date. The NDPSC denied the petition. On April 1, 2011, NSP terminated the PSA and thus the EPCA as well after the Long-Stop Date passed. enXco nonetheless obtained the CSC on June 8, 2011.

From execution of the contracts in October 2008 until their termination in April 2011, wind-energy-generation profit prospects declined such that NSP stood to lose significant amounts of money should it proceed with the Project. Apparently the market for wind turbines dried up significantly during this time. As a result, NSP had the economic incentive to avoid the contract—a fact that enXco emphasizes. Because the particular wind turbines that enXco purchased were already outdated, enXco could not resell them on the secondary market. Therefore, enXco redeployed them for use in a different project in Texas.

enXco purchased the turbines for $216 million. Experts testified that the turbines' post-termination value was between $83.3 million and $123 million, minus the $10 million cost enXco incurred to relocate them. Thus, the turbines diminished in value between $93 million and $141 million. enXco's valuation expert determined that the value of the Project's assets like real estate and permits totaled $0 because of the lack of market for the Project and the $15 million cost in maintaining the assets. However, enXco representatives testified that enXco still hoped the Project site would eventually be profitable.

enXco sued NSP on May 4, 2011, in response to a declaratory judgment action that NSP filed based on its termination of the contracts. The district court consolidated the cases, staying NSP's declaratory-judgment action pending the resolution of enXco's suit. enXco sued for declaratory relief and damages for breach of contract. The parties agreed, and the district court concluded, that Minnesota law applied to their contracts.

enXco argued that the doctrines of temporary impracticability and disproportionate forfeiture should apply to prevent strict enforcement of the condition precedent. The district court granted NSP's motion for summary judgment. The district court determined that NSP did not breach the contracts. The district court concluded that the conditions precedent and termination clause expressly permitted NSP to terminate the contracts if enXco failed to satisfy any condition precedent. Furthermore, the district court found that the parties were sophisticated and reached agreement after substantial arms-length negotiation. Thus, according to the district court, enXco should have appreciated the risk that it assumed in the event that it failed to obtain the required permit. The district court declined to apply the doctrine of temporary impracticability to a condition precedent. Additionally, it found that enXco could not demonstrate that it suffered a disproportionate forfeiture because it kept all of the real estate and assets associated with the project and bestowed nothing to NSP. Finally, the district court determined that it need not consider the materiality of conditions precedent as it would typical contract terms. enXco appeals, seeking reversal of the district court's grant of summary judgment to NSP.

II. Discussion

A district court "shall grant summary judgment if the movant shows that there is no genuine dispute as to any material fact and the movant is entitled to judgment as a matter of law." Fed. R. Civ. P. 56(a). . . .

enXco concedes that it failed to obtain the CSC prior to the Long-Stop Date. Furthermore, enXco does not dispute that in so doing it failed to satisfy a condition precedent rather than an ordinary contract term. enXco agrees that if we strictly construe the condition precedent, then NSP had the contractual right to terminate the contracts. However, enXco contends that we should excuse its failure to obtain the CSC by the Long-Stop Date based upon the legal doctrines of temporary impracticability and disproportionate forfeiture.

A. Temporary Impracticability

enXco contends that the doctrine of temporary impracticability should excuse its failure to satisfy the condition precedent that it obtain the CSC by the Long-Stop Date. More specifically, enXco argues that it was impracticable for it to obtain the CSC by the Long-Stop Date because of delays from a snowstorm, a hearing location error, and state law notice requirements. enXco contends that "inclement weather and regulatory error," which delayed the NDPSC's processing of enXco's CSC application for five months, made it "impracticable to obtain the CSC." As a result of this alleged impracticability, enXco was excused from fulfilling the condition precedent, rendering NSP's termination of the PSA and EPCA a breach of contract. Additionally, enXco argues that Minnesota law recognizes the doctrine of temporary impracticability as applied to conditions precedent in a contract. Finally, enXco argues that Minnesota law allows plaintiffs to use the doctrine of temporary impracticability as a sword or offensive legal mechanism to pursue breach-of-contract claims in addition to defendants' use of the doctrine as a shield or defense against such actions.

The doctrine of impracticability applies:

> [w]here, after a contract is made, a party's performance is made impracticable without his fault by the occurrence of an event the non-occurrence of which was a basic assumption on which the contract was made, his duty to render that performance is discharged, unless the language or the circumstances indicate the contrary.

Restatement (Second) of Contracts §261. The Restatement also recognizes that impracticability may sometimes be only temporary:

> Impracticability of performance or frustration of purpose that is only temporary suspends the obligor's duty to perform while the impracticability or frustration exists but does not discharge his duty or prevent it from arising unless his performance after the cessation of the impracticability or frustration would be materially more burdensome than had there been no impracticability or frustration.

Restatement (Second) of Contracts §269. The Restatement further provides for application of the doctrine of temporary impracticability to situations where a promisor violates a condition precedent, stating, "Impracticability excuses the non-occurrence of a condition if the occurrence of the condition is not a material part of the agreed exchange and forfeiture would otherwise result." Restatement (Second) of Contracts §271.

Assuming, without deciding, that Minnesota courts would apply the doctrine of temporary impracticability to conditions precedent for use as a sword, we conclude that the doctrine has no application on these facts. enXco argues that the several delays in holding a proper public hearing produced temporary impracticability. However, enXco waited approximately two years before applying for the CSC. enXco could have applied as early as January 2009, yet it waited until October 2010. enXco submitted its application less than six months before the Long-Stop Date, and North Dakota law expressly authorizes the NDPSC to consider the application for up to six months. See N.D. Cent. Code §49-22-08(5). The PSA's time table contemplated and assumed that the NDPSC process could be lengthy and not entirely predictable.

The various sources of delay were all foreseeable and manageable in the time frame agreed to in the contracts. Although problems surfaced related to endangered birds, enXco likely could have pursued some type of accommodation with the USFWS or NDPSC in order to ensure a timely submission of its application. Or, it could have insisted on a later Long-Stop Date, especially since the actual date was not a point of contention between the parties. enXco could have also negotiated for a more flexible Long-Stop Date (e.g., "The Long-Stop Date shall be no earlier than one year after enXco submits its application for a CSC."). See Vill. Of Minn. v. Fairbanks, Morse & Co., 226 Minn. 1, 31 N.W.2d 920, 926 (1948) ("A man may contract to do what is impossible, as well as what is difficult, and be liable for failure to perform."). In sum, enXco, by exercise of appropriate diligence within the terms of the agreement, could likely have avoided the circumstances that caused it to fail a condition precedent.

Furthermore, Minnesota courts have expressly acknowledged that " '[i]t is well settled that a promise which cannot be performed without the consent or cooperation of a third party is not excused because of the promisor's inability to obtain such cooperation.' " D.H. Blattner & Sons, Inc. v. Firemen's Ins. Co. of Newark, N.J., 535 N.W.2d 671, 675 (Minn. Ct. App. 1995) (quoting St. Paul Dredging Co. v. State, 259 Minn. 398, 107 N.W.2d 717, 723-24 (1961)).[2] Finally,

2. Persuasive authorities confirm this sentiment. See, e.g., 6 Corbin on Contracts §1347 (Perillo rev. ed. 2010) ("[W]hen one contracts to render a performance for which a government license or permit is required, it is his duty to get the license or permit so that he can perform."). Other courts have explicitly recognized that the obtainment of a government permit is foreseeable, and thus the risk of failing to obtain it can be properly allocated to a certain party. See Harvey v. Lake Buena Vista Resort, LLC, 306 Fed. Appx. 471, 473 (11th Cir. 2009) (per curiam) (slow processing of road permit due to several hurricanes was foreseeable); 1700 Rinehart, LLC v. Advance Am., 51 So. 3d 535, 538-39 (Fla. Dist. Ct. App. 2010); Mortenson v. Scheer, 957 P.2d 1302, 1306 (Wyo.1998) ("The obligor is expected to provide in the contract for contingencies that are foreseeable. This is particularly true in an instance in which performance of the contract depends upon obtaining a governmental license or permit which is required." (citations omitted)).

in discussing the doctrines of impossibility and impracticability, Minnesota courts have stated that

> the problem becomes one of allocating between the parties the burden of unreasonably excessive risks which the parties have encountered but which they did not, at the time the contract was made, foresee or provide for and by reason of which a greatly increased burden is placed upon the promisor at the time of performance.

Powers v. Siats, 244 Minn. 515, 70 N.W.2d 344, 349 (1955).

Here, the parties specifically contemplated what would occur in the event that the CSC was not obtained by the Long-Stop Date: NSP could terminate the contract. The PSA language regarding the satisfaction of conditions precedent and the termination clause expressly say so. The parties foresaw the risk of regulatory and weather delays and accounted for them. Although they could not foresee the specific circumstances that led to the non-occurrence of the condition, it is clear that the parties anticipated that the CSC might not be obtained in time. Furthermore, the doctrine of temporary impracticability does not apply when the government fails to issue a permit in a timely manner, especially where the parties recognized this possibility. See D.H. Blattner, 535 N.W.2d at 675. Consequently, the district court correctly declined to apply the doctrine of temporary impracticability.

B. Disproportionate Forfeiture

enXco argues that it suffered a disproportionate forfeiture. enXco experienced an approximately $100 million diminution in value of its properties. On the other hand, NSP suffered no meaningful harm from enXco's tardy CSC. enXco further argues that Minnesota courts recognize that the doctrine of disproportionate forfeiture applies to the non-fulfillment of a condition precedent as well as for use as a sword rather than a shield. The district court determined that enXco did not suffer a disproportionate forfeiture because it retained title to all of the real estate and assets involved in the Project. enXco never transferred any of this property to NSP.

Assuming, without deciding, that Minnesota courts would apply the doctrine of disproportionate forfeiture to the non-occurrence of conditions precedent and for use as a breach-of-contract sword, we conclude that enXco has not suffered a disproportionate forfeiture. We reach this conclusion despite the alleged materiality of the condition precedent at issue. The Restatement notes that a "forfeiture" "refer[s] to the denial of compensation that results when the obligee loses his right to the agreed exchange after he has relied substantially, as by preparation or performance on the expectation of that exchange." Restatement (Second) of Contracts §229 cmt. b. The Restatement further states:

> In determining whether the forfeiture is "disproportionate," a court must weigh the extent of the forfeiture by the obligee against the importance to the obligor of the risk from which he sought to be protected and the degree to which that

> protection will be lost if the non-occurrence of the condition is excused to the extent required to prevent forfeiture.

Id. Weighing these competing interests as the Restatement suggests can be difficult.

Nevertheless, we have recognized that forfeitures may be appropriate where they are "consonant with notions of fairness and justice under the law." Klipsch, Inc. v. WWR Tech., Inc., 127 F.3d 729, 737 (8th Cir. 1997) (quotation and citation omitted) (applying Indiana law). This court in *Klipsch* noted that forfeiture may be fair and just where able counsel represented sophisticated parties. Id. Also, forfeitures are legitimate when the parties included an express termination clause in the contract. Id. Additionally, no forfeiture occurs where the breaching party maintained ownership of the assets comprising the contract. Id. at 738. Minnesota courts are more likely to enforce express terms in a contract where counsel represented sophisticated parties in the drafting of the contract at issue. *See* Metro. Sports Facilities Com'n v. Gen. Mills, Inc., 470 N.W.2d 118, 125 (Minn. 1991) (en banc) ("These sophisticated parties, presumably with the assistance of experienced and able counsel, exercised their liberty of contract and now are accountable for the product of their negotiations.")[3]

Here, enXco parted with nothing. It still maintained possession and ownership of the Project assets and real estate. enXco transferred the Project's physical capital for use in other projects, and it hopes to employ the real property associated with the Project in the future. NSP did not obtain ownership of any property as a result of termination. NSP therefore did not receive something for little or nothing. Cf. Hideaway, Inc. v. Gambit Invs. Inc., 386 N.W.2d 822, 824 (Minn. Ct. App. 1986) (disproportionate-forfeiture doctrine applied where contract allowed non-breaching party to retain a business worth $13,000 after paying only $500). Notably, both enXco and NSP are sophisticated parties who have developed similar projects in the past. They were both represented by counsel during contract negotiations, which took place over the course of several months. In conclusion, we leave the parties to their bargain and do not apply the doctrine of disproportionate forfeiture.

III. CONCLUSION

We affirm the judgment of the district court.

BEAM, Circuit Judge, concurring specially.

I concur in Parts I, II, IIA and III. The issues arising from the contracts at work in this dispute are continuing evidence of the country's unforeseen and unfortunate economic turndown commencing in or about 2006 or 2007. There

3. See also Harleysville Ins. Co. v. Physical Distribution Servs., Inc., 716 F.3d 451, 462 (8th Cir. 2013) (applying Minnesota law) ("Both [parties] were sophisticated parties — each was in the business of providing products and services in exchange for fees according to terms set by contract. In this context, common sense weighs most heavily in favor of giving the parties the benefits — and misfortunes — of the clear terms of their bargain."); 13 Williston on Contracts §38:12 (4th ed. 2014) ("Although the court may regret the harshness of an express condition, as it may regret the harshness of a promise, it must nevertheless generally enforce the will of the parties unless to do so will violate public policy." (footnote omitted)).

has been, as a result, a clearly disproportionate forfeiture suffered by enXco, possibly aided and abetted by NSP as it saw an obvious need to abandon this unneeded project. In my view, however, such a consequence is insufficient to allow enXco to overcome the force and effect of the "condition precedent" in dispute as contractually agreed upon by the parties.

NOTES AND QUESTIONS

1. *Language sufficient to create an express condition.* The *enXco* court stated briefly at the beginning of its legal discussion that enXco conceded that it "failed to satisfy a condition precedent rather than an ordinary contract term" and that "strict" enforcement would mean that the defendant was entitled to terminate the contract. Thus, the court's opinion focused primarily on enXco's arguments for "excuse" from the express condition rather than whether such a condition existed. It should be noted, however, that in many cases involving an express condition as a defense to liability for nonperformance, a threshold and fiercely debated issue will be whether the duty in question was indeed so conditioned. The Restatement (Second) §224 defines a condition as "an event, not certain to occur, which must occur . . . before performance under a contract becomes due." Courts are typically emphatic that an "express condition" must be stated in unambiguous language because express conditions must be literally performed or satisfied; substantial performance will not suffice. See, e.g., MHR Capital Partners LP v. Presstek, Inc. 912 N.E.2d 43 (N.Y. 2009) (noting that courts have recognized that the use of terms such as "if," "unless," and "until" constitutes "unmistakable language of condition").

In making the determination whether a term is an express condition, it is important to note that the Restatement (Second) §227 prefers an interpretation that a term or event is not an express condition in order to reduce the risk of forfeiture. In Solar Applications Eng'g, Inc. v. T.A. Operating Corp., 327 S.W.3d 104 (Tex. 2010), the court relied heavily on that interpretive preference in concluding that a "lien-release affidavit" required before final payment to the builder in a construction project was only a promise and not an express condition. The court noted that whether a term is an express condition depends on the intent of the parties, but such a finding requires clear, unambiguous language. An express condition will not be found if there is another reasonable interpretation. Thus, the contractor could satisfy its obligation to deliver a lien-free property through other means and still be entitled to the final payment. Id. at 112-113. See also Lokan & Associates, Inc. v. American Beef, 311 P.3d 1285 (Wash. Ct. App. 2013) (doubtful language concerning receipt of federal funding by client would not be construed as an express condition to recruiter's right to payment).

2. *Strict enforcement of express conditions.* Once the court has determined that the contract term in question really does expressly condition the obligor's duty of performance on the occurrence of some event, what will be the effect

of its nonoccurrence? Until the conditioning event does occur, the duty does not arise; at the point when it cannot (or for some reason clearly will not) occur, the obligor is discharged from its performance obligations under the contract. Restatement (Second) §225. Although the "strict enforcement" approach to express conditions may be characteristic of classical contract law, it is alive and well today, as the *enXco* opinion demonstrates. Another example of the rule is found in Maxton Builders v. Lo Galbo, 502 N.E.2d 184 (N.Y. 1986) in which the buyers entered into a real estate contract that included a handwritten term providing that they could cancel the contract "upon written notice to the seller within three days" if the real estate taxes were determined to exceed $3,500. Upon discovering the next day that the taxes exceeded the stated amount, the buyers' attorney telephoned the seller's counsel and informed him that the contact was being cancelled. The buyers' attorney also sent a certified letter giving notice on the second day following contract formation but it was not received until the sixth day. The court held that it was "settled law" that a written notice required by a contract would be ineffective unless actually received within the stated time. Id. at 186. (You might be interested to know that the attorney in *Maxton* who failed to give the requisite written notice of cancellation on behalf of his clients was later held to have thereby committed actionable malpractice as a matter of law, despite assertions that he relied on the other attorney's assurances that oral notice was sufficient. Lo Galbo v. Plishkin, Rubano & Baum, 558 N.Y.S.2d 185 (App. Div. 1990).)

The Restatement (Second) endorses the general rule of strict enforcement of express conditions and Comment *d* to §237 rejects the application of a "substantial performance" qualification to that rule. See also Sun Valley, Ltd. v. Galyan's Trading Co., LLC, 2014 WL 1030956 (E.D. Mich.) (express condition in lease requiring a "Sears Great Indoors" store as anchor tenant in mall could not be satisfied by "Sears outlet store"; substantial performance rule does not apply to essential contract term).

3. *Distinction between express conditions and promises.* As suggested by the preceding notes, one issue of interpretation that frequently arises concerning contract terms involves the distinction between a condition and a promise. The difference is critically important because while an express condition requires strict compliance, a promise generally requires only "substantial performance," a concept explored in more detail in the Jacob & Youngs, Inc. v. Kent case in the following section of this chapter. If a condition fails, the obligor is discharged from further obligations under the contract. On the other hand, the breach of a promise does not necessarily discharge the obligor and may only give rise to a claim for damages for breach of the promise. As analyzed by the *enXco* court, the plaintiff's failure to acquire the permit by the stated date amounted to failure of a condition, releasing the defendant from any duty to proceed with the transactions. Could the term requiring the permit also be interpreted as a promise by the plaintiff to make timely application with the state agencies, the breach of which would give rise to a cause of action against enXco for breach of contract? It is clear that NSP was delighted to simply have the contracts discharged because they had become financially

disadvantageous, but suppose the contract had been profitable to NSP, could NSP have held enXco liable for damages because of the unreasonable delay in seeking the permits?

However one interprets the provision in *enXco*, there is no principled reason why a contractual term cannot be interpreted as *both* a promise and an express condition. See, e.g., Weber v. North Loup River Public Power and Irrigation Dist., 854 N.W.2d 263 (Neb. 2014) (farmer's obligation to pay annual fees to irrigation district was both a promise and an express condition precedent to district's obligation to deliver water in succeeding irrigation season). If an event is a "promissory condition," failure of the event to occur justifies the obligor in treating her obligations as discharged, and also subjects the obligee to liability for damages.

4. *"Pay-when-paid" clauses.* The preceding discussion indicates that a contract term might be interpreted by a court as either an express condition or as a promise, or possibly as both. Yet another possibility is that a term that defines a performance obligation by reference to the happening of some event may be *neither* a promise nor a condition. Thus, in cases where the language of the contract in some fashion links a subcontractor's right to payment for work performed to the general contractor's receipt of payment from the owner (sometimes referred to as a "pay-when-paid" clause), the majority of courts have preferred to interpret such language as merely calling for payment within a reasonable time, and not as also conditioning the subcontractor's right to payment on such prior receipt of payment by the general contractor. To rule otherwise, the courts have pointed out, would require the subcontractor to assume the risk of the owner's credit, with the accompanying possibility of forfeiture. To achieve that result, strong language will be needed (and even then may not be effective). See Superior Steel, Inc. v. Ascent at Roebling's Bridge, Inc., 540 S.W.3d 770 (Ky. 2018) (acknowledging that a "pay-when-paid" clause will usually be interpreted as mere timing mechanism and not as a term placing risk of nonpayment on subcontractor, but explicit "pay-*if*-paid" clause in construction subcontract would be given effect as express condition precedent under principle of freedom of contract). Some states regulate such clauses by statutes, which generally protect the subcontractor in varying degrees. See generally Margie Alsbrook, Contracting Away an Honest Day's Pay: An Examination of Conditional Payment Clauses in Construction Contracts, 58 Ark. L. Rev. 353 (2005).

There are a variety of other situations in which a duty to make payment is expressly conditioned on the happening of some event or the receipt of some funding by the obligor. See, e.g., P & E Properties, Inc. v. United Natural Foods, Inc., 713 F. Supp. 2d 262 (S.D.N.Y. 2010) (right of provider of administrative services to receive reimbursement from client for "extraordinary expenses" was expressly conditioned on prior written approval of such expenditures by client); Ferguson Advisors, LLC v. Malherbe, 274 P.3d 839 (Okla. Civ. App. 2011) (realtor who agreed to delay portion of broker's fee otherwise due at closing until buyer paid deferred portion of purchase price assumed risk that payment by buyer would not be made).

5. *Conditions precedent and subsequent.* The *enXco* court classifies the requirement of the permit as a "condition precedent." The phrasing intimates a distinction that courts traditionally made between conditions *precedent* and conditions *subsequent.* A condition precedent refers to an event that must exist or occur *before* a duty to perform will arise. A condition subsequent contemplates that a duty would be owed but subject to discharge on the happening of an event *after* that duty had originally arisen. See Joseph M. Perillo, Contracts §11.5, §11.7 (7th ed. 2014). If *enXco* illustrates a condition precedent, an example of a condition subsequent, in effect, is found in Jenkins v. Eckerd Corp., 913 So. 2d 43 (Fla. Dist. Ct. App. 2005), in which the tenant drug store had a long-term lease in a shopping center that allowed the tenant to terminate on 90-day notice if the anchor supermarket ever ceased operations. After operating for almost 20 years, the supermarket closed as part of bankruptcy proceedings and the tenant was allowed to terminate. The more modern view, however, reflected in the Restatement (Second) §224, Comment *e*, is that the distinction between conditions precedent and subsequent is unhelpful and should not be generally recognized. See also Gingras v. Avery, 878 A.2d 404, 408 n.4 (Conn. App. Ct. 2005) (modern view is that condition precedent versus subsequent distinction obscures more than it clarifies and results in confusion).

6. *Excuses due to impracticability and similar contract defenses.* Much of the *enXco* opinion is focused on the plaintiff's arguments for excusing the nonoccurrence of the express condition and enforcing the contract against the defendant notwithstanding the fact that the permit was not obtained by the deadline. The court indicated a general receptiveness to the theory that the impracticability doctrine might serve to excuse nonoccurrence of an express condition. The plaintiff needed to establish, however, that the elements of an impracticability defense were met. (Recall the discussion of impracticability in the *Hemlock* case in Chapter 8.) The *enXco* court found the plaintiff's impracticability claim lacking in at least two respects: The nonoccurrence was largely the fault of enXco and the contract assigned to enXco the risk that governmental approval might not be granted by the deadline. Note that a party might also seek to excuse an express condition based on other grounds for refusing enforcement to a term, such as inconsistency with public policy, unconscionability or mistake, if the elements of those doctrines can be shown. See generally Joseph M. Perillo, Contracts §11.36 (7th ed. 2014).

7. *Excuse to avoid disproportionate forfeiture.* The *enXco* court considered at length the possibility that the contract might be enforced, despite the failure of express condition, to avoid forfeiture. Even though enXco allegedly lost more than $100 million due to a decrease in value of the real property and other assets, the court identified a number of reasons to reject enXco's claim of disproportionate forfeiture – enXco still owned the property and assets and it did not transfer anything to NSP, the contract was negotiated by sophisticated parties with the assistance of counsel, the bargain expressly allowed for termination by NSP under the circumstances, and NSP did not obtain valuable property from enXco for little or nothing. Thus, the court left the parties to their bargain. The possibility of excuse due to forfeiture is also advanced, with

more success, by the plaintiff in J. N. A. Realty Corp. v. Cross Bay Chelsea Inc., the next case in these materials. We will further address the forfeiture theory in the notes following the *JNA* case.

8. *Excuse due to immateriality.* In recounting the trial court decision, the appellate court in *enXco* briefly mentions that the lower court had declined to consider an argument that the condition should be excused because it was not a material term of the contract. In fact, the trial court considered the argument at length before concluding that under the traditional requirement of strict compliance with express conditions, materiality is not a factor. See enXco Dev. Corp. v. Northern States Power Co., 2013 WL 1364242 (D. Minn.). The argument that immateriality should be a recognized excuse was forcefully made in an article by Professor Robert Childres, Conditions in the Law of Contracts, 45 N.Y.U. L. Rev. 33 (1970). After examining scores of decisions citing the conditions provisions of the first Restatement, Childres concluded that almost all modern courts (as of 1970, that is) would actually insist on strict performance of conditions only when the conditioning events are material to the agreement of the parties. Conditions that are merely "technical" he found to be generally excused under various theories such as adverse interpretation, waiver, prevention, or avoidance of forfeiture. Professor Childres recommended that courts abandon these theories in favor of a broader rule: Only material conditions should be strictly enforced. At least some courts appear to share Professor Childres's belief that the issue of materiality should be relevant to the question of how strictly a condition should be enforced. See, e.g, Sahadi v. Continental Illinois Nat'l Bank & Trust Co., 706 F.2d 193, 198 n.2 (7th Cir. 1983) (slight delay in making interest payments would not trigger failure of condition, accelerating payment of entire debt obligation; earlier precedents to the contrary were "decided in the salad days of American legal formalism which were marked by an unprecedented adherence to the letter of contractual text — a jurisprudential posture that has since been eclipsed by the kind of materiality approach embodied in [later Illinois cases]"). Adopting *arguendo* Professor Childres's approach, does it appear to you that the condition involved in the *enXco* case was material?

9. *Waiver and estoppel of condition.* An obligor whose duty is expressly dependent on a condition may be under a duty to perform despite the nonoccurrence of that condition, if a court finds that he has, by word or conduct, "waived" the right to insist on fulfillment of the condition before performing the duty. Restatement (Second) §84(1) expresses the concept of waiver (the term itself is not used in the section, but see Comment *b*). As usually defined, waiver is "an intentional relinquishment of a known right." As expressed in §84(1), a waiver is effective without either consideration or reliance, but only if the condition waived was not either a material part of the performance that the obligor was to receive in exchange or a material part of the risk assumed. Compare Savre v. Santoyo, 865 N.W.2d 419 (N.D. 2015) (affirming trial court conclusion that landlord waived express condition in lease-to-purchase option that required monthly lease payments for property to be made on time), with Fitzpatrick v. American Intern. Group, Inc., 2013 WL 709048 (S.D.N.Y.) (rejecting waiver

claim related to express condition requiring former employee to give notice of alleged breach by employer within 30 days of occurrence to be entitled to future profits; waiver will not be lightly inferred and continuing discussions with employee did not amount to intentional waiver by employer).

If the condition in *enXco* was merely minor — "procedural or technical" — it could be waived by the defendant-obligor's expression of intention to do so. If it were not minor, but material, it could still be overcome by an estoppel, based on the obligor's expression of intention not to insist on it, followed by the plaintiff-obligee's prejudicial reliance on that manifestation of intention. Note that the courts are not always precise in categorizing the type of excuse being recognized. See, e.g., In re Transact, Inc., 2014 WL 3888230 (C.D. Cal.) (lender "waived" express condition that contractor be "in good standing in California and Nevada" by disbursing first two draws of funds, knowing that condition was not satisfied; contractor relied to its substantial detriment on continued funding by incurring construction expenses).

10. *Prevention of condition.* Another potential basis for excuse is the doctrine of "prevention," which states that a condition is excused if the promisor wrongfully hinders or prevents the condition from occurring. E.g., United Partition Systems, Inc. v. United States, 90 Fed. Cl. 74 (2009) (stating that federal government like any other contracting party has an implied duty not to prevent or delay performance by the other party). See Restatement (Second) §245. Where the conditioning event is to some extent within the obligor's control, the obligor is likely to have at least the obligation to attempt to cause the condition to occur. E.g., Stendig, Inc. v. Thom Rock Realty Co., 558 N.Y.S.2d 917 (App. Div. 1990) (where both parties' obligations under lease of showroom space in design center were conditioned on landlord's having rented minimum amount of square feet of space, landlord subject to implied duty to use "good faith best efforts" to obtain tenants, citing Wood v. Lucy, Lady Duff-Gordon). Even if the event is not within the obligor's control, she may be under an obligation (express or implied) to cooperate with the obligee in causing the condition to happen, or at the minimum not to impede those efforts. E.g., Fateh v. Rich, 481 A.2d 464 (D.C. 1984) (defendant buyers of restaurant business wrongfully prevented condition that liquor authority give its consent to transfer of liquor license by engaging person with criminal record as manager of restaurant business, in violation of liquor authority policy). The question is often a difficult one, however, and courts have frequently held that the possibility of prevention of the condition by the obligor was a risk assumed by the obligee, and thus not "wrongful."

J. N. A. Realty Corp. v. Cross Bay Chelsea, Inc.

New York Court of Appeals 42 N.Y.2d 392, 366 N.E.2d 1313, 397 N.Y.S.2d 958 (N.Y. 1977)

WACHTLER, Judge.

J. N. A. Realty Corp., the owner of a building in Howard Beach, commenced this proceeding to recover possession of the premises claiming that the lease has expired. The lease grants the tenant, Cross Bay Chelsea, Inc., an option to renew and although the notice was sent, through negligence or inadvertence, it was not sent within the time prescribed in the lease. The landlord seeks to enforce the letter of the agreement. The tenant asks for equity to relieve it from a forfeiture.

The Civil Court, after a trial, held that the tenant was entitled to equitable relief. The Appellate Term affirmed, without opinion, but the Appellate Division, after granting leave, reversed and granted the petition. The tenant has appealed to this court.

Two primary questions are raised on the appeal. First, will the tenant suffer a forfeiture if the landlord is permitted to enforce the letter of the agreement. Secondly, if there will be a forfeiture, may a court of equity grant the tenant relief when the forfeiture would result from the tenant's own neglect or inadvertence.

At the trial it was shown that J. N. A. Realty Corp. (hereafter JNA) originally leased the premises to Victor Palermo and Sylvester Vascellero for a 10-year term commencing on January 1, 1964. Paragraph 58 of the lease, which was attached as part of 12-page rider, granted the tenants an option to renew for a 10-year term provided "that Tenant shall notify the landlord in writing by registered or certified mail six (6) months prior to the last day of the term of the lease that tenant desires such renewal." The tenants opened a restaurant on the premises. In February, 1964 they formed the Foro Romano Corp. (Foro) and assigned the lease to the corporation.

By December of 1967 the restaurant was operating at a loss and Foro decided to close it down and offer it for sale or lease. In March, 1968 Foro entered into a contract with Cross Bay Chelsea, Inc. (hereafter Chelsea), to sell the restaurant and assign the lease. As a condition of the sale Foro was required to obtain a modification of the option to renew so that Chelsea would have the right to renew the lease for an additional term of 24 years.

The closing took place in June of 1968. First JNA modified the option and consented to the assignment. The modification, which consists of a separate document to be attached to the lease, states: "the Tenant shall have a right to renew this lease for a further period of Twenty-Four (24) years, instead of Ten (10) years, from the expiration of the original term of said lease. . . . All other provisions of Paragraph #58 in said lease, . . . shall remain in full force and effect, except as hereinabove modified." Foro then assigned the lease and sold its interest in the restaurant to Chelsea for $155,000. The bill of sale states that "the value of the fixtures and chattels included in this sale is the sum of $40,000 and that the remainder of the purchase price is the value of the leasehold and possession of the restaurant premises." At that point five and one-half years remained on the original term of the lease.

In the summer of 1968 Chelsea reopened the restaurant. JNA's president, Nicholas Arena, admitted on the stand that throughout the tenancy it regularly informed Chelsea in writing of its obligations under the lease, such as the need to pay taxes and insurance by certain dates. For instance on June 13, 1973 JNA sent a letter to Chelsea informing them that certain taxes were due to be paid. When that letter was sent the option to renew was due to expire in approximately two weeks but JNA made no mention of this. A similar letter was sent to Chelsea in September, 1973.

Arena also admitted that throughout the term of the tenancy he was "most assuredly" aware of the time limitation on the option. In fact there is some indication in the record that JNA had previously used this device in an attempt to evict another tenant. Nevertheless it was not until November 12, 1973 that JNA took any action to inform the tenant that the option had lapsed. Then it sent a letter noting that the date had passed and, the letter states, "not having heard from you as prescribed by paragraph #58 in our lease we must assume you will vacate the premises" at the expiration of the original term, January 1, 1974. By letter dated November 16, 1973 Chelsea, through its attorney, sent written notice of intention to renew the option which, of course, JNA refused to honor.

At the trial Chelsea's principals claimed that they were not aware of the time limitation because they had never received a copy of paragraph 58 of the rider. They had received a copy of the modification but they had assumed that it gave them an absolute right to retain the tenancy for 24 years after the expiration of the original term. However, at the trial and later at the Appellate Division, it was found that Chelsea had knowledge of, or at least was "chargeable with notice" of, the time limitation in the rider and thus was negligent in failing to renew within the time prescribed.

Chelsea's principals also testified that they had spent an additional $15,000 on improvements, at least part of which had been expended after the option had expired. Toward the end of the trial JNA's attorney asked the court whether it would "take evidence from" Arena that he had negotiated with another tenant after the option to renew had lapsed. However, the court held that this testimony would be immaterial.

It is a settled principle of law that a notice exercising an option is ineffective if it is not given within the time specified (see, e.g., Restatement, Contracts 2d [Tent. Draft No. 1, 1964], §64, subd. [b]; 1A Corbin, Contracts [1963], §264; 1 Williston, Contracts [3d ed. 1957], §87; Sy Jack Realty Co. v. Pergament Syosset Corp., 27 N.Y.2d 449, 318 N.Y.S.2d 720, 267 N.E.2d 462). "At law, of course, time is always of the essence of the contract" (De Funiak, Modern Equity, §80, p. 223). Thus the tenant had no legal right to exercise the option when it did, but to say that is simply to pose the issue; it does not resolve it. Of course the tenant would not be asking for equitable relief if it could establish its rights at law.

The major obstacle to obtaining equitable relief in these cases is that default on an option usually does not result in a forfeiture. The reason is that the option itself does not create any interest in the property, and no rights accrue until the condition precedent has been met by giving notice within the time specified. Thus equity will not intervene because the loss of the option does not ordinarily result in the forfeiture of any vested rights. . . . It has been suggested that even when the option has been paid for, nothing is forfeited when it expires, because the amount paid "is the exact agreed equivalent" of the power to exercise the right for the time allotted (see 1 Corbin, Contracts, §35, p. 147).

But when a tenant in possession under an existing lease has neglected to exercise an option to renew, he might suffer a forfeiture if he has made valuable improvements on the property. This of course generally distinguishes the lease option, to renew or purchase, from the stock option or the option to buy goods. This was a distinction which some of the older cases failed to recognize. . . . More recently it has been noted that "although the tenant has no legal interest in the renewal period until the required notice is given, yet an equitable interest is recognized and protected against forfeiture in some cases where the tenant has in good faith made improvements of a substantial character, intending to renew the lease, if the landlord is not harmed by the delay in the giving of the notice and the lessee would sustain substantial loss in case the lease were not renewed" (2 Pomeroy, Equity Jurisprudence [5th ed.], §453b, p. 296).

The leading case on this point is Fountain Co. v. Stein, 97 Conn. 619, 118 A. 47, 27 A.L.R. 976 and the rule has been accepted by noted commentators (see, e.g., 1 Corbin, op. cit., §35, p. 146; 1 Williston, Contracts [3d ed.], §76, p. 249, n.4; 2 Pomeroy, op. cit., §453b, p. 296). It has also been accepted and applied by this court. In Jones v. Gianferante, 305 N.Y. 135, 138, 111 N.E.2d 419, 420, citing the *Fountain* case we held that the tenant was entitled to "the benefit of the rule or practice in equity which relieves against such forfeitures of valuable lease terms when default in notice has not prejudiced the landlord, and has resulted from an honest mistake, or similar excusable fault." The rule was extended in Sy Jack Realty Co. v. Pergament Syosset Corp., 27 N.Y.2d 449, 453, 318 N.Y.S.2d 720, 722, 267 N.E.2d 462, 464, supra to preserve the tenant's interest in a "long-standing location for a retail business" because this is "an important part of the good will of that enterprise, [and thus] the tenant stands to lose a substantial and valuable asset."

In neither of those cases were we asked to consider whether the tenant would be entitled to equitable relief from the consequences of his own neglect or "mere forgetfulness" as the court had held in the *Fountain* case, supra. In *Gianferante* the default was due to an ambiguous lease, and in *Sy Jack* the notice was mailed but never delivered. . . . But the principle involved is well established in this State. A tenant or mortgagor should not be denied equitable relief from the consequences of his own neglect or inadvertence if a forfeiture would result (Giles v. Austin, 62 N.Y. 486; Noyes v. Anderson, 124 N.Y. 175, 26 N.E. 316. . . .) The rule applies even though the tenant or mortgagor, by his inadvertence, has neglected to perform an affirmative duty and thus breached a covenant in the agreement (Giles v. Austin, supra; Noyes v. Anderson, supra).

On occasion the court has cautioned that equitable relief would be denied where there has been a willful or gross neglect (Noyes v. Anderson, supra, 124 N.Y. p. 179, 26 N.E. p. 317), but it has been reluctant to employ the sanction when a forfeiture would result. In Giles v. Austin, supra, p. 491, for instance, the landlord sought to recover possession of the premises after the tenant had neglected to pay the taxes as required by a covenant in the lease. We held that although the tenant had not paid the taxes since the inception of the lease in 1859, and had only paid them after suit was commenced in 1868, the tenant's default was not "so willful, or his neglect so inexcusable, that a court of equity should have denied him any relief."

There are several cases in which this court has denied a tenant or mortgagor equitable relief because of his own neglect to perform within the time fixed in the lease or mortgage, but only when it has found that there was "no penalty, no forfeiture" (Graf v. Hope Bldg. Corp., 254 N.Y. 1, 4, 171 N.E. 884, 885 . . .). Cardozo took a different view. He felt that even though there may be no penalty or forfeiture "in a strict or proper sense" equity should "relieve against it if default has been due to mere venial inattention and if relief can be granted without damage to the lender." Even in those cases he would apply the general equitable principle that "the gravity of the fault must be compared with the gravity of the hardship" (Graf v. Hope Bldg. Corp., supra, 254 N.Y. pp. 9-10, 13, 171 N.E. p. 888 [Cardozo, Ch. J., dissenting]; see, also, 2 Pomeroy, Equity Jurisprudence [5th ed.], §439, p. 220).

Here, as noted, the tenant has made a considerable investment in improvements on the premises — $40,000 at the time of purchase, and an additional $15,000 during the tenancy. In addition, if the location is lost, the restaurant would undoubtedly lose a considerable amount of its customer good will. The tenant was at fault, but not in a culpable sense. It was, as Cardozo says, "mere venial inattention." There would be a forfeiture and the gravity of the loss is certainly out of all proportion to the gravity of the fault. Thus, under the circumstances of this case, the tenant would be entitled to equitable relief if there is no prejudice to the landlord.

However, it is not clear from the record whether JNA would be prejudiced if the tenant is relieved of its default. Because of the trial court's ruling, JNA was unable to submit proof that it might be prejudiced if the terms of the agreement were not enforced literally. Its proof of other negotiations was considered immaterial. It may be that after the tenant's default the landlord, relying on the agreement, in good faith, made other commitments for the premises. But if JNA did not rely on the letter of the agreement then, it should not be permitted to rely on it now to exact a substantial forfeiture for the tenant's unwitting default. This, however, must be resolved at a new trial.

Finally we would note, as the dissenters do, that it is possible to imagine a situation in which a tenant holding an option to renew might intentionally delay beyond the time prescribed in order to exploit a fluctuating market. However, as the dissenters also note, there is no evidence to suggest that that is what occurred here. On the contrary there has been an affirmed finding of fact that the tenant's late notice was due to negligence. Of course a tenant who has intentionally delayed should not be relieved of a forfeiture simply because this tenant, who was merely inadvertent, may be granted equitable relief. But, on the other hand, we do not believe that this tenant, or any tenant, guilty only of negligence should be denied equitable relief because some other tenant, in some other case, may be found to have acted in bad faith. By its nature equitable relief must always depend on the facts of the particular case and not on hypotheticals.

Accordingly, the order of the Appellate Division should be reversed and a new trial granted.

BREITEL, Chief Judge (dissenting). . . .

In this State, as in others, relief has been afforded tenants threatened with loss of an expected renewal period (see, generally, Effect of Lessee's Failure or Delay in Giving Notice Within Specified Time, of Intention to Renew Lease, Ann., 44 A.L.R.2d 1359, esp. 1362-1369). But in New York, as elsewhere, the circumstances conditioning such relief have been carefully limited. It is only where the tenant can show, not mere negligence, but an excuse such as fraud, mistake, or accident, that is, one or more of the categories common and integral to invocation of equity, that courts have, despite the literal agreement and intention of the parties, stepped in to prevent a loss (see, e.g., Jones v. Gianferante, 305 N.Y. 135, 138-139, 111 N.E.2d 419, 420, supra; 1 McAdam, Landlord and Tenant [5th ed.], §156, pp. 721-722).

Even in the case of excusable default by the tenant the court looks to the investment the tenant has made to bolster his right to equitable relief. But the fact of tenant investment alone is not enough to justify intervention. . . . In no case of accepted or acceptable authority . . . were improvements alone enough to help the negligent tenant. . . .

. . . For reasons that are not persuasive [the majority] would distinguish, however, between mere neglect or forgetfulness and gross or willful negligence, whatever that might be. . . . This is not a distinction generally accepted and is hardly a pragmatic one to apply in an area where the opportunities for distortion and manipulation are so great. The instability and uncertainty would be dangerous and would allow for ad hoc dispensations in particular cases without reliable rule so essential to commercial enterprise.

To begin with, under the guise of sheer inadvertence, a tenant could gamble with a fluctuating market, at the expense of his landlord, by delaying his decision beyond the time fixed in the agreement. The market having resolved in favor of exercising the option, the landlord, even though the day appointed in the agreement has passed, could be held to the return set out in the option, although if the market had resolved otherwise, the tenant could not be held to the renewal period.

None of this is to say that the tenant in this case was guilty of any manipulation. Hardly so. But what the court is concerned with is a rule for this case which perforce must cover other cases of like kind, where there will be no assurance that the "forgetfulness" is no more than that. The worst of the matter is that the kind of paltry record made in this case is hardly one on which a new rule with potential for mischief should be based. When the option, especially one requiring notice well in advance of the expiration of the lease, permits of economic manipulation, in commercial fairness the parties, especially if represented by counsel, should be held to their bargain, if plainly expressed.

Considering investments in the premises or the renewal term a "forfeiture" as alone warranting equitable relief would undermine if not dissolve the general rule upon which there is agreement. For, it is difficult to imagine a dilatory commercial tenant, particularly one in litigation over a renewal, who would not or could not point, scrupulously or unscrupulously, to some threatened investment in the premises, be it a physical improvement or the fact of good will. As a practical matter, it is not unreasonable to expect the commercial tenant, as compared with his residential counterpart, to protect his business interests with meticulousness, a meticulousness to which he would hold his landlord. All he, or his lawyer, need do is red-flag the date on which he has to act.

Having established no excuse, other than its own carelessness, Chelsea's claim is unfounded. Even if Chelsea honestly thought it enjoyed a 30-year lease, it does not change the result. Nor is it helpful to argue that Chelsea, always represented by a lawyer, was unable to procure a copy of the entire lease agreement. Indeed, it borders on the utterly incredible that experienced, sophisticated businessmen and their lawyers would not have assembled and scrutinized every relevant document affecting a longterm lease covering, with a renewal, a 30-year period.

That adherence to well-settled principles, like a Statute of Limitations or a Statute of Frauds, works a hardship on some does not, alone, permit a court to depart from sound doctrine and principles. Even if precedent did not control the same doctrines and principles discussed should be applied.

Accordingly, I dissent and vote that the order of the Appellate Division should be affirmed, and the landlord awarded possession of the premises.

GABRIELLI, FUCHSBERG and COOKE, JJ., concur with WACHTLER, J.

BREITEL, C.J., dissents and votes to affirm in a separate opinion in which JASEN and JONES, JJ., concur.

Order reversed, with costs, and a new trial granted.

NOTES AND QUESTIONS

1. *Meaning of forfeiture.* In §229, the Restatement (Second) states as a general proposition that a court may excuse the nonoccurrence of a condition where disproportionate forfeiture would otherwise result, unless the conditioning event was a material part of the parties' exchange. In Comment *b* to §229, quoted in the *enXco* opinion, the Restatement (Second) defines "forfeiture" as "the denial of compensation that results when the obligee loses [its] right to the agreed exchange after [it] has relied substantially, as by preparation or performance on the expectation of that exchange." See, e.g., Aeolus Down, Inc. v. Credit Suisse Int'l, 2011 WL 5570062 (S.D.N.Y.) (plaintiff creditor stated plausible case for disproportionate forfeiture through loss of more than $650,000 premium paid for $2 million insurance protection if claim was barred because of failure to give notice to insurer within 25 days of debtor's bankruptcy filing; notice did not appear to be material part of exchange).

As suggested by the Restatement (Second) §229, however, not every loss or forfeiture will provide grounds to justify excuse of nonoccurrence of an express condition. The *enXco* court concluded that the alleged loss of more than $100 million was not a forfeiture or, at least, was a risk assigned to the plaintiff in a bargain made by sophisticated parties. Is it possible to reconcile the decisions in *enXco* and *JNA* regarding the existence of a forfeiture?

2. *Forfeiture in lease renewal cases.* Despite the close division of the court, *JNA* appears to have become a leading case for the principle of equitable relief against forfeiture, for tenants seeking to renew and in some other types of cases as well. A number of later New York decisions have followed *JNA* in lease renewal cases, despite late notice of intent to renew or other obstacles to extension; others have distinguished it on various grounds. Compare 135 East 57th Street LLC v. Daffy's Inc., 934 N.Y.S.2d 112 (App. Div. 2011) (excusing renewal notice given four days late due to honest mistake; no prejudice to landlord and risk of forfeiture by tenant in loss of goodwill from having retail location for 15 years, even though no building improvements; equity would also consider that more than 100 employees might lose jobs if store closed), with 95 East Main Street Serv. Station, Inc. v. H & D All Type Auto Repair, Inc., 556 N.Y.S.2d 385 (App. Div. 1990) (lease required nine months' notice of renewal but tenant gave notice only one day before expiration of term; no showing of investment that would be forfeited or long-standing interest in location, and indication that tenant deliberately delayed renewing while looking for another location). Courts in other states are divided on the issue whether a tenant's negligent failure to give timely notice to renew should be excusable on some basis. E.g., Heartland Delaware Inc. v. Rehoboth Mall Ltd. P'ship, 57 A.3d 917 (Del. Ch. 2012) (noting split among courts on equitable relief when delay is slight, harm to lessor is small, and hardship on lessee would be unconscionable, before deciding not to grant relief in the absence of waiver, estoppel, fraud, or similar excuse; equity respects freedom of contract and will not save party from its own negligence).

3. *Conditions of timely notice in options to purchase real estate.* In cases involving options to purchase real estate (as opposed to options to renew leases) courts almost uniformly have denied equitable relief to an option holder who fails to comply with the time period set forth in the option. E.g., Livesey v. Copps Corp., 280 N.W.2d 339 (Wis. Ct. App. 1979) (exercise of option expiring November 15 ineffective when notice of exercise received November 16; deposited acceptance rule does not apply to options). Are there factors that justify treating options to purchase real estate differently from options for lease renewal? A different problem is presented when the option to purchase is contained in a lease, and the prospective purchaser has already been in possession as a lessee. Here some courts have followed *JNA* by giving the prospective purchaser an enforceable right despite some defect in her exercise of the option. E.g., Pitkin Seafood, Inc. v. Pitrock Realty Corp., 536 N.Y.S.2d 527 (A.D. 1989) (lessee's exercise of option to purchase would be upheld despite fact letter was mistakenly sent in individual name of original tenant instead of name of closely held corporation to which she had assigned leasehold; valuable improvements had been

made to premises and landlord not misled or prejudiced by honest error). See also Bachorz v. Miller-Forslund, 812 F. Supp. 2d 83 (D. Mass. 2011) (lessee's exercise of option to purchase would be upheld despite "inconsequential and immaterial" failures to comply with lease by not getting written permission for sublease and improvements to property and by minor noncompliance with municipal ordinances; no harm of any kind to lessor who had also waived some defaults).

4. *Waiver by party with conditional duty?* The *JNA* court notes that the landlord regularly gave notice to the tenant of important performance dates under the lease. Recalling the discussion of excuse due to waiver or estoppel found in the notes after the *enXco* case, could either of those theories have been helpful to the tenant in JNA?

In some cases, the court must decide whether a given event stated as a condition should be regarded as conditioning *both* parties' duties of performance under the contract, in which case either one can insist on its nonoccurrence as a ground for nonperformance, or whether it properly conditions the duty of only one party, in which case it is waivable by that party acting alone. See, e.g., De Freitas v. Cote, 174 N.E.2d 371 (Mass. 1961) (where contract stated "this sale is subject to [federal] loan," buyer who obtained financing from other sources could enforce contract against seller; condition was clearly for benefit of buyer only and thus waivable by him); Howard v. Youngman, 81 S.W.3d 101 (Mo. Ct. App. 2002) (buyer had waived mortgage financing contingency included for his benefit and thus vendors were obligated to perform).

5. ***JNA** from the perspective of legal theory.* As the lengthy and vigorously presented views of the majority and dissenting members of the New York Court of Appeals demonstrate, there are persuasive reasons for granting the relief requested by the tenant in the *JNA* case but also persuasive reasons for withholding it. In an article inspired by the presentations of the participants at a 1988 conference at New York University Law School on the general topic "Contract Law: From Theory to Practice," Professor Knapp reviewed the facts and procedural history of the *JNA* case (including facts not contained in the above opinions), in order to consider whether the insights of modern legal theory could inform the decision-making process for a judge faced with a case like *JNA*. Charles L. Knapp, Judgment Call: Theoretical Approaches to Contract Decision-Making, 1988 Ann. Surv. Am. L. 307. (The papers and proceedings of the N.Y.U. conference can be found in the 1988 Ann. Surv. Am. L. 1-351. In addition to articles by Professors Crystal and Knapp, the proceedings include principal papers by Professors James J. White (Legal Realism), Jeffrey L. Harrison (Economic Analysis), Peter Linzer (Relational Theory), and Girardeau A. Spann (Critical Legal Studies).) Professor Knapp concluded that each of these theoretical perspectives can contribute to the court's understanding of the values and interests at stake in the decision, but that none appears to provide a sure answer for the judge in search of a just and principled outcome. No rule, no policy, no principle of justice inevitably controls the judge's action in such a case, he observed; in the end, it comes down to a moral decision by the individual judge. If you had sat on the court that decided *JNA*, what would your choice have been?

6. *Counseling clients facing* ***JNA****-type issues.* In evaluating the result and reasoning of the *JNA* decision, a factor one might consider is its effect on the ability of attorneys effectively to counsel their clients in transactions of this type. Suppose you had represented the landlord, JNA, at the time when Chelsea's exercise of its renewal option was about to be due (i.e., *before* the New York Court of Appeals had handed down the above opinion). If your client, aware of the fact that Chelsea was in the process of making some improvements to the property but desiring for some reason to terminate that tenancy, had asked you whether it should remind Chelsea of the necessity for timely written exercise of the option, what would you have said? Would it have mattered why your client wanted to terminate that lease? If the time for exercise of the renewal option came and went, with no word from Chelsea, would you have advised JNA that it was then free to rerent the premises to someone else, effective at the expiration of Chelsea's present term? (In preparing his article on the *JNA* case, Professor Knapp surveyed some practicing attorneys on these questions; the results are summarized in 1988 Ann. Surv. Am. L. 321-323.) Suppose you were representing a New York commercial landlord (residential tenancies may have different rules) in a similar situation today. In light of the *JNA* decision, how would you now advise your client, as the time for exercise of the option was approaching? What would you advise if that time had passed and no notice of renewal had been received from Chelsea?

7. *Settlement of* ***JNA****.* In addition to surveys of practicing lawyers, Professor Knapp also interviewed the attorneys who represented Chelsea and JNA in the litigation. According to the lawyer for JNA, a substantial increase in property values motivated JNA to claim that Chelsea had lost its right to renew. The increase in property values (as well as the trouble and expense associated with moving) could also explain Chelsea's determination to try to enforce the renewal provision. The parties eventually settled the case by negotiating a long-term lease at an increased rental. See Knapp, 1988 Ann. Surv. Am. L. at 327 n.86.

PROBLEM 9-1

In our discussion of express conditions, we suggested a number of respects in which the proper treatment of conditions might be problematic: The extent to which one party might have the ability by "waiving" the condition to hold the other to her performance obligation; the possibility that one party or the other (or both) might have a duty to cause the conditioning event to happen, or at least to cooperate in bringing it about; the point at which nonoccurrence of the conditioning event might release a party from his duty to perform, etc. The questions below pursue some of these issues, by posing a set of variations based on a simple underlying fact pattern.

BASIC FACTS: Robert Sellar is the owner of a house and lot in the residential area of Smalltown. On March 15, Sellar and Bonnie Byer entered into a written agreement by the terms of which Sellar agreed to sell the house and lot ("the Property") to Byer for a total purchase price of $65,000, and Byer agreed to buy the property for that price. By the terms of the Sellar-Byer agreement, the closing (transfer of title in exchange for payment of the purchase price) was to take place on or about June 15. In addition, the agreement also contained the following language:

> It is agreed that this transaction is conditioned on the ability of Byer to obtain by June 1, from the Smalltown Zoning Board, a variance permitting Byer to operate on the premises a drug rehabilitation outpatient clinic, of the type currently operated by Byer in Middleburg [a nearby city].

(a) In March, Byer applies to the zoning board of Smalltown for a variance as described above. The board formally denies that request on May 25. On May 26, Byer notifies Sellar of this fact by letter, and states in her letter, "As you can see, this means that my projected purchase of your property will not take place." On June 20, Sellar sells his property to Frank Fallbach for $60,000. Is Byer liable to Sellar in damages for breach of contract?

(b) In March, Byer makes a preliminary application to the zoning board for a variance as described above. In early April, the board furnishes Byer with a set of application forms and a list of documents to be furnished in order for her application to be processed. Byer never completes and files those forms and other papers. On June 5, Byer advises Sellar by letter that no variance was granted, and states, "As you can see, this means that my projected purchase of your property will not take place." On June 20, Sellar sells his property to Fallbach for $60,000. Is Byer liable to Sellar in damages for breach of contract?

(c) In March, Byer makes a preliminary application to the zoning board for a variance as described above. In early April, the board furnishes Byer with a set of application forms and a list of supporting papers to be furnished in order for her application to be processed. Byer completes the forms and files them with the board, and supplies the board with as many of the requested additional documents as she can. However, one of the papers requested by the board is a written statement from each adjoining landowner, either giving consent to the variance or specifying the reasons for objection. One of the pieces of adjoining land is also owned by Sellar. At Byer's request, Sellar files with the zoning board a written statement. In his statement, however, Sellar states that he does not consent to the requested variance, but strongly opposes it, because of the negative impact such a clinic would in his opinion have on the neighborhood. The Board denies Byer's request on May 25. On June 10, Sellar sells the property to Fallbach for $75,000. Is Sellar liable to Byer in damages for breach of contract?

(d) In March, Byer applies for the zoning variance described above, but her application is denied in early May. In the meantime, Byer has entered into negotiations with Fallbach concerning the Property. On May 25, Byer and Fallbach enter into an agreement whereby Byer agrees to sell the Property to Fallbach for $75,000, closing to take place on June 30. That agreement contains a clause conditioning Byer's obligation to sell on the consummation and closing of her purchase from Sellar on or before June 25. On May 26, Byer writes Sellar requesting that closing of Byer's purchase of the Property take place on June 15, at a specified time and place. On June 10, Sellar notifies Byer by letter that due to Byer's failure to obtain a zoning variance, the Sellar-Byer contract is terminated. On June 15, Sellar sells the property to Fallbach for $70,000. Is anybody liable to anyone else for anything?

B. MATERIAL BREACH

In earlier chapters, we addressed a variety of reasons why the parties may have failed to create an enforceable agreement, or why an apparently complete and binding agreement might be subject to some defense having to do with either the circumstances of its making or some change in circumstances since that time. At this point, however, we are assuming an agreement that meets all the conventional tests for enforceability, binding both parties to an exchange of performances. At some point in the life of such a contract, one party may completely fail to render a performance then due and owing under the contract. Or, she may render that performance, but in an incomplete, defective or untimely manner. The following case is a classic examination of the issue thus raised: When does one party's failure to perform justify the other party in refusing to render a performance of his own?

Jacob & Youngs, Inc. v. Kent

New York Court of Appeals 230 N.Y. 239, 129 N.E. 889 (1921)

CARDOZO, J. The plaintiff built a country residence for the defendant at a cost of upwards of $77,000, and now sues to recover a balance of $3,483.46, remaining unpaid. The work of construction ceased in June, 1914, and the defendant then began to occupy the dwelling. There was no complaint of defective performance until March, 1915. One of the specifications for the plumbing work provides that —

"All wrought-iron pipe must be well galvanized, lap welded pipe of the grade known as 'standard pipe' of Reading manufacture."

The defendant learned in March, 1915, that some of the pipe, instead of being made in Reading, was the product of other factories. The plaintiff was accordingly directed by the architect to do the work anew. The plumbing was then encased within the walls except in a few places where it had to be exposed. Obedience to the order meant more than the substitution of other pipe. It meant the demolition at great expense of substantial parts of the completed structure. The plaintiff left the work untouched, and asked for a certificate that the final payment was due. Refusal of the certificate was followed by this suit.

The evidence sustains a finding that the omission of the prescribed brand of pipe was neither fraudulent nor willful. It was the result of the oversight and inattention of the plaintiff's subcontractor. Reading pipe is distinguished from Cohoes pipe and other brands only by the name of the manufacturer stamped upon it at intervals of between six and seven feet. Even the defendant's architect, though he inspected the pipe upon arrival, failed to notice the discrepancy. The plaintiff tried to show that the brands installed, though made by other manufacturers, were the same in quality, in appearance, in market value, and in cost as the brand stated in the contract — that they were, indeed, the same thing, though

The George Edward Kent estate, circa 1906.

manufactured in another place. The evidence was excluded, and a verdict directed for the defendant. The Appellate Division reversed, and granted a new trial.

We think the evidence, if admitted, would have supplied some basis for the inference that the defect was insignificant in its relation to the project. The courts never say that one who makes a contract fills the measure of his duty by less than full performance. They do say, however, that an omission, both trivial and innocent, will sometimes be atoned for by allowance of the resulting damage, and will not always be the breach of a condition to be followed by a forfeiture. Spence v. Ham, 163 N.Y. 220, 57 N.E. 412, 51 L.R.A. 238. . . . The distinction is akin to that between dependent and independent promises, or between promises and conditions. Anson on Contracts (Corbin's ed.) §367; 2 Williston on Contracts, §842. Some promises are so plainly independent that they can never by fair construction be conditions of one another. . . . Others are so plainly dependent that they must always be conditions. Others, though dependent and thus conditions when there is departure in point of substance, will be viewed as independent and collateral when the departure is insignificant. 2 Williston on Contracts, §§841, 842; Eastern Forge Co. v. Corbin, 182 Mass. 590, 592, 66 N.E. 419. . . . Considerations partly of justice and partly of presumable intention are to tell us whether this or that promise shall be placed in one class or in another. The simple and the uniform will call for different remedies from the multifarious and the intricate. The margin of departure within the range of normal expectation upon a sale of common chattels will vary from the margin to be expected upon a contract for the construction of a mansion or a "skyscraper." There will be harshness sometimes and oppression in the implication of a condition when the thing upon which labor has been expended is incapable of surrender because united to the land, and equity and reason in the implication of a like condition when the subject-matter, if defective, is in shape to be returned. From the conclusion that promises may not be treated as dependent to the extent of their uttermost minutiae without a sacrifice of justice, the progress is a short one to the conclusion that they may not be so treated without a perversion of intention. Intention not otherwise revealed may be presumed to hold in contemplation the reasonable and probable. If something else is in view, it must not be left to implication. There will be no assumption of a purpose to visit venial faults with oppressive retribution.

Those who think more of symmetry and logic in the development of legal rules than of practical adaptation to the attainment of a just result will be troubled by a classification where the lines of division are so wavering and blurred. Something, doubtless, may be said on the score of consistency and certainty in favor of a stricter standard. The courts have balanced such considerations against those of equity and fairness, and found the latter to be the weightier. The decisions in this state commit us to the liberal view, which is making its way, nowadays, in jurisdictions slow to welcome it. Dakin & Co. v. Lee, 1916, 1 K.B. 566, 579. Where the line is to be drawn between the important and the trivial cannot be settled by a formula. "In the nature of the case precise boundaries are impossible." 2 Williston on Contracts, §841. The same omission may take on one aspect or another according to its setting. Substitution of equivalents may not have the same significance in fields of art on the one side and in those of mere utility on the other. Nowhere will change be tolerated, however, if it is so dominant or pervasive as in any real or substantial measure to frustrate the purpose of the contract. Crouch v. Gutmann, 134 N.Y. 45, 51, 31 N.E. 271, 30 Am. St. Rep. 608. There is no general license to install whatever, in the builder's judgment, may be regarded as "just as good." Easthampton L. & C. Co., Ltd., v. Worthington, 186 N.Y. 407, 412, 79 N.E. 323. The question is one of degree, to be answered, if there is doubt, by the triers of the facts (Crouch v. Gutmann; Woodward v. Fuller, supra), and, if the inferences are certain, by the judges of the law (Easthampton L. & C. Co., Ltd., v. Worthington, supra). We must weigh the purpose to be served, the desire to be gratified, the excuse for deviation from the letter, the cruelty of enforced adherence. Then only can we tell whether literal fulfillment is to be implied by law as a condition. This is not to say that the parties are not free by apt and certain words to effectuate a purpose that performance of every term shall be a condition of recovery. That question is not here. This is merely to say that the law will be slow to impute the purpose, in the silence of the parties, where the significance of the default is grievously out of proportion to the oppression of the forfeiture. The willful transgressor must accept the penalty of his transgression. Schultze v. Goodstein, 180 N.Y. 248, 251, 73 N.E. 21; Desmond-Dunne Co. v. Friedman-Doscher Co., 162 N.Y. 486, 490, 56 N.E. 995. For him there is no occasion to mitigate the rigor of implied conditions. The transgressor whose default is unintentional and trivial may hope for mercy if he will offer atonement for his wrong. Spence v. Ham, supra.

In the circumstances of this case, we think the measure of the allowance is not the cost of replacement, which would be great, but the difference in value, which would be either nominal or nothing. Some of the exposed sections might perhaps have been replaced at moderate expense. The defendant did not limit his demand to them, but treated the plumbing as a unit to be corrected from cellar to roof. In point of fact, the plaintiff never reached the stage at which evidence of the extent of the allowance became necessary. The trial court had excluded evidence that the defect was unsubstantial, and in view of that ruling there was no occasion for the plaintiff to go farther with an offer of proof. We think, however, that the offer, if it had been made, would not of necessity have been defective because directed to difference in value. It is true that in most cases the cost of replacement is the measure. Spence v. Ham, supra. The owner is entitled to the money which will permit him to complete, unless the cost of completion is grossly and unfairly out of proportion to the good to be attained. When that is true, the measure is the difference in value. Specifications call, let us say, for a foundation built of granite quarried in Vermont. On the completion of the building, the owner learns that through the blunder of a subcontractor part of the foundation has been built of granite of the same quality quarried in New Hampshire. The measure of allowance is not the cost of reconstruction. "There may be omissions of that which could not afterwards be supplied exactly as called for by the contract without taking down the building to its foundations, and at the same time the omission may not affect the value of the building for use or otherwise, except so slightly as to be hardly appreciable." Handy v. Bliss, 204 Mass. 513, 519, 90 N.E. 864, 134 Am. St. Rep. 673. . . . The rule that gives a remedy in cases of substantial performance with compensation for defects of trivial or inappreciable importance has been developed by the courts as an instrument of justice. The measure of the allowance must be shaped to the same end.

The order should be affirmed, and judgment absolute directed in favor of the plaintiff upon the stipulation, with costs in all courts.

McLaughlin, J. I dissent. The plaintiff did not perform its contract. Its failure to do so was either intentional or due to gross neglect which, under the uncontradicted facts, amounted to the same thing, nor did it make any proof of the cost of compliance, where compliance was possible.

Under its contract it obligated itself to use in the plumbing only pipe (between 2,000 and 2,500 feet) made by the Reading Manufacturing Company. The first pipe delivered was about 1,000 feet and the plaintiff's superintendent then called the attention of the foreman of the subcontractor, who was doing the plumbing, to the fact that the specifications annexed to the contract required all pipe used in the plumbing to be of the Reading Manufacturing Company. They then examined it for the purpose of ascertaining whether this delivery was of that manufacture and found it was. Thereafter, as pipe was required in the progress of the work, the foreman of the subcontractor would leave word at its shop that he wanted a specified number of feet of pipe, without in any way indicating of what manufacture. Pipe would thereafter be delivered and installed in the building, without any examination whatever. Indeed, no examination, so far as appears, was made by the plaintiff, the subcontractor, defendant's architect, or any one else, of any of the pipe except the first delivery, until after the building had been completed. Plaintiff's architect then refused to give the certificate of completion, upon which the final payment depended, because all of the pipe used in the plumbing was not of the kind called for by the contract. After such refusal, the subcontractor removed the covering or insulation from about 900 feet of pipe which was exposed in the basement, cellar, and attic, and all but 70 feet was found to have been manufactured, not by the Reading Company, but by other manufacturers, some by the Cohoes Rolling Mill Company, some by the National Steel Works, some by the South Chester Tubing Company, and some which bore no manufacturer's mark at all. The balance of the pipe had been so installed in the building that an inspection of it could not be had without demolishing, in part at least, the building itself.

I am of the opinion the trial court was right in directing a verdict for the defendant. The plaintiff agreed that all the pipe used should be of the Reading Manufacturing Company. Only about two-fifths of it, so far as appears, was of that kind. If more were used, then the burden of proving that fact was upon the plaintiff, which it could easily have done, since it knew where the pipe was obtained. The question of substantial performance of a contract of the character of the one under consideration depends in no small degree upon the good faith of the contractor. If the plaintiff had intended to, and had, complied with the terms of the contract except as to minor omissions, due to inadvertence, then he might be allowed to recover the contract price, less the amount necessary to fully compensate the defendant for damages caused by such omissions. Woodward v. Fuller, 80 N.Y. 312; Nolan v. Whitney, 88 N.Y. 648. But that is not this case. It installed between 2,000 and 2,500 feet of pipe, of which only 1,000 feet at most complied with the contract. No explanation was given why pipe called for by the contract was not used, nor was any effort made to show what it would cost to remove the pipe of other manufacturers and install that of the Reading Manufacturing Company. The defendant had a right to contract for what he wanted. He had a right before making payment to get what the contract called for. It is no answer to this suggestion to say that the pipe put in was just as good as that made by the Reading Manufacturing Company, or that the difference in value between such pipe and the pipe made by the Reading Manufacturing Company would be either "nominal or nothing." Defendant contracted for pipe made by the Reading Manufacturing Company. What his reason was for requiring this kind of pipe is of no importance. He wanted that and was entitled to it. It may have been a mere whim on his part, but even so, he had a right to this kind of pipe, regardless of whether some other kind, according to the opinion of the contractor or experts, would have been "just as good, better, or done just as well." He agreed to pay only upon condition that the pipe installed were made by that company and he ought not to be compelled to pay unless that condition be performed. . . . Smith v. Brady, 17 N.Y. 173, and authorities cited on page 185, 72 Am. Dec. 442. The rule, therefore, of substantial performance, with damages for unsubstantial omissions, has no application. . . .

What was said by this court in Smith v. Brady, supra, is quite applicable here:

> I suppose it will be conceded that every one has a right to build his house, his cottage or his store after such a model and in such style as shall best accord with his notions of utility or be most agreeable to his fancy. The specifications of the contract become the law between the parties until voluntarily changed. If the owner prefers a plain and simple Doric column, and has so provided in the agreement, the contractor has no right to put in its place the more costly and elegant Corinthian. If the owner, having regard to strength and durability, has contracted for walls of specified materials to be laid in a particular manner, or for a given number of joists and beams, the builder has no right to substitute his own judgment or that of others. Having departed from the agreement, if performance has not been waived by the other party, the law will not allow him to allege that he has made as good a building as the one he engaged to erect. He can demand payment only upon and according to the terms of his contract, and if the conditions on which payment is due have not been performed, then the right to demand it does not exist. To hold a different doctrine would be simply to make another contract, and would be giving to parties an encouragement to violate their engagements, which the just policy of the law does not permit. [17 N.Y. 186, 72 Am. Dec. 442].

I am of the opinion the trial court did not err in ruling on the admission of evidence or in directing a verdict for the defendant.

For the foregoing reasons I think the judgment of the Appellate Division should be reversed and the judgment of the Trial Term affirmed.

HISCOCK, C.J., and HOGAN and CRANE, JJ., concur with CARDOZO, J.

POUND and ANDREWS, JJ., concur with MCLAUGHLIN, J.
Order affirmed, etc.

NOTES AND QUESTIONS

1. *Commercial context.* Does the opinion of the court adequately explain the reasons for the dispute? Richard Danzig's research into the background of the case is revealing. Danzig tried to find out why the contract specified Reading pipe. At that time, two types of pipe, steel and wrought iron, were commonly used in construction. Although wrought iron was approximately 30 percent more expensive, its manufacturers claimed that use of the pipe would achieve substantial savings because of durability and low maintenance. Several companies manufactured wrought iron pipe, but evidence indicates that all of their pipe was of the same quality. However, manufacturers of wrought iron pipe cautioned buyers to specify a particular manufacturer in order to avoid receiving "wrought pipe," a cheaper product produced by steel companies using scrap steel. Considering this background, the contractor's deviation from the specifications seems immaterial since genuine wrought iron pipe (although not of Reading manufacture) was in fact used. Why then did Kent continue to insist on Reading pipe if genuine wrought iron pipe had in fact

been used? Kent moved into the house in June 1914, after substantial construction delays. According to Danzig's research, Kent was probably disenchanted with the contractor because of the delay, as well as some other mistakes in the work, and may have been searching for some reason to withhold the balance due on the contract. Richard Danzig & Geoffrey R. Watson, The Capability Problem in Contract Law 109-116 (2d ed. 2004). For further background on the Kent contract and the ensuing litigation, see Victor P. Goldberg, Rethinking Jacob & Youngs v. Kent, 66 Case W. Res. L. Rev. 111 (2015). Professor Goldberg finds that the doctrine of substantial performance was already established by the time Judge Cardozo wrote the opinion, and defends both the rule and the result.

2. *The doctrine of constructive conditions.* In deciding the *Jacob & Youngs* case, Judge Cardozo uses the notion of "dependent promises," promises that are treated like "conditions." We have already considered cases where one party's duty of performance has been expressly conditioned on the occurrence of some specified event, in which case that duty of performance will not arise (absent some excuse of the condition) unless and until the conditioning event occurs. In cases like *Jacob & Youngs*, the courts use similar terminology to answer a somewhat different question: When will one party's duty of performance be dependent on (thus in effect "conditioned" on) some performance by the other party? The doctrine of "constructive conditions" was developed over the years by English and American courts in order to achieve just results in cases where it seemed to the court that one party's failure to perform (or even to "tender" performance) should constitute a sufficient justification for the other party's withholding of its performance in return. (The history of the doctrine is discussed further in the Comment that follows these Notes.)

3. *Possible application of rules governing express conditions.* In the course of his opinion, Cardozo indicates that the case involves an implied, or "constructive" condition, rather than an express one: "This is not to say that the parties are not free by apt and certain words to effectuate a purpose that performance of every term shall be a condition of recovery. That question is not here." However, the case could easily have been treated as involving an express rather than a constructive condition. Article IX of the contract provided that the contractor was to be paid by the owner "only upon certificates of the Architect." Richard Danzig & Geoffrey R. Watson, The Capability Problem in Contract Law 98 (2d ed. 2004). The contractor brought suit when the architect failed to issue a final certificate because the contractor refused to replace the non-Reading pipe. Under New York law the result in the case would probably have been the same whether the case was treated as involving an express condition of the architect's certificate or a constructive condition of performance by the contractor. An earlier New York case had held that an architect could not properly refuse to issue a certificate if the contractor had substantially performed. Nolan v. Whitney, 88 N.Y. 648 (1882). In other jurisdictions, however, the result might well be different. According to the majority view, if the contractor's right to receive payment is expressly conditioned on the issuance of the architect's certificate, the condition will be strictly enforced and the contractor denied recovery unless the contractor shows some ground for excuse of the condition such as fraud, bad faith, or waiver. See, e.g., Glenn Constr. Co., LLC v. Bell Aerospace Services, Inc., 2009 WL 5174209 (M.D. Ala.); Town of Plainfield v. Paden Eng'g Co., Inc., 943 N.E.2d 904 (Ind. Ct. App. 2011).

4. *Principle of substantial performance.* Even though *Jacob & Youngs* could have been treated as a case involving express conditions, instead it is recognized as the leading case adopting the principle of "substantial performance." Substantial performance can best be understood as one aspect of the doctrine of constructive conditions. The principle provides that each party's duty of performance is implicitly conditioned on there being no uncured material failure of performance by the other party. Restatement (Second) §237. Minor or immaterial deviations from the contractual provisions do not amount to failure of a condition to the other party's duty to perform. As Justice Cardozo recognizes, even a minor deviation will give the other party a right to recover damages for that nonperformance, but those damages may be negligible. (Was the house worth less on the market because non-Reading pipe was used, when all manufacturers of wrought iron pipe made a product of the same quality?) Does the dissenting judge disagree with Justice Cardozo on the recognition of the doctrine of substantial performance or merely on its application?

5. *Standard for substantial performance.* When is performance "substantial"? In Thomas Haverty Co. v. Jones, 197 P. 105 (Cal. 1921) the California Supreme Court defined substantial performance as follows:

> [T]here is substantial performance where the variance from the specifications of the contract does not impair the building or structure as a whole, and where after it is erected the building is actually used for the intended purpose, or where the defects can be remedied without great expenditure and without material damage to other parts of the structure, but . . . the defects must not run through the whole work, so that the object of the owner to have the work done in a particular way is not accomplished . . . nor be so substantial [that] . . . the allowance out of the contract price will not give the owner essentially what he contracted for.

Id. at 108. In Flynn Builders, L.C. v. Lande, 814 N.W.2d 542 (Iowa 2012), the Iowa Supreme Court held that the contractor had not substantially performed when he had completed about 80 to 85 percent of the work on the house under a contract that had a total price of about $260,000. The unfinished work included doors, cabinets, drywall, flooring, painting, concrete work, and heating and air conditioning, and it was estimated to require about 5 to 7 weeks to complete. The court noted that while no mathematical rule can be stated regarding the percentage of completion required by a builder, the unfinished work in the case "materially affected the habitability of the house" and precluded a finding that substantial performance had been rendered. Id. at 547. On remand, however, the trial court found that the contractor's failure to render substantial performance was excused by the owner's previous failure to make payments when due; this ruling was affirmed by the Iowa Supreme Court, Flynn Builders, L.C. v. Lande, 814 N.W.2d 542 (2012).

The substantial performance doctrine applies to all types of agreements, not just to construction contracts. See Nature's Plus Nordic A/S v. Natural Organics, Inc., 980 F. Supp. 2d 400 (E.D.N.Y. 2013) (exclusive distributor who purchased at least 99.5 percent of required annual amount of $600,000 had substantially performed as a matter of law; manufacturer was not excused from contract on basis of immaterial breach); Hull v. Giesler, 331 P.3d 507 (Idaho 2014) (buyer substantially performed contract to purchase one-half interest in parcel of land by paying amount due in installments over five-year period even though some payments were late; material breach is one that "touches fundamental purpose of contract" and "defeats the purpose of the parties"); Viacom International Inc. v. MGA Entertainment, Inc., 2016 WL 7448142 (C.D. Cal.) (plaintiff entitled to summary judgment where it had substantially performed contract to broadcast TV series internationally by achieving at least 96 percent compliance with its contractual obligation).

6. *Measure of damages.* The notion of "substantial performance" as the fulfillment of a "constructive condition" to the other party's duty of performance may be important where the person rendering defective performance is attempting to enforce the other party's return performance, as was the case in *Jacob & Youngs.* But as that case illustrates, this is not the only issue that may turn on the degree and quality of performance rendered. Whether performance is deemed "substantial" or not, it may still be defective in important ways, requiring the court to consider what damage measure will appropriately remedy those defects. Sometimes courts will measure damages in cases of defective performance by the cost of completion or repair. E.g., Lewis Electric Co. v. Miller, 791 N.W.2d 691 (Iowa 2011) (electrical contractor who substantially performed but whose work was defective was entitled to recover remaining amount of contract price less cost to complete or repair incurred by owner; owner entitled to judgment for excess if costs to repair exceeded balance of contract price). In *Jacob & Youngs*, what measure of damages did Cardozo employ? We will return to this issue in Chapter 10, in our discussion of expectation damages.

7. *Effect of willful breach.* In his *Jacob & Youngs* opinion, Cardozo states that the "willful transgressor" will not be entitled to recover under the substantial performance doctrine. Professor Corbin criticized this limitation, arguing that willfulness was a vague concept and that even a willful breach should not necessarily prevent recovery. 3A Corbin on Contracts §707 (1960). The Second Restatement adopts Professor Corbin's view: A willful breach does not automatically bar recovery, but the motive of the breaching party is a factor to be considered in determining whether performance was substantial. Restatement (Second) §241(e) and Comment *f.* In Roudis v. Hubbard, 574 N.Y.S.2d 95 (App. Div. 1991), plaintiffs sought damages for defendant builder's failure to install styrofoam insulation and footing drains in plaintiffs' new home. The parties' contract provided that if the final product substantially complied with the plans and specifications, the owners' sole remedy should be market-value damages; defendant argued that because the defects in his performance did not diminish the value of the house, plaintiffs had suffered no compensable damages. The trial court's judgment for plaintiffs was affirmed. Relying on *Jacob & Youngs*,

the court held that since defendant apparently had intentionally omitted the drains and insulation called for because he thought them "unnecessary," the proper remedy was the cost of completion. Even if the contractor has substantially performed, it declared, a "diminution in value" measure should be applied only where the contractor's breach was unintentional and constituted substantial performance in good faith. Cf. First Nat'l Bank of Omaha v. Centennial Park, LLC, 303 P.3d 705 (Kan. Ct. App. 2013) (rule of substantial performance will not apply when the breach is a willful, intentional deviation from contract terms; borrower willfully breached loan repayment terms).

8. *Other grounds for recovery: restitution and divisibility.* If the contractor has not substantially performed, other bases for recovery may nonetheless exist. Many courts will allow a contractor that has committed a material breach to recover in restitution (quantum meruit) for the reasonable value of its services, less any harm resulting from the breach. See Kreyer v. Driscoll, 159 N.W.2d 680 (Wis. 1968). If the contract is "divisible," a court may allow recovery for the portions that have been completed. See Carrig v. Gilbert-Varker Corp., 50 N.E.2d 59 (Mass. 1943) (contract for construction of 35 houses in groups of 10; contractor who completed 20 houses allowed to recover because contract was divisible). The Restatement (Second) §240 defines the doctrine of divisibility. It provides that two requirements must be met in order for a contract to be divisible. First, it must be possible to apportion the performances of the parties into corresponding pairs of part performances. Second, it must be proper to treat these pairs of part performances as "agreed equivalents." Comment *e* to §240 explains that the second requirement is designed to protect the expectations of the contracting parties:

> This is because fairness requires that a party, having received only a fraction of the performance that he expected under a contract, not be asked to pay an identical fraction of the price that he originally promised on the expectation of full performance, unless it appears that the performance that he actually received is worth to him roughly that same fraction of what full performance would have been worth to him.

Comment: The Doctrine of Constructive Conditions

We have seen in *Jacob & Youngs* that the courts may use the terminology of "conditions" in deciding the consequences of one party's nonperformance or defective performance on the other party's contractual obligations. The use of the "condition" concept here is quite different from the idea of "express" conditions that we studied in the first section of this chapter. While express conditions result from the agreement of the parties, "constructive conditions" are judicially created devices, used to determine the consequences of breach when the parties have failed to spell that out in their agreement. (It is, of course, possible to argue that the rules of constructive conditions actually reflect the agreements that the parties probably would have reached had they actually bargained about the matter.)

The modern rules of constructive conditions examined in these materials have a long lineage. The English courts of the early seventeenth century originally rejected the idea that one party's duty to perform was conditioned on performance by the other, holding that mutual promises in bilateral contracts were "independent." Under this view, even if one party failed to perform his promise, the other was not justified in refusing to perform. An early case exemplifying this approach was Nichols v. Raynbred, 80 Eng. Rep. 238 (K.B. 1615), where the Court of King's Bench held that in an action by a seller against a buyer for the purchase price of a cow, the seller was not required to plead that the cow had been delivered. The buyer could, of course, bring an independent action against the seller for breach of his promise to deliver the cow, but the buyer could not raise that fact as a defense in the seller's action to recover the price. The promises of the buyer and seller were said to be "independent."

There is some evidence that the rule of independent promises was not firmly established in the English common law. William H. McGovern, Jr., Dependent Promises in the History of Leases and Other Contracts, 52 Tul. L. Rev. 659 (1978) (contending that the English courts in fact held that promises in many types of contracts were dependent). Nevertheless, the conventional view is that the rule of independent promises remained the law until Lord Mansfield decided the case of Kingston v. Preston, reported as part of the argument in Jones v. Barkley, at 99 Eng. Rep. 437 (K.B. 1773). In *Kingston* the defendant, a silk merchant, agreed to sell his business to the plaintiff, his apprentice, who promised in return to pay the purchase price in monthly installments and to provide "good and sufficient security" to be approved by the defendant. The buyer brought suit, alleging that the seller had failed to honor his promise to complete the sale of the business. The seller pleaded in response that the buyer had failed to provide the promised security for his payment of the purchase price. The buyer demurred to this defense, arguing that the covenants were independent. Lord Mansfield's analysis of the case is reported as follows:

> There are three kinds of covenants: 1. Such as are called mutual and independent, where either party may recover damages from the other, for the injury he may have received by a breach of the covenants in his favour, and where it is no excuse for the defendant, to allege a breach of the covenants on the part of the plaintiff. 2. There are covenants which are conditions and dependent, in which the performance of one depends on the prior performance of another, and, therefore, till this prior condition is performed, the other party is not liable to an action on his covenant. 3. There is also a third sort of covenants, which are mutual conditions to be performed at the same time; and, in these, if one party was ready, and offered, to perform his part, and the other neglected, or refused, to perform his, he who was ready, and offered, has fulfilled his engagement, and may maintain an action for the default of the other; though it is not certain that either is obliged to do the first act. — His Lordship then proceeded to say, that the dependence, or independence, of covenants, was to be collected from the evident sense and meaning of the parties. . . . That, in the case before the Court, it would be the greatest injustice if the plaintiff should prevail: the essence of the agreement was, that the defendant should not trust to the personal security of the plaintiff, but, before he delivered up his stock and business, should have good security for the payment of the money. The giving of such security, therefore, must necessarily be a condition precedent. — Judgment

> was accordingly given for the defendant, because the part to be performed by the plaintiff was clearly a condition precedent.

A subsequent English case, Morton v. Lamb, 101 Eng. Rep. 890 (K.B. 1797), added an important refinement to Mansfield's doctrine of conditions. In *Morton* the plaintiff brought an action for failure to deliver corn. The defendant argued in arrest of judgment that the plaintiff had not declared that he was ready to pay for the corn. The court held that when two performances can be rendered at the same time, it should be presumed (in the absence of express agreement otherwise) that the parties intended them to be performed simultaneously, so that neither party would be required in effect to extend credit to the other. In such a case the party who sues for nonperformance must declare that he either performed, or at least was ready to perform, his own obligation. In other words, if acts can be performed at the same time, the readiness of each party to perform is a "concurrent condition" to the other party's duty of performance. The court noted that in some kinds of contracts — construction and service contracts, for example — performances could not be rendered simultaneously. In such cases the performance requiring the longer period of time (rendering of services) is a "condition precedent" to the performance requiring the shorter period of time (payment of money).

Except for changes in terminology, the Restatement (Second) continues the rules of "constructive conditions" developed by Lord Mansfield and subsequent English cases. The revised Restatement abandons the use of the terms *independent covenant, concurrent condition, condition precedent*, and *condition subsequent.* Following an analysis developed by Professor Corbin, the Restatement divides conditions into three categories: express conditions, implied-in-fact conditions (inferred from the conduct of the parties), and constructive conditions (created by a court for reasons of justice). Restatement (Second) §226, Comments *a, b.*

Restatement (Second) §234 sets forth the conventional rules on order of performance, as developed in Morton v. Lamb. Performances that can be rendered at the same time are due simultaneously. Restatement (Second) §234(1). See also Restatement (Second) §238. Under §234(2), if performances cannot be rendered at the same time, the performance requiring the longer period of time must be rendered before the performance requiring the shorter period of time will be due. Contracts for the conveyance of land or for the sale of goods are viewed by the law as being capable of simultaneous performance; absent agreement otherwise, they will be construed as calling for simultaneous rendition of performances. Under the rule of §234(1), it will thus be necessary for either party to such a contract — buyer or seller — to show that she has at least tendered performance on her part, in order to maintain an action for breach against the other party. To the same effect are UCC §§2-507 (tender of delivery a condition to buyer's duty to accept and pay for goods) and 2-511 (tender of payment a condition to seller's duty to deliver). Like the Restatement rules, the UCC provisions are rules of construction only and are not applicable if the parties' agreement provides otherwise. (Note that Comment 1 to §2-511 observes that the requirement of payment against delivery has "no application" to most commercial contracts for the sale of goods, which commonly extend credit to the buyer.) On the other hand, construction contracts and employment contracts are ordinarily construed as requiring performance of the work to be completed before payment is due, under the rule of §234(2). Again, it must be remembered that this is merely a rule of construction, applicable unless the language of the contract itself or the circumstances indicate otherwise; ordinarily such contracts do call for payment at stated intervals as the services are performed, or the work progresses.

As thus elaborated, the doctrine of constructive conditions provides an analytic framework for the courts in various cases where one party claims he did not yet have a duty to perform because of the other party's failure to render her performance. Use of the "condition" device in this fashion has had other consequences, however, and in some cases it has appeared to work against the interests of justice. A well-known early example is Stark v. Parker, 19 Mass. 267 (1824). Plaintiff Stark had contracted to work for a year as a laborer on defendant Parker's farm, in exchange for the sum of $120. (A seemingly trivial sum, but this was 1824, remember; also, plaintiff probably received room and board.) For some reason not disclosed in the report of the case, the plaintiff had left the defendant's service shortly before the year was up. Plaintiff was held not entitled to recover any part of his wages for the year and was also denied any recovery in quantum meruit for the value of the services performed. Full rendition of the entire performance contracted for, the court held, was a condition precedent to the right to recover *any* of the promised compensation, either "on the contract" or on a quantum meruit (restitutionary) basis. Stark v. Parker was generally followed, although some courts did hold otherwise on similar facts, permitting the employee at least to bring an action in quantum meruit for the reasonable value of the work performed, less damages for any loss that the employer could show was suffered as a result of the employee's breach. E.g., Britton v. Turner, 6 N.H. 481 (1834). As exemplified in Britton v. Turner, the doctrine of restitution thus offers one way to ameliorate the possible harshness of the "constructive condition" approach. (We will return to this point in Chapter 11.) For a recent discussion of Britton v. Turner, see Charles A. Sullivan, Mastering the Faithless Servant?: Reconciling Employment Law, Contract Law, and Fiduciary Duty, 2011 Wis. L. Rev. 777. The other method devised by the courts to temper the effect of the doctrine of constructive conditions is of course the concept of "substantial performance" (which we saw in action in *Jacob & Youngs*), permitting recovery "on the contract" by a party whose breach is not material.

Sackett v. Spindler

California Court of Appeal 248 Cal. App. 2d 220, 56 Cal. Rptr. 435 (1967)

MOLINARI, Presiding Justice.

Plaintiff and cross-defendant, Sheldon Sackett, appeals from the judgment of the trial court determining that he take nothing on his complaint for money had and received and further awarding defendant and cross-complainant, Paul

Spindler, $34,575.74 plus interest on his cross-complaint against Sackett for breach of contract. Sackett's contentions on appeal are as follows: (1) the evidence reveals no "actionable breach" on his part; (2) damages were incorrectly computed; (3) certain evidence was improperly excluded; (4) the trial court's findings as to mitigation of damages by Spindler are not supported by the evidence; and (5) the trial court erred in awarding interest to Spindler.

THE RECORD

As of July 8, 1961, Spindler was the owner of a majority of the shares of S & S Newspapers, a corporation which, since April 1, 1959, had owned and operated a newspaper in Santa Clara known as the Santa Clara Journal. In addition, Spindler, as president of S & S Newspapers, served as publisher, editor, and general manager of the Journal. On July 8, 1961, Spindler entered into a written agreement with Sackett whereby the latter agreed to purchase 6,316 shares of stock in S & S Newspapers, this number representing the total number of shares outstanding. The contract provided for a total purchase price of $85,000 payable as follows: $6,000 on or before July 10, $20,000 on or before July 14, and $59,000 on or before August 15. In addition the agreement obligated Sackett to pay interest at the rate of 6 percent on any unpaid balance. And finally, the contract provided for delivery of the full amount of stock to Sackett free of encumbrances when he made his final payment under the contract.

Sackett paid the initial $6,000 installment on time and made an additional $19,800 payment on July 21. On August 10 Sackett gave Spindler a check for the $59,200 balance due under the contract; however, due to the fact that the account on which this check was drawn contained insufficient funds to cover the check, the check was never paid. Meanwhile, however, Spindler had acquired the stock owned by the minority shareholders of S & S Newspapers, had endorsed the stock certificates, and had given all but 454 shares to Sackett's attorneys to hold in escrow until Sackett had paid Spindler the $59,200 balance due under the contract. However, on September 1, after the $59,200 check had not cleared, Spindler reclaimed the stock certificates held by Sackett's attorney.

Thereafter, on September 12 Spindler received a telegram from Sackett to the effect that the latter "had secured payments our transaction and was ready, willing and eager to transfer them" and that Sackett's new attorney would contact Spindler's attorney. In response to this telegram Spindler, by return telegram, gave Sackett the name of Spindler's attorney. Subsequently, Sackett's attorney contacted Spindler's attorney and arranged a meeting to discuss Sackett's performance of the contract. At this meeting, which was held on September 19 at the office of Sackett's attorney, in response to Sackett's representation that he would be able to pay Spindler the balance due under the contract by September 22, Spindler served Sackett with a notice to the effect that unless the latter paid the $59,200 balance due under the contract plus interest by that date, Spindler would not consider completing the sale and would assess damages for Sackett's breach of the agreement. Also discussed at this meeting was the newspaper's urgent need for working capital. Pursuant to this discussion Sackett on the same date paid Spindler $3,944.26 as an advance for working capital. However, Sackett failed to make any further payments or to communicate with Spindler by September 22, and on that date the latter, by letter addressed to Sackett, again extended the time for Sackett's performance until September 29. Again Sackett failed to tender the amount owing under the contract or to contact Spindler by that date, the next communication between the parties occurring on October 4 in the form of a telegram by which Sackett advised Spindler that Sackett's assets were now free as a result of the fact that his wife's petition to impress a receivership on his assets had been dismissed by the trial court in which divorce proceedings between Sackett and his wife were pending; that he was "ready, eager and willing to proceed to . . . consummate all details of our previously settled sale and purchase"; and that the decision of the trial court dismissing his wife's petition for receivership "will clear way shortly for full financing any unpaid balance." Accordingly, Sackett, in this telegram, urged Spindler to have his attorney contact Sackett's attorney "regarding any unfinished details." In response to this telegram Spindler's attorney, on October 5, wrote a letter to Sackett's attorney stating that as a result of Sackett's delay in performing the contract and his unwillingness to consummate the agreement, "there will be no sale and purchase of the stock. . . ." Following this letter Sackett's attorney, on October 6, telephoned Spindler's attorney and offered to pay the balance due under the contract over a period of time through a "liquidating trust." This proposal was rejected by Spindler's attorney, who, however, informed Sackett's attorney at that time that Spindler was still willing to consummate the sale of the stock provided Sackett would pay the balance in cash or its equivalent. No tender or offer of cash or its equivalent was made and Sackett thereafter failed to communicate with Spindler until shortly before the commencement of this action.

Beginning during the period scheduled for Sackett's performance of the contract Spindler found it increasingly difficult to operate the paper at a profit, particularly due to the lack of adequate working capital. In an attempt to remedy this situation Spindler obtained a loan of approximately $4,000 by mortgaging various items of personal property owned by him. In addition, in November, Spindler sold half of his stock in S & S Newspapers for $10,000. Thereafter, in December, in an effort to minimize the cost of operating the newspaper, Spindler converted the paper from a daily to a weekly. Finally, in July 1962 Spindler repurchased for $10,000 the stock which he had sold the previous November and sold the full 6,316 shares for $22,000, which sale netted Spindler $20,680 after payment of brokerage commission.

Breach of Contract

. . . To begin with, the undisputed evidence shows that of the $85,000 due from Sackett to Spindler under the purchase agreement the total amount which the former paid to the latter up to the time of trial was $29,744.26. Moreover, the purchase agreement reveals that Sackett's promise to pay Spindler $85,000 was an unconditional one once the respective dates on which the payments were due had arrived. Accordingly, since the trial court found that it was not impossible for Sackett to perform the subject contract either by virtue of his illness and hospitalization or his pending divorce litigation, it is clear that his failure to tender the balance due under the contract constituted a breach of the agreement, a breach being defined as an unjustified or unexcused failure to perform all or any part of what is promised in a contract. (Rest., Contracts, §§312, 314, pp. 462, 465.) The question remains, therefore, as to whether Sackett's duty to consummate the contract or to respond to Spindler in damages for the former's failure to perform the subject contract was in any way discharged by Spindler's conduct. . . .

. . . [W]ith regard to Sackett's claim that Spindler "repudiated" the contract on October 5, it is clear that the letter which Spindler's attorney wrote to Sackett's attorney on that date informing the latter that as a result of the "many delays" on the part of Sackett "there will be no sale and purchase of the [newspaper] stock" constituted notification to Sackett that Spindler considered his own duty of performance under the contract discharged as a result of Sackett's breach of the contract and that Spindler was thereby terminating the contract and substituting his legal remedies for his contractual rights. Such action was justifiable on Spindler's part if, but only if, Sackett's breach could properly be classified as a total, rather than a partial, breach of the contract. (Rest., Contracts, §313, p. 464; 4 Corbin on Contracts, §946, p. 809.) If, on the other hand, Sackett's breach at that time was not total so that Spindler was not entitled to consider himself discharged under the contract, then Spindler's action would constitute an unlawful repudiation of the contract, which would in turn be a total breach of the contract sufficient to discharge Sackett from any further duty to perform the contract. (6 Corbin on Contracts, §1253, pp. 7, 13-16.)

Whether a breach of contract is total or partial depends upon its materiality. (Rest., Contracts, §317, p. 471.) In determining the materiality of a failure to fully perform a promise the following factors are to be considered:

> (1) The extent to which the injured party will obtain the substantial benefit which he could have reasonably anticipated; (2) the extent to which the injured party may be adequately compensated in damages for lack of complete performance; (3) the extent to which the party failing to perform has already partly performed or made preparations for performance; (4) the greater or less hardship on the party failing to perform in terminating the contract; (5) the wilful, negligent, or innocent behavior of the party failing to perform; and (6) the greater or less uncertainty that the party failing to perform will perform the remainder of the contract. (Rest., Contracts, §275, pp. 402-403.)

In the instant case, although Sackett had paid part of the purchase price for the newspaper stock and although his delay in paying the balance due under the contract could probably be compensated for in damages, we are of the opinion that Spindler was justified in terminating the contract on October 5 on the basis that despite Sackett's "offers" to perform and his assurances to Spindler that he would perform, it was extremely uncertain as to whether in fact Sackett intended to complete the contract. In addition, in light of Spindler's numerous requests of Sackett for the balance due under the contract, the latter's failure to perform could certainly not be characterized as innocent; rather it could be but ascribed to gross negligence or wilful conduct on his part. . . .

. . . [I]n the instant case although Sackett at no time repudiated the contract and although he frequently expressed willingness to perform, the evidence was such as to warrant the inference that he did not intend to perform the subject contract. Certainly, the state of the record was such as to justify the conclusion either that it was unlikely that Sackett would tender the balance due or that he would do so at his own convenience. Spindler was not required to endure the uncertainty or to await Sackett's convenience and was therefore justified in treating the latter's nonperformance as a total breach of the contract. Accordingly, we conclude that the letter which Spindler's attorney wrote to Sackett's attorney on October 5 did not constitute an unlawful repudiation of the contract on Spindler's part, was therefore not a breach of the contract by him, and thus did not discharge Sackett's duty to perform the contract or, alternatively, to respond to Spindler in damages.

In any event, even if Spindler was not justified in treating Sackett's breach as total as of October 5, the latter's contention that his duty to perform was discharged by Spindler's repudiation of the contract as of that date is untenable. Since Spindler was not obligated to perform his promise at that time due to Sackett's failure to tender the balance due under the contract, Spindler's repudiation was, at best, anticipatory in nature. Its effect was nullified by Sackett's disregard of it and his treating the contract as still in force as evidenced by his attempt, through his attorney, to arrange an alternative method of financing the balance due under the agreement. (See Cook v. Nordstrand, 83 Cal. App. 2d 188, 195, 188 P.2d 282; Rest., Contracts, §319, p. 481.) Moreover, Spindler's repudiation was itself retracted by his attorney who, on Spindler's behalf, told Sackett's attorney in the same conversation at which the latter suggested an alternative method of financing that Spindler was still willing to consummate the sale provided Sackett would pay the balance due in cash or its equivalent. Such a retraction constitutes a nullification of the original effectiveness of the repudiation. (Rest., Contracts, §319, p. 481.) . . .

The judgment is modified by deleting therefrom the award of interest from September 29, 1961 to the date of the entry of judgment. As so modified, the judgment is affirmed. Respondent Spindler to recover costs.

SIMS and BRAY, JJ., concur.
Hearing denied; SULLIVAN, J., not participating.

NOTES AND QUESTIONS

1. *Total and partial breach.* The court holds that Sackett committed a breach when he failed to tender the balance due under the contract. The court indicates, however, that once this breach had occurred, Spindler's rights depended on whether the breach was "total" or "partial." The term *total breach* does not mean

that a party has breached all of her obligations under the contract. A breach is total if the breach is sufficiently serious to justify discharging the nonbreaching party from her obligations to perform the contract. Restatement (Second) §242 identifies various factors to guide courts in making this determination. The distinction between total and partial breach is significant in two ways: It determines the effect of the breach on the performance obligations of the nonbreaching party; it also affects the measurement of that party's damages. First, a total breach relieves or "discharges" the nonbreaching party from his duties under the contract; after a total breach the nonbreaching party is justified in refusing to perform his obligations and may even enter into alternative contracts. (Spindler, for example, was justified in selling his stock to another purchaser.) See Restatement (Second) §243(1). A partial breach does not discharge the nonbreaching party, who must continue to perform his obligations under the contract. Second, after a total breach, the injured party is entitled to recover not only actual damages accrued as a result of the breach but also any future damages that will reasonably flow from the breach; a partial breach produces a right to damages only for the actual harm that has resulted to date, not for future harm. Restatement (Second) §243(4).

2. *Material and total breach.* Although the terms "material" and "total" breach are often used interchangeably, the Restatement (Second) distinguishes between them in terms of the effect on the other party: When an uncured "material" breach by one party occurs, Restatement (Second) §237 treats this as in effect the nonoccurrence of a (constructive) condition to the other party's duty to render any performance not yet due, and performance by that party may therefore be suspended until the breach is cured. The materiality of a breach is to be decided in light of the factors listed in Restatement (Second) §241. When a material breach becomes "total," under the rule of Restatement (Second) §242 it has the effect of discharging the other party's remaining duties of performance and permitting that party to proceed immediately to pursue a claim for damages from total breach (§236(1)).

You may also find it helpful to consider the relationship between the concept of total breach and the substantial performance doctrine announced by *Jacob & Youngs.* If performance is substantial but defective, nonperformance would be only a partial breach. The breaching party must answer in damages for the partial breach, but the nonbreaching party is not discharged. Thus, Kent could not refuse to pay Jacob & Youngs the balance of the purchase price. Kent had the theoretical right to recover damages for Jacob & Youngs's partial breach, its failure to use Reading pipe. The measure of damages for partial breach used by the court, however, did not result in Kent receiving any actual damages.

The first question to be addressed in such cases, therefore, is: Is the other party's breach material? In *Sackett* the court refers to §275 of the first Restatement for a list of factors to be used in deciding whether a breach is material. Section 241 of the revised Restatement adopts a similar list. How would the factors in §241 apply to the facts of *Sackett*? Does the Restatement (Second) test offer sufficient guidance to the court in determining whether a breach was material? A careful application of the §241 test can be found in Norfolk Southern Ry. Co. v. Basell, U.S.A., 512 F.3d 86 (3d Cir. 2008), in which the Third Circuit reversed the district court's decision to grant summary judgment for defendant Basell. The trial court held as a matter of law that Basell did not materially breach its contract with Norfolk Southern requiring it to use the railroad for 95 percent of its deliveries. The Third Circuit found that the district court had erroneously focused almost exclusively on the second Restatement factor dealing with the extent to which the nonbreaching party can be adequately compensated for the loss of benefit. The court found that all the other Restatement factors could have supported a finding of material breach, including the inquiry whether the nonbreaching party "was substantially deprived of the benefit that it had reasonably expected when entering into the . . . contract." Id. at 94. See, e.g., M & M Elec. Contractor, Inc. v. Cumberland Electric Membership Corp., 529 S.W.3d 413 (Tenn. Ct. App. 2016) (contractor could treat sub's willful disregard of safety procedures as material breach even though no injury resulted therefrom); Boston LLC v. Juarez, 199 Cal. Rptr. 3d 452 (Ct. App. 2016) (landlord could not enforce forfeiture clause against tenant for breach of obligation to procure renter's insurance; trivial breach did not justify eviction of tenant in violation of statutory policy protecting tenants against arbitrary termination).

3. *When does a material breach become total?* Having determined that the breaching party's failure to perform was indeed material, justifying the other party's suspension of performance, the next step for a court in applying the Restatement (Second) analysis is to determine whether the material breach had become total, entitling the other party to be released from its obligations under the contract. Section 242 indicates that the totality of a breach will depend on the existence of an uncured material breach, based on the factors listed in §241, plus two other considerations: the extent to which further delay appears likely to prevent or hinder the making of substitute arrangements by the nonbreaching party, and the degree of importance that the terms of the agreement attach to performance without delay. Comment *b* to §242 suggests an additional relevant consideration: In applying the discharge rule of that section, "the reasonableness of the injured party's conduct in communicating his grievances and in seeking satisfaction is a factor to be considered." See Bates v. Benedetti, 2011 WL 978195 (Tenn. Ct. App.) (common law requires notice of material breach and an opportunity for the nonperforming party to cure before termination of a contract). It should be noted that agreements often provide for notice of material breach and an opportunity to cure before an injured party may terminate the agreement. See, e.g., L-7 Designs, Inc. v. Old Navy, LLC, 647 F.3d 419, 434 (2d Cir. 2011) (Old Navy provided only notice of termination, but contract required (1) notice of material breach, (2) 30 days' opportunity to cure, (3) failure to cure the material breach, and (4) notice of termination); Arbor Windsor Court, Ltd. v. Weekly Homes, Inc., 403 S.W.3d 131 (Tex. Ct. App. 2015) (contract required lot vendor to give purchaser notice of default before pursuing remedy). Under the rule of Restatement (Second) §242, at what point (if any) did Sackett's breach become total, justifying Spindler in

treating his further duties under their contract as discharged and entitling Spindler to seek damages for total breach?

The Restatement (Second) §242 distinction between material and total breach, including the emphasis on the right to cure, has generated some criticism and the degree of its acceptance by the courts has been questioned. See Amy B. Cohen, Reviving Jacob and Youngs, Inc. v. Kent: Material Breach Doctrine Reconsidered, 42 Vill. L. Rev. 65, 81 n.53 (1997). Many court decisions seem to view a material breach as giving the nonbreaching party the ability to cancel the contract and sue for damages without applying the "total breach" analysis. See, e.g., Barbagallo v. Marcum LLP, 925 F. Supp. 2d 275 (E.D.N.Y. 2013) (under New York law, after material breach, nonbreaching party may elect to terminate or to continue contract and sue for damages in either event; accountant committed egregious, material breach by covertly working for another firm and was not entitled to retirement benefits from defendant employer). Perhaps those cases can be explained, however, on the ground that the breach was so serious that the possibility of cure was remote or nonexistent.

4. *Risks facing the nonbreaching party.* As the *Sackett* opinion demonstrates, there are substantial risks involved for the party who elects to treat the other party's nonperformance as a material or total breach, justifying suspension of performance or even termination on her part. In the *Sackett* case, it came out (except for the costs of litigation) satisfactorily for Spindler; not all litigating parties are as fortunate. E.g., Health Related Services, Inc. v. Golden Plains Convalescent Center, Inc., 806 S.W.2d 102 (Mo. Ct. App. 1991) (although management company may have performed defectively in various ways, convalescent center failed to demonstrate material breach by management company, justifying its discharge; center liable for damages for total breach). Suppose Spindler had been found to have "jumped the gun" in treating Sackett's breach as total: What effect would that have had on Spindler's rights and obligations?

5. *Effect of "time of essence" clause.* If you had represented Spindler at the time he entered into the contract with Sackett, could you have helped him avoid the necessity for litigation with Sackett by providing that timely performance by Sackett was to be "of the essence" under their contract? Comment *d* to Restatement (Second) §242 suggests that such "stock phrases" as "time is of the essence" in the contract will not necessarily mean that any delay in performance must be deemed material; such phrases are to be considered "along with other circumstances" in deciding this question. See, e.g., Foundation Dev. Corp. v. Loehmann's, Inc., 788 P.2d 1189 (Ariz. 1990) (en banc) ("time is of the essence" clause in lease did not entitle landlord to terminate commercial lease; two-day delay in paying common area charge both inadvertent and trivial); ADC Orange, Inc. v. Coyote Acres, Inc., 857 N.E.2d 513 (N.Y. 2006) (term in land sale contract requiring that buyer make interim payment of $250,000 "in no event later than December 31, 2001" was not enough to make time of the essence; payment made two weeks late was not material breach and contract was not discharged).

On the other hand, Comment *d* to Restatement (Second) §242 also indicates that the parties may make performance by a stated date a "condition to their agreement," in which case delay beyond that date (unless the condition is excused) will result in discharge. See *enXco*, in the first part of this chapter; Elda Arnhold and Byzantio, L.L.C. v. Ocean Atlantic Woodland Corp., 284 F.3d 693 (7th Cir. 2002) ("drop dead" clause in settlement agreement enforced even though purchaser missed deadline for closing by only one day and would suffer $1.7 million loss if contract not enforced; court uses two-part test focusing on intention of parties and equitable factors in deciding whether to enforce time-of-essence clause). Would a clear express condition of timely performance have provided Spindler with full protection against the adverse consequences of delayed performance by Sackett? Can you think of other provisions that might have helped Spindler avoid his dispute with Sackett? Do you think Sackett would have agreed to their inclusion in the agreement?

C. ANTICIPATORY REPUDIATION

By virtue of the rules of constructive conditions, if one party commits a total breach when his performance is due, the other party is justified in treating her performance obligations as discharged. Suppose, however, that something happens *before* the date specified for performance – something that causes the second party to have serious doubts about either the willingness or the ability of the first party to perform. For example, the first party could clearly indicate that he will not perform; this advance refusal to perform, or "anticipatory repudiation," could be expressed orally, in writing, or by conduct showing an unwillingness to perform. Or, even if the first party does not actually repudiate his obligations, circumstances might give the second party reasonable grounds for "insecurity" about the ability of the first party to perform on time (financial difficulty or shortage of materials, for example). In such cases must the party who learns of an anticipatory repudiation, or who has reasonable grounds for insecurity of performance, wait until the time specified for performance to exercise her legal rights, or does the law give her the right to act immediately? The materials that follow address this question.

Truman L. Flatt & Sons Co. v. Schupf

Appellate Court of Illinois 271 Ill. App.3d 983, 649 N.E.2d 990 (1995)

Presiding Justice KNECHT delivered the opinion of the court:

Plaintiff Truman L. Flatt & Sons Co., Inc., filed a complaint seeking specific performance of a real estate contract made with defendants Sara Lee Schupf, Ray H. Neiswander, Jr., and American National Bank and Trust Company of Chicago (American), as trustee under trust No. 23257. Defendants filed a motion for summary judgment, which the trial court granted. Plaintiff now appeals from the trial court's grant of the motion for summary judgment. We reverse and remand.

In March 1993, plaintiff and defendants entered a contract in which defendants agreed to sell plaintiff a parcel of land located in Springfield, Illinois. The contract stated the purchase price was to be $160,000. The contract also contained the following provisions:

> 1. This transaction shall be closed on or before June 30, 1993, or upon approval of the relief requested from the Zoning Code of the City of Springfield, Illinois, whichever first occurs ("Closing Date"). The closing is subject to contingency set forth in paragraph 14.
>
> . . .
>
> 14. This Contract to Purchase Real Estate is contingent upon the Buyer obtaining, within one hundred twenty (120) days after the date hereof, amendment of, or other sufficient relief of, the Zoning Code of the City of Springfield to permit the construction and operation of an asphalt plant. In the event the City Council of the City of Springfield denies the request for such use of the property, then this contract shall be voidable at Buyer's option and if Buyer elects to void this contract Buyer shall receive a refund of the earnest money paid.

On May 21, plaintiff's attorney sent a letter to defendants' attorney informing him of substantial public opposition plaintiff encountered at a public meeting concerning its request for rezoning. The letter concluded:

> The day after the meeting all of the same representatives of the buyer assembled and discussed our chances for successfully pursuing the re-zoning request. Everyone who was there was in agreement that our chances were zero to none for success. As a result, we decided to withdraw the request for rezoning, rather than face almost certain defeat.
>
> The bottom line is that we are still interested in the property, but the property is not worth as much to us a 35-acre parcel zoned I-1, as it would be if it were zoned I-2. At this juncture, I think it is virtually impossible for anyone to get that property re-zoned I-2, especially to accommodate the operation of an asphalt plant. In an effort to keep this thing moving, my clients have authorized me to offer your clients the sum of $142,500.00 for the property, which they believe fairly represents its value with its present zoning classification. Please check with your clients and advise whether or not that revision in the contract is acceptable. If it is, I believe we can accelerate the closing and bring this matter to a speedy conclusion. Your prompt attention will be appreciated. Thanks.

Defendants' attorney responded in a letter dated June 9, the body of which stated, in its entirety:

> In reply to your May 21 letter, be advised that the owners of the property in question are not interested in selling the property for $142,500 and, accordingly, the offer is not accepted.
>
> I regret that the zoning reclassification was not approved.

Plaintiff's attorney replied back in a letter dated June 14, the body of which stated, in its entirety:

> My clients received your letter of June 9, 1993[,] with some regret, however upon some consideration they have elected to proceed with the purchase of the property as provided in the contract. At your convenience please give me a call so that we can set up a closing date.

After this correspondence, plaintiff's attorney sent two more brief letters to defendants' attorney, dated June 23 and July 6, each requesting information concerning the status of defendants' preparation for fulfillment of the contract. Defendants' attorney replied in a letter dated July 8. The letter declared it was the defendants' position plaintiff's failure to waive the rezoning requirement and elect to proceed under the contract at the time the rezoning was denied, coupled with the new offer to buy the property at less than the contract price, effectively voided the contract. Plaintiff apparently sent one more letter in an attempt to convince defendants to honor the contract, but defendants declined. Defendants then arranged to have plaintiff's earnest money returned.

Plaintiff filed a complaint for specific performance and other relief against defendants and American, asking the court to direct defendants to comply with the terms of the contract. Defendants responded by filing a "motion to strike, motion to dismiss or, in the alternative, motion for summary judgment." The motion for summary judgment sought summary judgment on the basis plaintiff repudiated the contract.

Prior to the hearing on the motions, plaintiff filed interrogatories requesting, among other things, information concerning the current status of the property. Defendants' answers to the interrogatories stated defendants had no knowledge of any third party's involvement in a potential sale of the property, defendants had not made any offer to sell the property to anyone, no one had made an offer to purchase the property or discussed the possibility of purchasing the property, and defendants had not sold the property to, received any offer from, or discussed a sale of the property with, any other trust member.

After a hearing on the motions, the trial court granted the defendants' motion for summary judgment without explaining the basis for its ruling. Plaintiff filed a post-trial motion to vacate the judgment. The trial court denied the post-trial motion, declaring defendants' motion for summary judgment was granted because plaintiff had repudiated the contract. Plaintiff now appeals the trial court's grant of summary judgment, arguing the trial court erred because (1) it did not repudiate the contract, and (2) even if it did repudiate the contract, it timely retracted that repudiation.

Plaintiff contends the trial court erred in granting summary judgment. Summary judgment is proper when the resolution of a case hinges on a question of law and the moving party's right to judgment is clear and free from doubt. . . . Here, there are no facts in dispute. Thus, the question is whether the trial court erred in declaring defendant was entitled to judgment as a matter of law based on those facts.

Plaintiff first argues summary judgment was improper because the trial court erred in finding plaintiff had repudiated the contract.

> The doctrine of anticipatory repudiation requires a clear manifestation of an intent not to perform the contract on the date of performance. . . . That intention must be a definite and unequivocal manifestation that he will not render the promised performance when the time fixed for it in the contract arrives. [Citation.] Doubtful and indefinite statements that performance may or may not take place are not enough to constitute anticipatory repudiation. (In re Marriage of Olsen (1988), 124 Ill. 2d 19, 24, 123 Ill. Dec. 980, 982, 528 N.E.2d 684, 686.)

These requirements exist because "[a]nticipatory breach is not a remedy to be taken lightly." (*Olsen,* 124 Ill. 2d at 25, 123 Ill. Dec. at 983, 528 N.E.2d at 687.) The Restatement (Second) of Contracts adopts the view of the Uniform Commercial Code (UCC) and states "language that under a fair reading 'amounts to a statement of intention not to perform except on conditions which go beyond the contract' constitutes a repudiation. Comment 2 to Uniform Commercial Code §2-610." (Restatement (Second) of Contracts §250, Comment *b,* at 273 (1981).) Whether an anticipatory repudiation occurred is a question of fact and the judgment of the trial court thereon will not be disturbed unless it is against the manifest weight of evidence. . . .

As can be seen, whether a repudiation occurred is determined on a case-by-case basis, depending on the particular language used. Both plaintiff and defendants, although they cite Illinois cases discussing repudiation, admit the cited Illinois cases are all factually distinguishable from the case at hand because none of those cases involved a request to change a term in the contract. According to the commentators, a suggestion for modification of the contract does not amount to a repudiation. (J. Calamari & J. Perillo, Contracts §12-4, at 524-525 n.74 (3d ed. 1987) (hereinafter Calamari), citing Unique Systems Inc. v. Zotos International, Inc. (8th Cir. 1980), 622 F.2d 373.) Plaintiff also cites cases in other jurisdictions holding a request for a change in the price term of a contract does not constitute a repudiation. (Wooten v. DeMean (Mo. Ct. App. 1990), 788 S.W.2d 522; Stolper Steel Products Corp. v. Behrens Manufacturing Co. (1960), 10 Wis. 2d 478, 103 N.W.2d 683.) Defendants attempt to distinguish these cases by arguing here, under the totality of the language in the letter and the circumstances surrounding the letter, the request by plaintiff for a decrease in price clearly implied a threat of nonperformance if the price term was not modified. We disagree.

The language in the May 21 letter did not constitute a clearly implied threat of nonperformance. First, although the language in the May 21 letter perhaps could be read as implying plaintiff would refuse to perform under the contract unless the price was modified, given the totality of the language in the letter, such an inference is weak. More important, even if such an inference were possible, Illinois law requires a repudiation be manifested clearly and unequivocally. Plaintiff's May 21 letter at most created an *ambiguous implication* whether performance would occur. Indeed, during oral argument defense counsel conceded the May 21 letter was "ambiguous" on whether a repudiation had occurred. This is insufficient to constitute a repudiation under well-settled Illinois law.

Therefore, the trial court erred in declaring the May 21 letter anticipatorily repudiated the real estate contract as a matter of law.

Moreover, even if plaintiff had repudiated the contract, the trial court erred in granting summary judgment on this basis because plaintiff timely retracted its repudiation. Only one published decision has discussed and applied Illinois law regarding retraction of an anticipatory repudiation, Refrigeradora Del Noroeste, S.A. v. Appelbaum (1956), 138 F. Supp. 354 (holding the repudiating party has the power of retraction unless the injured party has brought suit or otherwise materially changed position), aff'd in part & rev'd in part on other grounds (1957), 248 F.2d 858. The Restatement (Second) of Contracts states:

> The effect of a statement as constituting a repudiation under §250 or the basis for a repudiation under §251 is nullified by a retraction of the statement if notification of the retraction comes to the attention of the injured party before he materially changes his position in reliance on the repudiation or *indicates* to the other party that he considers the repudiation to be final. (Emphasis added.) (Restatement (Second) of Contracts §256(1), at 293 (1981).)

The UCC adopts the same position:

> **Retraction of Anticipatory Repudiation.**
>
> (1) Until the repudiating party's next performance is due he can retract his repudiation unless the aggrieved party has since the repudiation cancelled or materially changed his position or otherwise *indicated* that he considers the repudiation final. (Emphasis added.) (810 ILCS 5/2-611(1) (West 1992).)

Professors Calamari and Perillo declare section 2-611 of the UCC:

> . . . is in general accord with the common law rule that an anticipatory repudiation may be retracted until the other party has commenced an action thereon or has otherwise changed his position. The Code is explicit that no other act of reliance is necessary where the aggrieved party *indicates* "that he considers the repudiation final." (Emphasis added.) (Calamari §12.7, at 528.) The majority of the common law cases appear to be in accord with this position. (Calamari §12.7, at 528 n.93.)

Other commentators are universally in accord. Professor Farnsworth states: "The repudiating party can prevent the injured party from treating the contract as terminated by retracting before the injured party has *acted* in response to it." (Emphasis added.) (2 E. Farnsworth, Contracts §8.22, at 482 (1990).) Professor Corbin declares one who has anticipatorily repudiated his contract has the power of retraction until the aggrieved party has materially changed his position in reliance on the repudiation. (4 A. Corbin, Corbin on Contracts §980, at 930-931 (1951) (hereinafter Corbin).) Corbin goes on to say the assent of the aggrieved party is necessary for retraction only when the repudiation is no longer merely anticipatory, but has become an actual breach at the time performance is due. (4 Corbin §980, at 935.) Williston states an anticipatory repudiation can be retracted by the repudiating party "unless the other party has, before the withdrawal, *manifested* an election to rescind the contract, or changed his position in reliance on the repudiation." (Emphasis added.) 11 W. Jaeger, Williston on Contracts §1335, at 180 (3d ed. 1968) (hereinafter Williston).

Defendants completely avoid discussion of the common-law right to retract a repudiation other than to say Illinois is silent on the issue. Defendants then cite . . . [three Illinois decisions] as well as Williston §1337, at 185-186. These authorities stand for the proposition that after an anticipatory repudiation, the aggrieved party is entitled to choose to treat the contract as rescinded or terminated, to treat the anticipatory repudiation as a breach by bringing suit or otherwise changing its position, or to await the time for performance. The UCC adopts substantially the same position. (810 ILCS 5/2-610 (West 1992).) Defendants here assert they chose to treat the contract as rescinded, as they had a right to do under well-settled principles of law.

Plaintiff admits the law stated by defendants is well settled, and admits if the May 21 letter was an anticipatory breach, then defendants had the right to treat the contract as being terminated or rescinded. However, plaintiff points out defendants' assertions ignore the great weight of authority, discussed earlier, which provides a right of the repudiating party to retract the repudiation *before* the aggrieved party has chosen one of its options allowed under the common law. . . . Plaintiff argues defendants' letter of June 9 failed to treat the contract as rescinded, and absent *notice* or *other manifestation* defendants were pursuing one of their options, plaintiff was free to retract its repudiation. Plaintiff is correct.

Defendants' precise theory that plaintiff should not be allowed to retract any repudiation in this instance is ambiguous and may be given two interpretations. The first is Illinois should not follow the common-law rule allowing retraction of an anticipatory repudiation before the aggrieved party elects a response to the repudiation. This theory warrants little discussion, because the rule is well settled. Further, defendants have offered no public policy reason to disallow retraction of repudiation other than the public interest in upholding the "sanctity of the contract."

The second possible interpretation of defendants' precise theory is an aggrieved party may treat the contract as terminated or rescinded *without* notice or other indication being given to the repudiating party, and once such a decision is made by the aggrieved party, the repudiating party no longer has the right of retraction. It is true no notice is required to be given to the repudiating party if the aggrieved party materially changes its position as a result of the repudiation. (See, e.g., Calamari §12-7, at 528 n.92, citing Bu-Vi-Bar Petroleum Corp. v. Krow (10th Cir. 1930), 40 F.2d 488, 493.) Here, however, the defendants admitted in their answers to plaintiff's interrogatories they had not entered another agreement to sell the property, nor even discussed or considered the matter with another party. Defendants had not changed their position at all, nor do defendants make any attempt to so argue. As can be seen from the language of the Restatement, the UCC, and the commentators, shown earlier, they are in accord that where the aggrieved party has not otherwise undergone a material change in position, the aggrieved party must *indicate to the other party* it is electing to treat the contract as rescinded. This can be accomplished either by bringing suit, by notifying the repudiating party, or by in some other way manifesting an election to treat the contract as rescinded. Prior to such indication, the repudiating party is free to retract its repudiation. The Restatement (Second) of Contracts provides the following illustrations:

> 2. On February 1, A contracts to supply B with natural gas for one year beginning on May 1, payment to be made each month. On March 1, A repudiates. On April 1, before B has taken any action in response to the repudiation, A notifies B that he retracts his repudiation. B's duties under the contract are not discharged, and B has no claim against A.
>
> . . .
>
> 4. The facts being otherwise as stated in Illustration 2, on March 15, B *notifies* A that he cancels the contract. B's duties under the contract are discharged and B has a claim against A for damages for total breach. . . ." (Emphasis added.) Restatement (Second) of Contracts §256, Comments *a, c* (1981).

This rule makes sense as well. If an aggrieved party could treat the contract as rescinded or terminated without notice or other indication to the repudiating party, the rule allowing retraction of an anticipatory repudiation would be eviscerated. No repudiating party ever would be able to retract a repudiation, because after receiving a retraction, the aggrieved party could, if it wished, simply declare it had already decided to treat the repudiation as a rescission or termination of the contract. Defendants' theory would effectively rewrite the common-law rule regarding retraction of anticipatory repudiation so that the repudiating party may retract an anticipatory repudiation only upon assent from the aggrieved party. This is not the common-law rule, and we decline to adopt defendants' proposed revision of it.

Applying the actual common-law rule to the facts here, plaintiff sent defendants a letter dated June 14, which clearly and unambiguously indicated plaintiff intended to perform under the contract. However, defendants did not notify plaintiff, either expressly or impliedly, of an intent to treat the contract as rescinded until July 8. Nor is there anything in the record demonstrating any indication to plaintiff, prior to July 8, of an intent by defendants to treat the contract as rescinded or terminated. Thus, assuming plaintiff's May 21 request for a lower purchase price constituted an anticipatory repudiation of the contract, plaintiff successfully retracted that repudiation in the letter dated June 14 because defendants had not yet materially changed their position or indicated to plaintiff an intent to treat the contract as rescinded. Therefore, because plaintiff had timely retracted any alleged repudiation of the contract, the trial court erred in granting summary judgment for defendants on the basis plaintiff repudiated the contract. Defendants were not entitled to judgment as a matter of law.

The trial court's grant of summary judgment for defendants is reversed, and the cause is remanded.

Reversed and remanded.

COOK and MCCULLOUGH, JJ., concur.

NOTES AND QUESTIONS

1. *History of anticipatory repudiation.* The doctrine of anticipatory repudiation is usually traced to the English case of Hochster v. De La Tour, 118 Eng. Rep. 922 (Q.B. 1853). In *Hochster*, defendant had contracted to employ plaintiff as a courier for three months beginning June 1. On May 11 defendant informed plaintiff that he had changed his mind and that plaintiff's services were not required. Plaintiff brought suit on May 22. Between May 22 and June 1 plaintiff obtained other employment. The court held that in light of defendant's unequivocal repudiation of the contract, the plaintiff had the right to bring suit even before the date set for performance. The court reasoned that unless the plaintiff could bring suit at once, he would be required to hold himself ready to perform; instead, the law should allow the injured party to enter into substitute contracts after the other party clearly expressed the intention not to perform.

The doctrine is generally accepted by American courts; it is included in both Restatement (Second) §253(1) and UCC §2-610. See Keith A. Rowley, A Brief History of Anticipatory Repudiation in American Contract Law, 69 U. Cin. L. Rev. 565 (2001).

2. *Expressions sufficient to be an anticipatory repudiation.* In discussing whether the plaintiff's communication to the defendants amounted to a repudiation of his contract to purchase their land, the court quotes authority to the effect that a manifestation of intent not to perform must be "definite and unequivocal" to constitute an anticipatory breach; mere "doubtful and indefinite statements that performance may or may not take place" will not be so regarded. The Restatement takes the same approach. Restatement (Second) §250, Comment *b*. Why does the law apply so stringent a test? The cases generally reflect this approach. See, e.g., Officemax, Inc. v. NHS Human Services, Inc., 2017 WL 1022078 (E.D. Ill.) (indication that defendant might seek bids from alternate suppliers not a clear and unequivocal anticipatory repudiation of supply contract with plaintiff; "doubtful and indefinite" statements do not sufficiently express intent to breach); Sunesis Trucking Co., Inc. v. Thistledown Racetrack, L.L.C., 22 N.E.3d 190 (Ohio Ct. App. 2014) (letter asking for new fee for horse manure hauling service was mere request for modification of contract terms and did not constitute repudiation, especially when service was never stopped and parties negotiated toward modification). On the other hand, an anticipatory repudiation can occur even if the party does not say in so many words that she will not perform the contract. The Restatement (Second) in Comment *b* to

§250 goes on to echo the Uniform Commercial Code (Comment 2 to UCC §2-610) in declaring that "language that under a fair reading 'amounts to a statement of intention not to perform except on conditions which go beyond the contract' constitutes a repudiation." In Millis Constr. Co. v. Fairfield Sapphire Valley, Inc., 358 S.E.2d 566 (N.C. Ct. App. 1987), plaintiff contractor sued for wrongful termination of its building contract with defendant real estate developer. The trial court's judgment on a jury verdict for plaintiff was reversed on appeal because of the trial court's refusal to charge the jury that it could find plaintiff was the first party in material breach of contract. Before defendant terminated plaintiff's work on the job, plaintiff had told defendant he was "belly up" and "busted," and would be financially unable to complete the job unless he was given advance payments to which he was not yet entitled; this could have been viewed as a refusal to perform except on a condition outside the terms of the contract and therefore as an anticipatory breach.

3. *Conduct amounting to an anticipatory repudiation.* Although a repudiation must be sufficiently definite and unequivocal to justify treating it as a breach, it may consist of conduct rather than words. Suppose the defendants in the *Truman L. Flatt* case had regarded the plaintiff's letter of May 21 as a repudiation, and contracted to sell their property to someone else. What would have been the respective rights of the parties? As Restatement (Second) §250(b) indicates, conduct that "renders the obligor unable or apparently unable to perform" may amount to a repudiation. For mere conduct to constitute an anticipatory repudiation, however, it must indicate that performance is a practical impossibility. See, e.g., Wallace v. Smith, 2014 WL 4810304 (Nev.) (plaintiff agent pled facts sufficient to establish that defendant recording artist repudiated seven-year exclusive representation contract by moving from Las Vegas to Los Angeles, cutting off all communication with plaintiff, and pursuing record deals without plaintiff's assistance; fact-finder could reasonably conclude that alleged conduct made plaintiff's performance impossible).

Financial difficulty that might impair performance, even to the level of insolvency, does not constitute an anticipatory repudiation. Restatement (Second) §252, Comment *a*. However, insolvency does constitute a ground for demand of adequate assurance of performance. (Hornell Brewing Co. v. Spry, the next principal case, examines the doctrine of adequate assurances of performance.) If a party files a petition in bankruptcy, federal law determines the effect of the bankruptcy on the rights of the other party to the contract. See Restatement (Second) §250, Comment *c*.

4. *Retraction of anticipatory repudiation.* As the *Truman L. Flatt* case amply demonstrates, a party who commits an anticipatory repudiation may change her mind and retract the repudiation so long as the other party has not relied to his detriment on the repudiation or notified the repudiating party that he is treating the repudiation as final. Restatement (Second) §256(1), UCC §2-611. Suppose you had represented the defendants at the time plaintiff's letter of May 21 was received, and that the defendants by that time had received inquiries from another buyer who was apparently prepared to pay somewhat more

for the property than the $142,500 that plaintiff had agreed to pay. You would of course be aware that if the plaintiff had effectively repudiated its obligation by the letter of May 21, the defendants could make that repudiation final and nonretractible, either by notifying the plaintiff of their intent to do so, or simply by selling their property to someone else. On the other hand, you would also be aware that if the plaintiff had *not* effectively repudiated by the letter of May 21, such an action by the defendants would constitute a repudiation by them, entitling plaintiff to treat them as having materially breached, and to claim damages flowing from their breach. How would you proceed?

5. *Effect of express condition in parties' agreement.* The court's opinion in *Truman L. Flatt* suggests that both parties, and the court as well, treated the plaintiff's letter of May 21 as one that might have been an anticipatory repudiation, except for its lack of definiteness. But even if the letter of May 21 had been an unequivocal "repudiation," asserting clearly plaintiff's intention not to proceed with the purchase of defendant's property, would that repudiation necessarily have been a wrongful breach of the contract? Or should the plaintiff have been able to argue successfully that in the circumstances of the case, Paragraph 14 of their contract released it from further obligation?

Hornell Brewing Co. v. Spry

Supreme Court of New York County 174 Misc. 2d 451, 664 N.Y.S.2d 698 (1997)

Louise GRUNER GANS, Justice.

Plaintiff Hornell Brewing Co., Inc. ("Hornell"), a supplier and marketer of alcoholic and non-alcoholic beverages, including the popular iced tea drink "Arizona," commenced this action for a declaratory judgment that any rights of defendants Stephen A. Spry and Arizona Tea Products Ltd. to distribute Hornell's beverages in Canada have been duly terminated, that defendants have no further rights with respect to these products, including no right to market and distribute them, and that any such rights previously transferred to defendants have reverted to Hornell.

In late 1992, Spry approached Don Vultaggio, Hornell's Chairman of the Board, about becoming a distributor of Hornell's Arizona beverages. Vultaggio had heard about Spry as an extremely wealthy and successful beer distributor who had recently sold his business. In January 1993, Spry presented Vultaggio with an ambitious plan for distributing Arizona beverages in Canada. Based on the plan and on Spry's reputation, but without further investigation, Hornell in early 1993 granted Spry the exclusive right to purchase Arizona products for distribution in Canada, and Spry formed a Canadian corporation, Arizona Iced Tea Ltd., for that express purpose.

Initially, the arrangement was purely oral. In response to Spry's request for a letter he needed to secure financing, Hornell provided a letter in July 1993 confirming their exclusive distributorship arrangement, but without spelling out the details of the arrangement. Although Hornell usually had detailed written distributorship agreements and the parties discussed and exchanged drafts of such an agreement, none was ever executed. In the meantime, Spry, with Hornell's approval, proceeded to set himself up as Hornell's distributor in Canada. During 1993 and until May 1994, the Hornell line of beverages, including the Arizona beverages, was sold to defendants on 10-day credit terms. In May 1994, after an increasingly problematic course of business dealings, Hornell de facto terminated its relationship with defendants and permanently ceased selling its products to them.

The problem dominating the parties' relationship between July 1993 and early May 1994 was defendants' failure to remit timely payment for shipments of beverages received from plaintiff. Between November and December 1993, and February 1994, defendants' unpaid invoices grew from $20,000 to over $100,000, and their $31,000 check to Hornell was returned for insufficient funds. Moreover, defendants' 1993 sales in Canada were far below Spry's initial projections.

In March and April 1994, a series of meetings, telephone calls, and letter communications took place between plaintiff and defendants regarding Spry's constant arrearages and the need for him to obtain a line and/or letter of credit that would place their business relationship on a more secure footing. These contacts included a March 27, 1994 letter to Spry from Vanguard Financial Group, Inc. confirming "the approval of a $1,500,000 revolving credit facility" to Arizona Tea Products Ltd., which never materialized into an actual line of credit; Spry sent Hornell a copy of this letter in late March or early April 1994.

All these exchanges demonstrate that during this period plaintiff had two distinct goals: to collect the monies owed by Spry, and to stabilize their future business relationship based on proven, reliable credit assurances. These exchanges also establish that during March and April, 1994, Spry repeatedly broke his promises to pay by a specified deadline, causing Hornell to question whether Vanguard's $1.5 million revolving line of credit was genuine.

On April 15, 1994, during a meeting with Vultaggio, Spry arranged for Vultaggio to speak on the telephone with Richard Worthy of Metro Factors, Inc. The testimony as to the content of that brief telephone conversation is conflicting. Although Worthy testified that he identified himself and the name of his company, Metro Factors, Inc., Vultaggio testified that he believed Worthy was from an "unusual lending institution" or bank which was going to provide Spry with a line of credit, and that nothing was expressly said to make him aware that Worthy represented a factoring company. Worthy also testified that Vultaggio told him that once Spry cleared up the arrears, Hornell would provide Spry with a "$300,000 line of credit, so long as payments were made on a net 14 day basis." According to Vultaggio, he told Worthy that once he was paid in full, he was willing to resume shipments to Spry "so long as Steve fulfills his requirements with us."

Hornell's April 18, 1994 letter to Spry confirmed certain details of the April 15 conversations, including that payment of the arrears would be made by April 19, 1994. However, Hornell received no payment on that date. Instead, on April 25, Hornell received from Spry a proposed letter for Hornell to address to a company named "Metro" at a post office box in Dallas, Texas. Worthy originally sent Spry a draft of this letter with "Metro Factors, Inc." named as the addressee, but in the copy Vultaggio received the words "Factors, Inc." were apparently obliterated. Hornell copied the draft letter on its own letterhead and sent it to Metro over Vultaggio's signature. In relevant part, the letter stated as follows:

> Gentlemen:
>
> Please be advised that Arizona Tea Products, Ltd. (ATP), of which Steve Spry is president, is presently indebted to us in the total amount of $79,316.24 as of the beginning of business Monday, April 25, 1994. We sell to them on "Net 14 days" terms. Such total amount is due according to the following schedule: . . .
>
> Upon receipt of $79,316.24. (which shall be applied to the oldest balances first) by 5:30 p.m. (EST) Tuesday, May 2, 1994 by wire transfer(s) to the account described below, we shall recommence selling product to ATP on the following terms:
>
> 1) All invoices from us are due and payable by the 14th day following the release of the related product.
>
> 2) We shall allow the outstanding balance owed to us by ATP to go up to $300,000 so long as ATP remains "current" in its payment obligations to us. Wiring instructions are as follows: . . .

Hornell received no payment on May 2, 1994. It did receive a wire transfer from Metro of the full amount on May 9, 1994. Upon immediate confirmation of that payment, Spry ordered 30 trailer loads of "product" from Hornell, at a total purchase price of $390,000 to $450,000. In the interim between April 25, 1994 and May 9, 1994, Hornell learned from several sources, including its regional sales manager Baumkel, that Spry's warehouse was empty, that he had no managerial, sales or office staff, that he had no trucks, and that in effect his operation was a sham.

On May 10, 1994, Hornell wrote to Spry, acknowledging receipt of payment and confirming that they would extend up to $300,000 of credit to him, net 14 days cash "based on your prior representation that you have secured a $1,500,000. US line of credit." The letter also stated,

> Your current balance with us reflects a 0 balance due. As you know, however, we experienced considerable difficulty and time wasted over a five week time period as we tried to collect some $130,000 which was 90-120 days past due.
>
> Accordingly, before we release any more product, we are asking you to provide us with a letter confirming the existence of your line of credit as well as a personal guarantee that is backed up with a personal financial statement that can be verified. Another option would be for you to provide us with an irrevocable letter of credit in the amount of $300,000.

Spry did not respond to this letter. Spry never even sent Hornell a copy of his agreement with Metro Factors, Inc., which Spry had signed on March 24, 1994 and which was fully executed on March 30, 1994. On May 26, 1994, Vultaggio met with Spry to discuss termination of their business relationship. Vultaggio presented Spry with a letter of agreement as to the termination, which Spry took with him but did not sign. After some months of futile negotiations by counsel this action by Hornell ensued.

At the outset, the court determines that an enforceable contract existed between plaintiff and defendants based on the uncontroverted facts of their conduct. Under Article 2 of the Uniform Commercial Code, parties can form a contract through their conduct rather than merely through the exchange of communications constituting an offer and acceptance. . . . Section 2-204(1) states: "A contract for sale of goods may be made in any manner sufficient to show agreement, including conduct by both parties which recognizes the existence of such a contract." Sections 2-206(1) and 2-207(3) expressly allow for the formation of a contract partly or wholly on the basis of such conduct. 1 White & Summers, Uniform Commercial Code, ibid.

Here, the conduct of plaintiff and defendants which recognized the existence of a contract is sufficient to establish a contract for sale under Uniform Commercial Code sections 2-204(1) and 2-207(3). Both parties' undisputed actions over a period of many months clearly manifested mutual recognition that a binding obligation was undertaken. Following plaintiff's agreement to grant defendant an exclusive distributorship for Canada, defendant Spry took certain steps to enable him to commence his distribution operation in Canada. These steps included hiring counsel in Canada to form Arizona Tea Products, Ltd., the vehicle through which defendant acted in Canada, obtaining regulatory approval for the labelling of Arizona Iced Tea in conformity with Canadian law, and obtaining importation approvals necessary to import Arizona Iced Tea into Canada. Defendants subsequently placed orders for the purchase of plaintiff's products, plaintiff shipped its products to defendants during 1993 and early 1994, and defendants remitted payments, albeit not timely nor in full. Under the Uniform Commercial Code, these uncontroverted business dealings constitute "conduct . . . sufficient to establish a contract for sale," even in the absence of a specific writing by the parties. UCC §2-207(3). . . .

Notwithstanding the parties' conflicting contentions concerning the duration and termination of defendants' distributorship, plaintiff has demonstrated a basis for lawfully terminating its contract with defendants in accordance with section 2-609 of the Uniform Commercial Code. Section 2-609(1) authorizes one party upon "reasonable grounds for insecurity" to "demand adequate assurance of due performance and until he receives such assurance . . . if commercially reasonable suspend any performance for which he has not already received the agreed return." The Official Comment to section 2-609 explains that this

> section rests on the recognition of the fact that the essential purpose of a contract between commercial men is actual performance and they do not bargain merely for a promise, or for a promise plus the right to win a lawsuit and that a continuing sense of reliance and security that the promised performance will be forthcoming when due, is an important feature of the bargain. If either the willingness or the ability of a party to perform declines materially between the

> time of contracting and the time for performance, the other party is threatened with the loss of a substantial part of what he has bargained for. A seller needs protection not merely against having to deliver on credit to a shaky buyer, but also against having to procure and manufacture the goods, perhaps turning down other customers. Once he has been given reason to believe that the buyer's performance has become uncertain, it is an undue hardship to force him to continue his own performance.

McKinney's Consolidated Laws of NY, Book 62 1/2, UCC §2-609 Official Comment 1, at 488.

Whether a seller, as the plaintiff in this case, has reasonable grounds for insecurity is an issue of fact that depends upon various factors, including the buyer's exact words or actions, the course of dealing or performance between the parties, and the nature of the sales contract and the industry. White & Summers, Uniform Commercial Code, supra §6-2 at 286; see also, Phibro Energy, Inc. v. Empresa De Polimeros De Sines Sarl, 720 F. Supp. 312, 322 (S.D.N.Y. 1989); S & S Inc. v. Meyer, 478 N.W.2d 857, 863 (Iowa App. 1991); AMF, Inc. v. McDonald's Corp., 536 F.2d 1167, 1170 (7th Cir. 1976). Subdivision (2) defines both "reasonableness" and "adequacy" by commercial rather than legal standards, and the Official Comment notes the application of the good faith standard. White & Summers, id., at 287; McKinney's Consolidated Laws of NY, Book 62 1/2, UCC §2-609 Official Comment at 488, 489; Turntables, Inc. v. Gestetner, 52 A.D.2d 776, 382 N.Y.S.2d 798 (1st Dep't 1976).

Once the seller correctly determines that it has reasonable grounds for insecurity, it must properly request assurances from the buyer. Although the Code requires that the request be made in writing, UCC §2-609(1), courts have not strictly adhered to this formality as long as an unequivocal demand is made. White & Summers, Uniform Commercial Code, supra §6-2 at 288; see, e.g., ARB, Inc. v. E-Systems, Inc., 663 F.2d 189 (D.C. Cir. 1980); Toppert v. Bunge Corp., 60 Ill. App. 3d 607, 18 Ill. Dec. 171, 377 N.E.2d 324 (1978); AMF, Inc. v. McDonald's Corp., supra. After demanding assurance, the seller must determine the proper "adequate assurance." What constitutes "adequate" assurance of due performance is subject to the same test of commercial reasonableness and factual conditions. McKinney's Consolidated Laws of NY, Book 62 1/2, UCC §2-609 Official Comment at 489.

Applying these principles to the case at bar, the overwhelming weight of the evidence establishes that at the latest by the beginning of 1994, plaintiff had reasonable grounds to be insecure about defendants' ability to perform in the future. Defendants were substantially in arrears almost from the outset of their relationship with plaintiff, had no financing in place, bounced checks, and had failed to sell even a small fraction of the product defendant Spry originally projected.

Reasonable grounds for insecurity can arise from the sole fact that a buyer has fallen behind in his account with the seller, even where the items involved have to do with separate and legally distinct contracts, because this "impairs the seller's expectation of due performance." McKinney's Consolidated Laws of NY, Book 62 1/2, UCC §2-609 Official Comment 2, at 488; see also

Waldorf Steel Fabricators, Inc. v. Consolidated Systems, Inc., 1996 WL 480902 (S.D.N.Y.) (n.o.r.); Turntables, Inc. v. Gestetner, supra; American Bronze Corp. v. Streamway Products, 8 Ohio App. 3d 223, 456 N.E.2d 1295 (1982).

Here, defendants do not dispute their poor payment history, plaintiff's right to demand adequate assurances from them and that plaintiff made such demands. Rather, defendants claim that they satisfied those demands by the April 15, 1994 telephone conversation between Vultaggio and Richard Worthy of Metro Factors, Inc., followed by Vultaggio's April 18, 1994 letter to Metro, and Metro's payment of $79,316.24 to Hornell, and that thereafter plaintiff had no right to demand further assurance.

The court disagrees with both plaintiff and defendants in their insistence that only one demand for adequate assurance was made in this case to which there was and could be only a single response. Even accepting defendants' argument that payment by Metro was the sole condition Vultaggio required when he spoke and wrote to Metro, and that such condition was met by Metro's actual payment, the court is persuaded that on May 9, 1994, Hornell had further reasonable grounds for insecurity and a new basis for seeking further adequate assurances.

Defendants cite White & Summers, Uniform Commercial Code, §6-2 at 289, for the proposition that "[i]f a party demands and receives specific assurances, then absent a further change of circumstances, the assurances demanded and received are adequate, and the party who has demanded the assurances is bound to proceed." Repeated demands for adequate assurances are within the contemplation of section 2-609. See McKinney's Consolidated Laws of NY, Book 62 1/2, UCC §2-609 Official Comment at 490.

Here, there was a further change of circumstances. Vultaggio's reported conversation with Worthy on April 15 and his April 25 letter to Metro both anticipate that once payment of defendants' arrears was made, Hornell would release *up to* $300,000 worth of product on the further condition that defendants met the 14 day payment terms. The arrangement, by its terms, clearly contemplated an opportunity for Hornell to test out defendants' ability to make payment within 14-day periods.

By placing a single order worth $390,000 to $450,000 immediately after receipt of Metro's payment, Spry not only demanded a shipment of product which exceeded the proposed limit, but placed Hornell in a position where it would have *no* opportunity to learn whether Spry would meet the 14-day payment terms, before Spry again became indebted to Hornell for a very large sum of money.

At this point, neither Spry nor Worthy had fully informed Hornell what assurance of payment Metro would be able to provide. Leaving aside the question whether the factoring arrangement with Metro constituted adequate assurance, Hornell never received any documentation to substantiate Spry's purported agreement with Metro. Although Spry's agreement with Metro was fully executed by the end of March, Spry never gave Hornell a copy of it, not even in response to Hornell's May 10, 1994 demand. The March 27, 1994 letter from Vanguard coincided with the date Spry signed the Metro agreement, but contained only a vague reference to a $1.5 million "revolving credit facility," without mentioning Metro Factors, Inc. Moreover, based on the Vanguard letter, Hornell had expected that payment would be forthcoming, but Spry once again offered only excuses and empty promises.

These circumstances, coupled with information received in early May (on which it reasonably relied) that Spry had misled Hornell about the scope of his operation, created new and more acute grounds for Hornell's insecurity and entitled Hornell to seek further adequate assurance from defendants in the form of a documented line of credit or other guarantee. Cf. Creusot-Loire Int'l Inc. v. Coppus Engineering Corp., 585 F. Supp. 45, 50 (S.D.N.Y. 1983). Defendants' failure to respond constituted a repudiation of the distributorship agreement, which entitled plaintiff to suspend performance and terminate the agreement. UCC §2-609(4); Turntables, Inc. v. Gestetner, supra; Creusot-Loire Int'l v. Coppus Engineering Corp., supra; AMF, Inc. v. McDonald's Corp., supra; ARB, Inc. v. E-Systems, Inc., supra; Toppert v. Bunge Corp., supra; Waldorf Steel Fabricators, Inc. v. Consolidated Systems, Inc., supra.

Even if Hornell had seen Spry's agreement with Metro, in the circumstances of this case, the agreement did not provide the adequate assurance to which plaintiff was entitled in relation to defendants' $390,000-$450,000 order. Spry admitted that much of the order was to be retained as inventory for the summer, for which there would be no receivables to factor within 14 days. Although the question of whether every aspect of Hornell's May 10 demand for credit documentation was reasonable is a close one, given the entire history of the relationship between the parties, the court determines that the demand was commercially reasonable. This case is unlike Pittsburgh-Des Moines Steel Co. v. Brookhaven Manor Water Co., 532 F.2d 572 (7th Cir. 1976), cited by defendants, in that plaintiff's demand for credit assurances does not modify or contradict the terms of an elaborated written contract.

The court notes in conclusion that its evaluation of the evidence in this case was significantly influenced by Mr. Spry's regrettable lack of credibility. See Spanier v. New York City Transit Authority, 222 A.D.2d 219, 634 N.Y.S.2d 122 (1st Dep't 1995). The court agrees with plaintiff, that to an extent far greater than was known to Hornell in May 1994, Mr. Spry was not truthful, failed to pay countless other creditors almost as a matter of course, and otherwise engaged in improper and deceptive business practices.

For the foregoing reasons, it is hereby

Ordered and adjudged that plaintiff Hornell Brewing Co., Inc. have a declaratory judgment that defendants Stephen A. Spry and Arizona Tea Products, Ltd. were duly terminated and have no continuing rights with respect to plaintiff Hornell Brewing Co.'s beverage products in Canada or elsewhere.

NOTES AND QUESTIONS

1. *Right to demand adequate assurances of performance.* As the cases in this chapter show, under common law doctrine it was often difficult to determine when a party had committed a total breach of a contract. Was a nonperformance material or insubstantial? What type of conduct was sufficient to amount

to an anticipatory repudiation? Such uncertainty meant that a party to a contract ran the risk that she would be held to have breached the contract by acting in response to what she perceived to be a material breach or anticipatory repudiation. Aware of this dilemma, the drafters of the Uniform Commercial Code created a new right, codified in §2-609, by which a party who has "reasonable grounds for insecurity" can demand "adequate assurance of due performance" from the other party. The failure to give such assurances constitutes an anticipatory repudiation of the contract. UCC §2-609(4). Although §2-609 only applies to contracts for the sale of goods, the Restatement has adopted a similar concept. Restatement (Second) §251. A comprehensive account of the history and application of these two provisions is given by Professor R. J. Robertson, Jr., in The Right to Demand Adequate Assurance of Due Performance: Uniform Commercial Code Section 2-609 and Restatement (Second) of Contracts Section 251, 38 Drake L. Rev. 305 (1988-1989). See also Michael J. Borden, The Promissory Character of Adequate Assurances of Performance, 76 Brook. L. Rev. 167 (2010).

2. *Reasonable grounds for insecurity.* The case law and comments to the UCC and the Restatement provide some guidance as to the factors that will give the other party reasonable grounds for insecurity. Significant financial difficulties will ordinarily amount to reasonable grounds for insecurity. Starchem Laboratories, LLC v. Kabco Pharm., Inc., 988 N.Y.S.2d 525 (Sup. Ct. 2014) (buyer's poor payment record with seller and its sister company, and request for more credit in response to seller's expressed concerns, gave grounds to seller for insecurity and suspension of performance). Failure to perform important obligations under the contract may be a reasonable basis for insecurity. AMF, Inc. v. McDonald's Corp., 536 F.2d 1167 (7th Cir. 1976) (seller's failure to deal with product defects, coupled with evidence that further deliveries would be substantially late). On occasion courts have found that circumstances having nothing to do with the other party's conduct can give rise to reasonable grounds for insecurity. See Top of Iowa Co-op. v. Sime Farms, Inc., 608 N.W.2d 454 (Iowa 2000) (jury question whether buyer had reasonable grounds for insecurity when, due to market conditions, producer would face significant loss if it chose to deliver grain under contracts and attorney general had publicly questioned legality of contracts). On the other hand, unreliable rumors or insignificant risks do not constitute reasonable grounds for insecurity. Compare BAII Banking Corp. v. UPG, Inc., 985 F.2d 685 (2d Cir. 1993) (oil company did not have reasonable grounds for insecurity based on rumors about processor's bankruptcy when boats containing oil had arrived or were about to arrive in port), with Clem Perrin Marine Towing, Inc. v. Panama Canal Co., 730 F.2d 186 (5th Cir. 1984) (phone call from individual who had played major role in brokering deal for sale of vessel stating his company rather than seller was making mortgage payments gave buyer reasonable ground for insecurity).

The demand for adequate assurance must be based on circumstances that arise after the contract was formed, not on the situation that was known when the contract was formed. In the *Pittsburgh-Des Moines Steel* case, cited and distinguished by the court in *Hornell*, the party demanding adequate assurances had earlier agreed to extend credit to the buyer, and failed to show a sufficient change in circumstances since the making of the contract to justify a demand for additional security or payment in advance of delivery.

3. *Assurances that may be demanded.* Assuming that a party has reasonable grounds for insecurity, what assurances may she demand? UCC §2-609, Comment 4 indicates that an "adequate assurance" may range from a mere verbal guarantee to the posting of a bond, depending on the circumstances. Restatement (Second) §251, Comment *d* adopts a similar "facts and circumstances" approach. See, e.g., Rocheux Int'l of N.J., Inc. v. U.S. Merchants Fin. Group, Inc., 741 F. Supp. 2d 651 (D.N.J. 2010) (holding that demand for letter of credit rather than acceptance of buyer's assurance of cash payment on delivery was not unreasonable when buyer had failed to pay outstanding invoices); Hope's Architectural Products, Inc. v. Lundy's Constr., Inc., 781 F. Supp. 711 (D. Kan. 1991) (seller not justified in withholding delivery of windows merely because buyer threatened to withhold part of purchase price to compensate for late delivery; buyer's action probably justified under UCC §2-717, and in any event seller's demand for payment before delivery went beyond what was needed for adequate assurance of buyer's performance). In addition, both the UCC and the Restatement indicate that a demand for assurances must be made in good faith. UCC §2-609, Comment 4; Restatement (Second) §251, Comment *d*.

4. *Necessity for a written demand.* Must a demand for adequate assurances be made in writing? UCC §2-609(1) states that a party who has reasonable grounds for insecurity may "in writing" demand adequate assurances. Courts are divided on whether a written demand is mandatory or optional. See Atwood-Kellogg, Inc. v. Nickeson Farms, 602 N.W.2d 749, 753 (S.D. 1999) (reviewing authorities and concluding that "more convincing authority exists that a written demand for adequate assurances is not necessary . . . as long as the demand provides a 'clear understanding' of the insecure party's intent to suspend performance until receipt of adequate assurances"). But see Koursa, Inc. v. Manroland, Inc., 971 F. Supp. 2d 765 (N.D. Ill. 2013) (Illinois law strictly requires that demand under UCC §2-609 must be in writing and clearly state it is demand for assurances). The Restatement adopts a flexible approach: "The demand need not be in writing. Although a written demand is usually preferable to an oral one, if time is of particular importance the additional time required for a written demand might necessitate an oral one." Restatement (Second) §251, Comment *d*. Where justice appears to favor the party seeking assurances, a court may be lenient in interpreting communications to satisfy the §2-609 requirement. E.g., Smyers v. Quartz Products Works Corp., 880 F. Supp. 1425 (D. Kan. 1995) (in some circumstances, a demand for payment may be construed as a demand for adequate assurances); cf. James J. White, Eight Cases and Section 251, 67 Cornell L. Rev. 841 (1982) (courts may use "right to adequate assurances" as tool for achieving substantial justice where issue is which party was first in material breach).

5. *Whether demand is permissive or compulsory.* Professor Robert Hillman has argued that in some circumstances the demand should be required:

> Where the aggrieved party could otherwise cancel or seek damages under the Code, the policies of the Code will be greatly served by holding that Section 2-609 requires the aggrieved party to demand adequate assurance first. A party who is in a position to explain the difficulties which have caused the insecurity and to give adequate assurance should have the opportunity to do so. The alternative — permitting the injured party to cancel arbitrarily — is inconsistent with the Code's policy of fostering the completion of commercial agreements and with the mitigation principles urged as proper in this article.

Robert A. Hillman, Keeping the Deal Together After Material Breach — Common Law Mitigation Rules, the UCC, and the Restatement (Second) of Contracts, 47 U. Colo. L. Rev. 553, 591-592 (1976). Compare Northwest Lumber Sales, Inc. v. Continental Forest Products, Inc., 495 P.2d 744 (Or. 1972) (dictum that demand for adequate assurances required), with Copylease Corp. of America v. Memorex Corp., 403 F. Supp. 625 (S.D.N.Y. 1975) (demand optional). Which view is more consistent with the language of UCC §2-609 and Restatement (Second) §251? As a matter of policy, should demand be mandatory?

6. *Time allowed for reasonable assurances.* Under the Code, after a justified demand for adequate assurances, the demanding party must wait a reasonable time not to exceed 30 days. (Note that this is the maximum period; circumstances may well make it reasonable to demand a faster response.) If adequate assurances are not given within that time, the demanding party may treat the failure to respond as an anticipatory repudiation. UCC §2-609(4). The Restatement requires a party to respond to a demand for assurances within a "reasonable time" but does not set a maximum time period.

PROBLEM 9-2

David Mason is a well-known producer of entertainment programs for stage and screen. NBS is a major television network. In early 2018, Mason acquired the motion picture and television rights to the novel, *Blood, Gore and More.* NBS negotiated with Mason for the right to do a miniseries based on the novel and on August 1, 2018, the parties entered into a written agreement. Mason agreed to grant NBS the right to do a miniseries based on the novel and to supervise production of the series. NBS agreed to pay Mason $1.5 million, $500,000 at the time the agreement was signed and the balance in installments as various stages of production were completed. The agreement provided that NBS would employ a writer and engage in preproduction preparation for the series. Paragraph 14 of the agreement provided as follows:

> 14. NBS shall notify Mason by August 1, 2019, whether it plans to proceed with production of the series. In the event NBS so notifies Mason, it shall submit the screenplay and preproduction report to him for his approval. In the event NBS decides not to proceed with the series (or fails to notify Mason of its intent to proceed), this agreement shall terminate and the parties shall have no further obligations hereunder. In no event, however, shall Mason be required to refund the Advance Payment.

If NBS decided to proceed with the series, the agreement provided that the parties would meet within 30 days to develop a budget and production schedule.

In May 2019, NBS notified Mason that the preparation of the screenplay and other preproduction work had been delayed; NBS sent Mason an agreement modifying the original contract by extending the notification date from August 1, 2020, to February 1, 2017. Mason returned the modification agreement unsigned to NBS.

On August 1 NBS notified Mason that it had elected to proceed with the series, but NBS failed to submit either the screenplay or the preproduction report because both were incomplete. NBS then asked Mason to meet with its representatives to discuss budget and planning. On August 24 Mason met with representatives of NBS to discuss these issues. At the meeting Mason asked when the screenplay and preproduction report could be expected. NBS informed Mason that they expected these documents to be completed within three months. Mason informed NBS that the delay caused him problems because he had "other commitments." One week after the August 24th meeting, Mason's lawyers wrote to NBS to inform it that because of NBS's failure to submit the screenplay or preproduction report on time, Mason had no further obligations under the contract. The letter stated that because the contract was terminated, all rights to the book had reverted to Mason.

NBS has retained your firm in connection with this matter and informs you that it could employ someone other than Mason to supervise the production. It is primarily interested in determining whether it has any legal basis for claiming the television rights to the book or recovering the $500,000 paid to Mason.

PROBLEM 9-3

The class has been divided into two-lawyer teams representing Mason and NBS. Secret written instructions have also been given to each of the teams. The teams should meet and attempt to negotiate a settlement of the dispute consistent with their instructions. If a settlement is reached, the teams should prepare and sign a written settlement agreement.

REVIEW QUESTIONS – CHAPTER NINE

1. Homer planned to retire during the coming months from his career as a factory supervisor in Chicago and he wanted to move to Arizona. On January 15, he met with Donna who owned a senior housing development near Phoenix. Homer and Donna agreed in writing that same day to a sales contract for a recently constructed home at a price of $400,000 with closing set for April 1. Homer paid a deposit of $10,000. The contract included a provision that read:

   > This contract is conditional upon purchaser obtaining approval no later than March 1 for a 30-year fixed loan for 90 percent of the purchase price ($360,000)

from a federally insured bank at an interest rate no higher than 5 percent. Deposit shall be returned to buyer and this contract shall be terminated if financing is not obtained by the stated date.

The week after signing the contract with Donna, Homer completed a loan application with First Bank and provided all necessary information except for his Federal Income Tax returns for the two preceding years which he accidentally forgot to retrieve from his file cabinet. On February 1, First Bank informed Homer that he had been provisionally approved for a loan in the amount of $360,000 at an interest rate of 5 percent, subject to Homer providing the missing documentation. The very next day Homer learned that his largest retirement investment account, which he thought was worth almost $1 million, had announced a projected loss of value of about 20 percent over the coming year. Consequently, Homer decided to postpone his retirement and he was no longer interested in buying the home in Arizona. Homer ignored multiple requests from First Bank for the tax returns and on February 22, First Bank withdrew the provisional approval for the loan. Homer then notified Donna that he would not close on the home purchase contract. If Donna sues Homer for breach of contract, will Homer have a good defense?

A. Yes, Homer has a good defense because his investment account loss would give him grounds for a claim of impracticability.
B. Yes, Homer has a good defense because his contract with Donna included a condition that was not satisfied.
C. No, Homer does not have a good defense because the financing condition was substantially satisfied by the provisional approval.
D. No, Homer does not have a good defense because he failed to provide the documentation needed for the loan and thereby prevented the loan from being approved.

2. Teri worked for Acme Drug Stores for 20 years, eventually becoming director of marketing. On August 10, Teri was contacted by a professional staffing agency about an executive position with Paragon Pharmaceutical Co., a regional wholesale supplier for drug stores in the Midwest. Teri interviewed with Paragon's president, Pat Park, and was offered a position as sales manager at a salary of $200,000 per year for a five-year period, starting September 15. Teri accepted the offer on August 24 and signed a written contract for the five-year agreement. On September 1, Teri gave two weeks notice to Acme that she would be leaving to work for Paragon. Acme senior management was very concerned about losing Teri and immediately offered to raise her annual salary to $230,000 if she would stay with Acme. On the morning of September 2, Teri called Pat and told him that she would come to work for Paragon only if they were willing to match the $230,000 salary that Teri was now being offered by Acme. Pat responded, "Let me think about it." After further thought, Teri called back to Pat's office two hours later and said, "Forget about my earlier call. I will come to work for Paragon

on the terms we agreed to." Pat had been busy with other matters had not done anything about Teri's earlier call. If Paragon should now refuse to employ Teri, would Teri have a viable legal claim that she has a right to the job under contract law?

A. No, Teri does not have a right to the job because she repudiated the contract.
B. No, Teri does not have a right to the job because she committed a material breach.
C. Yes, Teri has a right to the job because she retracted her repudiation.
D. Yes, Teri has a right to the job because she never stated absolutely that she would not work for Paragon and therefore she never repudiated the contract.

3. On October 4, Carl Contractor entered into a written contract to build a two-car garage for Haley, a homeowner. The price was $20,000, with half paid at the signing of the contract and the remaining $10,000 to be paid upon completion of the garage. The contract stated in part, "All work to be completed no later than December 1." Carl obtained the necessary building permits by November 2 after some delay due to a backlog in the municipal permits office. Carl then began actual work on November 4 and by December 1 the garage was completed in accordance with the plans, except that Carl needed to apply a second coat of paint to the garage door. Carl completed the remaining painting process on the morning of December 2. If Haley should refuse to pay Carl the second half of the price, would Carl have a valid, legal basis to seek the money?

A. Yes, because Carl has the right to recover for benefit conferred to Haley.
B. Yes, because Carl rendered substantial performance of the contract by being only one day late in completing the work.
C. No, because Carl committed a willful breach by not managing to finish the job by the stated date.
D. No, because the contract included an express condition to Carl's right to payment that was not satisfied.

4. Bob, owner of a local hotel, became interested in buying an adjacent lot of land that was vacant so that he could expand his building and become part of a national hotel chain. He contacted Owen, the owner of the vacant lot, and learned that Owen was interested in selling it. Bob met with Owen on February 15 at a realty office and they both signed a brief contract that stated that Bob would have the exclusive right for six months to buy the parcel of land for $45,000, plus a nonrefundable deposit of $5,000. The contract also stated that "the buyer must give written notice to the seller of the decision to purchase by August 15, or the right to purchase will terminate." Bob paid the $5,000 deposit to Owen at the time of signing the agreement. Over the next six months, Bob spent about 50 hours meeting with an architect and national chain hotel representatives and he paid the architect $2,500 to draft preliminary plans for the building expansion. Ultimately,

Bob decided to buy the land. Late in the day on August 15, Bob realized that he needed to give notice about his decision to Owen. Bob immediately drafted and signed a brief note to Owen which said, "I will buy the parcel of land." He dropped the letter in a U.S. Postal Service mailbox on the way home that night. Owen received the letter on August 17. Does Bob have a legal right to purchase the land?

A. Yes, because he mailed his notice by August 15.
B. Yes, because he substantially complied with the notice requirement.
C. No, because Bob's actions related to the potential purchase were not part of the bargain.
D. No, because Bob did not strictly comply with the notice requirement.

5. Vic Vintner, sales manager of ABC Wine Co., agreed with Mike Mills, owner of Mike's Cafes, to sell Mike 50 cases of wine per week for 6 months, beginning July 1, at 5 percent below list price. The contract provided that Mike would submit an order one week in advance and would pay for each shipment within 30 days after delivery. When Vanna Vintner, the business manager for ABC, saw the first order from Mike for July 1 she was surprised to learn Vic had agreed to sell to Mike on credit, because it had been widely reported during the preceding month in newspapers and trade magazines that Mike had closed two of his ten restaurants because of financial difficulty and that Mike was having trouble paying his suppliers. When Vanna asked him about the contract, Vic simply said, "I think Mike will be good for it." Vanna immediately sent an email message to Mike informing him that the wine would not be delivered unless Mike provided a current financial report showing his ability to pay. Mike wrote back to Vanna, reminding her that he had been in business for 20 years, telling her that he was insulted by the request, and saying that he would sue if delivery was not made. Vanna calls you and wants to know if ABC or Mike will be in breach if the wine is not delivered on credit?

   A. Mike will be in breach because his financial difficulties would amount to an anticipatory repudiation of the credit contract.
   B. Mike will be in breach because he failed to give proper assurances to ABC about the concerns regarding his finances.
   C. ABC will be in breach because its demand for assurances was based on information about Mike's financial situation that it had before it made the contract.
   D. ABC will be in breach because their concerns about Mike's finances were based on mere news reporting.

CHAPTER 10

Expectation Damages: Principles and Limitations

Until now, our study has focused for the most part on the process by which contractual agreements are reached, the methods courts use to interpret (and, where appropriate, supplement) those agreements, and the possible justifications for their nonperformance. In this chapter and the next, we address generally the question of what remedies should be available to a party who has been injured by the other party's unjustified failure to perform her contractual obligation. For this purpose, we will assume a binding contract has been made and that one party has committed an actionable "breach" — unjustified nonperformance — of some duty imposed by that contract. This assumption of breach does not mean that the court necessarily will or should be indifferent to the cause of the nonperformance, as we shall see; it does mean, however, that the party aggrieved by that nonperformance will ordinarily be entitled to some remedy, even if only "nominal damages." Restatement (Second) §346(2) ("a small sum fixed without regard to the amount of loss"). See MBM Financial Corp. v. The Woodlands Operating Co., L.P., 292 S.W. 3d 660 (Tex. 2009) (nominal damages are awarded for breach when there are no actual damages or none than can be proved; $1, $10, or even $100 may be nominal damages but $1,000 was too much). Except where the plaintiff is seeking some sort of vindication (e.g., the plaintiff in a libel action who has been publicly and wrongly accused of some criminal or unsavory activity), lawsuits are not brought with the aim of recovering merely nominal damages, nor is it likely that any plaintiff would regard such an outcome as anything more than a Pyrrhic victory. Much more interesting and significant, therefore, is the follow-up question: What kinds of remedies are available to give the plaintiff not merely symbolic justice but actual redress for the injury caused by the defendant's breach?

In Chapter 11, we will consider the possibility that a court may be willing to order "specific performance" of the defendant's promise. In the majority of cases arising out of breach of contract, however, specific relief is not at issue because the plaintiff merely seeks (and in any event, would probably only be awarded) money damages. A question of prime importance, then, is the way in which such damages are to be computed.

In 1936 Professor Lon Fuller and his associate William Perdue advanced the thesis that there are three basic interests that the law may seek to protect in fashioning remedies for breach of contract. Their analysis has become the standard exposition of what might be considered the "modern" approach to contract remedies.

> It is convenient to distinguish three principal purposes which may be pursued in awarding contract damages. These purposes, and the situations in which they become appropriate, may be stated briefly as follows:
>
> *First,* the plaintiff has in reliance on the promise of the defendant conferred some value on the defendant. The defendant fails to perform his promise. The court may force the defendant to disgorge the value he received from the plaintiff. The object here may be termed the prevention of gain by the defaulting promisor at the expense of the promisee; more briefly, the prevention of unjust enrichment. The interest protected may be called the *restitution interest.* For our present purposes it is quite immaterial how the suit in such a case be classified, whether as contractual or quasi-contractual, whether as a suit to enforce the contract or as a suit based upon a rescission of the contract. These questions relate to the superstructure of the law, not to the basic policies with which we are concerned.
>
> *Secondly,* the plaintiff has in reliance on the promise of the defendant changed his position. For example, the buyer under a contract for the sale of land has incurred expense in the investigation of the seller's title, or has neglected the opportunity to enter other contracts. We may award damages to the plaintiff for the purpose of undoing the harm which his reliance on the defendant's promise has caused him. Our object is to put him in as good a position as he was in before the promise was made. The interest protected in this case may be called the *reliance interest.*
>
> *Thirdly,* without insisting on reliance by the promisee or enrichment of the promisor, we may seek to give the promisee the value of the expectancy which the promise created. We may in a suit for specific performance actually compel the defendant to render the promised performance to the plaintiff, or, in a suit for damages, we may make the defendant pay the money value of this performance. Here our object is to put the plaintiff in as good a position as he would have occupied had the defendant performed his promise. The interest protected in this case we may call the *expectation interest....*
>
> It is obvious that the three "interests" we have distinguished do not present equal claims to judicial intervention. It may be assumed that ordinary standards of justice would regard the need for judicial intervention as decreasing in the order in which we have listed the three interests. The "restitution interest," involving a combination of unjust impoverishment with unjust gain, presents the strongest case for relief....

> On the other hand, the promisee who has actually relied on the promise, even though he may not thereby have enriched the promisor, certainly presents a more pressing case for relief than the promisee who merely demands satisfaction for his disappointment in not getting what was promised him. . . . It is as a matter of fact no easy thing to explain why the normal rule of contract recovery should be that which measures damages by the value of the promised performance. Since this "normal rule" throws its shadow across our whole subject it will be necessary to examine the possible reasons for its existence.

Lon L. Fuller & William R. Perdue, Jr., The Reliance Interest in Contract Damages I, 46 Yale L.J. 52, 53-57 (1936).

Some scholars have questioned the usefulness of Fuller and Perdue's three interests. See Richard Craswell, Against Fuller and Perdue, 67 U. Chi. L. Rev. 99 (2000); W. David Slawson, Why Expectation Damages for Breach of Contract Must Be the Norm: A Refutation of the Fuller and Perdue "Three Interests" Thesis, 81 Neb. L. Rev. 839 (2003). However, in Restatement (Second) §344, the drafters have adopted the Fuller and Perdue analysis and terminology. As Chapter 11 will demonstrate, both the reliance and restitution interests can be, and often are, a basis for assessing damages against a breaching defendant. It has long been the policy, however, for the court in a breach-of-contract suit to attempt, if possible, to compute and award damages so as to give plaintiff her expectation of gain under the contract: the "benefit of the bargain" that plaintiff would have realized had the agreement been fully performed. See Restatement (Second) §347. This strong preference for expect-ation damages means that an award may be revised on appeal if it appears that the court below has awarded the plaintiff less than the value of her lost expectation. See, e.g., Sampley Enterprises, Inc. v. Laurilla, 404 So. 2d 841 (Fla. Dist. Ct. App. 1981) (error to restrict plaintiff contractor to recovery of out-of-pocket expenses when amount of expected profit on contract with defendant had been proven with sufficient certainty). On the other hand, it may also be reversible error to render judgment for *more* than the injury to plaintiff's expectation. See, e.g., Wright v. Stevens, 445 So. 2d 791 (Miss. 1984) (error to award damages of $13,000 based on jury's verdict for defects in swimming pool construction when evidence only supported recovery of something less than $10,000).

In this chapter we survey the particular rules by which expectation damages are commonly computed in various types of cases and note some important limitations on such awards. Our discussion below demonstrates that the law is not always as rigid in this regard as the "general rule" might suggest; nevertheless, the rule of expectation damages survives as the stated norm for contract actions. As we proceed, keep in mind two questions raised by this historical preference for protection of the "expectation interest": Why should the law regard the value of the plaintiff's lost expectation as the minimum amount that plaintiff should receive as damages for defendant's breach? Conversely, why should the law regard the value of that lost expectation as the *maximum* permissible award? In the last section of this chapter, we return to these two questions.

A. COMPUTING THE VALUE OF PLAINTIFF'S EXPECTATION

As suggested above, the "expectation" that the court seeks to protect in its award of contract damages is the gain the plaintiff would have realized if the contract between plaintiff and defendant had been fully performed, as promised by both parties. Where the plaintiff has fully performed her obligation under the contract and the only unperformed obligation of the defendant is to pay a stated amount of money in return, the injury to the plaintiff's expectation ordinarily is simply the defendant's failure to pay the promised sum; that amount (perhaps with interest) is therefore a sufficient award of damages to compensate the injury to the plaintiff's expectation. (The judgment in such a case is also a kind of "specific performance," since it orders the defendant to do precisely what he promised.) Where the performance defendant has failed to render is something other than the payment of money (the conveyance of property, perhaps, or the performance of service), it may be more difficult to place a dollar value on the plaintiff's expectation of gain. The case will be further complicated if the plaintiff's own performance was incomplete when the defendant's breach occurred and remains incomplete when the plaintiff's claim for damages is adjudicated. Because the aim of the law is to put the plaintiff in as good a position as she would have occupied had the contract been fully performed *on both sides*, the "expectation" to be protected is the plaintiff's "net" expectation — the value of the performance defendant had promised to render, less the cost of the performance plaintiff had promised in return as the "price" of defendant's performance.

In §347 the Restatement (Second) states a formula by which damages based on the injury to the plaintiff's expectation interest may be computed. In his treatise, Professor Farnsworth (who served as Reporter for the revised Restatement) elaborates on the various components of the Restatement formula.

> **General Measure of Damages.** How is the injured party's expectation to be measured in terms of money? What sum will put the injured party in as good a position as if the contract had been performed? The answer depends on whether the injured party has terminated the contract, refused to render any further return performance, and is claiming damages for total breach or has not terminated, stands ready to perform to render any remaining return performance, and is claiming damages for partial breach.
>
> . . .
>
> A claim of damages for total breach may have four elements because the breach may affect an injured party in four ways. . . .
>
> First, the breach may cause the injured party a loss by depriving that party, at least to some extent, of the performance expected under the contract. The difference between the value to the injured party of the performance that should have been received and the value to that party of what, if anything,

actually was received will be referred to as the *loss in value*. If, for example, a buyer of goods has a claim for damages for partial breach because the goods were nonconforming, the *loss in value* equals the difference between the value to the buyer of the goods that were to have been delivered and the value of the goods that were actually delivered. (In addition the Vienna Convention gives a buyer in this situation a right to price reduction, a remedy unknown to the common law, as an alternative to damages for partial breach.[4]) If the buyer has a claim for damages for total breach because no goods were tendered or goods tendered were not accepted, the *loss in value* is simply the value to the injured party of the goods that were to have been tendered. . . . In many situations the *loss in value* depends on the circumstances of the injured party or those of that party's enterprise. If the injured party's expected advantage consists of the realization of profit, it may not be difficult to express that party's *loss in value* in terms of money. In other situations, such as those involving personal satisfaction, the task may be virtually impossible. . . .

Second, the breach may cause the injured party loss other than *loss in value,* and the party is also entitled to recovery for this, subject again to limitations such as that of unforeseeability. Such loss will be referred to as *other loss* and is sometimes said to give rise to "incidental" and "consequential" damages. Incidental damages include additional costs incurred after the breach in a reasonable attempt to avoid loss, even if the attempt is unsuccessful. If, for example, the injured party who has not received the promised performance pays a fee to a broker in a reasonable but unsuccessful attempt to obtain a substitute, that expense is recoverable. Consequential damages include such items as injury to person or property caused by the breach. If, for example, services furnished to the injured party are defective and cause damage to that party's property, that loss is recoverable. The terms used to characterize the loss should not, however, be critical, for the general principle is that all loss, however characterized, is recoverable.

What has been said in the two preceding paragraphs applies regardless of whether or not the injured party chooses to treat the breach as total. It applies to both claims for partial breach and claims for total breach. If the injured party does terminate the contract, however, the breach may have a third or fourth effect, because that party is relieved of the duty of rendering whatever remains of its own performance. What is said in the two following paragraphs applies only to claims for total breach.

Third, then, if the injured party terminates and claims damages for total breach, the breach may have a beneficial effect on that party by saving it the further expenditure that would otherwise have been incurred. This saving will be referred to as *cost avoided.* If, for example, the injured party is a builder that stops work after terminating a construction contract because of the owner's breach, the additional expenditure the builder saves is *cost avoided.*

Fourth, if the injured party terminates and claims damages for total breach, the breach may have a further beneficial effect on that party by allowing it to avoid some loss by salvaging and reallocating some or all of the resources that otherwise it would have had to devote to performance of the contract.

4. CISG 50. . . .

The saving that results will be referred to as *loss avoided*. If, for example, the injured party is a builder that, after stopping work after terminating a construction contract, uses some of the leftover materials on another contract, the resulting saving to the builder is *loss avoided*. Or if the injured party is an employee who, after being wrongfully discharged by an employer, takes other employment, the net amount that has been earned or will be earned from that employment is *loss avoided*. If the injured party has actually saved money, the saving is treated as *loss avoided* even though another person might not have been able to effect that saving. If, for example, the injured party happens to make especially favorable arrangements to dispose of leftover materials, and thereby avoids more loss than another person might have succeeded in doing, the *loss avoided* will be based on the actual favorable arrangements. . . .

The general measure of damages for total breach can therefore be expressed in terms of these four effects, two of which (*loss in value* and *other loss*) are adverse to the injured party and therefore increase damages, and two of which (*cost avoided* and *loss avoided*) are beneficial to the injured party and therefore decrease that party's damages. Formula (A) therefore reads:

(A) *general measure* = *loss in value* + *other loss* – *cost avoided* – *loss avoided*

In the case of claim for damages for partial breach, only the first two terms apply.

E. Allan Farnsworth, Contracts §12.9, at 764-768 (4th ed. 2004).

Using Professor Farnsworth's formula, how would you compute the plaintiff's expectation damages in the following hypothetical cases:

Case 1. Owner hires builder to construct a building for a total price of $200,000. The estimated total cost of construction is $180,000. The owner breaches by unjustifiably terminating the contract when the work is partly done. At the time of termination the owner has paid the builder $70,000 for work done, and the builder has spent a total of $95,000 for labor and materials (some of which are incorporated in the partially completed building). After the owner's breach the builder is able to resell $10,000 of materials purchased for the project.

Case 2. Employer hires employee under a two-year employment contract for a salary of $50,000 per year, payable in installments at the end of each month. Six months after the employee starts work, the employer wrongfully discharges her. The employee looks for work for three months, but is unable to find a job. Finally, she hires an employment agency, paying it a fee of $1,000. Three months later she obtains a job (similar to the one from which she was fired) paying $45,000 per year.

In this chapter we try generally to use the terminology employed in Restatement (Second) §347 to describe the process by which the plaintiff's damages are computed. It should be noted, however, that the computation of expectation damages may be articulated in different ways, although the end results should be identical. For example, in contracts for the sale of real estate, courts often state that expectation damages are measured by the *difference between the contract price and the market price at the time of breach*. In construction contracts, the measure of expectation damages for a breach by the owner is frequently stated to be the builder's *expected net profit on the entire contract plus the builder's unreimbursed expenses at the time of breach.* In the material that follows we will consider these and other alternative statements of the expectation damage measure.

Case 3. Compute the builder's expectation damages in Case 1, using the formula of expected net profit on the entire contract plus unreimbursed expenses at the time of breach.

The formula of Restatement (Second) §347, while not without its problems in application, works relatively easily in cases where the party in breach is the "paying" party: the one whose promised performance was to consist of one or more payments of money. Thus, where the plaintiff is a wrongfully discharged employee, the first factor, "loss in value," will simply be the excess of salary originally promised over the salary actually paid. Where the defendant is the defaulting buyer of property, the "loss in value" will be the difference between the amount the purchaser promised to pay and the amount (if any) the vendor has actually received. It should not be assumed, of course, that this calculation fixes the amount of the plaintiff's damage, as the rest of the Restatement's formula indicates. In any of these cases, there may in addition be items of "consequential" loss (sometimes referred to as "special" damages); on the other hand, from the aggregate of "total loss" there are likely to be deductions based on the amounts that plaintiff saved (or reasonably should have saved) either as costs avoided or by operation of the principle of "mitigation of damages" (discussed later in this chapter).

Where the defendant's promised performance is to be something other than payment of money, however, the threshold question of loss in value is not so easily answered. Suppose, in Case 1 above, that the breaching party is not the owner, but the builder. If the builder repudiates before construction even begins, then the owner has received no performance at all; how should we compute his loss in value? Is it simply an amount equal to the full contract price? Or should we somehow attempt to put a "value" on the building that was to be constructed? If performance has begun, and the builder unjustifiably stops work halfway through, the situation is even more complicated: How can we put a price tag on the half-completed building that the owner has received? The same question may arise where an employee has rendered part of the service called for by a contract and then wrongfully stops performance. If the loss in value is the difference in value between what was promised and what was performed, how can those two be computed? The cases that follow illustrate some of the approaches that may be used in such cases.

Crabby's, Inc. v. Hamilton

Missouri Court of Appeals 244 S.W.3d 209 (2008)

GARY W. LYNCH, Chief Judge:

Buyers under a contract for sale of real estate appeal the trial court's judgment awarding Seller damages due to Buyers' breach of that contract. We affirm.

Crabby's Seafood Bar & Grill, in Joplin, Missouri, in 2018.

STANDARD OF REVIEW

This case was tried before the court without a jury. . . . The judgment will be affirmed unless it is against the weight of the evidence, there is insufficient evidence to support it, or it erroneously declares or applies the law. . . .

FACTUAL AND PROCEDURAL BACKGROUND

Fred and Carolyn Billingsly are the shareholders of a Missouri corporation called Crabby's, Inc. ("Seller"), which owned and operated Crabby's restaurant in Joplin, Missouri, for several years. In 2003, Seller listed the restaurant and accompanying real property with Dee Kassab of Pro 100 Realty. The original listing price was $325,000, and Seller rejected an initial purchase offer for $275,000. James Hamilton, through his real estate agent Kent Eastman of Pro 100 Realty,[1] then offered to purchase the property for $290,000, and this offer was accepted on May 17, 2003. Hamilton thereafter assigned his interest in the contract to Paragon Ventures, L.L.C. ("Paragon"), a business that Hamilton and Richard Worley set up to operate a restaurant. Hamilton also remained as an individual buyer on the contract. Hamilton and Paragon are hereinafter referred to collectively as "Buyers."

The contract contained the following financing contingency provision:

> This contract is contingent on Buyer's [sic] ability to obtain a conventional loan or loans in the amount of $232,000, payable over a period of not less than

1. The contract discloses that Pro 100 Realty served as the Dual Agent of Seller and Buyers.

> 15 years and bearing interest at a rate of not more than 5.5% per annum. Seller shall not be obligated to pay any of the expenses incidental to the obtaining of such loan or loans. Buyer shall use reasonable diligence in seeking to obtain such loan or loans, and if Buyer does not furnish seller with a copy of an effective written loan commitment within 30 days from the Effective Date, then this Contract shall automatically terminate and the Earnest Money shall be returned to Buyer.

Buyers never furnished Seller with a copy of an effective written loan commitment within 30 days of the effective date of the contract.

After entering into the contract on May 17, 2003, Buyers made arrangements for financing at the Bank of Joplin. Buyers applied for and were approved by the bank for a loan in the amount of $340,000.00. The bank agreed to loan them $225,000.00 amortized over fifteen years on the real estate, $65,000.00 amortized over seven years on the equipment, and a $50,000.00 revolving line of credit all at the rate of interest of prime plus 1.5%. Buyers did not apply for a loan with any other financial institution.

On June 10, 2003, Buyers' real estate agent was furnished a title insurance commitment from Jasper County Title showing sales tax liens attached to the property.

The contract originally specified a June 30, 2003 closing date. Following an inspection of the property, certain repairs were made, and an appraisal was performed as a requirement of the financing by Bank of Joplin. As a result of some appraisal requirements, the parties, on a date not disclosed by the record, entered into an agreement extending the closing date to July 14, 2003. Following this extension, the parties discussed other additional repairs and this led to an agreement whereby Buyers would receive a credit of $1,373.54 against the purchase price in lieu of additional repairs being made.

By a second extension agreement dated July 18, 2003, the closing date was again extended, this time to August 1, 2003. On that same date the parties also entered into an agreement that allowed Buyers to take possession of the property prior to closing so that they could start cleaning it. Also around this same time period, Buyers made application for appropriate licenses to operate a restaurant on the property and had the utilities for the property transferred into Buyers' name.

Nothing in any of the subsequent agreements entered into between the parties altered any of the terms of the financing contingency contained in the original contract.

Immediately prior to July 30, 2003, all documentation was in place at the title company and ready for closing on August 1, 2003. Financing was in place from the Bank of Joplin. All parties were ready to close. The tax liens, mentioned in the title commitment provided to Buyers, were satisfied on the morning of August 1, as contemplated by the July 18 extension agreement between the parties, and Sellers obtained a certificate of "No Sales Tax Due" from the state. U.S. Bank (Seller's lender) had agreed to accept $266,000.00 to apply on Sellers' indebtedness and release its lien on the property. According to the closing statement prepared by the realtor, after payment of mortgages, real estate taxes, and liens, Seller was to receive a cash balance of $1,757.72 when the transaction closed.

On July 30, 2003, Buyers sent a letter to the realtor and Seller stating their intention not to close the transaction. In this letter, Buyers claimed "items, which we consider fixtures, have been taken from the premises." This missing property consisted of two used televisions, a couple of mirrors, a set of stereo speakers, and a computerized cash register. These items were not part of the list of personal property that was to be transferred in the sale, which was itemized and attached to the contract. This letter also specified the existence of the tax liens as an additional reason for Buyers' refusal to close the transaction as scheduled. Buyers made no mention of any inability to obtain satisfactory financing. Buyers failed to appear for closing as scheduled on August 1, 2003.

On August 5, 2003, Paragon offered to buy a building at 520 Main Street in Joplin, Missouri, for the purpose of establishing a restaurant. This offer was accepted by those sellers on August 6, 2003 and closed September 22, 2003. The purchase price for that property was $170,000.00.

After Buyers refused to close the sale with Seller on August 1, 2003, Seller's realtor continuously tried to sell the property. However, no offers were received until May of 2004, when J and A Cafe of Kansas, L.L.C., offered to purchase the property for $235,000.00. Sellers accepted this offer, and the transaction closed on July 15, 2004.

Seller thereafter filed suit against Buyers for breach of contract. As part of its damages, Seller claimed the difference in sales price between Buyers' $290,000 contract price which should have closed on August 1, 2003, and the $235,000 price actually obtained when the property subsequently sold eleven and one-half months later on July 15, 2004. Seller also claimed real estate and personal property taxes, utilities, and mortgage interest accruing during that period as damages.

The trial court entered judgment in favor of Seller and against Buyers in the total amount of $95,547.30. Buyers timely appeal this judgment.

Additional facts will hereinafter be disclosed as needed to appropriately discuss Buyers' points relied on.

DISCUSSION

BUYERS WAIVED THE FINANCING CONTINGENCY

Buyers' first point claims that the trial court erred in finding they breached the contract, "because the contract terminated pursuant to its own financing contingency provision when [Buyers] could not obtain financing." Buyers initially argue that as a matter of law they could not have breached the contract by refusing to close on August 1, 2003, because by its explicit terms the contract automatically terminated when Buyers did not "furnish Seller with a copy of an effective written loan commitment," as required by the financing contingency provision in the contract. Buyers alternatively argue that "if the trial court's judgment rests on an implicit finding that the contract had not automatically terminated under the financing contingency provision, then the trial court erred in interpreting the term 'reasonable diligence' and finding that the defendants had not used such diligence in finding a loan." Seller counters Buyers' point, contending that Buyers, by their conduct after entering into the contract, waived the financing contingency provisions in the contract.

"A provision in a real estate contract that makes the contract contingent upon the buyer's obtaining financing is a condition." Howard v. Youngman, 81 S.W.3d 101, 110 (Mo. App. 2002). Because such conditions are meant to protect the buyer, they are a condition of the buyer's duty, but not a condition of the seller's duty under the contract. Id. "[I]n a real estate contract containing a contingency clause, upon the nonoccurrence of the condition (i.e., the buyers obtaining financing), the buyer is *ipso facto* excused from performance." Id. However, "the buyer can elect to waive the contingency and proceed with the contract under the rule that a party may waive any condition of a contract in that party's favor." Id.

"Parties to an agreement may by their oral agreement or their conduct waive the provisions of a contract between them. This doctrine applies equally to provisions requiring written communications." Pilla v. Estate of Pilla, 689 S.W.2d 727, 730 (Mo. App. 1985).

Waiver of rights under a contract has been defined as follows:

> "Waiver" has been defined as an intentional relinquishment of a known right, on the question of which intention of the party charged with waiver is controlling and, if not shown by express declarations but implied by conduct, there must be a clear, unequivocal, and decisive act of party showing such purpose, and so consistent with intention to waive that no other reasonable explanation is possible.

Keltner v. Sowell, 926 S.W.2d 528, 531 (Mo. App. 1996). . . .

The contract in the instant case defines its Effective Date as "the date and time of final acceptance on the signature page." Seller finally accepted the contract by signing the signature page on May 17, 2003. Thus, the effective date of the contract was May 17, 2003. The financing contingency in paragraph five of the contract provided: "if Buyer does not furnish Seller with a copy of an effective written loan commitment within 30 days from the Effective Date, then this Contract shall automatically terminate and the Earnest Money shall be returned to Buyer." . . . Yet, Buyers' actions after that date were inconsistent with such a termination.

On July 17, 2003, a month after the contract supposedly automatically terminated, Buyers executed a written amendment to the contract extending the closing date from July 14, 2003 to August 1, 2003. This amendment additionally provided for the assignment of the contract to Paragon as a buyer in addition to Hamilton and for a $1,373.54 credit against the purchase price in exchange for Buyers releasing Seller from any obligation to perform any further repairs to the property. Finally this amendment provided: "IT IS UNDERSTOOD BY ALL PARTIES THAT ALL OTHER TERMS AND CONDITIONS OF THE CONTRACT REMAIN UNCHANGED." Buyers entered into this amendment with the intention of closing the contract on August 1, 2003.

Also on July 17, 2003, Buyers executed an "Agreement for Possession Prior to Closing — Contract Rider," which granted them the right to take possession of the property as a tenant on July 21, 2003. This agreement provided that "this Rider shall become a part of the Contract" and "[p]ossession is for the sole purpose of cleaning only." To effectuate their possession, Buyers accepted a key to the property from Seller. During this time period, Buyers had the utilities to the property switched over and put in their name. Also during this time, and as late as July 25, 2003, Buyers were in the process of securing appropriate licenses to operate their restaurant on the property after closing. . . .

Nevertheless, Buyers argue that, regardless of their waiver of the automatic termination provision in the financing contingency, their inability to obtain financing on the terms otherwise set forth in the financing contingency relieved them of their obligations under the contract. However, Seller counters that Buyers' conduct evidenced a clear and unequivocal intention to waive all of the financing terms in the financing contingency.

Initially, there is no evidence in the record that Buyers ever made any application for a loan "in the amount of $232,000, payable over a period of not less than 15 years and bearing interest at a rate of not more than 5.5% per annum," as provided in the financing contingency. Chris Crouch, the loan officer at Bank of Joplin testified that Buyers applied for a loan in the amount of $340,000.00. Other than this one application, Buyers did not apply for any other loans. Failing to seek a loan on the terms set forth in the financing contingency evidences Buyers' failure to use reasonable diligence to obtain such financing as required by the contingency. Goldberg v. Charlie's Chevrolet, Inc., 672 S.W.2d 177, 179 (Mo. App. 1984). We need not address that issue, however, because such action, coupled with Buyers' conduct on July 17, 2003, and thereafter, also evidences Buyers' waiver of the entire financing contingency. . . .

All of these actions by Buyers are clear, unequivocal, and decisive acts showing Buyers' intentional relinquishment of the benefit of the entire financing contingency, and are so consistent with the intention to waive that contingency that no other reasonable explanation is possible. . . . Point I is denied.

The Trial Court's Determination of Fair Market Value is Supported by Substantial Evidence

The Buyers' second point claims that the trial court's judgment is not supported by substantial evidence of the fair market value of the property as of the date the contract was breached by the Buyers — August 1, 2003 — in that Seller did not offer any direct evidence of the fair market value of the property on that date. Buyers contend that the actual sale price of $235,000.00 received by Seller on July 15, 2004, is not substantial evidence of the fair market value of the property on August 1, 2003 for two reasons: first, being eleven and one-half months after the relevant date, it is too remote in time; and, second, it was the product of a distress sale in that the Seller was compelled to sell the property in that transaction. We disagree with both contentions.

A seller's measure of damages for a buyer's breach of a contract for the sale of land with a structure on it is the difference between the purchase price and the fair market value of the property on the date of breach. Wooten v. DeMean, 788 S.W.2d 522, 527-528 (Mo. App. 1990). That is, the measure of damages is the difference between the contract price and the fair market value of the property on the date the sale should have been completed. Leonard v. American Walnut Co., Inc., 609 S.W.2d 452, 455 (Mo. App. 1980). "An essential element of the seller's case is proof of market value, and if he does resell within a reasonable time after the breach, the price obtained is some evidence of market value." Id. Conflicts in the evidence concerning real estate values are for resolution by the fact finder. State ex rel. Kansas City Power & Light Co. v. Salmark Homebuilders, Inc., 375 S.W.2d 92, 100 (Mo. 1964). It is sufficient if the value set by the fact finder is "within the range" of the evidence. City of Lee's Summit v. Hinck, 618 S.W.2d 719, 721 (Mo. App. 1981).

While Buyers acknowledge that the sale price received by a seller from a subsequent sale of the property is substantial evidence to support a trial court's determination of the fair market value of a property as of the date of the breach if the subsequent sale occurs within a reasonable time after the date of the breach, they claim that a sale eleven and one-half months after the breach, as occurred in this case, is not within a reasonable period of time as a matter of law. Buyers cite no Missouri cases supporting their contention. They cite only Chris v. Epstein, 113 N.C. App. 751, 440 S.E.2d 581 (N.C. App. 1994), for the proposition that a resale of realty that occurred an entire year after the contract breach was not only not representative of fair market value a year earlier, but irrelevant.

Seller points us to Hawkins v. Foster, 897 S.W.2d 80 (Mo. App. 1995), where we held that the price obtained in a subsequent sale which occurred a little over eleven and one-half months after the date of the buyer's breach of a real estate contract supported an award of damages in favor of the seller based upon the fair market value of the property. Buyers have failed to distinguish how the time period approved by us in *Hawkins* materially differs from the essentially same time period in the instant case. Thus, Buyers have not convinced us that we should depart from our holding in *Hawkins*. Based upon that holding, the subsequent sale by Seller in the case at bar on July 15, 2004, occurred within a reasonable time after the date of Buyers' breach of the contract, such that it provided substantial evidence to support the trial court's determination of the fair market value of the property on the date of Buyer's breach of the contract. See also Hoelscher v. Schenewerk, 804 S.W.2d 828 (Mo. App. 1991) (subsequent sale approximately nine months after date of breach).

Buyers next contend that the subsequent sale price received by Seller is not substantial evidence of the fair market value of the property as of the date of the breach because the subsequent sale was a distress sale in that Seller was "compelled" to sell the property. Buyers claim that because fair market value is defined as "the price which property will bring when it is offered for sale by an owner who is willing but *under no compulsion to sell* and is bought by a buyer who is willing or desires to purchase but is not compelled to do so[,]" Turner v. Shalberg, 70 S.W.3d 653, 659 (Mo. App. 2002) (quoting Carter v. Matthey Laundry & Dry Cleaning Co., 350 S.W.2d 786, 794 (Mo. 1961)) (emphasis added), and because Seller was compelled to sell the property, then the sale price could not, by definition, reflect the fair market value of the property. The flaw in Buyers' argument is that the evidence they cite in support of their claim does not exist.

Buyers direct us to the testimony of Carolyn Billingsly, one of Seller's owners, to support their contention. Buyers' trial counsel asked Billingsly: "And so, you were compelled to sell it, I mean, you wanted to sell it bad; true?" She responded: "We did." Counsel's question was a compound question — "you were compelled to sell it" and "you wanted to sell it bad." The wording of her response — "We did" — corresponded to the latter question and not the former. If she had been responding to the first question, her answer would have been in the form "We were." Thus, while Billingsly's testimony supports that Seller wanted badly to sell the property at the time of the subsequent sale, it does not support that Seller was compelled to do so.

Buyers fail to cite to any authority for the proposition that a sale in which the seller is highly motivated or badly wants to sell, as opposed to being compelled to sell, eliminates that sale from being considered as a fair market value sale of the property. Their reliance on *Carter*, 350 S.W.2d 786, is misplaced. In *Carter*, the sale was made pursuant to a plan of liquidation which had to be completed within a one-year period under a provision of the tax code, and, in addition, the property was under the threat of condemnation which would have compelled a forced sale. Id. at 794. While Seller here was financially motivated to sell and was highly desirous of selling the property at the time of the subsequent sale, it was not compelled to sell as was the seller in *Carter*.

Point II is denied.

DECISION

The trial court's judgment is affirmed.

GARY W. LYNCH, Chief Judge. BARNEY, P.J., and BARNES, Sr. J., concur.

NOTES AND QUESTIONS

1. *Measure of damages for breach of real estate contracts.* Assuming that the seller or purchaser has proved a breach of a land sale contract, how should such damages be computed to protect the plaintiff's expectation interest? As stated in the *Crabby's* opinion, damages for the loss of bargain in such cases are ordinarily calculated as the difference between the contract price and the

market value of the property at the time of breach. Thus, where the seller claims damages for the purchaser's wrongful repudiation, she must show that at the time of the breach the property was in fact worth less (on the market) than the contract price. See, e.g., Lawson v. Menefee, 132 S.W.3d 890 (Ky. Ct. App. 2004) (contract price was $265,000 and market value was $274,000, based on resale price as best evidence, thus seller suffered no damages). Conversely, when it is the seller who has breached, the disappointed purchaser must show that at the time of breach the property had a market value of *more* than the contract price. See, e.g., Horning v. Shilberg, 29 Cal. Rptr. 3d 717 (Ct. App. 2005) (non-breaching buyer entitled to damages based on "contract price-market value" differential but failed to present evidence of value on date set for performance). Moreover, in many cases the contract price and market value at the time of the breach will be reasonably close or perhaps the same. See the *Lawson* case above. Why would this equivalence in contract and market prices often be the case?

2. *Waiver of express condition.* The buyers in *Crabby's* attempted to justify their failure to complete the purchase of property on two theories. First, in a letter of repudiation the buyers made claims that the sellers committed a prior breach of the contract by improperly removing property from the restaurant building or by allowing tax liens to exist on the property. Those claims seemed to be abandoned by the time of the appeal. Second, the buyers asserted that an express condition — the "financing contingency" — was not satisfied and that resulted in discharge of the contract. Is the court's conclusion that the buyers waived the financing contingency consistent with the discussion of express conditions and excuses for noncompliance found in the *enXco* case and the accompanying notes in Chapter 9?

3. *Proof of market value.* The contract price minus market value formula requires proof of market value. Real estate appraisers or others who are qualified by education, training, or experience can provide testimony about market value. Courts also usually allow the owner of property to testify about its market value even though the owner may not be qualified as an expert on real estate values. See RWH Homebuilders, L.P. v. Black Diamond Dev. LLP, 2015 Tex. App. LEXIS 8876 (Tex. Ct. App.) (recognizing the owner-opinion rule but requiring owner to provide factual basis for opinion). Can you think of any disadvantage to using an owner's testimony rather than that of a real estate expert?

As in *Crabby's*, many courts have also allowed the resale price of the property as evidence of its market value at the time of the breach, provided the resale takes place within a reasonable period of time in an arm's length transaction. See, e.g., Kemp v. Gannett, 365 N.E.2d 1112 (Ill. 1977). The court in *Crabby's* rejects the argument that a resale taking place eleven and one-half months after breach is too remote to be evidence of the value at the time set for closing. In contrast, a later Texas appellate court decision expressed concern that a resale coming more than one year after breach might not be sufficient evidence of the value at the time for closing, especially in light of the upheaval in the United States housing market that began in 2008. Barry v. Jackson, 309 S.W.3d 135, 141 (Tex. App. 2010). The Texas court emphasized that the burden of proof was on the plaintiff-seller to establish that the price obtained a year later was within a reasonable time and therefore effective evidence of value at the time of breach. Id. at 142.

4. *English and American rules when seller breaches.* As indicated above, the "benefit of the bargain" rule of damages could be applied equally to cases of breach by the purchaser and to cases where the seller is the breaching party. Where the seller is in breach, however, many courts have traditionally restricted the plaintiff purchaser to restitution of any payments made on the purchase price, unless the defendant seller has breached in "bad faith." This rule, known as the "English rule," appears to have grown up at a time when searching land titles was an extremely difficult process, and a seller frequently contracted to sell in ignorance of some later-discovered "cloud" on title, which prevented him from conveying the good (or "marketable") title called for by the contract. See In re Std. Jury Instructions-Contract & Bus. Cases, 116 So. 3d 284 (Fla. 2013) (Florida has long recognized the English rule).

The competing "American rule" would generally award expectation damages for any unexcused failure to convey, regardless of the good faith or bad faith of the seller. The English rule has been generally criticized by American commentators, and the American rule appears to be gaining adherents. See, Donovan v. Bachstadt, 453 A.2d 160 (N.J. 1982). The latter rule is of course in line with the traditional general rule of contract law that unless the cause of nonperformance falls within one of the recognized categories of legal excuse, an expectation-based remedy will normally be available. On the other hand, the English rule does have the potentially attractive feature of adjusting the remedy for breach in light of the willfulness of the breaching party, an approach that some modern commentators have advocated. See Steve Thel & Peter Siegelman, Willfulness Versus Expectation: A Promisor-Based Defense of Willful Breach Doctrine, 107 Mich. L. Rev. 1517 (2009).

5. *Consequential damages.* Of course, the contract/market differential is not the exclusive measure of damages for breach of a land sale contract; an aggrieved plaintiff (buyer or seller) may seek damages based on injuries to her reliance or restitution interests, as discussed above. The Father's House Internat'l, Inc., v. Kurguz, 71 N.E.3d 711, 718-719 (Ohio Ct. App. 2016). (Both of these types of damages are discussed in Chapter 11.) Plaintiff may also seek "incidental damages" as part of a recovery of expectation damages. In the *Crabby's* case, based on the award to the seller of more than $95,000 in total damages, it is apparent that the trial court allowed the seller to recover "other losses" beyond the difference in contract price and fair market value (about $55,000). The appellate court states that the seller sought recovery for "real estate and personal property taxes, utilities, and mortgage interest" accruing during the time between the buyers' breach and the resale of the property eleven and one-half months later. Such damages are often labeled as "consequential" or "incidental" damages and are subject to certain requirements and limitations, including:

(a) the requirement that damages be reasonably foreseeable (i.e., breaching party had reason to foresee the harm as a probable result at the time of the contract);
(b) the harm must be measured with reasonable certainty (i.e., the amount of damages cannot be speculative); and
(c) the duty to mitigate damages (i.e., damages may not be recovered to the extent that they could have been avoided or minimized by reasonable efforts).

These concepts are examined in more detail in subsequent sections of this chapter. Based on the general descriptions of these limitations above, would it appear that the trial court correctly awarded these "other loss" damages to Crabby's?

6. *UCC damage rules.* Damages for breach of a contract to buy or sell goods under the UCC may also be measured by the difference between the market price and the contract price of the goods. UCC §2-708(1) measures the seller's damages for nonacceptance or repudiation by buyer as "the difference between the market price at the time and place for tender and the unpaid contract price together with any incidental damages provided in this Article (§2-710), but less expenses saved in consequence of the buyer's breach." Similarly, UCC §2-713 provides that the measure of the buyer's damages for nondelivery or repudiation by the seller is "the difference between the market price at the time when the buyer learned of the breach and the contract price together with any incidental and consequential damages provided in this Article (§2-715), but less expenses saved in consequence of the seller's breach." The UCC provides some flexibility on proof of market price. See §2-723.

The drafters of the Code thought, however, that application of the market measure of damages often did not accurately determine the loss suffered because the reaction of the nonbreaching party will often involve making a substitute contract that may be at a price other than the market value. In the case of breach by the buyer, UCC §2-706 provides for "seller's resale." That section allows the seller who complies with its provisions to recover from a breaching buyer damages measured by the difference between the contract price and the seller's resale price. Similarly, in the case of breach by the seller, UCC §2-712(1) allows the buyer to "cover" her loss by purchasing substitute goods and to measure her damages by the difference between the cost of those goods and the contract price. Section E of this chapter further explores these rules along with other remedies available to buyers and sellers under the UCC.

Handicapped Children's Education Board v. Lukaszewski

Supreme Court of Wisconsin 112 Wis. 2d 197, 332 N.W.2d 774 (1983)

CALLOW, Justice.

This review arises out of an unpublished decision of the court of appeals which affirmed in part and reversed in part a judgment of the Ozaukee county circuit court, Judge Warren A. Grady.

In January of 1978 the Handicapped Children's Education Board (the Board) hired Elaine Lukaszewski to serve as a speech and language therapist for the spring term. Lukaszewski was assigned to the Lightfoot School in Sheboygan Falls which was approximately 45 miles from her home in Mequon. Rather than move, she commuted to work each day. During the 1978 spring term, the Board offered Lukaszewski a contract to continue in her present position at Lightfoot School for the 1978-79 school year. The contract called for an annual salary of $10,760. Lukaszewski accepted.

In August of 1978, prior to the beginning of the school year, Lukaszewski was offered a position by the Wee Care Day Care Center which was located not far from her home in Mequon. The job paid an annual salary of $13,000. After deciding to accept this offer, Lukaszewski notified Thomas Morrelle, the Board's director of special education, that she intended to resign from her position at the Lightfoot School. Morrelle told her to submit a letter of resignation for consideration by the Board. She did so, and the matter was discussed at a meeting of the Board on August 21, 1978. The Board refused to release Lukaszewski from her contract. On August 24, 1978, the Board's attorney sent a letter to Lukaszewski directing her to return to work. The attorney sent a second letter to the Wee Care Day Care Center stating that the Board would take legal action if the Center interfered with Lukaszewski's performance of her contractual obligations at the Lightfoot School. A copy of this letter was sent to the Department of Public Instruction.

Lukaszewski left the Wee Care Day Care Center and returned to Lightfoot School for the 1978 fall term. She resented the actions of the Board, however, and retained misgivings about her job. On September 8, 1978, she discussed her feelings with Morrelle. After this meeting Lukaszewski felt quite upset about the situation. She called her doctor to make an appointment for that afternoon and subsequently left the school.

Dr. Ashok Chatterjee examined Lukaszewski and found her blood pressure to be high. Lukaszewski asked Dr. Chatterjee to write a letter explaining his medical findings and the advice he had given her. In a letter dated September 11, 1978, Dr. Chatterjee indicated that Lukaszewski had a hypertension problem dating back to 1976. He reported that on the day he examined Lukaszewski she appeared agitated, nervous, and had blood pressure readings up to 180/100. It was his opinion that, although she took hypotensive drugs, her medical condition would not improve unless the situation which caused the problem was removed. He further opined that it would be dangerous for her to drive long distances in her agitated state.

Lukaszewski did not return to work after leaving on September 8, 1978. She submitted a letter of resignation dated September 13, 1978, in which she wrote:

> I enclose a copy of the doctor's statement concerning my health. On the basis of it, I must resign. I am unwilling to jeopardize my health and I am also unwilling to become involved in an accident. For these reasons, I tender my resignation.

A short time later Lukaszewski reapplied for and obtained employment at the Wee Care Day Care Center.

After Lukaszewski left, the Board immediately began looking for a replacement. Only one qualified person applied for the position. Although this applicant had less of an educational background than Lukaszewski, she had more teaching experience. Under the salary schedule agreed upon by the Board and the teachers' union, this applicant would have to be paid $1,026.64 more per year than Lukaszewski. Having no alternative, the Board hired the applicant at the higher salary.

In December of 1978 the Board initiated an action against Lukaszewski for breach of contract. The Board alleged that, as a result of the breach, it suffered damage in the amount of the additional compensation it was required to pay Lukaszewski's replacement for the 1978-79 school year ($1,026.64). A trial was held before the court. The trial court ruled that Lukaszewski had breached her contract and awarded the Board $1,249.14 in damages ($1,026.64 for breach of contract and $222.50 for costs).

Lukaszewski appealed. The court of appeals affirmed the circuit court's determination that Lukaszewski breached her contract. However, the appellate court reversed the circuit court's damage award, reasoning that, although the Board had to pay more for Lukaszewski's replacement, by its own standards it obtained a proportionately more valuable teacher. Therefore, the court of appeals held that the Board suffered no damage from the breach. We granted the Board's petition for review.

There are two issues presented on this review: (1) whether Lukaszewski breached her employment contract with the Board; and (2) if she did breach her contract, whether the Board suffered recoverable damages therefrom.

I

It is undisputed that Lukaszewski resigned before her contract with the Board expired. The only question is whether her resignation was somehow justified. Lukaszewski argues that, because she resigned for health reasons, the trial court erred in finding a breach of contract. According to Lukaszewski, the uncontroverted evidence at trial established that her employment with the Board endangered her health. Therefore, her failure to fulfill her obligation under the employment contract was excused. . . .

. . . In order to excuse Lukaszewski's nonperformance, the trial court would had to have made a factual finding that she resigned for health reasons. The oral decision and supplemental written decision of the trial court indicate that it found otherwise. . . .

. . . We conclude that the trial court's findings of fact are not against the great weight and clear preponderance of the evidence and, therefore, must be upheld. Accordingly, we affirm that portion of the court of appeals' decision which affirmed the circuit court's determination that Lukaszewski breached her employment contract.

II

This court has long held that an employer may recover damages from an employee who has failed to perform an employment contract. Walsh v. Fisher, 102 Wis. 172, 179, 78 N.W. 437 (1899). Damages in breach of contract cases are ordinarily measured by the expectations of the parties. The nonbreaching party is entitled to full compensation for the loss of his or her bargain — that is, losses necessarily flowing from the breach which are proven to a reasonable certainty and were within contemplation of the parties when the contract was made. Lommen v. Danaher, 165 Wis. 15, 19, 161 N.W. 14 (1917); Pleasure Time, Inc. v. Kuss, 78 Wis. 2d 373, 385, 254 N.W.2d 463 (1977). Thus damages for breach of an employment contract include the cost of obtaining other services equivalent to that promised but not performed, plus any foreseeable consequential damages. Roth v. Speck, 126 A.2d 153, 155 (D.C. 1956); Annot., 61 A.L.R.2d 1008 (1958).

In the instant case it is undisputed that, as a result of the breach, the Board hired a replacement at a salary exceeding what it had agreed to pay Lukaszewski. There is no question that this additional cost ($1,026.64) necessarily flowed from the breach and was within the contemplation of the parties when the contract was made. Lukaszewski argues and the court of appeals held, however, that the Board was not damaged by this expense. The amount a teacher is paid is determined by a salary schedule agreed upon by the teachers' union and the Board. The more education and experience a teacher has the greater her salary will be. Presumably, then, the amount of compensation a teacher receives reflects her value to the Board. Lukaszewski argues that the Board suffered no net loss because, while it had to pay more for the replacement, it received the services of a proportionately more valuable teacher. Accordingly, she maintains that the Board is not entitled to damages because an award would place it in a better position than if the contract had been performed.

We disagree. Lukaszewski and the court of appeals improperly focus on the objective value of the services the Board received rather than that for which it had bargained. Damages for breach of contract are measured by the expectations of the parties. The Board expected to receive the services of a speech therapist with Lukaszewski's education and experience at the salary agreed upon. It neither expected nor wanted a more experienced therapist who had to be paid an additional $1,026.64 per year. Lukaszewski's breach forced the Board to hire the replacement and, in turn, to pay a higher salary. Therefore, the Board lost the benefit of its bargain. Any additional value the Board may have received from the replacement's greater experience was imposed upon it and thus cannot be characterized as a benefit. We conclude that the Board suffered damages for the loss of its bargain in the amount of additional compensation it was required to pay Lukaszewski's replacement.

This is not to say that an employer who is injured by an employee's breach of contract is free to hire the most qualified and expensive replacement and then recover the difference between the salary paid and the contract salary. An injured party must take all reasonable steps to mitigate damages. Kuhlman,

Inc. v. G. Heileman Brewing Co., 83 Wis. 2d 749, 752, 266 N.W.2d 382 (1978). Therefore, the employer must attempt to obtain equivalent services at the lowest possible cost. In the instant case the Board acted reasonably in hiring Lukaszewski's replacement even though she commanded a higher salary. Upon Lukaszewski's breach, the Board immediately took steps to locate a replacement. Only one qualified person applied for the position. Having no alternative, the Board hired this applicant. Thus the Board properly mitigated its damages by hiring the least expensive, qualified replacement available.

We hold that the Board is entitled to have the benefit of its bargain restored. Therefore, we reverse that portion of the court of appeals' decision which reversed the trial court's damage award.

The decision of the court of appeals is affirmed in part and reversed in part.

DAY, Justice (dissenting).

I dissent. The majority opinion correctly states, "The only question is whether her resignation is somehow justified." I would hold that it was.

Elaine Lukaszewski left her employment with the school board. She suffered from high blood pressure and had been treated for several years by her physician for the condition. She claimed her hypertension increased due to stress caused when the Board refused to cancel her teaching contract. Stress can cause a precipitous rise in blood pressure. High blood pressure can bring on damage to other organs of the body. . . .

It seems clear from the trial judge's comments that if he had found her physical condition had been caused by the Board's "harassment," he would have let her out of the contract. This is the only logical conclusion from the statement by the trial judge that, "The Court finds that the defendant's medical excuse was a result of the stress condition she had created by an attempted repudiation of her contract, and was not the product of any unsubstantiated, so-called, harrassment [sic] by the plaintiff's board."

In either instance, whether "caused" by the Board or "self induced" because of her gnawing feeling of being unfairly treated, the objective symptoms would be the same.

Either, in my opinion, should justify termination of the contract where the physical symptoms are medically certifiable as they admittedly are here. . . .

What the trial court said was that the desire to take the better job brought on the physical symptoms when release from her contract by the Board was refused.

If the trial court had found that she quit merely for the better job and *not* because of her health problems brought on by the high blood pressure, this would be an entirely different case. However, that is *not* what the trial court found in my opinion. The trial court found her medical problems were self induced and concluded they were therefore unworthy of consideration.

I would reverse the court of appeals decision that held she breached her contract.

Because I would hold that on this record there was no breach, I would not reach the damage question.

NOTES AND QUESTIONS

1. *Measurement of damages in **Lukaszewski**.* As we shall see, the courts will almost never order "specific performance" by an employee of the services promised in a contract of employment. The measure of damages applied in *Lukaszewski* is therefore probably the only potentially useful remedy in most cases where an employee "walks off" the job without legal justification. Is it appropriate? Would some other measure of damages (or no damages at all) be a better solution?

You will recall that many employment contracts are "at will." As we have seen, there are a number of potential limitations on the employer's right to terminate such at will relationships; however, there appears to be no movement toward similar restrictions on termination by the employee. The rule applied in *Lukaszewski* will thus have application only in cases where the employee has by contract bound herself to the employer for some stated period of time. In what fields of employment are such fixed-term contracts likely to be common?

2. *Illness as a defense to breach of an employment contract.* In Chapter 8 we examined the doctrine of impracticability and related concepts. In a personal service contract, the death or incapacity of a person necessary for performance may excuse nonperformance. See Baptist Mem. Hospital-North Mississippi, Inc. v. Lambert, 157 So. 3d 109, 114 (Miss. Ct. App. 2015); Restatement (Second) §262. Moreover, performance may be impracticable because it will involve undue risk of injury to a person. Restatement (Second) §261, Comment *d.* Do you agree with the dissent that even if Ms. Lukaszewski's high blood pressure was "self induced" by "her gnawing feeling of being unfairly treated," she should have been excused from performance? If so, should that feeling have to meet an objective "reasonableness" test? Or should it be enough that she did indeed suffer from such a condition because of her honest belief that she had been dealt with unjustly?

3. *Prejudgment and postjudgment interest.* Note that a considerable amount of time passed between the breach of the contract in 1978 and the final resolution of the *Lukaszewski* case in 1983. In such situations, the prevailing party will often request interest on the amount recovered for the period of time they did not have use of the funds at issue. The successful party will usually accrue *postjudgment interest* under local law (whether for breach of contract or on other grounds) at least from the date judgment is entered, perhaps from the date of the verdict. See, e.g., 28 U.S.C. §1961; N.Y. Civ. Prac. Law §§5003, 5004.

Should the plaintiff also be entitled to *prejudgment interest* with respect to the period between the accruing of the cause of action and the date of judgment? Sometimes an agreement will provide for the payment of interest in the event of breach (for example, in a promissory note). Otherwise, a prevailing party usually will be able to recover prejudgment interest only in cases where at the time of the breach the plaintiff's claim was for a "liquidated" sum. In Blair Constr., Inc. v. McBeth, 44 P.3d 1244 (Kan. 2002), the court stated: "A claim becomes liquidated when both the amount due and the date on which such amount is due are fixed and certain or when the same become definitely ascertainable by mathematical calculation." Id. at 1251. The court also ruled that the award of prejudgment interest was discretionary and that the existence of a good faith controversy about the amount of damages would not necessarily preclude prejudgment interest. Do you think the claim in *Lukaszewski* would have been viewed as liquidated or unliquidated?

American Standard, Inc. v. Schectman

New York Supreme Court 80 A.D.2d 318, 439 N.Y.S.2d 529 (App. Div.), appeal denied, 427 N.E.2d 512 (1981)

HANCOCK, Justice.

Plaintiffs have recovered a judgment on a jury verdict of $90,000 against defendant for his failure to complete grading and to take down certain foundations and other subsurface structures to one foot below the grade line as promised. Whether the court should have charged the jury, as defendant Schectman requested, that the difference in value of plaintiffs' property with and without the promised performance was the measure of the damage is the main point in his appeal. We hold that the request was properly denied and that the cost of completion — not the difference in value — was the proper measure. Finding no other basis for reversal, we affirm.

Until 1972, plaintiffs operated a pig iron manufacturing plant on land abutting the Niagara River in Tonawanda. On the 26-acre parcel were, in addition to various industrial and office buildings, a 60-ton blast furnace, large lifts, hoists and other equipment for transporting and storing ore, railroad tracks, cranes, diesel locomotives and sundry implements and devices used in the business. Since the 1870's plaintiffs' property, under several different owners, had been the site of various industrial operations. Having decided to close the plant, plaintiffs on August 3, 1973 made a contract in which they agreed to convey the buildings and other structures and most of the equipment to defendant, a demolition and excavating contractor, in return for defendant's payment of $275,000 and his promise to remove the equipment, demolish the structures and grade the property as specified.

We agree with Trial Term's interpretation of the contract as requiring defendant to remove all foundations, piers, headwalls, and other structures, including those under the surface and not visible and whether or not shown on the map attached to the contract, to a depth of approximately one foot below the specified grade lines.[2] The proof from plaintiffs' witnesses and the exhibits,

2. Paragraph 7 of the Agreement states in pertinent part:

> 7. After the Closing Date, Purchaser shall demolish all of the Improvements on the North Tonawanda Property included in the sale to Purchaser, cap the water intake at the pumphouse end, and grade and level the property, all in accordance with the provisions of Exhibit "C" and "C1" attached hereto.

Exhibit "C" (Notes on demolition and grading) contains specifications for the grade levels for four separate areas shown on Map "C1" and the following instruction:

> Except as otherwise excepted all structures and equipment including foundations, piers, headwalls, etc. shall be removed to a depth approximately one foot below grade lines as set forth above. Area common to more than one area will be faired to provide reasonable transitions, it being intended to provide a reasonably attractive vacant plot for resale.

showing a substantial deviation from the required grade lines and the existence above grade of walls, foundations and other structures, support the finding, implicit in the jury's verdict, that defendant failed to perform as agreed. Indeed, the testimony of defendant's witnesses and the position he has taken during his performance of the contract and throughout this litigation (which the trial court properly rejected), viz., that the contract did not require him to remove all subsurface foundations, allow no other conclusion.

We turn to defendant's argument that the court erred in rejecting his proof that plaintiffs suffered no loss by reason of the breach because it makes no difference in the value of the property whether the old foundations are at grade or one foot below grade and in denying his offer to show that plaintiffs succeeded in selling the property for $183,000 — only $3,000 less than its full fair market value. By refusing this testimony and charging the jury that the cost of completion (estimated at $110,500 by plaintiffs' expert), not diminution in value of the property, was the measure of damage the court, defendant contends, has unjustly permitted plaintiffs to reap a windfall at his expense. Citing the definitive opinion of Chief Judge Cardozo in Jacob & Youngs, Inc. v. Kent, 230 N.Y. 239, 129 N.E. 889, he maintains that the facts present a case "of substantial performance" of the contract with omissions of "trivial or inappreciable importance" (p. 245, 129 N.E. 889), and that because the cost of completion was "grossly and unfairly out of proportion to the good to be attained," (p. 244, 129 N.E. 889), the proper measure of damage is diminution in value.

The general rule of damages for breach of a construction contract is that the injured party may recover those damages which are the direct, natural and immediate consequence of the breach and which can reasonably be said to have been in the contemplation of the parties when the contract was made (see 13 N.Y. Jur., Damages, §§46, 56; Chamberlain v. Parker, 45 N.Y. 569; Hadley v. Baxendale, 9 Exch. 341, 156 Eng. Reprint 145; Restatement, Contracts, §346). In the usual case where the contractor's performance has been defective or incomplete, the reasonable cost of replacement or completion is the measure (see, Bellizzi v. Huntley Estates, 3 N.Y.2d 112, 164 N.Y.S.2d 395, 143 N.E.2d 802; . . . Restatement, Contracts, §346). When, however, there has been a substantial performance of the contract made in good faith but defects exist, the correction of which would result in economic waste, courts have measured the damages as the difference between the value of the property as constructed and the value if performance had been properly completed. . . . *Jacob & Youngs* is illustrative. There, plaintiff, a contractor, had constructed a house for the defendant which was satisfactory in all respects save one: the wrought iron pipe installed for the plumbing was not of Reading manufacture, as specified in the contract, but of other brands of the same quality. Noting that the breach was unintentional and the consequences of the omission trivial, and that the cost of replacing the pipe would be "grievously out of proportion" (Jacob & Youngs, Inc. v. Kent, supra, 230 N.Y. p. 244, 129 N.E. 889) to the significance of the default, the court held the breach to be immaterial and the proper measure of damage to the owner to be not the cost of replacing the pipe but the nominal difference in value of the house with and without the Reading pipe.

Not in all cases of claimed "economic waste" where the cost of completing performance of the contract would be large and out of proportion to the resultant benefit to the property have the courts adopted diminution in value as the measure of damage. Under the Restatement rule, the completion of the contract must involve "unreasonable economic waste" and the illustrative example given is that of a house built with pipe different in name from but equal in quality to the brand stipulated in the contract as in Jacob & Youngs, Inc. v. Kent (supra) (Restatement, Contracts, §346, subd. [1], par. [a], cl. [ii], p. 573; Illustration 2, p. 576). In Groves v. John Wunder Co., 205 Minn. 163, 286 N.W. 235, plaintiff had leased property and conveyed a gravel plant to defendant in exchange for a sum of money and for defendant's commitment to return the property to plaintiff at the end of the term at a specified grade — a promise defendant failed to perform. Although the cost of the fill to complete the grading was $60,000 and the total value of the property, graded as specified in the contract, only $12,160 the court rejected the "diminution in value" rule, stating:

> The owner's right to improve his property is not trammeled by its small value. It is his right to erect thereon structures which will reduce its value. If that be the result, it can be of no aid to any contractor who declines performance. As said long ago in Chamberlain v. Parker, 45 N.Y. 569, 572: "A man may do what he will with his own, . . . and if he chooses to erect a monument to his caprice or folly on his premises, and employs and pays another to do it, it does not lie with a defendant who has been so employed and paid for building it, to say that his own performance would not be beneficial to the plaintiff."

(Groves v. John Wunder Co., supra, 205 Minn., p. 168, 286 N.W. 235).

The "economic waste" of the type which calls for application of the "diminution in value" rule generally entails defects in construction which are irremediable or which may not be repaired without a substantial tearing down of the structure as in *Jacob & Youngs*. . . .

Where, however, the breach is of a covenant which is only incidental to the main purpose of the contract and completion would be disproportionately costly, courts have applied the diminution in value measure even where no destruction of the work is entailed (see, e.g., Peevyhouse v. Garland Coal & Min. Co., 382 P.2d 109 [Okla.], *cert. denied,* 375 U.S. 906, 84 S. Ct. 196, 11 L. Ed. 2d 145, holding [contrary to Groves v. John Wunder Co., supra] that diminution in value is the proper measure where defendant, the lessee of plaintiff's lands under a coal mining lease, failed to perform costly remedial and restorative work on the land at the termination of the lease. The court distinguished the "building and construction" cases and noted that the breach was of a covenant incidental to the main purpose of the contract which was the recovery of coal from the premises to the benefit of both parties; and see Avery v. Fredericksen & Westbrook, 67 Cal. App. 2d 334, 154 P.2d 41).

It is also a general rule in building and construction cases, at least under *Jacob & Youngs* in New York . . . , that a contractor who would ask the court to apply the diminution of value measure "as an instrument of justice" must not have breached the contract intentionally and must show substantial performance made in good faith (Jacob & Youngs, Inc. v. Kent, supra, 230 N.Y. pp. 244, 245, 129 N.E. 889).

In the case before us, plaintiffs chose to accept as part of the consideration for the promised conveyance of their valuable plant and machines to defendant his agreement to grade the property as specified and to remove the foundations, piers and other structures to a depth of one foot below grade to prepare the property for sale. It cannot be said that the grading and the removal of the structures were incidental to plaintiffs' purpose of "achieving a reasonably attractive vacant plot for resale" (compare Peevyhouse v. Garland Coal & Min. Co., supra). Nor can defendant maintain that the damages which would naturally flow from his failure to do the grading and removal work and which could reasonably be said to have been in the contemplation of the parties when the contract was made would not be the reasonable cost of completion (see 13 N.Y. Jur., Damages, §§46, 56; Hadley v. Baxendale, supra). That the fulfillment of defendant's promise would (contrary to plaintiffs' apparent expectations) add little or nothing to the sale value of the property does not excuse the default. As in the hypothetical case posed in Chamberlain v. Parker, 45 N.Y. 569, supra (cited in Groves v. John Wunder Co., supra), of the man who "chooses to erect a monument to his caprice or folly on his premises, and employs and pays another to do it," it does not lie with defendant here who has received consideration for his promise to do the work "to say that his own performance would not be beneficial to the plaintiff[s]" (Chamberlain v. Parker, supra, p. 572).

Defendant's completed performance would not have involved undoing what in good faith was done improperly but only doing what was promised and left undone (compare Jacob & Youngs, Inc. v. Kent, supra; Restatement, Contracts, §346, Illustration 2, p. 576). That the burdens of performance were heavier than anticipated and the cost of completion disproportionate to the end to be obtained does not, without more, alter the rule that the measure of plaintiffs' damage is the cost of completion. Disparity in relative economic benefits is not the equivalent of "economic waste" which will invoke the rule in Jacob & Youngs, Inc. v. Kent (supra) (see Groves v. John Wunder Co., supra). Moreover, faced with the jury's finding that the reasonable cost of removing the large concrete and stone walls and other structures extending above grade was $90,000, defendant can hardly assert that he has rendered substantial performance of the contract or that what he left unfinished was "of trivial or inappreciable importance" (Jacob & Youngs, Inc. v. Kent, supra, 230 N.Y. p. 245, 129 N.E. 889). Finally, defendant, instead of attempting in good faith to complete the removal of the underground structures, contended that he was not obliged by the contract to do so and, thus, cannot claim to be a "transgressor whose default is unintentional and trivial [and who] may hope for mercy if he will offer atonement for his wrong" (Jacob & Youngs, Inc. v. Kent, supra, p. 244,

129 N.E. 889). We conclude, then, that the proof pertaining to the value of plaintiffs' property was properly rejected and the jury correctly charged on damages.

The judgment and order should be affirmed.

Judgment and order unanimously affirmed with costs.

SIMONS, J.P., and DOERR, DENMAN and SCHNEPP, JJ., concur.

NOTES AND QUESTIONS

1. *Rationale for cost-to-complete measure of damages.* As we have seen, the basic principle for determining damages for breach of contract allows the injured party to recover an amount sufficient to give that party the benefit of the bargain. As a general matter, the cost-to-complete measure of damages seems more consistent with this principle than the diminution-in-value measure because the injured party can expend the damages to receive the bargained-for performance. Another reason for choosing the cost-to-complete measure is that the actual injury to the plaintiff may not be adequately reflected by the market-value comparison. Thus, where the plaintiff contemplates a personal use for the property (e.g., personal residence, family farm), it may be that the property has "idiosyncratic" value to the plaintiff that is not reflected in the market value of the property, in which case damages based on diminished value will clearly undercompensate the plaintiff, perhaps by a substantial but unquantifiable amount. On the other hand, where the plaintiff is a business enterprise, idiosyncratic value is much less likely, and the diminished market value of the property may appear more likely to be an accurate measure of the plaintiff's true injury. If this factor should be viewed as controlling, was *American Standard* correctly decided? Professor Timothy Muris argued that in choosing between remedies in such cases the courts should take into account the presence of "nonpecuniary" (or "subjective") value to the plaintiff; his survey of the decided cases suggests that indeed courts frequently do so, without necessarily adverting to that factor in their opinions. Timothy J. Muris, Cost of Completion or Diminution in Market Value: The Relevance of Subjective Value, 12 J. Legal Stud. 379 (1983). Are there any other factors that would favor cost-to-complete over diminution in market value?

2. *Justification for diminution in market value damages.* Using the *Groves* case (also discussed in *American Standard*) as his example, Judge Posner has suggested that in such cases damages should be based on the diminished value of the land, on grounds of efficiency. Richard A. Posner, Economic Analysis of Law 132 (9th ed. 2014). Posner argues that the award of cost-to-restore damages overcompensates the owner; if the owner had truly wanted restoration of the property, he could have brought an action for specific performance. Posner notes that in *Groves* the plaintiff, who received a cost-to-restore award, did not in fact use the money to restore the land to its original condition. This argument is a corollary of the general notion of encouraging the "efficient breach," a topic to which we return later in this chapter.

If the injured party does not use the award to restore the property, does it follow that the injured party has been overcompensated, as Posner suggests? In Emery v. Caledonia Sand & Gravel Co., 374 A.2d 929 (N.H. 1977), the defendant road construction company had breached a contract to restore the excavated area on defendant's farm. The trial court awarded the plaintiffs damages in the amount necessary to complete the restoration as promised. The Supreme Court of New Hampshire affirmed. While recognizing that there were some cases in which an award of cost-to-complete damages could result in overcompensation or economic waste, the court rejected the argument that the mere fact that the plaintiffs might pocket the money was sufficient to show unjust enrichment: "A valuable income-producing asset has been rendered unproductive; the damages awarded constitute a reasonable means of bringing that asset back to life. If the plaintiffs choose to 'pocket' their recovery, they will have foregone the restoration of their land; they will not have been unjustly enriched." Id. at 933.

In *American Standard* the court indicates that in some cases "economic waste" would justify an award of diminution in market value rather than cost to complete. When would the economic waste doctrine apply? See also Alan Schwartz & Robert E. Scott, Market Damages, Efficient Contracting, and the Economic Waste Fallacy, 108 Colum. L. Rev. 1610 (2008) (arguing that claims of economic waste and windfall recovery against awarding cost of completion damages are unsound).

By the time of the decision in *American Standard*, the plaintiffs had sold the land at only $3,000 less than its market value. Did the court give too little weight to this fact? Why? Should the cost-to-restore remedy be limited to cases in which it appears that the plaintiff can and will use the damages recovered for this purpose? See Bannum, Inc. v. 2210 Adams Place, N.E., LLC, 4 A.3d 431 (D.C. 2010) (limiting damages to diminution in market value and distinguishing *American Standard* because plaintiff did not pay specifically for restoration of the property).

3. *The **Peevyhouse** case.* Peevyhouse v. Garland Coal & Mining Co., the Oklahoma case cited and discussed in *American Standard*, is the leading case applying the diminished-value measure of damages for the defendant's failure to restore the plaintiffs' land as promised after completion of its strip-mining operations. In a comprehensive case study, Professor Judith Maute provides important insights about the background and litigation of *Peevyhouse*. Judith L. Maute, *Peevyhouse v. Garland Coal & Mining Co.* Revisited: The Ballad of Willie and Lucille, 89 Nw. U. L. Rev. 1341 (1995). Professor Maute's monograph explores the negotiations leading up to the lease, the context of strip mining in Oklahoma, the lawyering strategies and failures at various levels of the case, allegations of bribery that have surrounded the case for many years, and the continuing impact of the decision. For scholars who have long complained that appellate opinions are an inadequate source for teaching law, Professor Maute's article provides a rich resource.

Maute's research supplies factual background that bears on the choice between diminution in market value or cost to restore as the measure of damages for breach of contract:

> The Peevyhouses were opposed to permitting any mining on their land. An earlier mining operation stopped at their property line, leaving behind the disturbed land, including a dangerous pit, high wall, and unsightly burden. . . . Because they wanted the land restored to usable condition after the mining, they agreed to forego payment of $3000 . . . in exchange for Garland's promise to do remedial work. Willie explained his view that it was not right to take money for land and allow work to be done on it that would make the land worthless in the future.

Id. at 1358-1363. The Peevyhouses obtained a judgment of $300, far less than the $3,000 amount that they had waived. After payment of litigation costs, they received nothing. As of 1995, the Peevyhouses still lived on the property, which had not been restored. Id. at 1348, 1405. For Maute's discussion of the remedial issues in *Peevyhouse,* see 89 Nw. U. L. Rev. at 1426-1446.

4. *The Restatement approach.* The Restatement (Second) provides in §348(2) that if the loss in value to the injured party is not proved with sufficient certainty, damages may be measured by either (a) the diminution in market value or (b) by the reasonable cost of completing performance or of remedying the defects if that cost "is not clearly disproportionate to the probable loss in value to him." How does the Restatement rule compare to the holding in *American Standard*? More recently, the Restatement (Third) of Restitution §39, Illustration 5, takes the position that the cost of repair is the appropriate remedy in a hypothetical case drawn from the *Peevyhouse* and *American Standard* type of scenario, based on the reasoning that such costs had factored into the price set by the parties.

5. *Case law and scholarly analysis.* In ordinary cases of defective or unfinished construction work, the courts appear to be generally inclined to award cost-to-complete damages, so long as completion does not involve economic waste; e.g., Nippo Corporation/International Bridge Corp. v. AMEC Earth & Envtl., Inc., 2013 U.S. Dist. LEXIS 47232, at 63-65 (E.D. Pa.). See also Carol Chomsky, Of Soil Pits and Swimming Pools: Reconsidering the Measure of Damages for Construction Contracts, 75 Minn. L. Rev. 1445 (1991) (arguing that courts should generally award cost-to-complete damages because that measure ordinarily provides full compensation for loss, but recognizing that in some cases cost-to-complete measure may overcompensate).

Other commentators have suggested that the courts have been too rigid in restricting the choice to either cost to complete or diminution in market value. See E. Allan Farnsworth, Legal Remedies for Breach of Contract, 70 Colum. L. Rev. 1145, 1175 (1970) (trier of fact should have discretion to fix any "not unreasonable" compromise award between two extremes). See also Peter Linzer, On the Amorality of Contract Remedies — Efficiency, Equity, and the Second *Restatement*, 81 Colum. L. Rev. 111, 134-138 (1981) (suggesting that courts should award specific performance rather than damages; in cases where owner wants restoration, specific performance will provide full compensation; in other cases, parties will negotiate a buy-out of owner's right to specific performance).

B. RESTRICTIONS ON THE RECOVERY OF EXPECTATION DAMAGES: FORESEEABILITY, CERTAINTY, AND CAUSATION

In its formula for calculating expectation damages, Restatement (Second) §347 distinguishes between two positive components of plaintiff's recovery: "loss in value" (computed with respect to the value of the performance actually received from the defendant) and "other loss." For example, when the paying party is in breach, the "loss in value" is the unpaid contract amount. When the performing party is in breach, the loss in value to the injured party is the difference between the value of what the injured party expected to receive and what he actually received.

There are many types of "loss" that are in a sense extrinsic to the valuation of the defendant's performance, but that nevertheless are significant. Losses of this sort are commonly referred to as "consequential," and recovery for such losses is subject to certain controls not applied to ordinary damages. A typical type of consequential damage is loss in profits that the nonbreaching party expected to receive from the transaction. For example, if a seller breaches a contract to sell commercial property, consequential damages could include the loss in rental income that the buyer expected to receive. These restrictions are traditionally said to originate with the following English decision, one of the few cases that probably all students of contract law have learned to remember by name, even if (as may be likely) they eventually forget what it stands for.

Joseph and Jonah Hadley's flour mill, as operated by Priday Metford & Co. in the 1920s.

Hadley v. Baxendale

Court of Exchequer 156 Eng. Rep. 145 (1854)

At the trial before Crompton, J., at the last Gloucester Assizes, it appeared that the plaintiffs carried on an extensive business as millers at Gloucester; and that, on the 11th of May, their mill was stopped by a breakage of the crank shaft by which the mill was worked. The steam-engine was manufactured by Messrs. Joyce & Co., the engineers, at Greenwich, and it became necessary to send the shaft as a pattern for a new one to Greenwich. The fracture was discovered on the 12th, and on the 13th the plaintiffs sent one of their servants to the office of the defendants, who are the well known carriers trading under the name of Pickford & Co., for the purpose of having the shaft carried to Greenwich. The plaintiffs' servant told the clerk that the mill was stopped, and that the shaft must be sent immediately; and in answer to the inquiry when the shaft would be taken, the answer was, that if it was sent up by twelve o'clock any day, it would be delivered at Greenwich on the following day. On the following day the shaft was taken by the defendants, before noon, for the purpose of being conveyed to Greenwich, and the sum of 2*l*. 4s. [2 pounds, 4 shillings — Eds.] was paid for its carriage for the whole distance; at the same time the defendants' clerk was told that a special entry, if required, should be made to hasten its delivery. The delivery of the shaft at Greenwich was delayed by some neglect; and the consequence was, that the plaintiffs did not receive the new shaft for several days after they would otherwise have done, and the working of their mill was thereby delayed, and they thereby lost the profits they would otherwise have received.

On the part of the defendants, it was objected that these damages were too remote, and that the defendants were not liable with respect to them. The learned Judge left the case generally to the jury, who found a verdict with 25*l*. damages beyond the amount paid into Court.

Whateley, in last Michaelmas Term, obtained a rule nisi for a new trial, on the ground of misdirection.

ALDERSON, B. We think that there ought to be a new trial in this case; but, in so doing, we deem it to be expedient and necessary to state explicitly the rule which the Judge, at the next trial, ought, in our opinion, to direct the jury to be governed by when they estimate the damages.

It is, indeed, of the last importance that we should do this; for, if the jury are left without any definite rule to guide them, it will, in such cases as these, manifestly lead to the greatest injustice. The Courts have done this on several occasions; and, in Blake v. Midland Railway Company (18 Q.B. 93), the Court granted a new trial on this very ground, that the rule had not been definitely laid down to the jury by the learned Judge at Nisi Prius.

"There are certain established rules," this Court says, in Alder v. Keighley (15 M. & W. 117), "according to which the jury ought to find." And the Court, in that case, adds: "and here there is a clear rule, that the amount which would have been received if the contract had been kept, is the measure of damages if the contract is broken."

Now we think the proper rule in such a case as the present is this: — Where two parties have made a contract which one of them has broken, the damages which the other party ought to receive in respect of such breach of contract should be such as may fairly and reasonably be considered either arising naturally, i.e., according to the usual course of things, from such breach of contract itself, or such as may reasonably be supposed to have been in the contemplation of both parties, at the time they made the contract, as the probable result of the breach of it. Now, if the special circumstances under which the contract was actually made were communicated by the plaintiffs to the defendants, and thus known to both parties, the damages resulting from the breach of such a contract, which they would reasonably contemplate, would be the amount of injury which would ordinarily follow from a breach of contract under these special circumstances so known and communicated. But, on the other hand, if these special circumstances were wholly unknown to the party breaking the contract, he, at the most, could only be supposed to have had in his contemplation the amount of injury which would arise generally, and in the great multitude of cases not affected by any special circumstances, from such a breach of contract. For, had the special circumstances been known, the parties might have specially provided for the breach of contract by special terms as to the damages in that case; and of this advantage it would be very unjust to deprive them. Now the above principles are those by which we think the jury ought to be guided in estimating the damages arising out of any breach of contract. It is said, that other cases such as breaches of contract in the non-payment of money, or in the not making a good title to land, are to be treated as exceptions from this, and as governed by a conventional rule. But as, in such cases, both parties must be supposed to be cognisant of that well-known rule, these cases may, we think, be more properly classed under the rule above enunciated as to cases under known special circumstances, because there both parties may reasonably be presumed to contemplate the estimation of the amount of damages according to the conventional rule. Now, in the present case, if we are to apply the principles above laid down, we find that the only circumstances here communicated by the plaintiffs to the defendants at the time the contract was made, were, that the article to be carried was the broken shaft of a mill, and that the plaintiffs were the millers of that mill. But how do these circumstances shew reasonably that the profits of the mill must be stopped by an unreasonable delay in the delivery of the broken shaft by the carrier to the third person? Suppose the plaintiffs had another shaft in their possession put up or putting up at the time, and that they only wished to send back the broken shaft to the engineer who made it; it is clear that this would be quite consistent with the above circumstances, and yet the unreasonable delay in the delivery would have no effect upon the intermediate profits of the mill. Or, again, suppose that, at the time of the delivery to the carrier, the machinery of the mill had been in other respects defective, then, also, the same results would follow. Here it is true that the shaft was actually sent back to serve as a model for a new one, and that the want of a new one was the only cause of the stoppage of the mill, and that the loss of profits really arose from not sending down the new shaft in proper time, and that this arose from the delay in delivering the broken one to serve as a model. But it is obvious that, in the great multitude of cases of millers sending off broken shafts to third persons by a carrier under ordinary circumstances, such consequences would not, in all probability, have occurred; and these special circumstances were here never communicated by the plaintiffs to the defendants. It follows, therefore, that the loss of profits here cannot reasonably be considered such a consequence of the breach of contract as could have been fairly and reasonably contemplated by both the parties when they made this contract. For such loss would neither have flowed naturally from the breach of this contract in the great multitude of such cases occurring under ordinary circumstances, nor were the special circumstances, which, perhaps, would have made it a reasonable and natural consequence of such breach of contract, communicated to or known by the defendants. The Judge ought, therefore, to have told the jury, that, upon the facts then before them, they ought not to take the loss of profits into consideration at all in estimating the damages. There must therefore be a new trial in this case.

Rule absolute.

NOTES AND QUESTIONS

1. *What did the clerk know?* The Hadley v. Baxendale opinion has had universal acceptance in Anglo-American law as stating an appropriate rule of limitation on damages that would otherwise be recoverable under an unrestricted "expectation" rule. Does the decision itself appear to be sustainable on the facts of the *Hadley* case? In Victoria Laundry (Windsor) Ltd. v. Newman Industries, Ltd., [1949] 2 K.B. 528, 537 (C.A.), a later English court expressed the opinion that the headnote to *Hadley* is "definitely misleading in so far as it says that the defendants' clerk, who attended at the office, was told that the mill was stopped and that the shaft must be delivered immediately." If the court in *Hadley* had actually regarded that as established, it was asserted, then it is "reasonably plain" from Baron Alderson's opinion in *Hadley* that it would have decided that case "the other way round." On the other hand, it has been suggested that the opinion in *Hadley* can be viewed as consistent with the facts as stated in the headnote if one assumes that the clerk was not told either that the stoppage of the mill was solely due to the shaft's being broken or that no other shaft was available in the meantime. Charles T. McCormick, The Contemplation Rule as a Limitation upon Damages for Breach of Contract, 19 Minn. L. Rev. 497, 500-501 (1935). Richard Danzig concludes that there is evidence both ways on the question of whether the Hadleys indeed "served notice on the . . . clerk of their extreme dependence on the shaft," but suggests that in any event the

"rudimentary law of agency" as it then existed might have required notice to be served on Baxendale himself, or at least on some agent more exalted than a mere receiving clerk. Richard Danzig, Hadley v. Baxendale, A Study in the Industrialization of the Law, 4 J. Legal Stud. 249, 262-263 (1975). Danzig's article (substantially incorporated also in his book with Geoffrey R. Watson, The Capability Problem in Contract Law (2d ed. 2004)) explores the context in which the *Hadley* case was decided. Besides the now conventional notion that the *Hadley* decision was more or less consciously an attempt to protect infant industries in the early stages of the industrial revolution, Danzig sees a number of other factors reflected in that decision: tensions between Parliament and the courts, between different courts, and between judge and jury; differences over the proper extent of liability of common carriers, and about the way in which their activities should be regulated; and the still rudimentary state in 1854 of both commercial and agency law. Id. at 64-79.

2. *General and consequential damages.* In *Hadley* the court refers to two types of damages: those that arise naturally from the breach of contract and those that result from special circumstances communicated at the time the contract was formed. These two types of damages have various labels. Damages that arise naturally are often referred to as "general" or "direct" damages. Damages flowing from special circumstances are usually called "consequential" damages although the term "special" damages is sometimes used. (You should also be aware that in tort law a different terminology is employed. Special damages in tort refer to out-of-pocket medical expenses, while general damages refer to pain and suffering.)

The plaintiff need not make any special showing to recover general damages. For example, in a contract for the sale of land, the difference between the contract price and the market value constitutes general damages. Using the terminology of the Restatement formula discussed at the beginning of this chapter, general damages are called "loss in value."

The most important type of consequential damages in commercial cases is lost profits arising from collateral contracts. (Note that lost profit on the contract that is breached, as opposed to other contracts, is treated as general rather than consequential damages). Consequential damages also include injury to person or property caused by goods that fail to comply with contractual warranties. On the distinction between general and consequential damages, see American List Corp. v. U.S. News & World Report, Inc., 549 N.E.2d 1161 (N.Y. 1989) (lost profits on contract that was breached rather than on collateral contract are general damages not subject to rule of Hadley v. Baxendale).

3. *Foreseeability.* The modern formulation of the rule of Hadley v. Baxendale is now stated in terms of the foreseeability of the loss. See Restatement (Second) of Contracts §351 and UCC §2-715(2). Several aspects of the foreseeability standard should be noted. As the court in *Hadley* states, the recoverability of consequential damages depends on whether such damages

were in the contemplation of the parties "at the time they made the contract." It might plausibly be contended that liability for the foreseeable consequences of breach of contract ought to be based on the breacher's knowledge as of the time the *breach* occurs, just as the law of torts generally makes the tortfeasor's knowledge at the time of the tortious conduct the test for liability based on foreseeability of harm. However, application of the *Hadley* test is uniformly understood to depend on the defendant's knowledge at the time the contract is made. Why should this be so?

Second, it is only necessary that the type of loss be foreseeable, not the manner in which the loss occurs. E.g., Kraatz v. USAA Cas. Ins. Co., 2017 WL 876187 (W.D. N.Y.) (breaching insurer liable to insured for costs incurred in obtaining a second mortgage on home to finance necessary repairs and replacements; such expenses should have been reasonably foreseen by insurer); Williams v. Gray Group, L.L.C., 79 N.E.3d 1146 (Ohio Ct. App. 2016) (breaching contractor should have foreseen that defective home renovation would occasion plaintiffs' withdrawal of money from retirement account, incurring substantial IRS penalties). Third, while courts sometimes refer to risks that are within the contemplation of both parties, the focus of foreseeability is on the breaching party. Fourth, the standard for foreseeability is at least in part objective. The breaching party is liable for losses about which it had reason to know. Finally, the loss must be foreseeable as a "probable" result of the breach. Core-Mark Midcontinent Inc. v. Sonitrol Corp., 370 P.3d 353, 360 (Colo. Ct. App. 2016) (loss must be foreseeable as "probable" result of breach; standard for recovery is more restrictive than tort rule of "reasonable foreseeability"). Liability is not limited to losses that are necessary or inevitable, but it does not extend to remote losses. See E. Allan Farnsworth, Contracts §12.14, at 795-796 (4th ed. 2004); Restatement (Second) Contracts §351, Comment *a*.

4. *The Hadley rule under the CISG.* With regard to international transactions, Article 74 of the CISG provides as follows:

> Damages for breach of contract by one party consist of a sum equal to the loss, including loss of profit, suffered by the other party as a consequence of the breach. Such damages may not exceed the loss which the party in breach foresaw or ought to have foreseen at the time of the conclusion of the contract, in the light of the facts and matters of which he then knew or ought to have known, as a possible consequence of the breach of contract.

See Delchi Carrier SpA v. Rotorex Corp., 71 F.3d 1024 (2d Cir. 1995) (applying CISG Article 74 and finding that seller from U.S. was liable to buyer in Italy after defective compressors delivered under contract led to cancellation of the agreement and buyer lost sales to third parties). How does this principle compare to the *Hadley* rule?

5. *The tacit agreement test.* At the beginning of the twentieth century, Justice Holmes advocated a "tacit agreement" test for recovery of consequential damages. This test would have limited the availability of consequential damages

even more than the rule of Hadley v. Baxendale. Under the tacit agreement test the injured party would have been required to show not only that the special circumstances were brought to the attention of the other party, but also that the other party "assumed consciously" the liability in question. Globe Refining Co. v. Landa Cotton Oil Co., 190 U.S. 540, 544 (1903). Modern contract law has largely rejected the tacit agreement test. See Rexnord Corp. v. DeWolff Boberg & Assoc., Inc., 286 F.3d 1001 (7th Cir. 2002); Restatement (Second) of Contracts §351, Comment *a*; UCC §2-715, Comment 2; but see Sunnyland Farms, Inc. v. Central New Mexico Electrical Cooperative, Inc., 255 P.3d 324 (N.M. Ct. App. 2011) (New Mexico common law still requires that breaching party must "explicitly or tacitly" agree to be responsible for consequential damages likely to occur in event of breach).

Professor Richard Epstein has criticized the modern rejection of the "tacit agreement" test and the general application of the rule of Hadley v. Baxendale. He argues that determination of the amount of contract damages should be viewed as a question of contract interpretation. When the contract specifies the measure of damages, the contractual provision should be enforced, absent fraud, duress, or some other invalidating conduct. When the contract is silent on the measure of damages, the court should adopt the "default rule" of damages that the parties would most likely have agreed on had they considered the issue of damages. Relying on commercial practice, reflected in various types of contracts, which limits expectation damages below the amount that would be fixed by the *Hadley* rule (for example, consumer goods are typically sold with a "repair or replace" warranty), Epstein argues that the appropriate default rule will often be less than the amount determined under a *Hadley* approach. Richard A. Epstein, Beyond Foreseeability: Consequential Damages in the Law of Contract, 18 J. Legal Stud. 105 (1989).

By contrast, Professor Melvin Eisenberg reaches conclusions that are diametrically opposed to Epstein's. Melvin A. Eisenberg, The Principle of *Hadley v. Baxendale*, 80 Cal. L. Rev. 563 (1992). Eisenberg argues that the utility of the *Hadley* rule depends on communication of information by buyers and use by sellers of such information in setting prices to reflect risk. Id. at 587-588. This process is unlikely to occur, however, particularly with regard to standardized products, because of the costs of communicating and utilizing information. Id. at 592. Thus, Eisenberg concludes, the costs of the *Hadley* rule are likely to exceed its benefits. Id. at 597-598. He advocates a rule that would allow recovery of all losses that are proximately caused by a breach (in essence, the tort standard), subject to contractual allocation of risk and principles of fair disclosure of contractual limitations on liability. Id. at 598. For other scholarly commentary on the *Hadley* rule, see Eric A. Posner, Essay: Economic Analysis of Contract Law After Three Decades: Success or Failure? 112 Yale L.J. 829, 836-839 (2003); George S. Geis, Empirically Assessing Hadley v. Baxendale, 32 Fla. St. U. L. Rev. 897 (2005).

Florafax International, Inc. v. GTE Market Resources, Inc.

Supreme Court of Oklahoma 933 P.2d 282 (1997)

LAVENDER, Justice.

We consider the appropriateness of a jury award of lost profits over a two year time period in favor of . . . Florafax International, Inc. against . . . GTE Market Resources, Inc., for breaching a contract requiring GTE to provide telecommunication and/or telemarketing services for Florafax. The profits were those Florafax claimed it stood to make from a collateral contract it had with a third party, but allegedly lost when the collateral contract was canceled purportedly because GTE breached its contract with Florafax. . . .

I. STANDARD OF REVIEW. . . .

II. Facts

Florafax is generally a flowers-by-wire company acting as a clearinghouse to allow the placement and receipt of orders between florists throughout the United States and internationally. . . .

In addition to the above activities, Florafax solicits agreements with third party clients such as supermarket chains, American Express and other entities that advertise the sale of floral products by various methods (e.g., television, radio, newspapers, billing circulars, mass mailings to consumers) which allow a consumer to order floral arrangements via the use of a 1-800 telephone call, with Florafax agreeing to handle the actual inbound and outbound communication aspects of the transactions. . . .

One client that signed up for an arrangement like that described immediately above was Bellerose Floral, Inc., d/b/a Flora Plenty, a leading marketer of floral products advertising sales through use of the telephone number 1-800-FLOWERS. Florafax and Bellerose entered a contract in early October 1989 whereby Florafax and/or its designee would accept direct consumer orders (i.e. inbound calls and orders) placed via the 1-800-FLOWERS number and, of course, it also agreed to handle the outbound placement of orders either by telephone or computer transmission. The Florafax/Bellerose contract provided Florafax would be paid certain fee(s) per order. As we read the contract its initial term was for one year, to be automatically renewed from month to month thereafter, but that either party, with or without cause, could terminate the agreement upon sixty (60) days written notice.

GTE, on the other hand, was a company providing telecommunication and/or telemarketing services for other businesses. It provided for other businesses a call answering center where telemarketing sales representatives (TSRs) physically answered telephones when orders from promotional activities came in from consumers and took care of transmitting the orders by telephone or computer for fulfillment. For certain management and business-related reasons Florafax subcontracted out much of the telecommunication and telemarketing services of its business.

In mid-October 1989, about two weeks after Florafax signed its agreement with Bellerose, the Florafax/GTE contract was entered. In essence, it provided GTE would via a call answering center (apparently located in the Dallas, Texas area) handle much, if not all, of the activities connected with taking incoming orders and placing outgoing calls or computer transmissions directed to it by Florafax associated with the purchase and fulfillment of floral orders throughout the United States and internationally. The agreement required Florafax to pay GTE certain fees for this service depending on the type of order.

The Florafax/GTE contract generally ran for a term of three years from the effective date the parties anticipated Florafax would begin directing calls to GTE for floral orders — a date anticipated to be in early December 1989. It also contained certain provisions that in essence might result in termination after a two year period based upon application of a price/fee renegotiation clause. In answer to one of the questions submitted via a special verdict form, the jury determined the Florafax/GTE contract could be terminated after two years based on this clause.

The contract further contained a clause concerning lost profits providing in pertinent part:

> 20. Termination
>
> *a. Termination for cause.* Any non-defaulting party shall have the right to terminate this agreement at any date not less than forty-five (45) days after an event of default occurs and so long as it continues. In the event GTE [] ceases to perform its duties hereunder after a notice of termination is given or otherwise, Florafax may suffer tremendous damage to its business. GTE [] agrees to pay Florafax consequential damages and lost profits on the business lost.

The contract also specifically noted GTE would be providing services not only for Florafax, but for others.

In addition to the above express contractual provisions, evidence was presented that officials with GTE knew prior to signing the contract that GTE would be providing its services not only directly for Florafax, but that Florafax had been soliciting business from entities such as Bellerose, business that was anticipated to be at least partially directed through GTE's call answering center. In fact, competent evidence exists in this record showing GTE specifically knew when it signed the contract with Florafax that Bellerose was considering turning over a portion of its inbound and outbound business to Florafax, and that Bellerose received somewhere between 100,000-200,000 orders annually. Evidence was also presented that showed GTE, prior to contract execution, considered it a positive aspect of entering the agreement that Florafax was constantly marketing and promoting its business by the addition of outside clients and that this addition of clients would lead to revenue increases. Evidence also existed that Bellerose was Florafax's largest customer and that it had been an ongoing business for at least sixteen (16) years prior to the date of trial.

Evidence was also submitted showing that before GTE entered the contract, its director of finance and administration did a financial analysis of the Florafax/

GTE contract and determined GTE would make little or no money from it. His immediate supervisor (the general manager of GTE) was informed of the analysis. GTE, however, made the decision to enter the contract, apparently because it needed new customers and/or in the hope this financial analysis was wrong.

Although from December 1989 through Valentine's Day in February 1990 certain problems surfaced in regard to the adequacy of GTE's performance, at some point after Valentine's Day the problems appeared to worsen. At some time after Valentine's Day and leading up to Mother's Day in May 1990, the latter holiday being described as the largest floral holiday of the year, the adequacy of GTE's performance became subject to serious question. What appears from the evidence to be the most glaring breach on GTE's part was a failure during the week leading up to Mother's Day to provide sufficient TSRs to answer calls anticipated to be directed to it by Florafax, including calls from Bellerose. Without adequate TSRs to take the calls, floral product orders would obviously be lost and Florafax income lost in the process.

Coupled with this evidence of a failure to adequately staff for anticipated calls, there was also evidence that during the term of the contract GTE's project manager for the Florafax account admitted to Florafax's off-site manager stationed at the GTE facility to look out for Florafax's interests there, that GTE no longer wanted the Florafax account — in essence, because GTE was not making money under the contract's pricing scheme. . . .

In addition, evidence was presented that GTE's failure to perform caused Bellerose to terminate its agreement with Florafax and Bellerose ceased its relationship with Florafax apparently some time in July 1990, directing no more calls from its 1-800-FLOWERS number through GTE after that time. The President of Bellerose essentially testified that he anticipated his agreement with Florafax to be a long-term relationship if things worked out and, although his testimony was not absolute in such regard, that he pulled out of his relationship with Florafax because of the poor performance of GTE. . . .

As a result of GTE's breach, in addition to losing Bellerose as a client, Florafax incurred costs primarily associated with taking steps necessary to set up its own call answering center in Tulsa to perform the duties GTE was supposed to handle so that it would not lose other clients or business relationships as it had lost Bellerose. Florafax finally left the GTE facility at the end of September 1990.

In addition to seeking damages attributable to costs associated with performing the services GTE was supposed to perform, Florafax sought lost profits it claimed would have been realized from the Florafax/Bellerose contract. In support of and in opposition to the lost profit claim the parties presented conflicting economic projections through expert witnesses (Florafax through an economist, GTE through a Certified Public Accountant) as to how much profit, if any, Florafax would have made from the Bellerose contract over varying lengths of time. . . .

One major difference between the experts' projections was that the Florafax expert increased the Bellerose sales volume from 1990 to 1991 one hundred percent (100%), while the GTE expert kept the call and order volumes flat in his projections. The one hundred percent (100%) increase was based on evidence the Bellerose sales volume increased about this percentage over the 1990 year levels. GTE's expert, in contrast, used a flat growth rate because a general floral industry survey indicated declining volumes in the floral industry from the late 1980s through 1991.

The Florafax expert estimated the Bellerose loss at $1,921,028.00 for a period extended out to three years, i.e. for the period of time that remained in the term of the Florafax/GTE contract at the time Bellerose canceled. The GTE expert estimated the Bellerose loss over the same time frame to be $505,731.00 if the fees to be paid to GTE by Florafax remained constant for this period of time. The GTE expert also gave an alternative figure that coincided with the remaining part of a two year period beginning in December 1989 based on the view the Florafax/GTE contract would be subject to termination at such time in view of the price renegotiation provisions of that contract. The loss of profits for this period was estimated to be $294,044.00. These figures of the two experts took into consideration that the fees Florafax had to pay to GTE for its services would have to be deducted from the income or revenue Florafax would have received from Bellerose orders.[5]

The jury determined GTE breached its contract with Florafax and, in addition to other damages, awarded Florafax $750,000.00 in lost profits that would have been earned under the Florafax/Bellerose contract over a two year period of time. Other damages awarded to Florafax included a little over $820,000.00, the majority of which reflected costs and expenses associated with setting up and/or expanding a call center in Tulsa, Oklahoma to perform those functions GTE was supposed to perform under the Florafax/GTE contract. On appeal, GTE, although not admitting liability — i.e. that it breached its contract with Florafax — does not contest the jury determination that it did breach the contract. We now turn to the lost profit damage issues to be reviewed.

III. Lost Profits from a Collateral Contract May Be Recovered as a Proper Element of Damage for Breach of Contract

GTE raises two basic arguments on the propriety of the recovery of lost profits. These are: 1) lost profit damages cannot include profits from third-party collateral contracts or, if they are recoverable, Florafax failed to prove entitlement to them because it failed to show the prospect of profits from the Florafax/Bellerose contract or, conversely, the loss of such profits upon GTE's breach, were in the contemplation of GTE and Florafax at the time they entered the Florafax/GTE contract; and, 2) if lost profits from the Florafax/Bellerose

5. Although there was some dispute as to whether Florafax's expert properly deducted all of the expenses that should have been deducted to reach a net lost profit figure, it is clear from the evidence that the amounts reflected in the text from both experts did take into consideration the necessity of deducting the fees that Florafax would have had to pay to GTE for its services. Of course, only net profits — as opposed to gross profits — are recoverable and depending on the particular transactions involved, what does or does not have to be deducted to reach a net lost profit figure may vary. See H. Hunter, Modern Law of Contracts, Breach & Remedies, ¶7.03[4][c] at 7-20/7-23 (1986). GTE, on appeal, does not attack the lost profit award on the basis that it is not a net figure. . . .

contract are recoverable they must be limited to a sixty (60) day period, because profits beyond this time must be deemed too remote, speculative or uncertain, and Florafax could not be said to be reasonably assured of any profits from its relationship with Bellerose for any longer period, given the Florafax/Bellerose contract clause allowing either Florafax or Bellerose the right to terminate that contract upon sixty (60) days notice. In our view, each argument is without merit.

III(A). Collateral Contracts and Lost Profits

GTE asserts Oklahoma jurisprudence has not squarely addressed the question of whether a party suing for breach of contract may recover lost profits arising from a collateral contract. Although this Court may not have used the exact phrase "lost profits from third-party collateral contracts" a review of Oklahoma law makes clear if such damages are properly proved they are recoverable. Thus, GTE's apparent view that lost profits from a collateral contract are never recoverable for breach of contract because as a matter of law they are inherently too remote, speculative and/or unforeseeable, is mistaken.

The time-honored general rules on recovery of damages for breach of contract are found in Hadley v. Baxendale, 9 Ex. 341, 156 Eng. Rep. 145 (1854). . . . The lost profits involved here fall under the second branch of the Hadley v. Baxendale formulation.

Generally speaking, this Court has long espoused the view that loss of future or anticipated profit — i.e. loss of expected monetary gain — is recoverable in a breach of contract action: 1) if the loss is within the contemplation of the parties at the time the contract was made, 2) if the loss flows directly or proximately from the breach — i.e. if the loss can be said to have been caused by the breach — and 3) if the loss is capable of reasonably accurate measurement or estimate. Groendyke Transport, Inc. v. Merchant, 380 P.2d 682 Second Syllabus (Okla. 1962). An award in the form of a loss of profits, in fact, is generally considered a common measure of damages for breach of contract, it frequently represents fulfillment of the non-breaching party's expectation interest, and it often closely approximates the goal of placing the innocent party in the same position as if the contract had been fully performed. H. Hunter, Modern Law of Contracts, Breach & Remedies, ¶7.02[2] at 7-5/7-6 (1986).

Our cases also recognize that where there is sufficient evidence presented on the issue of the recovery of special damages — including lost profits — what was or was not in the contemplation of the parties at the time of contracting is a question of fact to be determined by the trier of fact. Home-Stake Production Company v. Minnis, 443 P.2d 91, 103 (Okla. 1968). . . .

Here, there is clearly sufficient competent evidence to show GTE had within its contemplation at the time of contracting the potential for profits from a Florafax association with Bellerose. As we noted in section II. FACTS above, GTE knew it would be providing services not only directly for Florafax, but for others on behalf of Florafax. It knew Florafax was soliciting other entities to use the services of a call answering center like GTE's and, in fact, GTE looked upon Florafax's solicitation of these other entities as a positive aspect of a contractual relationship with Florafax because of the potential for increased revenue.

Trial evidence also showed the Florafax/Bellerose contract was entered two weeks prior to the Florafax/GTE agreement and that GTE officials knew either before or contemporaneously with signing the latter contract that Bellerose was considering turning over a portion of its inbound and outbound business via its 1-800-FLOWERS network to Florafax — business GTE also knew consisted of 100,000-200,000 orders annually. Further, as already noted, a clause in the Florafax/GTE contract itself expressly reflects the parties' contemplation of the recovery of lost profits by Florafax should GTE cease to perform its duties and obligations during the term of the contract — and, as also noted, evidence exists in this record that GTE intentionally failed to perform during part of the term of the contract, a failure on its part we conclude would support a determination the lost profit clause of the Florafax/GTE contract was implicated. . . .

III(B). The Sixty (60) Day Termination Clause in the Florafax/Bellerose Contract Does not Preclude the Recovery of Lost Profits Beyond the Sixty (60) Day Period

GTE, in addition to arguing no lost profits are proper, alternatively asserts that if their recovery is appropriate, they must be limited to a period of sixty (60) days because of the termination notice clause of the Florafax/Bellerose contract which allowed either party to that agreement to terminate that contract, with or without cause, upon sixty (60) days written notice. For this position prime reliance is placed on Osborn v. Commanche Cattle Industries, Inc., 545 P.2d 827 (Okla. Ct. Civ. App. 1975), an opinion of the Oklahoma Court of Civil Appeals. Although we believe the rule of law laid down in *Osborn* is sound, the rule is not controlling here.

Osborn involved a situation where plaintiff had contracted with a feedlot to perform certain [services]. The contract was for a term of three years, but contained a clause allowing either party to terminate the agreement by giving the other thirty (30) days advance notice. . . . The trial court allowed the lost profit issue to go to the jury with instructions allowing their recovery for the entire three year period, over defendant's objection only nominal damages were appropriate because either party to the contract had the right to terminate it upon thirty (30) days notice.

The *Osborn* court found error in submitting the lost profit issue to the jury for a longer period than the thirty (30) day notice time frame based on the following rule of law: no party to a contract may recover more in damages for a breach of the contract than might have been gained by full performance. *Osborn,* supra, 545 P.2d at 831. . . . In other words, in *Osborn* it was absolutely certain plaintiff could not establish lost profits for any greater period of time because the defendant had an absolute right to terminate the contract upon giving the agreed notice and exercise of this right would have provided full performance on the defendant's part.

The situation here is quite different. . . . GTE had no right to terminate either the Florafax/GTE or Florafax/Bellerose contracts upon any short specified notice provision. That right belonged only to Florafax and Bellerose, and only in relation to the latter contract. Thus, full performance could not have been supplied by the simple expediency of GTE giving sixty (60) days notice to Florafax that it was terminating their agreement. Instead, the Florafax/GTE contract, according to the unchallenged finding of the jury, had a minimum term of two years based on the effect of the price renegotiation provisions of the contract, i.e. Florafax was guaranteed performance by GTE for a full two years.

. . . In fact, competent evidence exists supporting the view it is probable some additional profits would have been made from the Bellerose relationship for a longer period of time. Further, application of the *Osborn* rule here would improperly allow GTE to benefit from a cancellation right it had no ability to exercise. Accordingly, the rule of *Osborn* does not preclude Florafax's recovery of lost profit damages associated with the loss of the Bellerose relationship in excess of a sixty (60) day period.

III(C). Competent Evidence Exists to Support the Award of Lost Profit Damages to a Reasonable Certainty

Even though the rule of *Osborn* is inapplicable, GTE's arguments as to the termination notice clause of the collateral contract do, however, implicate the legal principle that before lost profit damages are recoverable it must be adequately shown such profits were reasonably certain to have been made by the non-breaching party absent breach. We believe the answer to the reasonable certainty question is not one subject to decision as a matter of law under this record, but was one of fact to be decided by the trier of fact — here the jury.

In order for damages to be recoverable for breach of contract they must be clearly ascertainable, in both their nature and origin, and it must be made to appear they are the natural and proximate consequence of the breach and not speculative and contingent. Chorn v. Williams, 186 Okla. 646, 99 P.2d 1036, 1037 (1940). It is not necessary, however, for the recovery of lost profits shown to have been caused by a breach of contract, that the profits be established with absolute certainty and barring any possibility of failure, but it is only required that it be established with reasonable certainty that profits would have been made had the contract not been breached. Megert v. Bauman, 206 Okla. 651, 246 P.2d 355, 358 (1952). In essence, what a plaintiff must show for the recovery of lost profits is sufficient certainty that reasonable minds might believe from a preponderance of the evidence that such damages were actually suffered. . . .

Once it is made to clearly appear that loss of business profits has been suffered by virtue of the breach, it is proper to let the jury decide what the loss is from the best evidence the nature of the case admits. . . . When a breach of a contractual obligation with resulting damages has been established, although the amount of damages may not be based on mere speculation, conjecture and surmise alone, the mere uncertainty as to the exact amount of damages will not preclude the right of recovery. . . . It is sufficient if the evidence shows the extent of damage by just and reasonable inference. . . . We believe sufficient evidence was presented so that Florafax carried its burden to prove the fact, cause and amount of its lost profit damages with the requisite degree of reasonable certainty.

The fact of lost profit damage beyond merely a sixty (60) day period is shown by the testimony of Bellerose's President. Although not absolute, his testimony was, in essence, he considered the relationship with Florafax a long-term one had things worked out and that the most important issues to him in making the decision to terminate were issues concerning performance. This testimony showed the relationship in all probability would have continued long after it was terminated had GTE adequately performed. Although it is true — given the existence of the sixty (60) day notice provision — Bellerose might have terminated the Florafax/Bellerose contract at some point in time even had GTE performed, the state of this record does not require a conclusion Bellerose would have exercised its right of termination for some other reason.

We are also of the view the fact of damage is partially shown by the projections for profits of both the damage experts presented by the parties. Although they differed in their ultimate conclusions as to the extent or amount of lost profits, both presented estimates that Florafax could have made profits from the Florafax/Bellerose relationship had it survived.

Causation is also shown by sufficient competent evidence, evidence that partially overlaps with that of the fact of damage in this case. There is enough evidence to support a reasonable determination that Bellerose's decision to cancel or terminate its relationship with Florafax was the direct result of GTE's failure to render adequate performance and, that GTE's breach of the Florafax/GTE contract caused the cancellation. Therefore, there is sufficient evidence in this record upon which reasonable minds might rely that profits from the Florafax/Bellerose relationship would have actually been made by Florafax beyond a sixty (60) day period and that GTE's breach of its contract with Florafax caused the loss of Bellerose as a client.

As to the exact extent or amount of damages, the record contains sufficient evidence to take the matter out of the realm of mere speculation, conjecture or surmise. A track record existed which showed the calls coming to GTE from Bellerose during the five to seven months Bellerose business was actually being routed to GTE. There was also evidence that although the business relationship between Florafax and Bellerose was relatively new, Bellerose had been in business for a number of years, and it had experienced 100,000-200,000 orders annually. Such evidence clearly was appropriate to consider on the issue of the extent of lost profits. Although this case is not exactly like our cases dealing with the destruction of an established business by a breach of contract, it is sufficiently close to be analogized to the established business situation, where we have allowed the recovery of lost profits. . . .

Evidence also existed which showed that Bellerose, after terminating its relationship with Florafax, experienced a substantial increase in its sales volume in 1991. In other words, there was not only evidence tending to show a certain volume of orders prior to the breach, but evidence tending to show that level of sales would have in all probability increased substantially during part of the term of the Florafax/GTE contract had Bellerose continued its relationship with Florafax. This post-breach evidence is proper to be considered at arriving at a reasonable estimate of the loss caused by a breach of contract . . . because all facts which would reasonably tend to make certain the amount of injury inflicted are admissible. . . . Although the jury apparently did not totally credit the testimony or documentation presented by either Florafax's or GTE's experts as to their projections of profits lost, the $750,000.00 awarded for the two year period was within the range of the estimates of the two experts. Accordingly, not only was the fact and causation of lost profit damages adequately shown to a reasonable certainty, but the amount of lost profit damages awarded was sufficiently shown through competent evidence contained in this record to take the matter out of the realm of mere speculation, conjecture and surmise.

IV. Conclusion

The award of the jury of lost profit damages associated with the Florafax/Bellerose contract was an appropriate remedy for GTE's breach of its contract with Florafax. It was consistent with our substantive law as to the recovery of lost profits for a breach of contract and was supported by competent evidence.

. . . Trial court judgment is affirmed as to the award of lost profits.

KAUGER, C.J., SUMMERS, V.C.J., and WILSON and WATT, JJ., concur.

HODGES, SIMMS and HARGRAVE, JJ., dissent.

NOTES AND QUESTIONS

1. *Applying Hadley v. Baxendale.* In applying the rule of Hadley v. Baxendale, the court in *Florafax International* points out that the Florafax/Bellerose contract was signed two weeks before the Florafax/GTE agreement. Would the result in the case have been different if the Florafax/Bellerose contract had been signed after the Florafax/GTE agreement?

Lost profits from the Bellerose contract were subject to the second prong of the *Hadley* test because they arose from a *collateral contract* rather than from breach of the Florafax/GTE agreement itself. Since Florafax was a recipient rather than a provider of telecommunications services, it did not expect to receive a profit on its contract with GTE. In cases where the plaintiff seeks lost profits it would have made *on the contract sued on*, these damages will be subject to the first rather than the second prong of the *Hadley* test, and will be recoverable (as "general" or "direct" damages) without the need to show foreseeability. It may also be easier to prove such damages with reasonable certainty. See Lewis Jorge Construction Management, Inc. v. Pomona Unified School Dist., 102 P.3d 257 (Cal. 2004) (contractor could recover lost profits on contract breached by school district but not for alleged lost profits on future, collateral contracts that were never made due to loss in bonding capacity; other types of transactions might justify lost profits on collateral contracts).

2. *Contractual limitations on consequential damages.* How can a contracting party avoid potentially large liability for consequential damages flowing from the breach of a contract? In *Florafax International* the Florafax/GTE contract specifically provided that GTE would be liable for consequential damages in the event the contract was terminated for cause. Was this provision essential to Florafax International's recovery of lost profits? Contractual assumptions of liability for consequential damages are, however, somewhat unusual. Much more common are contractual disclaimers or limitations of liability for consequential damages. Transactions governed by the UCC have specific rules governing contractual disclaimers of warranties or limitations of remedies for breach of warranty. See UCC §§2-316 (exclusion or modification of warranty), 2-719 (modification or limitation of remedy). Courses on UCC Article 2 examine these concepts in more detail. Statutes at both the federal and state level may regulate disclaimers and limitations of remedies in consumer transactions. For transactions in which the UCC and other statutory law are not applicable, general contractual principles apply. Can you think of any reason why GTE would have agreed to assume liability of a potentially unknown amount for consequential damages? As a lawyer for GTE could you have suggested a modification of this clause that would provide it protection against catastrophic damages?

3. *Requirement of certainty.* As the court points out, an injured party cannot recover damages that are "speculative." Plaintiffs must prove their damages with "reasonable certainty." See Restatement (Second) of Contracts §352. In applying this limitation, courts often draw a distinction between uncertainty about the *fact* of damage and uncertainty regarding the *amount* of damage. When the plaintiff establishes the fact of damage, the jury is given wide leeway in awarding compensation. See Pharmathene, Inc. v. Siga Techs., Inc., 2014 Del. Ch. LEXIS 142 (Del. Ch.) (while proof of the fact of damages must be certain, proof of the amount of damage does not require mathematical precision as long as the court has a reasonable basis for awarding damages). Consider Contemporary Mission, Inc. v. Famous Music Corp., 557 F.2d 918 (2d Cir. 1977), in which the plaintiff claimed that the defendant had breached a contract to produce and promote

recordings of songs composed by members of the plaintiff (a nonprofit corporation formed by a small group of Roman Catholic priests). The Court of Appeals held that the plaintiff could recover lost profits resulting from the defendant's failure to promote plaintiff's record, "Fear No Evil," noting that "[e]ven after the promotional efforts ended, [and] the record was withdrawn from the marketplace, it was carried, as a result of its own momentum, to an additional 10,000 sales and to a rise from approximately number 80 on the 'Hot Soul Singles' chart of Billboard magazine to number 61." These facts established that it was "certain" that the plaintiff had suffered some damage, even though the amount was unclear. On the other hand, the court ruled that claimed damages for lost tours were too speculative to be recovered:

> The same is not true, however, of the existence of damage in the form of lost opportunities for concert tours, theatrical tours or similar benefits. While it is certain that some sales were lost as a result of the failure to promote, we cannot believe that . . . the New York courts would accept what Famous' counsel aptly described at trial as Contemporary's "domino theory" of prospective damages. The theory is that if "Fear No Evil" had become a "hit," its success would have stimulated additional sales of the full two-record VIRGIN album and would have generated sufficient popular acceptance to enable Contemporary to obtain bookings for a nationwide concert tour. We hold that these additional benefits are too dependent upon taste or fancy to be considered anything other than speculative and uncertain, and, therefore, proof of damage in the form of such lost benefits was properly excluded by Judge Owen.

Id. at 926-927. Was the distinction between fact and amount of damage significant in *Florafax International*?

4. *Limitation of consequential damages to prevent injustice.* In subsection (3) of §351, the drafters of Restatement (Second) have proposed a limitation on consequential damages (and perhaps on other forms of damage as well) in addition to the *Hadley* rule, in cases where "justice so requires in order to avoid disproportionate compensation." Comment *f* expands somewhat on this open-ended criterion, by indicating that the limitation is intended to apply in cases where there is extreme disproportion between the price charged by the defendant under the contract in question and the liability sought to be imposed on it. The comment also suggests that informality of agreement and a noncommercial setting ought to be factors tending toward application of the suggested limitation. Professor Farnsworth, Reporter for this portion of Restatement (Second), concedes that §351(3)'s "frank recognition of the judicial reluctance" to award damages that are disproportionate to the consideration paid is "untraditional." He explains the proposed rule as being designed to permit the courts to do overtly what they have in many cases accomplished covertly through particularly rigorous application of the foreseeability and certainty tests. E. Allan Farnsworth, Contracts §12.17, at 808-810 (4th ed. 2004). Because Section 351(3) is unconventional, only a few courts have relied on it to

limit recovery of consequential damages. See Totaro, Duffy, Cannova and Co., L.L.C. v. Lane, Middleton & Co., L.L.C., 921 A.2d 1100 (N.J. 2007).

5. *Proof of lost profits.* As *Florafax International* shows, proof of lost profits typically requires expert testimony, and experts can vary widely in their assumptions and in their resulting projections of future lost profits. In computing expected lost profits, the plaintiff is only entitled to recover net as opposed to gross profits. See footnote 5 of the opinion. Why should this be the case? The court in *Florafax International* affirmed the jury's award of $820,000 in expenses for setting up a call center to perform functions that GTE had contracted to perform. Was the award of these expenses inconsistent with the principle that the injured party is only entitled to recover net profits?

Breach of a commercial contract can lead to lost profit as in *Florafax International.* Sometimes the injured party will claim that the breach of contract resulted in a decline of the value of that party's business. In such cases care must be taken to avoid double recovery. The plaintiff is generally not entitled to recover both the decline in market value of its business and the present value of the future net income from the business because these two methods are normally alternative ways of measuring the same injury. "According to economic theory, . . . market price should be approximately equal to the present value of all the income that can be derived far into the future from the business." Johnson v. Oroweat Foods Co., 785 F.2d 503, 507 (4th Cir. 1986). In practice, however, these two measures may differ quite substantially. For example, in Protectors Insurance Service, Inc. v. U.S. Fidelity & Guar. Co., 132 F.3d 612 (10th Cir. 1998), the plaintiff's expert testified that the decline in market value of the plaintiff's insurance agency resulting from the defendant's breach of contract was $35,000. Other evidence projected plaintiff's lost profits at $809,650. The Tenth Circuit reversed the jury's special verdict allowing both measures of damages and instead awarded the plaintiff $35,000. The court indicated that decline in market value was the preferred measure, and that lost profits should be awarded only "where no other reliable method of valuing the business is available." Id. at 618.

6. *The new business rule.* Plaintiffs have traditionally encountered great difficulty in recovering lost profits in a new business venture, or at least a new one for the plaintiff, with no history of prior profitability. Over the years courts have been unreceptive to such claims, often denying recovery as a matter of law for lost profits suffered by new businesses, an approach that came to be referred to as the "new business rule." Many recent decisions, however, have rejected a strict application of this rule and have allowed new businesses to recover lost profits provided that they are proved with reasonable certainty. See Erdman Co. v. Phoenix Land & Acquisition, LLC, 2013 U.S. Dist. LEXIS 100434 (W.D. Ark.) (recognizing that majority of courts have rejected strict application of a new business rule).

7. *Consequential damages in other cases.* Consequential damage claims can arise in a wide variety of cases. In a lending contract, the borrower may claim that

the lender's breach of the contract caused it to lose not only a favorable interest rate on the loan (general damages) but also profits from transactions that were prevented because the funds from the loan were unavailable. Such claims may run afoul of the requirements of mitigation (the borrower should have and could have borrowed money elsewhere, even if it had to pay a higher rate of interest, to mitigate the injury from the lender's breach) or foreseeability (the lender did not have reason to foresee that the borrower would be unable to obtain needed funds from any other source). The Restatement in Comment *e* to §351 indicates that consequential damages may be recovered in some cases for breach of a contract to lend money, and courts have allowed such awards if the requirements of mitigation, foreseeability, and certainty have been met. See, e.g., Basic Capital Management, Inc. v. Dynex Commercial, Inc., 348 S.W.3d 894 (Tex. 2011) (consequential damages may be recovered as foreseeable result of breached financing agreement if lender knew purpose of loan at time contract was made and that only less favorable financing alternatives would likely be available).

In some cases employees have claimed as consequential damages harm to their reputation flowing from the employer's breach. Such claims have usually been made by employees in professions where reputation is particularly important, such as acting or the media. English courts have allowed such claims, but American courts have been much less willing to do so unless the employee can show the loss of a particular opportunity, not simply harm to the employee's general reputation. Compare Herbert Clayton & Jack Waller, Ltd. v. Oliver, [1930] A.C. 209 (employee entitled not only to lost salary but also to compensation for the loss of valuable publicity), with Ericson v. Playgirl, Inc., 140 Cal. Rptr. 921, 926 (Ct. App. 1977) (defendant not liable to plaintiff for failure to feature his nude photo on cover of its Best of Playgirl magazine, as promised; value to plaintiff of lost publicity too "speculative and conjectural" — "as unpredictable as the lottery and the roulette wheel"), and Redgrave v. Boston Symphony Orchestra, Inc., 855 F.2d 888 (1st Cir. 1988), *cert. denied,* 488 U.S. 1043 (1989) (actress could recover consequential damages for loss of "identifiable professional opportunities," as contrasted with harm to her general reputation, when symphony canceled her appearance allegedly because of political statements; recovery of damages not subject to higher standard applicable to First Amendment claims because BSO's cancellation was not "symbolic speech").

C. RESTRICTIONS ON THE RECOVERY OF EXPECTATION DAMAGES: MITIGATION OF DAMAGES

In the preceding section we considered various rules that courts may employ to calculate the amount of the plaintiff's "loss in value" or "other loss," as Restatement (Second) §347 uses those terms. There are, however, a number of off-setting factors that may have the effect of reducing the plaintiff's recovery or even eliminating it altogether. At this point, we turn our attention to those minus factors, items that are to be subtracted from "total loss" in calculating the damages the plaintiff ought to receive. Restatement (Second) §347 refers to these generally as "cost avoided" and "loss avoided"; they are often referred to in the cases and commentary as instances of "mitigation of damages."

The field of tort law is studded with principles that — whether expressed in terms of "contributory negligence," "comparative negligence," "assumption of the risk," or some other label — reflect a common theme: Even if the defendant's actions have caused harm to the plaintiff, the defendant need not compensate the plaintiff to the extent that the plaintiff's own actions were a contributing cause of her injury. Given the apparent strength of this principle in Anglo-American jurisprudence, it should not be surprising to find the same notion expressed in the rules of contract law. Here, however, the principle is commonly stated as one of "mitigation" (sometimes "minimization") of damages: The plaintiff may not recover for those injurious consequences of the defendant's breach that the plaintiff herself could by reasonable action have avoided. This principle is also referred to — for obvious reasons — as the doctrine of "avoidable consequences."

We have seen in the example considered earlier that when the owner without justification repudiates a partially completed construction contract, the breach will represent a "loss in value" to the builder (the unpaid portion of the total price), but it will also present an opportunity for savings. Thus, the builder will be freed from the necessity of expending whatever additional sums it would have cost to complete its own performance ("cost avoided"); it may also have the ability to recoup some of the expenditures already made, by reselling materials purchased, or by applying them to some other job ("loss avoided"). These savings are to be deducted from the aggregate loss suffered in order to compute the plaintiff's net recovery.

These principles of loss avoidance will be honored throughout the area of contract remedies, but their application will vary according to the type of case under consideration. Thus, personal service contracts present different opportunities for loss avoidance than do other types of contracts; land transactions have their own traditional governing rules; difficult problems of cost allocation may be presented where an enterprise is involved in performing several different contracts at once. The cases and materials below explore some of these problems.

Rockingham County v. Luten Bridge Co.

United States Court of Appeals 35 F.2d 301 (4th Cir. 1929)

PARKER, Circuit Judge.

This was an action at law instituted in the court below by the Luten Bridge Company, as plaintiff, to recover of Rockingham county, North Carolina, an amount alleged to be due under a contract for the construction of a bridge.

The county admits the execution and breach of the contract, but contends that notice of cancellation was given the bridge company, before the erection of the bridge was commenced, and that it is liable only for the damages which the company would have sustained, if it had abandoned construction at that time.

[Plaintiff Luten Bridge Co. had entered into a contract to build a bridge for Rockingham County. This contract had been originally authorized by a 3 to 2 vote of the Rockingham County Commission. For some reason, feelings apparently ran high on this topic within the Commission — so high, in fact, that one of the three-member majority that voted for the Luten contract resigned his seat shortly thereafter. Although he later changed his mind and attempted to retract that resignation, neither he nor the other two proponents of the Luten contract attended any further meetings. As a result, the two-person minority, augmented by a new third member, undertook to function as the County Commission. Instructing Luten to stop work on the bridge contract, they took the position that the contract was not binding on the county and that in any case it would not be honored. Luten, gambling perhaps on the possibility that the earlier majority would act to regain control of the Commission, continued with the construction of the bridge. In Luten's eventual suit to recover damages for the county's asserted breach of contract, it was held on appeal that the repudiation of Luten's contract amounted to a total breach of contract on the

Mebane Bridge, in Rockingham County, North Carolina, in 2016.

part of the county. The court then had to consider what damages the plaintiff should recover for this breach. — EDS.]

Coming, then, to the third question — i.e., as to the measure of plaintiff's recovery — we do not think that, after the county had given notice, while the contract was still executory, that it did not desire the bridge built and would not pay for it, plaintiff could proceed to build it and recover the contract price. It is true that the county had no right to rescind the contract, and the notice given plaintiff amounted to a breach on its part; but, after plaintiff had received notice of the breach, it was its duty to do nothing to increase the damages flowing therefrom. If *A* enters into a binding contract to build a house for *B*, *B*, of course, has no right to rescind the contract without *A's* consent. But if, before the house is built, he decides he does not want it, and notifies *A* to that effect, *A* has no right to proceed with the building and thus pile up damages. His remedy is to treat the contract as broken when he receives the notice, and sue for the recovery of such damages as he may have sustained from the breach, including any profit which he would have realized upon performance, as well as any other losses which may have resulted to him. In the case at bar, the county decided not to build the road of which the bridge was to be a part, and did not build it. The bridge, built in the midst of the forest, is of no value to the county because of this change of circumstances. When, therefore, the county gave notice to the plaintiff that it would not proceed with the project, plaintiff should have desisted from further work. It had no right thus to pile up damages by proceeding with the erection of a useless bridge.

The contrary view was expressed by Lord Cockburn in Frost v. Knight, L.R. 7 Ex. 111, but, as pointed out by Prof. Williston (Williston on Contracts, vol. 3, p. 2347), it is not in harmony with the decisions in this country. The American rule and the reasons supporting it are well stated by Prof. Williston as follows:

> There is a line of cases running back to 1845 which holds that, after an absolute repudiation or refusal to perform by one party to a contract, the other party cannot continue to perform and recover damages based on full performance. This rule is only a particular application of the general rule of damages that a plaintiff cannot hold a defendant liable for damages which need not have been incurred; or, as it is often stated, the plaintiff must, so far as he can without loss to himself, mitigate the damages caused by the defendant's wrongful act. The application of this rule to the matter in question is obvious. If a man engages to have work done, and afterwards repudiates his contract before the work has been begun or when it has been only partially done, it is inflicting damage on the defendant without benefit to the plaintiff to allow the latter to insist on proceeding with the contract. The work may be useless to the defendant, and yet he would be forced to pay the full contract price. On the other hand, the plaintiff is interested only in the profit he will make out of the contract. If he receives this it is equally advantageous for him to use his time otherwise.

The leading case on the subject in this country is the New York case of Clark v. Marsiglia, 1 Denio (N.Y.) 317, 43 Am. Dec. 670. In that case defendant had employed plaintiff to paint certain pictures for him, but countermanded the order before the work was finished. Plaintiff, however, went on and completed the work and sued for the contract price. In reversing a judgment for plaintiff, the court said:

> The plaintiff was allowed to recover as though there had been no countermand of the order; and in this the court erred. The defendant, by requiring the plaintiff to stop work upon the paintings, violated his contract, and thereby incurred a liability to pay such damages as the plaintiff should sustain. Such damages would include a recompense for the labor done and materials used, and such further sum in damages as might, upon legal principles, be assessed for the breach of the contract; but the plaintiff had no right, by obstinately persisting in the work, to make the penalty upon the defendant greater than it would otherwise have been.

And the rule as established by the great weight of authority in America is summed up in the following statement in 6 R.C.L. 1029, which is quoted with approval by the Supreme Court of North Carolina in the recent case of Novelty Advertising Co. v. Farmers' Mut. Tobacco Warehouse Co., 186 N.C. 197, 119 S.E. 196, 198:

> While a contract is executory a party has the power to stop performance on the other side by an explicit direction to that effect, subjecting himself to such damages as will compensate the other party for being stopped in the performance on his part at that stage in the execution of the contract. The party thus forbidden cannot afterwards go on, and thereby increase the damages, and then recover such damages from the other party. The legal right of either party to violate, abandon, or renounce his contract, on the usual terms of compensation to the other for the damages which the law recognizes and allows, subject to the jurisdiction of equity to decree specific performance in proper cases, is universally recognized and acted upon.

. . . We have carefully considered the cases . . . upon which plaintiff relies; but we do not think that they are at all in point. . . . In the opinions in all of these some language was used which lends support to plaintiff's position, but in none of them was the point involved which is involved here, viz. whether, in application of the rule which requires that the party to a contract who is not in default do nothing to aggravate the damages arising from breach, he should not desist from performance of an executory contract for the erection of a structure when notified of the other party's repudiation, instead of piling up damages by proceeding with the work. As stated above, we think that reason and authority require that this question be answered in the affirmative. It follows that there was error in directing a verdict for plaintiff for the full amount of its claim. The measure of plaintiff's damage, upon its appearing that notice was duly given not to build the bridge, is an amount sufficient to compensate plaintiff for labor and materials expended and expense incurred in the part performance of the contract, prior to its repudiation, plus the profit which would have been realized if it had been carried out in accordance with its terms. See Novelty Advertising Co. v. Farmers' Mut. Tobacco Warehouse Co., supra.

Our conclusion, on the whole case, is that there was error in failing to strike out the answer of Pruitt, Pratt, and McCollum, and in admitting same as evidence against the county, in excluding the testimony offered by the county to which we have referred, and in directing a verdict for plaintiff. The judgment below will accordingly be reversed, and the case remanded for a new trial.

Reversed.

NOTES AND QUESTIONS

1. *Counseling Luten.* As noted in the summary of facts above, plaintiff Luten appears to have gambled that its friends would be able to reestablish their control over the Rockingham County Commission. While that never happened, the action of the remaining county commissioners in repudiating the county's contract with the plaintiff was held eventually to have been a breach of that contract (albeit a valid exercise of governmental authority). If the court had held instead that this attempted repudiation of the Luten contract was not in legal contemplation an act of the county commission, what would have been the outcome of this suit? If you represented a modern-day Luten Bridge Co., facing such turmoil in the county commission, what course of action would you advise?

2. *The mitigation principle.* The principle applied by the court in *Rockingham County* is often referred to as the "duty to mitigate damages." As numerous commentators have pointed out, however, it is not strictly speaking a "duty" at all, in the legal sense, any more than the plaintiff in a tort action has a "duty" not to add to his own injury by being contributorily negligent. It is rather a limitation on the plaintiff's right to recover damages. If the plaintiff in a contract action reasonably could have mitigated his damages, but fails to do so, then — as in the *Rockingham County* case — he will be unable to shift that portion of his loss to the defendant and will be forced to absorb it himself. See Joseph M. Perillo, 11 Corbin on Contracts §57.11 (2005 ed.), Restatement (Second) §350, Comment *b.*

Maness v. Collins

Tennessee Court of Appeals 2010 WL 4629614 (2010)

HOLLY M. KIRBY, J., delivered the opinion of the Court, in which DAVID R. FARMER, J., and J. STEVEN STAFFORD, J., joined.

HOLLY M. KIRBY, J:

This appeal involves an employment contract. The plaintiff employee owned a manufacturing business. He sold the business to the defendant new owners, and agreed to stay on as a management-level employee. To that end, the plaintiff entered into a three-year employment agreement with the company, and signed a non-competition agreement. After a few months, the company's new owners terminated the plaintiff employee on the basis that he had not fulfilled his job duties. The plaintiff filed this lawsuit against the company and the new owners, alleging breach of the employment agreement. . . .

FACTS AND PROCEEDINGS BELOW

Plaintiff/Appellant Sammie Maness ("Maness"), in his 50s at all pertinent times, lived most of his life in McNairy County, Tennessee. Much of his work life was spent doing hourly work, such as construction, maintenance, working as a mill operator, or working as a carpenter. In 1997, Maness incorporated his own wood manufacturing business in Adamsville, Tennessee, making table tops for a local sewing company. For a couple of years, Maness worked part-time for his new business. In time, the sewing company business diminished, but Maness's new company began making wooden bases and support parts for bath tubs for Aqua Glass, a local company whose business apparently involved manufacturing bath tubs. As the work from Aqua Glass increased, by 1999, Maness's company became his full-time occupation. In 2001, Maness's manufacturing company, Plaintiff SKM Wood Products, LLC ("SKM"), moved to a new facility in Adamsville. Within several years, SKM grew to have annual sales of several million dollars, with approximately twenty-five employees. SKM's primary customer remained bath tub manufacturer Aqua Glass.

In 2005, Defendant/Appellee Joannie Collins ("Collins") approached Maness about the possibility of purchasing SKM.[1] After several meetings, Collins told Maness that her brother-in-law, Defendant/Appellee Mike Smith ("Mike Smith"), and his son, Collins' nephew, Defendant/Appellee Josh Smith ("Josh Smith"), would be her partners in purchasing and operating the business. Mike Smith took the lead role in negotiating the sale. Not long before the negotiations began, Josh Smith was hospitalized for treatment for drug addiction issues; this fact was not disclosed to Maness during the negotiations.

The three purchasers expected to take on different roles in the newly acquired business. Collins, a certified public accountant, expected to maintain her full-time employment as a financial advisor and handle the new business's payroll and financial matters on a part-time basis. Similarly, Mike Smith expected to keep his full-time employment elsewhere and work part-time at SKM. Josh Smith had a college degree in business and marketing and had worked for a woodworking company; he was expected to be the "managing member," that is, to work full-time at SKM, supervising and managing

1. Collins had been a friend of Maness's deceased wife. Maness had known both Collins and Mike Smith for many years. Prior to 2005, Collins and Mike Smith, with others, approached Maness about investing in SKM, but nothing was done at that time.

the day-to-day operations. Part of Mike Smith's motivation in acquiring SKM was to have a business for Josh Smith as well as his other son. All parties expected that, after the acquisition, Maness would remain with SKM as an employee.

In anticipation of the acquisition, in the fall of 2005, Josh Smith was hired by SKM and began working under Maness's supervision. Maness was somewhat disappointed by Josh Smith's job performance at that point, but the record does not indicate that he voiced any concerns about Josh Smith to any of the purchasers.

On January 13, 2006, the parties executed an asset purchase agreement under which [SKM Wood Products, LLC's] assets were sold to SKM, LLC, with Collins, Mike Smith, and Josh Smith as guarantors.[2] Part of the total $1,300,000 purchase price was paid by a $300,000 promissory note guaranteed by Collins, Mike Smith, and Josh Smith. The new ownership of SKM was structured such that Collins owned one-third, Mike Smith owned one-third, and Josh Smith owned one-third.

The asset purchase agreement provided for SKM to employ Maness for three years, at an annual salary of $67,600. It stated:

> As an integral part of this Agreement, the Purchaser [SKM, LLC] agrees to employ Sammie Maness, with the beginning date of such employment to be the date of the closing of this transaction for a period thereafter of not less than three (3) years, provided that the Company shall maintain the current sales volume and for so long as the Company shall not suffer any material interruption of its business by causes beyond its control. During the term of Maness' employment, he shall generally serve as the Company's Production Manager and shall be paid an annual salary of Sixty-Seven Thousand Six Hundred Dollars ($67,600.00). . . .

Attached to the asset purchase agreement was a job description for Maness as an employee of SKM.[3]

On the same day, in conjunction with the asset purchase agreement, Maness also signed a non-competition and non-solicitation agreement. The non-competition provision stated that Maness would not:

> . . . for a period of five (5) years following his termination of employment, for whatever reasons, with SKM, LLC by himself or by or through any other person or entity, whether as a shareholder, owner partner, joint venturer, employee, agent, contractor, consultant, directly or indirectly compete with the Company within the Restricted Area. The "Restricted Area" shall mean within the continental United States of America.

2. After the acquisition, the name of the business was changed to SKM, LLC. For simplicity, in this opinion, we shall continue to refer to the business as "SKM."

3. The job description states that Maness was to: [1] Schedule the cutting department; [2] Work with Josh Smith on purchasing and scheduling incoming materials; [3] Coordinate maintenance on all equipment, forklifts, and vehicles; [4] Work with Chad Smith on maintenance and training on safety and OSHA compliance; [5] Work with Josh Smith, so he can schedule the frame-line, panel saw, and CNC; [6] Work on special projects; [7] Work with Josh Smith on developing new business; and [8] Train all new hires.

Thus, the noncompetition agreement had a geographic area of the entire continental United States, for a time period of five years after Maness's employment with SKM ended.

On the effective date of the asset purchase agreement, in mid-January 2006, Maness began his employment as SKM's Production Manager. As expected, Collins and Mike Smith worked at SKM no more than a few hours per week. Josh Smith worked full-time at SKM. At the time of the purchase, most of SKM's sales came from customer Aqua Glass. A primary aim of purchasers Collins, Mike Smith and Josh Smith was to bring in additional customers and to diversify SKM's customer base.

Initially, the parties' working relationship was reasonably harmonious. However, conflicts quickly arose. As Maness continued to discipline employees as he always had, the new owners perceived his interactions with the employees as unacceptably confrontational. Maness felt that, under the new ownership, SKM's employees became increasingly disrespectful toward him.

The problems came to a head in March 2006, when Maness fired an employee after a heated confrontation in which the employee spoke to Maness in a manner that he perceived as disrespectful of his authority. Afterward, the new owners admonished Maness for the termination and rehired the employee. The new owners indicated to Maness that he did not have the authority to discharge employees.

Maness's working relationship with the new owners deteriorated precipitously after that. By all accounts, Maness became unhappy and did much less work, spending considerable time in his office, essentially idle. The parties disputed the reason for Maness's behavior.

Finally, on May 16, 2006, the new owners terminated Maness's employment with SKM. As reason for termination, the termination notice stated: "Have not fulfilled job duties, according to our original agreement, your actions and attitude have been detrimental to the success of this Company."

On July 6, 2006, Maness filed a lawsuit in the Chancery Court of McNairy County against Collins, Mike Smith, Josh Smith, and SKM, LLC. The complaint alleged breach of Maness's employment agreement, and asserted that the non-competition agreement was unenforceable. The complaint sought a judgment for the unpaid compensation under Maness's employment contract, prejudgment interest, post-judgment interest, attorney fees and costs, as well as a declaration that the non-competition agreement was unenforceable. . . .

Maness testified at the outset of the trial. Prior to the acquisition, Maness said, Josh Smith was not a particularly good employee, but Maness was able to work with him on some tasks. After the acquisition, as Maness would walk through the plant correcting employees on transgressions such as safety violations, Maness noticed that the employees acted in an increasingly disrespectful and belligerent manner towards him. After Maness fired the disrespectful problem employee and the new owners reinstated him, Maness said, he told the new owners that they had undercut his authority. Maness said that the new owners responded by telling him that he no longer had the authority to discipline or terminate employees.

After that, Maness claimed, Josh Smith held a meeting with the SKM employees in which he told them that Maness no longer had any authority to correct employees or tell them what to do. Josh Smith did not inform Maness of this meeting. Maness alleged that "every time [he] tried to do anything, correct people, quality, safety or anything, [he] was told that wasn't [his] job, [and] not to do it." When he complained, Maness claimed, Mike Smith told him to just stay in his office at his desk and draw his money.

Subsequently, on an occasion when Maness came to SKM at an unusually early hour, he observed Josh Smith in what appeared to be a drug transaction. He told Collins what he had seen. Not long after that, the new owners terminated Maness's employment.

On cross-examination, Maness conceded that the new owners told him that his management style was too confrontational; Maness disagreed with their characterization. He also admitted that the new owners wanted to expand SKM's customer base beyond Aqua Glass, and that he did not care about such expansion.

Since his employment with SKM ended, Maness said, he had not been employed. Maness conceded that, after his termination, he did not seek new employment, but instead focused on building a new house for himself.

After Maness's testimony, a former SKM employee testified that Josh Smith talked with him about ideas for getting Maness to leave SKM. The former employee corroborated Maness's testimony that Josh Smith held a meeting at which SKM employees were told that Maness was no longer an owner, so they did not need to listen to him. Another former SKM employee testified that, several weeks after the acquisition, Josh Smith told employees that Maness would not be with SKM much longer. Both former employees described Josh Smith's extensive drug use while on the job at SKM and his drug transactions with SKM employees. That concluded Maness's case-in-chief.

Collins and Mike Smith both testified that the working relationship with Maness started amicably, but soon inexplicably deteriorated. Both acknowledged that their work time at the SKM plant was limited; for information on Maness's job performance, they relied in part on Josh Smith and others. . . .

Collins and Mike Smith both testified that Maness was resistant to the new owners' efforts to get customers beyond Aqua Glass. Both maintained that, after SKM decided to rehire the problem employee whom Maness had fired, Maness's work attitude soured and he essentially stopped working. Collins testified that Maness "sulked up like an old possum." Mike Smith denied telling Maness to just sit in his office and draw his pay. Both Collins and Mike Smith insisted that there was just cause to terminate Maness's employment.

Josh Smith testified as well. He said that his drug problems begin in 2005, and that he was addicted to a variety of drugs, prescription and otherwise. . . . Josh Smith admitted that he used drugs on the premises of SKM throughout his employment there. He denied buying or selling drugs on the premises of SKM, and maintained that his drug use did not affect his work performance.

. . . [Josh Smith] maintained that Maness was often confrontational with the employees, and that Maness made no attempt to get new customers. After the new owners rehired the employee Maness had fired, Josh Smith testified, Maness did little work, and began spending most of his work time in his office playing solitaire, and repeatedly asking Collins, Mike Smith, and Josh Smith to buy out the remainder of his contract. Josh Smith confirmed that, at this point, he did not want Maness dealing directly with the employees. He testified that the decision to terminate Maness's employment was made by he, Collins and Mike Smith together, and that the decision was not made hastily.

At the conclusion of the testimony, the trial court issued an oral ruling. At the outset of its ruling, the trial court noted that no proof had been presented on the enforceability of the noncompete agreement. Consequently, Maness's claim for declaratory relief on the noncompetition agreement was dismissed without prejudice. The trial court then addressed whether the defendants had breached the employment agreement by terminating Maness's employment.

The trial judge found that Josh Smith was responsible for the daily operations of SKM, and that he suffered from "extreme drug addiction." It found that Maness's work performance was generally satisfactory until the new owners rescinded Maness's firing of the problem employee. After that, the trial court said, "everything went downhill." The trial judge credited the testimony of witnesses who testified that, unbeknownst to Mike Smith and Collins, Josh Smith attempted to undercut Maness's authority and to have Maness's employment terminated. The trial judge observed that Maness, by "sulk[ing] up and sitting at a desk, and saying send me home," conducted himself in a less-than-professional manner, but the trial judge noted as well that Maness was dealing daily with "a drug-addicted business owner," namely, Josh Smith. The trial court found that the defendants did not meet their burden of proof to show just cause for terminating Maness's employment under the employment agreement.

Regarding the issue of damages, the trial court noted that, after his termination, Maness spent a year building a house and did not take any action to seek employment. The trial court found that Maness, as a wrongfully terminated employee, had a duty to mitigate his damages, but instead took no action. At that point, the trial court asked the attorneys for argument on the issue of mitigation of damages. Maness's attorney argued that the defendants' attorney had the burden to show that there was comparable, suitable employment available to Maness, had he looked for a job. Especially in light of the noncompetition agreement, he contended, the defendants' burden was not met. In response, the defendants' attorney argued that, since Maness made no effort to find work, employer SKM had no obligation to show the availability of substantially similar employment in the geographic area. After hearing the arguments, the trial judge determined that, in light of Maness's failure to make any effort to find work, Maness failed to mitigate his damages. It concluded that Maness's failure to mitigate damages prohibited any award for damages. . . .

Maness now appeals, and Collins, Mike Smith, and Josh Smith cross-appeal. . . .

ANALYSIS

BREACH OF EMPLOYMENT CONTRACT

We consider first the issue raised on appeal by [the defendants], that the trial court erred in determining that SKM breached the employment agreement with Maness by terminating Maness's employment without cause. They assert that Maness was terminated for cause, citing the description of good cause for termination contained in Biggs v. Reinsman Equestrian Products, Inc., 169 S.W.3d 218, 221 (Tenn. Ct. App. 2004) . . . ("good cause exists . . . where the discharge is objectively reasonable.").

SKM, Collins, Mike Smith, and Josh Smith acknowledge that the trial court's finding of no cause was based in part on the trial court's assessment of the credibility of the witnesses. They argue that Josh Smith's admitted drug use was no excuse for Maness to "sulk" and refuse to do his job. Relying on Maness's own testimony and the testimony of witnesses credited by the trial court, they argue that the undisputed proof shows that Maness utilized an inappropriately confrontational management style when dealing with SKM employees, and that he spent most of his time at work doing nothing or playing games on his computer. They assert that Maness's "failure to perform express or implied duties" gave SKM the right to terminate his employment contract for cause, prior to the expiration of its term, without incurring liability, citing *Biggs*, 169 S.W.3d at 221. . . .

Tennessee has long adhered to the doctrine of employment-at-will, which recognizes the right of either the employer or the employee to terminate the employment relationship at any time, for good cause, bad cause, or no cause at all, without being guilty of a legal wrong. . . . Cummings, Inc. v. Dorgan, 320 S.W.3d 316, 332 (Tenn. Ct. App. 2009). In Tennessee, employees are presumed to be employed at will in the absence of an agreement for employment for a term certain. [Id.]. . . .

In the case at bar, the asset purchase agreement provides for Maness's employment by SKM for a term of three years. Often, an employment contract for a term certain will expressly provide that the employee may be terminated "for cause" or "for good cause." See, e.g., Worley v. Lister Distribution, Inc., No. E2005-02932-COA-R3-CV, 2006 Tenn. App. LEXIS 419, 2006 WL 1684748 (Tenn. Ct. App. June 20, 2006). In this case, the employment agreement contains no such language. It states only that SKM "agrees to employ [Maness] for a period . . . of not less than three (3) years . . . ." The only stated proviso to SKM's obligation to employ Maness is that SKM maintain its sales volume and not suffer any "material interruption of its business." The record contains no indication of a business interruption for SKM, and the trial court specifically found that SKM's sales volume had increased. The contract indicates no other circumstance under which SKM is relieved of its obligation to employ Maness for the mandated term. Thus, under the plain language of the employment agreement, SKM had an essentially unqualified obligation to employ Maness for a period of three years, at a salary of $67,600 per year. . . .

However, there is authority in Tennessee to the effect that, even where an employment agreement is for a definite term, the employer may nevertheless discharge the employee for just cause. See Trabue, Inc. v. Professional Management-Automotive, Inc., 589 S.W.2d 661, 663 (Tenn. 1970); . . . . Thus, we assume that, despite the unambiguous language in Maness's employment agreement, SKM retained the right to terminate his employment for just cause.

As noted by SKM and the new owners, the trial court found that Maness "was sulked up and sitting at a desk," and "saying send me home." We agree that this indicates that Maness did not perform his job duties under the employment contract. Viewed in isolation, this could be seen as cause for termination under the case law cited by SKM, Collins, Mike Smith, and Josh Smith. See *Biggs*, 169 S.W.3d at 221 ("Sub-performance that compromises the employer's interest or impedes the company's progress will justify the termination for cause.") (citations omitted); . . . .

The trial court, however, did not view Maness's actions in isolation; rather, it viewed Maness's failure to perform his function as Production Manager in the context of the workplace disruption it found that Josh Smith created. . . .

Our courts have recognized that each party to a contract is "under an implied obligation to restrain from doing any act that would delay or prevent the other party's performance of the contract" and that "[e]ach party has the right to proceed free of hindrance by the other party." ACG, Inc. v. Southeast Elevator, Inc., 912 S.W.2d 163, 168 (Tenn. Ct. App. 1995). In German v. Ford, 300 S.W.3d 692, 706 (Tenn. Ct. App. 2009), this Court elaborated on this principle:

> [E]very contract imposes on the parties a duty of good faith and fair dealing in its performance. RESTATEMENT (SECOND) OF CONTRACTS §205 (1981). For example, every contract includes an implied condition that one party will not prevent performance by the other party. See Moody Realty Co. v. Huestis, 237 S.W.3d 666, 678 (Tenn. Ct. App. 2007) (citation omitted). This is easily seen where the prevention of the other party's performance takes the form of active hindrance:
>
> In any kind of contract, if the right of one party to compensation is conditional upon the rendition of some service or other performance by him . . . , it is nearly always a breach of contract for the other party to act so as to prevent . . . the performance of the condition. It is a breach of duty, only because the court finds a promise by implication not to prevent or hinder.
>
> . . .

[300 S.W.3d at 706.] The *German* Court noted the consequence of such active hindrance of the other party's performance of his contractual obligations: "[A]ctive prevention of another's performance . . . may excuse performance by the other party." Id. at 707; . . . .

In the instant case, the trial court made a factual finding that Josh Smith's actions effectively prevented Maness from functioning as a Production Manager for SKM. This factual finding hinged on the trial court's assessment of the witnesses' credibility. Josh Smith's disavowal of any such actions was not credited by the trial court. Instead, the testimony of Maness and the former SKM employees, that Josh Smith fomented dissent against Maness, undercut his authority, and sought to get rid of him, was credited. . . . This means that SKM and the new owners were without cause to terminate his employment, and that Maness may recover under the contract. Therefore, we affirm the finding of the trial court that Maness was terminated from his employment without cause.

MITIGATION OF DAMAGES

. . .

On the substantive issue of mitigation of damages, Maness asserts that the trial court erred in declining to award Maness damages where there was no evidence at trial that comparable, suitable employment was available to Maness. Maness maintains that, under Frye v. Memphis State Univ., 806 S.W.2d 170 (Tenn. 1991), it would have been futile for Maness to seek other employment. Id. at 173. He contends that the noncompetition agreement, prohibiting employment with a competitor anywhere in the United States for a period of five years, prevented him from seeking comparable employment.

Maness asserts that, under *Frye*, "the employer must prove both the availability of suitable and comparable substitute employment and a lack of reasonable diligence on the part of the employee." Id. (citing Rasimas v. Michigan Dep't of Mental Health, 714 F.2d 614, 624 (6th Cir. 1983). Maness argues that at no point during the trial did SKM and the new owners offer evidence of comparable, suitable employment for Maness.

In response, SKM and the new owners note that, without question, Maness had a duty to mitigate his damages, and that it is undisputed that he made no effort whatsoever to find substitute employment. They acknowledge candidly that they offered no proof of suitable, comparable alternative employment available to Maness. They argue somewhat hopefully on appeal that this case would be an excellent opportunity for this Court to adopt the exception noted in the case of Barnes v. Goodyear Tire and Rubber Co., No. W2000-01607-COA-RM-CV, 2001 Tenn. App. LEXIS 384, 2001 WL 568033 (Tenn. Ct. App. May 25, 2001). In *Barnes*, the Court stated:

> Some courts have carved out another exception to the general rule, holding that an employer is released from the duty to prove the availability of substantially equivalent employment if the employer proves that an employee has not made any reasonable efforts to obtain such work. . . . This exception has not been addressed in Tennessee.

2001 Tenn. App. LEXIS 384, [WL] at *6 (citations omitted). The *Barnes* Court declined to adopt the exception based on the facts in that case. 2001 Tenn. App. LEXIS 384, [WL] at *7.

In the alternative, SKM and the new owners argue that Maness should be bound by the following language in the noncompetition agreement: "Maness acknowledges that his skills are such that he could easily find alternative, commensurate employment or work that would not violate the provisions of this Agreement. . . ."

In the instant case, Maness seeks damages for the breach of his employment contract; he contends that, had his employment not been wrongfully terminated, he would have been paid the agreed-upon salary for three years. "Although liability for breach of contract is primarily based on a no-fault principle, . . . a party who has been wronged by a breach of contract may not unreasonably sit idly by and allow damages to accumulate." [Joseph M. Perillo, Calamari And Perillo On Contracts 584 Thomson West (5th ed. 2003).] This is the doctrine of avoidable consequences, often referred to as the plaintiff's obligation to mitigate his damages. See 22 Am. Jur. 2d Damages §§340, 345, 360 (2010). Thus, where a party seeks damages for breach of contract, courts will enforce the plaintiff's duty to mitigate or reduce his damages incurred after the other party's breach. See Feldman 22 Tenn. Prac. Contract Law And Practice §2:32 (2010). In the context of the breach of an employment contract by the employer, the terminated employee's damages "consist of compensation that the employee who has been wrongfully discharged would have received if the contract had been carried out according to its terms, provided that the employee has been unable to find comparable employment . . . ." 22 Am. Jur. 2d §101 (2010). See *Frye*, 806 S.W.2d at 173. . . .

The failure to mitigate damages is an affirmative defense. Id. In Tennessee, "the employer must prove both availability of suitable and comparable substitute employment and a lack of reasonable diligence on the part of the employee." *Frye*, 806 S.W.2d at 173. In light of their failure to proffer evidence of suitable comparable substitute employment for Maness, SKM and the new owners urge this Court to adopt the exception referred to in *Barnes*. We must respectfully decline to do so. First, adopting such an exception renders problematic the calculation of the plaintiff employee's damages. The plaintiff's failure to mitigate his damages does not *per se* preclude him from recovering any damages whatsoever; rather, "recovery is diminished only to the extent that the plaintiff fails to mitigate the damages as they would be mitigated by an ordinary, reasonable person under similar circumstances." 22 Am. Jur. 2d §336 (2010). Thus, only the amount that the plaintiff would have earned in the exercise of reasonable diligence is applied to reduce his contractual damages. See, e.g., *Barnes*, 2001 Tenn. App. LEXIS 384, 2001 WL 568033, at *5 ("A back pay award must be reduced by any . . . amounts that [the employee] could have earned had the employee exercised reasonable diligence.") (citations omitted). Therefore, the plaintiff is precluded from recovering damages *only* if the proof shows that the amount he would have earned in the exercise of reasonable diligence equaled or exceeded the amount he would have earned under the original employment agreement. See, e.g., *Denney*, 2006 Tenn. App. LEXIS 469, 2006 WL 1915303, at *10. If no proof of comparable, suitable substitute employment is presented to the trial court, then the trial court has no basis on which to determine the amount by which the plaintiff's damages should be reduced.

In the alternative, SKM and the new owners argue that the language in the noncompetition agreement, in which Maness "acknowledges . . . that he could easily find alternative, commensurate employment or work," relieves them of the burden of proving suitable, comparable substitute employment for the purpose of mitigation of damages. First, this argument was not raised in the trial court, and consequently cannot appropriately be raised for the first time on appeal. See Coleman Management, Inc. v. Meyer, 304 S.W.3d 340, 355 (Tenn. Ct. App. 2009). Here, not only was the argument not raised to the trial court, but in this case the trial court expressly declined to consider the noncompetition agreement or Maness's request for declaratory relief that it was unenforceable.[8]

Moreover, whatever the effect of such a provision in the consideration of whether the noncompetition agreement is enforceable, it does not obviate the need for the employer to submit evidence of suitable, comparable employment to prove the plaintiff's failure to mitigate damages. As noted above, the plaintiff's recovery is only diminished by the amount he would have earned in the exercise of reasonable diligence. A contractual acknowledgement that he could find "alternative, commensurate employment or work" is not equivalent to a stipulation that Maness would have earned compensation that equaled or exceeded the compensation he would have received pursuant to the employment agreement with SKM. Thus, even if the trial court had been presented with this argument, consideration of the language in the noncompete provision would not have enabled the trial court to determine the *amount* by which Maness's damages should be reduced. Therefore, in the absence of evidence that suitable alternative employment was available to Maness, [the defendants] cannot rely on the affirmative defense of mitigation of damages. . . .

Conclusion

Accordingly, we affirm the trial court's holding that the termination of Maness's employment was a breach of the employment provisions contained in Article 8 of the parties' asset purchase agreement. We reverse the trial court's holding that Maness's failure to mitigate his damages precludes him from recovering any damages for the breach of his employment contract. The cause must be remanded to the trial court for entry of judgment in favor of Maness and for calculation of Maness's damages resulting from the breach of Article 8 of the asset purchase agreement. The Appellees, having failed to offer proof of suitable alternative employment available to Maness in the proceedings below, are precluded on remand from submitting such proof. . . .

8. Such circumstances present particular problems where, as here, the noncompetition agreement is likely unenforceable. While it is conceivable that a draconian noncompetition agreement such as the one in this case might be enforceable in a case involving a high-level executive with a global corporation, it is difficult to imagine that a 25-employee manufacturing company could assert a protectable business interest that would justify a noncompetition agreement with a geographic area of the entire United States for a time period of five years. See generally Columbus Med. Servs., LLC v. Thomas, 308 S.W.3d 368 (Tenn. Ct. App. 2009); . . .

The decision of the trial court is affirmed in part, reversed in part, and remanded, as set forth above. Cost on appeal are to be taxed to Appellees SKM, LLC, Joannie Collins, Mike Smith, and Josh Smith, for which execution may issue, if necessary.

NOTES AND QUESTIONS

1. *Measuring damages for breach by an employer.* The *Maness* court found that the conduct of Sammie Maness in "sulking" and spending long hours "playing solitaire" resulted from his employer's prior bad faith conduct. In that regard, is the court's discussion of the implied duty of good faith consistent with the approach to that concept found in Chapter 6? Are you convinced that the employer breached the contract by terminating Maness?

Once the courts found that the employer breached the contract in this case, the measurement of damages for Sammie Maness appeared rather simple: The amount of salary he would have received during the rest of the contract term minus any sum that was earned or reasonably could have been earned through mitigation. In other cases of employer breach, however, there can be complicated issues concerning how many years an employee would have worked before retirement, whether the employee would have received raises or bonuses, what to do about vacation pay, etc. See, e.g., Havill v. Woodstock Soapstone Company, Inc., 865 A.2d 335 (Vt. 2004).

2. *Employer's burden of proof regarding mitigation.* As a general rule, most courts agree with the *Maness* court that the burden of proving that the employee failed to mitigate damages rests with the employer. See, e.g., Howard Univ. v. Roberts-Williams, 37 A.3d 896 (D.C. 2012) (mitigation is an affirmative defense with burden on the employer). The trial court in *Maness* found that Sammie Maness had failed to make any efforts to mitigate his damages and therefore should recover no damages. Accord, Mihalik v. Credit Agricole Chevreux North America, Inc., 2015 WL 13699239 (S.D.N.Y.). Consistent with the approach of the appellate court in *Maness*, however, many other courts have imposed on the employer the burden of showing not only that the employee failed to act reasonably in seeking other jobs but also that there were comparable positions that could have been obtained. See Ascare v. Mastercard Int'l, Inc., 2012 U.S. Dist. LEXIS 115427 (E.D. Mo. 2012); Bolanos v. Priority Business Services, Inc., 2018 WL 1224655 (Cal. Ct. App.). Do you agree that the burden of proof regarding mitigation should be allocated to the employer even when the employee makes no effort at all?

3. *Statutory rights and mitigation.* The *Maness* case involved a claim by the employee for common law breach of contract. Since the 1960s there has been a proliferation of federal and state statutes intended to protect employees from discrimination on certain prohibited bases. See generally Marcia L. McCormick, The Truth Is Out There: Revamping Federal Antidiscrimination Enforcement

for the Twenty-First Century, 30 Berkeley J. Emp. & Lab. L. 193, 200-204 (2009) (noting federal and sometimes state law offer employee protection based on a number of factors including race, color, religion, national origin, sex, age, and disability). Thus, employees will frequently seek to recover on a statutory basis in addition to or in lieu of breach of contract. In those cases courts tend to require employee mitigation similar to that expected under the common law. See Arbercheski v. Oracle Corp., 650 F. Supp. 2d 309 (S.D.N.Y. 2009) (employee pursuing Title VII discrimination claim had obligation to make reasonable efforts to obtain comparable employment).

4. *Breaching party's offer to mitigate.* In Fair v. Red Lion Inn, 943 P.2d 431 (Colo. 1997) (en banc), Red Lion discharged Fair when she attempted to return to work from a medical leave granted to allow recovery from injuries suffered in an automobile accident. With the assistance of legal counsel, Fair challenged the grounds for her termination and Red Lion offered her old job back. Fair declined the offer because she feared she would be fired again in retaliation for the dispute, she had concerns about physical aspects of her job due to having become pregnant, and she had doubts about her benefits under the proposed reinstatement. Fair brought suit; the jury found Red Lion liable for $140,000 plus interest. The Colorado Supreme Court reversed. The court stated that it did not "question the reasonableness of Fair's apprehensions," but any employee (or for that matter any contracting party) would have apprehensions about the other party' performance after a breach. The court concluded:

> Nonetheless, sound principles of contract law in the commercial and employment setting . . . ordain the principles we acknowledge today: The injured party claiming breach of an employment agreement has a duty to mitigate or minimize damages. In the employment agreement context, such duty includes the acceptance of an unconditional offer of reinstatement where no special circumstances exist to justify rejection.

Id. at 442. What "special circumstances" would justify rejection of an employer's unconditional offer of reemployment? See Restatement (Second) of Contracts §350(1) (damages are not recoverable if they can be avoided without "undue risk, burden or humiliation"); Pyramid Printing Co. v. Alaska State Commission, 153 P.3d 994 (Alaska 2007) (constructively discharged employee not obligated to accept reinstatement offer that would involve substantial contact with supervisor who caused hostile working environment).

5. *The **Parker** case.* In discussing the issue of mitigation, the court in *Maness* also espouses the commonly held view that the employee need only mitigate with alternative work that is "comparable" to the position lost. This limitation on the duty to mitigate was the central issue in the widely discussed decision of the California Supreme Court in Parker v. Twentieth Century-Fox Film Corp., 474 P.2d 689 (Cal. 1970) (en banc). In *Parker*, plaintiff (known professionally as Shirley MacLaine) sued to recover damages for the defendant's breach of a contract to employ her as the star of a major musical motion picture entitled

"Bloomer Girl"; the defendant argued that the plaintiff had rejected a post-breach offer from the defendant to star in a nonmusical motion picture for identical compensation and for that reason should not recover any damages. A majority of the California Supreme Court upheld the trial court's ruling that the second offer was not a truly comparable one, principally because the two pictures were of different types and because the second opportunity did not provide the plaintiff with the same approvals of director, and the like, that she would have had under the first one. In a vigorous dissent, Justice Sullivan had the following to say about the extent of the plaintiff's "duty" to mitigate the loss of her contracted-for employment:

> [The employee need not accept] employment which is of a *different kind*. . . . It has never been the law that the mere existence of *differences between two jobs in the same field* is sufficient, as a matter of law, to excuse an employee wrongfully discharged from one from accepting the other in order to mitigate damages. Such an approach would effectively eliminate any obligation of an employee to attempt to minimize damage arising from a wrongful discharge. The only alternative job offer an employee would be required to accept would be an offer of his former job by his former employer.
>
> Although the majority appear to hold that there was a difference "in kind" between the employment offered plaintiff in "Bloomer Girl" and that offered in "Big Country" . . . , an examination of the opinion makes crystal clear that the majority merely point out differences between the two *films* (an obvious circumstance) and then apodically [sic — apodictically?] assert that these constitute a difference in the *kind* of *employment*. The entire rationale of the majority boils down to this: that the "*mere circumstances*" that "Bloomer Girl" was to be a musical review while "Big Country" was a straight drama "demonstrates the difference in kind" since a female lead in a western is not "the equivalent of or substantially similar to" a lead in a musical. This is merely attempting to prove the proposition by repeating it. . . .

Id. at 696. Justice Sullivan also observed that many of the early cases held that an employee is not required to accept employment in an "inferior rank or position nor work which is more menial or arduous." He suggested that the rule may therefore "have had its origin in the bourgeois fear of resubmergence in lower economic classes." Id. at 695 n.2. Is the dissenting justice in *Parker* right in suggesting that this rule is an outmoded relic of concern for "bourgeois" interests? Or are there persuasive reasons for maintaining such an approach today?

The facts of *Parker* are more complex than the opinions in that case suggest. The original "Bloomer Girl" was a 1944 Broadway musical comedy set at the time of the Civil War and suggested by the career of Amelia Jenks ("Dolly") Bloomer, a nineteenth-century crusader for women's rights. Although essentially light entertainment, it did have strong themes of both feminism and racial justice. Plaintiff Parker (MacLaine) has publicly professed strong commitment to both causes. Would these facts have been relevant to the question of whether for her the second film was indeed a "comparable employment"? (It might also be noted that the full title of the substitute, "western-type" film offered to MacLaine was "Big Country, *Big Man*" (emphasis supplied).) For further discussion of the issues in *Parker*, see Mary Joe Frug, Re-Reading Contracts: A Feminist Analysis of a Contracts Casebook, 34 Am. U. L. Rev. 1065, 1114-1125 (1985).

Professor Victor Goldberg has argued that the *Parker* court was wrong even to apply the doctrine of mitigation of damages, because her contract had a "pay-or-play" clause. Such clauses, which are common in many fields, give one party (Fox in this case) what amounts to an option to either perform under the contract or to pay the amount set forth in the clause. (Recall Sondra Locke's agreement with Warner Brothers discussed in the *Locke* case in Chapter 6.) As Professor Goldberg sees the case, Fox had the right to have MacLaine perform in "Bloomer Girl" or to pay her the contractually agreed upon amount; application of the doctrine of mitigation would have been inappropriate because it would have deprived Parker of a contractual entitlement. Victor P. Goldberg, Bloomer Girl Revisited or How to Frame an Unmade Picture, 1998 Wis. L. Rev. 1051.

6. *Effect of other income.* Even though the wrongfully discharged plaintiff has no "duty" to mitigate by taking employment that is not comparable to that promised by the defendant, if she does indeed take another different job, the amounts earned there from are likely to be set off against her damages recoverable for breach of contract. See, e.g., Marshall School District v. Hill, 939 S.W.2d 319 (Ark. Ct. App. 1997) (wrongfully discharged teacher's recovery reduced by income earned from other jobs, including work in shirt factory); Cheathem v. Los Angeles Unified Sch. Dist., 2017 WL 3498917 (Cal. Ct. App.) (rejecting conflicting authority, court holds amount employee earned from other employment, whether comparable or not, should be deducted from recovery to avoid "windfall"). Why should this be the case? Does this rule undercut the policy, discussed above, of not requiring an employee to seek dissimilar employment when wrongfully discharged? There are, however, some situations in which a new contract entered into after breach will not be considered to be a mitigating one. The next principal case, Jetz Service Co. v. Salina Properties, explores this issue.

7. *Mitigation in the UCC.* Although the Uniform Commercial Code has no provision imposing a general responsibility of mitigation on the parties to a sales contract, Comment 1 to UCC §1-305 indicates this notion was intended to be subsumed in the more general principle that remedies are to be limited to compensation. The Comment also suggests that minimization of damages may be implicit in the more general obligation of good faith imposed by §1-304. The remedies provisions of Article 2 contain a number of specific references to actions by the buyer or the seller intended to have the effect of minimizing the loss or damage incurred by reason of the other party's breach, most specifically §2-715(2)(a), which states that a buyer is not entitled to consequential damages

unless loss could not have been reasonably prevented by making "cover" or a substitute contract. The remedies under Article 2 are discussed in more detail in Section E of this chapter.

8. *Mitigation in real estate leases.* The duty to mitigate has generally not been applied to real estate leases. Reflecting the principle that a lease of land was considered as a conveyance of an interest in real property (rather than merely a contract to permit its occupancy by someone other than the owner), defaulting tenants were traditionally held to their duty to pay the rent in full, with no obligation on the landlord's part to minimize loss by attempting to re-rent to another. See Restatement (Second) of Property §12.1(3) (1977). More recently, most American jurisdictions have by decision or statute adopted the position that real estate leases should be treated more like other contracts, with the landlord in the event of the tenant's abandonment having a "duty to mitigate" similar to that imposed on other contracting parties. See Frenchtown Square Partnership v. Lemstone, 791 N.E.2d 417 (Ohio 2003) (asserting that majority trend favors imposing duty to mitigate in all real property leases).

Not all courts agree with the modern trend, however. In 1995 a unanimous New York Court of Appeals adhered to the traditional rule that a landlord does not have a duty to mitigate damages. Holy Properties Ltd. v. Kenneth Cole Productions, Inc., 661 N.E.2d 694 (N.Y. 1995). See Jeremy Sheff, A Tale of Two Cities: The Residential Landlord's Duty to Mitigate in New York, 25 J. Civ. Rts. & Econ. Dev. 673 (2011) (advocating for equitable flexibility by courts in deciding whether particular residential landlord should have duty to mitigate).

Jetz Service Co. v. Salina Properties

Kansas Court of Appeals 19 Kan. App. 2d 144, 865 P.2d 1051 (1993)

LARSON, Judge:

Salina Properties appeals the damages awarded to Jetz Service Co., Inc., resulting from breach of the parties' lease of space in which coin-operated laundry equipment was installed in an apartment complex.

Jetz Service supplies and maintains coin-operated laundry equipment in approximately 2,000 locations in an eight-state area. It constantly seeks locations for installation of laundry equipment which is furnished from several warehouses in which an inventory of approximately 1,500 used washers and dryers is always available.

In May of 1987, Salina Properties' predecessor in title leased 175 square feet of an apartment complex to Jetz Service for use as a coin-operated laundry facility. Five washing machines and five dryers were installed in November of 1987.

The lease was for a six-year term. Jetz Service paid an initial $3,000 decorating allowance and was entitled to the first $300 per month or 50%, whichever was greater, of the gross receipts from the machines during the term of the lease. The lease stated the parties assumed the duties of a landlord and tenant under the laws of Kansas.

In July of 1992, with 16 months remaining on the term of the lease, Salina Properties disconnected all of Jetz Service's equipment and replaced it with its own laundry equipment.

Jetz Service retrieved its property at a cost of $187.50 and stored the washers and dryers in one of its warehouses. Four sets of the laundry equipment were re-leased in the Kansas City area in January 1993, although other suitable laundry equipment was available to complete this transaction.

Jetz Service sued Salina Properties to recover its lost profits for the remaining 16 months of the lease. It requested damages equal to one-half of the anticipated gross income for the remainder of the lease. Salina Properties raised numerous defenses but essentially relied on its argument that Jetz Services had failed to mitigate its damages and should only recover the cost of moving its equipment.

The trial court determined Jetz Service was a "lost volume" lessee and had sustained loss of profits and damages in the amount Jetz Service requested. Salina Properties received credit for one month of unpaid rent but Jetz Service was granted judgment for damages of $6,383.08 and $2,165 in attorney fees.

Salina Properties appeals the award of damages. It does not contest the trial court's finding that it was subject to the lease and that its actions in removing Jetz Service's property constituted a breach of the lease agreement.

The two principal contentions Salina Properties raises by this appeal are that Jetz Service (1) failed, as a matter of law, to mitigate its damages and (2) failed to prove the requisite elements to recover lost profits. The underlying issue of most importance, however, is the trial court's finding that Jetz Service should be treated as a "lost volume" lessee and is entitled to recover its expected gross receipts for the remaining term of the lease notwithstanding the fact it utilized part of the laundry equipment before the term of the Salina lease expired.

In deciding this case, we must remain mindful of several basic concepts in the assessment of damages.

> The purpose of awarding damages is to make a party whole by restoring that party to the position he or she was in prior to the [breach]. Cerretti v. Flint Hills Rural Electric Co-op Ass'n, 251 Kan. 347, Syl. P 6, 837 P.2d 330 (1992). [T]he injured party should be placed, so far as can be done by a money award, in the same position that he or she would have occupied if the contract had been performed. M & W Development, Inc. v. El Paso Water Co., 6 Kan. App. 2d 735, Syl. P 4, 634 P.2d 166 (1981).

. . .

Kansas courts have long held that lost profits may be recoverable as damages.

> This court follows the general rule that loss of profits resulting from a breach of contract may be recovered as damages when such profits are proved with reasonable certainty, and when they may reasonably be considered to have been within the contemplation of the parties. [Citations omitted.] Recovery for loss of profits caused by a breach of contract depends upon the facts and circumstances of each particular case. Vickers v. Wichita State University, 213 Kan. 614, 618, 518 P.2d 512 (1974).

. . .

Our courts further recognize the general rule of law "that one injured by reason of a breach of contract by another is under a duty to exercise reasonable care to avoid loss or to mitigate and minimize the resulting damage. The injured party is bound to protect himself if he can do so with reasonable exertion or at trifling expense, and can recover from the delinquent party only such damages as he could not, with reasonable effort, have avoided." In re Estate of Stannard, 179 Kan. 394, Syl. P 1, 295 P.2d 610 (1956).

. . .

If we assume a factual finding that Jetz Service made reasonable efforts to reuse the laundry equipment but was unable to do so until January of 1993, the trial court's award of damages for the first six months subsequent to the breach is easily affirmed. We would be required, however, to reduce the award for the damages awarded for the breach of the final 10 months of the lease because 80% (8 of the 10 machines) of the laundry equipment was placed into usage in the Kansas City area lease. We are not willing to reach this result because we agree with the trial court's determination that Jetz Service is a "lost volume" lessee, a concept which has not previously been considered by our Kansas courts.

The term "lost volume" seller is credited to Professor Robert J. Harris of the University of Michigan Law School. See Harris, A Radical Restatement of the Law of Seller's Damages: Sales Act and Commercial Code Results Compared, 18 Stan. L. Rev. 66 (1965); . . . Snyder v. Herbert Greenbaum & Assoc., 38 Md. App. 144, 154 n.3, 380 A.2d 618 (1977).

The "lost volume seller" measure of damages "refers to the lost volume of business the non-breaching seller incurs on buyer's breach. When the seller resells the entity he expected to sell to the original buyer, he usually deprives himself of something of value — the sale to a new buyer of another similar entity." 38 Md. App. at 154 n.3, 380 A.2d 618.

The meaning of the term is shown by the following example:

> To illustrate, assume a contract for the sale of a washing machine with a list price of $500. Assume further that the seller has or can obtain more machines than he can sell. The buyer breaches, and the seller resells that washing machine at the same list price the buyer had been willing to pay. However, the resale buyer is one of seller's regular customers who had intended to purchase a washing machine from him anyway. If the seller's total cost per machine was $300, he stood to gain an aggregate profit of $400, that is, $200 profit from each of two sales. Clearly the 2-708 contract-market differential formula is inadequate in this situation since it gives no damages to the seller who has lost a $200 profit because of the breach. In such a case the damage award should be the lost profit, that is, $200, for this will place the seller "in as good a position as performance would have done." 1 White & Summers, Uniform Commercial Code §7-9, p. 358 (3d ed. 1988).

Salina Properties argues forcefully that the lost volume theory of damage recovery may only be invoked where K.S.A. 84-2-708(2) of the Uniform Commercial Code applies, which it does not in this case because we are dealing with a provider of "services" and not a seller of "goods." K.S.A. 84-2-102.

We agree that Jetz Service does not sell goods, but the underlying concept is analogous; adequate authority exists to apply the lost volume rule to volume providers of services.

. . .

The Restatement (Second) of Contracts §350 Comment *d* (1979) has this to say:

> *Lost volume.* The mere fact that an injured party can make arrangements for the disposition of the goods or services that he was to supply under the contract does not necessarily mean that by doing so he will avoid loss. If he would have entered into both transactions but for the breach, he has "lost volume" as a result of the breach. See Comment *f* to §347. In that case the second transaction is not a "substitute" for the first one.

Section 347 Comment *f* of the Restatement (Second) of Contracts (1979) provides:

> *Lost volume.* Whether a subsequent transaction is a substitute for the broken contract sometimes raises difficult questions of fact. If the injured party could and would have entered into the subsequent contract, even if the contract had not been broken, and could have had the benefit of both, he can be said to have "lost volume" and the subsequent transaction is not a substitute for the broken contract. The injured party's damages are then based on the net profit that he has lost as a result of the broken contract. Since entrepreneurs try to operate at optimum capacity, however, it is possible that an additional transaction would not have been profitable and that the injured party would not have chosen to expand his business by undertaking it had there been no breach. It is sometimes assumed that he would have done so, but the question is one of fact to be resolved according to the circumstances of each case. See Illustration 16. . . .
>
> **Illustration:** 16. A contracts to pave B's parking lot for $10,000. B repudiates the contract and A subsequently makes a contract to pave a similar parking lot for $10,000. A's business could have been expanded to do both jobs. Unless it is proved that he would not have undertaken both, A's damages are based on the net profit he would have made on the contract with B, without regards to the subsequent transaction.

We were not furnished nor did our research reveal any Kansas cases directly on point. We therefore turn to several cases from other jurisdictions, the first being startlingly similar factually.

Although not so named, the status of lost volume lessor was found to apply to a plaintiff who was engaged in the business of leasing coin-operated equipment in Seaboard Music Co. v. Germano, 24 Cal. App. 3d 618, 101 Cal. Rptr. 255 (1972). Seaboard's lease of a coin-operated juke box and pool table was breached by a tavern operator. The tavern owner claimed that Seaboard was required to mitigate damages by re-leasing the equipment. The California court determined the duty to minimize damages did not apply to contracts " 'which do not preclude plaintiff from undertaking and being engaged in the performance contemporaneously of other contracts.' " 24 Cal. App. 3d at 623, 101 Cal. Rptr. 255.

The court found the evidence showed that Seaboard "was engaged in the business of leasing coin-operated equipment; it had a warehouse full of equipment similar to that leased to Ohmer from which it serviced its customers and from which it could service any additional leases negotiated, irrespective of whether Ohmer fulfilled or breached his obligation." 24 Cal. App. 3d at 623, 101 Cal. Rptr. 255.

The court concluded the duty to mitigate damages could not be imposed to deprive Seaboard of the benefit of subsequent contracts which would had been available to it irrespective of the original breach, and the defendants' liability would not be reduced by requiring Seaboard to forego profits that it would otherwise have made in the normal course of business.

In Wired Music, Inc. v. Clark, 26 Ill. App. 2d 413, 168 N.E.2d 736 (1960), the Appellate Court of Illinois determined that when a distributor of music by telephone wires had an unlimited supply of music and was limited in its distribution only by the number of contracts it could secure, the distributor could recover lost profits for the remaining months under a contract from a customer who discontinued service before expiration of the contract period. The fact that the distributor entered into another contract for service at the same location with a new tenant for a higher fee did not relieve the original customer of liability for damages.

. . .

Here, there was substantial competent evidence to support the trial court's determination that Jetz Service was a "lost volume" lessee. The evidence showed that Jetz Service is in the business of supplying coin-operated laundry equipment; it has several warehouses in which it has available for lease about 1,500 used washers and dryers; it continually looks for new locations in which to install laundry equipment; it would have been able to fulfill the Kansas City lease without using the machines from Salina Properties; and it is uncontroverted Jetz Service would have been able to enter into both transactions irrespective of the breach by Salina Properties.

Under appropriate facts such as exist here, lost volume status should be conferred upon one engaged in a service-oriented business. As a lost volume lessee, Jetz Service was not required to mitigate damages by using the equipment in another lease and Salina Properties is not relieved of the liability to pay damages even though Jetz Service did utilize four of the five sets of laundry equipment six months after Salina Properties' breach.

In Haag v. Dry Basement, Inc., 11 Kan. App. 2d 649, 654, 732 P.2d 392, rev. denied 241 Kan. 838 (1987), we stated:

> The determination of the amount of damages is a factual issue, and the trial court's calculation will be upheld if supported by substantial competent evidence. In order for the evidence to be sufficient to warrant a recovery of damages, there must be some reasonable basis for computation which will enable the factfinder to arrive at an approximate estimate thereof.

The calculation of lost future profits was based upon historical past profits generated during the seven month period preceding Salina Properties' breach. We find the amount claimed was proven with reasonable certainty.

Although the parties did not discuss lost profits when the lease was executed, lost profits are presumed to have been contemplated by the parties. The written agreement shows that the lease payments to Salina Properties were based upon the profits expected to be generated under the lease agreement. In this situation, lost profits would have naturally flowed from a breach of the lease agreement. See Farnsworth, Young & Jones, Cases and Materials on Contracts p. 527 (2d ed. 1972).

Salina Properties claims the trial court erred by failing to reduce the damage award by the direct costs of maintenance and insurance Jetz Service saved by its breach. The record shows these were fixed costs not affected by Salina Properties' breach. Fixed expenses or overhead are the continuous expenses of the business, irrespective of the outlay on a particular contract, and includes such expenses as executive and clerical salaries, property taxes, general administrative expenses, etc. Farnsworth, Young & Jones, pp. 474-475. Fixed expenses or overhead are not deducted when computing lost profits. Farnsworth, Young & Jones, p. 475.

We hold the trial court properly applied the status of lost volume lessee to Jetz Service under the facts of this case. There was substantial competent evidence to justify the trial court's findings and judgment.

Affirmed.

NOTES AND QUESTIONS

1. *Mitigating versus additional contracts.* In order for the breaching party to obtain a deduction from its damage liability for income received by the plaintiff from another contract, the breaching party must show that the other contract was a *mitigating contract*, that is, a contract that the plaintiff was able to perform only because the defendant's breach freed the plaintiff from the obligation to perform the original contract. If the court finds that the new contract is an *additional contract* rather than a mitigating one, however (as was the case in *Jetz Service*), the plaintiff is entitled to the profit from both contracts, and the defendant will not have the benefit of any deduction from its damage liability. As the court in *Jetz Service* indicates, whether the contract is mitigating or additional is a question of fact. In Rodriguez v. Learjet, Inc., 946 P.2d 1010 (Kan. Ct. App. 1997), the Kansas Court of Appeals amplified its holding in *Jetz Service.* To establish its status as a lost volume seller, the plaintiff must prove "(1) that it possessed the capacity to make an additional sale, (2) that it would have been profitable for it to make an additional sale, and (3) that it probably would have made an additional sale absent the buyer's breach." Id. at 1015. *Rodriguez* involved a breach of contract to purchase a commercial jet airplane. On the facts of the case Learjet was able to establish that it was a lost volume seller because: (1) it was operating at 60 percent of capacity, (2) accounting

evidence showed that additional sales could be made profitably, and (3) the company sold the jet that was the subject of the contract to another purchaser at a profit.

2. *Lost volume sellers under the UCC.* The Learjet contract in *Rodriguez* was governed by Article 2 of the Uniform Commercial Code since the plane was an item of "goods" as defined in UCC §2-105(1). The courts have been almost unanimous in holding that lost volume sellers of goods, such as Learjet, are entitled to recover their profit under UCC §2-708(2). See James J. White & Robert S. Summers, Uniform Commercial Code §8-9 (6th ed. 2010) (listing cases that have applied §2-708(2) to lost volume sellers). The various remedies available to sellers and buyers under the UCC are discussed later in this chapter.

3. *Application of the mitigation principle to service contracts.* The application of the mitigation principle to service contracts turns on several factors. If the contract is for personal services or employment (as in the *Maness* case), a new contract entered into after the breach will generally be considered to be a mitigating one since an individual has a limited capacity to perform personal services. In some cases, however, it may be possible for the employee or other provider of services to perform both contracts; in that case the second contract will not be considered a mitigating one. For example, in Gianetti v. Norwalk Hosp., 833 A.2d 891 (Conn. 2003), the plaintiff was a staff plastic surgeon at the defendant hospital, but was also on staff at four other hospitals. The defendant hospital was held to have breached its contract with the plaintiff by failing to renew his appointment. The Connecticut Supreme Court then rejected the defendant's argument that the physician could not possibly be a "lost volume seller" as a matter of law. The court held that the plaintiff, as a general proposition, could have continued to perform his contract with the defendant hospital in addition to his contracts with the other hospitals. 833 A.2d at 902. See also Restatement (Second) §347, Comment *e,* Illustration 13. Ultimately, after remand the Connecticut Supreme Court affirmed the award of lost volume seller's damages to the plaintiff, although for a limited number of years. 43 A.3d 567 (Conn. 2012).

When the contract does not require personal services (as was the case in *Jetz Service*), the courts may find it even easier to conclude that a second contract entered into after breach of the first contract is not a mitigating one because the provider of services has the capacity to perform both contracts. The Restatement supports this view. Illustration 10 to §350 provides: "*A* contracts to pay *B* $20,000 for paving *A*'s parking lot, which would give *B* a net profit of $3,000. *A* breaks the contract by repudiating it before *B* begins work. If *B* would have made the contract with *A* in addition to other contracts, *B*'s efforts to obtain other contracts do not affect his damages. *B*'s damages for *A*'s breach of contract include his $3,000 loss of profit." The courts have reached similar decisions. See, e.g., Harvey v. Timber Resources, Inc., 37 S.W.3d 814 (Mo. Ct. App. 2001) (plaintiff contractor entitled to lost profits on timber cutting contract; could have performed both the breached contract and a subsequent contract in the requisite time frame); Kllm Transport Services, LLC

v. JBS Carriers, Inc., 2015 WL 11005024 (S.D. Miss.) (question of fact whether trucking company could and would have performed other contracts in addition to the breached one; different tests for "lost volume seller" status discussed and compared).

4. *Calculation of lost profit.* If the new contract is viewed as an additional rather than a mitigating contract, the plaintiff is entitled to her "lost profit" from the original contract without deduction of the amount received from the new contract. The determination of lost profit, however, can be tricky. According to standard accounting principles, "profit" means gross income minus cost of the transaction. What is included in the term "cost"? Certain types of costs vary with the particular transaction ("variable costs," in accounting terminology), while other costs, such as mortgage expenses, officers' salaries, and general administrative expenses are "fixed costs." The court in *Jetz Service* awarded the plaintiff its "gross profit," defined as gross income less variable costs but without any deduction for a portion of fixed costs that could be allocated to the transaction. However, the determination of lost profits will inevitably turn on the facts of each case. See Gianetti v. Norwalk, Hosp., 43 A.3d 567, 598-601 (Conn. 2012) (adopting "average market approach" to determine plaintiff's net profits).

D. NONRECOVERABLE DAMAGES: ITEMS COMMONLY EXCLUDED FROM PLAINTIFF'S DAMAGES FOR BREACH OF CONTRACT

It was earlier suggested that the conventional rule governing contract damages implies both a floor and a ceiling: A plaintiff should ordinarily recover *at least* her expectation damages; on the other hand, a plaintiff should not recover anything *more* than that. As we have seen, a plaintiff's claim for expectation damages will be weighed in light of the doctrine of avoidable consequences; it will also be limited by the requirement that damages be foreseeable (at least where they are "special" or "consequential") and proven with reasonable certainty. As a result, in many cases the damages actually recoverable will in fact fall short of the true "expectation" of gain that the contract created.

In this section, we consider three types of damage recovery usually denied to a plaintiff in ordinary actions at common law for breach of contract (although they may be recoverable in other kinds of actions or specifically provided for by statute): damages to compensate the plaintiff for amounts expended on attorney fees; damages for mental distress (and related types of intangible, "noneconomic" injury); and "punitive" (or "exemplary") damages. In some instances, denial of such recovery will further depress the plaintiff's award of damages below the level that true expectation would require. (E.g., inability of the plaintiff to recover the full cost of litigation occasioned by the breach means that even if an otherwise fully compensatory damage award is granted, the plaintiff necessarily will be left worse off than she would have been if the contract had been performed.) In other cases, to award such damages might well bring the plaintiff's recovery *above* the net-expectation level. (This is particularly likely to be true of a sizeable award of punitive damages.) Recent developments suggest that these conventional rules of nonliability are not beyond question. Some evidence of this gradual shift in attitudes may be seen in the materials that follow.

Zapata Hermanos Sucesores, S.A. v. Hearthside Baking Company, Inc.

United States Court of Appeals 313 F.3d 385 (7th Cir. 2002), cert. denied, 540 U.S. 1068 (2003)

POSNER, Judge.

Zapata, a Mexican corporation that supplied Lenell, a U.S. wholesale baker of cookies, with cookie tins, sued Lenell for breach of contract and won. The district judge ordered Lenell to pay Zapata $550,000 in attorneys' fees. From that order, which the judge based both on a provision of the Convention on Contracts for the International Sale of Goods, Jan. 1, 1988, 15 U.S.C. App., and on the inherent authority of the courts to punish the conduct of litigation in bad faith, Lenell appeals.

The Convention, of which both the U.S. and Mexico are signatories, provides, as its name indicates, remedies for breach of international contracts for the sale of goods. Zapata brought suit under the Convention for money due under 110 invoices, amounting to some $900,000 (we round liberally), and also sought prejudgment interest plus attorneys' fees, which it contended are "losses" within the meaning of the Convention and are therefore an automatic entitlement of a plaintiff who prevails in a suit under the Convention. At the close of the evidence in a one-week trial, the judge granted judgment as a matter of law for Zapata on 93 of the 110 invoices, totaling $850,000. Zapata's claim for money due under the remaining invoices was submitted to the jury, which found in favor of Lenell. Lenell had filed several counterclaims; the judge dismissed some of them and the jury ruled for Zapata on the others. The jury also awarded Zapata $350,000 in prejudgment interest with respect to the 93 invoices as to which Zapata had prevailed, and the judge then tacked on the attorneys' fees — the entire attorneys' fees that Zapata had incurred during the litigation.

Article 74 of the Convention provides that "damages for breach of contract by one party consist of a sum equal to the loss, including loss of profit, suffered by the other party as a consequence of the breach," provided the consequence was foreseeable at the time the contract was made. Article 7(2) provides that "questions concerning matters governed by this Convention which are not expressly settled in it are to be settled in conformity with the general principles on which it is based or, in the absence of such principles, in conformity with the law applicable by virtue of the rules of private international law [i.e., conflicts of law rules]." There is no suggestion in the background of the Convention or the cases under it that "loss" was intended to include attorneys' fees, but no suggestion to the contrary either. Nevertheless it seems apparent that "loss" does not include attorneys' fees incurred in the litigation of a suit for breach of contract, though certain prelitigation legal expenditures, for example expenditures designed to mitigate the plaintiff's damages, would probably be covered as "incidental" damages. Sorenson v. Fio Rito, 90 Ill. App. 3d 368, 45 Ill. Dec. 714, 413 N.E.2d 47, 50-52 (1980); cf. Tull v. Gundersons, Inc., 709 P.2d 940, 946 (Colo. 1985); Restatement (Second) of Contracts §347, comment *c* (1981).

The Convention is about contracts, not about procedure. The principles for determining when a losing party must reimburse the winner for the latter's expense of litigation are usually not a part of a substantive body of law, such as contract law, but a part of procedural law. For example, the "American rule," that the winner must bear his own litigation expenses, and the "English rule" (followed in most other countries as well), that he is entitled to reimbursement, are rules of general applicability. They are not field-specific. There are, it is true, numerous exceptions to the principle that provisions regarding attorneys' fees are part of general procedure law. For example, federal antidiscrimination, antitrust, copyright, pension, and securities laws all contain field-specific provisions modifying the American rule (as do many other field-specific statutes). An international convention on contract law *could* do the same. But not only is the question of attorneys' fees not "expressly settled" in the Convention, it is not even mentioned. And there are no "principles" that can be drawn out of the provisions of the Convention for determining whether "loss" includes attorneys' fees; so by the terms of the Convention itself the matter must be left to domestic law (i.e., the law picked out by "the rules of private international law," which means the rules governing choice of law in international legal disputes).

U.S. contract law is different from, say, French contract law, and the general U.S. rule on attorneys' fee shifting (the "American rule") is different from the French rule (loser pays). But no one would say that French contract law differs from U.S. *because* the winner of a contract suit in France is entitled to be reimbursed by the loser, and in the U.S. not. That's an important difference but not a contract-law difference. It is a difference resulting from differing procedural rules of general applicability.

The interpretation of "loss" for which Zapata contends would produce anomalies; this is another reason to reject the interpretation. On Zapata's view the prevailing plaintiff in a suit under the Convention would (though presumably subject to the general contract duty to mitigate damages, to which we referred earlier) get his attorneys' fees reimbursed more or less automatically (the reason for the "more or less" qualification will become evident in a moment). But what if the defendant won? Could he invoke the domestic law, if as is likely other than in the United States that law entitled either side that wins to reimbursement of his fees by the loser? Well, if so, could a winning plaintiff waive his right to attorneys' fees under the Convention in favor of domestic law, which might be more or less generous than Article 74, since Article 74 requires that any loss must, to be recoverable, be foreseeable, which beyond some level attorneys' fees, though reasonable ex post, might not be? And how likely is it that the United States would have signed the Convention had it thought that in doing so it was abandoning the hallowed American rule? To the vast majority of the signatories of the Convention, being nations in which loser pays is the rule anyway, the question whether "loss" includes attorneys' fees would have held little interest; there is no reason to suppose they thought about the question at all.

For these reasons, we conclude that "loss" in Article 74 does not include attorneys' fees, and we move on to the question of a district court's inherent authority to punish a litigant or the litigant's lawyers for litigating in bad faith. The district judge made clear that he was basing his award of attorneys' fees to Zapata in part on his indignation at Lenell's having failed to pay money conceded to be owed to Zapata. Although the precise amount was in dispute, Lenell concedes that it owed Zapata at least half of the $1.2 million that Zapata obtained in damages (not counting the attorneys' fees) and prejudgment interest. Lenell had no excuse for not paying that amount, and this upset the judge.

Firms should pay their debts when they have no legal defense to them. *Pacta sunt servanda*, as the saying goes ("contracts are to be obeyed"). In the civil law (that is, the legal regime of Continental Europe), this principle is taken very seriously, as illustrated by the fact that the civil law grants specific performance in breach of contract cases as a matter of course. But under the common law (including the common law of Illinois, which is the law that choice of law principles make applicable to any issues in this case not covered in express terms by the Convention), a breach of contract is not considered wrongful activity in the sense that a tort or a crime is wrongful. When we delve for reasons, we encounter Holmes's argument that practically speaking the duty created by a contract is just to perform or pay damages, for only if damages are inadequate relief in the particular circumstances of the case will specific performance be ordered. In other words, and subject to the qualification just mentioned, the entire practical effect of signing a contract is that by doing so one obtains an option to break it. The damages one must pay for breaking the contract are simply the price if the option is exercised. See Oliver Wendell Holmes, Jr., The Common Law 300-302 (1881); Holmes, "The Path of the Law," 10 Harv. L. Rev. 457, 462 (1897).

Why such lenity? Perhaps because breach of contract is a form of strict liability. Many breaches are involuntary and so inapt occasions for punishment. Even deliberate breaches are not necessarily culpable, as they may enable an improvement in efficiency — suppose Lenell had a contract to take a certain quantity of tins from Zapata and found that it could buy them for half the price from someone else. Some breaches of contract, it is true, are not only deliberate but culpable, and maybe this was one — Lenell offers no excuse for failing to pay for tins that it had taken delivery of and presumably resold with its cookies in them. Refusing to pay the contract price after the other party has performed is not the kind of option that the performing party would willingly have granted when the contract was negotiated. The option of which Holmes spoke was the option not to perform because performance was impossible or because some more valuable use of the resources required for performance arose after the contract was signed. Zapata argues, moreover, perhaps correctly (we need not decide), that Lenell refused to pay in an effort to extract a favorable modification of the terms of the parties' dealings, which would be a form of duress if Zapata somehow lacked an effective legal remedy. Professional Service Network, Inc. v. American Alliance Holding Co., 238 F.3d 897, 900-901 (7th Cir. 2001); Alaska Packers' Ass'n v. Domenico, 117 F. 99, 100-104 (9th Cir. 1902). But Zapata did not charge duress, and probably couldn't, since it had a good remedy — this suit.

It is true that nowadays common law courts will sometimes award punitive damages for breach of contract in bad faith. But outside the field of insurance, where refusals in bad faith to indemnify or defend have long been punishable by awards of punitive damages to the insured, the plaintiff must show that the breach of contract involved tortious misconduct, such as duress or fraud or abuse of fiduciary duty. See, e.g., Miller Brewing Co. v. Best Beers of Bloomington, Inc., 608 N.E.2d 975, 982-983 (Ind. 1993); Story v. City of Bozeman, 242 Mont. 436, 791 P.2d 767, 776 (1990); E. Allan Farnsworth, Contracts §12.8, pp. 788-789 (3d ed. 1999). This is the rule in Illinois, Morrow v. L.A. Goldschmidt Associates, Inc., 112 Ill. 2d 87, 96 Ill. Dec. 939, 492 N.E.2d 181, 183-186 (1986), and Zapata has not tried to come within it. For that matter, it did not ask for punitive damages, and the judge had no authority to award attorneys' fees in lieu of such damages. He could not have awarded punitive damages if Zapata had asked for them but had been unable to prove tortious misconduct by Lenell, and even more clearly he could not award them when they had not been requested.

The decision whether punitive damages shall be a sanction for a breach of contract is an issue of substantive law, and under the *Erie* doctrine a federal court is not authorized to apply a different substantive law of contracts in a diversity case from the law that a state court would apply were the case being litigated in a state court instead. And obviously that rule must not be circumvented by renaming punitive damages "attorneys' fees." United States ex rel. Treat Bros. Co. v. Fidelity & Deposit Co. of Maryland, 986 F.2d 1110, 1119-1120 (7th Cir. 1993); see also Chambers v. NASCO, Inc., 501 U.S. 32, 52-55 (1991). . . . It is true that this is not a diversity case, but the *Erie* doctrine applies to any case in which state law supplies the rule of decision, see, e.g., O'Melveny & Myers v. FDIC, 512 U.S. 79, 83-85, 87-88 (1994), here by incorporation in the Convention.

The inherent authority of federal courts to punish misconduct before them is not a grant of authority to do good, rectify shortcomings of the common law (as by using an award of attorneys' fees to make up for an absence that the judge may deem regrettable of punitive damages for certain breaches of contract), or undermine the American rule on the award of attorneys' fees to the prevailing party in the absence of statute. Morganroth & Morganroth v. DeLorean, 213 F.3d 1301, 1318 (10th Cir. 2000); Association of Flight Attendants, AFL-CIO v. Horizon Air Industries, Inc., supra, 976 F.2d at 548-550 (9th Cir. 1992); Shimman v. International Union of Operating Engineers, Local 18, 744 F.2d 1226, 1232-1233 and n.9 (6th Cir. 1984) (en banc). These cases and others we could cite make clear that it is a residual authority, to be exercised sparingly, to punish misconduct (1) occurring in the litigation itself, not in the events giving rise to the litigation (for then the punishment would be a product of substantive law — designed, for example, to deter breaches of contract), and (2) not adequately dealt with by other rules, most pertinently here Rules 11 and 37 of the Federal Rules of Civil Procedure, which Lenell has not been accused of violating.

Insofar as he focused on Lenell's behavior in the litigation itself, which, to repeat, is the only lawful domain of the relevant concept of "inherent authority" — the authority could not constitutionally be extended to give parties remedies not available to them under the law of the state that furnishes the substantive rules of decision in the case — the judge punished Lenell for having failed to acknowledge liability and spare Zapata and the judge and the jury and the witnesses and so on the burden of a trial. But as it happens, the fault here was in no small measure the judge's. Well before the trial, and long, long before Zapata's lawyers had run the tab up to $550,000, they had moved for partial summary judgment, claiming that Lenell in answer to Zapata's requests for admission had acknowledged liability for $858,000 of the $890,000 sought in the complaint. The judge had denied the motion on the ground that partial summary judgment cannot be granted unless the grant would give rise to an appealable judgment. This was error. [The court then discusses how Rule 56 allows for partial summary judgment whether the judgment is appealable or not. — EDS.]

Since the challenged award of $550,000 in attorneys' fees cannot stand, we need not pick through the record to see whether some of the counterclaims or other moves by Lenell during the trial were sanctionable apart from Rule 11 and Rule 37. But it may be useful in guiding further proceedings on remand to point out that to the extent that those rules place limits on the award of sanctions under them (for example by the provision of safe harbors in Rule 11), those limitations are equally limitations on inherent authority, which may not be used to amend the rules. Kovilic Construction Co. v. Missbrenner, 106 F.3d 768, 772-773 (7th Cir. 1997). For federal rules of procedure have the force of statutes. See id.; 28 U.S.C. §2072(b).

One issue remains for discussion. Although we have treated the appeal so far as if the only issues concerned attorneys' fees, Lenell also argues that the jury verdict should be set aside because the judge by his comments in open court signaled to the jury his scorn for Lenell's case. There were only a couple of such comments (many more, however, at sidebars outside the jury's hearing), and we do not think they could have changed the outcome. But we also think that judges should be very cautious about making comments in the hearing of a jury about the quality of a party's case or lawyers. For if he signals to the jury his opinion as to how the case should be decided, he undermines the jury's authority. . . .

From what we have just reported about the judge's statements during the trial and from the tone of a number of other statements that he made in the course of this litigation, we think it best that the further proceedings that we are ordering be conducted before a different judge, in accordance with 7th Cir. R. 36.

AFFIRMED IN PART, REVERSED IN PART, AND REMANDED.

NOTES AND QUESTIONS

1. *CISG as grounds for recovery of attorney fees.* As stated by the *Zapata* court, the "English (or British)" rule concerning attorney fees is that the loser in litigation pays those fees for the prevailing party. This "fee-shifting" approach is also found in most civil law countries. In contrast, the "American rule" dictates that parties pay their own attorney fees. As detailed below, there are exceptions to the American rule that allow the awarding of attorney fees to the prevailing party when the parties have a valid contract term allowing for attorney fees, when there is an applicable statute granting such fees, or when there is an established court rule that allows for recovery. The primary issue facing the court in *Zapata* was whether the Convention for the International Sale of Goods (CISG), as a treaty that is tantamount to federal legislation, should be interpreted to provide for recovery of attorney fees.

The CISG applied in *Zapata*, of course, because the plaintiff had its place of business in Mexico, the defendant had its place of business in the United States, and both countries are signatories to the CISG. (Most of the United States' major trading partners, with the exception of the United Kingdom, are parties to the CISG. See the Rules of Contract Law supplement, Editors' Note on Convention on Contracts for the International Sale of Goods.) The trial court in *Zapata* held that attorney fees are recoverable under CISG Article 74 if they are foreseeable, and the defendant in *Zapata* stipulated that attorney fees were a foreseeable result of its failure to pay for the tins that it ordered. Perhaps more importantly, the trial court based its decision on the considerations that the "American rule" on attorney fees is a minority rule in the world community and, as reflected in its Preamble and Article 7, the CISG has a goal of promoting uniformity and certainty in the law. See Zapata Hermanos Sucesores, S.A. v. Hearthside Baking Company, Inc., 2001 WL 1000927 (N.D. Ill.). Thus, one could argue that the trial court's decision to allow attorney fees was consistent with central tenets of the CISG.

The Court of Appeals reversed the trial court's grant of attorney fees, with Judge Posner's opinion fitting nicely into a syllogism: The CISG deals with the substantive law of contracts, not procedure; attorney fees are a matter of procedure, not substance; therefore, the CISG does not authorize the recovery of attorney fees. It is unclear whether the decision in *Zapata* will be followed by other courts. Compare Stemcor United States v. Miracero, S.A. de C.V., 66 F. Supp. 3d 394 (S.D.N.Y. 2014) (citing scholarly criticism and contrary decisions and upholding an arbitration decision to award attorney fees under Article 74) with Victory Foodservice Distribs. Corp. v. N. Chr.

Laitsos & Co. Ltd., 2017 U.S. Dist. LEXIS 187203 (S.D.N.Y.) (denying recovery).

2. *Statutory exceptions for attorney fees, including the UCC.* As noted above, attorney fees may be awarded when a statute specifically provides for such recovery. Numerous federal and state statutes, covering the entire range of economic activity — consumer protection, civil rights, environmental protection, employment law, and securities regulation, to name just a few — authorize courts to grant attorney fees. See generally John F. Vargo, The American Rule on Attorney Fee Allocation: The Injured Person's Access to Justice, 42 Am. U. L. Rev. 1567, 1587-1588 (1993) (noting there are more than 200 federal statutes and almost 2,000 state statutes providing for attorney fees).

While the transaction in *Zapata* came under the CISG, a sale of goods between two American companies would be governed by the UCC. It has been occasionally contended that the UCC Article 2 provides for, or at least permits, the award of attorney fees to a victorious plaintiff, either as incidental or consequential damages. UCC §§2-710, 2-715. Such claims have almost always been unsuccessful. Indiana Glass Co. v. Indiana Mich. Power Co., 692 N.E.2d 886, 888 (Ind. Ct. App 1998) ("overwhelming weight of authority from other jurisdictions indicating that attorney's fees are not recoverable under §2-715"). In contrast, UCC §2A-108(4) explicitly authorizes the award of attorney fees for unconscionable terms or conduct in inducing or enforcing consumer leases only.

3. *Court rules as basis for attorney fees.* In addition to the statutory provisions discussed in the previous note, court rules may also allow the recovery of attorney fees. The Federal Rules of Civil Procedure, which constitute the model for most state procedural systems, contain a number of provisions allowing courts to award attorney fees against an attorney or party who engages in improper litigation conduct. Probably the best known of these is Rule 11 of the Federal Rules of Civil Procedure. Rule 11 provides, essentially, that by presenting a pleading, written motion, or paper to a court, an attorney or unrepresented party is certifying "to the best of the person's knowledge, information, and belief formed after an inquiry reasonable under the circumstances" that the litigation is not being presented for any improper purpose, that the claims and legal contentions are not frivolous and supported by the available evidence, and that any denials of factual contentions are warranted. Similar to Rule 11, a federal statute, 28 U.S.C. §1927, provides for sanctions against an attorney who "multiplies the proceedings in any case unreasonably and vexatiously." As an alternative basis for awarding attorney fees, the trial court in *Zapata* relied on 28 U.S.C. §1927 and Chambers v. NASCO, Inc., 501 U.S. 32 (1991), a Supreme Court decision that established that federal courts have inherent power to impose sanctions for bad faith conduct in specific situations. State courts have reached a similar conclusion. See, e.g., Maris v. McGrath, 850 A.2d 133 (Conn. 2004) (state courts have inherent authority to impose attorney fees as sanction for dilatory, bad faith, and harassing litigation even in absence of violation of a specific rule or order).

Apart from the question of CISG interpretation, the Seventh Circuit held that the trial court also erred in awarding attorney fees to sanction bad faith or vexatious conduct by the defendant. The Seventh Circuit concluded that a federal court's inherent authority to award fees is limited to conduct occurring during the course of the litigation and not covered by other rules of procedure or statutes. See also Centex v. U.S., 486 F.3d 1369 (Fed. Cir. 2007) (aligning with eight other circuits holding that attorney fees cannot be awarded based solely on pre-litigation conduct); but see Chambers v. NASCO, Inc., 501 U.S. 32 (1991) (5-4 decision affirming award of sanctions for litigation abuse, including fraud, even when conduct occurred outside the courtroom and holding that federal courts have inherent authority to award sanctions).

4. *Contract terms as basis for attorney fees.* Since a principal policy of contract law is to enforce the reasonable expectations created by the contract, it would appear that where the contract at issue expressly provides for an award of attorney fees to the prevailing party in a dispute, the court should enforce that promise so long as the fees are reasonable. See McMullen v. Kutz, 985 A.2d 769 (Pa. 2009). In a notable combination of the statutory and contract exceptions, California has enacted legislation which provides that if a contract grants attorney fees to one party, the agreement will be applied to also allow attorney fees for the other party if it should prevail in litigation. See Cal. Civ. Code §1717(a).

5. *Attorney fees available in other situations.* While contract provision, statutory mandate, and court rule constitute the three major exceptions to the American rule, some courts have recognized other exceptions. When the defendant's breach of contract causes the plaintiff to engage in "collateral litigation," the plaintiff may recover as consequential damage for breach of the principal contract the attorney fees incurred in the collateral litigation. The American rule only bars recovery of the litigation expenses in the case against the defendant. See, e.g., Eastern Shore Title Co. v. Ochse, 160 A.3d 1238 (Md. 2017) (recognizing the "collateral litigation" exception to the American Rule). Can you offer any justification for this distinction?

In some states courts have allowed an insured who incurs attorney fees in forcing an insurance company to honor its contractual obligations to recover these expenses. These courts usually rely on the special relationship that exists between insurer and insured. See Preferred Mutual Insurance Co. v. Gamache, 686 N.E.2d 989 (Mass. 1997) (attorney fees incurred by insured in obtaining declaratory judgment that insured had coverage under homeowners policy were recoverable).

6. *Justifications and criticisms of the American rule.* The American rule denying recovery of attorney fees has usually been defended on the basis of access to the court system and the burden on judicial administration:

> [S]ince litigation is at best uncertain one should not be penalized for merely defending or prosecuting a lawsuit, and . . . the poor might be unjustly discouraged from instituting actions to vindicate their rights if the penalty for losing included the fees of their opponents' counsel. . . . Also, the time, expense,

> and difficulties of proof inherent in litigating the question of what constitutes reasonable attorney's fees would pose substantial burdens for judicial administration.

Fleischmann Distilling Corp. v. Maier Brewing Co., 386 U.S. 714, 718 (1967). The American rule has been subject to extensive criticism, however. Among other arguments, opponents claim that the rule fails to provide full compensation for the prevailing party and prevents the assertion of meritorious small claims. See W. Kent Davis, The International View of Attorney Fees in Civil Suits: Why Is the United States the "Odd Man Out" in How It Pays Its Lawyers? 16 Ariz. J. Intl. & Comp. L. 361 (1999). Moreover, critics point out that the failure to require the loser to pay attorney fees for the other side may actually encourage frivolous litigation by parties who realize they have little chance of winning. See Jonathan Fischbach & Michael Fischbach, Rethinking Optimality in Tort Litigation: The Promise of Reverse Cost-Shifting, 19 BYU J. Pub. L. 317 (2005).

7. Ethical obligations of lawyers regarding litigation. Lawyers who engage in improper litigation tactics may be subject to professional discipline as well as sanctions under the rules of civil procedure. Rule 3.1 of the American Bar Association's Model Rules of Professional Conduct states that a "lawyer shall not bring or defend a proceeding, or assert or controvert an issue therein, unless there is a basis in law and fact for doing so that is not frivolous, which includes a good faith argument for an extension, modification or reversal of existing law." Rule 3.2 requires lawyers to "make reasonable efforts to expedite litigation consistent with the interests of the client." Rule 3.4(d) states that a lawyer shall not "in pretrial procedure, make a frivolous discovery request or fail to make reasonably diligent effort to comply with a legally proper discovery request by an opposing party." Rule 4.4(a) provides that in "representing a client, a lawyer shall not use means that have no substantial purpose other than to embarrass, delay, or burden a third person, or use methods of obtaining evidence that violate the legal rights of such a person." See generally Nathan M. Crystal, Limitations on Zealous Representation in an Adversarial System, 32 Wake Forest L. Rev. 671 (1997).

Erlich v. Menezes

Supreme Court Of California 21 Cal. 4th 543, 981 P.2d 978, 87 Cal. Rptr. 2d 886 (1999)

BROWN, J.

We granted review in this case to determine whether emotional distress damages are recoverable for the negligent breach of a contract to construct a house. A jury awarded the homeowners the full cost necessary to repair their home as well as damages for emotional distress caused by the contractor's negligent performance. Since the contractor's negligence directly caused only economic injury and property damage, and breached no duty independent of the contract, we conclude the homeowners may not recover damages for emotional distress based upon breach of a contract to build a house.

I. Factual and Procedural Background

Both parties agree with the facts as ascertained by the Court of Appeal. Barry and Sandra Erlich contracted with John Menezes, a licensed general contractor, to build a "dreamhouse" on their ocean-view lot. The Erlichs moved into their house in December 1990. In February 1991, the rains came. "[T]he house leaked from every conceivable location. Walls were saturated in[an upstairs bedroom], two bedrooms downstairs, and the pool room. Nearly every window in the house leaked. The living room filled with three inches of standing water. In several locations water 'poured in[] streams' from the ceilings and walls. The ceiling in the garage became so saturated . . . the plaster liquefied and fell in chunks to the floor."

Menezes's attempts to stop the leaks proved ineffectual. Caulking placed around the windows melted, " 'ran down [the] windows and stained them and ran across the driveway and ran down the house [until it] . . . looked like someone threw balloons with paint in them at the house.' " Despite several repair efforts, which included using sledgehammers and jackhammers to cut holes in the exterior walls and ceilings, application of new waterproofing materials on portions of the roof and exterior walls, and more caulk, the house continued to leak — from the windows, from the roofs, and water seeped between the floors. Fluorescent light fixtures in the garage filled with water and had to be removed.

"The Erlichs eventually had their home inspected by another general contractor and a structural engineer. In addition to confirming defects in the roof, exterior stucco, windows and waterproofing, the inspection revealed serious errors in the construction of the home's structural components. None of the 20 shear, or load-bearing walls specified in the plans were properly installed. The three turrets on the roof were inadequately connected to the roof beams and, as a result, had begun to collapse. Other connections in the roof framing were also improperly constructed. Three decks were in danger of 'catastrophic collapse' because they had been finished with mortar and ceramic tile, rather than with the light-weight roofing material originally specified. Finally, the foundation of the main beam for the two-story living room was poured by digging a shallow hole, dumping in 'two sacks of dry concrete mix, putting some water in the hole and mixing it up with a shovel.' " This foundation, required to carry a load of 12,000 pounds, could only support about 2,000. The beam is settling and the surrounding concrete is cracking.

According to the Erlichs' expert, problems were major and pervasive, concerning everything "related to a window or waterproofing, everywhere that there was something related to framing," stucco, or the walking deck.

Both of the Erlichs testified that they suffered emotional distress as a result of the defective condition of the house and Menezes's invasive and unsuccessful repair attempts. Barry Erlich testified he felt "absolutely sick" and had to be "carted away in an ambulance" when he learned the full extent of the structural problems. He has a permanent heart condition, known as superventricular tachyarrhythmia, attributable, in part, to excessive stress. Although the condition can be controlled with medication, it has forced him to resign his positions as athletic director, department head and track coach.

Sandra Erlich feared the house would collapse in an earthquake and feared for her daughter's safety. Stickers were placed on her bedroom windows, and alarms and emergency lights installed so rescue crews would find her room first in an emergency.

Plaintiffs sought recovery on several theories, including breach of contract, fraud, negligent misrepresentation, and negligent construction. Both the breach of contract claim and the negligence claim alleged numerous construction defects.

Menezes prevailed on the fraud and negligent misrepresentation claims. The jury found he breached his contract with the Erlichs by negligently constructing their home and awarded $406,700 as the cost of repairs. Each spouse was awarded $50,000 for emotional distress, and Barry Erlich received an additional $50,000 for physical pain and suffering and $15,000 for lost earnings.

By a two-to-one majority, the Court of Appeal affirmed the judgment, including the emotional distress award. The majority noted the breach of a contractual duty may support an action in tort. The jury found Menezes was negligent. Since his negligence exposed the Erlichs to "intolerable living conditions and a constant, justifiable fear about the safety of their home," the majority decided the Erlichs were properly compensated for their emotional distress.

The dissent pointed out that no reported California case has upheld an award of emotional distress damages based upon simple breach of a contract to build a house. Since Menezes's negligence directly caused only economic injury and property damage, the Erlichs were not entitled to recover damages for their emotional distress.

We granted review to resolve the question.

II. Discussion

A. In an action for breach of contract, the measure of damages is "the amount which will compensate the party aggrieved for all the detriment proximately caused thereby, or which, in the ordinary course of things, would be likely to result therefrom" (Civ. Code, §3300), provided the damages are "clearly ascertainable in both their nature and origin" (Civ. Code, §3301). In an action not arising from contract, the measure of damages is "the amount which will compensate for all the detriment proximately caused thereby, whether it could have been anticipated or not" (Civ. Code, §3333).

"Contract damages are generally limited to those within the contemplation of the parties when the contract was entered into or at least reasonably foreseeable by them at that time; consequential damages beyond the expectation of the parties are not recoverable. [Citations.] This limitation on available damages serves to encourage contractual relations and commercial activity by enabling parties to estimate in advance the financial risks of their enterprise." (Applied Equipment Corp. v. Litton Saudi Arabia Ltd. (1994) 7 Cal. 4th 503, 515, 28 Cal. Rptr. 2d 475, 869 P.2d 454 *(Applied Equipment)*.) "In contrast, tort damages are awarded to [fully] compensate the victim for [all] injury suffered. [Citation.]" (Id. at p. 516, 28 Cal. Rptr. 2d 475, 869 P.2d 454.)

" '[T]he distinction between tort and contract is well grounded in common law, and divergent objectives underlie the remedies created in the two areas. Whereas contract actions are created to enforce the intentions of the parties to the agreement, tort law is primarily designed to vindicate "social policy." [Citation.]' " (Hunter v. Up-Right, Inc. (1993) 6 Cal. 4th 1174, 1180, 26 Cal. Rptr. 2d 8, 864 P.2d 88, quoting Foley v. Interactive Data Corp. (1988) 47 Cal. 3d 654, 683, 254 Cal. Rptr. 211, 765 P.2d 373 (*Foley*).) While the purposes behind contract and tort law are distinct, the boundary line between them is not (Freeman & Mills, Inc. v. Belcher Oil Co. (1995) 11 Cal. 4th 85, 106, 44 Cal. Rptr. 2d 420, 900 P.2d 669 (conc. and dis. opn. of Mosk, J.) (*Freeman & Mills*)) and the distinction between the remedies for each is not " 'found ready made.' " (Ibid., quoting Holmes, The Common Law (1881) p.13.) These uncertain boundaries and the apparent breadth of the recovery available for tort actions create pressure to obliterate the distinction between contracts and torts — an expansion of tort law at the expense of contract principles which Grant Gilmore aptly dubbed "con*torts*." In this case we consider whether a negligent breach of a contract will support an award of damages for emotional distress — either as tort damages for negligence or as consequential or special contract damages.

B. In concluding emotional distress damages were properly awarded, the Court of Appeal correctly observed that "the same wrongful act may constitute both a breach of contract and an invasion of an interest protected by the law of torts." . . . Here, the court permitted plaintiffs to recover both full repair costs as normal contract damages and emotional distress damages as a tort remedy.

The Court of Appeal also noted that "[a] contractual obligation may create a legal duty and the breach of that duty may support an action in tort." This is true; however, conduct amounting to a breach of contract becomes tortious only when it also violates a duty independent of the contract arising from principles of tort law. (*Applied Equipment,* supra, 7 Cal. 4th at p. 515, 28 Cal. Rptr. 2d 475, 869 P.2d 454.) " ' "An omission to perform a contract obligation is never a tort, unless that omission is also an omission of a legal duty." ' " (Ibid., quoting Jones v. Kelly (1929) 208 Cal. 251, 255, 280 P. 942.)

Tort damages have been permitted in contract cases where a breach of duty directly causes physical injury . . . ; for breach of the covenant of good faith and fair dealing in insurance contracts . . . ; for wrongful discharge in violation of fundamental public policy . . . ; or where the contract was fraudulently induced. . . . In each of these cases, the duty that gives rise to tort liability is either completely independent of the contract or arises from conduct which is both intentional and intended to harm. . . .

Plaintiff's theory of tort recovery is that mental distress is a foreseeable consequence of negligent breaches of standard commercial contracts. However, foreseeability alone is not sufficient to create an independent tort duty. " 'Whether a defendant owes a duty of care is a question of law. Its existence depends upon the foreseeability of the risk and a weighing of policy considerations for and against imposition of liability.'[Citation.]" (Burgess v. Superior Court (1992) 2 Cal. 4th 1064, 1072, 9 Cal. Rptr. 2d 615, 831 P.2d 1197.) Because the consequences of a negligent act must be limited to avoid an intolerable burden on society . . . , the determination of duty "recognizes that policy considerations may dictate a cause of action should not be sanctioned no matter how foreseeable the risk." . . . "[T]here are clear judicial days on which a court can foresee forever and thus determine liability but none on which that foresight alone provides a socially and judicially acceptable limit on recovery of damages for [an] injury." (Thing v. La Chusa (1989) 48 Cal. 3d 644, 668, 257 Cal. Rptr. 865, 771 P.2d 814.) In short, foreseeability is not synonymous with duty; nor is it a substitute.

The question thus remains: is the mere negligent breach of a contract sufficient? The answer is no. It may admittedly be difficult to categorize the cases, but to state the rule succinctly: "[C]ourts will generally enforce the breach of a contractual promise through contract law, except when the actions that constitute the breach violate a social policy that merits the imposition of tort remedies." (*Freeman & Mills,* supra, 11 Cal. 4th at p. 107, 44 Cal. Rptr. 2d 420, 900 P.2d 669 (conc. and dis. opn. of Mosk, J.).) The familiar paradigm of tortious breach of contract in this state is the insurance contract. There we relied on the covenant of good faith and fair dealing, implied in every contract, to justify tort liability. . . . In holding that a tort action is available for breach of the covenant in an insurance contract, we have "emphasized the 'special relationship' between insurer and insured, characterized by elements of public interest, adhesion, and fiduciary responsibility." (*Freeman & Mills,* supra, 11 Cal. 4th at p. 91, 44 Cal. Rptr. 2d 420, 900 P.2d 669. . . .)

The special relationship test, which has been criticized as illusory and not sufficiently precise . . . has little relevance to the question before us. Menezes is in the business of building single-family homes. He is one among thousands of contractors who provide the same service, and the Erlichs could take their choice among any contractors willing to accept work in the area where their home would be constructed. Although they undoubtedly relied on his claimed expertise, they were in a position to view, inspect, and criticize his work, or to hire someone who could. Most significantly, there is no indication Menezes sought to frustrate the Erlichs' enjoyment of contracted-for benefits. He did build a house. His ineptitude led to numerous problems which he attempted to correct. And he remains ultimately responsible for reimbursing the cost of doing the job properly.

Moreover, since, as *Foley* noted, the insurance cases represented "a major departure from traditional principles of contract law," any claim for automatic extension of that exceptional approach whenever "certain hallmarks and similarities can be adduced in another contract setting" should be carefully considered. (*Foley,* supra, 47 Cal. 3d at p. 690, 254 Cal. Rptr. 211, 765 P.2d 373.)

Our previous decisions detail the reasons for denying tort recovery in contract breach cases: the different objectives underlying tort and contract breach; the importance of predictability in assuring commercial stability in contractual dealings; the potential for converting every contract breach into a tort, with accompanying punitive damage recovery, and the preference for legislative action in affording appropriate remedies. . . . The same concerns support a cautious approach here. Restrictions on contract remedies serve to protect the " 'freedom to bargain over special risks and [to] promote contract formation by limiting liability to the value of the promise.' " . . .

Generally, outside the insurance context, "a tortious breach of contract . . . may be found when (1) the breach is accompanied by a traditional common law tort, such as fraud or conversion; (2) the means used to breach the contract are tortious, involving deceit or undue coercion or; (3) one party intentionally breaches the contract intending or knowing that such a breach will cause severe, unmitigable harm in the form of mental anguish, personal hardship, or substantial consequential damages." (*Freeman & Mills,* supra, 11 Cal. 4th at p. 105, 44 Cal. Rptr. 2d 420, 900 P.2d 669 (conc. and dis. opn. of Mosk, J.).) Focusing on intentional conduct gives substance to the proposition that a breach of contract is tortious only when some independent duty arising from tort law is violated. . . . If every negligent breach of a contract gives rise to tort damages the limitation would be meaningless, as would the statutory distinction between tort and contract remedies.

In this case, the jury concluded Menezes did not act intentionally; nor was he guilty of fraud or misrepresentation. This is a claim for negligent breach of a contract, which is not sufficient to support tortious damages for violation of an independent tort duty.

It may ultimately be more useful, in attempting to develop a common law of tortious breach, to affirmatively identify specific practices utilized by contracting parties that merit the imposition of tort remedies (*Freeman & Mills,* supra, 11 Cal. 4th at p. 107, 44 Cal. Rptr. 2d 420, 900 P.2d 669 (conc. and dis. opn. of Mosk, J.)) instead of comparing each new claim to a template for exceptions. In the interim, however, it is sufficient to note that more than mere negligence has been involved in each case where tort damages have been permitted. The benefits of broad compensation must be balanced against the burdens on commercial stability. "[C]ourts should be careful to apply tort remedies only when the conduct in question is so clear in its deviation from socially useful business practices that the effect of enforcing such tort duties will be . . . to aid rather than discourage commerce." (*Freeman & Mills,* supra, 11 Cal. 4th at p. 109, 44 Cal. Rptr. 2d 420, 900 P.2d 669 (conc. and dis. opn. of Mosk, J.).)

C. Even assuming Menezes's negligence constituted a sufficient independent duty to the Erlichs, such a finding would not entitle them to emotional distress damages on these facts. "The fact that emotional distress damages may be awarded in some circumstances (see Rest. 2d Torts, §905, pp. 456-457) does not mean they are available in every case in which there is an independent cause of action founded upon negligence." (Merenda v. Superior Court (1992) 3 Cal. App. 4th 1, 7, 4 Cal. Rptr. 2d 87 (*Merenda*).) "No California case has allowed recovery for emotional distress arising solely out of property damage" (Cooper v. Superior Court (1984) 153 Cal. App. 3d 1008, 1012, 200 Cal. Rptr. 746); moreover, a preexisting contractual relationship, without more, will not support a recovery for mental suffering where the defendant's tortious conduct has resulted only in economic injury to the plaintiff. . . .

[The court then discussed with approval two decisions of the California Court of Appeals denying recovery for emotional distress damages to clients who had been injured by their attorneys' negligence. One case involved litigation; the other dealt with tax planning. The court of appeals concluded in both cases that damages for emotional distress could not be recovered because the harm flowed from inherently economic activity. — EDS.]

In Lubner v. City of Los Angeles (1996) 45 Cal. App. 4th 525, 53 Cal. Rptr. 2d 24, two artists lost a substantial portion of their life's work when a city trash truck, which had been parked on a hilltop, rolled down and crashed into their home, damaging the house, two cars, and much of their artwork. The Lubners filed a negligence action and sought damages for their emotional distress. Recognizing that the artwork may have been extremely important to the Lubners, the court nevertheless found they were not entitled to recover for emotional distress caused by injury to property. (Id. at p. 532, 53 Cal. Rptr. 2d 24.) The court based its ruling primarily on the absence of a preexisting relationship between the parties, but separately considered whether the defendant breached a duty of care to the plaintiffs. Noting that the moral blame on the defendant was only that which attends ordinary negligence and nothing in the record indicated bad faith or reckless indifference to the Lubners' emotional tranquillity, the court concluded liability for negligent infliction of emotional distress was unwarranted. (Id. at p. 534, 53 Cal. Rptr. 2d 24.)

Public policy supports a similar limit where the negligence concerns the construction of a home. In Blagrove v. J.B. Mechanical, Inc. (Wyo. 1997) 934 P.2d 1273 (*Blagrove*), the homeowners sued a plumbing contractor to recover damages for mental anguish caused when flooding from a faulty plumbing connection damaged their home and destroyed personal possessions. The Wyoming Supreme Court held that, absent physical injury, emotional distress damages can be recovered only in limited circumstances involving intentional torts, constitutional violations, and the breach of the covenant of good faith and fair dealing in insurance contracts, and concluded a contrary rule would be poor public policy.

. . .

Here, the breach — the negligent construction of the Erlichs' house — did not cause physical injury. No one was hit by a falling beam. Although the Erlichs state they feared the house was structurally unsafe and might collapse in an earthquake, they lived in it for five years. The only physical injury alleged is Barry Erlich's heart disease, which flowed from the emotional distress and not directly from the negligent construction.

The Erlichs may have hoped to build their dream home and live happily ever after, but there is a reason that tag line belongs only in fairy tales. Building a house may turn out to be a stress-free project; it is much more likely to be the stuff of urban legends — the cause of bankruptcy, marital dissolution, hypertension and fleeting fantasies ranging from homicide to suicide. As Justice Yegan noted below, "No reasonable homeowner can embark on a building project with certainty that the project will be completed to perfection. Indeed, errors are so likely to occur that few if any homeowners would be justified in resting their peace of mind on [its] timely or correct completion. . . ." The connection between the service sought and the aggravation and distress resulting from incompetence may be somewhat less tenuous than in a malpractice case, but the emotional suffering still derives from an inherently economic concern.

D. Having concluded tort damages are not available, we finally consider whether damages for emotional distress should be included as consequential or special damages in a contract claim. "Contract damages are generally limited to those within the contemplation of the parties when the contract was entered into or at least reasonably foreseeable by them at the time; consequential damages beyond the expectations of the parties are not recoverable. [Citations.] This limitation on available damages serves to encourage contractual relations and commercial activity by enabling parties to estimate in advance the financial risks of their enterprise." (*Applied Equipment,* supra, 7 Cal. 4th at p. 515, 28 Cal. Rptr. 2d 475, 869 P.2d 454.)

" '[W]hen two parties make a contract, they agree upon the rules and regulations which will govern their relationship; the risks inherent in the agreement and the likelihood of its breach. The parties to the contract in essence create a mini-universe for themselves, in which each voluntarily chooses his contracting partner, each trusts the other's willingness to keep his word and honor his commitments, and in which they define their respective obligations, rewards and risks. Under such a scenario, it is appropriate to enforce only such obligations as each party voluntarily assumed, and to give him only such benefits as he expected to receive; this is the function of contract law.' " (*Applied Equipment,* supra, 7 Cal. 4th at p. 517, 28 Cal. Rptr. 2d 475, 869 P.2d 454.)

Accordingly, damages for mental suffering and emotional distress are generally not recoverable in an action for breach of an ordinary commercial contract in California. (Kwan v. Mercedes-Benz of North America, Inc. (1994) 23 Cal. App. 4th 174, 188, 28 Cal. Rptr. 2d 371) (*Kwan*). . . . "Recovery for emotional disturbance will be excluded unless the breach also caused bodily harm or the contract or the breach is of such a kind that serious emotional disturbance was a particularly likely result." (Rest. 2d Contracts, §353.) The Restatement specifically notes the breach of a contract to build a home is not "particularly likely" to result in "serious emotional disturbance." (Ibid.)

Cases permitting recovery for emotional distress typically involve mental anguish stemming from more personal undertakings the traumatic results of which were unavoidable. (See, e.g., Burgess v. Superior Court, supra, 2 Cal. 4th 1064, 9 Cal. Rptr. 2d 615, 831 P.2d 1197 [infant injured during childbirth]; Molien v. Kaiser Foundation Hospitals (1980) 27 Cal. 3d 916, 167 Cal. Rptr. 831, 616 P.2d 813 [misdiagnosed venereal disease and subsequent failure of marriage]; Kately v. Wilkinson (1983) 148 Cal. App. 3d 576, 195 Cal. Rptr. 902 [fatal waterskiing accident]; Chelini v. Nieri (1948) 32 Cal. 2d 480, 196 P.2d 915 [failure to adequately preserve a corpse].) Thus, when the express object of the contract is the mental and emotional well-being of one of the contracting parties, the breach of the contract may give rise to damages for mental suffering or emotional distress. (See Wynn v. Monterey Club (1980) 111 Cal. App. 3d 789, 799-801, 168 Cal. Rptr. 878 [agreement of two gambling clubs to exclude husband's gambling-addicted wife from clubs and not to cash her checks]; Ross v. Forest Lawn Memorial Park (1984) 153 Cal. App. 3d 988, 992-996, 203 Cal. Rptr. 468 [cemetery's agreement to keep burial service private and to protect grave from vandalism]; Windeler v. Scheers Jewelers (1970) 8 Cal. App. 3d 844, 851-852, 88 Cal. Rptr. 39 [bailment for heirloom jewelry where jewelry's great sentimental value was made known to bailee].)

Cases from other jurisdictions have formulated a similar rule, barring recovery of emotional distress damages for breach of contract except in cases involving contracts in which emotional concerns are the essence of the contract. (See, e.g., Hancock v. Northcutt (Alaska 1991) 808 P.2d 251, 258 ["contracts pertaining to one's dwelling are not among those contracts which, if breached, are particularly likely to result in serious emotional disturbance"; typical damages for breach of house construction contracts can appropriately be calculated in terms of monetary loss]. . . .

Plaintiffs argue strenuously that a broader notion of damages is appropriate when the contract is for the construction of a home. Amici curiae urge us to permit emotional distress damages in cases of negligent construction of a personal residence when the negligent construction causes gross interference with the normal use and habitability of the residence.

Such a rule would make the financial risks of construction agreements difficult to predict. Contract damages must be clearly ascertainable in both nature and origin. (Civ. Code, §3301.) A contracting party cannot be required to assume limitless responsibility for all consequences of a breach and must be advised of any special harm that might result in order to determine whether or not to accept the risk of contracting. . . .

Moreover, adding an emotional distress component to recovery for construction defects could increase the already prohibitively high cost of housing in California, affect the availability of insurance for builders, and greatly diminish the supply of affordable housing. The potential for such broad-ranging economic consequences — costs likely to be paid by the public generally — means the task of fashioning appropriate limits on the availability of emotional distress claims should be left to the Legislature. (See Tex. Prop. Code Ann. §27.001 et seq. (1999); Hawaii Rev. Stat. §663-8.9 (1998).)

Permitting damages for emotional distress on the theory that certain contracts carry a lot of emotional freight provides no useful guidance. Courts have carved out a narrow range of exceptions to the general rule of exclusion where emotional tranquillity is the contract's essence. Refusal to broaden the bases for recovery reflects a fundamental policy choice. A rule which focuses not on the risks contracting parties voluntarily assume but on one party's reaction to inadequate performance, cannot provide any principled limit on liability.

The discussion in *Kwan,* a case dealing with the breach of a sales contract for the purchase of a car, is instructive. "[A] contract for [the] sale of an automobile is not essentially tied to the buyer's mental or emotional well-being. Personal as the choice of a car may be, the central reason for buying one is usually transportation. . . . In spite of America's much-discussed 'love affair with the automobile,' disruption of an owner's relationship with his or her car is not, in the normal case, comparable to the loss or mistreatment of a family member's remains [citation], an invasion of one's privacy [citation], or the loss of one's spouse to a gambling addiction [citation]. In the latter situations, the contract exists primarily to further or protect emotional interests; the direct and foreseeable injuries resulting from a breach are also primarily emotional. In contrast, the undeniable aggravation, irritation and anxiety that may result from [the] breach of an automobile warranty are secondary effects deriving from the decreased usefulness of the car and the frequently frustrating process of having an automobile repaired. While [the] purchase of an automobile may sometimes lead to severe emotional distress, such a result is not ordinarily foreseeable from the nature of the contract." (*Kwan,* supra, 23 Cal. App. 4th at p. 190, 28 Cal. Rptr. 2d 371.)

Most other jurisdictions have reached the same conclusion. (See . . . City of Tyler v. Likes (Tex. 1997) 962 S.W.2d 489, 497 [mental anguish based solely on property damage is not compensable as a matter of law].)

We agree. The available damages for defective construction are limited to the cost of repairing the home, including lost use or relocation expenses, or the diminution in value. . . . The Erlichs received more than $400,000 in traditional contract damages to correct the defects in their home. While their distress was undoubtedly real and serious, we conclude the balance of policy considerations — the potential for significant increases in liability in amounts disproportionate to culpability, the court's inability to formulate appropriate limits on the availability of claims, and the magnitude of the impact on stability and predictability in commercial affairs — counsel against expanding contract damages to include mental distress claims in negligent construction cases.

Disposition

The judgment of the Court of Appeal is reversed and the matter is remanded for further proceedings consistent with this opinion. . . .

NOTES AND QUESTIONS

1. *Amicus curiae. Erlich* was a significant case not only for the parties but also for builders, insurance companies, and consumer advocates. The case attracted *amicus curiae* briefs from, among others: the American Insurance Association, the National Association of Independent Insurers, the Association for California Tort Reform, the Building Industry Legal Defense Foundation, the California Building Industry Association, and Consumer Attorneys of California. Do you think the case would have been decided differently if there had been no amicus briefs for the court to consider?

2. *Scope of court's holding on tort liability.* In part II(B) of the opinion, the court holds that negligent breach of a contract is not sufficient to justify recovery of damages for emotional distress. Do you agree that negligent performance of a residential construction contract should never be sufficient to justify an award of damages for emotional distress? Consider Restatement (Third) of Torts §47, which deals with negligent infliction of emotional distress.

> An actor whose negligent conduct causes serious emotional harm to another is subject to liability to the other if the conduct:
>
> (a) places the other in danger of immediate bodily harm and the emotional harm results from the danger; or
>
> (b) occurs in the course of specified categories of activities, undertakings, or relationships in which negligent conduct is especially likely to cause serious emotional harm.

Under the Restatement test, would either or both of the Erlichs have been entitled to recover tort damages for emotional distress? Suppose a builder's breach goes beyond ordinary negligence to gross negligence or recklessness. Would a higher level of negligence support a recovery of damages for emotional distress? Consider Restatement (Third) of Torts §46, which provides as follows:

> An actor who by extreme and outrageous conduct intentionally or recklessly causes severe emotional harm to another is subject to liability for that emotional harm and, if the emotional harm causes bodily harm, also for the bodily harm.

Cf. Robinson Helicopter Co., Inc. v. Dana Corp., 102 P.3d 268 (Cal. 2004) (tort damages would be available when seller breached contract by intentionally providing false certificates of conformance for helicopter parts; fraud is a tort independent of contract breach). Would you characterize Menezes's breach of contract as merely negligent or does it rise to a higher level?

3. *Mitigation of damages.* In part II(C) of the opinion, the court makes the following point: "Although the Erlichs state they feared the house was structurally unsafe and might collapse in an earthquake, they lived in it for five years." The court seems to be suggesting that the Erlichs could have avoided emotional distress by moving out of the house. Should the Erlichs have moved out? Consider the following background information:

> Why didn't they move out, rather than remaining in perpetual fear for their safety, and if the house was in imminent danger of collapse? The simple reality was that the Erlichs could not afford to mitigate their damages, even though they might properly have recovered the expenses incurred for doing so. (Respondent's Brief at 14; (R.T. 478-479). It was a practical impossibility for them to achieve real mitigation, because they were effectively trapped in their nightmare home.
>
> The Erlichs had taken out a loan from the San Luis Obispo School District Credit Union for $300,000 to pay for the $258,000 house construction and

> for the separate contract to build a swimming pool. The land itself was still encumbered by a $300,000 loan.

Ronnie Wagner, Sand Castles: A Case Study of *Erlich v. Menezes* 22 (unpublished student paper on file with Professor Knapp).

4. *Contract cases in which damages for emotional distress may be recovered.* In part II(D), the court cites Restatement (Second) §353 as identifying two types of cases in which damages for emotional distress may be recovered in an action for breach of contract. In the first type of case, the breach of contract also causes bodily harm. E.g., Sullivan v. O'Connor, 296 N.E.2d 183 (Mass. 1973) (breach of contract action against surgeon who had promised to enhance appearance of plaintiff's nose; damages for emotional distress recoverable when operation disfigured nose). In the second category of cases, emotional distress is a "particularly likely" consequence of the breach. Comment *a* to §353 sets forth certain types of contracts in which the courts have found emotional distress to be particularly likely: contracts of carriers and innkeepers with passengers and guests, contracts dealing with the carriage or disposition of dead bodies, and contracts for the delivery of messages concerning death. The court's opinion gives several other examples. See also Miranda v. Said, 836 N.W.2d 8 (Iowa 2013) (holding that emotional distress was a particularly likely result of breach of attorney-client contract for immigration services when the breach resulted in separation of family members).

Outside of these established exceptions, numerous contract cases have denied such recovery even though the breach appears to have caused the plaintiff substantial emotional distress. See, e.g., In re Educ. Testing Serv. Praxis Principles of Learning & Teaching: Grades 7-12 Litig., 517 F. Supp. 2d 832 (E.D. La. 2007) (test takers could not recover damages for emotional distress resulting from scoring errors by Educational Testing Service); St. Charles v. Kender, 646 N.E.2d 411 (Mass. App. Ct. 1995) (damages for emotional distress may not be recovered from physician who breached contract with patient by not returning telephone calls for two days while patient was having miscarriage).

5. *Restatement test.* As noted above, Restatement (Second) §353 suggests that unless bodily harm was also caused by the defendant's breach, recovery for emotional disturbance should be granted only where either the contract or the breach in question was "of such a kind that serious emotional disturbance was a particularly likely result." In Illustration 1 to §353, the drafters suggest that recovery for "nervousness and emotional distress" resulting from "delays and departures from specifications" in the building of a house should be denied, even where the defendant had notice that the plaintiff buyer was "in delicate health."

In Brooks v. Hickman, 570 F. Supp. 619, 620 (W.D. Pa. 1983), plaintiff sought damages for emotional distress resulting from the defendant's breach of its contract to provide investment management services, causing loss of the plaintiff's savings. In denying recovery, the District Court observed:

> Plaintiffs argue that emotional distress was a particularly likely result of a breach in this case because plaintiffs sought to build a nest egg for retirement, and defendants were aware of this goal. The instant case is simply not of the same class as the cases cited above. The plaintiffs have not suffered disfigurement, anxiety over death or the birth of an unwanted, crippled child. They have only lost money, and not so much of it as to force personal bankruptcy or impoverishment. See, Restatement (Second) of Contracts, §353, comment. Although loss of money is often disturbing, it does not ordinarily give rise to a claim of emotional distress. We find no Pennsylvania decision permitting recovery of such damages on breach of a contract which caused only a monetary loss, and we hesitate to so extend the rule. Furthermore, even if recovery for emotional distress on such a breach is permitted as intimated in the Comment to §353, the plaintiffs have not alleged such an extreme loss from the breach, and while loss of a nest egg may cause anxiety, it does not appear particularly likely to cause *serious* emotional distress.

What test does the *Erlich* court use to determine when contract damages for emotional distress may be awarded? How does this test compare to the one in the Restatement?

6. *Scholarly commentary.* Commentators have generally favored liberalization of the rules dealing with recovery of damages for emotional distress in actions for breach of contract. See, e.g., Ronnie Cohen & Shannon O'Byrne, Cry Me a River: Recovery of Mental Distress Damages in a Breach of Contract Action — A North American Perspective, 42 Am. Bus. L. J. 97 (2005)(reviewing U.S. and Canadian reluctance to award mental distress damages for breach of contract and asserting the approach fails to recognize that many contracts contain promise of nonpecuniary benefit).

Scholars who employ principles of economic analysis have also argued that the rule denying recovery of damages for emotional distress is unsound because it allows a breaching party to avoid the full costs of his breach and thus produces "inefficient breach." (The concept of "efficient breach" is examined in Section F of this chapter.) E.g., John A. Sebert, Jr., Punitive and Nonpecuniary Damages in Actions Based upon Contract: Toward Achieving the Objective of Full Compensation, 33 UCLA L. Rev. 1565 (1986).

Comment: Recovery of Punitive Damages for Bad Faith Breach of Contract

In *Erlich* the California Supreme Court concluded that damages for emotional distress should not be awarded to compensate for a negligent breach of contract under either a tort or a contract theory of recovery. The relationship between tort and contract law also arises with regard to the possible recovery of punitive damages.

In a tort action, an injured party may recover punitive damages in addition to actual damages when the wrongdoer's conduct is "outrageous, because of the defendant's evil motive or his reckless indifference to the rights of others." Restatement (Second) of Torts §908(2). Punitive damages are generally not available, however, for an ordinary breach of contract. Restatement (Second) of Contracts §355 states: "Punitive damages are not recoverable for a breach of contract unless the conduct constituting the breach is also a tort for which punitive damages are recoverable."

Why should punitive, or exemplary, damages be available in tort actions, but not for breach of contract? The standard answer is twofold: First, the damage remedies available in contract are only such as will compensate the plaintiff for harm actually caused and should not put the injured party in a better position than she would have occupied if the contract had been performed. Second, contract law is a system founded not on "fault" but on "strict liability" for the consequences of breach; since culpability plays no part in determining liability it should also play no part in fashioning the remedy. See E. Allan Farnsworth, Contracts §12.8, at 760-761 (4th ed. 2004). To these observations, many modern commentators would add a third: Contract remedies (like the law of contract in general) should promote "efficiency," and therefore should deter only "inefficient" breaches of contract; punitive damage awards (or, for that matter, any award of more than pure "expectation" damages) could deter even "efficient" breaches, which ought rather to be encouraged. See id. §12.3, at 736. We return to this notion of "efficient breach" in the final section of this chapter.

One of the major exceptions to the principle that punitive damages are not recoverable for breach of contract involves insurance contracts. Courts around the country have held insurance companies liable in tort to their insureds for bad faith refusal to honor claims brought by third parties. See Douglas R. Richmond, An Overview of Insurance Bad Faith Law and Litigation, 25 Seton Hall L. Rev. 74 (1994).

In justifying the imposition of tort liability on insurance companies, the courts have focused on several factors, including the special nature of the relationship between the insurer and the insured, and the insured's expectation of coverage in the event of a loss. See Noble v. National American Life Insurance Co., 624 P.2d 866, 867-868 (Ariz. 1981) (en banc).

Courts have been very reluctant, however, to extend the tort of bad faith breach of contract beyond the insurance setting. See Freeman & Mills, Inc. v. Belcher Oil Co., 900 P.2d 669 (1995) (holding that recovery of punitive damages for bad faith breach of contract was limited to insurance contracts).

In The Case for Punitive Damages in Contracts, 48 Duke L.J. 629 (1999), Professor William Dodge argues that economic efficiency supports a rule that allows punitive damages for any willful breach of contract. Professor Dodge divides willful breaches into two categories: opportunistic and efficient. An opportunistic breach involves an attempt by the breaching party to gain at the expense of the nonbreaching party, for example, by coercing a settlement because the breaching party knows that the other party cannot afford to litigate. An efficient breach occurs when the breaching party seeks to engage in another transaction that is more profitable than the existing contract. Professor Dodge agrees with a number of other commentators who have concluded that punitive damages should be awarded to deter opportunistic breaches because such breaches by definition do not increase social wealth. He goes further, however, and argues that punitive damages should be available even in cases of efficient breach because the imposition of punitive damages gives the breaching party an incentive to negotiate with the nonbreaching party to obtain a release from the contract. From an efficiency perspective, negotiation of a release is likely to involve fewer transaction costs than assessment of the nonbreaching party's damages through litigation. Negotiation of a release also forces the breaching party to share some of the efficiency gains from the new transaction with the nonbreaching party, rather than capturing all of those gains for itself.

While recovery of punitive damages for bad faith breach of a noninsurance contract is unlikely in almost all jurisdictions, it should be remembered that punitive damages can be recovered if the defendant's conduct goes beyond bad faith to amount to an independent tort for which punitive damages are recoverable. Cases that involve fraud or breach of fiduciary duty are likely candidates for such treatment. See, e.g., Formosa Plastics Corp. U.S.A. v. Presidio Engineers & Contractors, Inc., 960 S.W.2d 41 (Tex. 1998) (claim that one party fraudulently induced other party to enter into contract states cause of action in tort justifying award of punitive damages).

PROBLEM 10-1

In 1987, Gordon and Amy Tan opened a drug store in the city of Newton. During the next 30 years, the Tans devoted themselves to developing their business and to raising their four children. In 2017, when their youngest child graduated from college, the Tans decided that it was time to sell their business, which had grown to 12 stores, and to retire. Through their lawyer, Stewart Taylor, the Tans employed Miranda Evans, a business broker, to assist them in the sale of the business. The Tans and Evans entered into a brokerage contract in which the Tans agreed to pay Evans 5 percent of the sales price of their business as a commission. Under the terms of the contract, 25 percent of the commission was due when the contract was signed, with the balance payable at the closing of the sale.

In June 2018, Evans succeeded in finding a purchaser, Simpson's, Inc., a large regional chain of drug stores. On June 19, 2018, the parties signed a contract of sale in which Simpson's agreed to purchase the Tan's 12 stores for a price of $4.5 million. The contract provided for a closing on October 15, 2018. Simpson's paid an earnest money deposit to Taylor of $250,000. With the approval of the Tans and Simpson's, Taylor paid from this deposit $56,250 to Evans as payment of the commission due Evans, leaving a balance held by Taylor of $193,750.

On September 15, 2018, the Tans received a letter from Simpson's stating that as a result of its due diligence investigation of the Tan's business, it would no longer be in a position to go forward with the purchase of the Tan's stores. The Tans immediately consulted with Taylor and Evans about how to proceed. Evans suggested that she would investigate informally what had happened to cause Simpson's to change its plans. Taylor advised the Tans that they should write to Simpson's to put it on formal notice that the Tans would insist on their contract rights. They decided, however, to delay this letter for a few days pending the results of Evans's contacts.

A few days later Evans met with Taylor and the Tans. Evans informed them that she had learned that a dramatic restructuring of the retail drug industry was under way, with many existing companies and new entrants beginning to offer drugs over the Internet. Apparently, Simpson's had decided to follow this route and would be closing, rather than opening or acquiring, new retail outlets.

Taylor immediately wrote to Simpson's stating that Simpson's was bound contractually to purchase the Tan's stores, that the Tans insisted on strict compliance with the contract, and that the Tans were ready, willing, and able to proceed with the sale. He demanded that Simpson's proceed with the closing as scheduled. They received no response to this letter.

On October 15, the Tans and Taylor appeared at the closing, but no one appeared on behalf of Simpson's. Taylor immediately wrote to Simpson's informing it that Simpson's had committed a total breach of the contract by failing to appear at the scheduled closing. Taylor informed Simpson's that the Tans would use their best efforts to attempt to resell the business, but that their sales efforts were with full reservation of all rights to seek to enforce the contract against Simpson's by action for specific performance or damages.

After consultation with Taylor and Evans, the Tans decided to place their stores on the market again and to proceed with a lawsuit against Simpson's seeking to enforce the contract. The Tans signed a new commission contract with Evans, which contained terms identical to the first contract. Taylor filed suit on behalf of the Tans against Simpson's for breach of contract.

In January 2019, Evans informed the Tans that she had received an offer to purchase their stores from Rite-Buy, a large national chain of retail drug stores for a price of $2.5 million. Evans told the Tans that she thought that Rite-Buy was "bottom fishing" because it knew about the failed deal with Simpson's.

The Tans were in a state of shock and bewilderment from this news. They both believed that the price was grossly inadequate. But, after talking with Taylor and being advised of the "uncertainties of litigation," they finally concluded that they couldn't take a chance on being able to find a better offer. They decided to sell to Rite-Buy and to try to hold Simpson's responsible for damages.

The Tan's sale to Rite-Buy was originally scheduled to close on March 3, 2019, but it was twice delayed, finally closing on May 15, 2019. Meanwhile, the lawsuit against Simpson's proceeded through discovery toward trial. The stress of these matters had an effect on the Tans, both of whom worried constantly about Rite-Buy changing its mind and about the lawsuit. Gordon was especially affected by these events. He treated Simpson's refusal to go forward with the contract as a personal insult. In late May, shortly after he gave a deposition in the case, Gordon suffered a heart attack, which was fortunately a relatively mild one.

As part of discovery, Simpson's has served interrogatories on the Tans. One of the interrogatories asks them to state the amount and basis of the damages that they claim in the case. In answer to this interrogatory, Taylor has listed the following elements of damage:

1. The purchase price of the contract totaling $4.5 million.
2. Interest on this amount from October 15, 2019, at the market rate of interest available on U.S. Treasury bonds on that date (approximately 3 percent).
3. Loss of the investment appreciation on the purchase price of $4.5 million if this amount had been invested in the Chambers U.S. Treasury Bond Mutual Fund on October 15, 2019, as the Tans planned to do. Taylor's answer showed that had the Tans invested $4.5 million in that fund on October 15, 2019, the amount would have appreciated by $326,000 as of the time the answer to the interrogatory was given.
4. Commissions paid to Evans totaling $181,250.
5. Attorney fees incurred in litigation with Simpson's.
6. Damages for emotional distress suffered by the Tans as a result of the willful breach of contract by Simpson's in an amount determined by the jury.
7. Punitive damages for fraudulent, willful, and malicious breach of contract in an amount to be determined by the jury.

Assuming the Tans can establish a breach of contract by Simpson's, how should their damages be computed?

E. BUYERS' AND SELLERS' REMEDIES UNDER THE UNIFORM COMMERCIAL CODE

In the previous sections we have studied the general principles governing remedies for breach of contract with only brief references to the Uniform Commercial Code. In this section we study buyers' and sellers' remedies for breach of contracts governed by UCC Article 2. While the Code continues many of the basic principles concerning remedies that we have already studied, it also includes several innovative provisions that have generated a number of interpretive questions. See Victor Goldberg, Remedies in the UCC: Some Critical Thoughts, 23 Barry L. Rev. 155 (2018).

1. Buyers' Remedies

A seller may commit a breach of contract in two general ways. First, a seller may deliver goods that fail to "conform" to the contract in some way (breach of an express or implied warranty relating to the "quality" of the goods, most likely). Second, the seller may fail to make a proper "tender" of the goods, such as failing to deliver on time, delivering too few or too many, or failing to deliver at all.

The buyers' remedies turn on whether the buyer has "accepted" the goods. §2-608. Acceptance and possession are often, but not always the same. In other words, a buyer may sometimes retain possession of the goods even if the buyer has not accepted the goods; conversely, a buyer's refusal to take possession may nonetheless legally amount to acceptance under §2-608.

When the buyer does not have the goods because the seller fails to deliver or the buyer rightfully rejects (§§2-601, 2-602) or revokes acceptance (§2-608), the buyer may recover any part of the price that has been paid under §2-711 and also obtain cover damages under UCC §2-712 or market damages under UCC §2-713. Alternatively, the buyer may pursue specific performance to compel delivery of the goods under §2-716.

When the buyer has accepted and retained goods despite a nonconformity, the buyer's damages are determined under §2-714.

Regardless of the type of breach and in addition to the above remedies, the buyer may be able to recover consequential and incidental damages under §2-715.

a. Cover, UCC §2-712

The traditional rule for measuring damages for a seller's breach is the contract price–market price difference, similar to that applied to the land sale contract in the *Crabby's* case earlier in this chapter. The drafters of Article 2 thought that the market measure of damages was often arbitrary in its application, sometimes overcompensating the buyer who purchased substitute goods at a price lower than the relevant market price, and sometimes undercompensating the buyer when the buyer bought substitute goods at a price greater than the relevant market price. Accordingly, the drafters created a new "cover" measure of damages in UCC §2-712. Roy R. Anderson, The Cover Remedy, 6 J.L. & Commerce 155 (1986). If the buyer complies with the requirements of §2-712, she may recover the difference between the cover price and the contract price, plus incidental and consequential damages. UCC §2-715.

To recover damages under §2-712, the covering purchase must be made "in good faith and without unreasonable delay." As Comment 2 indicates, the buyer need not purchase identical goods, only commercially reasonable substitutes. If the buyer purchases superior or significantly different goods, the purchase will not qualify as cover. Some courts have been willing to expand the scope of the cover section to include situations in which the buyer internally manufactures substitute goods rather than purchase the goods on the market. See Cives Corp. v. Callier Steel Pipe & Tube, Inc., 482 A.2d 852 (Me. 1984) (after seller failed to deliver steel tubing under contract and buyer was unable to locate another supplier, buyer allowed to recover the difference between the cost of manufacturing the tubing in-house and the contract price); but see

Chronister Oil Co. v. UNOCAL Refining & Marketing, 34 F.3d 462 (7th Cir. 1994) (criticizing courts that allow the buyer to "self-cover" because buyer cannot make a "purchase" from itself).

UCC 2-712(3) provides that cover is elective and failure to cover does not bar the buyer from any other remedy. However, this section must be read in light of the principle of mitigation of damages, expressed in UCC §2-715(2)(a), which allows a buyer to recover consequential damages that meet the foreseeability test of Hadley v. Baxendale, provided the damages "could not reasonably be prevented by cover or otherwise." Thus, the buyer's failure to cover will preclude recovery of consequential damages only if she fails to act reasonably.

b. Market Damages, UCC §2-713

If the buyer has elected not to purchase substitute goods as cover under UCC §2-712, the buyer may instead recover damages under UCC §2-713. That section provides a basic measure of damages based on the "difference between the market price at the time when the buyer learned of the breach and the contract price." Under §2-713(2) the relevant market is the place for tender and the place of tender depends on where the seller completes its delivery obligations with respect to the goods. In "shipment" contracts the seller tenders by placing the goods in the hands of a carrier, while in "destination" contracts tender takes place when the goods are delivered to a designated point, often the buyer's place of business or locale. UCC §§2-503, 2-504. The typical commercial contract will contain a delivery term that will define the seller's delivery obligations and thereby identify the relevant market price for measuring damages.

Suppose the buyer has covered, but the market price at the time and place of delivery is more than the cover price. May the buyer elect to forgo damages under the cover section and recover the greater amount of damages under the market damage section? The Code seems unclear on this point. Comment 3 to §2-712 states, "The buyer is always free to choose between cover and damages for nondelivery under the next section." However, Comment 5 to §2-713 provides that the market value rule applies "only when and to the extent that the buyer has not covered." Moreover, UCC §1-305 provides that the purpose of remedies under the Code is to place "the aggrieved party . . . in as good a position as if the other party had fully performed." Most commentators agree that in this situation the buyer should be limited to damages measured under the cover section. See, e.g., John A. Sebert, Jr., Remedies Under Article Two of the Uniform Commercial Code: An Agenda for Review, 130 U. Pa. L. Rev. 360, 380-383 (1981).

Suppose the seller has committed an anticipatory repudiation and the buyer fails or elects not to cover. As of what point in time should the market measure of damages be determined? This question has proved difficult for the courts because of uncertainty about the meaning of the phrase *learned of the breach* in §2-713. Three interpretations have been offered, each of which has its scholarly advocates and its support in case law:

1. the date when the buyer learns of the repudiation;
2. the date when the buyer learns of the repudiation plus a commercially reasonable time thereafter;
3. the date when actual performance by the seller is due under the contract.

The plain meaning of the section supports the first interpretation. The buyer's right to await performance by a repudiating party for a commercially reasonable time under UCC §2-610(a) supports the second approach. White and Summers argue for the third alternative based on legislative history and comparison with other Code provisions. See White & Summers, Uniform Commercial Code (6th ed. 2010) §7-7, at 332-333. For a discussion of the issue, particularly with regard to long-term contracts, see Victor Goldberg, Remedies in the UCC: Some Critical Thoughts, 23 Barry L. Rev. 155, 157-161 (2018).

c. Damages for Accepted Goods, UCC §2-714

Even though nonconforming goods have been accepted, the buyer may still be entitled to recover damages under §2-714(1). Under that section, the buyer may recover those damages that result "in the ordinary course of events from the seller's breach." More specifically, if the damages are caused by a breach of warranty, UCC §2-714(2) provides that the measure of damages is "the difference at the time and place of acceptance between the value of the goods accepted and the value they would have had if they had been as warranted, unless special circumstances show proximate damages of a different amount." For example, if an automobile is delivered with a different and lower priced set of tires than specified in the contract, the buyer would be able to recover the difference in the value (probably based on market prices) between the two sets of tires. Section 2-714(3) goes on to authorize incidental and consequential damages. It is important to note that if the buyer retains the goods despite nonconformity in the goods or the seller's tender, the buyer must give notice to the seller within reasonable period of time, under §2-607(3)(a), in order to preserve the right to collect a remedy.

d. Specific Performance, UCC §2-716

You may recall from an earlier overview of remedies in Chapter 2 and other discussion in this book that the principal alternative remedies for a nonbreaching party are money damages or equitable relief. The most common form of equitable remedy is specific performance, a judicial decree compelling the breaching party to render the performance required by the contract. In Chapter 11 we will see that the common law imposes various restrictions on the award of specific performance, particularly the requirement that the remedy of money damages be inadequate. In §2-716 the drafters of the Code made an effort to liberalize the award of specific performance. Under that section, specific performance "may" be decreed in the buyer's favor where the goods are "unique," or in "other proper circumstances." If goods are readily available on the market, a court applying the Code is likely to deny specific performance. Klein v. Pepsico, Inc., 845 F.2d 76 (4th Cir. 1988) (error to award specific performance of contract to sell airplane when comparable planes available on the market). Where substitute goods or a substitute contract are not available, the courts may be more willing to grant the remedy. See, e.g., Laclede Gas Co. v. Amoco Oil Co., 522 F.2d 33 (8th Cir. 1975) (specific performance granted of long-term requirements contract to supply propane; while propane was currently available to plaintiff under short-term contracts with other suppliers, it had "no assurance" that this situation would continue).

e. Incidental and Consequential Damages, UCC §2-715

After breach by the seller, the buyer is entitled to recover both incidental and consequential damages under UCC §2-715 in addition to other more immediate damages. Incidental damages consist of out-of-pocket expenses incurred by the buyer to deal with the consequences of the seller's breach. UCC §2-715(1). Consequential damages include:

> a) any loss resulting from general or particular requirements and needs of which the seller at the time of contracting had reason to know and which could not reasonably be prevented by cover or otherwise; and
>
> (b) injury to person or property proximately resulting from any breach of warranty.

UCC §2-715(2).

The section makes a distinction between economic or commercial loss, such as lost profits (subsection (a)), and damage to person or property (subsection (b)). The former is subject to the foreseeability test of Hadley v. Baxendale, which we studied in Section B of this chapter ("which the seller at the time of contracting had reason to know") and to the mitigation principle ("could not reasonably be prevented by cover or otherwise"). The Code rejects the "tacit agreement" formulation of the foreseeability test as discussed in the notes after the *Hadley v. Baxendale* case. UCC §2-715, Comment 2. Under subsection (b), damages for injury to person or property are not subject to the foreseeability test. Comment 4 to §2-715 states that damages must be proved by the buyer with reasonable certainty but not mathematical precision.

PROBLEM 10-2

Bing Industries is engaged in the manufacturing and fabrication of parts and components for the automotive industry. Last August it ordered 98,195 pounds of high-carbon cold-rolled steel from Southern Steel, Inc., for use in the fabrication of springs used in the assembly of automobile clutches. The purchase order set forth the specifications of the steel, which were critical because of the requirements for manufacture of the springs. Southern delivered the steel in coils to Bing on January 26 and 28. In accordance with its usual practice, Bing checked the steel for dimensional accuracy and chemical content and began partial fabrication of the steel into "blanks." It then stored the blanks, awaiting orders from its customers. Recently Bing removed the pieces from storage and resumed the fabrication process. During this processing, Bing noticed that the springs exhibited cracks and other failures. Bing immediately gave notice of the problem to Southern, which did extensive testing of the steel. A dispute has developed: Southern claims that Bing improperly processed the steel, while Bing contends that the steel was defective. Because of the problem with the steel, Bing is late on delivery of springs under a contract and runs the risk of having the contract canceled. Bing has sought your advice about how to proceed legally. What advice would you give?

2. Sellers' Remedies

In the section on buyers' remedies, we saw that the Code has modified the common law rules in several ways; in particular, a buyer has the option of recovering damages under the Code's rule on cover rather than under the traditional rule of market damages. For sellers, the Code adopts a similar provision, the right of "resale." UCC §2-706. In addition, the Code includes a new rule allowing a seller, under certain circumstances, to recover damages based on his lost profit. UCC §2-708(2). Analysis of sellers' remedies begins with §2-703, which outlines the seller's rights in the event the buyer breaches the contract. The measurement of the seller's damages depends partly on whether the buyer has accepted the goods based on the definition of acceptance in §2-606. If not, the seller may recover either resale damages, UCC §2-706, market damages, UCC §2-708(1), or lost profit, UCC §2-708(2). If the goods have been accepted, or are not reasonably subject to resale, the seller may recover the contract price under UCC §2-709.

a. Resale Damages, UCC §2-706

Section 2-706 allows a seller to resell goods after a breach by the buyer and "recover the difference between the resale price and the contract price." This remedy is the equivalent of the buyer's right to cover. The seller must follow three basic steps to recover damages under §2-706. First, the seller must identify the goods being resold as the same ones under the contract that was breached. Second, the seller must give the buyer proper notice of resale. For private sales, "the seller must give the buyer reasonable notification of his intention to resell." UCC §2-706(3). For public sales, the seller must give the buyer reasonable notice of the time and place of the resale except in the case of goods which are perishable or otherwise may quickly decline in value. UCC §2-706(4)(b).

Third, the seller's resale must be made in good faith and in a commercially reasonable manner. UCC §2-706(1). If the seller engages in a "sham" resale to a friendly purchaser or an affiliated entity, the court should not allow the seller to recover damages under the section. E.g., Coast Trading Co. v. Cudahy Co.,

592 F.2d 1074 (9th Cir. 1979) (seller entered into a "paper contract apparently intended to serve only as basis for calculating resale damages"). The fact that in hindsight a better price could have been obtained, however, does not make a sale unreasonable. Finnish Fur Sales Co. v. Juliette Shulof Furs, Inc., 770 F. Supp. 139 (S.D.N.Y. 1991) (seller sold at regularly scheduled auctions at prevailing prices; unreasonable for seller to suspend its operations to await higher world prices).

b. Market Damages, UCC §2-708(1)

As is the case with buyers, the Code contains a traditional contract price minus market value damage formula for sellers in UCC §2-708(1). The major problem in interpreting this section is the interrelationship between it and §2-706, the resale section. Suppose a seller has in fact resold goods identified to the contract. May the seller recover damages under §2-708(1) if that section would produce a greater recovery than the formula of §2-706? This situation can arise when the market price at the time and place for tender is less than the resale price. On the one hand, Comment 2 to §2-706 suggests that a seller who fails to follow the requirements for resale under that section is left to the remedy under §2-708(1). On the other hand, Professors White and Summers argue that a seller who has resold should not be entitled to recover greater damages under §2-708(1) than under §2-706. In their view, such a result would contravene the principle of awarding only compensatory damages as expressed in §1-305. White & Summers, §8-7, at 362. See Tesoro Petroleum Corp. v. Holborn Oil Co., 547 N.Y.S.2d 1012 (Sup. Ct. 1989) (following the White and Summers approach).

Professor Roy Anderson agrees that the nonbreaching party, whether a buyer or a seller, should not be able to receive greater damages under the market damages section than the party would have received by cover or resale. See Roy R. Anderson, A Look Back at the Future of UCC Damages Remedies, 71 SMU L. Rev. 185 (2018). By contrast, Professor Jennifer Martin argues for a more balanced approach to "section 2-708(1) that preserves the aggrieved seller's right to elect its remedy in most cases, subject to a limit of the seller achieving the position equivalent to full contractual performance only." See Jennifer S, Martin, Opportunistic Resales and the Uniform Commercial Code, 2016 U. Ill. L. Rev. 487, 525.

c. Lost Profits, UCC §2-708(2)

As an alternative to the market price measure of damages, UCC §2-708(2) authorizes courts to award lost profits to sellers if the market measure of damages set forth in §2-708(1) is "inadequate to put the seller in as good a position as performance would have done." Case law and commentary have identified three situations in which §2-708(2) should apply. The first of these is usually referred to as the case of the "lost volume seller." Recall the *Jetz Service* case earlier in this chapter. If the buyer breaches and the seller makes a resale of the same item, the seller may collect lost profits if it can prove that it had the capacity to make both sales and that both sales would have been profitable.

For example, a dealer who sells rather fungible new cars may argue that it has practically unlimited supply. The burden of proving its status as a lost volume seller is on the seller. See Razorback Concrete Co. v. Dement Constr. Co., LLC, 688 F.3d 346, 352 (8th Cir. 2012). Professor Goldberg argues that recovery of lost profits overcompensates the lost volume seller; instead, he contends that these cases should be treated as ones in which the buyer has an implied option to cancel, and damages should be measured by a cancellation charge. Further, "[i]n the absence of an explicit option price, the default rule should set the price at zero." Goldberg, Remedies in the UCC: Some Critical Thoughts, 23 Barry L. Rev. at 161-164.

Note that Section 2-708(2) requires "due credit for payments or proceeds of resale." This phrase has proved troublesome in the "lost volume seller" cases. If the total proceeds of the seller's resale are deducted, the profit recovery under §2-708(2) would be negated because the resale price also includes seller's profit. Courts have avoided this problem by interpreting the "due credit" language to apply only when the seller sells uncompleted or otherwise unmarketable goods for scrap. See R.E. Davis Chemical Corp. v. Diasonics, Inc., 826 F.2d 678, 684 (7th Cir. 1987).

The second situation in which §2-708(2) has been applied involves a seller who is in the process of assembling a product for sale when the buyer breaches. While the seller could complete manufacture of the product and attempt to resell it on the open market, it might not be commercially reasonable to do this (for example, if the goods were specialty items without an established market). See UCC §2-704(2). Awarding lost profits based on the contract price minus the cost of production would be perhaps the only way to compensate the seller.

Finally, §2-708(2) has been applied in the case of the "jobber," a middle person who purchases goods for resale. If the buyer from a jobber breaches before the jobber has acquired the goods, courts may award lost profits as the best measure of the seller's harm. See Blair International, Ltd. v. LaBarge, Inc., 675 F.2d 954 (8th Cir. 1982) (jobber of oil casings allowed to recover lost profits); TCP Industries, Inc. v. Uniroyal, Inc., 661 F.2d 542 (6th Cir. 1981) (intermediary for chemicals allowed to recover lost profits).

Section 2-708(2) states that it applies if the market value measure of damages is "inadequate" to put the seller in as good a position as full performance by the buyer. May a seller elect to recover market value damages under §2-708(1), if the measure of recovery under that section *exceeds* his lost profit in the transaction? We have previously encountered similar questions concerning whether a covering buyer or a reselling seller elect market damages if that measure would produce a greater recovery? In each situation, the same arguments have reappeared. The language and legislative history of the Code favor allowing the election by the nonbreaching party, while the principle of compensation supports the opposite view. The courts are divided. See Nobs Chemical, U.S.A., Inc. v. Koppers Co., 616 F.2d 212 (5th Cir. 1980) (acknowledging ambiguity in §2-708 and limiting seller to lost profit even though market damages would have been greater).

d. Seller's Action for the Price, UCC §2-709

The seller may recover the price of the goods from the buyer as damages under §2-709 in three situations. First, if the buyer has accepted the goods, then the seller may recover the price under §2-709(1)(a). Second, under the same section, the seller may recover the price if the goods are damaged after the risk of loss has passed to the buyer. In both of these situations, the buyer has effectively received the goods and thus should pay the contract price. Third, the seller may recover the price under §2-709(1)(b), and essentially force the goods onto the buyer, if the seller is unable to resell the goods with reasonable effort. Although neither §2-709(1)(b) nor its comments use the phrase *specific performance*, it appears that the section is the analogue of §2-716, which makes specific performance available to the buyer. See Schumann v. Levi, 728 F.2d 1141 (8th Cir. 1984) ("the equitable remedy of specific performance and the Uniform Commercial Code's action for the price are virtually identical").

e. Seller's Incidental and Consequential Damages, UCC §2-710

All of the above remedial sections also allow the seller to recover incidental damages under §2-710. Incidental damages include a variety of out-of-pocket expenses incurred by the seller to deal with the buyer's breach, such as cost of storage or transportation of the goods. Section 2-710 does not contain any reference to consequential damages, perhaps because the drafters of the Code were persuaded that sellers rarely suffer consequential damages that would not be compensated by the damage measures discussed above. White and Summers argue that, despite the language of §2-710, courts should rely on common law principles via §1-103(b) and allow sellers to recover consequential damages in appropriate cases. White & Summers, §8-16, at 393-395.

PROBLEM 10-3

On July 1, Henry T. Johnson Food Distributors, Inc., entered into a written contract with McBride Farms to purchase 5,000 bushels of "large" peaches at $4 per bushel, delivery to be made on or before August 15. At 9 A.M. on August 15 McBride's truck pulled up at the Johnson facility. The delivery driver, Charlotte McBride, gave an invoice to the Johnson agent at the unloading docks. She pointed out that the invoice showed 4,800 bushels of "large" peaches and 200 bushels of "small" peaches. (In the trade, small peaches are not as marketable as large ones, selling to buyers like Johnson Food for approximately $2 per bushel.) She also noted that the invoice price ($19,600) had been adjusted by $400 to reflect the small peaches. The agent said he would have to "check with the boss." He returned a few minutes later to say that the peaches were unacceptable and could not be unloaded. McBride asked to talk with the boss, who told her that he was "sick and tired" of "farmers making deliveries any way they wanted." He said that McBride should have obtained approval first, not just "showed up" with the small peaches. McBride offered to leave only the large peaches, but the Johnson agent refused and ordered her to leave. McBride returned with the peaches to her farm, and left them at the McBride Cannery, a subsidiary operation that cans unmarketable peaches. On its books, the Cannery recorded a credit of $5,000 for McBride Farms, treating the peaches as costing $1 per bushel. Subsequently, the Cannery completed canning the peaches; its manufacturing costs for doing so were $3,000. McBride has now brought suit against Johnson Food Distributors for breach of contract. Analyze McBride's rights to recover damages. If additional facts are needed, explain what they are and why they are legally significant.

F. JUSTIFICATIONS FOR THE EXPECTATION DAMAGE RULE

At the beginning of our survey of the rules governing contract damages, we posed — but did not then attempt to answer — two questions about the expectation-damage principle: Why should contract law allow recovery of the plaintiff's full expectation of gain under the breached contract, even in cases where the plaintiff has not yet performed, expended any resources in preparations for performance, or substantially relied in any other way on the contract at issue? Conversely, why should the law ordinarily award *no more than* expectation damages for breach of contract, denying to most contract plaintiffs the sorts of exemplary or punitive damages often available in tort actions? In this section, we will consider some answers that have been given to these questions.

1. Protecting the Expectation Interest Under a Wholly Executory Contract

In many cases where enforcement of a contractual obligation is sought, it is clear that the party seeking enforcement has relied in a variety of ways, substantial and insubstantial, on her expectation that the defendant's promised performance would be rendered. In many such cases, the defendant promisor has also received some benefit from the plaintiff's actions, so that the defendant would be unjustly enriched if his promise were to go completely unenforced. In such cases, the plaintiff's reliance or restitution interest may therefore appear to require compensation in damages. But not every breach of contract will necessarily involve such injury. Since the law recognizes an exchange of purely executory promises as sufficient in itself to create a contract, there is no theoretical barrier to enforcement where the defendant promisor has breached his promise at a time when the plaintiff promisee had neither performed nor relied (in any but a purely psychological way) on the defendant's promise of performance. In such a case, the only remedial interest that has been injured is the plaintiff's expectation interest. Aside from the internal logic of the rule-structure itself, what justifies the law's willingness to award an expectation-based remedy to a plaintiff who has not been demonstrably injured in any quantifiable or even tangible way by the defendant's breach?

In their landmark 1936 article, Professor Lon Fuller and his associate William Perdue attempted to answer that question. After rejecting the "psychological" explanation for the award of expectation damages, Fuller and Perdue argue that expectation damages can be justified to compensate for what could be called "hidden reliance":

> It is a cure for these losses in the sense that it offers the measure of recovery most likely to reimburse the plaintiff for the (often very numerous and very difficult to prove) individual acts and forbearances which make up his total reliance on the contract. . . . Physicians with an extensive practice often charge their patients the full office call fee for broken appointments. Such a charge looks on the face of things like a claim to the promised fee; it seems to be based on the "expectation interest." Yet the physician making the charge will quite justifiably regard it as compensation for the loss of the opportunity to gain a similar fee from a different patient. This foregoing of other opportunities is involved to some extent in entering most contracts, and the impossibility of subjecting this type of reliance to any kind of measurement may justify a categorical rule granting the value of the expectancy as the most effective way of compensating for such losses. . . .

Fuller and Perdue go on to offer a second justification for expectation damages: "a policy in favor of promoting and facilitating reliance on business agreements." Lon L. Fuller & William R. Perdue, Jr., The Reliance Interest in Contract Damages (Pt. I), 46 Yale L.J. 52, 57-62 (1936).

In contrast to Fuller and Perdue, English historian P.S. Atiyah has asserted that the law's readiness to protect a promisee's expectation under a completely executory bilateral contract (i.e., one that has been neither performed nor relied on) is a relatively recent development. Atiyah has also argued that cases where enforcement of a completely executory contract is sought are much rarer in real life than in contract theory:

> It is, I think, worth observing that wholly executory contracts are generally nothing like as binding in practice as legal theory might suggest. Consumers and even business men often expect to be able to cancel executory agreements with the minimum of penalty, paying perhaps only for actual expenses laid out in reliance on the promise. And such reliance expenditures would, by definition, not exist if the arrangement were still wholly executory. . . . Where there is no difference in the market price of the goods or services which are the subject of the contract, and the market price of comparable goods or services, the contract may in law be broken with impunity. In practice this must comprise a high proportion of cases in which executory arrangements are broken. Then again, the binding force of wholly executory contracts is normally of an ephemeral nature. Executory contracts do not normally remain executory for very long. Even if made well before the time for performance, the whole purpose of making them is frequently to enable the parties to make preliminary arrangements in confident reliance on reciprocal performance. Thus action in reliance is likely to follow hard on the heels of the making of most executory contracts. . . .

P.S. Atiyah, Contracts, Promises and the Law of Obligations, 94 L.Q. Rev. 193, 211-212 (1978).

In a 1982 article, The Bargain Principle and Its Limits, 95 Harv. L. Rev. 741, Professor Melvin Eisenberg critically examines in a variety of situations the principle that bargained-for promises should be enforced to the full extent of the expectation created thereby. In the half-completed contract, when one party has rendered full performance and seeks the return performance or its value from the breaching party, both fairness and efficiency support an award of expectation damages. By contrast, when the contract is infected by some form of overreaching, such as unconscionability, neither fairness nor efficiency justify expectation damages: Either restitution or no remedy are likely to be more appropriate.

Eisenberg then addresses the "pure" case for the recovery of expectation damages, where the plaintiff has not performed at all, even partially. Assuming that the contract in question is not in any degree tainted by some form of unconscionability, should the plaintiff's expectation interest be protected by enforcing the contract? Eisenberg asserts that at least three policies can be identified that may justify full-bargain enforcement: (1) assured protection of the full cost of reliance (which Eisenberg calls the "surrogate-cost theory"); (2) facilitation of planning (by deterring breach in most cases); (3) protection of a risk-allocation that the contract was created to effectuate (e.g., a contract for future delivery at a fixed price, made in order to allocate the risk of price changes between the time of contract and the time set for performance). He then applies this analysis to a number of contracts between business concerns and concludes that in most cases full-bargain enforcement can be justified on the basis of one or more of these policies. Melvin A. Eisenberg, The Bargain Principle and Its Limits, 95 Harv. L. Rev. 741, 788-789 (1982).

Suppose, however, that the contract at issue is not between two commercial concerns, but between a merchant and a consumer. Here Eisenberg's analysis produces somewhat different results. In contracts for services to consumers (e.g., education, fitness, language) Eisenberg's policies do not support an award to businesses of full expectation damages; in these situations the seller's interest in planning and the buyer's expectations would justify an award of a cancellation charge, which could be set by the seller in the contract provided it was reasonable. Id. at 794-797.

If Professor Atiyah's observations above are as correct as intuitively they seem to be, the number of cases in which a court is asked to enforce a completely executory agreement (both unperformed and unrelied on) will be relatively few. In the absence of injury to either the reliance or the restitution interest of the plaintiff, the arguments for full-bargain enforcement seem much less compelling. When such a case does arise, therefore, it should not be surprising to find the court seeking some basis for denying enforcement – particularly where the defendant is a consumer who may not have prepared for or even foreseen the possibility of substantial liability.

2. Encouraging or Deterring Breach of Contract: The Concepts of "Efficient Breach" and Disgorgement

The rules governing remedies for breach of contract have often been referred to (sometimes with favor, sometimes not) as "amoral." Perhaps the most frequently quoted passage in support of this view is from an address delivered in 1897 by Oliver Wendell Holmes, then Justice of the Massachusetts Supreme Judicial Court, at the dedication of a new hall at the Boston University School of Law. Speaking first of the necessity for law students to avoid the fallacy of assuming "law" and "morality" to be synonymous, Holmes went on to give some examples of the divergence between them.

> Nowhere is the confusion between legal and moral ideas more manifest than in the law of contract. . . . The duty to keep a contract at common law means a prediction that you must pay damages if you do not keep it — and nothing else. If you commit a tort, you are liable to pay a compensatory sum. If you commit a [breach of] contract, you are liable to pay a compensatory sum unless the promised event comes to pass, and that is all the difference. But such a mode of looking at the matter stinks in the nostrils of those who think it advantageous to get as much ethics into the law as they can.

Oliver Wendell Holmes, The Path of the Law, in Collected Legal Papers 174-175 (1920). Holmes voiced similar views elsewhere: "It is true," he observed in his lecture on the Elements of Contract,

> that in some instances equity does what is called compelling specific performance. But . . . [t]his remedy is an exceptional one. The only universal consequence of a legally binding promise is, that the law makes the promisor pay damages if the promised event does not come to pass. In every case it leaves him free from interference until the time for fulfillment has gone by, and therefore free to break his contract if he chooses.

Oliver Wendell Holmes, The Common Law 236 (Mark DeWolfe Howe ed. 1963).

To Holmes, it may be that these statements represented an effort to direct our thinking toward the possibility that law is primarily the product of social forces whose nature as "good" or "evil" may be debatable, but whose existence and effect cannot be denied. This thought is most pithily expressed in what are perhaps Holmes's best-known words: "The life of the law has not been logic; it has been experience." Id. at 1. Others, however, have seen in Holmes's observations about contract law a challenge to both morals and logic. If indeed the law of contract does take an "amoral" view of contract-breaking behavior, why has this been so? And, indeed, *should* it be so?

The view that Holmes's observation is correct both historically and philosophically has been most energetically advanced by writers of the law and economics school, led by Richard Posner. Holmes's statement that the breaching party is merely required to choose between performance and compensation contains, Posner asserts, "an important economic insight." Richard A. Posner, Economic Analysis of Law 128-129 (9th ed. 2014). "In many cases," Posner continues,

> it is uneconomical to induce completion of performance of a contract after it has been broken. I agree to purchase 100,000 widgets custom-ground for use as components in a machine that I manufacture. After I have taken delivery of 10,000, the market for my machine collapses. I promptly notify my supplier that I am terminating the contract and admit that my termination is a breach. When notified of the termination he has not yet begun the custom grinding of the other 90,000 widgets, but he informs me that he intends to complete his performance under the contract and bill me accordingly. The custom-ground widgets have no use other than in my machine and a negligible scrap value. To give the supplier a remedy that induced him to complete the contract would cause a waste of valuable resources. The law is alert to this danger and, under the rubric of mitigation of damages, would deny the supplier damages for costs he incurred in continuing production after the notice of termination. . . .
>
> Suppose the contract is broken by the seller rather than by the buyer. I really need those 100,000 custom-ground widgets for my machine, but the supplier, after producing 50,000, is forced to suspend production. Other sellers are in a position to supply the remaining widgets that I need, but I insist that the promisor complete his performance of the contract. If the law compels completion, the supplier will have to make arrangements with other producers in order to be able to complete the performance of his contract with me. Probably it will be more costly for him to procure an alternative supplier than for me to do so directly (after all, I know my own needs best); otherwise he would have done it voluntarily, to minimize his liability for the breach. To compel completion of the contract (or costly negotiations to discharge the promisor) in such a case would again waste resources, and so again the law limits the victim to seeking damages.
>
> What should those damages be? The objective of giving the promisor an incentive to fulfill his promise unless the result would be an inefficient use of resources can be achieved by giving the promisee his expected profit on the transaction. If the supplier in the first example (buyer breach) receives his expected profit from making 10,000 [sic 100,000?] widgets, he will have no incentive to make the unwanted 90,000. We do not want him to make them; no one wants them. In the second example (seller breach), if I receive my expected profit from dealing with the original seller, I become indifferent to whether he completes his performance.

Id. at 129-131.

It should be remembered at this point that in many cases where performance is in some sense "impossible" or even "impracticable," the law will in fact excuse the nonperforming party from the duty of performance, in which case no damages at all would be awarded. (Recall our discussion in Chapter 8.) But Posner's analysis is not limited to cases where the breach is "involuntary." The same result should follow, he continues, even in some cases where the breaching party could perform, but chooses not to do so.

> [I]n some cases a party is tempted to break his contract simply because his profit from breach would exceed his profit from completing performance. He will do so if the profit would also exceed the expected profit to the other party from completion of the contract, and hence the damages from breach. So

> in this case awarding damages will not deter a breach of contract. It should not. It is an efficient breach. Suppose I sign a contract to deliver 100,000 custom-ground widgets at 10¢ apiece to *A* for use in his boiler factory. After I have delivered 10,000, *B* comes to me, explains that he desperately needs 25,000 custom-ground widgets at once since otherwise he will be forced to close his pianola factory at great cost, and offers me 15¢ apiece for them. I sell him the widgets and as a result do not complete timely delivery to *A*, causing him to lose $1,000 in profits. Having obtained an additional profit of $1,250 on the sale to *B*, I am better off even after reimbursing *A* for his loss, and *B* is also better off. The breach is therefore Pareto superior. True, had I refused to sell to *B* he could have gone to *A* and negotiated an assignment to him of part of *A*'s contract with me. But this would have introduced an additional step, with additional transaction costs. . . .

Id. at 131.

Many commentators have echoed Posner's view that when nonperformance (in order to permit entry into a substitute, more profitable transaction) would be "efficient," the law should not only permit breach but indeed regard it as appropriate behavior to be encouraged rather than condemned. See Charles J. Goetz & Robert E. Scott, Liquidated Damages, Penalties, and the Just Compensation Principle: Some Notes on an Enforcement Model and a Theory of Efficient Breach, 77 Colum. L. Rev. 554, 558 (1977). See also Richard Caswell, Contract Remedies, Renegotiation, and the Theory of Efficient Breach, 61 S. Cal. L. Rev. 629 (1988); and Robert L. Birmingham, Breach of Contract, Damage Measures, and Economic Efficiency, 24 Rutgers L. Rev. 273, 291 (1970) (applying the theory of efficient breach to personal service contracts to allow an employer in a market of falling wages to discharge an employee and hire a new employee at a lower wage, so long as the fired employee is compensated for his loss of wages).

Criticism of the doctrine of efficient breach has taken a number of forms. Many writers emphasize that the theory of efficient breach ignores "transaction costs," particularly attorney fees incurred by the nonbreaching party for litigation or negotiation of a settlement. As we saw in the previous section, such fees are ordinarily not recoverable as damages for breach of contract. As a result, application of the principle of efficient breach will often undercompensate the nonbreaching party. Critics also point to the traditional limitations on expectation damages (including not only the denial of reimbursement for litigation costs, but also the requirements of foreseeability and certainty) as virtually guaranteeing that the nonbreaching party will be undercompensated if breach does occur. See generally Daniel A. Farber, Reassessing the Economic Efficiency of Compensatory Damages for Breach of Contract, 66 Va. L. Rev. 1443 (1980); Richard Schiro, Prospecting for Lost Profits in the Uniform Commercial Code: The Buyer's Dilemmas, 52 S. Cal. L. Rev. 1727 (1979).

To remedy these defects, the theory of efficient breach would need to be modified to allow for compensation for transaction costs and to loosen the rules limiting the recovery of "nonforeseeable" or "speculative" damages, to increase the likelihood that the actual injury resulting from breach will be fully compensated. See Farber, supra at 1443-1445 (calling for the recovery of "supercompensatory" damages, calculated to compensate the plaintiff for some of the major transaction costs incurred as a result of breach) and Schiro, supra (suggesting a substantial modification of the rules limiting the recovery of "nonforeseeable" or "speculative" damages, to increase the likelihood that the actual injury resulting from breach will be fully compensated).

Another thread of criticism of the theory of efficient breach focuses on specific performance as an alternative to damages as a remedy for breach of contract. Professor Ian Macneil argues that if courts award specific performance (i.e., a breaching party will be ordered to specifically perform his contractual duty), rather than expectation damages, the result will be both efficient and fairer to the nonbreaching party. When a court orders specific performance, the parties will bargain among themselves to reach this result: The party who has available a more profitable second contract will buy his way out of the first one (rather than simply breaching it). Thus, the goods will still end up being allocated to their most highly valued use, but some of the resulting gain will have gone to the other party to the original contract. Ian R. Macneil, Efficient Breach of Contract: Circles in the Sky, 68 Va. L. Rev. 947, 951-952 (1982). See also Alan Schwartz, The Case for Specific Performance, 89 Yale L.J. 271 (1979).

More fundamentally, a number of critics question the moral foundations of the theory of efficient breach. Professor Daniel Friedman argues that the theory of efficient breach fails to recognize that contractual rights, like property rights, are entitlements of which a person should not be deprived without his consent. Daniel Friedmann, The Efficient Breach Fallacy, 18 J. Legal Stud. 1, 6-7 (1989) (arguing also that the theory is itself inefficient because it often produces multiple transactions including "protracted negotiations, or even litigation, over difficult questions of fact and law" and sometimes "an expensive tort action for inducement of breach of contract"). Professor Macneil points out that the theory is founded on a "bias is in favor of individual, uncooperative behavior as opposed to behavior requiring the cooperation of the parties." Macneil, supra at 968-969. Professor Patricia Marschall contends that promotion of economic efficiency is neither a "realistic" nor a "proper" goal for contract law. She urges courts to distinguish between willful and nonwillful breaches, awarding either specific performance or the highest measure of compensatory damages for the former. In addition, punitive damages should be available when the breach is not only willful, but also made in unreasonable disregard of the other party. Patricia H. Marschall, Willfulness: A Crucial Factor in Choosing Remedies for Breach of Contract, 24 Ariz. L. Rev. 733, 761 (1982). Professor Peter Linzer stresses that while economic efficiency is an important value in the law, fairness and justice are more important. He calls on courts to award specific performance for breach of promise rather than a "diluted substitute" of money damages. Peter Linzer, On the Amorality of Contract Remedies—Efficiency, Equity and the Second Restatement, 81 Colum. L. Rev. 111, 139 (1981). See also George M. Cohen, The Fault Lines in Contract Damages, 80 Va. L. Rev. 1225 (1994) (arguing for a fault-based theory of contract damages).

In a review of the results produced by scholars applying principles of economic analysis to contract law generally, one of the leading scholars in the field, Professor Eric Posner, points to some successes but ultimately reaches a surprisingly negative conclusion: "[T]he economic approach does not explain the current system of contract law, nor does it provide a solid basis for criticizing and reforming contract law." Eric A. Posner, Economic Analysis of Contract Law after Three Decades: Success or Failure? 112 Yale L.J. 829, 830 (2003).

Notwithstanding Professor Posner's criticism, there appears to be a growing number of court decisions explicitly recognizing the efficient breach concept and using the theory to support a denial of punitive or enhanced damages for breach of contract, often referring to Holmes' amoral view of contract law. For example, in TruGreen Companies., L.L.C. v. Mower Brothers, 199 P.3d 929 (Utah 2008), the Supreme Court of Utah answered a certified question from the federal district court concerning the proper measurement of damages for a former employee's breach of non-competition, non-solicitation and non-disclosure covenants, stating:

> [A]s a policy matter, we do not wish to adopt a remedy for breach of contract that punishes the breaching party. Rather, our focus is on placing "the non-breaching party in as good a position as if the contract had been performed." . . . Contract law is amoral and, therefore, appropriate in a business setting in which efficiency is valued. See Marcus, Stowell & Beye Gov't Secs., Inc. v. Jefferson Inv. Corp., 797 F.2d 227, 232 (5th Cir. 1986) (discussing the appropriateness of efficient breaches of contract) . . . We have also held that punitive damages for breach of contract, by themselves, are inappropriate "even if [the breach was] intentional and unjustified." Hal Taylor Assocs. v. Unionamerica, Inc., 657 P.2d 743, 750 (Utah 1982). "[S]uch damages are [only] allowable if there is some independent tort indicating malice, fraud or wanton disregard for the rights of others." Id. Thus, we confirm our earlier holdings that any measure of damages that punishes a breaching party is inappropriate. Id. at 933.

See also Mission Beverage Co. v. Pabst Brewing Co., LLC, 223 Cal. Rptr. 3d 547, 562 (Ct. App. 2017) (recognizing that the concept of efficient breach allows one party to a contract to breach and pay damages rather than perform, but does not support a rule that allows the breaching party to avoid paying damages by having someone else pay a portion of those damages); Am. Capital Acquisition Partners, LLC v. LPL Holdings, Inc., 2014 Del. Ch. LEXIS 12 (Del. Ch.) (stating that Delaware recognizes the concept of "efficient breach"). But see Sundberg v. TTR Realty, LLC, 109 A.3d 1123 (D.C. 2015) (criticizing the concept of "efficient breach" because it recognizes a "right" to breach a contract by paying damages).

The concept of efficient breach is, of course, only one topic among many that have been the subject of theoretical analysis by contact scholars. For recent books about contract theory, with extensive bibliography to other works, see Douglas G. Baird, Reconstructing Contracts (2013); Brian H. Bix, Contract Law: Rules, Theory, and Context (2013); Melvin Eisenberg, Foundational Principles of Contract Law (2013); and Nathan B. Oman, The Dignity of Commerce: Markets and the Moral Foundations of Contract Law (2017). Professor Oman's book is the subject of a Symposium, Morality, Markets, and Contract Law, 9 Wm. & Mary Bus. L. Rev. #2 (2018).

Roth v. Speck

District of Columbia Municipal Court of Appeals 126 A.2d 153 (1956)

QUINN, Associate Judge.

This suit was brought by plaintiff (employer) against defendant (employee) for breach of a written contract of employment. Trial by the court resulted in a finding and judgment for plaintiff for one dollar. Plaintiff appeals.

Plaintiff testified that he was the owner of a beauty salon in Silver Spring, Maryland; that his business was seasonal; and that on April 15, 1955, by a written contract he agreed to employ defendant as a hairdresser for one year. Defendant's salary was to be $75 a week or a commission of fifty percent on the gross receipts from his work, whichever sum was greater. Defendant remained in his employ for approximately six and one-half months and then left. Plaintiff testified that from the beginning defendant earned his salary, needed no special training, and soon built up and maintained a following because of his exceptional skill and talent.

Plaintiff also testified that his net profit was seven percent of the gross receipts per hairdresser. To substantiate this he introduced defendant's statement of earnings, which reflected gross receipts and salary paid to him. Plaintiff testified that in an effort to mitigate his damages he employed another person "to whom he paid $350, which was a complete loss and he had to let this employee go." He then hired still another operator who even at the date of trial was not earning his salary, and was thus employed at a loss to plaintiff. A witness for plaintiff testified that he had been the owner of a beauty salon for many years; that defendant had been in his employ since November 1, 1955, at a weekly salary of $100; and that defendant was a very good operator.

Defendant testified that he left because conditions in plaintiff's shop were unbearable; that he complained to plaintiff on numerous occasions; that he had asked for more money but that salary was not the main reason for his leaving; and that he was presently earning $100 per week.

The sole question presented is what damages plaintiff was entitled to under these circumstances. Plaintiff argues that the trial court did not consider the value of defendant's services or the profits lost by plaintiff and therefore erroneously limited the award to nominal damages. It is established law that where a plaintiff proves a breach of a contractual duty he is entitled to damages; however, when he offers no proof of actual damages or the proof is vague and speculative, he is entitled to no more than nominal damages. While the facts warrant application of this principle to plaintiff's claim concerning lost profits, we think there was proof of actual damage and that the evidence with regard to the value of defendant's services provided an accurate measure of such damage.

The measure of damages for breach of an employment contract by an employee is the cost of obtaining other service equivalent to that promised and not performed. Compensation for additional consequential injury may be recovered if at the time the contract was made the employee had reason to foresee that such injury would result from his breach. However, we need not concern ourselves with the foreseeability of lost profits resulting from defendant's breach since plaintiff's proof on this point was at most conjectural and speculative. He introduced defendant's statement of earnings, which reflected gross receipts and salary paid to defendant, and testified that his net profit was seven percent of such gross receipts per hairdresser. However, he also testified that his business was seasonal. The matter was further complicated by the testimony of both plaintiff and defendant to the effect that an employee assigned the customers and that some customers requested a particular operator. It can be seen then that defendant's gross receipts, and hence plaintiff's seven percent profit, depended on a number of contingencies — the seasonal fluctuations of business, defendant's skill and industry, and the judgment of the employee who assigned the operators. There was no criterion by which the trial court could have estimated plaintiff's profits with the degree of certainty necessary to allow their recovery; therefore they were not within the range of recoverable damages.

There remains the question as to the value of defendant's services. Defendant was evidently a hairdresser of exceptional talent. This is demonstrated not only by the fact that he experienced no difficulty in securing and retaining another position at a higher salary, but also by plaintiff's own testimony that he was unable to hire a satisfactory substitute. Defendant did not claim that he was required to render services other than those in his original contract with plaintiff in order to obtain a higher salary from his new employer, nor did plaintiff prove by expert testimony how much such services would bring in the market. But plaintiff did prove the amount defendant actually received. Under such circumstances, there was some evidence of the value of defendant's services and therefore of the cost of replacement. As was said in Triangle Waist Co. v. Todd, 223 N.Y. 27, 119 N.E. 85, 86:

> If one agrees to sell something to another, and then, the next day, sells it to someone else at an advance, the new transaction is not to be ignored in estimating the buyer's loss. . . . The rule is not different when one sells one's labor. The price received upon a genuine sale either of property or of service is some evidence of value. . . .

Twenty-four weeks yet remained when defendant abandoned his contract and obtained employment elsewhere at a higher salary. Until this new compensation is disproved as the value of his services, it may be presumed to be the fair value. That it was the fair value of defendant's services was partially supported by plaintiff's unsuccessful efforts to obtain a comparable replacement. Seemingly, plaintiff would have had to pay $100 a week in order to obtain an equally talented hairdresser, if one could have been found. If this be so, plaintiff, having contracted for defendant's services at a guaranteed wage of $75 per week, would be entitled to the difference between the two salaries for the remainder of the contract period. The fact that defendant was entitled to a fifty-percent commission on his gross receipts — if such receipts were more than his salary — should not be a deterrent to the application of this measure of damages. It was defendant's duty to prove facts in mitigation of the damage he caused by his breach. If he believed his damages would be lessened by proving that if he had stayed for the remainder of his contract the fifty-percent commission on his gross receipts would have been higher than his guaranteed salary, it was his burden to offer such proof. Though such facts may be difficult to prove, one who breaches his contract " 'cannot wholly escape on account of the difficulty which his own wrong has produced of devising a perfect measure of,' or method of proving, damages."

The judgment will be reversed with instructions to grant a new trial, limited to the issue of damages.

Reversed with instructions.

NOTES AND QUESTIONS

1. ***Roth and Lukaszewski compared.*** Recall the measure of damages employed in Handicapped Children's Education Board v. Lukaszewski, section A of this chapter. Does the court in *Roth* recognize that rule? Should that measure have been used to compute the plaintiff's damages in *Roth*? Conversely, could the measure employed in *Roth* have been used in *Lukaszewski*? Should it have been?

2. *Use of market value measure of damages.* In computing damages for a seller's wrongful refusal to convey land, the court may employ as a measure of "market value" the higher price that the seller received in selling to another (a sale that would not have been possible, of course, if the seller had not breached his earlier contract with the plaintiff). See Ament v. One Las Olas, Ltd., 898 So. 2d 147 (Fla. 2005) (long-standing precedent establishes that breaching seller should be liable to buyer for any profit made on subsequent sale). This result shifts to the innocent original purchaser the gain that the seller was able to realize as a result of the seller's breach. In *Roth*, the court carries that approach over to a case involving breach of an employment contract. Is this appropriate? Or are there factors, not present in the sale-of-land cases, that militate against using this approach to computation of damages in cases like *Roth*? See also Trilogy Network Systems, Inc. v. Johnson, 172 P.3d 1119 (Ida. 2007) (amount of profit made from breach by employee is relevant to measure of damages if it is shown by evidence to correspond with loss incurred by nonbreaching employer).

3. *The disgorgement principle.* Should the measure of damages used in *Roth* and in the sale-of-land cases be more generally employed, so as to give the plaintiff in most breach-of-contract cases the option of having her damages computed with reference to the gain the defendant was enabled to realize by virtue of his breach? Some commentators have argued that the principle of "disgorgement" traditionally employed in cases of tortious conversion and breach of fiduciary duty should be further extended into the area of breach of

contract. See Daniel Friedmann, Restitution of Benefits Obtained Through the Appropriation of Property or the Commission of a Wrong, 80 Colum. L. Rev. 504 (1980). (This form of remedy is commonly referred to as a species of "restitution," although it is clear that this is to some extent a misnomer, since the gain realized by the defendant was not received from the plaintiff.) Professor Friedmann argues that such restitution of gain may be proper in two types of cases: those involving appropriation of some "property" or "quasi-property" interest rightly belonging to the plaintiff and those in which "deterrence" is a major factor.

Professor Allan Farnworth has taken issue with Friedman's general conclusions and instead advocates a more cautious approach. He stresses that in many cases it is at least an oversimplification, if not an outright inaccuracy, to say that the defendant's gain is the "result" of his breach of contract. E. Allan Farnsworth, Your Loss or My Gain? The Dilemma of the Disgorgement Principle in Breach of Contract, 94 Yale L.J. 1339, 1343-1350 (1985). Farnsworth also notes that where there is a functioning market for the goods or services involved, application of market-value remedies will frequently result in effect in disgorgement of substantially all of the breacher's gain. Id. at 1370-1378. He concludes, however, that a limited extension of the disgorgement principle would be appropriate in cases of what he called "abuse of contract." He gives as an example a situation in which a builder intentionally substitutes less costly building materials in a structure in breach of the contract saving $25,000. The cost to remedy the defect is $60,000, which many courts would not allow because of "economic waste" (Recall *Jacob & Youngs, Inc. v. Kent* in Chapter 9) and the decline in market value of the property is $10,000. Farnsworth argues that there is a "strong moral argument" for allowing the owner to recover the builder's profit of $25,000 to prevent the builder from profiting from his own wrong. In addition, the award of $10,000 has a "significant risk of undercompensation." Id. at 1384-1386. For a case relying on Professor Farnsworth's analysis, see Earthinfo, Inc. v. Hydrosphere Resource Consultants, Inc., 900 P.2d 113 (Colo. 1995) (en banc) (in software development contract, defendant's conscious and intentional breach by refusing to make royalty payments justified plaintiff's rescission of contract and also disgorgement of profits received by defendant under derivative software contracts; case remanded for apportionment of profits between parties).

4. *Disgorgement under the Restatement (Third) of Restitution and Unjust Enrichment.* The Restatement (Third) of Restitution and Unjust Enrichment has adopted the disgorgement principle in §39, Profit from Opportunistic Breach:

> (1) If a deliberate breach of contract results in profit to the defaulting promisor and the available damage remedy affords inadequate protection to the promisee's contractual entitlement, the promisee has a claim to restitution of the profit realized by the promisor as a result of the breach. Restitution by the rule of this section is an alternative to a remedy in damages.

(2) A case in which damages afford inadequate protection to the promisee's contractual entitlement is ordinarily one in which damages will not permit the promisee to acquire a full equivalent to the promised performance in a substitute transaction.

(3) Breach of contract is profitable when it results in gains to the defendant (net of potential liability in damages) greater than the defendant would have realized from performance of the contract. Profits from breach include saved expenditure and consequential gains that the defendant would not have realized but for the breach, as measured by the rules that apply in other cases of disgorgement (§51(5)).

In Southwestern Energy Prod. Co. v. Berry-Helfand, 491 S.W.3d 699 (Tex. 2016), the Texas Supreme Court, while citing several provisions of the Restatement (Third) of Restitution and Unjust Enrichment, including §39, indicated that previous Texas lower court decisions had refused to allow disgorgement as a remedy for breach of contract. Id. at 728, n.13.

In light of the materials we have studied in this chapter, does it appear that a deliberate breach of contract will in many types of cases also create "inadequate protection to the promisee's contractual entitlement?" In the next chapter, we consider some of the more orthodox applications of the restitutionary principle in the area of contract damages, along with other alternatives to the award of expectation damages.

PROBLEM 10-4

You are an attorney representing a variety of clients involved in different phases of the motion picture and television industries. Not long ago you assisted one of your clients, Robin Green, with the negotiation of a contract for her services next season as a performer in a weekly dramatic television series, "Operating Room," in which she was to play the continuing featured role of a doctor, for a salary of $30,000 per week, for a minimum of 13 and maximum of 39 weeks of installments. Before that contract was negotiated and signed, Green had performed a featured role in a theatrical motion picture, *Frat Men in Space.* When *Frat Men* was subsequently released, it became the surprise hit of the summer season, grossing many millions of dollars for its producers and winning acclaim and attention for all its featured performers, particularly Green. Green has now received informal and indirect word from the producer of an established television comedy series, "Flying High," that she is being considered to replace one of the three principal players in that series, in the role of an airline pilot. She has been led to believe (and your experience confirms this) that such a role would be compensated at $75,000 or more per weekly episode. However, Green's fulfillment of her existing contract for "Operating Room" would be inconsistent with a role in "Flying High," both legally and practically, since either role would require a full-time commitment to filming during the coming television season. Green now asks you whether she can and should pursue the possibility of a role in "Flying High." Specifically, she asks you what would be the legal consequences if she breached her contract for "Operating Room," and – in light of your conclusions on that point – whether you would advise her to do so, if necessary, in order to obtain the better and more remunerative contract.

In light of the preceding material on damage remedies, what would you tell her?

REVIEW QUESTIONS – CHAPTER TEN

1. Gabriela Santos moved to the United States three years ago as an economist with the World Bank in Washington, DC. She purchased a single family home in the Georgetown area for $1,800,000. She is now ending her assignment in Washington and will be returning to her native country of Brazil. Gabriela entered into a contract to sell her home to Francesco Romano, an Italian economist, who is also coming to the United States to take a position with the World Bank. The price was $1,900,000. The contract called for closing within 90 days. Gabriella's real estate broker is entitled to a commission of 5 percent ($95,000) payable by Gabriella when and if the sale closes. Unfortunately, shortly before the closing Francesco was told by the Italian Government that he would not be coming to the United States for at least a year and perhaps not at all. If Gabriella brings suit against Francesco, which of the following is most likely to be a correct statement?
   - A. Gabriella must hire an expert to establish the fair market value of the property.
   - B. Gabriella will be entitled to recover prejudgment interest on her damages.
   - C. If Gabriella rents the property before reselling it, the amount of rental income that she receives will reduce the amount of her damages.
   - D. Gabriella will be entitled to recover the amount of the real estate commission that she contracted to pay.

2. Mega University, a major urban college, wanted to expand its campus to add more student housing. Mega was bordered by residential and commercial buildings on all sides. Janet Smith owned two modest-sized apartment buildings near the east side of campus. After negotiations, Janet signed a contract with officials from Mega agreeing to sell the two buildings to Mega for $1 million, with closing in 60 days. When it was announced that the sale was taking place, there was immediate protest from activists about the loss of affordable housing. The activists rallied and protested both on campus and near Janet's buildings. There were newspaper articles with data showing that the two buildings were worth only $700,000 on the open market. After six weeks, Mega announced that due to the protest, it would not go through with the purchase of Janet's buildings. Instead, Mega would on the west side of campus buy warehouse space, of comparable size, for $1.2 million that would not lead to the same community protests. Assuming that Mega does not have a valid excuse for nonperformance and Janet sues for money damages, what would be Janet's measure of recovery?

A. $1 million, as the full measure of the promised performance because Mega's breach was willful.
B. $300,000, as the best measure of the benefit of the bargain for Janet.
C. $200,000, as the difference between the original contract price and Mega's mitigating contract.
D. Nothing, because there is no evidence that Janet has acted in reliance on the contract and thus she has suffered no harm.

3. Tremont Howard is the owner of a family farm in western Pennsylvania. Tremont would like to bring his family property into the twenty-first century while preserving its historical significance. He has hired Modern but Faithful, Inc. (MBF), a construction company that specializes in what it calls "modern preservation." Under MBF's approach, which Tremont loves, property is equipped with all modern features while the exterior and much of the look of the interior is preserved. Under the terms of the contract between Howard and MBF, MBF was required to follow various detailed specifications for the work. When MBF had largely completed the project, with only painting and decoration left to be done, Howard discovered that MBF had used wiring for the farm that did not meet the contract specifications. It appears that the subcontractor hired by MBF used the wrong brand of wiring, although the quality of wiring appears to be equivalent to the contract specifications. MBF was unaware of the subcontractor's error. Howard has demanded that MBF install wiring that complies with the contract, even if it means tearing open walls to do so. MBF has refused to do this work. Expert testimony would show that the use of the wrong brand of wiring has a *de minimis* effect on the fair market value of the property; however, the cost to repair the problem would be several hundred thousand dollars. If Howard brings suit against MBF seeking to recover the cost of the repair, which of the following is probably correct?
   A. Howard will not be able to recover the cost of repair because repair would involve economic waste and MBF appears to have acted in good faith.
   B. Howard will not be able to recover the cost of repair because a risk exists that he would pocket the award rather than using it for repair.
   C. Howard may recover the cost of repair because the property has idiosyncratic value to him.
   D. Howard may recover the cost of repair because that is the basic measure of damages for breach of a construction contract under the Restatement.

4. Stephanie Zinn was a law professor with the Southeastern Law School, a for-profit law school created about seven years ago. Two years ago Stephanie received tenure from the Law School, which means that she could be discharged only for good cause or for bona fide reductions in staff due to financial exigencies. In awarding her tenure, the school noted that Stephanie was a recognized expert in data privacy and was working on a book on the subject. Many other professors at the law school publish books and obtain royalties from their publications. Six months ago Southeastern notified

Stephanie that her employment with the school was being terminated effective at the end of the current school year. The school claims that the termination was proper because it faced financial exigencies due to declining enrollment. However, Stephanie contends that the owners of the school simply wanted to reduce expenses and increase their profits, and this motivation does not satisfy the contractual requirement of a "financial exigency." Several months after Stephanie received her notice of termination, she received another shock. The publisher of her data privacy book notified her that it was cancelling her contract to publish the book on the ground that she failed to meet one of the requirements for publication – being a tenured professor at an accredited law school. Stephanie tried without success to find another publisher for the book. Assume that Stephanie brings suit against Southeastern for breach of contract and is able to establish that the school breached the contract, will she probably be able to recover damages for lost royalties from her book?

A. No, she will not be able to recover the lost royalties from the book because such profits are inherently speculative.
B. No, she will not be able to recover the lost royalties because Southeastern did not "tacitly agree" to be liable for the lost profits in the event of breach.
C. Yes, if Stephanie can prove that the amount of her lost royalties was reasonably foreseeable at the time of breach by Southeastern.
D. Yes, because at the time the school awarded Stephanie tenure, it was reasonably foreseeable that the breach of her contract could result in a loss of royalties.

5. Consider again the situation of law professor Stephanie Zinn in Question 4 above. Assume that prior to her discharge, her annual salary was $150,000 per year. Assume that after Southeastern gave Professor Zinn a notice of discharge, she considered whether to look for another position as a law professor, but she finally decided that the job market was so tight that it was very unlikely that she would obtain another position. She also considered private employment with a law firm, but the only position that she was able to obtain was that of a contract attorney doing document review work. She was told that she could anticipate 1,000 hours of work over the next year at a rate of $30 per hour, total $30,000. Stephanie concluded that accepting such employment would be so damaging to her reputation and future prospects that even though she needed the money, she would not accept employment doing document review work. She does have some savings and family support that enable her to get by for a while and fortunately she also has a good friend/lawyer who will handle her lawsuit against Southeastern without charge except for court-awarded fees. Several months after filing suit, her lawyer tells her that the Southeastern has offered to reinstate her at a salary of $75,000 per year. Stephanie rejects the offer saying, "I will never work for those people again." Assume that Stephanie is able to establish that they breached her employment contract – what would be the measure

of her damages for the first year of breach? (Note that she might be entitled to damages for future years depending on her job prospects, discounted to present value).

A. $150,000, because Southeastern acted in bad faith.
B. $120,000, because Stephanie did not accept employment as a contract attorney.
C. $75,000, because Stephanie should have accepted the offer of reinstatement.
D. Nothing, because Stephanie failed to make any effort to mitigate her damages.

6. Exorbitant Motors, LLC (EM) is the local distributor of the new Exorbitant E85, an all-electric vehicle that is revolutionizing the automotive market. The E85, as the name of the company indicates, is pricey, starting at $150,000. Nathan Orsinski, a car enthusiast, places an order for a new E85 on the first day that the car is offered for sale. With various options and add-ons, Orsinski's contract price is $175,000. EM tells Orsinski that because the car is in such high demand, EM has a back order of vehicles for more than a year. Six months after placing his order, Orsinski receives a notice from EM that his order is being cancelled because of "supply difficulties." Orsinski has learned, however, that EM has delivered the E85 to some "favored buyers" in the area. Orsinski searches in vain to find an E85 available for sale. Assume that Orsinski brings suit against EM for specific performance, or in the alternative, damages. Which of the following is the most accurate statement about Orsinski's possible recovery?

   A. He will not be able to obtain specific performance because that remedy is limited to real estate contracts.
   B. He will not be able to obtain specific performance because the E85 is not unique.
   C. He will not be able to obtain specific performance because his damage remedy is adequate.
   D. He will be able to obtain specific performance if he can show that the E85 is not readily available on the market.

7. Assume the reverse of the situation in the Question 6 above. Six months after Orsinski enters into the contract with EM, EM notifies Orsinski that his new E85 is available for delivery. However, Orsinski notifies EM that he is no longer interested in the vehicle because of the delay in delivery. EM is able to find another purchaser for Orsinski's car but had to cut the price a little (to $170,000) because some of Orsinski's extras were not ones that the new purchaser wanted. Assume that EM would have obtained a net profit of $25,000 from Orsinski if he had gone through with the sale. Assume that EM brings suit against Orsinski for breach of contract. How would EM's damages be measured?

   A. $5,000 plus incidental damages (e.g. storage costs, etc.) that EM can prove.
   B. $25,000 expected profit on the Orsinski sale.

C. $0, because EM failed to resell at a public sale.
D. $0, if EM failed to offer proof of market price.

8. Ramon Sanchez and his wife Esmerala have lived at their home in Jackson, Texas for more than 35 years. This year their youngest child Sofia was married and moved to live with her husband in Atlanta. Being "empty nesters," the Sanchezes decided that it was time to move to a much smaller house. Over the next few months they began cleaning out the tangible results of their more than three decades in their current home. In the process of doing so they discovered a treasure trove of old family photographs and papers going back at least 100 years. They decided that they wanted to preserve this material for their children and future generations. After talking with friends, seeking advice from local librarians, and conducting Internet searches, they decided to hire Family Preservation Specialists (FPS), a company that focuses on preservation of materials like the ones found by the Sanchezes. They paid a fee of $7,500 to turn all of the material into digital form, to make it searchable, and to preserve the physical copies in the most protective way. However, to their great sadness, the Sanchezes received a call about two months later from FPS reporting to its great regret that due to a flash flood at its headquarters, all of the Sanchezes' property had been destroyed. At first the Sanchezes were saddened by the news, but their sadness turned to anger as they learned more about the flash flood and FPS's failure to institute reasonable precautions to protect the irreplaceable property FPS had received. Suppose the Sanchezes have brought suit against FPS for breach of contract, intentional infliction of emotional distress, and negligence including negligent infliction of emotional distress because of FPS's failure to preserve their irreplaceable family material. Assume that the Sanchezes are able to establish that FPS breached its contract with them and that FPS was also negligent (but that it did not act intentionally and was not grossly negligent) in failing to preserve and protect their material. Which of the following is the most accurate statement about the remedy available to the Sanchezes?
   A. They will be able to recover punitive damages for breach of contract under the bad faith exception to general prohibition against recovery of punitive damages for breach of contract.
   B. Unless their contract with FPS provides for the award of attorney fees, they will be unable to recover the fees that they incurred in the litigation.
   C. They will be able to recover damages for emotional distress for breach of contract only if they are able to show that they suffered some bodily harm as a result of FPS's breach of contract.
   D. They will be unable to recover damages in tort from FPS because they failed to prove that FPS's conduct was either intentional or grossly negligent.

Alternatives to Expectation Damages: Reliance and Restitutionary Damages, Specific Performance, and Agreed Remedies

In Chapter 10 we examined the principles governing the award of expectation damages in actions for breach of contract. In this chapter we will analyze several alternatives to expectation damages: reliance and restitutionary damages, specific performance, and agreed remedies. In addition, we will consider the measure of recovery when the basis of liability is either the doctrine of promissory estoppel or restitution, rather than conventional breach of contract.

A. RELIANCE DAMAGES

We have seen that modern contract law recognizes three interests as the basis for awarding damages: expectation, reliance, and restitution. (Recall the excerpt from the Fuller and Perdue article quoted in the introduction to Chapter 10.) When and how should damages be determined based on the reliance interest rather than the expectation interest? The following materials explore these questions.

Wartzman v. Hightower Productions, Ltd.

Court of Special Appeals of Maryland 53 Md. App. 656, 456 A.2d 82 (1983)

JAMES S. GETTY, Judge (Specially Assigned).

Woody Hightower did not succeed in breaking the Guinness World Record for flagpole sitting; his failure to accomplish this seemingly nebulous feat, however, did generate protracted litigation. We are concerned here with whether Judge Robert L. Karwacki, presiding in the Superior Court of Baltimore City, correctly permitted a jury to consider the issue of "reliance damages" sustained

Alvin "Shipwreck" Kelly achieved fame in the 1920s as one of the most well-known pole sitters, setting the world record at 49 days in 1930.

by the appellees. Additionally, we are requested by the appellees, as cross-appellants, to determine if the trial court's refusal to permit the jury to consider prejudgment interest is error.

Hightower Productions Ltd. (appellees and cross-appellants) came into being in 1974 as a promotional venture conceived by Ira Adler, Frank Billitz and J. Daniel Quinn. The principals intended to employ a singer-entertainer who would live in a specially constructed mobile flagpole perch from April 1, 1975, until New Years Eve at which time he would descend in Times Square in New York before a nationwide television audience having established a new world record for flagpole sitting.

The young man selected to perform this feat was to be known as "Woody Hightower." The venture was to be publicized by radio and television exposure, by adopting a theme song and by having the uncrowned champion make appearances from his perch throughout the country at concerts, state fairs and shopping centers.

In November, 1974, the three principals approached Michael Kaminkow of the law firm of Wartzman, Rombro, Rudd and Omansky, P.A., for the specific purpose of incorporating their venture. Mr. Kaminkow, a trial attorney, referred them to his partner, Paul Wartzman.

The three principals met with Mr. Wartzman at his home and reviewed the promotional scheme with him. They indicated that they needed to sell stock to the public in order to raise the $250,000 necessary to finance the project. Shortly thereafter, the law firm prepared and filed the articles of incorporation and Hightower Productions Ltd. came into existence on November 6, 1974. The Articles of Incorporation authorized the issuance of one million shares of stock of the par value of 10 cents per share, or a total of $100,000.00.

Following incorporation, the three principals began developing the project. With an initial investment of $20,000, they opened a corporate account at Maryland National Bank and an office in the Pikesville Plaza Building. Then began the search for "Woody Hightower." After numerous interviews, twenty-three year old John Jordan emerged as "Woody Hightower."

After selecting the flagpole tenant, the corporation then sought and obtained a company to construct the premises to house him. This consisted of a seven foot wide perch that was to include a bed, toilet, water, refrigerator and heat. The accommodations were atop an hydraulic lift system mounted upon a flat bed tractor trailer.

Hightower employed two public relations specialists to coordinate press and public relations efforts and to obtain major corporate backers. "Woody" received a proclamation from the Mayor and City Council of Baltimore and after a press breakfast at the Hilton Hotel on "All Fools Day" ascended his home in the sky.

Within ten days, Hightower obtained a live appearance for "Woody" on the Mike Douglas Show, and a commitment for an appearance on the Wonderama television program. The principals anticipated a "snowballing" effect from commercial enterprises as the project progressed with no substantial monetary commitments for approximately six months.

Hightower raised $43,000.00 by selling stock in the corporation. Within two weeks of "Woody's" ascension, another stockholders' meeting was scheduled, because the corporation was low on funds. At that time, Mr. Wartzman informed the principals that no further stock could be sold, because the corporation was "structured wrong," and it would be necessary to obtain the services of a securities attorney to correct the problem. Mr. Wartzman had acquired this information in a casual conversation with a friend who recommended that the corporation should consult with a securities specialist.

The problem was that the law firm had failed to prepare an offering memorandum and failed to assure that the corporation had made the required disclosures to prospective investors in accordance with the provisions of the Maryland Securities Act Article 32A. (The Act was repealed and re-enacted in 1975 as CA Sec. 11-101 to 11-805). Mr. Wartzman advised Hightower that the cost of the specialist would be between $10,000.00 and $15,000.00. Hightower asked the firm to pay for the required services and the request was rejected.

Hightower then employed substitute counsel and scheduled a shareholders' meeting on April 28, 1975. At that meeting, the stockholders were advised that Hightower was not in compliance with the securities laws; that $43,000.00, the amount investors had paid for issued stock, had to be covered by the promoters and placed in escrow; that the fee of a securities specialist would be $10,000.00 to $15,000.00 and that the additional work would require between six and eight weeks. In the interim, additional stock could not be sold, nor could "Woody" be exhibited across state lines. Faced with these problems, the shareholders decided to discontinue the entire project.

On October 8, 1975, Hightower filed suit alleging breach of contract and negligence for the law firm's failure to have created a corporation authorized to raise the capital necessary to fund the venture. At the trial, Hightower introduced into evidence its obligations and expenditures incurred in reliance on the defendant law firm's creation of a corporation authorized to raise the $250,000.00, necessary to fund the project. The development costs incurred included corporate obligations amounting to $155,339 including: initial investments by Adler and Billitz, $20,000; shareholders, excluding the three promoters, $43,010; outstanding liabilities exclusive of salaries, $58,929; liability to talent consultants, $25,000; and accrued salaries to employees, $8,400.

Individual liabilities to the three promoters, Adler, Billitz and Quinn, totaled $88,608, including loans to the corporation $44,692; repayment of corporate debt to Maryland National Bank, $8,016; and loss of salaries $36,000. The trial court disposed of the individual suit filed by the promoters, Adler, Billitz and Quinn and the cross complaint filed by the appellants. The only claim submitted for the jury's consideration was the claim of the corporation, Hightower, against the defendant law firm.

The jury returned a verdict in favor of Hightower in the amount of $170,508.43. Wartzman, Rombro, Rudd and Omansky, P.A., appealed to this Court. Hightower filed a cross appeal alleging that the jury should have been permitted to consider prejudgment interest.

The appellants raise four issues for our consideration:

1. The trial court erred in permitting Hightower to recover "reliance damages" or "development costs."

2. If "reliance damages" were recoverable, the trial court failed to properly instruct the jury on the law concerning their recovery.

3. The trial court erred in refusing to instruct the jury on the duty to mitigate damages.

4. The trial court erroneously permitted a member of the plaintiff's law firm to testify as a witness in the case.

RELIANCE DAMAGES

The appellants first contend that the jury verdict included all of Hightower's expenditures and obligations incurred during its existence resulting in the law firm being absolute surety for all costs incurred in a highly speculative venture. While they do not suggest the analogy, the appellants would no doubt equate the verdict as tantamount to holding the blacksmith liable for the value of the kingdom where the smith left out a nail in shoeing the king's horse, because of which the shoe was lost, the horse was lost, the king was lost and the kingdom was lost. Appellants contend that there is a lack of nexus or causation between the alleged failure of Mr. Wartzman to discharge his duties as an attorney and the loss claimed by Hightower. Stated differently, an unjust result will obtain where a person performing a collateral service for a new venture will, upon failure to fully perform the service, be liable as full guarantor for all costs incurred by the enterprise.

Ordinarily, profits lost due to a breach of contract are recoverable. Where anticipated profits are too speculative to be determined, monies spent in part performance, in preparation for or in reliance on the contract are recoverable. 5 Corbin, Contracts, Sec. 1031, Restatement of Contracts, Sec. 333, cited with approval in Dialist Co. v. Pulford, 42 Md. App. 173, 399 A.2d 1374 (1979).

In *Dialist,* supra, a distributor, Pulford, brought suit for breach of an exclusive contract that he had with Dialist. Pulford paid $2500.00 for the distributorship, terminated his employment with another company and expended funds in order to begin developing the area where the product was to be sold. When Pulford learned that another distributor was also given part of his territory he terminated his services.

This Court upheld the award of development costs to Pulford which included out of pocket expenses, telephone installation, office furniture, two months of forfeited salary and the value of medical insurance lost. The Court determined that the expenditures were not in preparation for or part performance of a contract, but in reliance upon it. "Such expenditures are not brought about by reason of the breach. They are induced by reliance on the contract itself and rendered worthless by its breach." Id. at 181, 399 A.2d 1374.

Recovery based upon reliance interest is not without limitation. If it can be shown that full performance would have resulted in a net loss, the plaintiff cannot escape the consequences of a bad bargain by falling back on his reliance interest. Where the breach has prevented an anticipated gain and made proof of loss difficult to ascertain, the injured party has a right to damages based upon his reliance interest, including expenditures made in preparation for performance, or in performance, less any loss that the party in breach can prove with reasonable certainty the injured party would have suffered had the contract been performed. Restatement, Second, Contracts, Sec. 349, Holt v. United Security Life Ins. & Trust Co., 76 N.J. 585, 72 A. 301 (1909); In Re Yeager Company, 227 Fed. Supp. 92 (N.D. Ohio, E.D. 1963).

The appellants' contention that permitting the jury to consider that reliance damages in this case rendered the appellants insurers of the venture is without merit. Section 349 of the Restatement, cited above, expressly authorizes the breaching party to prove any loss that the injured party would have suffered had the contract been performed. Such proof would avoid making the breaching party a guarantor of the success of the venture.

As Judge Learned Hand stated in Albert & Son v. Armstrong Rubber Company, 178 F.2d 182 (2d Cir. 1949),

> It is often very hard to learn what the value of the performance would have been; and it is a common expedient, and a just one, in such situations to put the peril of the answer upon that party who by his wrong has made the issue relevant to the rights of the other. On principle therefore the proper solution would seem to be that the promisee may recover his outlay in preparation for the performance, subject to the privilege of the promisor to reduce it by as much as he can show that the promisee would have lost if the contract had been performed.

In the present case the appellants knew, or should have known, that the success of the venture rested upon the ability of Hightower to sell stock and secure advertising as public interest in the adventure accelerated. Appellants' contention that their failure to properly incorporate Hightower was collateral and lacked the necessary nexus to permit consideration of reliance damages is not persuasive. The very life blood of the project depended on the corporation's ability to sell stock to fund the promotion. This is the reason for the employment of the appellants. In reliance thereon, Hightower sold stock and incurred substantial obligations. When it could no longer sell its stock, the entire project failed. No greater nexus need be established. Aside from questioning the expertise of the promoters based upon their previous employment, the appellants were unable to establish that the stunt was doomed to fail. The inability to establish that financial chaos was inevitable does not make the appellants insurers and does not preclude Hightower from recovering reliance damages. The issue was properly submitted to the jury.

Appellants contend that the appellees should be limited to the recovery of damages under traditional contract and negligence concepts, citing Meyerberg, Sawyer and Rue v. Agee, 51 Md. App. 711, 446 A.2d 69 (1982).

Meyerberg, supra, involved a breach of contract action for certification of a title that was not marketable. The trial judge permitted the jury, in assessing damages, to consider:

1. Economic loss occasioned by increased costs of construction and financing.
2. Attorneys' fees expended to establish access to the property.
3. Capital gains taxes paid for failure to purchase another property within the time limitations prescribed by law.
4. The amount of earned hazard insurance premium the appellees were required to purchase.

In affirming the decision of the trial court, this Court acknowledged that a contracting party is expected to take account of only those risks that are foreseeable at the time he makes the contract and is not liable in the event of breach for loss that he did not at the time of contracting have reason to foresee as a probable result of such a breach. This limitation is set forth in Restatement, Contracts, (2d), Sec. 351.

In *Meyerberg,* we noted that exceptional perception is not relevant to the test of foreseeability when applied to an attorney who is relied upon by a layman to protect his investment from pitfalls which are not readily apparent to those in foreign fields of endeavor.

Relying on Cochrane v. Little, 71 Md. 323, 18 A. 698 (1889), we further stated:

> A client who has employed an attorney has a right to his diligence, his knowledge and his skill; and whether he had not so much of these qualities as he was bound to have, or having them, neglected to employ them, the law properly makes him liable for the loss that has accrued to his employer.

We find little solace for the appellants' cause in the cases cited above. . . .

INSTRUCTIONS ON RELIANCE DAMAGES

Appellants' primary exception to the court's damage instruction relates to the failure to include suggested instruction 23b which states:

> You are instructed that you may not award any damages for unpaid expense of Hightower unless you find that these expenses were incurred by Hightower in justifiable reliance on the defendant's causing Hightower to comply with the securities laws. If you find that the expenses were not incurred in reliance on the defendant's performance, or if such reliance was not justified, then you may not award unpaid expenses as damages.

The Court instructed the jury that in order to find liability that the plaintiff must prove three things:

> First, the employment of the defendants in behalf of the Plaintiff and the extent of the duties for which the Defendants were employed; secondly, that the Defendants neglected the duties undertaken in the employment and, thirdly, that such negligence resulted in and was the proximate cause of loss by the Plaintiff, that is that the Plaintiff was deprived of any right or parted with anything of value in reliance upon the negligence of the Defendants.

The instruction given fairly apprised the jury of the Plaintiffs' burden and adequately covered the reliance damage concept. Additionally, the court instructed the jury that they could not consider unpaid salaries due its officers or employees or amounts invested by stockholders as recoverable damages.

Appellants further object to the court's refusal to grant its suggested instructions 23C and D designed to forbid recovery if the jury found that Hightower would not have been able to secure funds to remain in business regardless of the defendants' breach. The instruction was properly refused. The very nature of reliance damages is that future gain cannot be measured with any reasonable degree of reliability. Had Hightower been able to show lost profits the theory of their right to recover may not have been development costs in reliance on the contract but loss based upon expectation interest instead. Appellants had the opportunity to minimize the recovery by showing that the venture could not succeed. This was difficult, but their failure to do so does not entitle them to an instruction that requires the jury to speculate on the ultimate success of the venture. We find no error in the instructions given by Judge Karwacki.

DUTY TO MITIGATE DAMAGES

Appellants further except to the trial court's refusal to grant any instruction on the issue of Hightower's obligation to mitigate its damages. The instruction offered by appellants is a correct statement of the law. Correctness alone, however, is insufficient to require the court to grant the prayer; there must be evidence to support the proposition to which it relates. Dorough v. Lockman, 224 Md. 168, 167 A.2d 129 (1961).

The evidence in this case establishes that Hightower did not have the $43,000.00 to place in escrow covering stock sold, did not have the $10,000.00 or $15,000.00 to employ a securities specialist and could not continue stock sales or exhibitions to obtain the necessary funds. Mr. Wartzman's offer to set up an appointment for Hightower with an expert in security transactions at Hightower's expense can hardly be construed as a mitigating device that Hightower was obligated to accept. The party who is in default may not mitigate his damages by showing that the other party could have reduced those damages by expending large amounts of money or incurring substantial obligations. *Meyerberg,* supra. Since such risks arose because of the breach, they are to be borne by the defaulting party. 22 Am. Jur. 2d, Damages, Sec. 37, Griffin v. Bredouw (Okla.), 420 P.2d 546 (1966).

The doctrine of avoidable consequences, moreover, does not apply where both parties have an equal opportunity to mitigate damages. Appellants had the same opportunity to employ and pay a securities specialist as they contend Hightower should have done. They refused. Having rejected Hightower's request to assume the costs of an additional attorney, they are estopped from asserting a failure by Hightower to reduce its loss. See D. Dobbs, Remedies, Sec. 37, (1973), 11 Williston, Contracts Sec. 1353, (1979).

There is no evidence in this case that the additional funds necessary to continue the operation pending a restructuring of the corporation were within the financial capabilities of Hightower. The Court properly declined to instruct the jury on the issue of mitigation. . . .

PREJUDGMENT INTEREST

Hightower, in its cross-appeal, alleges that the issue of pre-judgment interest should have been presented to the jury for its consideration. Applicable Maryland law provides that where a claim is for unliquidated damages, interest may run from the date of the judgment, but not before. *Affiliated Distillers,* 213 Md. 509, 132 A.2d 582 (1957), Taylor v. Wahby, 271 Md. 101, 314 A.2d 100 (1974).

The reliance damages sought in this case are not subject to pre-judgment valuation. "Reasonable and justified" damages incurred by reason of Mr. Wartzman's representation of Hightower were not reasonably ascertainable until the jury rendered its verdict. Refusal to permit the jury to consider pre-judgment interest, therefore, was not an abuse of discretion.

In conclusion, the final comment of Judge Lowe in *Meyerberg,* supra, is equally apposite here.

> The unfortunate oversight on which this case was based was a costly one, but it was made by one who was hired precisely for the purpose of averting the consequent losses. It is he, and his firm, who must bear them.

Judgment affirmed.
Costs assessed to appellants.

NOTES AND QUESTIONS

1. *Reliance damages as a substitute remedy.* Even if expectation damages would in theory be recoverable, they may not be proveable with reasonable certainty. In such a case, the plaintiff's fall-back position will usually be to seek recovery of reliance damages. See, e.g., Hollywood Fantasy Corp. v. Gabor, 151 F.3d 203 (5th Cir. 1998) (promoter of "fantasy vacations" for movie fans allowed to recover out-of-pocket expenses from breaching celebrity despite inability to prove lost profits for new venture); World of Boxing LLC v. King, 634 Fed. Appx. 1 (2nd Cir. 2015) (Russian boxing promoters unable to prove with certainty profits lost as a result of American promoter's breach of contract, but reliance damages for out-of-pocket expenses recoverable). The Restatement also adopts this rule in §349. In *Wartzman,* what could the plaintiff's expectation damages have consisted of? What were the obstacles to establishing a claim for such damages?

2. *Contract price as limit on reliance damages.* The report of the *Wartzman* case does not indicate the amount the defendants charged for their legal services, but in light of the indication that a "securities specialist" would have cost no more than $15,000, it seems obvious that the defendants' bill for legal fees was far less than the $170,000 awarded to the plaintiffs. Should this factor bear on the availability of reliance damages? Under the original Restatement, reliance damages as an alternative to expectation damages were stated to be "not recoverable in excess of the full contract price promised by the defendant." Restatement §333(a). Fuller and Perdue criticized this limitation. They argued that a distinction should be drawn between the costs of performance of the contract (which they labeled "essential reliance") and the costs incurred in collateral transactions related to the contract ("incidental reliance"). The contract price should limit the recovery only of essential reliance damages. To the extent that essential reliance exceeds the contract price, the contract would be a losing one. An award of essential reliance damages in excess of the contract price would put the injured party in a better position than if the contract had been fully performed. The contract price should not, however, limit the recovery of incidental reliance damages. Lon L. Fuller & William R. Perdue, Jr., The Reliance Interest in Contract Damages, 46 Yale L.J. 52, 77-78 (Pt. I) (1936). For example, in Maine Rubber International v. Environmental Management Group, Inc., 324 F. Supp. 2d 32 (D. Me. 2004), the plaintiff paid the defendant $1,900 to perform an environmental assessment of a prospective business site. After the defendant falsely reported that the property was free of problems, the federal and state governments found environmental hazards and the plaintiff lost more than $211,000 in wasted expenditures when a move to the site was aborted. The court held that these amounts could be recovered as reasonably foreseeable reliance damages even though their total greatly exceeded the contract price.

3. *Other limitations on recovery of reliance damages.* The Restatement indicates that the doctrines that normally apply to limit recovery of expectation

damages — foreseeability, causation, certainty, and mitigation — should also apply to recovery of reliance damages. E.g., Restatement (Second) §352, Comment *a* (requirement of certainty). See also L. Albert & Son v. Armstrong Rubber Co., 178 F.2d 182 (2d Cir. 1949) (in contract for sale of rubber reconditioning machines, buyer denied damages for investment in rubber reclaiming department and for cost of scrap rubber because of showing that delay in delivery by seller was only one of several possible causes of loss); Cities Services Co. v. Gulf Oil Corp., 980 P.2d 116 (Okla. 1999) (reliance damages have goal of undoing harm that was foreseeable and can be measured with reasonable certainty).

In Merry Gentleman, LLC v. George and Leona Productions, Inc., 799 F.3d 827 (7th Cir. 2015), plaintiff film producer sought to recover from actor-director Michael Keaton reliance damages claimed to have resulted from Keaton's failure to perform certain duties under his director's contract with respect to the film "Merry Gentleman." Affirming the district court's denial of recovery, the appellate court had this to say about the necessity for showing the causal link between the breaches complained of and the reliance losses asserted:

> In the typical case where reliance damages are sought, the defendant has simply repudiated the contract and walked away from the deal. This causal link will be straightforward in those cases. As the district court explained, in such cases the nonbreaching plaintiff is left "holding the bag after having made its expenditures." *Merry Gentleman,* 76 F. Supp. 3d at 763. In those cases, it is appropriate for the injured party to claim as damages all expenditures it made in preparation for performance because the other side failed to perform at all. In such cases, the complete loss of investment will often be the proximate result of the breach.
>
> But in cases like this one, where the breaching party has substantially performed and the alleged breaches have to do with the quality of the final product, the causal link between reliance damages and the breach is not so direct. An injured party cannot reasonably claim that *all* of its expenditures were caused by the other party's breach without some reason to think the breach destroyed the entire value of the breaching party's performance. In this context, the breach does not cause the complete loss of investment.
>
> Take this case, for example. Who can say why a critically praised movie did not make money? Merry Gentleman claims as damages all $5.5 million it spent to produce the movie. If Keaton had somehow prevented completion of the movie, Merry Gentleman might well have been entitled to all expenditures made in preparation for his performance (subject, of course, to the "losing contract" limitation in [Restatement (Second) of Contracts] §349). But here, Keaton actually made the movie. Merry Gentleman complains that Keaton slowed down the production process and failed to publicize the movie adequately after it was finished. No doubt, these services have economic value and, on a proper showing, Merry Gentleman might have been entitled to recover damages for these shortcomings. (Imagine, for instance, if Keaton's tardiness in submitting the first cut forced Merry Gentleman to pay the film editors for a longer period. Or, to take a more extreme example, imagine if Keaton had publicly criticized the film released to theaters so harshly that no one bought tickets to see it.) But no reasonable trier of fact

> could find that Merry Gentleman lost its entire investment of $5.5 million because Keaton failed to submit his first cut on time or failed to publicize the movie better. Merry Gentleman entered the directing contract to have Keaton deliver a finished movie, and he delivered one that showed well at Sundance and won some critical praise. The breaches by Keaton that Merry Gentleman alleges cannot reasonably be said to have rendered the investment completely worthless.

Id. at 830-831.

As we have seen, one of the principal damage-limiting factors is the possibility that the plaintiff could have mitigated the injury resulting from the defendant's breach. In *Wartzman*, the court held that the plaintiffs had no obligation to mitigate their damages by paying the amount necessary to hire an attorney specialized in securities law, because the defendants had the same opportunity as the plaintiffs to take that action. This "equal opportunity" exception to the requirement of mitigation has been applied by other courts, although some have expressed doubt about its utility. Compare Chicago Title Insurance Co. v. Huntington National Bank, 719 N.E.2d 955 (Ohio 1999) (failure to mitigate will not limit damages when defendant title company had equal opportunity to that of plaintiff bank to bid on foreclosed home to prevent sale below market value after title company breached contract), with Cates v. Morgan Portable Building Corp., 780 F.2d 683 (7th Cir. 1985) (plaintiff's obligation to mitigate not offset by fact that defendant had "equal opportunity" to complete performance of installing buildings for plaintiff's motel facility; defendant could mitigate only by performing as promised while plaintiff had variety of other options, and application of "questionable" equal opportunity rule would remove incentive for plaintiff to act reasonably in mitigation). Did the *Wartzman* court properly reject the defendant's mitigation argument?

4. *Losing contracts.* In the course of its opinion in *Wartzman*, the court notes another potential limitation on the recovery of reliance expenses, quoting from Restatement (Second) §349: recovery should be offset by "any loss that the party in breach can prove with reasonable certainty the injured party would have suffered had the contract been performed." The defendant, however, would have the burden of showing that the contract would have been a losing one for the plaintiff. Accord Agam v. Gavra, 186 Cal. Rptr. 3d 295 (Ct. App. 2015) (California adopts the "losing contract" limitation on the award of reliance damages). In a case like *Wartzman*, where expectation damages in the form of lost profits were impossible to show with reasonable certainty, shifting the burden to the defendant may at least permit the plaintiff to recover its reliance costs, because of the difficulty of showing that the plaintiff's venture would have been a losing one. That burden is not always an impossible one to carry, however. See, e.g., Home Depot USA, Inc. v. Cytec Indus., Inc., 2013 WL 388202 (Conn. Super. Ct.) (with aid of expert testimony, defendant proved that even if it had not breached contract to convey real property to plaintiff, projected real estate development could not have been completed and generated sufficient revenue to recoup plaintiff's reliance costs); St. Lawrence Factory Stores v. Ogdensburg Bridge and Port Auth., 994 N.Y.S.2d 704 (App.

Div. 2014) (following earlier proceedings in which appellate court ruled that plaintiff should be permitted to go to trial on its claim for reliance damages, trial court's denial of recovery upheld; defendant has only to show with "reasonable certainty" that plaintiff could not have recouped expenditures even if defendant had not breached).

5. *Precontract reliance.* Courts may not allow a party to recover for reliance costs incurred before the contract was made. See Chicago Coliseum Club v. Dempsey, 265 Ill. App. 542 (1932) (fight promoter not allowed to recover expenses incurred before defendant signed contract to perform); Drysdale v. Woerth, 153 F. Supp. 2d 678 (E.D. Pa. 2001) (tenant may not recover reliance damages for improvements made to property while tenant occupied property under one-year lease prior to negotiation of 20-year lease renewal, but tenant may recover in restitution for increase in market value of defendant's property as result of improvements); E. Allan Farnsworth, Contracts §12.16, at 805. But see Security Stove & Manufacturing Co. v. American Railway Express Co., 51 S.W.2d 572 (Mo. Ct. App. 1932) (shipper allowed to recover precontract expenses from carrier who failed to deliver goods to exhibition, thus causing expenses to be wasted); Gregory S. Crespi, Recovering Pre-Contractual Expenditures as an Element of Reliance Damages, 49 S.M.U. L. Rev. (1995) (generally supporting recovery of pre-contract expenditures when parties would reasonably contemplate that the expenses would be wasted in the event of breach and other limits on recovery do not apply).

6. *Forgone opportunities as reliance damages.* Ordinarily, reliance damages are thought of as out-of-pocket expenditures made by the plaintiff. Sometimes, however, protection of the injury to the plaintiff's reliance extends further, taking into account the gains the plaintiff would have made had she not relied on the promises of the defendant. See Dialist Co. v. Pulford, 399 A.2d 1374, 1382 (Md. Ct. Spec. App. 1979) (after breach of exclusive territory provision, plaintiff permitted to recover not only initial franchise fee but also amount of lost salary after quitting his original job until reemployed; court asserted that "giving up one's livelihood in reliance on, in preparation for and in performance of, a contractual obligation can be as real a detriment as out-of-pocket expenditures"); Bouton v. Byers, 321 P.3d 780 (Kan. Ct. App. 2015) (plaintiff daughter entitled to recover in action for promissory estoppel reliance damages based on the amount of salary she would have earned from teaching, employment she forwent in reliance on father's promise to leave ranch property to her if she would come and help him work the ranch).

Walser v. Toyota Motor Sales, U.S.A., Inc.

United States Court of Appeals 43 F.3d 396 (8th Cir. 1994)

HANSEN, Circuit Judge.

The plaintiffs, Paul Martin Walser and Philip Martin McLaughlin, appeal from a jury verdict in this diversity case awarding them $232,131 in damages on their promissory estoppel claim against Toyota Motor Sales. The plaintiffs argue that the district court erred by instructing the jury that the plaintiffs' damages on their promissory estoppel claim were limited to out-of-pocket expenses. The plaintiffs also argue that the district court erred in declining to award specific performance as an alternative remedy on their promissory estoppel claim, in denying their motion for judgment as a matter of law on their contract claim, in instructing the jury on their contract claim, in requiring them to accept payment from Toyota for $.89 less than the amount of damages and interest awarded, in granting summary judgment on their claim under the Minnesota Motor Vehicle Sale and Distribution Regulations, and in precluding them from taxing costs prior to a final determination of this case on appeal. We affirm.

I.

In 1987, Toyota Motor Sales, U.S.A., conducted market surveys throughout the United States to identify the best markets for the new line of "Lexus" automobiles that Toyota planned to introduce in 1989. The market studies identified the Minneapolis/St. Paul, Minnesota, metropolitan area as a two-dealership market and recommended establishing dealerships in two suburban areas — Wayzata and the Bloomington/Richfield area.

In April 1988, Toyota issued letters of intent for the prospective dealerships in the two locations. The recipient of the letter for the Bloomington/Richfield dealership was unwilling or unable to comply with the conditions of the letter of intent and returned it to Toyota in early 1989. Soon after, Toyota began to search anew for a dealer for the Bloomington/Richfield location. Lexus Central Region Area Manager, James Melton, asked Stephen Haag, the Central Region Market Manager, to contact Walser, who was then co-owner with McLaughlin of a BMW dealership and a Lincoln-Mercury dealership both located in Bloomington. Both Walser and McLaughlin met with Haag and indicated that they would be interested in obtaining the Lexus dealership.

Toyota had instituted a three-step process to establish dealerships. First, the prospective dealer would fill out a formal application and propose a dealership plan to Toyota. If acceptable, then Toyota would issue a letter of intent signed by the head of the Lexus division and to be signed by the prospective dealer, which would contain final conditions that had to be satisfied before the agreement was finalized. If all conditions were satisfied, then a formal dealership agreement would be approved by Toyota and signed by the parties to establish the dealership.

[After Walser and McLaughlin formally applied for the Lexus dealership, Haag told Walser in October 1989 that the letter of intent would soon be approved. Subsequently, in December 1989, Haag told Walser that "you're our dealer" and that the letter of intent had been formally approved by Lexus management. A few days later Haag called Walser to tell him that a mistake had been made, that the letter had not been finally approved, and that additional financial information would be necessary. In the meantime Walser's father, R.J. Walser, had agreed to purchase property for the proposed Lexus dealership. In February 1990, Haag informed Walser that Lexus would not be issuing the letter of intent to him and McLaughlin. — EDS.]

On March 7, 1990, Walser and McLaughlin filed a seven-count complaint in Minnesota state court against Toyota. Walser and McLaughlin sought relief under the following theories: breach of the Minnesota motor vehicle franchise statute (count I); breach of contract (count II); promissory estoppel (count III); joint venture (count IV); fraud (count V); intentional interference with contractual relations (count VI); and interference with a prospective business advantage (count VII). Toyota removed this action to the United States District Court for the District of Minnesota.

The district court granted Toyota's motion for partial summary judgment and dismissed the claims for breach of the Minnesota motor vehicle franchise statute and for recovery on a joint venture theory. Prior to trial, the parties filed a joint stipulation to dismiss without prejudice the claims for intentional interference with contractual relations and interference with a prospective business advantage. The case went to trial in February 1992 on the breach of contract, promissory estoppel, and fraud claims. Walser and McLaughlin sought approximately $7,600,000 in damages, which included expected lost profits. The jury returned a verdict in favor of Toyota on the contract and fraud claims but in favor of Walser and McLaughlin on the promissory estoppel claim. The jury awarded Walser and McLaughlin $232,131 in accordance with the district court's instruction to limit damages on the promissory estoppel claim to Walser and McLaughlin's out-of-pocket expenses.

. . .

II.

. . .

A.

Walser and McLaughlin's principal argument in this appeal is that the district court erred in instructing the jury that damages on their promissory estoppel claim were limited to the out-of-pocket expenditures they made in reliance on Toyota's promise. The jury awarded $232,131 in out-of-pocket expenses. Walser and McLaughlin argue that under Minnesota law, the court should have allowed the jury to consider awarding lost profits of up to $7,600,000 allegedly flowing from Toyota's failure to keep its promise.

Minnesota has adopted the statement of the doctrine of promissory estoppel found at Restatement (Second) of Contracts §90 (1981). Christensen v. Minneapolis Mun. Employees Retirement Bd., 331 N.W.2d 740, 749 (Minn. 1983). Section 90 provides, in relevant part:

> A promise which the promisor should reasonably expect to induce action or forbearance on the part of the promisee or a third person and which does induce such action or forbearance is binding if injustice can be avoided only by enforcement of the promise. The remedy granted for breach may be limited as justice requires.

Restatement (Second) of Contracts §90(1) (1981); see also Cohen v. Cowles Media Co., 479 N.W.2d 387, 391-392 (Minn. 1992) (relying on and quoting from portions of section 90); *Christensen,* 331 N.W.2d at 749 (quoting section 90). Of particular significance to this case is the meaning of the last phrase of the quoted section: "The remedy granted for breach may be limited as justice requires." The commentary to section 90 elaborates on the nature of the remedy available for breach based on promissory estoppel:

> A promise binding under this section is a contract, and full-scale enforcement by normal remedies is often appropriate. But the same factors which bear on whether any relief should be granted also bear on the character and extent of the remedy. *In particular, relief may sometimes be limited to restitution or to damages or specific relief measured by the extent of the promisee's reliance rather than by the terms of the promise.*

Restatement (Second) of Contracts §90 cmt. *d* (emphasis added). Minnesota courts have incorporated the underlined language stating: "When a promise is enforced pursuant to section 90 '[t]he remedy granted for breach may be limited as justice requires.' Relief *may be limited* to damages measured by the promisee's reliance." Grouse v. Group Health Plan, 306 N.W.2d 114, 116 (Minn. 1981) (alterations in original) (emphasis added). The Minnesota Court of Appeals, relying on *Grouse,* further stated that "relief *may be limited* to the party's out-of-pocket expenses made in reliance on the promise." Dallum v. Farmers Union Cent. Exch., Inc., 462 N.W.2d 608, 613 (Minn. Ct. App. 1990) (emphasis added).

The critical question in this case is whether the language of section 90 as interpreted by the Minnesota courts authorized the district court to limit damages to Walser and McLaughlin's out-of-pocket expenses. We conclude that it did. This language is permissive — courts *may* limit relief as justice requires. The Minnesota Court of Appeals specifically stated that "relief *may* be limited to the party's out-of-pocket expenses made in reliance on the promise." *Dallum,* 462 N.W.2d at 613 (emphasis added). This permissive language and the Minnesota courts' interpretation of it indicate to us that Minnesota courts, like the other courts addressing this issue, treat the damages decision under section 90 as being within the district court's discretion. See, e.g., Chedd-Angier Prod. Co., Inc. v. Omni Publications Int'l, Ltd., 756 F.2d 930, 937 (1st Cir. 1985) (in determining damages under section 90 "whether to charge full contract damages, or something less, is a matter of discretion delegated to district courts"); Green v. Interstate United Management Serv. Corp., 748 F.2d 827, 831 (3d Cir. 1984) (concluding that district court did not abuse its "equitable discretion" under section 90 "in refusing to allow full-scale enforcement of the promise"); Signal Hill Aviation Co. v. Stroppe, 96 Cal. App. 3d 627, 158 Cal. Rptr. 178, 186 (1979) ("California Supreme Court appeared to emphasize . . . the exercise of judicial discretion in promissory estoppel cases to fashion relief to do justice") (citing C & K Eng'g Contractors v. Amber Steel Co., 23 Cal. 3d 1, 151 Cal. Rptr. 323, 587 P.2d 1136 (1978)); Gerson Elec. Constr. Co. v. Honeywell, Inc., 117 Ill. App. 3d 309, 72 Ill. Dec. 851, 453 N.E.2d 726, 728 (1983) (decision under section 90 whether the damage award prevents injustice is a policy decision and "necessarily embraces an element of discretion").

We are left then to determine only whether the district court abused its discretion in limiting the damages to out-of-pocket expenses. We will not disturb a district court's discretionary decision if that decision remains within "the range of choice" available to the district court, accounts for all relevant factors, does not rely on any irrelevant factors, and does not constitute a "clear error of judgment." Kern v. TXO Prod. Corp., 738 F.2d 968, 970 (8th Cir. 1984). We cannot find that the district court abused its discretion in limiting the award of damages on the promissory estoppel claim to out-of-pocket expenses.

. . .

Our review of the record . . . also reveals that the district court did not make a "clear error of judgment" in finding that justice required limiting Walser and McLaughlin to out-of-pocket expenses. Toyota presented evidence that the dealership was far from a certainty and that Walser and McLaughlin would have great difficulty in meeting the capitalization requirements. The negotiations were still in a preliminary stage and broke down at that point. The promise on which they relied did not guarantee that they would get the dealership, as there were other conditions in the letter of intent that still would have had to be satisfied. Walser and McLaughlin could have relied on the promise for only a short period of time, as they were informed by Haag only a couple of days later that he had misinformed them about the status of the letter of intent. Moreover, Walser and McLaughlin have not demonstrated any opportunity they lost by virtue of relying on the promise by Toyota. Accordingly, the district court did not make a clear error of judgment in limiting Walser and McLaughlin's damages on their promissory estoppel claim to out-of-pocket expenses.

. . .

B.

Walser and McLaughlin next argue that the district court erred in limiting out-of-pocket expenses to "the difference between the actual value of the property and the price paid for it." (Jury Instr. No. 34.) They argue that they should have been allowed to "recoup" at least the full amount of the "unamortized capital investments" they made in attempting to obtain the dealership. They claim the full value of their investment totals more than $1,000,000 including the $676,864 they paid for the land and the various expenses in maintaining it.

. . .

. . . [W]e find no error in the district court's instruction to the extent that it defined their out-of-pocket expenses to be only the difference between the actual value and the amount paid for the property. Such an instruction reflects the amount of damage Walser and McLaughlin suffered from relying on Toyota's promise. For example, while the purchase price of the land totalled $676,864 Walser acknowledged in his trial testimony that the land still had significant value, worth at least $550,000. (Tr. Vol. VI at 23-24.) Their *damage* from relying on Toyota's promise is essentially the difference between the two amounts.

Accordingly, the district court committed no error in instructing the jury on how to determine the damage award.

. . .

III.

For the foregoing reasons, the judgment of the district court is affirmed.

NOTES AND QUESTIONS

1. *Measuring damages in promissory estoppel actions.* In the first case in this section, we saw that an injured party may recover reliance damages for breach of contract even if she is unable to prove expectation damages with reasonable certainty. Suppose, however, that liability is based on the doctrine of promissory estoppel and the plaintiff has suffered expectation damages (lost profits, for example), which the plaintiff is able to prove with reasonable certainty. Should the plaintiff be entitled to recover these expectation damages, or should the plaintiff's recovery always be limited to the amount of her actual reliance? Or is the best approach the one adopted by the *Walser* court, allowing the trial court discretion to award a full range of remedies for promissory estoppel, including expectation or reliance-based recovery, as justice seems to require?

In assessing the merits of these various remedial approaches, it may help to recall that the doctrine of promissory estoppel was viewed originally as a substitute for consideration rather than an independent theory of recovery. The logical consequence of this view was that the injured party would be entitled to recover full expectation damages.

2. *View that damages should be limited to protection of reliance interest.* As the use of promissory estoppel became more widespread, some commentators questioned whether recovery of expectation damages was just. Writing in 1950, Professor Benjamin Boyer stated: "There is no real need for the courts to restrict themselves to giving only complete enforcement. It is to be hoped that the trend will be towards a protection of the reliance interest of the promisee without the injustice to the promisor that is often patent when complete enforcement is granted." Benjamin F. Boyer, Promissory Estoppel: Requirements and Limitations of the Doctrine, 98 U. Pa. L. Rev. 459, 497 (1950). A number of significant, relatively early promissory estoppel cases did limit recovery to reliance damages. See Goodman v. Dicker, 169 F.2d 684 (D.C. Cir. 1948) (reliance on promise that radio franchise would be awarded; recovery limited to expenses incurred preparing to do business); Wheeler v. White, 398 S.W.2d 93 (Tex. 1965) (reliance on promise to procure or make a loan to develop property; recovery limited to losses incurred in reliance on promise); Hoffman v. Red Owl Stores, Inc., 133 N.W.2d 267 (Wis. 1965) (promissory estoppel adopted and applied to precontract reliance but recovery limited to reliance damages). The court in *Wheeler* explicitly stated that expectation damages would not be

recoverable even if they could be proven with reasonable certainty and based its holding, in part, on the reasoning that the promisee "in such cases is partially responsible for his failure to bind the promisor to a legally sufficient contract." 398 S.W.2d at 97. Accord, Bruce Foods Corp. v. Texas Gas Serv., 2014 WL 652312 (W.D. Tex.) (plaintiff may only recover reliance damages on its promissory estoppel claim, citing *Wheeler*).

3. *View that courts should have discretion in determining measure of damages.* As reflected by citations in its opinion, a number of other courts agree with the appellate court in *Walser* that a trial court has discretion to award expectation, reliance, or some other form of remedy when the basis of recovery is promissory estoppel. See, e.g., Woodland Harvesting, Inc. v. Georgia Pacific Corp., 2011 WL 4596041 (E.D. Mich.) (reliance damages typical remedy for promissory estoppel, but courts occasionally award lost profits); Nightingale v. Wal-Mart Stores, Inc., 2015 WL 6549364 (S.D. Ohio) (plaintiff employee could recover in promissory estoppel for expectancy of lost future wages). See also Restatement (Second) §90, Comment *d* ("full-scale enforcement by normal remedies is often appropriate"); Dynalectric Co. of Nevada, Inc. v. Clark & Sullivan Constructors, Inc., 255 P.3d 286 (Nev. 2011) (agreeing with Restatement §90 and majority of jurisdictions that remedy for promissory estoppel should be flexible; may be expectation, reliance, or restitution damages as justice requires); Grandoe Corp. v. Gander Mountain Co., 2013 WL 3353927 (D. Minn.) (plaintiff manufacturer left with warehouse full of specially-manufactured, unsaleable gloves entitled to recovery of lost profits; *Walser* discussed and distinguished), *aff'd*, 761 F.3d 876, 881 n.3 (8th Cir. 2014) (contract damages awarded; issue of damages for promissory estoppel not reached). See generally Charles L. Knapp, Reliance in the Revised *Restatement*: The Proliferation of Promissory Estoppel, 81 Colum. L. Rev. 52, 57-58 (1981) (noting lack of clarity in comments and illustrations to §90 regarding when expectancy damages should be available). If the court in *Walser* had been willing to give expectancy relief, could the plaintiffs' expectation interest have been measured with reasonable certainty?

4. *Scholarly commentary.* As discussion of the proper remedy for promissory estoppel has continued, some writers have argued that expectation damages may often be the appropriate remedy in promissory estoppel cases. These writers claim that an award of expectation damages may be the best way of compensating the injured party for reliance damages that may be difficult to prove. In commercial cases, such reliance could take the form of forgone contractual opportunities, including numerous and difficult to prove acts or forbearances that may be deemed to make up the "total reliance" of the plaintiff. Comment, Once More into the Breach: Promissory Estoppel and Traditional Damages Doctrine, 37 U. Chi. L. Rev. 559, 566-567 (1970).

In a 1987 study of this area, Professor Mary Becker found that expectation-based remedies are commonly and routinely awarded in promissory estoppel cases and concluded that where recovery is limited to reliance damages, this is usually not because promissory estoppel is the basis of recovery, but because an expectation-based recovery would fail to satisfy one of the other requirements, such as certainty or foreseeability. Mary E. Becker, Promissory

Estoppel Damages, 16 Hofstra L. Rev. 131 (1987). By contrast, Professor Robert A. Hillman observed that the cases did not clearly show a judicial preference for reliance or expectancy damages in promissory estoppel actions, but he did conclude that the cases establish "that courts take seriously the admonition of the second Restatement to award damages as justice requires." Robert A. Hillman, Questioning the "New Consensus" on Promissory Estoppel: An Empirical and Theoretical Study, 98 Colum. L. Rev. 580, 610 (1998). Professor Eric Holmes reached a similar conclusion that courts consider the remedy for promissory estoppel as discretionary and award a "full range of remedies" that includes expectation and reliance damages. Eric Mills Holmes, Restatement of Promissory Estoppel, 32 Willamette L. Rev. 263, 295-296 (1996).

5. *Specific performance in promissory estoppel actions.* As we shall see later in this chapter, cases involving land are usually good candidates for specific performance or other types of equitable relief. Such literal enforcement of the defendant's obligation is in one sense the most purely expectation-based remedy. The Restatement (Second) apparently contemplates the award of specific performance in promissory estoppel cases involving land (see §90, Illustration 11). Recall the Harvey v. Dow case from Chapter 3 in which the court granted specific performance relief to the plaintiff. See also Jackson v. Morse, 871 A.2d 47 (N.H. 2005) (full range of remedies are available for promissory estoppel, including specific performance in appropriate circumstances); Satcher v. Satcher, 570 S.E.2d 535 (S.C. Ct. App. 2002) (specific performance available for promise of land when established by clear and convincing evidence). Section C of this chapter will offer more detailed discussion of specific performance.

6. *Measure of recovery in construction bidding cases.* We saw in Chapter 3 that courts have generally followed the lead of the California Supreme Court in Drennan v. Star Paving Co., awarding damages on a promissory estoppel theory to the general contractor injured by the withdrawal of a subcontractor's bid, despite the failure of the parties to conclude a formal contract binding the general contractor as well. As the *Drennan* case itself illustrates, the damage award in such cases will typically be computed by subtracting the defendant's bid price from the price the plaintiff had to pay another subcontractor for the goods or services in question. Such a recovery might be regarded as reliance-based, but it seems apparent that the courts in such cases are really awarding a conventional expectation-based remedy, whatever the terminology they employ. In the *Dynalectric Co.* case cited in Note 3 above, the lower court had awarded to the plaintiff general contractor the difference between the defendant's bid and the amount that the plaintiff had to pay another subcontractor to complete the work. Affirming this decision, the Nevada Supreme Court observed:

> Interestingly, despite the consensus that the measure of damages adopted in *Drennan* is appropriate in the type of situation presented here, courts have not definitively labeled this measure "expectation" or "reliance" damages. . . . Scholars appear to agree, however, that the *Drennan* measure of damages is, in fact, expectation damages. See . . . W. David Slawson, *The Role of Reliance in Contract Damages.* 76 Cornell L. Rev. 197, 221-22 (1990) (discussing the near

> impossibility of proving true reliance damages in the subcontract-bidding context and indicating that the *Drennan* measure of damages represents expectation damages); Charles L. Knapp, *Reliance in the Revised Restatement: The Proliferation of Promissory Estoppel,* 81 Colum. L. Rev. 52, 57 n.35 (1981) (noting the ambiguity in the caselaw on this issue and stating that an award of damages based upon the difference between the nonperforming subcontractor's bid and the amount paid to a replacement subcontractor is "the classic expectation remedy").

Dynalectric Co. of Nevada, Inc. v. Clark & Sullivan Constructors, Inc., 255 P.3d 286, 290 (Nev. 2011).

B. RESTITUTIONARY DAMAGES

As we saw in the first section of this chapter, if a party cannot prove expectation damages with reasonable certainty, she may still recover damages measured by her reliance interest. Restatement (Second) §349. Modern contract law also allows a nonbreaching party to elect recovery of restitutionary rather than expectation damages for breach of contract. Restatement (Second) §373. Even a breaching party may in some cases be entitled to restitution by virtue of the benefit conferred on the other party by part performance. Restatement (Second) §374. Moreover, if the performance obligations imposed by the contract have been "discharged" for some reason, such as incapacity or impracticability, either or both of the parties may be entitled to restitutionary relief. Restatement (Second) §§375 (restitution when contract is unenforceable because of the statute of frauds); 376 (restitution when contract is voidable because of lack of capacity, mistake, misrepresentation, duress, undue influence, or breach of fiduciary duty); 377 (restitution when contract is discharged due to impracticability, frustration of purpose, or failure of condition).

The materials in this section explore the restitutionary principle at work in a variety of contractual situations. The principal cases address some of the possibilities enumerated above: restitution as a remedy for breach; the possibility of restitution in favor of a party who is herself in breach; and the role of restitution where the contract has been rendered unenforceable.

United States ex rel. Coastal Steel Erectors, Inc. v. Algernon Blair, Inc.

United States Court of Appeals 479 F.2d 638 (4th Cir. 1973)

CRAVEN, Circuit Judge:

May a subcontractor, who justifiably ceases work under a contract because of the prime contractor's breach, recover in quantum meruit the value of labor and equipment already furnished pursuant to the contract irrespective of whether he would have been entitled to recover in a suit on the contract? We think so, and, for reasons to be stated, the decision of the district court will be reversed.

The subcontractor, Coastal Steel Erectors, Inc., brought this action under the provisions of the Miller Act, 40 U.S.C.A. §270a et seq., in the name of the United States against Algernon Blair, Inc., and its surety, United States Fidelity and Guaranty Company. Blair had entered a contract with the United States for the construction of a naval hospital in Charleston County, South Carolina. Blair had then contracted with Coastal to perform certain steel erection and supply certain equipment in conjunction with Blair's contract with the United States. Coastal commenced performance of its obligations, supplying its own cranes for handling and placing steel. Blair refused to pay for crane rental, maintaining that it was not obligated to do so under the subcontract. Because of Blair's failure to make payments for crane rental, and after completion of approximately 28 percent of the subcontract, Coastal terminated its performance. Blair then proceeded to complete the job with a new subcontractor. Coastal brought this action to recover for labor and equipment furnished.

The district court found that the subcontract required Blair to pay for crane use and that Blair's refusal to do so was such a material breach as to justify Coastal's terminating performance. This finding is not questioned on appeal. The court then found that under the contract the amount due Coastal, less what had already been paid, totaled approximately $37,000. Additionally, the court found Coastal would have lost more than $37,000 if it had completed performance. Holding that any amount due Coastal must be reduced by any loss it would have incurred by complete performance of the contract, the court denied recovery to Coastal. While the district court correctly stated the " 'normal' rule of contract damages," we think Coastal is entitled to recover in quantum meruit.[2]

In United States for Use of Susi Contracting Co. v. Zara Contracting Co., 146 F.2d 606 (2d Cir. 1944), a Miller Act action, the court was faced with a situation similar to that involved here — the prime contractor had unjustifiably breached a subcontract after partial performance by the subcontractor. The court stated:

> For it is an accepted principle of contract law, often applied in the case of construction contracts, that the promisee upon breach has the option to forego any suit on the contract and claim only the reasonable value of his performance.

146 F.2d at 610. The Tenth Circuit has also stated that the right to seek recovery under quantum meruit in a Miller Act case is clear. Quantum meruit recovery is not limited to an action against the prime contractor but may also be brought against the Miller Act surety, as in this case. Further, that the complaint is not

2. Where there is a distinction between federal and state substantive law, federal law controls in actions under the Miller Act. United States for Use and Benefit of Astro Cleaning & Packaging Co. v. Jamison Co., 425 F.2d 1281, 1282 n.1 (6th Cir. 1970). But in this case the result would be the same, we think, under either state or federal law. Compare United States for Use of Susi Contracting Co. v. Zara Contracting Co., 146 F.2d 606 (2d Cir. 1944), with Gantt v. Morgan, 199 S.C. 138, 18 S.E.2d 672 (1942).

clear in regard to the theory of a plaintiff's recovery does not preclude recovery under quantum meruit. Narragansett Improvement Co. v. United States, 290 F.2d 577 (1st Cir. 1961). A plaintiff may join a claim for quantum meruit with a claim for damages from breach of contract.

In the present case, Coastal has, at its own expense, provided Blair with labor and the use of equipment. Blair, who breached the subcontract, has retained these benefits without having fully paid for them. On these facts, Coastal is entitled to restitution in quantum meruit.

> The "restitution interest," involving a combination of unjust impoverishment with unjust gain, presents the strongest case for relief. If, following Aristotle, we regard the purpose of justice as the maintenance of an equilibrium of goods among members of society, the restitution interest presents twice as strong a claim to judicial intervention as the reliance interest, since if *A* not only causes *B* to lose one unit but appropriates that unit to himself, the resulting discrepancy between *A* and *B* is not one unit but two.

Fuller and Perdue, The Reliance Interest in Contract Damages, 46 Yale L.J. 52, 56 (1936).

The impact of quantum meruit is to allow a promisee to recover the value of services he gave to the defendant irrespective of whether he would have lost money on the contract and been unable to recover in a suit on the contract. Scaduto v. Orlando, 381 F.2d 587, 595 (2d Cir. 1967). The measure of recovery for quantum meruit is the reasonable value of the performance, Restatement of Contracts §347 (1932); and recovery is undiminished by any loss which would have been incurred by complete performance. 12 Williston on Contracts §1485, at 312 (3d ed. 1970). While the contract price may be evidence of reasonable value of the services, it does not measure the value of the performance or limit recovery.[7] Rather, the standard for measuring the reasonable value of the services rendered is the amount for which such services could have been purchased from one in the plaintiff's position at the time and place the services were rendered.

Since the district court has not yet accurately determined the reasonable value of the labor and equipment use furnished by Coastal to Blair, the case must be remanded for those findings. When the amount has been determined, judgment will be entered in favor of Coastal, less payments already made under the contract. Accordingly, for the reasons stated above, the decision of the district court is

Reversed and remanded with instructions.

---

7. . . .

> It should be noted, however, that in suits for restitution there are many cases permitting the plaintiff to recover the value of benefits conferred on the defendant, even though this value exceeds that of the return performance promised by the defendant. In these cases it is no doubt felt that the defendant's breach should work a forfeiture of his right to retain the benefits of an advantageous bargain.

Fuller and Perdue, supra, at 77.

NOTES AND QUESTIONS

1. *Actions under the Miller Act.* Plaintiff's claim was based on the Miller Act, which provides that in any contract for construction, alteration, or repair of any public building or public work of the United States in an amount in excess of $100,000 the contractor is required to furnish both "performance" and "payment" bonds issued by satisfactory sureties (normally insurance companies). 40 U.S.C. §3131. A performance bond protects the government against the contractor's improper performance; if the contractor breaches, the government may demand that the surety complete or pay for performance of the contract. A payment bond protects subcontractors who supply labor or materials to the project against nonpayment by the contractor. If a subcontractor is not paid, he may bring suit against the contractor and surety under the payment bond. The suit is styled on behalf of the United States for the use of the subcontractor. As the court points out in footnote 2, while federal rather than state law governs claims brought under the Miller Act, both federal and state law recognize the right of the injured party to elect to recover restitutionary rather than expectation damages.

2. *Market value restitution.* The court of appeals in *Algernon Blair* held that when a plaintiff elects restitution as a remedy for breach of contract by the defendant, the "measure of recovery . . . is the reasonable value of the performance . . . and recovery is undiminished by any loss which would have been incurred by complete performance." Several arguments have been made to support the rule of "market value restitution" followed by the court. If the plaintiff elects to rescind the contract and recover in restitution, the contract no longer legally "exists"; any loss that would have resulted from performance of the contract, therefore, should not act as a limitation on the amount of recovery. George E. Palmer, The Contract Price as a Limit on Restitution for the Defendant's Breach, 20 Ohio St. L.J. 264, 273 (1959). In addition, it seems unfair to allow the defendant, who is after all the breaching party, to retain the benefit of the bargain. 1 George E. Palmer, Law of Restitution §4.4 at 393 (1978). See also Andrew Kull, Restitution as a Remedy for Breach of Contract, 67 S. Cal. L. Rev. 1465 (1994) (criticizing remedy on both historical and efficiency grounds). A majority of courts apparently follows the rule of market value restitution applied in *Algernon Blair.* See Bausch & Lomb Inc. v. Bressler, 977 F.2d 720 (2d Cir. 1992) (restitution looks to value of benefit conferred and is not governed by terms of agreement; therefore, restitution is available even if nonbreaching party would have lost money on contract); IT Corp. v. Motco Site Trust Fund, 903 F. Supp. 1106 (S.D. Tex. 1994) (after breach of environmental remediation contract for $32 million, nonbreaching contractor allowed to recover more than $43 million in restitution; no Texas authority to limit recovery to contract price). See also Restatement (Second) §373, Comment *d* (adopting majority rule permitting restitution in excess of contract price).

3. *Full performance exception to market value restitution.* The right of a nonbreaching party to elect restitution in situations like that presented in *Algernon Blair* is subject to an important exception. If the nonbreaching party has fully

performed his obligations under the contract and the breaching party's only remaining duty of performance is the payment of a liquidated or specified sum of money, the nonbreaching party may not elect a restitutionary recovery but is limited to expectation damages. Restatement (Second) §373(2). A leading case applying this "full performance" exception is Oliver v. Campbell, 273 P.2d 15 (Cal. 1954). In *Oliver* an attorney agreed for a fee of $750 to defend a husband in an action for separate maintenance brought by his wife. After the husband discharged the lawyer at the end of the trial, the lawyer sued to recover $10,000 in restitution as the reasonable value of his services. Although the California Supreme Court recognized the general rule of market value restitution as an alternative remedy for breach of contract, the court held that the full performance exception applied and limited recovery to the contract price. Id. at 20. But see Chodos v. West Publishing Co., Inc., 292 F.3d 992 (9th Cir. 2002) (after defendant breached contract by declining to publish finished manuscript, plaintiff author could elect to recover in quantum meruit because publisher's obligation to pay percentage of gross revenue was not a "liquidated" debt). The Restatement asserts that the exception is justified because it protects the nonbreaching party's expectation interest while eliminating the judicial burden of determining the market value of the performance. Restatement (Second) §373, Comment *b*. Is this persuasive?

Lancellotti v. Thomas

Superior Court of Pennsylvania 341 Pa. Super. 1, 491 A.2d 117 (1985)

SPAETH, President Judge.

This appeal raises the question of whether a defaulting purchaser of a business who has also entered into a related lease for the property can recover any part of his payments made prior to default. The common law rule precluded a breaching buyer from recovering these payments. Today, we reject this rule, which created a forfeiture of the breaching buyer's payments and unjustly enriched the nonbreaching seller, and adopt §374 of the Restatement (Second) Contracts (1979), which permits limited restitution. This case is remanded for further proceedings so that the trial court may apply the Restatement rule.

1

On July 25, 1973, the parties entered into an agreement in which appellant agreed to purchase appellees' luncheonette business and to rent from appellees the premises on which the business was located. Appellant agreed to buy the name of the business, the goodwill, and equipment; the inventory and real estate were not included in the agreement for the sale of the business. Appellees agreed to sell the business for the following consideration: $25,000 payable on signing of the agreement; appellant's promise that only he would own and operate the business; and appellant's promise to build an addition to the existing building, which would measure 16 feet by 16 feet, cost at least $15,000, and be 75 percent complete by May 1, 1973.[1]

It was also agreed that appellees would lease appellant the property on which the business was operated for a period of five years, with appellant having the option of an additional five-year term. The rent was $8,000 per year for a term from September 1, 1973, to August 31, 1978. A separate lease providing for this rental was executed by the parties on the same date that the agreement was executed. This lease specified that the agreement to build the existing building [sic – the addition?] was a condition of the lease. In exchange for appellant's promise to build the addition, there was to be no rental charge for the property until August 31, 1973. Further, if the addition was not constructed as agreed, the lease would terminate automatically. An addendum, executed by the parties on August 14, 1973, modified this agreement, providing that "if the addition to the building as described in the Agreement is not constructed in accordance with the Agreement, the Buyer shall owe the Sellers $6,665 as rental for the property . . ." for the period from July 25, 1973, to the end of that summer season. The addendum also provided that all the equipment would revert to appellees upon the appellant's default in regard to the addition.

Appellant paid appellees the $25,000 as agreed, and began to operate the business. However, at the end of the 1973 season, problems arose regarding the construction of the addition. Appellant claims that the building permit necessary to construct the addition was denied. Appellees claim that they obtained the building permit and presented it to appellant, who refused to begin construction. Additionally appellees claim that appellant agreed to reimburse them if they built the addition. At a cost of approximately $11,000, appellees did build a 20 feet by 40 feet addition. In the spring of 1974 appellees discovered that appellant was no longer interested in operating the business. There is no evidence in the record that appellant paid any rent from September 1, 1973, as the first rental payment was not due until May 15, 1974. Appellees resumed possession of the business and, upon opening the business for the 1974 summer season, found some of their equipment missing.

Appellant's complaint in assumpsit demanded that appellees return the $25,000 plus interest. Appellees denied that appellant was entitled to recovery of this sum and counterclaimed for damages totalling $52,000; $6,665 as rental for the property for the 1973 summer season and the remainder as compensation for "grievous damage to [appellees'] business, its good-will and its physical operation . . ." and appellee Lillian Thomas suffering "nervous illness, pain and suffering inclusive of serious bodily injury and necessitating bed rest and physicians' supervision for one year after [appellant's] default." Defendants' Counterclaim and New Matter, paras. 9-11. In his answer, Appellant only conceded liability for the $6,665 rent under the terms of the addendum. Plaintiff's

1. The parties agree that this date was incorrect, and that the date the parties intended was May 1, 1974.

Answer to Counterclaim and New Matter, para. 9. The trial court, sitting without a jury, found against appellant on the original claim, allowing appellees to retain the $25,000 paid by appellant, and for appellees on the counterclaim, allowing them to recover the $6,665 rent.

2

At one time the common law rule prohibiting a defaulting party on a contract from recovering was the majority rule. J. Calamari and J. Perillo, The Law of Contracts §11-26, at 427 (2d ed. 1977). However, a line of cases, apparently beginning with Britton v. Turner, 6 N.H. 481 (1834), departed from the common law rule. The merit of the common law rule was its recognition that the party who breaches should not be allowed "to have advantage from his own wrong." Corbin, The Right of a Defaulting Vendee to the Restitution of Instalments Paid, 40 Yale L.J. 1013, 1014 (1931). As Professor Perillo states, allowing recovery "invites contract-breaking and rewards morally unworthy conduct." Restitution in the Second Restatement of Contracts, 81 Colum. L. Rev. 37, 50 (1981). Its weakness, however, was its failure to recognize that the nonbreaching party should not obtain a windfall from the breach. The party who breaches after almost completely performing should not be more severely penalized than the party who breaches by not acting at all or after only beginning to act. Under the common law rule the injured party retains more benefit the more completely the breaching party has performed prior to the default. Thus it has been said that "to allow the injured party to retain the benefit of the part performance . . . , without making restitution of any part of such value, is the enforcement of a penalty or forfeiture against the contract-breaker." Corbin, supra, at 1013.

Critics of the common law rule have been arguing for its demise for over fifty years. See Corbin, supra. See also Calamari and Perillo, supra, at §11-26; 5A Corbin on Contracts §§1122-1135 (1964); 12 S. Williston, A Treatise on the Law of Contracts §§1473-1478 (3d ed. 1970). In response to this criticism an alternative rule has been adopted in the Restatement of Contracts.

The first Restatement of Contracts (1932) adopted the following rule:

§357. Restitution in Favor of a Plaintiff Who is Himself in Default

(1) Where the defendant fails or refuses to perform his contract and is justified therein by the plaintiff's own breach of duty or non-performance of a condition, but the plaintiff has rendered a part performance under the contract that is a net benefit to the defendant, the plaintiff can get judgment, except as stated in Subsection (2), for the amount of such benefit in excess of the harm that he has caused to the defendant by his own breach, in no case exceeding a ratable proportion of the agreed compensation, if

(a) the plaintiff's breach or non-performance is not wilful and deliberate; or

(b) the defendant, with knowledge that the plaintiff's breach of duty or non-performance of condition has occurred or will thereafter occur, assents to the rendition of the part performance, or accepts the benefit of it, or retains property received although its return in specie is still not unreasonably difficult or injurious.

(2) The plaintiff has no right to compensation for his part performance if it is merely a payment of earnest money, or if the contract provides that it may be retained and it is not so greatly in excess of the defendant's harm that the provision is rejected as imposing a penalty.

(3) The measure of the defendant's benefit from the plaintiff's part performance is the amount by which he has been enriched as a result of such performance unless the facts are those stated in Subsection (1b), in which case it is the price fixed by the contract for such part performance, or, if no price is so fixed, a ratable proportion of the total contract price.

In 1979, this rule was liberalized. [The court quotes Restatement (Second) of Contracts §374 (1979). — EDS.] . . . Thus the first Restatement's exclusion of the willful defaulting purchaser from recovery was deleted, apparently in part due to the influence of the Uniform Commercial Code's permitting recovery by a buyer who willfully defaults.[2] Id., Reporter's Note at 218. Professor Perillo suggests that the injured party has adequate protection without the common law rule.[3] Choosing "the just path," he therefore rejects the common law rule, explaining this choice by saying that times have changed. "What appears to be just to one generation may be viewed differently by another." Perillo, supra, at 50. See also 12 S. Williston, supra, §1473, at 222 ("The mores of the time and place will often determine which policy will be followed.").

Many jurisdictions have rejected the common law rule and permit recovery by the defaulting party. See, e.g., Amtorg Trading Corp. v. Miehle Printing Press and Manufacturing Co., 206 F.2d 103 (2d Cir. 1953) (noting with approval §357 of Restatement (First) of Contracts); . . . Kulseth v. Rotenberger, 320 N.W.2d 920 (North Dakota 1982) (following rule in Restatement (Second) of Contracts §374); . . . Hartford Elevator, Inc. v. Lauer, 94 Wis. 2d 571, 289 N.W.2d 280 (1980) (approving of §357 of Restatement (First) of Contracts).

This development has been called the modern trend. See Quillen v. Kelley, 216 Md. 396, 140 A.2d 517 (1958). See also 12 S. Williston, supra, §1473, at 222 (cases permitting recovery are now the weight of the authority); 5A Corbin on Contracts, supra, §1122, at 3 (common law rule is broad statement not supported by the actual decisions). But see 1 G. Palmer, The Law of Restitution 568 (1978) (no valid generalization may be made regarding when a defaulting vendee can recover). It may be that the growing number of jurisdictions permitting recovery have been influenced by the widespread adoption of the Uniform Commercial Code §2-718. See, e.g., Maxey v. Glindmeyer, 379 So. 2d 297 (Miss. 1980) (allowing recovery of excess of seller's actual damages in land sale contract by following

2. [The court quotes UCC §2-718. — EDS.]

3. He identifies four types of protection:

> First, the defaulting party's right to recovery is subject to the aggrieved party's right to offset his damages. Second, the measure of benefit is limited to the actual enrichment and cannot exceed a ratable portion of the contract price. Third, restitution is denied to the extent that the criteria for a valid liquidated damages clause are present. Fourth, restitution is denied if the aggrieved party seeks and is entitled to specific performance.

Perillo, supra, at 50 (footnotes omitted).

the logic of the state statute equivalent to §2-718 of the Uniform Commercial Code). Indeed, the common law rule is no longer intact even with respect to land sales contracts. See, e.g., Honey v. Henry's Franchise Leasing Corp., 64 Cal. 2d 801, 415 P.2d 833, 52 Cal. Rptr. 18 (1966); . . . and see 1 G. Palmer, supra, at 596 n.15 (citing cases).

In Pennsylvania, the common law rule has been applied to contracts for the sale of real property. Kaufman Hotel & Restaurant Co. v. Thomas, 411 Pa. 87, 190 A.2d 434 (1963); Luria v. Robbins, 223 Pa. Super. 456, 302 A.2d 361 (1973). In such cases, however, the seller has several remedies against a breaching buyer, including, in appropriate cases, an action for specific performance or for the purchase price. See Trachtenburg v. Sibarco Stations, Inc., 477 Pa. 517, 384 A.2d 1209 (1978). See also 5A Corbin on Contracts, supra, §1145. As long as the seller remains ready, able, and willing to perform a contract for the sale of real property, the breaching buyer has no right to restitution of payments made prior to default. See 5A Corbin on Contracts, supra, at §1130.

The common law rule has also been applied in Pennsylvania to contracts for the sale of goods. Atlantic City Tire and Rubber Corp. v. Southwark Foundry & Machine Co., 289 Pa. 569, 137 A. 807 (1927). However, Pennsylvania has since adopted the Uniform Commercial Code, which, as to contracts for the sale of goods, has modified the common law rule by 13 Pa. C.S. §2718(b), which permits a breaching party to recover restitution. See note 2, supra.

The viability of the common law rule permitting forfeiture has also been undermined in other areas of Pennsylvania law. In Estate of Cahen, 483 Pa. 157, 168 n. 10, 394 A.2d 958, 964 n.10 (1978), the Supreme Court held that assuming that a breaching fiduciary could recover in unjust enrichment, the basis would be Restatement of Contracts §357 (1932), which allows recovery by a breaching party to the extent that the benefits exceed the losses sustained by the other party.[4]

3

In regard to the present case, §374 of the Restatement (Second) of Contracts represents a more enlightened approach than the common law rule. "Rules of contract law are not rules of punishment; the contract breaker is not an outlaw." Perillo, supra, at 50. The party who committed a breach should be entitled to recover "any benefit . . . in excess of the loss that he has caused by his own breach." Restatement (Second) of Contracts §374(1).

This conclusion leads to the further conclusion that we should remand this case to the trial court. The trial court rested its decision on the common law rule. Slip op. of trial court at 7-8. Thus it never considered whether appellant is entitled to restitution, Restatement (Second) of Contracts §374(1), nor, if

4. The assertion in the dissenting opinion that "the majority does not and cannot cite *any* Pennsylvania authority" allowing a breaching party recovery, dissent op. at 122, fails to acknowledge the Supreme Court's decision in *Cahen.* While not citing *Cahen,* the dissenting opinion does cite Luria v. Robbins, 223 Pa. Super. 456, 302 A.2d 361 (1973), but as we have already discussed, we find *Luria* distinguishable.

appellant is not entitled to restitution, whether retention of the $25,000 was "reasonable in the light of the anticipated or actual loss caused by the breach and the difficulties of proof of loss," id., §374(2).[5]

Remanded for further proceedings consistent with this opinion. Jurisdiction relinquished.

TAMILIA, Judge, dissenting:

I strongly dissent. In the first instance, the majority does not and cannot cite *any* Pennsylvania authority adopting the rule cited in §374 of the Second Restatement of Contracts. Although the ostensible basis for remand is the trial court's reliance on outmoded law, the majority relies on law so new as to be virtually unknown in this jurisdiction. The law in Pennsylvania has been and continues to be that where a binding contract exists, and there is no allegation that the contract itself is void or voidable, a breaching party is not entitled to recovery. Luria v. Robbins, 223 Pa. Super. 456, 302 A.2d 361 (1978). While our Supreme Court may yet abrogate the forfeiture principle in this Commonwealth, it has not yet seen fit to do so, and we may not usurp its prerogatives, particularly when the result would be unjust.

Secondly, the Uniform Commercial Code §2718, cited by the majority in (partial) support, is applicable only to the sale of goods, and, while it and some of the equally inapplicable cases referred to by the majority may be part of a trend, the mainstream of contract law in Pennsylvania has not yet been diverted by it. Indeed the identification of the jurisdictions cited as the vanguard of change is for the most part questionable, as of those states relied upon to confer legitimacy on the majority's somewhat arbitrary conclusion, only one may be termed authoritative.

Lastly, and given the current state of the law, the most important determinant of the proper result in this case is the trial judge's assessment of the witness' credibility, here resolved in appellee's favor. The majority, far from according these findings their due, ignores them, contrary to law and our mandate. Knepp v. Nationwide Insurance Co., 324 Pa. Super. 479, 471 A.2d 1257 (1984).

The trial court correctly points out that the understanding of the parties is clearly evidenced by the agreements they signed. In breaching those agreements, appellant has engaged in what might charitably be termed sharp practice. The facts reasonably support the inference that appellant learned the hoagie business, benefited from the acquired trade and good will at appellees' place of business, then conducted the hoagie business at its previously owned pizza

5. We do not share the view expressed in the dissenting opinion that "the most important determinant of the proper result in this case is the trial judge's assessment of the witness[es]' credibility." Dissent op., at 122. To the contrary, as we have discussed, the trial court did not base its decision on an assessment of credibility but on the common law rule. Thus the court did not even consider the possibility of recovery by the breaching plaintiff. We are remanding so that the trial court may consider whether appellant is entitled to restitution. If the trial court again finds that it was the intention of the parties that the $25,000 be retained in the event of a breach, see slip op. of trial court at 7, then the court must determine whether this sum is reasonable. If the sum is unreasonable, appellant is entitled to restitution. See Restatement (Second) of Contracts §374 Comment *c*.

shop in the following season. Restitution in this instance constitutes a wholly unmerited reward for bad faith. We do not feel that such a result is consistent with the intent of law or the expectations of equity.

NOTES AND QUESTIONS

1. *Origin of breaching party's right to restitution.* In 1931 Professor Arthur Corbin collected and analyzed the cases dealing with the right of a defaulting purchaser in a land contract to recover in restitution. He concluded that the right had been recognized in "too many thousands of cases to deny such a right to a vendee merely because he is in default." Arthur L. Corbin, The Right of a Defaulting Vendee to the Restitution of Installments Paid, 40 Yale L.J. 1013, 1015 (1931). Corbin's work led to the inclusion of §357 in the original Restatement, which recognized a general right to restitution in favor of a party in default. Section 374 of the Restatement (Second) is the current version of this doctrine.

2. *Case law.* The court in *Lancellotti* cites several modern cases allowing a breaching party to recover in restitution, and decisions adopting the rule of Restatement (Second) §374 have continued to appear. E.g., Alstom Power, Inc. v. RMF Industrial Contracting, Inc., 418 F. Supp. 2d 766 (W.D. Pa. 2006) (even if subcontractor breached contract for installation of boilers, it could recover in restitution for benefit conferred in excess of harm to other party); Roberts Contracting Co. v. Valentine-Wooten Road Public Facility Board, 320 S.W.3d 1 (Ark. Ct. App. 2009); Eker Bros., Inc. v. Rehders, 163 P.3d 319 (N.M. Ct. App. 2011) (New Mexico will follow Restatement (Second) §374; *Lancellotti* cited and quoted). Not all jurisdictions agree, however. Two notable exceptions are Massachusetts and New York. Albre Marble & Tile Co. v. Goverman, 233 N.E.2d 533 (Mass. 1968) (subcontractor not allowed to recover in quantum meruit for tile work that did not comply with contract specifications; quantum meruit recovery available only if party "can prove both substantial performance of the contract and an endeavor on his part in good faith to perform fully"); Intermetal Fabricators, Inc. v. Losco Group, Inc., 2000 WL 1154249 (S.D.N.Y.) (under New York law, builder who defaults on construction contract may not recover either under contract or on quantum meruit basis unless builder has substantially performed the contract). In support of the modern rule, the *Lancellotti* court also cites UCC §2-718, which provides for a right of restitution on behalf of a defaulting purchaser of goods. Notably, the Pennsylvania Supreme Court raised the question whether it should adopt the approach of §374 in a subsequent case, but it decided that dispute on other grounds without resolving the issue from *Lancellotti.* See Sevast v. Kakouras, 915 A.2d 1147 (Pa. 2007). Do you think the modern rule is superior to the common law rule? Why? Based on the Pennsylvania cases cited in the opinion, did the court in *Lancellotti* exceed its authority as an intermediate appellate court by adopting the modern rule?

3. *Effect of willful breach.* As the court points out, the original Restatement provided that a defaulting party could not recover in restitution if the breach was willful and deliberate. Professor Corbin took issue with this portion of the section; this requirement, he asserted, showed a "childlike faith in the existence of a plain and obvious line between the good and the bad, between unfortunate virtue and unforgiveable sin." 5A Corbin on Contracts §1123, at 7. Other commentators have agreed with Corbin. Robert J. Nordstrom & Irwin F. Woodland, Recovery by Building Contractor in Default, 20 Ohio St. L.J. 193, 211-224 (1959). The language of §374 of the Restatement (Second) does not mention willfulness. Comment *b* to that section indicates, however, that an intentional variation from the terms of the contract (as distinguished from an intentional nonperformance) will preclude restitution: "A party who intentionally furnishes services or builds a building that is materially different from what he promised is properly regarded as having acted officiously and not in part performance of his promise and will be denied recovery on that ground even if his performance was of some benefit to the other party." Does the dissenting opinion in *Lancellotti* suggest another possible doctrine that might limit the right of a breaching party to recover in restitution?

4. *Measure of restitution.* We have seen in the *Jacob & Youngs* case that a court may permit a party who has substantially performed a contract to recover "on the contract" even though his performance in some respect involves an immaterial breach. What should the measure of the restitutionary interest be when recovery is given to a party who has committed a material breach? Since the breaching party is seeking relief, not surprisingly, recovery is limited. The Restatement (Second) §374, Comment *b*, provides that recovery should be limited to the lesser of either (a) the value of the benefit conferred or (b) the defendant's increase in wealth. In addition, to prevent the breaching party from recovering more than her expectation interest, the Restatement also provides that "in no case will the party in breach be allowed to recover more than a ratable portion of the total contract price where such a portion can be determined." Restatement (Second) §374, Comment *b* and Illustration 3. Finally, to ensure protection of the nonbreaching party's expectation interest, any damages suffered by that party must be deducted from the amount of the restitutionary award. Restatement (Second) §374(1).

In some cases, a breaching party's recovery in restitution will not differ markedly from the recovery that would have followed if the plaintiff had the benefit of the doctrine of substantial performance. E.g., Kreyer v. Driscoll, 159 N.W.2d 680 (Wis. 1968) (trial court found contractor had substantially performed and awarded contract price of house, less deductions for work not performed; appellate court holds that magnitude of work not done precluded finding of substantial performance but affirms award below on quantum meruit theory). In many cases, however, the plaintiff even if eligible for §374 recovery will receive little on its quantum meruit claim. E.g., Denver Ventures, Inc. v. Arlington Lane Corp., 754 P.2d 785 (Colo. Ct. App. 1988) (subcontractor entitled to no quantum meruit recovery because in light of large cost of completion, damages from breach exceeded benefit conferred).

Ventura v. Titan Sports, Inc.

United States Court of Appeals 65 F.3d 725 (8th Cir. 1995)

MAGILL, Circuit Judge.

This appeal arises out of a match between wrestler/commentator Jesse "The Body" Ventura and Titan Sports, Inc., which operates "The World Wrestling Federation" (WWF). Titan appeals the district court's judgment in favor of Ventura, arguing that (1) Ventura was not entitled to recovery under quantum meruit because an express contract covers the subject matter for which Ventura sought recovery; and (2) the district court erroneously admitted and relied upon the testimony of Ventura's damages expert. Ventura cross-appeals the district court's denial of prefiling interest. We affirm in all respects.[1]

I. BACKGROUND

During July 1984, Titan entered into a licensing agreement with LJN Toys authorizing LJN Toys to manufacture dolls using the images of WWF wrestlers. Titan also entered a "master licensing" agreement with DIC Enterprises that resulted in WWF T-shirts, trading cards, calendars, a computer game and numerous other items. In December 1984, Titan entered into a licensing agreement with A & H Video Sales (d/b/a Coliseum Video) for the production of videotapes of WWF matches. Agreements with A & H and Columbia House resulted in the production of approximately ninety videotapes of WWF performances involving Ventura.

Ventura began wrestling for Titan in Spring 1984 under an oral contract with Vincent K. McMahon, Titan's President and sole shareholder. In late 1984,

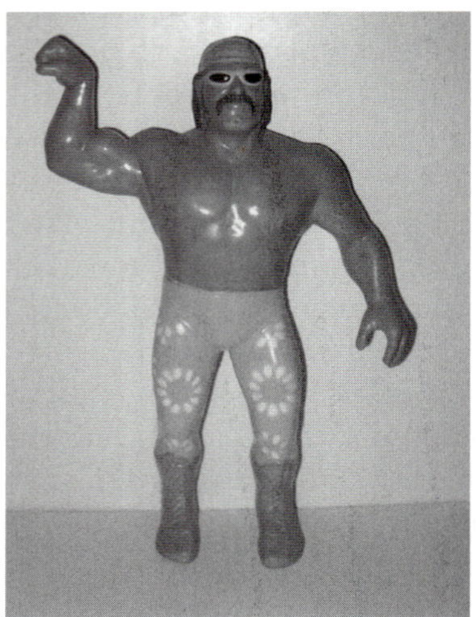

The Jesse "The Body" Ventura action figure was produced by LJN as part of their Wrestling Superstars toy line.

Jesse Ventura during his wrestling career.

1. We refer to the contracts negotiated by Ventura's agent, Barry Bloom, during the 1987-90 period as "post-Bloom" contracts. The earlier oral agreements between Ventura and [Vincent K.] McMahon we refer to as the "pre-Bloom" contracts.

Ventura suffered medical problems and ceased to work as a wrestler, although Titan continued to pay him during his convalescence. After Ventura recovered, he returned to work for Titan as a "color" or "heel"[2] commentator under an oral agreement with Titan. He was paid a flat rate of $1000 per week and there was no discussion of videotape royalties or licenses. Shortly after returning to work for Titan, Ventura executed a "Wrestling Booking Agreement" (WBA) with an effective date of January 1, 1985. Ventura subsequently resumed wrestling for Titan, for which he was paid according to the terms of the WBA. In March 1986, Ventura terminated his relationship with Titan in order to pursue an acting career.

Ventura's foray into movies was moderately successful, but in fall 1986 he returned to Titan as a commentator, again under an oral agreement that made no mention of videotape royalties or licenses. In fall 1987, Ventura hired Barry Bloom as his talent agent. Bloom negotiated on Ventura's behalf with Dick Ebersol, Titan's partner in producing the "Saturday Night's Main Event" show. However, the negotiations quickly broke down, and as a result, the first show of the 1987-88 season aired without Ventura. A few weeks later, Titan's Vice-President of Business Affairs, Dick Glover, contacted Bloom concerning Ventura and represented to Bloom that Titan's policy was to pay royalties only to "feature" performers. Because Ventura was interested in working for Titan, Bloom thought it wise not to attempt to "break the policy." Ventura returned to work for Titan under a new contract that waived royalties and continued to work as a commentator for Titan until August 1990. Since that time he has worked as a commentator for WCW, Titan's main competitor.

In December 1991, Ventura filed an action in Minnesota state court seeking royalties for the use of his likeness on videotapes produced by Titan. The original complaint contained causes of action for fraud,[3] misappropriation of publicity rights and quantum meruit. Titan removed the case to federal court, and the case was tried before a jury. Although only the quantum meruit claim was submitted to the jury, the jury was given a special verdict form concerning misrepresentation. Using this form, the jury found that Titan had defrauded Ventura and that $801,333.06 would compensate Ventura for Titan's videotape exploitation of his commentary. The jury also determined that Titan exploited Ventura's name, voice or likeness as a commentator in other merchandise and concluded that $8,625.60 would compensate Ventura for this exploitation.

After the jury rendered its verdict, the district court concluded that Ventura was not entitled to a jury trial on his quantum meruit claim. Accordingly, the court vacated the jury verdict and entered findings of fact and conclusions of law that were consistent with the verdict. The court denied Ventura's request for prefiling interest but granted prejudgment interest from the time the suit was filed. Titan appealed, and Ventura cross-appealed the denial of prefiling interest.

---

2. A color commentator provides the story of the wrestling match, which is in essence a stage show. A heel commentator is a color commentator who plays the role of "the bad guy."

3. The fraud pleaded in Ventura's Complaint and Second Amended Complaint is that Titan fraudulently misrepresented to Ventura that Ventura was employed for no purpose other than a live performance. Second Amended Complaint ¶42.

II. Discussion

Titan raises three claimed errors on appeal. First, Titan argues that Ventura was not entitled to quantum meruit recovery of royalties for the videotape[4] exploitation of his performance as color commentator during the 1985-87 (pre-Bloom) period because Ventura provided his commentating services under an express contract. Second, Titan claims that the district court erroneously applied the law of quantum meruit when it rescinded an express contract and awarded Ventura royalties for the videotape exploitation of his performance as color commentator during the 1987-90 (post-Bloom) period. Third, Titan alleges that the district court abused its discretion in qualifying and relying upon Ventura's expert witness in awarding damages. Ventura's cross-appeal presents a single issue: whether the district court clearly erred when it denied Ventura's request for prefiling interest. We address each of these issues in turn.

A. Is Quantum Meruit Available During the Pre-Bloom Period?

Minnesota law determines the rights of the parties in this diversity action, and we review the district court's interpretation of Minnesota law de novo. Salve Regina College v. Russell, 499 U.S. 225, 231, 111 S. Ct. 1217, 1221, 113 L. Ed. 2d 190 (1991). The basic contours of the law of quantum meruit, or unjust enrichment, are well settled under Minnesota law:

> An action for unjust enrichment may be based on failure of consideration, fraud, mistake, and situations where it would be morally wrong for one party to enrich himself at the expense of another. However, a claim of unjust enrichment does not lie simply because one party benefits from the efforts or obligations of others, but instead lies where one party was unjustly enriched in the sense that the term 'unjustly' could mean illegally or unlawfully.

Hesselgrave v. Harrison, 435 N.W.2d 861, 863-64 (Minn. App. 1989) (internal quotations and citation omitted). Although the applicable law is well settled, the facts of this case are rather unique and therefore require us to address some preliminary issues.

The first unique aspect of this appeal involves defining the benefit received (allegedly unjustly) by Titan. Titan makes much of the fact that Ventura provided no services for Titan other than pursuant to the Ventura-Titan contracts. While it is true that the Ventura-Titan contracts governed all the services provided by Ventura (i.e., his acts of appearing at the wrestling match and commentating), the agreements do not necessarily address all the benefits created by Ventura's services. Ventura's services created several varieties of intellectual property rights. In defining the "benefit" conferred upon Titan, the proper focus is not merely Ventura's labor as he performed, but must also include the intellectual property rights created by Ventura's performance. Thus, we find that the intellectual property rights to Ventura's commentary are benefits upon which an action for unjust enrichment may be based.

4. For the sake of simplicity, we discuss the issues only in terms of the videotapes. However, the principles applied to videotape licenses and royalties apply equally to other merchandise.

We next must determine whether Titan, in taking this benefit, was *unjustly* enriched. Ventura's quantum meruit claim may succeed only if Titan's rights to use Ventura's performance are limited so that Titan is not entitled to use the performance without Ventura's consent. We believe that Titan's rights are limited by Ventura's right to publicity. In determining the law of the State of Minnesota concerning publicity rights, we are bound by the decisions of the Minnesota Supreme Court. If the Minnesota Supreme Court has not addressed the issue, we must determine what that court would probably hold were it to decide the issue. The parties have identified, and we have discovered, no case in which the Minnesota Supreme Court has either accepted or rejected the tort of misappropriation of publicity rights. We must therefore attempt to predict the decision of the Minnesota Supreme Court. In making our prediction, we may consider relevant state precedent, analogous decisions, considered dicta, scholarly works and any other reliable data. B.B. v. Continental Ins. Co., 8 F.3d 1288, 1291 (8th Cir. 1993).

We believe that the Minnesota Supreme Court would recognize the tort of violation of publicity rights. . . . The right to publicity protects the ability of public personae to control the types of publicity that they receive. The right to publicity protects pecuniary, not emotional, interests. [Uhlaender v. Henricksen, 316 F. Supp. 1277, 1280-1281 (D. Minn. 1970)]. . . . Thus, we believe that the Minnesota courts would recognize the right to publicity, and Titan's violation of this right makes Titan's use of Ventura's commentary without his consent unjust.[6]

However, quantum meruit is not available simply because Titan may have been unjustly enriched. Minnesota law is clear that "[w]here an express contract exists, there can be no implied [in law] contract with respect to the same subject matter." Reese Design v. I-94 Highway 61 Eastview Center Partnership, 428 N.W.2d 441, 446 (Minn. App. 1988); accord Sharp v. Laubersheimer, 347 N.W.2d 268, 271 (Minn. 1984). On the other hand, if an existing contract does not address the benefit for which recovery is sought, quantum meruit is available regarding those items about which the contract is silent. Holman v. CPT Corp., 457 N.W.2d 740, 745 (Minn. App. 1990); Frankson v. Design Space Int'l, 394 N.W.2d 140, 145 (Minn. 1986); Sagl v. Hirt, 236 Minn. 281, 52 N.W.2d 721, 725 (1952).[7]

6. We are troubled by the fact that section 301(a) of the copyright code (Title 17) preempts Ventura's claims that are "equivalent to any of the exclusive rights within the general scope of copyright as specified by section 106," such as the production of videotapes of Ventura's televised commentary. Baltimore Orioles, Inc. v. Major League Baseball Players Ass'n, 805 F.2d 663, 675 (7th Cir. 1986) (baseball players' challenge to television broadcast of live games without their consent as a violation of their publicity rights preempted), cert. denied, 480 U.S. 941, 107 S. Ct. 1593, 94 L. Ed. 2d 782 (1987). However, Titan has not timely raised the issue of preemption on appeal, and has therefore waived it. . . .

7. A corollary of this rule is that quantum meruit is available if the benefit is conferred unknowingly, but not if the benefit is conferred merely as part of a bad bargain. Galante v. Oz, Inc., 379 N.W.2d 723, 726 (Minn. App. 1986). For the reasons discussed below, we conclude that Ventura conferred the videotape rights upon Titan unknowingly.

Between 1985 and 1987, Ventura performed services for Titan under two different agreements. Ventura's services as a wrestler are governed by the WBA; his services as a commentator are governed by his oral agreements with McMahon. Thus, two contracts existed between Ventura and Titan between 1985 and March 1986, when the WBA was terminated. Whether quantum meruit recovery was proper depends upon whether or not the two agreements between Ventura and Titan were of limited scope, addressing only televised live performances, or also included subsequent videotape releases of the performances. The district court found that the WBA precluded royalties for the videotape exploitation of Ventura's performance *as a wrestler*. The district court also found that Ventura and Titan had no agreement concerning the payment of royalties for videotape exploitation of Ventura's performance *as a commentator*. This finding concerns the intent of the parties, Cepeda v. Swift & Co., 415 F.2d 1205, 1207-1208 (8th Cir. 1969), and as such, is a factual finding which we review only for clear error. 1 Steven A. Childress & Martha S. Davis, Federal Standards of Review §2.23 (2d ed. 1991) ("The clearly erroneous rule generally applies to a finding regarding the intent of the contracting parties, at least where the contract is ambiguous.").

We have reviewed the record, and are left with no definite and firm conviction that a mistake has been made. From 1985 to 1987, there was no discussion of Titan's right to use Ventura's color commentary. At least initially,[8] Ventura was not aware of the impending videotape sales, as merchandising was not part of the industry practice. These facts support the conclusion that Ventura's contract for commentating services did not contemplate a license for videotape distribution. Accordingly, we hold that the district court's finding that the pre-Bloom Ventura-Titan contracts did not address videotape licenses or royalties is not clearly erroneous. See Anderson v. Bessemer City, 470 U.S. 564, 105 S. Ct. 1504, 84 L. Ed. 2d 518 (1985). We believe that the judgment of the district court was correct insofar as it awarded damages for the exploitation of Ventura's pre-Bloom commentating performances.

B. Is Quantum Meruit Available for the Post-Bloom Period?

The post-Bloom contracts pose different issues. It is clear that Ventura performed commentating services between 1987 and 1990 pursuant to a series of contracts with Titan. It is also clear that the post-Bloom Ventura-Titan contracts included an arrangement concerning videotape royalties. Bloom specifically inquired about royalties and was told of the Titan policy. In reliance upon this purported policy, Ventura waived his rights to royalties. Titan contends that Ventura is not entitled to recovery in quantum meruit for the post-Bloom period because of the existence of express contracts waiving royalties. See *Sharp*, 347 N.W.2d at 271 (" 'It is fundamental that proof of an express contract precludes recovery in quantum meruit.' " (quoting Breza v. Thaldorf, 276 Minn. 180, 149 N.W.2d 276 (Minn. 1967))). Thus, the question reduces to whether Ventura may avoid the express contract waiving royalties and recover these royalties under

8. Ventura stated that he was aware that tapes were being distributed in 1985. App. at 99-100.

quantum meruit. We believe that the district court correctly concluded that Ventura was entitled to avoid the fraudulently induced contracts and to recover the reasonable value of the royalties.

. . .

It is well established under Minnesota law that unjust enrichment and quantum meruit may arise from fraud or several other predicates. See, e.g., *Holman,* 457 N.W.2d at 745; *Hesselgrave,* 435 N.W.2d at 863; Timmer v. Gray, 395 N.W.2d 477, 478 (Minn. App. 1986); Anderson v. DeLisle, 352 N.W.2d 794, 796 (Minn. App. 1984). Nothing in these Minnesota cases requires that all elements of a cause of action for fraud must be proved in order to use fraud as a stepping stone for quantum meruit. However, we begin with the elements of a cause of action for fraud under Minnesota law as a useful guide. See Davis v. Re-Trac Mfg. Corp., 149 N.W.2d 37, 38-39 (Minn. 1967) (listing elements of cause of action for fraud). Titan argues that the evidence was insufficient to support the necessary findings of materiality, inducement, justifiable reliance, causation and damages. We disagree. . . .

The evidence demonstrates that in 1987, Ventura hired Bloom to negotiate with Titan on his behalf. During negotiations, Glover told Bloom that Titan's policy was to pay royalties only to talent featured in their own videotapes, such as the "Best of" videotapes. Believing it difficult to break Titan's policy, Bloom negotiated an agreement under which Ventura agreed to perform for Titan as a commentator. The agreement did not entitle Ventura to royalties for videotapes of his performances, unless he was the featured performer. Ventura's compensation did not include any payment based on videotape sales.

Between 1987 and 1990, Glover and Bloom met annually, in person or by telephone, to negotiate Ventura's performance fees for each broadcast season, and occasionally for special performances. During each negotiation, Bloom asked Glover whether Titan had changed its policy regarding the payment of videotape royalties, and each time Glover reiterated that no talent received videotape royalties unless they were the featured performer on a videotape. Glover also told Ventura of this policy. Bloom and Ventura relied on Glover's statements concerning Titan's royalty policy, and understood that by entering into fee agreements they waived any right Ventura had to royalties. Despite these representations, Titan simultaneously made numerous royalty payments which were inconsistent with the purported policy of not paying royalties except to featured performers.[10]

In light of this evidence concerning Titan's representations and its history of royalty payments, the district court concluded that from 1987 through 1990, Titan's representations to Ventura that its policy was to pay videotape royalties only to featured performers were false. The district court also found that had

10. In 1985, 1986 and 1987, Titan paid videotape royalties to Hulk Hogan and Marvel Comics for "Wrestlemania I," "II" and "III," despite the fact that there was no featured performer in these productions. During 1988, Titan paid videotape royalties to all 54 wrestlers appearing in the "Survivor Series," to all 57 wrestlers appearing in "Wrestlemania IV" and to all 38 wrestlers appearing in "Summer Slam '88." Again, these payments were inconsistent with Titan's stated policy because none of these videotapes had one featured performer. Beginning in December 1988, Titan paid royalties to all wrestlers appearing in videotapes of pay-per-view events.

Ventura known that Titan did not abide by its stated policy, he would not have accepted a deal which did not compensate him for the reproduction and sale of his performances on videotape. The court further found that Ventura justifiably relied on Titan's fraudulent misrepresentations of its royalty policy, and as a result Ventura suffered damages. Thus, the district court rescinded the 1987-1990 agreements, and permitted Ventura to recover in quantum meruit. In light of the abundance of supporting evidence, we find no basis for concluding the district court's findings were clearly erroneous or lacked sufficient evidentiary support.

C. Did the District Court Abuse Its Discretion When It Relied Upon the Testimony of Ventura's Damages Expert?

[The court first concluded that the testimony of Ventura's expert, Weston Anson, pertained to a material issue, the reasonable value of the services rendered by the plaintiff or the benefit to the defendant. — EDS.]

We now turn to the related question whether Anson's testimony was reliable. Titan argues that Anson's testimony is unreliable because it is impermissibly speculative. In order to assess whether Anson's testimony is reliable, we must focus on the methodology and principles underlying the testimony, not the conclusions they generate. *Sorensen,* 31 F.3d at 648. Anson arrived at his estimate of damages by applying a royalty percentage to Titan's revenues from wholesale distribution of the tapes. The sales figures for the ninety videotapes upon which Ventura appeared were not available, but net profits (a more conservative measure) were established to the penny ($25,733,527.94). The main dispute concerns the royalty rate applied to this figure to generate the royalty that is the measure of damages. Titan's expert figured damages in a similar fashion, applying varying royalty percentages and formulas to base amounts keyed to sales. Anson testified that a five percent royalty was the minimum that he would be satisfied with as an agent and was the single most likely rate, but that rates could range from 3.5% to 7.5%. When applied to the profits figure, these rates yield: $865,723.00 (3.5%), $1,236,747.00 (5%), and $1,855,121.00 (7.5%).

We believe that Anson's methodology in arriving at the royalty percentages was reliable. Anson based his opinion as to the reasonable royalty upon a survey of thousands of licensing agreements. It is common practice to prove the value of an article (e.g., a videotape license) by introducing evidence of transactions involving other "substantially similar" articles (i.e., other licenses). 2 John H. Wigmore, Wigmore on Evidence §463, at 616-630 (James H. Chadbourn rev. 1979). Anson surveyed licensing agreements involving numerous sports and entertainment figures, App. at 487a (NFL), 489a (major league baseball), as well as various other types of characters. Although no individual arrangement examined by Anson was "on all fours" with the predicted Ventura-Titan license, in the aggregate, the licenses provided sufficient information to allow Anson to predict a royalty range for a wrestling license. We believe that this methodology is sufficiently reliable to support the admission of Anson's testimony.

. . .

III. Conclusion

The district court did not clearly err when it determined that Ventura's pre-Bloom contracts did not address videotape licensing and royalties. Accordingly, it did not err in permitting quantum meruit recovery of videotape royalties for the pre-Bloom period. Nor did the district court err when it awarded quantum meruit recovery for the post-Bloom period. We also find that the district court did not abuse its discretion in qualifying Anson, nor did it abuse its discretion in determining that Anson's testimony was relevant and that the methods used by Anson were reliable. We further find that the district court did not clearly err in denying Ventura's request for prefiling interest where Ventura's potential damages varied by over 200% and where the amount was contingent upon the factfinder's determination of unresolved issues.

Morris Sheppard Arnold, Circuit Judge, dissenting.

I dissent from so much of the court's opinion as allows Mr. Ventura a recovery for royalties before Mr. Bloom negotiated a contract for him. To state a cause of action for unjust enrichment in Minnesota, a plaintiff must show either on legal or equitable grounds, or based on principles of natural justice, that a defendant's retention of a benefit would be unjust. Mehl v. Norton, 201 Minn. 203, 205-207, 275 N.W. 843, 844-845 (1937). In the court's view, Mr. Ventura was deprived of a legal right to additional compensation because Titan infringed his right of publicity. I believe that the court has mistakenly allowed this recovery, however, because I do not think that a right of publicity exists under Minnesota law.

The court finds a right of publicity under Minnesota law in the absence of any evidence that Minnesota's courts would welcome this cause of action — and, indeed, a Minnesota Supreme Court case indicates to me that they would not. Minnesota has not adopted the tort of appropriation of name or likeness or any of the other torts collectively known as invasion of privacy, Hendry v. Conner, 303 Minn. 317, 319, 226 N.W.2d 921, 922-923 (Minn. 1975), and a right to one's likeness is virtually indistinguishable from a right of publicity. . . . [I]t is highly significant that, in the year 1995, when everyone not only wants his or her fifteen minutes of fame but the concomitant television rights as well, no Minnesota state court has yet discovered a right of publicity in Minnesota law. The court has thus cited no "reliable data," B.B. v. Continental Ins. Co., 8 F.3d 1288, 1291 (8th Cir. 1993), to indicate that Minnesota would recognize such a right. Titan was therefore not enriched in violation of a legal right recognized in Minnesota.

Nor has Mr. Ventura shown that it would be inequitable or violate natural justice for Titan to reproduce and sell the videotapes that it produced and on which Mr. Ventura was already paid to appear as an announcer without paying him additional consideration. The doctrine of unjust enrichment, it is true, may provide recovery for performing extra services not specified in an original contract, Sagl v. Hirt, 236 Minn. 281, 287, 52 N.W.2d 721, 725 (1952), but

Mr. Ventura does not argue that he performed any duties in addition to his commentary. One may also recover to prevent unjust enrichment if a benefit is conferred "unknowingly" or "unwillingly," Galante v. Oz, Inc., 379 N.W.2d 723, 726 (Minn. App. 1986), but Mr. Ventura's own testimony shows that he did not confer the alleged benefit unknowingly or unwillingly. More important, it is hardly unjust, from an economic viewpoint, that Titan should receive the full benefit from selling copies of the videotapes that it created. Titan, as entrepreneur, staged the wrestling matches, hired the various wrestlers, hired the announcers, and, above all, took the risks that the venture would fail to turn a profit. Now that Titan has been successful, Mr. Ventura wants additional compensation for having performed no additional work. If there is any unjust enrichment in this case, it is in allowing Mr. Ventura a recovery under these circumstances.

Plaintiff cites Frankson v. Design Space Int'l, 394 N.W.2d 140, 145 (Minn. 1986), and Holman v. CPT Corp., 457 N.W.2d 740, 745 (Minn. App. 1990), for the proposition that when there is a lack of full agreement concerning compensation an employee may still recover in quantum meruit. That is no doubt so. But those cases are inapposite because each involved performances that had concededly not been compensated. The issue in each was whether sales employees would be allowed to recover commissions. In *Frankson,* the court held that the parties never reached an agreement about commissions and that therefore the plaintiff should be allowed a quantum meruit recovery. In *Holman,* plaintiff was terminated before she realized a commission on a sale that was virtually complete but still pending when she was fired, and the contract was silent with respect to whether a commission was due under the circumstances. Mr. Ventura, by contrast, performed and was compensated for his performances. He made an agreement to be paid a weekly sum rather than royalties for announcing wrestling events, and while he now regrets this less favorable arrangement, his regrets are not actionable under Minnesota law because one cannot recover for an unfavorable bargain. See *Galante,* 379 N.W.2d at 726.

Nelson v. Radio Corp. of Am., 148 F. Supp. 1 (S.D. Fla. 1957) is an instructive case. Nelson, a vocalist, was hired to perform with the Glenn Miller Orchestra. Miller paid him weekly according to union scale. Nelson sang six selections for a recording session and two more for a broadcast that also was recorded. Miller assigned all his rights in the records to the defendant, and in due course, defendant made copies of the recordings for sale. Nelson sued for an accounting for the sale of the recordings on which he sang, a 5 percent royalty on the records, as well as injunctive relief and damages. The evidence established that Nelson had no agreement with Miller entitling him to receive any royalties on the sale of phonograph records. The court ruled that "any right in and to phonograph records or other recordings in connection with the production of which plaintiff worked were the property of the plaintiff's employer Miller. . . ." 148 F. Supp. at 3. The court therefore rejected Nelson's claim for royalties.

The reasoning of *Nelson* is highly persuasive and our case is strikingly similar to it. Mr. Ventura agreed to receive weekly pay to perform wrestling commentary. He does not dispute, as far as I can discern, that the videotapes belong to Titan. Mr. Ventura; like Nelson, is suing for a royalty on the sales of the recordings on which he performed. And like Nelson, Mr. Ventura deserves no recovery because he and Titan both performed under their contract and the recordings of Mr. Ventura's performances now belong to Titan and it may profit from them as it sees fit.

Finally, even if Minnesota recognized a cause of action for the breach of a right of publicity, and even if this case could be properly characterized, as the court seems to believe, as a dispute over the scope of a license of intellectual property rights (that is, publicity rights), I still doubt that Mr. Ventura should recover. Mr. Ventura himself testified that he was employed to "broadcast wrestling." The agreement was therefore clearly susceptible to the construction that it authorized the sale of videotapes to end users. According to a leading copyright treatise, the preferred rule for copyright contracts when the intent of the parties is unclear is that the licensee may properly pursue any uses that may reasonably be said to fall within the medium as described in the license. 3 Melville B. Nimmer & David Nimmer, Nimmer on Copyright §10.10[B] at 10-93 (1993). It follows "that a grant of the right to exhibit a motion picture by 'television' in its unambiguous core meaning refers to over-the-air television broadcasts, but in its ambiguous penumbra includes any device by which the motion picture may be seen on television screens, including cable television and videocassette uses." Id. at 10-94. The ambiguity ought to favor the licensee because "it is surely more arbitrary and unjust to put the onus on the licensee by holding that he should have obtained a further clarification of a meaning that was already present than it is to hold that the licensor should have negated a meaning that the licensee might then or thereafter rely upon." Id. I believe that this principle is recommended by reason and is applicable here because a right of publicity does not differ in any material way from a copyright. See Baltimore Orioles, Inc. v. Major League Baseball Players Ass'n, 805 F.2d 663, 679 (7th Cir. 1986), cert. denied, 480 U.S. 941, 107 S. Ct. 1593, 94 L. Ed. 2d 782 (1987). Mr. Ventura testified that he was hired to perform commentary for television broadcasts. "Television broadcasts" under these circumstances must reasonably include dissemination of the videotapes containing the commentary that Mr. Ventura performed as part of his employment. Indeed, this seems to me utterly implicit in the original contractual arrangement.

For the foregoing reasons, I believe that Mr. Ventura's claim for additional compensation for his announcing duties in the period before Mr. Bloom negotiated a contract for him fails as a matter of law. I would therefore reverse that part of the judgment allowing Mr. Ventura's recovery for his role as a commentator before he entered into the written contract.

NOTES AND QUESTIONS

1. *Governor Ventura.* Plaintiff Jesse Ventura eventually left professional wrestling and entered the political arena where he served as mayor of Brooklyn Park, Minnesota, before being elected governor of Minnesota in 1998. After serving one term, he decided not to seek reelection.

2. *Types of restitutionary claims in Ventura.* The majority and the dissent make a distinction between plaintiff Ventura's claims for restitution arising during the time that he had oral contracts and his claims from the period when he had written contracts negotiated by Bloom. How do these two claims for restitution compare with the theories advanced in the first two cases in this section? The dissent disagrees with the majority only about the "pre-Bloom" claims for restitution. Part of the disagreement focuses on whether there is a right of publicity in Minnesota in the absence of a clear ruling by the state courts. Beyond that dispute about state law, however, the dissent also disagrees with the majority's holding on whether Titan was unjustly enriched. Are you more persuaded by the majority or the dissent? More specifically, are you persuaded that Ventura conferred an uncompensated benefit "unknowingly" in the pre-Bloom performances?

The "post-Bloom" claim exemplifies a case in which restitution is sought after a contract has been rendered unenforceable due to fraud. As noted in the introduction to this section, the same reasoning applies if a contract is unenforceable for other reasons, such as mistake, incapacity, impossibility, duress, etc. What measure of restitution would be appropriate in such cases? See the following note.

3. *Measuring the restitutionary interest: enrichment or benefit.* In the late nineteenth century, when commentators first began developing the theory of restitution, it was often said that the basis of restitution was "unjust enrichment." William A. Keener, A Treatise on The Law of Quasi-Contracts 19 (1893). See also Arthur L. Corbin, Quasi Contractual Obligations, 21 Yale L.J. 533, 550 (1912). Other commentators argued, however, that courts often awarded recovery in restitutionary actions even if the defendant was not in fact enriched. In his 1913 treatise on quasi contracts, Professor Woodward suggested that the measure of recovery should be based on the "receipt of benefit" rather than enrichment. Frederic C. Woodward, The Law of Quasi Contracts (1913). While the use of the word *benefit* seems to imply enrichment, the term was intended to refer to the value of what was received rather than the increase in the defendant's wealth. The Restatement of Restitution, which was published in 1937, adopted this concept of benefit as the measure of recovery. Comment *e* to §1 provided that "a person who has been unjustly deprived of his property or its value or the value of his labor may be entitled to maintain an action for restitution against another although the other has not in fact been enriched thereby."

The Restatement (Second) of Contracts §371 recognizes both means of measuring restitution (reasonable value of the performer's services and value of increase to the recipient's property) and indicates that relief may be measured as justice requires. Cf. Maglica v. Maglica, 78 Cal. Rptr. 2d 101 (Ct. App. 1998) (after jury awarded $84 million, appellate court reversed, holding that quantum meruit could be measured only by "reasonable value of the services rendered" and not by the "impact" on the business). Would these measures necessarily be different? Which measure would be more appropriate in *Ventura*?

4. ***Recovery of reliance damages in restitution.*** A number of commentators have argued that courts should have the power under the theory of restitution to compensate for reliance damages or order some other equitable adjustment of the rights of the parties when a contract has been discharged because of impracticability or other similar cause. See John P. Dawson, Restitution Without Enrichment, 61 B.U. L. Rev. 563 (1981); Jeffrey L. Harrison, A Case for Loss Sharing, 56 S. Cal. L. Rev. 573 (1983). The Restatement (Second) appears to authorize courts to engage in such loss sharing, albeit in a somewhat roundabout fashion. Section 371 provides that in an action for restitution a court may "as justice requires" measure recovery either by the value of the performance rendered (the benefit theory) or the increase in value of the defendant's property or interests (the enrichment theory). Comment *b* to §371 provides that the measure of recovery excludes expenditures "to the extent that they conferred no benefit." This comment notwithstanding, other sections of the Restatement allow a court to award reliance damages when a contract is discharged for reasons such as impracticability. See Restatement (Second) §§158 (mistake), 272 (impracticability). See generally Joseph M. Perillo, Restitution in the Second Restatement of Contracts, 81 Colum. L. Rev. 37 (1981); William F. Young, Half Measures, 81 Colum. L. Rev. 19 (1981). See, e.g., Hart v. Arnold, 884 A.2d 316 (Pa. Super. Ct. 2005) (even though acts in reliance did not benefit buyer, seller of parcel of land was entitled to restitution plus reliance damages after governmental regulations made performance by buyer of promise to build lake impracticable but buyer failed to timely inform seller of the changed circumstances).

5. ***Proving restitutionary damages with reasonable certainty.*** The defendant in *Ventura* challenged the sufficiency of the evidence offered to measure the restitutionary interest of the plaintiff. Is it surprising to find here the same problem of "certainty" that we have seen in connection with claims for expectation and reliance damages? Are you persuaded that the majority reached the correct conclusion on this issue? An example of the potential difficulty in measuring restitution damages with certainty is found in ATACS Corp. v. Trans World Communications, Inc., 155 F.3d 659 (3d Cir. 1998), *remanded at* 2002 U.S. Dist. LEXIS 15070 (E.D. Pa.). After the plaintiff subcontractor entered into a preliminary "teaming agreement" with the defendant to produce the successful bid for a Greek government contract worth more than $23 million, the defendant breached by unexpectedly awarding a contract to one of the plaintiff's competitors for the work the plaintiff expected to perform. After finding that the plaintiff's expectancy relief would be too speculative, the trial court also ruled that it could not quantify the value of the plaintiff's services rendered in enhancing the defendant's winning bid and thus awarded nominal damages of $1. The plaintiff did not seek and the trial court did not address a reliance-based measure of damages. Id. at 670. The Third Circuit Court of Appeals reversed on the issue of restitutionary damages, ruling that the trial court should have invited

the parties to offer expert evidence about the reasonable value of technical and consulting services in the market of government contracting and should have considered dollar savings realized by the defendant in later subcontracts made possible by the plaintiff's earlier services. In remanding and essentially urging the trial court to make a greater effort to give relief to the nonbreaching party, the court of appeals stated that "equitable considerations must predominate over a parochial approach" to the remedies issue. Id. at 671. On initial remand, the trial court rejected the plaintiff's request for more than $4 million in restitution damages as a disguised claim for lost profits and awarded the plaintiff only $18,900 based on the defendant's calculation of the plaintiff's costs in preparing technical submissions. After the appellate court rejected that award and remanded again, the trial court awarded the plaintiff restitutionary damages of $230,000 as a reasonable commission for facilitating the contract and another $20,000 as the reasonable value to the defendant of technical submissions provided by the plaintiff.

PROBLEM 11-1

Big Burger, Inc., is a corporation that franchises hamburger restaurants throughout the country. In June 2016 Emily Michaels approached Big Burger about obtaining a franchise. After reviewing literature from the company, Michaels visited several Big Burger franchises in other cities and hired a lawyer to represent her in negotiations; she spent a total of $15,000 in traveling expenses and legal fees.

In August the parties signed an agreement in which Big Burger granted Michaels a franchise to sell hamburgers under its corporate name and agreed to construct and lease a restaurant to her. Michaels agreed to pay Big Burger a franchise fee of $100,000 and to lease the restaurant for a ten-year term at a fixed rental plus a percentage of sales. After resigning her job as a manager of a local restaurant, where she had been earning $40,000 per year, to devote full time to her franchise, Michaels purchased equipment for the restaurant from suppliers approved by Big Burger at a cost of $50,000. In January 2017 the restaurant was ready for operation.

Within six months after the restaurant opened, disputes developed between Michaels and Big Burger. Michaels objected to the quality of some of the products she received from the company and to the company's failure to honor a commitment to run a major advertising campaign. She also complained that her income did not meet company projections. During negotiations Big Burger had shown Michaels financial reports from comparable restaurants indicating an average net profit of $75,000 per year in addition to an average owner's salary of $50,000 per year. After paying Michaels a salary of $20,000 per year, the restaurant was just breaking even.

By late 2018 Michaels had become so dissatisfied with her situation that she decided to give up the restaurant. When negotiations with the company were unsuccessful, she decided to bring suit.

(a) Assume Michaels can establish that Big Burger committed a material breach of the franchise agreement. How might her damages be computed?

(b) Suppose Michaels's complaint includes a count seeking rescission and restitution. At a pretrial conference the judge stated that he would require the plaintiff to "elect" between the claim for damages for breach of contract and the claim for rescission because the causes of action were inconsistent. In some jurisdictions a plaintiff must elect between inconsistent remedies in order to avoid double recovery and jury confusion. Which theory — restitution or damages — should Michaels's lawyer elect to pursue?

(c) At a pretrial conference the judge asks the lawyers for Michaels and Big Burger to prepare proposed jury instructions on the issue of damages for breach of contract. Write proposed jury instructions for either Michaels or Big Burger. In doing so, you may obtain guidance from model civil jury instructions for state or federal courts in your jurisdiction.

C. SPECIFIC PERFORMANCE

As we saw in Chapter 10, some types of injury are not compensable in money damages at all, while the doctrines of foreseeability, certainty, causation, and mitigation may prevent recovery of damages even for compensable types of harm. It seems natural to wonder whether the plaintiff should not be able to avoid all these problems by simply asking the court to order the defendant to perform as promised. In the Anglo-American legal tradition, however, "specific performance" is not a remedy to which the plaintiff is automatically entitled, even when an unexcused breach has been clearly established. The following discussion by Professor Farnsworth explains the nature and genesis of the various limitations on the availability of specific relief.

> The early common law courts did know specific relief, for many of the first suits after the Norman Conquest were proprietary in nature, designed to regain something of which the plaintiff had been deprived. Even the action of debt was of this character, since it was based on the notion of an unjust detention of something belonging to the plaintiff. But it became the practice in these actions to allow money damages for the detention in addition to specific relief, and with the development of new forms of action, such as assumpsit, that were in no way proprietary, substitutional relief became the usual form.
>
> The typical judgment at common law declared that the plaintiff recover from the defendant a sum of money, which in effect imposed on him a new obligation as redress for the breach of the old. The new obligation required no cooperation on his part for its enforcement since, if the sum was not paid, a writ of execution would issue empowering the sheriff to seize and sell so much of the defendant's property as was required to pay the plaintiff. . . . The judgment itself was seen as a mere declaration of rights as between the parties, and the process for its execution was directed not at the defendant but at the sheriff, ordering him to put the plaintiff in possession of real or personal property

or to seize the defendant's property and sell such of it as was necessary to satisfy a money judgment.

The enforcement of promises in equity developed along very different lines. . . .

Under the influence of the canon law (for the early chancellors were usually clerics), decrees in equity came to take the form of a personal command to the defendant to do or not to do something. His cooperation was assumed, and if he disobeyed he could be punished not only for criminal contempt, at the instance of the court, but also for civil contempt, at the instance of the plaintiff. This put into the plaintiff's hands the extreme sanction of imprisonment, which might be supplemented by fines payable to the plaintiff and sequestration of the defendant's goods. So it was said that equity acted in personam, against the person of the defendant, while the law acted in rem, against his property. But it did not follow that the chancellor stood ready to order every defaulting promisor to perform his promise. Equitable relief was confined to special cases in light of both practical and historical limitations.

The practical limitations grew out of the problems inherent in coercion. Our courts, like those of civil law countries, will not undertake to coerce a performance that is personal in nature — to compel an artist to paint a picture or a singer to sing a song. . . . Our courts have also been reluctant to order specific performance where difficulties of supervision or enforcement are foreseen, e.g., to order a building contractor specifically to perform his contract to repair a house. It has been suggested that in their origins these ideas carried a load of snobbery, expressed in distaste for menial tasks — "how can a Master judge of repairs in husbandry?" Today they are more often justified as a means of avoiding conflict and unfairness where no clear standards can be framed in advance. The practical exigencies of drafting decrees to guide future conduct under threat of contempt have also moved courts to require that contract terms be expressed with somewhat greater certainty if specific performance is to be granted than if damages are to be awarded. But these practical limitations are on the whole far less significant than the historical ones.

The most important of the historical limitations derives from the circumstance that, since the chancellor had first granted equitable relief in order to supply the deficiencies of the common law, equitable remedies were readily characterized as "extraordinary." When, during the long jurisdictional struggle between the two systems of courts, some means of accommodation were needed, an "adequacy" test was developed to prevent encroachment by the chancellor on the powers of the common law judges. Equity would stay its hand if the remedy at law was "adequate." To this test was added the gloss that the money damages awarded by the common law courts were ordinarily "adequate" — a gloss encouraged by the philosophy of free enterprise, since in a market economy money ought to enable an aggrieved promisee to arrange a substitute transaction. . . .

So it came to be that, in sharp contrast to the civil law approach, money damages were regarded as the norm and specific relief as the deviation, even where the law could easily have provided specific relief without any cooperation from the defaulting promisor.

> Land, which the common law viewed with particular esteem, was singled out for special treatment. Each parcel, however ordinary, was considered to be "unique," and from this it followed that if a vendor defaulted on his promise to convey land, not even money would enable an injured purchaser to find a substitute. The remedy at law being in this sense "inadequate," a decree of specific performance would ordinarily issue. Although the case for allowing the vendor to have specific performance when the purchaser defaulted was less compelling, equity also granted him relief. But no such reason applied to the contract for the sale of goods, for in a market economy it was supposed that, with rare exceptions for such "unique" items as heirlooms and objects of art, substantially similar goods were available elsewhere. . . .
>
> A second historical limitation, or group of limitations, is premised on the notion that equitable relief is "discretionary." Since the chancellor was to act according to "conscience" (a circumstance that prompted the famous charge that his conscience might vary with the length of his foot), he might withhold relief where considerations of "fairness" or "morality" dictated. Some of the most renowned of these equitable restrictions are embodied in equity's colorful maxims: "he who seeks equity must do equity"; "he who comes into equity must come with clean hands"; and "equity aids the vigilant." . . .
>
> The historical development of the parallel systems of law and equity may afford an adequate explanation of the reluctance of our courts to grant specific relief; it is scant justification for it. A more rational basis might be the severity of the sanctions available under the contempt power for their enforcement. In any event, the current trend is clearly in favor of the extension of specific relief. The fusion of law and equity into a single court system at least facilitates a major change in this direction, and commentators have urged such a change. . . .
>
> Still, for the present, the promisee must ordinarily be content with money damages.

E. Allan Farnsworth, Legal Remedies for Breach of Contract, 70 Colum. L. Rev. 1145, 1149-1156 (1970).

In 1991, Professor Douglas Laycock published a major study of equitable remedies entitled The Death of the Irreparable Injury Rule. As his title suggests, Professor Laycock contended that regardless of what courts say by way of justifying their decisions, they do not in fact limit access to equitable relief by requiring the plaintiff to demonstrate that otherwise an "irreparable injury" will result (or that there is "no adequate remedy at law," a principle that he equates with the requirement of "irreparable injury"). Instead, Laycock concluded that although this requirement is often invoked, it is virtually never decisive in fact: Courts grant or withhold equitable relief on the basis of a number of other, more particular policies, such as hardship to the defendant or others, hostility to the merits of the plaintiff's case, or values such as freedom of speech or freedom from compulsory service. The work of additional scholars is cited in the Notes that follow the cases below.

City Stores Co. v. Ammerman

United States District Court 266 F. Supp. 766 (D.D.C. 1967), aff'd, 394 F.2d 950 (D.C. Cir. 1968)

GASCH, District Judge.

The plaintiff, City Stores Company, seeks specific performance of a contract wherein defendants allegedly promised to offer plaintiff a lease as a major tenant in defendants' shopping center in Tyson's Corner, Fairfax County, Virginia. By the terms of the contract, the defendants were to give plaintiff an opportunity to accept a lease on terms at least equal to those offered to other major department stores in the center. The court granted a preliminary injunction to prevent the defendants from leasing the last available department store site to another department store. Now the court is called upon to decide whether there is a valid contract and, if so, whether it is sufficiently definite so that specific performance of it should be decreed.

Defendants desired to construct a large shopping center on a tract of land near Tyson's Corner, in Fairfax County, Virginia. In order to build the center, they had to persuade the Board of County Supervisors of Fairfax County to rezone the property for that use. By the time plaintiff came into the picture, defendants' prospects for securing the necessary zoning were not good: the Fairfax County Planning Commission and the Planning Commission Staff had voted against defendants' requested zoning. Defendants had to persuade the Board that these advisory groups were wrong in their recommendations. Moreover, defendants had an extremely strong competitor, the Rouse-Reynolds group, for another shopping center in the same general area. There was a zoning application for the Rouse-Reynolds center pending before the Board of Supervisors at the same time. Hearing on defendants' application was set for May 31, 1962.

During a period of time prior to May 31, Lansburgh's Department Store, which is owned by City Stores Company, the plaintiff herein, had been negotiating the terms of a lease of a store site in the Wheaton Plaza shopping center with defendants Lerner and Gudelsky. In the course of meetings with Mr. Lerner, or Messrs. Lerner and Gudelsky together, Lansburgh's president, Mr. Jagels, learned of the Tyson's Corner proposal. Mr. Lerner asked for a letter from Lansburgh's expressing a desire to participate in defendants' Tyson's Corner project, which could be used in the hearing before the Fairfax County Board of County Supervisors. Mr. Lerner had sought similar letters from other department stores in Washington, but found them unwilling to express a preference for defendants' Tyson's Corner site over the nearby proposed site of the Rouse-Reynolds group. Under normal circumstances, Lansburgh's also would have been unwilling to express a preference for one site over the other. It was eager to obtain suburban department store sites for expansion purposes. But, for a reason which is a matter of dispute between plaintiff and defendants, Mr. Jagels wrote a letter to Mr. Lerner and Mr. Gudelsky (Plaintiff's Exhibit E) in which he stated that it was Lansburgh's conclusion that the Tyson's Corner site was preferable to any other in the area and expressing Lansburgh's great interest in becoming a major tenant at a Lerner-Gudelsky shopping center if they were successful in their zoning application.

Defendants contend that plaintiff wrote this letter in order to secure defendants' help in obtaining necessary permission from other department store tenants in the Wheaton Plaza shopping center for plaintiff to become another major tenant there. However, I find that this contention is not supported by the evidence. The evidence shows that during the period in question, plaintiff and Lerner-Gudelsky had not themselves reached agreement on rental and other terms for plaintiff to become a tenant in the Wheaton Plaza center, and that they were engaged in negotiations. It was not until November of 1962, by defendant Lerner's own correspondence records, which are part of the evidence herein, that either plaintiff or defendants became aware that there would be an objection raised to plaintiff's tenancy by Montgomery Ward, one of the major tenants at Wheaton Plaza with right of approval of other lessees.

Plaintiff contends, on the other hand, that the Jagels letter to Lerner and Gudelsky was written at Lerner's request in exchange for a promise that plaintiff would be given an opportunity to become a major tenant at Tyson's Corner on terms at least equal to those of other major tenants at the center.

I find that on or about May 29, 1962, the Lerner-Gudelsky interests promised to give Lansburgh's an opportunity to become a major tenant at the Tyson's Corner center on terms at least equal to those granted other major department store tenants in exchange for assistance from Lansburgh's in securing the necessary zoning for the tract. I further find that on or about May 29, 1962, the defendants Lerner and Gudelsky signed and gave to Lansburgh's president Jagels the following letter concerning the defendants' promise, and that this letter, together with plaintiff's full performance of the requested services, is a sufficient writing to satisfy the Statute of Frauds, §12-302 D.C. Code. The letter is Plaintiff's Exhibit B, and states:

> Dear Mr. Jagels:
>
> We very much appreciate the efforts which you have expended in endeavoring to assist Mr. Gudelsky and me in our application for zoning at Tyson's Corner for a Regional Shopping Center.
>
> You have our assurance that in the event we are successful with our application, that we will give you the opportunity to become one of our contemplated center's major tenants with rental and terms at least equal to that of any other major department store in the center.
>
> Sincerely yours,
> /s/*Isadore M. Gudelsky*
> /s/*Theodore N. Lerner*

I also find that the services plaintiff performed for defendants, particularly the letter from Mr. Jagels which defendants used to support their case in the zoning hearing on May 31, constituted adequate consideration for a valid unilateral contract which was binding on defendants thereafter.

I

The plaintiff contends that this unilateral contract is an option for an opportunity to accept or reject a lease for a store at Tyson's Corner on terms at least equal to those granted to other major tenants. Defendants deny that the agreement is an option contract and contend that, even if it were, it would not be sufficiently definite to be specifically enforced by this court.

In determining the nature and consequences of this contract, it should be observed first that a typical option contract is a continuing offer for a fixed period of time (or a reasonable time if no time is specified) which is binding on the offeror because given for a valuable consideration. As noted by Williston, the word "option" is a business and not a strictly legal term. 5 Williston on Contracts §1441 (Rev. ed. 1937). An option contract is a unilateral contract as is the contract at issue. Generally, however, an option contract describes specifically the subject offered and all its material terms. The offeree knows at the time he receives the option exactly what has been offered and what he may accept or reject. It is obvious that the contract between Lerner-Gudelsky and Lansburgh's is not of this description, and further analysis is needed to decide whether or not it may be classified as an option, despite its superficial dissimilarity to the usual form.

In this case, it is clear that an option in typical form could not have been offered by Lerner-Gudelsky, because they had nothing but a contingency to offer at the time the contract was made. Any specific terms they might have included in their letter to Jagels would have been meaningless in view of the fact that they had neither received the necessary permission to construct their center, nor had they entered into leases with other major tenants which were to be the measure of the lease offered to Lansburgh's. Yet it does not follow from this that what they did promise to offer Lansburgh's was without substance. What we have here is a contract with certain conditions precedent to its operation.

The first condition precedent to the Lerner-Gudelsky obligation to Lansburgh's was the securing of necessary zoning for its Tyson's Corner tract, without which it could not construct a shopping center at all. The second condition precedent was its entering into leases with other major tenants for stores in the center, so the terms of those leases could provide the essential terms of a lease to be offered to plaintiff. Defendants did secure the zoning, and they did, in the latter half of 1965, enter into leases with Woodward & Lothrop and Hecht department stores. At the time it secured those leases, defendants were under an immediate contractual obligation to tender plaintiff a lease which in all its material terms would be at least as favorable to plaintiff as the two other leases were to their respective stores. That this would have been possible is entirely clear from the record: both the Hecht and Woodward & Lothrop leases, Plaintiff's Exhibit F, contain clauses to the effect that their terms will be at least equal to those offered to other lessees in the center. Thus, even though none of the stores in the center will be identical in design, it is apparent from defendants' own leases that complete equality of material terms governing occupancy, including amount of space and cost per square foot, and substantially equal terms on less material aspects of the lease, is within the customary contemplation of parties entering into shopping center agreements of the type at issue in this case. When it is recognized that a lessor's success in a shopping center is directly tied to the success of all of his lessees, it must be conceded that as a practical business matter it is to the lessor's advantage that one tenant be given no distinct competitive advantage over another traceable to the terms of the leases entered into.

I therefore hold as a matter of law that the Lerner-Gudelsky letter was a binding unilateral contract, which gave plaintiff an option to accept a lease at Tyson's Corner, and that the existence of express and implied conditions precedent did not render it invalid or too indefinite to be a contract. . . .

II

Whether the option contract secured by plaintiff in this case is sufficiently definite to be the subject of a decree for specific performance is quite another question, which does not concern the validity or existence of the contract but only the nature of the remedy available to plaintiff.

It is not contested by the plaintiff that if it were to accept a lease tendered by defendants in accordance with the contract, there would be numerous complex details left to be worked out. The crucial elements of rate of rental and the amount of space can readily be determined from the Hecht and Woodward & Lothrop leases. But some details of design, construction and price of the building to be occupied by plaintiff at Tyson's Corner would have to be agreed to by the parties, subject to further negotiation and tempered only by the promise of equal terms with other tenants. The question is whether a court of equity will grant specific performance of a contract which has left such substantial terms open for future negotiation.

The defendants have cited a number of cases in support of their argument that a court of equity will not grant specific performance of a contract in which some terms are left for further negotiations by the parties, or which would require a great deal of supervision by the court. I have examined those cases cited which were decided in this jurisdiction, because unless the precedents here establish a clear policy one way or the other, this court may exercise its discretion in fashioning an equitable decree. Moreover, this is an area of law in which not all jurisdictions are in agreement, and whichever way this court were to decide the case, there would be cases holding to the contrary in other parts of the country. . . .

Thus, defendants have cited no cases in this jurisdiction that would support the contention that an option contract involving further negotiations on details and construction of a building may not be specifically enforced.

On the other hand, the 1926 case of Morris v. Ballard, 56 App. D.C. 383, 16 F.2d 175, 49 A.L.R. 1461, held that an option to purchase property which contained a provision as to price "on terms to be agreed upon" was specifically enforceable by a court of equity. The court in that case held that "it became the duty of defendant, upon proper demand, either to accept the agreed purchase price in cash or to specify such terms as were acceptable to him. He had no right to refuse arbitrarily and unconditionally to accept payment solely for the purpose of defeating the option. Such a refusal would operate as a fraud upon the plaintiff." The court further held that the clause "on terms to be agreed upon" *"was in good conscience a stipulation that he would in fact agree with plaintiff upon reasonable terms of payment, and would not arbitrarily refuse to proceed with the sale. . . ."* [Emphasis added.] 56 App. D.C. 383, 384, 16 F.2d 175, 176. The court also quoted Pomeroy, Specific Performance §145 to the following effect: "when a contract has been partly performed by the plaintiff, and the defendant has received and enjoys the benefits thereof, and the plaintiff would be virtually remediless unless the contract were enforced, the court, from the plainest considerations of equity and common justice, does not regard with favor any objections raised by the defendant merely on the ground of the incompleteness or uncertainty of the agreement." 56 App. D.C. 383, 384, 16 F.2d 175, 176. I therefore hold as a matter of law that the mere fact that a contract, definite in material respects, contains some terms which are subject to further negotiation between plaintiff and defendant will not bar a decree for specific performance, if in the court's discretion specific performance should be granted. Walsh v. Rundlette, supra, adds further support to this position. See also 5 Williston on Contracts §1424 (Rev. ed. 1937).

The question whether a contract which also calls for construction of a building can or should be specifically enforced apparently never has been decided before in this jurisdiction. The parties have cited no cases on this point.

At the outset, it should be noted that where specific performance of such contracts has been granted the essential criterion has not been the nature or subject of the contract, but rather the inadequacy or impracticability of legal remedies. See 5 Williston on Contracts §1423 (Rev. ed. 1937); 4 Pomeroy's Equity Jurisprudence §§1401-1403 (5th ed. 1941). Contracts involving interests in land or unique chattels generally are specifically enforced because of the clear inadequacy of damages at law for breach of contract. As Pomeroy says:

> The foundation and measure of the jurisdiction is the desire to do justice, which the legal remedy would fail to give. . . .
>
> . . . The jurisdiction depending upon this broad principle is exercised in two classes of cases: 1. Where the subject-matter of the contract is of such a special nature, or of such a peculiar value, that the damages, when ascertained according to legal rules, would not be a just and reasonable substitute for or representative of that subject-matter in the hands of the party who is entitled to its benefit; or in other words, where the damages are *inadequate;* 2. Where, from some special and practical features or incidents of the contract inhering either in its subject matter, in its terms, or in the relations of the parties, it is impossible to arrive at a legal measure of damages at all, or at least with any sufficient degree of certainty, so that *no* real compensation can be obtained by means of an action at law; or in other words, where damages are *impracticable.*

It is apparent from the nature of the contract involved in this case that even were it possible to arrive at a precise measure of damages for breach of a contract to lease a store in a shopping center for a long period of years — which it is not — money damages would in no way compensate the plaintiff for loss of the right to participate in the shopping center enterprise and for the almost incalculable future advantages that might accrue to it as a result of extending its operations into the suburbs. Therefore, I hold that the appropriate remedy in this case is specific performance.

Some jurisdictions in the United States have opposed granting specific performance of contracts for construction of buildings and other contracts requiring extensive supervision of the court, but the better view, and the one which increasingly is being followed in this country, is that such contracts should be specifically enforced unless the difficulties of supervision outweigh the importance of specific performance to the plaintiff. 5 Williston on Contracts §1423 (Rev. ed. 1937). This is particularly true where the construction is to be done on land controlled by the defendant, because in that circumstance the plaintiff cannot employ another contractor to do the construction for him at defendant's expense. In the case at bar, the fact that more than mere construction of a building is involved reinforces the need for specific enforcement of the defendants' duty to perform their entire contractual obligation to the plaintiff.

Cases from an early date have granted specific performance of construction contracts. In Jones v. Parker, 163 Mass. 564, 40 N.E. 1044 (1895), Justice Holmes commented:

> There is no universal rule that courts of equity never will enforce a contract which requires some building to be done. They have enforced such contracts from the earliest days to the present time. [163 Mass. 564, 40 N.E. 1044, 1045.]

Joy v. City of St. Louis, 138 U.S. 1, 11 S. Ct. 243, 34 L. Ed. 843 (1890), is the leading Supreme Court case on specific performance of contracts where the relations between the parties were of a complex nature and might require continuous supervision by the court granting the decree. The Court said on this point:

> In the present case, it is urged that the court will be called upon to determine from time to time what are reasonable regulations to be made by the Wabash Company for the running of trains upon its tracks by the Colorado Company. But this is no more than a court of equity is called upon to do whenever it takes charge of the running of a railroad by means of a receiver. Irrespectively of this, the decree is complete in itself, and disposes of the controversy; and it is not unusual for a court of equity to take supplemental proceedings to carry out its decree, and make it effective under altered circumstances. 138 U.S. 1, 47, 11 S. Ct. 243, 257.

. . . See also Union Pacific Railway Co. v. Chicago, Rock Island & Pacific Railway Co., 163 U.S. 564, 16 S. Ct. 1173, 41 L. Ed. 265 (1896), where the Supreme Court commented in a case involving a similarly complex situation: "It must not be forgotten that, in the increasing complexities of modern business relations, equitable remedies have necessarily and steadily been expanded, and no inflexible rule has been permitted to circumscribe them. . . ."

The defendants contend that the granting of specific performance in this case will confront the court with insuperable difficulties of supervision, but after reviewing the evidence, I am satisfied that the standards to be observed in construction of the plaintiff's store are set out in the Hecht and Woodward & Lothrop leases with sufficient particularity (Plaintiff's Ex. F) as to make design and approval of plaintiff's store a fairly simple matter, if the parties deal with each other in good faith and expeditiously, as I shall hereafter order.

For example, Article VIII, Sec. 8.1, Paragraph (G) of the Hecht lease (the Woodward & Lothrop lease contains a similar provision) says:

> The quality of (i) the construction, (ii) the construction components, (iii) the decorative elements (including landscaping irrigation systems for the landscaping) and (iv) the furnishings; and the general architectural character and general design, the materials selection, the decor and the treatment values, approach and standards of the Enclosed Mall shall be comparable, at minimum, to the qualities, values, approaches and standards as of the date hereof of the enclosed mall at Topanga Plaza Shopping Center, Los Angeles, California. . . .

The existing leases contain further detailed specifications which will be identical to those in the lease granted to plaintiff. The site for plaintiff's store has already been settled by the design of the center. Although the exact design of plaintiff's store will not be identical to the design of any other store, it must be remembered that all of the stores are to be part of the same center and subject to its overall design requirements. If the parties are not in good faith able to reach an agreement on certain details, the court will appoint a special master to help settle their differences, unless they prefer voluntarily to submit their disagreements to arbitration.

III

The defendants contend that specific performance of this contract will result in hardship to them, and invoke the maxim that equity will not grant specific performance if the hardship to the defendants is greater than the potential benefit to the plaintiff. Defendants point to the fact that they agreed with Woodward & Lothrop and Hecht in their leases to limit the number of major department stores in the center to three. That means that if a lease is granted to Lansburgh's, defendants will be unable to negotiate a lease with Sears, which has expressed a willingness to be the center's third department store tenant. The Sears lease would be more valuable to them, defendants claim, because the lease would be for a larger amount of space, and also because Sears would be expected to do a larger business than Lansburgh's, and defendants would receive a percentage share of its profits over a certain minimum amount as part of the agreed rental.

The defendants have not contended that performance of their obligation to Lansburgh's would be impossible or would ruin them financially. In effect, their contention is only that they can make more money by dealing with Sears than with Lansburgh's. This is not a reason for denying specific performance. Willard v. Tayloe, 75 U.S. 557, 8 Wall. 557, 19 L. Ed. 501 (1869). 5 Williston on Contracts §1425 (Rev. ed. 1937).

Moreover, the defendants need not have executed leases with both Hecht and Woodward & Lothrop to the exclusion of Sears as a possible additional tenant; nor need they have agreed with Hecht and Woodward & Lothrop that there would be no more than three stores in the center. Plaintiff was not responsible for these actions of defendants and should not be made to suffer irreparable loss due to the limitations which defendants have written into their contracts with Hecht and Woodward & Lothrop and which they now assert as a basis for their refusal to honor their obligation to plaintiff.

The defendants do contend that plaintiff was indirectly responsible, however, in failing to "press its claim" in May of 1964 when defendants advised it by letter that they considered themselves under no contractual obligation to plaintiff. First of all, I find from the record that at all material times the plaintiff through its officers did inform the defendants that it intended to hold them to their contract. Secondly, the defendants in effect imply that the plaintiff, by not "pressing its claim," gave up its rights under the contract, or waived them. But it is elementary contract law that a release of a contractual right (as distinguished from waiver of a condition) is not valid unless made for a valuable consideration. Finally, in May of 1964 defendants' obligation to tender a lease to plaintiff had not yet ripened because one of the conditions precedent to that obligation — execution of leases with other major tenants — had not yet been satisfied. Plaintiff could not have brought an action for anticipatory breach because of the impossibility of assessing damages; it certainly could not have brought an action for specific performance because as yet there was no specifically enforceable contract right. Plaintiff did contact defendants again when it learned that the Hecht and Woodward & Lothrop leases had been executed; and it brought this suit in a timely manner to prevent the defendants from entering into a lease with Sears which would have precluded them from performing their contract with plaintiff. I therefore hold that plaintiff neither gave up its contractual rights nor unnecessarily delayed its assertion of them in this court. . . .

During the course of this proceeding, the plaintiff has examined the leases executed between defendants and Hecht and Woodward & Lothrop and has indicated its willingness to accept a lease with terms equal to the Hecht lease. I therefore find that the plaintiff has exercised its option, and is entitled to specific performance of a lease on terms equal to those contained in the Hecht lease.

NOTES AND QUESTIONS

1. *Effect of indefiniteness on specific performance.* The court in *City Stores* begins its analysis by determining that an enforceable contract did exist, utilizing concepts familiar to us from our earlier discussions of agreement formation and consideration. The court then proceeds to decide whether the obligations imposed by the contract were sufficiently certain and definite to be susceptible to specific performance. Specific relief will not be denied merely

because the parties have left some matters out of their agreement, or left some issues to be agreed on in the future, particularly when the parties have agreed on all material terms and other equitable factors are present. See Restatement (Second) §362 and Comment *b*. See also Stanford Hotels Corp. v. Potomac Creek Assocs., L.P., 18 A.3d 725 (D.C. 2011) (where defendant seller breached obligation to bargain in good faith by refusing to sign negotiated contract for sale of hotel, court could order it to enter into contract and then order specific performance of the sale; *City Stores* cited and quoted). On the other hand, failure to agree on material terms may result in the denial of specific relief, though lines are difficult to draw. Compare Oglebay Norton Co. v. Armco, Inc., 556 N.E.2d 515 (Ohio 1990) (long-term contract for shipping of iron ore on Great Lakes specifically enforceable despite failure of agreed-on pricing mechanism; injury to plaintiff impossible to remedy by damages), with Honolulu Waterfront Ltd. Partnership v. Aloha Tower Development Corp., 692 F. Supp. 1230 (D. Haw. 1988), *aff'd*, 891 F.2d 295 (9th Cir. 1989) (four-page letter agreement did constitute binding agreement for real estate development but left too many material matters for future agreement to be specifically enforceable; virtually every provision contemplated further negotiation). Does the court in *City Stores* adequately weigh the indefiniteness factor in granting the relief requested?

2. *Inadequacy of damages at law.* As the discussion by Professor Farnsworth indicated, contracts involving land are prime candidates for specific enforcement because land has been regarded in the Anglo-American legal tradition as unique, presumptively justifying equitable relief under the traditional rule that equity will act only where the remedy at law is "inadequate." Modern American courts will routinely grant specific performance to purchasers of real estate. See, e.g., Sullivan v. Porter, 861 A.2d 625 (Me. 2004) (court may assume inadequacy of money damages in contract for purchase of real estate and order specific performance without actual showing of singular character of the realty); but see Meikle v. Watson, 69 P.3d 100 (Idaho 2003) (denying specific performance to buyer who merely planned to resell land). Restatement (Second) §360, Comment *e* indicates that specific performance has traditionally been available to both buyers and sellers. Cases awarding specific performance to sellers, however, are not very common. Compare Humphries v. Ables, 789 N.E.2d 1025 (Ind. Ct. App. 2003) (granting specific performance to sellers of property with a liquor store, based on mutuality of remedy principle and contract term that contemplated specific performance for the sellers, but also noting that only small number of cases grant the remedy to sellers), with Wolf v. Anderson, 334 N.W.2d 212 (N.D. 1983) (specific performance available to sellers only when equitable considerations warrant award).

Besides the possibility that a land-related contract will be specifically enforced because of the "uniqueness" of its subject matter, the Restatement (Second) in §360 identifies other circumstances which support a claim that damages are inadequate. These include the difficulty of proving damages with certainty, the difficulty of procuring a suitably equivalent substitute performance, and the likelihood that a damage award would not be collectible. See, e.g., Sokoloff v. Harriman Estates Development Corp., 754 N.E.2d 184 (N.Y.

2001) (plaintiffs properly stated cause of action for specific performance to obtain allegedly unique architect plans that were based on plaintiffs' concept). To what extent are these factors concerning adequacy of money damages at work in the *City Stores* decision?

3. *Specific performance of development contract.* Another example of a court balancing the potential harm to the nonbreaching party with difficulty of court supervision is found in Franklin Point, Inc. v. Harris Trust & Savings Bank, 660 N.E.2d 204 (Ill. App. Ct. 1995). *Franklin Point* involved a plan to develop a parcel of land near downtown Chicago, pursuant to which the defendant, Harris Bank, agreed to purchase a portion of the property and construct a high-rise office building. Not surprisingly, many details of the construction plans were not established by the contract, but the agreement did establish an architectural review board to approve construction decisions not within the discretion of Harris Bank. Harris Bank purchased the property but failed to construct the building and the remainder of the project was not developed. The appellate court decided that the trial court erred in its ruling that "specific performance of a construction contract is barred as a matter of law." Id. at 206. Citing *City Stores* and similar precedent, the court held that specific performance might be available if the presence of the review board would prevent the court from becoming embroiled in ongoing supervision of construction disputes. Id. at 208. Cf. Mayor's Jewelers, Inc. v. State of California Employees' Retirement System, 685 So. 2d 904 (Fla. Ct. App. 1996) (denying request for specific performance of lease by tenant because court would be required to supervise future performance). If it is assumed that Harris Bank was expected to be the "anchor" business of the Franklin Point development, how does the case for specific performance compare to that in *City Stores*?

Ordinary building contracts are unlikely to be specifically enforced, both because of the difficulties of supervision and because construction services can readily be purchased on the market with a money award in damages. As cases such as *City Stores* and *Franklin Point* suggest, however, the courts are probably more willing than they were at an earlier day to decree specific performance in cases where some degree of service or labor will have to be performed by the defendant. See E. Allan Farnsworth, Contracts §12.7, at 754 (4th ed. 2004). Drawing a comparison to complex civil rights cases, Professor Farnsworth suggests that courts have discovered that the burden of supervision is not as great as might be feared. How does the test used by the *City Stores* court compare to that prescribed in Restatement (Second) §366 to determine when to grant specific performance even though court supervision will be required?

4. *Other factors affecting award of specific performance.* Besides the question of adequacy of the remedy "at law" and the problem of difficulty of supervision, courts of equity traditionally consider various other factors in deciding whether specific relief should be available. Some of these are listed in Restatement (Second) §364. These include the possibility that the contract was the product of mistake or unfair practices, or that the exchange it calls for is grossly inadequate or the terms of the contract are otherwise unfair. These factors are reflected in the doctrine that equity will not aid one who comes to the

court with "unclean hands." See, e.g., Ingram v. Kasey's Associates, 531 S.E.2d 287 (S.C. 2000) (tenant denied specific performance of option contract because he had unclean hands; tenant misled landlord into believing that he would not exercise option and he had ulterior motive for doing so).

Another factor to be considered is the question whether specific relief would cause unreasonable hardship or loss to the party in breach. See, e.g., Webster Trust v. Roly, 802 A.2d 795 (Conn. 2002) (denying specific performance of "right of first refusal" contract allegedly triggered by intra-family transfer for $100,000 while land had $340,000 fair market value; sale to plaintiffs at lower price would have been "inequitable" and plaintiffs could still exercise option if land was sold in "market place" before the right's expiration); Kilarjian v. Vastola, 877 A.2d 372 (N.J. Super. Ch. Div. 2004) (declining to award specific performance for buyers where seller's health had declined significantly due to spinal muscular atrophy after contract was made, even though buyers were faultless and there is virtual presumption that nonbreaching buyers should receive specific performance). Should the potential hardship to the defendants have militated against the grant of specific relief to the plaintiff in *City Stores*?

5. *Effect on third parties.* Besides the possibility that specific relief may disproportionately affect the defendant, the court in some cases must consider the possible impact of its decree on third parties. Restatement (Second) §364(1)(b). Compare Craven v. TRG-Boyton Beach, Ltd., 925 So. 2d 476 (Fla. Ct. App. 2006) (denying award of specific performance to tenant in building project where enforcing commitment for location of plaintiff's store would have required destruction of five new townhouses valued at $5 million, dispossessing the residents, and would have required judicial supervision), with Ruddock v. First National Bank of Lake Forest, 559 N.E.2d 483 (Ill. App. Ct. 1990) (specific performance of contract to purchase rare clock improperly denied where subsequent purchaser from defendant took with notice of plaintiff's claim). The court in *City Stores* had previously granted a temporary injunction to prevent the defendants from leasing to someone else the last available site suitable for the plaintiff's department store in the Tyson's Corner shopping center, pending disposition of the plaintiff's claim. If in the absence of such an order the defendants had actually entered into a binding lease agreement with another tenant, should that fact have precluded specific relief for plaintiff City Stores?

6. *Scholarly analysis.* A number of writers have addressed the question whether there should be greater availability of specific performance as a remedy for breach. Favoring the traditional approach: Anthony T. Kronman, Specific Performance, 45 U. Chi. L. Rev. 351, 360-361 (1978); Edward Yorio, In Defense of Money Damages for Breach of Contract, 82 Colum. L. Rev. 1365 (1982). Arguing that specific performance should be the normal remedy for breach of contract because money damages are often undercompensatory: Alan Schwartz, The Case for Specific Performance, 89 Yale L.J. 271, 276-277 (1979); Peter Linzer, On the Amorality of Contract Remedies — Efficiency, Equity, and the Second *Restatement*, 81 Colum. L. Rev. 111 (1981).

7. *Specific performance under the UCC.* In §2-716 the UCC declares that specific performance "may" be decreed for a buyer where the goods are "unique,"

or "in other proper circumstances." Comment 1 to §2-716 states that the section is intended generally to continue "prior policy," but with a "more liberal attitude than some courts have shown" toward the granting of specific performance of contracts for the sale of goods. The comparable provision for sellers, §2-709(1)(b), allows goods to be forced on the buyer and the price obtained when the goods are not reasonably subject to resale to others. Under the Code's approach, courts will still face the question whether the goods contracted for are sufficiently "unique" to justify specific enforcement. Compare International Casings Group, Inc. v. Premium Standard Farms, Inc., 358 F. Supp. 2d 863 (W.D. Mo. 2005) (specific performance of contract for hog casings appropriate for buyer where comparable goods were not available in market place and harm to buyer could be irreparable), with I. Lan Systems, Inc. v. Netscout Service Level Corp., 183 F. Supp. 2d 328 (D. Mass. 2002) (if UCC is treated as applicable by analogy to software licensing agreements, software at issue was not sufficiently unique to warrant specific performance). See also JNS Power and Control Systems, Inc. v. 350 Green, LLC, 624 Fed. Appx. 439 (7th Cir. 2015) (buyer properly granted specific performance of contract to purchase electric vehicle charging equipment in Chicagoland area together with leases for host locations; purpose of contract would be frustrated without transfer of actual chargers).

Reier Broadcasting Company, Inc. v. Kramer

Supreme Court of Montana 316 Mont. 301, 72 P.3d 944 (2003)

Justice W. WILLIAM LEAPHART delivered the Opinion of the Court.

Reier Broadcasting Company, Inc., appeals from the order of the Eighteenth Judicial District Court, Gallatin County, denying Reier's motion for relief from judgment. We affirm.

The following issue is raised on appeal:

Whether the District Court correctly concluded that Reier Broadcasting was not entitled to injunctive relief to prevent a breach of its employment agreement with Michael Kramer.

FACTUAL AND PROCEDURAL BACKGROUND

Appellant, Reier Broadcasting Company, Inc., owns several radio stations in Gallatin County and, until 2002, had exclusive rights to broadcast Montana State University athletic events. Respondent, Michael Kramer, is the head football coach at MSU. In January 2001, Reier Broadcasting and Kramer entered into an employment contract at the behest of MSU, whereby Reier agreed to pay Kramer $10,020 per year in exchange for exclusive broadcast rights with Kramer. Pursuant to the contract, Reier agreed to employ Kramer as an announcer and talent on the weekly, one-hour "Cat Chat" program, which airs during the MSU football season. [The Montana State football team is known as the "Bobcats." — EDS.] In addition, Kramer agreed to record commercials for several of Reier's advertisers. The agreement remains in force and effect until November 2004. Section Two of the contract contains an exclusivity clause that provides the following:

> That Coach shall diligently and faithfully serve Station in such capacity, shall devote his entire skill and energies to such service, and shall not perform on or permit his name to be used in connection with any other radio or television station or program, or to accept any other engagement which will conflict with his performance or effectiveness for Station, without prior approval and consent in writing by the Station.

Reier Broadcasting had earlier purchased exclusive broadcast rights to all MSU athletic events. These rights expired in the summer of 2002, at which time MSU began seeking competitive bids from other broadcasting companies. After reviewing MSU's Request for Proposal, under which these bids were to be obtained, Reier notified the university that there was a potential conflict between the Request for Proposal and Reier's contract with Kramer. According to Reier, the Request for Proposal required the successful offeror to broadcast interviews and conduct a commentary program with Kramer in violation of Section Two of the Reier-Kramer employment agreement, under which Kramer was contractually prohibited from announcing, or otherwise providing talent for Reier's competitors.

MSU declined to amend the Request for Proposal to address this conflict. MSU then disqualified Reier Broadcasting as a potential bidder, and awarded broadcast rights to the university's athletic events to Clear Channel Communications. MSU also notified Kramer that he was expected to provide interviews to Clear Channel despite the exclusivity clause contained in his contract with Reier.

Reier Broadcasting subsequently filed a Complaint and Application for Temporary Restraining Order with the Eighteenth Judicial District Court in an effort to protect its rights under the employment agreement, and to prevent Kramer from providing services to Clear Channel. The District Court granted the request for a TRO, pending an evidentiary hearing on the matter. In August 2002, the court held an evidentiary hearing on the question of whether or not to convert the TRO into a preliminary injunction. The TRO was later amended to allow Kramer to "engage in audio, video or printed media obligations in connection with his coaching job. . . ."

After hearing testimony and reviewing the parties' pleadings, the court concluded that §27-19-103(5), MCA [Montana Code Annotated], prohibited the issuance of an injunction under the circumstances. The court also dissolved the TRO. Reier Broadcasting moved to alter or amend the court's judgment. The court denied the motion, and Reier appealed.

STANDARD OF REVIEW

Generally, when reviewing a trial court's grant or denial of an injunction, our standard of review is for abuse of discretion. Spoklie v. Montana Dep't of Fish, Wildlife & Parks, [311 Mont. 427, 56 P.3d 349]. However, when a trial court

" 'bases its decision to grant such relief upon its interpretation of a statute, no discretion is involved and we review the [ ] court's conclusion of law to determine whether it is correct.' " [*Spoklie,* 56 P.3d 352-353]. . . .

DISCUSSION

This appeal concerns the scope and effect of §27-19-103(5), MCA, which provides the following: "An injunction cannot be granted: . . . (5) to prevent the breach of a contract the performance of which would not be specifically enforced. . . ." The paramount issue raised by the appellant, Reier Broadcasting, is whether, within the context of a personal services contract such as the employment agreement between Reier and Kramer, the language of §27-19-103(5), MCA, may be interpreted as prohibiting the use of injunctive relief to prevent one of the contracting parties (in this case, Kramer) from performing services elsewhere during the life of the contract.

Characterizing the Reier-Kramer employment agreement as a personal services contract and not subject to specific enforcement, the District Court concluded that the prohibition contained in §27-19-103(5), MCA, precluded the issuance of the injunction sought by Reier. The court relied, in part, on §27-1-412(1), MCA, which states that, "[t]he following obligations cannot be specifically enforced: (1) an obligation to render personal service. . . ." Combining this restriction with the language of §27-19-103(5), MCA, the court concluded that it "may not enjoin one from doing something in violation of a contract if the [c]ourt cannot enforce the contract by specific performance. . . . The [a]greement between Kramer and [Reier] is a personal services contract and cannot be enforced by specific performance." The court explained that it could not prevent Kramer from violating the terms of that contract without improperly enforcing the affirmative obligations of the Reier-Kramer agreement through indirect means.

Reier Broadcasting argues that neither §27-1-412(1), MCA, nor §27-19-103(5), MCA, applies in the present case. Reier contends that by seeking an injunction, the company did not intend to require Kramer to render personal services, but rather to prevent Kramer from providing the same services to Clear Channel. Accordingly, Reier asserts that §27-1-412(1), MCA, and its prohibition against the specific enforcement of personal services contracts, has no bearing on the present case, and thus §27-19-103(5), MCA, is equally irrelevant.

Reier characterizes its request for an injunction as an attempt to enforce a negative covenant which, according to Reier, is appropriate given that Kramer's services are special or unique. According to Reier, contracts based on special or unique personal services, or in which a person holds a unique position, may be indirectly enforced by restraining the person from providing services to another. In support of this, Reier cites Volume 71, Section 165 of the American Jurisprudence, Second Edition, which states the following:

> Contracts calling for personal services or acts of a special, unique, or extraordinary character, or by persons in eminence in their profession or calling who

> possess special and extraordinary qualifications, may be indirectly enforced by restraining the person employed from rendering services to another. . . .

71 Am. Jur. 2d Specific Performance §165, 213 (1973).

Reier also cites a 1972 decision, Nassau Sports v. Peters (E.D.N.Y. 1972), 352 F. Supp. 870, 875 (citations omitted), in which the federal district court for the eastern district of New York noted that "it has long been settled that injunctive relief may be granted to restrain an employee's violation of negative covenants in a personal services contract. . . ." On this basis, Reier concludes that although Kramer should not be forced to fulfill his contractual obligations to the company, he nonetheless may be prevented from providing his unique services to Reier's competitors until the employment agreement expires in 2004.

We discussed the proper application of §27-19-103(5), MCA, in Westland Enterprises, Inc. v. Boyne, USA, Inc. (1989), 237 Mont. 186, 772 P.2d 309. Although we held that an injunction against the defendant was improperly issued for reasons not associated with §27-19-103(5), MCA, we set forth the rationale for the statute, and articulated the circumstances under which it would apply. We stated the following:

> Injunctions are rarely used to enforce contract rights or prevent breaches, and applicable court decisions concerning the propriety of this tactic are scarce. However, the legislature has set forth statutory guidelines for the use of injunctions. An applicable guideline is found at §27-19-103(5), MCA. Under this section, an injunction cannot be obtained "to prevent the breach of a contract the performance of which would not be specifically enforced." A list of "obligations which cannot be specifically enforced" is found at §27-1-412, MCA.

Westland Enterprises, 237 Mont. at 191, 772 P.2d at 312.

Reier appears to accept this general premise from *Westland* that §27-1-412(1), MCA, identifies those contracts that cannot be specifically enforced, and that §27-19-103(5), MCA, prohibits the use of injunctive relief to enforce the affirmative covenants contained in such agreements. That said, the point of contention, here, is whether these statutory prohibitions also apply to the enforcement of negative covenants, such as the exclusivity clause contained in the Reier-Kramer employment agreement. Given the absence of any relevant Montana case law, we turn to the California and Arizona courts, which have interpreted statutes similar to §27-19-103(5), MCA, to prevent the enforcement of negative covenants in personal services contracts.

In Anderson v. Neal Institutes Co. (1918), 37 Cal. App. 174, 173 P. 779, the California Court of Appeals construed an early version of §3423 of the California Civil Code, which provided that "[a]n injunction may not be granted . . . to prevent the breach of a contract the performance of which would not be specifically enforced. . . ." In *Anderson,* the court of appeals identified two conflicting lines of authority under which §3423 could have been construed at the time. The first suggested that although a court cannot specifically enforce an affirmative agreement by compelling one party to perform, the court can enjoin a party from breaching a negative covenant and performing elsewhere. *Anderson,* 37 Cal. App. at 177, 173 P. at 780. The second line of authority suggested that since a court cannot enforce the positive part of a personal services contract, it cannot restrain by injunction the negative part. 37 Cal. App. at 178, 173 P. at 780. The court of appeals adopted the later rationale, concluding that in light of the unambiguous language of §3423, a court cannot "interfere by injunction to prevent the violation of an agreement of which, from the nature of the [contract], there could be no decree of specific enforcement." 37 Cal. App. at 178-179, 173 P. at 781.[1]

The Arizona Supreme Court followed *Anderson* in Titus v. Superior Court, Maricopa County (1962), 91 Ariz. 18, 368 P.2d 874. The court reasoned that §12-1802(5) of the Arizona Revised Statutes, like §3423 in California, was intended "to deprive the court of jurisdiction to enjoin breaches of covenants not to compete during the original term of the contract (where enforcement would indirectly enforce the promise to render services)." *Titus,* 91 Ariz. at 23, 368 P.2d at 878. The court noted that the purpose of this rule is to prevent parties from "seeking injunctive relief to force the course of affirmative action." *Titus,* 91 Ariz. at 21, 368 P.2d at 876.

We determine that §27-19-103(5), MCA, like its California and Arizona counterparts, prohibits the use of injunctive relief to prevent a party to a personal services contract from performing services elsewhere during the life of the contract. The exclusivity clause in the Reier-Kramer employment agreement, if enforced vis a vis an injunction, would prevent Kramer from performing for Clear Channel or any of Reier's other competitors until the summer of 2004 when the Reier-Kramer agreement expires. Thus, if Kramer were to perform at all, he would have to perform for Reier. In that sense, an injunction would amount to the indirect enforcement of the affirmative part of the contract. It was this sort of indirect enforcement that the California court sought to avoid in *Anderson,* stating that "to enjoin one from doing something in violation of his contract is an indirect mode of enforcing the . . . contract." *Anderson,* 37 Cal. App. at 178, 173 P. at 780.

Following the lead of California and Arizona, we conclude that the issuance of an injunction, preventing Kramer from working for Clear Channel during the period remaining on his contract with Reier, would result in the indirect specific enforcement of the Reier-Kramer employment agreement. Contrary to the dissent's characterization, we do not hold that the underlying contract was invalid. The issue presented is not whether the contract is valid, but rather, whether the

1. Immediately following *Anderson,* the California Legislature modified §3423 to allow for the use of injunctive relief to enforce a negative covenant where the promised service is of a unique character the loss of which cannot be adequately compensated in damages. In its current form, the statute states, "[a]n injunction may not be granted . . . to prevent the breach of a contract the performance of which would not be specifically enforced . . . other than a contract in writing for the rendition of personal services . . . where the promised service is of a special, unique, [or] unusual . . . character, which gives it peculiar value. . . ." Construing this new version of the statute in Motown Record Corp. v. Brockert (1984), 160 Cal. App. 3d 123, 138, 207 Cal. Rptr. 574, 584, the California Court of Appeals stated that for reasons of public policy, a negative covenant (an exclusivity clause in that case), can be enforced by injunction when the contract is with a performer of requisite distinction as measured by the compensation the employer is willing to pay. Although *Motown* establishes the appropriate application of §3423 in its current form, that case is of no consequence here given that §27-19-103(5), MCA, is identical to the earlier version of §3423.

contract can be specifically enforced by means of an injunction. We conclude that pursuant to the explicit language of §27-19-103(5), MCA, Montana courts may not enjoin the violation of a contract, the specific enforcement of which is barred by Montana law. The issue of whether Reier has other legal remedies for the alleged breach of contract is not before the Court.

CONCLUSION

In summary, we hold that §27-19-103(5), MCA, prohibits the use of injunctive relief to enforce negative covenants contained in personal services contracts. Accordingly, the District Court correctly concluded that Reier Broadcasting was not entitled to enjoin Kramer from performing services elsewhere during the life of the contract.

We concur: KARLA M. GRAY, C.J., JAMES C. NELSON and JIM REGNIER, J.J.

Justice PATRICIA O. COTTER dissents.

I dissent. As requested by RBC, I would reverse the District Court's order dissolving the TRO and remand this case for a determination of whether or not a preliminary injunction should issue to prevent Kramer from providing his services to others in violation of the agreement between Kramer and RBC.

I would conclude that the enforcement of the negative covenant in the contract between RBC and Kramer would not run afoul of §27-19-103(5), MCA. The court properly recognizes that the exclusivity clause in the agreement, if enforced by way of an injunction, would prevent Kramer from performing for Clear Channel or any of Reier's other competitors until the summer of 2004 when the Reier-Kramer agreement expires. I disagree, however, with the ensuing conclusion the Court reaches, which is that an injunction would amount to the indirect enforcement of the affirmative part of the contract because, if Kramer were to perform at all, he would have to perform for Reier. I respectfully submit that this is a stretch. RBC is not seeking to compel Kramer to perform under the contract. It is simply seeking to prevent him from violating the non-competition provisions of the contract-provisions which were specifically bargained for by Kramer, at the encouragement and behest of MSU.

In addition, I find the position taken by MSU in this litigation offensive. As the majority notes, RBC and Kramer entered into an employment contract "at the behest of MSU." RBC alleges, and MSU does not deny, that representatives of MSU approached RBC for purposes of securing additional compensation for Kramer, after Kramer had been hired by MSU. An agreement was reached whereby Kramer would receive $10,200 from RBC, and in exchange would broadcast with RBC and no one else. MSU actively sought this benefit for Kramer and approved of the terms of the contract. A little more than a year later, MSU decided to award the exclusive rights to broadcast its athletic events to RBC's competitor, Clear Channel Communications. It was only at this point — when the deal between RBC and Kramer ceased serving MSU's interests — that MSU began to cry foul, claiming that the contract, which it solicited in the first place, should be declared unenforceable. Laid bare, theirs is an argument born of convenience, not virtue.

RBC has fully and in good faith performed its obligations under its contract with Kramer, and for the first year, MSU and Kramer both accepted the benefits of the contract as well. Now, they want this Court to assist them in their breach. Many years ago this Court recognized that "[a] party who has secured to himself the benefits of a contract, and has accepted and used these benefits, has estopped himself in the courts from denying the validity or binding force of the instrument, or from setting up or asserting the contrary." Brundy v. Canby (1915), 50 Mont. 454, 148 P. 315 (citations omitted). Numerous other courts have embraced this same legal premise: Once a contract is performed and a party has received the benefits of it, that party is estopped from claiming invalidity in order to avoid the contract's burdens. See Seay v. Dodge (N.D. Ill. 1998), 1998 U.S. Dist. LEXIS 12005, 1998 WL 460273; Silling v. Erwin (S.D. W. Va. 1995), 885 F. Supp. 881; Smith v. Hornbuckle (1977), 140 Ga. App. 871, 232 S.E.2d 149.

Although the resolution I favor [allowing enforcement of the covenant not to compete for the duration of the contract] could stand alone, I would also conclude that MSU and Kramer were estopped from challenging the contract's enforceability. For these reasons, I dissent.

Justice Jim Rice concurs in the foregoing dissent.

NOTES AND QUESTIONS

1. *Equitable remedies and personal service contracts.* The parties in the *Reier Broadcasting* case did not dispute that the respondent Kramer contracted to provide services for the radio station or that he intended to breach that agreement. Rather, the dispute focused on whether an equitable remedy for breach would be available to Reier Broadcasting. You will recall from the *City Stores* case that one form of equitable relief is specific performance, in which a court compels a party to render a promised performance, based primarily on a showing that money damages would be an inadequate remedy. Without any need to address the adequacy of money damages, the *Reier Broadcasting* court briefly notes that Montana statutes prohibit specific enforcement of a personal services contract. The Restatement (Second) §367(1) is equally succinct: "A promise to render personal services will not be specifically enforced." Why should there be such an absolute ban on enforcement of a personal services contract through specific performance? Comment *a* to §367 states the prohibition is based on reasons of both policy and practicality: the undesirability of forcing parties to continue in a relationship that has soured, potential concerns about involuntary servitude, and the difficulty of a court enforcing a decree for specific performance. Considering the nature of the contract in *Reier Broadcasting*, is it possible that Kramer could have been compelled to render the promised performance?

While specific performance of a personal service contract will not be available, some courts have been willing to grant "negative enforcement" by way of injunction that prohibits a breaching party from performing for anyone other than the nonbreaching party. Such an injunction might be based on an implied promise that a party, such as the respondent in *Reier Broadcasting*, would not perform for another employer during the contract period. Alternatively, an injunction might be based on an express covenant not to work for others during the term of employment. See American Broadcasting Co. v. Wolf, 420 N.E.2d 363 (N.Y. 1981) (historically injunctions were initially available only if based on an express covenant not to compete with employer during the contract, but later became available if based on clear implication not to work elsewhere). The dissent in *Reier Broadcasting* founded its proposed resolution primarily on the presence of an express covenant not to compete. Is the dissent persuasive in its argument that Reier Broadcasting should have been allowed to seek an injunction?

2. *Historical perspective: Lumley v. Wagner.* The granting of relief by way of injunction may be traced back to the early English chancery case of Lumley v. Wagner, 42 Eng. Rep. 687 (1852). In that case, defendant Johanna Wagner had contracted to appear in several operas in London at the opera house of the plaintiff, Benjamin Lumley, during three months of the 1852 season; as part of that agreement she promised not to appear for any other opera company in London during that time. Wagner thereafter agreed, in violation of her contract with Lumley, to appear in the Royal Italian Opera at London's Covent Garden (for a salary higher than the sum that plaintiff had agreed to pay her). Lumley sought an injunction restraining Wagner from singing for his competitor, and the court granted him the requested relief. In the course of his decision, the Lord Chancellor conceded that under established principles his court would not have granted specific performance by ordering Wagner to sing for the plaintiff as promised. Nevertheless, the defendant had also expressly promised to refrain from singing for any competitor of the plaintiff during the period in question, which in the Lord Chancellor's opinion made the requested relief appropriate.

> It was objected that the operation of the injunction in the present case was mischievous, excluding the defendant J. Wagner from performing at any other theatre while this Court had no power to compel her to perform at Her Majesty's Theatre. It is true, that I have not the means of compelling her to sing, but she has no cause of complaint, if I compel her to abstain from the commission of an act which she has bound herself not to do, and thus possibly cause her to fulfil her engagement. The jurisdiction which I now exercise is wholly within the power of the Court, and being of opinion that it is a proper case for interfering, I shall leave nothing unsatisfied by the judgment I pronounce. The effect too of the injunction, in restraining J. Wagner from singing elsewhere may, in the event of an action being brought against her by the plaintiff, prevent any such amount of vindictive damages being given against her as a jury might probably be inclined to give if she had carried her talents and exercised them at the rival theatre; the injunction may also, as I have said, tend to the

> fulfilment of her engagement; though, in continuing the injunction, I disclaim doing indirectly what I cannot do directly.

Id. at 693. This portion of the Lumley v. Wagner opinion acknowledges that an injunction might force a party to perform a contract that could not be specifically enforced, but seems to permit that outcome. In contrast, the state law cited in *Reier Broadcasting* seems clearly to prohibit an injunction as an indirect way of compelling specific performance. See also Restatement (Second) §367(2) (injunction will not be issued if probable result would be to compel an "undesirable" continuance of personal relations or "to leave the employee without other reasonable means of making a living"). What do you think would have been the practical effect if an injunction had been issued against the respondent in *Reier Broadcasting*?

Whatever the artistic merits of Wagner's vocal performances, her dispute with Lumley has guaranteed her at least a kind of immortality in legal circles. Besides the decision quoted above, making injunctive relief available in such cases, Wagner's attempt to forsake Lumley for his competitor also generated a lawsuit by Lumley against that competing impresario, which culminated in the decision in Lumley v. Gye, 118 Eng. Rep. 749 (1853), establishing the modern tort of intentional interference with contract — and thus paving the way for Pennzoil v. Texaco, discussed in Chapter 2. See also Lea S. VanderVelde, The Gendered Origins of the Lumley Doctrine: Binding Men's Consciences and Women's Fidelity, 101 Yale L.J. 775 (1992) (discussing historical context of Lumley v. Wagner and observing that disproportionate number of early cases allowing injunctive relief in personal services contracts involved women defendants).

3. Requirement that services be unique. The majority opinion in *Reier Broadcasting* interpreted the applicable Montana statutes in a manner that would always bar injunctive relief in a personal services contract. While the court cited California statutes and case law as supporting its holding, the majority opinion also acknowledged in footnote 1 that the law in California was subsequently changed to allow for a possible injunction when an employee's "service is of a special, unique, [or] unusual . . . character, which gives it peculiar value." Indeed, in jurisdictions where injunctive relief is a possibility, courts will likely deny a request if the personal services are not unique. Injunctive relief may be available against employees whose services are not easily replaceable, such as athletes, artists, or media personalities, particularly when the employee plans to work for a competing enterprise. *Lumley* was such a case. See, e.g., Marchio v. Letterlough, 237 F. Supp. 2d 580 (E.D. Pa. 2002) (preliminary injunction issued against boxer to prevent breach of contract with promoter; boxer was unique talent and there existed risk of irreparable injury to plaintiff); Zomba Recording LLC v. Williams, 839 N.Y.S.2d 438 (Sup. Ct. 2007) (injunctive relief granted to record company to stop breach by artist with undisputed "special, unique and extraordinary" musical talents, as evidenced by Grammy Award nomination, pending determination whether plaintiff committed prior material breach).

Writing in 1967, Professor James Brennan concluded that the case law had reached a point where professional athletes of "better than average," "average," or even "marginal" ability would be held sufficiently "unique" to warrant their being judicially restrained from playing for any other team; he contended, however, that such judicial willingness to grant "indirect specific performance" is not justified:

> While the language of the cases speaks of exceptional knowledge, skill or ability, the cases in fact ignore the limitations inherent in this language. The reason appears to be an undemonstrated and unlitigated assumption on the part of the courts that professional athletics would collapse as an industry economically or competitively if injunctions against breach were not issued. Personally, I see little justification and no proof for this assumption.

James T. Brennan, Injunction Against Professional Athletes' Breaching Their Contracts, 34 Brooklyn L. Rev. 61, 70 (1967). See also Sharon F. Carton, Damning with Fulsome Praise: Assessing the Uniqueness of an Artist or Performer as a Condition to Enjoin Performance of Personal Service Contracts in Entertainment Law, 5 Vill. Sports & Ent. L.J. 197 (1998).

4. *Enforcement of post-employment covenants not to compete.* The *Reier* case involved a covenant restricting the coach from working for another radio broadcast *during* his three-year contract. You may recall from the Valley Medical Specialists v. Farber case in Chapter 7 that frequently employment contracts will include express *post-employment* covenants not to compete with the former employer. Such restrictions may be enforceable if the employer has a valid, protectable interest and the restrictions are reasonable. E.g., The 7's Enterprises, Inc. v. Rosario, 143 P.3d 23 (Haw. 2006) (injunction granted to enforce three-year express non-compete agreement against ex-employee where employer gave unique training that constituted a protectable interest and ex-employee was not precluded from pursuing other work); Pinnacle Healthcare, LLC v. Sheets, 17 N.E.3d 947 (Ind. Ct. App. 2014) (where plaintiff doctor sued purchaser of plaintiff's former practice for money owed, trial court erred in denying defendant's motion for enforcement of plaintiff's covenant not to compete; presence of liquidated damages clause did not preclude finding of inadequate remedy at law for defendant). Notably, California is a jurisdiction that has taken a policy position strongly in favor of the former employee's ability to pursue a trade or profession and severely restricting the employer's ability to enforce a covenant not to compete. See Edwards v. Arthur Andersen LLP, 189 P.3d 285 (Cal. 2008) (discussing California statute rejecting test of reasonableness and making noncompete covenants "void" except in limited situations).

5. *Specific performance or reinstatement on behalf of employees.* Can a court ever order, against a breaching employer, specific performance on behalf of a wrongfully discharged employee? Although some of the policy problems relating to specific enforcement *against* the employee would not apply in this reverse situation (most notably the prohibition against "involuntary servitude"), the courts have nevertheless traditionally been unwilling to grant such relief. See, e.g., Nicholas v. Pennsylvania State University, 227 F.3d 133 (3d Cir.

2000) (tenured professor could not obtain reinstatement under breach of contract claim because court of equity will not grant specific performance of personal service contracts); Quadron Software International Corp. v. Plotseneder, 568 S.E.2d 178 (Ga. Ct. App. 2002) (employee not entitled to specific performance of software development contract absent showing of irreparable harm or inadequacy of damage remedy). When the employee's claim is based on violation of a statutory provision prohibiting discrimination in employment, such as Title VII of the Civil Rights Act of 1964, 42 U.S.C. §2000e et seq., however, reinstatement is authorized and usually ordered. See generally Bergerson v. New York State Office of Mental Health, 652 F.3d 277 (2d Cir. 2011) (discussing award of reinstatement and alternative remedies).

6. *Problem 10-4 reconsidered.* Recall Problem 10-4. In light of the materials in this section, should injunctive relief be available to the producers of "Operating Room" if Green accepts a contract with "Flying High"?

D. AGREED REMEDIES

Once a nonperformance (or defective performance) of an existing contract has occurred, it is within the power of the parties to agree to compromise or "settle" their dispute. By doing so the parties will in effect be agreeing on the remedy for breach. Absent some element of fraud, mistake, or duress, that agreement will almost surely be the final settlement of the dispute, with no occasion for judicial readjustment. Alternatively, it would be possible in such a case for the parties to stipulate between them the amount of damages that the one party had suffered from the other's nonperformance, litigating only the issue of whether that nonperformance was indeed an unexcused breach of their contract. Again, if such an agreement is free from fraud, mistake, or other bargaining defects, it is unlikely to be judicially condemned: Such agreements save all those concerned — the parties and the court — the time and money that would otherwise have to be expended on a full trial of all the issues material to their dispute.

Suppose, however, that the parties as part of their original agreement (as opposed to a settlement agreement entered into after breach) specify the remedy to be awarded in the event of its breach. One might assume that such an agreement should simply be viewed as another bargained-out compromise of liability, to be accorded the respect that any freely bargained contract enjoys in our system. Indeed, in light of our studies so far, it could be plausibly contended that such an originally agreed-on remedy term represents the "expectation interest" in its purest, most easily ascertainable form and thus should enjoy the highest degree of enforceability. The agreed-remedy provision (often referred to as a "liquidated damages" clause, where a fixed or determinable sum of money has been specified in advance as the remedy for a particular type of breach) has not been so warmly received by the courts, however. Despite the obvious advantages that such terms can have for the parties and the court system, they are subject to judicial scrutiny and will not be enforced unless they meet certain traditional tests. As reflected in the following case, courts make a distinction between a term aimed at compensation, and therefore enforceable, and a clause intended to penalize, and therefore unenforceable.

Barrie School v. Patch

Court of Appeals of Maryland 401 Md. 497; 933 A.2d 382 (2007)

Judges: BELL, C.J., RAKER, WILNER, CATHELL, HARRELL, BATTAGLIA, GREENE, JJ. Opinion by RAKER, J. BELL, C.J., Dissents.

Opinion by RAKER, J.

The primary question we must decide in this case is whether a non-breaching party to a contract has a duty to mitigate damages where the contract between the parties contains a valid liquidated damages clause. We shall answer that question in the negative and hold that a non-breaching party has no duty to mitigate damages where the parties agree to a valid liquidated sum in the event of a breach.

I.

Petitioner, The Barrie School, is a private, non-profit Montessori school located in Silver Spring, Maryland. Respondents, Andrew and Pamela Patch, are parents who enrolled their daughter, Christiana, in The Barrie School for the 2004-2005 academic year. The Patches entered into a re-enrollment agreement (the "Agreement") with The Barrie School that contained a specific deadline for cancelling the Agreement. The Agreement stated that if respondents withdrew their child from The Barrie School after a specific date, respondents would pay tuition for the entire academic year as liquidated damages.

The Agreement provided for a $1,000.00 non-refundable deposit and payment of the remaining tuition balance of $13,490.00 in two installments. The Agreement contained an escape clause that allowed for unilateral cancellation, provided that the head of the school received written notice by certified letter before May 31, 2004. Under §3 of the Agreement, respondents were obligated to pay the full tuition if they failed to meet the May 31, 2004 deadline for withdrawal. Section 3 of the Agreement provided as follows:

> "I understand that unless the Student is withdrawn by written notice given by certified letter, return receipt requested, and received by the Head of School prior to May 31, 2004, I am liable for and agree to pay the entire year's charges for the academic year, including expenses, as later defined, incurred by the School for collection. Withdrawal, dismissal, absences or illness of Student during the year do not release me from any portion of this obligation."

The Patches did not cancel the Agreement on or before May 31, 2004.

On July 14, 2004, forty-four days after the withdrawal deadline noted in §3 of the Agreement, the Patches sent a cancellation notice via facsimile to The Barrie School's admissions office and demanded a refund of their initial deposit. Respondents refused to pay any of the remaining tuition balance to the school and enrolled Christiana in another school.

The Barrie School filed a breach of contract action against respondents in the District Court of Maryland, sitting in Montgomery County. The Barrie School sought the remaining tuition balance for the 2004-2005 academic year, plus 12% interest, and attorney's fees. In their notice of intent to defend, respondents claimed that the Agreement had been procured by fraud, that it was a contract of adhesion, that the damages constituted a penalty, that The Barrie School had a duty to mitigate any damages, and that the Agreement was unenforceable because it violated public policy and Maryland's anti-competition laws.[1] Respondents also filed a counter-claim, seeking the return of their $1,000.00 deposit, interest, and attorney's fees.

The case proceeded to trial before the District Court. Charles Shayler, the Chief Financial Officer of The Barrie School, testified for petitioner; Andrew and Pamela Patch testified on their own behalf. Respondents' major argument at the close of evidence was that The Barrie School had a duty to mitigate its damages, notwithstanding the language of §3 of the Agreement.

The District Court found that there was a valid contract between the parties, including a valid liquidated damages clause, that there was no fraud in the inducement to enter into the Agreement, and that the Agreement was not a contract of adhesion. Accordingly, the court denied respondents' counterclaim. With respect to the liquidated damages clause, the court reasoned as follows:

> "I am satisfied that it is a valid liquidated damages provision, that based on the testimony of Mr. Goss, that there was — it would have been next to impossible to assign an exact amount as to the impact of losing one child for the school year. And that in light of that, and the fact that A, it was agreed to by the parties, this was not a contract of adhesion, certainly as I understand a contract of adhesion to be. These people could simply have walked away from this. Their lives did not — did not depend on signing this contract. And that basing one year's tuition or using one year's tuition as the measure is certainly not unreasonable and in fact, Mr. Goss' testimony was that it — probably the one year's tuition probably represented less than the actual costs of educating the child at Barrie School. Okay, so I find the contract is okay, including the liquidated damages provision."

The court next addressed respondents' argument that, notwithstanding a valid liquidated damages clause, a non-breaching party has a duty to mitigate damages. The court concluded that The Barrie School's failure to mitigate damages was fatal to its claim, reasoning as follows:

> "There is obviously the issue that I was most concerned with, and that was the issue of what effect liquidated damages has on the general rule that a party in — Plaintiff in the face of a breach does have some duty to mitigate.
>
> * * *

1. Based on the record from the District Court proceedings, it appears that respondents abandoned this final claim.

> Even if the amount is difficult to determine, I don't see why in the world they still shouldn't do something to mitigate. And again, even if the tuition amount does not exactly hit the number, it sure comes close to it in terms of going toward making them whole.
>
> And it's unquestionable that they did absolutely nothing whatsoever to try to fill the space for this child once they got the word in July that she was — that she was not going to be there. They — they didn't go through their old applications, they didn't put out any advertisements. They did absolutely nothing. And I understand there is the black letter rule. But I think even black letter rules are subject to some exception, and I don't see why, under the circumstances of this case, when they — even if it couldn't exactly correspond to exact amount that they would have been harmed, they — again, could have done a lot to have helped themselves out, at least to the extent of the amount they're suing for in this case. And that their failure to do so I do find to be fatal.
>
> So for that reason I'm going to also grant a Defendants' verdict on The Barrie School as Plaintiff."

The court entered judgment in favor of respondents on The Barrie School claim.

The Barrie School noted a timely appeal. . . .

In a written opinion, the Circuit Court agreed with the District Court and held that even though the liquidated damages clause was valid and not a penalty, The Barrie School had a duty to mitigate damages. . . . The Circuit Court stated as follows:

> "The question is presented as to whether a party who is protected by a liquidated damages clause in a contract is excused of the normal contractual duty to mitigate its damages as a prerequisite to recovery. The court finds that such a duty does exist, notwithstanding the existence of a liquidated damages clause, and, thus, the District Court did not err as a matter of law in so finding. It is interesting to note that while no evidence of mitigation was presented, it would appear that mitigation had, in effect, already occurred when The Barrie School already enrolled more students than its budget projections called for."

We granted The Barrie School's petition for a writ of certiorari to this Court. . . .

II.

Before this Court, The Barrie School argues that a non-breaching party has no duty to mitigate damages where the parties have agreed to a valid liquidated sum in the event of breach. The school states that it is well settled that liquidated damages clauses are recognized and enforced in Maryland and that, when valid, such clauses do not require the injured party to reduce the agreed-upon amount by avoiding loss. . . .

Respondents do not appear to controvert petitioner's argument that there exists a liquidated damages clause in the Agreement. Rather, respondents argue that the general law of contracts, i.e., the general duty to mitigate damages in the event of a breach, applies to a contract containing a liquidated damages provision. Respondents argue that the purpose of a liquidated damages clause is "solely to agree on the *amount* of damages," stating that "it does not have and should not have any effect on whether avoidable damages should be mitigated."

In addition to their mitigation argument, respondents contend that The Barrie School suffered no actual damages from the breach because it enrolled more students than originally expected in the 2004-2005 enrollment projections. . . .

III.

Liquidated damages have been defined as a specific sum stipulated to and agreed upon by the parties at the time they entered into a contract, to be paid to compensate for injuries in the event of a breach of that contract. Board of Education v. Heister, 392 Md. 140, 155, 896 A.2d 342, 351 (2006) (stating that a liquidated damages clause is "a specific sum of money . . . expressly stipulated by the parties to a . . . contract as the amount of damages to be recovered by either party for a breach of the agreement by the other"). Whether a contract provision is a penalty or a valid liquidated damages clause is a question of law, reviewed *de novo* by this Court. Id. See also Hammaker v. Schleigh, 157 Md. 652, 667, 147 A. 790, 796 (1929).

Because respondents seek to set aside the bargained for contractual provision in the Agreement stipulating damages in the event of breach, respondents have the burden of proving that the clause should not be enforced. Placing the burden of proof on the challenger is consistent with giving the non-breaching party the advantage inherent in stipulated damages clauses, that of eliminating the need to prove damages, and with the general principle of Maryland law that assumes that bargains are enforceable and that the party asking the court to invalidate a bargain should demonstrate the justice of his or her view. See Dashiell v. Meeks, 396 Md. 149, 167, 913 A.2d 10, 20 (2006).

It has long been the rule in Maryland that valid liquidated damages provisions are enforceable. Our predecessors stated "the settled rule of law" with respect to liquidated damages as follows:

> "[W]here the parties, at or before the time of the execution of the contract, agree upon and name a sum therein to be paid as liquidated damages, in lieu of anticipated damages which are in their nature uncertain and incapable of exact ascertainment, that the amount so named in the agreement will be regarded as liquidated damages and not as a penalty, unless the amount so agreed upon and inserted in the agreement be grossly excessive and out of all proportion to the damages that might reasonably have been expected to result from such breach of the contract. And whether it is excessive or whether the damages are incapable of exact ascertainment should be determined from the subject-matter of the contract considered in the light of all the surrounding facts and circumstances connected therewith and known to the parties at the time of its execution. That these questions should be considered and determined from the contract itself, its subject-matter and the surrounding facts and circumstances connected therewith with which the parties are confronted at the time of its execution, is made necessary in order to ascertain the intention of the parties, which is one of the essential factors in deciding whether the stipulation is for liquidated damages or is a penalty. It may afterwards be disclosed that the damages actually sustained are more or less than those anticipated at the time of the execution of the contract. If more, this fact would not characterize or stamp the stipulation as a penalty unless it was so exorbitant as to clearly show that such

> amount was not arrived at in a *bona fide* effort, made at or before the execution of the contract, to estimate the damages that might have been reasonably expected to result from a breach of it, and that it was named as a penalty for such breach. And on the other hand, if the amount stipulated was found to be inadequate, a greater amount could not be recovered for such breach, because of the agreement between the parties that the amount so named should be in lieu of the damages resulting therefrom."

Balto. Bridge Co. v. U. Rwys. & E. Co., 125 Md. 208, 214-215, 93 A. 420, 422-423 (1915). This Court has not strayed from the notion that, absent specific statutory provisions, the time of contract formation is the appropriate point from which to judge the reasonableness of a liquidated damages provision.

Writing for this Court, Judge Harrell elucidated more recently the elements of a liquidated damages provision, stating as follows:

> "There are three essential elements of a valid and enforceable liquidated damages clause. First, such a clause must provide in clear and unambiguous terms for a certain sum. Secondly, the liquidated damages must reasonably be compensation for the damages anticipated by the breach. Thirdly, liquidated damage clauses are by their nature mandatory binding agreements before the fact which may not be altered to correspond to actual damages determined after the fact. While the language used by the parties is instructive in determining the validity of a liquidated damages clause, the decisive element is the intention of the parties — whether they intended that the sum be a penalty or an agreed-upon amount as damages in case of a breach and this is to be gleaned from the subject matter, the language of the contract and the circumstances surrounding its execution."

Heister, 392 Md. at 156, 896 A.2d at 352 (internal citations and quotations omitted). . . .

We have long recognized that "one of the most difficult and perplexing inquiries encountered in the construction of written agreements" is determining whether a contractual clause should be regarded as a valid and enforceable liquidated damages provision or as a penalty. Willson v. M. & C. C. of Baltimore, 83 Md. 203, 211, 34 A. 774, 775 (1896). Thus, "if there is doubt whether a contract provides for liquidated damages or a penalty, the provision will be construed as a penalty." Goldman v. Conn. Gen. Life Ins. Co., 251 Md. 575, 581, 248 A.2d 154, 158 (1968). . . .

As we have indicated, in the absence of a statute providing otherwise, Maryland courts determine the validity of a liquidated damages clause by looking to the stipulated loss at the time of the contract's formation, and not actual losses resulting from breach.[5] . . .

---

5. For statutory provisions providing otherwise, see, for example, the Uniform Commercial Code §2-718(1) and the corresponding Maryland provision applying to the sale of goods, Md. Code (1975, 2002 Repl. Vol.), §2-718(1) of the *Commercial Law Article* (stating that damages "may

In the case *sub judice*, the lower courts found correctly that §3 of the Agreement was a valid liquidated damages clause and not a penalty. The sum in §3 was a reasonable forecast of just compensation for potential harm caused by a breach of the Agreement. The damages contemplated in the Agreement were neither grossly excessive nor out of all proportion to those which might have been expected at the time of contracting.[6] See Lake Ridge Academy v. Carney, 66 Ohio St. 3d 376, 613 N.E.2d 183 (Ohio 1993) (finding that a year's tuition constitutes a reasonable liquidated sum for breach of a school enrollment contract); Wentworth Military Academy v. Marshall, 225 Ark. 591, 283 S.W.2d 868 (Ark. 1955) (same); Kentucky Military Institute v. Bramblet, 158 Ky. 205, 164 S.W. 808 (Ky. 1914) (same); Teeter v. Horner Military School, 165 N.C. 564, 81 S.E. 767 (N.C. 1914) (same).

The actual damages resulting from breach would have been very difficult to estimate at the time of contracting as well. The Barrie School's Chief Financial Officer testified to this effect before the District Court, stating as follows:

> "The budget's developed in November and December of the preceding year, and reviewed and approved in January of the preceding year. We determine the total number of expenses, faculty and otherwise, to instruct our students, and we then, because we're a non-profit and we try to have a balanced budget, we then determine what tuition level needs to be set, and the number of students to meet the revenue goal. So to parse out of that the effect of one student is very difficult."

As the Circuit Court noted, "it would be next to impossible to assign an exact amount as to the impact of losing one child for the school year." Section 3 of the Agreement constitutes a valid liquidated damages clause.

Respondents argue that there exists a duty to mitigate damages even in the face of a valid liquidated damages clause. Respondents would have us hold that there is such a duty because parties to a contract are required usually to minimize loss in the event of breach. In Circuit City v. Rockville Pike, 376 Md. 331, 829 A.2d 976 (2003), we addressed the concept of mitigation of damages, stating as follows:

> "We have recognized generally that, when one party breaches a contract, the other party is required by the 'avoidable consequences' rule of damages to make all reasonable efforts to minimize the loss sustained from the breach and can charge the defending party only with such damages as, 'with reasonable endeavors and expense and without risk of additional substantial loss or injury, he could not prevent.' "

Id. at 355, 829 A.2d at 990 (quoting Sergeant Co. v. Pickett, 285 Md. 186, 203, 401 A.2d 651, 660 (1979)). As we made clear in *Circuit City*, mitigation of

---

be liquidated in the agreement but only at an amount which is reasonable in the light of the anticipated or actual harm caused by the breach"), Md. Code (1975, 2005 Repl. Vol.), §14-1106(c) of the *Commercial Law Article* (noting that under Maryland's laws governing layaway sales, the seller may "retain as liquidated damages an amount not to exceed 10 percent of the layaway price or the total amount paid by the buyer to the date of default, whichever is less"). . . .

6. We do not address the enforceability of specific contractual provisions related to liability for school tuition and related charges in the event of nonattendance under circumstances related to serious illness, military transfers, and the like.

damages helps to determine the proper amount of damages resulting from a breach of contract. In other words, it is part of the law of court-assessed damages.

Liquidated damages differ fundamentally from mitigation of damages. While mitigation is part of a court's determination of actual damages that have resulted from a breach of contract, liquidated damages clauses are the remedy the parties to a contract have determined to be proper in the event of breach. Where the parties to a contract have included a reasonable sum that stipulates damages in the event of breach, that sum replaces any determination of actual loss. Professor Williston has explained this principle as follows:

> "[O]ne purpose of a liquidated damages provision is to obviate the need for the nonbreaching party to prove actual damages. Thus, where the liquidated damages clause represents a reasonable attempt by the parties to agree in advance upon a sum that will compensate the nonbreacher for any harm caused by the breach, in lieu of the compensatory contract damage to which the nonbreacher would otherwise be entitled, the clause will be upheld."

[Richard A. Lord, Williston on Contracts] §65:1, at 230 (internal citations and quotations omitted). See also 11 Arthur Linton Corbin, Corbin on Contracts §1062, at 307 (interim ed. 2002) (stating that a valid liquidation of damages makes other proof as to the amount of injury unnecessary). It follows naturally that once a court has determined that a liquidated damages clause is valid, it need not make further inquiries as to actual damages. This includes a determination of whether the parties attempted to mitigate damages resulting from breach.

Judge Richard Posner of the United States Court of Appeals for the Seventh Circuit noted the distinction between liquidated damages and the duty to mitigate in Lake River Corp. v. Carborundum Co., 769 F.2d 1284 (7th Cir. 1985). That case involved a shipping contract in which one party to the contract failed to fulfill the terms of the agreement after market prices shifted. Although the court found that the contractual clause at issue was invalid as a penalty, the court nonetheless explained the distinction between mitigation of damages and liquidated damages, stating as follows:

> "[M]itigation of damages is a doctrine of the law of court-assessed damages, while the point of a liquidated-damages clause is to substitute party assessment; and that point is blunted, and the certainty that liquidated-damages clauses are designed to give the process of assessing damages impaired, if a defendant can force the plaintiff to take less than the damages specified in the clause, on the ground that the plaintiff could have avoided some of them."

Lake River Corp., 769 F.2d at 1291.

As Judge Posner noted in *Lake River Corp.*, the purpose of §3 of the Agreement would be "blunted" if The Barrie School were required to mitigate damages. The parties to the Agreement determined that a certain sum would be paid in order to avoid the necessity of determining actual damages that might have resulted from breach. As a necessary conclusion, §3 of the Agreement was a comprehensive sum that eliminated the need to calculate actual losses, including any mitigation of damages that might have occurred. Maryland's approach to liquidated damages supports this conclusion, as we view such clauses as "binding agreements *before the fact* which may not be altered to correspond to actual damages determined after the fact." *Heister*, 392 Md. at 156, 896 A.2d at 352 (emphasis added) (internal citations and quotations omitted). Because mitigation of damages is part of a post-breach calculation of actual damages, in the absence of a statute mandating mitigation of damages, there exists no duty to mitigate damages where a valid liquidated damages clause exists.

Section 3 of the Agreement is a valid liquidated damages clause and not a penalty. Therefore, The Barrie School had no duty to mitigate damages and was entitled to the sum enumerated in §3 of the Agreement.

Finally, in addition to arguing the duty to mitigate, respondents claim the defense of no-actual-harm. Respondents contend that because The Barrie School filled their daughter's space and actually enrolled more students than anticipated originally, the school suffered no harm from its breach of the Agreement. We reject this defense in this context. The same rationale we rely on in rejecting the duty to mitigate in the face of a valid liquidated damages provision applies to the no-actual-harm defense. Such a defense negates the benefit of an agreed-upon or stipulated damages clause and deviates from our acceptance of the principle that the time of contract formation is the appropriate point from which to judge the reasonableness of a stipulated amount of damages. It would also breed uncertainty in the calculation of damages, because if we were to accept the no-actual-harm defense, why would courts not then give greater damages than contemplated when the damages actually exceeded the stipulated amount?. . .

IV.

We address respondents' remaining contentions. Respondents argue that the Agreement was a contract of adhesion because it specified, in bold, capital letters that "ANY ALTERATIONS OR MODIFICATIONS TO THIS AGREEMENT WILL NOT BE ACCEPTED BY THE SCHOOL." Respondents reason that because there was a gross inequity of bargaining power and The Barrie School imposed a liquidated damages provision in the Agreement, the provision was unenforceable. Both lower courts found that the Agreement was not a contract of adhesion. We agree with the lower courts.

We note that a contract of adhesion is not void per se. *Walther v. Sovereign Bank*, 386 Md. 412, 430, 872 A.2d 735, 746 (2005). A court will find a contract of adhesion unenforceable only if it is unconscionable. Id. In the instant case, the Agreement was neither a contract of adhesion nor unconscionable. An unconscionable contract involves extreme unfairness, "made evident by (1) one party's lack of meaningful choice, and (2) contractual terms that unreasonably favor the other party." Id. at 426, 872 A.2d at 743 (internal citations and quotations omitted). Respondents were not forced to enroll their child at The Barrie School. Moreover, the "escape clause" was put into the Agreement for the benefit of respondents. If respondents did not want to enroll their child at the school, all they needed to do was to notify school officials before May 31, 2004, and they would have incurred no financial liability. But for that provision respondents would have been bound to the Agreement without any opportunity for a refund. Respondents have not established that they had no choice but to enroll their child at The Barrie School, and the record does not suggest that the Agreement was anything but an arm's-length business transaction. Therefore, we conclude that the District Court did not err in concluding that the Agreement was not a contract of adhesion. . . .

[The Court of Appeals thus reversed the circuit court judgment and remanded for the trial court to enter judgment consistent with this opinion. — EDS.]

Dissenting Opinion by BELL, C.J.:

The Majority, agreeing that the liquidated damages clause embodied in §3 of the re-enrollment agreement ("the Agreement") between the appellant, The Barrie School ("the School"), and the appellees, Mr. and Mrs. Patch ("the Patches"), and on which the trial courts relied, is valid, reverses the judgment of the Circuit Court for Montgomery County because it concludes that where the liquidated damages clause is valid, there is no duty to mitigate. I disagree. I am troubled by the result reached by the Majority, as it undermines basic principles of contract law pertaining to the equity and reasonableness of contract remedies.

It is a long-held, and well-settled, general principle of contract law that contract remedies are to be compensatory, not punitive. Restatement (Second) of Contracts §356, comment *a* (1981) (stating that "the central objective behind the system of contract remedies is compensatory, not punitive). . . .

Integral to the inquiry into the validity of a liquidated damages clause is determining whether the clause is fair and reasonable. The vantage point from which that determination is made is critical to, and may be dispositive of, that inquiry. The Majority maintains that "the time of the contract formation is the appropriate point from which to judge the reasonableness of a liquidated damages provision." Focusing exclusively on this "prospective view" leads the Majority to the conclusion it reaches.

There is another "view," however. Because the validity of a liquidated damages does not become an issue until one of the parties breaches the contract to which it relates, it follows, logically, that the review of a liquidated damages clause to determine whether it is a penalty should include the effect of the breach, at the least, whether actual damages have been incurred. . . .

The second Restatement [states]:

> "[T]wo factors combine in determining whether an amount of money fixed as damages is so unreasonably large as to be a penalty. The first factor is the anticipated or actual loss caused by the breach. . . . The second factor is the difficulty of proof of loss. . . . If the difficulty of proof of loss is great, considerable latitude is allowed in that approximation of anticipated or actual harm. If, on the other hand, the difficulty of proof of loss is slight, less latitude if allowed in

> that approximation. If, to take an extreme case, it is clear that no loss at all has occurred, a provision fixing a substantial sum as damages is unenforceable."

§356 at comment *b* (emphasis added). See Mattingly Bridge Co. v. Holloway & Son Const. Co., 694 S.W.2d 702, 705 (Ky. 1985) in which the Supreme Court of Kentucky, adopting Restatement (Second) Contracts §356(1) (1981) "as a reasonable expression of the rule applicable to liquidated damages" acknowledged that liquidated damages clauses are "useful commercial tool[s] to avoid litigation to determine actual damages," subject, however, to two restrictions: "they should be used only (1) where the actual damages sustained from a breach of contract would be very difficult to ascertain and (2) where, after the breach occurs, it appears that the amount fixed as liquidated damages is not grossly disproportionate to the damages actually sustained." (emphasis added). . . .

The viability of a liquidated damages clause, thus, does not depend solely on the fixed amount for which the parties contracted; rather, all of the surrounding circumstances are important, those existing at the time of contracting, as well as those existing at the time of the breach, and they include consideration of the actual damages sustained. . . . This is, in my view, the only way in which to be completely fair to both parties.

In the case sub judice, there is no doubt that the Patches breached their Agreement with the School. On the other hand, the record indicates that the School did not suffer harm commensurate to the sum fixed as liquidated damages. While the Patches' daughter did not attend the School, it is undisputed that the School met its enrollment projections for that year; there was "no empty desk" for which budgetary projections were made, yet not realized. Looking at the provision retrospectively, it is clear that the School should not be awarded a full year's tuition, as this amount is grossly disproportionate to, and in excess of, the harm it actually suffered. . . .

The Majority rejects "no-actual-harm" as a defense. It argues that "[s]uch a defense negates the benefit of an agreed-upon or stipulated damages clause[.]" The Majority also believes that "[i]t would also breed uncertainty in the calculation of damages, because if we were to accept the no-actual-harm defense, why would courts not then give greater damages than contemplated when the damages actually exceeded the stipulated amount?" Id. This view is not supported by the precedent on which the Majority itself relies. In *Baltimore Bridge*, this Court opined:

> "It may afterwards be disclosed that the damages actually sustained are more or less than those anticipated at the time of the execution of the contract. If less, this fact would not characterize or stamp the stipulation as a penalty unless it was so exorbitant as to clearly show that such amount was not arrived at in a bona fide effort, made at or before the execution of the contract, to estimate the damages that might have been reasonably expected to result from a breach of it, and that it was named as a penalty for such breach. And, on the other hand, if the amount stipulated was found to be inadequate, a greater amount could not be recovered for such breach, because of the agreement between the parties that the amount so named should be in lieu of the damages resulting therefrom."

[Baltimore Bridge Co. v. United Railways & Electric Co., 125 Md. 208, 215, 93 A.2d 420, 422-423 (1915).] This is consistent with my position and with principles of fairness and equity; liquidated damages clauses limit recovery where the actual damages suffered are greater, while yet allowing exorbitant, excessive sums to be challenged. This is not at all contrary to the purpose of such clauses.

To be sure, the School is entitled to compensation for any and all damages it suffered as a result of the contract breach. When, however, considered retrospectively, it is determined that the School's recovery will be excessive, the liquidated damages clause that provides for that recovery is invalid and unenforceable. That simply means that the School will have to prove its actual damages as it would in any breach of contract action and will be required, moreover, to mitigate its damages, if the circumstances make that appropriate.

The purpose of imposing a duty to mitigate damages is to "encourag[e] the injured party to attempt to avoid loss." Restatement (Second) of Contracts §350 at comment *a*. This Court has held, in accordance with this general "avoidable consequences" rule of damages, that "the ordinary rule with respect to minimization of damages . . . [is] that 'damages are not recoverable if the consequences of a breach are avoidable. . . .' "

I do not agree [with the Majority that there is no duty to mitigate]. The liquidation of damages and the mitigation of damages are, indeed, distinct and separate concepts, which must be treated as such, i.e., there is no exception to the general contractual duty to mitigate simply because a fixed sum has been agreed upon by the parties in advance. That is to say, whether mitigation of damages applies, or not, should be determined when, post-breach, a court considers whether there have been actual damages incurred at all. . . .

To uphold the liquidated damages clause in the case sub judice would be unfair to the Patches. General contract principles make that clear. I would affirm the judgment of the Circuit Court.

For the foregoing reasons, I dissent.

NOTES AND QUESTIONS

1. *Test for enforcement of liquidated damages clauses.* Courts traditionally have used a three-pronged test to determine the validity of clauses providing for agreed remedies: (1) the damages to be anticipated from the breach must be uncertain in amount or difficult to prove; (2) the parties must have intended the clause to liquidate damages rather than operate as a penalty; and (3) the amount set in the agreement must be a reasonable forecast of just compensation for the harm flowing from the breach. See Orr v. Goodwin, 953 A.2d 1190 (N.H. 2008). Similarly, Restatement (Second) §356 states a two-part test: A provision for liquidated damages will be enforceable if the amount fixed is reasonable in light of the "anticipated or actual loss" and the "difficulties of proof of loss." Comment *b* to §356 provides, "[t]he greater the difficulty either of proving that loss has occurred or of establishing its amount with the requisite

certainty . . . , the easier it is to show that the amount fixed is reasonable." Thus, the difficulty in quantifying harm resulting from a breach is pivotal in many cases. See, e.g., Radisson Hotels Int'l, Inc. v. Majestic Towers, Inc., 488 F. Supp. 2d 953 (C.D. Cal. 2007) (liquidated damages clause in hotel licensing agreement enforceable in light of difficulty estimating future profitability of hotel at time contract was made); City of Davenport v. Shewry Corp., 674 N.W.2d 79 (Iowa 2004) (enforcing liquidated damages in economic development contract; it would be difficult, if not impossible, to measure harm resulting to plaintiff city from defendant company's failure to create jobs that would contribute to city's economy and tax base).

Many courts have also adopted the position expressed in *Barrie School* that a liquidated damage clause is presumed to be valid and the burden of proof is on the party seeking to invalidate the provision. This presumption is seen as a corollary of the "freedom of contract" principle. See, e.g., Carrothers Construction Co. v. City of S. Hutchinson, 207 P.3d 231 (Kan. 2009) (burden of proving that liquidated damage clause is unenforceable penalty falls on party challenging the provision; this approach promotes public policy favoring settlement, avoidance of litigation, and allowing parties to live by their own contracts); TAL Financial Corp. v. CSC Consulting, Inc., 844 N.E.2d 1085 (Mass. 2006) (majority of states place burden of proof on party seeking to avoid clause; doubts resolved in favor of enforcement).

2. *Evaluating provision in light of anticipated or actual harm.* The majority and dissenting opinions in *Barrie School* disagree on a number of issues, including whether a liquidated damage clause should be judged *only* from the perspective of the parties at the time that the contract was made or *dually* from both the time of contracting and after the breach. Traditionally, courts used only the prospective view and many still adhere to this approach. For these courts, proof of a low amount of actual damage would have only limited relevance. See, e.g., Kelly v. Marx, 705 N.E.2d 1114 (Mass. 1999) (noting sharp division among jurisdictions on the issue but holding that stipulated remedy should be evaluated only in light of circumstances at time of contract formation; the expectations of parties and efficiency considerations support "single look" approach). The dissent in *Barrie School*, however, reflects the more recent trend toward assessing reasonableness either at the time of formation or after the breach. See, e.g., Wasserman's Inc. v. Township of Middletown, 645 A.2d 100 (N.J. 1994) (adopting modern approach, noting "that hindsight is frequently better than foresight" and that a court cannot avoid being influenced by its knowledge of subsequent events).

As noted above, the Restatement (Second) §356 states that a liquidated damage clause must be reasonable in light of the "anticipated or actual loss." Also contributing to the current trend, UCC §2-718 provides that damages may be liquidated "only at an amount which is reasonable in the light of the anticipated or actual harm." The impact of this two-fold perspective, however, is less than clear. In Wassenaar v. Panos, 331 N.W.2d 357 (Wis. 1983), the court stated that a clause producing liquidated damages "grossly disproportionate to the actual harm" may thus be determined to be unreasonable. This approach suggests that a liquidated damages clause should be *denied* enforcement if it is unreasonable in light of the actual harm even if it appeared reasonable at contract formation. The Ninth Circuit court used a different approach in California & Hawaiian Sugar Co. v. Sun Ship, Inc., 794 F.2d 1433 (9th Cir. 1986), *cert. denied*, 484 U.S. 871 (1987). In that case, the court interpreted the disjunctive language in the Restatement (Second) and the UCC to mean that a liquidated damage clause should be *upheld* if the clause was reasonable either in light of anticipated harm or in light of the actual harm. Thus, the Ninth Circuit court enforced a clause resulting in recovery of more than $4 million because it was a reasonable forecast of what might have happened, even though the actual harm was apparently less than $400,000. The Ninth Circuit court also emphasized that the parties to the contract were sophisticated and that the precise extent of actual harm was difficult to measure. Id. at 1439. See also XCO International, Inc. v. Pacific Scientific Co., 369 F.3d 998 (7th Cir. 2004) (rule against penalty clauses is "anachronism," especially in contracts between commercial enterprises; clause will be enforceable if reasonable in light of actual harm even if not reasonable forecast at time contract was made).

3. *Necessity of actual loss.* The defendant parents in *Barrie School* argued that the plaintiff suffered no actual harm from their daughter's failure to attend the school. If it did appear that there had been no injury at all, should the liquidated damages clause have been enforced? Under the traditional approach of assessing enforceability solely at the time of contracting, as noted above, even a total absence of loss might well be irrelevant. See, e.g., Frick Co. v. Rubel Corp., 62 F.2d 765 (2d Cir. 1933) (actual harm not relevant); Wallace Real Estate Investment, Inc. v. Groves, 881 P.2d 1010 (Wash. 1994) (actual damage not prerequisite to upholding liquidated damages clause, but unconscionably disproportionate actual damage may be used in evaluating reasonableness of preestimate). A number of courts have held, however, that the complete absence of actual loss or injury will make a clause invalid as a penalty. See, e.g., Colonial at Lynnfield, Inc. v. Sloan, 870 F.2d 761 (1st Cir. 1989); Valentine's, Inc. v. Ngo, 251 S.W.3d 352 (Mo. Ct. App. 2008).

4. *Liquidated damages clauses and mitigation.* The majority opinion in *Barrie School* refused to impose on the plaintiff school a duty to mitigate, greatly relying on Judge Posner's reasoning in Lake River Corp. v. Carborundum Co., 769 F.2d 1284 (7th Cir. 1985). *Lake River* involved a contract for distribution services between two commercial entities and the court held that any savings from mitigation should not be deducted from recovery under a liquidated damages clause. As noted by the *Barrie School* majority, Judge Posner asserted that mitigation is inconsistent with the underlying premise that such clauses allow parties to fix the amount of damages with certainty. The rule that there is no duty to mitigate in the face of a valid liquidated damages clause appears to be the consensus view. See NPS, LLC v. Minihane, 886 N.E.2d 670 (Mass. 2008). On the other hand, the dissenting judge in *Barrie School* would have imposed a duty to mitigate and at least a few other courts seem to agree. See Southern Bldg. Services, Inc. v. City of Ft. Smith, 427 S.W.3d 763 (Ark. Ct. App. 2013)

(affirming denial of liquidated damages when plaintiff failed to mitigate after breach); Howard Sales Co., Inc. v. Bradley, 2008 WL 2930197 (Neb. Ct. App.) (noting that if circumstances of a contract and its breach lend themselves to mitigation, it is difficult to sustain a liquidated damages clause). See also Lisa A. Fortin, Why There Should Be a Duty to Mitigate Liquidated Damages Clauses, 38 Hofstra L. Rev. 285 (2009) (advocating for duty to mitigate despite liquidated damages clause to promote efficiency and good faith behavior, to avoid penalties and double recovery, and on other grounds).

5. *Liquidated damages in consumer contracts.* The majority opinion in *Barrie School* recognized in footnote 5 that a specific state statute regulates liquidated damages clauses in "layaway" sales. Similarly, statutory provisions in California create special rules limiting enforceability of liquidated damages clauses in consumer contracts involving goods or services obtained for personal, family, or household purposes and in residential leases. See Cal. Civ. Code §1671. The contract in the *Barrie School* case would be considered a "consumer" contract rather than a commercial contract. Should that fact have affected the willingness of the court to enforce the liquidated damages clause? See L & L Wings, Inc. v. Marco-Destin, Inc., 756 F. Supp. 2d 359 (S.D.N.Y. 2010) (in evaluating liquidated damages provision, court must consider whether parties were sophisticated, represented by counsel, negotiated at "arms-length" or had equal bargaining power).

6. *Liquidated damages in construction contracts.* Clauses providing for liquidated damages in the event of delay in completion are common in construction and similar contracts; such clauses typically measure the amount recoverable by some daily or weekly rate, with perhaps an outside time limit, and are usually held to be enforceable in light of the various kinds of injury — both tangible and intangible — that can result from such delays. See, e.g., Hutton Contracting Company, Inc. v. City of Coffeyville, 487 F.3d 772 (10th. Cir. 2007) (applying Kansas law in enforcing $500 per day delay damages in construction of new power and fiber optic lines); American Multi-Cinema, Inc. v. Southroads, L.L.C., 119 F. Supp. 2d 1190 (D. Kan. 2000) (enforcing portion of liquidated damage clause that allowed four days of free rent for each day that shopping center was late in turning over site for construction of movie "mega-plex" by tenant); but see Rohlin Construction Co. v. City of Hinton, 476 N.W.2d 78 (Iowa 1991) (provision in highway contract for $400 daily liquidated damages for delay held to be unenforceable penalty; while slight damage might have occurred, amount in contract bore no reasonable relation to anticipated or actual loss). In Cuesport Properties, LLC v. Critical Developments, LLC, 61 A.3d 91 (Md. Ct. Spec. App. 2013), a liquidated damages clause provided for per diem payments when the builder was late in completing construction. Rejecting the defendant builder's argument that the clause created a penalty because payments could continue indefinitely if the builder abandoned the project, the appellate court held that in such a case the builder's liability need be continued only for whatever time period would be necessary for the owner or another builder to complete the work. The court recognized the *Barrie* holding that generally mitigation would not be required where the parties had liquidated

damages in their agreement, but distinguished that case on its facts. Compare Dollar Tree Stores Inc. v. Toyama Partners LLC, 875 F. Supp. 2d 1058 (N.D. Cal. 2012), where the court disallowed as a penalty a clause providing a fixed sum per diem for delay in performance, because the payment rate was the same no matter how severe or minor the breach, and because the payments could continue indefinitely.

7. *Liquidated damages in employment contracts.* In the preceding section of this chapter we saw that courts will not grant specific performance of personal service contracts and are even reluctant to provide injunctive relief. Because of this judicial tendency, employment contracts may contain liquidated damage clauses that apply in the event of breach by the employee. See, e.g., Vanderbilt v. DiNardo, 174 F.3d 751 (6th Cir. 1999) (liquidated damage clause requiring college football head coach to pay sum equal to net annual salary for breach was enforceable; amount was reasonable in light of tangible and intangible harm resulting from discontinuity in football program if coach did not complete five-year term). Of course, such clauses must still survive judicial determination of whether they operate as a penalty. See Equity Enterprises, Inc. v. Milosch, 633 N.W.2d 662 (Wis. Ct. App. 2001) (forfeiture of sales commissions by former insurance agent for breach of covenant not to compete was not a reasonable liquidated damage provision).

Employment contracts may also include a liquidated damage clause that provides a remedy for the employee in the event of breach by the employer. In *Wassenaar*, cited in Note 2 above, the plaintiff entered into a three-year employment contract, agreeing to serve as the general manager of the defendant's hotel. If the defendant terminated the contract prior to its expiration, defendant agreed to be "responsible for fulfilling the entire financial obligation as set forth within this agreement for the full period of three (3) years." The employer discharged the plaintiff 21 months before the expiration of the contract. The plaintiff was unemployed for approximately two and one-half months, but then obtained a job, which he held until the time of trial. The Wisconsin Supreme Court held that the employee was entitled to his full compensation for the remainder of the three-year term as liquidated damages with no deduction for the pay he received from the other job. The court reasoned that the standard measure of damages for the employer's breach of an employment contract (the contract amount plus expenses of seeking other employment less earnings received from other employment) does not compensate for certain consequential damages, such as harm to reputation and emotional stress; accordingly, the clause could be upheld as a reasonable forecast of uncertain damages.

8. *Liquidated damages in real estate contracts and specific performance.* Real estate contracts typically require purchasers to make "earnest money" deposits and often provide for retention of the deposit by the seller if the purchaser breaches. Courts are divided on how to treat such provisions. Many courts will not allow a breaching purchaser to recover any portion of an earnest money deposit. See Star Financial Corp. v. Howard Nance Co., 508 S.E.2d 534 (N.C. Ct. App. 1998), *aff'd*, 516 S.E.2d 381 (1999) (North Carolina adheres to common law rule, followed by majority of jurisdictions, that breaching purchaser

cannot recover any portion of consideration paid). Other courts treat such provisions as liquidated damage clauses subject to judicial scrutiny under the tests discussed above. See, e.g., Palmieri v. Partridge, 853 A.2d 1076 (Pa. Super. Ct. 2004) (clause requiring forfeiture of $225,000 deposit on purchase price of $2,250,000 was a reasonable liquidated damage provision and not a penalty; forfeitures of up to 10 percent have often been found to be reasonable).

Should the presence of a liquidated damage clause bar the granting of specific performance of a real estate contract? The courts have been divided on this question. Compare Allen v. Smith, 114 Cal. Rptr. 2d 898 (Ct. App. 2002) (liquidated damage clause will not bar action for specific performance in real estate contract), with O'Shield v. Lakeside Bank, 781 N.E.2d 1114 (Ill. App. Ct. 2002) (liquidated damage clause does preclude action for specific performance in real estate contract, based on clear intent of parties). Professor Murray concluded that if specific performance or injunctive relief would otherwise be available, a liquidated damages clause will not bar such relief unless it is expressly excluded. John E. Murray, Jr., Murray on Contracts §126, at 800-801 (5th ed. 2011). Professor Murray further noted that courts will not allow the nonbreaching party to receive both liquidated damages and specific performance if the result would be overcompensation. Id.

9. *Underliquidated damages.* Most often, liquidated damage clauses are scrutinized in light of the possibility that they might greatly overcompensate the plaintiff for defendant's breach. The majority and dissenting opinions in *Barrie School*, relying on earlier precedent, clearly contemplate that a liquidated damages clause will not be rendered unenforceable merely because the actual damages greatly exceed the stipulated remedy. You should note, however, that Restatement (Second) §356, Comment *a*, suggests that a term fixing an "unreasonably small amount" of damages might be unenforceable because it is "unconscionable." UCC §2-718(1) and its Comment 1 are to the same effect as the Restatement on this point. Still, there is the possibility that a clause providing for a small amount of damages may reflect a rational agreement to limit liability in the event of breach. See Rainbow Country Rentals & Retails, Inc. v. Ameritech Publishing, Inc., 706 N.W.2d 95 (Wis. 2005) (agreeing with majority of jurisdictions that clause limiting liability for error in telephone directory is enforceable stipulated remedy in light of difficulty in assessing actual harm).

10. *Scholarly commentary.* A considerable body of scholarly writing has debated the wisdom of the "penalty" limitation on the enforceability of liquidated damage clauses. See, e.g., Charles J. Goetz & Robert E. Scott, Liquidated Damages, Penalties and the Just Compensation Principle: Some Notes on an Enforcement Model and a Theory of Efficient Breach, 77 Colum. L. Rev. 554 (1977) (penalty limitation on liquidated damage clauses should be abolished; such clauses should be enforced unless they are the product of some defect in the bargaining process); Kenneth W. Clarkson, Roger LeRoy Miller, & Timothy J. Muris, Liquidated Damages v. Penalties: Sense or Nonsense?, 1978 Wis. L. Rev. 351 (under economic analysis penalty limitation should be applied to situations where there may be opportunity and incentive to induce breach; in other cases clause should be upheld without regard to whether it is

penalty); Larry A. DiMatteo, A Theory of Efficient Penalty: Eliminating the Law of Liquidated Damages, 38 Am. Bus. L.J. 633 (2001) (advocating a strong presumption of enforceability for liquidated damage clauses, subject to the unconscionability doctrine as primary ground for avoidance).

PROBLEM 11-2

In June 2017, Waste Disposal, Inc. entered into a contract with Yamini Chemical Company, a chemical manufacturer, for the transportation and disposal of waste chemicals from Yamini's manufacturing operations. The contract was for a five-year term. Paragraph 7 of the agreement provided as follows:

> 7. *Price.* The price for the first year of this agreement has been set under paragraph 6 above. For subsequent years, the price shall be set by mutual agreement of the parties not more than thirty (30) days before the anniversary of the execution of this contract. Adjustment in price from the previous year's price shall be based on the amount of any cost increases incurred by Waste Disposal during the previous year. The parties agree to negotiate in good faith to agree on price.

In February 2019 Waste Disposal notified Yamini that it was terminating the contract effective June 30 of that year because changes in federal and state regulations governing waste disposal had made the business so difficult and expensive that Waste Disposal found it commercially impracticable to continue performance. After receiving this notification, Yamini contacted other waste disposal companies to determine if it could obtain alternative services. While two other companies are willing to enter into contracts with Yamini, both insist on a right of termination on 30 days' notice and demand that Yamini agree to indemnify them against any liability arising from the contract. (Yamini's contract with Waste Disposal does not have an indemnification provision.)

Yamini has asked your advice concerning its legal rights against Waste Disposal. In particular, Yamini wants to know whether it could require Waste Disposal to specifically perform the contract. What advice would you give?

PROBLEM 11-3

Albertson & Yee is a professional partnership of two doctors, Sally Albertson and Joanne Yee, engaged in the practice of medicine and specializing in dermatology. Albertson and Yee have decided to take in a third doctor, Ron Newsome, as an associate in the practice, with plans that he will eventually become a partner. The doctors have negotiated the terms of an employment contract, including salary and benefits. They have agreed that at the end of three years a decision will be made whether Newsome will be admitted as a partner. While Albertson and Yee expect that they will decide to admit Newsome into the partnership, they are concerned about the possible impact on their practice if they decide not to admit him, or if he leaves on his own, taking with him a number of their patients. Albertson and Yee want you to draft a provision for Newsome's employment contract to protect the partnership in the event Newsome leaves. Draft such a provision. In doing so you may obtain some guidance from form books such as Am. Jur. 2d, Legal Forms.

PROBLEM 11-4

Edith Evans owns and operates a private elementary school (the "Evans School") with approximately 200 students. In June 2017 Bryn Barnes enrolled her son, Kyle, in the Evans School and signed a contract agreeing to pay full tuition of $42,000 for the academic year. Tuition was payable in two equal installments, due in July and September. The written contract included a provision which read, "All tuition payments are nonrefundable and will be forfeited upon withdrawal from the Evans School for any reason whatsoever." The contract also had a clause stating, "This written contract contains the complete agreement of the parties."

In October 2017 the school sent a questionnaire form to all parents, including Bryn, inquiring if they had any skills they would be willing to perform for the school as a volunteer to help reduce school expenses. Bryn returned the form to the school, stating, "I build and design websites for a living." At the time, the Evans School had a very basic website.

After receiving Bryn's response, Edith asked Bryn to update the appearance of and make some new "posts" on the school's website. Bryn agreed and from November 2017 to May 2018, she spent about ten hours each month doing information technology (IT) work for the school. Bryn did not receive any monetary compensation for this work. In June 2018, Bryn re-enrolled Kyle for the 2018-2019 academic year, again signing a contract to pay yearly tuition of $42,000 in two installments. Bryn paid $21,000 at that time.

In August 2018 Edith told Bryn the school was planning to upgrade its IT systems in anticipation of an upcoming inspection by an accreditation committee and she wished to discuss how Bryn could help in that process. On August 21, Edith and Bryn met to discuss Bryn's possible role in improving the school's IT system. They discussed Bryn's educational background, work history, and qualifications. Edith told Bryn she wanted to improve the school's network and wireless system to allow use of iPads. Edith added that she wanted more interaction and communication with the parents through the school's website, and she wanted an upgraded electronic newsletter.

During the meeting, Edith said to Bryn, "This is a lot of work, and obviously, I wouldn't ask you to do this without some sort of arrangement of compensation." Edith told Bryn that with some other parents who perform services for the school, "we work out a tuition reimbursement." Edith explained she compensated other parents this way "for tax purposes." Bryn said that the value of her time to do all the tasks Edith had described would clearly exceed one year's tuition of $42,000, but Bryn also said that she was so happy with the school for her son that she would do the work for a tuition abatement of that amount, plus any expenses Bryn incurred. At Edith's request, Bryn sent her an e-mail the next day, outlining the services Bryn intended to perform. Bryn divided the work into three areas: website, network, and iPad rollout. Bryn described the work in each area in substantial detail. The email also stated, "The refund of Kyle's tuition for the year will be appreciated." Edith replied by e-mail, stating, "Terrific. A tall order, but let's go forward with this plan."

From September 2018 to the end of the academic year in June 2019, Bryn performed all the work described in her August 2018 e-mail. Bryn was also "the on-call IT person," receiving and responding to requests from students, parents, faculty, and staff about how to use certain computer applications and e-mail systems. She upgraded the school's newsletter and trained students to use the new applications. In materials submitted to the accreditation agency, the school referred to Bryn as its "Director of Information Technology." In the meantime, Bryn paid the 2018-2019 tuition balance of $21,000 for Kyle in September 2018 when billed. Bryn heard nothing from Edith about the tuition refund.

On July 1, 2019, Bryn went to the Evans School to sign the enrollment contract for Kyle for the 2019-2020 academic year. Before signing, Bryn told the school's financial manager that she was owed a rebate of the prior year's tuition and thus Bryn thought she should not need to pay for the coming year. The financial manager said he had not been informed about any tuition refund for Bryn and that he would speak with Edith about the tuition question.

On July 15, 2019, Bryn received a letter from the school's attorney, taking the position that the school did not agree to trade a tuition refund for Bryn's work. Responding, Bryn prepared an invoice, showing time spent and tasks performed under the August 2018 agreement pursuant to the email exchange with Edith. Bryn prepared the invoice by reviewing her e-mails, computer "log-ins," and other records to create an hourly spreadsheet showing the work she performed. The invoice totaled 1,247 hours, which Bryn said represented "everything that I did for the school over a 10-month period." Bryn billed her time at $100 per hour, the rate she charged in her business, and added $5,336 in costs she had advanced for travel, six iPads and other material, and certain internet fees.

The school refused to pay any part of Bryn's $130,036 invoice. When Bryn concluded the school was not going to honor the agreement, she enrolled Kyle in a different school for the 2019-2020 school year.

Bryn has now come to your law office and tells you all of the foregoing information. Bryn explains that she wants to bring suit against the Evans School for breach of August 2018 agreement and any related claims. Bryn also states that she wishes to claim payment for the work she did during Kyle's first year (2017-2018) at the Evans School. Bryn wants to know if she would be likely to succeed in a lawsuit and what remedies, if any, she might be able to recover. What is your assessment?

REVIEW QUESTIONS – CHAPTER ELEVEN

1. Cathy Coleman (CC) is an expert in refrigeration systems. Beginning in 2001, she was a salaried employee of Eezy Freezy, Inc. (EF), a manufacturer of refrigeration equipment for large commercial uses. CC had no written contract with EF, and worked on an at-will basis. Her salary steadily increased over time; by 2018 she was being paid by EF at an annual rate of $120,000. In late 2018, CC was offered a job by Absolute Zero, Inc. (AZ), a maker of household refrigerators and freezers, selling appliances in bulk to residential developers and large retail dealers. The offer was for a three-year full-time employment contract, with her compensation to be in the form of a 5% commission on all sales made by her annually up to $3,000,000. She would receive a $10,000 monthly advance against commissions to be earned. CC was assured that based on past experience of AZ sales agents she could easily make up to $3 million in annual sales, and also that if she was successful in making sales she would be considered for a stock bonus after one year. CC accepted the offer from AZ, and began working on Jan. 1, 2019, pursuant to a written contract signed by both parties. By the end of April, serious differences had developed between CC and AZ's vice-president in charge of sales. At the end of June 2019, CC had made sales of only $450,000 for AZ, and she was notified by AZ that her employment was being terminated for cause: insufficient productivity and refusal to follow established AZ procedures.

   It is now July of 2019. CC has inquired of EF whether her old job could be available to her again, but the answer was no. She is contemplating suing AZ for wrongful termination of her employment contract. A major issue in such a suit would obviously be whether AZ had sufficient legal cause to terminate her contract. Assuming CC could prevail on that issue, what damages could she expect to be awarded as the successful plaintiff?

   A. Damages for the period from July 1, 2019 to December 31, 2021 at the annual rate of $150,000, computed on the basis of 5% of $3 million in annual sales.
   B. Damages for the period from July 1, 2019 to December 31, 2021 at the annual rate of $120,000.
   C. Damages for the period from July 1, 2019 to December 31, 2021 at the annual rate of $150,000, offset by what she could reasonably earn at comparable employment during that period.
   D. Damages for the period from July 1, 2019 to December 31, 2021 at the annual rate of $120,000, offset by what she could reasonably earn from comparable employment during that period.

2. Assume the same facts as Question 1, except that AZ's offer to CC of a three-year contract did not include a sales commission as part of her compensation, but instead provided for a fixed annual salary of $100,000. CC decided to accept AZ's offer even though her salary at EF was higher, because a three-year contract with AZ would provide her with job security. But (as in

Question 1) CC was fired by AZ at the end of six months. Assuming again that AZ did not have sufficient cause to terminate her employment, what remedy could CC expect to receive in a lawsuit against AZ for wrongful termination?

A. Damages for the period from July 1, 2019 to December 31, 2021 at the annual rate of $100,000.
B. Damages for the period from July 1, 2019 to December 31, 2021 at the annual rate of $100,000, offset by what she could reasonably earn at comparable employment during that period.
C. Damages for the period from July 1, 2019 to December 31, 2021 at the annual rate of $120,000, offset by what she could reasonably earn at comparable employment during that period.
D. Reinstatement as an AZ employee at the annual salary rate of $100,000, computed from July 1, 2019.

3. Bonnie Berger is the owner of a popular barbeque restaurant in the city of Austen. On March 15, Bonnie made an oral agreement with Sara Smith, a local contractor, to build two customized "smokehouse sheds" on property in the rear of her restaurant. Bonnie already had plans for the two smokehouses of 10 feet by 20 feet with related equipment and storage bins. Bonnie and Sara agreed upon a price of $50,000 per smokehouse with 50% due at the beginning of construction of each smokehouse and the balance due upon completion of each unit. They agreed that Sara would complete the first unit before starting the second. The first smokehouse was to be completed by May 1 and the second smokehouse was to be completed by July 1. Sara started work on the first smokehouse on April 1 and Bonnie paid her $25,000 that week. Sara completed the first smokehouse on April 30 and gave an invoice to Bonnie for the $25,000 due upon completion. Before making that payment, Bonnie asked Sara when she would start the second smokehouse. Sara told Bonnie, "I just got a big cabinetry subcontract on an office building and I am not going to have time to build your second smokehouse. You need to get someone else." Bonnie then said, "I won't pay you another dime until you keep the contract to build the second smokehouse." After three months, Bonnie heard no more from Sara and got bids on the second smokehouse from two contractors who both quoted a price of $55,000. Bonnie comes to your law office and wants to know if she might be liable to Sara if Sara should bring suit for payment of the balance of $25,000 on the first smokehouse. Which of the following outcomes is most likely?

A. The agreement between Bonnie and Sara is not enforceable because it is not in a signed writing. Bonnie is entitled to a refund of her initial payment of $25,000 for the first smokehouse.
B. Sara committed a willful breach of the contract and therefore would not be able to recover any damages from Bonnie for nonpayment of the $25,000 balance for the first smokehouse.
C. Sara would be able to recover the $25,000 balance for the first smokehouse because she rendered substantial performance on a divisible part

of the contract, but would be liable to Bonnie for the additional cost of $5000 to build the second smokehouse.

D. Sara would be able to recover the reasonable value of her work on the first smokehouse, less the $25,000 she has been paid, without regard to the contract price.

4. Gateway Drug, Inc. (GD), is a corporation that owns and operates a national chain of retail pharmacies. Recently GD's staff competed a study showing that because of population growth in that area over the last five years, a new pharmacy on the west side of Smalltown would be a good investment, yielding profits at least at the average level for Gateway stores in that region of the country. GD's real estate agents identified in that area a three-acre lot of appropriate size and location for its proposed new store. The lot was owned by Rachel Robinson (RR), an elderly widow. RR had lived in a small house on that lot for over 25 years, but during that time the character of the neighborhood had changed from rural/residential to residential/commercial. After the death of her husband two years ago, RR began to feel the burden (financial and practical) of maintaining the house on her own, and finally decided to sell the property and move to live with her daughter in Capital City, some 200 miles to the east. After some negotiation, RR and GD's agents agreed that GD would buy RR's property for $455,000, the closing to be held within 60 days after the parties' signing of the agreement, at a time and place to be mutually agreed upon. The contract provided for a down payment of $25,000 by GD, with the balance to be paid at the closing. The agreement also provided that in the event the sale did not take place, RR would be entitled to retain the down payment as liquidated damages. GD's intention, of which RR was aware, was to demolish the house and erect on the lot a building suitable for a full-size retail pharmacy.

Six days after the signing of the contract, RR changed her mind about selling the property to GD, because she could not bear to think of her long-time home being demolished, and notified GD of this fact. Assuming that RR has committed a breach of this contract without legal excuse, which of the following statements is/are accurate description(s) of this situation?

A. GD will not be awarded specific performance, because RR is an elderly widow.

B. GD will not be awarded specific performance, because the parties have not made an agreement definite enough for a court to enforce specifically.

C. If GD seeks to recover full expectation damages including lost profits, it will be able to do so.

D. If GD is unable to recover lost profits because they are deemed too speculative, it should still be able to recover from RR both (1) its $25,000 down payment and (2) the difference between the contract price and the fair market value of the lot at the time of breach, if the latter is higher.

5. Assume all the facts in the first paragraph of Question 4, above. Assume also that six days after the signing of their contract, GD changed its mind about buying RR's property and repudiated their contract, because it had found an equally suitable property in the same general area for a substantially lower price, $400,000. Assuming that GD has thereby committed a breach of its contract with RR without legal excuse, which of the following statements is/are accurate description(s) of this situation?
   A. In a successful suit against GD for breach of contract, RR will (if she requests it) be awarded the remedy of specific performance.
   B. In a successful suit against GD for breach of contract, RR's remedy will include damages based on the difference between the sale price in their contract and the lower price that GD is going to pay for the other property.
   C. In a successful suit against GD for breach of contract, RR's remedy will include damages based on the difference between the sale price in their contract and the market value of the property at the time of GD's repudiation (if that latter figure is lower), plus incidental damages.
   D. If RR chooses to seek another buyer for her property, and finds one who is willing to pay $455,000 for it, she will have no effective damage claim against GD.

CHAPTER 12

Rights and Duties of Third Parties

In our study thus far of the various issues raised by the creation and enforcement of promissory obligations, we have been concerned almost entirely with the rights and obligations of the original parties — the ones who entered into the contract in question (or, in cases involving the protection of unbargained-for reliance, the promisor and promisee). In this chapter, we address the possibility that other persons may have rights or duties, or both, enforceable by or against them as a result of the making of contracts to which they were not themselves parties. Such persons are frequently referred to as "third parties," to distinguish them from the two persons who, by convention, are visualized as the original makers of a contract. (Of course, a contract may have any number of original parties, but two is the minimum for the making of either a contract or a promise.) In this chapter, we consider first the possibility that third-party rights may arise simply from the making of the original contract; then we discuss the extent to which the rights or duties of the original parties may be later "assigned" or "delegated" by them to other persons.

A. RIGHTS OF THIRD PARTIES AS CONTRACT BENEFICIARIES

In any system that allows persons to compete more or less freely for goods and services and to enter into binding contracts by which such commodities can be bought and sold, it is obvious that the making of a contract is often likely to have effects on persons who are not parties to it. If *A* agrees to construct a building on land owned by *B*, this building may have the practical effect of lessening the enjoyment or utility to *C* of an adjoining lot of land owned by her. In a loose sense, the "rights" of *C* in such cases may be adversely affected by the making of these contracts, if the word *rights* is used to mean simply the freedom to do as one pleases to the extent not forbidden by law. Such a characterization is not really accurate, however. When two persons contract, they do not ordinarily have the power under law to affect adversely any *right* of a person who is not a party to their contract, in the sense in which that word is usually employed by lawyers. In the above example if *C* actually had a legal right to the enjoyment of her property undiminished by the proximity of *B*'s building, then any invasion of those rights by *A* or *B* would be an actionable wrong — possibly a breach of contract, possibly a tort.

It does not follow from this proposition, however, that the parties to a contract should not be able, if they so desire, to *create* by contract a right in some third person. That was essentially the situation in the leading case of Lawrence v. Fox, decided by the New York Court of Appeals in 1859. In that case, plaintiff Lawrence had loaned money to one Holly; Holly later made a similar loan to Fox, who promised Holly that he (Fox) would make repayment to Lawrence. Fox did not keep that promise, however, and Lawrence sued Fox for the amount of the promised payment. Although Lawrence was not a party to the transaction between Holly and Fox — Lawrence was not in "privity" with Fox — the court nevertheless held that the cause of action would lie.

The court sought to justify the result by likening the case to ones in which the defendant had been a "trustee" of property under a trust created by another, with instructions to sell the trust property and convey the proceeds to the plaintiff. In such a case, the plaintiff as "beneficiary" of the trust would have the right to enforce the trust obligation against the promisor/trustee, should the latter fail to perform his promise to pay over those proceeds.

In Lawrence v. Fox, however, there was no property held in trust (no "res"), merely an in personam obligation imposed on the defendant by contract with the promisee. Nevertheless, a majority of the court held that the plaintiff could enforce the obligation created by that promise, as a kind of beneficiary of the right created by it. (Two judges concurred in the decision based on agency theory and two other judges dissented based on the lack of privity.) Lawrence v. Fox, 20 N.Y. 268 (1859). The majority opinion's analysis in *Lawrence* has been generally accepted, and the plaintiff in such cases is typically referred to as a "third-party beneficiary" of the defendant's promise.

In *Lawrence*, the promise sued on had its genesis in the promisee's desire to provide for the satisfaction of an obligation owed by him to a third party, the plaintiff Lawrence. Since the plaintiff in that case was a creditor of the promisee, the *Lawrence*-type plaintiff came to be called a "creditor beneficiary." (In §133(1)(b), the first Restatement defined the "creditor beneficiary" case as one where performance by the promisor would satisfy an "actual or supposed or asserted duty of the promisee to the beneficiary.")

In New York, it appeared during the latter part of the nineteenth century that recovery by third parties would be limited to the creditor-beneficiary case exemplified by Lawrence v. Fox. However, later decisions extended recovery to cases where the promisee had apparently sought to confer the benefit of the promisor's performance on a child, a parent, or some other member of the promisee's family. The 1918 New York case of Seaver v. Ransom has come to be the leading example of this latter type of case. In *Seaver* the promisee was Mrs. Beman, an elderly woman in ill health. Mrs. Beman was about to sign a will that had been prepared pursuant to her instructions by her husband, Judge Beman, when she realized that it made insufficient provision for a beloved niece. Mrs. Beman proposed that another will be prepared to remedy this omission, but it appeared that she might not live long enough to execute it. Judge Beman urged his wife to sign the will already prepared (which left him a life estate in certain real property), promising her solemnly that he would see that the niece was amply provided for in his own will. When Judge Beman himself later died, it was discovered that his will made no provision for the niece, and she therefore sued the Judge's estate to enforce the promise he had made to his dying wife.

The court pointed out that in similar cases a "constructive trust" had been imposed on the promisor's estate after his death; this was not feasible in *Seaver*, however, because his estate had not been enriched by the wife's actions. (Recall that Beman received only a life estate under his wife's will.) Nevertheless, the court allowed recovery by the niece, holding that the principle of Lawrence v. Fox should be extended to the facts of *Seaver*. In reaching this decision, the court observed that some earlier cases allowed third-party standing to children and wives on the basis of the "close relationship" they had with the promisee. Seaver v. Ransom, 120 N.E. 639 (N.Y. 1918). Many courts have since permitted third-party enforcement of promises where it appears that the promisee's intention was to make a gift to the plaintiff third party. Such plaintiffs are often referred to as "donee beneficiaries." (See the first Restatement §133(1)(a).)

The principle that a third party may have standing to recover on a contract is now universally accepted by American courts. See John E. Murray, Jr., Contracts §130[C], at 851 (5th ed. 2011). The Restatement (Second) continues its approval of this principle (§§302, 304), but the drafters attempted to deemphasize somewhat the distinction between "creditor" and "donee" beneficiaries, stating that the fundamental distinction is between "intended" beneficiaries (who enjoy a right of direct action) and "incidental" ones (who do not). Their aim apparently was to direct courts away from the somewhat mechanical application of those earlier categories, in the direction of more flexibility (particularly in the case of noncreditor beneficiaries, where "donative" intent in the altruistic sense may be lacking). See generally Harry G. Prince, Perfecting the Third Party Beneficiary Standing Rule under Section 302 of the Restatement (Second) of Contracts, 25 B.C.L. Rev. 919, 974-980 (1984).

This shift in emphasis is somewhat undercut by the appearance in §302(1)(a) and (b) of slightly altered versions of the old creditor and donee beneficiaries. See Comments *b* and *c*, and the Reporter's Note to §302 (stating somewhat ingenuously that the terms *creditor* and *donee beneficiary* are "not used"). From his survey of the cases decided since the appearance of §302, Professor Prince concluded in 1984 that its provisions had made relatively little impact on the courts' traditional approach to determining the ability of a third party to enforce a contract. 25 B.C.L. Rev. at 990-997. In a subsequent study, Professor

Eisenberg agreed that §302 preserves, in essence, the categorical aspects of the first Restatement; he also concluded that §302 adds an "intent to benefit" test that the courts had frequently used with little consistency because of inherent vagueness about how intent should be defined and proved. Melvin Aron Eisenberg, Third-Party Beneficiaries, 92 Colum. L. Rev. 1358, 1378-1384 (1992).

While third-party beneficiary doctrine is sometimes considered to be arcane, a recent study indicates that it is playing an increasingly important role in the law. Professors Alan Schwartz and Robert Scott found that economic actors are frequently forming networks, platforms, and other associations in which third party claims play an important role. They identify the following types of networks: credit cards, standard setting organizations, medical services, franchise networks, and construction projects. They discovered more than 1,400 cases in the decade between 2004 and 2014 that discussed the distinction between intended and incidental beneficiaries. Alan Schwartz & Robert E. Scott, Third Party Beneficiaries and Contractual Networks, 7 J. Leg. Analysis #2 (2015) (available online). See also George S. Geis, Broadcast Contracting, 106 Nw. U. L. Rev. 1153, 1156 (2012) (examining the widespread use of "broadcast contracting," which involves the "adoption of private agreements to create a heightened legal commitment to a defined class of third parties").

The cases that follow primarily address the threshold issue of third-party beneficiary standing. Apart from the determination of standing for third parties, other issues that may arise include the ability of the promisor and the promisee to vary the contract, the defenses that may be raised by the promisor in responding to an action by a third-party beneficiary, and the remedies that are appropriate in third-party beneficiary cases.

Vogan v. Hayes Appraisal Associates, Inc.

Supreme Court of Iowa 588 N.W.2d 420 (1999)

CARTER, Justice.

Hayes Appraisal Associates, Inc. (Hayes Appraisal), the defendant in the district court, had been hired by MidAmerica Savings Bank (MidAmerica) to monitor the progress of new home construction for plaintiffs, Susan J. Vogan and Rollin G. Vogan. The Vogans had obtained a construction loan from MidAmerica. The contractor defaulted after all of the original construction loan proceeds and a subsequent portion of a second mortgage loan had been paid out by the bank.

The Vogans recovered judgment against Hayes Appraisal on a third-party beneficiary theory based on its alleged failure to properly monitor the progress of construction, thus allowing funds to be improperly released by the lender to the defaulting contractor. The court of appeals reversed the judgment on the basis that erroneous progress reports by Hayes Appraisal were not the cause of any loss to the Vogans. After reviewing the record and considering the arguments of the parties, we vacate the decision of the court of appeals and affirm the judgment of the district court.

In June 1989 the Vogans moved to Des Moines. They wanted to build a home in West Des Moines. They met with builder Gary Markley of Char Enterprises, Inc. Markley agreed to build the home for $169,633.59. The Vogans contacted MidAmerica for a mortgage. MidAmerica orally contracted with Hayes Appraisal to do the initial appraisal and make periodic appraisals of the progress of the construction. The home, according to the plans, and lot were appraised at $250,000.

Thereafter, the Vogans obtained a $170,000 mortgage from MidAmerica. MidAmerica was to disburse progress payments to Markley based on progress reports received from Hayes Appraisal. On November 6, 1989, the Vogans purchased the lot for $66,000 with their own funds. Construction began on November 22, 1989. On December 28, 1989, Hayes Appraisal issued a progress report to MidAmerica that twenty-five percent of the home had been completed.

There were cost overruns on the job, and in February 1990 MidAmerica determined that there was less than $2000 remaining of the $170,000 loan proceeds. Markley determined that at this point it would take another $70,000 to complete the home. The Vogans then took out a second mortgage on the home for $42,050 and turned that money plus some of their own funds over to the bank to continue making progress payments to Markley based on Hayes Appraisal's progress reports. Prior to completion of the home, the Vogans decided to sell it rather than to occupy it.

On March 20, 1990, Hayes Appraisal certified that the home was sixty percent complete. Only eight days later, Hayes Appraisal issued another progress report indicating that ninety percent of the work had been completed on the home. During the trial, witnesses testified for the Vogans that this was an inaccurate report overstating the extent of the contractor's progress on the job. As late as October 1990, substantial additional work was required on the house. At this point, Markley defaulted on the job after having been paid all of the initial $170,000 and much of the additional monies raised by the Vogans. Another contractor estimated the completion of the home would cost an additional $60,000.

The Vogans stopped making mortgage payments, and MidAmerica brought an action to foreclose the mortgage. The Vogans counterclaimed, alleging that the bank had improperly authorized payment of funds to Markley. Allegedly, MidAmerica did not follow its loan procedure for disbursement of funds. At least thirty percent of the loan amount was to be retained until completion. An undisclosed settlement was reached in the litigation between Vogans and MidAmerica.

The Vogans then filed a petition against Hayes Appraisal, contending it negligently certified the extent of the construction that had been completed. Hayes Appraisal filed a motion for summary judgment, arguing, in part, that even if the March 28, 1990 appraisal was negligently issued, it could not have proximately caused harm to the Vogans because MidAmerica had already released most of the loan funds prior to receiving the March 1990 progress reports. The court denied the motion. On reconsideration, the court again denied the motion and stated that the Vogans' claims were based upon other oral and written appraisals that led to the disbursement of the additional money that had been raised to cover cost overruns.

The case proceeded to jury trial on a contract theory. The court denied Hayes Appraisal's motions for directed verdict in which it argued the Vogans were not third-party beneficiaries of its contract with MidAmerica and the March 1990 progress reports did not proximately cause the damages alleged. The jury returned a verdict for the Vogans. Hayes Appraisal's motion for judgment notwithstanding the verdict was denied.

Hayes Appraisal appealed. It contended the evidence was insufficient to prove the Vogans were third-party beneficiaries or that its conduct proximately caused any damage to the Vogans. It believed the trial court erred in failing to grant its motions for summary judgment, directed verdict, and judgment notwithstanding the verdict on these issues.

The court of appeals reversed. It concluded the March 1990 progress reports did not result in any damage to the Vogans because the bank had already released more funds than recommended in those reports. The court concluded the use of the appraisal was to manage the disbursement of only the $170,000 loan, not any monies above that amount. Based upon this disposition, the court of appeals did not address the third-party beneficiary issue. We granted further review.

I. Whether the Vogans Were Third-Party Beneficiaries of the Contract Between MidAmerica and Hayes Appraisal

A. Standard of Review

In assessing a motion for judgment notwithstanding the verdict, this court's only inquiry is whether there is sufficient evidence to justify submitting the case to the jury. Tredrea v. Anesthesia & Analgesia, P.C., 584 N.W.2d 276, 280 (Iowa 1998). If there is substantial evidence to support a plaintiff's claims, a motion for judgment notwithstanding the verdict should be denied. Id. Evidence is substantial when a reasonable mind would find the evidence presented adequate to reach the same findings. Id. In order to avoid a defendant's motion for judgment notwithstanding the verdict, a plaintiff must present more than a "mere scintilla of evidence." Id. . . . This court views the evidence in the light most favorable to the party against whom the motion was made and takes into consideration every legitimate inference that may fairly and reasonably be made. . . .

B. Arguments

The Vogans argue that they presented ample evidence to generate a jury question concerning whether they were third-party beneficiaries of the contract between MidAmerica and Hayes Appraisal. The Vogans assert that the court should look to the intent of the parties and the surrounding circumstances and argue that the bank's intent was to protect the Vogans' money as construction progressed. The Vogans claim that Hayes Appraisal knew they were owners of the property and that they would benefit from the progress reports.

Hayes Appraisal, however, claims that the verbal contract between MidAmerica and Hayes had no provision or intent to make the Vogans third-party beneficiaries. Hayes Appraisal claims that the Vogans presented no evidence of intent on behalf of the bank to benefit the Vogans and so failed to meet their burden of proof. Hayes Appraisal argues that this failure of proof entitles them to a directed verdict or judgment notwithstanding the verdict on this issue.

C. Analysis

This court has adopted the following principles from the Restatement (Second) of Contracts that are applicable to third-party beneficiary cases:

> (1) Unless otherwise agreed between promisor and promisee, a beneficiary of a promise is an intended beneficiary if recognition of a right to performance in the beneficiary is appropriate to effectuate the intention of the parties and either
> (a) the performance of the promise will satisfy an obligation of the promisee to pay money to the beneficiary; or
> (b) the circumstances indicate that the promisee intends to give the beneficiary the benefit of the promised performance.
> (2) An incidental beneficiary is a beneficiary who is not an intended beneficiary.

See *Tredrea,* 584 N.W.2d at 281 (quoting Restatement (Second) of Contracts §§302 (1979)) (emphasis added); Midwest Dredging Co. v. McAninch Corp., 424 N.W.2d 216, 224 (Iowa 1988) (same). This court has determined that the primary question in a third-party beneficiary case is whether the contract manifests an intent to benefit a third party. *Tredrea,* 584 N.W.2d at 281; *Midwest Dredging Co.,* 424 N.W.2d at 224. However, this intent need not be to benefit a third party directly. *Tredrea,* 584 N.W.2d at 281.

In *Tredrea* we explained

> [w]hen a contract is made, the two or more contracting parties have separate purposes; each is stimulated by various motives, some of which he may not be acutely conscious. . . . A third party who is not a promisee and who gave no consideration has an enforceable right by reason of a contract made by two others . . . if the promised performance will be of pecuniary benefit to [the third party] and the contract is so expressed as to give the promisor reason to know that such benefit is contemplated by the promisee as one of the motivating causes of his making the contract.

Id. at 281-282 (quoting 4 Arthur Linton Corbin, A Comprehensive Treatise on the Working Rules of Contract Law §776, at 15-16, 18 (1951)). In the present case, MidAmerica is the promisee, who stands to benefit from Hayes Appraisal's performance, and Hayes Appraisal is the promisor, who agreed to provide periodic inspections to the bank.

The promised performance of Hayes Appraisal to MidAmerica will be of pecuniary benefit to the Vogans, and the contract is so expressed as to give Hayes reason to know that such benefit is contemplated by MidAmerica as one of the motivating causes of making the contract. The inspection reports and invoices that Hayes

Appraisal provided MidAmerica contained not only the location of the project, but also the Vogans' name as the home purchasers. This information gave Hayes Appraisal reason to know that the purpose of MidAmerica obtaining the periodic progress reports from Hayes was to provide the Vogans with some protection for the money they had invested in the project. If we apply the *Tredrea* standard to these circumstances, the Vogans qualify as third-party beneficiaries of the agreement between MidAmerica and Hayes Appraisal.

II. Whether the Faulty Inspection Reports Were a Cause of Injury to the Vogans

The court of appeals determined that Hayes Appraisal did not cause any damage to the Vogans by reason of their faulty progress reports. That court found that the periodic completion reports submitted by Hayes Appraisal were only for purposes of disbursement of the initial $170,000 construction loan and did not pertain to the additional funds that the Vogans deposited with the bank for periodic disbursement to the contractor. The court of appeals concluded that the bank had already distributed the original $170,000 to the contractor prior to receiving the March 1990 periodic progress reports from Hayes Appraisal that were deemed to be erroneous.

Susan Vogan prepared a spreadsheet, admitted into evidence, that showed both debits and credits on the Vogans' construction account, including the monies added to the original $170,000. The Vogans testified that based on this analysis the bank disbursed a portion of the additional funds raised by the Vogans to cover cost overruns based on the March 1990 progress reports showing that the project was ninety percent completed.

Questions of proximate cause are ordinarily questions of fact that, only in exceptional cases, may be taken from the jury and decided as a matter of law. . . . We believe the facts that we have just detailed would permit the jury to find that the purpose of Hayes Appraisal's reports on the progress of the work was to assist the bank in disbursing all funds on deposit that were intended for application to the Vogans' home construction. Consequently, although the initial $170,000 construction loan might have been disbursed prior to the faulty completion estimate, the erroneous reporting of the project's completion in March 1990 caused the bank to disburse other funds of the Vogans that would have been retained had the report been accurate.

Consequently, we disagree with the conclusion of the court of appeals that the jury could not have found that Hayes Appraisal's faulty progress report caused any injury to the Vogans.

III. Whether the Vogans' Recovery Violates the Rule of Hadley v. Baxendale

Hayes Appraisal suggests that, even if its conduct could be found to be a proximate cause of injury to the Vogans, it should not be held liable for dissipation of any funds after the $170,000 construction loan had been exhausted. It bases this argument on the rule in Hadley v. Baxendale, 9 Exch. 341 (1854). In that case, the British Court of Exchequer stated:

> Where two parties have made a contract which one of them has broken, the damages which the other party ought to receive in respect of such breach of contract should be such as may fairly and reasonably be considered either arising naturally, *i.e.,* according to the usual course of things, from such breach of contract itself, or such as may reasonably be supposed to have been in the contemplation of both parties, at the time they made the contract, as the probable result of the breach of it. Now, if the special circumstances under which the contract was actually made were communicated by the plaintiffs to the defendants, and thus known to both parties, the damages resulting from the breach of such a contract, which they would reasonably contemplate, would be the amount of injury which would ordinarily follow from a breach of contract under these special circumstances so known and communicated.

Hadley, 9 Exch. at 344. We have approved this principle as a rule of Iowa law. . . .

In applying this rule to the circumstances of the present case, we are convinced that, to the extent the Vogans' recovery included sums advanced to Markley by the bank based on an inaccurate progress report from Hayes Appraisal, that element of recovery was not beyond Hayes' contemplation at the time its contract with the bank was made. If the bank had scrupulously honored its construction loan procedures and there had been no adjustments based on cost overruns, a substantial portion of the $170,000 construction loan would have been retained at the time that Hayes Appraisal inaccurately reported that the project was ninety percent completed. The portion of Vogans' recovery based on improper payments to the contractor by the bank thus did not violate the rule of Hadley v. Baxendale. Of course, much of the Vogans' recovery was for items of consequential damage. Hayes Appraisal has not lodged any challenge to the claims of consequential damage other than its general claim that the Vogans were not a third-party beneficiary of the bank's contract. We have previously rejected that contention.

We have considered all issues presented and conclude that the decision of the court of appeals should be vacated. We affirm the judgment of the district court.

Decision of Court of Appeals Vacated; District Court Judgment Affirmed.

NOTES AND QUESTIONS

1. *Whose intent determines standing?* Probably the most perplexing question involved in third-party beneficiary cases is determination of the intent necessary for a third party to be an intended beneficiary with rights under the contract. Restatement (Second) §302 is unclear. The section begins by indicating that the intention of both parties is necessary: "a beneficiary of a promise is an intended beneficiary if recognition of a right to performance in the beneficiary is appropriate to effectuate the *intention of the parties*" (emphasis added). But the section then focuses on the intention of the promisee: "(a) the performance of the promise will satisfy *an obligation of the promisee* to pay money to the

beneficiary; or (b) the circumstances indicate that the *promisee intends* to give the beneficiary the benefit of the promised performance" (emphasis added).

Three lines of authority have developed. Some courts have held that both the promisor and promisee must intend to give the third party rights under the contract. See Grigerik v. Sharpe, 721 A.2d 526 (Conn. 1998) (under dual intent standard, buyer of real property not third-party beneficiary of contract between seller and engineer to perform soil tests and design sewage system). Other courts have concluded that the intention of the promisee controls. See E. Allan Farnsworth, Contracts §10.3, at 658 (4th ed. 2004). Finally, a number of decisions hold that the promisor must know or at least have reason to know of the promisee's intent to benefit the third party, even if the promisor has no particular desire to confer a benefit on or create an obligation to the third person. See KMART Corp. v. Balfour Beatty, Inc., 994 F. Supp. 634, 637 (D.V.I. 1998) ("the increasingly more modern view hold[s] that it is enough that the promisor . . . understood that the promisee had an intent to benefit the third party"); Joseph M. Perillo, Contracts, §17.3, at 616 (7th ed. 2014) (modern cases require intent of promisee and promisor's knowledge of that intent). What test does the court use in *Vogan*? What arguments support each of the three positions?

Related to the question of whose intent controls is the issue of the nature of the benefit sufficient for a third party to be a beneficiary of a contract. The court in *Vogan* refers to the need for a "pecuniary benefit," but it might be argued that such a requirement is too restrictive. For example, the Restatement provides: "if the beneficiary would be reasonable in relying on the promise as manifesting an intention to confer a right on him, he is an intended beneficiary." Restatement (Second) §302, Comment *d*.

2. *Evidence of intent.* What evidence should be used to determine the intention of the parties? On occasion the contract will specifically confirm or negate standing for a third-party beneficiary. E.g., Buckhorn, Inc. v. Orbis Corp., 2015 U.S. App. Lexis 11409 (Fed. Cir.) (defendant in patent infringement case not entitled to recover attorney fees from plaintiff under indemnification provision in contract because that contract specifically denied third-party rights). Some courts have adopted a presumption that a third party is an incidental rather than an intended beneficiary. See Alan Schwartz & Robert E. Scott, Third Party Beneficiaries and Contractual Networks, 7 J. Leg. Analysis #2, at n.18 (2015) (available online). However, most cases indicate that in the absence of a clear contractual provision, a totality of the circumstances approach will often be used. Courts generally will consider the language and provisions of the agreement, the background of the contract, and considerations of fairness and practicality. One commentator has concluded that courts apply a "messy mix of strategies for giving content to the imprecise distinction between intended and incidental beneficiaries . . . that include a focus on the language of the promise, the intentions or purposes of the parties, vague notions of utility or fairness, and even less explicit assertions about the needs of various commercial settings." See George S. Geis, Broadcast Contracting, 106 Nw. U. L. Rev. 1153, 1167 (2012).

In light of these factors, how strong was the Vogan's claim for standing as an intended beneficiary? Recent developments in mortgage financing have highlighted the importance of the role played by professional appraisers of real estate. See generally Shelby D. Green, Re-appraising the Appraisers: Expanding Liability to Buyers and Borrowers in the Story of the 2008 Financing Industry Crisis, 25(6) Prob. & Prop. 10 (2011).

3. *Incidental beneficiaries.* In what may appear to be rather circular reasoning, the Restatement (Second) of Contracts §§302(2) and 315 provide, in essence, that an "incidental beneficiary" is a party who benefits from a contract between others but who is not an intended beneficiary. Illustration 16 to §302 provides an example of a party who is expected to benefit from a contract but clearly not intended by the contracting parties to have standing to enforce it:

> B contracts with A to erect an expensive building on A's land. C's adjoining land would be enhanced in value by the performance of the contract. C is an incidental beneficiary.

Cf. Devine v. Roche Biomedical Laboratories, 659 A.2d 868 (Me. 1995) (employee who received false positive drug test was not intended beneficiary of contract between employer and testing lab even though employee would clearly be affected by lab's breach; there was no evidence of intent to give employee standing to enforce contract); Daley v. Fryer, 30 N.E.3d 213 (Ohio Ct. App. 2015) (person who slipped and fell on natural accumulation of snow and ice outside of pharmacy was an incidental beneficiary of lease agreement between pharmacy and owner). See also Joseph M. Perillo, Contracts, §17-3, at 616 (7th ed. 2014) (observing that courts often determine third-party standing primarily on the basis of social and economic policy).

4. *Liability of attorneys for negligent will drafting.* Apart from "true creditor" and "true donee" cases, one can identify categories of recurrent third-party standing cases, including: will drafting contracts; construction contracts involving owners, contractors, and sureties; government contracts; and contracts affecting employees. See Harry G. Prince, Perfecting the Third Party Beneficiary Standing Rule under Section 302 of the Restatement (Second) of Contracts, 25 B.C.L. Rev. 919, 946-973 (1984). One frequently litigated issue is whether an intended beneficiary of a will or trust has standing as a third party beneficiary to sue an attorney for breach of contract with the testator or creator of the trust. While courts recognize that attorneys generally owe duties to their clients and not to third parties, the majority of courts have allowed such claims under limited circumstances. See, e.g., Paul v. Patton, 185 Cal. Rptr. 3d 830 (Ct. App. 2015) (discussing case law dealing with circumstances under which intended legatees or beneficiaries may sue attorney for malpractice or breach of contract). It should be noted that attorneys who engage in fraud can be held liable to third parties even without privity. See generally John P. Freeman & Nathan M. Crystal, Scienter in Professional Liability Cases, 42 S.C. L. Rev. 783 (1991).

5. *Defenses available to promisor.* Even if the court rules in favor of the plaintiff on the issue of third-party standing, this is not the end of the case. If a binding contract between the promisor and the promisee is not formed for any reason, such as lack of mutual assent or consideration, the promisor may raise this issue in a claim brought by the beneficiary. Restatement §309(1). In addition,

the claim of the beneficiary against the promisor is subject to any defense that the promisor could raise in a claim by the promisee, such as mistake, fraud, or impracticability of performance. Id. §309(2). The beneficiary must also prove that there has been a breach by the promisor. See Lucas v. Hamm, 364 P.2d 685 (Cal. 1961) (intended legatees had standing in tort and contract, but alleged error concerning obscure "rule against perpetuities" was mistake that might be made by lawyer using requisite level of skill, prudence, and diligence and thus was not a breach of contract). The third-party beneficiary's right may also be limited by provisions or conditions in the contract, such as the obligation to submit disputes to arbitration. See, e.g., Borsack v. Chalk & Vermillion Fine Arts, Ltd., 974 F. Supp. 293 (S.D.N.Y. 1997) (intended beneficiary of licensing contract must arbitrate dispute).

6. *Causation and foreseeability.* Having concluded that the Vogans were third-party beneficiaries of the contract between Hayes and MidAmerica, the court goes on to consider whether Hayes's breach of contract caused them damages and whether their damages were reasonably foreseeable at the time of contract formation under the doctrine of Hadley v. Baxendale. Chapter 10 examined these and other issues involved in determining damages. Is the remedial outcome in *Vogan* consistent with that discussion?

Chen v. Chen

Supreme Court of Pennsylvania 893 A.2d 87 (2006)

OPINION

Justice BAER.

We granted allowance of appeal to address a question of first impression before this Court concerning whether a child may bring suit or intervene in an action to enforce provisions of her parents' property settlement agreement. The Superior Court and the trial court below held that the child in this case could intervene in her mother's support action because the child was a third party intended beneficiary under her parents' property settlement agreement pursuant to the Restatement (Second) of Contracts §302, as adopted by this Court in *Guy v. Liederbach*, 501 Pa. 47, 459 A.2d 744 (1983). For the reasons that follow, we reverse.

Wheamei Chen ("Mother") and Richard Chen ("Father") were married on August 9, 1977. During the course of their six-year marriage, they had two children, Robert (Son), born in 1978, and Theresa (Daughter), born in 1982. At the time of the divorce in 1983, the parties entered into a property settlement agreement (the "Agreement"). The Agreement provided that Mother would have physical and legal custody of Daughter and that Father would have physical and legal custody of Son. The Agreement also contained the following provision:

> **9. Child Support**
> [Father] agrees and contracts to pay to [Mother] the sum of $25.00 per week as child support of the child, [Daughter] who will be in the custody of [Mother]. [Father] further agrees that upon obtaining regular employment or upon any

> increase in salary the aforementioned support award will be increased in accordance with the Northampton County Domestic Relations Guidelines. [Father] hereby waives, releases and renounces any and all claims to child support for [Son].

The Agreement was incorporated by reference but not merged into the divorce decree.

The parties do not contest that Father paid to Mother $25.00 weekly until Daughter's eighteenth birthday. Although Father obtained employment and increases in salary beginning in 1985, he never increased the amount of child support in accordance with the Domestic Relations Section Guidelines as specified in the Agreement. Furthermore, at no time did Mother seek an increase in the support amount.[1]

When Daughter turned eighteen in February 2000, the Domestic Relations Section of the Northampton County Court of Common Pleas notified Mother that support would be terminated. On April 27, 2000, Mother filed a petition for special relief in the Northampton County Court of Common Pleas requesting enforcement of the property settlement agreement and a finding of contempt of court. Mother sought to enforce the Agreement's provision for increases in child support and to collect "total support/arrearages" based upon Husband's salary increases over the almost eighteen years the agreement had been in effect and Father had been paying $25.00 per week. Petition for Special Relief, April 27, 2000, at 3.

On May 25, 2000, shortly after turning eighteen, Daughter filed a petition to intervene as a party to her mother's action. She asserted that intervention under Pa. R.C.P. 2327(4)[2] was appropriate because she had a "legally enforceable interest" as a third party intended beneficiary under the Agreement. Daughter relied upon this Court's adoption in *Guy* of the Restatement (Second) of Contracts §302 (Section 302), which expanded our prior rule that restricted an intended beneficiary's standing to recover under a contract to those contracts manifesting an express intention by the contracting parties to benefit the third party. See *Spires v. Hanover Fire Insurance Co.*, 364 Pa. 52, 70 A.2d 828 (1950). She contended that she satisfied the more liberal Section 302, which provides, in pertinent part, that "a beneficiary of a promise is an intended beneficiary if recognition of a right to performance in the beneficiary is appropriate to effectuate the intentions of the parties" and "circumstances indicate that

---

1. Mother testified that she ended the relationship days after Daughter's birth due to Father's physical abuse of Mother. Moreover, she asserted that she did not seek an increase in the support payments upon Father's employment due to her fear of Father. As noted in the body of the opinion, however, Mother quickly sought to enforce the relevant provision in April 2000, upon notification that the support would terminate due to Daughter reaching majority.

2. **Rule 2327. Who May Intervene:**

> At any time during the pendency of an action, a person not a party thereto shall be permitted to intervene therein, subject to these rules if . . .
>
> (4) the determination of such action may affect any legally enforceable interest of such person whether or not such person may be bound by a judgment in the action.

the promisee intends to give the beneficiary the benefit of the promised performance." Restatement (Second) of Contracts §302(1)(b).

On November 27, 2000, after conducting a hearing, the trial court found that the Daughter was an intended beneficiary to the Agreement and granted her petition to intervene. The court concluded that Daughter satisfied the *Guy* test because "recognition of [Daughter] as [an intended] beneficiary[5] to paragraph nine [of the Agreement] is appropriate to achieve what appears to be the parties' clear intention that the child support provision was to benefit [Daughter] throughout her minority." Tr. Ct. Order, Nov. 27, 2000, at 6.

After the trial court granted Daughter's intervention petition, Mother withdrew as party-petitioner, leaving Daughter and Father as party-opponents. A non-jury trial was held on January 28, 2002 on the merits of what was then Daughter's petition to enforce the Agreement. On June 28, 2002, the trial court entered an order in favor of Daughter and against Father. . . . The court calculated the amount of support allegedly due Mother from Father under the Domestic Relations Section Guidelines, subtracted the amount that had been paid by Father, and determined that Father owed $59,292.80. . . .

In a published decision affirming the trial court, the Superior Court observed that the specific question of whether a child can sue to enforce a support provision for her benefit based on her parents' property settlement agreement was an issue of first impression in the Commonwealth. *Chen v. Chen*, 840 A.2d 355, 359 (Pa. Super. 2003). To determine whether Daughter could enforce the provision as an intended beneficiary, the court applied the two-part test set forth in *Guy*:

(1) the recognition of the beneficiary's right must be "appropriate to effectuate the intention of the parties," and
(2) the performance must "satisfy an obligation of the promisee to pay money to the beneficiary" or "the circumstances indicate that the promisee intends to give the beneficiary the benefit of the promised performance."

Guy, 459 A.2d at 751. The Superior Court appropriately observed that this Court in *Guy* found that the application of the second part of the test was restricted by the first part, which implicated standing. See id.

Applying the test to the facts, the Superior Court found that Daughter was an intended beneficiary because Mother intended to give Daughter the benefit of the support payments and because "[t]he primary intent of the parties in paragraph [nine] of the [Agreement] was to help [Daughter] by providing for her financial support." *Chen*, 840 A.2d at 358. The court then determined that there was "nothing to prevent [Daughter] from enforcing her right under the

5. The trial court uses the term "third party beneficiary" rather than "intended beneficiary." We observe that the courts below and the parties, as well as some of this Court's precedent on which we rely today, have used the term "third party beneficiary" in reference to those third parties that have standing to enforce an agreement. See *Guy*, 459 A.2d at 751. We recognize that that term is merely a short hand reference to intended third parties beneficiaries who have the ability to enforce the agreement. We prefer to use the designations of intended and incidental beneficiaries, provided in Section 302, and will utilize the specific terms rather than the generalized "third party beneficiary."

[Agreement] to an increased amount of support based on her father's increased earning." Id. at 359.[10] In doing so, the court rejected Father's argument that Daughter had no direct right to the payments, but only to her parents' support. Father argued that Daughter received the benefit of the property agreement because she had led a "typical life." The Superior Court found this argument irrelevant to the question of breach of contract as claimed by Daughter, as the intended beneficiary. Although not stated by the Superior Court, one can infer that it believed that where Mother could have sought recovery regardless of whether Child had enjoyed a "typical life," so too could Daughter as an intervenor acting in Mother's stead. The Superior Court then reviewed the merits of Daughter's breach of contract claim, and affirmed the trial court's award of $59,292.

Father filed a petition for allowance of appeal, which we granted, limited to the question of whether the courts below erred in determining that Daughter was an intended beneficiary to her parents' settlement agreement. *Chen v. Chen*, 578 Pa. 433, 853 A.2d 1011 (2004). In his brief, Father maintains that although they obviously intended Daughter to benefit from the support obligations, neither Father nor Mother intended that Daughter be a direct recipient of cash payments. Consequently, Father contends that Daughter should have been denied intervention, because she was not an intended beneficiary of the payments. Father notes that the support guidelines . . . established by this Court pursuant to 23 Pa. C.S. §4322, do not provide for direct payment of funds between a parent and child, but rather provide for payment from the obligor to the custodial parent or guardian. Father asserts that if this Court upholds Daughter's intervention based on the Agreement's provision for increased payments to be made to Mother, we would open the door to a child suing one or both of her parents by equating the right to be supported with the right to support payments. Because he concludes that neither parent intended Daughter to receive the payments dollar for dollar, we read his argument to assert that Daughter is an incidental rather than intended beneficiary under the test set forth in Section 302.

Daughter counters that the trial court appropriately granted intervention to her as an intended beneficiary of her parents' agreement. In support, Daughter cites cases from other jurisdictions allowing children to enforce provisions of their parents' settlement agreements.[12] Without directly addressing whether she meets the test under the first part of *Guy* regarding the appropriateness of granting standing to third parties, she contends that to deny her the opportunity to intervene as a third party would be to treat children differently than other parties who meet the *Guy* test. She maintains that as an intended beneficiary she is

10. The Superior Court noted that some of our sister states have allowed children to enforce their parents' separation greements. . . .

12. Daughter cites several cases from our sister states . . . . [H]owever, . . . Daughter's cases are distinguishable from the case at bar. Many of the cases cited by Daughter involve provisions that involve special circumstances or agreements to provide a benefit directly to the children such as trust funds, insurance, or college education. . . .

able to intervene to enforce the Agreement.[13] Daughter therefore requests that this Court affirm the holdings of the trial court and the Superior Court.

Initially, we observe, as did the Superior Court, that whether a child is an intended or incidental beneficiary to the provisions of her parents' separation agreement regarding child support is a question of first impression in Pennsylvania, and is a pure question of law. Accordingly, our standard of review is *de novo*, and our scope of review is plenary. . . .

As previously noted, intervention by a person not a party to an action is appropriate where the determination of the action "may affect any legally enforceable interest of such person whether or not such person may be bound by a judgment in the action." Pa. R.C.P. 2327(4). Daughter asserts that she has a "legally enforceable interest" as an intended beneficiary to her parents' separation agreement.

To determine whether Daughter has a legally enforceable interest, we must evaluate the Agreement pursuant to contract principles because property settlement agreements incorporated but not merged into divorce decrees are considered independent contracts, interpreted according to the law of contracts. See *Nicholson v. Combs*, 550 Pa. 23, 703 A.2d 407, 412 (1997). "A fundamental rule in construing a contract is to ascertain and give effect to the intent of the contracting parties." *Mace v. Atlantic Refining Mktg. Corp.*, 567 Pa. 71, 785 A.2d 491, 496 (2001). "It is firmly settled that the intent of the parties to a written contract is contained in the writing itself. When the words of a contract are clear and unambiguous, the meaning of the contract is ascertained from the contents alone." Id. (citations and internal quotation marks omitted).

Our review of the Agreement is controlled by this Court's precedent regarding standing of third party beneficiaries. Before 1983, we relied exclusively upon the test set forth in *Spires*, 364 Pa. 52, 70 A.2d 828, holding that a person has standing to enforce provisions of a contract as an intended beneficiary only if both contracting parties "have expressed an intention that the third party be a beneficiary and that intention must have affirmatively appeared in the contract itself." *Scarpitti v. Weborg*, 530 Pa. 366, 609 A.2d 147 (1992). As the relevant paragraph nine of the Agreement in the case at bar does not contain an express intention to designate Daughter as an intended beneficiary of the child support payments to be paid to Mother, Daughter would fail to meet the *Spires* test.

Daughter, however, argues that she meets the less strict test enunciated by this Court in *Guy*. As previously noted, in *Guy*, we adopted the two-part test set forth in the Restatement (Second) of Contracts §302 for distinguishing intended beneficiaries from incidental beneficiaries, who cannot enforce the provisions of a contract. We concluded that the first part of the test sets forth a standing requirement that leaves "discretion with the court to determine whether recognition of [intended] beneficiary status would be appropriate," while the second part of the test defines "the two types of claimants who may be intended as third party beneficiaries." *Scarpitti*, 609 A.2d at 150.

13. There is no doubt Mother could have enforced her agreement with Father, subject to any relevant defenses including the statute of limitations. . . . As Mother voluntarily withdrew as a party-plaintiff, her claims are not before us.

We agree with the courts below and with Daughter that "circumstances indicate that [Mother] intend[ed] to give [Daughter] the benefit of the promised performance" as required by the second part of the *Guy* test, corresponding to Section 302(1)(b).[15] The question in this case concerns the standing portion of the test — whether recognition of a right in Daughter to seek performance of the provision to increase Father's weekly payments upon employment in accordance with the support guidelines is "appropriate to effectuate the intentions of the parties." *Guy*, 459 A.2d at 751.

This question implicates competing policy considerations. In favor of Daughter's position, the Legislature and the courts often have expressed the obligation of parents to support their children. See, e.g., 23 Pa. C.S. §4321(2) ("Parents are liable for the support of their children who are unemancipated and 18 years of age or younger."). Moreover, our Legislature has empowered this Court to set forth child support guidelines, in part to provide apportionment of the financial burdens of child support between the parents. . . . This Court also has stressed the importance of protecting the best interests of children through child support in its willingness to abandon contract principles in the application of support agreements where the agreed upon support amount is insufficient. See *Nicholson*, 703 A.2d at 412 . . . The peculiar best interests of a child passing through life's changes are not implicated in the proceeding at bar, however, because Daughter is grown. While we recognize that a lump sum award would be helpful to Daughter as she starts her adult life, this case nonetheless does not involve the same concerns underlying our requirement that parents provide ongoing support for children during their minority.

This case also raises parents' fundamental right to direct the care, custody, and control of their children. . . . As a society, we allow parents to make decisions concerning how to allocate their incomes between savings and spending, between themselves and their children, and between individual children. While parents may include their children in discussions of expenditures, especially as children age, the final decision regarding the family's budget is for the parent or parents.

A parent's control of the family's finances applies both to intact and divorced families. In this Court's collective experience, we have never seen a parental agreement or a court order providing for a non-custodial parent to pay generalized child support directly to a minor child. It stretches credibility to believe that parents would entrust a twelve-year-old, to say nothing of a four-year-old, with control of support payments. Instead, agreements and orders direct the non-custodial parent to pay support monies to the custodial parent. The rationale behind this is obvious: parents are better equipped to utilize support payments and to decide what is best for their children than are children

15. The parties have not discussed whether Daughter would satisfy Section 302(1)(a), which requires that "performance of the promise will satisfy an obligation of the promisee to pay money to the beneficiary." As it informs our consideration of the standing portion of the *Guy* test which considers the appropriateness of a beneficiary's right to performance of the contract, we note that Daughter would not satisfy Section 302(1)(a) because Mother is not obligated to "pay money" to Daughter but rather is obligated to support Daughter. Moreover, Father, as promisor, is not paying Mother, as promisee, money to satisfy Mother's obligation to support daughter, but rather to satisfy his own obligation to support his child.

themselves. Moreover, as a society, we assume that custodial parents will use the support payments as part of the custodial family budget as the parent sees fit, whether it be through direct expenditures for the child's clothing or extracurricular activities or on provisions for the benefit of the whole family. As a general rule, we do not put strings on the custodial parent's use of the money, confident that a parent's natural love will guide his or her motives as the family finances are apportioned among the many competing opportunities.

Along this same vein, . . . many courts are reluctant, absent unusual circumstances such as the death of a parent, to allow children to enforce their parents' agreements where the custodial parent was a signatory to the agreement and the designated recipient of the payments. See *Forman v. Forman*, 17 N.Y.2d 274, 270 N.Y.S.2d 586, 217 N.E.2d 645 (1966) (noting policy reasons in favor of not allowing children to enforce periodic support provisions of their parents' separation agreements absent special circumstances, but allowing children to enforce provisions for their direct benefit such as the establishment of life insurance policies) . . . . This reluctance is often rooted in a desire "to promote familial harmony and foster the parent-child relationship," neither of which are served when a child litigates support obligations against a parent. *Drake v. Drake*, 89 A.D.2d 207, 455 N.Y.S.2d 420, 424 (N.Y. App. Div. 1982) (holding that child did not have standing as third party beneficiary to enforce separation agreement relating to periodic support payments, but noting the children may enforce specific provisions made exclusively for their benefit such as promises to pay college tuition or in unusual situations such as the death or disability of the custodial parent).

We too refuse to enable a child to enforce her parents' settlement agreement where, as here, the agreement provides for support payments to the custodial parent. To construe the Agreement as providing Daughter a direct interest in the individual payments as opposed to support generally could open a Pandora's Box. Such a ruling could allow every child of divorced parents whose property agreement contained a provision for child support to bring suit against one or both parents, challenging the parents' compliance with the terms of the agreement. Indeed, such standing could allow a child as an intended beneficiary of the actual periodic support payments and not merely the beneficiary of support the right to demand from the payee-parent a dollar for dollar accounting of moneys paid for support pursuant to a separation agreement.

Accordingly, we conclude that strong public policy favors denying a child standing to seek the specific dollars one parent owes the other for the child's generalized support pursuant to a separation agreement, absent special circumstances such as a direct designation that a benefit be paid to the child or the custodial parent's inability to enforce the agreement due to death or disability. In doing so, we protect parents' rights to contract specifically for the direct payment of benefits to a child should they conclude that their circumstances warrant such a provision, but refuse to transform general language, providing a child with support by way of payments to one parent, into a provision permitting a child to claim direct payment from the payor-parent or a specific accounting from the payee-parent. While Mother and Father clearly intended to provide support for Daughter, they did not intend for her to receive payments directly. Instead, the Agreement left Mother to exercise her prerogative as a parent to direct the care, custody, and control of Daughter, and determine how to best use the support funds provided by Father. We will not rewrite the Agreement to provide otherwise. In doing so, we hold that Daughter is not an intended beneficiary under Section 302 and *Guy* because recognition of Daughter's right to performance is not "appropriate to effectuate the intention of the parties."

Based on the foregoing, the courts below erred in concluding that Daughter had a legally enforceable interest to justify intervention pursuant to Pa. R.C.P. §2327. Accordingly, we reverse.

Justice NEWMAN joins the majority opinion.

Former Justice NIGRO did not participate in the decision of this case.
Chief Justice CAPPY files a concurring opinion.
Justice CASTILLE files a concurring opinion.
Justice SAYLOR files a concurring opinion in which Justice EAKIN joins.

Chief Justice CAPPY, Concurring.

I join the Majority Opinion insomuch as it resolves this matter on principles of contract law. I, however, respectfully disassociate myself from the Majority's reliance on principles outside of contract law and its consideration of issues outside the scope of the issue to which this Court limited its review. See, e.g., Maj. Op. at 586 Pa. 308-311, 893 A.2d at 94-95 (discussing competing policy considerations); id. at 302-303, n.8, 893 A.2d at 90, n.8 (commenting on the trial court's calculation of child support).

Justice CASTILLE, Concurring.

I concur in the result since I believe that Theresa Chen ("Daughter") was not an intended beneficiary of her parents' property settlement agreement. I am in agreement with Chief Justice Cappy's Concurring Opinion that the Majority unnecessarily relies on principles outside of contract law in disposing of the issue presented, see Maj. Op. at 586 Pa. 308-311, 893 A.2d at 94-95, and considers extraneous issues unrelated to the limited issue upon which this Court granted review. . . . In my opinion, the issue presented in this case is easily resolved by a straightforward application of the two-part test presented in the Restatement (Second) of Contracts §302, as adopted by this Court in *Guy v. Liederbach*, 501 Pa. 47, 459 A.2d 744 (1983).

Like the Majority, I agree that Daughter satisfies the second prong of the §302 test because Wheamei Jenq Chen ("Mother"), as promisee, intended to give Daughter the benefit of the promised performance, i.e., the $25.00 weekly child support payments from Richard Chen ("Father"). See Restatement (Second) of Contracts §302(1)(b). I also agree that the central issue in this case concerns the first prong of the §302 test — whether recognition of a right to performance in Daughter is appropriate to effectuate the intention of the parties. See id. §302(1). In actually resolving this issue, however, the Majority, rather than applying this prong to the underlying facts, needlessly considers competing policy considerations in concluding that, "strong public policy favors denying a child standing to seek the specific dollars one parent owes the other for the child's generalized support pursuant to a separation agreement, absent special circumstances. . . ." Maj. op. at 586 Pa. 309-311, 893 A.2d at 95.

I believe that, based on the unambiguous words of the property settlement agreement, Mother and Father clearly intended for Mother to receive the child support payments for the benefit of Daughter, not for Daughter to be the direct recipient of the payments. Accordingly, Daughter is not an intended beneficiary under §302; rather, she is an incidental beneficiary. That is enough to decide this case and require reversal.

Justice SAYLOR, Concurring

Because the contract at issue is a child support agreement, it seems evident to me that Daughter was the intended beneficiary, at least during her minority. . . . Therefore, I am not as certain as the majority that it is appropriate to rely exclusively upon ordinary contract principles to resolve the specific question of whether Daughter had standing to sue Father to enforce the contract's terms. It seems to me that that essential question amounts to one of public policy resolvable even in the absence of the overlay provided by Section 302 of the Restatement of Contracts. Because I agree that, as a policy matter, minor children should not be accorded standing to initiate such legal actions absent express statutory authority, see Majority Opinion at 586 Pa. 308-313, 893 A.2d at 94-96, I join the majority opinion subject only to the above thoughts.

Justice EAKIN JOINS this concurring opinion.

NOTES AND QUESTIONS

1. *Competing bodies of law and policy.* The judges who decided the *Chen* case appear to agree on denying to the plaintiff a direct right of action on her father's promise, but they disagree among themselves as to the reasons for that result. Writing for the court, Justice Baer bases his opinion on prior Pennsylvania case law, the rule of Restatement (Second) of Contracts §302, and the state's public policy as to parents' responsibility for the support of their minor children; Justice Newman simply concurs. However, Justices Cappy and Castille while agreeing with the outcome disapprove of Justice Baer's reliance on principles of child support policy, while Justices Saylor and Eakin appear to feel that plaintiff could possibly be deemed an intended beneficiary under contract principles, but should still be denied her action because of other policy considerations. Based on the facts as recounted in the court's opinion, would you favor allowing the plaintiff her right to sue as an intended beneficiary of her parents' agreement? Why? If not, which arguments do you regard as decisive?

2. *Vesting of rights of third-party beneficiaries.* An important question concerning third parties is at what time the rights of an intended beneficiary "vest" and are therefore no longer subject to change by agreement of the promisor and promisee. The first Restatement of Contracts §142 provided that the rights of a donee beneficiary vested immediately upon the making of the contract,

but §143 stated that the rights of a creditor beneficiary did not vest until there was reliance. Given that Restatement (Second) §302 discards the distinction between creditor and debtor beneficiaries, §311 makes a complementary change by treating vesting for all intended beneficiaries essentially the way that creditor beneficiaries were treated under the first Restatement. Unless the contract prohibits modification by the promisor and promisee, §311 permits variation of the rights of the intended beneficiaries until the third party does one of three things: manifests assent at the invitation of the promisor or promisee, materially changes position in justifiable reliance on the promise, or brings suit on the promise. See Olson v. Etheridge, 686 N.E.2d 563 (Ill. 1997) (adopting §311). Contra Biggins v. Shore, 565 A.2d 737 (Pa. 1989) (immediate vesting of donee's rights found in First Restatement is more consistent with concept of gift than position of Second Restatement).

3. *Special requirements for third-party beneficiaries of government contracts.* Restatement (Second) §313 sets forth special rules making it more difficult for plaintiffs to establish they are third-party beneficiaries of government contracts. These appear to be concerned primarily with liability to third parties for consequential damage: A promisor contracting with a governmental entity may not reasonably expect to assume liability to members of the public who may be affected by a breach. The classic case dealing with this situation is H. R. Moch Co. v. Rensselaer Water Co., 159 N.E. 896 (N.Y. 1928), which appears as the following illustration in the Restatement:

> B, a water company, contracts with A, a municipality, to maintain a certain pressure of water at the hydrants on the streets of the municipality. A owes no duty to the public to maintain that pressure. The house of C, an inhabitant of the municipality, is destroyed by fire, owing to B's failure to maintain the agreed pressure. B is under no contractual duty to C.

Restatement (Second) §313, illus. 2. While some cases have reached contrary conclusions, most jurisdictions follow *Moch.* See, e.g., Clay Elec. Coop., Inc. v. Johnson, 873 So. 2d 1182 (Fla. 2003) (courts almost uniformly hold that utilities are not liable for nonfunctioning street lights, relying on *Moch*). In explaining in Comment *a* to §313 its continued adherence to the result in *Moch*, the Restatement (Second) identifies as relevant factors "arrangements for governmental control over the litigation and settlement of claims, the likelihood of impairment of service or of excessive financial burden, and the availability of alternatives such as insurance."

In some cases involving government benefit programs of various types, courts have been asked to allow individuals to sue as direct beneficiaries of contracts between a governmental unit and some private entity, to enforce the latter's promises of performance that would have benefited the plaintiffs in some way. Sometimes these efforts have been successful. E.g., Zigas v. Superior Court, 174 Cal. Rptr. 806 (Ct. App. 1981), *cert. denied*, 455 U.S. 943 (1982) (tenants could sue landlord to recover rent overcharges above amounts permitted by financing agreement between federal Department of Housing and Urban Development and landlord).

In his article, The Property in the Promise: A Study of the Third Party Beneficiary Rule, 98 Harv. L. Rev. 1109, 1176-1192 (1985), Professor Anthony Jon Waters analyzed *Zigas* and other cases as involving a new kind of "property," the right to various "statutory entitlements" created by federal laws affecting housing, education, welfare, and other public programs. For a more pessimistic analysis after Congress enacted welfare reform legislation in 1996, see Wendy Netter Epstein, Contract Theory and the Failures of Public-Private Contracting, 34 Cardozo L. Rev. 2211 (2013).

PROBLEM 12-1

Sandra Carson is the creator of a social media app for users of city bikes marketed by various companies. Having developed a fairly large following of 100,000 users, Sandra is now monetizing the app through advertising for restaurants, bars, etc., and the sale of various products for the biking community. Her company is named Biking4ever, LLC.

Sandra has agreed to sell her app to NewTech Investors, LLC, a company that acquires a portfolio of technology-related investments and capitalizes on the synergies among these companies, for $8 million. The principal owner of NewTech is Greg Bronson. The sale from Sandra to NewTech is contingent on NewTech obtaining financing for the acquisition. Bronson has financing arrangements with several hedge funds. One of the funds, Nakamoto Management, has agreed to finance NewTech's acquisition of Sandra's company.

Nakamoto issued a letter of intent to NewTech. The letter states "Nakamoto is delighted to confirm its decision to finance NewTech's acquisition of Biking4ever, LLC, or its assets in accordance with the terms of this letter of intent." The letter of intent provides a number of conditions to its agreement to close financing of the purchase. Among the conditions are the following:

> "Within sixty (60) days, NewTech must present to Nakamoto proof satisfactory to Nakamoto
>
> (1) of ownership by Biking4ever, LLC, of the intellectual property necessary to the operation of the Biking4ever app; and
>
> . . .
>
> (8) that Biking4ever has at least 95,000 genuine, nonduplicative members.

Greg and Sandra worked diligently to meet the conditions for the financing, in particular conditions (1) and (8) listed above. Both were disappointed, however, when Nakamoto informed them that their submissions did not meet the contractual conditions. In particular, Nakamoto stated that Greg and Sandra had failed to present certifications from independent auditors about both of these conditions. Greg and Sandra objected to Nakamoto's refusal to go forward with the financing. They noted that the contract did not call for independent, certified audits; that such audits were expensive (often costing more than $50,000); and that such audits could not have easily been accomplished within the 60-day period. Nonetheless, Nakamoto rejected these objections and has confirmed its refusal to finance the acquisition. Greg has expressed to

Sandra his regret that they could not do business together, but he has decided to move on to other opportunities.

(A) Sandra has consulted you for advice about her rights and the rights of her company against Nakamoto. (She does not want to sue Greg and NewTech even if there might be a nonfrivolous basis for a claim against him.) Analyze the rights of Sandra and her company, Biking4ever, LLC (You may treat these together as a single claim.) against Nakamoto for breach of contract. In analyzing their rights, please review material in Chapters 2 and 6 as well as the material in this chapter.

(B) If you were counsel for Nakamoto, what drafting suggestions could you make to Nakamoto?

B. ASSIGNMENT AND DELEGATION OF CONTRACTUAL RIGHTS AND DUTIES

As has been the case with other aspects of contract law discussed in these pages, we must begin by treating in a few sentences what took the English courts of law and equity hundreds of years and gallons of ink to accomplish. Just as a long period of growth proved necessary before the courts were willing to enforce the executory bilateral agreement, so there was an initial resistance on their part to the notion that rights of parties to any contract might be transferred, or "assigned," to persons not originally privy to the agreement. In the postfeudal age, when wealth and power were still largely bound up in land, it was undoubtedly natural to think of any contract as creating an essentially personal relationship between individuals, not as giving rise to rights that could be handed from person to person like cabbages. With the growth of mercantile capitalism, it became increasingly apparent that wealth could come from the production and distribution of goods, and also from the financing of such activity; the corporation, whose shareholders enjoy limited liability for corporate obligations, came to be the typical vehicle for such commercial enterprise. In such an environment, it became easier to think of a contract right — particularly the right to a payment of money — as constituting a kind of property, which could itself be the subject of sale or exchange.

Consider, for example, the merchant. One who sells goods is likely to find that more goods are sold, and sold more quickly, if credit is extended to buyers, allowing them to take delivery now and pay later. Of course, selling on credit requires the merchant to run the risk of getting no payment at all (although that risk may seem minimal in the case of customers whose solvency and integrity are beyond question); it also involves a delay in receipt of payment in any case. Since procuring more stock in trade may require cash, however, the merchant who sells on credit may be in a bind — may have, as we say, a "cash-flow" problem. One solution is to find someone who is willing to buy the credit accounts, for cash; this purchase will ordinarily be at something less than the face value of those accounts, to reflect the burden of collection and the risk of default. Or, the merchant may find a bank or other financer willing to lend money (to be repaid with interest) against the security of the accounts receivable (using them as "collateral"). Assignability of contract rights can thus serve as a lubricant to the production-distribution process. Indeed, in a modern credit economy, the availability of credit to commercial and consumer buyers and borrowers is more than just a lubricant; it has become an essential part of the economic machinery. However, for such transactions as these to be part of the accepted mode of doing business, they will generally require the backstop of potential legal enforceability by the "assignee" — the one to whom the merchant's accounts have been sold or pledged.

Given the commercial justification for assignability (at least of money obligations), it is not surprising that the English courts eventually came around to the notion that contract rights were indeed assignable. Equally unsurprising should be the fact that this process was long and tortuous, involving the interplay of law and equity courts and the use of legal fictions. Today in every American jurisdiction it is generally true that the assignee of a contract right may bring suit to enforce the assigned right; indeed, statutes or rules of court usually *require* that such a suit be brought in the name of the "real party in interest," the assignee.

Before proceeding to survey some of the ramifications of contract transferability, we should first note the terminology employed in this area, as developed in the writings of Professor Corbin and others. See Arthur L. Corbin, Assignment of Contract Rights, 74 U. Pa. L. Rev. 207 (1926). As we know, bilateral contracts create both "rights" and "duties" (both parties having one or more of each). A contract *right* (i.e., the ability to require the other party either to perform or to pay damages) can today be "assigned." Restatement (Second) §317(2). Such an assignment at once creates in the assignee a new right, while at the same time extinguishing the corresponding right previously held by the assignor. Restatement (Second) §317(1). The assignment of a right is thus in practical effect a transfer in the true sense: It results in the moving of something from one person to another, just as does the passing of a football or a baton.

The transferring of a contractual *duty*, however, is quite another matter. In many cases, a person who is subject to a duty of performance may properly "delegate" that duty, that is, may satisfy it by employing others to perform it for her. Restatement (Second) §318(1). (This is particularly true of a corporation, whose every performance must obviously be through agents of some kind.) Such delegation of performance is not always permissible, however; whether it is will depend in a given case on the degree to which individual performance was called for by the contract that created the duty in question. Restatement (Second) §318(2). In any event, the mere procuring of a substitute to render performance — even in a case where such delegation of performance is proper — does not by itself extinguish the duty of performance created by the contract. The person originally bound to perform will remain subject to that duty (unless released by the obligee) until performance is actually rendered. Restatement (Second) §318(3). Do you see why this should be so? The essential difference between assignment and delegation lies here, in its effect on the original party. If assigning a right is like passing a football, then delegating a duty resembles more the communication of a catchy tune or a bad cold: Passing it on is not the same as getting rid of it.

In any case where assignment or delegation has been attempted by one or both of the original contracting parties, sorting out the rights and duties of all concerned can be a complicated process. First, you must ascertain the nature of what has been done (or attempted): Was it an assignment of rights? A delegation of duties? Or both? Next, you must test its validity against the terms of the contract itself and also against any other applicable rules of law. As we shall see, an assignment or delegation may be improper even if not expressly forbidden by the terms of the original contract. Conversely, it may in some cases achieve its intended result — may be "effective," to use the terminology suggested by Restatement (Second) §317, Comment *a* — even though the terms of the contract *do* expressly forbid it. If the assignment or delegation is indeed effective, this will create a new set of rights and duties among three persons: the assigning/delegating party; the other original party to the contract; and the new, third party. The cases below illustrate some of the complexities of sorting out these rights and duties, under the rules of the common law and the UCC.

Herzog v. Irace

Maine Supreme Court 594 A.2d 1106 (Me. 1991)

BRODY, Justice.

Anthony Irace and Donald Lowry appeal from an order entered by the Superior Court (Cumberland County, Cole, J.) affirming a District Court (Portland, Goranites, J.) judgment in favor of Dr. John P. Herzog in an action for breach of an assignment to Dr. Herzog of personal injury settlement proceeds[1] collected by Irace and Lowry, both attorneys, on behalf of their client, Gary G. Jones. On appeal, Irace and Lowry contend that the District Court erred in finding that the assignment was valid and enforceable against them. They also argue that enforcement of the assignment interferes with their ethical obligations toward their client. Finding no error, we affirm.

The facts of this case are not disputed. Gary Jones was injured in a motorcycle accident and retained Irace and Lowry to represent him in a personal injury action. Soon thereafter, Jones dislocated his shoulder, twice, in incidents unrelated to the motorcycle accident. Dr. Herzog examined Jones's shoulder and concluded that he needed surgery. At the time, however, Jones was unable to pay for the surgery and in consideration for the performance of the surgery by the doctor, he signed a letter dated June 14, 1988, written on Dr. Herzog's letterhead stating:

1. This case involves the assignment of proceeds from a personal injury action, not an assignment of the cause of action itself.

> I, Gary Jones, request that payment be made directly from settlement of a claim currently pending for an unrelated incident, to John Herzog, D.O., for treatment of a shoulder injury which occurred at a different time.

Dr. Herzog notified Irace and Lowry that Jones had signed an "assignment of benefits" from the motorcycle personal injury action to cover the cost of surgery on his shoulder and was informed by an employee of Irace and Lowry that the assignment was sufficient to allow the firm to pay Dr. Herzog's bills at the conclusion of the case. Dr. Herzog performed the surgery and continued to treat Jones for approximately one year.

In May, 1989, Jones received a $20,000 settlement in the motorcycle personal injury action. He instructed Irace and Lowry not to disburse any funds to Dr. Herzog indicating that he would make the payments himself. Irace and Lowry informed Dr. Herzog that Jones had revoked his permission to have the bill paid by them directly and indicated that they would follow Jones's directions. Irace and Lowry issued a check to Jones for $10,027 and disbursed the remaining funds to Jones's other creditors. Jones did send a check to Dr. Herzog but the check was returned by the bank for insufficient funds and Dr. Herzog was never paid.

Dr. Herzog filed a complaint in District Court against Irace and Lowry seeking to enforce the June 14, 1988 "assignment of benefits." The matter was tried before the court on the basis of a joint stipulation of facts. The court entered a judgment in favor of Dr. Herzog finding that the June 14, 1988 letter constituted a valid assignment of the settlement proceeds enforceable against Irace and Lowry. Following an unsuccessful appeal to the Superior Court, Irace and Lowry appealed to this court. Because the Superior Court acted as an intermediate appellate court, we review the District Court's decision directly. See Brown v. Corriveau, 576 A.2d 200, 201 (Me. 1990). . . .

VALIDITY OF ASSIGNMENT

An assignment is an act or manifestation by the owner of a right (the assignor) indicating his intent to transfer that right to another person (the assignee). See Shiro v. Drew, 174 F. Supp. 495, 497 (D. Me. 1959). For an assignment to be valid and enforceable against the assignor's creditor [sic — debtor?] (the obligor), the assignor must make clear his intent to relinquish the right to the assignee and must not retain any control over the right assigned or any power of revocation. Id. The assignment takes effect through the actions of the assignor and assignee and the obligor need not accept the assignment to render it valid. Palmer v. Palmer, 112 Me. 149, 153, 91 A. 281, 282 (1914). Once the obligor has notice of the assignment, the fund is "from that time forward impressed with a trust; it is . . . impounded in the [obligor's] hands, and must be held by him not for the original creditor, the assignor, but for the substituted creditor, the assignee." Id. at 152, 91 A. 281. After receiving notice of the assignment, the obligor cannot lawfully pay the amount assigned either to the assignor or to his other creditors and if the obligor does make such a payment, he does so at his peril because the assignee may enforce his rights against the obligor directly. Id. at 153, 91 A. 281.

Ordinary rights, including future rights, are freely assignable unless the assignment would materially change the duty of the obligor, materially increase the burden or risk imposed upon the obligor by his contract, impair the obligor's chance of obtaining return performance, or materially reduce the value of the return performance to the obligor, and unless the law restricts the assignability of the specific right involved. See Restatement (Second) Contracts §317(2)(a) (1982). In Maine, the transfer of a future right to *proceeds* from pending litigation has been recognized as a valid and enforceable equitable assignment. McLellan v. Walker, 26 Me. 114, 117-118 (1896). An equitable assignment need not transfer the entire future right but rather may be a partial assignment of that right. Palmer, 112 Me. at 152, 91 A. 281. We reaffirm these well established principles.

Relying primarily upon the Federal District Court's decision in *Shiro,* 174 F. Supp. 495, a bankruptcy case involving the trustee's power to avoid a preferential transfer by assignment, Irace and Lowry contend that Jones's June 14, 1988 letter is invalid and unenforceable as an assignment because it fails to manifest Jones's intent to permanently relinquish all control over the assigned funds and does nothing more than request payment from a specific fund. We disagree. The June 14, 1988 letter gives no indication that Jones attempted to retain any control over the funds he assigned to Dr. Herzog. Taken in context, the use of the word "request" did not give the court reason to question Jones's intent to complete the assignment and, although no specific amount was stated, the parties do not dispute that the services provided by Dr. Herzog and the amounts that he charged for those services were reasonable and necessary to the treatment of the shoulder injury referred to in the June 14 letter. Irace and Lowry had adequate funds to satisfy all of Jones's creditors, including Dr. Herzog, with funds left over for disbursement to Jones himself. Thus, this case simply does not present a situation analogous to *Shiro* because Dr. Herzog was given preference over Jones's other creditors by operation of the assignment. Given that Irace and Lowry do not dispute that they had ample notice of the assignment, the court's finding on the validity of the assignment is fully supported by the evidence and will not be disturbed on appeal.

Ethical Obligations

Next, Irace and Lowry contend that the assignment, if enforceable against them, would interfere with their ethical obligation to honor their client's instruction in disbursing funds. Again, we disagree.

Under the Maine Bar Rules, an attorney generally may not place a lien on a client's file for a third party. M. Bar R. 3.7(c). The Bar Rules further require that an attorney "promptly pay or deliver to the client, as requested by the client, the funds, securities, or other properties in the possession of the lawyer which the client is entitled to receive." M. Bar R. 3.6(f)(2)(iv). [Substantially similar to Model Rule of Professional Conduct 1.15(b). — Eds.] The rules say nothing, however, about a client's power to assign his right to proceeds from a pending lawsuit to third parties. Because the client has the power to assign his right to funds held by his attorney, McLellan v. Walker, 26 Me. at 117-118, it follows that a valid assignment must be honored by the attorney in disbursing the funds on the client's behalf. The assignment does not create a conflict under Rule 3.6(f)(2)(iv) because the client is not entitled to receive funds once he has assigned them to a third party. Nor does the assignment violate Rule 3.7(c), because the client, not the attorney, is responsible for placing the incumbrance upon the funds. Irace and Lowry were under no ethical obligation, and the record gives no indication that they were under a contractual obligation, to honor their client's instruction to disregard a valid assignment. The District Court correctly concluded that the assignment is valid and enforceable against Irace and Lowry.

The entry is:

Judgment affirmed.

All concurring.

NOTES AND QUESTIONS

1. *Limitations on assignments in general; statutory restrictions.* As discussed previously, the law now generally recognizes the validity of assignments of contract rights, but various limitations remain. The Restatement (Second) §317(2) identifies three bases for restricting assignment of rights: conflict with statute or public policy, material adverse effect on the other party, and valid preclusion by contract term.

Assignment of some contract rights may be expressly prohibited either by state or federal statute. Almost every state has some form of statutory restriction on assignment of wages. Federal statutes restrict the assignment of any public contract or order and of any claim against the government. 41 U.S.C. §15; 31 U.S.C. §3727. See generally Statutory Note, Restatement (Second) of Contracts, ch. 15.

2. *Public policy limitations.* The *Herzog* opinion implicitly addresses a potential public policy limit in footnote 1 by underscoring that the assignment involves proceeds from a personal injury action and "not the cause of action itself." The distinction is important because courts are divided on the issue of assignability of personal injury claims. Traditionally, courts have been concerned that assignments of legal claims would promote "champerty" (stirring up lawsuits by financing litigation). Some courts have held that while parties may not assign personal injury claims, they may assign the *proceeds* of such claims. Other courts have held that this is a distinction without a difference. See A. Unruh Chiropractic Clinic v. De Smet Ins. Co., 782 N.W.2d 367 (S.D. 2010) (discussing two lines of authority and adopting nonassignability approach). In recent years, a business of funding litigation has grown up, testing the limits of the anti-champerty laws, and courts and litigators differ as to whether these practices should be either prohibited entirely or at least substantially restricted. See generally Victoria A. Shannon, Harmonizing Third-Party Litigation Funding Regulation, 36 Cardozo L. Rev. 861 (2015).

3. *Material adverse effect on obligor.* In addition to the statutory and public policy restrictions on assignment of rights, an assignment of a contract right may be invalid if the assignment would have a material adverse effect on the other party to the original contract (the obligor). Restatement (Second) §317(2)(a) provides that a contract can be assigned unless "the substitution of a right of the assignee for the right of the assignor would materially change the duty of the obligor, or materially increase the burden or risk imposed on him by his contract, or materially impair his chance of obtaining return performance, or materially reduce its value to him." See Allstate Ins. Co. v. Med. Lien Mgmt., Inc., 348 P.3d 943 (Colo. 2015) (holding that assignment of an ill-defined portion of claim was invalid because it materially increased the burden on the obligor to determine the amount of the assignment, possibly through litigation). UCC §2-210(2) contains similar limitations. In light of the public policy in favor of assignability, however, courts will generally be reluctant to find that the assignment would have a material adverse effect on the obligor. E.g., Clark v. B.P. Oil Co., 137 F.3d 386 (6th Cir. 1998) (assignment of gasoline supply contract from producer to regional distributor resulted only in immaterial price increases and credit term changes for retailer).

The assignment of rights under a personal services contract may raise questions of material adverse effect on the obligor because of the potential change in the performance to be rendered. See E. Allan Farnsworth, Contracts §11.4, at 693 (4th ed. 2004). See also Munchak Corp. v. Cunningham, 457 F.2d 721 (4th Cir. 1972) (purchasers of basketball franchise could enforce player's contract because he was not obligated to perform differently for the plaintiffs than for the previous owner of the same club).

Personal services or employment contracts often involve express covenants not to compete after termination (as discussed in the *Valley Medical* case in Chapter 7). The courts are divided on whether an employer may assign its rights under such a covenant to a successor that buys the business and for which the employee often continues to work for some period of time. See generally Adam Schneid, Assignability of Covenants Not to Compete: When Can a Successor Firm Enforce a Noncompete Agreement?, 27 Cardozo L. Rev. 1485 (2006).

Some early cases held that the typical requirements contract was not assignable because of the seller's substantial interest in the particular circumstances and creditworthiness of the buyer. E.g., Crane Ice Cream Co. v. Terminal Freezing & Heating Co., 128 A. 280 (Md. 1925). Without attempting to state a blanket rule applicable to all such cases, Comment 4 to UCC §2-210 suggests strongly that the application of §§2-306 and 2-609 should ordinarily overcome this objection, unless "material personal discretion" is involved. Questions related to the adverse impact of an assignment on the other original party are discussed further in the next case, Sally Beauty Co. v. Nexxus Products Co., and the accompanying notes.

4. *Partial assignments.* The *Herzog* facts also suggest the potential for adverse impact on the obligor that may result from a partial transfer of rights. At common law, the obligor's assent to a "partial assignment" was required to make it effective because of concerns about the inconvenience to the obligor of splitting its performance and the exposure of the obligor to multiple

lawsuits. Partial assignments, however, were enforceable in equity. See E. Allan Farnsworth, Contracts §11.3, at 689-690 (4th ed. 2004). In light of modern procedural rules allowing joinder of parties in a single action, the rationale for restricting enforcement of partial assignments has largely disappeared. Therefore, the *Herzog* opinion accurately reflects the willingness of many courts to enforce partial assignments in the same manner as a full transfer. The Restatement (Second) §326 also takes this approach, subject to some procedural limitations. Nevertheless, some courts still deny enforcement to partial assignments of rights made without the obligor's consent. See, e.g., Cincinnati Ins. Co. v. American Hardware Mfrs. Ass'n, 898 N.E.2d 216 (Ill. App. Ct. 2008) (although rationale for rule against partial assignments has been questioned, it is still applied in Illinois). The possibility also remains that the splitting of rights into many, partial assignments could impose a material adverse burden on the obligor and therefore be ruled ineffective.

5. *Contractual prohibitions on assignment.* Reflecting a huge departure from the common law position of general nonassignability of contract rights, both the UCC and the Restatement allow assignment of some contractual rights even in the face of contract language expressly providing otherwise. UCC §§2-210(2) and 9-406(d), (f) provide that in some cases the right to payment of money can always be assigned even though the contract may attempt to prohibit such transfer. While Restatement (Second) §317(2) suggests that contract terms may preclude assignment, §322 modifies that limitation. Under §322 a "no assignment" clause will be first construed only to prohibit delegation of duties, and, alternatively, will be read to constitute a promise not to assign rights that might lead to damages for breach but will not render the assignment ineffective. The Restatement (Second) §322 preference for interpreting a nonassignment clause would be applied "unless a different intention is manifested," suggesting that some language might be strong enough to actually prohibit assignment of rights. In Owen v. CNA Insurance/Continental Cas. Co., 771 A.2d 1208 (N.J. 2001), the New Jersey Supreme Court held that a clause limiting assignment of the proceeds of a structured settlement would be construed as a covenant not to assign, for which the assignor would be liable in damages, but not a prohibition on the assignment. To be effective to prevent assignment, the court indicated that the clause must use magic words:

> To meet that standard, the non-assignment provision generally must state that non-conforming assignments (i) shall be "void" or "invalid," or (ii) that the assignee shall acquire no rights or the non-assigning party shall not recognize any such assignment. Id. at 1214.

See also E. Allan Farnsworth, Contracts §11.4, at 694-695 (4th ed. 2004) (anti-assignment clauses are generally enforced but narrowly construed where possible).

6. *Defenses against assignee.* The *Herzog* decision reflects the basic principle that once the obligor receives notice of an effective assignment of rights, performance must be rendered to the assignee and payment to the assignor will not defeat the assignee's rights. See also UCC §9-406(a). Suppose that Mr. Jones

had informed his attorneys that he considered Dr. Herzog's services unsatisfactory. Would that make a difference in the attorneys' obligation to honor the assignment? See Restatement (Second) §336(4). What should the attorneys have done in such a situation?

Sally Beauty Co. v. Nexxus Products Co.

United States Court of Appeal 801 F.2d 1001 (7th Cir. 1986)

CUDAHY, Circuit Judge.

Nexxus Products Company ("Nexxus") entered into a contract with Best Barber & Beauty Supply Company, Inc. ("Best"), under which Best would be the exclusive distributor of Nexxus hair care products to barbers and hair stylists throughout most of Texas. When Best was acquired by and merged into Sally Beauty Company, Inc. ("Sally Beauty"), Nexxus cancelled the agreement. Sally Beauty is a wholly-owned subsidiary of Alberto-Culver Company ("Alberto-Culver"), a major manufacturer of hair care products and a competitor of Nexxus'. Sally Beauty claims that Nexxus breached the contract by cancelling; Nexxus asserts by way of defense that the contract was not assignable or, in the alternative, not assignable to Sally Beauty. The district court granted Nexxus' motion for summary judgment, ruling that the contract was one for personal

A Sally Beauty Supply store in Denton, Texas.

services and therefore not assignable. We affirm on a different theory — that this contract could not be assigned to the wholly-owned subsidiary of a direct competitor under section 2-210 of the Uniform Commercial Code.

I

Only the basic facts are undisputed and they are as follows. Prior to its merger with Sally Beauty, Best was a Texas corporation in the business of distributing beauty and hair care products to retail stores, barber shops and beauty salons throughout Texas. Between March and July 1979, Mark Reichek, Best's president, negotiated with Stephen Redding, Nexxus' vice-president, over a possible distribution agreement between Best and Nexxus. Nexxus, founded in 1979, is a California corporation that formulates and markets hair care products. Nexxus does not market its products to retail stores, preferring to sell them to independent distributors for resale to barbers and beauticians. On August 2, 1979, Nexxus executed a distributorship agreement with Best, in the form of a July 24, 1979 letter from Reichek, for Best, to Redding, for Nexxus:

> Dear Steve :
>
> It was a pleasure meeting with you and discussing the distribution of Nexus [sic] Products. The line is very exciting and we feel we can do a substantial job with it — especially as the exclusive distributor in Texas (except El Paso).
>
> If I understand the pricing structure correctly, we would pay $1.50 for an item that retails for $5.00 (less 50%, less 40% off retail), and Nexus will pay the freight charges regardless of order size. This approach to pricing will enable us to price the items in the line in such a way that they will be attractive and profitable to the salons.
>
> Your offer of assistance in promoting the line seems to be designed to simplify the introduction of Nexus Products into the Texas market. It indicates a sincere desire on your part to assist your distributors. By your agreeing to underwrite the cost of training and maintaining a qualified technician in our territory, we should be able to introduce the line from a position of strength. I am sure you will let us know at least 90 days in advance should you want to change this arrangement.
>
> By offering to provide us with the support necessary to conduct an annual seminar (i.e., mailers, guest artisit [sic]) at your expense, we should be able to reenforce our position with Nexus users and introduce the product line to new customers in a professional manner.
>
> To satisfy your requirement of assured payment for merchandise received, each of our purchase orders will be accompanied by a Letter of Credit that will become negotiable when we receive the merchandise. I am sure you will agree that this arrangement is fairest for everybody concerned.
>
> While we feel confident that we can do an outstanding job with the Nexus line and that the volume we generate will adequately compensate you for your continued support, it is usually best to have an understanding should we no longer be distributing Nexus Products — either by our desire or your request. Based on our discussions, cancellation or termination of Best Barber & Beauty Supply Co., Inc. as a distributor can only take place on the anniversary date of our original appointment as a distributor — and then only with 120 days prior

notice. If Nexus terminates us, Nexus will buy back all of our inventory at cost and will pay the freight charges on the returned merchandise.

Steve, we feel that the Nexus line is exciting and very promotable. With the program outlined in this letter, we feel it can be mutually profitable and look forward to a long and successful business relationship. If you agree that this letter contains the details of our understanding regarding the distribution of Nexus Products, please sign the acknowledgment below and return one copy of this letter to me.

Very truly yours,
/s/*Mark E. Reichek*
President

Acknowledged /s/ *Stephen Redding*
Date 8/2/79

Appellant's Appendix at 2-3.

In July 1981 Sally Beauty acquired Best in a stock purchase transaction and Best was merged into Sally Beauty, which succeeded to Best's rights and interests in all of Best's contracts. Sally Beauty, a Delaware corporation with its principal place of business in Texas, is a wholly-owned subsidiary of Alberto-Culver. Sally Beauty, like Best, is a distributor of hair care and beauty products to retail stores and hair styling salons. Alberto-Culver is a major manufacturer of hair care products and, thus, is a direct competitor of Nexxus in the hair care market.[1]

Shortly after the merger, Redding met with Michael Renzulli, president of Sally Beauty, to discuss the Nexxus distribution agreement. After the meeting, Redding wrote Renzulli a letter stating that Nexxus would not allow Sally Beauty, a wholly-owned subsidiary of a direct competitor, to distribute Nexxus products:

> As we discussed in New Orleans, we have great reservations about allowing our NEXXUS Products to be distributed by a company which is, in essence, a direct competitor. We appreciate your argument of autonomy for your business, but the fact remains that you are totally owned by Alberto-Culver. Since we see no way of justifying this conflict, we cannot allow our products to be distributed by Sally Beauty Company.

Appellant's Appendix at 475.

. . .

II

Sally Beauty's breach of contract claim alleges that by acquiring Best, Sally Beauty succeeded to all of Best's rights and obligations under the distribution agreement. It further alleges that Nexxus breached the agreement by failing to give Sally Beauty 120 days notice prior to terminating the agreement and by terminating it on other than an anniversary date of its formation. Complaint,

1. The appellant does not appear to dispute the proposition that Alberto-Culver is Nexxus' direct competitor, see Reply Brief at 8-10; rather it disagrees only with Nexxus' contention that performance by Sally Beauty would necessarily be unacceptable. See infra.

Count III, Appellant's Appendix at 54-55. Nexxus, in its motion for summary judgment, argued that the distribution agreement it entered into with Best was a contract for personal services, based upon a relationship of personal trust and confidence between Reichek and the Redding family. As such, the contract could not be assigned to Sally without Nexxus' consent.

In opposing this motion Sally Beauty argued that the contract was freely assignable because (1) it was between two corporations, not two individuals and (2) the character of the performance would not be altered by the substitution of Sally Beauty for Best. It also argued that "the Distribution Agreement is nothing more than a simple, non-exclusive contract for the distribution of goods, the successful performance of which is in no way dependent upon any particular personality, individual skill or confidential relationship." Appellant's Appendix at 119.

In ruling on this motion, the district court framed the issue before it as "whether the contract at issue here between Best and Nexxus was of a personal nature such that it was not assignable without Nexxus' consent." It ruled:

> The court is convinced, based upon the nature of the contract and the circumstances surrounding its formation, that the contract at issue here was of such a nature that it was not assignable without Nexxus's consent. First, the very nature of the contract itself suggests its personal character. A distribution agreement is a contract whereby a manufacturer gives another party the right to distribute its products. It is clearly a contract for the performance of a service. In the court's view, the mere selection by a manufacturer of a party to distribute its goods presupposes a reliance and confidence by the manufacturer on the integrity and abilities of the other party. . . . In addition, in this case the circumstances surrounding the contract's formation support the conclusion that the agreement was not simply an ordinary commercial contract but was one which was based upon a relationship of personal trust and confidence between the parties. Specifically, Stephen Redding, Nexxus's vice-president, travelled to Texas and met with Best's president personally for several days before making the decision to award the Texas distributorship to Best. Best itself had been in the hair care business for 40 years and its president Mark Reichek had extensive experience in the industry. It is reasonable to conclude that Stephen Redding and Nexxus would want its distributor to be experienced and knowledgeable in the hair care field and that the selection of Best was based upon personal factors such as these.

Memorandum Opinion and Order at 56 (citation omitted). The district court also rejected the contention that the character of performance would not be altered by a substitution of Sally Beauty for Best: "Unlike Best, Sally Beauty is a subsidiary of one of Nexxus' direct competitors. This is a significant distinction and in the court's view, it raises serious questions regarding Sally Beauty's ability to perform the distribution agreement in the same manner as Best." Id. at 7.

We cannot affirm this summary judgment on the grounds relied on by the district court. . . . Although it might be "reasonable to conclude" that Best and Nexxus had based their agreement on "a relationship of personal trust and confidence," and that Reichek's participation was considered essential to Best's performance, this is a finding of fact. . . . Since the parties submitted conflicting affidavits on this question,[3] the district court erred in relying on Nexxus' view as representing undisputed fact in ruling on this summary judgment motion. . . .

We may affirm this summary judgment, however, on a different ground if it finds support in the record. United States v. Winthrop Towers, 628 F.2d 1028, 1037 (7th Cir. 1980). Sally Beauty contends that the distribution agreement is freely assignable because it is governed by the provisions of the Uniform Commercial Code (the "UCC" or the "Code"), as adopted in Texas. Appellants' Brief at 46-47. We agree with Sally that the provisions of the UCC govern this contract and for that reason hold that the assignment of the contract by Best to Sally Beauty was barred by the UCC rules on delegation of performance, UCC §2-210(1), Tex. Bus. & Com. Code Ann. §2-210(a) (Vernon 1968).

III

[The court concluded that although the contract involved some services, it was predominantly a contract for the sale of goods and therefore came within the scope of Article 2 of the UCC. — EDS.]

IV

The fact that this contract is considered a contract for the sale of goods and not for the provision of a service does not, as Sally Beauty suggests, mean that it is freely assignable in all circumstances. The delegation of performance under a sales contract (whether in conjunction with an assignment of rights, as here, or not) is governed by UCC section 2-210(1), Tex. Bus. & Com. Code §2-210(a) (Vernon 1968). The UCC recognizes that in many cases an obligor will find it convenient or even necessary to relieve himself of the duty of performance under a contract, see Official Comment 1, UCC §2-210 ("[T]his section recognizes both delegation of performance and assignability as normal and permissible incidents of a contract for the sale of goods."). The Code therefore sanctions delegation except where the delegated performance would be unsatisfactory to the obligee: "A party may perform his duty through a delegate unless otherwise agreed to or unless the other party has a substantial interest in having his

3. Reichek stated the following in an affidavit submitted in support of Sally Beauty's Memorandum in Opposition to Nexxus' Motion for Summary Judgment:

> At no time prior to the execution of the Distribution Agreement did Steve Redding tell me that he was relying upon my personal peculiar tastes and ability in making his decision to award a Nexxus distributorship to Best. Moreover, I never understood that Steve Redding was relying upon my skill and ability in particular in choosing Best as a distributor.
>
> I never considered the Distribution Agreement to be a personal service contract between me and Nexxus or Stephen Redding. I always considered the Distribution Agreement to be between Best and Nexxus as expressly provided in the Distribution Agreement which was written by my brother and me. At all times I conducted business with Nexxus on behalf of Best and not on my own behalf. In that connection, when I sent correspondence to Nexxus, I invariably signed it as president of Best.
>
> Neither Stephen Redding nor any other Nexxus employee ever told me that Nexxus was relying on my personal financial integrity in executing the Distribution Agreement or in shipping Nexxus products to Best. . . .

Affidavit of Mark Reichek, pars. 19-21, Appellant's Appendix at 189-190.

original promisor perform or control the acts required by the contract." UCC §2-210(1), Tex. Bus. & Com. Code Ann. §2-210(a) (Vernon 1968). Consideration is given to balancing the policies of free alienability of commercial contracts and protecting the obligee from having to accept a bargain he did not contract for.

We are concerned here with the delegation of Best's duty of performance under the distribution agreement, as Nexxus terminated the agreement because it did not wish to accept Sally Beauty's substituted performance.[6] Only one Texas case has construed section 2-210 in the context of a party's delegation of performance under an executory contract. In McKinnie v. Milford, 597 S.W.2d 953 (Tex. Civ. App. 1980, *writ ref'd, n.r.e.*), the court held that nothing in the Texas Business and Commercial Code prevented the seller of a horse from delegating to the buyer a pre-existing contractual duty to make the horse available to a third party for breeding. "[I]t is clear that Milford [the third party] had no particular interest in not allowing Stewart [the seller] to delegate the duties required by the contract. Milford was only interested in getting his two breedings per year, and such performance could only be obtained from McKinnie [the buyer] after he bought the horse from Stewart." Id. at 957. In *McKinnie,* the Texas court recognized and applied the UCC rule that bars delegation of duties if there is some reason why the non-assigning party would find performance by a delegate a substantially different thing than what he had bargained for.

In the exclusive distribution agreement before us, Nexxus had contracted for Best's "best efforts" in promoting the sale of Nexxus products in Texas. UCC §2-306(2), Tex. Bus. & Com. Code Ann. §2-306(b) (Vernon 1968), states that "[a] lawful agreement by either buyer or seller for exclusive dealing in the kind of goods concerned imposes unless otherwise agreed an obligation by the seller to use best efforts to supply the goods and by the buyer to use best efforts to promote their sale." This implied promise on Best's part was the consideration for Nexxus' promise to refrain from supplying any other distributors within Best's exclusive area. See Official Comment 5, UCC §2-306. It was this contractual undertaking which Nexxus refused to see performed by Sally.

In ruling on Nexxus' motion for summary judgment, the district court noted: "Unlike Best, Sally Beauty is a subsidiary of one of Nexxus' direct competitors. This is a significant distinction and in the court's view, it raises serious questions regarding Sally Beauty's ability to perform the distribution agreement in the same manner as Best." Memorandum Opinion and Order at 7. In Berliner Foods Corp. v. Pillsbury Co., 633 F. Supp. 557 (D. Md. 1986), the court stated the same reservation more strongly on similar facts. Berliner was an exclusive distributor of Haagen-Dazs ice cream when it was sold to Breyer's, manufacturer

6. If this contract is assignable, Sally Beauty would also, of course, succeed to Best's rights under the distribution agreement. But the fact situation before us must be distinguished from the assignment of contract rights that are no longer executory (e.g., the right to damages for breach or the right to payment of an account), which is considered in UCC section 2-210(2), Tex. Bus. & Com. Code Ann. §2-210(b) (Vernon 1968), and in several of the authorities relied on by appellants. The policies underlying these two situations are different and, generally, the UCC favors assignment more strongly in the latter. See UCC §2-210(2) (non-executory rights assignable even if agreement states otherwise).

of a competing ice cream line. Pillsbury Co., manufacturer of Haagen-Dazs, terminated the distributorship and Berliner sued. The court noted, while weighing the factors for and against a preliminary injunction, that "it defies common sense to require a manufacturer to leave the distribution of its products to a distributor under the control of a competitor or potential competitor." Id. at 559-560. We agree with these assessments and hold that Sally Beauty's position as a wholly-owned subsidiary of Alberto-Culver is sufficient to bar the delegation of Best's duties under the agreement.

We do not believe that our holding will work the mischief with our national economy that the appellants predict. We hold merely that the duty of performance under an exclusive distributorship may not be delegated to a competitor in the market place — or the wholly-owned subsidiary of a competitor — without the obligee's consent. We believe that such a rule is consonant with the policies behind section 2-210, which is concerned with preserving the bargain the obligee has struck. Nexxus should not be required to accept the "best efforts" of Sally Beauty when those efforts are subject to the control of Alberto-Culver. It is entirely reasonable that Nexxus should conclude that this performance would be a different thing than what it had bargained for. At oral argument, Sally Beauty argued that the case should go to trial to allow it to demonstrate that it could and would perform the contract as impartially as Best. It stressed that Sally Beauty is a "multi-line" distributor, which means that it distributes many brands and is not just a conduit for Alberto-Culver products. But we do not think that this creates a material question of fact in this case. When performance of personal services is delegated, the trier merely determines that it is a personal services contract. If so, the duty is per se nondelegable. There is no inquiry into whether the delegate is as skilled or worthy of trust and confidence as the original obligor: the delegate was not bargained for and the obligee need not consent to the substitution. And so here: it is undisputed that Sally Beauty is wholly owned by Alberto-Culver, which means that Sally Beauty's "impartial" sales policy is at least acquiesced in by Alberto-Culver — but could change whenever Alberto-Culver's needs changed. Sally Beauty may be totally sincere in its belief that it can operate "impartially" as a distributor, but who can guarantee the outcome when there is a clear choice between the demands of the parent-manufacturer, Alberto-Culver, and the competing needs of Nexxus? The risk of an unfavorable outcome is not one which the law can force Nexxus to take. Nexxus has a substantial interest in not seeing this contract performed by Sally Beauty, which is sufficient to bar the delegation under section 2-210, Tex. Bus. Com. Code Ann. §2-210 (Vernon 1968). Because Nexxus should not be forced to accept performance of the distributorship agreement by Sally, we hold that the contract was not assignable without Nexxus' consent.[10]

The judgment of the district court is affirmed.

---

10. This disposition makes it unnecessary to address Nexxus' argument that Sally Beauty breached the distribution agreement by not giving Nexxus 120 days' notice of the Best-Sally Beauty merger.

Posner, Circuit Judge, dissenting.

My brethren have decided, with no better foundation than judicial intuition about what businessmen consider reasonable, that the Uniform Commercial Code gives a supplier an absolute right to cancel an exclusive-dealing contract if the dealer is acquired, directly or indirectly, by a competitor of the supplier. I interpret the Code differently.

Nexxus makes products for the hair and sells them through distributors to hair salons and barbershops. It gave a contract to Best, cancellable on any anniversary of the contract with 120 days' notice, to be its exclusive distributor in Texas. Two years later Best was acquired by and merged into Sally Beauty, a distributor of beauty supplies and wholly owned subsidiary of Alberto-Culver. Alberto-Culver makes "hair care" products, too, though they mostly are cheaper than Nexxus's, and are sold to the public primarily through grocery stores and drugstores. My brethren conclude that because there is at least a loose competitive relationship between Nexxus and Alberto-Culver, Sally Beauty cannot — as a matter of law, cannot, for there has been no trial on the issue — provide its "best efforts" in the distribution of Nexxus products. Since a commitment to provide best efforts is read into every exclusive-dealing contract by section 2-306(2) of the Uniform Commercial Code, the contract has been broken and Nexxus can repudiate it. Alternatively, Nexxus had "a substantial interest in having his original promisor perform or control the acts required by the contract," and therefore the delegation of the promisor's (Best's) duties to Sally Beauty was improper under section 2-210(1).

. . .

The fact that Best's president has quit cannot be decisive on the issue whether the merger resulted in a delegation of performance. The contract between Nexxus and Best was not a personal-services contract conditioned on a particular individual's remaining with Best. Compare Jennings v. Foremost Dairies, Inc., supra, 235 N.Y.S.2d at 574. If Best had not been acquired, but its president had left anyway, as of course he might have done, Nexxus could not have repudiated the contract.

No case adopts the per se rule that my brethren announce. The cases ask whether, as a matter of fact, a change in business form is likely to impair performance of the contract. . . .

My brethren find this a simple case — as simple (it seems) as if a lawyer had undertaken to represent the party opposing his client. But notions of conflict of interest are not the same in law and in business, and judges can go astray by assuming that the legal-services industry is the pattern for the entire economy. The lawyerization of America has not reached that point. Sally Beauty, though a wholly owned subsidiary of Alberto-Culver, distributes "hair care" supplies made by many different companies, which so far as appears compete with Alberto-Culver as vigorously as Nexxus does. Steel companies both make fabricated steel and sell raw steel to competing fabricators. General Motors sells cars manufactured by a competitor, Isuzu. What in law would be considered a fatal conflict of interest is in business a commonplace and legitimate practice. The lawyer is a fiduciary of his client; Best was not a fiduciary of Nexxus.

Selling your competitor's products, or supplying inputs to your competitor, sometimes creates problems under antitrust or regulatory law — but only when the supplier or distributor has monopoly or market power and uses it to restrict a competitor's access to an essential input or to the market for the competitor's output. . . . There is no suggestion that Alberto-Culver has a monopoly of "hair care" products or Sally Beauty a monopoly of distributing such products, or that Alberto-Culver would ever have ordered Sally Beauty to stop carrying Nexxus products. Far from complaining about being squeezed out of the market by the acquisition, Nexxus is complaining in effect about Sally Beauty's refusal to boycott it!

How likely is it that the acquisition of Best could hurt Nexxus? Not very. Suppose Alberto-Culver had ordered Sally Beauty to go slow in pushing Nexxus products, in the hope that sales of Alberto-Culver "hair care" products would rise. Even if they did, since the market is competitive Alberto-Culver would not reap monopoly profits. Moreover, what guarantee has Alberto-Culver that consumers would be diverted from Nexxus to it, rather than to products closer in price and quality to Nexxus products? In any event, any trivial gain in profits to Alberto-Culver would be offset by the loss of goodwill to Sally Beauty; and a cost to Sally Beauty is a cost to Alberto-Culver, its parent. Remember that Sally Beauty carries beauty supplies made by other competitors of Alberto-Culver; Best alone carries "hair care" products manufactured by Revlon, Clairol, Bristol-Myers, and L'Oreal, as well as Alberto-Culver. Will these powerful competitors continue to distribute their products through Sally Beauty if Sally Beauty displays favoritism for Alberto-Culver products? Would not such a display be a commercial disaster for Sally Beauty, and hence for its parent, Alberto-Culver? Is it really credible that Alberto-Culver would sacrifice Sally Beauty in a vain effort to monopolize the "hair care" market, in violation of section 2 of the Sherman Act? Is not the ratio of the profits that Alberto-Culver obtains from Sally Beauty to the profits it obtains from the manufacture of "hair care" products at least a relevant consideration?

Another relevant consideration is that the contract between Nexxus and Best was for a short term. Could Alberto-Culver destroy Nexxus by failing to push its products with maximum vigor in Texas for a year? In the unlikely event that it could and did, it would be liable in damages to Nexxus for breach of the implied best-efforts term of the distribution contract. Finally, it is obvious that Sally Beauty does not have a bottleneck position in the distribution of "hair care" products, such that by refusing to promote Nexxus products vigorously it could stifle the distribution of those products in Texas; for Nexxus has found alternative distribution that it prefers — otherwise it wouldn't have repudiated the contract with Best when Best was acquired by Sally Beauty.

Not all businessmen are consistent and successful profit maximizers, so the probability that Alberto-Culver would instruct Sally Beauty to cease to push Nexxus products vigorously in Texas cannot be reckoned at zero. On this record, however, it is slight. And there is no principle of law that if something happens that trivially reduces the probability that a dealer will use his best efforts, the supplier can cancel the contract. Suppose there had been no merger, but the only child of Best's president had gone to work for Alberto-Culver as a chemist. Could Nexxus have canceled the contract, fearing that Best (perhaps unconsciously) would favor Alberto-Culver products over Nexxus products? That would be an absurd ground for cancellation, and so is Nexxus's actual ground. At most, so far as the record shows, Nexxus may have had grounds for "insecurity" regarding the performance by Sally Beauty of its obligation to use its best efforts to promote Nexxus products, but if so its remedy was not to cancel the contract but to demand assurances of due performance. See UCC §2-609; Official Comment 5 to §2-306. No such demand was made. An anticipatory repudiation by conduct requires conduct that makes the repudiating party unable to perform. Farnsworth, Contracts 636 (1982). The merger did not do this. At least there is no evidence it did. The judgment should be reversed and the case remanded for a trial on whether the merger so altered the conditions of performance that Nexxus is entitled to declare the contract broken.

NOTES AND QUESTIONS

1. *Effect of general language.* The court noted that the attempted assignment in *Sally Beauty* included a transfer of both rights and duties of the assignor. The language used in assignments does not always make explicit whether the intent is to both assign rights and delegate duties. Restatement (Second) §328 states that general language of assignment will include both assignment of rights and delegation of duties unless the circumstances indicate otherwise. The UCC takes the same approach in §2-210(5). See, e.g., Kunzman v. Thorsen, 740 P.2d 754, 756 (Or. 1987) (stating that both the UCC and the Restatement adopt a presumption that an assignment of rights includes a delegation of duties because this presumption "most probably conforms to the parties' intent and to their understanding of the meaning of such broad language of assignment"). See also Pines Plaza Ltd. P'ship v. Berkley Trace, LLC, 66 A.3d 720, 730 (Md. 2013) (holding that delegation presumption applies to real estate contracts even though Restatement had adopted a caveat to the application of section §328 to such contracts).

2. *Delegation of personal service obligations.* Where a contract imposes on an individual the duty of personal service, that duty is almost always regarded as inherently undelegable, unless the other party (obligee) assents. See, e.g., Restatement (Second) §318, Illustrations 5 (school teacher) and 6 (radio singer); compare Illustration 3 (*A* will build a building "in accordance with specifications"; delegable by *A*) with Illustration 7 (*A* will "personally cut the grass on *B*'s meadow"; not delegable by *A*). The principle applies to contracts involving artists and professionals. See Rosetti v. City of New Britain, 303 A.2d 714 (Conn. 1972) (citing as nondelegable duties personal services of artists, physicians, lawyers, and possibly architects, depending upon intent of parties). It has also been extended to business contracts when the promisee has a substantial interest in performance by a particular individual. See R&B Appliance Parts,

Inc. v. Amana Co., L.P., 258 F.3d 783, 786-787 (8th Cir. 2001) (recognizing that the principle against delegation of personal service contracts applies to distribution contracts, but finding it inapplicable on the facts of the case); UCC §2-210(1); Restatement (Second) §318(2). The court in *Sally Beauty* appears to accept this principle, but it disagrees with the trial court's decision on motion for summary judgment that the distribution contract between Sally Beauty and Nexxus was a personal service contract as a matter of law. Do you agree with the appellate court on this point, or was the trial judge correct in finding as a matter of law that the contract was a personal service contract?

3. *Economic analysis.* In his stinging dissent Judge Posner characterizes the majority opinion as having "no better foundation than judicial intuition about what businessmen consider reasonable." Do you agree? Can you articulate a justification for the decision based on principles of economic analysis?

4. *Effect of clause requiring consent to delegation.* The contract in *Sally Beauty* did not expressly prohibit delegation of duties, but suppose that it had, would such a clause be effective? The notes after *Herzog* underscored the difficulty of prohibiting assignment of rights, but Restatement (Second) §322(1) and UCC §2-210(4) reflect the general view that courts are likely to enforce a clause prohibiting delegation of a duty. Real property leases and franchise agreements present settings in which the ability to assign rights and delegate duties is particularly important. If the clause requires the obligee's consent to the delegation but does not provide a standard for granting or withholding consent (often called a "silent" consent clause), courts are divided on the issue of how such a clause should be interpreted. Some courts interpret the clause to require the obligee to act reasonably and in good faith in refusing to grant consent. See Larese v. Creamland Dairies, Inc., 767 F.2d 716 (10th Cir. 1985) (transfer of franchise); Julian v. Christopher, 575 A.2d 735 (Md. 1990) (real property lease). Under these decisions, if a party wishes to avoid subjecting an assignment to a reasonableness requirement, it should "bargain for a provision expressly granting the right to withhold consent unreasonably, to insure that [the other party] is put on notice." Larese v. Creamland Dairies, 767 F.2d at 718. However, other courts interpret "silent" consent clauses to only require that the obligee act honestly in its decision whether to grant or withhold consent. See Taylor Equipment, Inc. v. John Deere Co., 98 F.3d 1028, 1034 (8th Cir. 1996) (implied obligation of good faith did not apply to manufacturer's refusal to consent to assignment of equipment dealership); First Federal Savings Bank v. Key Markets, Inc., 559 N.E.2d 600 (Ind. 1990) (landlord had unlimited right to withhold approval). See generally Terrence M. Dunn, The Franchisor's Control over the Transfer of a Franchise, 27 SPG Franchise L.J. 233 (2008).

5. *Effect of delegation or assignment on rights and duties of the parties.* In those situations that involve a permissible delegation of a duty, the obligee generally has rights against the original obligor and the delegate. The original obligor remains liable to the obligee until the performance is rendered by the delegate, unless the obligee agrees to release the original obligor (referred to as "novation"), but evidence of the novation must be clear. See Rosenberg v. Son, Inc., 491 N.W.2d 71 (N.D. 1992) (an obligor cannot escape its liability by merely

delegating duties); Restatement (Second) §§280, 318, Comment *d.* If the obligee is an intended beneficiary of the assignment, the obligee may also bring suit against the delegate as a third-party beneficiary of the agreement by which the delegate promises to assume the original obligor's duty. Compare Gateway Co. v. DiNoia, 654 A.2d 342 (Conn. 1995) (landlord as third-party beneficiary of lease assignment agreement could enforce against tenant's assignee) with Ames v. JP Morgan Chase Bank, N.A., 783 S.E.2d 614, 620 (Ga. 2016) (borrower does not have standing as third party beneficiary to challenge assignment of security deed "because the debtor . . . is not intended to directly benefit from the transfer of the power of sale").

If the transaction involves an assignment of rights rather than a delegation of duties, generally the assignee "stands in the shoes" of the assignor. See, e.g., Brown v. Bluecross Blueshield of Tenn., Inc., 827 F.3d 543, 548 (6th Cir. 2016). Thus, the assignee will be subject to any claims or defenses of the obligor that arise out of the contract assigned. See UCC §9-404(a)(1); Restatement (Second) §336(1).

When the assignor and the obligor have done business together over a period of time, it is possible that the obligor may also have claims against the assignor arising from contracts other than the one assigned. The rights of the assignee under the contract assigned will be subject as well to claims and defenses of the obligor arising from these other contracts, but only as to claims or defenses that "accrue" before the obligor receives notification of the assignment. E.g., Seattle-First National Bank v. Oregon Pacific Industries, Inc., 500 P.2d 1033 (Or. 1972) (assignee bank not subject to claim arising from unassigned plywood contract that accrued after notice of assignment; "accrue" defined to mean when breach of contract occurs); UCC §9-404(a)(2); Restatement (Second) §336(2).

PROBLEM 12-2

Recall the facts of Problem 6-3, following the *Geysen* case, in which you were asked by your client, Francis Fallon, to review the terms of his proposed contract with Captain Donut, Inc. Assume that you are visited again by Fallon, who has decided to retire after five years of the ten-year franchise period because his pension rights and savings will adequately support him and his household for the foreseeable future. Fallon poses to you a number of questions about his rights under the franchise agreement.

First, Fallon wants to know if he can simply retire from the doughnut business and terminate the franchise without liability to Captain Donut.

Second, since the franchise represents a considerable initial investment on Fallon's part, he is also interested in the possibility of selling the property and his business (including his rights under the franchise agreement) to Carlos Cruz, his assistant store manager for the last three years. Is Fallon likely to be able to make the sale to Cruz?

Third and last, Fallon is interested in the possibility of turning over the business to his daughter Teresa, who is now a 21-year old college senior. Is Fallon likely to be able to transfer the business to Teresa?

Fallon also mentions that six months ago Captain Donut was acquired by Gigantic Corporation through a stock purchase arrangement. To date, Gigantic has not made any changes in the standard operating procedures for franchisees except that franchise fees are now mailed directly to Gigantic's corporate offices. Does the change in ownership of Captain Donut have any relevance to Fallon's rights and duties?

You should consider the provisions of the franchise agreement as set out in Problem 6-3 in answering Fallon's questions.

REVIEW QUESTIONS – CHAPTER TWELVE

1. Two years ago Hirato Electrical Supplies, Inc. agreed to sell its business to Construction Supplies, Inc., a large international supplier of materials for home construction. The agreement between Hirato and Construction provided that Construction agreed to keep operating Hirato as a wholly-owned subsidiary of Construction for at least two years after the closing of the acquisition. While Hirato's current employees were all at-will (i.e., may be terminated regardless of cause), as part of Construction's agreement to continue to operate Hirato as a subsidiary for two years, Construction also agreed that it would continue to employ all of Hirato's current employees for two years, except those for whom good cause for discharge existed. However, one year after the closing of the acquisition Construction decided to merge Hirato's operations into the parent company. In connection with this transaction, approximately 100 of Hirato's employees were laid off. The discharged employees have brought suit against Construction claiming that it has breached a contractual duty owed to them. Which of the following statements best describes the legal position of the discharged employees?
   - A. They do not have any contractual rights against Construction because they were not signatories to the contract between Hirato and Construction.
   - B. They do not have any contractual rights against Construction because Hirato did not have a duty to continue their employment.
   - C. They have contractual rights against Construction because they would receive a benefit from the agreement between Construction and Hirato.
   - D. They have contractual rights against Construction because Hirato intended to provide a benefit to the employees and Construction was aware of and agreed to that intent.

2. O'Hara Construction, LLC is engaged in the business of construction of office buildings for private developers and governmental entities. From time to time, O'Hara needs capital to support its operations. O'Hara has a working relationship with Capitol City Bank under which O'Hara sells its rights to receive payment under specified contracts to Bank. In the standard transaction, O'Hara sells all of its payment rights under a specified contract to Bank, typically for about 80% of the contract amount. When the sale

involves a contract with the federal government, O'Hara usually receives about 90% of the face amount of the contract because the risk to the Bank is less in such transactions. Sometimes, the transaction involves a sale of only a portion of O'Hara's right to receive payment under a contract. Which of the following is the most accurate statement about transactions between Bank and O'Hara?

A. A sale by O'Hara to Bank of a right to receive payment under a contract with the federal government will probably be enforceable because of the public policy in favor of free markets.
B. A sale by O'Hara to Bank of a right to receive payment under a contract with a private developer is unenforceable without the consent of any developer because the sale affects the obligations of the developer.
C. A sale by O'Hara to Bank of a portion of its right to receive payment under a contract with a private developer will probably be enforceable.
D. If O'Hara fails to perform a contract when the right to receive payment has been sold to Bank, Bank will have the obligation to complete performance of the contract.

3. Livingston Management Services, LLC is an agent for developers of residential apartment buildings located in the Washington, DC area. Livingston provides a wide range of management services to the owners, including leasing, maintenance, and rent collection. National Leasing Management, Inc. is a large nationwide company that provides services similar to the ones offered by Livingston. National also operates in the Washington area in competition with Livingston. While National and Livingston are competitors, their competition has been "friendly." Recently, National approached Livingston about the possibility of acquiring Livingston's operations. After some negotiations, National agreed to acquire all of Livingston's Washington contracts with apartment owners. However, National will not purchase Livingston's facilities, and it will offer employment to only some of Livingston's personnel. Which of the following is the most correct statement about the relationship among Livingston, National, and the owners of the apartment buildings?

A. Because the contracts between Livingston and the owners involve personal services, Livingston may not transfer the contracts to National without the consent of the owners.
B. Livingston does not have the right to delegate performance of its contracts to National because the owners have a substantial interest in performance by Livingston due to the fact that National and Livingston were competitors.
C. After National acquires Livingston's contracts, Livingston will not be liable to the owners for nonperformance of those contracts.
D. After National acquires Livingston's contracts, National will be liable to the owners for any breach of those contracts.

ANSWERS TO REVIEW QUESTIONS

Chapter 1

1. A, B, and C. Clearly case law in your jurisdiction and also the Restatement (which reflects the general common law of contracts) could be relevant. Although this may be less likely, there might also be land use statutes relating to this kind of transaction. The parties both appear to be residents of the same American state, however, so the CISG could have no application or potential relevance.
2. None of these statements is definitely true. A: Since contract law is traditionally case law, it is in part the creation of courts over time, although legislatures can and sometimes do change the rules that the courts have developed. B: Although "classical" contract law was — ostensibly, at least — not concerned with "fairness" (the reality might not have been so clear-cut), modern courts usually do attempt to reach outcomes that are both consistent with the rules and fair to the parties involved. C: Although lower courts are probably not likely to refer to legal theory when deciding case disputes, higher courts may (frankly or tacitly) be influenced by various theoretical approaches to legal decision making.
3. Of these four statements, the one most likely to be accurate is B: Attorneys in large or specialized law firms may seldom if ever appear in court, although that is less likely to be true of a "general practice" firm, particularly in a smaller city or town. A is not accurate: an attorney must initially analyze problems objectively, although she may eventually have to argue on behalf of her client in a way that stresses favorable facts and arguments. C is sometimes true, but attorneys do often serve as negotiators of deals, and even a mere "drafter" is likely to do some negotiating over the language of the eventual agreement. D is clearly not true: When a dispute arises, an attorney will attempt to settle it in a way that is favorable or at least tolerable for her client, and will ordinarily see litigation as a last resort, even if sometimes a necessary one.
4. Probably not. The ease of communication might make it less likely that such a misunderstanding would arise in the first place, or that it would persist for as long as it did in *Allen*, but the court's reasoning in that case seems applicable to any exchange of letters, whether on paper or by e-mail.

Chapter 2

1. Yes, X has made an offer to Y. She identified the subject matter - a particular desk, probably known to Y (the next question confirms this) — and the price ($15,000). She expressed a willingness to commit herself to this bargain ("I'd certainly sell it for [$15,000] . . ."). The time and method of delivery and payment could have been stated also, but failure to include all possible terms does not prevent a communication from being complete enough to be legally an offer. She indicated a (somewhat soft?) time limit for acceptance. The fact that the parties are related does not keep her note from being an offer for an exchange. The fact that neither of them is (so far as we know) a "merchant" does not mean that the Uniform Commercial Code will not apply; it is still a sale of goods. However, the UCC does not have its own definition of "offer," so the common law rules will still apply. Also, the fact that X indicated willingness to entertain a lower offer from Y does not negate her expression of willingness to sell for $15,000; it simply reflects her understanding that the price she set may be too high for Y to accept her offer.
2. A and B. Y's communication, like X's earlier one, has enough detail, and evidences a possible willingness to commit to a purchase at the price of $12,000. Y's intent is not as clear as X's was, however, as Y says only "I guess I can go up to . . ." the lower price. And Y follows that with an inquiry "Would you take that for it?" which again is somewhat equivocal. So this note could be an offer, but this is less certain than was the answer to Question 1. Even if X's original note was not an offer, however, Y's response to it might still be characterized as one (Answer A). If X's note was an offer, then if Y's response is an "offer" at all, it will also be a "counter-offer" (Answer B). The outcome in question C could be a *possibility* also, because a counter-offer is ordinarily treated as a rejection, terminating the counter-offeror's power to accept the original offer. On these facts this is not a *necessary* outcome, however, because the counter-offeror seems to be indicating a possible continuing interest in the original offer, not actually rejecting it: He doesn't flatly reject buying for $15,000 ("pretty high for me . . .") and he seems to suggest an ongoing negotiation ("would you take . . .?").

3. All four answers are *potentially* accurate, depending on the way various issues are resolved. Answer B could be correct, if – as indicated might be the case in the answer to Question 2 – Y's first response is treated as a counter-offer and also as a rejection. Answer C could be correct if X's original reference to a response "by the end of the week" is treated as a firm deadline for acceptance, rather than merely a request for a reasonably prompt reply (". . . if possible"). Answer D could be correct if X's last note is interpreted as generally a revival of her earlier offer but without any particular firm deadline. ("I can't go as low as that" might imply a willingness to continue negotiation over her original price.) And Answer A also could be correct if outcomes B and C are both *in*correct (not a clear rejection; not a firm deadline).
4. Answer A is probably correct; B and C are both probably wrong. As for Answer B, the store's posted sign indicates that to be entered to win the prize, one must go to the customer service counter on the store's fourth floor. This could be merely a "condition" to the ability to enter (you have to go to the fourth floor only because that's where the box is). However, since going to the fourth floor means you have to enter and travel through the store itself, and given that getting customers inside the store is potentially a benefit to DDS, there should be little difficulty in treating this as consideration for the store's promise. Clearly the store's motive in making this offer is commercial gain; it's not just to give something away. Answer C is somewhat more likely than B. The store should be bound if Ashley both honestly and reasonably believed that the sign actually referred to a real, full-size Ford automobile, rather than just a plastic model of one. The first of those is a question of fact specific to Ashley (did she in fact honestly believe that?) and the second is a more general question – could a reasonable customer of the store have interpreted the sign that way? Answer A does seem to be the most likely outcome, if not an inevitable one.
5. Answer C is the one most likely to be correct. Answer A echoes the court's decision in the similar case of Walker v. Keith, but here the option provision in the lease does not condition the renewal on the parties' ability to agree on a new rental; it commits Lily to a renewal term at the stated price, and then adds the possibility that the parties might agree to a different amount. (Presumably this might happen if Chuck balks at renewing the lease at $2,250, and Lily offers to take some lower amount as an incentive.) Answer B correctly suggests that Chuck's three years of reliance on the renewal option is likely to be substantial, but proof of reliance should not be necessary for Chuck to prevail. Answer D could be correct if Lily had committed herself only to bargain in good faith to reach an amount for the renewal rental, but the lease provision appears to actually commit her to the stated amount.
6. Answer B comes closest to being sound advice. This question invokes the UCC, and specifically §2-207. If Bob signs onto a seller's form with disadvantageous terms, then for him the "battle of forms" is over, and he has surrendered. Section 2-207 has no work to do there. Answer C is misleading; if the seller has a strong form of its own and the seller's terms are additional to or different from the buyer's, then the likely outcome is that either the buyer's form prevails (because the seller's response is not considered to be an "expressly conditional acceptance" under §2-207(1) and the seller's terms are deemed to be "material" changes under §2-207(2)), or the forms cancel each other out, in which case under §2-207(3) the terms "implied by law" would remain, and those include the remedies that Bob is trying to preserve. D simply describes the former common law rule, which §2-207 is expressly designed to change. Answer A is too over-simplified to be good advice; even if it is generally accurate, there are too many exceptions and qualifications that it glosses over.

Chapter 3

1. Of the four possibilities, Answer B is the most likely outcome. A is not correct, because the mere fact that a promise is expressed in writing does not make it enforceable in the absence of consideration. Answer C does not apply because Rebecca did not make an "offer" to Myles; she made a gratuitous promise, not proposing the formation of a contract. Answer D may be a statement of desirable public policy, but the common law of contracts does not adopt that policy as a rule of law. It is possible that a court would be willing to consider the application to this case of the rule stated in Restatement (Second) of Contracts §86 (inspired by the *Webb* case), permitting enforcement of a promise made in recognition of a benefit conferred – a possibility not considered by the four answers proposed for this question – but the case law adopting §86 is sparse, and the facts of this case are nowhere near as compelling as those of *Webb*.
2. Answer C is the best answer because Ashley meets the requirement of promissory estoppel, as stated in Restatement (Second) §90. Answer A might be correct if promissory estoppel were not available to Ashley, although she might argue that her Aunt Ivy has specified Ashley's attendance at college and achievement of good grades as the consideration for Aunt Ivy's promise, which Ashley has accepted by performance, creating a unilateral contract. (Compare the *Hamer* case.) Answer B is wrong because Aunt Ivy is wealthy, and a blood relative of Ashley – her mother's sister. Not only that, she is an alumna of Stepford, and apparently a loyal one, anxious to have Ashley attend there as well. Absent additional facts that we do not have (which could be negative), there is every reason for Ashley to trust her aunt to keep her word. Answer D could also be the outcome, but that depends on more facts than we are given here. It is at least possible that Ashley's reliance would be seen as not sufficiently detrimental or unjust to require enforcement of her aunt's promise – Ashley does now have one year of achievement at a major university to her credit, so it is possible that indeed she can

get scholarship aid for the next year of her studies at Stepford as a result of that. In addition, whether she will receive a scholarship is speculative now (although the issue might be resolved before a court had to decide the case).

3. Answer C is the one most likely to be correct, because the school board can argue that the requirements of UCC §2-205 have all been met here, and an acceptance now would be within the two weeks specified in the offer. (This is well within the outside limit of three months of irrevocability that §2-205 can create.) Answer A is wrong because although §2-205 requires the offeror to be a "merchant," it does not require him to be in the business of selling goods of the kind; it applies to offers made by "business practice" merchants as well, which Hank surely would be. (See Comment 2 to UCC §2-104, defining "merchant.") Also, §2-205 applies to offers made by buyers as well as sellers. Answer D is wrong because the "signature" requirement of §2-205 can include more than just a hand-signing. See Comment 2 to §2-205. Answer B is somewhat more problematic, because whether the offer made by Hank was a "firm" one is matter of interpretation. It does not use the words "firm offer," but §2-205 does not require that; it simply requires that the offer give an "assurance that it will be held open." Saying that the offer "is good for the next two weeks" could conceivably be interpreted as meaning merely that it will expire automatically at the end of two weeks; it does seem, however, that saying the offer "is good" for two weeks could easily be seen as also a statement that it will not be revoked during that time.
4. B. The principle of restitution requires that Megan repay the money that was paid to her by mistake. This type of obligation is often referred to as an "implied-in-law" contract, or sometimes "quasi-contract." It does not depend on the making of a promise, but rather on the law's desire to prevent unjust enrichment. This is true whether the mistake was her fault or not, so Answer C is incorrect. Answer A states the correct result, but not the correct reason: Megan would be liable to repay even if she had not promised to do so.

Chapter 4

1. Answer A is the best answer. The majority and traditional view is that a contract of indefinite duration can be terminated at any time and thus fully performed in less than a year. Therefore, such contracts do not come within the one-year category of the statute of frauds. The agreement for Anne to serve as Bill's agent for as long as Bill performed professionally could have lasted less than a year because at any time Bill could have easily decided to discontinue his career. He also might at any time have been disabled from performing. Therefore, his oral promise need not be in writing to be enforceable. For similar reasons, Answer C would not be correct. The prevailing approach to the one-year category is that a contract falls outside of it even if performance lasts for more than year if it could have been fully performed in less than a year. Answer B would not be correct because there is not any conduct that is tantamount to a signature under statute of frauds analysis. While the Restatement (Second) §139 does protect reasonable reliance on an oral contract in some situations, it is not based on a theory that conduct is the equivalent to a signature. Answer D is not correct because Anne would be suing for compensation for future performances under an executory contract.
2. Answer C is the best answer. As indicated in the *Buffaloe* decision, the UCC §2-201(1) minimal writing requirement can be satisfied by a personal check, with a notation of the goods on the memo line, signed by the party against whom enforcement is sought. This outcome would be true even if the check is not cashed or payment is stopped by Donna. Thus, Answer B is not correct. It should be noted, however, that the part payment exception to the UCC statute of frauds under §2-201(3)(c) would probably also apply to these facts. Similarly, Answer A is not correct because Carl does not need Donna to admit the making of the contract under §2-201(3)(a) in order to enforce the contract. Answer D is not correct because uniqueness of the goods is the basis for an exception to the writing requirement only under the "specially manufactured goods" rule in UCC §2-201(3)(a).
3. Answer D is the best available answer. This question focuses on the "suretyship" category of the statute of frauds, or promises to answer for the debt or duty of another, as discussed in Note 3 following the *Crabtree* case. This category is covered by the Restatement (Second) of Contracts §§112-123. The promise here is made to the creditor and is for the benefit of Megan's daughter and does not benefit Megan herself. Thus, the promise from Megan to Carl would come within the suretyship category and would require a writing signed by Megan. Answer A would not be correct because, while it is true that the promise would not fall within the one-year category, it does fall within the suretyship category. Answer B would not be correct because, while the promise from Megan was reflected in the writing, Megan did not sign it. There is no indication that Dina signed on Megan's behalf. Answer C would not be correct because Carl's contract was for construction services and was not one for transfer of an interest in real property as discussed in Note 1 following the *Beaver* case. Carl would be left to his contract claim against Dina. Carl might pursue a reliance claim against Megan under Restatement (Second) of Contracts §139, but Comment *a* to Restatement (Second) of Contracts §112 gives a strong indication that a reliance argument should not prevail in a suretyship situation.
4. Answer B is the best answer. Answer B would likely be true in most jurisdictions because the writing contains sufficient terms and the presence of the letterhead would amount to a signature under the lenient view of that element in both the Restatement (Second) of Contracts and the UCC. Furthermore, Gina's email would arguably constitute an authenticated record under cur-

rent law on electronic communications, as provided in the federal E-SIGN Act and the state law counterpart, the Uniform Electronic Transactions Act (UETA), and her email explicitly references the contract reflected by the terms in the written note. As in the *Crabtree* case, Ed could argue that the two documents related to the same transaction make a strong case for a sufficient writing. Moreover, the email message concedes that a contract had been made while explaining a breach of it. For the foregoing reasons, Answer C would likely be incorrect; the writing and the email message would provide a strong case for satisfying the statute of frauds even without every detail of the contract being stated. Similarly, Answer D would be incorrect because a formal signature is not necessary to satisfy the requirement that a writing be "signed" by the party against whom enforcement is sought. Answer A would not be correct because the fact that a two-year contract might be breached in less than one year is not the same thing as full performance. Thus, the contract is not one that can be fully performed within one year from the date of making. See the notes after *Crabtree*.

5. Answer D is the best answer. The UCC §2-201(1) applies to contracts for the sale of goods for a price of $500 or more. Sam never signed anything that would satisfy the writing requirement of UCC §2-201(1), and thus the question is whether one of the exceptions in the section is satisfied. No exception applies and therefore the correct answer is D. Answer A is not correct because the exception in UCC §2-201(3)(a) requires that the goods be "specially manufactured for the buyer" and a unique heirloom would not qualify. Answer B raises the possible application of UCC §2-201(2), the "between merchants" exception, but Sam Seller is a school teacher and does not appear to be a merchant with regard to antique furniture. Answer C is not correct because while UCC §2-201(3)(c) creates a part performance exception to the statute of frauds, it requires *either* that payment have been "made and accepted" by the seller *or* that goods have been "received and accepted" by the buyer, not both, and neither of which have occurred here.

Chapter 5

1. A. The email would be relevant negotiating history, under the majority and traditional view, and should be admissible to explain a term in the written contract. Jim would argue that he shared a mutual understanding with Ann that bills would be mailed each Wednesday and that the ultimate goal of contract interpretation is to determine the shared intent of the parties. While one could argue that B is also correct and many courts use a "plain meaning approach," it is a less persuasive argument than the use of extrinsic evidence to pursue the ultimate goal of identifying what the parties reasonably understood the term to mean. Answer C should not be correct because extrinsic evidence for purposes of interpretation should not be barred by a merger clause or integrated agreement under the better approach to interpretation. Answer D would be illogical, in fact, because a party cannot unilaterally deviate from contract terms because they believe an alternative performance would be better. (Contract modification will be discussed in Chapter 8.)
2. C. If properly considered, the parol evidence rule should not be a bar to evidence of the oral agreement concerning debris removal because it is a "separate contract" with separate consideration. See Restatement (Second) §216(2)(a). It should be noted, however, that some courts would have difficulty with this analysis because of the proximity of the subject matter of the written and oral contracts. Answer A would not be correct because the alleged oral agreement in no sense contradicts or is in direct opposition to any term in the writing. Answer B would not be correct because the evidence does not purport to interpret any provision in the writing. Answer D is not correct because the presence or absence of a merger clause does not necessarily determine whether a writing is a complete or partial integration.
3. D. From the available information, it appears that the oil paintings and sketches together would be worth at least $800,000. To sell them for only $280,000 would be clearly an irrational bargain and it appears that Grant should have known that. Answer C is also a plausible answer because under a standard maxim of interpretation, the listing of specific items will define a more general item. The maxims, however, are often viewed by the courts as not being controlling and they tend to lend themselves to use by both sides to a dispute. Answer E is not a good answer because it appears that Grant should have been aware of Lucy's meaning and therefore would be bound by it under the Restatement (Second) of Contracts §201(2). Answer A would be incorrect because it is essentially a "plain meaning" argument and only the most formalistic of courts would adopt such an approach in the face of two plausible interpretations. The alleged ambiguity could be established by relatively objective evidence and thereby preclude any plain meaning approach to the dispute. Answer B would not be correct because the rule of "contra proferentem" would not be applicable. The contract is not a formalized agreement with drafting attributable to one party. Furthermore, the rule of construction against the drafter is a rule of last resort, typically used only when other means of interpretation do not resolve the dispute.
4. B would likely be correct in those jurisdictions that have adopted a broad version of the reasonable expectations doctrine because Olga received an oral promise of coverage that would have been disproved only by reading through the lengthy standardized policy. Her situation is exactly the kind that the broad form of the reasonable expectations doctrine would address. It should be noted, however, that some states do require that the objectionable term be ambiguous or hidden before the reasonable expectations doctrine will apply. The term at issue for Olga is probably not ambiguous,

but it may be considered to have been hidden since it was on page 7 of a 20-page contract. Answer A would not be correct because insurance contracts are a type where parties frequently contemplate that the detailed terms will arrive after formation and the insured party will be able to cancel the contract if they disagree with the terms. Answer C would not be correct because the premise of the reasonable expectations doctrine is its recognition that adherents to standardized agreements will frequently not read the fine print in the contract. Answer D would not be correct in a state with a broad version of the reasonable expectations doctrine because an ambiguity is not required to apply the doctrine. Moreover, even if an ambiguity is required, one would expect that courts would recognize the possibility of a latent ambiguity.

5. B. Generally speaking, the parol evidence rule should not be a bar to evidence offered to prove fraud for the purpose of invalidating the agreement. See Restatement (Second) §214(d). The California Supreme Court took that position in the *Riverisland* case, discussed in Note 1 following the *Sherrodd* case. It should be noted from the *Sherrodd* case, however, that some jurisdictions will add a qualification that the alleged fraud cannot be based on something specifically disclaimed in the writing. If Bob were located in such a jurisdiction, then Answer C would most likely be the correct response. While the parol evidence rule does not bar evidence of a modification, the statement about the roof came before the written contract was executed and therefore Answer A would not be correct. Answer D would not be correct because it is in fact possible for a buyer to reasonably rely on an oral statement from a seller, depending on the context.

Chapter 6

1. B. UCC §2-313 on express warranties makes a distinction between factual representations about goods and mere sales talk or "puffery." Answer B is correct because the statement in the magazine about the water-resistant characteristics of the watch would clearly fall on the factual side. See Note 1 after the *Bayliner Marine* case. For the same reasons, the statements by Sam referred to in Answer A would be mere puffery and would not give rise to an express warranty. It also follows that Answer C would not be correct because the statement in the magazine would not be sales talk. Answer D would be incorrect because there is not a requirement in UCC §2-313 that express warranties be made in writing.
2. C. As discussed in the introduction to Chapter 6, Section B, the essence of the implied duty of good faith is the prohibition on one party engaging in conduct that frustrates the reasonable expectations of the other party to the contract. Answer C reflects that central tenet. As explained in the *Seidenberg* case and the following notes, conduct may violate the implied duty of good faith even if the express terms have not been contravened. Thus, Answer A would not be correct. Answer B is incorrect because it is directly at odds with the holding in Wood v. Lucy, Lady Duff-Gordon concerning the enforceability of a promise to use best efforts in performance of a contract. See also UCC §2-306(2) on exclusive dealings contracts and reasonable efforts. Answer D would be incorrect because it reflects a fundamental misconception of the doctrine of equitable estoppel which protects reasonable reliance on a misstatement of fact by a party to a contract. See the notes after Harvey v. Dow in Chapter 3. It does not appear that Empire made a misstatement of fact at contract formation.
3. D. As explained in the notes following the *Geysen* case, there is a very strong presumption of at-will employment when a contract is of indefinite duration. With an at-will contract, the employee can be terminated at any time, absent some exceptional rule. Thus, Answer D is correct unless an exception applies. Answer A would not be correct because most courts interpret permanent employment to be employment at-will. See Note 1 after *Geysen*. Answer B is almost certainly incorrect because courts very narrowly interpret the public policy limitation on termination of at-will employees and would not protect them from retaliation based on political discussion. See Note 3 after *Geysen*. Likewise, Answer C would be incorrect because the promissory estoppel limitation on at-will employment, when recognized, is narrowly limited to situations where there is a clear promise of secure employment or compelling acts in reliance. Merely passing up another job is not likely to be enough to make a good promissory estoppel case.
4. A. It appears from the facts that both parties had an intent to be bound to the sales contract, even though they did not agree on the time for performance. See UCC §2-204(3). As provided in UCC §2-309(1), if a contract is otherwise enforceable but fails to state a time for performance, then performance is due in a "reasonable time." See the notes following the *Leibel* case. The contract would be enforceable with that implied term added and that means that Answer A is correct. For the same reason, Answer C would be incorrect. Answer D would not be correct because the parties did not intend to create an option contract for Bob as that concept is explained in the notes following the Berryman v. Kmoch case in Chapter 3. Answer B states that the contract would include an implied option for the seller unilaterally to set a date for performance. While UCC §2-311(1) allows for the possibility that one party will be given an option to specify a term of performance, there is not any basis in the facts here to suggest such an implied term for the seller. In fact, Bob may have had such a right to set the date for performance, but he would have needed to exercise that option in good faith and within commercially reasonable limits under UCC §2-311(1). Delaying performance for about nine months, again, would appear to be clearly unreasonable.
5. B. As explained in Note 1 following the *Morin* case, courts almost uniformly apply a subjective, good faith

standard to a condition of satisfaction when it is a third party who must be satisfied. Such a third party must be honestly dissatisfied. Here that appears not to be the case and Answer B is therefore correct. The given facts strongly suggest collusion between Second Bank and the architect, and thus the condition would be excused. (This concept of excuse of conditions is explored further in Chapter 9.) Answer A refers to the interpretive principle of contra proferentem (construe against the drafter) as discussed in Note 3 following the Joyner v. Adams case in Chapter 5. As indicated there, however, the rule is used when there is an ambiguity that cannot otherwise be resolved. There are clear rules of construction for conditions of satisfaction that would make resort to contra proferentem unnecessary. Answer C would be incorrect because conditions of satisfaction are never construed to allow completely unfettered discretion. There is always at a minimum the constraint of the implied duty of good faith. Answer D would not be correct because it is perfectly clear from the *Morin* case, its notes, and the Restatement (Second) §228 that conditions of satisfaction are not deemed too uncertain to be enforceable even though there is some inherent indefiniteness in those terms.

Chapter 7

1. Answer B is the best answer. Although the courts are not entirely consistent in determining what is a "necessary," they tend to include the necessities of life: food, shelter, medical care, etc. Adam's use of transportation to support his ability to obtain those necessities would arguably be a necessary as well. Answer A is clearly not correct because mere depreciation of the motorcycle will not preclude the ability to disaffirm the contract, though some jurisdictions would require compensation by the minor to the other party for use or benefit received, as in the *Dodson* case. Similarly, answer D is not correct because the ability of a minor to disaffirm clearly extends to fully executed contracts. Answer C is not correct because there is no requirement that the contract be unfair in order for the minor to disaffirm, though that requirement does apply to cases of mental incapacity in some situations. Note that Adam might be emancipated since his parents are deceased and he supports himself, but that is not clear from the facts.
2. Answer B is the best answer. Natalie lacks volitional capacity because she is unable to act in a reasonable manner in the transaction. Note that rescission on the basis of volitional incapacity generally requires a showing that the counterparty had reason to know of the condition. See Restatement (Second) of Contracts §15(1)(b). See also §15(2) (providing that a contract resulting from mental incapacity is not voidable if the contract is on fair terms, the counterparty does not know of the incapacity, and avoidance would be unjust based on the circumstances). Some courts, like the court in Sparrow v. Demonico, require the mental incapacity to be established by medical evidence. A person lacks cognitive capacity if the person is unable to understand the transaction that the person is entering into. Natalie does not appear to lack cognitive capacity because she understands that she has been purchasing many items that she does not need. Therefore, choice A is incorrect. Answer C is incorrect because the expiration of the return period might bar a claim for breach of contract, but would not affect a right to rescind the contract because of incapacity. Answer D is also incorrect. Even though it may be difficult for a store to know of incapacity, the sale will be subject to rescission only if the store had reason to know of the incapacity. See §15(1)(b). Moreover, the burden of proving incapacity will rest on the person claiming incapacity. See Sparrow v. Demonico.
3. Answer A is the best answer. To establish duress to avoid a contract, a party must show an improper threat by the other party, manifestation of assent induced by the threat, and the absence of a reasonable alternative. See Restatement (Second) of Contracts §175(1). Unless SEC was in desperate need of funds, it is likely that it had a reasonable alternative to accepting RAB's offer, for example, by filing a lawsuit. Even if it did establish this element, SEC still might fail in a claim for duress because RAB's threat may not have been improper, for example, if RAB had a good faith belief that SEC breached the contract. Answer B is incorrect because a threat may be improper even if it is not illegal, for example, a threat to breach a contract in bad faith. See Restatement (Second) of Contracts §176(1)(d). While some jurisdictions may require a wrongful threat to be illegal, this is a minority view. Answer C is incorrect because it does not appear that SEC was under the domination of RAB; compare the facts of this situation with the *Odorizzi* case. In addition, domination is only one element of undue influence; SEC would also need to establish unfair persuasion. See Restatement (Second) of Contracts §177(1). Answer D is incorrect because an arm's length business transaction will rarely if ever amount to a fiduciary relationship.
4. FALSE. Under general contract principles, a party may rescind a contract if the party's assent was induced by a material false representation by the counterparty on which the recipient was justified in relying, even if the representation was made innocently. In other words, it is not necessary to show fraud or negligence by the counterparty to rescind the contract based on a material misrepresentation. See Restatement (Second) of Contracts §164(1). In this case, the representation that the painting was an "original" by Caldo seems clearly material because it goes to the essence of the bargain. Moreover, the Buyer would be justified in relying on the Dealer's representation because Dealer is in the art business. Note that if the Buyer brought suit in tort rather than to rescind the contract, it would probably be necessary for the Buyer to establish negligence or fraudulent intent (scienter) to recover from the Dealer. Note also that because the painting is movable personal property it would be classified as a "good" under the Uniform Commercial Code. Buyer could also seek to

recover damages or rescind the contract for breach of an express warranty by the Dealer. See UCC §2-313.

5. Answer C is the best answer. While there are different formulations of the doctrine of unconscionability, the most frequently stated elements of the doctrine come from the *Williams* case: "an absence of meaningful choice on the part of one of the parties together with contract terms which are unreasonably favorable to the other party." See note 1 following *Williams*. Answer A is incorrect. While some courts have held that unconscionability cannot be the basis of an affirmative claim, a number of courts have held the doctrine can be used as either a shield or a sword, particularly when the party seeking to recover would not otherwise have a basis for relief from unconscionable behavior. See *In re Checking Account Overdraft Litigation* discussed in note 5 following the *McFarland* case. Answer B is incorrect because a number of court decisions have allowed claims of unconscionability based on excessive price. See note 4 following *Williams*. Answer D is incorrect. While fraud may be a basis of a claim for damages, an incorrect prediction in itself would be insufficient to establish unconscionability or fraud; it would probably be treated as a mere expression of opinion unless there was some evidence that the repairman did not in fact hold the opinion that he was expressing. See Restatement (Second) of Contracts §168.
6. Answer C is the best answer. Rule 5.6(a) of the ABA Model Rules of Professional Conduct, which are followed in almost all jurisdictions, provide that it is unethical for a lawyer to "participate in offering or making . . . (a) . . . a[n] . . . employment, or other similar type of agreement that restricts the right of a lawyer to practice after termination of the relationship, except an agreement concerning benefits upon retirement." While Rule 5.6 is an ethics rule, most courts would probably enforce the rule by invalidating any agreement that violated its provisions. See note 6 following Valley Medical Specialists v. Farber. Answer A is incorrect because covenants not to compete must be reasonable not only as to time but also geographically. Here there is no geographical limitation on the covenant. Answer B is incorrect. While a law firm, indeed any business, may have a legitimate interest in protecting its investment in an employee, the employer's interest is only one factor in determination of the reasonableness of a covenant. In addition, Answers A and B are incorrect for another reason: Covenants not to compete by lawyers are unethical and therefore probably unenforceable. Answer D is not the best answer. An agreement restricting a lawyer's right to practice law may or may not interfere with the judicial process. In addition, the fundamental reason for the ethical prohibition against lawyers' entering into restrictive covenants is protection of clients' right to engage lawyers of their choice rather than protection of the judicial process.
7. Answer D is the best answer. Covenants not to compete must contain reasonable restrictions regarding scope, duration, and geography. In addition, the covenantee must have a legitimate interest in the covenant. Therefore, answers A, B, and C all contain information that would be relevant to determination of the enforceability of the covenant. The salesman's current salary might be relevant to damages, but it does not appear to have any relevance to the reasonableness of the covenant, or in any event less relevance that the other choices.
8. Answer A is the best answer because it is not a correct statement of the law. Most courts would permit payment to the surrogate mother for reasonable expenses as well as compensation for the time involved in the pregnancy, as long as the payment is not contingent on surrender of parental rights. Answers B and C are correct statements of the law and therefore not a correct choice. See *P.M. v. T.B.* and the notes following the case. Answer D is also a correct statement of the law and therefore not a correct choice. See *P.M. v. T.B.* and the discussion of the *Johnson v. Calvert* case in that opinion and the following notes.

Chapter 8

1. Answer B is the best answer. The Buyer probably bears the risk of the mistake because the Buyer could have inquired into the zoning of the property. See Restatement §154. Answer A is incorrect because the doctrine of mutual mistake can encompass legal as well as factual mistakes. The text of Restatement §152 does not limit the concept of mutual mistake to factual mistakes. See also note 1 following *Lenawee*. Of course, a party is more likely to bear the risk of a legal mistake because a court is more likely to assign the risk to the party that failed to investigate the law, but there is not a per se prohibition on the application of the doctrine of mistake to legal mistakes. Answer C is probably not the best answer because mutual mistake in itself is not sufficient to avoid the contract; the doctrine of mutual mistake requires the showing of several other elements, including that the buyer does not bear the risk of the mistake. Recall, however, that mutual mistake cases are known to reach inconsistent outcomes and some courts might accept the mutual mistake argument. Answer D is incorrect. In some cases a contract will have an "as is" clause, as in *Lenawee*, and such a clause may be the basis of risk allocation, but risk of the mistake can be allocated in other ways beyond agreement of the parties.
2. Answer C is the best answer. Proof of unilateral mistake requires a special showing of circumstances not required to establish mutual mistake. The circumstances set forth in Answer C are found in Restatement (Second) of Contracts §153(a) and (b). Answer A is incorrect because unilateral mistake is generally grounds for avoidance of a contract but not a basis of affirmative relief (except if based in restitution). Thus, if a party to a contract encounters circumstances that could be the grounds of a claim for relief based on either mutual or unilateral mistake and the party completes performance, it will not be able to recover the

increased cost. An alternative is for the party to refuse to perform, claiming that its performance is excused because of mistake. However, this strategy runs the risk that the party claiming relief may be sued by the counterparty and found to be in breach. Answer B is also incorrect because a party may bear the risk of mistake if it should have discovered and protected against the circumstance that is the claimed basis of mistake. Answer D is not the best answer. Some courts have limited the grounds for relief based on unilateral mistake to mistakes that are palpable or based on computational errors, but this is an older view. The Restatement and most modern courts would allow relief based on unilateral mistake on broader grounds. See notes 1 and 2 following *BMW Financial.*

3. Answer C is the best answer. See note 3 following *Mel Frank* with regard to force majeure clauses and the common inclusion of a strike provision as grounds for excuse. Answer A is not correct. While impossibility of performance is one basis for relief from a contract, excuse based on changed circumstances is not limited to that ground. See *Hemlock* and *Mel Frank* and related notes. Since AutoParts is supplying "goods" to FM, the UCC applies to the contract. UCC §2-615 expressly applies to sellers. However, most courts have applied the section also to buyers. See comment 9 to §2-615 and note 2 following the *Mel Frank* case. Therefore, answer B is not the best advice. Answer D is incorrect. An increase in the cost of performance by the buyer will not be sufficient grounds for the excuse of impracticability except if it is an "extreme and unreasonable" change that renders the performance fundamentally different from what the parties expected. See notes 1 and 2 following *Hemlock*. Excuse on this later basis is rare, and the buyer would not be likely to meet that standard.
4. Answer A is the best answer. While National Artists' purpose has been frustrated to some extent, it seems unlikely that the performance has been substantially frustrated. As the comment to Restatement §265 states: "It is not enough that the transaction has become less profitable for the affected party or even that he will sustain a loss. The frustration must be so severe that it is not fairly to be regarded as within the risks that he assumed under the contract." In fact, it is not at all clear that the absence of the drummer would cause lost ticket sales since sales have been slow even before the problem with the drummer arose. Answer B is probably incorrect. The fact that the parties did not specify that all original band members must be present would not be taken to mean that any band members could simply drop out. The tour promoter would have a strong argument that it was a basic assumption of the contract that the essential band members would be present. The band's argument would be that the drummer was not essential to performance. Answer C is incorrect because the existence of governmental action that prohibits performance may be the basis of relief from a contract on the ground of impracticability or frustration, but relief will not be available merely because governmental action affects the value or performance of a contract to some extent. See the *Mel Frank* case. Answer D is incorrect. If a party is at fault, it will probably prevent that party from claiming excuse on the ground of frustration (and related theories of excuse). See Restatement (Second) §265. However, fault of one party is alone insufficient to excuse the other party if the contract can still be performed.
5. Answer D is the best answer. Answer A is incorrect because the contract is governed by the UCC and under §2-209(1) a modification of a contract "needs no consideration to be binding." Answer C is probably incorrect. The fact that the seller would have faced an increase in the cost of performance would almost certainly not qualify for excuse under the impracticability standard stated in UCC §2-615, Comment 4, which requires an extreme change in cost that changes the essential nature of that performance. While a modification of a contract under the UCC does not require consideration, it still must satisfy the statute of frauds if the contract comes within the scope of the UCC §2-201 or there is a "no oral modification" clause. See §§2-209(2) and (3) and the notes following Brookside Farms v. Mama Rizzo's, Inc. The contract here is for a price of more than $500 and thus, under the majority view, the modification would need to be in writing or otherwise fall within one of the excuses for a writing in §2-201. See Note 1 following *Brookside Farms*. However, UCC §§2-209(4) and (5) go on to provide, in essence, that an oral modification will be enforceable if material reliance on the oral modification has occurred and would make a retraction of the oral agreement unjust. See Note 3 following *Brookside Farms*. The reliance by the seller on the buyer's oral agreement to accept delayed delivery cannot be reversed and thus there will be injustice if the oral modification is not enforced, making D the best answer and making answer B incorrect.

Chapter 9

1. D. The sales contract included an express condition that financing needed to be approved before Homer would be obligated to go forward with the house purchase. The condition was not satisfied because Homer failed to provide necessary documentation. The nonoccurrence of the express condition resulted from intentional "prevention" by Homer and the nonoccurrence would be excused. See Note 10 after the *enXco* case. Thus, Homer would be obligated to go forward with the purchase even without the loan approval. If Homer had applied for the loan in good faith and still been denied, then Answer B would have been correct, but since he did not, his prevention of the condition makes Answer B incorrect. While impracticability could be grounds for nonperformance of a contract, including failure to perform an implied duty to pursue the loan in good faith, it is very unlikely that Homer could establish the elements for an impracticability defense based on a drop in his investment account. See the *Hemlock* case in Chapter 8. Therefore, Answer

A would not be correct. Answer C would not be correct because express conditions require strict compliance; substantial compliance is not enough. See Note 2 after the *enXco* case.

2. C. Teri repudiated her employment contract when she stated that she would perform only if she was paid additional salary. An unequivocal statement that a party will perform only if they are given additional consideration beyond that called for by the contract is a classic form of repudiation. See Note 2 after the *Truman L. Flatt* case. Therefore, Teri did repudiate the contract and Answer D is incorrect. Teri retracted her repudiation, however, before Paragon did anything in response to that repudiation and therefore she had that ability. See Note 2 after the *Truman L. Flatt* case. Thus, Answer C is correct and Answer A is incorrect for that same reason. Answer B could have been correct, since a repudiation of the entire contract is a material breach, but since such a breach can be "cured" by an effective retraction, Answer B is not correct.
3. B. Because express conditions are not favored in the law, courts are reluctant to interpret language as having that effect unless it is quite clear. See Note 1 after the *enXco* case. This reluctance to find an express condition is particularly true when the finding of an express condition would create a risk of forfeiture. See Note 5 after the *Sackett* case. Thus, Answer D would be incorrect. The performance date in the contract would only be a promise of performance to which the constructive condition of substantial performance would apply. See Note 4 following the *Jacob & Youngs* case. For that reason, Answer B would be correct. Answer A suggests a fundamental misperception; because there is a valid contract with mutual assent and consideration, there would not be a need for Carl to resort to a claim in restitution to recover his payment. Note, however, that if Carl had committed a material breach and was not entitled to recover the contract price, he might still recover in restitution. See Note 8 following the *Jacob & Youngs* case. While some courts persist in the approach that a willful breach must always be a material breach, Professor Corbin and others have criticized that view. See Note 7 following the *Jacob & Youngs* case. In any event, there is nothing in the facts that indicate a purposeful deviation or delay in Carl's performance; therefore his breach would not be deemed willful and Answer C is incorrect.
4. D. The courts almost uniformly treat the time period in an option to purchase land as an express condition that requires receipt of notice by the optionor or seller by the stated deadline. See Note 3 following the *JNA Realty* case. For the same reason, Answer A would not be correct; the mailbox rule does not apply to option contracts in most jurisdictions. See also the notes on option contracts following the *Berryman* case in Chapter 3. Answer B raises the possible application of the substantial performance rule to an express condition. That idea has been clearly rejected by most courts and the Restatement (Second). See Note 2 following the *enXco* case. Answer C suggests the prospect of excuse due to risk of forfeiture, but as indicated by Note 3 following the *JNA Realty* case, courts have not been receptive to such equitable claims in an option to purchase rather an option to renew a lease as in *JNA Realty*. The $5,000 down payment and other expenses incurred would most likely be deemed to be the price that Bob paid to have the six-month period to decide whether he wanted to buy the land.
5. C. As stated in Note 3 following the *Truman L. Flatt* case, financial difficulties alone, even to the point of insolvency, will not be deemed to amount to an anticipatory repudiation of a contract. Thus, Answer A is not correct. Such financial difficulties, however, may well provide grounds for a right to demand adequate assurances. See Note 2 after the *Hornell Brewing* case and Comments 3 and 4 to UCC §2-609. The subsequent failure to give adequate assurances within a reasonable time would mean a repudiation under UCC §2-609(4). The flaw with the demand for assurances in this problem is that the Seller, ABC, already had the information about Mike's financial difficulties before making the contract. The right to demand adequate assurances requires that there be a change in circumstances that arise "after" the contract is made. See Note 2 after the *Hornell Brewing* case and Comment 1 to UCC §2-609. Thus, Answer C is correct; ABC would not be justified in its demand for assurances. It follows then that Mike's response would not be a failure to give required assurances and Answer B would not be the best answer. Note that if the demand had been justified, Mike's response would likely not have been sufficient. While Comment 4 to UCC §2-609 does not establish any specific requirements for what constitutes adequate assurances, Mike's defiant and threatening response would almost certainly not have been adequate. Answer D is incorrect because Comments 3 and 4 to UCC §2-609 indicate that a "rumor" from a reliable or trustworthy source may in fact provide reasonable grounds for insecurity. The newspaper and trade magazines would be sufficient sources for the information if the reports had first surfaced after the contract was made.

Chapter 10

1. C. The general formula for expectation damages contains two items for reduction of damages, one of which is loss avoided, often referred to as mitigation. See the introductory text to section A on Computing the Value of Plaintiff's Expectation. It should be noted that Gabriella would be entitled to post-judgment interest at the statutory rate until Francesco paid the judgment, reflecting the fact that Gabriella did not have the investment use of the damage amount until Francesco paid her the amount of the judgment. On post-judgment interest see note 3 following Handicapped Children's Education Board v. Lukaszewski. Answer A is incorrect. While it may be desirable to hire an expert to establish her damages, an expert is not essential. If Gabriella resells the property in an arm's length transaction within a reasonable time, the amount of the real sale price will

be presumptive evidence of its fair market value. In addition, in most jurisdictions Gabriella, as the owner of the property, is qualified to testify about its fair market value. See note 3 following Crabby's Inc. v. Hamilton. Answer B is incorrect. To recover prejudgment interest, a party must show that the damages were a "liquidated" amount. Damages are liquidated when both the amount due and the due date are fixed and certain, or when the damages can be determined by mathematical calculation. Gabriella's damages depend on a determination of the fair market value of the property at the date of breach. This amount is not fixed or certain nor can it be determined by mathematical calculation because it depends on a number of facts and circumstances which the trier of fact must evaluate. Answer D is incorrect for two reasons. First, Gabriella did not pay the commission because the commission was only due on closing. Second, even if she had paid the commission she would not have been entitled to recover the amount because the commission was a cost that she had to pay in order to receive the purchase price. In fact, Francesco has the right to have the damages that he must pay reduced by the amount of the commission that she would have had to pay to receive the purchase price.

2. B. The measure of damages for breach of a land sale contract would generally be the difference between the contract price and the fair market value on the date for performance. See the *Crabby's* case and Note 1 following it. Answer A would not be correct because it would be overcompensation and perhaps punitive damages for Janet to keep the land and get the full contract price, too. Answer C would not be applicable because Mega is the party in breach and Janet is not mitigating. If Janet had breached, then Mega's substitute contract might have been made in mitigation. Answer D is not correct because the nonbreaching party does not have to show reliance to collect damages where the promise is enforced because there is a contract with consideration and mutual assent.
3. A. As discussed by the court in *American Standard*, when repair would involve economic waste in the sense of undoing work that has been done and the breaching party substantially performed in good faith, the measure of damages is the diminution in market value caused by the breach rather than the cost of repair. See the discussion of Jacob & Youngs v. Kent in *American Standard*. Answer B is incorrect. While it is true that Howard might pocket a damage award, that fact is not a sufficient reason to deny recovery because he will have foregone restoration of the property. See Emery v. Caledonia Sand & Gravel Co., note 3 following *American Standard*. Answer C is incorrect. While the family farm as a whole may have idiosyncratic value, the type of wiring in the walls does not seem to have been a matter of personal value to Howard. Answer D is incorrect. Under Restatement §348(2) damages may be measured either by the diminution in market value or the reasonable cost of completing performance if that cost "is not clearly disproportionate to the probable loss in value to him." In this case, the cost of completion seems clearly disproportionate because the effect on market value is *de minimis* while the cost of repair is several hundred thousand dollars.
4. D. As stated above, foreseeabilty is determined at the time the contract is made. Perhaps the school could argue that it was not foreseeable at the time of her tenure with the school that her publication contract required her to be a tenured professor at an accredited law school, but it is doubtful that foreseeability would be interpreted to require the breaching party to have such detailed information. Note also that Stephanie has taken reasonable efforts to mitigate her damages. Answer A is incorrect. While a plaintiff must establish damages with reasonable certainty, Restatement (Second) of Contracts §352, royalties are not inherently speculative. If Zinn is able to establish the fact of damage – perhaps she can obtain testimony that people would have purchased the book if it had been published – then a court or jury will generally be able to determine damages even if they are uncertain in amount. Answer B is incorrect because modern contract law has largely rejected the "tacit agreement" test. See note 5 following Hadley v. Baxendale. Answer C is also incorrect because foreseeability is determined at the time the contract is made in order to enable the parties to contract out of or limit damage liability. See note 3 following Hadley v. Baxendale. In addition, foreseeability does not require the nonbreaching party to prove that the amount of damages was foreseeable.
5. C. While it may not have been palatable to Stephanie to accept an offer of reinstatement, this concern probably does not rise to the level of "special circumstances" justifying rejection of Southeastern's offer. See Fair v. Red Lion discussed in note 4 after *Maness*. Perhaps Stephanie could argue that accepting her old job at one-half her original salary amounts to "undue humiliation," and this constitutes "special circumstances." While this is a plausible argument, Answer C is the best choice among the answers offered. Answer A is incorrect. While contract law imposes a duty of good faith in the performance and enforcement of contracts, the general rule with regard to contract damages is that the nonbreaching party is only entitled to compensation for her loss of the benefit of the bargain regardless of the willfulness of the breach. The last section of this chapter examines the theoretical basis of this principle, including the economic theory of efficient breach. Answer B is incorrect because an employee only has an obligation to accept "comparable" employment. See the *Parker* case discussed in note 5 following *Maness*. Employment as a contract attorney would be considered to be significantly inferior employment by almost all law professors. Answer D is incorrect because the failure of the employee to make any effort to seek comparable employment is insufficient to establish a reduction in damages for lack of mitigation. The employer has the burden of proving that the employee failed to

make reasonable efforts to seek comparable employment *and* the availability and suitability of comparable employment. See *Maness.*

6. D. Lack of availability of the car on the market is a "proper circumstance" supporting the remedy of specific performance under UCC §2-716. Answer A is incorrect. While historically specific performance developed in contracts for the sale of land, it is not limited to that type of contract as shown by UCC §2-716. Answer B is incorrect because specific performance of contracts for the sale of goods under UCC §2-716 is not limited to situations where the goods are unique. It also applies "in other proper circumstances." Answer C is incorrect. When a seller breaches a contract for the sale of goods, the basic damage remedy for the buyer is "cover," UCC §2-712, measured by the difference between the cover price for the goods and the contract price, plus incidental and consequential damages. Unfortunately for Orsinski, he is unable to find a replacement E85 on the market. In the absence of cover, an injured buyer may recover the difference between the market price for the goods and the contract price, plus incidental and consequential damages. UCC §2-713. If the price that Orsinski contracted to pay for the E85 is the market price, this remedy will also not be adequate.
7. Answer A is the best answer. Of course, the seller (EM) must prove that it gave proper notice under UCC §2-706 and that the sale was made in good faith and was commercially reasonable. If so, EM may recover the difference between the contract price and the resale price plus incidental damages. Answer B is incorrect because the right to recover profit under UCC §2-708(2) is dependent on the seller being a "lost volume seller." Cf. *Jetz Service.* To establish that it is a lost volume seller, the seller must show that it had: (1) the capacity to make an additional sale; (2) that the additional sale would have been profitable; and (3) that it probably would have made an additional sale absent the buyer's breach. See note 2 following *Jetz Service.* In this case because of the limited supply of E85s, it is highly unlikely that EM could establish that it had the capacity to make an additional sale. Answer C is incorrect because under the UCC the seller may sell at either a public or a private sale, although the notice requirements are different. See UCC §2-706(2). Answer D is incorrect. Lack of proof of market price would probably be fatal to a seller's attempt to recover market damages under UCC 2-708(1). However, an arm's length resale within a reasonable time after the breach would probably be evidence of market price. In addition, even if the seller does not offer proof of market price, the seller may still recover resale damages under UCC §2-706.
8. B. The "American rule" provides that a prevailing party in litigation is generally not allowed to recover its attorney fees. There are exceptions to the American rule that allow the awarding of attorney fees to the prevailing party when the parties have a valid contract term allowing for attorney fees, when there is an applicable statute granting such fees, or when there is an established court rule that allows for recovery. None of these exceptions appear to be applicable on these facts. See the notes following the *Zapata* case. Answer A is incorrect because the "bad faith" exception to the recovery of punitive damages applies to insurance contracts and has not been extended beyond that particular type of contract. See the Comment above about the Recovery of Punitive Damages for Bad Faith Breach of Contract. Answer C is incorrect. Under the Restatement test, damages for emotional distress may be recovered for breach of contract if *either* the plaintiff suffered bodily harm *or* where either the contract or the breach in question was "of such a kind that serious emotional disturbance was a particularly likely result." Restatement (Second) §353. Of course, whether this contract meets the "particularly likely result" standard is arguable. See notes 4-5 following *Erlich.* Answer D is incorrect because under the Restatement (Third) of Torts §47 it is possible in some cases to recover damages for emotional distress as a result of negligence. See note 2 following *Erlich.*

Chapter 11

1. The best answer is D. Answers A and B do not allow for the possibility of an offset for reasonable mitigation by CC, so in that respect C and D are better answers. Although CC knows her previous job at EF is now not available, given her experience and expertise it may well be that there are other reasonable employment opportunities open to her. Answer C would be a claim of expectation damages, based on the maximum amount of income she could have earned at AZ from commissions on sales. Since she had performed poorly during her first six months at AZ, it is likely that a court would regard that latter claim as being too speculative. In that case reliance damages should be an alternative claim available to CC, based on the amount of annual salary from EF she gave up to accept AZ's offer. (Recall the *Dialist* case, discussed in the Notes following *Wartzman.*) This is what Answer D calls for. AZ might argue against that claim on the basis that as an at-will employee CC could have been dismissed by EF any time; there appears to be no reason why that would have happened, however. Answers B and D are thus better answers than A and C, but D is the better of the two because it contemplates the possibility of mitigation by CC.
2. The best answer is B, because it provides CC with a full expectation damages remedy. Here, as in the first two answers to Q. 1, above, Answer A does not allow for the possibility of mitigation by CC, so Answer B is better than A. Answer C, reliance damages based on her higher salary at EF, is not appropriate in Question 2, because the value of CC's lost expectation can be calculated and is not speculative. To award CC damages measured by her former salary at EF in this case would be to overcompensate her. Although she elected to accept AZ's offer because she wanted job security, the remedy of specific performance, as in Answer D, is rarely available to an aggrieved employee as a remedy

in a common law suit for wrongful termination of an employment contract.

3. The best answer is C. Answer A would not be correct because although the agreement between them is oral, this fact does not keep it from being enforceable. (Recall our discussion of the statute of frauds in Chapter 4.) No ordinary statute of frauds applies here: the agreement is to be performed in less than a year and it is not for a sale of goods, since a contract of this sort is commonly considered to be one primarily for construction services, not covered by UCC Article 2. Nor does it involve the transfer of an interest in land. Moreover, allowing Bonnie to keep the smokehouse without paying anything for it would likely be deemed unjust enrichment, despite any possible writing requirement. See Note 3 following the *Alaska Democratic Party* case in Chapter 4. Answer B is a plausible answer, given the historical practice among courts to deny any recovery to a breaching party, but the tendency of modern courts and the Restatement (Second) is not to preclude recovery even by a party who commits an intentional, material breach. See the *Lancellotti* case and the notes following it. Answer C is supported by *Lancellotti* and the Restatement (Second) §374 in allowing recovery to the party in breach for benefit conferred, less any harm caused by the breach. The contract may also be deemed divisible into two parts, thus allowing recovery for the part performed, minus any harm caused by the breach. See Note 8 following the *Jacob & Youngs* case in Chapter 9 and the Restatement (Second) §240. The *Lancellotti* case and cited authority therein are clear, however, that recovery by the party in breach cannot exceed a ratable portion of the contract price. See footnote 3 in *Lancellotti*. Answer D is incorrect because it would allow recovery in restitution without the limitation of the contract rate.
4. Answer D is the most likely remedy of the four possible answers. It calls for application of the conventional rule which measures damages by the difference between the contract price and the fair market value in a breach of contract to sell real property (recall the discussion in Note 1 after the *Crabby's* case in Chapter 10), and it also calls for restitution to GD of its down payment. Answer A is a plausible answer but not clearly correct. The remedy of specific performance, which will ordinarily be limited to situations where money damages are for some reason inadequate, is commonly available to a disappointed purchaser of real property, each parcel of which is deemed to be "unique" for this purpose. Answer A asserts that this remedy will not be granted against an elderly widow. While it is true that specific performance is an equitable remedy over which the court has considerable discretion, the fact that RR was aware of GD's plans when she made the contract makes it unlikely that her regret about selling would keep a court from awarding specific performance to GD. (Note: The facts do not say that she would have nowhere else to go to live; that might be a more difficult case for the court.) Answer B is correct in suggesting that even an agreement which is not too indefinite to be a binding contract might nevertheless be deemed too indefinite for a court to enforce specifically. However, mere postponement of agreement on the time and place of closing is not likely to be seen as creating a substantial problem in that regard; such provisions are common. Thus, Answer B is not correct. Answer C is probably not correct because consequential damages, including lost profits, must be measurable with reasonable certainty. Based on the given facts, future profits are likely to be considered too speculative. On the other hand, however, (1) GD is an established business with a track record of operating successful pharmacies and (2) before contracting with RR, GD did a study indicating that a pharmacy at this location would be a profitable one. These factors make it plausible that a court would consider an award of lost profits (at least for a reasonable period of time) to be appropriate, but Answer D is the more likely outcome.
5. Answer C is the best answer. It correctly states the conventional rule applicable to a breach by the seller of real property. Answer A is plausible but probably not accurate. Although courts do routinely award specific performance to disappointed buyers of real property, they are less likely to award that remedy to a disappointed seller even though all land is considered unique. See Note 2 after the *City Stores* case. The seller can usually resort to a sale to another buyer, with a damage claim if necessary, making the seller's remedy "at law" against the first buyer an adequate one. That might well be the case here, particularly if GD has already contracted to buy a different property. On the other hand, GD's breach has no legal or (arguably) moral excuse, so a court might award RR specific performance, thus giving her a stronger bargaining chip if GD really wants to get out of its deal with her. Answer B might reach the same result as C, if the price that GD pays for a comparable property is deemed to be sufficient evidence of the market value of RR's property as well, but it is not the rule articulated by the courts for cases like this. Answer D is generally a correct one, except that under the conventional rule (see Answer C), the non-breaching party will have a claim for consequential or incidental damages even if she makes a substitute contract to resale at the same price as in the contract with the defendant.

Chapter 12

1. D. The promisee, Hirato, intended to benefit the employees, and enforcement of the promise is appropriate to carry out that intent. See Restatement (Second) §302(1)(b). Answer A is incorrect because a person can have rights under a contract even if the person is not a signatory to the contract if the person qualifies as an intended third-party beneficiary. Answer B is incorrect. While Hirato may not have had a duty to continue the employment of the workers, Hirato could intend to provide them with a benefit of Construction's promised performance. Under the traditional terminol-

ogy of third-party beneficiaries, the workers would be viewed as third-party donee beneficiaries. Answer C is also incorrect. Receipt of a benefit is insufficient to establish a person as an intended beneficiary because the person may be an incidental beneficiary. See Restatement (Second) of Contracts §302(2).

2. C. At one time partial assignments were unenforceable, but today such assignments are generally enforceable, subject to the requirement of joinder of all interested parties. See note 4 following *Herzog* and Restatement §326. Answer A is incorrect. The transaction between O'Hara and Bank is an assignment because O'Hara is selling its right to receive payment under a development contract to Bank. The sale will be governed by general contract law rather than Article 2 of the UCC because the sale involves contractual rights arising out of development of real estate contracts, rather than contracts for the sale of goods. Note that it is possible that Article 9 of the UCC dealing with secured financing could also apply to this transaction. Under Restatement (Second) §317, there are three basic grounds by which an assignment may be unenforceable: violation of statute or public policy, material adverse effect on the other party, and valid preclusion by contract term. While there is a public policy in favor of free markets, federal statutes restrict the assignment of any federal government contract or order and of any claim against the federal government probably because of the volume of contracts in which the federal government is involved. See note 1 following *Herzog*. Answer B is incorrect. In the absence of a clause prohibiting assignment of a contract right, and the facts do not refer to such a clause, an assignment is valid unless it will have a material adverse effect on the obligor (i.e., the developer). An assignment to a bank does not appear to have such a material adverse effect because it will not change the performance by the developer other than the entity to which payment will be made. Answer D is incorrect. The sale of a right to receive payment under a contract is an assignment but not a delegation of performance. Therefore, Bank would not have any performance obligation if O'Hara breaches a contract. Note that the situation might be different if the transaction between O'Hara and Bank involved a sale of "the contract" or of "all my rights under the contract" or an assignment in similar general terms. See Restatement §328 and the following problem.

3. D. When a person acquires the "contract rights" of another person, the acquisition operates as an assignment of rights, a delegation of duties, and as assumption by the assignee/delegate of the duties under the contract. See Restatement (Second) of Contracts §328(1), (2). Answer A is incorrect. While it is true that some of Livingston's services involve personal services by its employees, the restriction on delegation of personal service contracts applies to personal services by an individual, not to a business, unless the obligee has a substantial interest in performance of personal services by a particular individual in the business. See note 2 following *Sally Beauty Co.* Here there is no indication that the owners have a substantial interest in personal services by a particular individual at Livingston. Answer B is incorrect because it misconceives the holding in *Sally Beauty*. In that case, the court held that the obligee (Nexxus) was not bound to Sally Beauty as an assignee/delegate of a contract between Nexxus and Best because Sally Beauty was owned by a competitor of Nexxus. This problem does not involve an agreement to distribute products and there is no reason to think that National will have any competitive reason not to use its best efforts to provide management services to its new obligees, the owners. Answer C is incorrect. Delegation of a duty does not relieve the delegating party of its contractual duties to the obligee unless the contract specifically relieves the delegating party of those duties or the obligee agrees to release the original obligor. See Restatement (Second) of Contracts §318(3).

TABLE OF CASES

Principal cases are indicated by italics.

A&A Mech., Inc. v. Thermal Equip. Sales, Inc., 507
A & M Land Dev. Co. v. Miller, 724-726, 727, 728
A & M Produce v. FMC Corp., 676
Aaron E. Levine & Co. v. Calkraft Paper Co., 178
Aas v. Superior Court, 560
Abdelrhman v. Ackerman, 413
Academy Chi. Publishers v. Cheever, 152
Aceves v. U.S. Bank, N.A., 255, 262, 264
ACG, Inc. v. Southeast Elevator, Inc., 932
Action Eng'g v. Martin Marietta Aluminum, 509
Adamar of N.J., Inc. v. Luber, 589
Adam Metal Supply, Inc. v. Electrodex, Inc., 189
Adams v. Underwood, 327
Adams v. Whitmore, 581, 583
ADC Orange, Inc. v. Coyote Acres, Inc., 848
Addington v. Texas, 584
Addyston Pipe & Steel Co.; United States v., 691
Adkins v. Labor Ready, Inc., 660
Adolph Coors Co. v. Rodriguez, 794
Adoption of. *See name of party*
Advanced Choices, Inc. v. State Dep't of Health Servs., 258, 259
Advanced Cleanup Techs., Inc. v. BP Am., 601
Advanced Mobilehome Sys. of Tampa, Inc. v. Alumax Fabricated Prods., Inc., 187
Aeolus Down, Inc. v. Credit Suisse Int'l, 824
Aerel, S.R.L. v. PCC Airfols, L.L.C., 778
Aetna Cas. & Sur. Co. v. Murphy, 527
Affiliated Distillers Brands Corp. v. R.W.L. Wine & Liquor Co., 1008
Agam v. Gavra, 1011
A.G. Edwards & Sons, Inc. v. Hilligoss, 637
Ahern v. Knecht, 133-134, 135, 136, 646
A.J. Amer Agency, Inc. v. Astonish Results, LLC, 484
Alaska Airlines, Inc. v. Stephenson, 374
Alaska Democratic Party v. Rice, 368, 375, 376
Alaska Packers' Ass'n v. Domenico, 774, 777-780, 787, 950
Albrecht v. Clifford, 564, 566
Albre Marble & Tile Co. v. Goverman, 1030
Alder v. Keighley, 903
Alfa Life Ins. Corp. v. Lewis, 620
Al-Ibrahim v. Edde, 710
Allapattah Servs., Inc. v. Exxon Corp., 472
Allegheny Coll. v. National Chautauqua Cnty. Bank, 245, 276
Allen v. Bissinger & Co., 18, 32, 33, 34, 44
Allen v. Metropolitan Life Ins. Co., 420
Allen v. Smith, 1085
Allied Van Lines, Inc. v. Bratton, 188
Alligood v. Procter & Gamble Co., 70, 157
Allstate Ins. Co. v. Medical Lien Mgmt., Inc., 1121
Alstom Power, Inc. v. RMF Indus. Contracting, Inc., 1030
Alta Vista Props., LLC v. Mauer Vision Ctr., PC, 486
Alvarez v. Alvarez, 360
Ament v. One Las Olas, Ltd., 991
American Airlines, Inc. v. American Coupon Exch., Inc., 69
American Broad. Co. v. Wolf, 1066
American Bronze Corp. v. Streamway Prods., 159, 863
American Capital Acquisition Partners, LLC v. LPL Holdings, Inc., 988
American Cyanamid Co. v. Stephen, 635
American Dredging Co. v. Miller, 167
American Exp. Lines, Inc., In re, 168
American Express Co. v. Italian Colors Rest., 663
American Fin. Servs. Ass'n v. FTC, 679
American Home Improvement, Inc. v. MacIver, 647
American List Corp. v. U.S. News & World Report, Inc., 906
American Multi-Cinema, Inc. v. Southroads, LLC, 1083
American Standard, Inc. v. Schectman, 895, 899, 900, 901
American Strategic Ins. Co. v. Lucas-Soloman, 186
American Trading & Prod. Corp. v. Shell Int'l Marine, Ltd., 753-754
Ames v. JP Morgan Chase Bank, N.A., 1134
Amex Distrib. Co. v. Mascari, 684, 686, 688, 690
AMF, Inc. v. McDonald's Corp., 862, 864, 865
AM Int'l, Inc. v. Graphic Mgmt. Assocs., Inc., 414
Amtorg Trading Corp. v. Miehle Printing Press & Mfg. Co., 1027
Anderson v. Bessemer City, 159, 1036
Anderson v. DeLisle, 1037
Anderson v. Neal Insts. Co., 1062, 1063
Anderson, Estate of, 606
APAC-Se., Inc. v. Coastal Caisson Corp., 283
Applied Equip. Corp. v. Litton Saudi Arabia Ltd., 958, 959, 962
ARB, Inc. v. E-Sys., Inc., 862, 864
Arbeeny v. Kennedy Exec. Search, Inc., 531
Arbercheski v. Oracle Corp., 936
Arbitron, Inc. v. Tralyn Broad., Inc., 86
Arbor Windsor Court, Ltd. v. Weekly Homes, Inc., 847
Arcadian Phosphates, Inc. v. Arcadian Corp., 94
Architectural Metal Sys., Inc. v. Consolidated Sys., Inc., 157
Arko v. Cirou, 631

Armendariz v. Foundation Health Psychcare Servs., Inc., 654-655, 657-658, 661
Arnold v. United Cos. Lending Corp., 667-668
Aronsohn v. Mandara, 564
Arrowood Indem. Co. v. King, 527
Arrowsmith v. Mercantile-Safe Deposit & Trust Co., 239
Arthur v. Microsoft Corp., 676
A/S Apothekernes Laboratorium for Specialpraeparater v. I.M.C. Chem. Grp., Inc., 88
Ascare v. Mastercard Int'l, Inc., 936
Asmus v. Pacific Bell, 74, 780
Association of Flight Attendants, AFL-CIO v. Horizon Air Indus., Inc., 951
ATACS Corp. v. Trans World Commc'ns, Inc., 1043-1044
AT&T Mobility LLC v. Concepcion, 24
AT&T Mobility, LLC, State ex rel., v. Wilson, 670
Atlantic City Tire & Rubber Corp. v. Southwark Foundry & Mach. Co., 1028
Atlas Roofing Corp. Chalet Shingle Prods. Liab. Litig., In re, 554
ATS-1 Corp. v. Rodriguez, 739
Atwater Creamery Co. v. Western Nat'l Mut. Ins. Co., 424
Atwood-Kellogg, Inc. v. Nickeson Farms, 866
A. Unruh Chiropractic Clinic v. De Smet Ins. Co., 1120
Austin Instrument, Inc. v. Loral Corp., 595, 596, 785, 788
Autonation U.S.A. Corp. v. Leroy, 199
Avedon Eng'g, Inc. v. Seatex, 187
Avery v. Fredericksen & Westbrook, 897
Avery v. State Farm Mut. Auto. Ins. Co., 151
Avola v. Louisiana-Pac. Corp., 553
Axelson, Inc. v. McEvoy-Willis, Div. of Smith Int'l (N. Sea), Ltd., 203

B.A.A. v. University of Iowa Hosps., 302
Babcock & Wilcox Co. v. Hitachi Am., Ltd., 158
Baby Boy J. v. Johnson, 709
Baby, In re, 700, 701
Baby M, In re, 702, 703, 708-709
Bachorz v. Miller-Forslund, 826
Bagby Land & Cattle Co. v. California Livestock Comm'n Co., 795
BAII Banking Corp. v. UPG, Inc., 865
Bak-A-Lum Corp. v. Alcoa Bldg. Prods., Inc., 497, 498
Baker v. Bailey, 454
Balandran v. Labor Ready, Inc., 654
Ball v. District No. 4, Area Bd., 318
Balla v. Gambro, Inc., 537
Ballesteros v. Johnson, 688
Balogh v. Balogh, 644
Baltazar v. Forever 21, Inc., 660, 661
Baltimore Bridge Co. v. United Rys. & Elec. Co., 1074, 1079-1080
Baltimore Orioles, Inc. v. Major League Baseball Players Ass'n, 1035, 1041
Banbury v. Omnitrition Int'l Inc., 459
Bank of Montreal v. Signet Bank, 631
Bankey v. Storer Broad., 780
Banning Co. v. California, 276
Bannum, Inc. v. 2210 Adams Place, N.E., LLC, 900
Baptist Mem'l Hosp.-N. Miss., Inc. v. Lambert, 894
Barbagallo v. Marcum LLP, 848
Bard v. Kent, 281
Barinaga v. JP Morgan Chase & Co., 797
Barnes v. Goodyear Tire & Rubber Co., 933, 934
Barnes v. Lopez, 624
Barnes v. Michalski, 490
Barrie School v. Patch, 1070, 1081-1083, 1085
Barry v. Jackson, 887
Barton v. Sclafani Invs., Inc., 126
Bashas' Inc., In re, 244-245
Basic Capital Mgmt., Inc. v. Dynex Commercial, Inc., 920
Bates v. Benedetti, 847
Bates & O'Steen v. State Bar, 633
Batsakis v. Demotsis, 137, 138
Batty v. Arizona State Dental Bd., 625
Bausch & Lomb Inc. v. Bressler, 1023
Bayer, State ex rel. v. Funk, 335, 336
Bayliner Marine Corp. v. Crow, 546, *548*, 552, 553, 554
Bayway Ref. Co. v. Oxygenated Mktg. & Trading, 186, 187, 188
B.B. v. Continental Ins. Co., 1035, 1039
Beacon Hill Civic Ass'n v. Ristorante Toscano, Inc., 691
Beacon Theatres, Inc. v. Westover, 367
Beal v. Beal, 323
Bean v. BAC Home Loans Servicing, L.P., 768
Bearden v. Honeywell Int'l Inc., 630
Beastie Boys v. Monster Energy Co., 57
Beaver v. Brumlow, 357, 365-367
Beckwith v. Talbot, 350, 351
Beidel v. Sideline Software, Inc., 504
Belk v. Martin, 737, 739
Bellamah v. Schmider, 362
Belleville Toyota, Inc. v. Toyota Motor Sales, U.S.A., Inc., 151
Bellizzi v. Huntley Estates, 896
Beltran v. InterExchange, Inc., 660
Bende & Sons, Inc. v. Crown Recreation, Inc., 743
Benjamin v. Koeppel, 693
Bennett v. Bailey, 621
Bennett v. Coors Brewing Co., 621
Bennett Heating & Air Conditioning, Inc. v. NationsBank of Md., 314
Benya v. Stevens & Thompson Paper Co., 55
Berg v. Hudesman, 442
Bergerson v. New York State Office of Mental Health, 1069
Berglund v. American Multigraph Sales Co., 574
Berkson v. Gogo LLC, 26, 219
Berliner Foods Corp. v. Pillsbury Co., 1128
Bernard v. IMI Sys., Inc., 534
Berrey v. Jeffcoat, 85
Berryman v. Kmoch, 266, 271, 272, 273, 274, 282
BH 329 NB LLC v. CBRE, Inc., 291
Biakanja v. Irving, 281
Biggins v. Shore, 1113

Biggs v. Reinsman Equestrian Prods., Inc., 930, 931, 932
Bill's Coal Co. v. Board of Pub. Utils. of Springfield, 977
Blagg v. Fred Hunt Co., 560
Blagrove v. J.B. Mech., Inc., 961
Blair Constr., Inc. v. McBeth, 894
Blair Int'l, Ltd. v. LaBarge, Inc., 978
Blake v. Midland Ry. Co., 903
Blanshan v. Russell, 116
Blumenthal v. Brewer, 326
BMW Financial Services NA LLC v. Deloach, 730, 737-738, 739, 740
Board of Control of E. Mich. Univ. v. Burgess, 271
Board of Educ. v. Heister, 1073, 1074, 1077
Board of Educ. v. Weiland, 602
Bob McKiness Excavating & Grading, Inc. v. Morton, 562, 563
Boese-Hilburn Co. v. Dean Mach. Co., 177
Bohatch v. Butler & Binion, 537
Bohler-Uddeholm Am., Inc. v. Ellwood Grp., Inc., 413-414
Bolanos v. Priority Bus. Servs., Inc., 936
Bollinger v. Fall River Rural Elec. Co-op., Inc., 535
Bonds, In re, 609
Bonebrake v. Cox, 168, 169
Bonner v. Westbound Records, Inc., 135
Boothe v. Fitzpatrick, 334
Borg-Warner Corp. v. Anchor Coupling Co., 88
Borsack v. Chalk & Vermillion Fine Arts, Ltd., 1104
Boston Helicopter Charter, Inc. v. Augusta Aviation Corp., 647
Boston LLC v. Juarez, 847
Boud v. SDNCO, Inc., 553
Bouton v. Byers, 235, 1012
Bracale v. Gibbs, 231
Braka v. Travel Assistance Int'l, 338
Brakke v. Iowa Dep't of Natural Res., 704
Bresnahan v. McAuliffe, 584
Brewer v. J-Six Farms, L.P., 753
Breza v. Thaldorf, 1036
Britton v. Turner, 841, 1026
Brochsteins, Inc. v. Whittaker Corp., 795
Brooklyn Bagel Boys, Inc. v. Earthgrains Refrigerated Dough Prods., Inc., 507
Brooks v. Hickman, 967
Brookside Farms v. Mama Rizzo's, Inc., 789, 796-798
Brooks Peanut Co. v. Great S. Peanut, LLC, 389
Brower v. Gateway 2000, Inc., 201, 204
Brown v. Bluecross Blueshield of Tenn., Inc., 1134
Brown v. Corriveau, 1118
Brown v. Genesis Healthcare Corp., 665, 668
Brown v. United States Fid. & Guar. Co., 585
Brown Dev. Corp. v. Hemond, 435
Brown Machine, Inc. v. Hercules, Inc., 165, *174*, 180, 182, 183, 191, 207
Bruce Foods Corp. v. Texas Gas Serv., 1018
Brundy v. Canby, 1065
Brunzell Constr. Co. v. G.J. Weisbrod, Inc., 280
Bruyn v. Russell, 116
Bruzesse v. Chesapeake Exploration, LLC, 146
Bryceland v. Northey, 684, 686, 687-688
Buckeye Check Cashing, Inc. v. Cardegna, 654
Buckhorn, Inc. v. Orbis Corp., 1102
Buffaloe v. Hart, 366, *382*, 387-388
Bull Motor Co. v. Murphy, 414-415
Burgess v. Superior Court, 959, 963
Burke v. Gould, 784
Burkons v. Ticor Title Ins. Co., 445
Burnham v. Karl & Gelb, P.C., 525
Burns v. McCormick, 360, 365
Burriss v. Starr, 385
Bush, In re Estate of, 327
Bush v. ProTravel Int'l, Inc., 754
Bustamante v. Intuit, Inc., 72, 73
Butcher v. Stapley, 365
Butitta v. First Mortg. Corp., 601
Butler v. Balolia, 98
Buttorff v. United Elec. Labs., Inc., Ky., 487
Bu-Vi-Bar Petroleum Corp. v. Krow, 854
Byrd v. Byrd, 170

Cabot Corp. v. AVX Corp., 599
Caceci v. DiCanio Constr. Corp., *566*
Cadle Co. v. Vargas, 407
Cahen, Estate of, 1028
C.A.I., Inc. v. Vitex Packaging Grp., Inc., 191
California & Hawaiian Sugar Co. v. Sun Ship, Inc., 1082
California Lettuce Growers, Inc. v. Union Sugar Co., 73
Cambridge Plating Co. v. Napco, Inc., 168
Campbell v. Robinson, 119
Campbell Soup Co. v. Wentz, 641
Campeggi v. Arche Inc., 535
C & J Fertilizer Inc. v. Allied Mutual Insurance Co., 416, 424, 425, 426, 649, 660
C & K Eng'g Contractors v. Amber Steel Co., 1015
Cao v. Nguyen, 621
Cape-France Enters. v. Estate of Peed, 753
Capital One Bank USA N.A. v. Ponte, 748
Capps v. Georgia Pac. Corp., 596
Capson Physicians Ins. Co. v. MMIC Ins. Inc., 629
Carideo v. Dell, Inc., 202
Carlisle v. T & R Excavating, Inc., 110
Carey v. New England Organ Bank, 580
Carma Developers (Cal.), Inc. v. Marathon Dev. Cal., Inc., 519, 520
Carmona v. Lincoln Millennium Car Wash, Inc., 660
Carnival Cruise Lines, Inc. v. Shute, 576
Carr v. Arthur D. Little, Inc., 243
Carrig v. Gilbert-Varker Corp., 43, 838
Carrothers Constr. Co. v. City of S. Hutchinson, 1081
Carter v. Matthey Laundry & Dry Cleaning Co., 885, 886
Cassinari v. Mapes, 84, 85
Caterpillar, Inc. v. Usinor Industeel, 264
Cates v. Morgan Portable Bldg. Corp., 1011
Centex v. United States, 954
Central Bearings Co. v. Wolverine Ins. Co., 422
Central Transp., Inc. v. Cleveland Metallurgical Supply Co., 159

Centron DPL Co. v. Tilden Fin. Corp., 403
Century Commc'ns v. Housing Auth. of City of Wilson, 401
Cepeda v. Swift & Co., 1036
Ceramic & Metal Coatings Corp. v. Hizer, 695
Ceres Ill., Inc. v. Illinois Scrap Processing, Inc., 88
Cerretti v. Flint Hills Rural Elec. Co-op Ass'n, 941
Chainworks, Inc. v. Webco Indus., Inc., 748, 749
Challenge Mach. Co. v. Mattison Mach. Works, 178
Chamberlain v. Parker, 896, 897, 898
Chambers v. NASCO, Inc., 951, 954
Chandelor v. Lopus, 556
Chang v. First Colonial Sav. Bank, 170
Chang v. Pacificorp, 751
Chariton Feed & Grain, Inc. v. Harder, 303
Chateau Des Charmes Wines Ltd. v. Sabate USA, Inc., 192
Cheathem v. Los Angeles Unified Sch. Dist., 939
Checking Account Overdraft Litig., In re, 674, 676
Chedd-Angier Prod. Co. v. Omni Publ'ns Int'l, Ltd., 1015
Chelini v. Nieri, 963
Chemical Distribs., Inc. v. Exxon Corp., 508
Chen v. Chen, 1104, 1106, 1107, 1112
Chesus v. Watts, 263
Chevalier v. Lane's, Inc., 376
Chicago Coliseum Club v. Dempsey, 1012
Chicago Inv. Corp. v. Dolins, 88, 89
Chicago Title Ins. Co. v. Huntington Nat'l Bank, 1011
Childers v. Talbott, 360
Chodos v. West Publ'g Co., 1024
Chorn v. Williams, 915
Chris v. Epstein, 885
Christensen v. Minneapolis Mun. Emps. Ret. Bd., 1014, 1015
Christy v. Heil, 618
Chronister Oil Co. v. UNOCAL Ref. & Mktg., 972
Ciardi v. Laurel Media Inc., 534
Cincinnati Ins. Co. v. American Hardware Mfrs. Ass'n, 1122
Circuit City v. Rockville Pike, 1075
CitaraManis v. Hallowell, 710
Cities Servs. Co. v. Gulf Oil Corp., 1010
C. Itoh & Co. (Am.) v. Jordan Int'l Co., 170
City of. *See name of city*
City Stores Co. v. Ammerman, 1048, 1055-1058, 1065
City Univ. of N.Y. v. Finalco, Inc., 295
Cives Corp. v. Callier Steel Pipe & Tube, Inc., 972
Clark v. B.P. Oil Co., 1121
Clark v. Marsiglia, 923
Clark v. Wallace Cnty. Coop. Equity Exch., 757
Claude v. Guaranty Nat'l Ins., 702
Clay Elec. Coop., Inc. v. Johnson, 1113
Clem Perrin Marine Towing, Inc. v. Panama Canal Co., 168, 865
Clifford-Jacobs Forging Co. v. Capital Eng'g & Mfg. Co., 179
C.M. v. M.C., 706
CNA Int'l Reinsurance Co. v. Phoenix, 755
Coakley & Williams, Inc. v. Shatterproof Glass Corp., 168, 169, 170
Coast Trading Co. v. Cudahy Co., 976
Coastal Steel Erectors, Inc., United States ex rel. v. Algernon Blair, Inc., 1020, 1023
Cobaugh v. Klick-Lewis, Inc., 112
Coburn v. Lenox Homes, Inc., 560
Coca-Cola Co. v. Babyback's Int'l, Inc., 375
Cochran v. Norkunas, 93
Cochran v. Quest Software, Inc., 530
Cochrane v. Little, 1006
Coddington; State v., 626
Coffman v. Fleming, 386
Coffman Indus., Inc. v. Gorman-Taber Co., 63
Cohen v. Cowles Media Co., 263, 1014
Cohen v. Lord, Day & Lord, 685, 693
Colcott v. Sutherland, 362
Coleman Mgmt., Inc. v. Meyer, 934
Colley v. Benson, Young & Downs Ins. Agency, Inc., 580
Collins v. Allied Pharmacy Mgmt., Inc., 370
Collins v. City of Newton, 536
Colonial at Lynnfield, Inc. v. Sloan, 1082
Columbus Med. Servs., LLC v. Thomas, 934
Commerce Partnership 8098 Ltd. Partnership v. Equity Contracting Co., 309, 314
Complete Gen. Constr. Co. v. Kard Welding, Inc., 284
Comstock v. North, 277
Comunale v. Traders & Gen. Ins. Co., 520
Confederate Motors, Inc. v. Terny, 57
Congregation Kadiman Toras-Moshe v. DeLeo, 239, 240, 241
Conklin v. Hurley, 567
Conklin v. Silver, 762, 763
ConocoPhillips Alaska, Inc. v. Williams Alaska Petro., Inc., 180
Conservatorship of. *See name of ward*
Consolidated Data Terminals v. Applied Digital Data Sys., Inc., 554
Contempo Design v. Chicago & Ne. Ill. Dist. Council of Carpenters, 779-780
Contemporary Mission, Inc. v. Famous Music Corp., 918
Continental Oil Co. v. Bell, 453, 456
Conway v. Cutler Grp., Inc., 565
Cook v. Coldwell Banker/Frank Laiben Realty Co., 59, 61, 64, 65, 66, 282
Cook v. Nordstrand, 845
Cooper v. Superior Court, 961
Copylease Corp. of Am. v. Memorex Corp., 867
Cordova v. World Fin. Co. of N.M., 645
Core-Mark Midcontinent Inc. v. Sonitrol Corp., 907
Corestates Bank, N.A. v. Cutillo, 108
Cort v. Bristol-Myers Co., 530
Cosmopolitan Homes, Inc. v. Weller, 560
Costco v. World Wide, 797
Council Bros., Inc. v. Ray Burner Co., 189
Cox v. United States, 585
CPG Int'l LLC v. Georgelis, 694
C.R. Anthony Co. v. Loretto Mall Partners, 442

Crabby's, Inc. v. Hamilton, 879, 886, 887, 888, 972
Crabtree v. Elizabeth Arden Sales Corp., 347, 352, 354, 355, 356
Crane Co., United States ex rel. v. Progressive Enters., Inc., 789
Crane Ice Cream Co. v. Terminal Freezing & Heating Co., 1121
Craven v. TRG-Boyton Beach, Ltd., 1058
Creative Demos, Inc. v. Wal-Mart Stores, Inc., 263
Credit Bureau Enterprises, Inc. v. Pelo, 297, 304-305, 339
Creery v. Holly, 430
Creusot-Loire Int'l Inc. v. Coppus Eng'g Corp., 864
Crisan, In re Estate of, 304
Crook v. Mortenson-Neal, 283
Crouch v. Gutmann, 831
Crowder v. Vandendeale, 560
CRS Proppants LLC v. Preferred Resin Holding Co., LLC, 753
Crum v. McCollum, 617
Cruz v. Visual Perceptions, LLC, 405
C. Szabo Contracting, Inc. v. Lorig Constr. Co., 314
Cuesport Props., LLC v. Critical Devs., LLC, 1083
Cullinane v. Uber Techs., Inc., 32, 33
Culver v. Castro, 784
Cummings, Inc. v. Dorgan, 931
Cunnison v. Richardson Greenshields Sec., Inc., 370

Daigle Commercial Grp., Inc. v. St. Laurent, 231
Dakin & Co. v. Lee, 831
Dale R. Horning Co. v. Falconer Glass Indus., Inc., 187, 188
Daley v. Fryer, 1103
Daley v. People's Bldg., Loan & Sav. Ass'n, 642
Dallum v. Farmers Union Cent. Exch., Inc., 1015
Danann Realty Corp. v. Harris, 631
D & N Boening, Inc. v. Kirsch Beverages, Inc., 353
Daniel v. Snowdoun Ass'n, 142
Daniels-Hall v. National Educ. Ass'n, 67
Dan Ryan Builders, Inc. v. Nelson, 667, 668-669
Darner Motor Sales, Inc. v. Universal Underwriters Ins. Co., 444
Dashiell v. Meeks, 1073
Daughtrey v. Ashe, 550, 552-553
Davenport, City of v. Shewry Corp., 1081
Davis v. Re-Trac Mfg. Corp., 1037
Davis & Warde, Inc. v. Tripodi, 109
Davis, Matter of the Marriage of, 582
Dawson v. General Motors Corp., 152, 153
DeArmitt v. New York Life Ins. Co., 436
DeCicco v. Schweizer, 116
DeFontes v. Dell, Inc., 197, 205, 206, 207, 208
De Freitas v. Cote, 826
DeKalb Agresearch, Inc. v. Abbott, 555
De La Concha of Hartford, Inc. v. Aetna Life Ins. Co., 528, 529
De La Torre v. CashCall Inc., 675-676
Delchi Carrier SpA v. Rotorex Corp., 907
Delta Servs. & Equip., Inc. v. Ryko Mfg. Co., 491-492
Demasse v. ITT Corp., 780
Deni Assocs. of Fla., Inc. v. State Farm Fire & Cas. Ins. Co., 425
Denney v. Lovett, 934
Denver Ventures, Inc. v. Arlington Lane Corp., 1032
Deom v. Walgreen Co., 504
De Petris v. Union Settlement Ass'n, Inc., 536
DePrince v. Starboard Cruise Services, 738
Desmond-Dunne Co. v. Friedman-Doscher Co., 831
Deutsch v. Barsky, 692
Devine v. Notter, 146
Devine v. Roche Biomed. Labs., 1103
DF Activities Corp. v. Brown, 388
D.H. Blattner & Sons, Inc. v. Firemen's Ins. Co. of Newark, N.J., 810, 811
Dialist Co. v. Pulford, 1005, 1012
Diamond Fruit Growers, Inc. v. Krack Corp., 170, 181, 182
Diaz-Amador v. Wells Fargo Home Mortg., 375
Dick Broad. Co. of Tenn. v. Oak Ridge FM, Inc., 493, 522
Dickens v. Quincy Coll. Corp., 370
Dickinson v. Dodds, 56, 273
Dier v. Peters, 702
DiPadova; Commonwealth v., 584
Dixon v. Wells Fargo Bank, N.A., 262
DK Arena, Inc. v. EB Acquisitions I, LLC, 375
Dodson v. Shrader, 572, 576, 578
Doerr v. Hibben Hollweg & Co., 636
Dohrmann v. Swaney, 129, 137, 138, 647
Dollar Tree Stores Inc. v. Toyama Partners LLC, 1084
Donohue v. Picinich, 730
Donovan v. Bachstadt, 888
Donovan v. RRL Corp., 69, 70, 71, 72, 733-737, 738-740
Dorough v. Lockman, 1007
Dorton v. Collins & Aikman Corp., 178, 181
Dougherty v. Salt, 101, *115*, 116, 117, 118, 120, 145
Doyle v. Holy Cross Hosp., 780
Dracopoulas v. Rachal, 792
Drake v. Drake, 1110
Drennan v. Star Paving Co., 277, 282, 283, 284, 292, 740, 1019, 1020
Drogorub v. Payday Loan Store of WI, Inc., 675
Drysdale v. Woerth, 1012
Duck Creek Tire Serv., Inc. v. Goodyear Corners, L.C., 365
Duffey v. Twentieth Century Fox Film Corp., 472
Dukowitz v. Hannon Sec. Servs., 536
Dulany Foods v. C.M. Ayers, Inc., 125-126
Dunbar v. United States Ins. Co. of Am., 784
Dunes Hospitality, L.L.C. v. Country Kitchen Int'l, Inc., 600
Du Pont v. Claiborne-Reno Co., 146, 490-491
Durham v. National Pool Equip. Co. of Va., 170
Dutton v. Gerrish, 431
Dwyer v. Jung, 685, 686
Dynalectric Co. of Nev., Inc. v. Clark & Sullivan Constructors, Inc., 1018, 1019-1020
Dynamic Mach. Works, Inc. v. Machine & Elec. Consultants, Inc., 798
Dyno Constr. Co. v. McWane, Inc., 158

Earl of Chesterfield v. Janssen, 641-642
Earthinfo, Inc. v. Hydrosphere Res. Consultants, Inc., 993
Eastern Air Lines, Inc. v. Gulf Oil Corp., 506
Eastern Forge Co. v. Corbin, 830
Eastern Shore Title Co. v. Ochse, 954-955
Easthampton L. & C. Co. v. Worthington, 831
East River Energy, Inc. v. Gaylord Hosp., Inc., 389
Eavenson v. Lewis Means, Inc., 369, 370
E.C. Styberg Engineering Co. v. Eaton Corp., 154, 159, 160
Edie v. East India Co., 410
Educational Testing Serv. Praxis Principles of Learning & Teaching: Grades 7-12 Litig., In re, 966
Edwards v. Arthur Andersen LLP, 1068
Edwards v. Tobin, 81, 82
Ehlen v. Melvin, 57
E.I. Du Pont de Nemours & Co. v. Claiborne-Reno Co., 146, 490-491
E.I. Du Pont de Nemours & Co. v. Pressman, 535
1861 Grp., L.L.C. v. Wild Oats Mkts., Inc., 292
E.K.D. v. Facebook, Inc., 576
Eker Bros., Inc. v. Rehders, 1030
Elda Arnhold & Byzantio, L.L.C. v. Ocean Atl. Woodland Corp., 849
Electrical Constr. & Maint. Co. v. Maeda Pac. Corp., 277
Electro-Lab of Aiken, Inc. v. Sharp Constr. Co. of Sumter, Inc., 277
1119 Del. v. Continental Land Title Co., 521
Elliott v. Duke Univ., 401
Ellis v. Ellis, 609
Elm St. Builders, Inc. v. Enterprise Park Condo. Ass'n, Inc., 529
Emerson Radio Corp. v. Orion Sales, Inc., 498, 499, 501
Emery v. Caledonia Sand & Gravel Co., 899-900
Empire Gas Corp. v. American Bakeries, Inc., 507
Empower Health, LLC v. Providence Health Sols., LLC, 530
Environmental Servs., Inc. v. Hull Forest Prods., 738
enXco Development Corp. v. Northern States Power Co., 805, 813-818, 824, 825, 826, 849
Equity Enters., Inc. v. Milosch, 1084
Erdman Co. v. Phoenix Land & Acquisition, LLC, 919-920
Ericson v. Playgirl, Inc., 920
Erie R.R. Co. v. Tompkins, 950
Erlich v. Menezes, 956, 965, 967, 968
Essco Geometric v. Harvard Indus., 507
Estate of. *See name of estate*
Etherton, In re Estate of, 306
Evans, Inc. v. Tiffany & Co., 91
Everbank v. Marini, 598

Fair v. Red Lion Inn, 936
Falcon Tankers, Inc. v. Litton Sys., Inc., 178
Farnum v. Silvano, 581, 582, 585, 587
Fast Ball Sports, LLC v. Metropolitan Entm't & Convention Auth., 375
Fateh v. Rich, 818
Father's House Int'l, Inc. v. Kurguz, 888
Fattah v. Bim, 566
Faulkner v. United Techs. Corp., 532
Federal Ins. Co. v. P.A.T. Homes, Inc., 443
Federal Ins. Co. v. Village of Westmont, 551
Federal Signal Corp. v. Safety Factors, Inc., 551
FEI Enters., Inc. v. Kee Man Yoon, 512
Feinberg v. Pfeiffer Co., 250, 251
Feld v. Henry S. Levy & Sons, Inc., 508
Ferguson Advisors, LLC v. Malherbe, 815
Ferguson; State v., 422
Field's Will, In re, 241
Fink v. Cox, 116
Fink v. DeClassis, 151
Finnish Fur Sales Co. v. Juliette Shulof Furs, Inc., 976
Finora Co. v. Amitie Shipping, Ltd., 168
Fire Ins. Ass'n v. Wickham, 116
Fire Ins. Exch. v. Bell, 636, 637
First Baptist Church of Moultrie v. Barber Contracting Co., 739
First Fed. Sav. Bank v. Key Mkts., Inc., 1133
Firstmerit Bank, N.A. v. Vision Fin. Grp., Inc., 729
First Nat'l Bank of Cincinnati v. Pepper, 595
First Nat'l Bank of Omaha v. Centennial Park, LLC, 838
First Nat'l Bankshares of Beloit, Inc. v. Geisel, 282
Firth v. Lu, 365
Fisher v. Bartlett, 336
Fishman v. LaSalle Nat'l Bank, 407
FI-Tampa, LLC v. Kelly-Hall, 643
Fitz v. NCR Corp., 658, 659
Fitzgerald v. Hutchins, 354
Fitzpatrick v. American Int'l Grp., Inc., 817
Fitzpatrick v. Teleflex, Inc., 491
Flathead-Mich. I, LLC v. Penninsula Dev., LLC, 749, 750
Fleischmann Distilling Corp. v. Maier Brewing Co., 955
Fleming v. AT&T Info. Servs., Inc., 536
Flom v. Stahly, 559
Florafax International, Inc. v. GTE Market Resources, Inc., 908, 917-919
Flores v. Transamerica HomeFirst, Inc., 654
Florida Bar v. Went For It, Inc., 633
Flower City Painting Contractors, Inc. v. Gumina Constr. Co., 472
Flynn Builders, L.C. v. Lande, 836
Foakes v. Beer, 799
Foley v. Interactive Data Corp., 958, 960
Fontbank, Inc. v. CompuServe, Inc., 433
Ford Motor Credit Co. v. Ryan, 233
Forman v. Benson, 513
Forman v. Forman, 1110
Formosa Plastics Corp. U.S.A. v. Presidio Eng'rs & Contractors, Inc., 969
Fortune v. National Cash Register Co., 529-530, 531, 535
Foster v. Mutual Sav. Ass'n, 792
Foundation Dev. Corp. v. Loehmann's, Inc., 848
Fountain Co. v. Stein, 821

1464-Eight, Ltd. v. Joppich, 272
Fournier v. Burby, 386
Fowler v. Mumford, 785
Franklin Point, Inc. v. Harris Trust & Sav. Bank, 1057
Frankson v. Design Space Int'l, 1035, 1040
Freedman v. Chemical Constr. Corp., 352
Freeman v. State Farm Mut. Auto. Ins. Co., 212
Freeman & Mills, Inc. v. Belcher Oil Co., 958-961, 968
Frenchtown Square P'ship v. Lemstone, 939
Frick Co. v. Rubel Corp., 1082
Fried v. Fisher, 251
Frigaliment Importing Co. v. B.N.S. International Sales Corp., 401, *408*, 413, 414, 415, 434, 449, 471, 720
Frost v. Knight, 923
Frostifresh Corp. v. Reynoso, 647
Frye v. Memphis State Univ., 933, 934
Fteja v. Facebook, Inc., 26, 28
F.T.R., In re Paternity of, 699, 700, 702, 707
Fuller v. Terrell, 327

Galante v. Oz, Inc., 1035, 1040
Galardi v. Naples Polaris, LLC, 415
Gallagher Switchboard Corp. v. Heckler Elec. Co., 596
Gallo v. PHH Mortg. Corp., 505
Galloway v. Methodist Hosps., Inc., 301, 304
Galloway v. State of Iowa, 578
Ganss v. Guffey Petroleum Co., 277
Gantt v. Morgan, 1021
Garay v. Overholtzer, 577
Garcia v. World Sav., FSB, 258, 260
Gartner v. Eikill, 728
Gateway Co. v. DiNoia, 1134
Gateway Exteriors, Inc. v. Suntide Homes, Inc., 62
Gene B. Glick Co. v. Sunshine Ready Concrete Co., 312
General Dynamics Corp. v. Superior Court, 537
Genesco, Inc. v. T. Kakiuchi & Co., 25
Genesee Merchs. Bank & Trust Co. v. Tucker Motor Sales, 784
Geneva Pharms. Tech. Corp. v. Barr Labs., 263
George M. Morris Constr. Co. v. Four Seasons Motor Inn, Inc., 315
German v. Ford, 932
Gerson Elec. Constr. Co. v. Honeywell, Inc., 1015
Geysen v. Securitas Security Services, USA, Inc., 523, 534, 535, 780, 1134
Gianetti v. Norwalk Hosp., 945, 946
Gibbs v. American Sav. & Loan Ass'n, 50
Gibli v. Kadosh, 730
Gibson v. Arnold, 388
Gibson v. Cranage, 510
Giddings & Lewis, Inc. v. Industrial Risk Insurer, 556
Gilbert & Bennett Mfg. Co. v. Westinghouse Elec. Corp., 177, 178
Giles v. Austin, 821
Gingras v. Avery, 816
Ginsberg v. Northwest, Inc., 69
Givan v. Masterson, 636
Glanski v. Ervine, 626
Glasgo v. Glasgo, 318, 321
Glasscock v. Wilson Constructors, Inc., 370
Glenn Constr. Co., LLC v. Bell Aerospace Servs., Inc., 836
Globe Ref. Co. v. Landa Cotton Oil Co., 907
Goddard v. Stabile, 631
Godfrey v. Navratil, 627
Goeckel v. Stokely, 54, 56
Goldberg v. Charlie's Chevrolet, Inc., 884
Golding v. Golding, 609
Goldman v. Connecticut Gen. Life Ins. Co., 1074
Goodman v. Dicker, 1017
Goodwin v. Durant Bank & Trust Co., 553
Gore v. Gadd, 582
GPL Treatment, Ltd. v. Louisiana-Pac. Corp., 390
Graf v. Hope Bldg. Corp., 822
Graham v. Scissor-Tail, Inc., 655
Grandoe Corp. v. Gander Mountain Co., 1018
Grand Prospect Partners, L.P. v. Ross Dress for Less, Inc., 660
Graves v. Berkowitz, 314
Gray v. Zurich Ins. Co., 420
Greaves v. Medical Imaging Sys., Inc., 370
Green v. Interstate United Mgmt. Serv. Corp., 1015
Greer v. Tweed, 642
Gregerson v. Jensen, 355
Greiner v. Greiner, 234, 235, 236
Griffin v. Bredouw, 1008
Grigerik v. Sharpe, 1102
Grindlinger v. Grindlinger, 585
Groendyke Transp., Inc. v. Merchant, 913
Groothand v. Schlueter, 620
Grossman's Estate, In re, 327
Gross Valentino Printing Co. v. Clarke, 789
Group Hosp. Servs., Inc. v. One & Two Brookriver Ctr., 792
Grouse v. Group Health Plan, 1015
Groves v. John Wunder Co., 897-899
Gruen Indus., Inc. v. Biller, 292
Guerrant v. Roth, 404
Gutierrez v. Autowest, Inc., 659
Guy v. Liederbach, 1104-1109, 1111
Guyther v. Nationwide Mut. Fire Ins. Co., 386

Haag v. Dry Basement, Inc., 944
Hackley v. Headley, 784
Hadley v. Baxendale, 896, 898, *902*, 905-908, 912, 917-918, 973, 975, 1100-1101, 1104
Hagan v. Val-Hi, Inc., 760
Halbman v. Lemke, 574, 576
Hall v. Butterfield, 574
Hall v. Hall, 604
Hall v. Weatherford, 81
Hal Taylor Assocs. v. Unionamerica, Inc., 988
Hamer v. Sidway, 101, *102*, 106, 116, 117, 120, 125, 146, 227, 228
Hamilton v. Suntrust Mortg. Inc., 505
Hammaker v. Schleigh, 1073
Hammes v. JCLB Props., L.L.C., 630
Hancock v. Northcutt, 963

Handicapped Children's Education Board v. Lukaszewski, 889, 893-895, 991
Handle Constr. Co. v. Norcon, Inc., 740
Handy v. Bliss, 832
Hanscom v. Gregorie, 512
Hanson v. Williams Cnty., 563
Harley v. Indian Spring Land Co., 271
Harleysville Ins. Co. v. Physical Distribution Servs., Inc., 812
Harper v. Battle, 385
Harper v. Ultimo, 657
Harrington v. Taylor, 337
Harris v. Axline, 723
Harris v. Clark, 116
Harris v. Rudin, Richman & Appel, 733
Harris v. Time, Inc., 69-70
Harriscom Svenska, AB v. Harris Corp., 766
Harrison v. Harrison, 327
Hart v. Arnold, 1043
Hart v. Strong, 124
Hartford Elevator, Inc. v. Lauer, 1027
Hartigan, People ex rel., v. Knecht Servs., Inc., 679
Harvey v. Dow, 226, *228,* 233, 234-236, 1019
Harvey v. Lake Buena Vista Resort, LLC, 810
Harvey v. Timber Res., Inc., 946
Havill v. Woodstock Soapstone Co., 936
Hawkins v. Foster, 885
Haydocy Pontiac Inc. v. Lee, 574
Hayes v. Plantations Steel Co., 254
HCA Health Servs. of Tenn., Inc.; Doe v., 304
Health Related Servs., Inc. v. Golden Plains Convalescent Ctr., Inc., 848
Hearn v. Stevens & Bros., 483
Heartland Del. Inc. v. Rehoboth Mall Ltd. P'ship, 825
Heartland Health Sys. v. Chamberlin, 301, 303
Hei v. Heller, 430
Hemlock Semiconductor Corp. v. Deutsche Solar GmbH, 756
Hemlock Semiconductor Corp. v. Kyocera Corp., 749, 750, 751
Hemlock Semiconductor Operations, LLC v. Solarworld Industries Sachsen GmbH, 744, 752, 753, 756, 757, 816
Hendry v. Conner, 1039
Henningsen v. Bloomfield Motors, Inc., 562, 641, 642
Henry v. Masson, 993
Henry M. Butler, Inc. v. Trizec Props., Inc., 310
Hensler v. City of Glendale, 255
Herbert Clayton & Jack Waller, Ltd. v. Oliver, 920
Herrod v. First Republic Mortg. Corp., 667
Herzog v. Irace, 1117, 1120, 1121, 1122, 1133
Hesselgrave v. Harrison, 1034, 1037
Hetchler v. American Life Ins. Co., 233
Hewitt v. Hewitt, 320, 321, 322, 325-326
Hideaway, Inc. v. Gambit Invs. Inc., 812
Higgins v. Disney/ABC Int'l Television, Inc., 659, 660
Higgins v. Superior Court of Los Angeles County, 650, 659-661, 674
Hill v. Gateway 2000, Inc., 201, 202-208
Hill v. Jones, 622, 629-632, 637
Hill v. Town of Hillsborough, 400
Hillman Constr. Corp. v. Wainer, 310
Hill-Shafer P'ship v. Chilson Family Trust, 398
Hilton Oil Transp. v. Oil Transp. Co., 755
HM DG, Inc. v. Amini, 24, 212, 214
Hochster v. De La Tour, 856
Hoelscher v. Schenewerk, 885
Hoffman v. Porter, 336
Hoffman v. Red Owl Stores, Inc., 290, 292, 1017
Holler v. Holler, 600
Hollowell v. Career Decisions, Inc., 784
Hollywood Fantasy Corp. v. Gabor, 1009
Holman v. CPT Corp., 1035, 1037, 1040
Holman Erection Co. v. Orville E. Madsen & Sons, Inc., 284
Holmes v. Roper, 116
Holt v. United Sec. Life Ins. & Trust Co., 1005
Holy Props. Ltd. v. Kenneth Cole Prods., Inc., 939
Home Depot USA, Inc. v. Cytec Indus., Inc., 1011
Home Elec. Co. v. Hall & Underdown Heating & Air Conditioning Co., 283
Home-Stake Prod. Co. v. Minnis, 913
Honey v. Henry's Franchise Leasing Corp., 1028
Honolulu Waterfront Ltd. P'ship v. Aloha Tower Dev. Corp., 1056
Hoover Universal, Inc. v. Brockway Imco, Inc., 555
Hope's Architectural Prods., Inc. v. Lundy's Constr., Inc., 866
Horace Mann Ins. Co. v. General Star Nat'l Ins. Co., 667
Horn & Hardart Co. v. Pillsbury Co., 355
Horne v. Peckham, 633
Hornell Brewing Co. v. Spry, 857, *858,* 865
Horner v. Bourland, 792
Horning v. Shilberg, 887
Horton v. Horton, 550
Horton v. Humble Oil & Ref. Co., 56
Hospodar v. Schick, 108
Hotchkiss v. National City Bank, D.C., 43
Hottinger Excavating & Ready Mix, LLC v. R.E. Crawford Constr., LLC, 283, 314
Hougland; State v., 422
Howard v. Babcock, 693
Howard v. Youngman, 826, 883
Howard Sales Co. v. Bradley, 1083
Howard Univ. v. Roberts-Williams, 936
Howell v. Smith, 56
Howse v. Crumb, 386
H.R. Moch Co. v. Rensselaer Water Co., 1113
Hull v. Giesler, 837
Human v. Hartsell, 573
Humantech, Inc. v. Caterpillar, Inc., 504
Humphries v. Ables, 1056
Hunt v. Walker, 627
Hunter v. Union State Bank, 300
Hunter v. Up-Right, Inc., 958
Huntington Nat'l Bank v. Toland, 587
Hurwitz v. Bocian, 377
Hutton Contracting Co. v. City of Coffeyville, 1083

Hyde v. Anania, 299
Hyman v. Ford Motor Co., 598

I & R Mech., Inc. v. Hazelton Mfg. Co., 295
Iannuccillo v. Material Sand & Stone Corp., 753
Idaho Lumber, Inc. v. Buck, 314
Idaho Power Co. v. Westinghouse Elec. Corp., 178
IDT Corp. v. Tyco Grp., 98
IIG Wireless, Inc. v. Yi, 457
I. Lan Sys., Inc. v. Netscout Serv. Level Corp., 1059
Indiana Glass Co. v. Indiana Mich. Power Co., 953
Indianapolis Morris Plan Corp. v. Sparks, 641
Indiana Tri-City Plaza Bowl, Inc. v. Estate of Glueck, 509
Ingram v. Kasey's Assocs., 1058
In re. *See name of party*
In re Estate of. *See name of estate*
In re Marriage of. *See name of party*
Insurance Agency v. Leasing Corp., 401
InterCall, Inc. v. Egenera, Inc., 611
Intermetal Fabricators, Inc. v. Losco Grp., Inc., 1030
International Casings Grp., Inc. v. Premium Standard Farms, Inc., 1059
Interway, Inc. v. Alagna, 88
Ionics, Inc. v. Elmwood Sensors, Inc., 181
Iowa Fuel & Minerals, Inc. v. Board of Regents, 766
Irish Oil & Gas, Inc. v. Riemer, 377
I. R. Kirk Farms, Inc. v. Pointer, 273
Irons v. Community State Bank, 300
Isbrandtsen v. North Branch Corp., 442
Italian & French Wine Co. v. Negociants USA, Inc., 491
IT Corp. v. Motco Site Trust Fund, 1023
Iuka Guar. Bank v. Beard, 144
Ives v. Sterling, 242, 243

Jackman Constr., Inc. v. Rock Springs Winnelson Co., 283
Jackson v. Morse, 1019
Jackson v. Pepper Gasoline Co., 80
Jacob & Youngs, Inc. v. Kent, 814, *829*, 835-838, 841, 846, 896-898, 1031
James v. National Fin., LLC, 676
James Baird Co. v. Gimbel Bros., Inc., 274, 277, 280, 282, 284, 740
Jamison's Estate, In re, 250
Jannusch v. Naffziger, 149, 153, 154, 160, 171, 172
Javins v. First Nat'l Realty Corp., 546
Jeanguneat v. Jackie Hames Constr. Co., 560
Jenkins v. Eckerd Corp., 816
Jennings v. Foremost Dairies, Inc., 1130
Jensen v. Taco John's Int'l, Inc., 291
Jetz Service Co. v. Salina Properties, 939, *940*, 945, 946, 977
J.F. v. D.B., 701
J. N. A. Realty Corp. v. Cross Bay Chelsea Inc., 817, *818*, 825-827
JNS Power & Control Sys., Inc. v. 350 Green, LLC, 1059
John Dyer's Case, 680
Johnson v. Calvert, 702, 704-705, 706, 708, 709
Johnson v. Cash Store, 675
Johnson v. Davis, 626
Johnson v. Dodgen, 303
Johnson v. Lowery, Ky., 80, 81
Johnson v. Mobil Oil Co., 676
Johnson v. Northwestern Mut. Life Ins. Co., 574
Johnson v. Oroweat Foods Co., 919
JOM, Inc. v. Adell Plastics, Inc., 187
Jones v. Barkley, 839
Jones v. Best, 263
Jones v. Gianferante, 821, 823
Jones v. Kelly, 959
Jones v. Parker, 1053
Jones, In re Estate of, 608
Jordan v. Knafel, 620
Jordan v. Mount Sinai Hosp. of Greater Miami, Inc., 239
Jorstad, In re Estate of, 272
Joseph v. Rottschafer, 784
Joseph Martin, Jr., Delicatessen, Inc. v. Schumacher, 85, 86
Joy v. City of St. Louis, 1053
Joyner v. Adams, 399, 402-404, 412-413
Julian v. Christopher, 1133
June Roberts Agency, Inc. v. Venture Props., Inc., 231

K&K Servs., Inc. v. City of Irwindale, 693
Kansas City Power & Light Co., State ex rel. v. Salmark Homebuilders, Inc., 885
Karlin v. Weinberg, 684, 689
Karl Wendt Farm Equip. Co. v. International Harvester Co., 748-750, 753
Kately v. Wilkinson, 963
Katz v. Danny Dare, Inc., 248, 253-254
Kaufman v. Solomon, 386
Kaufman Hotel & Rest. Co. v. Thomas, 1028
Keaster v. Bozik, 271
Keithley v. Civil Serv. Bd., 608
Kelly v. Marx, 1081
Kelly v. McCarthy, 604
Kelly v. Provident Life & Accident Ins. Co., 608
Kelsey-Hayes Co. v. Galtaco Redlaw Castings Corp., 782, 787-789
Kelso v. McGowan, 599
Keltner v. Sowell, 883
Kemp v. Gannett, 887
Kendall v. Ernest Pestana, Inc., 517
Kendrick v. Barker, 730
Kennedy Assocs., Inc. v. Fischer, 513
Kentucky Military Inst. v. Bramblet, 1075
Kern v. TXO Prod. Corp., 1016
Kerns v. Range Res.-Appalachia, LLC, 50
Keystone Eng'g Corp. v. Sutter, 43
Kham & Nate's Shoes No. 2, Inc. v. First Bank of Whiting, 501
Kilarjian v. Vastola, 1058
Kilby v. Charles City W. Ry. Co., 617
Kimmel & Silverman, P.C. v. Porro, 436
King v. Railway Co., 776

King v. Texacally Joint Venture, 792
King v. Trustees of Boston University, 237, 243, 245
King Constr. Co. v. W.M. Smith Elec. Co., 785
Kingston v. Preston, 839
Kirk v. Ridgway, 559, 560
Kirke La Shelle Co. v. Paul Armstrong Co., 493
Kirksey v. Kirksey, 226, *227,* 228
Klamen v. Genuine Parts Co., 62
Klein v. Pepsico, Inc., 974
Klinke v. Famous Recipe Fried Chicken, Inc., 375
Klipsch, Inc. v. WWR Tech., Inc., 812
Kllm Transp. Servs., LLC v. JBS Carriers, Inc., 946
Klocek v. Gateway, Inc., 200, 202, 203, 207-208
KMART Corp. v. Balfour Beatty, Inc., 1102
K.M.C. Co. v. Irving Trust Co., 505
Knepp v. Nationwide Ins. Co., 1029
Knott v. Racicot, 119, 272, 273
Kohn Nast & Graf; Doe v., 523
Kolkman v. Roth, 375
Kolodziej v. Mason, 76
Koursa, Inc. v. Manroland, Inc., 866
Kovilic Constr. Co. v. Missbrenner, 951-952
Kozlowski v. Kozlowski, 318, 321
Kraatz v. USAA Cas. Ins. Co., 906
Kramer, In re, 245
Kramer v. Kramer, 116
Krasner v. Berk, 581, 582, 583, 584
Krebs ex rel. Krebs v. Strange, 143
Krell v. Henry, 743
Kreyer v. Driscoll, 838, 1031
Krueger v. Home Depot USA, Inc., 537
Kruse v. Bank of Am., 259
Kuhlman, Inc. v. G. Heileman Brewing Co., 892
Kulseth v. Rotenberger, 1027
Kunzman v. Thorsen, 1132
Kwan v. Mercedes-Benz of N. Am., Inc., 963, 964

Laclede Gas Co. v. Amoco Oil Co., 974
Ladies Collegiate Inst. v. French, 243
La Farge v. Rickert, 430
Lafayette Dramatic Prod. v. Ferentz, 784
Lahr Constr. Corp. v. J. Kozel & Son, Inc., 283-284
Laidlaw v. Organ, 628, 629
Laird v. Scribner Coop, Inc., 551
Lake Ridge Acad. v. Carney, 1075
Lake River Corp. v. Carborundum Co., 1076, 1082
Lakota v. Newton, 105
Laks v. Coast Fed. Sav. & Loan Ass'n, 258-259
L. Albert & Son v. Armstrong Rubber Co., 1005, 1010
Lamborn v. Slack, 311
Lancellotti v. Thomas, 1024, 1030, 1031
Land Baron Inv. v. Bonnie Springs Family LP, 729
L & L Wings, Inc. v. Marco-Destin, Inc., 1083
Landry v. Spitz, 528
Langemeier v. National Oats, Inc., 676
Larese v. Creamland Dairies, Inc., 1133
Latham v. Latham, 321
La Trace v. Webster, 555
Lawrence v. Fox, 1094, 1095
Lawson v. Menefee, 886, 887
Layne-Atl. Co. v. Koppers Co., 552
Lee v. Clark & Assocs. Real Estate, Inc., 560
Leeper v. Beltrami, 602
Leeson v. Etchison, 62
Lee's Summit, City of v. Hinck, 885
Lefkowitz v. Great Minneapolis Surplus Store, 51
Leibel v. Raynor Manufacturing Co., 486, 490, 491, 533
Leigh v. Loyd, 625
Leigh v. Wadsworth, 561
Lemoge Elec. v. San Mateo Cnty., 281
Lempke v. Dagenais, 561
Lenawee County Board of Health v. Messerly, 720, 722, 725, 727-728, 729, 741
Leo Eisenberg & Co. v. Payson, 445
Leo F. Piazza Paving Co. v. Bebek & Brkich, 281
Leonard v. American Walnut Co., 885
Leonard v. Pepsico, Inc., 46, 70, 76, 106
Lerner v. DMB Realty, LLC, 630
Lesher v. Strid, 729
Levar v. Elkins, 370
Lewis Elec. Co. v. Miller, 837
Lewis Jorge Constr. Mgmt., Inc. v. Pomona Unified Sch. Dist., 917
Licitra v. Gateway, Inc., 202
Liggett Rest. Grp., Inc. v. City of Pontiac, 750
Light v. Centel Cellular Co., 144
Lindell v. Rokes, 105
Lindley v. Lacey, 431
Lindy Lu LLC v. Illinois Cent. R.R. Co., 138
Lingenfelder v. Brewing Co., 776, 778
Lingsch v. Savage, 626
Litman v. Massachusetts Mut. Life Ins. Co., 435
Little Beaver Enters. v. Humphreys Rys., 168
Little Caesar Enters., Inc. v. Bell Canyon Shopping Ctr., L.C., 85
Livesey v. Copps Corp., 825
Locke v. Warner Bros. Inc., 503, *513,* 521, 522, 523, 938
Lo Galbo v. Plishkin, Rubano & Baum, 814
Lokan & Assocs., Inc. v. American Beef, 813
Lommen v. Danaher, 892
Lonergan v. Scolnick, 47, 49, 50, 60, 75
Long v. Dell, Inc., 197
Long v. Provide Commerce, Inc., 32, *209,* 218
Lopez v. Kmart Corp., 577
Lowe v. Smith, 154
Lowndes Coop. Ass'n v. Lipsey, 142, 143, 144
L-7 Designs, Inc. v. Old Navy, LLC, 847
Luana Sav. Bank v. Pro-Build Holdings, Inc., 565
Lubner v. City of L.A., 961
Lucas v. Hamm, 1104
Lucy v. Zehmer, 45, 106
Lufty v. R. D. Roper & Sons Motor Co., 624
Luke v. Smith, 627
Lumber Mut. Ins. Co. v. Clarklift of Detroit, Inc., 555
Lumley v. Gye, 1067
Lumley v. Wagner, 1066, 1067
Luria v. Robbins, 1028, 1029

Lynn v. Taylor, 627
Lyon Metal Prods., Inc. v. Hagerman Constr. Corp., 283

Mace v. Atlantic Ref. Mktg. Corp., 1108
Mack v. Coker, 272
MacKenzie v. Flagstar Bank, FSB, 262
Madison Indus., Inc. v. Eastman Kodak Co., 472
Maestro W. Chelsea SPE LLC v. Pradera Realty Inc., 485
Magee v. Garreau, 151
Maglica v. Maglica, 326, 1042
Magnan v. Anaconda Indus., Inc., 528, 529, 530
Maimonides Sch. v. Coles, 581
Maine Rubber Int'l v. Environmental Mgmt. Grp., Inc., 1009
Maintenance Enters., LLC v. Orascom E & C USA, Inc., 314
Malaker Corp. Stockholders Protective Comm. v. First Jersey Nat'l Bank, 288, 289, 290
Mallet v. Pickens, 669
Malone v. Malone, 604-605
Maloney v. Sargisson, 728
Maloney v. Therm Alum Indus. Corp., 311-312, 313
M.A. Mortenson Co. v. Timberline Software Corp., 201, 203, 204
Mandel v. Liebman, 642
Mandeville v. Harman, 683-684, 687
M&M Elec. Contractor, Inc. v. Cumberland Elec. Membership Corp., 847
M & W Dev., Inc. v. El Paso Water Co., 941
Maness v. Collins, 925, 936-937, 945
Man Indus. (India), Ltd. v. Midcontinent Express Pipeline, LLC, 788
Manyon v. Graser, 385
Marchio v. Letterlough, 1067
Marcoux v. Shell Oil Prod. Co., LLC, 505
Marcus, Stowell & Beye Gov't Sec., Inc. v. Jefferson Inv. Corp., 988
Margeson v. Artis, 782
Maris v. McGrath, 954
Marker v. Preferred Fire Ins. Co., 268
Marks v. Cowdin, 349, 350, 352
Maronda Homes, Inc. of Fla. v. Lakeview Reserve Homeowners Ass'n, Inc., 564, 566
Marshall Durbin Food Corp. v. Baker, 102, *139*, 145, 146
Marshall Sch. Dist. v. Hill, 938-939
Mart v. Forest River, Inc., 534
Martin v. New York Life Ins. Co., 352
Martocci v. Greater N.Y. Brewery, 352
Marvin v. Marvin, 318, 321, 322, 325
Marvin Lumber & Cedar Co. v. PPG Indus., Inc., 187
Maryatt v. Hubbard, 386
Maryland Nat'l Bank v. United Jewish Appeal Fed'n, 243-244
Mathis v. Exxon Corp., 503, 504
Mattei v. Hopper, 518
Mattingly Bridge Co. v. Holloway & Son Constr. Co., 1079
Maudlin v. Pacific Decision Scis. Corp., 710
Maurice Elec. Supply Co. v. Anderson Safeway Guard Rail Corp., 177
Maxey v. Glindmeyer, 1027
Maxon Corp. v. Tyler Pipe Indus., Inc., 182
Maxton Builders v. Lo Galbo, 814
Maxwell v. Fidelity Fin. Servs., Inc., 644
Mayor's Jewelers, Inc. v. State of Cal. Emps.' Ret. Sys., 1057
MBM Fin. Corp. v. The Woodlands Operating Co., L.P., 873
The McCaffrey Grp., Inc. v. Superior Court, 643-644
McCall Co. v. Wright, 483
McCalment v. Eli Lilly & Co., 147
McCarty v. Verson Alsteel Press Co., 178
McClain v. Octagon Plaza, LLC, 261
MCC-Marble Ceramic Ctr., Inc. v. Ceramica Nuova d'Agostino, S.p.A., 451
McDermott; Commonwealth v., 583
McDonald v. Acker, Merrall & Condit Co., 410
McDonald v. Mianecki, 564
McFarland v. Wells Fargo Bank, N.A., 664, 666, 673-675
McGinnis Piano & Organ Co. v. Yamaha Int'l Corp., 489
McGuire v. Ryland Grp., Inc., 566
McInerney v. Charter Golf, Inc., 353
McIntosh v. Murphy, 370
McKay v. Coleman, 725
McKinnie v. Milford, 1128
McLellan v. Walker, 1119, 1120
McMullen v. Kutz, 954
MDC Corp. v. John H. Harland Co., 485
M. DeMatteo Constr. Co. v. Daggett, 585
Medcom, Inc. v. C. Arthur Weaver Co., 552
Medical Specialists, Inc. v. Sleweon, 688
Megert v. Bauman, 915
Mehl v. Norton, 1039
Mehta v. Mehta, 621
Meier v. Sac & Fox Indian Tribe, 299
Meikle v. Watson, 1056
Meincke v. Northwest Bank & Trust Co., 112
Mel Frank Tool & Supply, Inc. v. Di-Chem Co., 752, 757, 766-767
Mercer v. Woodard, 627
Merenda v. Superior Court, 961
Merry Gentleman, LLC v. George & Leona Prods., Inc., 1010
Meserve v. Jordan Marsh Co., 583, 584
Metropolitan Sports Facilities Comm'n v. General Mills, Inc., 812
Metten v. Benge, 318
Meyer v. Kalanick, 24, 29
Meyer v. Uber Technologies, Inc., 21, 32, 33, 195, 196, 218
Meyerberg, Sawyer & Rue v. Agee, 1006, 1008
M.F. Kemper Constr. Co. v. City of L.A., 280
MHR Capital Partners LP v. Presstek, Inc., 813
Michels Corp. v. Resitech Indus., LLC, 180
Midwest Commerce Banking Co. v. Elkhart City Ctr., 636

Midwest Dredging Co. v. McAninch Corp., 1099
Midwest Family Mut. Ins. Co. v. Wolters, 424
Mihalik v. Credit Agricole Chevreux N. Am., Inc., 936
Miller v. Rhode Island Hosp., 589
Miller v. Sears, 630
Miller v. Wooters, 386
Miller Brewing Co. v. Best Beers of Bloomington, Inc., 950
Millis Constr. Co. v. Fairfield Sapphire Valley, Inc., 857
Mills v. Wyman, 328, 331, 332, 337, 339
Mimica v. Area Interstate Trucking, Inc., 134, 135
Mineral Park Land Co. v. Howard, 744, 753
Minneota, Village of v. Fairbanks, Morse & Co., 810
Miranda v. Said, 966
Mitchell v. BBB Servs. Co., 554
Mitchell v. Mitchell, 578
M.J. Paquet, Inc. v. N.J. DOT, 766
M'Naghten's Case, 588
Molien v. Kaiser Found. Hosps., 963
Montanaro Bros. Builders, Inc. v. Snow, 376
Moody Realty Co. v. Huestis, 932
The Moorcock, 483
Moore v. Moore, 606
Moore v. Warr Acres Nursing Ctr., LLC, 535
"Moore" Burger, Inc. v. Phillips Petroleum Co., 792, 793
Moran v. NAV Servs., 370
Moran v. Standard Oil Co., 483
Morgan Bldgs. & Spas, Inc. v. Humane Soc'y of Se. Tex., 433
Morganroth & Morganroth v. DeLorean, 951
Morin Building Products Co. v. Baystone Construction, Inc., 503, *508*, 512, 513, 521
Morris v. Ballard, 1051
Morris v. Hartford Courant Co., 529, 532
Morris v. Redwood Empire Bancorp, 660
Morrison v. Rossingnol, 83
Morrissey v. United States, 699
Morrow v. L.A. Goldschmidt Assocs., Inc., 950
Morse v. Cremer, 453
Mortenson v. Scheer, 810
Morton v. Lamb, 840
Morton's of Chi./Great Neck LLC v. Crab House, Inc., 50
Morton 1200 Shoe Co., In re, 239
Moses v. Macferlan, 308
Moses H. Cone Mem'l Hosp. v. Mercury Constr. Corp., 24
Moss v. Olson, 81
Mostek Corp., In re, 182
Motown Record Corp. v. Brockert, 1063
Moulton v. Kershaw, 49
Mousel, In re Estate of, 325
Moxley v. Laramie Builders, Inc., 561
Mueller v. Bethesda Mineral Spring Co., 483
Mullowney v. Data Gen. Corp., 527, 530
Munchak Corp. v. Cunningham, 1121
Munoz v. Kaiser Steel Corp., 370, 376
Murfreesboro Med. Clinic, P.A. v. Udom, 692
Muriithi v. Shuttle Express, Inc., 661
Murphy v. White Hen Pantry Co., 511
Murray; State v., 422
Mytych v. May Dep't Stores Co., 526-527, 533

Nalle Clinic Co. v. Parker, 692
Nanakuli Paving & Rock Co. v. Shell Oil Co., 460, 472, 473, 503
N & D Fashions, Inc. v. DHJ Indus., Inc., 179
Nappi v. Nappi Distribs., 231, 232, 234
Narragansett Improvement Co. v. United States, 1022
Nashan v. Nashan, 361
Nassau Sports v. Peters, 1062
National Bank of Ky. v. Louisville Trust Co., 80
National Credit Mgmt. Grp., LLC, In re, 679
National Hous. Indus. Inc. v. E. L. Jones Dev. Co., 625
Nature's Plus Nordic A/S v. Natural Organics, Inc., 837
Nauga, Inc. v. Westel Milwaukee Co., 741
Naumberg v. Young, 430, 431
Neal v. Farmers Ins. Exch., 737
Neal v. State Farm Ins. Cos., 426, 655
Neilson Bus. Equip. Ctr., Inc. v. Monteleone, 554
Nelson v. Radio Corp. of Am., 1040-1041
Nelson v. Town of Johnsbury Selectboard, 537
Nelson, Estate of v. Rice, 729
Ner Tamid Congregation v. Krivoruchko, 755
New Jersey Bank v. Palladino, 498
Newman & Snell's State Bank v. Hunter, 137
Nguyen v. Barnes & Noble, Inc., 25, 26, 212-215, 217
Nicholas v. Pennsylvania State Univ., 1068-1069
Nichols v. City of Evansdale, 728
Nichols v. Raynbred, 839
Nicholson v. Combs, 1108, 1109
Nicosia v. Amazon.com, Inc., 25, 26-27, 28
Nieto v. Litton Loan Servicing, LP, 375
Nightingale v. Wal-Mart Stores, Inc., 1018
Niles v. Hancock, 49
Nilsson v. Cherokee Candy & Tobacco Co., 62
95 East Main St. Serv. Station, Inc. v. H & D All Type Auto Repair, Inc., 825
Nippo Corp./Int'l Bridge Corp. v. AMEC Earth & Envtl., Inc., 901
Nix v. Whiteside, 633
NLRB v. *See name of opposing party*
Noble v. Bruce, 443
Noble v. National Am. Life Ins. Co., 968
Nobs Chem., U.S.A., Inc. v. Koppers Co., 978
Nolan v. Whitney, 833, 835
Norfolk S. Ry. Co. v. Basell, U.S.A., 847
Normile v. Miller, 51, 57, 58, 59, 225, 266, 271, 273
Northern Fabrication Co. v. UNOCAL, 601
Northern Ind. Pub. Serv. Co. v. Carbon County Coal Co., 756
Northrop Corp. v. Litronic Indus., 191
Northview Motors v. Chrysler Motors Corp., 501
Northwest Acceptance Corp. v. Almont Gravel, Inc., 784
Northwest Lumber Sales, Inc. v. Continental Forest Prods., Inc., 867
Northwestern Eng'g Co. v. Ellerman, 280

Novelty Adver. Co. v. Farmers' Mut. Tobacco Warehouse Co., 924
Noyes v. Anderson, 821
NPS, LLC v. Minihane, 1082
NRG Sols. v. Neurogistics Corp., 534
Nursing Care Servs. v. Dobos, 300, 301

Obde v. Schlemeyer, 627
Obermeier, In re Estate of, 588
O'Connor v. Harger Constr., Inc., 729
O'Connor, Conservatorship of, 737
Odorizzi v. Bloomfield School District, 601, 607-609
Officemax, Inc. v. NHS Human Servs., Inc., 856
Oglebay Norton Co. v. Armco, Inc., 1056
O'Grady v. Bank, 401
Ohanian v. Avis Rent A Car Sys., Inc., 353
Ohio Urology, Inc. v. Poll, 683-685, 687
O'Keefe v. Aptos Land & Water Co., 363
Okoboji Camp Owners Coop. v. Carlson, 300
Olander v. Compass Bank, 143-144
Oliver v. Campbell, 1024
Ollerman v. O'Rourke Co., 625
Olliver/Pilcher Ins. v. Daniels, 686, 690
Olsen, In re Marriage of, 852
Olson v. Etheridge, 1113
O.M. Droney Beverage Co. v. Miller Brewing Co., 489
O'Melveny & Myers v. FDIC, 951
Omnitrus Merging Corp. v. Illinois Tool Works, Inc., 133
Onderdonk v. Presbyterian Homes, 496, 498
135 E. 57th St. LLC v. Daffy's Inc., 825
Opera Co. of Boston, Inc. v. Wolf Trap Found. for the Performing Arts, 730, 754
Operating Eng'rs Local 324 Health Care Plan v. G & W Constr. Co., 746
Operating Tech. Elecs., Inc. v. Generac Power Sys., 191
Option Wireless, Ltd. v. Openpeak, Inc., 181
O'Quin v. Verizon Wireless, 201
Orange, City of, v. San Diego Cty. Emps. Ret. Ass'n, 733
Original Great Am. Chocolate Chip Cookie Co. v. River Valley Cookies, Ltd., 501
O'Rourke v. Hunter, 584
Orr v. Goodwin, 1080
Ortelere v. Teachers' Ret. Bd., 581, 582, 584, 586
Osborn v. Commanche Cattle Indus., Inc., 913-914
Oscar v. Simeonidis, 778
O'Shield v. Lakeside Bank, 1085
Owen v. CNA Ins./Cont'l Cas. Co., 1122
Owen v. Kroger Co., 356

Pacific Gas & Elec. Co. v. G.W. Thomas Drayage & Rigging Co., 442
Packgen v. BP Exploration, Inc., 388
PAK Foods Houston, LLC v. Garcia, 578
Palisades Props., Inc. v. Brunetti, 496
Palmer v. Palmer, 581, 1118, 1119
Palmieri v. Partridge, 1085
Pancakes of Haw., Inc. v. Pomare Props. Corp., 457
P & E Props., Inc. v. United Natural Foods, Inc., 815
Paradine v. Jane, 742
Parente v. Pirozzoli, 526, 528
Parker, Estate of v. Dorchak, 428
Parker v. Twentieth Century-Fox Film Corp., 937, 938
Park 100 Investors, Inc. v. Kartes, 634, 637, 638, 741
Paschall's Inc. v. Dozier, 312
Patterson v. Patterson's Estate, 300
Paul v. Patton, 1103
The Paul & Irene Bogoni Found. v. St. Bonaventure Univ., 245
Paul Gottlieb & Co. v. Alps South Corp., 165, 182, *184*, 190-192, 207
PayoutOne v. Coral Mortg. Bankers, 356
Payson, In re, 245
Payton v. Abbott Labs, 584
Pearson v. Norton, 603
Pearson v. Simmonds Precision Prods., Inc., 630
Peevyhouse v. Garland Coal & Mining Co., 897, 898, 900, 901
Peninsular Supply Co. v. C.B. Day Realty of Fla., Inc., 313
Pennsylvania Acad. of Fine Arts v. Grant, 273
Pennsy Supply, Inc. v. American Ash Recycling Corp. of Pennsylvania, 102, *107*, 112, 125, 228, 571
Pennzoil Co. v. Texaco, Inc., 95, 96, 1067
People ex rel. v. *See name of principal party*
Pepsi-Cola Co. v. Steak 'N Shake, Inc., 507
Perdue v. Crocker Nat'l Bank, 517
Petermann v. International Bhd. of Teamsters, 535
Peterson v. Ellebrecht, 604
Pettit v. Liston, 574
Petty v. Countrywide Home Loans, Inc., 669
Pharmathene, Inc. v. Siga Techs., Inc., 918
Phibro Energy, Inc. v. Empresa De Polimeros De Sines Sarl, 862
Philpot v. Gruninger, 116
Phoenix Hermetic Co. v. Filtrine Mfg. Co., 483
Phoenix Orthopaedic Surgeons, Ltd. v. Peairs, 683, 685, 686, 687, 688, 690
Pickett v. Lloyd's, 496
Pick Kwik Food Stores, Inc. v. Tenser, 147
Pierce v. Farm Bureau Mut. Ins. Co., 760
Pierson v. Medical Health Ctrs., P.A., 692
Pilla v. Estate of Pilla, 883
Pine River State Bank v. Mettille, 780
Pines Plaza Ltd. P'ship v. Berkley Trace, LLC, 1132
Pingley v. Perfection Plus Turbo-Dry, LLC, 670
Pinnacle Healthcare, LLC v. Sheets, 1068
Pitkin Seafood, Inc. v. Pitrock Realty Corp., 825
Pitts v. McGraw-Edison Co., 252
Pittsburgh-Des Moines Steel Co. v. Brookhaven Manor Water Co., 864, 865
Pittsburgh Steel Co. v. Hollingshead & Blei, 785
Plainfield, Town of v. Paden Eng'g Co., 836
Pleasure Time, Inc. v. Kuss, 892
Plowman v. Indian Refining Co., 120, 125, 126, 127, 129, 247, 327, 331
P.M. v. T.B., 695, 707-708, 709

Poeppel v. Lester, 436
Polk v. BHRGU Avon Props, LLC, 271, 445
Pop's Cones, Inc. v. Resorts International Hotel, Inc., 285, 291, 292
Porter v. Wilson, 574
Poulsen v. Treasure State Indus., 455
Power Eng'g & Mfg., Ltd. v. Krug Int'l, 767
Powers v. Siats, 811
PPG Indus., Inc. v. Shell Oil Co., 767
Preferred Mut. Ins. Co. v. Gamache, 955
Premix-Marbletite Mfg. Corp. v. SKW Chems., Inc., 183
Presten v. Sailer, 364-365
Princess Cruises, Inc. v. General Electric Co., 153, *165,* 171, 172-174, 181, 191, 192
ProCD, Inc. v. Zeidenberg, 200-208
Professional Prop. Servs., Inc. v. Agler Green Townhouses, Inc., 693
Professional Serv. Network, Inc. v. American Alliance Holding Co., 599, 950
Progressive Enters.; United States v., 786
Protectors Ins. Serv., Inc. v. U.S. Fid. & Guar. Co., 919
Prudential Ins. Co. of Am. v. Clark, 459
Pugh's IGA v. Super Food Servs., Inc., 635
Puttkammer v. Minth, 314, 323
Pyramid Printing Co. v. Alaska State Comm'n, 937

Quadron Software Int'l Corp. v. Plotseneder, 1069
Quake Construction, Inc. v. American Airlines, Inc., 86, 93, 94, 95, 96, 160, 293
Quaker State Mushroom Co. v. Dominick's Finer Foods, Inc., 177
Quality Liquid Feeds, Inc. v. Plunkett, 695
Quashnock v. Frost, 625
Quicken Loans, Inc. v. Brown (Quicken Loans I), 667, 671-673, 674
Quicken Loans, Inc. v. Brown (Quicken Loans II), 669
Quicken Loans, Inc. v. Walters for Walters, 673
Quigley v. KPMG Peat Marwick, LLP, 598
Quillen v. Kelley, 1027

Racine & Laramie, Ltd. v. California Dep't of Parks & Recreation, 519, 736
Radisson Hotels Int'l, Inc. v. Majestic Towers, Inc., 1081
Raffles v. Wichelhaus, 396, 398
Ragen v. Hancor, Inc., 403
Rainbow Country Rentals & Retails, Inc. v. Ameritech Publ'g, Inc., 1085
Rainwater v. Hobeika, 81
R&B Appliance Parts, Inc. v. Amana Co., L.P., 1132-1133
R & B Farms, Inc. v. Cedar Valley Acres, Inc., 729
Rash v. Toccoa Clinic Med. Assocs., 685
Rasimas v. Michigan Dep't of Mental Health, 933
R.A. Weaver & Assocs., Inc. v. Asphalt Constr., Inc., 507
Rawlings v. John Hancock Mut. Life Ins. Co., 588
Ray v. Montgomery, 626
Ray v. William G. Eurice & Bros., Inc., 37, 44, 45, 60, 76, 106, 638, 740-741
RBS Citizens Bank, N.A. v. Purther, 433
R.E. Davis Chem. Corp. v. Diasonics, Inc., 977
Redarowicz v. Ohlendorf, 560
Reddington v. Staten Island Univ. Hosp., 534
Redgrave v. Boston Symphony Orchestra, Inc., 920
Reed v. Mattapan Deposit & Trust Co., 581
Reese Design v. I-94 Highway 61 Eastview Ctr. P'ship, 1035
Refrigeradora Del Noroeste, S.A. v. Appelbaum, 853
Regency Outdoor Adver., Inc. v. Carolina Lanes, Inc., 521
Reger Dev., LLC v. National City Bank, 505
Register.com, Inc. v. Verio, Inc., 25-26, 29
Reier Broadcasting Co. v. Kramer, 1059, 1065-1068
Reliford v. United Parcel Serv., 600
ReMapp Int'l Corp. v. Comfort Keyboard Co., 388
Remillard Brick Co. v. Dandini, 733
Rent-A-Ctr., W., Inc. v. Jackson, 663
Retail Assocs., Inc. v. Macy's E., Inc., 491
Rexnord Corp. v. DeWolff Boberg & Assoc., Inc., 907
Ricci v. Key Bancshares of Me., Inc., 523
Rich & Whillock v. Ashton Dev., Inc., 608, 784
Richards v. Powercraft Homes, Inc., 560, 625
Richardson v. Greensboro Warehouse & Storage Co., 53
Richardson Lumber Co. v. Hoey, 723
Ricketts v. Scothorn, 234
Ricks, Estate of, 604
Riley v. California, 27
Ring v. State Farm Mut. Auto. Ins., 444
Ring v. Taylor, 438
Riverisland Cold Storage Inc. v. Fresno-Madera Prod. Credit Ass'n, 457-458
Rizzitiello v. McDonald's Corp., 523
R.J. Daum Constr. Co. v. Child, Utah, 280
R.J. Gaydos Ins. Agency, Inc. v. National Consumer Ins. Co., 498
Robert Gordon, Inc. v. Ingersoll-Rand Co., 280, 281
Roberts v. Farmers Ins. Exch., 748
Roberts Contracting Co. v. Valentine-Wooten Rd. Pub. Facility Bd., 1030
Robertson v. Robertson, 608
Robert's River Rides v. Steamboat Dev. Corp., 300
Robinson v. Food Serv., 578
Robinson Helicopter Co. v. Dana Corp., 965
Roby v. Corp. of Lloyd's, 30
Rocheux Int'l of N.J., Inc. v. U.S. Merchs. Fin. Grp., Inc., 866
Rockingham County v. Luten Bridge Co., 921, 925
Rodman v. State Farm. Mut. Ins. Co., 420, 422
Rodriguez v. Learjet, Inc., 945
Rogers v. Dell Computer Corp., 202
Rohlin Constr. Co. v. City of Hinton, 1083
Romano v. Site Acquisitions, LLC, 253
Rooney v. Tyson, 534
Root v. Insurance Co., 402
Rosauer Corp. v. Sapp Dev., L.L.C., 565
Rose v. Vulcan Materials Co., 785
Rosen v. Bank of Am., N.A., 262
Rosenberg v. Son, Inc., 1133
Rosenfeld v. Basquiat, 356

Rosenthal v. Great W. Fin. Sec. Corp., 637
Rosetti v. City of New Britain, 1132
Rosewood Care Ctr., Inc. v. Caterpillar, Inc., 354
Ross v. Forest Lawn Mem'l Park, 963
Ross Sys. v. Linden Dari-Delite, Inc., 595, 785
Rotenberry v. Hooker, 142
Roth v. Speck, 892, *989,* 991
Roth Steel Prods. v. Sharon Steel Corp., 786, 787-788
Roto-Lith, Ltd. v. F.P. Bartlett & Co., 181
Roudis v. Hubbard, 837
Roussalis v. Wyoming Med. Ctr., Inc., 781
Route 6 Outparcels, LLC v. Ruby Tuesday, Inc., 767
Rubin v. Irving Trust Co., 408-409
Rucker v. Sanders, 54
Ruddock v. First Nat'l Bank of Lake Forest, 1058
Russell v. Allerton, 483
RWH Homebuilders, L.P. v. Black Diamond Dev. LLP, 887

Sabo v. Delman, 631
Sackett v. Spindler, 841, 846, 848
Sagl v. Hirt, 1035, 1039
Sahadi v. Continental Ill. Nat'l Bank & Trust Co., 817
St. Charles v. Kender, 966
St. Charles Foods, Inc. v. America's Favorite Chicken Co., 404
St. James Mut. Homes v. Andrade, 433
St. Lawrence Factory Stores v. Ogdensburg Bridge & Port Auth., 1011-1012
St. Paul Dredging Co. v. State, 810
St. Regis Paper Co. v. Quality Pipeline, Inc., 312
Sales Serv., Inc. v. Daewoo Int'l (Am.) Corp., 370
Sally Beauty Co. v. Nexxus Products Co., 1121, *1123,* 1132-1133
Salsbury v. Northwestern Bell Tel. Co., 243
Salve Regina Coll. v. Russell, 1034
Samica Enters., LLC v. Mail Boxes Etc. USA, Inc., 485
Sampley Enters., Inc. v. Laurilla, 875
Sandlin v. Weaver, 54
Sands v. Menard, 326
S & S Inc. v. Meyer, 862
Sarvis v. Vermont State Colls., 620
Sass v. Thomas, 386
Satcher v. Satcher, 1019
Sateriale v. R.J. Reynolds Tobacco Co., 66, 75, 77, 146
Savre v. Santoyo, 817
Sawyer v. Mills, 353
Scaduto v. Orlando, 1022
Scarpitti v. Weborg, 1108
Scherk v. Alberto-Culver Co., 24
Schlaifer Nance & Co. v. Estate of Andy Warhol, 621
Schmidt, In re, 243
Schnabel v. Trilegiant Co., 24, 25, 26, 27, 28, 29
Schroeder v. Fageol Motors, Inc., 647
Schultze v. Goodstein, 831
Schumann v. Levi, 978
Schumm by Whymer v. Berg, 138, 602-603
Schuyler v. Pantages, 518
Schwartzreich v. Bauman-Basch, Inc., 781
The Score Bd., Inc., In re, 577
Scott v. Grow, 724
Scott v. Pacific Gas & Elec. Co., 537
Scott v. United States, 641
Seaboard Lumber Co. v. United States, 749
Seaboard Music Co. v. Germano, 943
Seattle-First Nat'l Bank v. Oregon Pac. Indus., Inc., 1134
Seaver v. Ransom, 1095
Seay v. Dodge, 1065
Security Bank & Trust Co. v. Bogard, 291
Security Stove & Mfg. Co. v. American Ry. Express Co., 1012
Sedmak v. Charlie's Chevrolet, Inc., 387
Seidel v. Gordon A. Gundaker Real Estate Co., 62
Seidenberg v. Summit Bank, 485, *494,* 503, 504
Seixas v. Woods, 556
Selcke v. New England Ins. Co., 490
Selmer Co. v. Blakeslee-Midwest Co., 601, 778
Semitekol v. Monaco Coach Corp., 555
Sergeant Co. v. Pickett, 1075
Sevast v. Kakouras, 1030
1700 Rinehart, LLC v. Advance Am., 810
7200 Scottsdale Rd. Gen. Partners v. Kuhn Farm Mach., 754
7's Enters., Inc. v. Rosario, 1068
SFEG Corp. v. Blendtec, Inc., 183
Sgouros v. TransUnion Corp., 26, 29
Shadow Lakes, Inc. v. Cudlipp Constr. & Dev. Co., 189
Shadwell v. Shadwell, 105
Sharon v. City of Newton, 577
Sharp v. Laubersheimer, 1035, 1036
Sharp Elecs. Corp. v. Deutsche Fin. Servs. Corp., 173
Shay v. Aldrich, 449-450
Sheets v. Teddy's Frosted Foods, Inc., 532
Shell Oil Co. v. HRN, Inc., 505
Sheppard v. Morgan-Keegan, 536
Sherrodd, Inc. v. Morrison-Knudsen Co., 436, *451,* 457, 458, 459
Sherwood v. Walker, 723, 724-726, 728
Shields v. Clifton Hill Land Co., 124
Shimman v. International Union of Operating Eng'rs, Local 18, 951
Shirley v. Christian Episcopal Methodist Church, 141
Shiro v. Drew, 1118, 1119
Shore Builders, Inc. v. Dogwood, Inc., 729
Shulse v. City of Mayville, 323
Shultz v. Shultz, 598
Siegel v. Spear & Co., 276
Sierra Fria Corp. v. Evans, 633
Signal Hill Aviation Co. v. Stroppe, 1015
Silchia v. MCI Telecomms. Corp., 536
Silling v. Erwin, 1065
Silvestri v. Optus Software, Inc., 512
Simcala, Inc. v. American Coal Trade, Inc., 507
Simpson v. Murkowski, 234
Sixta v. Ochsner, 603
Skrbina v. Fleming Cos., 45

Sky Angel U.S., LLC v. Discovery Commc'ns, LLC, 512
Slade's Case, 307
Slayter v. Pasley, Or., 81, 83
Smith v. Brady, 833, 834
Smith v. Hornbuckle, 1065
Smith v. Melson, Inc., 440, 442
Smith v. Smith, 361
Smith v. Wheeler, 272
Smith, Estate of v. Samuels, 142
Smyers v. Quartz Prods. Works Corp., 866
Snaith v. Snaith, 109
Snyder v. Herbert Greenbaum & Assoc., 941
Snyder v. Nixon, 300
Sofa Gallery, Inc. v. Stratford Co., 491
Sokoloff v. Harriman Estates Dev. Corp., 1056-1057
Solar Applications Eng'g, Inc. v. T.A. Operating Corp., 813
Solymar Invs., Ltd. v. Banco Santander S.A., 457
Sonfast Corp. v. York Int'l Corp., 789
Sons of Thunder v. Borden, Inc., 496, 497-498, 503
Sorensen v. Fio Rito, 948, 1038
Southern Bldg. Servs., Inc. v. City of Ft. Smith, 1082
Southern Concrete Servs., Inc. v. Mableton Contractors, Inc., 472
Southworth Mach. Co. v. F/V Corey Pride, 168
Spanier v. New York City Transit Auth., 864
Sparrow v. Demonico, 579, 586-589, 638
Specht v. Netscape Commc'ns Corp., 24, 25, 26, 209, 213, 214-216, 218
Speedway Motorsports Int'l Ltd., v. Bronwen Energy Trading, Ltd., 404
Speight v. Walters Development Co., 558, 564, 565
Spence v. Ham, 830, 831, 832
Spiegel v. Lowenstein, 349
Spires v. Hanover Fire Ins. Co., 1105, 1108
Spivack v. Berks Ridge Corp., 565
Spoklie v. Montana Dep't of Fish, Wildlife & Parks, 1060-1061
Standard Jury Instructions — Contract & Bus. Cases, In re, 888
Stanford Hotels Corp. v. Potomac Creek Assocs., L.P., 1056
Stannard, In re Estate of, 941
Starchem Labs., LLC v. Kabco Pharm., Inc., 865
Star Fin. Corp. v. Howard Nance Co., 1084
Stark v. Parker, 841
Starkville, City of v. 4-County Elec. Power Ass'n, 142, 143, 767
State v. *See name of opposing party*
State ex rel. v. *See name of principal party*
State Farm Mut. Auto. Ins. Co. v. Anderson-Weber, Inc., 562
State Farm Mut. Auto. Ins. Co. v. Wilson, 441, 443
Stearns v. Emery-Waterhouse Co., 370
Steel v. Eagle, 269, 270
Steffen v. Dumke, 85
Steffes, In Matter of Estate of, 321, 322, 323-324
Steinberg v. Chicago Med. Sch., 133, 152
Stelluti Kerr, L.L.C. v. Mapei Corp., 180
Stelmack v. Glen Alden Coal Co., 109
Stemcor United States v. Miracero, S.A. de C.V., 953
Stendig, Inc. v. Thom Rock Realty Co., 818
Stenzel v. Dell, Inc., 201
Step-Saver Data Sys., Inc. v. Wyse Tech., 183, 202, 203
Stewart v. Marvin, 605
Stewart v. Wilmington Trust SP Servs., 710
Stitch Ranch v. Double B.J. Farms, 398
Stolper Steel Prods. Corp. v. Behrens Mfg. Co., 852
Stone v. Harmon, 430
Stone Mountain Props., Ltd. v. Helmer, 509
Stones v. Sears, Roebuck & Co., 552
Storti v. University of Wash., 64
Story v. City of Bozeman, 454, 950
Strand v. U.S. Bank Nat'l Ass'n ND, 647
Strata Prod. Co. v. Mercury Exploration Co., 282, 369, 370
Strickland v. Henry, 116
Sudamax Industria E Comercio De Cigaros, LTDA v. Buttes & Ashes, Inc., 767
Sullivan v. Boston Gas Co., 584
Sullivan v. O'Connor, 966
Sullivan v. Porter, 1056
Sully-Miller Contracting Co. v. Gledson/Cashman Constr., Inc., 69
Sumerel v. Goodyear Tire & Rubber Co., 737
Sun City Pet Mkt., LLC v. Honest Kitchen, Inc., 154
Sundberg v. TTR Realty, LLC, 988
Sunesis Trucking Co. v. Thistledown Racetrack, L.L.C., 856
Sunnyland Farms, Inc. v. Central N.M. Elec. Coop., Inc., 907
Sunshine Imp & Exp Corp. v. Luxury Car Concierge, Inc., 755
Sun Trust Bank v. Harper, 587
Sun Valley, Ltd. v. Galyan's Trading Co., LLC, 814
Superior Oil Co. v. Vanderhoof, 453
Superior Steel, Inc. v. Ascent at Roebling's Bridge, Inc., 815
The Superlative Grp., Inc. v. WIHO, L.L.C., 263
Surrogate Parenting Assocs., Inc. v. Commonwealth ex rel. Armstrong, 704
Susi Contracting Co., United States ex rel. v. Zara Contracting Co., 1021
Sutcliffe v. Heatley, 582
Sutton v. Banner Life Ins. Co., 426
Suzy Phillips Originals, Inc. v. Coville, Inc., 187
Swavely v. Freeway Ford Truck Sales, Inc., 691
Swick v. Seward Sch. Bd., 371
Sy Jack Realty Co. v. Pergament Syosset Corp., 820, 821
Syester v. Banta, 611, 620, 621, 629, 637
Systems Tech. Assocs., Inc. v. United States, 784

Talbott v. Nibert, 269
Talbott v. Stemmons, 105
TAL Fin. Corp. v. CSC Consulting, Inc., 1081
Tallmadge v. Aurora Chrysler Plymouth, Inc., 551
Tamayo v. CGS Tires US, Inc., 554
T & M Solar & Air Conditioning, Inc. v. Lennox Int'l Inc., 554

T & S Brass & Bronze Works, Inc. v. Pic-Air, Inc., 789
Tardy v. Wills, 353
Taylor v. Caldwell, 742, 743
Taylor v. State Farm Mutual Automobile Insurance Co., 438, 439, 442-443, 445, 447-448, 449, 451
Taylor v. Wahby, 1008
Taylor Equip., Inc. v. John Deere Co., 1133
TCP Indus., Inc. v. Uniroyal, Inc., 978
Teeter v. Horner Military Sch., 1075
Tenzer v. Superscope, Inc., 521
Terraces of Sunset Park, LLC v. Chamberlin, 271
Tesoro Petroleum Corp. v. Holborn Oil Co., 977
Thermal Sys. of Ala., Inc. v. Sigafoose, 491
Thing v. La Chusa, 959
Third Story Music, Inc. v. Waits, 519, 520
1324 W. Pratt Condo. Ass'n v. Platt Constr. Grp., Inc., 566
Thomas v. General Motors Acceptance Corp., 157
Thomas v. Progressive Cas. Ins., 705
Thomas Haverty Co. v. Jones, 836
Thomas J. Duggan, LLC v. Peacock Point, LLC, 728
Thompson v. Libby, 429, 432, 433, 434, 437, 447-448, 449, 457
Thompson v. St. Regis Paper Co., 535
Thorne v. Walker-Thomas Furniture Co., 646
Thrifty Rent-A-Car Sys., Inc. v. South Fla. Transp., Inc., 754
Tigg Corp. v. Dow Corning Corp., 472, 485
Timmer v. Gray, 1037
Tisher v. California Horse Racing Bd., 521
Titus v. Superior Court, Maricopa Cnty., 1063
T. K. v. Adobe Sys. Inc., 576
TKO Equip. Co. v. C & G Coal Co., 398
TLG Elecs, Inc. v. Newcome Corp., 158
TMG Kreations, LLC v. Seltzer, 484
Top of Iowa Co-op. v. Sime Farms, Inc., 865
Toppert v. Bunge Corp., 862, 864
Torres v. D'Alesso, 435
Totaro, Duffy, Cannova & Co. L.L.C. v. Lane, Middleton & Co., L.L.C., 919
Totem Marine Tug & Barge, Inc. v. Alyeska Pipeline Service Co., 591, 598-601, 788
Toussaint v. Blue Cross & Blue Shield, 536
Town of. *See name of town*
Tozier v. Tozier, 232
Trabue, Inc. v. Professional Mgmt.-Auto., Inc., 931
Trachtenburg v. Sibarco Stations, Inc., 1028
Transact, Inc., In re, 818
Transatlantic Fin. Corp. v. United States, 755
Treat Bros. Co., United States ex rel. v. Fidelity & Deposit Co. of Md., 950-951
Tredrea v. Anesthesia & Analgesia, P.C., 1098-1100
Trees v. Kersey, 710
Trexler's Estate, 251, 252
Triangle Waist Co. v. Todd, 990
Trilogy Network Sys., Inc. v. Johnson, 991
Tri-State Roofing Co. of Uniontown v. Simon, 595
Tri-Town Constr. Co. v. Commerce Park Assocs. 12, LLC, 768
TRT Transp., Inc. v. Aksoy, 98
Truax v. Corrigan, 502
TruGreen Cos., LLC v. Mower Bros., 988
Truhe v. Turnac Grp., LLC, 797
Truman L. Flatt & Sons Co. v. Schupf, 849, 857, 858
Trustees of Amherst Acad. v. Cowls, 242
Tuck v. Payne, 573
TufAmerica, Inc. v. Codigo Music LLC, 638
Tull v. Gundersons, Inc., 948
Tuomala v. Regent Univ., 550
Turner v. Shalberg, 885
Turntables, Inc. v. Gestetner, 862, 863, 864
Tusch Enters. v. Coffin, 560, 561, 567
Twin City Fire Ins. Co. v. Philadelphia Life Ins. Co., 291
Twyman v. Roell, 189
Tyler v. Iowa Dep't of Revenue, 706-707
Tyler, City of v. Likes, 964
Tyranski v. Piggins, 321, 322

Uhar & Co. v. Jacob, 356
Uhlaender v. Hendricksen, 1035
Union Carbide Corp. v. Oscar Mayer Foods Corp., 187-188
Union Pac. Ry. Co. v. Chicago, Rock Island & Pac. Ry. Co., 1053
Unique Sys. Inc. v. Zotos Int'l, Inc., 852
United Bank v. Ashland Dev. Corp., 729
United Parcel Serv. Co. v. Rickert, 293
United Partition Sys., Inc. v. United States, 818
United States v. *See name of opposing party*
United States ex rel. v. *See name of principal party*
United States for Use & Benefit of Astro Cleaning & Packaging Co. v. Jamison Co., 1021
United States for Use of Susi Contracting Co. v. Zara Contracting Co., 1021
Universal Inv. Co. v. Sahara Motor Inn, Inc., 626
Uniwill v. City of L.A., 600
U.S. Bank, N.A. v. Aceves, 257
USEMCO, Inc. v. Marbro Co., 177

Valencia v. White, 574
Valentine's, Inc. v. Ngo, 1082
Valley Medical Specialists v. Farber, 681, 683, 684, 687, 691-694, 1068, 1121
Van Buren v. Pima Cmty. Coll. Dist. Bd., 625
Vanderbilt v. DiNardo, 1084
Vastoler v. American Can Co., 253
Venable v. Hickerson, Phelps, Kirtley & Assoc., Inc., 370
Ventura v. Titan Sports, Inc., 1032, 1042, 1043
Venture Assocs. Corp. v. Zenith Data Sys. Corp., 98
Viacom Int'l Inc. v. MGA Entm't, Inc., 837
Vickers v. Wichita State Univ., 941
Victoria Laundry (Windsor) Ltd. v. Newman Indus., Ltd., 905
Victory Foodservice Distribs. Corp. v. N. Chr. Laitsos & Co. Ltd., 953
Viking Supply v. National Cart Co., 492
Vilella v. AT&T, 647
Village of. *See name of village*

Vitek v. Jones, 584
Vivaro Corp. v. Raza Commc'ns, Inc. (In re Vivaro Corp.), 988
VLM Food Trading Int'l, Inc. v. Illinois Trading Co., 192
Vogan v. Hayes Appraisal Associates, Inc., 1096, 1102, 1104

Waage v. Borer, 326
Wade v. Kessler Inst., 501
Wakefield v. Northern Telecom, Inc., 530-531
Waldorf Steel Fabricators, Inc. v. Consolidated Sys., Inc., 863, 864
Walker v. Keith, 78, 84, 85, 93
Wallace v. Smith, 857
Wallace Real Estate Inv., Inc. v. Groves, 1082
Waller v. Truck Ins. Exch., Inc., 517, 520
Walls v. Bailey, 410
Walser v. Toyota Motor Sales, U.S.A., Inc., 1012, 1017-1018
Walsh v. Fisher, 891
Walsh v. Rundlette, 1052
Walther v. Sovereign Bank, 1077
Ward v. Albertson, 55
Warden v. Warden, 318, 323
Warner v. Kaplan, 755
Warner Ins. Co. v. Commissioner of Ins., 581
Wartzman v. Hightower Productions, Ltd., 1001, 1009, 1011
Warwick; State v., 241
Wassenaar v. Panos, 1081, 1084
Wasserman's Inc. v. Township of Middletown, 1081
Waste Mgmt. of Mass., Inc. v. Carver, 620
Water Dev. Co. v. Lankford, 705
Watson v. Cal-Three, LLC, 993
Watts v. Watts, 315, 325, 326, 522
Weavertown Transp. Leasing, Inc. v. Moran, 109
Webb v. McGowin, 333, 336-339
Webb v. Saunders, 605
Weber v. North Loup River Pub. Power & Irrigation Dist., 815
Webster Trust v. Roly, 1058
Weed v. Weed, 118
Weger v. Rocha, 606
Wehry v. Daniels, 388
Weitz Co. v. Hands, Inc., 283
Wells v. Weston, 171
Wentworth Military Acad. v. Marshall, 1075
West Branch State Bank v. Gates, 300
Western Sling & Cable Co. v. Hamilton, 404
Westland Enters., Inc. v. Boyne, USA, Inc., 1062
Weston Invs., Inc. v. Domtar Indus., Inc., 407
W.G. Taylor Co. v. Bannerman, 483
Wheaton v. East, 573
Wheelabrator Envtl. Sys. v. Galante, 766
Wheeler v. White, 1017
Wheeling-Pittsburgh Steel Corp., In re, 295
Whirlpool Corp. v. Grigoleit Co., 599, 788
White v. State of Washington, 537
White City Shopping Ctr., LP v. PR Rests., LLC, 415
Whiteco Indus., Inc. v. Kopani, 370
Whitlock v. Burke, 587
Wholey v. Sears, Roebuck & Co., 535
Wieder v. Skala, 537
Wil-Fred's, Inc. v. Metropolitan Sanitary Dist., 739, 740
Wilkinson v. Carpenter, 631
Willard v. Tayloe, 1054
Wille v. Southwestern Bell Tel. Co., 645
Willett v. Webster, 582
Williams v. AT&T Mobility Servs., 747
Williams v. Curtin, 415
Williams v. Gray Grp., L.L.C., 906
Williams v. Insurance Co., 401
Williams v. Walker-Thomas Furniture Co., 639, 640, 643-646, 648, 674, 678
Willson v. M. & C. C. of Baltimore, 1074
Wilson v. Amerada Hess Corp., 498-502, 504
Wilson v. Career Educ. Corp., 535
Wilson v. McCann, 631
Wilson v. W. M. Storey Lumber Co., 53
Windeler v. Scheers Jewelers, 963
Windsor Mills, Inc. v. Collins & Aikman Corp., 25, 213
Winternitz v. Summit Hills Joint Venture, 366
Winthrop Towers; United States v., 1127
Wired Music, Inc. v. Clark, 943
Wisconsin & Mich. Ry. Co. v. Powers, 109, 116, 276
Wisconsin Knife Works v. National Metal Crafters, 797
Witten, In re Marriage of, 705
Wolens v. American Airlines, Inc., 70, 71
Wolf v. Anderson, 1056
Wolfe v. Welton, 555
Wolfeld v. Hanika, 637
Wood v. Lucy, Lady Duff-Gordon, 146, *482*, 484-486, 818
Woodland Harvesting, Inc. v. Georgia Pac. Corp., 1018
Woodmere Acad. v. Steinberg, 245
Woodward v. Fuller, 831, 833
Woolley v. Stewart, 360
Wooten v. DeMean, 852, 885
World of Boxing LLC v. King, 1009
Worley v. Lister Distribution, Inc., 931
Worley v. Wyoming Bottling Co., 534
Worms v. Burgess, 273
W.R. Grimshaw Co. v. Nevil C. Withrow Co., 594-595
Wreglesworth v. Arctco, Inc., 578
Wright v. Newman, 234, 236
Wright v. Stevens, 875
Wright v. Wright, 581
W.S. Carnes, Inc. v. Board of Supervisors of Chesterfield County, 550
W.T. Rawleigh Co. v. Snider, 636
Wynn v. Monterey Club, 963

XCO Int'l, Inc. v. Pacific Scientific Co., 1082

Yeager Co., In re, 1005

Zaleznik v. Gulf Coast Roofing Co., 310, 313
Zanakis-Pico v. Cutter Dodge, Inc., 51

Zapata Hermanos Sucesores, S.A. v. Hearthside Baking Co., *947*, 952-954
Zelnick v. Adams, 577
Zemco Mfg., Inc. v. Navistar Int'l Transp. Corp., 796, 797
Zigas v. Superior Court, 1113, 1114
Zinn v. Ex-Cell-O Corp., 603
Zivich v. Mentor Soccer Club, Inc., 578
Zomba Recording LLC v. Williams, 1067
Zuk v. Zuk, 365

TABLE OF UNIFORM COMMERCIAL CODE PROVISIONS (UCC)

Note: The ALI and the NCCUSL completed a revision of Article 1 in 2001 that has now been adopted by a substantial majority of states. Any references to sections in pre-revised Article 1 are noted as "pre-revised." The same organizations proposed an amended version of Article 2 but withdrew it in 2011 after it failed to be adopted by any state.

Article 1 148, 415, 492, 493
§1-103, *pre-revised* 177
§1-103(b) 147, 149, 389, 978
§1-201(b)(20) 492, 504
§1-201(b)(20), Official Comment 492
§1-201(b)(31) 389
§1-201(b)(37) 295, 356, 387, 389
§1-201(b)(37), Comment 387
§1-201(b)(43) 295, 356, 389
§1-203, *pre-revised* 471, 492
§1-203, *pre-revised,* Comment 471
§1-205, *pre-revised* 415, 468, 471
§1-205(1), *pre-revised* 465
§1-205(2), *pre-revised* 465
§1-207(1), *pre-revised* 799
§1-207(2), *pre-revised* 799
§1-302 161, 489
§1-303 183, 415, 471
§1-304 492, 493, 939
§1-304, Comment 493
§1-305 973, 977
§1-305, Comment 1 939
§1-306 799
§1-308(a) 799
§1-308(b) 799
§1-309, Official Comment 505
Article 2 86, 111, 147, 148, 149, 151, 153, 157, 159, 160, 161, 165, 172, 173, 176, 183, 191, 192, 194, 209, 221, 294, 295, 381, 387, 389, 437, 473, 487, 488, 489, 491, 492, 787, 788, 789, 861, 917, 939, 945, 953, 971, 972, 1127
§2-102 148, 149, 160, 176
§2-104 546
§2-104, Comment 2 247
§2-104(1) 149, 295, 388, 554
§2-105(1) 148, 209, 295, 387, 945
§§2-201 to 2-210 147
§2-201 151, 154, 346, 347, 380, 381, 387, 389, 796
§2-201, Comment 1 387
§2-201, Comment 2 387
§2-201, Comment 3 389
§2-201(1) 387, 389, 796, 797
§2-201(2) 388, 390
§2-201(3)(a) 388
§2-201(3)(b) 388
§2-201(3)(c) 387, 388
§2-202 415, 428, 434, 437, 472, 555
§2-202, Comment 1(a) 433
§2-202, Comment 2 472
§2-202, Comment 3 437
§2-202(b) 437
§2-203 119
§2-204 93, 152, 157, 159, 160, 200
§2-204(1) 205, 861
§2-204(2) 153, 159
§2-204(3) 93, 153
§2-205 273, 295
§2-205, Comment 2 295
§2-205, Comment 3 295
§2-205, Comment 4 295, 296
§2-206 200, 206
§2-206(1) 160, 202, 861
§2-206(1)(b) 65
§2-207 165, 167, 168, 172, 173-174, 178, 179, 180-183, 185, 186, 187, 188, 190-193, 200, 202, 203, 389
§2-207, Comment 1 174
§2-207, Comment 3 179, 191
§2-207, Comment 4 187
§2-207, Comment 5 187, 188, 190, 202, 203
§2-207, Comment 7 183
§2-207(1) 172, 178, 179, 180-181, 191, 194
§2-207(2) 172, 179, 181-182, 190, 191, 207
§2-207(3) 183, 861
§2-208 415, 468
§2-209 200, 787, 797
§2-209, Comment 1 787
§2-209, Comment 2 787
§2-209, Comment 3 797
§2-209(1) 781, 785, 787, 788
§2-209(2) 797
§2-209(3) 796, 797
§2-209(4) 797
§2-209(5) 798
§2-210 1121, 1124, 1128, 1129
§2-210, Comment 1 1127
§2-210, Comment 4 1121
§2-210(1) 1127, 1128, 1130, 1133
§2-210(2) 1121, 1122, 1128

§2-210(4) 1133
§2-210(5) 1132
§2-302 296, 639, 641-643, 646, 647, 649, 650, 672, 676, 738
§2-302, Comment 641, 642
§2-305 85, 86, 470, 504
§2-305, Comment 3 470, 504
§2-306 491, 506, 507, 1121, 1132
§2-306, Comment 2 507
§2-306, Comment 3 507
§2-306, Comment 5 1128, 1132
§2-306(1) 507
§2-306(2) 485, 1128, 1130
§2-307 183
§2-307, Comment 642
§2-308 183, 489
§2-309 489, 491
§2-309, Comment 8 488, 491
§2-309(3) 488, 489, 492
§2-310 489
§2-313 546, 552, 553
§2-313, Comment 3 553
§2-314 183, 546, 553
§2-314(2) 554
§2-315 183, 546, 554
§2-316 489, 554, 555, 567, 917
§2-316(1) 554, 555
§2-316(1), Comment 1 554
§2-316(2) 555
§2-316(3) 555
§2-326 484
§2-503 973
§2-504 973
§2-507 840
§2-509 489
§2-511 840
§2-511, Comment 1 840
§2-513 489
§§2-601 to 2-608 208
§2-601 972
§2-602 972
§2-602(1) 152
§2-606 976
§2-607(3)(a) 974
§2-608 972
§2-609 788, 861, 863, 865, 866, 867, 1121, 1132
§2-609, Comment 1 862
§2-609, Comment 2 788, 862
§2-609, Comment 4 866
§2-609, Official Comment 861, 862, 863
§2-609(1) 861, 862, 866
§2-609(2) 862
§2-609(4) 864, 865, 867
§2-610 852, 856
§2-610, Comment 2 852, 857
§2-610(a) 973
§2-611 853, 857
§2-613 743, 744, 755, 757
§2-615 744, 752, 753, 756, 757, 766, 767, 788
§2-615, Comment 1 756
§2-615, Comment 9 757, 767
§2-615, Comment 10 743
§2-615(a) 743
§2-616 744, 788
§2-703 976
§2-704(2) 977
§2-706 889, 976, 977
§2-706, Comment 2 977
§2-706(1) 976
§2-706(3) 976
§2-706(4)(b) 976
§2-708 942, 978
§2-708(1) 889, 976, 976, 977, 978
§2-708(2) 945, 976, 977, 978
§2-709 976, 978
§2-709(1)(a) 978
§2-709(1)(b) 978, 1059
§2-710 192, 889, 953, 978
§2-711 972
§2-712 972, 973
§2-712, Comment 2 972
§2-712, Comment 3 973
§2-712(1) 889
§2-712(3) 972
§2-713 889, 972, 973-974
§2-713, Comment 5 973
§2-713(2) 973
§2-714 208, 972, 974
§2-714(1) 974
§2-714(2) 974
§2-714(3) 974
§2-715 183, 192, 208, 889, 953, 972, 975
§2-715, Comment 2 907, 975
§2-715, Comment 4 975
§2-715(1) 975
§2-715(2) 906, 975
§2-715(2)(a) 939, 972, 975
§2-715(2)(b) 975
§2-716 972, 974, 978, 1058-1059
§2-716, Comment 1 1059
§2-717 866
§2-718 1027, 1028, 1029, 1030, 1081
§2-718, Comment 1 1085
§2-718(1) 1074, 1085
§2-719 917
§2-719(3) 489
§2-723 889
§2-725 563
§2-725(1) 556
Article 2A 111, 148
§2A-108(4) 953
§3-104 381

Article 5	492	§9-404(a)(1)	1134
§5-104	381	§9-404(a)(2)	1134
§7-202	381	§9-406(a)	1122
Article 9	148	§9-406(d)	1122
§9-203	381	§9-406(f)	1122

TABLE OF PROVISIONS FROM RESTATEMENT (SECOND) OF CONTRACTS

§1, Comment *f*, Reporter's Note 66
§2 232
§2(1) 232
§12, Comment *f* 577
§13 587
§14 577
§15 304, 586, 588
§15, Illus. 1 586
§15(2) 587
§16 588
§16, Comment *a* 589
§17 35
§19(1) 171, 173
§20 401
§21 44
§24 49, 50, 177
§25 58
§26 49, 50, 51
§26, Comment *b* 51, 70
§26, Illus. 4 50
§27 93
§27, Comment *c* 94
§29, Comment *a* 50
§30 50
§32 65
§33 86
§33, Comment *a* 73, 407
§33, Comment *b* 73
§33, Comment *e* 86
§35 53
§36 57, 273-274
§37 274
§39 54, 57, 172
§39(2) 58
§41 53
§42 56, 270
§42, Comment *a* 270
§43 56, 273
§45 64, 65
§45, Comment *a* 70
§45, Comment *d* 64
§45(2) 64
§57 57
§58 57
§59 57, 170, 172, 178
§59, Comment *a* 172
§61 172
§63 50
§63(b) 273
§63(b), Comment *f* 273
§64(b) (draft) 820
§65 50
§66 50
§69 57, 172
§71 102, 111, 113, 118, 146, 272
§71, Comment *b* 113, 118
§71, Comment *c* 110
§71(2) 112
§74(2) 138
§77 113, 506
§77, Comment *a* 146
§77, Comment *b* 506
§79 137, 138
§79, Comment *d* 272
§79, Comment *e* 138
§79(c) 75, 147
§81 126
§81, Comment *b* 126
§82 331
§82(2) 331
§83 332
§83, Comment *a* 332
§84(1) 817
§84(1), Comment *b* 817
§86 337, 339
§86, Comment *f* 338
§86, Comment *i* 337
§86, Comment *i*, Illus. 12 338
§86, Comment *i*, Illus. 13 338
§86, Illus. 1 337
§87, Comment *c* 272
§87(1)(a) 272-273
§87(1)(b) 294
§87(2) 282, 284, 291
§89 781
§89, Comment *b* 781
§89, Illus. 1 781
§89(a) 780
§89(c) 781
§90 226, 231, 233, 235, 236, 239, 245, 248, 251-254, 263, 285, 289, 290, 291, 781, 792, 1014, 1015, 1018
§90, Comment *a* 232
§90, Comment *a*, Reporter's Note 232
§90, Comment *b* 235, 245, 291
§90, Comment *d* 233, 1015, 1018
§90, Comment *d*, Illus. 10 290, 292
§90, Comment *f* 232

§90, Comment *f*, Illus. 16 233
§90, Illus. 11 1019
§90(1) 231, 239, 243, 244, 245, 1014
§90(2) 239, 243, 244, 245, 246
§95 119
§110 346, 347
§§110-150 346
§112 354
§115 354
§116 354
§124 354
§124, Comment *c* 354
§129 365-366
§129, Comment *a* 366
§129, Comment *c* 366
§130, Comment *a* 353
§130, Comment *b* 353
§§131-137 356
§132 354
§132, Comment *c* 355
§133 355
§133, Comment *b* 355
§133, Comment *c* 355
§133, Illus. 355-356
§139 369-373, 375-376, 389
§139, Illus. 4 376
§139(2) 369, 371
§139(2)(c) 371
§151 723
§152 725-726
§152(1) 726
§152(2) 726
§153 625, 733-734, 737
§153(a) 738
§153(b) 737, 738
§154 726, 727, 734
§154, Comment *a* 735
§154, Comment *d* 734, 735
§154, Comment *d*, Illus. 4 735
§154(a) 727
§154(b) 729
§157 735, 736, 739
§157, Comment *a* 736
§158 1043
§159, Comment *d* 620
§160 629
§161 625, 629
§161, Comment *d* 627
§161(a) 629
§161(b) 629
§161(c) 629
§161(d) 629, 630
§162(1)(b) 620
§162(1)(c) 620
§162(2) 620
§162(2), Comment *c* 620
§163 637
§163, Comment *a* 637
§164 629
§164(1) 611, 619, 626, 629
§166 637
§168(1) 620
§169 621
§173 630
§174 598
§174, Comment *a* 598
§§174-177 304
§175 598, 600
§175, Comment *b* 600
§175, Comment *b*, Illus. 5 785
§175, Comment *c* 600
§175(1) 784
§176 598, 599
§176(1)(c) 599
§176(1)(d) 599
§177(1) 607
§178 710
§178, Comment *a* 693
§178, Comment *b* 320
§178, Comment *e* 320
§178, Comment *f* 792
§179 691
§179, Comment *b* 693
§184 694
§184, Comment *b* 694
§184, Reporter's Note 694
§187 692
§188 683, 690, 692
§188, Comment *a* 686, 687
§188, Comment *d* 692
§188, Comment *f* 692
§188, Comment *g* 692
§188, Comment *h* 684
§189 708
§190 708
§191 708
§197 710
§200 398, 439
§201 401, 451
§201, Comment *c* 414
§201(1) 398
§201(2) 398, 401
§201(2)(b) 398, 403
§201(3) 398
§201(3), Comment *d* 398
§202 413
§202(4) 471
§203, Comment *a* 445
§203, Comment *b* 445
§203, Comment *c* 398
§203, Illus. 1 406-407
§203(a) 406
§204 407, 490
§205 492, 789, 932
§205, Comment *a* 500
§205, Comment *d* 522, 529
§206 402
§206, Comment *a* 402

§208 639, 647, 649, 738
§208, Comment *c* 647
§§209-218 428
§210 432, 434
§210, Comment *b* 433
§211 426
§211, Comment *f* 425
§211(3) 426
§212 451
§212, Comment *b* 440, 441
§212, Comment *d* 757
§212, Illus. 3 441
§212, Illus. 4 441
§213 434
§214 451
§214, Comment *b* 434, 439, 449
§214, Comment *c* 435
§214(c) 434, 439, 449
§214(d) 435, 457
§214(e) 436
§215, Comment *b* 442
§216, Comment *e* 433
§216(2) 437
§217 435
§220, Comment *d* 415
§222 471
§223 471
§224 813, 816
§224, Comment *e* 816
§225 814
§226, Comment *a* 840
§226, Comment *b* 840
§227 813
§227, Comment *b,* Illus. 3 512
§228 509, 512, 513
§228, Comment *a* 512, 517
§228, Comment *b* 512, 513, 517
§229 824, 825
§229, Comment *b* 513, 811, 824
§234 840
§234(1) 840
§234(2) 840, 841
§235(2) 803
§235(2), Comment *b* 803
§236(1) 846
§237 420-421, 425, 814, 836, 846
§237, Comment *d* 814
§237, Comment *e* 420
§237, Comment *f* 420, 421
§238 840
§240 838
§240, Comment *e* 838
§241 846, 847
§241, Comment *f* 837
§241(e) 837
§242 846, 847-848
§242, Comment *b* 847
§242, Comment *d* 848
§243(1) 846
§243(4) 846
§245 818
§250 853, 857
§250, Comment *b* 852, 856-857
§250, Comment *c* 857
§250(b) 857
§251 853, 865, 867
§251, Comment *d* 866
§252, Comment *a* 857
§253(1) 856
§256, Comment *a* 855
§256, Comment *c* 855
§256, Illus. 2 855
§256, Illus. 4 855
§256(1) 853, 857
§261 744, 752, 755, 809
§261, Comment *b* 748
§261, Comment *c* 755
§261, Comment *d* 748, 754, 894
§262 743, 744, 755, 894
§263 743, 744, 755
§264 743, 744, 766
§265 744, 761, 752
§265, Comment *a* 750, 752, 761, 762
§265, Comment *a,* Illus. 6 762
§266 744
§269 754, 810
§271 810
§272 1043
§280 1134
§281 799
§302 1095, 1096, 1099, 1101-1102, 1104-1106, 1108, 1111, 1112, 1113
§302, Comment *b* 1095
§302, Comment *c* 1095
§302, Comment *d* 1102
§302, Illus. 16 1103
§302, Reporter's Note 1095
§302(1)(a) 1095, 1109
§302(1)(b) 1095, 1106, 1109, 1111
§302(2) 1103
§304 1095
§309(1) 1103
§309(2) 1104
§311 1113
§313 1113
§313, Comment *a* 1113
§313, Illus. 2 1113
§315 1103
§317, Comment *a* 1117
§317(1) 1116
§317(2) 1116, 1120, 1122
§317(2)(a) 1119, 1121
§318, Comment *d* 1134
§318, Comment *e* 595
§318, Illus. 3 1132
§318, Illus. 5 1132
§318, Illus. 6 1132
§318, Illus. 7 1132

§318(1) 1116
§318(2) 1116, 1133
§318(3) 1116
§322 1122
§322(1) 1133
§328 1132
§336(1) 1134
§336(2) 1134
§336(4) 1123
§344 875
§346(2) 873
§347 189, 875, 876, 878, 879, 901, 920-921
§347, Comment *a* 189
§347, Comment *c* 948
§347, Comment *e* 946
§347, Comment *f* 942
§347, Illus. 13 946
§347, Illus. 16 943
§348(2) 901
§349 1005, 1009, 1010, 1011, 1020
§350, Comment *a* 1080
§350, Comment *b* 925
§350, Comment *d* 942
§350, Illus. 10 946
§350(1) 937
§351 906, 1006
§351, Comment *a* 907
§351, Comment *e* 920
§351, Comment *f* 918
§351(3) 918, 919
§352 917
§352, Comment *a* 1010
§353 963, 966, 967
§353, Comment 967
§353, Comment *a* 966
§353, Illus. 1 967
§355 968
§356 1080, 1081
§356, Comment *a* 1078, 1085
§356, Comment *b* 1079, 1080
§356(1) 1079
§360 1056
§360, Comment *e* 1056
§362 1056
§362, Comment *b* 1056
§364 1057
§364(1)(b) 1058
§366 1057
§367 1065
§367, Comment *a* 1065
§367(1) 1065
§367(2) 1067
§371 1042, 1043
§371, Comment *b* 1043
§373 1020
§373, Comment *b* 1024
§373, Comment *d* 1023
§373(2) 1024
§374 1020, 1024, 1027-1032
§374, Comment *b* 1031
§374, Comment *c* 1029
§374, Illus. 3 1031
§374(1) 1028, 1031
§374(2) 1029
§375 376, 1020
§376 1020
§377 1020

TABLE OF PROVISIONS FROM RESTATEMENT (FIRST) OF CONTRACTS

§20 43
§25 48
§35 275
§45 64, 65, 279, 282
§45, Comment *b* 63, 279
§60 172
§70 42, 642
§75 118, 142
§75, Illus. 2 124
§90 226, 228, 231, 248, 250, 251, 276, 279-282, 792
§133(1)(a) 1095
§133(1)(b) 1094, 1095
§142 1112
§143 1113
§178, Comment *f* 374, 375, 792
§208(a) 350
§208(b)(iii) 350
§209 349
§210 349
§214 349
§228 432
§230 43, 397
§230, Comment *b* 397
§230, Illus. 1 397
§233 397
§261 744
§262 744
§263 744
§264 744
§265 744
§266 744
§275 844, 846
§288 743
§312 844
§313 844
§314 844
§317 844
§319 845
§333 1005
§333(a) 1009
§346 896
§346, Illus. 2 897, 898
§346(1)(a)(i) 43
§346(1)(a)(ii) 897
§347 1022
§357 1026-1027, 1028, 1030
§455 743
§471 603
§492 602
§492, Comment *g* 595
§492(b) 594
§493 602
§497, Comment *c* 607
§502, Comment *e* 603-604
§589 321

TABLE OF PROVISIONS FROM OTHER RESTATEMENTS

Restatement (Third) of Agency
§1.01 127
§2.01, Comment *b* 128
§2.02, Comment *b* 128
§2.02(1) 128
§2.03 129
§2.05 129
§2.05, Comment *d* 129
§3.03, Comment *e* 129
§4.01 129
§4.06 129
§6.01 128
§8.01 127

Restatement of Employment Law
§2.01, Comment *b* 534
§2.02(b) 537

Restatement (Second) of Property
§12.1(3) 939

Restatement (First) of Restitution
§1 300
§1, Comment *e* 1042
§2 300
§2, Comment *a* 300
§116 300-301, 304, 305, 339
§116, Comment *b* 301, 303
§116, Comment *b*, Illus. 4 301

Restatement (Third) of Restitution and Unjust Enrichment
§1 297
§20 304-305, 339
§20, Comment *b* 339
§21 306
§21, Illus. 1 306
§28 326
§28, Comment *e* 326
§39 993-994
§39, Illus. 5 901
§51(5) 994
§66 611
§107 305
§107, Comment *b* 305
§107(2) 305

Restatement (Second) of Torts
§530 262
§549 611
§551 625, 630
§552 611
§552(1) 373
§552B 611
§552C 611
§905 961
§908(2) 968

Restatement (Third) of Torts
§46 965
§47 965

TABLE OF OTHER ACTS, CODES, AND RULES

Americans with Disabilities Act, 523

Bankruptcy Code, 256, 264, 332

Civil Rights Act of 1964, Title VII, 1069
Consumer Credit Protection Act, 677-678
Copyright Code, 1035
Credit Practices Rule, 679

Dodd-Frank Wall Street Reform and Consumer Protection Act, 679

Electronic Signatures in Global and National Commerce Act (E-Sign Act), 356

Federal Arbitration Act (FAA), 24, 199, 210, 653-655, 662-663
Federal Trade Commission (FTC) Act, 679
Federal Trade Commission Improvement Act, 678
Foreign Corrupt Practices Act, 535

Magnuson-Moss Warranty Act, 555, 678
Married Women's Property Acts, 590
Miller Act, 1021, 1023
Model Act Governing Assisted Reproductive Technology, 701, 708
Model Penal Code, 588
Model Rules of Professional Conduct, 600, 621, 622, 632-634, 693, 955, 1119

Sherman Act, 1131

Truth-in-Lending Act, 677, 678

Uniform Computer Information Transactions Act, 203
Uniform Consumer Credit Code (UCCC), 644-645, 647, 672, 678
Uniform Electronic Transactions Act (UETA), 356
Uniform Parentage Act, 701
Uniform Premarital and Marital Agreements Act, 609-610
Uniform Probate Code, 587
Uniform Residential Landlord Tenant Act, 547
Uniform Sales Act, 553, 557
United Nations Convention on Contracts for the International Sale of Goods (CISG), 12, 50-51, 160-161, 192, 263-264, 266, 295, 381, 389-390, 450-451, 599, 756, 877, 907, 947-949, 952-954

TABLE OF SECONDARY AUTHORITIES

Acret, James, *Construction Law Digests,* 560, 561
Administrative Law—Agency Design—Dodd-Frank Act Creates the Consumer Financial Protection Bureau, 680
Alderman, Richard M., Pre-Dispute Mandatory Arbitration in Consumer Contracts: A Call for Reform, 661-662
ALI, Principles of the Law of Nonprofit Organizations, Donor's Failure To Perform A Pledge, 246
Alsbrook, Margie, Contracting Away an Honest Day's Pay: An Examination of Conditional Payment Clauses in Construction Contracts, 815
American & English Encyclopedia of Law, 123
Ames, James B., The History of Assumpsit (Pt. II), 308
Ancheta, Angelo N., *Race, Rights and the Asian American Experience,* 590
Anderson, Eugene R., & Fournier, James J., Why Courts Enforce Insurance Policyholder's Objectively Reasonable Expectations of Insurance Coverage, 424-425
Anderson, Roy R., The Cover Remedy, 972
Anderson, *UCC,* 487, 488-489
Annot., Effect of Lessee's Failure or Delay in Giving Notice Within Specified Time, of Intention to Renew Lease, 823
Annot., Lack of Consideration as Barring Enforcement of Promise to Make Charitable Contribution or Subscription—Modern Cases, 239
Annot., What Constitutes Acceptance "Expressly Made Conditional" Converting it to Rejection and Counteroffer under UCC §2-207(1), 178
Anson, *Contracts* (Corbin's ed.), 830
Anson, *Principles of Contract,* 104
Aoki, Keith, Direct Democracy, Racial Group Agency, Local Government Law and Residential Racial Segregation: Some Reflections on Radical and Plural Democracy, 590
Appleman, *Insurance Law and Practice,* 423
Atiyah, P.S., Contracts, Promises and the Law of Obligations, 981, 982
Atiyah, P.S., & Summers, Robert S., *Form and Substance in Anglo-American Law,* 395
Atwood, Barbara A., & Bix, Brian H., A New Uniform Law for Premarital and Marital Agreements, 610
Axelrod, Elliot, The Requirements Contract—What Is Required?, 507
Ayres, Ian, & Gertner, Robert, Filling Gaps in Incomplete Contracts: An Economic Theory of Default Rules, 490
Baird, Douglas G., *Reconstructing Contracts,* 988
Barnett, Randy E., Consenting to Form Contracts, 206
Baron, Jane B., Gifts, Bargains, and Form, 118
Baron, Noah, & Bazzell, Jennifer, eds., Fifteenth Annual Gender and Sexuality Law: Annual Review Article: Assisted Reproductive Technologies, 709-710
Becker, Mary E., Promissory Estoppel Damages, 1018-1019
Beh, Hazel G., Curing the Infirmities of the Unconscionability Doctrine, 648
Ben-Shahar, Regulation Through Boilerplate: An Apologia, 16
Berg, Paula, Judicial Enforcement of Covenants not to Compete Between Physicians: Protecting Doctors' Interests at Patients' Expense, 684, 685, 687, 689
Bernstein, Lisa, Merchant Law in a Merchant Court: Rethinking the Code's Search for Immanent Business Norms, 415-416
Bernstein, Lisa, Social Norms and Default Rules Analysis, 490
Birmingham, Robert L., Breach of Contract, Damage Measures, and Economic Efficiency, 985
Birmingham, Robert L., The Duty to Disclose and the Prisoner's Dilemma: *Laidlaw v. Organ,* 632
Bix, Brian H., *Contract Law: Rules, Theory, and Context,* 988
Blake, Harlan M., Employee Agreements not to Compete, 683, 684, 685, 686, 687, 688, 690
Bodie, Matthew T., The Best Way Out Is Always Through: Changing the Employment-At-Will Default Rule to Protect Personal Autonomy, 537-538
Borden, Michael J., The Promissory Character of Adequate Assurances of Performance, 865
Bowers, James W., Murphy's Law and the Elementary Theory of Contract Interpretation: A Response to Schwartz and Scott, 416
Boyer, Benjamin F., Promissory Estoppel: Principle from Precedents (Pt. 1), 236-237, 248
Boyer, Benjamin F., Promissory Estoppel: Requirements and Limitations of the Doctrine, 1017
Braucher, Robert, Freedom of Contract and the Second Restatement, 338
Brennan, James T., Injunction Against Professional Athletes' Breaching Their Contracts, 1068
Brody, Evelyn, The Charity in Bankruptcy and Ghosts of Donors Past, Present, and Future, 244

Brook, James, Conditions of Personal Satisfaction in the Law of Contract, 512
Brown, Ray A., *The Law of Personal Property,* 119, 239
Bruch, Property Rights of De Facto Spouses Including Thoughts on the Value of Homemakers' Services, 322
Burton, Steven J., Breach of Contract and the Common Law Duty to Perform in Good Faith, 493
Burton, Steven J., A Lesson on Some Limits of Economic Analysis: Schwartz and Scott on Contract Interpretation, 416
Burton, Steven J., Racial Discrimination in Contract Performance: *Patterson* and a State Law Alternative, 523
Burton, Steven J., & Andersen, Eric G., *Contractual Good Faith,* 493

Calamari, John D., & Perillo, Joseph M., The Law of Contracts, 440, 852, 853, 854, 933, 1026
Caplan, Gerald, Legal Autopsies: Assessing the Performance of Judges and Lawyers Through the Window of Leading Contract Cases, 228
Carton, Sharon F., Damning with Fulsome Praise: Assessing the Uniqueness of an Artist or Performer as a Condition to Enjoin Performance of Personal Service Contracts in Entertainment Law, 1068
Casto, William R., & Ricks, Val D., "Dear Sister Antillico . . .": The Story of *Kirksey v. Kirksey,* 228
Caswell, Richard, Contract Remedies, Renegotiation, and the Theory of Efficient Breach, 985
Cender, Joshua, Knocking Opportunism: A Reexamination of Efficient Breach of Contract, 986
Charny, David, Hypothetical Bargains: The Normative Structure of Contract Interpretation, 490
Chase, Anthony R., Race, Culture, and Contract Law: From the Cottonfield to the Courtroom, 590
Childres, Robert, Conditions in the Law of Contracts, 817
Childress, Steven A., & Davis, Martha S., *Federal Standards of Review,* 1036
Chomsky, Carol L., Casebooks and the Future of Contracts Pedagogy, 338-339
Chomsky, Carol L., Of Soil Pits and Swimming Pools: Reconsidering the Measure of Damages for Construction Contracts, 901
Chused, Richard H., Married Women's Property Law: 1800-1850, 590
Circo, Carl J., The Evolving Role of Relational Contract in Construction Law, 284
Clarkson, Kenneth W., Miller, Roger LeRoy, & Muris, Timothy J., Liquidated Damages v. Penalties: Sense or Nonsense?, 1085
Cohen, Amy B., Reviving *Jacob and Youngs, Inc. v. Kent:* Material Breach Doctrine Reconsidered, 848
Cohen, George M., The Fault Lines in Contract Damages, 987-988
Cohen, Ronnie, & O'Byrne, Shannon, Cry Me a River: Recovery of Mental Distress Damages in a Breach of Contract Action—A North American Perspective, 967
Colby, Eben, What Did the Doctrine of Unconscionability Do to the Walker-Thomas Furniture Company?, 646
Collier on Bankruptcy, 261
Comment, *Marvin v. Marvin:* Five Years Later, 322
Comment, Once More into the Breach: Promissory Estoppel and Traditional Damages Doctrine, 1018
Construction and Design Law, 312
Contract Law Present and Future: A Symposium to Honor Professor Charles L. Knapp on Fifty Years of Teaching Contract Law, 648
Corbin, Arthur L., Assignment of Contract Rights, 1116
Corbin, Arthur L., *A Comprehensive Treatise on the Working Rules of Contract Law,* 1099
Corbin, Arthur L., Offer and Acceptance, and Some of the Resulting Legal Relations, 53
Corbin, Arthur L., Quasi Contractual Obligations, 1042
Corbin, Arthur L., The Right of a Defaulting Vendee to the Restitution of Installments Paid, 1026, 995, 1030
Corbin on Contracts, 63, 69, 70, 72, 73, 74, 78, 143, 269, 280, 300, 310, 311, 349, 350, 351, 352, 370, 385, 397-398, 401, 402, 413, 414, 418, 419, 420, 433, 437, 439, 440-442, 464, 506, 519, 641, 642, 655, 693, 725, 726, 810, 820, 821, 837, 844, 853, 925, 1005, 1026-1027, 1028, 1031, 1076
Couch, *Cyclopedia of Insurance Law,* 423
Coyle, John F., The Role of the CISG in U.S. Contract Practice: An Empirical Study, 161
Craswell, Richard, Against Fuller and Perdue, 875
Craswell, Richard, Contract Remedies, Renegotiation, and the Theory of Efficient Breach, 985
Craswell, Richard, Offer, Acceptance, and Efficient Reliance, 284
Crespi, Gregory S., Recovering Pre-Contractual Expenditures as an Element of Reliance Damages, 1012
Crystal, Nathan M., Limitations on Zealous Representation in an Adversarial System, 956
Crystal, Nathan M., *Professional Responsibility: Problems of Practice and the Profession,* 449
Crystal, Nathan M., & Giannoni-Crystal, Francesca, Contract Enforceability During Economic Crisis: Legal Principles and Drafting Solutions, 262, 599
Dalzell, John, Duress By Economic Pressure I, 595
Dalzell, John, Duress By Economic Pressure II, 596
Dalzell, Julia, The Enforcement of Selective Reduction Clauses in Surrogacy Contracts, 708
Danzig, Richard, *Hadley v. Baxendale,* A Study in the Industrialization of the Law, 905
Danzig, Richard, & Watson, Geoffrey R., *The Capability Problem in Contract Law: Further Readings on Well-Known Cases,* 336, 337, 586, 835
Davis, Adrienne D., The Private Law of Race and Sex: An Antebellum Perspective, 590

Davis, Wendy B., Corrosion by Codification: The Deficiencies in the Statutory Versions of the Implied Warranty of Workmanlike Construction, 566
Davis, W. Kent, The International View of Attorney Fees in Civil Suits: Why Is the United States the "Odd Man Out" in How It Pays Its Lawyers?, 955
Dawson, John P., Duress and the Fair Exchange in French and German Law, 649
Dawson, John P., Economic Duress—An Essay in Perspective, 591, 594, 597
Dawson, John P., Restitution Without Enrichment, 1043
Dawson, John P., Unconscionable Coercion: The German Version, 649
De Funiak, *Modern Equity,* 820
DeJarnatt, Once Is Not Enough: Preserving Consumers' Rights to Bankruptcy Protection, 260
Difonzo, J. Herbie, & Stern, Ruth C., The Children of Baby M., 709
DiMatteo, Larry A., Contractual Excuse Under the CISG: Impediment, Hardship, and the Excuse Doctrines, 756
DiMatteo, Larry A., Reason and Context: A Dual Track Theory of Interpretation, 473
DiMatteo, Larry A., A Theory of Efficient Penalty: Eliminating the Law of Liquidated Damages, 1086
DiMatteo, Larry A., et al., *Contract Law: Transatlantic Perspectives,* 664
DiMatteo, Larry A., et al., Justice, Employment, and the Psychological Contract, 538
DiSabatino, Michael A., Annot., Liability of Builder of Residence for Latent Defects Therein as Running to Subsequent Purchasers from Original Vendee, 560
Dobbs, Dan B., *Dobbs' Law of Remedies,* 364, 1008
Dodge, William S., The Case for Punitive Damages in Contracts, 969
Dodge, William S., Teaching the CISG in Contracts, 51, 192, 390, 451
Dunn, Terrence M., The Franchisor's Control over the Transfer of a Franchise, 1133

Eisenberg, Melvin A., The Bargain Principle and Its Limits, 981, 982
Eisenberg, Melvin A., Donative Promises, 117-118
Eisenberg, Melvin A., Expression Rules in Contract Law and Problems of Offer and Acceptance, 58, 70
Eisenberg, Melvin A., *Foundational Principles of Contract Law,* 988
Eisenberg, Melvin A., Impossibility, Impracticability, and Frustration, 744
Eisenberg, Melvin A., The Principle of *Hadley v. Baxendale,* 908
Eisenberg, Melvin A., The Principles of Consideration, 484
Eisenberg, Melvin A., Third-Party Beneficiaries, 1096
Epstein, David G., Arbuckle, Melinda, & Flanagan, Kelly, Contract Law's Two "P.E.'s": Promissory Estoppel and the Parol Evidence Rule, 459
Epstein, Richard A., Beyond Foreseeability: Consequential Damages in the Law of Contract, 907-908
Epstein, Richard A., In Defense of the Contract At Will, 538
Epstein, Richard A., Unconscionability: A Critical Reappraisal, 648
Epstein, Wendy Netter, Contract Theory and the Failures of Public-Private Contracting, 1114
Estlund, Cynthia L., Wrongful Discharge Protections in an At-Will World, 537

Farber, Daniel A., Reassessing the Economic Efficiency of Compensatory Damages for Breach of Contract, 985, 986
Farber, Daniel A., & Matheson, John H., Beyond Promissory Estoppel: Contract Law and the "Invisible Handshake," 265
Farnsworth, E. Allan, *Contracts,* 56, 71, 74, 75, 111, 113, 300, 365, 396, 402, 428, 432, 433, 440, 509, 576, 630, 649, 680, 739, 742, 752, 778, 799, 853, 876-878, 907, 918-919, 950, 968, 1012, 1057, 1102, 1121, 1122, 1132
Farnsworth, E. Allan, Developments in Contract Law During the 1980s: The Top Ten, 264-265, 650
Farnsworth, E. Allan, Legal Remedies for Breach of Contract, 901, 1045-1047, 1056
Farnsworth, E. Allan, On Trying to Keep One's Promises: The Duty of Best Efforts in Contract Law, 486
Farnsworth, E. Allan, Precontractual Liability and Preliminary Agreements: Fair Dealing and Failed Negotiations, 91, 92, 97
Farnsworth, E. Allan, Promises and Paternalism, 244
Farnsworth, E. Allan, Your Loss or My Gain? The Dilemma of the Disgorgement Principle in Breach of Contract, 992-993
Farnsworth, Young, & Jones, *Cases and Materials on Contracts,* 944
Feinman, Jay M., The Last Promissory Estoppel Article, 265
Feinman, Jay M., Relational Contract and Default Rules, 490
Feinman, Jay M., Un-Making Law: The Classical Revival in the Common Law, 459
Feldman, Steven W., *Tenn. Prac. Contract Law And Practice,* 933
Fisch, E.L., Freed, D.J., & Schacter, E.R., *Charities and Charitable Foundations,* 239
Fischbach, Jonathan, & Fischbach, Michael, Rethinking Optimality in Tort Litigation: The Promise of Reverse Cost-Shifting, 955
Fleming, Anne, The Rise and Fall of Unconscionability as the "Law of the Poor," 650
Floresta1, Marjorie, Is a Burrito a Sandwich? Exploring Race, Class and Culture in Contracts, 415
Fortin, Lisa A., Why There Should Be a Duty to Mitigate Liquidated Damages Clauses, 1083
Franklin, John Hope, & Moss, Alfred A., Jr., *From Slavery to Freedom,* 590

Frantz, John P., Market Ordering Versus Statutory Control of Termination Decisions: A Case for the Inefficiency of Just Cause Dismissal Requirements, 538
Freeman, John P., & Crystal, Nathan M., Scienter in Professional Liability Cases, 1103
Fried, Charles, *Contract as Promise,* 126-127
Friedman, Lawrence M., *A History of American Law,* 590
Friedmann, Daniel, The Efficient Breach Fallacy, 987
Friedmann, Daniel, Restitution of Benefits Obtained Through the Appropriation of Property or the Commission of a Wrong, 991-992
Frug, Mary Joe, Re-Reading Contracts: A Feminist Analysis of a Contracts Casebook, 938
Fuller, Lon L., Consideration and Form, 115, 395, 571
Fuller, Lon L., & Perdue, William R., Jr., The Reliance Interest in Contract Damages, 874-875, 980-981, 1001, 1009, 1022

Gan, Orit, Contractual Duress and Relations of Power, 600-601
Gan, Orit, The Justice Element of Promissory Estoppel, 255, 265
Gan, Orit, Promissory Estoppel: A Call for a More Inclusive Contract Law, 265
Garrison, Michael J., & Wendt, John T., The Evolving Law of Employee Noncompete Agreements: Recent Trends and an Alternative Policy Approach, 694
Geis, George S., Broadcast Contracting, 1096, 1102
Geis, George S., Empirically Assessing *Hadley v. Baxendale,* 908
Giesel, Grace McLane, *Corbin on Contracts,* 693
Goetz, Charles J., & Scott, Robert E., Liquidated Damages, Penalties and the Just Compensation Principle: Some Notes on an Enforcement Model and a Theory of Efficient Breach, 984-985, 1085
Goldberg, Victor P., Bloomer Girl Revisited or How to Frame an Unmade Picture, 938
Goldberg, Victor P., Rethinking Jacob & Youngs v. Kent, 835
Goldberg, Victor P., Traynor (*Drennan*) versus Hand (*Baird*): Much Ado About (Almost) Nothing, 284
Green, Milton D., Proof of Mental Incompetency and the Unexpressed Major Premise, 583
Green, Shelby D., Re-appraising the Appraisers: Expanding Liability to Buyers and Borrowers in the Story of the 2008 Financing Industry Crisis, 1103
Gregory, Donald W., & Travers, Eric B., Ethical Challenges of Bid Shopping, 284

Hamilton, Walton H., The Ancient Maxim Caveat Emptor, 556
Harris, Robert J., A Radical Restatement of the Law of Seller's Damages: Sales Act and Commercial Code Results Compared, 941
Harrison, Jeffrey L., A Case for Loss Sharing, 1043
Harrison, Jeffrey L., Economic Analysis, 826
Helveston, Max N., Judicial Deregulation of Consumer Markets, 493
Henderson, Roger C., The Doctrine of Reasonable Expectations in Insurance Law After Two Decades, 426
Henderson, Stanley D., Promises Grounded in the Past: The Idea of Unjust Enrichment and the Law of Contracts, 336
Henderson, Stanley D., Promissory Estoppel and Traditional Contract Doctrine, 248
Hillman, Robert A., Debunking Some Myths about Unconscionability: A New Framework for U.C.C. Section 2-302, 647-648, 677
Hillman, Robert A., Keeping the Deal Together After Material Breach—Common Law Mitigation Rules, the UCC, and the Restatement (Second) of Contracts, 866-867
Hillman, Robert A., Online Boilerplate: Would Mandatory Website Disclosure of E-standard Terms Backfire?, 219
Hillman, Robert A., Policing Contract Modifications under the UCC: Good Faith and the Doctrine of Economic Duress, 787
Hillman, Robert A., Questioning the "New Consensus" on Promissory Estoppel: An Empirical and Theoretical Study, 265, 1019
Hillman, Robert A., A Study of Uniform Commercial Code Methodology: Contract Modification under Article Two, 787
Hillman, Robert A., & Rachlinski, Jeffrey J., Standard-Form Contracting in the Electronic Age, 209
Hillman, Robert W., *Law Firm Breakups,* 694
Holdsworth, William S., *A History of English Law,* 366-367
Holmes, Eric Mills, Restatement of Promissory Estoppel, 265, 1019
Holmes, Eric Mills, Stature and Status of a Promise under Seal as a Legal Formality, 114, 119
Holmes, Oliver Wendell, The Common Law, 44, 111, 949-950, 958, 982-983
Holmes, Oliver Wendell, The Path of the Law, 368, 408, 950, 982
Holmes, Oliver Wendell, The Theory of Legal Interpretation, 44, 397, 413
Horwitz, Morton J., The Transformation of American Law, 1780-1860, 138
Houh, Emily M.S., Critical Race Realism: Re-Claiming the Antidiscrimination Principle Through the Doctrine of Good Faith in Contract Law, 523
Houh, Emily M.S., The Doctrine of Good Faith in Contract Law: A (Nearly) Empty Vessel?, 493
Hunter, H., *Modern Law of Contracts, Breach & Remedies,* 911, 913
Hurst, Freedom of Contract in an Unstable Economy: Judicial Reallocation of Contractual Risks Under UCC Section 2-615, 730
Huxley, Aldous, *Brave New World,* 699

Jaeger, W., *Williston on Contracts,* 594, 785, 854
Jimenez, Marco J., The Many Faces of Promissory Estoppel: An Empirical Analysis Under the Restatement (Second) of Contracts, 265
Joo, Thomas W., New "Conspiracy Theory" of the Fourteenth Amendment: Nineteenth Century Chinese Civil Rights Cases and the Development of Substantive Due Process Jurisprudence, 590

Kafker, Serena L., Golden Handcuffs: Enforceability of Noncompetition Clauses in Professional Partnership Agreements of Accountants, Physicians, and Attorneys, 683, 685, 689
Katz, Avery W., When Should an Offer Stick? The Economics of Promissory Estoppel in Preliminary Negotiations, 284
Kaye, Joshua, Disclosure, Information, the Law of Contracts, and the Mistaken Use of *Laidlaw v. Organ,* 629
Keener, William A., *A Treatise on The Law of Quasi-Contracts,* 1042
Keeton, R., Insurance Law Rights At Variance With Policy Provisions, 418, 419
Keeton, Robert E., Insurance Law Rights at Variance with Policy Provisions, 425
Keeton, W. Page, Fraud—Concealment and Non-disclosure, 629, 630
Keeton, W. Page, et al., *Prosser and Keeton on the Law of Torts,* 629
Keren, Hila, Textual Harassment: A New Historicist Reappraisal of the Parol Evidence Rule with Gender in Mind, 428
Kessler, F., Contracts of Adhesion—Some Thoughts About Freedom of Contract, 418, 426
Kim, Nancy S., *Wrap Contracts: Foundations and Ramifications,* 16, 209
Kindregan, Charles P., Jr. & Snyder, Steven H., Clarifying the Law of ART: The New American Bar Association Model Act Governing Assisted Reproductive Technology, 708
Kirst, Roger W., Usage of Trade and Course of Dealing: Subversion of the UCC Theory, 468, 469-470, 472
Knapp, Charles L., Blowing the Whistle on Mandatory Arbitration: Unconscionability as a Signaling Device, 648, 650, 663
Knapp, Charles L., Cases and Controversies: Some Things to Do with Contracts Cases, 339, 621
Knapp, Charles L., Contract Law Walks the Plank: *Carnival Cruise Lines, Inc. v. Shute,* 577
Knapp, Charles L., Enforcing the Contract to Bargain, 91, 94, 96-97, 293
Knapp, Charles L., Is There a "Duty to Read?", 45
Knapp, Charles L., Judgment Call: Theoretical Approaches to Contract Decision-Making, 826, 827
Knapp, Charles L., An Offer You Can't Revoke, 473
Knapp, Charles L., Opting Out or Copping Out?, 648
Knapp, Charles L., Reliance in the Revised *Restatement:* The Proliferation of Promissory Estoppel, 263, 264, 781, 1018, 1020
Knapp, Charles L., Rescuing Reliance: The Perils of Promissory Estoppel, 236, 254, 264, 458-459, 798
Knapp, Charles L., Taking Contracts Private: The Quiet Revolution in Contract Law, 661
Knapp, Charles L., Unconscionability in American Contract Law: A Twenty-first Century Survey, 663-664
Kniffin, Margaret N., Conflating and Confusing Contract Interpretation and the Parol Evidence Rule: Is the Emperor Wearing Someone Else's Clothes?, 448
Kniffin, Margaret N., *Corbin on Contracts,* 398, 413, 414
Konefsky, Alfred S., Freedom and Interdependence in Twentieth-Century Contract Law: Traynor and Hand and Promissory Estoppel, 284
Korobkin, Russell, Bounded Rationality, Standard Form Contracts, and Unconscionability, 648
Kostritsky, Juliet P., Bargaining with Uncertainty, Moral Hazard, and Sunk Costs: A Default Rule for Precontractual Negotiations, 293
Kostritsky, Juliet P., Plain Meaning v. Broad Interpretation: How the Risk of Opportunism Defeats a Unitary Default Rule for Interpretation, 416
Kostritsky, Juliet P., The Rise and Fall of Promissory Estoppel or Is Promissory Estoppel Really as Unsuccessful as Scholars Say It Is: A New Look at the Data, 265
Kovacic, Candace S., A Proposal to Simplify Quantum Meruit Litigation, 305
Kronman, Anthony T., Mistake, Disclosure, Information and the Law of Contracts, 631-632
Kronman, Anthony T., Specific Performance, 1058
Kull, Andrew, Rationalizing Restitution, 308
Kull, Andrew, Reconsidering Gratuitous Promises, 115, 118
Kull, Andrew, Restitution as a Remedy for Breach of Contract, 1023
Kunz, Christina L., et al., Browse-wrap Agreements: Validity of Implied Assent in Electronic Form Agreements, 219

Lawrence, William H., Rolling Contracts Rolling over Contract Law, 206
Laycock, Douglas, The Death of the Irreparable Injury Rule, 1047
Leff, Arthur Allen, Unconscionability and the Code—The Emperor's New Clause, 643, 644, 650
Leff, Arthur Allen, Unconscionability and the Crowd—Consumers and the Common Law Tradition, 677
Levie, J. H., Trade Usage and Custom Under the Common Law and the Uniform Commercial Code, 468, 470
Levin, Alisa M., Condo Developers and Fiduciary Duties: An Unlikely Pairing?, 564
Levit, Nancy, Familial and Matrimonial Agreements: An Annotated Bibliography, 710

Lewis, Michael, *The Big Short: Inside the Doomsday Machine*, 675
Linzer, Peter, *Corbin on Contracts,* 433, 437
Linzer, Peter, The Decline of Assent: At-Will Employment as a Case Study of the Breakdown of Private Law Theory, 538
Linzer, Peter, On the Amorality of Contract Remedies—Efficiency, Equity, and the Second *Restatement,* 901, 987, 1058
Linzer, Peter, Relational Theory, 826
Linzer, Peter, Uncontracts: Context, Contorts and the Relational Approach, 473
Llewellyn, Karl N., Book Review, 650
Llewellyn, Karl N., *The Common Law Tradition,* 420, 642
Llewellyn, Karl N., On Our Case-Law of Contract: Offer and Acceptance (Pts. 1 & 2), 65-66
Llewellyn, Karl N., On Warranty of Quality, and Society (Pts. I & II), 557
Llewellyn, Karl N., What Price Contract?—An Essay in Perspective, 381, 419
Lord, Richard A., *Williston on Contracts,* 559, 582, 1076

Macaulay, Stewart, Bambi Meets Godzilla: Reflections on Contracts Scholarship and Teaching vs. State Unfair and Deceptive Trade Practices and Consumer Protection Statutes, 679
Macneil, Ian R., Economic Analysis of Contractual Relations: Its Shortfalls and the Need for a "Rich Classificatory Apparatus," 987
Macneil, Ian R., Efficient Breach of Contract: Circles in the Sky, 986, 987
Malloy, S. Elizabeth Wilborn, Physician Restrictive Covenants: The Neglect of Incumbent Patient Interests, 692-693
Marks, Colin P., Not What, but When Is an Offer: Rehabilitating the Rolling Contract, 206
Marschall, Patricia H., Willfulness: A Crucial Factor in Choosing Remedies for Breach of Contract, 987
Maute, Judith L., *Peevyhouse v. Garland Coal & Mining Co.* Revisited: The Ballad of Willie and Lucille, 900-901
Maute, Judith L., Race Politics, O'Hare Airport Expansion, and Promissory Estoppel: The More Things Change, the More They Stay the Same, 95
Mazower, Mark, *Inside Hitler's Greece,* 137
McAdam, *Landlord and Tenant,* 823
McClintock, Henry L., *Principles of Equity,* 363
McCormick, Charles T., The Contemplation Rule as a Limitation upon Damages for Breach of Contract, 905
McCormick, Marcia L., The Truth Is Out There: Revamping Federal Antidiscrimination Enforcement for the Twenty-First Century, 936
McDaniel, Amy L., Note, The New York Housing Merchant Warranty Statute: Analysis and Proposals, 566
McDonald, Michelle Z., The Complicated World of Lender Liability, 505
McGovern, William H., Jr., Dependent Promises in the History of Leases and Other Contracts, 839
McLaughlin, Katie, Another Argument "Pops Up" Against Reliance in Express Warranty Law, 553
Meyer, Contracts of Adhesion and the Doctrine of Fundamental Breach, 419
Miller, Meredith R., Contract Law, Party Autonomy and the New Formalism, 404
Miller, Meredith R., Contract Law, Party Sophistication and the New Formalism, 293
Miller, Meredith R., Revisiting *Austin v. Loral:* A Study in Economic Duress, Contract Modification and Framing, 788
Miller, Zachary, Comment, Best Efforts?: Differing Judicial Interpretations of a Familiar Term, 485
Mnookin, Robert H., & Wilson, Robert B., Rational Bargaining and Market Efficiency: Understanding *Pennzoil v. Texaco,* 96
Mooney, Ralph James, The New Conceptualism in Contract Law, 459
Morey, Alexander C., & Grossman, Dixie, Property Rights of Unmarried Cohabitants—Nothing New under the Sun, 325
Moringiello, Juliet M., Signals, Assent and Internet Contracting, 26
Morriss, Andrew P., Bad Data, Bad Economics, and Bad Policy: Time to Fire the Wrongful Discharge Law, 538
Muris, Timothy J., Cost of Completion or Diminution in Market Value: The Relevance of Subjective Value, 899
Murray, John E., Jr., Contract Theories and the Rise of Neoformalism, 15
Murray, John E., Jr., The Dubious Status of the Rolling Contract Formation Theory, 206
Murray, John E., Jr., ed., *Grismore on Contracts,* 418, 419
Murray, John E., Jr., *Murray on Contracts,* 109-110, 147, 172-173, 191, 354, 388, 435, 691, 751-752, 1085, 1095

NeJaime, Douglas, The Nature of Parenthood, 700
New York, State of, Law Revision Commission, Report and Record of Hearings on the Uniform Commercial Code, 641
Nimmer, Melville B., & Nimmer, David, *Nimmer on Copyright,* 1041
Nordstrom, Robert J., & Woodland, Irwin F., Recovery by Building Contractor in Default, 1031
Note, The $10.53 Billion Question—When Are the Parties Bound?: Pennzoil and the Use of Agreements in Principle in Mergers and Acquisitions, 92
Note, Unconscionable Contracts: The Uniform Commercial Code, 419

Oakley, Robert L., Fairness in Electronic Contracting: Minimum Standards for Non-Negotiated Contracts, 209
O'Brien, Sean M., Note, Caveat Venditor: A Case for Granting Subsequent Purchasers a Cause of Action

Against Builder-Vendors for Latent Defects in the Home, 559, 560, 561
O'Gorman, Daniel P., The Statute of Frauds and Oral Promises of Job Security: The Tenuous Distinction Between Performance and Excusable Nonperformance, 353-354
Oldfather, C., Toward a Usable Method of Judicial Review of the Adhesion Contractor's Lawmaking, 418, 419
Oldham, Theodore H., Letters of Intent in Business Transactions, 96
Oldham & Caudill, A Reconnaissance of Public Policy Restrictions upon Enforcement of Contracts between Cohabitants, 322
O'Neill, Ann W., Locke Feels Vindicated After Lawsuit, 522

Palmer, George E., The Contract Price as a Limit on Restitution for the Defendant's Breach, 1023
Palmer, George E., *Law of Restitution,* 308, 314, 1027, 1028
Park, Arthur J., What to Reasonably Expect in the Coming Years from the Reasonable Expectations of the Insured Doctrine, 425
Parsons on Contracts, 104
Patterson, Dennis M., *Good Faith and Lender Liability,* 493
Patterson, Edwin W., The Interpretation and Construction of Contracts, 405-406
Perillo, Joseph M., *Calamari and Perillo on Contracts,* 933
Perillo, Joseph M., *Contracts,* 413, 428, 472, 649, 710, 816, 1102, 1103
Perillo, Joseph M., *Corbin on Contracts,* 925
Perillo, Joseph M., Misreading Oliver Wendell Holmes on Efficient Breach and Tortious Interference, 985
Perillo, Joseph M., Restitution in the Second Restatement of Contracts, 1026, 1027, 1028, 1043
Perillo, Joseph M., UNIDROIT Principles of International Commercial Contracts: The Black Letter Text and a Review, 649
Perillo, Joseph M., & Bender, Helen H., *Corbin on Contracts,* 75
Perkins, Rollin M., & Boyce, Ronald, *Criminal Law,* 588
Pettit, Mark, Jr., Modern Unilateral Contracts, 66
Pew Research Center, U.S. Smartphone Use in 2015, 27
Pollock, Principles of Contract, 104
Pomeroy, *Equity Jurisprudence,* 821, 822, 1052
Pomeroy, *Specific Performance,* 1052
Pomeroy, John Norton, & Mann, John C., *Specific Performance of Contracts,* 362-363
Posner, Eric A., Economic Analysis of Contract Law After Three Decades: Success or Failure?, 908, 988
Posner, Richard A., *Economic Analysis of Law,* 306-307, 899, 983-984
Posner, Richard A., The Law and Economics of Contract Interpretation, 407
Posner, Richard A., & Rosenfeld, Andrew M., Impossibility and Related Doctrines in Contract Law: An Economic Analysis, 756
Powell, Frona M., & Mallor, Jane P., The Case for an Implied Warranty of Quality in Sales of Commercial Real Estate, 567
Pratt, Walter F., Jr., American Contract Law at the Turn of the Century, 484
Preston, Cheryl B., CyberInfants, 576
Preston, Cheryl B., & Crowther, Brandon T., Infancy Doctrine Inquiries, 577, 578
Pridgen, Mary Dee, *Consumer Protection and the Law,* 560, 561
Prince, Harry G., Contract Interpretation in California: Plain Meaning, Parol Evidence and Use of the "Just Result" Principle, 407, 448
Prince, Harry G., Perfecting the Third Party Beneficiary Standing Rule under Section 302 of the Restatement (Second) of Contracts, 1095, 1103
Prince, Harry G., Public Policy Limitations in Cohabitation Agreements: Unruly Horse or Circus Pony, 320, 322
Prince, Harry G., Unconscionability in California: A Need for Restraint and Consistency, 648, 676
Prosser, W., and Keeton, W., *The Law of Torts,* 626

Radin, Margaret Jane, *Boilerplate: The Fine Print, Vanishing Rights, and the Rule of Law,* 16, 209
Rakoff, Todd D., Contracts of Adhesion: An Essay in Reconstruction, 426-427
Rawls, Amelia, Contract Formation in an Internet Age, 50
Rendleman, Doug, Quantum Meruit for the Subcontractor: Has Restitution Jumped Off Dawson's Dock?, 314
Richmond, Douglas R., An Overview of Insurance Bad Faith Law and Litigation, 448, 968
Ritter, Lowell, Payday Lending: Friend or Foe?, 675
Roberts, The Case of the Unwary Home Buyer: The Housing Merchant Did It, 559
Robertson, R. J., Jr., The Right to Demand Adequate Assurance of Due Performance: Uniform Commercial Code Section 2-609 and Restatement (Second) of Contracts Section 251, 865
Rowley, Keith A., A Brief History of Anticipatory Repudiation in American Contract Law, 856
Rowley, Keith A., You Asked for It, You Got It . . . Toy Yoda: Practical Jokes, Prizes, and Contract Law, 45
Russell, Irma S., Reinventing the Deal: A Sequential Approach to Analyzing Claims for Enforcement of Modified Sales Contracts, 787

Saito, Natsu Taylor, Alien and Non-Alien Alike: Citizenship, "Foreignness," and Racial Hierarchy in American Law, 590
Scalia, Antonin, *A Matter of Interpretation: Federal Courts and the Law,* 10

Schiro, Richard, Prospecting for Lost Profits in the Uniform Commercial Code: The Buyer's Dilemmas, 985-986
Schneid, Adam, Assignability of Covenants Not to Compete: When Can a Successor Firm Enforce a Noncompete Agreement?, 1121
Schwartz, Alan, The Case for Specific Performance, 986, 1058
Schwartz, Alan, & Scott, Robert E., Contract Theory and the Limits of Contract Law, 416
Schwartz, Alan, & Scott, Robert E., Market Damages, Efficient Contracting, and the Economic Waste Fallacy, 900
Schwartz, Alan, & Scott, Robert E., Precontractual Liability and Preliminary Agreements, 293
Schwartz, Alan, & Scott, Robert E., Third Party Beneficiaries and Contractual Networks, 1096, 1102
Schwartz, David S., Enforcing Small Print to Protect Big Business: Employee and Consumer Rights Claims in an Age of Compelled Arbitration, 663
Schwartz, Dudi, Interpretation and Disclosure in Insurance Contexts, 425
Seavey, Warren A., & Scott, Austin W., Restitution, 308
Sebert, John A., Jr., Punitive and Nonpecuniary Damages in Actions Based upon Contract: Toward Achieving the Objective of Full Compensation, 967
Sebert, John A., Jr., Remedies Under Article Two of the Uniform Commercial Code: An Agenda for Review, 973
Shannon, Victoria A., Harmonizing Third-Party Litigation Funding Regulation, 1120
Sheff, Jeremy, A Tale of Two Cities: The Residential Landlord's Duty to Mitigate in New York, 939
Shell, Substituting Ethical Standards for Common Law Rules in Commercial Cases: An Emerging Statutory Trend, 91-92
Sherwin, Emily L., Law and Equity in Contract Enforcement, 649
Siegel, Steven A., The Federal Government's Power to Enact Color-Conscious Laws: An Originalist Inquiry, 590
Simpson, Alfred W. B., *A History of the Common Law of Contract*, 107, 308, 556, 589-590, 680, 742
Simpson, Alfred W. B., The Horwitz Thesis and the History of Contracts, 138
Slawson, W. David, The Role of Reliance in Contract Damages, 1019
Slawson, W. David, Standard Form Contracts and Democratic Control of Lawmaking Power, 418, 419
Slawson, W. David, Why Expectation Damages for Breach of Contract Must Be the Norm: A Refutation of the Fuller and Perdue "Three Interests" Thesis, 875
Smith, Barbara Jo, Note: Tenants in Search of Parity with Consumers: Creating a Reasonable Expectations Warranty, 547
Solan, Lawrence M., Contract as Agreement, 398
Sorkin, Andrew Ross, *Too Big to Fail*, 675
Spann, Girardeau A., Critical Legal Studies, 826
Speidel, Richard E., Revising Article 2: A View from the Trenches, 148
Spence, Muriel Morisey, Teaching *Williams v. Walker-Thomas Furniture Co.*, 646
Stempel, Jeffrey W., Bootstrapping and Slouching Toward Gomorrah: Arbitral Infatuation and the Decline of Consent, 663
Stern, Stephanie, Temporal Dynamics of Disclosure: The Example of Residential Real Estate Conveyancing, 630
Stipanowich, Thomas J., Reconstructing Construction Law: Reality and Reform in a Transactional System, 284
Strasser, Mark, Traditional Surrogacy Contracts, Partial Enforcement, and the Challenge for Family Law, 710
Sullivan, Charles A., Mastering the Faithless Servant?: Reconciling Employment Law, Contract Law, and Fiduciary Duty, 841
Sullivan, Timothy J., Innovation in the Law of Warranty: The Burden of Reform, 557
Symposium, Contract Law Present and Future: A Symposium to Honor Professor Charles L. Knapp on Fifty Years of Teaching Contract Law, 648
Symposium, The Enduring Legacy of *Wood v. Lucy, Lady Duff-Gordon*, 484
Symposium: Restitution and Unjust Enrichment, 308
Symposium, Restitution Rollout: The Restatement (Third) of Restitution and Unjust Enrichment, 308

Teeven, Kevin M., Consensual Path to Abolition of Preexisting Duty Rule, 778
Teeven, Kevin M., A History of Promissory Estoppel: Growth in the Face of Doctrinal Resistance, 264
Teeven, Kevin M., Moral Obligation Promise for Harm Caused, 337
Tennyson, Sharon, & William J. Warfel, The Law and Economics of First-Party Bad Faith Liability, 448
Thel, Steve, & Siegelman, Peter, Willfulness Versus Expectation: A Promisor-Based Defense of Willful Breach Doctrine, 888
Thel, Steve, & Siegelman, Peter, You Do Have to Keep Your Promise: A Disgorgement Theory of Contract Remedies, 993
Thompson, G., *Commentaries on the Modern Law of Real Property*, 54, 56
Threedy, Debora L., Dancing Around Gender: Lessons from Arthur Murray on Gender and Contracts, 228, 621
Threedy, Debora L., A Fish Story: *Alaska Packers' Association v. Domenico*, 779
Tinio, Ferdinand S., Annotation, Validity and Construction of Contractual Restrictions on Right of Medical Practitioner to Practice, Incident to Partnership Agreement, 686
Tousey, Clay B., III, Exceptional Circumstances: The Material Benefit Rule in Practice and Theory, 337

Van Alstine, Michael P., Of Textualism, Party Autonomy, and Good Faith, 493
VanderVelde, Lea S., The Gendered Origins of the Lumley Doctrine: Binding Men's Consciences and Women's Fidelity, 1067
van Ee, Daun, *David Dudley Field and the Reconstruction of the Law,* 367
Vargo, John F., The American Rule on Attorney Fee Allocation: The Injured Person's Access to Justice, 953

Wagner, Ronnie, Sand Castles: A Case Study of *Erlich v. Menezes,* 966
Walsh, Thomas J., Wisconsin's Undeveloped Surrogacy Law, 699
Waters, Anthony Jon, The Property in the Promise: A Study of the Third Party Beneficiary Rule, 1114
Watson, Geoffrey, In the Tribunal of Conscience: *Mills v. Wyman* Reconsidered, 332
Watson, Geoffrey R., The Capability Problem in Contract Law, 905
Webster, J., *North Carolina Real Estate for Brokers and Salesmen,* 53, 54
Weiskopf, Nicholas R., Frustration of Contractual Purpose—Doctrine or Myth?, 744
White, James J., Eight Cases and Section 251, 866
White, James J., Legal Realism, 826
White, James J., & Summers, Robert S., *Uniform Commercial Code,* 12, 157, 181, 182-183, 464, 465, 468, 861, 862, 863, 942, 945, 973-974, 977, 978-979
Whitford, William C., & Macaulay, Stewart, *Hoffman v. Red Owl Stores:* The Rest of the Story, 292
Wigmore, John H., *Evidence,* 409, 410, 1038
Williams, Neil G., Offer, Acceptance, and Improper Considerations: A Common Law Model for the Prohibition of Racial Discrimination in the Contracting Process, 523, 590
Willis, Hugh E., The Statute of Frauds—A Legal Anachronism, 380
Williston on Contracts, 42, 43, 53, 54, 55, 63, 64, 79, 80, 109, 112, 124, 137, 144, 241, 269, 279, 300, 303, 349, 350, 352, 397, 418, 421, 432, 559, 582, 594, 595, 607, 642, 785, 812, 820, 821, 830-831, 853-854, 923, 1008, 1022, 1026, 1027, 1050, 1052, 1053, 1054, 1076
Williston, Samuel, & Jaeger, W., *Williston on Contracts,* 785, 853-854
Wilmarth, Arthur E., Jr., The Dark Side of Universal Banking: Financial Conglomerates and the Origins of the Subprime Financial Crisis, 767-768
Winn, Jane K., & Bix, Brian H., Diverging Perspectives on Electronic Contracting in the U.S. and E.U., 209
Witkin, *Summary of California Law,* 517, 518
Wood, Gordon S., The Creation of the American Republic 1776-1787, 367
Woodward, Frederic C., The Law of Quasi Contracts, 1042
Woodward, William J., Jr., "Contraps," 209
Wormser, I. Maurice, The True Conception of Unilateral Contracts, 65
Wright, C., & Miller, A., *Federal Practice and Procedure,* 597

Yorio, Edward, In Defense of Money Damages for Breach of Contract, 1058
Yorio, Edward, & Thel, Steve, The Promissory Basis of Section 90, 265
Young, William F., Jr., Half Measures, 1043

INDEX

Acceptance, liability in absence of, 265-296
Accord and satisfaction, 798-799
Accounting as remedy, 308
Acts of God, 767
Additional terms, 181-183, 190-193
Adequate assurances of performance, 864-867
  assurances that may be demanded, 866
  compulsory demands, 866-867
  conduct as anticipatory repudiation, 857
  permissive demands, 866-867
  reasonable ground for insecurity, 865-866
  right to demand, 864-865
  time allowed, 867
  written demand requirement, 866
Adhesion contracts, 15, 404, 426-427, 660, 661, 662, 663
ADR (Alternative Dispute Resolution). *See* Arbitration; Mediation
Advertisements
  attorneys, 633-634
  as invitations to receive offers, 51
  mistake, 740
  as offers, 51
Agents and principals, 127-129
Agreed remedies, 1069-1086
Agreement to agree, 77-101
  classical approach, 78
  contract to bargain, 94, 96-98
  formal contract contemplated, 93-94
  good faith bargaining, 94, 96-98
  intention to be bound, 93-94
  letters of intent, 93-98
  open price terms, 85-86
  Pennzoil-Texaco litigation, 95-96
  promissory estoppel and, 94
  Quake, insight into background of, 95
  reliance, protection of, 94
  UCC, 85-86, 93
Alternative Dispute Resolution (ADR). *See* Arbitration; Mediation
Ambiguity, 413-414
American Arbitration Association, 23, 32, 212
American Law Institute (ALI), 8, 10-11, 148, 246, 308. *See also* Restatements
American rule for recovery of attorney fees, 955-956
Ancillary covenants, 691-692
Anticipatory repudiation, 849-868
  adequate assurances of performance. *See* Adequate assurances of performance
  communicating, 856-857
  conduct as, 857
  expressions, sufficiency of, 856-857
  history of, 856
  retraction of, 857-858
  withdrawal of, 857-858
"Apps" on smartphones, 21-31
Arbitration
  consumer contracts, 660-664
  enforceability, 660-664
  substantive unconscionability, 660-661
  terms of service, 21-31
  terms of use, 209-218
  unconscionability of agreements, 660-664
"As is" disclaimers, 631, 728-729
"Assent-based" theories of liability, 265
Assignment and delegation of rights and duties, 1115-1134
  consent required, 1133
  contractual prohibitions on, 1122
  defenses against assignee, 1122-1123
  economic analysis, 1133
  employment contracts, 1121
  government contracts, limitations on, 1120
  language, 1132
  limitations on assignments, 1120-1122
  material adverse effect on obligor, 1121
  partial assignment, 1121-1122
  personal services contracts, 1121, 1132-1133
  public policy limitations, 1120
  requirements contracts, 1121
  rights and duties of parties, effect on, 1133-1134
  rights of parties after, 1133-1134
  validity of assignment, 1117
Assumpsit, 107, 307-308
Attorney-client relationship. *See* Ethics, attorney
Attorney fees, recovery, 952-955
At-will doctrine. *See* Employment at will

"Baby M" case, 708-709
Bad faith, 493, 504. *See also* Good faith
  insurance contracts, damages, 968-969
  modification of contract, protest, 789
  noninsurance contracts, 969
  role of, 608-609
Bankruptcy
  debts discharged in, 332
  promissory estoppel and, 264
Bargaining power, disparity in, 45

Bargain theory of consideration, 112-113
"Battle of the forms," 163-194
  additional terms, 181-183, 190-193
  classical view, 165
  common law vs. UCC Article 2, 171-174
  confirmation, 173-174, 190-193
  drafting, 163-165
  first offer, 180
  formation of contract, 163-165
  indemnification clauses, 182, 183
  "knock-out" rule, 191
  "last shot" rule, 172-173
  materiality of terms, 191
  mirror image rule. *See* Mirror image rule
  response to offer, testing of, 180-181
  under Revised Article 2, 190-193
  supplementary terms, 183
  terms included in contracts, 190-193
Best efforts, 484-485
Bidding
  bidding statutes, 284
  unilateral mistake in construction bidding cases, 739-740
Bilateral contracts
  consumer rewards program, 69
  defined, 46
  distinguished from unilateral contract, 60, 65-66
  offer and acceptance, 46-60, 282
  subcontractors, 277
"Black Codes," 590
"Blue pencil" theory, 694-695
Boilerplate clauses, 164, 180, 181
Bonds, public works construction contractors, 1023
Breach of contract
  anticipatory repudiation. *See* Anticipatory repudiation
  buyers' remedies, 971-975
  constructive conditions, 835, 838-841, 858
  divisible contracts, 837
  efficient breach theory, 982-994
  employment contract, 894
  illness as defense to breach of employment contract, 894
  material. *See* Material breach
  nonbreaching party, risks, 848
  partial breach, 845-846
  promise to marry, 354
  punitive damages, 968-969
  remedies generally, 59-60, 873-875
  restitution, 1020, 1031
    material breach, 837-838
  sellers' remedies, 976-979
  substantial performance, 836-837, 838
  timely performance, 848-849
  total breach, 845-848
  willful breach, 837-838, 969, 1031
"Browsewrap" terms, 26, 195, 196, 209-218, 218-219
Burden of proof
  mental incapacity, 588
  mitigation of damages, 936
  trade usage, 472

Capacity to contract, 138
  history, 589-591
  intoxication, 588-589
  medical testimony/evidence, 586-587
  mental incapacity, 572-589
  minors, 332, 572-589
Caveat emptor, 556
Changed circumstances, 741-771
Charitable subscriptions, promissory estoppel, 236-247
"Chestnut" cases, 338-339
Chicago School. *See* Contract theory, *subheading:* economic analysis
Child custody, public policy, 708
Children. *See* Minors
Choice of law, 32, 195, 756
CISG. *See* Convention on the International Sale of Goods
"Clickthrough" terms, 26, 195, 213
"Clickwrap" terms, 26, 195, 210, 213, 219
Cognitive tests, mental incapacity, 586-587
Collateral agreements, parol evidence rule, 437
Collateral litigation, recovery of attorney fees, 954-955
Collateral source rule, 938-939
Commercial buildings, implied warranties, 567
Commercial promises, promissory estoppel, 247-265
Computers
  electronic contracting, 195-221, 356
Conditions. *See* Constructive conditions; Express conditions
Confirmation
  "battle of the forms," 173-174, 190-193
  statute of frauds and, 388-389
Consent to assignment and delegation of rights and duties, 1133
Consequential damages, 888-889, 906, 917, 920
Consideration, 101-147
  accord and satisfaction, 798-799
  adequacy, 129-138
  authority, issue of, 127
  bargained-for exchange, 126
  benefit to promisor or detriment to promisor, 107, 112-113, 125
  condition vs., 125-126
  criticism of, 115
  definition of, 101-102
  donative promises, 117-118
  fairness, change in law's concern for, 138-139
  formalities, 113-115, 571
  gift vs., 112
  grossly inadequate, 137
  history of, 106-107
  modification. *See* Modification of contracts
  moral obligation, 126-127
  mutuality of obligation, 146-147
  no consideration, 137
  nominal, 118, 271-272

options, 270-271
past consideration, 126-127
quitclaim deed and, 138
requirements contracts, 506
services as, 272
tests for, 113
Construction contracts. *See also* Subcontractors
bidding and, 284
bonds for public works, 1023
computation of expectation damages, 878-879, 901
liquidated damages, 1083-1084
specific performance, 1057
Constructive conditions, 835, 838-841, 858. *See also* Breach of contract
Constructive trusts, 308
Consumer contracts
arbitration agreements, 660-664
legislation, 677-680
liquidated damages, 1083
Truth-in-Lending Act, 677-678
Consumer Credit Protection Act, 677-678
Consumer Financial Protection Bureau, 679-680
Consumer rewards program, 69
Contemporary contracting, 195-219. *See also* Electronic contracting
Contract, defined, 2
Contract law
"chestnut" cases, 338-339
defined, 2-4
in law schools, 1-2, 3
sources of, 8-12
commentary, 11-12
international commercial law, 12
judicial opinions, 8-9
legal commentary, 11-12
Restatements, 10-11
statutory law, 9-10
UCC, 10, 11, 12
structure of, 5-8
defenses to enforcement, 6-7
formation of agreement, 6
interpretation and implication, 6
nonperformance and its consequences, 7
third-party rights and duties, 7-8
Contractors. *See also* Construction contracts; Subcontractors
public works, bonds, 1023
restitution, 314-315
Contract theory, 12-16
choice of law, 32
classical, 165
Critical Legal Studies, 15
economic analysis, 14
duress, 598
efficient breach theory, 982-994
frustration of purpose, 756-757
impracticability, 756-757
liquidated damages, 1085
nondisclosure, 631-632
restitution, 306-307
specific performance, 1057
feminist and radical perspectives, 937-938
formalism, 13, 15
lawyering perspectives, 32-33
Legal Realists, 13, 15, 33, 59, 113
merit and procedure, questions of, 32
morality, fairness, and consent, 15
consideration, 138-139
damages encouraging breach, 982-994
enforcement of moral obligation, 126-127
obligation to honor promises, 126-127
past consideration, 126-127
promissory restitution, 331
objective theory of contractual intent, 44
race and gender, 15
theoretical perspectives, 33
Contra proferentem, 404, 405
Convention on the International Sale of Goods (CISG). *See also Other Acts Table preceding Index*
attorney fees, recovery, 952-953
contract formation under, 161
damages, 907
deposited acceptance rule under, 50-51
failure to perform obligations, 756
nonperformance, excuses for, 756
parol evidence and interpretation, 450-451
promissory estoppel, 263-264
scope of, 160-161
statute of frauds and, 381, 389-390
UCC compared, 12
Counteroffers
assent, 182-183
conditional acceptance, 180-181, 182-183
options and, 58
qualified acceptance, 57, 172, 173, 183
Course of dealing, 183, 471
Course of performance, 183
Covenants not to compete, 691-695. *See also* Public policy
Cover, 972-973
Credibility of parties, 44-45
Creditor, third party beneficiary, as, 1094
Criminal law, mental incapacity, 588
Critical Legal Studies, 15

Damages, 873-1092
attorney fees, recovery, 952-955
buyers' remedies, 971-975
CISG, 907
consequential damages, 888-889, 906, 917, 920
construction contracts
computation of expectation damages, 878-879, 901
liquidated damages, 1083-1084
emotional distress, 965-967
employment contracts, 894, 920, 936
expectation damages. *See* Expectation damages
fraud, remedy, 610

Damages (*cont'd*)
- general damages, defined, 906
- generally, 59-60
- incidental damages, 978-979
- insurance contracts, bad faith, 968-969
- liquidated damages. *See* Liquidated damages
- market value, computation, 886, 887, 991
- material breach, 837-838
- mitigation of. *See* Mitigation of damages
- nominal damages, 873
- nondisclosure, 629, 631
- nonrecoverable damages, 946-971
- promissory estoppel, 293, 1017-1020
- punitive damages
  - breach of contract, 968-969
  - willful breach, 969
- real estate contracts
  - computation, 886-887
  - disgorgement principle, 991-994
  - market value, 886, 887, 899-901, 991
- real property leases, 939
- reliance damages. *See* Reliance damages
- restitution. *See* Restitution
- sellers' remedies, 976-979
- special damages, defined, 906
- speculative damages, 917-918
- torts, 906
- UCC. *See* Uniform Commercial Code, *subheadings:* buyers' remedies, *and* sellers' remedies

Debt, revival of, 332
Defenses. *See specific topics*
Definition of contract, 2
Delegation of rights and duties. *See* Assignment and delegation of rights and duties
Deposited acceptance rule, 50-51
Detrimental reliance, 113, 234-235, 236, 253-254
Dictum, 245
Disclaimers
- "as is" disclaimers, 631, 728-729
- express warranties, 554-555
- fraud, 631
- implied warranties, 555, 566-567

Disclosure requirements. *See* Nondisclosure
Discretionary rights, good faith obligations, 521-522
Disgorgement principle, 991-994
"Distributive" justice, 255
Distributorships, implied terms, 490-491
Divisibility doctrine, 838
Dodd-Frank Wall Street Reform and Consumer Protection Act of 2010, 679
Drafting forms. *See* "Battle of the forms"
Duress, 15, 36, 45, 591-610
- defining, 607-608
- economic, 459, 598, 599, 601
- force, use of, 598
- hardship, threat causing, 601
- history of, 591
- inducement of involuntary assent, 600-601
- market changes, 599
- marriage agreements, 609-610
- modification of contracts, 788-789
- no reasonable alternative, 600
- parol evidence rule, 435, 459
- restitution, 1042
- threat of criminal prosecution by attorney, 599-600
- void vs. voidable contract, 598
- wrongful or improper threat, 598-599

"Duty to read" what is signed, 45, 638

Earnest money, 1084
Economic approach. *See* Contract theory, *subheading:* economic analysis
Economic crisis (2008) and foreclosures, 262, 767-768
Economic duress/coercion, 459, 598, 599, 601
modification of contract, 788-789
Economic loss rule, 555-556
Ejusdem generis, 405
Electronic contracting, 195-219
- "apps" on smartphones, 21-31
- "browsewrap" terms, 26, 195, 196, 209-218, 218-219, 219
- "clickthrough" terms, 26, 195, 213
- "clickwrap" terms, 26, 195, 196, 210, 213, 219
- E-Sign Act and, 356
- forum selection clause, 576-577
- mailbox rule and, 50
- minority doctrine, 576-577
- offer and acceptance, 205-207
- public policy considerations, 207-208
- "scrollwrap" terms, 26, 219
- "shrinkwrap" terms, 195, 196, 209
- signed writing requirement under UCC, 389
- "sign-in wrap" terms, 26
- smartphone "apps," 21-31
- standard-form contracting, 208-209
- terms of service, notice of and assent to, 21-31
- terms of use, assent to, 209-218
- terms of use, mandatory disclosure of, 219
- UCC, applicability of, 209, 389
- unfair terms, 208-209

Electronic Signatures in Global and National Commerce (E-Sign) Act of 2000, 356
Emancipation of minors, 578
Emotional distress, damages, 965-967
Employment at will, 533-538
- additional consideration as basis of "for cause" term, 534
- attorney, termination of, 537
- commission provision contrary to public policy, 523-533
- detrimental reliance by discharged employee, 536-537
- efficiency of, 538
- employee manuals, 536
- ethical duties of lawyers, 537
- exceptions, 534-538

good faith duty, 533-538
handbooks and personnel manuals, 536
limitations, 533-534
personnel actions other than discharge, 537
presumption, 533-534
promissory estoppel, 536-537
public policy exception, 535-536
Employment contracts
assignability, 1121
damages, 894, 920, 936
employment at will, 536
expectation damages, 894
liquidated damages, 1084
minors, 578
mitigation of damages, 936-939
modification of contracts, 779-780
promissory estoppel and, 254-255
specific performance, 1065-1069
damages, 894
statute of frauds, 353-354
Equitable estoppel, 233-234
Equity, history of, 366-368
E-Sign (Electronic Signatures in Global and National Commerce) Act of 2000, 356
Estoppel
agency law, under, 129
equitable estoppel, 233-234
in pais, 233
promissory estoppel. *See* Promissory estoppel
Ethics, attorney
communication with opposing party, 621-622
covenants not to compete, 693
fiduciary duty, 630-631, 632-633
litigation tactics, 955-956
rules, 630-631, 632-634
termination of attorney, 537
threat of criminal prosecution, 599-600
Executed gifts, 119
Executory contracts, 4, 980-982
Expectation damages, 873-999
attorney fees, recovery, 952-955
certainty
fact vs. amount of damage, 917-918
new business rule, 919-920
collateral source rule, 938-939
computation of, 876-901
consequential damages, 888-889
construction contracts, 878-879
cost-to-complete, 899, 901
diminished value, 899-900
English vs. American rule, 887-888
general formula, 876-901
market value, 886, 887, 899-901
real estate contracts, 886-887
real estate leases, 939
conventional approach to contract enforcement and, 59
disgorgement principle, 991-994
efficient breach theory, 982-994
employment contracts, 894
encouraging breach, 982-994
exclusions, 946-971
foreseeability, 906-907
gains obtained from breach, 982-994
general damages, defined, 906
justification for, 979-994
limitation on, 901-920
lost profits, 917, 919, 946
lost volume sellers, 945
mitigation. *See* Mitigation of damages
nonrecoverable damages, 946-971
promissory estoppel, 293, 1017-1020
special damages. *See* Consequential damages
special damages, defined, 906
tacit agreement test, 907-908
UCC, 889
wholly executory contracts, 980-982
Express conditions, 805-828
conditions precedent, 805-813, 816
conditions subsequent, 816
constructive conditions vs., 835-836
estoppel, 817-818
excuse to avoid disproportionate forfeiture, 816-817, 824
forfeiture, 816-817, 819, 824-825
immateriality, excuse due to, 817
impracticability, excuse due to, 816
language, 813
material vs. technical, 817, 818
minor condition, 818
nonoccurrence of condition, 816
overview, 803-804
"pay-if-paid" clauses, 815
"pay-when-paid" clauses, 815
prevention of, 818
"procedural or technical" condition, 818
promises vs., 814-815
strict enforcement, 813-814
waiver of, 817-818, 887
Expressio unius exclusio alterius, 405
Express warranties. *See* Warranties

Fairness. *See* Contract theory
Family members' claims, promissory estoppel, 226-236
Federal Arbitration Act of 1925 (FAA), 24, 662-663
Federal Rules of Civil Procedure, attorney fees, 953
Federal Trade Commission (FTC), 678-679
Fiduciary duty
agency relationship, 127-129
attorney and client, 630-631, 632-633
disclosure, standard for, 630-631
Financial crisis (2008) and foreclosures, 262, 674-675, 679, 767-768
FindLaw terms of use, 196
Firm offers, 295
Fitness for particular purpose, implied warranty of, 546, 554

Force majeure clauses, 767
Foreclosures
  impracticability and, 767-768
  promissory estoppel and, 262
Foreseeability
  expectation damages, 906-907
  frustration of purpose, 755
  impracticability, 755
  modification of contracts, 780-781
  standard for, 906-907
  third party beneficiaries, 1104
  type of loss vs. manner in which loss occurs, 907-908
Forms, drafting. *See* "Battle of the forms"
Fraud, 4, 15, 36, 45, 138, 610-638
  consumer protection legislation, 677-680
  damages as remedy, 610
  disclaimers, 631
  execution, in, 457, 637-638
  false opinion or prediction, 620-621
  inducement, in, 457, 637
  meaning of, 629-630
  merger clause, effect of, 631
  nondisclosure. *See* Nondisclosure
  opinions vs. representations of fact, 620-621
  parol evidence rule, 435-436, 457-458, 459
    fraud in the execution, 436, 457
    fraud in the factum, 436
    fraud in the inducement, 436, 457
    promissory fraud, 457
  promissory fraud, 262, 376-377, 457
  reasonable reliance, 621
  rescission as remedy for, 610-611
  types of, 629-630
  unconscionability, interrelationship with, 674
  voidable contracts, 619-620
Frequent flyer programs, 69
Frustration of purpose, 741-771. *See also* Impracticability
  change in market conditions, 744-752, 753
  economic downturn, 767-769
  foreseeability, 755-756
  governmental regulation, 766-767
  impracticability doctrine vs., 752
  judge or jury, decision by, 757
  natural disaster or war, 753-754
  nature of relief, 767
  terrorism, 754
FTC (Federal Trade Commission), 678-679
"Full payment check" rule, 798-799

Gender. *See also* Women
  bias, 522-523
  contract theory and, 15
Gestational surrogacy contract, 695-708, 709
Gifts
  condition to, 112
  consideration vs., 112
  executed gifts, 119
  made in contemplation of death, 119-120
  testamentary gifts, 119-120
  in trust, 120
Good faith
  agreement to agree, 94, 96-98
  application of, 503
  at-will employment and, 534-535
  bad faith or ill motive, showing of, 504
  conditions of satisfactory performance, 512-513
  definitions, 492-493
  discretionary rights, 521-522
  employment at will, 533-538
  express terms vs., 503-504
  gender discrimination, 522-523
  implied obligation of, 492-546
  lender liability, 505
  meanings of, 492-493
  modification of contracts, 787-788
  open price terms, 504-505
  output contracts, 507
  parol evidence rule and, 503
  racial discrimination, 522-523
  reasonable expectations, 503, 504
  requirements contracts, 507
Governmental regulation, impracticability claims, 766-767
Government contracts
  assignment limitations, 1120
  third party beneficiaries, 1113-1114
"Gratuitous" promises, reliance on, 226. *See also* Promissory estoppel
Guardians, effect of mental incapacity, 587

Habitability, warranty of, 546-547
  disclaimers, 566-567
  latent defects, 565-566
  privity requirement, 565
  skillful construction vs., 564-565
Home foreclosures
  impracticability and, 767-768
  promissory estoppel and, 262
Home sales, implied warranty of quality in sale of new home, 564, 565-566

Illegality, 435. *See also* Public policy
Illusory promises, 146, 484
Implied contracts, 234, 305-306, 307
Implied contractual provisions, 481-570
  default rules, 490
  factual context, 484
  gap-filling provisions, 489-490
  good faith, 492-546
  illusory promises, 484
  in-fact vs. in-law, 486
  rationale for, 481-492
  UCC providing, 489-490
Implied warranties, 546-547. *See also* Warranties
  commercial buildings, 567
  disclaimers, 555

extended application of, 565-566
fitness for particular purpose, 546, 554
habitability. *See* Habitability, warranty of
latent defects, 565-566
merchantability, of, 546, 553-554, 566
quality in sale of new home, 564
subsequent purchasers, 565
workmanlike construction, 558-564, 564-565

Impossibility of performance, 741-771. *See also* Impracticability
death or incapacity of person, 755, 894
destruction of thing necessary for performance, 755
nature of relief, 767
personal services contracts, 743, 894
restitution, 1020, 1042
specific performance, 742
UCC, 744

Impracticability, 741-771
change in market conditions, 744-752, 753
death or incapacity of person, 755, 894
economic analysis, 756-757
economic downturn, 767-768
express condition, excuse of, 816-817
failure of basic assumption of contract, 753
force majeure clauses, 767
foreclosures and, 767-768
foreseeability, 755-756
frustration doctrine vs., 752
governmental regulation, 766-767
increased costs, 753
judge or jury, decision by, 757
market failure, 753
natural disaster, 753-754
nature of relief, 767
performance made impracticable, 752-753
personal services contract, 743, 894
restitution, 1020, 1042
terrorism, 754
UCC, 744, 767
undue risk of injury to person, 894
war, 753-754

Incapacity to contract. *See* Capacity to contract

Incidental damages, 978-979

Incomplete bargaining, 93-94. *See also* Agreement to agree

Indemnification clauses, 182, 183

Insurance contracts
ambiguity, 424-425
bad faith, 448-449
attorney fees, recovery, 954
damages, 968-969
reasonable expectation doctrine, 424-426

Integration, 631
parol evidence rule, 432-434, 449

Intent, 35-101

International commercial law, 12. *See also* Convention on the International Sale of Goods

International Institute for the Unification of Private Law (UNIDROIT), 12

Internet. *See* Electronic contracting

Interpretation, 396-427
adhesion contracts, 426-427
ambiguity, 413-414
construction against drafter, 404-407
contextual approach, 416
contract as whole, 405
contra proferentem, 404, 405
ejusdem generis, 405
expressio unius exclusio alterius, 405
extrinsic evidence, admission of, 413-414, 447-448, 449
handwritten or typed provisions control printed provisions, 406
insurance contracts, 424-425
know or have reason to know, 398, 402-404
modified objective theory, 397-398
noscitur a sociis, 405
objective theory, 397-398
omitted terms, 407
omnia praesumuntur contra proferentem, 405
parol evidence and, under CISG, 450-451
patent and latent ambiguity, 413-414
plain meaning, 413
prevailing meaning, 413
principles of, 396-427
public interest preferred, 406
purpose of parties, 405-406
reasonable, lawful, and effective, 406
reasonable expectation, 424-426
specific provision as exception to general one, 406
standard maxims, 405-406
strict formalist approach, 416
subjective theory, 396-397
supplementation, 447-448
trade usage, 415
traditional approach, 416
unconscionability, 427
ut magis valeat quam pereat, 405

Intoxication, capacity to enter into contract, 588-589

Intra-family claims for restitution, 327

Joke, promise made as, 45-46

Justice
"corrective," 255
"distributive," 255
promissory estoppel, element of, 254-255

"Knock-out" rule, 191

Land contracts. *See* Real estate contracts

"Last shot" rule, 172-173

Late charges, liquidated damages as, 1083

Lawyering skills
as advocate, 17-18, 32-33
as counselor, 16, 32, 33, 118-120
as drafter, 17, 32, 33
as negotiator, 16, 32

Layered contracts, 195

Leases
  goods, 148
  real property
    damages, 939
    forfeiture in lease renewal cases, 825
    mitigation, 939
    warranty of habitability, 546-547
  renewal options, 85, 825
  restitutionary liability of lessors, 314
  UCC, 148
Legal commentary, 11-12
Legal formalities, function of, 113-115, 571
Legal Realists, 13, 15, 33, 59, 113
Lender liability, good faith, 505
Letters of intent, 93-98
Liens, 314-315
Liquidated damages, 1068, 1069-1086
  actual loss requirement, 1082
  anticipated vs. actual harm, 1081-1082
  construction contracts, 1083-1084
  consumer contracts, 1083
  earnest money, 1084
  economic analysis, 1085
  employment contracts, 1084
  late charges, as, 1083
  mitigation, 1082-1083
  penalty limitation, 1085
  real estate contracts, 1084-1085
  test for enforcement, 1080-1081
  UCC, 1081-1082
  underliquidated damages, 1085
Loans
  lender liability, 505
  mortgage lending, 664-673, 674-675, 767-768
  Truth-in-Lending Act, 677-678
Lost profits
  expectation damages, 917, 919, 946
  seller's remedies, 977-978

Magnuson-Moss Act of 1975, 678-679
Mailbox rule, 50, 51, 273
Marital agreements, 609-610
Market value
  damages computation, 886, 887, 991
  restitution, 1023-1024
Marriage
  contracts made upon consideration of, 354
  minors, effect on capacity to contract, 578
  undue influence and duress in agreements, 609-610
Married women, capacity to contract, 590
Material benefit rule, 336-337
Material breach, 829-849. *See also* Breach of contract
  commercial context, 834-835
  damages, 837-838
  overview, 804
  remedies, 837-838
  restitution, 838
  test to determine, 846-847
  total breach vs., 846-847
  willful, 837-838
Mechanic's liens, 314-315
Mediation, 579-586, 589
Medical practice covenants, public policy, 692-693
"Meeting of the minds," 32, 36, 44, 58
Mental incapacity, 572-589
  burden of proof, 588
  cognitive and volitional tests, 586-587
  in criminal cases, 588
  guardianship, effect, 587
  medical testimony, requirement of, 586-587
  minority doctrine vs., 587
  vulnerability, 587-588
Merchant
  defined, 388
  statute of frauds exception, 388-389
Merchantability, implied warranty of, 546, 553-554, 566
Merger clauses, 432-433, 435, 457, 631
Miller Act of 1935, 1023
Minors
  age of majority, reduction to 577
  capacity to contract, 572-589
  child custody, public policy, 708
  disaffirming minor's restoration or restitution, 576-578
  emancipation, 578
  employment contract provisions, 578
  enforcement of contracts, 332, 576
  injury release agreements, 578
  Internet world, 576-577
  liability for "necessaries" and tortious conduct, 577
  marriage, effect, 578
  mental incapacity vs. minority doctrine, 587
  ratification after reaching majority, 577
Mirror image rule, 172, 180, 192
Misrepresentation. *See* Fraud; Nondisclosure
Mistake, 45, 720-741
  advertisement, 740
  "as-is" clause, 728-729
  clerical errors, 739
  conscious ignorance, 729
  construction bidding cases, 739-740
  content of writing, 740-741
  equitable relief, 729-730
  express condition, excuse of, 816
  fact vs. judgment mistake, 739
  judge or jury, decision by, 757
  mutual mistake, 459, 728, 730
  negligence, effect, 739
  "palpable" nature of, 737-738
  parol evidence rule, 435, 459
  personal injury settlement cases, 730
  reformation of contract, 729, 730
  releases and settlements, 730
  remedies, 741
  requirement that benefitting party cause or induce the mistake, 738-739
  rescission, 728, 729, 730

restitution, 729, 1020, 1042
tests for unilateral mistake, 737-738
unconscionable effect of, 737-738
unilateral mistake, 277, 730-741
written expression, in, 729
Mitigation of damages, 920-946
additional vs. mitigating contracts, 945
burden of proof, 936
duty, 925
employment contracts, 936-939
leases, 939
liquidated damages, 1082-1083
personal service contracts, 945-946
reliance damages, 1009-1011
statutory rights, 936
UCC, 939
M'Naghten test, 588
Modification of contracts, 771-799
bad faith modification, protest, 789
coercive behavior, policing, 778-779
duress and, 788-789
employment contracts, 779-780
foreseeability, 780-781
good faith, 787-788
historical context, 779
mutual release, 781-782
no-oral-modification provision, 797
"no-waiver" clause, 798
one-sided modifications, 778
preexisting duty rule, 771, 777-778
reliance and oral modifications, 797-798
settlements, through, 798-799
statute of frauds, applicability of, 796-797
UCC, 787-789
unforeseen circumstances, 780-781
"Money now, terms later" contracts, 195
Mortgage lending, 664-673, 674-675, 679, 767-768
Mutual assent, 35-101. *See also* Offer and acceptance
application of
agreement to agree, 77-101
"battle of the forms," 163-194
electronic contracting, 195-221
firm offer, 295
unaccepted offer, effect of offeree's reliance on, 274-294
bilateral contracts, 46-60
"duty to read" what is signed, 45, 638
presumption of knowing assent, 45
objective theory of contract, 36-46
terms of service, 21-31
UCC Article 2, 147-161
acceptance through conduct, 160
common law vs., 153
contract formation, 153-154
offer and acceptance, 159-160
open terms, 160
relaxed rules for contract enforcement, 154
statute of frauds and, 154
unilateral contracts, 60-77
Mutuality of obligation
consideration, 146-147
requirements contracts, 506-507
unilateral contracts, 75
Mutual mistake, 459, 728

National Conference of Commissioners on Uniform State Laws (NCCUSL), 147, 148, 557, 644, 678. *See also specific Uniform Law*
Natural disasters, impracticability claims, 753-754
Negligence
emotional distress, negligent infliction of, 965
mistake and, 739
will drafting, 1103
Negotiations, promissory estoppel, 293
New business rule, lost profits, 919-920
Nominal consideration, 118, 271-272
Noncompetition covenants, 691-695
Nondisclosure. *See also* Fiduciary duty
attorneys, breach of fiduciary duty, 632-633
consumer protection legislation, 677-680
damages, 629, 631
economic analysis, 631-632
fiduciary relationship, effect of, 630-631
fraud in execution, 637-638
historical perspective on, 628-629
innocent, 629
modern approach to, 629
negligent, 630
real estate, 622-628, 630
rescission as remedy, 629, 631
tort liability, 630
Truth-in-Lending Act, 677-678
Nonprofessional employment, covenants not to compete, 694
Nonprofit corporations, 246
Nonrecoverable damages, 946-971
Noscitur a sociis, 405
Notice to terminate, 491

Objective theory of contract, 36-46
Offer and acceptance
additional terms, 181-182, 190-193
advertisements, offers as, 51
bilateral contracts, 46-60
classical principles of, 57, 165
deposited acceptance rule, 50-51
different terms, 191
electronic contracting, 195-221
firm offer, 295
first offer, 180
invitation for offer, 49, 51, 180
irrevocable offers, 294-295
"lost acceptance," 51
mailbox rule, 50, 51, 273
multiple acceptances, 58-59
offer defined, 49-50
promise vs. offer, 60
qualified acceptance, 57, 163-194

Offer and acceptance (*cont'd*)
- response to offer as conditional acceptance, 180-181, 182-183
- under Restatements, 57
- revocation of offer, 46, 50, 57, 64-65, 274-294
- Section 2-207, applicability, 190-193
- supplementary terms, 183
- time of acceptance, 50-51
- UCC Article 2, 159-160
- unaccepted offer and promissory estoppel, 283, 284
- unaccepted offer, offeree's reliance on, 274-294
- unilateral contracts, 60-77
- varying acceptance, 172, 180

Omnia praesumuntur contra proferentem, 405

Open price terms
- agreements, 85-86
- good faith, 504-505
- UCC Article 2 and, 160

Opinions vs. representations of fact, misrepresentation, 620-621

Option contract, 266-274
- consideration, 270-271
- counteroffers and, 58
- enforceability, 58, 84-85
- formality rules, 272-273
- lease-renewal, 85
- mailbox rule and, 273
- performance inviting acceptance, 64
- real estate, time period to exercise, 825-826
- Restatement and, 58, 65, 272
- revocation and, 273, 277
- termination of, 273-274

Output contracts, 507

Palimony, 522

Parental rights, 707, 709

Parol evidence rule, 427-476
- classical vs. modern approach, 449-450
- collateral agreements, 437
- debate over use of, 449-450
- defined, 427
- exceptions to rule, 434-437
- express warranties, 555
- formalities, 571
- "four corners," 432-433
- fraud, duress, undue influence, incapacity, mistake, or illegality, 435-436, 457-458, 459
  - fraud in the execution, 436, 457
  - fraud in the factum, 436
  - fraud in the inducement, 436, 457
  - promissory fraud, 457
- good faith and, 503
- integration, 432-433, 449
- interpretation under CISG, 450-451
- later written agreements, 435
- merger clause, 432-433, 457
- operation of, 427-429
- oral condition precedent, 435
- partial integration, 432-433, 434
- plain meaning, 449
- promissory estoppel and, 459-460
- rationale for, 432
- reformation of contract, 436-437
- right to equitable remedy, 436-437
- supplementation, 447-448
- trade usage, 471-473
- UCC Comments, 437

Partial assignment, 1121-1122

Partial breach, 845-846

Partial integration, 432-433, 434

Parties to contract
- credibility of, 44-45
- nature of, 45, 292-293

Part performance, 63, 64, 365-366, 387-388

Past consideration, 126-127

"Payday loans," 675-676

Payment bonds, public works contractors, 1023

"Pay-if-paid" clauses, 815

"Pay-or-play" clause, 938

"Pay-when-paid" clauses, 815

"Peerless Case," 396

Pennzoil-Texaco litigation, 95-96

Performance bonds, public works contractors, 1023

Personal injury release agreements of minors, 578

Personal injury settlement cases
- mutual mistake, claims of, 730
- relief for mutual mistake, 730

Personal services contracts
- assignability and delegation, 1121, 1132-1133
- impossibility to perform, 743, 755
- mitigation of damages, 945-946
- specific performance, 1065-1069

Plain meaning rule, 413

Policy. *See* Public policy

Postjudgment interest, 894-895

Postponed bargaining. *See* Agreement to agree

Precedents, judicial system based on, 8-9

Preemption of state law, 263-264

Preexisting duty rule, 771, 778, 780-782

Prejudgment interest, 894-895

Premarital agreements, 609-610

Preservation of goods, restitutionary liability, 306

Prevailing meaning, 413

Prevention, doctrine of, 818

Price term unconscionability, 646-647

Principals and agents, 127-129

Prior course of dealing, 183, 471

Privity, warranties, 565

Professional services, recovery in absence of promise, 339-340

Promise
- "clear and definite," 291
- donative promises, 117-118
- express conditions vs., 814-815
- gratuitous, 226
- implied, 64, 234
- made as joke, 45-46

marriage, breach of, 354
offer vs., 60
oral, 235, 354, 365, 375, 459, 797
promissory estoppel and, 291
under seal, 106, 114, 118-119
Promissory estoppel, 225-265
assurances, sufficiency of, 291-292
bankruptcy and, 264
charitable subscriptions, 236-247
CISG and, 263-264
"clear and definite promise," 291
commercial promises, 247-265
damages, 293, 1017-1020
detrimental reliance, 234-235, 236, 253-254
employment at will, 536-537
evolution of, 233-234
express promise, 234
family members' claims, 226-236
foreclosures and, 262
implied promise, 234
incomplete bargaining and, 94
injustice, role in avoidance of, 254-255
justice element of, 254-255
nature of parties, 292-293
parol evidence rule, 459-460
preemption, 263-264
promise requirement, 291-292
race politics, 95
reasonableness of reliance, 234-236
Restatement (Second) view, 263
specific performance, 1019
status and future of the principle, 264-265
statute of frauds, 375-376, 389
unaccepted offer, offeree's reliance on, 274-294
bid by subcontractor, 284
negotiations, 293
Promissory fraud, 262, 376-377, 457
Promissory note, 119
Promissory restitution, 327-342
"Prove me wrong" cases, 76
Public policy, 680-715
assignment limitations, 1120
"blue pencil" theory, 694-695
charitable subscription and, 245
child custody, 708
commission provision in at-will employment agreement, 523-533
conflict with statutory law, 693
covenants not to compete, 691-695
electronic contracting, 207-209
employment at will and, 523-533, 535-536
express condition, excuse of, 816
family relations, 708
generally, 7
gestational surrogacy and, 709
history of, 680
invalidating contracts, 680-715
medical practice, covenants restraining, 692-693
parental rights, 707, 709
in pari delicto, 710
remedial options, 710
restraint of trade agreements, 691-695
surrogacy contracts, 695-708, 709
wrongful conduct of parties and, 710
Public works, contractor bonds, 1023
Punitive damages
breach of contract, 968-969
willful breach, 969

Quantum meruit, 305, 307, 1024, 1030, 1032
Quantum valebat, 307
Quasi contracts, 305-306, 307-308
Quitclaim deed, 138

Race, contract theory, 15
Racial discrimination
breach of contract, 522-523
breach of duty of good faith, 522-523
Real estate contracts. *See also* Leases
commercial buildings, implied warranties, 567
damages
computation, 886-887
disgorgement principle, 991-994
liquidated damages, 1084-1085
market value, 886, 887, 899-901, 991
habitability warranty vs. skillful construction, 564-565
implied warranties, new home sales, 564-567
liability of party other than builder-vendor, 565
nondisclosure and, 630
restitution, 1023-1024, 1030
specific performance, 1056-1057, 1084-1085
statute of frauds, 364-365
time period to exercise option, 825-826
warranties associated with, 564-567
Real property
leases
damages, 939
time period to exercise option, 825
warranty of habitability, 546-547
mortgage lending, 664-673, 674-675, 679, 767-768
sale of. *See* Real estate contracts
warranties, 564-567
Reasonable expectations
adhesion contracts, 426-427
good faith obligation, 503, 504
insurance policies, 424-426
Restatement approach to, 425-426
Recession
impracticability and, 767-768
mortgage loans, 673-674, 679, 767-768
promissory estoppel and, 262
Reformation of contracts
mutual mistake, 729, 730
parol evidence rule, 436-437
Rejection, buyers' remedies, 972
Releases, mistake, 730

Reliance
  detrimental reliance, 113, 234-235, 236, 253-254
  letters of intent and, 94
  protection of, 94
  reasonableness of, 234-236
  unaccepted offer, effect of reliance on, 274-294
Reliance damages, 1001-1020
  essential reliance, 1009
  expectation damages not proven with reasonable certainty, 1009
  incidental reliance, 1009
  limitations on, 1009-1011
  loss of contracts and, 1011-1012
  lost opportunities, as, 1012
  mitigation, 1009-1011
  out-of-pocket expenditures as, 1012
  precontract reliance, 1012
  promissory estoppel, 293, 1017-1020
  restitution, 1043
  subcontractors' withdrawal of bid, 1019-1020
Remedies, 59-60, 741, 873-875. *See also specific remedy*
Rent-to-own cases, 646
Requirements contracts, 505-507, 1121
Rescission
  fraud, remedy, 610-611
  misrepresentation as grounds for, 620
  mutual mistake, 728, 729, 730-737
  nondisclosure as grounds for, 629, 631
Restatements. *See also Tables preceding Index*
  offer and acceptance, 57-58
  options, 58, 65, 272
  as source of contract law, 10-11
  UCC and, 10
Restitution, 296-342, 1020-1045
  in absence of promise, 297-327
  bankruptcy, debts discharged in, 332
  breach of contract, 1020, 1031
    material breach, 837-838
  contractors and, 314-315
  debts barred by time, 331
  development of law of, 307-308
  disaffirming minor's restoration or restitution, 576-578
  duress, 1042
  economic analysis, 306-307
  emergency services and, 304-305
  history, 307-308, 1042-1043
  impossibility of performance, 1020, 1042
  impracticability, 1020, 1042
  intra-family claims, 327
  lessor's liability in, 314
  market value, 1023-1024
  material benefit rule, 336-337
  measure of, 1031-1032
  mistake, 729, 1020, 1042
  nonmarried cohabitants, 325-326
  owner's liability in, 314
  promises to revive debts, 332
  promissory restitution, 327-342
  proving with reasonable certainty, 1043-1044
  public works contractors, bonds, 1023
  real estate contracts, 1023-1024, 1030
  reliance damages and, 1043
  subcontractors and, 314-315
  terminology, 307-308
  transaction costs, 307
  unjust enrichment, as, 1042-1043
  willful breach, 1031
Revive debt, promises to, 332
Revocation of offer
  bilateral contracts, 46
  classical contract theory and, 57
  explicit reservation of power to revoke, 64-65
  limitations on, 270-271, 274-296
  mailbox rule and, 50
  part performance or tender, effect of, 63, 64
  protection against, 65
  reliance and, 274-294
  reservation of power to revoke, 64-65
  statutory limits on, 294-296
  unaccepted offer, offeree's reliance on, 274-294
"Rolling" contracts, 195, 206-207, 208. *See also* Electronic contracting

Sale of goods. *See* Uniform Commercial Code
Sale of real property. *See* Real estate contracts
"Scrollwrap" terms, 26, 219
Seals, 106, 114, 118-119
Services as consideration, 272
Settlements
  mistake, 730-737
  modification of contract, 798-799
  personal injury settlement and mistake, 730
  rescission of agreement based on mistake, 730-737
"Shrinkwrap" terms, 195, 196, 209
"Sign-in wrap" terms, 26
"Slave Codes," 590
Slavery, capacity to contract, 590
Smartphone "apps," 21-31
Software under UCC, 209
"Special manufacture" exception to statute of frauds, 388
Specific performance
  construction contracts, 1057
  economic analysis, 1057
  employment agreements, 1065-1069
    damages, 894
  impossibility to perform, 742
  inadequacy of damages at law, 1056-1057
  indefiniteness, 1055-1056
  land contracts, 1056-1057
  limitations on, 1045-1047
  personal services, 1065-1069
  promissory estoppel, 1019
  real estate contracts, 1056-1057, 1084-1085
  remedy, as, 59, 1045-1069

third parties and, 1058
third party beneficiaries, 1058
UCC, 974, 1058-1059
Speculative damages, 917-918
Sports, minors' injury release agreements, 578
Standard forms, 164, 208-209
Stare decisis, 8-9
Statute of frauds, 345-394, 571
admissions of defendants, 388
application, 347-380
CISG and, 381, 389-390
confirmations and, 388-389
contracts made upon consideration of marriage, 354
electronic transactions, requirement of signed writing in, 389
employment contracts, 353-354
history of, 9-10, 345-347
land transfers, 364-365
lifetime contracts, 353-354
linking documents, 354-355
marriage category, scope of, 354
memorandum of contract, 356
merchant exception, 388-389
modification of contracts, applicability, 796-797
one-year provision, 352-353, 354
oral contracts and, 154, 374, 375, 376, 377, 389
oral promises, 375
part performance and, 365-366, 387-388
promise to answer for the debt of another, 354
promissory estoppel, 375-376, 389
scope, 347-380
signed writing, 356, 387, 571
"special manufacture" exception, 388
suretyship contracts, 354
UCC, 380-391
mutual assent, 153-154
writing requirement, 345, 346, 354-356, 387, 389, 571
Subcontractors
bidding statutes, 284
bid shopping and, 284
bilateral contracts, 277
payment bonds, 1023
reliance damages for withdrawal of bid, 1019-1020
restitution and, 314-315
Substantial performance, 64, 836-837, 838. *See also* Breach of contract
Supplementary terms, 183
Surrogacy contracts, 695-710

Termination
express provisions, 491-492
notice, 491
Terms of service, notice of and assent to, 21-31
Terms of use
assent to, 209-218
FindLaw, 196
mandatory disclosure of, 219
Terrorism, impracticability claims, 754
Testamentary gifts, 119-120
Tests
consideration, 113
liquidated damages, 1080-1081
material breach, 847-848
mental incapacity, 586-587
M'Naghten test, 588
tacit agreement test, 907-908
unconscionability, 645
Third-party beneficiaries, 1093-1115
adverse effect on obligor, 1121
assignment and delegation of rights and duties. *See* Assignment and delegation of rights and duties
causation and foreseeability, 1104
as contract beneficiaries, 1093-1115
creditor-beneficiary, 1094, 1095
defenses available to promisor, 1103-1104
donee beneficiary, 1095
evidence of intent and, 1102-1103
government contracts, 1113-1114
incidental, 1095, 1103
intended, 1095
rights of, 1093-1136
specific performance and, 1058
standing of, 1095, 1096, 1101-1102, 1103
vesting of rights, 1112-1113
wills, 1095, 1103
Threats. *See* Duress
"Time of essence" clauses, 848-849
Torts
damages, 906, 965
emotional distress, damages for, 965
minors, liability for, 577
negligent infliction of emotional distress, 965
nondisclosure, liability for, 630
Total breach, 845-848
Trade usage, 183, 415
burden of proof, 472
establishing existence of, 472
express terms and, 472
negation of, 472-473
parol evidence, 471-473
Trust, gifts in, 120
Truth-in-Lending Act of 1968, 677-678

UCC. *See* Uniform Commercial Code
UCCC (Uniform Consumer Credit Code), 678
UETA (Uniform Electronic Transactions Act), 356
Unaccepted offer, offeree's reliance on, 274-294
bid by subcontractor, 284
negotiations, 293
UNCITRAL (United Nations Commission on International Trade Law), 12

Unconscionability, 14, 45, 638-680
  adhesion contracts, 660
  affirmative relief, 676
  arbitration agreements, enforceability, 660-664
    consumer contracts, 660-664
    substantive unconscionability, 660-661
  as basis for affirmative relief, 676
  commercial cases, 676-677
  consumer protection legislation, 677-680
  contract law, 676
  excessive loan amounts, 673-674
  express condition, excuse of, 816
  fraud, interrelationship with, 674
  history, 639, 649-650
  interpretation and, 426-427
  mortgage lending, 664-673, 674-675
  "payday loans," 675-676
  price term, 646-647
  procedural vs. substantive, 643-645, 647, 660-661
  rent-to-own cases, 646
  tests for, 645
  UCC, 639, 646, 676
Undue influence, 138, 607-610
  defining, 607-608
  factors indicating undue influence, 608
  marriage agreements, 609-610
  overview, 591
  parol evidence rule, 435
Unforeseen circumstances, modification of contracts, 780-781
UNIDROIT. *See* International Institute for the Unification of Private Law (UNIDROIT)
Uniform Commercial Code (UCC). *See also Tables preceding Index*
  accord and satisfaction, 799
  additional terms in acceptance of confirmation (§2-207), 181-183, 190-193
  adequate assurances of performance. *See* Adequate assurances of performance
  agreement to agree, 85-86, 93
  assignment, 1122
  assignment and delegation of rights and duties. *See* Assignment and delegation of rights and duties
  attorney fees, recovery, 953
  "battle of the forms." *See* "Battle of the forms"
  best efforts, 484-485
  buyers' remedies, 971-975
    accepted goods, damages for, 974
    cover, 972-973
    damages, 972-975
    incidental and consequential damages, 975
    market damages, 973-974
  CISG compared, 12
  collateral agreements, parol evidence, 437
  common law vs., 171-173
  damages, 889
  electronic contracting, applicability to, 209, 389
  expectation damages, 889
  frustration of purpose, 767
  good faith, 492
  goods, applicability to, 148-149
  history of, 10, 147-148
  implied contractual provisions, providing, 489-490
  impossibility, 744
  impracticability of performance, 744, 767
  liquidated damages, 1081-1082
  mitigation of damages, 939
  modification of contracts, 787-789
  mutual assent
    acceptance through conduct, 160
    common law vs., 153
    contract formation, 153-154
    offer and acceptance, 159-160
    open price terms, 160
    relaxed rules for contract enforcement, 154
    statute of frauds, 154
  offer and acceptance, 159-160
  open price terms, 85-86
  output contracts, 507
  parol evidence rule, Comments, 437
  requirements contracts, 507
  Restatements and, 10
  sellers' remedies, 976-979
    action for price, 978
    damages, 976-979
    incidental and consequential damages, 978-979
    lost profits, 977-978
    market damages, 976-977
    resale damages, 976
  software, status of, 209
  as source of contract law, 10, 11, 12
  specific performance, 974, 1058-1059
  statute of frauds, 380-391
    mutual assent, 154
  unconscionability, 639, 646
  varying acceptance, 172, 180
  warranties, 111-112, 546
Uniform Consumer Credit Code (UCCC), 644, 678
Uniform Electronic Transactions Act (UETA), 356
Uniform Law Commission, 147, 148, 557, 644, 678
Uniform laws. *See Other Acts Table preceding Index*
Uniform Premarital and Marital Agreements Act, 609-610
Uniform Residential Landlord Tenant Act, 547
Unilateral contracts, 60-77
  history, 65-66
  illusory promises and, 146
  mutuality of obligation and, 75
  offer and acceptance, 60-77
  part performance, 63, 64
  "prove me wrong" cases, 76
  revocation, 64-65
Unilateral mistake, 277, 730-741

United Nations Commission on International Trade Law (UNCITRAL), 12
United Nations Convention on the International Sale of Goods. *See* Convention on the International Sale of Goods
Unjust enrichment, 297, 1042-1043
Ut magis valeat quam pereat, 405

Volitional tests of mental incapacity, 586-587

Waivers
  express conditions, 817-818, 887
  modification of contracts, "no-waiver" clause, 798
War, impracticability claims, 753-754
Warranties
  disclaimers, 554-555, 566-567
  economic loss rule, 555-556
  elements, 552-553
  habitability. *See* Habitability, warranty of
  history of, 546-547
  implied. *See* Implied warranties
  parol evidence and, 555
  privity, 565
  real property, 564-567
  UCC, 111-112, 546
Wills, liability of attorney for negligent drafting, 1103
Women
  contract law and feminist perspectives, 937-938
  contract theory and, 15
  gender discrimination, 522-523
  married woman's capacity to enter into contracts, 590
  surrogacy contracts, 695-710
World Wide Web. *See* Electronic contracting